Continued

Anxiety Disorders

Panic Disorder Without Agoraphobia
Panic Disorder with Agoraphobia
Agoraphobia Without History of Panic
  Disorder
Specific Phobia
Social Phobia
Obsessive-Compulsive Disorder
Posttraumatic Stress Disorder
Acute Stress Disorder
Generalized Anxiety Disorder

Somatoform Disorders

Somatization Disorder
Undifferentiated Somatoform Disorder
Conversion Disorder
Pain Disorder
Hypochondriasis
Body Dysmorphic Disorder

Factitious Disorder

Factitious Disorder
Factitious Disorder NOS

Dissociative Disorders

Dissociative Amnesia
Dissociative Fugue
Dissociative Identity Disorder
Depersonalization Disorder

Sexual and Gender Identity Disorders

Sexual Dysfunctions
  Sexual Desire Disorders
    Hypoactive Sexual Desire Disorder
    Sexual Aversion Disorder
  Sexual Arousal Disorders
    Female Sexual Arousal Disorder
    Male Erectile Disorder

Orgasmic Disorders
  Female Orgasmic Disorder
  Male Orgasmic Disorder
  Premature Ejaculation
Sexual Pain Disorders
  Dyspareunia (Not Due to a General
    Medical Condition)
  Vaginismus (Not Due to a General
    Medical Condition)
Paraphilias
  Exhibitionism
  Fetishism
  Frotteurism
  Pedophilia
  Sexual Masochism
  Sexual Sadism
  Transvestic Fetishism
  Voyeurism
Gender Identity Disorders
  Gender Identity Disorder in Children
  Gender Identity Disorder in Adolescents
    or Adults

Eating Disorders

Anorexia Nervosa
Bulimia Nervosa

Sleep Disorders

Primary Sleep Disorders: Dyssomnias
  Primary Insomnia
  Primary Hypersomnia
  Narcolepsy
  Breathing-Related Sleep Disorder
  Circadian Rhythm Sleep Disorder
Primary Sleep Disorders: Parasomnias
  Nightmare Disorder
  Sleep Terror Disorder
  Sleepwalking Disorder

Impulse-Control Disorders Not Elsewhere Classified

Intermittent Explosive Disorder
Kleptomania
Pyromania
Pathological Gambling
Trichotillomania

Adjustment Disorders

Adjustment Disorder
  With Depressed Mood
  With Anxiety
  With Mixed Anxiety and Depressed
    Mood
  With Disturbance of Conduct
  With Mixed Disturbance of Emotions and
    Conduct Unspecified

Personality Disorders

Note: These are coded on Axis II.
Paranoid Personality Disorder
Schizoid Personality Disorder
Schizotypal Personality Disorder
Antisocial Personality Disorder
Borderline Personality Disorder
Histrionic Personality Disorder
Narcissistic Personality Disorder
Avoidant Personality Disorder
Dependent Personality Disorder
Obsessive-Compulsive Personality Disorder

Abnormal Psychology

Abnormal Psychology

Susan Nolen-Hoeksema
University of Michigan

Boston, Massachusetts Burr Ridge, Illinois Dubuque, Iowa
Madison, Wisconsin New York, New York San Francisco, California St. Louis, Missouri

McGraw-Hill

*A Division of The **McGraw·Hill** Companies*

ABNORMAL PSYCHOLOGY

 This book is printed on recycled, acid-free paper containing 10% postconsumer waste.

1 2 3 4 5 6 7 8 9 0 QPD/QPD 9 0 9 8 7

ISBN 0-697-23118-6

Publisher: Jane E. Vaicunas
Sponsoring Editor: Meera Dash
Marketing Manager: James Rozsa
Project Manager: Gloria G. Schiesl
Production Supervisor: Sandy Ludovissy
Cover and interior design: Jeff Storm
Cover image: "In the Field" © Daniel Nivens/SUPERSTOCK
Photo research coordinator: Carrie K. Burger
Compositor: GAC Shepard Poorman
Typeface; 10/12 Minion
Printer: Quebecor Printing Book Group/Dubuque

Library of Congress Cataloging-in Publication Data
Nolen-Hoeksema, Susan, 1959–
        Abnormal psychology / Susan Nolen-Hoeksema.
                p.   cm.
        Includes bibliographical references and index.
        ISBN 0-697-23118-6 (alk. paper)
        1.   Psychology, Pathological.   I.   Title.
RC454.N64   1997
616.89—dc21   97–16976
                                                                CIP

www.mhhe.com

To Michael and Richard

Brief Contents

Contents

Part Two
Disorders of Anxiety, Mood, Psychosis, and Personality

6 The Schizophrenias 214

7 Dissociative and Somatoform
Disorders 252

8 Personality Disorders 280

Part Three
Developmental and
Health-Related Disorders

Part Four
The Methods, Ethics, and Policy of Abnormal Psychology

Preface

Writing this book has been a joy. It has provided me with the opportunity to integrate years of scholarly work and teaching in abnormal psychology into a tool that can help students understand abnormal psychology better. In writing this book, I have had the following goals:

1. To address students' various interests in taking a course in abnormal psychology.
2. To call attention to issues of gender as well as culture in discussions of psychological disorders.
3. To present ground-breaking biological research on abnormal psychology in an understandable way, and to provide students with an integrated bio-psycho-social understanding of each of the disorders.
4. To organize the book in a way that matches the approach that many instructors take in organizing their courses.
5. To give students a respect for traditional approaches to understanding abnormal psychology as well as an excitement for the new research and paradigms that are greatly expanding our knowledge.

Addressing Students' Various Interests

Students take a course on abnormal psychology for various reasons. Some students find the phenomena of abnormal psychology interesting and want to know more about what science has discovered about these phenomena. Others think they may want to become mental health professionals who treat people with psychological problems. Still others want to gain an understanding of troubling behaviors or feelings that they or people close to them have experienced.

During my 12 years of teaching abnormal psychology, I have learned to address each of these motivations. It is not easy to maintain a scholarly research focus while addressing clinical issues and students' personal concerns; but I feel I have been fairly successful at attaining a balance, and my students have recognized and appreciated my efforts. In writing this book, I hope I have brought that balanced approach to students' various interests to the written page.

Students interested in the science of psychopathology will appreciate the research focus of this book. Discussions of the causes and treatments for each of the psychological disorders focus on those that have received the most empirical support. For many disorders, I describe critical experiments that have shaped our understanding of those disorders. These descriptions give students a sense of the excitement of doing ground-breaking research in psychology. Throughout each chapter are critical thinking questions, which are referred to as "Questions for the Mind." They are designated by the icon you see in the margin. These questions are designed to challenge students to think like a theorist and researcher of abnormal psychology.

Students who want to become mental health practitioners will appreciate the many case studies and autobiographical accounts of people with psychological problems. These are meant to give students a feel for what it is like to have these problems and to work with people who have these problems. The best treatments for psychological problems are described so that students know what types of therapy they will be learning if they become therapists. Excerpts of conversations between therapists and clients bring psychotherapies to life for students. Finally, throughout the book appear critical thinking questions , which are referred to as "Questions for the Heart." They are designated by the icon you see in the margin. These questions challenge students to consider what it is like to be a person with a disorder, a close friend or family member of such a person, or a therapist trying to provide treatment.

Students who come to this course to understand troubling feelings, thoughts, or behaviors in themselves or their families or friends will appreciate the *Application* sections at the end of each chapter, which address personal questions or concerns students bring to this course. These sections aim to give students useful information that addresses their concerns, and many of them provide students with ideas for how to seek more information from mental health professionals about their concerns. Examples of some topics covered in the *Application* sections are "When You Wonder If You Are Abnormal" (Chapter 1), "Is Self-Assessment a Good Idea?" (Chapter 2), "How to Look for a Therapist" (Chapter 3), "Relaxation Exercises" (Chapter 4), "Seeing Oneself in the Personality Disorders" (Chapter 8), "If Your Parent has a Psychological Disorder" (Chapter 9) and "Promoting Responsible Alcohol Use in Young Adults" (Chapter 12).

Focusing on Gender as Well as Culture

Many abnormal psychology textbooks now acknowledge the importance of gender and culture in shaping people's experience of psychological problems. In many textbooks, however, issues of gender and culture are raised only sporadically and are often relegated to "boxes" as if they are peripheral issues. In addition, most textbooks attend primarily to culture, and give only cursory attention to gender. This is unfortunate because there are substantial gender differences in the prevalence of most psychopathologies. Gender also influences the ways people manifest psychological problems and perhaps their response to certain treatments for disorders.

A unique feature of this book is its attention to gender as well as cultural influences on abnormal psychology. For example, in Chapters 1 and 2, I discuss how people's gender and cultural background influence whether their behaviors are labeled as abnormal, and the particular diagnoses they might receive. Then in each of the chapters on specific disorders, I discuss the way that people's gender and cultural background influence their vulnerability to the disorders, the manifestation of the disorders, and the effectiveness of treatments for the disorders.

I have integrated these discussions of gender and culture into each chapter. Information on the differences between genders or between people of various cultures in the experience of disorders can give us clues to the causes of disorders. Integrating this information into the ongoing discussions of the disorders will help students learn to treat this information as central to their understanding of the disorders and to their critique of various theories and treatments for the disorders.

I am in a unique position to bring in-depth discussions of gender into an abnormal psychology textbook. I have spent my career researching gender issues in psychopathology, writing and speaking about these issues for various audiences, and teaching students how to think critically about gender and mental health.

Integrating Biology, Psychology, and Social Context

Biological approaches are at the forefront of new work in abnormal psychology. This book emphasizes ground-breaking biological theories and treatments for psychological disorders, and makes these theories and treatments accessible and exciting for students, and easy for instructors to present. Chapters 2 and 3 describe the fundamentals of these theories and treatments, and some of the new methods used to research biological factors in abnormal psychology, including MRI, PET, and CT technologies. The remainder of the book includes discussions of biological approaches to each of the psychological disorders. These theories and treatments are examined critically in light of the evidence for and against them, rather than simplistically as some textbooks do. Throughout the book, the role of biology in producing the gender and cultural differences in psychological disorders is addressed.

Psychological and social factors also play roles in all psychological disorders. A theme throughout this book is that most psychological problems probably have multiple causes; they are the result of a complex interplay of biological, social, and psychological causes. For example, Chapter 6 discusses evidence that people with schizophrenia, a disorder strongly influenced by biological factors, show greater relapse rates if they live in families or cultures that do not provide positive social support. In addition, the fact that women with schizophrenia have a better prognosis than men with schizophrenia is discussed in light of psychological and social differences between the genders, as well as biological differences.

Throughout each chapter, and in the *Bio-Psycho-Social Integration* section at the end of each chapter, I weave together the strongest biological, psychological, and social theories into an integrated framework for understanding each disorder. These frameworks are not simply my own opinions about these disorders, but a description of the best integrative thinking about the disorders currently in the field.

Organizing the Book's Chapters

Students in an abnormal psychology course want to begin talking about disorders on the first day of class. Many textbooks, however, have several chapters of introductory material before getting to specific disorders. I have found that this arrangement of material frustrates students and instructors alike, particularly because the introductory material is repeated in chapters on the individual disorders.

I have condensed the introductory material on definitions of abnormality, historical perspectives, assessment, diagnosis, and overviews of biological and psychosocial theories into the first three chapters of this book, under Part I, "Understanding and Treating Abnormality." This section covers all the subject matter necessary to prepare students for the remainder of the book, without giving them a great deal of material that is unnecessary or better introduced in the context of specific disorders.

Part II, "Disorders of Anxiety, Mood, Psychosis, and Personality," covers the anxiety and mood disorders, schizophrenia, the dissociative and somatoform disorders, and the personality disorders. These disorders are grouped together because they are the ones that most instructors discuss in their classes, and because they form the major focus of many theories and research on abnormal psychology.

Part III, "Developmental and Health-Related Disorders," discusses the childhood disorders, eating disorders, sexual and substance use disorders, the role of personality and behavior in physical health, and cognitive disorders. These disorders are grouped together because they occur in a developmental context and often involve people's physical health as well as their mental health.

Part IV, "The Methods, Ethics, and Policy of Abnormal Psychology," addresses the methods and ethical questions in doing research on psychopathology and social policy issues in the field. I have put the chapter on research methods near the end of the book, rather than at the beginning, because some instructors choose not to teach this material directly but refer students to the material in the textbook. The chapter is written so that students can understand it whether they are reading it at the beginning, middle, or end of the course. The chapter on "Abnormality and Social Policy" highlights the roles mental health professionals are increasingly playing in family law (such as in child abuse cases), as well as the traditional issues of involuntary commitment, the insanity defense, and patients' rights.

The organization into 16 chapters should make the book easy to use in the average semester or quarter. Knowing how pressed students and instructors are for time, I have striven to include all the material necessary for students to gain a thorough understanding of abnormal psychology, without including a lot of peripheral material.

Respecting Tradition While Pushing the Boundaries

Abnormal psychology is a field deeply rooted in theoretical traditions that still influence practice today. It is also a field being reshaped and expanded by important new research on biology, cognitive processes, and the impact of contextual factors on abnormal psychology. This book presents a balanced view of the continuing impact of traditional theories in abnormal psychology and the emerging impact of new research and paradigms, and it integrates these traditional and emerging views wherever possible.

For example, Chapter 2 discusses the standard assessment methods that have been used in clinical psychology for years. It also discusses the role of state-of-the-art neuroimaging techniques in assessment and research. Later the chapter presents a detailed description of DSM-IV and its development, but this presentation includes questions that have been raised about gender biases in the development of the DSM-IV and the sociopolitical context surrounding the DSM-IV. In each of the chapters on disorders, DSM-IV criteria are presented as the basis for defining and describing the disorders, but issues of gender bias in the application of DSM-IV criteria are discussed when appropriate. Culture-bound syndromes and manifestations of disorders are discussed in each chapter as well.

Chapter 8 on "Personality Disorders" emphasizes the influence of traditional psychodynamic conceptualizations of personality disorders. It also describes newer ideas on how biological vulnerabilities (such as genetics and temperamental factors) might interact with early childhood experiences emphasized in psychodynamic theories to produce some of the personality disorders. Chapter 10 on "Eating Disorders" integrates traditional psychodynamic and family systems theories of anorexia and bulimia nervosa with more recent cognitive theories and new research on the biological contributors to disordered eating patterns.

As a final example, Chapter 13, "Personality, Behavior, and the Body," describes some of the historical perspectives on the effects of personality on physical health (such as the idea that repression is bad for your health), and then describes new, state-of-the-art psycho-biological research that is directly testing some of these perspectives. This chapter goes beyond the brief and often outdated treatment of health psychology given in many abnormal psychology textbooks and gives students an excitement for one of the fastest growing subfields in psychology.

Thus, throughout the book, I have attempted to give students a respect for the traditions in abnormal psychology, particularly those that still influence clinical theory and practice today. At the same time, I have attempted to give students a sense of the excitement many clinicians and researchers have over the new knowledge and paradigms that are changing our understanding of psychopathology.

Pedagogical Features

This book includes a number of pedagogical features designed to make learning easier and more enjoyable for students.

- **Annotated Chapter Outlines.** Each chapter begins with an annotated outline that provides students with a stimulating framework for approaching the chapter.
- **Key Terms Defined in Margin.** All of the key terms are defined in the margin near where they first appear in the chapter. The margin glossary provides students with an explicit definition of each term and a running glossary of important terms.
- **Gender and Cultural Influences Sections.** Although discussions of the roles of gender and culture are woven throughout the chapters, each chapter also has separate sections that explicitly bring together facts and hypotheses about the roles of gender and culture.
- **Case Studies.** Case studies are presented for almost every disorder to provide students with a better sense of how the disorder is manifested in real people. Rather than relying only on my own clinical experience to provide the most illustrative cases for each disorder, I have gleaned cases from dozens of colleagues, books, and articles, as well as from clients I have known.
- **Autobiographical Accounts of People with Disorders.** Several chapters highlight excerpts from autobiographies of people with a disorder (for example, Kay Redfield Jamison, Donna Williams, William Styron). These excerpts take students into the minds and lives of people living with psychological disorders.
- **"Heart" and "Mind" Critical Thinking Questions.** This book has two types of critical thinking questions. "Questions for the Heart" challenge students to reflect on the personal experiences of people with psychopathology, their family members, and therapists. "Questions for the Mind" challenge students to think analytically about specific theoretical or research issues.
- **Summing Up Sections.** Each major section of a chapter ends with a feature that summarizes, in bullet form, the major points of that section.
- **Chapter Summaries.** Each chapter ends with an integrative summary of the major points of the chapter.
- **Bio-Psycho-Social Integrations.** Distinctively designed sections at the end of each chapter explicitly integrate the various biological, psychological, and social theories and treatments described in the chapter.
- **Application Sections.** Practical sections at the end of each chapter address personal issues or concerns that students often bring to a course on abnormal psychology, such as fears that they are suffering from a disorder, the experience of having a parent with a disorder, and questions about how to achieve healthy behaviors and attitudes toward eating.

Ancillary Package

This book is supported by a number of ancillaries that will help students and instructors move through the abnormal psychology course.

Clashing Views on Abnormal Psychology: A Taking Sides® Custom Reader is a debate-style reader designed to introduce students to controversies in abnormal psychology. I have compiled issues of current concern to mental health professionals and lay people. Each issue is explored by two articles that represent "Yes" and "No" responses. By requiring students to analyze opposing viewpoints and reach considered judgments, *Clashing Views* actively engages students' critical thinking skills.

The **Study Guide** provides students with a thorough review of the material in the textbook. Each chapter of the study guide includes learning objectives, a list of essential ideas from the chapter in the textbook, a guided review through all of the major sections, a case example with questions about the case, a 20-item practice multiple-choice exam with answers, and a practice essay exam with answers. I coauthored this study guide with Robert Davis. Students can be assured that it accurately and thoroughly represents the most important material in the textbook.

The **Instructor's Course Planner** includes an overview of each chapter, learning objectives, suggestions and resources for lecture topics, classroom activities, between-class projects, suggestions for video and media that will enhance lectures and discussions, and essay questions that will help students think about material between classes. A special section of the planner includes an instructor's manual for the reader, *Clashing Views on Abnormal Psychology: A Taking Sides Custom Reader*. The course planner was written by Dr. Anita Rosenfield at Chaffey Community College. With more than ten years of teaching experience, Dr. Rosenfield has taught abnormal psychology at both California State University, Los Angeles, and Chaffey Community College.

The **Test Item File**, also compiled by Dr. Rosenfield, includes 1,600 multiple-choice and essay items. Multiple-choice items are classified as factual, conceptual, or applied, and referenced to the appropriate learning objective and textbook page number.

Computerized Test Item Files are available in MicroTest, a powerful but easy-to-use test-generating program by Chariot Software Group. MicroTest is available for DOS, Windows, and Macintosh. MicroTest enables you to select questions easily from the Test Item File and print a test and answer key. It also lets you customize questions, headings, and instructions, add or import questions of your own, and print your test in a choice of fonts if your printer supports them.

Annual Editions: Abnormal Psychology 97/98 brings together a wide range of more than 40 carefully selected articles on topics related to the latest research and thinking on abnormal behavior, its causes, and therapies. Compiled by Joseph Palladino at the University of Southern Illinois, this volume's sources include *Scientific American, Schizophrenia Bulletin, Psychology Today,* and *Newsweek*.

Psych Online 97: Abnormal, Clinical and Counseling Psychology Edition is a reference guide that points students and instructors to electronic resources in abnormal, clinical, and counseling psychology. Prepared by Patricia Wallace, Director of Information Technologies and psychologist at the University of Maryland, *Psych Online 97* includes general help in using the Internet and specific sites for academic and professional resources as well as self-help and support.

Videotapes that can support the textbook include *DSM-IV Videotaped Clinical Vignettes*, as well as *The World of Abnormal Psychology, The Brain,* and *Madness* series. These videotapes are available to instructors based on the number of textbooks ordered from McGraw-Hill by your college bookstore.

Acknowledgments

Writing a textbook is a big undertaking. I am deeply grateful to the dozens of people who have provided me editorial, scholarly, technical, clerical, and emotional support as I wrote this book.

Michael Lange first approached me about writing an abnormal psychology textbook that dealt seriously with issues of gender as well as culture in psychopathology. His vision and enthusiasm made me think it was possible, and certainly interesting, to attempt this task while maintaining my research, teaching, and family life. Ted Underhill and Steven Yetter provided invaluable, persistent, and patient editorial advice and support. Sarah Lane and Julie Hall did a wonderful job in copy editing the manuscript. The McGraw-Hill team—Jane Vaicunas, Meera Dash, Jim Rozsa, Susan Kunchandy, Gloria Schiesl, Mary Christianson, Carrie Burger, and Sandy Ludovissy—put the finishing touches on the book. And I had a fabulous time working with Toni Michaels in choosing the photography for this book. Toni's great eye and quick wit made those hours and hours of looking at images pure fun, resulting in an attractive, compelling, and upbeat (for an abnormal psychology textbook) set of photos.

Reviewers contributed to the development of this book at every stage. The prospectus for this book was reviewed by instructors and researchers of abnormal psychology and by a focus group, and substantial changes in the organization and focus of the book were made as a result of these reviewers' comments:

John Belmont
University of Kansas Medical Center

Gayle Iwamasa
Ball State University

Michael Lambert
Brigham Young University

Jennifer Langenrichsen-Rohling
University of Nebraska

David Mastofsky
Boston University

Janet Matthews
Loyola University

Lily McNair
University of Georgia

Jodi Mindell
St. Joseph's University

Lynne Rehm
University of Houston

David Allen Smith
Ohio State University

Michael W. Vasey
Ohio State University

Janet Wollersheim
University of Maryland

Teresa Wozencraft
Midwestern State University

The first draft of each chapter was reviewed for both style and content by expert teachers and writers. Each chapter was then thoroughly rewritten to reflect these additional reviewers' suggestions for new pedagogical features and ways of making material more accessible to students:

Gerianne Alexander
University of New Orleans

L. E. Banderet
Northeastern University

Salvatore Catanzaro
Illinois State University

Patricia DiBartolo
Smith College

Jacqueline Horn
University of California–Davis

Diane Pfahler
University of California, San Bernadino

Anita Rosenfield
Chaffey Community College

Timothy Trull
University of Missouri, Columbia

Fred Whitford
Montana State University

Later drafts of the chapters were reviewed by experts in research on the specific disorders. These experts checked accuracy and comprehensiveness, and often provided new data and papers in press that were incorporated into the chapters. The following people provided in-depth attention to chapters of their specialties:

John Belmont
University of Kansas Medical Center
(mood disorders)

Paul Garfinkel
University of Toronto (eating disorders)

Jill Goldstein
Harvard Medical School (schizophrenia)

John Helzer
University of Vermont School of Medicine
(substance abuse)

Chris Hayward
*Stanford University Department of
Psychiatry* (dissociative and somatoform
disorders)

Stephen Hinshaw
University of California at Berkeley
(assessment)

Nadine Kaslow
Emory University (childhood disorders)

Terence Keane
National Center for Post-Traumatic Stress Disorder (anxiety disorders)

Robert Sapolsky
Stanford University (disorders of stress and health)

Richard Kluft
Temple University School of Medicine (dissociative and somatoform disorders)

Kathleen Blindt Segraves
Case Western Reserve University (sexual disorders)

Gary Melton
Institute for Families in Society at the University of South Carolina (legal issues)

I also wish to thank the following expert reviewers for reviewing excerpts of chapters, citing their work, and providing me with additional material:

Nancy Andreasen
University of Iowa

Alan Marlatt
University of Washington

Thomas Borkovec
The Pennsylvania State University

Andrew Matthews,
MRC Applied Psychology Unit

Jeanne Brooks-Gunn
Columbia University

Edward Mulvey
University of Pittsburgh

Glorisa Canino
University of Puerto Rico

Carol Nemeroff
Arizona State University

Shelly Chaiken
New York University

Michael O'Hara
University of Iowa

Christopher Davis
University of Michigan

Harrison Pope
McLean Hospital

Adam Drewnowski
University of Michigan

Norman Rosenthal
National Institute of Mental Health

L. Erlenmeyer-Kimling
Columbia University

Marc Schuckit
University of California, San Diego

Christopher Fairburn
Oxford University

Ruth Striegel-Moore
Wesleyan University

Irving Gottesman
University of Virginia

Albert Stunkard
University of Pennsylvania

Peter Guarnaccia
Rutgers University

Lenore Terr
University of California, San Francisco

Steven Hollon
Vanderbilt University

Joseph Westermeyer
University of Minnesota

Barbara Lex
McLean Hospital

Valerie Whiffen
University of Ottawa

Spero Manson
University of Colorado Health Sciences Center

Kimberly Yonkers
University of Texas SW Medical Center

I'd like to thank Lorry Cology, Owens Community College, and Beth Menees Rienzi, California State University–Bakersfield, for their invaluable comments and suggestions as they reviewed the Test Item File. Beth Rienzi also offered valuable input to the Instructor's Course Planner.

My colleagues at Stanford University and the University of Michigan created an environment of vigorous scholarly activity and rigorous critical thinking, and a devotion to educating students, which I learned from and is reflected in this book. I want to thank all of them collectively and single out the following people with whom I have had many formative discussions: Albert Bandura, Laura Carstensen, David Rosenhan, Leonard Horowitz, Gordon Bower, and Eleanor Maccoby of Stanford University, and Christopher Peterson, Jacquelynne Eccles, Abigail Stewart, Randy Larsen, and Elizabeth Young of the University of Michigan. I also wish to thank my long-time collaborators Joan Girgus of Princeton University and Martin Seligman of the University of Pennsylvania for their support and mentorship over the years.

Writing a textbook requires endless computer searches for information, runs to the library, phone calls to researchers to follow-up on their written work, typing of manuscripts, tracking down references, and so on. Many people helped me with these tasks, most notably Robert Davis, Jennifer Schneps, Leslie Smithline, and Leonor Diaz. They were patient and diligent, and even managed to turn many tasks into fun learning experiences.

My dear friend and colleague Judith Larson also helped on these tasks. Judi contributed much more to this book, however, by simply being my dear friend, listening to my ramblings about the book, and helping me sort them out, and keeping my lab running while I wrote the book. I could not have written the book without her, and I sure could not have kept my own mental health stable during the process if I hadn't had her shoulder to lean on.

Finally, my family has contributed to this book more than they can know. My son Michael was born during the period I was writing this book. Although juggling new motherhood along with writing this book and my other career activities was a challenge, experiencing the joys and stresses of parenthood gave me new perspectives on much of the material I was writing about (such as theories of the impact of temperament and early childhood experiences), and greatly deepened my commitment to educating young people. Coming home to my wonderful little boy each evening also relieved a lot of the stresses of the workday and added the kind of meaning to my life that only children can bring.

My husband Richard has been an unfailing source of support throughout this process. His generosity and trust in me over the years has been astounding. My parents, Catherine and John Nolen, prepared me in so many ways for this task—by encouraging my interests, providing the resources to pursue those interests, teaching me that working hard for a good cause was important and fun, and offering nearly unconditional positive regard. My parents-in-law, Marjorie and Renze Hoeksema, and siblings and siblings-in-law, have also been stalwart supporters as I wrote this book, and long before. All of us should be so lucky as to have these kind of people in our lives.

Susan Nolen-Hoeksema
University of Michigan

About the Author

Susan Nolen-Hoeksema received her B.A. in 1982 from Yale University and her Ph.D. in 1986 from the University of Pennsylvania. She then taught at Stanford University for nine years, where she received tenure. Dr. Nolen-Hoeksema currently teaches in the Psychology Department at the University of Michigan. She is well-known across the world for her work on gender differences in mood disorders, coping with depression, bereavement, and childhood depression. During the last twelve years she has published four books and over thirty-five articles and chapters. Many of Dr. Nolen-Hoeksema's research and theoretical articles have been published in the leading journals in psychology, including the *Journal of Abnormal Psychology, Journal of Consulting and Clinical Psychology, Journal of Personality and Social Psychology*, and *Psychological Bulletin.*

Dr. Nolen-Hoeksema has received numerous awards for her research and writing. These include the David Shakow Early Career Award from the American Psychological Association, the W. T. Grant Foundation Faculty Scholars Award, and an Independent Scientist Award from the National Institute of Mental Health. She serves on a panel that reviews research proposals at the National Institute of Mental Health, and as a Consulting Editor for the *Journal of Abnormal Psychology.*

Dr. Nolen-Hoeksema has received two university-wide awards for her teaching of abnormal psychology. She is currently Director of the *Gender and Mental Health Training Program* at the University of Michigan. This program trains predoctoral and postdoctoral students to conduct research on the role of gender in mental health and to practice gender-sensitive interventions for people with psychological problems. Dr. Nolen-Hoeksema also gives workshops to more than 2,000 health care professionals each year, focusing on gender and mood disorders.

Abnormal Psychology

Part One

Understanding and Treating Abnormality

What is abnormality? Throughout history, whether a person's behavior is labeled abnormal often has depended on the culture's norms for appropriate behavior and the gender and ethnicity of the person. Current definitions of abnormality focus on the person's ability to function in daily life and his or her level of distress and grasp of reality. Many biological and psychological tests are used to assess people's functioning and well-being. The information gathered in these tests is compared to criteria for diagnosing psychological disorders provided in guidebooks such as the *Diagnostic and Statistical Manual of Mental Disorders* (DSM). Several modern biological and psychological theories provide different ways of understanding and treating people with psychological disorders. Most disorders appear to be influenced both by biological and psychosocial factors, and theories integrating these factors have proven most useful in understanding and treating abnormality.

You can be totally rational with a machine. But if you work with people, sometimes logic often has to take a backseat to understanding.

—Akio Morita

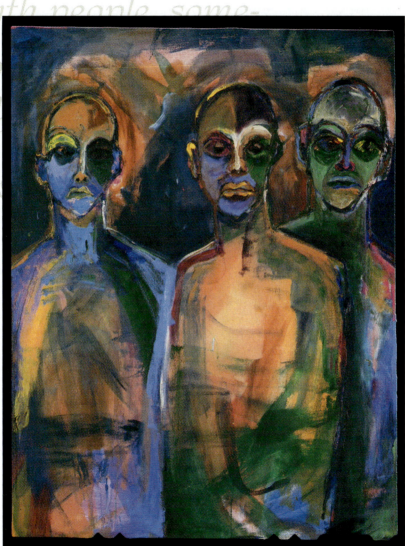

Michelle Puleo
Heart of the Hunter

chapter 1

Looking at Abnormality

Defining Abnormality

The context for a behavior often determines whether it is considered abnormal. Other criteria that have been used to determine the normality of behaviors are the societal norms for behaviors, how unusual the behaviors are, whether the behaviors cause the person discomfort, the presence of an identifiable illness, and whether the behaviors interfere with the person's functioning.

Historical Perspectives on Abnormality

Theories of abnormality across the ages have included biological theories, supernatural theories, and psychological theories. These theories led to very different modes of treatment for people who exhibited abnormal behaviors.

Ancient Theories

References to madness, insanity, and other forms of mental disorder can be found throughout written history. Some of the most ancient writings are from Chinese texts around 2674 B.C. Other prominent writings include the papyri of Egypt and Mesopotamia, the Old Testament, and the works of Greek and Roman philosophers and physicians.

The Middle Ages

Many people with mental disorders may have been accused of being witches and killed out of fear. Other people without mental disorders were also probably accused of being witches to punish or silence them.

The Growth of Asylums in Europe and America

The treatment of people who acted abnormally was often deplorable. They were imprisoned, tortured, or cast out. In the eighteenth and nineteenth centuries, however, several advocates of more gentle treatment of people with mental disorders helped to establish asylums where they could be treated with kindness.

The Humanitarian Movement

The eighteenth and nineteenth centuries saw a movement toward more humane treatment of the mentally ill. Patients were provided with clean and safe living conditions and the best care available at the time.

Psychic Epidemics and Mass Hysteria

Over history there have been many examples of groups of people simultaneously developing strange psychological and behavioral symptoms that were probably the result of common stressors or belief systems.

Looking Ahead

Biological and psychosocial theories of abnormality predominate in mainstream science and practice in abnormal psychology. Some clients still bring their own lay and supernatural theories of abnormality into their interactions with therapists, however.

Professions Within Abnormal Psychology

The professions in abnormal psychology include psychiatry, clinical psychology, clinical social work, and psychiatric nursing.

Chapter Summary
Key Terms
Application: *When You Wonder If You Are Abnormal*

Who, except the gods, can live time through forever without any pain.

Aeschylus

Peter Sickles
People Flying

Singing in a town square is not considered abnormal if it is done by a folk singer intending to entertain an audience.

Singing in a open square may be considered abnormal if the singer's intent is to communicate with imaginary spirits.

Consider the following behaviors. Do you think these behaviors are abnormal?

1. A man wearing a bright red skirt
2. A person sitting in the middle of a town square swaying back and forth and singing loudly
3. A man kissing another man
4. A parent slapping a child
5. A man driving a nail through his hand
6. A woman refusing to eat for several days
7. A college student refusing to study medicine as his parents wish, because he would rather study art
8. A man barking like a dog and crawling on the floor on his hands and knees
9. A woman building a shrine to her dead husband in a corner of her living room and leaving food and gifts for him at the shrine
10. A woman who works fourteen hours a day to build her career, hardly ever seeing her husband or her children

Some of these behaviors clearly seem abnormal, such as the man driving the nail through his hand. However, some of the behaviors are not clearly abnormal or normal. The man singing in the town square may be out of touch with reality, trying to communicate with spirits he sees floating in the sky above him. If so, many people would think his behavior is abnormal. If he is a budding folk singer trying to earn money and fame by singing to lunch-hour audiences, we would probably not label his behavior abnormal. What about the man wearing a bright red skirt? Few people would have questioned the behavior of a woman wearing a bright red skirt, but many people consider the same behavior by a man to be abnormal.

Defining Abnormality

These examples illustrate that an important factor influencing whether a given behavior is labeled abnormal is the *context* for the behavior. Sometimes the context for a behavior is determined by the intent behind a behavior: the folk singer's intent to entertain a noontime audience seems normal, but the intent to communicate with spirits may not seem normal. Often the context for a behavior is determined by the norms or traditions of the *culture* in which a person lives. Most of the behaviors in our list are considered perfectly normal and indeed are prescribed for specific situations by some culture in the world. In Scotland, men playing traditional music on bagpipes will often wear bright red skirts, known as *kilts*. In Mexico, some Christians have themselves nailed to crosses at Easter to commemorate the crucifixion of Jesus. The traditional greeting between men in many European countries is a kiss. Among Caucasians in North America, a college student defying his parents' wishes is considered quite normal, but in some Asian cultures, such behavior is considered disgraceful. Among the Yoruba of Africa, healers act like dogs, barking and crawling on the floor, during healing rituals (Murphy, 1976). In Shinto and Buddhist religions, it is customary to build altars to dead loved ones, to offer them food and gifts, and to speak with them as if they were in the room.

The context for a behavior can also be influenced by the *gender* of the person displaying the behavior. Women wear skirts in most cultures, but men do not. In the United States and Japan, men often work long hours to build their careers, and may be with their families infrequently, but most women do not. What about the woman who refuses to eat for several days? You might have said that this behavior is normal, because many women go on crash diets. If this had been a man refusing to eat, might you have been more likely to label the behavior abnormal, because it is less common for men to go on crash diets?

Many different criteria have been suggested for labeling a behavior abnormal. Let us discuss five criteria that have often been used.

Some behaviors—like one man kissing another man—are considered normal in some cultures but not in others.

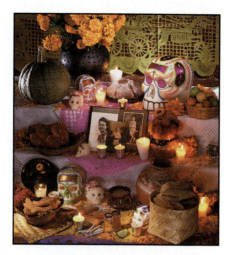

People in some cultures build altars to dead loved ones, leave them food and gifts, and speak to the dead. In other cultures these practices are considered highly abnormal.

Cultural Relativism

First, some theorists have argued that abnormality can only be defined in reference to the norms of a culture or society (Scheff, 1966). This perspective is often known as **cultural relativism.** A central argument of this perspective is that behaviors are never abnormal in the sense of an immutable, objective reality. They are only abnormal relative to cultural norms (Schur, 1971). Thus, cultural relativists believe that there is no single, universal definition of abnormality but different definitions within different cultures.

Opponents of cultural relativism argue that there are some behaviors or experiences that almost all cultures consider abnormal, or at least undesirable. For example, many different cultures recognize experiences of severe emotional pain, which we label *anxiety* or *depression,* as undesirable states that need to be treated by healers. Similarly, most cultures define sane behaviors as those under the control of the individual and guided by societal norms, and insane behaviors as those not under the individual's control and not enacted for some social function. For example, among the Yoruba people of Africa, a healer who acts like a dog during healing rituals but clearly understands that he is not truly a dog is considered sane. However, a man who believes that he is truly possessed by a dog and is not able to control when he does and does not act like a dog is considered insane.

Opponents of cultural relativism have also pointed to the dangers that arise when societal norms are allowed to dictate what is normal and abnormal. Throughout history, societies have labeled individuals and groups abnormal in order to justify controlling or silencing them. Hitler branded Jews abnormal and used this as one justification for the Holocaust. The former Soviet Union branded political dissidents mentally ill and jailed them in mental hospitals. When the slave trade was active in the United States, slaves who tried to escape their masters were diagnosed as having *drapetomania,* a sickness that caused them to desire freedom. This provided a justification for capturing them and returning them to their masters (Szaz, 1971). In 1851, Dr. Samuel Cartwright, a prominent physician, published an essay in the prestigious *New Orleans Medical and Surgical Journal* titled "Report on the Diseases and Physical Peculiarities of the Negro Race," in which he argued that

> The cause, in most cases, that induces the Negro to run away from service, is as much a disease of the mind as any other species of mental alienation, and much more curable, as a general rule. With the advantages of proper medical advice, strictly followed, this troublesome practice that many Negroes have of running away, can be almost entirely prevented.

cultural relativism
view that norms among different cultures set the standard for what counts as normal behavior, which implies that abnormal behavior can only be defined relative to these norms; no universal definition of abnormality is therefore possible; only definitions of abnormality relative to a specific culture are possible

One problem with cultural relativism is that societies can brand some groups as abnormal to justify persecuting them, as Hitler did against the Jews.

Cartwright also described a disease called *dysaesthesia Aethiopis,* the refusal to work for one's master. To cure this "disease," Cartwright prescribed the following:

> The liver, skin and kidneys should be stimulated to activity, and be made to assist in decarbonising the blood. The best means to stimulate the skin is, first, to have the patient well washed with warm water and soap; then to anoint it all over with oil, and to slap the oil with a broad leather strap; then to put the patient to some hard kind of work in the open air and sunshine, that will compel him to expand his lungs, as chopping wood, splitting rails, or sawing with the cross-cut or whip saw.

Thus, using medical terminology, Cartwright recommended whipping slaves who refused to work and then assigning them to hard labor to "revitalize" their lungs and bring them back to their senses. We might like to believe that Cartwright's essay represented the extreme views of just one person, but he was writing on behalf of the Medical Association of London. Although most modern psychologists acknowledge that culture and societal norms can influence labels of abnormality, they do not accept the cultural relativist view that abnormality can only be defined as what deviates from societal norms.

Statistical Deviance

statistical deviance
view that normal behaviors are those performed by a statistical majority of people and that abnormal behaviors are those that deviate from the majority, occurring only rarely or infrequently

A second criterion that has been suggested for designating behaviors abnormal is **statistical deviance**. Under this criterion, behaviors that are rare or unusual are considered abnormal, whereas behaviors that are typical or usual are considered normal. There are at least two major problems with this criterion, however. First, although the criterion may seem objective, someone still has to decide how rare a behavior must be in order to call it abnormal. Are behaviors that only 10 percent of the population exhibits abnormal? Or do we want to set a more strict cutoff and say that only behaviors that 1 percent or less of the population exhibits are abnormal? Choosing a cutoff is as subjective a judgment as relying on people's personal opinions as to what is abnormal and normal. The second major problem with the statistical deviance criterion is that most people would not want to label rare positive behaviors abnormal. For example, we don't label the playing of a piano virtuoso abnormal; we label it gifted.

Subjective Discomfort

subjective discomfort
view that a person must both suffer as a result of a certain behavior and wish to be rid of it in order for it to qualify as abnormal

A third criterion that has been suggested for labeling behaviors abnormal is the **subjective discomfort** criterion. Proponents of this view suggest that behaviors should only be considered abnormal if the individual suffers as a result of the behaviors and wishes to be rid of them. This criterion avoids, to some extent, the problems of using societal norms as the criterion for abnormality. If a person's behaviors violate societal norms but do not cause him or her any discomfort, then perhaps the behaviors should not be considered abnormal. This viewpoint contributed to a change in how psychologists and psychiatrists viewed one behavior pattern—homosexuality. Gays and lesbians argued that their sexual orientaton is a natural part of themselves and a characteristic that causes them no discomfort and that they don't wish to alter or eliminate. In addition, despite the stress that gays and lesbians endure because of prejudice against them, homosexuals are no more likely than heterosexuals to experience serious forms of psychological distress (Herek, 1990). Partially based on these arguments, the American Psychiatric Association removed homosexuality from its list of recognized psychological disorders in 1973 (Spitzer, 1981).

Some therapists have objected to the subjective discomfort criterion, however, because people are not always aware of severe problems their behaviors create for themselves or for others. For example, some people who have lost touch with reality wander the streets aimlessly, not eating or taking care of themselves, in danger of starvation or exposure to the elements. These people may not be fully aware that they have severe problems and often do not seek help. If we require that people acknowledge and seek help for their behaviors before we call those behaviors abnormal, some people who could benefit greatly from help might never get it.

Although extremely talented people like Ray Charles are rare, we do not label them as abnormal; we think of them as gifted.

Mental Disease or Illness Criterion

A fourth way of defining abnormality is as behaviors that result from mental disease or illness. This **mental disease** or **mental illness criterion** begs the question, however, of how we define *mental disease* or *illness*. The terms imply that there is a clear, identifiable physical process or structure that is deviant from "health" and that leads to specific behaviors or symptoms. However, to date, there is no medical test that people can take that definitively indicates whether they have a mental illness. Instead, biologically oriented clinicians infer that there is some sort of physical process underlying a set of observed symptoms, and they search for that physical process. The mental disorder or illness is simply a hypothetical construct or conceptual abstraction used as a label or description of this set of symptoms. Thus, for example, the term *obsessive compulsive disorder* is a construct or label used to designate a certain set of symptoms. When we say someone "has" obsessive compulsive disorder, we can only mean that he or she is exhibiting this set of symptoms. The term *obsessive compulsive disorder* does not refer to some identifiable physical entity that is found in all people who exhibit these symptoms.

mental disease or mental illness criterion
view that abnormal behaviors are those that result from a mental illness; this view does not explain how "mental illness" is itself defined

 Think about people whom you have considered abnormal, unusual, disturbed. What criteria were you using to make this judgment?

The Consensus

So how do the majority of researchers and clinicians in the mental health field decide whether a behavior or set of behaviors is abnormal? The consensus is that behaviors that cause people to *suffer distress* and that *prevent them from functioning in daily life* are abnormal and should be the focus of research and intervention (Spitzer, 1981). Such behaviors are often described as **maladaptive** or *dysfunctional*. Of course, what is maladaptive and what makes people suffer is in part determined by the norms of society. Psychologists have tried to reserve the label *maladaptive* for behaviors that have one or more of the following characteristics:

1. They are physically damaging to the individual.
2. They cause the individual emotional suffering or harm.

maladaptive
term referring to behaviors that cause people who have them physical or emotional harm, prevent them from functioning in daily life, and/or indicate that they have lost touch with reality and/or cannot control their thoughts and behavior (also called *dysfunctional*)

3. They severely interfere with the individual's ability to function in daily life.
4. They indicate that the individual has lost touch with reality and cannot control his or her behaviors or thoughts.

Still, most psychologists recognize that culture and gender can influence many aspects of abnormal or maladaptive behavior. First, culture and gender influence how likely it is that a given maladaptive behavior will be shown. These differences in vulnerabilities to different types of abnormality can provide clues as to the causes of a given type of abnormality. For example, the fact that men are nearly twice as likely as women to suffer problems due to alcohol suggests that something about being male—something about male biology, male personality, or the social pressures put on men—contributes to the development of alcoholism. Second, culture and gender can influence the ways people express distress or lose touch with reality. For example, people who lose touch with reality will often believe that they are deities, but whether an individual believes he is Jesus Christ or the Buddha depends on his religious background. Third, culture and gender can influence people's willingness to admit to certain types of maladaptive behaviors. For example, people in Eskimo and Tahitian cultures may be reluctant to admit to angry feelings because of strong cultural norms against the expression of anger. However, the Kaluli of New Guinea and the Yanamamo of Brazil value the expression of anger and have elaborate and complex rituals for expressing anger (Jenkins, Kleinman, & Good, 1990). Fourth, culture and gender can influence the types of treatments that are deemed acceptable or helpful for maladaptive behaviors. For example, women may be more willing than men to accept psychological treatments for problems. Throughout this book, we will explore these influences of culture and gender on maladaptive behaviors.

 What are some of the ways the current consensus definitions of abnormality could be misused or exploited?

Before we discuss how modern psychology views maladaptive behaviors, we shall review how abnormality has been viewed historically and the major events leading to our current perspectives on abnormality.

Historical Perspectives on Abnormality

References to madness, insanity, or other forms of mental disorder can be found throughout the history of humankind. Three types of theories of the causes of mental disorders have competed for dominance across time. The *natural theories* saw mental disorders as similar to physical diseases, caused by the breakdown of some system in the body. The appropriate cure for mental disorders, according to the natural theories, was the restoration of the body to good health. The *supernatural theories* saw mental disorders as the result of divine intervention, curses, demonic possession, and personal sin. To rid the person of the disorder, religious rituals, exorcisms, confessions, and atonement were prescribed, although people who were thought to be possessed or otherwise touched by magic or the gods were sometimes simply ostracized or killed. The third type of theory of mental disorder consisted of *psychological or stress-related theories,* which saw mental disorders as the result of traumas, such as bereavement, or chronic stress. According to these theories, rest, relaxation, a change of environment, and certain herbal medicines were sometimes helpful to the afflicted person. These different theories influenced how people afflicted with disorders were regarded and treated in the society. Obviously, a person thought to be insane because she was a sinner would be treated differently from a person thought to be insane because of a physiological problem.

Ancient Theories

Some of the earliest written sources on mental disorders are ancient Chinese texts on medicine (Tseng, 1973). *Nei Ching* (Classic of Internal Medicine) was probably written by Huang Ti, the third legendary emperor of China, around 2674 B.C. Chinese medicine was based on the concept of yin and yang; the human body was said to contain a positive force and a negative force that both confront and complement each other. If the two forces are in balance, the individual is healthy. If not, illness, including insanity, can result. For example, insane excitement was considered the result of an excessive positive force:

Some of the earliest medical writings on mental disorders come from ancient Chinese texts.

> The person suffering from excited insanity initially feels sad, eating and sleeping less; he then becomes grandiose, feeling that he is very smart and noble, talking and scolding day and night, singing, behaving strangely, seeing strange things, hearing strange voices, believing that he can see the devil or gods, etc. As treatment for such an excited condition withholding food was suggested, since food was considered to be the source of positive force and the patient was thought to be in need of a decrease in such force. (Tseng, 1973, p. 570)

Another theory in ancient Chinese medical philosophy is that various kinds of emotion in humans are affected by specific visceral organs. When the "vital air" is flowing on one of these organs, emotion ensues. For example, when air flows on the heart, a person feels joy; when on the lungs, sorrow; when on the liver, anger; when on the spleen, worry; and when on the kidney, fear. This theory encourages people to live in an orderly and harmonious way, particularly in the areas of eating and sex, so as to maintain proper movement of vital air. Thus, the Chinese perspective on psychological symptoms was largely a natural theory in ancient times.

Although Chinese medicine was never as strongly influenced by supernatural theories as Western medicine was, during the Chin and T'ang dynasties (A.D. 420 to 618, respectively), the rise of Taoism and Buddhism led to some religious interpretations of mental disorders. Evil winds and ghosts were blamed for bewitching people, erratic emotional displays, and uncontrolled behavior. Religious theories of abnormality declined in China after this period, however.

Other ancient writings on mental disorders are found in the papyri of Egypt and Mesopotamia (Veith, 1965). The oldest of these is a document known as the Kahun Papyrus, after the ancient Egyptian city in which it was found, and dates from about 1900 B.C. This document lists a number of disorders, each followed by a physician's judgment of the cause of the disorder and the appropriate treatment. Several of the disorders apparently left people with unexplainable aches and pains, sadness or distress, and apathy about life. Some illustrative cases are "a woman who loves bed; she does not rise and she does not shake it"; "a woman who is pained in her teeth and jaws; she knows not how to open her mouth"; and "a woman aching in all her limbs with pain in the sockets of her eyes" (Veith, 1965, p. 3).

These disorders were said to occur only in women and were attributed to a "wandering uterus." Apparently, the Egyptians believed that the uterus could become dislodged and wander throughout a woman's body, interfering with her other organs and causing these symptoms. Later the Greeks, holding to the same theory of the anatomy of women, named this disorder **hysteria** (derived from the Greek word *hysteria*, which means *uterus*). In the Egyptian papyri, the prescribed treatment for this disorder involved the use of strong-smelling substances to drive the uterus back to its proper place. Another and more complete papyrus, the Papyrus Ebers, recommends a combination of physiological interventions and incantations to the gods to assist in the healing process (Veith, 1965). One

hysteria

term used by the ancient Greeks and Egyptians to describe what is now referred to as conversion disorder (a disorder in which a person loses functioning in some part of his or her body following a stressful event); the Ancients believed that hysteria was caused by a woman's uterus, which would wander throughout the body and interfere with other organs

In the Bible, David played his harp as the evil spirits departed from Saul, relieving Saul of his emotional and physical distress.

astounding feature of the Papyrus Ebers is that it provides a detailed description of the brain, and clearly ascribes mental functioning to the brain. Thus, the perspective of the ancient Egyptians on mental disorders was driven largely by natural theories of these disorders, although the Egyptians clearly believed that supernatural powers could intervene in the cure of (and perhaps cause) disorders.

The Old Testament holds several references to madness. In Deuteronomy, which dates from the seventh century B.C., Moses warns his people that if they "will not obey the voice of the Lord your God or be careful to do all his commandments and his statutes . . . the Lord will smite you with madness and blindness and confusion of the mind . . ." (Deuteronomy 28:15, 28). Thus, the Hebrews saw madness as a punishment from God. People stricken with madness were to confess their sins and repent in order to achieve relief. There are several passages in the Old Testament in which people thought to be mad were also attended by physicians, however (e.g., Job 13:4). So the Hebrews believed that physicians could at least comfort, if not cure, people of madness.

 Biological theories and treatments of abnormality were sometimes seen as evil or blasphemous in ancient days. Why might this have happened?

Beginning with Homer, the Greeks wrote frequently of people thought to be mad (Veith, 1965). Flute music played an important role in religious rituals, and there are accounts of people hearing and seeing phantom flute players by day and night. The physician Hippocrates (460–377 B.C.) describes a case of a common phobia. A man could not walk alongside a cliff, or pass over a bridge, or jump over even a shallow ditch without feeling unable to control his limbs and having his vision impaired. Another physician, Aretaeus (A.D. 50–130), describes an artisan who appears to have had symptoms of what we now call *agoraphobia* (people with this disorder become housebound because they experience episodes of panic when away from their safe abodes): "If at any time he went away to the market, the bath, or on any other engagement, having laid down his tools, he would first groan, then shrug his shoulders as he went out. But when he had got out of sight of the domestics, or of the work and the place where it was performed, he became completely mad; yet if he returned speedily he recovered his reason again" (cited in Veith, 1965, p. 96). The traditional interpretation of madness throughout much of Greek and Roman history was that it was an affliction from the gods. The afflicted would retreat to temples honoring the god Aesculapius, where priests would hold healing ceremonies. Plato (429–347 B.C.) and Socrates (384–322 B.C.) argued that some forms of madness were divine and could be the source of great literary and prophetic gifts.

For the most part, however, Greek physicians rejected supernatural explanations of mental disorders. Hippocrates, often referred to as the father of medicine, argued that mental disorders were like other diseases of the body. According to Hippocrates, the body is composed of four basic humors: blood, phlegm, yellow bile, and black bile. All diseases, including mental disorders, were caused by imbalances in the body's essential humors, typically an excess of one of the humors. Based on careful observation of his many patients, including listening to their dreams, Hippocrates classified mental disorders into epilepsy, mania, melancholia, and brain fever. He also recognized hysteria, although he did not view it as a mental disease. Like others, he thought that this was a disorder confined to women and caused by a wandering uterus.

The treatments prescribed by the Greek physicians were intended to restore the balance of the humors. Sometimes these treatments were physiological and intrusive; for example, bleeding a patient was a common practice for disorders thought to result from an excess of blood. Other times, treatments involved rest, relaxation, change of climate or scenery, change of diet, and a temperate life. Some of the nonmedical treatments prescribed by these physicians sound remarkably like prescriptions made by modern psychotherapists. For example, Hippocrates believed that removing a patient from a difficult family could help to restore mental health.

It is clear in the writings of Hippocrates, Plato, Socrates, and other writers of the Graeco-Roman era that these physicians and philosophers believed madness is not a disgrace and that people who are mad should not be held accountable for their behaviors. Relatives of people considered mad were encouraged to confine the afflicted person to the home and care for him or her in a humane manner. The state claimed no responsibility for insane people; there were no asylums or institutions, other than the religious temples, to house and care for them. The state could, however, take rights away from people declared mad. Relatives could bring suit against those they considered mad, and the state could award the property of the insane person to the relatives. People declared mad could not marry or acquire or dispose of their own property. Poor people who were considered mad were simply left to roam the streets if they were not violent. If they were violent, they were locked away in stocks and chains. The general public greatly feared madness of any form, and people thought to be mad, even if divinely mad, were often shunned or even stoned.

The Middle Ages

Although some psychiatric historians have characterized the Middle Ages (around A.D. 400–1400) as being dominated by supernatural theories of mental disorders (e.g., Zilboorg & Henry, 1941), even within Europe, supernatural theories of mental disorders did not predominate until late in the Middle Ages, between the eleventh and fifteenth centuries. Prior to the eleventh century, witches and witchcraft were accepted as real but considered merely nuisances that were overrated by superstitious people. Physical illness or injury or severe emotional shock were most often seen as the causes of bizarre behaviors. For example, English court records of examinations of persons thought to be mentally ill attributed their illnesses to factors such as a "blow received on the head" or explained that they were "induced by fear of his father." They explained of a person that "he has lost his reason owing to a long and incurable infirmity" and referred to "an illness which he had before that time" (Neugebauer, 1979, p. 481). Lay people probably did believe in demons and curses as causes of mental disorders, but there is strong evidence that physicians and government officials attributed mental disorders to physical causes or traumas.

Beginning in the eleventh century, however, the Church faced a number of threats to its power, owing largely to rebellions caused by the economic and political inequalities of the times and the breakdown of feudalism. The Church chose to interpret these threats in terms of heresy and satanism. The Inquisition was established originally to rid the earth of religious heretics, but eventually those practicing witchcraft or satanism were also the focus of hunts. The witch hunts continued long after the Reformation and were perhaps at their height during the fifteenth and seventeenth centuries, the period known as the Renaissance (Kroll, 1973).

Some psychiatric historians have argued that persons accused of witchcraft must have been mentally ill (Veith, 1965; Zilboorg & Henry, 1941). Accused witches sometimes confessed to speaking with the devil, flying on the backs of animals, and other unusual behaviors. Such people may have been experiencing delusions (false beliefs) or hallucinations (unreal perceptual experiences), which are signs of the disorder schizophrenia. Accused witches were also said to have a devil's mark on their bodies, which was often invisible but was insensitive to even the most severe pain. Professional "witch prickers" would poke accused witches all over their bodies to find the devil's mark, and areas of insensitivity were found in some of the accused. Psychiatric historians have interpreted this insensitivity as a sign of hysteria or self-hypnosis.

Some people burned at the stake as witches may have been suffering from mental disorders that caused them to act abnormally.

Many of the confessions of accused witches may have been extracted through brutal torture or under the promise of a stay of execution in exchange for confession (Spanos, 1978). The accused witches' purported insensitivity to pain indeed could have been real but may have been due to poor nutrition and ill health, common in medieval times, as opposed to any influence of the devil. Professional witch prickers were also known to use techniques to make it falsely appear that a person was insensitive to pain. For example, some witch prickers used collapsible needles attached to hollow shafts. When the needle was pressed against the accused's body, it collapsed into the hollow shaft, making it appear that the needle pierced deeply into the accused's flesh without inducing pain.

Accusations of being a witch were often leveled by officials against certain citizens or by one citizen against another as a means of social punishment or control. For example, in 1581, Johann Klenke was accused of witchcraft by the mayor of his town. This accusation came after Klenke had lent the mayor money and then insisted on having it paid back (Rosen, 1968). In England, during the sixteenth and seventeenth centuries, persons accused of being witches were typically older women, unmarried and poor, who often begged for food and money, and were considered by their neighbors to be foul mouthed and disgusting. These women sometimes cultivated the myth that they were witches to frighten their neighbors into giving them money. If some misfortune befell one of these neighbors, however, one of these older women might be accused of casting a spell on the neighbor and then remanded to authorities for prosecution. The neighbor thus had an explanation (other than personal misdeeds or other behavior) for his or her misfortune and could be rid of the troublesome old woman.

Still, there were some people who truly believed they themselves were witches. These people may have been suffering from mental disorders. Indeed, even during the witch hunts, some physicians risked condemnation by the Church and even death by arguing that accused witches were suffering from mental illnesses. In 1563, Johann Weyer published *The Deception of Dreams,* in which he argued that the people accused of being witches were women suffering from melancholy (depression) and senility. The Church banned Weyer's writings, however, and he was scorned by many of his peers. Reginald Scot in his *Discovery of Witchcraft* (1584) vehemently argued that accused witches were women suffering from mental disorders: "These women are but diseased wretches suffering from melancholy, and their words, actions, reasoning, and gestures show that sickness has affected their brains and impaired their powers of judgment" (in Castiglioni, 1946, p. 253). Again, the Church, and this time the State, refuted the arguments and banned Scot's writings.

As is often the case, change came from within. In the sixteenth century, Teresa of Avila, a Spanish nun who was later canonized, explained that the mass hysteria that had broken out among a group of nuns was not the work of the devil but the effect of infirmities or sickness. She argued that these nuns were *comas enfermas,* or "as if sick." She sought out natural causes for the nuns' strange behaviors and concluded that they were due to melancholy, a weak imagination, or drowsiness and sleepiness (Sarbin & Juhasz, 1967).

However, it is also possible that some people who truly believed they were witches were not suffering from mental disorders. The culture in which they lived so completely accepted the existence of witches and witchcraft that these people may simply have used these cultural beliefs to explain their own feelings and behaviors, even when these feelings and behaviors were not components of some type of mental disorder. In addition, most writings of medieval times and Renaissance times, including writings from the witch-hunt period in Salem, Massachusetts, clearly distinguish between people who are mad and people who are witches. This distinction between madness and witchcraft continues to this day in cultures that believe in witchcraft.

What are the modern equivalents of the witch hunts—the singling out of certain groups of people to blame for current societal problems?

The Growth of Asylums in Europe and America

As early as the twelfth century, many towns in Europe took some responsibility for housing and caring for people considered mentally ill (Kroll, 1973). Remarkable among these towns was Gheel, in Belgium, where townspeople regularly took into their homes the mentally ill who came to the shrine of Saint Dymphna for cures.

General hospitals began to include special rooms or facilities for people with mental disorders in about the eleventh or twelfth century. In 1326 a *Dollhaus* (madhouse) was constructed as part of the Georgehospital at Elbing. In 1375 a *Tollkiste* (mad cell) was mentioned in the municipal records of Hamburg (Kroll, 1973). Unlike the humane treatment people with mental disorders received in places like Gheel, treatment in these early hospitals was far from humane. The mentally ill were little more than inmates, housed against their will, often in extremely harsh conditions. One of the most famous of these hospitals was the Hospital of Saint Mary of Bethlehem, in London, which officially became a mental hospital in 1547. This hospital, nicknamed *Bedlam*, was famous for its deplorable conditions, which were highlighted in Shakespeare's *King Lear:*

> "Bedlam beggers, who, with roaring voices . . . Sometimes with lunatic bans, sometimes with prayers enforce their charity" (*King Lear,* Act II, Scene iii)

Shakespeare is referring to the practice of forcing patients at this hospital to beg in the streets for money. At Bedlam and other mental hospitals established in Europe in the sixteenth, seventeenth, and eighteenth centuries patients were exhibited to the public for a fee. They lived in filth and confinement, often chained to walls or locked in small boxes. The following description of the treatment of patients in La Bicêtre Hospital in Paris provides an example of typical care:

> The patients were ordinarily shackled to the walls of their dark, unlighted cells by iron collars which held them flat against the wall and permitted little movement. Ofttimes there were also iron hoops around the waists of the patients and both their hands and feet were chained. Although these chains usually permitted enough movement that the patients could feed themselves out of bowls, they often kept them from being able to lie down at night. Since little was known about dietetics, and the patients were presumed to be animals anyway, little attention was paid to whether they were adequately fed or whether the food was good or bad. The cells were furnished only with straw and were never swept or cleaned; the patient remained in the midst of all the accumulated ordure. No one visited the cells except at feeding time, no provision was made for warmth, and even the most elementary gestures of humanity were lacking. (Adapted from Selling, 1940, pp. 54–55)

The laws regarding the confinement of the mentally ill in Europe were concerned with the protection of the public and the ill person's relatives. For example, Dalton's 1618 edition of the *Common Law* states that "It is lawful for the parents, kinsmen or other friends of a man that is mad, or frantic . . . to take him and put him into a house, to bind or chain him, and to beat him with rods, and to do any other forcible act to reclaim him, or to keep him so he shall do no hurt" (in Allderidge, 1979). The first *Act for Regulating Madhouses* in England was not passed until 1774, with the intention of cleaning up the deplorable conditions in hospitals and madhouses and protecting people from being

"Bedlam"—the Hospital of St. Mary of Bethlehem—was famous for the chaotic and deplorable conditions in which people with mental disorders were kept.

unjustly jailed for insanity. This act provided for the licensing and inspection of madhouses and required that a physician, surgeon, or apothecary sign a certificate before a patient could be admitted. These provisions applied only to paying patients in private madhouses, however, and not to the poor people confined to workhouses for lunatics.

The conditions of asylums in America were not much better. In 1756, Benjamin Franklin helped to establish the Pennsylvania Hospital in Philadelphia, which included some cells or wards for mental patients. In 1773, the Public Hospital in Williamsburg, Virginia, became the first hospital exclusively for the mentally ill. The treatment of patients, although designed to restore health and balance to the mind, included powerful electrical shocks, bleeding, plunging into ice water or hot water, starvation, and heavy use of restraints (Bennett, 1947).

It is worth noting that these asylums typically were established and run by people who thought that mental disorders were medical illnesses. Thus, although the demonology and witchcraft theories of the Middle Ages have often been decried as leading to brutal treatment of people with mental illnesses, the medical theories of the times did not necessarily lead to much more gentle treatment, largely because these treatments were based on beliefs and understandings about anatomy and physiology that we now know to be incorrect.

What are some ways that people considered abnormal in our modern culture are mistreated and ostracized?

The Humanitarian Movement

Fortunately, the eighteenth and nineteenth centuries saw the growth of a movement toward a more humane treatment of the mentally ill. This new form of treatment was based on the philosophy that people become mad because they are separated from nature and succumb to the stresses imposed by the rapid social changes of the period (Rosen, 1968). This was a heavily psychological theory of mental disorders, which suggested that the appropriate treatment for madness is rest and relaxation in a serene and physically appealing place, an *asylum* from the chaotic world. Patients were released from their chains and allowed to walk freely around the asylum estates set aside for them. They were provided with clean and sunny rooms, comfortable sleeping quarters, and good food. Nurses and professional therapists were trained to work with the patients, to help them restore their sense of tranquillity, and to help them engage in planned social activities. This *moral management* of mental hospitals became widespread in Europe and the United States. Leaders in this movement included Phillipe Pinel in France, William Tuke in England, and Benjamin Rush in the United States.

Dorothea Dix crusaded for moral treatment of mental patients in the United States.

One of the most militant crusaders for a moral treatment of the insane was Dorothea Dix. A retired schoolteacher living in Boston in 1841, Dix discovered the negligence and brutality that characterized the treatment of poor people with mental disorders, who were often locked away in prisons in the mid-nineteenth century. She began a crusade to free these people from the prisons and to establish state hospitals where the indigent insane could receive humane treatment. Over the next forty years, she helped to establish over thirty mental institutions in the United States, Canada, Newfoundland, and Scotland.

In the late nineteenth century, the moral management approach to the treatment of mental patients was supplanted by the *mental hygiene movement,* which argued again that all mental disorders are medical diseases that should be treated biologically. Although this was certainly not a new idea, it gained tremendous force during this period because of the great strides that were being made in the prevention of major medical diseases that had previously claimed the lives of large segments of the population, such as cholera and typhus (Deutsch, 1937). One of the founders of this movement was Clifford Beers. During his undergraduate days at Yale, Beers' brother developed epilepsy. Beers was overcome with fear that he would also develop this disease. In June 1900, Beers threw himself from a fourth-floor window, in a suicide attempt prompted by his false belief that he had become an epileptic. He escaped with only broken bones. Beers' obsession with becoming epileptic passed with this incident but was replaced with other delusions of persecution and grandeur. As a result, he spent three years as a patient in three mental hospitals in Connecticut. Unfortunately for Beers, these hospitals did not practice moral treatment. Beers was beaten, choked, locked away for long periods in dark, padded cells, and put in a strait-jacket for up to twenty-one days.

Phillipe Pinel, a leader in the moral movement in France, helped to free mental patients from the horrible conditions of the hospitals.

In 1903 Beers was released, somehow a healthy man. He vowed to change the way mental patients were treated. He began to do so by writing a personal account of these institutions, which was published in 1908 as *A Mind That Found Itself.* In this book, Beers outlined a plan for reforms in the treatment of the mentally ill and for the prevention of mental illness. He advocated public education about mental illness and early treatment for those who were afflicted. One of Beers' supporters was Dr. Adolph Meyer, who was himself revolutionizing the treatment of mental patients by advocating the treatment of the "whole individual," including assisting former mental patients in their reintegration into society.

Unfortunately, however, effective biological treatments were not developed for most major mental disorders until well into the twentieth century. Until these treatments were developed, mental patients who could not afford private care were basically warehoused in large state institutions and not given the psychological and social rehabilitation prescribed by the moral management theories. These institutions were often overcrowded and isolated far from cities or towns. The physical isolation of the mental hospitals contributed to the slow progress in the application of medical advances to the treatment of mental disorders (Deutsch, 1937).

Psychic Epidemics and Mass Hysteria

Throughout the recorded history of abnormality, one of the most interesting phenomena has been the *psychic epidemic* or *mass madness.* During such epidemics, large groups of people apparently are afflicted with the same set of bizarre behavioral symptoms and may seem to lose touch with reality. *Dance frenzies* or *manias* were observed in regions of Germany over a four-month period in 1374. A monk, Peter of Herental, described one such instance:

> Both men and women were abused by the devil to such a degree that they danced in their homes, in the churches and in the streets, holding each other's hands and leaping in the air. While they danced they called out the names of demons, such as Friskes and others, but they were unaware of this nor did they pay attention to modesty even though people watched them. At the end of the dance, they felt such pains in the chest, that if their friends did not tie linen clothes tightly around their waists, they cried out like madmen that they were dying (in Rosen, 1968, pp. 196–197).

This picture of "moonstruck" women dancing frenetically in seventeenth-century France illustrates one type of psychic epidemic.

Other instances of dance frenzy were reported in 1428 during the feast of Saint Vitus, at Schaffhausen, at which a monk danced himself to death. Again in 1518, a large epidemic of uncontrolled dance frenzy occurred at the chapel of Saint Vitus at Hohlenstein, near Zabern. According to one account, more than 400 people danced during the four-week period the frenzy lasted. Some writers of the time began to call the frenzied dancing *Saint Vitus' dance.*

A similar phenomenon was *tarantism,* which was seen in Italy as early as the fourteenth century but became prominent in the seventeenth century. People would suddenly develop an acute pain, which they attributed to the bite of a tarantula. They would jump around and dance wildly in the streets, tearing at their clothes and beating each other with whips. Some people would dig holes in the earth and roll on the ground; others howled and made obscene gestures.

Many people interpreted dance frenzies and tarantism as the results of possession by the devil. The behaviors may have been the remnants of ancient rituals performed by people worshipping the Greek god Dionysus. Other groups in which dance frenzies or similar behavior patterns were observed later, in the eighteenth century, were religious sects. These included the Shakers, the mystical Russian sects such as the Chlysti, certain Jewish sects, congregations of the early Methodist movement, and the Quakers. During religious services, members of these sects might become so emotionally charged that they would jerk around violently, running, singing, screaming, and dancing. This type of religious service tended to be more popular among people suffering great economic and social deprivation and alienation. The enthusiastic behavioral expression of religious fervor can act as a welcome release from the tensions and stresses of simply trying to survive in a hostile world.

Modern cases of mass hysteria have tended to focus on modern concerns, such as environmental toxins and terrorist plots. For example, in 1982, the media reported the poisoning of some Chicago-area residents by Tylenol capsules laced with cyanide. Soon after, approximately 200 people attending a high school football game reported sudden illness after drinking soda. No reason for the illnesses could be found, and some officials believed that the illnesses were related to the Tylenol scare. In 1983, a case of mass hysteria nearly had serious political repercussions. Hundreds of school girls on the West Bank of Palestine developed the same mysterious physical symptoms. At first, some Arab and Israeli leaders thought that the girls had been poisoned by Israeli forces. Later, it was determined that these girls were showing psychological symptoms due to the chronic unrest in their communities (Hefez, 1985).

More recently, an episode of mass hysteria in the United States was attributed to the stress caused by the Persian Gulf War of 1991 (Rockney & Lemke, 1992). One of the great fears during that war was that the Iraqis would use chemical weapons either on the military troops fighting against them in the Persian Gulf or even in a terrorist attack in the United States. On February 8, 1991, a number of students and teachers in a high school in Rhode Island thought they smelled noxious fumes coming from the ventilation system. The first person to detect these fumes, a 14-year-old girl, fell to the floor, crying and saying that her stomach hurt and her eyes stung. Other students and the teacher in that room then began to experience symptoms. They were moved into the hallway with a great deal of commotion. Soon, students and teachers from adjacent rooms, who could clearly see into the hallway, began to experience symptoms. Eventually, 21 people (17 students and 4 teachers) were admitted to the local hospital emergency room. All were hyperventilating, and most complained of dizziness, headache, and nausea. Although some of them initially showed symptoms of mild carbon monoxide intoxication in blood tests, no evidence of toxic gas in the school could be found. The physicians treating the children and teachers concluded that the outbreak was a case of mass hysteria prompted by the fear of chemical warfare during the Persian Gulf War.

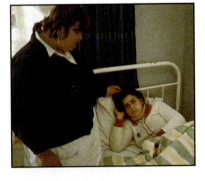

In 1983, hundreds of school girls on the West Bank of Palestine thought they had been poisoned. Their symptoms were later attributed to psychological distress due to the unrest in their communities.

- There are three types of theories that have influenced the definition and treatment of abnormality over the ages: the natural theories, the psychological theories, and the supernatural theories.

- The supernatural theories have been rejected in most modern, developed countries, at least by scientists and mental health professionals, but are still accepted in many developing countries. Over the ages, believers in the supernatural have often been very tolerant of some very bizarre behaviors (by modern standards), if those behaviors are considered "gifts" from the gods or used as part of religious rituals. Supernatural theories have also led, however, to the killing or banning of people thought to be cursed or possessed.

- Psychological theories of abnormality have been around for most of written history, although they appear not to have been as prominent as the supernatural or natural theories until the last century. These theories recognize that humans are social and emotional creatures, who are impacted by events in the environment and by their relationships with others. One advantage of these theories, in terms of the types of treatments they often lead to, is that they view abnormal behavior as changeable. People can be helped to overcome distress or disorder by helping them restore a good relationship with their environment or with other people. The psychological theories, however, have sometimes been used to "blame the victims" of psychological disorders. That is, proponents of these theories have sometimes suggested—wrongly—that people have control over their abnormality and thus can be held responsible for their abnormal behavior.

- The natural, or biological, theories of mental disorders are often considered to be the most advanced and the most objective of theories. Certainly, proponents of the biological theories have rescued many people suffering from mental disorders from harm or even death at the hands of believers in the supernatural theories and have argued that people cannot be blamed for having a medical disease that happens to result in abnormal behaviors. As we have seen, however, "bad medicine" in the form of incorrect theories of anatomy and disease has led to treatments that are often worse than the symptoms for which the person is being treated. Biological theories have also been misused by people wishing to argue that a certain group of people is biologically inferior and therefore deserves to be treated in deplorable ways.

Looking Ahead

In modern, mainstream research and practice in abnormal psychology, biological and psychosocial theories predominate. Chapter 3 will provide an overview of these theories. Throughout this book we will discuss the application of these theories to specific disorders. Although biological and psychosocial theories traditionally have been viewed as competing with each other for which one *best* explains psychological disorders, many clinicians and researchers now believe that theories that integrate biological, psychological, and social perspectives on abnormality will prove most valid and useful. We will highlight these integrated theories throughout each chapter of this book and in special *Bio-Psycho-Social Integrations*, at the end of each of the following chapters.

What about supernatural theories? Most cultures still have *spiritual healers* of one type or another. As we consider cross-cultural perspectives on psychological disorders, we will note the supernatural theories some cultures hold about abnormality and the healing rituals that emerge from these theories. However, even in cultures in which most healers do not subscribe to supernatural theories of abnormality, laypeople often still believe in the power of supernatural forces to cause or cure their psychological problems. These lay beliefs influence what type of healer a person with a psychological problem might seek out and how he or she might present the psychological problem to a potential therapist. Thus, even though supernatural theories may not be believed by therapists, they arise in the practice of treating people with psychological problems because these clients bring them into discussions with their therapists.

 Clients bring with them into therapy their own conceptualizations of their disorders, which often are different from the therapists' conceptualizations of disorders. To what extent do you think therapists should "go along" with clients' conceptualizations of disorders?

Professions Within Abnormal Psychology

In our times, there are a number of different professions that are concerned with abnormal or maladaptive behavior. Psychiatry is a branch of medicine that focuses on psychological disorders. Psychiatrists have an M.D. degree and have specialized in the treatment of psychological problems. Psychiatrists can prescribe medications for the treatment of these problems; some also have been trained to conduct psychotherapies that involve talking with people about their problems. Clinical psychologists typically have a Ph.D. in psychology, with a specialization in psychological problems. Clinical psychologists can conduct psychotherapy, but they do not currently prescribe medications. Many clinical psychologists also conduct research on the causes and appropriate treatments of psychological problems. Clinical social workers have a master's degree in social work and often focus on helping people with psychological problems to overcome social conditions contributing to their problems, such as joblessness or homelessness. Psychiatric nurses have a degree in nursing, with a specialization in the treatment of people with severe psychological problems. They often work on inpatient psychiatric wards in hospitals, delivering medical care and certain forms of psychotherapy, such as group therapy to increase patients' contacts with one another.

Each of these professions has its rewards and its limitations. Students who are interested in one or more of these professions often find it helpful to volunteer to be a research assistant in studies of psychological problems or to volunteer to work in a psychiatric clinic or hospital, to learn more about these professions. This type of volunteering can help students determine what type of work within abnormal psychology is most comfortable for them. Some students find tremendous gratification working with people with psychological problems, whereas other students find it more gratifying to conduct research that might answer important questions about psychological problems.

 Based on your current knowledge, what type of mental health professional would you seek out first if you felt you needed help for a psychological disturbance? What does this choice indicate about your beliefs about the causes of psychological disturbances?

Chapter Summary

The context for a behavior influences whether it is deemed abnormal. Two factors that determine the context for a behavior are the culture of the person exhibiting the behavior and his or her gender. Various criteria have been used to determine whether a behavior is abnormal. Cultural relativists argue that the norms of a society must be used to determine the normality of a behavior. Others have suggested that statistically deviant behaviors, or behaviors that cause subjective discomfort in a person, should be labeled abnormal. Still others have suggested that only behaviors resulting from mental illness or disease are abnormal. All these criteria have serious limitations, however. Currently, the consensus among professionals in the mental health field is that behaviors that cause people to suffer distress or that prevent them from functioning in daily life are abnormal. Often these behaviors are referred to as *maladaptive* or *dysfunctional.*

Historically, theories of abnormality have fallen into one of three categories. Natural or biological theories saw mental disorders as similar to physical diseases, caused by the breakdown of some system of the body. Supernatural theories saw mental disorders as the result of divine intervention, curses, demonic possession, and personal sin. Psychological or stress-related theories saw mental disorders as the results of stress. These three types of theories led to very different types of treatment of people who acted abnormally.

Even well into the nineteenth and twentieth centuries, people who acted abnormally might be shut away in prisonlike conditions, tortured, starved, and ignored. As part of the humanitarian and mental hygiene movements, however, the moral management of mental hospitals became more widespread. Patients in these hospitals were treated with kindness and the best biological treatments available. Effective biological treatments were not available until the mid-twentieth century for most psychological problems, however.

Throughout history, there have been many accounts of psychic epidemics and mass hysteria. Groups of people have shown similar psychological and behavioral symptoms, which usually have been attributed to common stresses or beliefs.

The different professions within abnormal psychology include psychiatrists, psychologists, clinical social workers, and psychiatric nurses.

Key Terms

cultural relativism 7	mental disease or mental	hysteria 11
statistical deviance 8	illness criterion 9	
subjective discomfort 8	maladaptive 9	

Application   When You Wonder If You Are Abnormal

Most students reading a book on abnormal psychology will recognize in themselves some behaviors that are labeled as abnormal. In fact, it is often easy to see signs in oneself (or one's close friends or relatives) of almost every type of abnormality discussed in this book! This type of perception is referred to as *medical student's disease.*

Be aware that many of the behaviors discussed in this book occur occasionally, in mild form, in many people. For example, many people between the ages of 18 and 25, even when not under the influence of some drug, have brief "out of body" experiences, in which they feel their "soul" or "self" is floating out of their body. It is even more common for people of all ages to have periods of sad or anxious moods or times when they feel that life is "out of control." For most people, these periods are relatively brief, and these behaviors or feelings do not severely interfere with their ability to function in life.

Yet, if you have been behaving in ways that have been interfering with daily functioning for a long time or that have been causing you or others much suffering, it is a good idea to talk with a professional about these experiences. Your instructor may be willing to speak with you or to provide you with referrals to professionals with whom you may speak. Many colleges offer confidential counseling for students at no cost or minimal cost. Some counties have mental health associations that provide information on professionals or groups that serve people with specific types of problems; the phone number for your local mental health association may be in the *Yellow Pages* or available through an operator. ■

chapter 2 Assessing and Diagnosing Abnormality

Gathering Information

Assessment is the process of gathering information about what is wrong with a person and the possible causes of his or her symptoms. Many types of information are gathered during an assessment, including information about current symptoms, recent events and physical condition, drug and alcohol use, personal and family history of psychological disorders, and cognitive functioning. This helps in making a diagnosis. In addition, information about coping styles, social resources, self-concept, and sociocultural background helps in planning treatment.

Assessment Tools

There are many types of assessment tools clinicians use. Any assessment tool should provide valid and reliable information. Biological tests such as CT, PET, and MRI scans, and neuropsychological tests, can help detect neurological problems that may be causing symptoms. Intellectual tests give an indication of cognitive functioning. Structured clinical interviews and symptom questionnaires provide direct information about symptoms. Personality inventories, behavioral observations, self-monitoring, and projective tests can indicate personality styles and behavioral deficits.

Problems in Assessing Adults and Children

Certain problems frequently complicate the assessment process. Clients may be resistant to providing information. Countertransference occurs when clinicians read their own concerns into clients' situations. Some clients may be unable to provide information because of cognitive impairment or youth. Children's manifestation of distress can change significantly with age. Cultural biases can impair the accuracy of clinicians' assessments of clients from other cultures.

Diagnosis

The *Diagnostic and Statistical Manual of Mental Disorders* (DSM) is the primary set of rules used for diagnosing psychological disorders in the United States. The first two editions of the DSM had diagnostic criteria that were vague and based on psychodynamic theory. Beginning with the third edition of the DSM in 1980, the diagnostic criteria were revised to be as observable and atheoretical as possible. The current edition, DSM-IV, specifies five axes to be used in making diagnoses.

Gender and Cultural Bias in Diagnosis

Critics of the DSM have charged that it reflects Western, masculine ideals for a "healthy" person and thus pathologizes normal behaviors of women and people from other cultures.

The Dangers of Diagnosis

The subjectivity inherent in psychiatric diagnoses and the stigma attached to these diagnoses make the application of these diagnoses dangerous. Yet having clear criteria for diagnosis is necessary for the progress of research on psychological disorders and for communication among clinicians.

Bio-Psycho-Social Integration
Chapter Summary
Key Terms
Application: *Is Self-Assessment a Good Idea?*

Beauty cannot disguise nor music melt
A pain undiagnosable but felt.

—Anne Morrow Lindbergh
The Unicorn and Other Poems, 1935–1955 (1956)

Andre Rouillard
Essor

It is the year 2023, and Jackson Alexander has a problem. For the last several weeks, he has been feeling anxious and agitated most of the time. He cannot concentrate on his work and is so distracted that he has had several accidents. Jackson's thoughts seem to jump from one subject to another.

Jackson goes to see his therapist. The therapist first administers psychological tests to identify all of Jackson's symptoms. Then the therapist administers a series of brain scans and blood tests to determine the causes of these symptoms. The brain scans indicate that Jackson has a deficit in neurotransmitter functioning in the lateral thalamus, combined with abnormal electrical activity in the prefrontal cortex, suggesting that Jackson is suffering from Bindle's Disorder. The blood tests confirm this diagnosis.

The brain scan and blood data suggest the specific type of drug therapy and psychotherapy that will be most useful in treating Jackson's symptoms. The therapist prescribes this drug and begins working with Jackson using the psychotherapy that Jackson needs.

assessment
process of gathering information about a person's symptoms and their possible causes

What you have just read is a wishful depiction of what assessment and diagnosis will be like in the future. **Assessment** is the process of gathering information about what is wrong with a person and the possible causes of his or her symptoms. In the future, we may be able to administer psychological and biological tests that pinpoint the nature and causes of people's psychological problems and determine the most appropriate treatment for these problems. Today we have psychological and biological tests that *suggest* the nature and causes of these problems. These tests can provide vital information, although they are not always foolproof or definitive.

diagnosis
label affixed to a set of symptoms that tend to occur together

The information gathered in an assessment is used to determine the appropriate diagnosis for a person's problems. A **diagnosis** is a label we attach to a set of symptoms that tend to occur with one another. Most of the chapters of this book address specific diagnoses, such as schizophrenia or depression or eating disorders. Before we discuss these specific diagnoses, however, we must discuss how clinicians and researchers go about assessing what is wrong with a person and making a diagnosis.

tools of assessment
measurements of personality characteristics, cognitive deficits, emotional well-being, and biological functioning that clinicians use to pinpoint psychological problems and their possible causes

In this chapter, we discuss the modern **tools of assessment** and how they are used to determine the proper diagnosis of psychological symptoms and to understand the nature and causes of psychological problems. Some of these tools are very new, and some have been around for many years. These tools provide information on the individual's personality characteristics, cognitive deficits (such as learning disabilities or problems in maintaining attention), emotional well-being, and biological functioning.

We also consider modern systems of diagnosing psychological problems. There are a number of dangers and problems inherent in applying a psychiatric diagnosis to a person, such as the stigmatizing effects of having a psychiatric diagnosis. We will discuss these dangers. Still, having a standardized **system of diagnosis** is crucial to communication among mental health professionals and to good research on psychological problems. We must agree on what we mean when we use a label such as *Bindle's Disorder* (which, by the way, is a fictitious disorder), and a standardized diagnostic system provides agreed-upon definitions of disorders.

system of diagnosis
set of agreed-upon definitions and criteria that mental health professionals use to pinpoint psychological problems for purposes of research and treatment

First, however, we will explore the types of information a clinician will want to gather during an assessment. Then we will review several psychological and biological tests that can be used to gather this information. Throughout the process of gathering information, the clinician must watch for many pitfalls in the assessment process, and we will examine several of these in the next sections.

Gathering Information

If Jackson showed up at a therapist's office today, what kind of information would the therapist want to know about Jackson? Let us look first at seven types of information that will guide the therapist to a diagnosis (see Table 2.1). After that, we will consider four additional types of information that will help in formulating a treatment plan.

Table 2.1   Information Gathered During Assessment That Is Important to Diagnosis

These seven types of information provide important clues to diagnosis.

Type of Information	Types of Questions Asked
Current symptoms	What are the symptoms?
	How severe are they?
	How chronic or acute are they?
	When did they begin?
	How much are they interfering with functioning?
	Are they specific to certain situations or are they global?
Recent events	Have any negative or positive events happened lately?
	Are there ongoing stressors in the client's life?
Physical condition	Can any medical conditions account for the symptoms?
Drug and alcohol use	Is the client taking any drugs that could cause symptoms?
	Is the client taking drugs that could interact with medications prescribed to treat the symptoms?
History of psychological disorders	Has the client experienced symptoms similar to or different from current symptoms at some time in the past?
Family history of psychological disorders	Does the client's family have a history of any psychological disorders or symptoms?
Intellectual and cognitive functioning	What are the client's strengths and deficits?
	Could the symptoms be caused by cognitive deficits?

First, the therapist will want to know more about Jackson's *current symptoms*, including their severity and chronicity. Jackson may be able to describe his symptoms in detail and may know exactly when these symptoms began, especially if the onset of the symptoms was associated with a specific event, such as being fired from a job. However, he may only complain of feeling "out of it" or "upset" and may not be able to pinpoint when he first began experiencing these feelings. It may take some gentle prodding by the therapist to determine the exact nature of these symptoms.

The therapist will try to ascertain how much the symptoms are interfering with Jackson's *ability to function* in the different domains in his life (such as in his work, his relationships with others, his role as a parent). Jackson will also be asked whether he experiences the symptoms across a wide variety of situations or only in specific types of situations. For example, does he feel anxious only at work or both at work and at home? The criteria for diagnosing most of the major psychological disorders require that the symptoms be severe and pervasive enough that they are interfering with the person's ability to function in daily life. If the symptoms are not that severe and are specific to one situation, then a diagnosis may not be warranted. Information about the pervasiveness and duration of Jackson's symptoms will also help the therapist formulate a plan for treatment that addresses all the areas in which Jackson is having problems.

Second, the therapist will want to know about any *recent events* in Jackson's life. Major negative life events, such as the death of a loved one or a divorce, can be associated with a variety of psychological problems. However, positive changes can also create stress that is associated with psychological symptoms. For example, perhaps Jackson was recently promoted at work and is experiencing his new responsibilities as extremely stressful. Symptoms that arise in response to a specific event are often given a different diagnosis (or in some cases no diagnosis) from the same ones when they arise with no apparent trigger. For example, a child who becomes depressed after his parents separate might be given a diagnosis of Adjustment Disorder with Depressed Mood, whereas a child who gradually becomes more and more depressed for no apparent reason might be given a diagnosis of Major Depressive Disorder. This distinction is made because symptoms that are triggered by a specific event often have a different prognosis and require different treatment than do symptoms that arise "out of the blue." A child whose symptoms of depression are triggered by a specific event is more likely to recover from these symptoms after a few talks with a supportive counselor than is a child who gradually becomes more and more depressed for no apparent reason. Similarly, if a therapist knows that Jackson's symptoms were triggered by some specific life event, she can address the meanings and consequences of the event in working with Jackson.

Third, the therapist should ask Jackson to obtain a complete *physical examination* to determine if he is suffering from any medical conditions that can create psychological symptoms. For example, some brain tumors can create the kind of disorientation and agitation that Jackson is reporting. In our case study about Jackson at the beginning of this chapter, the therapist pinpointed a specific brain abnormality that was causing Jackson's symptoms. As we will discuss next, medical technology and our understanding of the underlying neurology of psychological disorders are not yet developed enough for us to pinpoint the biological underpinnings of most disorders. That is, we do not know what the biological causes of most disorders are, and we don't have definitive tests of most of the biological causes we think exist.

What biological tests can sometimes tell us today, however, is whether there is some medical disease that is causing psychological symptoms as side effects. Thyroid disorders can cause people to experience the classic symptoms of depression, but most people who get depressed do not have a thyroid disorder. However, if an individual's depression is caused by a thyroid disorder, we can often simply treat the thyroid disorder and the symptoms of depression will also disappear without any additional antidepressant treatment. Thus, it is important to determine whether a medical disease such as a thyroid disorder might be causing a person's psychological symptoms.

Fourth, therapists need to know about any *drugs*—legal or illegal—their clients may be taking. Many drugs can induce distressing psychological symptoms as side effects during drug use or withdrawal from the drug. In such cases, a different diagnosis is given from that given when the symptoms are not the consequence of some drug. Therapists also need to know about any drugs a client is taking to protect against interactions between those drugs and medications the therapist might prescribe for the client's symptoms.

Fifth, the therapist will seek out Jackson's *past history of psychological problems*. This information is especially relevant if Jackson has symptoms that suggest different diagnoses. For example, imagine that Jackson reports, in addition to the symptoms described earlier, that he believes he has extraordinary powers or talents. He has also heard voices telling him that he has a special mission. These are core symptoms of both schizophrenia and mania, two disorders that require different treatments. Thus, it is crucial to make a **differential diagnosis** to determine which of two or more disorders might be causing Jackson to suffer. One of the best ways to determine whether Jackson is suffering from schizophrenia or from mania is to examine his past history of psychological problems. If Jackson has a clear history of severe mood swings, in which he alternated between elated moods and extremely depressed moods, then the chances are good that his current symptoms are symptoms of mania instead of schizophrenia, and he will respond well to the treatments for mania. If he has no history of mood swings and has responded well in the past to drugs for schizophrenia, then the chances are good that he is currently suffering from schizophrenia. This example also illustrates why it is important that we have a standardized and reliable system of diagnosis. We need to be sure that the diagnoses people such as Jackson received in the past were based on the same criteria we are using to diagnose his current episode. Otherwise, the information we have on Jackson's past diagnoses will give us no clues as to how to interpret his current symptoms.

Sixth, the therapist will ask Jackson about his *family history of psychological disorders*. Again, family history can be extremely helpful when we are unsure of which of two disorders Jackson may have. Some disorders "run true" in a family, meaning that there is a high incidence of that particular disorder in a family but not a high incidence of other disorders in the same family. For example, some families tend to have a high incidence of schizophrenia among their members but not a high incidence of mania. Thus, if Jackson has a strong family history of schizophrenia, the chances are higher that he is suffering from schizophrenia than mania. In contrast, if he has a strong family history of mania, then the chances are that his current symptoms represent mania.

differential diagnosis
determination of which of two or more possible diagnoses is most appropriate for a client

These types of information do not always influence diagnosis but can be helpful in planning treatment.

Type of Information	Types of Questions Asked
Coping style	Is the client engaging in adaptive or maladaptive coping strategies?
Social resources	Does the client have supportive family or friends? How supportive are the client's work relationships?
Self-concept and concept of symptoms	Does the client have a strong or weak sense of self-efficacy? What are the client's beliefs about what is wrong with him or her? What are the client's beliefs about the appropriate treatment for his or her symptoms?
Sociocultural background	In what culture was the client raised? How long has the client been in this country? Why did the client come to this country? What are the client's connections to his or her homeland? What is the client's level of acculturation??

Seventh, the therapist may need to assess Jackson's *cognitive functioning* and *intellectual abilities.* This information can be crucial to making differential diagnoses. For example, the kinds of symptoms Jackson is showing—disorientation and agitation—can be psychological signs of neurological disorders such as Alzheimer's disorder. Cognitive tests can help to determine the extent of Jackson's disorientation and cognitive deficits. As another example, among the elderly, undetected problems in short-term memory can lead to the symptoms of paranoia. Some older people who cannot remember conversations they had with other people or where they have left items begin to believe that other people are doing things behind their backs. Determining that symptoms of paranoia are due to memory deficits rather than to other causes can have a major impact on the diagnosis and type of treatment the person receives.

These seven types of information are essential for making an accurate diagnosis of Jackson's current condition. There are at least four other types of information that the therapist may also want to have to facilitate planning for successful treatment. First, it is helpful to know how Jackson tends to *cope* with stressful circumstances, including how he copes with his own symptoms (see Table 2.2). Does he seek out people whom he trusts to talk about his stresses, or does he retreat to his apartment and drink heavily when stressed? Sometimes the person's ways of coping with his symptoms and stressors create significant problems that must also be addressed in therapy.

Second, the therapist may want to know about the *social resources* Jackson has available to him—the numbers of friends and family members he has contact with and the quality of his relationships with these people. Social isolation can make it much more difficult for people to overcome psychological problems; on the other hand, friends and family members can also be burdens for the person when these relationships are marked by conflict or create unreasonable demands on the person.

Third, the therapist should explore Jackson's *self-concept* and his *concept of his symptoms.* Does Jackson have a strong sense of himself and his ability to overcome his symptoms, or is his self-esteem low and does he feel hopeless and helpless to overcome his symptoms? A client's sense of **self-efficacy**—ability to overcome the troubles he or she is faced with—is an important ingredient in therapy (Bandura, 1995). Also, as we will discuss more in Chapter 3, how a client conceives of his or her symptoms and problems will affect how he or she reacts to the therapist's interventions. If a client believes her symptoms have biological origins, she may be resistant to psychotherapy. Similarly, if a client believes his symptoms are tied to his relationships to others, he may not want to take pills to get rid of the symptoms.

Having good social support can help people cope with difficult times.

self-efficacy
person's belief that he or she can execute the behaviors necessary to control desired outcomes

Fourth, the therapist must obtain information on Jackson's *sociocultural background.* This is an important step for therapists working with a culturally diverse clientele. For immigrant clients, this background includes the specific culture where they were raised, the number of years they have been in this country, the circumstances that brought them to this country (to escape war or oppression, to seek work), their continuing connections to their homeland, and whether they are currently living with people from their homeland (Westermeyer, 1993). As we shall see, immigrants who left their homeland under difficult circumstances and who do not have a strong support system of people from their culture in their new homes are at especially high risk for disorders such as posttraumatic stress disorder (see Chapter 4). It is also useful to know as much as possible about the clients' socioeconomic status and occupation in their homeland—perhaps they were physicians in their homeland and now they are street cleaners—because the contrast between their lives in the homeland and their current lives can be a source of difficulty.

Immigrants and other members of ethnic minority groups differ in their levels of **acculturation.** Acculturation is the extent to which a person identifies with her or his group of origin and its culture or with the mainstream dominant culture (Westermeyer, 1993). Some members of ethnic minority groups retain as much of their culture of origin as possible and reject the dominant mainstream culture. They may continue to speak their language of origin and refuse to learn the dominant language. Other members fully identify with the dominant culture and reject their culture of origin. Still others are bicultural—they continue to identify with their culture of origin and celebrate it but also assimilate as necessary to the dominant culture.

Therapists need to understand their clients' level of acculturation because this can affect how clients talk about and present their problems, the kinds of stresses clients will be exposed to, and clients' responses to interventions therapists might make. We will discuss these issues in more depth in Chapter 3 and in later chapters on specific disorders, but let us briefly examine three examples. First, members of some cultures often experience psychological distress in somatic symptoms such as headaches and stomachaches. Knowing that a client remains fully identified with a culture that tends to present psychological symptoms in somatic terms can help a therapist interpret a client's complaints.

Second, when members of a family differ in their levels of acculturation, this can cause significant stress for family members. For example, an adolescent who is fully acculturated to the dominant culture may have many conflicts with a parent who remains identified with his or her culture of origin and does not want the adolescent to adopt the mainstream culture. Third, a client who is acculturated to the mainstream American culture will respond differently to certain suggestions a therapist might make, such as to confront an abusive boss, than will a client who remains identified with a culture in which authority figures are never questioned.

In sum, there are eleven types of information that make up a comprehensive assessment. For those clinicians who do both the assessment and treatment of clients, this assessment process can familiarize them with the details of clients' lives and functioning and facilitate a positive relationship between themselves and clients.

acculturation
extent to which a person identifies with his or her group of origin and its culture or with the mainstream dominant culture

Differences between parents and children in levels of acculturation can create family stress.

Assessment Tools

interview
method for gathering information from a client and/or his or her family in which a therapist asks questions and examines the content of answers as well as nonverbal behaviors

How does a clinician gather all this information? Much of it is gathered in an initial **interview,** often called an *intake interview,* when the clinician first meets the client. The interview may be an **unstructured interview,** with only a few questions that are open-ended such as, "Tell me about yourself." Or the interview may be a **structured interview,** with a list of questions that are asked of every client. The therapist will listen to the client's answers to the questions and observe how the client answers the questions—does the client hesitate when talking about her marriage, does she avoid questions about her drinking habits, does she look sad when talking about her career—to obtain nonverbal indicators of what is bothering the client.

The clinician may also interview the client's family members for information about the family's history of psychological problems, the client's past history, and the client's current symptoms. Information from family members is especially important if the client is a child or an adult who cannot or will not report on his or her own symptoms.

Clinicians have a number of tests that are used to aid in the gathering of information from clients, and we will discuss several of these tests shortly. First, however, let us define two criteria that are used to evaluate the quality of any test: validity and reliability.

Validity

If you administer a test to determine what is wrong with a client, you obviously want assurances that the test is a valid or accurate measure of what it is supposed to measure. The best way to determine the **validity** of a test would be to see if the results of the test yielded the same information as some objective and accurate indicator of what the test is supposed to measure. For example, if there were a blood test that definitively proved whether a person had Bindle's Disorder, you would want any other test for Bindle's Disorder (such as a questionnaire) to yield the same results when administered to the person.

Unfortunately, there are no definitive blood tests, brain scans, or otherwise objective tests for any of the psychological disorders we will discuss in this book. There are a number of other ways that the validity of a test can be estimated, however (see Table 2.3). A test is said to have **face validity** when, on face value, the items seem to be measuring what the test is intended to measure. For example, a questionnaire for anxiety that includes questions such as, "Do you feel jittery much of the time?", "Do you feel like you can't sit still?", and "Do you worry about many things?" has face validity because it seems obvious that it assesses symptoms of anxiety.

Content validity is the extent to which a test assesses all the important aspects of a phenomenon that it purports to measure. For example, if our measure of anxiety included only questions about the physical symptoms of anxiety (nervousness, restlessness, stomach distress, rapid heart beat) and none of the cognitive symptoms of anxiety (apprehensions about the future, anticipation of negative events), then we might question whether it is a good measure of anxiety.

Concurrent validity is the extent to which a test yields the same results as other measures of the same behavior, thoughts, or feelings. A person's scores on our anxiety questionnaire should bear some relation to information gathered from the client's family members and friends about his or her typical level of anxiety. Information from family members and friends may not be completely accurate or valid, so this is not a definitive standard against which to judge our anxiety questionnaire. However, the notion behind concurrent validity is that any new measure of a variable should yield similar results to established measures of that variable.

unstructured interview
meeting between a clinician and a client or a client's associate(s) that consists of open-ended, general questions that are particular to each person interviewed

structured interview
meeting between a clinician and a client or a client's associate(s) in which the clinician asks questions that are standardized, written in advance, and asked of every client

validity
degree of correspondence between a measurement and the phenomenon under study

face validity
extent to which a measure *seems* to measure a phenomenon on face value, or intuition

content validity
extent to which a measure assesses all the important aspects of a phenomenon that it purports to measure

concurrent validity
extent to which a test yields the same results as other measures of the same phenomenon

Table 2.3 Types of Validity	
The validity of a test can be evaluated in several different ways.	
Face validity	Test *appears* to measure what it is supposed to measure
Content validity	Test assesses all important aspects of a phenomenon
Concurrent validity	Test yields the same results as other measures of the same behavior, thoughts, or feelings
Predictive validity	Test predicts the behavior it is supposed to measure
Construct validity	Test measures what it is supposed to measure and not something else

A test that has **predictive validity** is good at predicting how a person will think or act or feel in the future. Our anxiety measure has good predictive validity if it correctly predicts which people will behave in anxious ways when confronted with stressors in the future and which people will not be anxious.

Construct validity is the extent to which the test measures what it is supposed to measure and not something else altogether (Cronbach & Meehl, 1955). Consider the construct validity of multiple-choice exams given in courses. These exams are supposed to be measuring a student's knowledge and understanding of what was taught in a course. What they may often be measuring, however, is the student's ability to take multiple-choice examinations—to determine what the instructor is trying to get at with the questions and to recognize any tricks or distractors in the questions. The construct validity of achievement tests and intelligence tests has been questioned, as we will discuss later in this chapter (Helms, 1992). Critics have questioned whether these tests really measure what a student knows and how intelligent a student is or just how well the student has been taught to answer the odd types of questions posed on these tests.

Reliability

The **reliability** of a test is an indicator of the consistency of a test. As with validity, there are several types of reliability (see Table 2.4). **Test-retest reliability** is an index of how consistent the results of a test are over time. If a test supposedly measures some enduring characteristic of a person, then the person's scores on that test should be similar when he or she takes the test at two different points in time. So if our anxiety questionnaire is supposed to measure people's general tendencies to be anxious, then their scores on this questionnaire should be similar if they complete the questionnaire once this week and then again next week. On the other hand, if our anxiety questionnaire is a measure of people's current symptoms of anxiety (with questions such as, "Do you feel jittery right now?") then we might expect low test-retest reliability on this measure. Typically, measures of general and enduring characteristics should have higher test-retest reliability than measures of momentary or transient characteristics.

When people take the same test a second time, they may remember their answers from the first time and try to repeat these answers to seem consistent. Thus, researchers will often develop two or more forms of a test. When people's answers to these different forms of a test are similar, the tests are said to have **alternate form reliability.** Similarly, a researcher may simply split a test into two or more parts to determine if people's answers to one part of a test are similar to their answers to another part of the test. When there is similarity in people's answers to different parts of the same test, the test is said to have high **internal reliability.**

Finally, many of the tests we will examine in this chapter are not self-report questionnaires but interviews or observational measures that require the therapist or researcher to make judgments about the people being assessed. These tests should have high **interrater** or *interjudge* **reliability.** That is, different raters or judges who administer and score the interview or test should come to similar conclusions when they are evaluating the same people.

With that background on how the quality of tests is determined, let us discuss several types of tests used in the assessment process.

Table 2.4 Types of Reliability	
The reliability or consistency of a test is an important indicator of its value.	
Test-retest reliability	Test produces similar results when given at two points in time
Alternate form reliability	Two versions of the same test produce similar results
Internal reliability	Different parts of the same test produce similar results
Interrater or interjudge reliability	Two or more raters or judges who administer and score a test to an individual come to similar conclusions

Biological Tests

In the imaginary case study that began this chapter, Jackson underwent brain scans and blood tests to determine what disorder he had. There is hope that, in the future, we will understand the biological underpinnings of psychological disorders well enough and our biological technologies will be sensitive enough that we will have definitive biological tests that determine whether a person has a specific psychological disorder. We are not at that stage now, however. That is, there currently are no brain scans or blood tests that can definitively diagnose the disorders we will discuss in this book.

Still, biological tests can provide crucial information about individual patients and are useful research tools. In clinical practice, brain scans and blood tests are used to determine if a patient has some brain injury or tumor or a medical disease that can be detected in the blood (such as low blood sugar) that might be contributing to his or her psychological symptoms. Researchers use brain scans and blood tests to search for differences in biochemicals or in brain activity or structure between people with a psychological disorder and people with no disorder. Ideally, this research will tell us enough about the biology of psychological disorders that we can develop valid and reliable biological tests for these disorders in the future.

Indeed, both technology and our understanding of the biology of disorders are advancing so rapidly that there will probably be major breakthroughs in biological techniques for assessing and diagnosing psychological disorders in the near future. Thus, let us review the existing technologies and what they can tell us now (Beatty, 1995). We will focus on brain scanning technology because this technology is providing some of the most exciting new findings in the search for biological underpinnings of psychological disorders.

Computerized tomography (CT) is an enhancement of X-ray procedures. In CT, narrow X-ray beams are passed through the person's head in a single plane from a variety of angles, as shown in Figure 2.1. The amount of radiation absorbed by each beam is measured, and from these measurements a computer program can construct an image that looks like a slice of the brain (see Figure 2.2). By taking many different slices of the brain, the computer can reconstruct a three-dimensional image, showing the major structures of the brain. A CT scan can reveal brain injury, tumors, and structural abnormalities (see Figure 2.2). The two major limitations of CT technology are that it exposes patients to X rays, which can be harmful, and it provides only an image of the structure of a brain, rather than an image of the activity in the brain.

computerized tomography (CT) method of analyzing brain structure by passing narrow X-ray beams through a person's head from several angles to produce measurements from which a computer can construct an image of the brain

Positron emission tomography (PET) can provide a picture of activity in the brain. PET requires injecting the patient with a harmless radioactive isotope such as fluorodeoxyglucose (FDG). This is a substance that travels through the blood to the brain. The parts of the brain that are active need the glucose in FDG for nutrition, and thus FDG accumulates in active parts of the brain. Subatomic particles in FDG called *positrons* are emitted as the isotope decays. These positrons collide with electrons; both are annihilated and are converted to two photons traveling away from each other in opposite directions (Beatty, 1995). The PET scanner detects these photons and the point at which they are annihilated and constructs an image of the brain showing areas that are most active. PET scans can be used to show differences in the activity levels of specific areas of the brain between people with a psychological disorder and people without a disorder (see Figure 2.3).

positron emission tomography (PET) method of localizing and measuring brain activity by detecting photons that result from the metabolization of an injected isotope

Magnetic resonance imaging (MRI) is the newest of the brain imaging techniques and holds several advantages over both CT and PET technology (Beatty, 1995). It does not require exposing the patient to any form of radiation or injection of radioisotopes. It is safe to use repeatedly in the same patient. It provides much more finely detailed pictures of the anatomy of the brain than do other technologies, and it can image the brain at any angle. It can also provide pictures of the activity and functioning in the brain.

MRI involves creating a magnetic field around the brain of the patient that is so powerful that it causes realignment of hydrogen atoms in the brain. When the magnetic field is turned off and on, the hydrogen atoms change position, causing them to emit magnetic signals. These signals are read by a computer, which reconstructs a three-dimensional

magnetic resonance imaging (MRI) method of measuring both brain structure and function through construction of a magnetic field that affects hydrogen atoms in the brain, emitting signals that a computer then records and uses to produce a three-dimensional image of the brain

Figure 2.1

CT Images. A CT image is formed by passing X-ray beams through a person's head from several angles and measuring the amount of radiation absorbed.

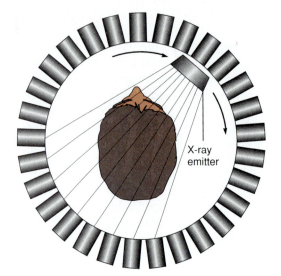

X-ray emitter

X-ray detector array

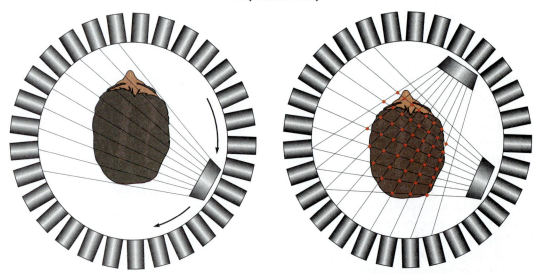

Figure 2.2

CT Scan of Human Head. From measures of the amount of radiation absorbed in a CT scan, computers can construct an image of the major structures of the brain.

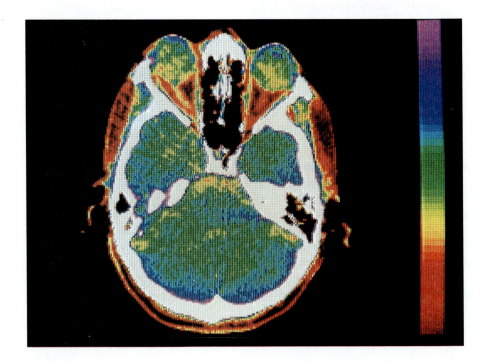

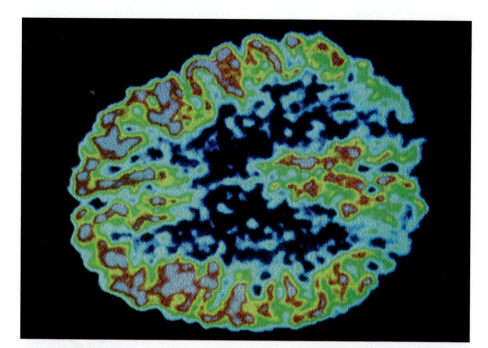

Figure 2.3

PET Scan of a Human Brain. PET scans provide a picture of activity in the brain. This scan was taken of a patient with Alzheimer's disease.

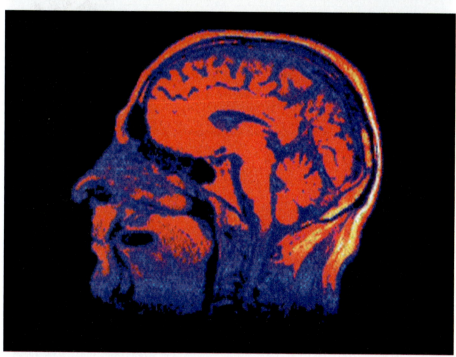

Figure 2.4

Magnetic Resonance Image (MRI). An MRI can provide pictures of the structure and activity of the brain.

image of the brain. Researchers are using MRI to study functional and structural brain abnormalities in almost every psychological disorder (see Figure 2.4).

Two other tests that are sometimes used to record brain activity are the **electroencephalogram (EEG)** and **event-related potential (ERP).** EEG is a graph of the electrical activity in the brain, recorded from electrodes placed on the surface of the scalp. Hans Berger, a German psychiatrist, first recorded EEG activity in 1924 (Brazier, 1960). He identified different patterns of EEG activity, which he labeled *alpha, beta, theta,* and *delta* and which differ in frequency and amplitude (see Figure 2.5). These different patterns of activity are correlated with human behavior. In normal waking, EEG activity alternates between alpha and beta activity. Theta activity is prominent when we are drowsy, and large delta waves are seen during dreamless sleep. EEGs have been useful in studying people with sleep disorders, who often show abnormalities in EEG activity, and with

electroencephalogram (EEG)
graph of the electrical activity in the brain, recorded from electrodes placed on the surface of the scalp

event-related potential (ERP)
EEG measure of the brain's electrical activity (potentials) as it corresponds to stimuli (events) in the environment

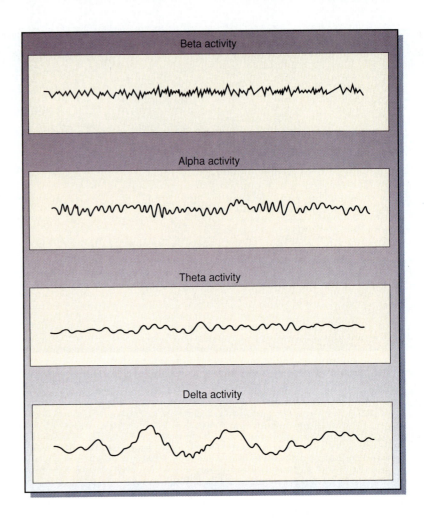

Figure 2.5

Typical EEG Patterns. When we are awake, EEG activity alternates between alpha and beta activity. Theta activity is prominent when we are drowsy, and large delta waves occur during dreamless sleep.

epilepsy, a disorder in which people experience sudden bursts of electrical activity in the brain (see Figure 2.6).

Event-related potential (ERP) is a component of EEG activity that is elicited by mental events. When a person has a thought or senses something in the environment, there is electrical activity associated with that mental event. By exposing a person to something like the flash of a word on a screen while recording brain activity with an EEG, a researcher can examine the extent and nature of the electrical activity associated with the stimulus. ERP technology is being used to help diagnose attentional difficulties in children suspected of having attention deficit disorder (see Figure 2.7 and Chapter 9).

In summary, CT, PET, MRI, EEG, and ERP technologies are being used to investigate the structural and functional differences between the brains of people with psychological disorders and those of people without disorders. Sometimes these technologies can also be used to identify gross structural or functional abnormalities such as a brain tumor or severe atrophy (deterioration) in the brain of an individual patient. For the most part, however, we cannot yet use these technologies to diagnose specific psychological disorders in individual patients, largely because we do not yet understand the biological underpinnings of these disorders.

 Would you submit to one of these biological tests purely for research purposes? Why or why not?

In addition to these biological tests, there are several psychological tests used to assess possible brain damage. Let us examine some of the most popular of these tests.

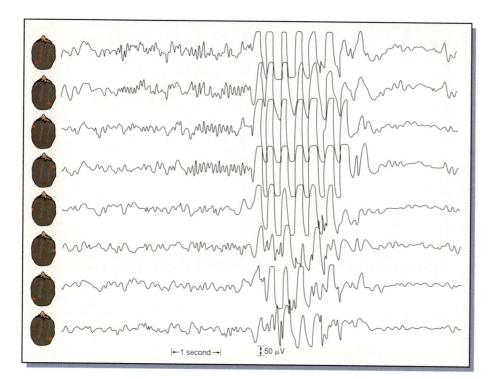

Figure 2.6
Electroencephalogram Showing a Grand Mal Seizure. The red dots on the heads indicate the positions of the electrodes. The violent swings of the recording indicate electrical activity during the seizure.

←1 second→ ↕50 μV

Figure 2.7
EEG and ERP techniques safely provide information about activity levels in specific areas of the brain.

Neuropsychological Tests

If some sort of neurological impairment is suspected in a client, the clinician may use paper-and-pencil tests that may detect specific cognitive and fine-motor deficits, such as an attentional problem or a tendency to ignore items in one part of the visual field. One frequently used **neuropsychological test** is the Bender-Gestalt Test (Bender, 1938). This test assesses clients' sensorimotor skills by having them reproduce a set of nine drawings (see Figure 2.8). Clients with brain damage may rotate or change parts of the drawings or be unable to reproduce the drawings. When asked to remember the drawings after a delay, they may show significant memory deficits. The Bender-Gestalt Test appears to be good at differentiating people with brain damage from those without brain damage, but it does not reliably identify the specific type of brain damage a person has (Goldstein & Hersen, 1990).

More extensive batteries of tests have been developed to pinpoint type of brain damage. Two of the most popular batteries are the Halstead-Reitan Test (Reitan & Davidson, 1974) and the Luria-Nebraska Test (Luria, 1973). These batteries contain several tests that provide specific information about an individual's functioning in several skill areas, such as concentration, dexterity, and speed of comprehension. Increasingly, these

neuropsychological test
test of cognitive, sensory, and/or motor skills that attempts to differentiate people with deficits in these areas from normal people

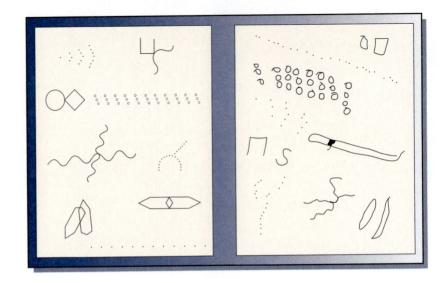

Figure 2.8

The Bender-Gestalt Test. On the left are the figures presented to clients. On the right are the figures as copied by a child with a brain tumor that is creating perceptual-motor difficulties.

neuropsychological tests are used in conjunction with brain imaging techniques such as CT, PET, and MRI to identify specific deficits and possible brain abnormalities.

Intelligence Tests

In clinical practice, intelligence tests are used to get a sense of a client's intellectual strengths and weaknesses, particularly when mental retardation or brain damage are suspected. Intelligence tests are also used in school settings to identify children with intellectual difficulties or to place children in "gifted" classrooms. They are used in occupational settings and the military to evaluate adults' capabilities for certain jobs or types of service. Some examples of these tests are the Wechsler Adult Intelligence Scale—Revised, the Stanford-Binet Intelligence Test, and the Wechsler Intelligence Scale for Children—Third Edition. These tests were designed to measure basic intellectual abilities such as the ability for abstract reasoning, verbal fluency, and spatial memory. The term *IQ* is used to describe a method of comparing an individual's score on an intelligence test with the performance of average individuals of the same age group. An IQ score of 100 means that the person performed similarly to the average performance of other people his or her age (see Figure 2.9).

Intelligence tests are controversial in part because there is little consensus as to what is meant by intelligence. The most widely used intelligence tests assess verbal and analytical abilities but do not assess other talents or skills such as artistic and musical ability. Some psychologists argue that success in life is as strongly influenced by social skills and other talents not measured by intelligence tests as it is by verbal and analytical skills (Sternberg, 1988).

Another important criticism of intelligence tests is that they are biased in favor of middle- and upper-class educated European Americans because these people have more familiarity with the kinds of reasoning that are assessed on the intelligence tests (Helms, 1992). In addition, educated European Americans may be more comfortable in taking intelligence tests because testers are often also European Americans, and the testing situation resembles testing situations in their educational experience. In contrast, different cultures within the United States and in other countries may emphasize other forms of reasoning over those assessed on intelligence tests and may not be comfortable with the testing situations of intelligence tests.

A classic example involves the interpretation of syllogisms, logical problems often used in intelligence tests. A typical syllogism runs like this: All bears in the North are white. My friend saw a bear in the North. What color was that bear? The "right" answer according to intelligence tests is that the bear is white. A subject's ability to infer that the bear must be white is taken as an indication of his or her deductive reasoning skills.

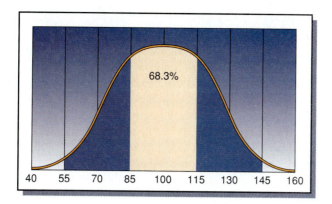

68.3%

40 55 70 85 100 115 130 145 160

Figure 2.9

If the entire population took an IQ test, the scores would fall into a bell-shaped curve around the most frequent score of 100. More than two-thirds of people score between 85 and 115 on IQ tests.

When researchers asked peasant farmers in Central Asia to solve these syllogisms, however, they discovered that this form of reasoning violated a social norm that you never state something you do not know from firsthand experience (Luria, 1976, pp. 108–109):

[Experimenter]:   In the Far North, where there is snow, all bears are white. Novaya Zemlya is in the Far North and there is always snow there. What color are the bears there?

"... We always speak only of what we see; we don't talk about what we haven't seen."

[E]:   But what do my words imply? [The syllogism is repeated.]

"Well, it's like this: our tsar isn't like yours, and yours isn't like ours. Your words can be answered only by someone who was there, and if a person wasn't there he can't say anything on the basis of your words."

[E]:   ... But on the basis of my words—in the North, where there is always snow, the bears are white, can you gather what kind of bears there are in Novaya Zemlya?

"If a man was 60 or 80 and had seen a white bear and had told about it, he could be believed, but I've never seen one and hence I can't say. That's my last word."

"YOU CAN'T BUILD A HUT, YOU DON'T KNOW HOW TO FIND EDIBLE ROOTS AND YOU KNOW NOTHING ABOUT PREDICTING THE WEATHER. IN OTHER WORDS, YOU DO TERRIBLY ON OUR I.Q. TEST."

© 1997 by Sidney Harris.

This man may have been interpreted as unintelligent by the rules of the test, but he was only following a social convention of his culture in his answer to the experimenter. Critics of intelligence tests argue that similar cultural clashes happen in more subtle ways whenever persons not of the dominant, educated culture that created intelligence tests are asked to take these tests. A "culture-fair" test would have to include items that are equally applicable to all groups or items that are different for each culture but are psychologically equivalent for the groups being tested. Attempts have been made to develop "culture-fair" tests, but the results have been disappointing. Even if a universal test were created, it would be difficult to make statements about intelligence in different cultures because different nations and cultures vary in the emphasis they place on "intellectual achievement."

 If you have ever taken SATs or another standardized test of ability, what do you think the test assessed? How valid a test of ability do you think that test was?

So far, we have focused on tests to assess brain abnormalities and cognitive and intellectual functioning. Much of the information that must be gathered in an assessment, however, has to do with the client's emotional, social, and behavioral functioning. Let us turn to tools that help the clinician assess these characteristics.

Structured Clinical Interviews

We mentioned earlier that a clinician will often attempt to gather information about a client in an interview. Sometimes these interviews are informal and unstructured. Increasingly, however, clinicians and researchers are using what is known as a *structured interview*. In a structured clinical interview, the clinician asks the respondent a series of questions about symptoms he or she may be experiencing, or may have experienced in the past. The format of the questions and the entire interview are highly structured and standardized, and the person's answers to each question are scored by the clinician according to concrete criteria (see Table 2.5). At the end of the interview, the clinician should have enough information from the respondent to determine whether he or she has symptoms that qualify for a diagnosis of any of the major types of psychological problems. Several such interviews have been developed in recent decades, including the Diagnostic Interview Schedule, or DIS (Robins, Helzer, Croughan, & Ratcliff, 1981), and the Structured

Table 2.5 Sample Structured Clinical Interview

F. ANXIETY DISORDERS PANIC DISORDER	PANIC DISORDER CRITERIA					
Have you ever had a panic attack, when you *suddenly* felt frightened, anxious or extremely uncomfortable?	A. At some time during the disturbance, one or more panic attacks (discrete periods of intense fear or discomfort) have occurred that were (1) unexpected, i.e., did not occur immediately before or on exposure to a situation that almost always causes anxiety, and (2) not triggered by situations in which the person was the focus of others' attention.	?	1	2	3	16
IF YES: Tell me about it. When does that happen? (Have you ever had one that just seemed to come on out of the blue?) IF PANIC ATTACKS IN EXPECTED SITUATIONS: Did you ever have one of these attacks when you weren't in (EXPECTED SITUATION)?						
Have you ever had four attacks like that in a four-week period?	B. Either four attacks, as defined in criterion A, have occurred within a four-week period, or one or more attacks have been followed by a period of at least a month of persistent fear of having another attack.	?	1	2	3	17
IF NO: Did you worry a lot about having another one? (How long did you worry?)						
When was the last bad one (EXPECTED OR UNEXPECTED)?	C. At least four of the following symptoms developed during at least one of the attacks:					
Now I am going to ask you about that attack. What was the first thing you noticed? Then what? During the attack . . .						
. . . were you short of breath? (Have trouble catching your breath?)	(1) shortness of breath (dyspnea) or smothering sensations	?	1	2	3	18
. . . did you feel dizzy, unsteady, or like you might faint?	(2) dizziness, unsteady feelings, or faintness	?	1	2	3	19
. . . did your heart race, pound or skip?	(3) palpitations or accelerated heart rate (tachycardia)	?	1	2	3	20
. . . did you tremble or shake?	(4) trembling or shaking	?	1	2	3	21
. . . did you sweat?	(5) sweating	?	1	2	3	22
. . . did you feel as if you were choking?	(6) choking	?	1	2	3	23
. . . did you have nausea or upset stomach or the feeling that you were going to have diarrhea?	(7) nausea or abdominal distress	?	1	2	3	24
. . . did things around you seem unreal or did you feel detached from things around you or detached from part of your body?	(8) depersonalization or derealization	?	1	2	3	25

Source: Data from R. L. Spitzer, et al., 1992.

? = inadequate information   1 = absent or false   2 = subthreshold   3 = threshold or true

Clinical Interview for DSM (Spitzer, Williams, Gibbon, & First, 1992). Structured clinical interviews have also been adapted for diagnosing children's problems. Often, however, much of the information about a child's symptoms must come from parents and other sources, as we shall discuss shortly.

The standard set of questions and scoring system for structured clinical interviews increases the reliability of information gathered from these interviews. Still, the interviews rely on the willingness and ability of respondents to tell interviewers about their symptoms. Differences between the interviewer and respondent in age, gender, and ethnicity can affect the accuracy of the information obtained during these interviews, as we shall discuss in greater detail shortly. In addition, these interviews can take hours to administer and thus can be costly to use.

Symptom Questionnaires

Often when a therapist or researcher wants a quick way to assess what symptoms a person is experiencing, he or she will ask the person to complete a symptom questionnaire. These questionnaires may cover a wide variety of symptoms, representing several different disorders. Others focus on the symptoms of specific disorders. One of the most common depression inventories is the Beck Depression Inventory, or BDI (Beck & Beck, 1972). The long form of the BDI has 21 items, each of which describes four levels of a given symptom of depression (see Table 2.6). The respondent is asked to indicate which of the descriptions best fits how he or she has been feeling in the last week. The items are scored to indicate the level of depressive symptoms the person is experiencing. Cutoff scores have been established to indicate moderate and severe levels of depressive symptoms.

Critics of the BDI have argued that it does not differentiate well between the clinical syndrome of depression and the general distress that may be related to an anxiety disorder or several other disorders (see Kendall, Hollon, Beck, Hammen, & Ingram 1987). The BDI also cannot indicate whether the respondent would qualify for a diagnosis of depression. But the BDI is extremely quick and easy to administer and has good test-retest reliability. Hence, it is widely used, especially in research on depression. Clinicians treating depressed people will also use the BDI to keep track of their clients' symptom levels from week to week; that is, as a monitoring tool rather than as a diagnostic tool. A client may be asked to complete the BDI at the beginning of each therapy session; both the client and the therapist then have a concrete indicator of the progress of the client's symptoms.

A frequently used measure of anxiety is the Spielberger State-Trait Anxiety Scale or STAI (Spielberger, Gorsuch, & Lushene, 1970). This self-report questionnaire is comprised of two separate self-report scales for measuring state anxiety and trait anxiety. The

---

Table 2.6 Items from the Beck Depression Inventory

The Beck Depression Inventory is one of several self-report questionnaires to assess psychological symptoms.

Instructions: Please read each group of statements carefully. Pick out the one statement in each group that best describes the way you have been feeling the past week, including today.

1. I do not feel sad.
   I feel sad.
   I feel sad all the time and I can't snap out of it.
   I am so sad or unhappy that I can't stand it.

2. I am not particularly discouraged about the future.
   I feel discouraged about the future.
   I feel I have nothing to look forward to.
   I feel that the future is hopeless and that things cannot improve.

3. I do not feel like a failure.
   I feel I have failed more than the average person.
   As I look back on my life, all I can see is a lot of failures.
   I feel I am a complete failure as a person.

From A. T. Beck, et al., *Cognitive Therapy of Depression.* Copyright © 1979 Guilford Press.

STAI trait scale consists of 20 items describing how a person might generally feel. The STAI state scale consists of 20 items that assess the respondent's current level of anxiety at a particular moment in time. Like the BDI, this scale has been used widely in research because of its ease of administration and good test-retest reliability.

One of the most commonly used questionnaires for assessing symptoms in children is the Child Behavior Checklist, or CBCL (Achenbach & Edelbrock, 1983). The CBCL presents the parent with a list of over 100 behaviors, thoughts, or feelings that the child may be experiencing and asks the parent to rate how frequently a child shows them. The CBCL can be used to assess specific symptom domains (such as aggression and depression) and prosocial or adaptive behavior (such as peer interaction skills). The CBCL has been administered to thousands of healthy children in the general population, so the researcher or clinician can compare an individual child's scores on the CBCL to the scores of children who are functioning well to determine how much the child's functioning is deviating from these norms.

 Do you think there are some symptoms of psychological disorders that can never be defined by objective, observable criteria but must always rely on people's subjective self-reports?

Personality Inventories

Personality inventories are usually questionnaires that are meant to assess people's typical ways of thinking, feeling, and behaving. These inventories are used as part of an assessment procedure to obtain information on people's well-being, their self-concept, their attitudes and beliefs, their ways of coping, their perceptions of their environment and social resources, and their vulnerabilities.

The most widely used personality inventory is the *Minnesota Multiphasic Personality Inventory (MMPI),* which has been translated into over 150 languages and used in over 50 countries (Dana, 1995) (see Figure 2.10). The original MMPI was first published in 1945 and contained 550 items. In 1989, an updated version published under the name MMPI-2 contained 567 items (Butcher, 1990). Both versions of the MMPI present respondents with sentences describing moral and social attitudes, behaviors, psychological states, and physical conditions and ask them to respond either "true," "false," or "can't say" to each sentence. Some examples of items from the MMPI follow:

I would rather win than lose in a game

I am never happier than when alone.

My hardest battles are with myself.

I wish I were not bothered by thoughts about sex.

I am afraid of losing my mind.

When I get bored, I like to stir up some excitement.

People often disappoint me.

The MMPI was developed *empirically,* meaning that a large group of possible items were given to psychologically "healthy" people and people suffering from different psychological problems. Then the items that reliably differentiated among groups of people were included in the inventory. The items on the original MMPI cluster into 10 scales that measure different types of psychological characteristics or problems, such as paranoia, anxiety, and social introversion. An additional four scales have been added to the MMPI-2 to assess vulnerability to eating disorders, substance abuse, and poor functioning at work. A respondent's scores on each of the scales are compared to scores from the normal population, and a profile of the respondent's personality and psychological problems is derived. There are also four validity scales that determine whether the person tends to respond to the items on the scale in an honest and straightforward manner or tends

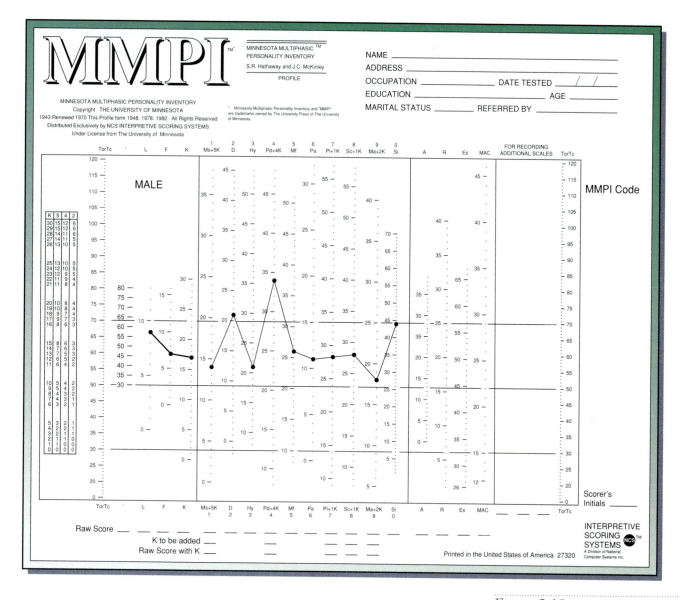

Figure 2.10

An MMPI profile (from MMPI, 1982)

to distort his or her answers in a way that might invalidate the test (see Table 2.7). For example, the Lie Scale measures the respondent's tendency to respond to items in a socially desirable way that makes him or her look unusually positive or good.

Because the items on the MMPI were chosen for being those that best differentiated people with specific types of psychological problems from people without psychological problems, the concurrent validity of the MMPI scales was "built into" the scales in their development. The MMPI may be especially useful as a general screening device for detecting people who are functioning very poorly psychologically. The test-retest reliability of the MMPI has also proven quite high (Parker, Hanson, and Hunsley, 1988).

Many criticisms have been raised about the use of the MMPI in culturally diverse samples, however (Dana, 1995). The norms for the original MMPI—the scores that were considered "healthy" scores—were based on samples of people in the United States that were not representative of people from a wide range of ethnic and racial backgrounds, age groups, and social classes. In response to this problem, the publishers of the MMPI established new norms based on more representative samples of eight communities across the United States. Still, there are concerns that the MMPI norms do not reflect variations across cultures in terms of what is considered normal or abnormal. In addition, the linguistic accuracy of the translated versions of the MMPI and the comparability of these versions to the English version have been questioned (Dana, 1995).

Table 2.7 Clinical and Validity Scales of the Original MMPI

The MMPI is one of the most widely used questionnaires to assess people's symptoms and personalities. It also includes scales to assess whether respondents are lying or trying to obfuscate their answers.

Clinical Scales

Scale Number	Scale Name	What It Measures
Scale 1	Hypochondriasis	Excessive somatic concern and physical complaints
Scale 2	Depression	Symptomatic depression
Scale 3	Hysteria	Hysterical personality features and tendency to develop physical symptoms under stress
Scale 4	Psychopathic deviate	Antisocial tendencies
Scale 5	Masculinity-femininity	Sex-role conflict
Scale 6	Paranoia	Suspicious, paranoid thinking
Scale 7	Psychasthenia	Anxiety and obsessive behavior
Scale 8	Schizophrenia	Bizarre thoughts and disordered affect
Scale 9	Hypomania	Behavior found in mania
Scale 0	Social introversion	Social anxiety, withdrawal, overcontrol

Validity Scales

Scale Name	What It Measures
Cannot say scale	Total number of unanswered items
Lie scale	Tendency to present favorable image
Infrequency scale	Tendency to falsely claim psychological problems
Defensiveness scale	Tendency to see oneself in unrealistically positive manner

From *Minnesota Multiphasic Personality Inventory.* Copyright © the University of Minnesota, 1942, 1943, 1951, 1967 (renewed 1970), 1983.

behavioral observation
method for assessing the frequency of a client's behaviors and the specific situations in which they occur

self-monitoring
method of assessment in which a client records the number of times per day that he or she engages in a specific behavior and the conditions surrounding the behavior

Behavior Observations and Self-Monitoring

Clinicians will often use **behavioral observation** of clients to assess deficits in their skills or ways of handling situations. For example, a clinician might watch a child interact with other children to determine what situations seem to provoke the child to act aggressively. The clinician can then use information from behavior observations to help the client learn new skills, to stop negative habits, and to understand and change the way he or she reacts to certain situations.

The advantages of direct behavioral observations are that they do not rely on the clients' reporting and interpretation of their behaviors. Instead the clinician sees just how skilled the client is or is not in handling important situations. One disadvantage is that different observers may draw different conclusions about an individual's skills. That is, direct behavioral observations may have low interrater reliability, especially when no standard means of making the observations is established.

In addition, it can be time-consuming and sometimes impossible for a clinician to observe a client's behaviors in key situations. If direct observation is not possible, the clinician may require client **self-monitoring;** that is, ask the client to keep track of the number of times per day he or she engages in a specific behavior (e.g., smoking a cigarette) and the conditions under which this behavior happens. Self-monitoring is open to biases in what the client notices about his or her behavior and is willing to report. However, the client can gain valuable insight into the triggers of unwanted behaviors through self-monitoring, which can lead to changing these behaviors.

By observing children's or adults' behavior directly, a clinician can obtain information about their strengths and weaknesses in various settings.

Projective Tests

A **projective test** is based on the assumption that when people are presented with an ambiguous stimulus, such as an oddly shaped inkblot or a captionless picture, they will interpret the stimulus in line with their current concerns and feelings, their relationships with others, and conflicts or desires of which they may not even be aware. The people are said to project these issues as they describe the "content"

Figure 2.11

Clinicians analyze people's answers to the Rorschach Ink Blot test for particular themes or concerns.

of the stimulus, hence the name *projective tests*. Proponents of these tests argue that they are useful in uncovering unconscious issues or motives of a person or when the person is resistant or heavily biasing the information he or she presents to the assessor. Four of the most frequently used projective tests are the Rorschach Inkblot Test, the Thematic Apperception Test (TAT), the Sentence Completion Test, and the Draw-a-Person Test.

The *Rorschach Inkblot Test*, commonly referred to simply as the *Rorschach*, was developed in 1921 by the Swiss psychiatrist Hermann Rorschach. The test consists of 10 cards, each containing a bilaterally symmetrical "inkblot" in black, gray, and white or in color (see Figure 2.11). The examiner tells the respondent, "I would like you to look at each card and tell me what it looks like, what it could be." If the respondent further questions how to proceed, the examiner says, "It's up to you." After the response is given, the card is removed and the examiner inquires, "What made it look like that?" followed by, "Was there anything else that made it look like that?" (Allison, Blatt, & Zimet, 1968).

Clinicians are interested in both the content of the clients' responses to the inkblots and the style of their responses. In the content of responses, they will look for particular themes or concerns, such as frequent mentions of aggression or fear of abandonment. Important stylistic features may include the clients' tendency to focus on small details of the inkblot rather than the inkblot as a whole or the clients' hesitations in responding to certain inkblots.

The *Thematic Apperception Test (TAT)* consists of a series of pictures. The client is asked to make up a story about what is happening in the pictures (Murray, 1943). Proponents of the TAT argue that the stories clients give reflect their concerns and wishes and their personality traits and motives. As with the Rorschach, clinicians are interested in both the content and style of clients' responses to the TAT cards. Some cards may stimulate more emotional responses than others or no responses at all. These cards are considered to tap the clients' most important issues. The following is a story that a person made up about a picture of a man and young woman (Allison, Blatt, & Zimet, 1968):

> This looks like a nice man and—a sweet girl—They look like this is a happy moment—Looks like he's telling her that he loves her—or something that's tender and sweet. She looks very confident and happy! It looks nice; I like it. Hm! Wait now! Maybe—well—that's right—he looks kind of older—but she looks efficient—and sweet. [Efficient?] Yes [laughs]. Doesn't look particularly efficient at the moment, but I imagine—[puts card away]. [What led up to this?] Well—I think maybe he taught school nearby, and she was a girl in the village—It strikes me as a sort of sweet, old fashioned romance. Maybe she's seen him a long time, and now it has just come to the state where he tells her that he loves her. [What will the outcome be?] I think they will get married, get some children and be happy—not that they will live happily ever after, not like a fairy tale. They look like ordinary people.

In interpreting the client's story, the clinician might note that it exhibits a romanticized, naive, and childlike quality. The client presents a very conventional scenario but

projective test

presentation of an ambiguous stimulus, such as an inkblot, to a client, who then projects unconscious motives and issues onto the stimulus in his or her interpretation of its content

with moral themes and much emotional expression. The clinician might interpret these tendencies as part of the client's basic personality style (Allison, Blatt, & Zimet, 1968).

A third test that is based on the idea that people project their concerns and wishes onto ambiguous stimuli is the *Sentence Completion Test.* Sentence completion tests have been designed for children, adolescents, and adults. The tests provide a "stem," which is the beginning of a sentence, such as, "My mother is . . ." or "I wish . . .". The individual is asked to complete the sentence. While more structured than the Rorschach and TAT, sentence completion tests are also interpreted subjectively by the examiner. Clinicians might look for indications of the person's concerns both in what he or she says in response to the sentence stem and in what he or she avoids saying in response to the stem. For example, a clinician might find it interesting that the person seems unable to come up with any response to the stem "Sex is . . .".

A fourth test is the *Draw-a-Person Test* (Machover, 1949). The client is asked to draw a picture of the self and then to draw a picture of another person of the opposite sex. The clinician examines how the client depicts the self: Does he draw himself as a small figure huddled in the corner of the page or as a large figure filling the page? The drawings of self are thought to reflect the client's self-concept as a strong person or weak person, a smart person or unintelligent person, and so on. The drawing of the other person is thought to reflect the client's attitudes toward the opposite sex and his or her relationships with important members of the opposite sex.

When assessing children, clinicians may also ask the children to play with toys that might elicit play organized around important themes, such as the functioning of their families or their relationship with specific family members. Clinicians then observe the children's drawings or play for these themes and attempt to engage the children in conversations about these themes to learn more about their concerns and needs.

Clinicians from psychodynamic perspectives see projective tests as valuable tools for assessing the underlying conflicts and concerns that clients cannot or will not report directly. Clinicians from other perspectives question the usefulness of these tests. The validity and reliability of all of the projective tests have not proven strong in research (Kline, 1993). In addition, because these tests rely so greatly on subjective interpretations by clinicians, they are open to a number of biases.

 If clinicians feel they get a strong sense of a client's personality and concerns from projective tests, do you think it matters that research has not provided evidence these tests are valid or reliable?

Summing Up | Assessment Tools

- Numerous biological and psychological tests are available for the assessment of psychological problems and their possible causes.
- Brain-imaging tests, including the CT, PET, MRI, EEG, and ERP tests, can help to identify significant brain pathology that may be contributing to psychological problems. They cannot definitively diagnose a psychological disorder, however.
- Paper-and-pencil neuropsychological tests can help to identify specific cognitive deficits that may be tied to brain damage.
- Intelligence tests can indicate a client's general level of intellectual functioning in verbal and analytic tasks.
- Structured clinical interviews provide a standardized way to assess in an interview format people's symptoms.
- Symptom questionnaires allow for mass screening of large numbers of people to determine self-reported symptoms.
- Personality inventories assess stable personality characteristics.
- Behavioral observation and self-monitoring can help detect behavioral deficits and the environmental triggers for symptoms.
- Projective tests are used to uncover unconscious conflicts and concerns but are open to interpretive biases.

Problems in Assessing Adults and Children

The assessment process as laid out seems straightforward enough. The assessor simply interviews the individual, asking direct questions to elicit the relevant information. Then he or she writes down a diagnosis and sends the patient off for treatment. Of course nothing is ever that easy, and the assessment endeavor is no exception; a number of problems and barriers plague those who seek accurate assessment.

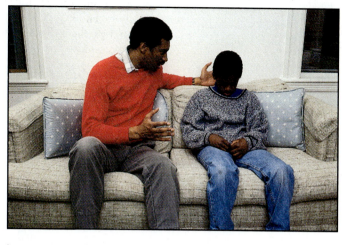

Just as youngsters can be resistant to talking with their parents about their concerns, clients can be resistant to talking with therapists about their concerns.

Resistance

One of the barriers to accurate assessment arises ironically from the very person who is there for help. It is **resistance.** Sometimes the individual being assessed does not want to be assessed or treated. For example, the parents of a teenager may have forced him to see a psychologist because they are worried about recent changes in his behavior. This teenager may be resistant to providing any information to the assessor, however.

Since much of the information a clinician needs must come directly from the person being assessed, resistance to providing that information can be a formidable problem. Even when the person is not completely resistant to being assessed, he or she may have a strong interest in the outcome of that assessment and thus may be highly selective in the information provided, may bias his or her presentation of the information, or may even lie to the assessor. Such problems often arise when assessments are being done as part of a legal case, such as when parents are fighting for custody of their children in divorce. Each parent will want to present him- or herself in the best light but may negatively bias his or her reports on the other parent when speaking to psychologists who have been appointed to assess each parent's fitness for custody of the children.

resistance
client's avoidance of assessment or treatment

 If you were forced against your will (by your parents, your spouse, the court) to see a therapist, how would you handle the interaction with the therapist? Why?

Countertransference

Clinicians themselves can introduce a variety of biases into the assessment process. One of the most difficult of these biases is known as **countertransference.** This occurs when the person being assessed reminds the clinician of an important person in his or her life, and the clinician reacts to the client as if the client were that important person. For example, imagine that the clinician is a psychiatrist named Marge who has recently broken off a dating relationship with a man. This man accused Marge of being unfair, of not being willing to work on the relationship with him. The next day, Marge interviews a client, named Joel, who has come to her for help with his feelings about the breakup of a relationship in his life. Joel tells Marge that the woman he was dating broke off their relationship suddenly and would not discuss how to improve the relationship with him. Marge begins to react to Joel in unsympathetic ways—she "sides" with his former partner and begins to see problems in Joel's behavior that are really problems she had with the behavior of her former partner. This is a case of countertransference, in which Marge is transferring her feelings about her former partner onto Joel and incorporating these feelings into her assessment of him. Clinicians must always watch for such processes in their

countertransference
bias that occurs when a therapist reacts to a client as if the client were a particularly important person in his or her life and incorporates these feelings into his or her assessment of the client

work, which is why they often continue to seek supervision of their work by other psychologists or psychiatrists even when they are highly experienced. Other professionals can help them check personal biases that may be entering into their work.

Inability to Provide Information

Many clients being assessed cannot articulate their concerns or symptoms. This is especially true of children, as the following conversation between a mother and her 5-year-old son illustrates. The son, Jonathon, was sent home from preschool for fighting with another child.

Mom:	Jonathon, why did you hit that other boy?
Jonathon:	I dunno. I just did.
Mom:	But I want to understand what happened. Did he do something that made you mad?
Jonathon:	Yeah, I guess.
Mom:	What did he do? Did he hit you?
Jonathon:	Yeah.
Mom:	Why did he hit you?
Jonathon:	I dunno. He just did. Can I go now?
Mom:	I need to know more about what happened.
Jonathon:	[Silence]
Mom:	Can you tell me more about what happened?
Jonathon:	No. He just hit me and I just hit him. Can I go now?

Anyone who has tried to have a conversation with a distressed child about why he or she misbehaved has some sense of how difficult it can be to engage a child in a discussion about emotions or behaviors. Even when a child readily engages in such a conversation, his or her understanding of the causes of his or her behaviors or emotions may not be very well-developed.

Children, particularly preschool-aged children cannot describe their feelings, or the events associated with these feelings as easily as adults can (Achenbach, McConaughy, & Howell, 1987). Young children do not differentiate among different types of emotions, often just saying that they feel "bad," for example (Harter, 1983). When distressed, children may talk about physical aches and pains rather than the emotional pain they are feeling. Or a child might not verbalize that he or she is distressed and only show this distress in nonverbal behavior, such as making a sad face, withdrawing or behaving aggressively. Children who have behavioral problems, such as excessive distractibility or lack of control over their anger, may not believe that they have problems and thus may deny that anything is wrong when asked (Kazdin, 1991).

These problems with children's self-reporting of emotional and behavioral problems have led clinicians and researchers to rely on other people, usually adults in children's lives, to provide information about children's functioning. Parents are often the first source of information about a child's functioning. A clinician may interview a child's parents when the child is brought for treatment, asking the parents about changes in the child's behavior and corresponding events in the child's life. A researcher studying children's functioning may ask parents to complete questionnaires assessing the children's behavior in a variety of settings.

Because parents typically spend more time with their child than any other person does, they potentially have the most complete information about the child's functioning and a sense of how the child's behavior has or has not changed over time. Unfortunately, however, parents are not always accurate in their assessments of their children's functioning. Parents' perceptions of their children's well-being can be influenced by their own symptoms of psychopathology and by parental self-esteem, expectations for their children's behavior, and marital discord (Forehand, Lautenschlager, Faust, & Graziano, 1986; Lambert et al., 1992). Indeed, sometimes parents bring children for assessment and treatment of psychological problems as a way of seeking treatment for themselves.

Clinicians must often engage parents in assessing young children.

Parents may also be the source of a child's psychological problems and, as a result, unwilling to acknowledge or seek help for the child's problems. The most extreme example of this is the parent who is physically or sexually abusing a child. Such a parent is unlikely to acknowledge the psychological or physical harm he or she is causing the child or to seek treatment for that harm. A less extreme example is the parent who does not want to believe that some action he or she has taken, such as filing for a divorce or moving the family across the country, is the cause of the child's emotional or behavioral problems. Again, such parents may be slow in taking a child who is distressed to a mental health professional or in admitting to the child's problems when asked by a researcher.

Cultural norms for children's behaviors differ, and parents' expectations for their children and their tolerance of "deviant" behavior in children will be affected by these norms. For example, Jamaican parents appear more tolerant than American parents of unusual behaviors in children, including both aggressive behavior and behavior indicating that a child is shy and inhibited. In turn, Jamaican parents have a higher threshhold than American parents in terms of the appropriate time to take a child to a therapist (Lambert et al., 1992).

How might you frame questions to a parent to get information that is as accurate as possible about a child?

Teachers are another source of information about children's functioning. Teachers and other school personnel (such as guidance counselors or coaches) are often the first to recognize that a child has a problem and to initiate an intervention for the problem (Tuma, 1989). Teachers' assessments of children, however, are often discrepant with the assessments given by other adults, including parents and trained clinicians who rate children's behavior. Such discrepancies may arise because these other adults are providing invalid assessments of the children while the teachers are providing valid assessments. The discrepancies may also arise because children function at different levels in different settings. At home, a child may be well-behaved, quiet, and withdrawn, while at school, the same child may be impulsive, easily angered, and distractible. These differences in a child's actual behavior in different settings might make it seem that either a parent's report of the child's behavior or the teacher's report is invalid, when the truth is that the child simply acts differently depending on the situation.

Problems in obtaining information do not only occur when the client is a child. Some adults are so impaired that they cannot provide adequate information to the assessor. They may be so depressed or anxious or confused that they cannot properly answer questions. In such cases, the assessor may be able to obtain much of the information from family members or friends, but again, these sources of information are not always available or reliable.

Cultural Biases

A number of challenges to assessment arise when there are significant cultural differences between the assessor and the person being assessed (Manson, in press; Westermeyer, 1993). Imagine having to obtain all the information needed to assess what is wrong with someone from a culture very different from your own. The first problem you may run into is that the client does not speak the same language that you do or speaks your language only partially (and you do not speak his or hers at all). There is evidence that symptoms can go both underdiagnosed and overdiagnosed when the client and assessor do not speak the same language (Altarriba & Santiago-Rivera, 1994). Overdiagnosis often occurs because a client tries to describe his or her symptoms in the assessor's language, but the assessor interprets a client's slow and somewhat confused description of symptoms as indicating more pathology than is really present. Underdiagnosis can occur when the client cannot articulate complex emotions or strange perceptual experiences in the assessor's language and thus does not even try.

One solution is to find an interpreter to translate between the therapist and the client. Interpreters can be invaluable to good communication. However, interpreters who are not trained assessors themselves can misunderstand and mistranslate a therapist's questions and the client's answers, as in the following example (Marcos, 1979, p. 173):

Clinician to Spanish-speaking patient: "Do you feel sad or blue, do you feel that life is not worthwhile sometimes?"

Interpreter to patient: "The doctor wants to know if you feel sad and if you like your life."

Patient's response: "No, yes, I know that my children need me, I cannot give up, I prefer not to think about it."

Interpreter to clinician: "She says that no, she says that she loves her children and that her children need her."

In this case the interpreter did not accurately reflect the client's answer to the therapist's question, giving the therapist a sense that the client was doing much better than the client reported she was. In addition, different people from the same country can speak different dialects of a language or may have different means of expressing feelings and attitudes. Mistranslation can occur when the interpreter does not speak the particular dialect spoken by the client or comes from a different subculture than the client.

Even when mistranslation is not a problem, some of the very questions that the assessor may ask or that may appear on a test or questionnaire that the client is asked to complete may be so culture-bound that they do not make sense to the client, or they can be interpreted by the client in ways the assessor did not anticipate (Manson, in press). This can happen on even the most "objective" of tests. For example, several assessment tests ask whether a client ever believes that forces or powers other than himself control his behavior or if he ever hears voices talking in his head. According to Western conceptualizations, these are signs of psychosis. Yet many cultures, such as the Xhosa of South Africa,

Translators can be invaluable in helping clients communicate with clinicians, but accurate translation is very difficult.

believe that ancestors live in the same psychic world as living relatives and that ancestors speak to the living and advise them on their behavior (Gillis, Elk, Ben-Arie, & Teggin, 1982). Thus, members of this culture might answer "yes" to questions intended to assess psychotic thinking, when they are really reporting on the beliefs of their culture.

Cultural biases can arise when everyone is supposedly speaking the same language but comes from quite different cultural backgrounds. There is evidence that African Americans in the United States are overdiagnosed as suffering from schizophrenia (Snowden & Cheung, 1990). For example, African Americans are more likely than whites to be misdiagnosed as schizophrenic when their symptoms actually fit the diagnosis of manic depression (Mukherjee, Shukla, Woodle, Rosen, and Olarte, 1983). Many investigators believe that cultural differences in the presentation of symptoms play a role (Neighbors, 1984). African Americans may present more intense symptoms than whites, which are then misunderstood by white assessors as representing more severe psychopathology. Another possibility is that some white assessors are too quick to diagnose severe psychopathology in African Americans because of negative stereotypes of them.

Finally, even when clinicians avoid all these biases, they are still left with the fact that people from other cultures often think about and talk about their psychological symptoms quite differently from members of their own culture. We will discuss several examples of cultural differences in the presentation of symptoms throughout this book. One of the most pervasive differences is the tendency among some cultures to experience and report psychological distress in emotional symptoms or in somatic (physical) symptoms. Following a psychologically distressing event, European Americans tend to report that they feel anxious or sad, but members of many other cultures will report having physical aches and maladies (Kleinman & Kleinman, 1985). To conduct an accurate assessment, clinicians must know about cultural differences in the manifestation of disorders and in the presentation of symptoms and correctly use this information in interpreting the symptoms that their clients report to them. This difference is further complicated by the fact that not every member of a culture will conform to what is known about that culture. That is, within every culture, people differ in their acceptance of cultural norms for behavior.

Training programs for clinicians are attempting to increase their sensitivity to biases and misunderstandings that can arise when they are interacting with people from cultures other than their own. There are a number of tests that clinicians can take themselves to assess their own cultural sensitivity (Dana, 1995). At the end of Chapter 16 are some guidelines from the American Psychological Association for how psychologists should provide assessment and service to culturally diverse populations.

 What kinds of psychological symptoms might be most vulnerable to misinterpretation due to cultural differences between a therapist and client?

Summing Up | Problems in Assessment

- During the assessment procedure, many problems and biases can be introduced.
- Clients may be resistant to being assessed and thus distort the information they provide.
- Clinicians may introduce their own bias into the assessment through countertransference.
- Clients may be too impaired by cognitive deficits, distress, or lack of development of verbal skills to provide information.
- Other sources of information, such as family members, may be called upon, but their reports are not always accurate.
- There are many biases that can arise when the clinician and client are from different cultures.

Diagnosis

As we suggested at the beginning of this chapter, a *diagnosis* is a label we attach to a set of symptoms that tend to occur together. This set of symptoms is referred to as a **syndrome.** In medical models of psychological disorders, a syndrome is thought to be the observable manifestation of an underlying biological disorder (see Figure 2.12). So if you have the symptoms that make up the syndrome we call *schizophrenia*, you are thought also to have a biological disorder we call *schizophrenia*. However, as mentioned repeatedly, there are no definitive biological tests for psychological disorders. Thus, it is impossible to

syndrome
set of symptoms that tend to occur together

Figure 2.12

Each syndrome is made up of a set of symptoms. Some of the symptoms of one syndrome may overlap with the symptoms of another syndrome. In addition, one person may have a different subset of symptoms within a syndrome than the other person.

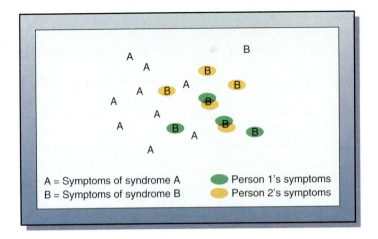

A = Symptoms of syndrome A   ● Person 1's symptoms
B = Symptoms of syndrome B   ● Person 2's symptoms

verify whether a given person *has* schizophrenia by giving him or her a biological test for schizophrenia.

Thus, we are left to observe humans and identify what symptoms typically co-occur in them, and then we call those co-occurring symptoms a *syndrome*. Identifying naturally occurring syndromes is no easy task. Typically, several symptoms will make up a syndrome, but there are differences among people in which of these symptoms they experience most strongly. Think about the last time you were in a sad or depressed mood. Did you also feel tired and have trouble sleeping? Do you always feel tired and have trouble sleeping every time you are in a sad or depressed mood or just sometimes? Does everyone you know also experience fatigue and sleeplessness when they are in a sad mood? Or do some of them simply lose their appetite and their ability to concentrate?

For centuries, humans have tried to organize the confusing array of psychological symptoms into a limited set of syndromes. This set of syndromes and the rules for determining whether an individual's symptoms are part of one of these syndromes are called a **classification system.** One of the first classification systems for psychological symptoms was proposed by Hippocrates in the fourth century B.C. Hippocrates divided all mental disorders into mania (states of abnormal excitement), melancholia (states of abnormal depression), paranoia, and epilepsy. Modern classification systems divide the world of psychological symptoms into a much larger number of syndromes than did Hippocrates. Let us focus on the classification system most widely used in the United States.

classification system
set of syndromes and criteria for determining whether a client's symptoms constitute a particular syndrome

The Development of the Diagnostic and Statistical Manual of Mental Disorders (DSM)

For over forty years, the official manual for diagnosing psychological disorders in the United States has been the ***Diagnostic and Statistical Manual of Mental Disorders*** of the American Psychiatric Association, referred to as the **DSM.** The first edition of the DSM was published in 1952. It outlined the diagnostic criteria for all the mental disorders recognized by the psychiatric community at the time. These criteria were somewhat vague descriptions of disorders that were heavily influenced by psychoanalytic theory. For example, the diagnosis of *Anxiety Neurosis* could have been manifested in a great variety of specific behavioral and emotional symptoms. The key to the diagnosis was whether the clinician inferred that unconscious conflicts were causing the client to experience anxiety. The second edition of the DSM, published in 1968, included some new disorders that had been recognized since the publication of the first edition but was not much different.

Because the descriptions of disorders were so abstract and theoretically based in the DSM-I and DSM-II, the reliability of the diagnoses was low. For example, one study found that four experienced clinicians using the DSM-I to diagnose 153 patients agreed on their diagnoses only 54 percent of the time (Beck et al., 1962). This eventually led psychiatrists and psychologists to call for a radically new system of diagnosing mental disorders that would be more reliable.

Diagnostic and Statistical Manual of Mental Disorders (DSM)
official manual for diagnosing mental disorders in the United States, containing a list of specific criteria for each disorder, how long a person's symptoms must be present to qualify for a diagnosis, and requirements that the symptoms interfere with daily functioning in order to be called disorders

The DSM-III, DSM-IIIR, and DSM-IV

In response to the reliability problems with the first and second editions of the DSM, in 1980 the American Psychiatric Association published the third edition of the DSM, known as DSM-III. This third edition was followed by a revised third edition, known as DSM-IIIR, published in 1987, and a fourth edition, known as DSM-IV, published in 1994. In these newer editions of the DSM, the developers replaced the vague descriptions of disorders with specific and concrete criteria for each disorder. These criteria are in the form of behaviors people must show or experiences or feelings they must report in order to be given a diagnosis. The developers tried to be as atheoretical and descriptive as possible in listing the criteria for each disorder. Good examples are the diagnostic criteria for Panic Disorder in the DSM-IV, which are given in Table 2.8. As you can see, a person must have 4 of 13 possible symptoms during at least one attack in order to be given the diagnosis of Panic Disorder, reflecting the fact that not all the symptoms of Panic Disorder are going to be present in every individual.

Two other elements distinguished the DSM-III, DSM-IIIR, and DSM-IV from their predecessors. First, these later editions specify how long a person must show symptoms of the disorder to be given the diagnosis (see Table 2.8B). Second, the criteria for most disorders require that symptoms interfere with occupational or social functioning for the person to be diagnosed. This emphasis on symptoms that are long-lasting and severe reflects the consensus among psychiatrists and psychologists that abnormality should be defined in terms of the impact of behaviors on the individual's ability to function and on his or her sense of well-being (see Chapter 1).

The DSM-III and its subsequent revisions also include information on how to make a differential diagnosis between a disorder and related disorders and on the course and prevalence of each disorder. The **course** of a disorder is the length of time the disorder

course
length of time that a disorder typically lasts and the likelihood that the client will relapse following the current episode of the disorder

---

Table 2.8 DSM-IV Diagnostic Criteria for Panic Disorder

These are the DSM-IV criteria for a diagnosis of Panic Disorder. They specify core symptoms that must be present and several other symptoms, a certain number of which must be present, for the diagnosis.

A. At some time during the disturbance, one or more panic attacks have occurred that were (1) unexpected, and (2) not triggered by situations in which the person was the focus of another's attention.

B. Either four attacks, as defined in criterion A, have occurred within a 4-week period, or one or more attacks have been followed by a period of at least a month of persistent fear of having another attack.

C. At least four of the following symptoms developed during at least one of the attacks:
1. shortness of breath or smothering sensations
2. dizziness, unsteady feelings, or faintness
3. palpitations or accelerated heart rate
4. trembling or shaking
5. sweating
6. choking
7. nausea or abdominal distress
8. depersonalization or derealization
9. numbness or tingling sensations
10. flushes or chills
11. chest pain or discomfort
12. fear of dying
13. fear of going crazy or doing something uncontrolled

D. During at least some of the attacks, at least four of the C symptoms developed suddenly and increased in intensity within 10 minutes of the beginning of the first C symptom.

E. It cannot be established that an organic factor initiated the disturbance, such as caffeine intoxication.

Reprinted with permission from the *Diagnostic and Statistical Manual of Mental Disorders*, Fourth Edition. Copyright © 1994 American Psychiatric Association, 1994.

typically lasts and the likelihood that the disorder will relapse in the future after the current episode of the disorder has ended.

The **prevalence** of a disorder is the number of people who have the disorder during a specified period of time. **Point prevalence** is the number of people who have the disorder at one given point in time. **Lifetime prevalence** is the number of people who will have the disorder at some time in their lives. So if the point prevalence of anxiety disorders is 8 percent and the lifetime prevalence is 20 percent, this means that 8 percent of people have an anxiety disorder at any given point in time, and 20 percent will develop an anxiety disorder at some time in their lives. Typically, the lifetime prevalence of a disorder is much higher than the point prevalence because disorders wax and wane, so that a person who is going to have a disorder at some time in his or her life may not be experiencing the disorder at a particular point in time.

Prevalence is often contrasted with the incidence of a disorder. **Incidence** is the number of new cases of a disorder that develop during a specific period of time. The 1-year incidence of a disorder is the number of people who develop the disorder during a 1-year period. Throughout this book, we will be quoting prevalence and incidence statistics for each of the disorders.

Reliability of the DSM

Despite the use of explicit criteria for disorders, the reliability of many of the diagnoses listed in the DSM-III and DSM-IIIR was disappointing. On average, experienced clinicians only agreed on their diagnoses using these manuals about 70 percent of the time (Kirk & Kutchins, 1992). The reliability for some of the diagnoses, particularly the personality disorder diagnoses, was much lower. Low reliability of diagnoses can be caused by many factors. Although the developers of the DSM-III and DSM-IIIR attempted to make the criteria for each disorder explicit, many of these criteria were still vague and required the clinician to make inferences about the client's symptoms or to rely on the client's willingness to report symptoms. For example, most of the symptoms of the mood disorders and anxiety disorders are subjective experiences (sadness, apprehensiveness, hopelessness); only clients can report whether they have these symptoms and how severe they are. To diagnose any of the personality disorders, the clinician must establish that the client has a lifelong history of specific dysfunctional behaviors or ways of relating to the world. Unless the clinician has known the client all his or her life, the clinician must rely on the client and his or her family to provide information about the client's history, and different sources of information can provide very different pictures of the client's functioning.

In an effort to increase the reliability of diagnoses in the DSM-IV, the task force that developed the DSM-IV conducted numerous field trials, in which the criteria for most of the diagnoses to be included in the DSM-IV were tested in clinical and research settings. In a **field trial**, testing determines if diagnostic criteria can be applied reliably, and if they fit clients' experiences. As a result, the reliability of the DSM-IV diagnoses are expected to be higher than the reliability of predecessors. We shall have to wait and see, however.

The Multiaxial System

Beginning with the third edition of the DSM, the manual has specified five *axes* or dimensions along which a clinician evaluates a client's behavior (see Table 2.9). Only the first two axes list actual disorders and the criteria required for their diagnoses. The other three axes are meant to provide information on physical conditions that might be affecting the person's mental health (Axis III), psychosocial and environmental stressors in the person's life (Axis IV), and the degree of impairment in the person's mental health and functioning (Axis V). Let us take a look at these five axes one by one as defined by the DSM-IV and then apply them to an actual case study.

On Axis I, a clinician lists any major DSM-IV disorders for which the person qualifies, with the exclusion of mental retardation and personality disorders (see Table 2.10). The clinician also notes whether these disorders are chronic or acute. Chronic disorders

prevalence
number of people who have a disorder during a specified period of time

point prevalence
number of people who have a disorder at one given point in time

lifetime prevalence
number of people who will have a disorder at some time in their lives

incidence
number of new cases of a disorder that develop during a specified period of time

field trial
way to increase the reliability of diagnostic criteria by testing proposed diagnostic criteria in applied settings to determine their fit with patients' symptoms and consistency across clinicians

Table 2.9 DSM-IV Axes

The DSM-IV has five axes along which each client should be evaluated.

Axis I	Clinical disorders
Axis II	Personality disorders
	Mental retardation
Axis III	General medical conditions
Axis IV	Psychosocial and environmental problems
Axis V	Global assessment of functioning

Reprinted with permission from the *Diagnostic and Statistical Manual of Mental Disorders*, Fourth Edition. Copyright 1994 American Psychiatric Association, 1994.

Table 2.10 Disorders Listed on Axis I

These disorders, most of which we will discuss in this book, represent conditions that typically cause people significant distress or impairment.

Disorders usually first diagnosed in infancy, childhood, or adolescence
- Attention-deficit disorder
- Hyperactivity
- Conduct and oppositional disorder
- Separation anxiety disorder
- Pervasive developmental disorder
- Learning disorders
- Feeding, tic, and elimination disorders

Delirium, dementia, and amnestic or other cognitive disorders

Substance-related disorders

Schizophrenia and other psychotic disorders

Mood disorders

Anxiety disorders

Somatoform disorders

Factitious disorders

Dissociative disorders

Sexual and gender identity disorders

Eating disorders

Sleep disorders

Adjustment disorders

Other conditions that may be a focus of clinical attention

Reprinted with permission from the *Diagnostic and Statistical Manual of Mental Disorders*, Fourth Edition. Copyright 1994 American Psychiatric Association, 1994.

are ones lasting for long periods of time. Acute disorders are ones that have a more recent and abrupt onset of severe symptoms.

On Axis II, the clinician lists mental retardation or any personality disorders for which the person qualifies (see Table 2.11). Mental retardation is listed on Axis II instead of Axis I because it is a lifelong condition, whereas most of the disorders on Axis I tend to wax and wane across the lifespan. Similarly, a personality disorder is characterized by a chronic and pervasive pattern of dysfunctional behavior that the person has shown since at least adolescence. For example, a person with an antisocial personality disorder has a lifelong pattern of being abusive toward others and violating basic norms of social relationships.

On Axis III, the clinician notes any medical or physical diseases from which the person is suffering. These diseases may or may not be directly related to the psychological

Table 2.11 Disorders Listed on Axis II

These disorders listed on Axis II typically represent lifelong disorders that pervade every area of the person's life.

Mental retardation

Personality disorders

- Paranoid personality disorder
- Schizoid personality disorder
- Schizotypal personality disorder
- Antisocial personality disorder
- Borderline personality disorder
- Histrionic personality disorder
- Narcissistic personality disorder
- Avoidant personality disorder
- Dependent personality disorder
- Obsessive-compulsive personality disorder

Reprinted with permission from the *Diagnostic and Statistical Manual of Mental Disorders,* Fourth Edition. Copyright 1994 American Psychiatric Association, 1994.

Table 2.12 Axis IV Psychosocial and Environmental Problems to Note

These are some of the important problems people might face that should be noted on Axis IV.

Problems with primary support group

Problems related to the social environment

Educational problems

Occupational problems

Housing problems

Economic problems

Problems with access to health care services

Problems related to interaction with the legal system and to crime

Reprinted with permission from the *Diagnostic and Statistical Manual of Mental Disorders,* Fourth Edition. Copyright 1994 American Psychiatric Association, 1994.

disorders from which the person is also suffering. For example, a person may have lung cancer, which has nothing to do with the fact that she also has schizophrenia. However, it is important for the clinician to know about any physical diseases for two reasons. First, these diseases could be related to the person's mental health. For example, a person might be depressed because she has lung cancer. As noted earlier, a clinician must guard against any interactions between the treatment the patient may be taking for her physical disease and the treatment the clinician will prescribe for her mental disorder.

On Axis IV, the clinician rates the severity of the psychosocial stressors the client is facing, such as those listed in Table 2.12. Again, these psychosocial stressors may be related to the client's mental disorder, as causes or consequences. Or they may merely be coincidental with the disorder. However, it is important for the clinician to know what types of stressors the client is facing in order to provide a successful treatment plan.

On Axis V, the clinician rates the level at which the client is able to function in daily life on the scale given in Table 2.13. This helps the clinician quantify and communicate the degree to which the disorder is impairing the client's functioning.

 What about people whose symptoms of distress do not quite meet the diagnostic criteria for any disorder? How should we think about their problems? Should they be treated?

Table 2.13 Axis V Global Assessment of Functioning Scale

This is the scale for indicating how well the person is functioning across different domains of his or her life.

Code	
100	Superior functioning in a wide range of areas
90	Absent or minimal symptoms; good functioning in all areas
80	If symptoms present, they are transient and expectable reactions to psychosocial stressors; only slight impairment in functioning
70	Some mild symptoms or difficulty in functioning
60	Moderate symptoms and difficulty in functioning
50	Serious symptoms and difficulty in functioning
40	Some impairment in reality testing or communication or major impairment in several domains
30	Considerable delusions and hallucinations or serious impairment in communication and judgment
20	Some danger of hurting self or others or gross impairment in communication
10	Persistent danger of severely hurting self or others

Reprinted with permission from the *Diagnostic and Statistical Manual of Mental Disorders*, Fourth Edition. Copyright 1994 American Psychiatric Association, 1994.

The Case of Jonelle

Consider the following case study of a woman who is seeking help for some distressing symptoms. We will see how the clinician incorporates all five of the DSM-IV axes in making a diagnosis.

> **Case Study** • Jonelle is a 35-year-old African-American woman who works as a manager of a large bank. She reports at least a dozen incidents in the last 6 weeks in which she has suddenly felt her heart pounding, her pulse racing, and her breathing become rapid and shallow, she has felt faint and dizzy, and she has been sure that she is about to die. These attacks have lasted for several minutes. Jonelle consulted with her physician who conducted a complete physical checkup and concluded that there was no evidence of cardiac problems or other physical problems that could be causing her symptoms. Jonelle is becoming so afraid of having one of these attacks that it is interfering with her ability to do her job. She is constantly vigilant for signs of an impending attack, and this vigilance is interfering with her concentration and her ability to converse with customers and employees. When she feels an attack may be coming on, she rushes to the restroom or out to her car and remains there, often for over an hour, until she is convinced she will not have an attack. Jonelle reports that the attacks began shortly after her mother died of a heart attack. She and her mother were extremely close, and Jonelle still feels devastated by her loss.

In consulting the five axes, Jonelle's therapist would likely come up with this list:

Axis I: Panic Disorder

Axis II: None

Axis III: None

Axis IV: Psychosocial and environmental stressors: recent bereavement

Axis V: Global functioning: 60 (moderate difficulty)

What is particularly interesting is that this case study provides a good example of the importance of Axes III (physical conditions) and IV (psychosocial and environmental stressors). The clinician would certainly want to know if Jonelle had some physical condition that was creating her panic attacks before diagnosing them as a psychological

At the beginning of this chapter, we discussed several types of information gathered during an assessment. This table outlines how each of these pieces of information is reflected across the five axes of diagnosis in the DSM.

Information Reflected on Axis I (clinical disorders):

Current symptoms
Recent events (e.g., diagnosis of Adjustment Disorder requires a recent event in client's life)
Physical condition (symptoms given different diagnosis if caused by general medical disorder than if not)
Drug and alcohol use (may indicate Substance Abuse or Dependence Disorder)
History of psychological disorders (used to make differential diagnosis)
Family history of psychological disorders (used to make differential diagnosis)
Intellectual and cognitive functioning

Information Reflected on Axis II (mental retardation and personality disorders):

Current symptoms
History of psychological disorders
Family history of psychological disorders
Intellectual and cognitive functioning
Coping style (some personality disorders have characteristic coping styles that are indicators of the disorder)

Information Reflected on Axis III (general medical conditions):

Physical condition
Drug and alcohol use

Information Reflected on Axis IV (psychosocial and environmental problems):

Recent events
Social resources
Sociocultural background

Information Reflected on Axis V (global assessment of functioning):

Incorporates all information from an assessment into one global rating

Reprinted with permission from the *Diagnostic and Statistical Manual of Mental Disorders*, Fourth Edition. Copyright 1994 American Psychiatric Association, 1994.

disorder. Similarly, knowing that the panic attacks began to occur shortly after the death of Jonelle's mother from a heart attack gives the clinician a good clue about their possible psychological origins. It is fairly common for people suffering from panic attacks to have lost a close relative or friend to a heart attack or stroke and to then experience symptoms mimicking a heart attack or stroke.

Table 2.14 outlines how the information gathered in an assessment is reflected in the five axes. Actually, every piece of information in an assessment may be used to make an accurate diagnosis on each of the five axes. However, Table 2.14 describes the information that is most crucial to making each of the five judgments in the multiaxial system of the DSM.

Summing Up   Diagnosis

- The *Diagnostic and Statistical Manual of Mental Disorders* (DSM) provides criteria for diagnosing all psychological disorders currently recognized in the United States.
- The first two editions of the DSM provided vague descriptions of disorder based on psychoanalytic theory, and thus the reliability of diagnoses made according to these manuals was low.
- More recent editions of the DSM contain more specific, observable criteria that are not as strongly based on theory for the diagnosis of disorders.

- Five axes or types of information are specified in determining a DSM diagnosis.
- On Axis I, clinicians list all significant clinical syndromes.
- On Axis II, clinicians indicate if the client is suffering from a personality disorder or mental retardation.
- On Axis III, clinicians list the client's general medical condition.
- On Axis IV, clinicians list psychosocial and environmental problems the client is facing.
- On Axis V, clinicians indicate the client's global level of functioning.

Gender and Cultural Bias in Diagnosis

So how do a disorder and the diagnostic criteria for that disorder become recognized and accepted as part of the DSM system? It happens largely by the consensus of clinicians and researchers in psychiatry and psychology. The diagnostic criteria for the DSM-III, DSM-IIIR, and the new DSM-IV were derived by committees of experts on each of the disorders. These committees conducted comprehensive and systematic reviews of the published literature to determine the evidence for and against the existence of the syndromes being considered for inclusion in the DSM. As noted, the developers of the DSM-IV also conducted field trials to determine the reliability and usefulness of criteria sets in clinical and research settings.

Despite the best efforts of the developers of the DSMs to be objective and accurate in their definitions of disorders, these definitions represent a process of consensus-building and compromise among experts with different opinions. The opportunity for political, cultural, and ideological influences on the establishment of the diagnostic criteria for disorders in such a process should be obvious.

One good example of the politicization of the DSM process was the debate over the addition of two personality disorders in the DSM-IIIR. Some members of the committee revising the DSM-IIIR argued for the inclusion of a disorder that they felt was very common and was distinct from all the disorders that were already recognized in the DSM-IIIR. People with this proposed disorder had a lifelong practice of getting themselves into and remaining in situations in which other people used and abused them. The proponents of this disorder suggested that it be labeled Masochistic Personality Disorder. When news of this proposed disorder became public, some psychologists and psychiatrists strongly objected to it (Caplan & Gans, 1991). They argued that it would be used to pathologize women who, because of their lack of power and their social upbringing, found themselves trapped in abusive relationships, such as wife-battering relationships. They demanded a hearing before the committee to discuss the scientific merits of the Masochistic Personality Disorder diagnosis and the social implications of including it as a disorder in the DSM. What some of the committee members suggested, to address the concerns of the opponents of the Masochistic Personality Disorder diagnosis, was to add yet another disorder, called Sadistic Personality Disorder, that then would pathologize the behavior of the abusers in wife-battering and other types of abusive relationships. Soon, however, several people pointed out that one of the political implications of this "solution" was that some wife-batterers could plead "not guilty" by reason of a mental disorder when charged with beating their wives. In the end, the committee could not reach consensus and simply voted on what to do. The Masochistic Personality Disorder was relabeled Self-Defeating Personality Disorder, and both it and Sadistic Personality Disorder were included in an appendix of the DSM-IIIR as "Proposed Diagnostic Categories Needing Further Study." The further study of these diagnoses after the publication of the DSM-IIIR did not strongly support the reliability or validity of the diagnoses. Thus, they were dropped altogether from the DSM-IV.

Some critics of the DSM have argued that it reflects only male, Western views of mental health and mental disorders. The model for healthy behavior for Western males is to be assertive and independent. People who appear unassertive and dependent on others—such as women and people from cultures that value interdependence among people—may be labeled as unhealthy. For example, some of the personality disorders, such as the Dependent Personality Disorder, have been said to pathologize behaviors associated with women's sex role, simply because they do not conform to male models of healthy behaviors (Caplan & Gans, 1991; Kaplan, 1983).

We noted in Chapter 1 that different cultures have different ways of conceptualizing mental disorders, and there are some disorders defined in one culture that do not seem to occur in other cultures. The developers of the DSM-IV included an appendix that lists many of these culture-specific disorders and brief guidelines for gathering information during the assessment process regarding a client's culture. The DSM-IV also includes short descriptions of cultural variation in the presentation of the each of the major mental disorders recognized in the manual. For example, it notes differences among cultures in the content of delusions (beliefs out of touch with reality) in schizophrenia. Some critics do not believe it goes nearly far enough in recognizing cultural and gender variation in what is "healthy" and "unhealthy" (see Dana, 1995). Throughout the remainder of this book, we comment on cultural and gender variations in the experience and prevalence of each of the disorders recognized by the DSM.

The Dangers of Diagnosis

The possibility of cultural and gender bias in the formulation and application of psychological diagnoses raises questions about the validity of these diagnoses. One influential critic of psychiatry, Thomas Szasz, has argued that there are so many biases inherent in who is labeled as having a mental disorder that the entire system of diagnosis is corrupt and should be abandoned. Szasz (1961) believes that people in power use psychiatric diagnoses to label and dispose of people who do not "fit in." He suggests that mental disorders do not really exist, and that people who seem to be suffering from mental disorders are only suffering from the oppression of a society that does not accept their alternative ways of behaving and looking at the world.

Even psychiatrists and psychologists who do not fully agree with Szasz's perspective on labeling recognize the great dangers of labeling behaviors or people abnormal. The person labeled abnormal is treated differently by society, and this treatment can continue long after the person stops exhibiting behaviors labeled abnormal. In a classic study of the effects of labeling, psychologist David Rosenhan and several of his research colleagues falsely told the admitting staff at a psychiatric hospital that they were hearing voices that said the words *empty, hollow,* and *thud* (Rosenhan, 1973). The researchers denied having any other symptoms, and when asked questions about their personal histories (which were quite normal by most criteria), they answered honestly. The researchers were admitted to the hospital, and most were given the diagnosis of schizophrenia. Once they were admitted, however, the researchers told the hospital staff that they no longer heard voices and acted in their usual, "normal" manner. Despite this, the researchers were kept in the hospital by the physicians for an average of 19 days. Although some of the "real" patients in the psychiatric hospitals detected that the pseudopatient researchers were fakes, none of the hospital staff did. Moreover, the behaviors and histories of the pseudopatients were interpreted in light of their status as patients. For example, most of the pseudopatients took notes frequently on the activities of the hospital ward. In their charts, nurses wrote that the patients "engaged in writing behavior." Rosenhan (1973, p. 253) also describes how one pseudopatient's rather unremarkable personal history was translated by the hospital staff in terms of his diagnosis:

> A clear example of such translation is found in the case of a pseudopatient who had a close relationship with his mother but was rather remote from his father during his early childhood. During adolescence and beyond, however, his father

became a close friend, while his relationship with his mother cooled. His present relationship with his wife was characteristically close and warm. Apart from occasional angry exchanges, friction was minimal. The children had rarely been spanked . . .

Observe, however, how such a history was translated in the psychopathological context, this from the case summary prepared after the patient was discharged:

This white 39-year-old male manifests a long history of considerable ambivalence in close relationships, which begins in early childhood. A warm relationship with his mother cools during his adolescence. A distant relationship to his father is described as becoming very intense. Affective stability is absent. His attempts to control emotionality with his wife and children are punctuated by angry outbursts and, in the case of the children, spankings. And while he says that he has several good friends, one senses considerable ambivalence embedded in those relationships also.

When the pseudopatients were discharged, it was with the diagnosis of "Schizophrenia, in remission," meaning that they still were considered to have schizophrenia, but their symptoms had subsided.

The label *abnormal* may be even more pernicious when it is applied to children, as is illustrated by a study of boys in grades 3 through 6 (Harris et al., 1992). Researchers paired boys who were the same age but who were previously unacquainted. In half of the pairs, one of the boys was told that his partner had a behavior problem that made him disruptive. In reality, only some of the boys labeled as having a behavior problem actually had a behavior problem. In the other half of the pairs, the boys were not told anything about each other, although some of the boys actually did have behavior problems. All the pairs worked together on a task while researchers videotaped their interaction. After the interaction, the boys were asked several questions about each other and about their enjoyment of the interaction.

The boys who had been told that their partners had a behavior problem were less friendly toward their partners during the task, talked with them less often, and were less involved in the interaction with their partners than were the boys who had been told nothing about their partners. In turn, the boys who had been labeled as having a behavior problem enjoyed the interaction less, took less credit for their performance on the task, and said their partners were less friendly toward them than did boys who had not been labeled as having a behavior problem. Most importantly, labeling a boy as having a behavior problem influenced his partner's behaviors toward him and his enjoyment of the task, regardless of whether he actually had a behavior problem. These results show that labeling a child abnormal strongly affects other children's behaviors toward him or her, even when there is no reason for the child to be labeled abnormal.

Should we avoid psychiatric diagnoses altogether? Probably not. Despite the potential dangers of diagnostic systems, they serve vital functions. The primary role of diagnostic systems is to organize the confusing array of psychological systems in an agreed-upon manner. This facilitates communication from one clinician to another and across time. So if Dr. Jones reads in a patient's history that he was diagnosed with schizophrenia according to the DSM-IIIR, she knows what criteria were used to make that diagnosis and can compare the patient's diagnosis then with his symptoms now. Such information can assist Dr. Jones in making an accurate assessment of the patient's current symptoms and in determining what the proper treatment for his symptoms might be. For example, if the patient's current symptoms also suggest schizophrenia and the patient responded to Drug X when he had schizophrenia a few years ago, this suggests that the patient might respond well to Drug X now.

Having a standard diagnostic system also greatly facilitates research on psychological disorders. For example, if a researcher at State University is using the DSM-IV criteria to identify people with obsessive-compulsive disorder, and a researcher at Private University is using the same criteria for the same purpose, the two researchers will be

The labels children acquire can affect other children's behaviors toward them.

better able to compare the results of their research than if they were using different criteria to diagnose obsessive-compulsive disorder. This can lead to faster advances in our understanding of the causes of and effective treatment for disorders.

After clinicians administer a battery of assessment tests to a client, they must then integrate the information from these tests to form a coherent picture of the client's strengths and weaknesses. This picture weaves together information on the client's biological functioning (major illnesses, possible genetic vulnerability to psychopathology), psychological functioning (personality, coping skills, intellectual strengths, symptoms), and social functioning (support networks, work relationships, social skills). The clinician comments on ways in which strengths or deficits in one domain are influencing functioning in another domain. For example, the clinician might note that a client with multiple sclerosis is having increasing difficulties performing her job and, as a result, has become anxious about losing her job. To cope with that anxiety, she has begun drinking heavily. This has caused conflict in her marriage, which then has made her even more anxious. The assessment process is thus inherently a process of bio-psycho-social integration of pieces of information about an individual.

The latest edition of the DSM was revised to reflect a more integrated and dynamic view of how biology, psychology, and social factors influence each other. The manual now includes information on cultural differences and similarities for each disorder and biological correlates for each disorder. In addition, the DSM-IV changed the label for an entire set of disorders to enhance an integrated bio-psycho-social view of disorders. The editions prior to DSM-IV included a category called *Organic Disorders*, which included delirium, dementia, and amnesia. These disorders are still included in the DSM-IV but not under a category labeled *Organic Disorders*. The developers of the DSM-IV wanted to drop the label *Organic Disorders* because having one category of disorders labeled as organic implied that these disorders were caused by biological factors but that other disorders listed in the manual under other labels were not.

Thus, both the assessment process and the DSM-IV itself reflect a bio-psycho-social approach to psychopathology. As we shall see as we discuss each of the major disorders recognized by the DSM-IV, this type of approach appears warranted.

Chapter Summary

Assessment is the process of gathering information about what is wrong with a person and the causes of his or her symptoms. Diagnosis is a label we attach to a set of symptoms that tend to co-occur with one another.

During an assessment, a clinician will want to gather at least eleven types of information about clients. First, clinicians need to find out about the nature, duration, and severity of their symptoms. Second, they need to know about any recent life events. Third, clients should have complete physical examinations to determine if they are suffering from any medical conditions that might be tied to their psychological symptoms. Fourth, therapists need information about any drugs clients are taking. Fifth, therapists will ask about clients' histories of psychological problems. Sixth, clinicians inquire about clients' families histories of psychological disorders. Seventh, clinicians may assess clients' cognitive and intellectual functioning. Eighth, clinicians will ask about clients' typical ways of coping with situations. Ninth, clinicians investigate the social resources available to the client. Tenth, clinicians assess clients' self-concepts and their concepts of their symptoms. Eleventh, clinicians assess the sociocultural backgrounds of clients, particularly of those who are from cultures different from those of the clinicians.

The validity and reliability of assessment tools are indices of their quality. Validity is the accuracy of a test in assessing what it is supposed to assess. Five different types of validity are face validity, content validity, concurrent validity, predictive validity, and construct validity. Reliability is the consistency of a test. Types of reliability include test-retest reliability, alternate form reliability, internal reliability, and interrater or interjudge reliability.

Biological tests for brain imaging include computerized tomography (CT), positron emission tomography (PET), magnetic resonance imagery (MRI), electroencephalogram (EEG), and event-related potential (ERP). These tests can suggest differences between people with psychological disorders and those without and can detect gross brain abnormalities in individuals. As yet, they cannot definitively diagnose psychological disorders in individuals.

Paper-and-pencil neuropsychological tests can assess specific cognitive deficits that may be related to brain damage in patients. Intelligence tests provide a more general measure of verbal and analytical skills.

To assess emotional and behavioral functioning, clinicians use structured clinical interviews, symptom questionnaires, personality inventories, behavioral observation and self-monitoring, and projective tests. Each of these tests has its advantages and disadvantages.

During the assessment procedure, many problems and biases can be introduced. Clients may be resistant to being assessed and thus distort the information they provide. Clinicians may introduce their own biases into the assessment through countertransference. Clients may be too impaired by cognitive deficits, distress, or lack of development of verbal skills to provide information. Finally, there are many biases that can arise when the clinician and client are from different cultures.

A classification system is a set of definitions for syndromes and rules for determining when a person's symptoms are part of each syndrome. The predominant classification system for psychological problems in the United States is the *Diagnostic and Statistical Manual of Mental Disorders* of the American Psychiatric Association. The most recent editions of the DSM have provided specific criteria for diagnosing each of the recognized psychological disorders. The DSM also provides information on the course of disorders and their prevalence. The explicit criteria in the DSM have increased the reliability of diagnoses in the DSM, but there is still room for improvement.

There are five axes along which clinicians should assess clients, according to the DSM. On Axis I, major clinical syndromes are noted. Axis II contains diagnoses of mental retardation and personality disorders. On Axis III, the clinician notes any medical conditions that clients have. On Axis IV, psychosocial and environmental stressors are noted. On Axis V, clients' general levels of functioning are assessed.

Critics have charged that the DSM reflects cultural and gender biases in its views of what is psychologically healthy and unhealthy. They also point to many dangers in labeling people with psychiatric disorders, including the danger of stigmatization. Diagnosis is important, however, to communication between clinicians and researchers. Only when a system of definitions of disorders is agreed upon can communication about disorders be improved.

Key Terms

assessment 24
diagnosis 24
tools of assessment 24
system of diagnosis 24
differential diagnosis 26
self-efficacy 27
acculturation 28
interview 28
unstructured
  interview 28

structured interview 28
validity 29
face validity 29
content validity 29
concurrent validity 29
predictive validity 30
construct validity 30
reliability 30
test-retest reliability 30

alternate form
  reliability 30
internal reliability 30
interrater reliability 30
computerized
  tomography (CT) 31
positron emission
  tomography (PET) 31
magnetic resonance
  imaging (MRI) 31

more on back page

Application
Is Self-Assessment a Good Idea?

Self-help books and magazine articles often feature questionnaires that allow readers to assess their own personal characteristics or weaknesses or the characteristics of their relationships with others. These self-assessment tools typically involve a set of questions that help readers "diagnose" problems and some guidelines as to how to interpret scores on the questionnaires. Are these self-assessment tools a good idea?

In this chapter, we have discussed the problems with the reliability and validity of many assessment tools. The tools that have been described in this chapter are the "best of the bunch"—those most widely used and accepted by professional psychologists and psychiatrists—and yet even these tools have many critics. The self-assessment questionnaires that appear in books and magazines are often not as well-tested or well-conceived as those we discussed in this chapter. In addition, the writers of these questionnaires often make claims about the diagnoses that they produce that are overly conclusive and extreme, such as, "If you scored between 10 and 20 on the Relationship Diagnostic Inventory, then your relationship is definitely going to fail. You might as well dump him and find someone else now!"

This does not mean that all self-assessment tools are a bad idea. People often want to deny their problems or are not aware that their symptoms are part of syndromes that can be successfully treated, and self-assessment tools can help people recognize their troubles and seek help. For example, questionnaires that lead people to recognize that they consume much more alcohol than the average person and that withdrawal from the effects of alcohol often interferes with their daily functioning can help these people to moderate their alcohol consumption or seek treatment for alcohol addiction if necessary. Similarly, questionnaires or guidelines that make people aware that the set of symptoms they have been experiencing add up to the syndrome of an anxiety disorder can lead these people into therapy.

One of the most important points to remember about any self-assessment tool is that the information it provides is only suggestive, not conclusive. If you are concerned about the outcome of any self-assessment tool—your score on a questionnaire or how you answered individual questions—it is a good idea to consult with a professional counselor about your concerns to obtain a more thorough and expert assessment of how you are doing. ■

chapter 3

Approaching and Treating Abnormality

Biological Theories of Abnormality

Biological theories ascribe psychological symptoms to structural abnormalities in the brain, dysfunctioning of brain neurotransmitter systems, or faulty genes. These three types of biological abnormalities may work independently of each other to create psychological symptoms, or genetic abnormalities may sometimes be the cause of other abnormalities.

Psychosocial Theories of Abnormality

Psychodynamic theories of abnormality ascribe psychological symptoms to unconscious conflicts. Behavioral theories say symptoms result from the reinforcements and punishments people have received for their behaviors. Cognitive theories say that people's ways of interpreting situations determine their emotional and behavioral symptoms. Humanist and existential theories suggest that symptoms arise when people are not allowed to pursue their potential and instead try to conform to others' wishes.

Treatments for Abnormality

Biological therapies most often involve the prescription of drugs. Psychodynamic therapies focus on uncovering and resolving unconscious conflicts. Humanist and existential therapies seek to help people discover their greatest potentials and self-heal. Behavior therapies try to reshape people's maladaptive behaviors. Cognitive therapies attempt to change people's maladaptive ways of thinking.

Modes of Delivering Psychosocial Therapy

Therapy can be delivered to individuals, to groups of people with similar problems, to couples, and to families.

Special Issues in Treating Children

A number of special issues arise in the treatment of children with psychological problems. First, therapies must be adapted so that they are appropriate to children's developmental levels. Second, there are concerns about the long-term effects of drug therapies on children's physical development. Third, it is often necessary to treat a child's family as well as the individual child. Fourth, children typically do not seek therapy for themselves but are brought to therapy by others.

Common Components of Therapy

All successful therapies share certain components, although their specific techniques may differ greatly. These common components include the development of a positive relationship with a therapist and the client believing that the therapy may help him or her.

Cultural and Gender Issues in Therapy

It may not be necessary for a therapist and client to be of the same gender and culture for a therapy to be successful, but a therapist must be sensitive to the cultural background and the gender of the client. Culturally specific therapies use the beliefs and rituals of a culture in treating clients of that culture.

Bio-Psycho-Social Integration
Chapter Summary
Key Terms
Application: *How to Look for a Therapist*

It can be no dishonor to learn from others when they speak good sense.

—Sophocles, *Antigone* (442–441 B.C.; translated by Elizabeth Wyckoff)

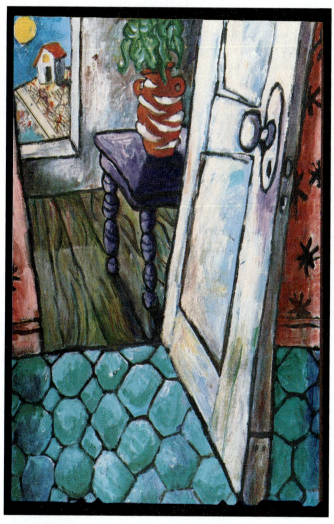

Christian Pierre
Window of Opportunity

> **Case Study** • Catherine, a 6-year-old girl, has been doing strange things lately. When she goes through the door to her bedroom, she stops, steps back into the hallway and reenters the door. She repeats this procedure six times. She cannot say why she feels she must do this. However, if she does not enter and reenter the door six times, she becomes very upset and nervous. Catherine has also begun to pull the hair on one section of her head so hard and often that she nearly has a bald spot there. Again, she cannot say why she does this; she just feels that she must.

biological approach
view that biological factors cause and should be used to treat abnormality

psychosocial approach
view that psychological characteristics and social events cause abnormality

What are the likely causes of Catherine's symptoms, and what would be an appropriate treatment for these symptoms? Your answer to this question depends on your *theoretical approach* to abnormality. A theoretical approach is a set of assumptions about the likely causes of abnormality and the appropriate treatments for abnormality. If you take a **biological approach** to abnormality, you probably suspect that Catherine's symptoms are caused by a biological factor, such as structural or functional deficits in the brain, biochemical imbalances, or genetics. The treatment you would prescribe, typically a medication, would be meant to alter or compensate for these biological abnormalities. If you take a **psychosocial approach** to abnormality, you suspect that Catherine's symptoms are rooted in early childhood experiences, more recent traumas, thinking styles, or other personality characteristics. The treatment you would prescribe, typically psychotherapy, would be meant to help her overcome the psychosocial issues in her life.

Chapter 1 emphasized that most forms of abnormality probably have both biological and psychosocial causes and that the integration of these two approaches has proven very useful. Historically, however, biological and psychsocial approaches to abnormality have developed separately. Today there are still many mental health experts who advocate one of these approaches over the other.

Before reading about modern conceptualizations of abnormality, take a moment to reflect on your own assumptions about the causes of abnormality. What is the basis for these assumptions?

In this chapter, we will examine the biological and psychosocial approaches that have dominated the field of abnormal psychology in its modern history. We begin by examining the general principles of the major biological and psychosocial theories of the causes of abnormality. Then we describe the most commonly used biological and psychosocial treatments. The details of these approaches and their application to specific disorders will be described in the remaining chapters of this book. We close the chapter with a discussion of the effects of gender and culture on the choice and effectiveness of treatment.

Biological Theories of Abnormality

On 13 September 1848, Phineas P. Gage, a 25-year-old construction foreman for the Rutland and Burlington Railroad in New England, became the victim of a bizarre accident. In order to lay new rail tracks across Vermont, it was necessary to level the uneven terrain by controlled blasting. Among other tasks, Gage was in charge of the detonations, which involved drilling holes in the stone, partially filling the holes with explosive powder, covering the powder with sand, and using a fuse and a tamping iron to trigger an explosion into the rock. On the fateful day, a momentary distraction let Gage begin tamping directly over the powder before his assistant had had a chance to cover it with sand. The result was a powerful explosion away from the rock and toward Gage. The fine-pointed, 3-cm-thick,

109-cm-long tamping iron was hurled, rocket-like, through his face, skull, brain, and then into the sky. Gage was momentarily stunned but regained full consciousness immediately thereafter. He was able to talk and even walk with the help of his men. The iron landed many yards away.

Phineas Gage not only survived the momentous injury, in itself enough to earn him a place in the annals of medicine, but he survived as a different man, and therein lies the greater significance of this case. Gage had been a responsible, intelligent, and socially well-adapted individual, a favorite with peers and elders. He had made progress and showed promise. The signs of a profound change in personality were already evident during the convalescence under the care of his physician, John Harlow. But as the months passed, it became apparent that the transformation was not only radical but difficult to comprehend. In some respects, Gage was fully recovered. He remained as able-bodied and appeared to be as intelligent as before the accident; he had no impairment of movement or speech; new learning was intact, and neither memory nor intelligence in the conventional sense had been affected. On the other hand, he had become irreverent and capricious. His respect for the social conventions by which he once abided had vanished. His abundant profanity offended those around him. Perhaps most troubling, he had taken leave of his sense of responsibility. He could not be trusted to honor his commitments. His employers had deemed him "the most efficient and capable" man in their "employ" but now they had to dismiss him. In the words of his physician, "the equilibrium or balance, so to speak, between his intellectual faculty and animal propensities" had been destroyed. In the words of his friends and acquaintances, "Gage was no longer Gage." (Damasio et al., 1994, p. 1102)

The story of Phineas Gage is one of the most dramatic examples of the effect of biological factors on psychological functioning. As a result of damage to his brain from the accident, Gage's basic personality seemed to change. Most stark was his transformation from a responsible, socially appropriate man to an impulsive, emotional, and socially inappropriate man.

Almost 150 years later, researchers using modern neuroimaging techniques of Gage's preserved skull and a computer simulation of the tamping-iron accident determined the precise location of the damage to Gage's brain (see Figure 3.1). (For a discussion of neuroimaging techniques such as MRI, CT, and PET scanning, see Chapter 2.) Studies of people today who suffer damage to this area of the brain reveal that these people have trouble making rational decisions in personal and social matters and have trouble processing information about emotions. They do not have trouble, however, in tackling the logic of an abstract problem, in performing calculations, or in memory. Thus, like Gage, their basic intellectual functioning remains intact, but their emotional control and judgment in personal and social matters is impaired (Damasio et al., 1994).

Gage's psychological changes were the result of damage to structures in his brain. Structural damage to the brain is one of three causes of abnormality on which biological approaches to abnormality often focus. The other two are biochemical imbalances and genetic abnormalities. We explore these three biological causes in this section.

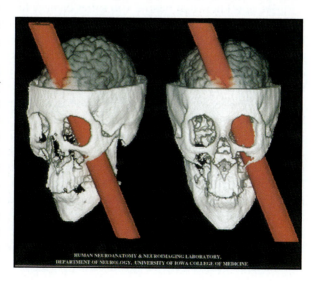

Figure 3.1

Phineas Gage's Brain Injury. Modern neuroimaging techniques have helped to identify the precise location of damage to Phineas Gage's brain.

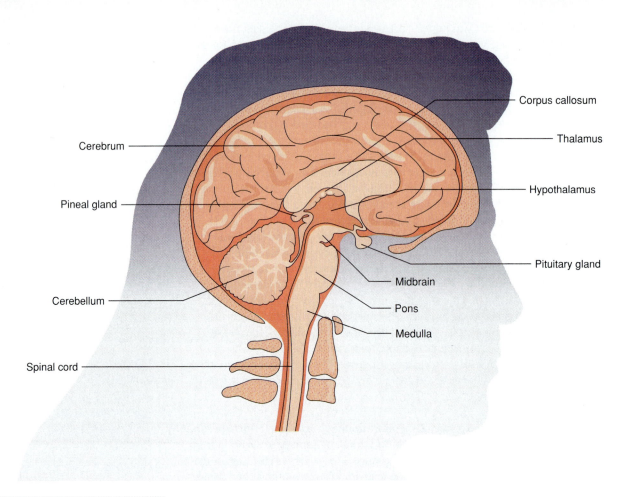

Labels in figure:
- Cerebrum
- Pineal gland
- Cerebellum
- Spinal cord
- Corpus callosum
- Thalamus
- Hypothalamus
- Pituitary gland
- Midbrain
- Pons
- Medulla

Figure 3.2

The Human Brain. These are some of the major structures of the brain. The cerebrum regulates many complex activities, such as speech and analytical thinking. The hypothalamus regulates eating, drinking, sexual desire, and emotions.

cerebrum

part of the brain that regulates complex activities such as speech and analytical thinking

Structural Brain Abnormalities

It seems obvious to us today that if areas of the brain responsible for personality and emotional functioning are damaged, this will result in psychological changes. In the days of Phineas Gage and for many years thereafter, however, this was not a popular perspective. More precisely, it was not popular to believe that a person's character and control over his or her behavior rested, at least in part, in biology, and were not completely the result of will and upbringing.

We now know that people who suffer damage to the brain (often referred to as lesions) or have major abnormalities in the structure of their brains often show problems in psychological functioning. The location of the structural damage influences the specific psychological problems they have. Figure 3.2 shows some of the major areas of the brain. The damage that Phineas Gage suffered was primarily to the frontal area of his **cerebrum**, a part of the brain that regulates many of the complex activities that make us human. The cerebrum is divided into two halves: the left and right hemispheres. The left hemisphere governs the ability to produce language and many complicated logical and analytic activities, such as mathematical computations. The right hemisphere is involved in spatial perception, pattern recognition, and the processing of emotion. It is important to note that, although certain functions such as language production may be localized in certain areas of the brain, the different structures of the brain are highly interrelated and must work together to produce the complex behaviors of which humans are capable.

One area of the brain that may be involved in several types of abnormal behavior is the hypothalamus (see Figure 3.2). The hypothalamus regulates eating, drinking, and

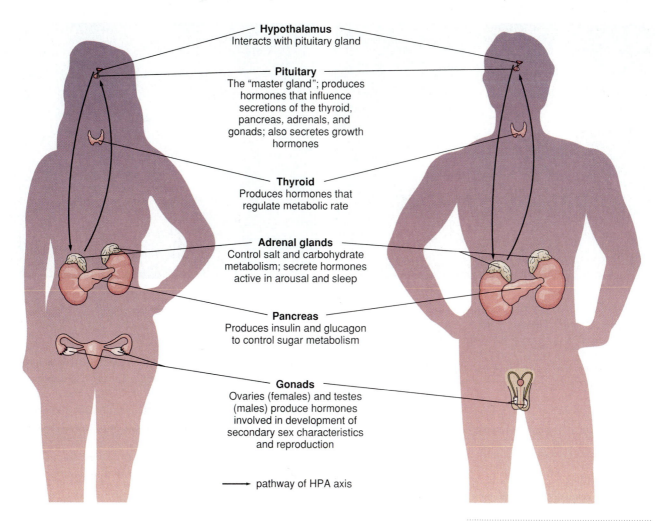

Hypothalamus
Interacts with pituitary gland

Pituitary
The "master gland"; produces hormones that influence secretions of the thyroid, pancreas, adrenals, and gonads; also secretes growth hormones

Thyroid
Produces hormones that regulate metabolic rate

Adrenal glands
Control salt and carbohydrate metabolism; secrete hormones active in arousal and sleep

Pancreas
Produces insulin and glucagon to control sugar metabolism

Gonads
Ovaries (females) and testes (males) produce hormones involved in development of secondary sex characteristics and reproduction

→ pathway of HPA axis

Figure 3.3

The Endocrine System. The hypothalamus regulates the endocrine system, which produces most of the major hormones of the body.
Source: Goldstein, 1994.

limbic system
brain region that regulates eating, sex, and reactions to stressful situations

ventricles
fluid-filled spaces of the brain

sexual behavior. Abnormal behaviors that involve any of these activities may be the result of dysfunctioning of the hypothalamus. Basic emotions may be influenced by the hypothalamus; stimulation of certain areas of the hypothalamus produces sensations of pleasure, while stimulation of other areas produces sensations of pain or unpleasantness. The hypothalamus also regulates the endocrine system, which is a system of glands that produce the hormones of the body (see Figure 3.3).

Another important area of the brain, the **limbic system** is a collection of structures that are closely interconnected with the hypothalamus and appear to exert additional control over some of the instinctive behaviors regulated by the hypothalamus, such as eating, sexual behavior, and reactions to stressful situations. Monkeys with damage to the limbic system sometimes become chronically aggressive, reacting with rage to the slightest provocation; at other times, they become excessively passive and do not react even to direct threats.

Structural damage to the brain can result from injury, such as from an automobile accident, and from disease processes that cause deterioration. In schizophrenia, a severe disorder in which people lose touch with reality, a disease process can cause deterioration in the frontal cortex of the brain and enlargement of fluid-filled spaces of the brain called the **ventricles** (see Figure 3.4). We will encounter other examples of psychological disorders that appear to be associated with structural abnormalities in the brain.

Often, however, even modern neuroimaging techniques detect no structural abnormalities in the brains of people with psychological disorders, even some severe disorders. Instead, these disorders may be tied to biochemical processes in the brain.

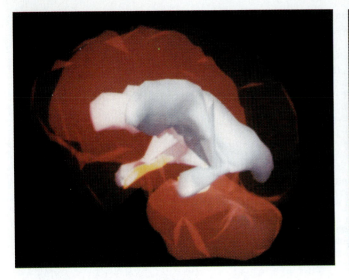 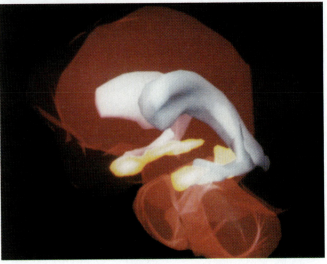

Figure 3.4

The Effects on the Brain of Schizophrenia. An MRI of the brain of a person with schizophrenia (left) shows a shrunken hippocampus (part of the limbic system) in yellow and enlarged, fluid-filled ventricles in gray. The MRI on the right is of a normal person.

neurotransmitters
biochemicals released from a sending neuron that transmit messages to a receiving neuron in the brain and nervous system

synapse
space between the sending neuron and the receiving neuron into which neurotransmitters are first released (also known as the *synaptic gap*)

reuptake
process in which the sending neuron reabsorbs some of the neurotransmitter in the synapse, decreasing the amount left in the synapse

degradation
process in which the receiving neuron releases an enzyme into the synapse, breaking down neurotransmitters into other biochemicals

endocrine system
system of glands that produces many different hormones

hormone
biochemical that sends messages regulating moods, levels of energy, and reactions to stress

Biochemical Causes of Abnormality

Most biochemical theories of abnormality focus on compounds called **neurotransmitters.** Neurotransmitters facilitate the transmission of signals from one neuron to another in the brain and in other parts of the nervous system (see Figure 3.5). These signals travel down the length of one neuron, through its axon, to the synaptic terminals at the end of the axon. Here the signals stimulate the release of neurotransmitters. A neurotransmitter is released through the axonal endings into the space between the axon and the dendrite of the next neuron. This space is known as the **synapse** or *synaptic gap*. The neurotransmitter binds to receptors on the exterior of the receiving dendrite, stimulating the receiving neuron to initiate an impulse.

Many of the biochemical theories of psychopathology suggest that too much or too little of certain neurotransmitters in the synapses causes specific types of psychopathology. The amount of a neurotransmitter available in the synapse can be affected by two processes. The process of **reuptake** occurs when the initial neuron releasing the neurotransmitter into the synapse reabsorbs the neurotransmitter, decreasing the amount left in the synapse. Another process, called **degradation,** occurs when the receiving neuron releases an enzyme into the synapse that breaks down the neurotransmitter into other biochemicals. Reuptake and degradation of neurotransmitters happen naturally. Sometimes one or both of these processes is out of kilter. When there is more than the normal amount of reuptake or degradation, abnormally low levels of a certain neurotransmitter in the synapse result. When there is less than the normal amount of reuptake or degradation, abnormally high levels of neurotransmitter in the synapse result.

Psychological symptoms may also be linked to the number and functioning of the receptors for neurotransmitters on the exterior of dendrites. If there are too few receptors or the receptors are not sensitive enough, the neuron will not be able to make adequate use of the neurotransmitter available in the synapse. If there are too many receptors or they are too sensitive, the neuron may be overexposed to the neurotransmitter that is in the synapse.

Other biochemical theories of psychopathology focus on the body's **endocrine system** (see Figure 3.3). This is a system of glands that produce many different chemicals called *hormones*, which are released directly into the blood. A **hormone** acts like a neurotransmitter, carrying "messages" throughout the system, potentially affecting people's moods, levels of energy, and reactions to stress. For example, some people with depression show an excessive secretion of the hormone cortisol from the adrenal gland in response to stress.

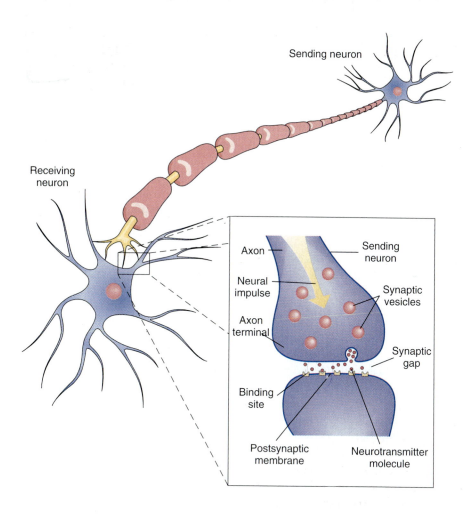

Figure 3.5

Neurotransmitters and the Synapse. The neurotransmitter is released into the synaptic gap. There it may bind with receptors on the postsynaptic membrane.

Sending neuron

Receiving neuron

Axon

Neural impulse

Axon terminal

Binding site

Postsynaptic membrane

Sending neuron

Synaptic vesicles

Synaptic gap

Neurotransmitter molecule

People are often relieved when they are told that a psychological disorder they are suffering from is due to a "chemical imbalance" in their brains. Why do you think this is so?

The proper working of neurotransmitter and neuroendocrine systems thus requires a delicate balance, and many forces can upset this balance. One of these is a genetic abnormality. Genetic abnormalities may cause biochemical systems to work improperly, and they can cause major structural anomalies in the brain. The end result is a psychological disturbance.

Genetic Factors in Abnormality

Genetic studies of personality and abnormality are a relatively new and a fast-growing area of research. This area, often referred to as **behavior genetics**, is concerned with two questions: (1) To what extent are behaviors or behavioral tendencies inherited and (2) What are the processes by which genes affect behavior?

Let us begin by reviewing the basics of genetic transmission. At conception, the fertilized embryo has 46 chromosomes, 23 from the female egg and 23 from the male sperm, making up 23 pairs of chromosomes (see Figure 3.6). One of these pairs is referred to as the *sex chromosomes* because it determines the sex of the embryo: The XX combination results in a female embryo, and the XY combination results in a male embryo. The mother of an embryo always contributes an X chromosome; the father can contribute an X or a Y.

behavior genetics
study of the processes by which genes affect behavior and the extent to which personality and abnormality are genetically inherited

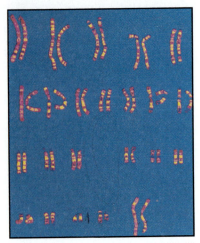

Figure 3.6

Human Chromosomes. The normal human has 23 pairs of chromosomes. In this photo, pair 23 is XX, so these are from a female.

polygenic
combination of many genes, each of which makes a small contribution to an inherited trait

predisposition
tendency to develop a disorder which must interact with other biological, psychological, or environmental factors for the disorder to develop

Down Syndrome is caused when chromosome 21 is present in triplicate instead of duplicate.

Alterations in the structure or number of chromosomes can cause major defects. For example, Down syndrome results when chromosome 21 is present in triplicate instead of as the usual pair. Down syndrome is characterized by mental retardation, heart malformations, and facial features such as a flat face, small nose, protruding lips and tongue, and slanted eyes.

Chromosomes are made up of individual genes, which are themselves segments of long molecules of DNA (deoxyribonucleic acid). Genes give coded instructions to cells to perform certain functions, usually to manufacture certain proteins. Genes, like chromosomes, come in pairs. One gene of each pair comes from the sperm chromosome and the other gene of the pair comes from the egg chromosome. Thus, a child receives only half of each parent's total genes. Abnormalities in genes that make up chromosomes are much more common than are major abnormalities in the structure or number of chromosomes.

Although you may often hear of scientists having discovered "the gene" for a major disorder, most disorders are not the result of single faulty genes but of combinations of altered genes. Each of these altered genes makes only a small contribution to vulnerability for the disorder. The more an individual has of the altered genes contributing to the disorder, the more likely he or she is to develop the disorder and the more severely he or she will manifest the disorder. There are a number of physiological disorders, such as diabetes, coronary heart disease, epilepsy, and cleft lip and palate, that are the result of such **polygenic,** or *multifactorial* processes. Most of the genetic models of the major types of mental disorder are also polygenic.

People who have disorders caused by polygenic processes often wonder why they have no family history of the disorder and why they are the only ones in their families to inherit the disorder. It may be because none of their relatives accumulated all the genes necessary for the disorder to develop fully. It just happens that when the people with disorders were conceived, all the genes necessary for the disorders were present in the chromosomes contributed by their mothers and fathers. When their brothers or sisters were conceived, however, different sets of chromosomes were contributed by their mothers and fathers, and these may not have contained all the necessary genes for the disorders, so their siblings did not develop the disorders.

Conversely, many people who have relatives with disorders that are heritable worry that they will inevitably develop the disorders. However, it is the case with most disorders, including psychological disorders, that the odds of an individual inheriting all the genes necessary for a disorder are fairly low, even if a relative who has the disorder is a parent or sibling. For example, the sibling of a person with schizophrenia, which is probably the psychological disorder in which genes play the strongest role, only has about a 9 percent chance of developing schizophrenia at some point in his or her life (see Chapter 6).

Another extremely important characteristic of polygenic disorders is that what is inherited is the **predisposition** to the disorder and not the inevitability of the disorder. Often, this predisposition must interact with other biological or environmental factors for the individual to fully develop the disorder. A good example from the medical field is coronary heart disease. A person can inherit a predisposition to coronary heart disease by inheriting the genes for hypertension, diabetes, or hyperlipidemia (too much fat in the blood). Whether he or she actually develops coronary heart disease depends, however, on a number of environmental and behavioral factors, such as obesity, smoking, exercise, alcohol abuse, hard-driving personality, and living in an industrialized society. The same characteristic may be true of many psychological disorders. What is inherited is a predisposition to the disorder. Whether an individual ever fully develops the disorder may depend on other biological risks (e.g., malnutrition or negative intrauterine experiences) and other psychosocial risks (e.g., growing up in a dysfunctional family) he or she is exposed to. As we discuss the specific psychological disorders in this textbook, we will consider the ways genetic predispositions and other biological or psychosocial factors may interact to increase an individual's risk for the disorder.

First, however, let us consider how we know whether a disorder is heritable. There are three basic types of studies scientists use to determine the heritability of a disorder: family history studies, twin studies, and adoption studies.

Could it be true that believing you are doomed by your genes to develop a psychological disorder actually contributes to your developing the disorder? If so, how would this happen?

Family History Studies

Disorders that are genetically transmitted should, on average, show up more often in the families of people who have the disorder than they do in families of people who do not have the disorder. This is true whether the disorder is caused by a single gene or by a combination of faulty genes. To conduct a **family history study**, scientists first identify people who clearly have the disorder in question; this group is called the **probands.** They also identify a control group of people who clearly do not have the disorder. They then trace the family pedigrees, or family trees, of these two groups of individuals and determine how many of their relatives have the disorder. Researchers are most interested in *first-degree* relatives, because these are the relatives who are most genetically similar to the probands and control subjects (unless they have identical twins, who will be genetically identical to them). Figure 3.7 illustrates the degree of genetic relationship between an individual and various categories of relatives. This figure gives you an idea of why the risk of inheriting the genes for a disorder quickly decreases as the relationship between an individual and the ill relative becomes more distant: It is because the percentage of genes the individual and ill relative have in common decreases greatly with distance.

Although family history studies provide very useful information about the possible genetic transmission of a disorder, they have their problems. The most obvious one is that families share not only genes but also environment. Thus, several members of a family could have a disorder because they share genes or because they share the same environmental stresses. Family history studies cannot tease apart genetic and environmental contributions to a disorder. Researchers often turn to twin studies to do this.

family history study
study of the heritability of a disorder involving identifying people with the disorder and people without the disorder and then determining the disorder's frequency within each person's family

probands
people who have the disorder under investigation in a family history study

Figure 3.7

Degrees of Genetic Relationship. Only monozygotic twins have 100 percent of their genes in common. People with whom you share 50 percent of your genes are your first-degree relatives. People with whom you share 25 percent of your genes are your second-degree relatives. People with whom you share 12.5 percent of your genes are your third-degree relatives.

100% of Genes in Common
Identical (monozygotic) twins
50% of Genes in Common
Parent–child
Full siblings (both parents in common)
Nonidentical (dizygotic) twins
25% of Genes in Common
Grandparent–grandchild
Uncle/aunt–Nephew/niece
Half siblings (one parent in common)
12.5% of Genes in Common
Great-grandparent–great-grandchild
Great-uncle/aunt–Grandnephew/niece
First cousins

Twin Studies

Notice in Figure 3.7 that identical, or **monozygotic (MZ) twins**, share 100 percent of their genes. This is because they came from a single fertilized egg that splits into two identical parts. In contrast, nonidentical or **dizygotic (DZ) twins** share, on average, 50 percent of their genes because they came from two separate eggs fertilized by separate sperm. Researchers have capitalized on this difference between MZ and DZ twins to investigate the contribution of genetics to many disorders through a **twin study**. If a disorder is determined *entirely* by genetics, then when one member of an monozygotic (MZ) twin pair has a disorder, the other member of the pair should always have the disorder. This probability that both twins will have the disorder if one twin has the disorder is called the **concordance rate** for the disorder. So if a disorder is entirely determined by genes, the concordance rate among MZ twins should be 100 percent. The concordance rate for the disorder among dizygotic (DZ) twins will be much lower than 100 percent. The actual concordance rate will depend on the number of faulty genes necessary for the disorder and

monozygotic (MZ) twins
twins who share 100 percent of their genes because they developed from a single fertilized egg

dizygotic (DZ) twins
twins who average only 50 percent of their genes in common because they developed from two separate fertilized eggs

twin study
study of the heritability of a disorder by comparing concordance rates between monozygotic and dizygotic twins

concordance rate
probability that both twins will develop a disorder if one twin has the disorder

the dominance of these genes. Even when a disorder is transmitted only partially by genetics, the concordance rate for MZ twins should be considerably higher than the concordance rate for DZ twins, because MZ twins are genetically identical but DZ twins share only about half the same genes.

Let us say that the concordance rate for Disorder X for MZ twins is 48 percent, whereas the concordance rate for DZ twins is 17 percent. These concordance rates tell us two things. First, because the concordance rate for MZ twins is considerably higher than the concordance rate for DZ twins, we have evidence that Disorder X is genetically transmitted. Second, because the concordance rate for MZ twins is well under 100 percent, we have evidence that it takes a combination of a genetic predisposition and other factors (biological or environmental) for an individual to develop Disorder X.

By now, you may be objecting that twin studies do not fully tease apart genetic factors from environmental factors, because MZ twins may have much more similar environments and experiences than do DZ twins. MZ twins typically look alike, whereas DZ twins often do not look alike, and physical appearance can strongly affect other people's reactions to an individual. MZ twins may also be more likely than DZ twins to share talents that influence the opportunities they are given in life. For example, MZ twins may both be athletic or very talented academically or musically, which then affects their treatment by others and their opportunities in life. In contrast, DZ twins much less often share the same talents and thus are less likely to be treated similarly by others. Finally, parents may simply treat MZ twins more similarly than they do DZ twins, for a variety of reasons.

Thus, researchers have turned to a third method for studying heritability, the adoption study, to try to tease apart fully the impacts of environmental and genetic factors.

Adoption Studies

adoption study
study of the heritability of a disorder by finding adopted people with a disorder and then determining the prevalence of the disorder among their biological and adoptive relatives, in order to separate out contributing genetic and environmental factors

An **adoption study** can be carried out in a number of ways. In the most common type of adoption study, researchers first identify people who have the disorder of interest who were adopted shortly after birth. Then they determine the rates of the disorder in the biological relatives of these adoptees and the adoptive relatives of the adoptees. If a disorder is strongly influenced by genetics, then researchers should see higher rates of the disorder among the biological relatives of the adoptee than among the adoptive relatives. If the disorder is strongly influenced by environment, then they should see higher rates of the disorder among the adoptive relatives than among the biological relatives.

The most interesting studies of the genetics of personality combine the strategies of the adoption study and the twin study. For example, researchers at the University of Minnesota identified several dozen pairs of MZ and DZ twins who were reared apart and brought them together at the laboratories to assess their personalities (Bouchard et al., 1990; Lykken et al., 1993; Tellegen et al., 1988). Some of the twins reared apart had never met each other and had not even known that they had a twin. The personalities of the MZ twins reared apart were compared to the personalities of the DZ twins reared apart and to MZ and DZ twins reared in the same households. The results of this study have provided evidence that some aspects of personality are substantially affected by genetics. For example, it appears that traits such as shyness or the tendency to become easily upset are between 30 and 50 percent caused by genetics (Bouchard et al., 1990).

There are startling examples of identical twins reared apart who are amazingly similar, even though they have never met each other. Consider, for example, the "Jim twins" (Holden, 1980). Jim Lewis and Jim Springer were identical twins reunited at the age of 39 after being separated since infancy. Both had married and later divorced women named Linda. Their second wives were both named Betty. Both had sons named James Allan and dogs named Toy. Both chain-smoked Salem cigarettes, worked as sheriffs' deputies, drove Chevrolets, chewed their fingernails, enjoyed stock car racing, had basement workshops, and had built circular white benches around trees in their yards. Genetic researchers do not argue that there are genes for marrying women named Linda or Betty or genes for having basement workshops. However, given similar circumstances, people with identical genes may choose the same activities and have the same likes and dislikes.

Question for the Heart: Many people are resistant to believing that much of personality is inherited. Why do you think this is so?

Thus, adoption studies, twin studies, and family history studies all help to determine whether a characteristic or disorder is influenced by genetics and the degree of this influence. Each type of study has its limitations. Family history and twin studies cannot fully tease apart the impacts of genetics and shared environment. Adoption studies suffer from the fact that it is difficult to find large numbers of adoptees with the disorder of interest, so the sample sizes in these studies tend to be very small.

Summing Up | Biological Theories

- The biological theories of psychopathology hold that psychological symptoms and disorders are caused by structural abnormalities in the brain, disordered biochemistry, or faulty genes.
- Structural abnormalities in the brain can be caused by injury or disease processes. The specific area of the brain damaged will influence the type of psychological symptoms shown.
- Most biochemical theories focus on neurotransmitters, the biochemicals that facilitate transmission of impulses in the brain. Some theories say that psychological symptoms are caused by too little or too much of a particular neurotransmitter in the synapses of the brain. Other theories focus on the number of receptors for neurotransmitters.
- Some people may be genetically predisposed to psychological disorders. Most of these disorders are probably linked not to a single faulty gene but to the accumulation of a group of faulty genes.
- Three methods of determining the heritability of a disorder are family history studies, twin studies, and adoption studies.

Psychosocial Theories of Abnormality

Psychosocial theories of abnormality vary greatly in the factors and processes they say are involved in the development of abnormal or maladaptive behavior. Some theories focus on unconscious conflicts and anxiety, some focus on the effects of rewards and

psychodynamic theory
theory that explains cognition, emotion, and behavior in terms of a system of unconscious drives; also known as *psychoanalytic theory*

libido
psychical energy derived from physiological drives

id
most primitive part of the unconscious that consists of drives and impulses seeking immediate gratification

superego
part of the unconscious that consists of absolute moral standards internalized from one's parents during childhood and one's culture

ego
part of the psyche that channels libido into activities in accordance with the superego and within the constraints of reality

unconscious
area of the psyche where memories, wishes, and needs are stored and where conflicts among the id, ego, and superego are played out

preconscious
area of the psyche that contains material from the unconscious before it reaches the conscious mind

conscious
mental contents and processes of which we are actively aware

repression
defense mechanism in which the ego pushes anxiety-provoking material back into the unconscious

punishments in the environment, some focus on thought processes, and some focus on the difficulties humans have in striving to realize their full potentials in a capricious world. There are many more specific psychosocial theories of abnormality than can be described in this book. We shall discuss the theories that have had the largest and most enduring impacts on how psychologists view abnormality and on the types of psychosocial therapies that are currently used to treat people with psychological disorders.

Psychodynamic Theories

Sigmund Freud is the person most associated with **psychodynamic** (also called *psychoanalytic*) **theory**. Although Freud's theory is categorized today as a psychosocial theory, he was a physician by training and thought of his theory as a neurological theory of the human psyche. He believed that behaviors and thoughts, whether normal or abnormal, were largely the results of physiological drives. Freud described a psychical form of energy, which he called **libido**, that derives from these drives and processes. This energy continually seeks to be released but can be channeled or harnessed by different psychological systems.

Three systems of the human psyche involved in the regulation of libido are the id, the ego, and the superego. The **id** is the system from which libido emanates, and its drives and impulses seek immediate release. The **superego** is the storehouse of rules and regulations for the conduct of behavior that are learned from one's parents and from society. These rules and regulations are in the form of absolute moral standards. The **ego** is the arbitrator between the id, the superego, and reality. The ego strives to allow the release of libidinal energy and the satisfaction of impulses and drives, within the constraints of reality and in accord with the superego's norms for acceptable behavior. The id, ego, and superego are not organs of the body or even areas of the brain but systems of the psyche.

Freud further categorized the psyche into the **unconscious**, the **preconscious**, and the **conscious** (see Figure 3.8). Most of what drives human thought and behavior goes on in the unconscious. Here is where conflicts between the id, ego, and superego are usually played out and where memories, wishes, and needs are stored. The preconscious is a way station or buffer between the unconscious and conscious. Some material (i.e., wishes, needs, or memories) from the unconscious can make its way into the preconscious, but it rarely makes its way in raw form into the conscious. The ego deflects this material back into the unconscious or changes the material in such a way as to protect the conscious from being fully aware of the unconscious material. This pushing material back into the unconscious is known as **repression**. Why must the conscious be protected from unconscious material? Because in their raw form, unconscious wishes, needs, and memories are often unacceptable to the individual or to society. They represent our basic instincts and drives, unrestrained and seeking to be satisfied in the quickest and fullest way possible. If these

Figure 3.8

Freud's Three Levels of Consciousness. Freud divided the human psyche into conscious, preconscious, and unconscious processes. Only a small amount of psychic activity is conscious.

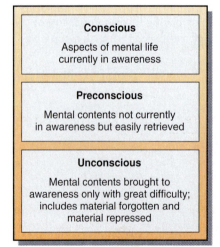

Conscious
Aspects of mental life currently in awareness

Preconscious
Mental contents not currently in awareness but easily retrieved

Unconscious
Mental contents brought to awareness only with great difficulty; includes material forgotten and material repressed

Sigmund Freud believed that normal and abnormal behavior was driven by needs and drives, most of which were unconscious.

Anna Freud, daughter of Sigmund Freud, was a major contributor to psychodynamic theory and described the basic defense mechanisms people use to control anxiety.

Adolescents with aggressive impulses may sublimate these impulses by taking up boxing.'

anxiety
unpleasant state of arousal that consists of symptoms such as rapid heartbeat, perspiration, and feelings of dread

regression
defense mechanism in which a person retreats to a behavior of an earlier developmental period in order to prevent anxiety and satisfy current needs

denial
defense mechanism in which a person refuses to perceive or accept reality

displacement
defense mechanism in which a person discharges unacceptable feelings against someone or something other than the true target of these feelings

rationalization
defense mechanism in which a person invents an acceptable motive to explain unacceptably motivated behavior

intellectualization
defense mechanism in which a person adopts a cold, distanced perspective on a matter that actually creates strong unpleasant feelings

projection
defense mechanism in which a person attributes his or her own unacceptable motives or wishes to someone else

reaction formation
defense mechanism in which a person adopts a set of attitudes and behaviors that are the opposite of his or her true dispositions

identification
defense mechanism in which a person adopts the ideas, values, and tendencies of someone in a superior position in order to elevate self-worth

sublimation
defense mechanism in which a person translates wishes and needs into socially acceptable behavior

neurotic paradox
situation of a person developing a means of avoiding anxiety that is itself maladaptive

drives begin to reach consciousness, the person experiences **anxiety,** and the ego goes into action to push the material back into the unconscious.

Freud described certain defense mechanisms that the ego uses to disguise or transform unconscious wishes. Later, his daughter Anna Freud expanded the list of defense mechanisms. The particular defense mechanisms a person uses shape his or her behavior and personality.

Regression is one of the most primitive defense mechanisms, involving retreating to earlier forms of behavior in order to satisfy one's needs. A woman who has been abandoned by her lover may experience regression, curling up in a chair, rocking and sucking her fingers. **Denial** is the simple refusal to perceive or accept reality. A husband whose wife has recently died may deny that she is gone and actively search for her. **Displacement** occurs when one discharges unacceptable feelings, often aggressive feelings, against someone other than the true target of these feelings. A woman who is angry at her children may kick her dog. **Rationalization** involves "explaining away" one's unacceptable motives or behavior. A soldier who killed innocent civilians may rationalize that he was only following orders. **Intellectualization** is adopting a cold, analytical perspective on a distressing situation. An emergency room physician who is extremely troubled by seeing young people with severe gunshot wounds every night may have discussions with colleagues that focus only on the technical aspects involved in treating various kinds of wounds. **Projection** is attributing one's own motives or wishes to someone else. A husband who is sexually attracted to a colleague may accuse his wife of cheating on him. **Reaction formation** involves adopting a set of behaviors or attitudes that is the polar opposite of one's true wishes or attitudes. A man who cannot accept his own homosexuality may become extremely homophobic. **Identification** is allying with others who can make one feel a greater sense of self-worth. Prisoners sometimes identify with their guards in order to overcome their powerless status. **Sublimation** involves channeling one's needs or wishes into a socially acceptable form of behavior. An adolescent with strong aggressive impulses may train to be a boxer.

Everyone uses defense mechanisms to one degree or another, because everyone must protect against awareness of unacceptable wishes in the unconscious and conform his or her behavior to societal norms. When our behavior becomes ruled by defense mechanisms or the specific mechanisms we use are in themselves maladaptive, then the defense mechanisms can result in abnormal, pathological behavior. Freud called this the **neurotic paradox**: Some people develop means of anxiety avoidance that are in themselves maladaptive. For example, a man whose father physically abused him as a child may develop the tendency to engage in displacement, because it was too dangerous to directly express his anger against his father. This displacement may take the form of beating his

Erik Erikson and his wife.

object relations school
group of modern psychodynamic theorists who believe that one develops a self-concept and appraisals of others in a four-stage process during childhood and retains them throughout adulthood; psychopathology consists of an incomplete progression through these stages or an acquisition of poor self- and-other concepts

wife or getting into frequent fistfights with other men. The displacement behavior is maladaptive in itself, and thus the man is stuck in the neurotic paradox.

 Do you recognize any of these defense mechanisms in your own behaviors and ways of thinking?

Freud's theories are some of the most intriguing and enduring in psychology, but they had critics even among Freud's followers. Freud viewed behavior and thought as the products of energies that were either contained or released. Where, many people asked, was the person, the self, in Freud's human being? Freud downplayed the roles of the environment and interpersonal relationships in the development of personality, and several of his students and contemporaries believed this was a mistake. Freud believed that personality was essentially fixed in childhood, with little opportunity for significant change later on, even with therapy. Many of his early critics believed that human personality continues to grow and change in response to changes in the environment and in personal relationships and that therapy did offer significant hope for people who wanted to change fundamental aspects of their personalities. Some of these critics developed their own theories of personality and psychopathology, which became the foci of more recent psychodynamic approaches.

For example, Erik Erikson proposed a developmental sequence through which a person passes on his or her way toward self-actualization (see Figure 3.9). Personal growth takes place in a series of stages from birth to death. Each stage involves the resolution of some type of conflict. In the first year of life, the conflict is between trust and mistrust. In years 2 through 3, the conflict is between autonomy and shame. In years 4 through 5, the conflict is between taking initiative and feeling guilt for that initiative. In years 6 through 11, the child faces conflicts between gaining a sense of industry or mastery and having a sense of inferiority. Ages 12 to 18 are characterized by a search for one's identity versus a confusion about one's role in society. During young adulthood, a person faces conflicts between intimacy and isolation. In middle age, the issue is whether one will evidence creative productivity or become stagnant. In old age, the individual can develop a sense of integrity or a sense of despair. We never fully resolve all of the conflicts of life, but some people make better resolutions than others, and these people tend to be happier and better adjusted.

One of the most influential schools of thought within modern psychodynamic theory is the **object relations school**. Object relations theory focuses on the role of early interpersonal relationships in the development of self-concept. According to proponents of this school, such as Melanie Klein, Margaret Mahler, Otto Kernberg, and Heinz Kohut, our early relationships create images or representations of ourselves and others that we carry throughout adulthood and that affect all subsequent relationships we have. There are four fundamental phases in the development of the self-concept (Figure 3.10). In the

Figure 3.9

Erikson's Stages of Psychosocial Development. Erikson proposed eight stages of psychosocial crises that can lead to positive or negative development across the life span.

Stage of life	Psychosocial crisis	Favorable outcome
I. Infancy	Trust vs. mistrust	Trust and hope
II. Early childhood	Autonomy vs. shame, doubt	Self-control, sense of adequacy
III. Years 3 to 5	Initiative vs. guilt	Purpose and direction, initiative
IV. Years 6 to puberty	Industry vs. inferiority	Competence
V. Adolescence	Identity vs. confusion	Integrated view of self as unique
VI. Early adulthood	Intimacy vs. isolation	Ability to form close relationships
VII. Middle adulthood	Generativity vs. stagnation	Concern for family, society
VIII. Old age	Integrity vs. despair	Fulfillment and satisfaction, willingness to face death

first phase, known as the *undifferentiated stage*, the newborn infant has only an image of the self and no sense that other people or objects are separate from the self. The infant believes that its caregiver and itself are one and that everything the infant feels or wants the caregiver feels or wants. In the second phase, known as *symbiosis*, the newborn infant still does not distinguish between self and other but does distinguish between good and bad aspects of the self-plus-other image. That is, the child has an image of the good self-plus-other and an image of the bad self-plus-other. These images are either all good or all bad. In the third phase, the *separation-individuation phase*, the child begins to differentiate between the self and the other. The child's image of the good self and the bad self are not integrated, however. The child either focuses on the good self or the bad self exclusively. Similarly, the child's image of the good other and the bad other are not integrated, and the child focuses on only the good other or the bad other. In the fourth stage, the *integration stage*, the child is able to distinguish clearly between the self and the other and is able to integrate the good and bad images of the self and the other into complex representations.

According to the object relations theorists, many people with psychopathology never fully resolve stages two or three, and are prone to seeing the self and others as all good or all bad. This is known as **splitting**, because the image of the self and other are split into the good image and the bad image, with no appreciation for the mixed qualities of good and bad that are true of all people. Also, a person stuck in stages two or three never fully differentiates between the self and other and thus expects the other to feel and want what the self feels and wants. As we shall see, this notion of splitting provides an intriguing explanation of the syndrome known as *borderline personality disorder*. People with this disorder tend to view themselves and other people as either all good or all bad and vacillate between these two images, either idealizing themselves and others or hating themselves and others to the point of wanting to commit violence to the self or others. People with borderline personality disorder also tend to have trouble accepting the boundaries between themselves and others and, when even slightly rejected by another, feel completely abandoned and empty.

Behavioral Theories

Behavioral theories of abnormality developed, in part, as an attempt to provide explanations for human behavior that could be tested through rigorous scientific methods. Behaviorists rejected claims that unconscious conflicts drove human behavior and focused on observable and replicable relationships between events in the environment and in human behavior.

Melanie Klein questioned some of the principles of Freudian psychoanalytic theory and helped to develop object relations theory.

Otto Kernberg is one of the leaders of the object relations school

splitting

in object relations theory, phenomenon wherein a person fails to resolve stages two or three of the self-concept acquisition process and splits conceptions of self and others into either all-good or all-bad categories, neglecting to recognize people's mixed qualities

Figure 3.10

Stages of Development of Self-Concept According to Object Relations Theory. Object relations theory suggests that infants begin with an undifferentiated sense of self and other and eventually develop an integrated sense of the positive and negative aspects of self and other.

S = Self
O = Other

1. Undifferentiated

+ S

2. Symbiosis

+
S-O

−
S-O

3. Separation, individuation

+
S

+
O

−
S

−
O

4. Integration

+ −
S

+ −
O

Ivan Pavlov

Classical Conditioning

Ivan Pavlov, a Russian physiologist, while conducting experiments on the salivary glands of dogs, made discoveries that would revolutionize psychological theory. Not surprisingly, his dogs would salivate when Pavlov or an assistant put food in their mouths. Pavlov noticed that, after a while, the dogs would begin to salivate when he or his assistant simply walked into the room. This phenomenon gained the name **classical conditioning**. Pavlov had paired a previously neutral stimulus (himself) with a stimulus that naturally leads to a certain response (the dish of food which leads to salivating), and eventually the neutral stimulus was able to elicit that response. He named the stimulus that naturally produced the desired response the **unconditioned stimulus** (**US**), and the response created by the unconditioned stimulus was named the **unconditioned response** (**UR**). So, in Pavlov's experiments, the dish of food was the US and salivation in response to this food was the UR. He named the previously neutral stimulus the **conditioned stimulus** (**CS**) and the response that it elicited the **conditioned response** (**CR**). Thus, Pavlov was the CS, and when the dogs salivated in response to seeing him, this salivation became the CR (see Table 3.1).

Classical conditioning has been used to explain people's seemingly irrational responses to a host of benign or neutral stimuli. For example, consider the following case study:

Case Study • A 2-year-old girl named Sarah had undergone major surgery for a congenital defect. The surgery was a success, and Sarah was recovering at home. Her Aunt Jean and Uncle Vern came to visit Sarah about one week after she returned home. Sarah had always adored Jean and Vern, but soon after they entered the house, Sarah showed great fear of Vern and began crying hysterically when he tried to console her. Vern and Jean left and came back a few days later. Once again, upon hearing Vern's voice, Sarah began sobbing and ran to her mother's arms in great fear. Vern was heartbroken at Sarah's response and did not understand how she could have suddenly become so fearful of him. After a while, Sarah's mother realized that Vern's voice was extremely similar to the voice of the doctor who had treated Sarah in the hospital. Although this doctor was a kind man, he had had to perform several very painful procedures on Sarah while she was in the hospital. Eventually, Sarah had come to shake and cry simply upon seeing the doctor enter the room and hearing his voice. Sarah had apparently generalized her learned fear of the doctor's voice to Vern's voice because of the similarities in the voices.

Classical conditioning can also explain why heroin addicts sometimes have physiological responses similar to those they have when they take heroin if they simply see a syringe. They have developed a conditioned physiological response to syringes (which have become a

classical conditioning
form of learning in which a neutral stimulus becomes associated with a stimulus that naturally elicits a response, thereby making the neutral stimulus itself sufficient to elicit the same response

unconditioned stimulus (US)
in classical conditioning, stimulus that naturally elicits a reaction, as food elicits salivation in dogs

unconditioned response (UR)
in classical conditioning, response that naturally follows when a certain stimulus appears, as a dog salivating when it smells food

conditioned stimulus (CS)
in classical conditioning, previously neutral stimulus that when paired with a natural stimulus becomes itself sufficient to elicit a response, as an empty dish will elicit salivation in dogs due to past association with food

conditioned response (CR)
in classical conditioning, response that first followed a natural stimulus but that now follows a conditioned stimulus

Table 3.1 Stimulus and Response in Classical Conditioning

Through classical conditioning, Pavlov's dogs came to associate Pavlov with food and thus began to salivate when Pavlov entered the room.

Term	Definition	Example from Pavlov's Experiment
Unconditioned stimulus (US)	Stimulus that naturally produces desired response	Dish of food
Unconditioned response (UR)	Response created by unconditioned stimulus	Salivation
Conditioned stimulus (CS)	Previously neutral stimulus paired with unconditioned stimulus	Pavlov
Conditioned response (CR)	Response elicited by conditioned stimulus	Salivation

conditioned stimulus), because of the frequent pairing of the syringes with the actual physiological action of the drugs.

Operant Conditioning

E. L. Thorndike observed that behaviors that are followed by a reward are strengthened, whereas behaviors that are followed by a punishment are weakened. This simple but important observation, which Thorndike labeled the **law of effect**, led to the development of the principles of **operant conditioning**. B. F. Skinner is the psychologist most strongly associated with operant conditioning. He showed that he could shape the behaviors of animals and humans by providing rewards for desired behaviors and punishments for undesired behaviors. For example, a pigeon will learn to press on a bar if pressing it is associated with the delivery of food, and it will learn to avoid pressing another bar if pressing it is associated with an electric shock. Similarly, a child will learn to make his bed if he receives a hug and kiss from his mother each time he makes the bed, and he will learn to stop hitting his brother if every time he hits his brother he loses one hour of television watching.

In operant conditioning, behaviors will be learned most quickly if they are paired with the reward or punishment every time the behavior is emitted. This consistent response is called a **continuous reinforcement schedule**. Behaviors can be learned and maintained, however, on a **partial reinforcement schedule**, in which the reward or punishment occurs only sometimes in response to the behavior. **Extinction**—getting rid of a learned behavior—is more difficult when the behavior was learned through a partial reinforcement schedule than it is when the behavior was learned through a continuous reinforcement schedule. This is because the organism will continue to emit the behavior learned through a partial reinforcement schedule in the absence of the reward, anticipating that the reward will eventually come. A good example is gambling behavior. People who frequently gamble are seldom rewarded, but they continue to gamble in anticipation of that occasional, unpredictable win.

law of effect
Thorndike's observation that behaviors followed by reward are strengthened and behaviors followed by punishment are weakened

operant conditioning
form of learning in which behaviors lead to consequences that either reinforce or punish the organism, leading to an increased or decreased probability of a future response

continuous reinforcement schedule
system of behavior modification in which certain behaviors are always rewarded or punished, leading to rapid learning of desired responses

partial reinforcement schedule
form of behavior modification in which a behavior is rewarded or punished only some of the time

extinction
abolition of a learned behavior

conditioned avoidance response
type of behavior in which a person avoids stimuli that he or she associates with anxiety-provoking symptoms, reducing anxiety, which then becomes a positive reinforcer for continuing avoidance

The practice of giving children "time outs" when they misbehave is based on what principles of conditioning?

Combinations of classical and operant conditioning can help to explain elaborate responses people develop to avoid situations that arouse fear in them. For example, consider a woman who developed a fear of bridges through classical conditioning: She fell off a bridge into icy waters as a child, and now anytime she nears a bridge, she feels very anxious. This woman has developed elaborate means of getting around her hometown without having to cross any bridges. Avoiding the bridges reduces her anxiety, and thus her avoidant behavior is reinforced. This woman has developed a **conditioned avoidance response** through operant conditioning. As a result, however, she never exposes herself to a bridge and thus never has the opportunity to extinguish her initial fear of bridges. As we shall see, many of the therapeutic techniques developed by behavioral

Edward L. Thorndike

B. F. Skinner

theorists are designed to extinguish conditioned avoidance responses, which can often interfere greatly with a person's ability to function in everyday life.

Modeling and Observational Learning

Skinner and other "pure" behaviorists argued that humans and animals learn behaviors only by directly experiencing the rewards or punishments for these behaviors. In the 1950s, however, psychologist Albert Bandura argued that people could also learn behaviors by watching other people, a view that came to be known as **social learning theory**. First, in **modeling**, people learn new behaviors from imitating the behaviors modeled by important people in their lives, such as their parents. Learning through modeling is more likely to occur when the person modeling the behavior is seen as an authority figure or is perceived to be like oneself. For example, Bandura (1969) argued that children are most likely to imitate the behaviors modeled by their same-sex parent, because this parent is an authority figure and because their same-sex parent seems more similar to them than does their opposite-sex parent. Both positive and negative behaviors can be learned through modeling and imitation. For example, children can learn kind and generous behaviors or cruel and aggressive behaviors from their parents.

Observational learning takes place when a person observes the rewards and punishments that another person receives for his or her behavior and then behaves in accord with those rewards and punishments. For example, a child who views her sibling being punished for dropping food on the floor will learn, through observation, the consequences of dropping food on the floor and thus will be less likely to engage in this behavior herself. Critics of television violence have argued that children learn aggressive behavior by observing television characters receiving rewards for engaging in violent behavior.

The movement that eventually supplanted behavioral theories of human behavior was the cognitive revolution in psychology. Cognitive psychologists made great strides in understanding the processes of memory, attention, and information processing, and by the late 1960s and early 1970s, much of the theorizing about the causes of abnormal behavior focused on the role of cognitions. The cognitive theorists argued that it is not just rewards, punishments, or even drives that motivate human behavior. Instead, humans actively construct meaning out of their experiences and act in accord with their interpretations of the world.

Cognitive Theories

Cognitions are thoughts or beliefs. There are many types of cognitions people can have about situations, and these cognitions can influence people's behaviors in the situations and the emotions they feel. Three types of cognitions that have been the focus of several theories of abnormal behavior are causal attributions, control beliefs, and dysfunctional assumptions.

Attribution theories suggest that, when we observe an event, we immediately ask why that event happened (Abramson, Metalsky, & Alloy, 1989; Abramson, Seligman, & Teasdale, 1978). The answer to this "why" question is our **causal attribution** for the event. The attributions we make for events can influence our behavior and emotions because they influence the meaning we ascribe to events and our expec-

Albert Bandura

Children tend to imitate the behaviors of their same-sex parents.

Children may learn aggressive behaviors by watching TV characters be rewarded for being aggressive.

tations for similar events in the future. For example, if we attribute a friend's rude behavior to temporary or situational factors, (he is under a lot of pressure) then we do not evaluate that friend too harshly and we do not expect the friend to act rudely again in the future. However, if we attribute the friend's behavior to dispositional factors (he is a mean guy), then our evaluations of the friend will be more harsh, and we will expect the friend to act rudely again. A dispositional attribution for the friend's behavior might lead us to avoid the friend or even break up the relationship, whereas a situational attribution would not.

The attributions we make for our own behavior in situations can have a strong effect on our emotions and self-concept. For example, if we act meanly toward another person and attribute this behavior to situational factors (the other person acted mean first), we may feel slightly guilty but we may also feel justified. However, if we attribute this behavior to dispositional factors (I am a mean person), then we may feel quite guilty and lose self-esteem. Our attributions for our performance in achievement settings can also affect our self-esteem, our emotions, and our willingness to continue striving. Attributing failure on an exam to situational factors (the exam was too hard) will result in less negative emotion and more persistence than attributing failure on an exam to dispositional factors (I am not very smart).

A **control theory** focuses on people's expectancies for their abilities to control important events (Bandura, 1977; Rotter, 1954; Seligman, 1975). When people believe they can control an important event, they will behave in ways to control that event. When they do not believe they can control an event, they will not attempt to control it or will easily give up when they have difficulty controlling it. Martin Seligman (1975) argued that repeated experiences with uncontrollable events lead a person to develop **learned helplessness**, the general expectation that future events will be uncontrollable. He described a set of learned helplessness deficits that resulted from this expectation, including lowered self-esteem, lowered persistence and motivation, and the inability to see opportunities for control when they do arise.

In an update of his social learning theory, Albert Bandura (1977) argued that a major contributor to people's sense of well-being, motivation, and persistence is their sense of self-efficacy. **Self-efficacy** is a person's belief that he or she can successfully execute the behaviors necessary to control desired outcomes. People with low self-efficacy expectations for a particular domain will be less likely than people with high expectations to try to control or cope with a situation and instead may avoid the situation. People with high self-efficacy expectations for a given situation exert more control over that situation, try harder, are more persistent, and are more successful in that situation than are people with low self-efficacy expectations (Bandura, 1986). High self-efficacy expectations also protect a person against negative emotional reactions to a situation. For example, consider a person whose home was ruined in a flood. If she has high self-efficacy, she will maintain her motivation to rebuild her home, will make better decisions about how to rebuild, and will be less likely to become depressed over the loss of her home than if she has a low sense of self-efficacy.

A different set of cognitive theories of psychopathology suggest that people prone to psychological disorders, particularly emotional problems, are plagued by **global assumptions** about themselves and the world that are **dysfunctional assumptions**. One of the earliest proponents of this view was Albert Ellis (1958). Ellis argued that most negative emotions or maladaptive behaviors are the result of

control theory
cognitive theory that explains people's variance in behavior in certain domains in terms of their beliefs that they can or cannot effectively control situations in that domain

learned helplessness
general expectation that one cannot control important events, leading to lowered persistence, motivation, self-esteem, and initiative

self-efficacy
person's belief that he or she can successfully execute the behaviors necessary to control desired outcomes

global assumptions
fundamental beliefs that encompass all types of situations

dysfunctional assumptions
fundamental beliefs that are irrational or maladaptive

Self-efficacy can help people cope with the aftermath of a trauma like a flood.

Albert Ellis

Aaron T. Beck

one or more dysfunctional assumptions that guide a person's life. Some of the most common dysfunctional assumptions Ellis identified follow:

1. I should be loved by everyone for everything I do.
2. Things should turn out the way I want them to turn out.
3. I should be terribly upset by dangerous situations.
4. It is better to avoid problems than to face them.
5. I need someone stronger and more powerful than me to rely on.
6. I should be completely competent, intelligent, and achieving in all I do.
7. Once something affects my life, it will affect it forever.
8. I must have perfect self-control.
9. I have no control over my emotions and cannot help feeling certain feelings.

People who hold these beliefs then interpret situations and react to situations in line with the beliefs, resulting in frequent negative emotions and irrational behaviors. For example, someone who believes that she must be completely competent, intelligent, and achieving in all domains in her life will be extremely upset by even minor failures or bad events, such as tearing her blouse or forgetting to return a phone call. Similarly, someone who believes that things should always turn out the way he wants them to may be unable to respond flexibly to the obstacles and setbacks that inevitably stand in the way of achieving goals in daily life. Rather than finding some way around these obstacles, he may focus on the obstacles, incredulous and distressed that things are not going his way.

Another influential cognitive theorist, Aaron Beck, developed an effective and widely used therapy for emotional disorders, which we will explore shortly. Beck distinguished between the kinds of dysfunctional beliefs or assumptions that Ellis described and automatic thoughts. **Automatic thoughts** are thoughts about specific situations we face. In people with emotional problems, these automatic thoughts are typically negative and often irrational. They bolster a person's dysfunctional global beliefs. For example, when a person who believes she must always be perfect scores poorly on an exam, she may have automatic thoughts such as "I am a total failure. I will never amount to anything. I should have gotten a perfect score on that exam." Beck's cognitive therapy helps clients identify and challenge these automatic thoughts, which then helps to tear down their dysfunctional belief systems.

automatic thoughts
thoughts processed without active effort

humanistic theory
view that people strive to develop their innate potential for goodness and self-actualization; abnormality arises as a result of societal pressures to conform to unchosen dictates that clash with a person's self-actualization needs and from an inability to satisfy more basic needs, such as hunger

existential theory
view that upholds personal responsibility for discovering one's personal values and meanings in life and then living in accordance with them; people face existential anxiety due to awareness of their life's finitude, and must overcome both this anxiety and obstacles to a life governed by the meanings they give to it, in order to achieve mental health and avoid maladaptive behavior

 Think back to a recent incident that left you feeling distressed. What were some of your thoughts about that incident that influenced your feelings? Do you think they were rational or irrational?

Humanistic and Existential Theories

The **humanistic theory** and **existential theory** of human behavior emerged in the 1950s and 1960s, partially in reaction to the pessimistic and deterministic view of human behavior provided by traditional psychodynamic theory and to the claims within traditional behavior theory that humans were only the product of their environment. The humanistic and existential perspectives focused on the human capacity for self-definition and self-direction. The human being has an innate capacity for goodness and for living a full life, according to these theories. What gets in the way of fulfilling this capacity is pressure from society to conform to certain norms rather than to seek one's most developed self.

Carl Rogers, one of the most influential humanists, believed that, without undue pressure from others, individuals naturally move toward personal growth, self-acceptance, and self-actualization, the fulfillment of their potential for love, creativity, and meaning. Under the stress of pressure from society and family, however, people can develop rigid and distorted perspectives on the self and can lose touch with their own values and needs. Rogers developed a form of therapy, called *client-centered therapy,* that is designed to free people to realize their genuine selves, to accept themselves entirely, and to begin growing toward self-actualization. This therapy is described later in this chapter.

Abraham Maslow argued that humans have a hierarchy of needs, and self-actualization can only occur after lower-order needs are satisfied. The most basic needs are physiological needs, such as hunger. Next is the need for safety and security. Next are needs for love from others and a sense of belongingness to a group. Next are needs for esteem from others. At the highest level of the hierarchy is the need to fulfill one's own personal values and to reach self-actualization. Maslow said that people who were at this highest level of the hierarchy "no longer strive in the ordinary sense, but rather develop. They attempt to grow to perfection and to develop more and more fully in their own style" (Maslow, 1954, p. 211). Maladaptive behavior and general distress can result from a person's inability to fulfill lower-order needs and reach a point of growth instead of striving.

The existential theories of Fritz Perls, Martin Heidegger, and Søren Kierkegaard were similar in many ways to the humanistic theories. They believed that our life is what we make of it—that humans have the capacity and the responsibility to direct their lives in meaningful and constructive ways. They also believed that the ultimate goal in human growth is the discovery of one's own values and meaning and living one's life by these values. The existentialists, however, held a view somewhat less positive than did the humanists of the human's natural tendency toward goodness and put more emphasis on the difficulties inherent in self-actualization. Society puts many obstacles in the way of living according to one's own values. Moreover, we all must face the *existential anxiety* created by the realization of our ultimate death. This anxiety leads many people to abandon their personal growth and search for meaning. We must overcome this anxiety by choosing to live full and meaningful lives, or our lives will be wasted and corrupted and likely filled with misery and maladaptive behaviors.

Carl Rogers

Summing Up Psychosocial Theories

- Psychodynamic theories of psychopathology focus on unconscious conflicts that cause anxiety in the individual and result in maladaptive behavior. These conflicts arise when the libidinal impulses of the id clash with the constraints on behavior imposed by the ego and superego. The ways people handle their conflicts are defined by the types of defense mechanisms they use.

- More recent psychodynamic theories focused less on the role of unconscious impulses and more on the development of the individual's self-concept in the context of interpersonal relationships. They see a greater role for the environment in the shaping of personality and have more hope for change in personality during adulthood than Freud did.

- The behaviorist theories of abnormality reject notions of unconscious conflicts and focus only on the rewards and punishments in the environment that shape and maintain behavior.

- Classical conditioning takes place when a previously neutral stimulus is paired with a stimulus that naturally creates a certain response; eventually the neutral stimulus will also elicit the response.

- Operant conditioning involves rewarding desired behaviors and punishing undesired behaviors.

- People also learn by imitating the behaviors modeled by others and by observing the rewards and punishments others receive for their behaviors.

- The cognitive theorists criticized behaviorist theorists for ignoring the subjective meanings people place on the events in their lives. Cognitive theories suggest that people's attributions for events, their perceptions of control and self-efficacy, and their beliefs about themselves and the world influence their behaviors and emotions in reaction to situations.

- Humanist and existential theories suggest that all humans strive to fulfill their potential for good and to self-actualize. The inability to fulfill one's potential arises from the pressures of society to conform to others' expectations and values and from existential anxiety.

Treatments for Abnormality

Each of these theoretical approaches to abnormality has led to a treatment approach. The majority of the biological treatments for abnormality are drugs. These drugs can relieve psychological symptoms by correcting imbalances of neurotransmitters. They also may compensate for structural deficits in the brain or the effects of genetic abnormalities. There are a few other biologically based therapies that are used for individual disorders. We will discuss these therapies when we discuss the disorders they are used to treat. Our focus in this chapter will be only the drug therapies.

The treatment usually prescribed by proponents of psychosocial approaches to abnormality is **psychotherapy**. There are many forms of psychotherapy, but most involve a therapist (psychiatrist, psychologist, social worker, family counselor) talking with the person suffering from the disorder (typically called a *client*) about his or her symptoms and what is contributing to those symptoms. The specific foci of these conversations depends on the therapists' theoretical approaches, as described next.

Both drug therapy and psychotherapy have proven effective in the treatment of many disorders. Drugs and psychotherapy may work on different aspects of a disorder, and they are increasingly used together in an integrated approach to psychological disorders.

Drug Therapies

As we discuss the use of specific types of drugs for specific disorders in upcoming chapters, we will discuss how each drug is thought to work biochemically for each specific disorder and the evidence for the effectiveness of the drug in treating a disorder. We will also discuss the major side effects of each drug. For now, we will briefly describe the five classes of drugs most commonly used to treat psychological symptoms.

As their name suggests, **antipsychotic drugs** are used to treat symptoms of psychosis: delusions (beliefs out of touch with reality), hallucinations (sensory experiences that are not real), and severe disorganization of thought. These drugs are sometimes referred to as the *major tranquilizers,* but their effects are mostly on psychotic symptoms, and they only tend to have a mild calming effect when given in appropriate dosages.

The first type of antipsychotic drug introduced was chlorpromazine (trade name Thorazine), in the 1950s. It is one of a group of drugs known as the *phenothiazines.* Chlorpromazine was originally used with animals as a preanesthetic sedative and to lower blood pressure (Bernstein, 1983). Psychiatrists thought it might reduce agitation in psychotic patients. As it turned out, chlorpromazine did not simply sedate psychotic patients, it actually reduced or eliminated their psychotic symptoms. This drug led to a revolution in the treatment and lives of people with psychosis. They had formerly been locked away in mental hospitals and state institutions, perhaps for life, often completely out of touch with reality and sometimes quite difficult to control. Physicians and nurses could do little more than provide for their basic needs and try to keep them from hurting themselves or others. Within days of receiving chlorpromazine, however, a patient might regain control of his or her behavior and grip on reality, and delusions and hallucinations would disappear.

Antidepressant drugs are used to treat the symptoms of depression: sad mood, loss of motivation, disturbances in sleep and appetite, and negative thinking. There historically have been two major classes of antidepressant drugs used: the *tricyclic antidepressants* and the *monoamine oxidase inhibitors,* or MAOIs. In the last decade, a new class of antidepressants, called the *selective serotonin reuptake inhibitors* (or SSRIs), have been introduced and have gained much public attention. One of the best known of these drugs is fluoxetine, which goes by the trade name Prozac. Although all of these drugs were initially introduced as treatments for depression, we shall see that they are currently being used to treat many different kinds of disorders, including anxiety disorders and eating disorders.

Anxiety and insomnia are the psychological symptoms for which drugs are most often prescribed. The first group of drugs developed for treating anxiety and insomnia were

---

psychotherapy

treatment for abnormality that consists of a therapist and client discussing the client's symptoms and their causes; the therapist's theoretical orientation determines the foci of conversations with the client

antipsychotic drugs

drugs used to treat psychotic symptoms such as delusions, hallucinations, and disorganized thinking

antidepressant drugs

drugs used to treat the symptoms of depression, such as sad mood, negative thinking, and disturbances of sleep and appetite; three common types are monoamine oxidase inhibitors, tricyclics, and serotonin reuptake inhibitors

the **barbiturates**, introduced at the beginning of the twentieth century. Barbiturates suppress the central nervous system, decreasing the activity of a variety of types of neurons. Although these drugs are effective for inducing relaxation and sleep, they are quite addictive, and withdrawal from them can cause life-threatening symptoms, such as increased heart rate, delirium, and convulsions.

Once these adverse side effects were recognized, scientists began searching for alternative antianxiety drugs. The **benzodiazepines**, a class of drugs with more specific neurological effects, were introduced in the mid 1950s. These drugs appear to reduce the symptoms of anxiety without interfering substantially with an individual's ability to function in daily life. The most frequent use of these drugs, accurately referred to as *minor tranquilizers*, is as sleeping pills. As many as 70 million prescriptions are written each year in the United States for benzodiazepines. Unfortunately, the benzodiazepines are also highly addictive, and up to 80 percent of people who take them for 6 weeks or more show withdrawal symptoms, including heart rate acceleration, irritability, and profuse sweating.

Finally, **stimulants** are used to treat some psychological problems. For example, stimulants are used to help children who suffer from attentional problems increase their attention and ability to focus. In turn, this helps the children control their behavior so that they become less impulsive and hyperactive.

Drugs can go a long way toward helping people with psychological problems. For many disorders, however, psychotherapy is an effective alternative to drugs (Seligman, 1995). Psychotherapy is often used even with people taking drugs for their symptoms, to help them learn to control their symptoms and to deal with issues in their lives that are contributing to the symptoms.

Psychodynamic Therapies

Psychodynamic therapies focus on relieving the unconscious conflicts driving psychological symptoms by helping people gain insight into their conflicts and then find ways of resolving these conflicts within the constraints of reality. It is not easy to uncover unconscious conflicts. Freud and others developed the method of *free association*, in which a client is taught to talk about whatever comes to her mind, trying not to censor any thoughts. By "turning off" her censor, a client might find herself talking about subjects or memories that she did not even realize were "on her mind." The therapist notices what themes seem to recur in a client's free associations, just how one thought seems to lead to another thought, and the specific memories that a client recalls. The material that the

barbiturates
drugs used to treat anxiety and insomnia that work by suppressing the central nervous system and decreasing the activity level of certain neurons

benzodiazepines
drugs that reduce anxiety and insomnia

stimulants
drugs used to increase attention, focus, and self-control

Traditional psychodynamic therapy involves listening for a client's unconscious conflicts and concerns.

resistance
in psychodynamic therapy, material that a client finds difficult or impossible to address; client's resistance signals an unconscious conflict that the therapist then tries to interpret

transference
in psychodynamic therapy, client's reaction to the therapist as if the therapist were an important person in his or her early development; the client's feelings and beliefs about this other person are transferred onto the therapist

client is reluctant to talk about when fully awake—that is, the client's **resistance** to certain material—is an especially important clue to the content of the client's most central unconscious conflicts, because the most threatening conflicts are the ones the ego tries hardest to repress. The therapist eventually puts together these pieces of the puzzle into a suggestion or interpretation of a conflict the client might be facing and voices this interpretation to the client. Sometimes the client accepts this interpretation as a revelation. Other times, the client is resistant to this interpretation. The therapist might interpret this resistance as a good indication that the interpretation identified an important issue in the client's unconscious.

The client's **transference** to the therapist is also a clue to his unconscious conflicts and needs. A transference occurs when the client reacts to the therapist as if the therapist were some important person in his early development, such as his father or mother. For example, a client may find himself reacting with rage or extreme fear when a therapist is just a few minutes late for an appointment, and this might stem from his feelings of having been emotionally abandoned by a parent during childhood. The therapist might point out the ways the client behaves that represent a transference and help the client explore the roots of his behavior in his relationships with significant others.

Some psychodynamic therapists also have their clients recount their dreams, and they use this material in analysis of their conflicts. Freud believed that during sleep, the ego loosens its control over the unconscious, and some unconscious material slips out in the form of dreams. These dreams are seldom direct representations of unconscious material, however, because this would be too threatening. Instead, dreams symbolize unconscious material in fascinating and creative ways.

Traditional psychodynamic therapy is still practiced today by a highly specialized core of psychiatrists and psychologists. It involves frequent sessions with the therapist, often several per week, over an extended period of time, even years. Many people find self-exploration under psychoanalysis to be extremely valuable. The long-term, intensive nature of psychodynamic therapy makes it unaffordable for many people, however. In addition, people suffering from acute problems, such as severe depression or anxiety, often cannot tolerate the lack of structure in traditional psychodynamic therapy and need more immediate relief from their symptoms. Finally, it is unclear whether traditional psychodynamic therapy is effective in the treatment of many mental disorders, largely because the therapy lasts so long that studies have not been conducted to test its effectiveness empirically.

For these reasons, modern psychodynamic therapists have developed some shorter-term, more structured versions of psychodynamic therapy (Luborsky, 1984). Many of these new therapies also have incorporated the revisions in psychodynamic theory offered by theorists who argued that interpersonal relationships throughout the lifespan can shape people's behaviors and self-concepts (Anderson & Lambert, 1995).

interpersonal therapy (IPT)
more structured and short-term version of psychodynamic therapy

One form of psychodynamically oriented therapy, **interpersonal therapy (IPT),** was developed for the treatment of depression but is now used to treat a variety of disorders (Klerman et al., 1984). IPT is similar to traditional psychodynamic therapies because it focuses on a patient's significant relationships as the source of psychological symptoms. IPT differs from other psychodynamic therapies in that the therapist is much more structuring and directive in the therapy, offering interpretations much earlier and focusing on how to change current relationships. IPT and other brief psychodynamically oriented therapies have been shown effective in the treatment of drug addiction, eating disorders, depression, and anxiety (Markowitz & Weissman, 1995).

Humanist-Existential Psychotherapies

The goal of humanist-existential therapy is to help the client discover his or her potentialities and place in the world and to accomplish self-actualization through self-exploration. The best known of these therapies is Carl Rogers's **client-centered therapy (CCT).** There are three essential ingredients to CCT, according to Rogers (1951). First, the therapist communicates a genuineness in her role as a helper to the client, acting as an authentic, real, living, behaving person rather than as an authority figure. Second, the therapist

client-centered therapy (CCT)
Carl Rogers's form of psychotherapy that consists of an equal relationship between therapist and client as the client searches for his or her inner self, receiving unconditional positive regard and an empathic understanding from the therapist

shows unconditional positive regard for the client, no matter how unattractive, disturbed, or difficult that person is. Third, the therapist communicates an empathic understanding of the client by making it clear that she understands and accepts the client's underlying feelings and search for the inner self. Through these conditions, the therapist helps the client know that she is fully there with the client, understanding what he or she is experiencing and feeling and what he or she is trying to bring forth and understand. Rogers believed that this experience of being understood helped clients bring forth their own self-healing powers and have the courage to recognize and pursue their potential. Rogers emphasized that the relationship between the therapist and client was one of equality, rather than a paternalistic relationship such as the kind fostered by traditional Freudian psychotherapy.

Client-centered therapy was adapted for use in group settings to help large numbers of people understand themselves in the context of a distressing modern world. These *encounter groups* are sometimes sponsored by mental health professionals but often are organized by nonprofessionals who accept Rogers' view that one does not necessarily need a professional to help in self-exploration—what it really takes is a listening, caring person. Many self-help groups of people who share a common experience or problem (such as a diagnosis of cancer or a history of sexual abuse) also follow the principles of client-centered therapy. In colleges, client-centered approaches are often taught in courses on *peer counseling*, in which students learn to counsel other college students. Client-centered therapy is considered appropriate for such situations because it does not require years of training for the counselor and is based on the premise that the counselor and client are equals.

Behavior Therapies

Just as behavior *theories* of psychopathology are radically different from psychodynamic and humanist-existential theories, behavior *therapies* would seem to be the polar opposite of these other therapies. Whereas psychodynamic therapies focus on uncovering unconscious conflicts and relational issues that developed during childhood and humanist-existential therapies focus on helping the client discover the inner self, behavior therapies focus only on changing a person's specific behaviors in the present day.

Although there are many specific techniques for behavior change (see Table 3.2), they can be grouped into two main categories: techniques that extinguish unwanted behaviors and techniques for teaching a person new, desired behaviors. We will discuss one example

Table 3.2 Types of Behavior Therapies

These are some of the several different methods used in behavior therapy.

Removal of reinforcements	Removes the individual from reinforcing situation or environment
Aversion therapy	Makes situation or stimulus that was once reinforcing no longer reinforcing
Relaxation exercises	Help the individual voluntarily control physiological manifestations of anxiety
Distraction techniques	Help the individual temporarily distract from anxiety-producing situations; divert attention from physiological manifestations of anxiety
Flooding or implosive therapy	Exposes individual to dreaded or feared stimulus while preventing avoidant behavior
Systematic desensitization	Pairs implementation of relaxation techniques with hierarchical exposure to aversive stimulus
Response shaping through operant conditioning	Pairs rewards with desired behaviors
Behavioral contracting	Provides rewards for reaching proximal goals
Modeling and observational learning	Models desired behaviors so that client may learn through observation

systematic desensitization therapy
type of behavior therapy that attempts to reduce client anxiety through relaxation techniques and progressive exposure to feared stimuli

in each of these categories in this chapter. The application of the other therapies listed in Table 3.2 to specific disorders will be discussed in later chapters on those disorders.

Systematic desensitization therapy is a gradual method for extinguishing anxiety responses to stimuli and the maladaptive behavior that often accompanies this anxiety (Wolpe, 1969). In systematic desensitization, the person first develops a hierarchy of feared stimuli, ranging from stimuli that would cause him only mild anxiety to stimuli that would cause him severe anxiety or panic. A person with a snake phobia might generate the hierarchy in Table 3.3. Then the therapist would help the person proceed through this hierarchy, starting with the least feared stimulus. The person would be instructed to vividly imagine the feared stimulus or even be exposed to the feared stimulus for a short period, while implementing relaxation exercises to control the anxiety he feels. When he gets to the point where he can imagine or experience the first and least feared stimulus without feeling anxious, he moves on to the next most feared stimulus, imagining or experiencing it while implementing relaxation exercises. This proceeds until he reaches the most feared stimulus on his list and is able to experience this stimulus without feeling extremely anxious. Thus, by the end of systematic desensitization therapy, a person with a snake phobia should be able to pick up and handle a large snake without becoming very anxious. Often, systematic desensitization therapy is combined with modeling—the client might watch a therapist pick up a snake, pet it, and play with it, observing that the therapist is not afraid, is not bitten or choked, and seems to enjoy playing with the snake. Eventually, the client is encouraged to model the therapist's behaviors with and reactions to the snake.

 What kind of motivation do you think a person would need to have to be willing to undergo systematic desensitization therapy for a phobia?

These techniques are designed to extinguish maladaptive responses or behaviors. Often, however, a person wishes to learn a new set of behaviors. A student of B. F. Skinner's named Ogden Lindsley first conceived of using the methods of operant conditioning to create new positive behaviors in people with serious mental disorders. He began working with severely impaired mental patients in the Metropolitan State Hospital just outside Boston, setting up a system whereby they were given rewards for positive, nonpsychotic behavior and rewards were withheld when they exhibited psychotic behavior. This method of shaping the responses of severely impaired people proved extremely successful. Soon, during the 1950s and 1960s, whole wards of state hospitals were being turned over to behavior therapists. In these wards, a **token economy** was often set up in which a patient would receive a small chip or token each time he or she exhibited a desired behavior (e.g., spoke to another person, made his or her bed). These tokens could be exchanged for priv-

token economy
application of operant conditioning in which patients receive tokens for exhibiting desired behaviors that are exchangeable for privileges and rewards; these tokens are withheld when a patient exhibits unwanted behaviors

Table 3.3   Hierarchy of Fears for Snake Phobia

This is a hierarchy of feared stimuli for a person with a snake phobia, ranging from the least feared stimulus to the most feared stimulus.

1. Hearing the word *snake*
2. Imagining a snake in a closed container at a distance
3. Imagining a snake uncontained at a distance
4. Imagining a snake nearby in a closed container
5. Looking at a picture of a snake
6. Viewing a movie or video of a snake
7. Seeing a snake in a container in the same room
8. Seeing a snake uncontained in the same room
9. Watching someone handle a snake
10. Touching a snake
11. Handling a snake
12. Playing with a snake

ileges, such as a walk on the hospital grounds, or desired objects, such as special food. Although this technique may sound simplistic and manipulative, it is credited, along with the introduction of antipsychotic drugs, with helping to cut the populations of inpatient mental hospitals by 67 percent between 1955 and 1980 (Bellack, Morrison, & Meuser, 1992). This type of operant conditioning is frequently used to treat children with severe disorders such as autism, as we shall discuss in Chapter 9.

Cognitive Therapies

Cognitive therapies focus on challenging maladaptive interpretations of events or ways of thinking and replacing them with more adaptive ways of thinking. One of the most widely used forms of **cognitive therapy** was developed by Aaron Beck (1976). There are three basic techniques involved in this type of cognitive therapy.

In the first technique, clients are assisted in *identifying* their irrational or maladaptive thoughts. People often do not recognize the negative thoughts that are swirling in their minds and affecting their emotions and behaviors. Cognitive therapists encourage clients to pay attention to the thoughts that are associated with their moods or with unwanted behaviors, to write these thoughts down, and to bring the thoughts into the therapy session.

In the second technique, clients are taught to *challenge* their irrational or maladaptive thoughts and to consider alternative ways of thinking. The therapist might ask the client to consider the answers to three types of questions about his or her thoughts.

The therapist might first ask, "What's the evidence for your perspective or interpretation of this situation?" Sometimes a client will have no evidence for his of her belief about a situation. For example, a man who feels that his wife may be seeing another man may have absolutely no evidence of this and just a nagging fear that it might happen. Other times, a client will have identified pieces of evidence for his or her perspective. For example, suppose an elderly woman believes that her children do not love her anymore. When asked for the evidence for this, she may state that her children do not call her or come to visit her often. In response to this, a therapist might ask the client how often her children do visit or call, to get a sense of what the client's expectations are.

If the client's children call at least once a week and visit her about once a month, the therapist might ask the second question "Are there other ways of looking at this evidence or this situation?" Here the therapist is encouraging the client to think of alternative perspectives to her own. The elderly client in our example may answer, "Well, they are very busy, and they have children and lives of their own. Maybe they are calling me as often as they can." Of course, it is not always as easy as this for a client to think of alternative viewpoints to her own. The therapist may have to suggest alternatives, by saying, for example, "What do your children do for a living? Do they have children of their own? How difficult do you think it would be for them to call you or visit you more often?" In her responses to these questions, the client might reveal that she believes that her children should find the time to visit and call her more often, even if they are extremely busy. The therapist might then ask the client once again to consider alternative viewpoints to her own. For example, the therapist might suggest that if the client wants to see her children more often, she call them or visit them rather than waiting for them to call and visit her.

The third question or set of questions the cognitive therapist might ask a client is, "What's the worst that could happen?" and "What could you do if the worst did happen?" The point of these questions is to get the client to face her worst fears about a situation and recognize ways she could cope with even her worst fears. The elderly client in our example may say that her worst fear is that her children truly do not need her or love her as much as they used to. The therapist will then help her explore ways of coping with this if it were true. For example, the client might ask her children if there is anything she needs to change about her behavior to improve their relationship. Or the client might accept that grown children simply do not need their mothers as much as when they were young and find other sources of gratification in her life.

In the third of Beck's cognitive therapy techniques, *behavioral assignments* are used to help the client gather evidence concerning his or her beliefs, to test alternative viewpoints

cognitive therapy
therapeutic approach that focuses on changing people's maladaptive thought patterns

about a situation, and to try new methods of coping with difficult situations. These assignments are presented to the client as ways of testing hypotheses and gathering information that will be useful in therapy regardless of the outcome. Therapists also often use role-plays during therapy sessions to elicit the client's reactions to feared situations and to help the client rehearse positive responses to these situations. For example, a therapist might engage our elderly client in a role-play in which the therapist plays the part of one of the client's children and the client rehearses how she might talk with her child about her concerns about their relationship. This additional focus on shaping adaptive behaviors as well as on changing cognitions has led many proponents of this therapy to call it cognitive-*behavioral* therapy.

Cognitive therapies have proven effective in the treatment of depression, anxiety, and interpersonal problems. Although the founders of cognitive-behavior therapy have argued that their therapies work by changing the *content* of people's negative beliefs and thoughts, Barber and DeRubeis (1989) have suggested that these therapies work more by changing the *process* by which people think about situations in their lives. That is, people who undergo cognitive-behavioral therapy may still have negative thoughts or beliefs in response to situations, but they learn through therapy not to assume these thoughts and beliefs are true, as they once assumed. They then are free to question their thoughts and beliefs and to consider alternative, more positive thoughts and beliefs.

Modes of Delivering Psychosocial Therapy

The psychosocial therapies just described were discussed in terms of their applications in one-on-one therapist-client interactions. All of these therapies, however, can and have been delivered to families, couples, and groups of strangers in addition to individuals. One type of therapy that *requires* focusing on a group rather than an individual is **family systems therapy**.

Family systems theorists believe that an individual's problems are always rooted in interpersonal systems, particularly in the systems we call *families*. According to this viewpoint, you cannot help an individual without treating the entire family system that created and is maintaining the individual's problems. In fact, these theorists argue that the individual may not actually even have a problem but has become the "identified patient" in the family, carrying the responsibility or blame for the dysfunction of the family system.

Two of the most frequently used types of family systems therapy are Virginia Satir's Conjoint Family Therapy (1967) and Salvador Minuchin's Structural Family Therapy (1981). Satir's therapy focuses on the patterns and processes of communication between family members. The therapist identifies and points out dysfunctional communication

family systems therapy
psychotherapy that focuses on the family, rather than a single individual, as the source of problems; family therapists challenge communication styles, disrupt pathological family dynamics, and challenge defensive conceptions in order to harmonize relationships among all members and within each member

Family therapists believe that individuals' problems are rooted in patterns of interaction among family members.

patterns and teaches family members to communicate better by modeling for them effective communication and by teaching members to be clear and to refrain from inferring meaning.

Minuchin's Structural Family Therapy focuses more on the role each member of the family has come to play in the family system and on changing the structure and dynamics of the relationships among family members. The therapist attempts to "join" with the family, becoming a part of the family so as to exert influence over the processes by which family members interact. By questioning family members about their feelings about one another's behaviors and commenting on the behaviors and feelings of the members, the therapist attempts to bring the family dynamics into the open. What follows is an example of an interchange between Minuchin and a husband and wife with whom he was working (1981, adapted from pp. 35–36).

Husband:	I think when something irritates me, it builds up and I hold it in until some little thing will trigger it, and then I'll be very, very critical and get angry. Then I'll tell her that I just don't understand why it has to be this way. But then I try to be very careful not to be unreasonable or too harsh because when I'm harsh, I feel guilty about it.
Minuchin:	So, sometimes the family feels like a trap.
Husband:	It's not the family so much; it's just—(Indicates wife).
Minuchin (completing husband's gesture):	Your wife?
Husband (looking at wife):	No, not her either. It's just the things she doesn't do versus the things she does in terms of how she spends her time. Sometimes I think her priorities should be changed.
Minuchin:	I think you are soft-pedaling.
Wife:	About being trapped?
Minuchin:	Yes, about being trapped. I think people sometimes get depressed when they are, like your husband, unable to be direct. He's not a straight talker. There's a tremendous amount of indirection in your family, because you are essentially very good people who are very concerned not to hurt one another. And you need to tell white lies a lot. . . .
Wife (to husband):	Am I indirect?
Husband:	I don't really know. Sometimes you seem very direct, but I find myself wondering if you are telling me everything about what's bothering you. You know, if you seem upset, I'm not always sure that I know what's bugging you.
Wife:	That I can be upset for something like that because it wouldn't upset you?
Husband:	Maybe that's part of it.
Wife (smiling, but at the same time her eyes are watering):	Because you always seem to know better than I do what is really upsetting me, what my problem is at the moment.

Minuchin (to husband): You see what's happening now? She's talking straight, but she's afraid that if she talks straight, you will be hurt, so she begins to cry and she begins to smile. So she's saying, "Don't take my straight talk seriously, because it is just the product of a person who is under stress." And that is the kind of thing you do to each other. So you cannot change too much. Because you don't tell each other in what direction to change.

The goal of the therapist is to challenge and disrupt the current dysfunctional dynamics of the family, so that the family is forced to change these dynamics, ideally toward more adaptive dynamics. Three primary strategies of family therapy are (1) to challenge the family's assumption that "the problem" lies in one member of the family rather than in the family dynamics, (2) to challenge dysfunctional family structures, such as those in which members of the family are overinvolved with each other and do not allow each other sufficient autonomy, and (3) to challenge the family's defensive conception of reality, such as in challenging the belief of two parents that there is nothing wrong with their daughter when she is suffering from a serious eating disorder.

Special Issues in Treating Children

Every therapy we have described has probably been used at one time or another to treat children and adolescents with psychological disorders. Studies of the effectiveness of psychosocial and biological therapies generally show that children and adolescents receiving therapy have better outcomes than those receiving no therapy (Weisz, Donenberg, Han, & Kauneckis, 1995). The effectiveness of any specific type of therapy may depend largely on the type of disorder the child or adolescent has.

Designing and applying effective therapies for children and adolescents are made difficult by problems similar to those that arise in assessing and diagnosing children's and adolescents' disorders (refer to Chapter 2). These include the need to match the therapy to the child's developmental level; the possibility that a therapy, especially a drug therapy, will have long-term negative effects on the child's development; the fact that children are embedded in families, and often the family as well as the child must be treated; and the fact that children and adolescents seldom refer themselves for treatment and thus are often not motivated to engage in treatment.

Therapists use play to elicit children's concerns and help children work through these concerns.

Matching Psychotherapies to Children's Developmental Levels

As we discussed in Chapter 2, children can have difficulty expressing their feelings and concerns in words, particularly when they are very distressed. Thus, therapists use a variety of methods to elicit information from children about their feelings, such as having children draw pictures or engage in play that might symbolize how they are feeling.

Psychodynamically oriented therapists believe that expressing feelings and concerns through play can help the child master these feelings and concerns and overcome negative behaviors. Their therapy with a child may consist primarily of helping the child engage in this indirect expression and exploration of feelings and concerns. Other therapists use play or other projective techniques only as tools to assess a child's feelings and concerns.

Can children participate in talking therapies such as cognitive-behavioral therapy? It seems that the answer is "yes," although the conversations between the therapist and child must be at a level that is appropriate for the child's age (Craighead, Meyers, & Craighead, 1985). However, many therapists believe that for children behaviorally oriented therapies are more appropriate than are talking therapies because behavior therapies are not as dependent on children's verbal abilities. Moreover, children may have trouble changing their behaviors only by changing their thinking—it may take repeated practicing of new behaviors and reinforcement for these behaviors for children to learn them. Comparisons of behavioral and nonbehavioral therapies for children have suggested that behavioral therapies produce a larger and more reliable effect, although nonbehavioral therapies do have positive effects on children (Weiss & Weisz, 1995; Weisz, Weiss, Alicke, & Klotz, 1987).

 How would you go about adapting cognitive therapy for use with elementary-school children?

Effects of Drugs on Children and Adolescents

Drug therapies are becoming increasingly popular in treating children and adolescents with psychological problems (Gadow, 1991). Drugs were initially used to treat only the most severe disorders in children, such as autism, but are now being used to treat disorders such as depression and phobias. The use of drugs in children has been extremely controversial, largely because of fears that drugs will have toxic effects both in the short term and in the long term. Finding a safe dosage of psychotropic drugs for children is initially tricky, because body size, age, and hormones all affect the metabolism of drugs, and there is more variability in the proper dosage of a drug among children than there is among adults. We do not know the long-term effects of most drugs on children's physical or psychological development because the studies necessary to understand these effects have not been done. Such studies would require administering drugs to thousands of children and following these children (and control groups of children with disorders who do not receive drugs) throughout their development. These studies have not been done partly because of fears about the effects of drugs on children's development and because researchers have only begun to study children's disorders recently (Gadow, 1991).

The Need to Treat the Child's Family

Children are almost always living in some sort of family, whether in the traditional two-parent family, with a single parent or perhaps a grandparent, in a foster-care family, or in some other configuration. Many clinicians believe that children's disorders cannot be effectively treated outside of the context of the family (Kaslow & Racusin, 1990). The family may be the direct cause of a child's disorder, such as in the case when one parent is physically abusive to the child and perhaps to other members of the family. In such cases, treating the child without correcting the cause of the child's problem (i.e., the parental abuse) is ineffective. Indeed, sometimes it is a parent who needs therapy even more than the child. In other cases, the family may not have directly caused the child's problem but may be reinforcing or supporting the child's problem in some way. For example, a child may have trouble controlling aggressive behavior, perhaps because of a biological dysfunction, but the family reinforces the child's aggressivity by allowing her to have what she wants when she threatens to lose control. In such cases, teaching family members how to extinguish the child's aggressive behavior can help the child gain control over that behavior, even if the initial cause of the behavior is biological (Estrada & Pinsof, 1995). Children and their families are sometimes treated with the techniques of family systems therapy, but all the psychotherapies we explored earlier in this chapter have been adapted for application to children and families.

Incorporating the family into a child's treatment creates many difficulties, however. A child may not want his or her family involved in treatment. For example, an adolescent who is depressed because her mother is emotionally abusive may not want to confront her mother in therapy and may instead want an exclusive relationship with the caring therapist. The therapist may still choose to meet with the parent, apart from the adolescent, if the therapist believes the parent must be dealt with in order for the adolescent's problems to be overcome. The adolescent must know the therapist is meeting with the parent, however, and must be helped to trust that her relationship with the therapist is not compromised by these meetings with the parent. Family members may themselves not want to join therapy, particularly if they feel they are being blamed for the child's problems. If they do join therapy, they may not be cooperative with the therapist in overcoming the child's and family's problems.

Therapists are sometimes faced with extremely difficult decisions about whether to remove children from their families such as when a therapist believes a family poses a danger to a child. They also must decide when to allow a child to return to a family from which he or she has been removed because of a perceived danger. A therapist's perceptions of the danger a family poses to a child can be influenced by the therapist's biases against the ethnicity or culture of the family or misunderstandings of the parenting practices of that ethnic or cultural group. For example, Gray and Cosgrove (1985) note that spanking is an accepted form of discipline in some ethnic and socioeconomic groups in the United States but can be taken as evidence of child abuse by social workers and therapists who do not believe spanking is appropriate. There may be some parenting practices that are accepted by certain cultures that therapists never want to endorse; but therapists must be careful to take into account the cultural context of a parent's behaviors before passing judgment.

Children Often Do Not Seek Therapy Themselves

Most children and adolescents who enter therapy do not seek it for themselves (Kendall & Morris, 1991). They may be taken by their parents, who are overwhelmed by their children's behavioral or emotional difficulties. Often, troubled children are first identified by school officials, by their pediatricians, by social service agents (e.g., welfare workers), or by the criminal justice system (Tuma, 1989). Children who enter psychotherapy through any of these avenues may enter it reluctantly and thus may not participate wholeheartedly in therapy. Little research has been done on the effects of the relationship between a child and a therapist on the outcome of child psychotherapy, but it is likely that a warm, positive relationship with a therapist is as important in therapy with children as it is in therapy with adults. Therapists usually must work against a child's initial reluctance to enter therapy in order to establish a good therapeutic relationship.

 Is it ethical to force a child or adolescent to receive treatment?

Unfortunately, most children who could benefit from therapy do not receive any therapy. Treatment facilities specializing in children's problems are unavailable in many parts of the United States and other industrialized countries and nonexistent in other parts of the world. Perhaps 50 percent of psychologically disturbed children receive advice or medications only from their family physicians, who are untrained in the assessment and treatment of psychological disorders (Tuma, 1989). The child welfare system sees many troubled children, often the victims of abuse and neglect. Such children are increasingly placed in long-term foster care rather than given specialized psychological treatment. Many children in the juvenile justice system suffer from psychological disorders, including conduct disorders, depression, and drug addiction, but few receive long-term intensive treatment (Tuma, 1989). There is much room for the expansion of services to psychologically disturbed children.

Summing Up | Treatments for Children

- Treatments for children must take into account their cognitive skills and developmental levels and adapt to their ability to comprehend and participate in therapy.
- There are reasons to be concerned about the possible toxic effects of drugs on children.
- Often, a child's family must be brought into therapy, but the child or the family may object.
- Most children who enter therapy do not seek it out themselves but are brought by others, raising issues about children's willingness to participate in therapy.

Common Components of Therapy

The several theoretical approaches to and modes of delivery of therapy described in this chapter may seem radically different. Indeed, proponents of a given approach have often been vociferous in their opposition to other approaches, decrying these other approaches as useless or even harmful to clients. There is increasing evidence, however, that there are some common components to successful therapies, even when the specific techniques of the therapies differ greatly. The first of these is a *positive relationship* with the therapist (Crits-Cristoph et al., 1991). Clients who trust their therapists and believe that the therapists understand them are more willing to reveal important information, engage in homework assignments, and try out new skills or coping techniques that the therapists suggest. In addition, simply having a positive relationship with a caring and understanding human being goes a long way toward helping people overcome distress and change their behaviors.

 Why would clients who develop a warm and trusting relationship with a therapist recover more fully? What would each of the psychological theories discussed in this chapter say are the reasons?

A second, related component of most successful therapies is a client's *belief that the therapy will help* him or her (Frank, 1978). For example, studies of cognitive-behavior therapy for depression have found that the extent to which clients believe and accept the rationale behind this therapy is a significant predictor of the effectiveness of the therapy (Fennell & Teasdale, 1987). Clients to whom the rationale behind cognitive therapy makes sense engage more actively in therapy and are less depressed after a course of therapy than are those who don't "buy" the rationale for the therapy from the outset. A major problem in drug therapies is the high dropout rate from these therapies. Often people drop out because they do not experience quick enough relief from the drugs and therefore believe the drugs will not work or because they feel they need to talk about problems to overcome them.

It seems likely that two factors affecting the therapeutic relationship and a client's beliefs about the usefulness of a therapy are culture and gender. When a therapist and client come from very different cultures, can the therapist fully understand the client's problems and the client fully trust the therapist? What do different cultures believe about the effectiveness of different therapies? Do clients work better with therapists of their same gender? Do men and women have different beliefs about the appropriateness of certain therapies?

Cultural and Gender Issues in Therapy

Several recommendations have been made about what types of psychotherapy are most acceptable to specific ethnic groups or to a gender. More structured and action-oriented therapies, such as behavior and cognitive-behavior therapies, have been recommended for Hispanics, African Americans and Asian Americans, on the premise that these groups may be less inclined to the intrapsychic explorations of psychodynamic therapies. Asian Americans are said to prefer therapists who provide structure, guidance, and direction, rather than nondirective therapies such as psychoanalysis or client-centered therapy (Atkinson, Maruyama, & Matsui, 1978). Most of these assertions have not been put to rigorous empirical tests, however. Similarly, although some clinicians have suggested that women find therapies that focus on interpersonal relationships and expression of feelings more appealing and helpful than other types of therapies, there is little evidence for or against this assertion (McGrath et al., 1990).

The specific form of therapy may not matter so much as the cultural sensitivity the therapist shows the client, whatever therapy is being used (Allison et al., 1994). Sue and Zane (1987, pp. 42–43) give the following example of the importance of cultural sensitivity in the interaction between a client and a therapist. First, they describe the problems the client faced, and second, they describe how the therapist (one of the authors) responded to these problems:

Case Study • At the advice of a close friend, Mae C. decided to seek services at a mental health center. She was extremely distraught and tearful as she related her dilemma. An immigrant from Hong Kong several years ago, Mae met and married her husband (also a recent immigrant from Hong Kong). Their marriage was apparently going fairly well until six months ago when her husband succeeded in bringing over his parents from Hong Kong. While not enthusiastic about having her parents-in-law live with her, Mae realized that her husband wanted them and that both she and her husband were obligated to help their parents (her own parents were still in Hong Kong).

After the parents arrived, Mae found that she was expected to serve them. For example, the mother-in-law would expect Mae to cook and serve dinner, to wash all the clothes, and to do other chores. At the same time, she would constantly complain that Mae did not cook the dinner right, that the house was always messy, and that Mae should wash certain clothes separately. The parents-in-law also displaced Mae and her husband from the master bedroom. The guest room was located in the basement, and the parents refused to sleep in the basement because it reminded them of a tomb.

Mae would occasionally complain to her husband about his parents. The husband would excuse his parent's demands by indicating "They are my parents and they're getting old." In general, he avoided any potential conflict; if he took sides, he supported his parents. Although Mae realized that she had an obligation to his parents, the situation was becoming intolerable to her.

I (the therapist) indicated (to Mae) that conflicts with in-laws were very common, especially for Chinese, who are obligated to take care of their parents. I attempted to normalize the problems because she was suffering from a great deal of guilt over her perceived failure to be the perfect daughter-in-law. I also conveyed my belief that

---

in therapy we could try to generate new ideas to resolve the problem—ideas that did not simply involve extreme courses of action such as divorce or total submission to the in-laws (which she believed were the only options).

I discussed Mae during a case conference with other mental health personnel. It is interesting that many suggestions were generated: Teach Mae how to confront her parents-in-law; have her invite the husband for marital counseling so that husband and wife could form a team in negotiation with his parents; conduct extended family therapy so that Mae, her husband, and her in-laws could agree on contractual give-and-take relationships. The staff agreed that working solely with Mae would not change the situation. However, these options entailed extreme response costs. Confronting her in-laws was discrepant with her role of daughter-in-law, and she felt very uncomfortable in asserting herself in the situation. Trying to involve her husband or in-laws in treatment was ill-advised. Her husband did not want to confront his parents. More important, Mae was extremely fearful that her family might find out that she had sought psychotherapy. Her husband as well as her in-laws would be appalled at her disclosure of family problems to a therapist who was an outsider. . . .

How could Mae's case be handled? During the case conference, we discussed the ways that Chinese handle interpersonal family conflicts which are not unusual to see. Chinese often use third-party intermediaries to resolve conflicts. The intermediaries obviously have to be credible and influential with the conflicting parties.

At the next session with Mae, I asked her to list the persons who might act as intermediaries, so that we could discuss the suitability of having someone else intervene. Almost immediately, Mae mentioned her uncle (the older brother of the mother-in-law) whom she described as being quite understanding and sensitive. We discussed what she should say to the uncle. After calling her uncle, who lived about 50 miles from Mae, she reported that he wanted to visit them. The uncle apparently realized the gravity of the situation and offered to help. He came for dinner, and Mae told me that she overheard a discussion between the uncle and Mae's mother-in-law. Essentially, he told her that Mae looked unhappy, that possibly she was working too hard, and that she needed a little more praise for the work that she was doing in taking care of everyone. The mother-in-law expressed surprise over Mae's unhappiness and agreed that Mae was doing a fine job. Without directly confronting each other, the uncle and his younger sister understood the subtle messages each conveyed. Older brother was saying that something was wrong and younger sister acknowledged it. After this interaction, Mae reported that her mother-in-law's criticisms did noticeably diminish and that she had even begun to help Mae with the chores.

If Mae's therapist had not been sensitive to Mae's cultural beliefs about her role as a daughter-in-law and had suggested some of the solutions put forward by his colleagues in the case conference, Mae may have even dropped out of therapy. People from ethnic minority groups in the United States are much more likely than European Americans to drop out of psychosocial therapy (Sue & Zane, 1987). One study of 13,450 therapy clients found that the dropout rate for Hispanics was 42 percent, American Indians 55 percent, and African Americans 52 percent, compared to only 30 percent for European Americans (Sue, Allen, & Conway, 1978). Ethnic minority clients often find the suggestions of therapists strange, unhelpful, and even insulting. Because Mae's therapist was willing to work within the constraints of her cultural beliefs, he and Mae found a solution to her situation that was acceptable to her.

In treating children, cultural norms about child-rearing practices and the proper role of doctors can make it difficult to include the family in a child's treatment (Tharp, 1991). For example, a study of behavior therapy for children found that Hong Kong Chinese parents were very reluctant to be trained to engage in behavioral techniques, such as responding contingently with praise or ignoring certain behaviors. Such techniques violated the parents' views of appropriate child-rearing practices and their expectations that the therapist should be the person "curing" the child (Lieh-Mak, Lee, & Luk, 1984).

However, several clinicians argue that family-based therapies are more appropriate than individual therapy in cultures that are highly family-oriented, including Native-American, Hispanic, African-American, and Asian-American cultures (see Tharp, 1991). In the treatment of Latin-American children and their families, Vazquez-Nuttal, Avila-Vivas, and Morales-Barreto (1984) argued that the therapist should help the family reinforce the importance of ethnic and family values and explore the conflicts between these values and those of mainstream American culture that could be contributing to the psychological problems a child or family is experiencing. One therapeutic program, the Homebuilders Program, takes the further step of placing the therapist in the home of the troubled child and family, so that therapy is delivered completely in the context of the family and community (Kinney, Haapala, & Booth, 1991). Most of the children in this program are at risk for being placed in foster care because of the severity of their problems or the family's dysfunctions. This program has proven effective for children in many ethnic groups, but African-American and Hispanic children and families have seemed to benefit from this approach even more than have European-American children and families (Fraser, Pecora, & Haapala, 1991).

Matching Therapist and Client

Must a therapist come from the same culture or be of the same gender as the client to fully understand the client? Cultural and gender sensitivity can probably be acquired through training and experience to a large degree (D'Andrea & Daniels, 1995). In fact, Sue and Zane (1987) warn that just because a therapist is from the same ethnic or racial group as the client does not mean that therapist and client share the same value system. For example, a fourth-generation Japanese American who has fully adopted American competitive and individualistic values may clash with a recent immigrant from Japan who ascribes to the self-sacrificing, community-oriented values of Japanese culture. Similarly, a woman therapist who has strong feminist values may clash with a woman client who holds very traditional sex-role expectations. These value differences among people of the same ethnic/racial group or of the same gender may explain why studies show that matching the ethnicity, race, or gender of the therapist and client does not necessarily lead to a better outcome for the client (Atkinson, 1983, 1986; Jones, 1978; Lerner, 1972).

Some people seeking therapy certainly prefer therapists of their ethnic group or gender. African Americans are especially likely to prefer African-American therapists (Atkinson, Furlong, & Poston, 1986). In general, college students prefer counselors of their same ethnicity and gender and are more likely to use counseling services when their preferences are met (Tharp, 1991). Studies of noncollege adults do not find that they prefer counselors of their same gender, however (e.g., DeHeer, Wampold, & Freund, 1992). The important finding from many studies of clients' preferences for therapists is that there are large individual differences in these preferences (Atkinson, Furlong, & Poston, 1986; Pomales, Claiborn, & LaFromboise, 1986; Sue, 1988). While some clients care deeply about having a therapist of the same ethnic group or gender, some only trust a therapist who corresponds to their stereotype of a "doctor," and some have no preferences regarding the ethnicity or gender of their therapist. For clients who wish to be matched with therapists of the same ethnic or gender group, this matching may be necessary for a client to trust the therapist and have faith in the therapy. As noted earlier, the relationship between a client and therapist, and a client's beliefs about the likely effectiveness of a therapy contribute strongly to a client's full engagement in the therapy and the effectiveness of the therapy.

Culturally Specific Therapies

Our review of the relationships between culture and gender and therapy has focused on the forms of therapy most often practiced in modern industrialized cultures, such as psychodynamic, behavioral, and cognitive therapies. Cultural groups, even within modern industrialized countries, often have their own forms of therapy for distressed people, however. Let us examine two of these.

Native American Indian healing processes simultaneously focus on the physiology, psychology, and religious practices of the individual (LaFromboise, Trimble, & Mohatt, 1990). "Clients" are encouraged to transcend the self and experience the self as embedded in the community and as an expression of the community. Family and friends are brought together with the individual in traditional ceremonies involving prayers, songs, and dances that emphasize Native American cultural heritage and the reintegration of the individual into the cultural network. These ceremonies may be supplemented by a variety of herbal medicines used for hundreds of years to treat people with physical and psychological symptoms.

Hispanics in the southwestern United States and in Mexico suffering from psychological problems may consult folk healers, known as *curanderos* or *curanderas* (Martinez, 1993; Rivera, 1988). One survey of urban Hispanic-American women in Colorado found that 20 percent had consulted a curandero for treatment (Rivera, 1988). Curanderos use religiously based rituals to overcome the folk illnesses believed to cause psychological and physical problems. These illnesses may be the result of hexes placed on the individual or of soul loss or magical fright. These healing rituals include prayers, use of holy palm, and incantations. Curanderos may also apply healing ointments or oils and prescribe herbal medicines.

Native Americans and Hispanics often seek both folk healers and psychiatric care from mental health professionals practicing the therapies described earlier in this chapter. Mental health professionals need to be aware of the practices and beliefs of folk healing when treating clients from these cultural groups and of the possibility that clients will combine these different forms of therapy, following some of the recommendations of both types of healers.

Bio-Psycho-Social INTEGRATION

Some psychologists and psychiatrists tend to practice only one type of therapy, believing that this type of therapy is effective for all the problems that they treat. Other psychologists and psychiatrists apply different types of therapy for different problems, based on their own clinical experience and research showing what type of therapy works best for a given type of problem. Increasingly, psychologists and psychiatrists are working together and in conjunction with social workers, psychiatric nurses, and other mental health professionals in teams that take a comprehensive approach to the treatment of client's problems. For example, a depressed client may receive antidepressant therapy from a psychiatrist, cognitive-behavior therapy from a psychologist, and help in finding a new job and place to live from a social worker. This team-oriented approach will probably become more common as more people are treated in health maintenance organizations or other comprehensive care facilities rather than in private practice.

Chapter Summary

Psychodynamic theories of psychopathology focus on unconscious conflicts that cause anxiety in the individual and result in maladaptive behavior. These conflicts arise when the libidinal impulses of the id clash with the constraints on behavior imposed by the ego and superego. The ways people handle their conflicts are defined by the types of defense mechanisms they use. More recent psychodynamic theorists focus less on the role of unconscious impulses and more on the development of the individual's self-concept in the context of interpersonal relationships. They see a greater role for the environment in the shaping of personality and have more hope for change in personality during adulthood than Freud did.

The behaviorist theories of abnormality reject notions of unconscious conflicts and focus only on the rewards and punishments in the environment that shape and maintain behavior. Classical conditioning takes place when a previously neutral stimulus is paired with a stimulus that naturally creates a certain response; eventually, the neutral stimulus will also elicit the response. Operant conditioning involves rewarding desired behaviors and punishing undesired behaviors. People also learn by imitating the behaviors modeled by others and by observing the rewards and punishments others receive for their behaviors.

Cognitive theories suggest that people's attributions for events, their perceptions of control and self-efficacy, and their global beliefs or assumptions influence the behaviors and emotions they have in reaction to situations.

Humanist and existential theories suggest that all humans strive to fulfill their potential for good and to self-actualize. The inability to fulfill one's potential arises from the pressures of society to conform to others' expectations and values and from existential anxiety.

A wide variety of biological and psychosocial approaches to the treatment of psychological disorders have been developed in line with different theories of the causes of these disorders. Biological therapies most often involve drugs intended to regulate the functioning of brain neurotransmitters associated with a psychological disorder or to compensate for structural brain abnormalities or the effects of genetics.

Psychosocial therapies include (1) psychodynamic therapy, which focuses on unconscious conflicts and interpersonal conflicts that lead to maladaptive behaviors and emotions; (2) humanist existential therapies, which intend to help a client realize his or her potential for self-actualization; (3) behavior therapies, which focus on changing specific maladaptive behaviors and emotions by changing the contingencies for them; and (4) cognitive therapies, which focus on changing the way a client thinks about important situations. All of these therapies can be delivered to individual clients or in a group setting. One form of therapy that requires a group focus is family systems therapy, which intends to alter the communication patterns and family dynamics that create and sustain maladaptive behaviors in members of the family. Common components of effective therapy seem to be a good therapist-client relationship and the client's belief that the therapy can be effective.

Therapy with children has its own set of challenges. First, a therapy must be matched to a child's developmental level for the child to be able to participate fully. Second, therapists must be concerned about the short-term and long-term effects of drugs on children's development. Third, children's families may often need to be brought into therapy. Fourth, children do not tend to seek therapy for themselves and thus are sometimes reluctant to participate.

Some clients may wish to work with therapists of the same culture or gender, but it is unclear whether matching therapist and client in terms of culture and gender is necessary for therapy to be effective. It is important for therapists to be sensitive to the influences of culture and gender on a client's attitudes toward therapy and on the acceptability to the client of different types of solutions to problems.

Key Terms

biological approach 66
psychosocial
    approach 66
cerebrum 68
limbic system 69
ventricles 69
neurotransmitters 70
synapse 70
reuptake 70
degradation 70
endocrine system 70
hormone 70
behavior genetics 71

polygenic 72
predisposition 72
family history study 73
probands 73
monozygotic (MZ)
    twins 73
dizygotic (DZ) twins 73
twin study 73
concordance rate 73
adoption study 74
psychodynamic
    theory 76
libido 76

id 76
superego 76
ego 76
unconscious 76
preconscious 76
conscious 76
repression 76
anxiety 77
regression 77
denial 77
displacement 77
rationalization 77
intellectualization 77

44

Application

How to Look for a Therapist

How do you know when you or someone you care about needs a therapist? How do you find a therapist once you decide to seek one? The American Psychological Association has published the following guidelines for evaluating whether you should seek a therapist and for finding a therapist (from *Choosing a Therapist Who Is Right for You*, distributed by the Practice Directorate of the American Psychological Association).

Consider Therapy If . . .

- You feel helpless and problems do not seem to get better despite your efforts.
- You feel sad or blue, nervous, or tense for a prolonged period of time.
- You or others notice changes in your mood or behavior or a decrease in your ability to carry out everyday activities.
- You are concerned about the emotional health of a family member or partner.
- You want to look at life and make decisions in a different way.
- You want to find ways of changing your life to feel more satisfied.

How Do You Find a Therapist?

- Talk to friends and family.
- Call your local or state psychological association.
- Contact your community mental health center.
- Inquire at your church or synagogue.
- Ask your physician or other health professional.
- Consult counseling centers at local colleges and universities.
- Consult your local Yellow Pages.

What Should You Consider When Making a Choice?

A therapist and client work together. The right match is important. The following are sample questions that may be useful when considering a particular psychologist:

- Are you a licensed psychologist?
- How many years have you been practicing psychology?
- I've been feeling (anxious, tense, depressed, etc.). I'm having problems (with my job, my marriage, eating, sleeping, etc.). What kind of experience do you have helping people with these types of problems?

- What are your specialty areas? (children, marriage, etc.).
- What might I expect during our sessions?
- What are your fees? (Fees are usually based on a 45-minute to 50-minute session).
- Do you use a sliding-fee scale? Please explain how this works.
- What types of insurance do you accept?
- Do you accept Medicare/Medicaid patients?
- How do you bill for services? Will you bill my insurance company directly or do I bill for reimbursement?

Interview several therapists—by telephone or in person—before making a choice. Following the initial contact, you may want to meet two or three times before you decide to work together. These sessions, called *consultation sessions*, will help you determine if the therapist is right for you.

For further information on choosing a therapist, you can contact the American Psychological Association, Practice Directorate, 1200 Seventeenth Street, N.W., Washington, DC 20036. The telephone number is 202-955-7618. ■

Part Two

Disorders of Anxiety, Mood, Psychosis, and Personality

The disorders in Part II involve maladaptive and distressing emotions, thoughts, and behaviors that are often chronic and pervade every aspect of people's lives.

People with anxiety disorders and mood disorders frequently experience extreme emotional distress that severely interferes with their ability to function in life. Biology, stressful experiences, and maladaptive ways of thinking all appear to contribute to the anxiety and mood disorders. Fortunately, there are several effective biological and psychosocial treatments for these disorders.

Psychosis is loss of touch with reality, and is the hallmark of the disorder called schizophrenia. Schizophrenia probably has strong biological roots, but can be influenced by environmental stress. People with the dissociative disorders respond to stress by experiencing a fragmentation of their sense of self, sometimes developing separate personalities and often developing amnesia for important information about themselves. People with personality disorders maintain a consistent personality style, but it is a highly maladaptive style for them and for people around them.

If misery loves company, misery has company enough.

—Henry David Thoreau, *Journal* (1851, September 1)

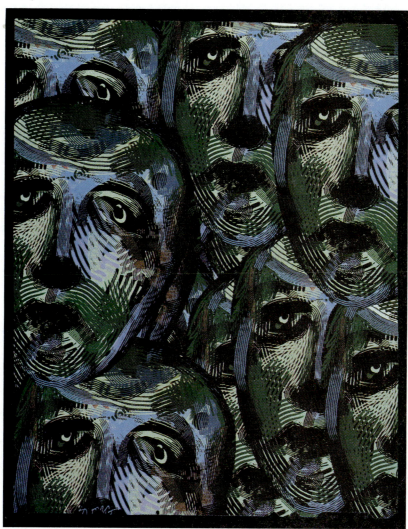

Diana Ong
Grey Clowns

chapter 4 Anxiety Disorders

Panic and Agoraphobia

People with panic disorder experience sudden bursts of anxiety symptoms, feel out of control, and think they are dying. People with agoraphobia fear being in places where they might be trapped or unable to get help in an emergency. The emergency they often fear is having a panic attack. People prone to panic may have an overreactive autonomic nervous system that easily goes into a fight-or-flight response. They also may tend to catastrophize their symptoms. Agoraphobia may develop as people learn they can reduce their anxiety by remaining in certain kinds of places. Antidepressant and antianxiety drugs can reduce symptoms of panic. Cognitive-behavioral treatments are highly effective for panic and agoraphobia.

Specific Phobias and Social Phobia

The specific phobias focus on animals, elements of the environment (such as water), certain situations (such as flying), and blood or injections. Social phobia involves a pervasive fear of scrutiny by others. Psychodynamic theories attribute phobias to the displacement of unconscious conflicts onto symbolic objects. Behavioral theories argue that phobias develop from straightforward classical and operant conditioning. Biological theories attribute phobias to genetics. The most effective treatments for phobias are behavioral treatments that expose people to their phobic objects and teach them skills for reducing their anxiety.

Post-Traumatic Stress Disorder

Post-traumatic stress disorder (PTSD) is a set of symptoms experienced by trauma survivors, including hypervigilance, reexperiencing of the trauma, and emotional numbing. People who have experienced either human-created or natural disasters are at high risk for PTSD. Some predictors of people's vulnerability to PTSD are the proximity, duration, and severity of the stressor; the availability of social support; pretrauma distress; and coping strategies. Treatment generally involves exposing people to their fears, challenging cognitions, and helping them manage ongoing problems.

Generalized Anxiety Disorder

People with generalized anxiety disorder have chronic and pervasive anxiety about most aspects of their lives. Both consciously and unconsciously they are hypervigilant for threat. Cognitive-behavioral therapies have proven most effective for generalized anxiety disorder.

Gender Differences in Anxiety Disorders

Women are more likely than men to have any of the anxiety disorders discussed to this point. Theories have attributed this likelihood to a greater genetic vulnerability among women, the effects of hormonal fluctuation on anxiety, personality characteristics that predispose women to anxiety, and the objective threats that women face in everyday life.

Cultural Differences in Anxiety Disorders

Anxiety may have different manifestations and conceptualizations across cultures. For example, Puerto Ricans have a syndrome called *ataque de nervios* that shares many symptoms of anxiety but is distinct.

Obsessive-Compulsive Disorder

Obsessive-compulsive disorder is classified as an anxiety disorder but has many distinct characteristics. Obsessions are unwanted, intrusive thoughts that the individual feels are uncontrollable. Compulsions are ritualized behaviors that the individual feels forced to engage in. Biological theories attribute obsessive-compulsive disorder to genetics and to dysfunction in areas of the brain regulating primitive impulses. Psychodynamic theories view obsessions and compulsions as symbols of unconscious conflicts. Cognitive-behavioral theories attribute obsessions to absolutist thinking and compulsions to operant conditioning. Treatment for obsessive-compulsive disorder generally involves a combination of drug therapy and cognitive-behavioral therapy.

Bio-Psycho-Social Integration
Chapter Summary
Key Terms
Application: *Relaxation Exercises*

All emotions are pure which gather you and lift you up; that emotion is impure which seizes only one side of your being and so distorts you.

—Rainer Maria Rilke, *Letters to a Young Poet*
(1904, November 4; translated by M. D. Herter)

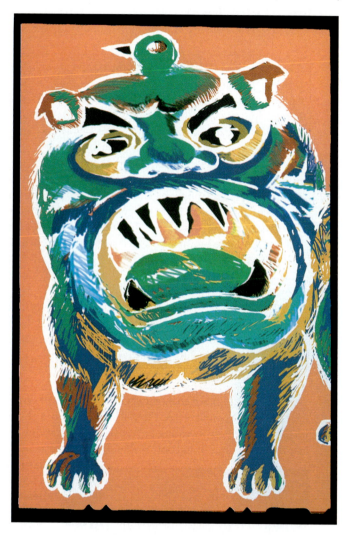

Diana Ong
Birddog

Fears are common in everyday life. As children, we may have been fearful of dogs or of strangers. As adults, we may have been fearful when we were nearly in a car accident or when we were walking alone at night down a narrow and deserted street. Our parents, friends, and other loved ones may have not understood why we were so fearful and may have admonished us to be less fearful, saying things like, "Be brave!" "There's nothing to be scared of!" "Relax!" "Don't be such a scaredy-cat!"

Most of us have grown out of our childhood fears, and our adult fear responses are mild, transient (ending when the situation ends), or reasonable, given the circumstances. People with anxiety disorders live with fears that are neither mild, transient, nor reasonable, given their circumstances. The fears of people with anxiety disorders are severe and lower the quality of their lives. Their fears are chronic, either occurring all day long every day or recurring frequently enough to interfere with their functioning. Finally, their fears are out of proportion to the dangers that they truly face. The following case study illustrates the debilitating fears that one person with an anxiety disorder lived with (adapted from Spitzer et al., 1987, p. 262).

Case Study • Fredrick is sitting in the waiting room of a cardiologist, hoping that this time, he has found a physician who can do something about his symptoms. Every day for about two years, Fredrick has experienced periods of dizziness, sweating palms, heart palpitations, and ringing of the ears. He has a chronically dry mouth and throat, periods of uncontrollable shaking, and a constant "edgy" and watchful feeling that often interferes with his ability to concentrate.

Because of these symptoms, Fredrick has seen a family practitioner, a neurologist, a neurosurgeon, a chiropractor, and an ear, nose, and throat specialist. He has been placed on a hypoglycemic diet, received physiotherapy for a pinched nerve, and told he might have "an inner ear problem." Nothing has seemed to help, however.

Fredrick has many worries. He constantly worries about the health of his parents. His father, in fact, had a heart attack two years before, but now is feeling well. Fredrick has also worried about whether he is "a good father," whether his wife will ever leave him (there is no indication that she is dissatisfied with the marriage), and whether he is liked by coworkers.

For the past two years, Fredrick has had few social contacts because of his nervous symptoms. Although he has sometimes had to leave work when the symptoms became intolerable, he continues to work for the same company he joined for an apprenticeship following high school graduation.

Fredrick is experiencing four different types of symptoms that make up what clinicians refer to as *anxiety* (see Table 4.1). First, he has physiological or *somatic symptoms*, including dizziness, sweating palms, heart palpitations, ringing of the ears, dry mouth and throat, periods of uncontrollable shaking, and a constant "edgy" feeling. Second, he

has *emotional symptoms*—primarily a sense of fearfulness and watchfulness. Third, he has *cognitive symptoms*, including unrealistic worries that something bad is happening (that his father is ill) or is about to happen (that his wife will leave him). Finally, he has *behavioral symptoms*—primarily avoidance of situations because of his fears.

The physiological and behavioral symptoms listed in Table 4.1 make up what is known as the **fight-or-flight response** (also called the *emergency reaction*). Evolution has prepared our

The symptoms of anxiety are emotional, somatic, behavioral, and cognitive.

fight-or-flight response
physiological and behavioral symptoms of the autonomic nervous system used to fight off or flee threats to one's safety

Table 4.1 Symptoms of Anxiety

Somatic	Behavioral	Emotional	Cognitive
Goosebumps emerge	Escape	Sense of dread	Anticipation of harm
Muscles tense	Avoidance	Terror	Exaggerating of danger
Heart rate increases	Aggression	Restlessness	Problems in concentrating
Respiration accelerates	Freezing	Irritability	Hypervigilance
Respiration deepens	Decreased appetitive responding		Worried, ruminative thinking
Spleen contracts			Fear of losing control
Peripheral blood vessels dilate	Increased aversive responding		Fear of dying
Liver releases carbohydrates			Sense of unreality
Bronchioles widen			
Pupils dilate			
Perspiration increases			
Adrenaline is secreted			
Stomach acid is inhibited			
Salivation decreases			
Bladder relaxes			

bodies to mobilize resources so that we can fight off or flee from threats to our safety, such as hungry lions (in ancient times) or knife-wielding muggers. Our heart rate increases and our blood vessels widen to allow more oxygen to be pumped through our bloodstream to our muscles and brain. Our breathing becomes deeper, and air passages widen so that more oxygen gets into our blood. Our liver releases sugar for use by our muscles. We sweat so that we can be more quickly cooled.

There are several differences between the adaptive fear response that we have developed through evolution and the maladaptive anxiety that some people suffer:

- In adaptive fear, people fear something that truly could hurt them, but in maladaptive anxiety, people's perception of threat is *unrealistic*. What they are anxious about cannot hurt them or is very unlikely to come about. For example, a person with obsessive-compulsive disorder may worry that her mother will die if she does not say a specific sequence of words at a specific time of the day, every day.
- In adaptive fear, the amount of fear people experience is in proportion to the real threat they face, but in maladaptive anxiety, the amount of fear experienced is *out of proportion* to the harm the threat could cause. For example, a person with a social phobia may become absolutely panicked over the thought that he could say something that would embarrass him if he were called on in class, and he therefore avoids going to class at all.
- In adaptive fear, people's fear response subsides when the threat ends, but in maladaptive anxiety, people's concern is *persistent* when a threat passes, and they may have a great deal of *anticipatory anxiety* about the future. For example, Fredrick continues to worry about his father's health after his heart attack, even though his father now seems healthy, and he worries in anticipation that his wife might become dissatisfied with their marriage.

Chronic or frequent anxiety may not only interfere with a person's ability to enjoy and prosper in life. As we shall discuss in Chapter 13, excessive arousal of the physiological systems that make up the fight-or-flight response may also create wear and tear on the body, increasing risk for serious medical illness.

Anxiety is also a prominent feature in many other psychological disorders. For example, the majority of people with serious depression also report bouts of anxiety.

People with schizophrenia often feel anxious when they believe they are slipping into a new episode of psychosis. Many people who abuse alcohol and other drugs do so to dampen anxious symptoms. Indeed, Freud and many other theorists believed that anxiety resulting from internal conflicts was the underlying cause of most forms of psychopathology.

In this chapter, however, we focus on disorders in which the primary symptoms are anxiety symptoms. We begin with a discussion of panic, which can be a part of many of the anxiety disorders or, when frequent, a disorder in itself. We then discuss agoraphobia, which usually develops in response to a history of panic attacks. Next, we discuss the other phobias: simple phobias and social phobias. We move on to discuss post-traumatic stress disorder and then generalized anxiety disorder. There are gender differences in the prevalence of these anxiety disorders and cultural differences in the focus of anxieties—that is, what people get anxious about—and we will discuss these differences. Finally, we end with a discussion of obsessive-compulsive disorder, which is categorized as an anxiety disorder but which has some intriguing features that distinguish it from the other anxiety disorders.

Panic and Agoraphobia

> **Case Study** • The first time Celia had a panic attack, she was working at McDonald's. It was two days before her 20th birthday. As she was handing a customer a Big Mac, she had the worst experience of her life. The earth seemed to open up beneath her. Her heart began to pound, she felt she was smothering, she broke into a flop sweat, and she was sure she was going to have a heart attack and die. After about twenty minutes of terror, the panic subsided. Trembling, she got in her car, raced home, and barely left the house for the next three months.
>
> Since that time, Celia has had about three attacks a month. She does not know when they are coming. During an attack she feels dread, searing chest pain, smothering and choking, dizziness, and shakiness. She sometimes thinks this is all not real and she is going crazy. She always thinks she is going to die. (Seligman, 1993, p. 61).

panic attacks
short, intense periods during which an individual experiences physiological and cognitive symptoms of anxiety, characterized by intense fear or discomfort

Celia is suffering from **panic attacks**, short but intense periods in which she experiences many symptoms of anxiety: heart paliptations, trembling, feeling of choking, dizziness, intense dread, and so on (see Table 4.2). Celia's panic attacks appear to occur in the absence of any environmental triggers; they come "out of the blue." Simply handing a customer a hamburger should not cause such terror. This is one of the baffling characteristics of some panic attacks.

Other people have panic attacks that are situationally bound, that is, they are triggered by specific situations or events. For example, people with a social phobia may have panic attacks when forced into a social situation. Most commonly, panic attacks are situationally predisposed: The person is more likely to have them in certain situations but does not always have them when in those situations. In all these cases, however, the panic attack is a terrifying experience, characterized by intense fear or discomfort, the physiological symptoms of anxiety, and the feeling of losing control, going crazy, or dying.

 Have you ever had a panic attack? If so, think back to what kinds of symptoms you experienced and what was going on in your life at the time.

Panic Disorder

Between 8 and 12 percent of people have occasional panic attacks, especially during times of intense stress, such as exams week (Telch, Lucas, & Nelson, 1989). For most of these people, the panic attacks are annoying but isolated events and do not change how they live

Table 4.2   Symptoms of a Panic Attack

These are the common symptoms of a panic attack. Occasional experiences of these symptoms are common. When the symptoms occur frequently and interfere with daily living, the individual may be diagnosed with panic disorder.

Heart palpitations
Pounding heartbeat
Numbness or tingling sensations
Chills or hot flashes
Sweating
Trembling or shaking
Sensations of shortness of breath or smothering
Feeling of choking
Chest pain or discomfort
Nausea and upset stomach
Feeling dizzy, unsteady, lightheaded, or faint
Feelings of unreality or being detached from oneself
Fear of losing control or going crazy
Fear of dying

their lives. When panic attacks become a common occurrence and a person begins to worry about having attacks and changes behaviors as a result of this worry, a diagnosis of **panic disorder** may be given (APA, 1994).

panic disorder
disorder characterized by recurrent, unexpected panic attacks

Some people with panic disorder will have many attacks in a short period of time, such as every day for a week, and then go for weeks or months without having another attack, followed by another period in which the attacks come often. Other people will have attacks less frequently but more regularly such as once a week every week for months. In between full-blown panic attacks, they might have more minor bouts of panic.

People who have panic disorder will often fear that they have life-threatening illnesses. However, even after such illnesses are ruled out, people with panic disorder may continue to believe that they are about to die of a heart attack, a seizure, or some other physical crisis. They may seek medical care very frequently, going from physician to physician to find out what is wrong with them. Another common but erroneous belief among people with panic disorder is that they are "going crazy" or "losing control." Many people with panic disorder feel ashamed of their disorder and try to hide it from others. If left untreated, they may become demoralized and depressed.

The lifetime prevalence of panic disorder appears to be between 1.5 and 3.5 percent, according to studies done in many different countries (APA, 1994). Most people who develop panic disorder usually do so sometime between late adolescence and their mid-30s. The disorder tends to be chronic once it begins. One study found that 92 percent of patients with panic disorder continued to experience panic attacks for at least 1 year, and among those whose symptoms subsided at some time during the year, 41 percent relapsed into panic attacks within the year (Ehlers, 1995).

Panic disorder can be debilitating in its own right. However, as we discuss in the next section, it is often accompanied by another syndrome known as *agoraphobia*.

Agoraphobia

About one-third to one-half of people diagnosed with panic disorder develop **agoraphobia** (APA, 1994). The term *agoraphobia* is from the Greek for "fear of the marketplace." People with agoraphobia fear crowded, bustling, places, such as the marketplace or, in our times, the shopping mall. They also fear enclosed spaces, such as buses, subways, or elevators. Finally, they fear wide open spaces, such as open fields, particularly if they are alone. In general, people with agoraphobia fear any places where they might have trouble escaping or getting help in an emergency (see Table 4.3). The particular emergency that they fear is usually a panic attack. Thus, the person with agoraphobia will think, "If I have a panic

agoraphobia
anxiety disorder characterized by fear of places and situations in which it would be difficult to escape in a panic attack, such as enclosed places, wide open spaces, and crowds

Table 4.3 Places Avoided by People with Agoraphobia

People with agoraphobia avoid situations in which they would have trouble getting help or would be embarrassed if they had an emergency, such as a panic attack.

Shopping malls	Theaters
Automobiles	Supermarkets
Buses	Stores
Trains	Crowds
Subways	Planes
Tunnels	Elevators
Restaurants	Escalators

Source: Adapted from Barlow & Craske, 1994.

attack while I'm in this mall (or on this airplane, or in this movie theatre, or on this deserted beach), it will be hard for me to get away quickly or to find help." People with agoraphobia also often fear that they will embarrass themselves if others see their symptoms of panic or their frantic efforts to escape during a panic attack. Actually, other people can rarely tell when a person is having a panic attack.

Agoraphobia can occur in people who do not have panic attacks, but the vast majority of people with agoraphobia do experience either full-blown panic attacks, more moderate panic attacks, or severe social phobia in which they experience panic-like symptoms in social situations (Barlow, 1988). In most cases, agoraphobia begins within one year of the onset of recurrent panic attacks.

The lives of people with agoraphobia can be terribly disrupted, and even brought to a complete halt. Just think how difficult it would be to carry on daily life if you could not ride in a car, bus, train, or airplane; you could not go into a store; you could not stand being in any kind of crowd. Lia's case illustrates how debilitating agoraphobia can be:

> **Case Study** • Lia was a graduate student who was conducting research on children's styles of learning in the classroom. For her research, Lia needed to travel to local elementary schools and observe children in certain classrooms for a couple of hours each day. Lia had spent months developing good relationships with the schools, teachers, and children who were participating in her research. Everyone was excited about the potential for Lia's research to improve classroom teaching. It seemed that Lia was on her way toward a promising career as an educational researcher.
>
> The only problem was that Lia could not leave her apartment. Over the last year, she had become terrified at the idea of driving her car, convinced that she would have a panic attack while driving and have a fatal car accident. She had tried to ride the public bus instead, but when she got onto the bus, she felt like she was choking, and she was so dizzy she almost missed her stop. So she began walking everywhere she went. The elementary schools participating in her research were too far away for her to walk to them, however. Moreover, Lia was becoming afraid even when she stepped out of her apartment. When she walked onto her street, it seemed to open into a big chasm. The thought of being confined in a small elementary school classroom for two hours was just intolerable.
>
> Lia was beginning to believe that she was going to have to abandon her research and her degree. She could not see any way to finish her work. Even if she did get her degree, how could she possibly hold a job if she could not even leave her apartment?

Like Lia, people with agoraphobia often get to the point where they will not leave their own homes. Sometimes, they can venture out with a close family member who makes them feel "safe." However, often family members and friends have trouble understanding their anxiety and may not be willing to chaperone them everywhere they go. People with agoraphobia may force themselves to enter situations that frighten them, as Lia had been forcing herself to travel for her research. The persistent and intense anxiety

People with agoraphobia fear both crowded places they may not be able to escape, and wide open places where they may not be able to get help, if they should panic.

they experience in these situations can be miserable, however, and like Lia, many people just give up and remain confined to their homes. Some agoraphobics turn to alcohol and other substances to dampen these anxiety symptoms.

Agoraphobia strikes people in their youth. In one large study, more than 70 percent of people who developed agoraphobia did so before the age of 25, and 50 percent developed the disorder before the age of 15 (Bourden, Boyd, Rae, & Burns, 1988).

There have been tremendous strides in the last several years in our understanding of panic and agoraphobia. These disorders are probably best explained by a vulnerability-stress model. In many cases, people who develop these disorders may have biological vulnerability to panic attacks, as we will describe next. For panic disorder and agoraphobia to develop out of this vulnerability, certain psychological factors may also need to be present.

Biological Theories

People prone to panic attacks seem to have an overreactive fight-or-flight response (McNally, 1994). A full panic attack can be induced easily by having them engage in certain activities that stimulate the initial physiological changes of the fight-or-flight response. For example, when people with panic disorder purposely hyperventilate, breathe into a paper bag, or inhale a small amount of carbon dioxide, they experience an increase in subjective anxiety, and many will experience a full panic attack (Rapee, Brown, Antony, & Barlow, 1992). In contrast, people without a history of panic attacks may experience some physical discomfort while doing these activities but rarely experience a full panic attack (see Figure 4.1).

Just how do these procedures trigger panic attacks in people prone to them? One theory is that people who develop panic disorder may have poorly regulated autonomic nervous systems (Gorman, Liebowitz, Fyer, Fyer, & Klein, 1986; Margraf, 1993). The **autonomic nervous system** is made up of the **sympathetic nervous system**, which when activated creates physiological arousal, and the **parasympathetic nervous system**, which generally works to dampen physiological arousal. These two systems typically work to balance each other. In people with panic disorder, this balance may be easily lost, and their bodies go into a full, uncontrollable fight-or-flight response.

Another theory of why panic patients have panic attacks when they hyperventilate, inhale carbon dioxide, or breathe into a paper bag is the **suffocation false alarm theory** (Klein, 1993). Each of these procedures elevates levels of carbon dioxide in the blood and brain. People who develop panic disorder may be hypersensitive to carbon dioxide. When their brains detect even small increases in carbon dioxide, the brain registers "suffocation!!!" and this triggers the autonomic nervous system into a full fight-or-flight response.

autonomic nervous system
system that regulates the functions of the adrenals, heart, intestines, and stomach (*see also* **parasympathetic nervous system** and **sympathetic nervous system**)

sympathetic nervous system
part of the autonomic nervous system that creates physiological arousal, such as an increased heart rate when experiencing fear

parasympathetic nervous system
part of the autonomic nervous system that lessens physiological arousal (*see also* **autonomic nervous system**)

suffocation false alarm theory
the theory that people who develop panic disorder are hypersensitive to carbon dioxide and when they are exposed to carbon dioxide (e.g., breathe into a paper bag), their body triggers the autonomic nervous system into a full fight-or-flight response

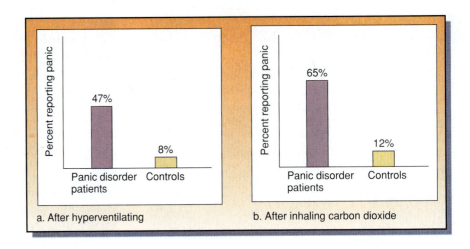

Figure 4.1

Panic Attacks of Patients and Controls. People with panic disorder are much more likely than people without panic disorder to have a panic attack when made to hyperventilate or inhale small amounts of carbon dioxide in laboratory experiments.
Source: Rapee et al., 1992.

limbic system
part of the brain that relays information from the primitive brain stem about changes in bodily functions to the cortex where the information is interpreted (*see also* **brain stem** and **cortex**)

brain stem
primitive brain structure lying near the core of the brain

cortex
surface layer of the cerebral hemispheres

serotonin
neurotransmitter that is involved in the regulation of mood and impulsive responses

norepinephrine
neurotransmitter that is involved in the regulation of mood

In contrast, people who are not prone to panic disorders are not as sensitive to carbon dioxide, and therefore small increases in brain levels of carbon dioxide do not trigger a sense of suffocation or the full fight-or-flight response.

The area of the brain that has been studied most extensively in relation to anxiety is the **limbic system**. The limbic system relays information from the primitive **brain stem** about changes in bodily functions to the **cortex** where that information is interpreted. Neuropsychologist Jeffrey Gray (1982, 1985) suggests that people prone to panic disorders may have deficiencies in the neurotransmitter **serotonin** in the limbic system and other brain circuits involved in the fight-or-flight response (see also Deakin & Graeff, 1991). Serotonin deficiencies cause chronic hyperactivation of these areas of the brain, putting the individual on the verge of a panic attack most of the time. Other researchers argue that the neurotransmitter GABA (gamma-aminobutyric acid) or one of several noradrenergic neurotransmitters, such as **norepinephrine**, are involved in anxiety disorders. One study using positron emission tomography (PET) found higher levels of activity in the limbic areas of the brains of panic attack patients who were having panic attacks than in the brains of controls (Reiman, Raichle, & Robins, 1986). Whether this higher level of activity is involved in causing panic attacks or results from the arousal of a panic attack is unknown.

Finally, panic disorder and agoraphobia appear to run in families. One family history study of panic disorder found that nearly one-fourth of the first-degree relatives of patients with panic disorder also had a history of panic disorder, compared to only about 2 percent of people in the general population (Crowe, 1990). Twin studies of panic disorder find a concordance rate of 24 percent in monozygotic twins but 11 percent in dizygotic twins (Kendler, Neale, Kessler, & Heath, 1992, 1993). These studies suggest that a biological vulnerability to panic disorder may be transmitted at least in part through disordered genes.

Psychological Theories

Although many people who develop panic and agoraphobia may have biological vulnerability to these disorders, psychological factors also appear to play a heavy role in determining who will develop the disorders. The *cognitive model* of panic disorder argues that people prone to panic attacks tend to (1) pay very close attention to their bodily sensations, (2) misinterpret bodily sensations in a negative way, and (3) engage in snowballing catastrophic thinking (Barlow, 1988; Clark, 1988). So when a person prone to panic disorder feels a bit dizzy because she stood up too quickly, she might think, "I'm really dizzy. I think I'm going to faint. Maybe I'm having a seizure. Oh God, what's happening!" This kind of thinking increases the subjective sense of anxiety and sympathetic nervous system activity. These feelings then are interpreted catastrophically, and the person is on her way into a full panic attack. In between full panic attacks, the person is hypervigilant for any bodily sensations (Ehlers & Breuer, 1992). She worries about her health generally and about having more panic attacks specifically. This constant arousal makes it more likely that she will have more panic attacks.

The fear of panic attacks also leads the individual to search for safe people and places that are associated with a low risk of panic attacks. These safe people and places have been referred to as *safety signals*. According to the **safety signal hypothesis** (Seligman & Binik, 1977), people remember vividly the places in which they have had panic attacks, even if the panic attacks have come on by surprise, with no obvious environmental triggers. They associate these places with their symptoms of panic and may begin to feel these symptoms again if they return to these places. By avoiding these places, they reduce their symptoms, and their avoidance behavior is thus highly reinforced. So if a man has a panic attack while sitting in the theater, he may later associate the theater with his panic symptoms and begin to feel anxious whenever he is near the theater. He can reduce his anxiety by avoiding the theater. In addition, other places, such as his own home or perhaps a specific room in his home, may become associated with lowered anxiety levels, and being in these places is thus reinforcing. So through straightforward classical and operant conditioning, the person's behavior becomes shaped in ways that lead to the development of agoraphobia.

 What are some of your "safety signals"—situations in which you feel you can relax completely and not be anxious? Why are these situations safety signals for you?

Evidence for the role of these psychological factors in panic and agoraphobia comes from several studies (see McNally, 1994, for a review). In one study, researchers examined the influence of panic patients' beliefs about the controllability of their panic symptoms on their actual experience of panic in the laboratory. Two groups of panic patients were asked to wear breathing masks, through which they would inhale air enriched slightly with carbon dioxide. They were warned that inhaling carbon dioxide could induce a panic attack. One group was told that they could not control the amount of carbon dioxide that came through their masks. The other group was told they could control the amount of carbon dioxide that came through their masks by turning a knob. Actually, neither group had any control over the amount of carbon dioxide they inhaled. Eighty percent of the patients who believed they had no control experienced a panic attack, but only 20 percent of the patients who believed they could countrol the carbon dioxide had a panic attack. This occurred despite the fact that both groups inhaled the same amount of carbon dioxide. These results strongly suggest that beliefs about the uncontrollability of panic symptoms play a strong role in panic attacks (Sanderson, Rapee, & Barlow, 1989).

In another study, researchers examined whether people with panic disorder could avoid having a panic attack, even after inhaling carbon dioxide, by having a "safe person" nearby. Panic patients exposed to carbon dioxide with their safe person present were much less likely to experience the emotional and physical symptoms of anxiety than were panic patients exposed to carbon dioxide without their safe person present. Indeed, the panic patients who had their safe person with them did not experience signficantly more anxiety than a control group of people who were not prone to any type of anxiety disorder. In addition, the panic patients who did not have their safe person nearby when inhaling carbon dioxide reported many more catastrophic cognitions such as "I'm losing control," and "I'm having a heart attack" than did the panic patients who did have their safe person nearby and than did the control subjects. It seemed that having the safe person nearby reduced the tendency of the panic patients to interpret the bodily changes they were experiencing as dangerous (Carter, Hollon, Carson, & Shelton, 1995).

Thus, the biological and psychological theories of panic and agoraphobia can be integrated to suggest the following vulnerability-stress model of these disorders (Barlow,

safety signal hypothesis
the hypothesis that people vividly remember the places in which they have been anxious and associate such locations or situations with symptoms of anxiety, while seeking out situations associated with lowered anxiety

1988): Many people who develop these disorders have a biological vulnerability to a hypersensitive fight-or-flight response. With just a mild stimulus, these people's hearts begin to race, their breathing begins to become rapid, and their palms begin to sweat. However, they typically will not develop frequent panic attacks or a panic disorder unless they also engage in catastrophizing cognitions about their physiological symptoms. These cognitions will increase the intensity of their initially mild physiological symptoms to the point of a panic attack. They will also cause them to become hypervigilant for signs of another panic attack and to search for safety signals that will help them predict when they are safe from another attack. Agoraphobia then develops as they begin avoiding situations that might induce new attacks and stick close to environments in which they feel less likely to have attacks.

Biological Treatments for Panic and Agoraphobia

Surprisingly, some of the most effective drugs for the treatment of panic and agoraphobia are classified as antidepressant drugs. For example, the **tricyclic antidepressants** such as imipramine can reduce panic attacks in 60 to 90 percent of patients (Lydiard, Brawman-Mintzer, & Ballenger, 1996; Rapee, 1994). Agoraphobic behaviors are also reduced in these patients, in large part because they no longer fear having panic attacks.

You might wonder why a drug classified as an antidepressant would reduce an anxiety disorder. Recall that one of the neurotransmitters that may be involved in panic disorder is norepinephrine. The tricyclic antidepressants are thought to improve the functioning of this neurotransmitter system, and this may be why they are effective in treating anxiety. These drugs also may affect levels of a number of other neurotransmitters, including serotonin, thereby affecting levels of anxiety. The disadvantages of the tricyclic antidepressants are their side effects and the relapse rate once patients discontinue the drugs. Common side effects include blurred vision, dry mouth, and urinary retention. In addition, between 20 and 50 percent of patients relapse into panic attacks when they discontinue the tricyclics (Telch, 1988).

The second class of drugs used to treat panic disorder and agoraphobia is the **benzodiazepines,** which suppress the central nervous system and influence functioning in the GABA, norepinephrine, and serotonin neurotransmitter systems. The benzodiazepine most commonly used to treat panic is alprazolam (trade name Xanax). This drug works quickly to reduce panic attacks and general symptoms of anxiety in 60 to 80 percent of persons with panic disorder (Ballenger, Burrows, Dupont, & Lesser, 1988; Klosko, Barlow, Tassinari, & Cerny, 1990). Unfortunately, the benzodiazepines have three major disadvantages.

First, they are physically (and psychologically) addictive. People build up a tolerance to these drugs so that they need increasing dosages of the drug to get a positive effect. In turn, when they stop using the drug, they experience difficult withdrawal symptoms, including irritability, tremors, insomnia, anxiety, tingling sensations, and more rarely seizures and paranoia. These withdrawal symptoms can occur even if people are tapered off the drug gradually.

The second major disadvantage of benzodiazepines is that they can interfere with cognitive and motor functioning. People's ability to drive or to avoid accidents is impaired, and their performance on the job, at school, and in the home suffers. These impairments can be especially severe if the benzodiazepines are combined with alcohol.

The third major disadvantage of the benzodiazepines in the treatment of panic and agoraphobia is that about 90 percent of patients relapse after being taken off these drugs (Fyer et al., 1987). Relapse rates can be greatly diminished, however, if cognitive-behavior therapies, to be described next, are combined with the benzodiazepines (Otto, Pollack, Meltzer-Brody, & Rosenbaum, 1992; Spiegel, Bruce, Gregg, & Nuzzarello, 1994).

A third class of drugs that is increasingly being used to treat people experiencing situational anxiety or chronic mild anxiety is the **selective serotonin reuptake inhibitors**

tricyclic antidepressants
group of drugs that reduces symptoms of depression and anxiety by affecting the functional levels of norepinephrine, serotonin, and other neurotransmitters.

benzodiazepines
drugs that reduce anxiety and insomnia

selective serotonin reuptake inhibitors (SSRIs)
group of drugs that reduces symptoms of depression and anxiety by affecting the functional levels of serotonin

(**SSRIs**). These drugs increase the functional levels of the neurotransmitter serotonin in the brain. They are not physically addictive or sedating as are the benzodiazepines. In addition, some people can tolerate the side effects of these drugs, which include gastrointestinal upset and irritability, better than they can the side effects of the benzodiazepines or the tricyclic antidepressants. The use of these drugs for panic attacks is relatively new, however, and more research is needed on their efficacy for panic (den Boer, Westenberg, de Leeuw, & van Vliet, 1995).

Psychological Treatments for Panic and Agoraphobia

Psychological treatments for all the anxiety disorders, including panic and agoraphobia, involve getting clients to confront the situations or thoughts that arouse anxiety in them. Confrontation seems to help in two ways: Irrational thoughts about these situations can be challenged and changed, and anxiety reactions to the situations can be extinguished.

Cognitive behavioral therapies appear to be highly effective in eliminating panic and agoraphobia (Clark, 1991). There are a number of components to these cognitive-behavioral interventions.

First, clients are taught relaxation and breathing exercises such as those described in the Application section at the end of this chapter. These exercises are useful in therapy for anxiety disorders because they give clients some control over their symptoms, which then permits them to engage in the other components of the therapy.

Second, the clinician guides clients in identifying the catastrophizing cognitions they have about changes in bodily sensations. Clients may do this by keeping diaries of the cognitions they have about their bodies on days between therapy sessions, particularly when they begin to feel they are going to panic. Figure 4.2 illustrates the entries in one man's panic thoughts diary. He noted that he had mild symptoms of panic while in his office at work but more severe symptoms while riding the subway home. In both situations, he had thoughts about feeling trapped and suffocating and thought he was going to faint. Many clients need to experience real panic symptoms in the presence of their therapist before they can begin to identify their catastrophizing cognitions. They are too overwhelmed by their symptoms when they are having them outside the therapy office to pay attention to their thoughts. Thus, the therapist may try to induce panic symptoms in clients during therapy sessions, by having clients exercise to elevate their heart rates or spin to get dizzy or put their heads between their knees and then stand up quickly so they get lightheaded (due to sudden changes in blood pressure). None of these activities is dangerous but all are likely to produce the kind of symptoms that clients catastrophize. As clients are experiencing these symptoms and their catastrophizing cognitions, the therapist helps them "collect" these thoughts.

Situation	Symptoms and severity	Thoughts
Office at work	Choking (mild) Dizziness (mild) Heart racing (mild)	Oh, I can't have an attack here. People will see me and I might get fired. I'm suffocating! I'm going to faint.
Riding subway home	Sweating (severe) Choking (severe) Shaking (severe) Heart racing (severe) Dizziness (severe)	I can't stand this! I've got to get out of here. I'm going to choke to death. I'm trapped. I'm going to faint!
At home	Sweating (mild) Heart still racing (moderate) A little faintness	I can't believe I made it home.

Figure 4.2

A Panic Thoughts Diary. This man recorded the thoughts he had during panic attacks and then worked on these thoughts in cognitive therapy.

Third, clients practice using their relaxation and breathing exercises while experiencing panic symptoms in the therapy session. If the panic attacks occur during sessions, the therapist will talk clients through them, coaching them in the use of relaxation and breathing skills, suggesting ways of improving their skills, and noting successes clients have in using these skills to stop the attacks.

Fourth, the therapist will challenge clients' catastrophizing thoughts about their bodily sensations and teach them to challenge their thoughts for themselves, using the cognitive techniques described in Chapter 3. The therapist might help clients reinterpret bodily sensations accurately. For example, the client whose thoughts are illustrated in Figure 4.2 frequently felt he was choking. His therapist might explore whether his choking sensation might be due to the stuffiness of a small office or a subway on a warm summer day. If he interprets the increase in his heart rate as a heart attack, the therapist might have him collect evidence from his physician that he is in perfect cardiac health. The therapist and client might also explore the the client's expectations that he is sure to die of a heart attack because a relative of his did. If the therapist induces panic symptoms in the client during a therapy session, and the client is able to reduce these symptoms with relaxation or breathing skills, the therapist will use this success to challenge the client's belief that there is nothing that can be done to control the panic symptoms once they begin.

Fifth, to reduce agoraphobic behaviors the therapist will use **systematic desensitization** techniques to gradually expose clients to those situations they most fear while helping them maintain control over their panic symptoms. Clients and therapist will compose a list of panic-inducing situations, from most threatening to least threatening. Then, after learning relaxation and breathing skills and perhaps gaining some control over panic symptoms induced during therapy sessions, clients will begin to expose themselves to their panic-inducing situations, beginning with the least threatening. The therapist may accompany the client on trips to the panic-inducing situations, coaching them in the use of their relaxation and breathing skills and their skills in challenging catastrophic cognitions that arise in these situations. Here is an example of an interchange between a therapist and client as they ride together in the client's car.

Client:	I really don't think we should be doing this. I might have a panic attack while I'm driving. I wouldn't want to be responsible for an accident while you're in the car.
Therapist:	Do you think I would have gotten in the car if I thought that it was likely you would have a panic attack and wreck the car?
Client:	No, probably not, but I'm really scared.
Therapist:	Yes, I understand. Have you ever had a car wreck?
Client:	No, I just always worry about one.
Therapist:	Remember, our worries are not reality. Tell me what else is going through your mind.
Client:	I feel like my chest is about to cave in. I'm having trouble breathing. Oh no, here I go. . . .
Therapist:	Okay, let's begin using some of your exercises. Try counting backwards from 100 by 7s. Breathe in deeply with the first count, then out with the second count, and so on.
Client:	Okay, I'll try. (Breathes in.) One hundred. (Breathes out.) Ninety-three. (Breathes in.) Eighty-six. (Breathes out.)
Therapist:	How are you feeling now?
Client:	Better. I'm not as panicked. Oh my gosh, here comes a bridge. I hate bridges.
Therapist:	What do you hate about bridges?

systematic desensitization
type of behavior therapy that attempts to reduce client anxiety through relaxation techniques and progressive exposure to feared stimuli

Client: If I ever had an accident on a bridge, I'd be more likely to die.

Therapist: What do you think is the likelihood that you are going to have an accident on a bridge?

Client: Well, sometimes it feels like it's 100%!

Therapist: But what do you think it really is?

Client: Probably very low. Hey, we're already over that bridge!

Therapist: Okay, there's another bridge coming up in a couple of miles. I want you to decide what strategies you're going to use to help yourself feel less panicked as we approach the bridge.

Eighty-five to 90 percent of panic and agoraphobia patients treated with this combined cognitive and behavioral treatment experience complete relief from their panic attacks within 12 weeks (Barlow, Craske, Cerny, & Klosko, 1989; Klosko, Barlow, Tassinari, & Cerny, 1990). Follow-up studies of patients receiving this combined treatment have found that nearly 90 percent are classified as panic-free 2 years after the treatment (Craske, Brown, & Barlow, 1991; Margraf, Barlow, Clark, & Telch, 1993). Comparisons of cognitive-behavioral therapy to antidepressant therapy (tricyclics) or relaxation therapy found that 85 percent of the patients in cognitive-behavioral therapy were classified as panic-free at a follow-up 15 months after the therapy compared to 60 percent of the tricyclics patients and 47 percent of the patients receiving only relaxation therapy (Clark et al., 1994). These relatively new treatments for panic and agoraphobia hold much hope for people suffering from these debilitating conditions.

Summing Up	Panic and Agoraphobia

- Panic attacks are acute experiences of most of the physiological and psychological symptoms of anxiety. People who have frequent panic attacks and begin to worry about these attacks may be diagnosed with a panic disorder.
- People with agoraphobia fear being in open places or enclosed places in which they may be trapped or not able to get help in an emergency. These people usually have a history of panic attacks and the emergency they fear is having a panic attack.
- People prone to panic disorder may have exaggerated physiological responses to perceived threats; but only those people who also catastrophize their physiological reactions may go on to develop frequent panic attacks.
- Agoraphobia may develop through operant conditioning as people learn that they can reduce their anxiety by remaining in certain "safe" places.
- Antidepressant and antianxiety drugs can relieve symptoms of panic temporarily. Cognitive-behavior therapies are more effective in reducing panic and agoraphobia over the long-term.

Specific Phobias and Social Phobia

Agoraphobia is different from many people's conception of a phobia, because people with agoraphobia fear such a wide variety of situations. In contrast, the specific phobias and social phobia conform more to popular conceptions of phobia. People with a **specific phobia** become so anxious when confronted with a specific object or situation (such as dogs or flying in an airplane) that they organize their lives around avoiding that object or situation. People with **social phobia** become so anxious when they feel they are being scrutinized or judged by others that they may avoid all social situations, especially ones that involve performing in front of others. In this section, we will discuss the characteristics of specific and social phobias and what we know about their causes and appropriate treatments.

specific phobia
extreme fear of a specific object or situation that causes an individual to routinely avoid that object or situation

social phobia
extreme fear of being judged or embarrassed in front of people that causes the individual to avoid social situations

Table 4.4 Types of Phobias

People can have phobias of all sorts of animals, places, and situations.

Claustrophobia (closed places)	Ailurophobia (cats)
Arachnophobia (spiders)	Cynophobia (dogs)
Ophidiophobia (snakes)	Insectophobia (insects)
Acrophobia (heights)	Avisophobia (birds)
Nosophobia (illness/injury)	Equinophobia (horses)
Mysophobia (dirt)	Thanatophobia (death)
Brontophobia (storms)	Xenophobia (strangers)
Nyctophobia (darkness)	Autophobia (oneself)

Specific Phobias

People can develop phobias of many things. Medical-sounding names have been created for many of these phobias (see Table 4.4). Most phobias fall into one of four categories, however (APA, 1994): animal type, natural environment type, situational type, and blood-injection-injury type. When people with these phobias encounter their feared objects or situations, their anxiety is immediate and intense, and they may even have full panic attacks. They also become anxious if they believe there is any chance they might encounter their feared objects or situations, and will go to great lengths to avoid the objects or situations. Adults with phobias recognize that their anxieties are illogical and unreasonable. Children may not have this insight, however, and just have the anxiety. As many as one in ten people will have a specific phobia at some time, making it one of the most common disorders (Kessler et al., 1994). Most phobias develop during childhood.

Animal type phobias are focused on specific animals or insects, such as dogs, cats, snakes, and spiders. A snake phobia appears to be the most common type of animal phobia in the United States (Agras, Sylvester, & Oliveau, 1969). Other animals or insects, such as scorpions, may be more commonly feared in other countries. Many people fear certain animals or insects, such as snakes or spiders, and if they come across one of these they may startle and move away quickly. Most of these people would not be diagnosed with a phobia because they do not live in terror of encountering a snake or spider or organize their lives around avoiding snakes or spiders. People with phobias go to great lengths to avoid the objects of their fear. For example, one woman with a severe spider phobia would spray powerful insecticide around the perimeter of her apartment (which was in a pristine, new apartment building) once a week to prevent spiders from coming in. The fumes from this insecticide made her physically ill, and her neighbors complained of the smell. However, this woman was so fearful of encountering a spider that she withstood the fumes and her neighbors' complaints, remaining vigilant for any signs of a spider web in her apartment. She refused to go into older buildings because she believed they were more likely to hold spiders. Since she lived in a city with many old buildings, this meant that she could not go into the homes of many of her friends or into establishments where she might want to do business.

Natural environment type phobias are focused on events or situations in the natural environment, such as storms, heights, or water. As

animal type phobias
extreme fear of specific animals that may induce immediate and intense anxiety and cause the individual to go to great lengths to avoid the animals

natural environmental type phobias
extreme fear of events or situations in the natural environment that causes impairment in one's ability to function normally

One of the most common specific phobias is a snake phobia.

with fears of animals or insects, mild to moderate fears of these natural events or situations are extremely common. Again, however, these fears do not usually cause people much inconvenience or concern in their daily lives and thus would not be considered phobias. It is only when people begin reorganizing their lives to avoid their feared situations or having severe anxiety attacks when confronted with the situations that a diagnosis of phobia is warranted.

Situational type phobias usually involve fear of public transportation, tunnels, bridges, elevators, flying, and driving. Claustrophobia, or fear of enclosed spaces, is a common situational phobia. People with situational phobias believe they might have panic attacks in their phobic situations, and indeed often have had panic attacks when forced into those situations. Unlike people with agoraphobia, people with situational phobias tend to have panic attacks only in the specific situations they fear. Situational phobias often arise in people between 2 and 7 years of age, but another common period of onset is the mid-20s.

The final type, **blood-injection-injury type** phobias, was first recognized in DSM-IV. People with this type of phobia fear seeing blood or an injury or receiving an injection or experiencing some other invasive medical procedure.

> **Case Study** • When her son José was born, Irene decided to quit her job and become a full-time mother. She had enjoyed José's infancy tremendously. He was a happy baby and had hardly been ill for the first two years of his life. Now that he was a toddler, however, José was beginning to get the usual skinned knees and bumps and bruises that small children do. Irene had always been squeamish about blood, but she thought she could overcome this when it came to caring for her son. The first time José scraped his knee seriously enough for it to bleed, however, Irene became dizzy upon seeing it and fainted. José screamed and cried in terror at seeing his mother faint. Fortunately, a neighbor saw what happened and quickly came over to comfort José and see that Irene was okay. Since then, Irene has fainted three more times upon seeing José injured. She has begun to think that she will not be able to care for José by herself any longer.

Irene's reaction to seeing José's scraped knee illustrates the unusual physiological reaction of people with blood-injection-injury type phobias to their feared objects. Whereas people with one of the other specific phobias typically experience increases in heart rate, blood pressure, and other fight-or-flight physiological changes when confronted with their feared objects or situations, people with a blood-injection-injury type of phobia experience significant *drops* in heart rate and blood pressure when confronted with their feared stimuli and are likely to faint. This type of phobia runs more strongly in families than do the other types (Ost, 1992).

Social Phobia

Social phobia is not categorized as a specific phobia because, rather than fearing a specific (often inanimate) object or situation, people with social phobia fear being judged or embarrasing themselves in front of other people. Social phobia also differs from the specific phobias in that it is more likely to create severe disruption in a person's daily life. It is easier in most cultures to avoid snakes or spiders than it is to avoid social situations in which you might embarrass yourself. Consider the inner pain that this social phobic suffers and the way that he has organized his life to avoid social situations:

> **Case Study** • Malcolm was a computer expert who worked for a large software firm. One of the things he hated to do most was ride the elevator at the building where he worked when there were other people on it. He felt that everyone was watching him, commenting silently on his ruffled clothes, and noticing every way he moved his body.

situational type phobias
extreme fear of stiuations such as public transportation, tunnels, bridges, elevators, flying, driving, and enclosed spaces.

blood-injection-injury type phobias
extreme fear of seeing blood or an injury or receiving an injection or other invasive medical procedures, which causes a drop in heart rate and blood pressure and fainting

He held his breath for almost the entire elevator ride, afraid that he might say something or make some sound that would embarrass him. Often, he would walk up the eight flights of stairs to his office rather than take the risk that someone might get on the elevator with him.

Malcolm rarely went anywhere except to work and home. He hated even to go to the grocery store for fear he would run his cart into someone else or say something stupid to a grocery clerk. He found a grocery store and several restaurants that allowed customers to send orders for food over the computer to be delivered to their homes. He liked this service because he could use it to avoid even talking to someone over the phone to place the order. He often placed the money for his food in an envelope and left it by his front door, so he did not have to interact with the delivery person.

In the past, Malcolm's job had allowed him to remain quietly in his office all day, without interacting with other people. Recently, however, his company was reorganized and it took on a number of new projects. Malcolm's supervisor said that everyone in Malcolm's group needed to begin to work together more closely to develop these new products. Malcolm was supposed to make a presentation to his group on some software he was developing, but he called in sick the day of the presentation because he could not face it. Malcolm was thinking that he had to change jobs and that perhaps he would go into private consulting so he could work from his home rather than having to work with anyone else.

Most people get a little nervous when they are speaking in front of a group of people or must join a group of people already engaged in conversation. However, people like Malcolm get more than a little nervous. If they find themselves in social situations, they may begin trembling and perspiring, feel confused and dizzy, have heart palpitations, and eventually a full panic attack. Like Malcolm, they are sure that others see their nervousness and judge them as inarticulate, weak, stupid, or "crazy." Malcolm avoided public speaking or having conversations with others for fear of being judged. People with a social phobia may avoid eating or drinking in public, for fear they will make noises when they eat, drop food, or otherwise embarrass themselves. They may avoid writing in public, including signing their name, for fear that others will see their hand tremble. Men with social phobia will often avoid urinating in public bathrooms for fear of embarrassing themselves. Some people with social phobia fear only one of these types of social situations. People like Malcolm who fear many social situations, from public speaking or attending a party to just having a conversation with another person, are said to have a generalized type of social phobia.

Social phobia is relatively common, with about 8 percent of the U.S. adult population qualifying for the diagnosis in a 12-month period (Schneier et al., 1992). Social phobia typically begins in the adolescent years, when many people become excessively self-conscious and concerned about others' opinions of them (Blazer et al., 1991). Some people report humiliating experiences that triggered their social phobia. Some children seem excessively shy and fearful of others from a very young age, however, and these children may be more prone to develop social phobia (Biederman, Bolduc-Murphy, & Faraone, 1993). Once it develops, social phobia tends to be a chronic problem if untreated.

 How do you think most people overcome their anxiety about speaking in front of other people?

Psychodynamic Theories of Phobias

Freud's theory of the development of phobias is one of his most well-known. He argued that phobias are the result of the displacement of unconscious anxiety onto a neutral or symbolic object (Freud, 1909). That is, people become phobic of objects not because they have any real fear of the objects, but because they have displaced their anxiety over other issues onto the object. This theory is detailed in a 150-page case history of a little boy named Hans who had a phobia of horses after seeing a horse fall on the ground and writhe around violently. How did Hans's phobia develop? According to Freud, young boys have a sexual desire for their mother and jealously hate their father, but fear that their fathers will castrate them in retaliation for this desire. This phenomenon is known as the **Oedipus complex.** In Freud's interpreation, little Hans found the anxiety created by this conflict so unbearable that he unconsciously displaced this anxiety onto horses, which somehow symbolized his father for him. Freud's evidence for this formulation came from Little Hans's answers to a series of leading questions asked by Freud and by Hans's father. After long conversations about horses and what Hans was "really" afraid of, Hans reportedly became less fearful of horses because, according to Freud, he had gained insight into the true source of his anxiety.

There is little reason to accept Freud's theory of phobias, either in the case of Hans or in general. Hans never provided any spontaneous or direct evidence that his real concerns were Oedipal concerns instead of fear of horses. In addition, Hans's phobia of horses decreased slowly over time rather than suddenly in response to some insight. Many children have specific fears that simply fade with time with no intervention. In general, psychodynamic therapy for phobias is not highly effective, suggesting that insight into unconscious anxieties is not what is needed in treating phobias.

Behavioral Theories of Phobias

In contrast to the psychodynamic theories, the behavioral theories have been very successful in explaining the onset of at least some phobias. According to these theories, classical conditioning leads to the fear of the phobic object, and operant conditioning helps to maintain that fear. Recall that in classical conditioning a previously neutral object (the conditioned stimulus) is paired with an object that naturally elicits a reaction (an unconditioned stimulus that elicits an unconditioned response) until the previously neutral object elicits the same reaction (which is now called the conditioned response). So when a tone is paired with an electric shock, the conditioned stimulus is the tone, the electric shock is the unconditioned stimulus, the unconditioned response is anxiety in response to the shock, and the conditioned response is anxiety in response to the tone (Figure 4.3).

The first application of these theories to phobias came in a series of studies done 80 years ago by a philosopher turned behaviorist, John Watson, and a graduate student named Rosalie Raynor (1920). Their subject in these studies was an 11 month-old boy named Little Albert. One day, Watson and Raynor placed a white rat in front of Little Albert. As Little Albert playfully reached for the white rat, they banged a metal bar loudly just above his head. Naturally, Little Albert was completely startled, nearly jumped out of his diapers, quickly pulled his hand away from the rat, and then broke down whimpering. This only encouraged Watson and Raynor to continue their study, however. After several more pairings of the white rat with the loud noise from the metal bar, Little Albert would have nothing to do with the creature, in effect developing a fear of the white rat. When presented with it, he would retreat and show distress. Little Albert's fear also generalized to other white furry animals—he would not approach white rabbits either. Although by today's standards, this experiment with Little Albert would raise serious

Oedipus complex
conflict in little boys between their love for their mothers, their jealousy of their fathers, and their fear that their fathers will punish them for loving their mothers

1. Unconditioned stimulus	naturally leads to	Unconditioned response
Banged bar	naturally leads to	Startle
2. Unconditioned stimulus	paired with	Conditioned stimulus
Banged bar	paired with	White rat
3. Conditioned stimulus	then leads to	Conditioned response
White rat	then leads to	Startle

Figure 4.3

The Behavioral Account of Little Albert's Phobia. The behavioral account of Little Albert's phobia of the white rat is that the pairing of the banged bar (the US), which naturally leads to a startle response (the UR), and the white rat (the CS) leads eventually to the white rat producing the same startle response (now referred to as the CR)

ethical questions, it did lay the groundwork for the behavioral theories of phobias by showing powerfully that a phobia could easily be created through classical conditioning. In the case of Little Albert, the unconditioned stimulus (US) was the loud noise from the banged bar, and the unconditioned response (UR) was his startle response to the loud noise. The conditioned stimulus (CS) was the white rat, and the conditioned response (CR) was the startle and fear response to the white rat.

If Little Albert were subsequently presented with the white rat several times without the bar being banged behind his head, his fear of white rats should have been extinguished, according to what we know about classical conditioning. Most people who develop a phobia, however, will try to avoid being exposed to their feared object. Thus, they avoid the exposure that could extinguish their phobia. In addition, if they are suddenly confronted with their feared object, they will experience extreme anxiety and run away as quickly as possible. The running away, or avoidance, is reinforced by the subsequent reduction of their anxiety. Thus, through operant conditioning, behaviors that help to maintain the phobia are reinforced.

For example, Malcolm, the social phobic previously described, had developed a wide array of avoidant behaviors to prevent exposing himself to what he feared most: the possibility of scrutiny by others. He would walk up several flights of stairs rather than be trapped in an elevator for a few minutes with another person who might notice something odd about Malcolm's clothes or mannerisms. He paid a great deal of money to have his groceries delivered rather than risk going to a crowded grocery store where he might embarrass himself in front of other people. He was even prepared to quit his job to avoid having to make presentations and work closely with others on projects. These avoidant behaviors created much hardship for Malcolm, but they reduced his anxiety and therefore were greatly reinforced. Also, as a result of this avoidance, Malcolm never had the opportunity to extinguish his anxiety about social situations.

The behavioral theory of phobias was one of the most elegant examples of the application of basic learning principles to understanding of a mysterious psychological disorder. Many people with phobias can recount the specific traumatic experiences that triggered their phobias: being bitten by a dog, being trapped in an elevator, nearly drowning in a lake, humiliating themselves while speaking in public. For them, the behavioral accounts of their phobias seem to ring true. In an extension of the behavioral theory, some argued that phobias can develop through observational learning and not just through direct classical conditioning. According to this theory, people can develop phobias by watching someone else experience extreme fear in response to a situation. For example, small children may learn that snakes are to be feared when their parents have severe fright reactions upon seeing snakes (Bandura, 1969; Mineka et al., 1984).

Another extension of the behavioral theory of phobias seems to answer an interesting question about phobias: Why do humans develop phobias to some objects or situations and not to others (deSilva, Rachman, & Seligman, 1977; Mineka, 1985; Seligman, 1970)? For example, phobias of spiders, snakes, and heights are common, but phobias of flowers are not. The common characteristic of many phobic objects appears to be that these are things whose avoidance, over evolutionary history, has been advantageous for humans. Our distant ancestors had good reason to be fearful of insects, snakes, heights, loud noises, and strangers. Those who learned quickly to avoid these situations were more likely to survive and bear offspring. Thus, evolution may have selected for rapid conditioning of fear to certain objects or situations. Although these objects or situations are not as likely to cause us harm today, we carry the vestiges of our evolutionary history and are biologically prepared to learn certain associations quickly. This preparedness is known as **prepared classical conditioning**. In contrast, many objects that are more likely to cause us harm in today's world (such as guns and knives) have not been around long enough, evolutionarily speaking, to be selected for rapid conditioning, so phobias of these objects should be relatively difficult to create.

How would you go about proving this idea of prepared classical conditioning? Researchers presented subjects with pictures of objects that theoretically should be evolutionarily selected for conditioning (snakes or spiders) or objects that should not be selected (houses, faces, and flowers) and paired the presentation of these pictures with

prepared classical conditioning
theory that evolution has prepared us to be easily conditioned to fear objects or situations that were dangerous in ancient times

short but painful electric shocks. The subjects developed anxiety reactions to the pictures of snakes and spiders within one or two pairings with shock, but it took four to five pairings of the pictures of houses, faces, or flowers with shock to create a fear reaction to these pictures. In addition, it was relatively easy to extinguish the subjects' anxiety reactions to houses or faces once the pictures were no longer paired with shock, but the anxiety reactions to spiders and snakes were difficult to extinguish (Hugdahl & Ohman, 1977; Ohman, et al., 1976).

Thus, particularly with the addition of principles of observational learning and prepared classical conditioning, the behavioral theory of phobias seems to provide a compelling explanation for this disorder. As we shall see, the behavioral theory has also led to very effective therapies for phobias. The most significant problem with these theories is that many people with phobias can identify no traumatic event in their own lives or in the lives of people they are close to that triggered their phobias. Without conditioned stimuli, it is hard to argue that they developed their phobias through classical conditioning or observational learning.

 If the preparedness theory of phobias is correct, what are some of the objects that are likely to be the focus of phobias among people in the very distant future?

Biological Theories of Phobias

Family history studies provide some reason to think that phobias may be transmitted genetically, at least in part. About 30 percent of the first-degree relatives of people with specific phobias have the same phobias or phobias in the same category (Fyer et al., 1990). About 16 percent of the first-degree relatives of people with social phobia have an increased risk of social phobia, compared to 5 percent of the relatives of people without social phobia (Fyer et al., 1993). Of course, family history data cannot separate the influence of genes from the influence of shared environments. It may be that some children are born with a general tendency toward anxious reactions but learn their specific fears through their own difficult experiences or by modeling their parents, as illustrated by the case of Jennifer (adapted from Silverman & Ginsburg, 1995, pp. 169–170).

Case Study • Jennifer, an 8-year-old girl, was referred to a psychiatric clinic by her pediatrician because of her severe fear of insects, excessive worrying, and somatic complaints. Her pediatrician ruled out an organic basis for her symptoms. Jennifer was extremely frightened of insects and avoided places where she had previously seen insects. She would no longer go into the kitchen of her home because she had seen an ant there once. When she saw an insect, Jennifer reported headaches, stomachaches, sweating, and a racing heart. Jennifer also worried a great deal about "not being good enough" (e.g., in her school performance), "making mistakes," "being teased by others," and "being in accidents" in which she or her parents would be hurt. Jennifer's mother described herself as "chronically anxious" and reported that she too had a fear of insects, though not as severe as her daughter's. She also stated that her daughter had always been a "worrier," needing constant reassurance.

In sum, although there is some evidence that genetics may play a role in susceptibility to phobias, the behavioral theories have proven most useful in explaining the development of these disorders. As we shall see in the next section, the behavioral therapies have proven most consistently and powerfully effective in the treatment of phobias, as well.

Treatments for Phobias

The goal of behavioral therapies for phobias is to extinguish fear of the feared object or situation by exposing the phobic person to the object or situation. There are three basic forms of therapy in which this is done: systematic desensitization, modeling, and flooding.

As we discussed earlier in this chapter, in systematic desensitization clients formulate lists of situations or objects they fear, ranked from most feared to least feared. They learn relaxation techniques that will reduce the symptoms of anxiety they will experience when they are exposed to their feared objects. They then begin to expose themselves to the items on their "hierarchy of fears," beginning with the least feared item. For example, a person with a severe dog phobia might have as the first item on his list "seeing a picture of a dog in a magazine." This client might then first visualize a picture of a dog. As the client begins to feel anxious, the therapist will coach him to use his relaxation techniques to quell his anxious feelings. The point is to help the client replace his anxious reaction with the calm that comes with the relaxation techniques. When the client can visualize a picture of a dog without experiencing anxiety, he might move on to actually looking at a picture of a dog in a magazine, again using relaxation techniques to lower his anxiety reaction and replace it with a calm reaction. Gradually, the client and therapist will move through the entire list, until the client is able to pet a big dog without feeling overwhelming anxiety. Eighty to 90 percent of phobias can be cured with this treatment, with little risk of relapse after the therapy (Kazdin & Wilcoxon, 1976).

Modeling techniques are often used in conjunction with systematic desensitization techniques in the treatment of phobias. The therapist models the behaviors most feared by the client before the client attempts them himself. For example, if a therapist is treating a person with a snake phobia, she may perform each of the behaviors on the client's hierarchy of fears before asking the client to perform them: The therapist will stand in the room with the snake before asking the client to do so, the therapist will touch the snake before the client is asked to do so, the therapist will hold the snake before the client does, and eventually the therapist will allow the snake to crawl around on her before asking the client to attempt this. Through observational learning, the client begins to associate these behaviors with a calm, nonanxious response in the therapist, which reduces the client's own anxiety about engaging in the behaviors. Modeling is as effective as systematic desensitization in reducing phobias (Bandura, 1969).

The idea behind **flooding** is to intensively expose a client to his or her feared object until anxiety extinguishes. Thus, in a flooding treatment, a person with claustrophobia might lock herself in a closet for several hours, a person with a dog phobia might spend the night in a dog kennel, and a person with social phobia might volunteer to teach a class that meets every day for a semester. The therapist will typically prepare clients with relaxation techniques they can use to reduce their fear during the flooding procedure. Flooding is as effective as systematic desensitization or modeling and often works more quickly. It is more difficult to get clients to agree to this type of therapy, though, because it is frightening to contemplate.

One of the specific phobias, blood-injection-injury phobia, requires a different approach from the other phobias (Ost & Sterner, 1987). Recall that, unlike people with other specific phobias whose blood pressure and heart rate increase when they confront their phobic objects, people with a blood-injection-injury phobia experience severe decreases in heart rate and blood pressure when confronted with their phobic objects. Sometimes, because less blood is circulating to their heads, they faint. Relaxation techniques would only exacerbate these people's natural response to their phobic object because such techniques also decrease blood pressure and heart rate. Thus, therapists must take the opposite approach with people with this phobia and teach them to tense the muscles in their arms, legs, and chest until they feel the warmth of their blood rising in their faces. This **applied tension technique** increases blood pressure and heart rate. When a person with a blood-injection-injury phobia learns this technique, she can use it when confronted with her phobic object to counteract her typical biological response and prevent fainting. Then systematic desensitization, modeling, or flooding can be implemented to extinguish her fear of blood, injury, or injections.

Many therapists will combine these behavioral techniques with cognitive techniques that help clients identify and challenge negative, catastrophizing thoughts they are having when they are anxious (Beck & Emery, 1985). For example, when the snake phobic is saying, "I just can't do this, I can't stand this anxiety, I'll never get over this," the therapist might point out the progress the client has already made on his hierarchy of fears and

modeling
technique used to learn new behaviors through observational learning and imitation techniques

flooding
behavioral technique in which a client is intensively exposed to the feared object until the anxiety diminishes

applied tension technique
technique used to alleviate blood-injection-injury phobias in which the therapist teaches the client to increase his or her blood pressure and heart rate, thus preventing the client from fainting

Group therapy can give people with social phobia an opportunity to gain experience and confidence in being with other people.

Some people drinking heavily on an airplane may be trying to quell a phobia of flying.

the client's previous statements that the relaxation techniques have been a great help to him. Creating the expectations in clients that they can master their phobias, known as *self-efficacy expectations*, is a potent factor in curing the phobias (Bandura et al., 1977).

In the treatment of social phobia, it is often useful to implement systematic desensitization, modeling, and flooding techniques in a group setting, where all the members, except the therapist, suffer from a social phobia (Heimberg et al., 1990). The group members are an audience for one another, providing exposure to the very situation that each member fears. An individual group member can practice his feared behaviors in front of the other members while the therapist coaches him in the use of relaxation techniques to quell his anxiety. The group can also help the therapist challenge the client's negative, catastrophizing thoughts about his behavior (e.g., "I'm stuttering. I'm being incoherent. My voice is quavering. They probably think I'm stupid."). The group can report to the individual client that he was actually quite coherent in his speech and that his comments seemed intelligent. Through observational learning, the group members' cognitions about incompetence and embarrassment are challenged as they challenge one another. Group-administered cognitive-behavioral therapy has proven effective even for people with generalized social phobia (Foa, Franklin, Perry, & Herbert, 1996).

Drug therapies have not proven as useful as behavioral therapies for the treatment of specific phobias or social phobia. Some people will use the benzodiazepines to reduce their anxiety when forced to confront their phobic objects. For example, when people with a phobia of flying are forced to take a flight, they might take a high dose of the benzodiazepine Valium to relieve their anxiety. These drugs produce some temporary relief, but the phobia remains. Antidepressants are more effective than placebos in the treatment of social anxiety, but people relapse soon after discontinuing use of the drug (Liebowitz et al., 1992). Of course, these drugs also have significant side effects, and the benzodiazepines are addictive. For now, it appears that the old advice to "confront your fears" through behavioral therapy is the best advice for people with phobias.

Summing Up   Specific and Social Phobias

- People with specific phobias have excessive anxiety reactions to animals or insects; events in the natural environment; specific situations; or blood, injections, or injuries.
- People with social phobia have excessive anxiety over being scrutinized or judged by others.
- Freud argued that phobias represent the displacement of unconscious anxiety onto neutral objects. This theory and the therapy it suggests have not been well-supported.

- Behavioral theories suggest that phobias develop through classical and operant conditioning. Through prepared classical conditioning, people may more easily develop phobias of objects or situations that have been dangerous to people over evolutionary history.
- Some people may have biological predispositions to phobias or, more generally, to be excessively shy or chronically anxious, which increases their vulnerability to phobias.
- Behavioral treatments have proven most effective for phobias. They focus on extinguishing anxiety reactions.
- Drug therapies have not proven very useful for phobias.

Post-Traumatic Stress Disorder

No one except someone who has experienced rape can know the late night, quiet playback and the thousands of stirring memories ready to rear up their ugly heads at the slightest incitement. Even almost a year later, as the "anniversary" draws near, I can feel all of my own original reactions once again full force, and they are something which will not recede in time. Only women who have spent lonely nights such as this one trying to exorcise the ghosts can truly comprehend the insolence and hideousness of rape. And our number is growing, faster all the time (J. Pilgrim, letter quoted by Thom, 1987)

post-traumatic stress disorder (PTSD) anxiety disorder characterized by (a) repeated mental images of experiencing a traumatic event, (b) emotional numbing and detachment, and (c) hypervigilance and chronic arousal

This rape survivor is describing symptoms of **post-traumatic stress disorder (PTSD)**, a syndrome experienced by many people who have survived traumas. The diagnosis of PTSD requires that three types of symptoms be present (see Table 4.5).

The first set of PTSD symptoms is repeated *reexperiencing of the traumatic event*, through intrusive images or thoughts, recurring nightmares, flashbacks in which they are reliving the event, and psychological and physiological reactivity to stimuli that remind them of the event. The rape survivor just quoted vividly remembers to the point of reliving her traumatic event. Memories of her rape intrude into her consciousness against her

---

Table 4.5 Symptoms of Post-Traumatic Stress Disorder

Three categories of symptoms characterize PTSD:

Reexperiencing the Event:

Distressing memories of the event
Distressing dreams about the event
Reliving the event by acting or feeling as if the event were recurring
Intense psychological and physiological distress when exposed to situations reminiscent of the event

Emotional Numbing and Detachment:

Avoiding thoughts, feelings, or conversations about the event
Avoiding activities, places, or people associated with the event
Having trouble recalling important aspects of the event
Loss of interest in activities
Feelings of detachment from others
Inability to have loving feelings toward others and a general restriction of feelings
Sense that the future is bleak

Hypervigilance and Chronic Arousal:

Difficulty falling or staying asleep
Irritability or outbursts of anger
Difficulty concentrating
Hypervigilance
Exaggerated startle response

will, particularly when she encounters something that reminds her of the event. She also relives her emotional reaction to the event, and since the event she has chronically experienced negative emotions that have not diminished with time.

The second set of symptoms in PTSD involves *emotional numbing and detachment.* People become avoidant and withdrawn, reporting that they feel numb and detached from others, and want to avoid anything that might arouse memories of the event.

The third set of symptoms involves *hypervigilance and chronic arousal.* PTSD sufferers are always on guard for the traumatic event to recur.

In addition to the symptoms listed in the diagnostic criteria for PTSD, suffers of this disorder may report "survivor guilt," painful guilt feelings over the fact that they survived or about things that they had to do to survive. For example, one survivor of a flood reported tremendous guilt over not having responded when a neighbor called to him for help (Erikson, 1976). Instead, he chose to save his own family. One Vietnam veteran with PTSD said, "I am a killer. No one can forgive me. I—we—should be shot. There should be a Nuremberg trial for us" (quoted in Langone, 1985). Many Holocaust survivors report guilt for having survived when their families did not or for not having fought more strongly against the Nazis (Krystal, 1968).

Children can experience PTSD in much the same way that an adult can, but they may have their own particular ways of manifesting PTSD (LaGreca, Silverman, Vernberg, & Prinstein, 1996). Children's memories and fears of a traumatic event may generalize to fears of a wide range of stimuli. One 12-year-old girl who was kidnapped along with several of her friends spoke of her feelings several months later (Terr, 1981, p. 18):

> I don't like to turn off the lights. I'm afraid someone would come in and shoot and rob us. When I wake up I turn on the light. . . . I've been in Bakersfield helping my brother. . . . At night in Bakersfield it feels like someone broke in. Nothing is there. I hear footsteps again. I keep going to check. . . . I check where the sound is coming from. . . . I'm very frightened of the kitchen because no one's there at all. I completely avoid it. At home I kept feeling someone was looking in and watching me. I kept the light on. I was afraid they'd come in and kill us all or take us away again.

Children may also show "regressive" behavior, such as bed-wetting, may repeatedly play out the trauma with dolls or other toys, and may express their distress through aches and pains. Children who have been sexually abused may engage in age-inappropriate sexual behavior.

The Role of Trauma in PTSD

A wide variety of traumatic events can induce post-traumatic stress disorder. Natural disasters, such as floods, earthquakes, fires, hurricanes, and tornadoes, can trigger a wave of PTSD among the survivors. In 1972, a flood wiped out the community of Buffalo

Women who have suffered violence often experience symptoms of post-traumatic stress disorder.

Natural disasters like floods or earthquakes leave behind people with post-traumatic stress symptoms.

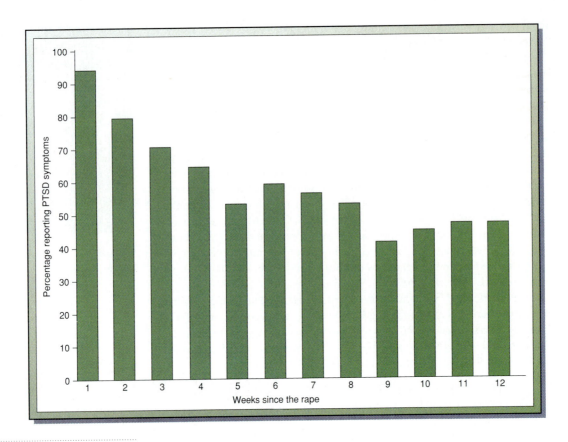

Figure 4.4

Post-Traumatic Symptoms in Rape. Almost all women show symptoms of post-traumatic stress disorder severe enough to be diagnosed with PTSD in the first or second week following a rape. Over the 3 months following a rape, the percentage of women continuing to show PTSD declines. However, almost 50 percent of women continue to be diagnosed with PTSD 3 months after a rape.

Source: Adapted from Foa & Riggs, 1995.

Human-made disasters like the war in Bosnia may more likely lead to post-traumatic stress disorder than natural disasters like floods or earthquakes.

Creek, West Virginia. Shortly after the flood, 60 percent of the 193 survivors of the flood were suffering from PTSD. Fourteen years later, 25 percent still suffered from PTSD (Green, Lindy, Grace, & Leonard, 1992). A study of Florida children who lived through Hurricane Andrew in 1992 found that nearly 20 percent were still suffering from PTSD a year after the disaster (La Greca et al., 1996).

Traumas for which humans are responsible, such as sexual or physical assault, terrorist attacks, and war, may be even more likely to cause PTSD than natural disasters for at least two reasons. First, human-made disaster can challenge our basic beliefs about the goodness of life and other people, and when these beliefs are shattered, PTSD appears to be more likely. Second, human-made disasters often strike individuals rather than whole communities, and suffering through a trauma alone seems to increase a person's risk for PTSD.

Severe human-made traumas are shockingly common. One study of 4,000 randomly selected women in the United States found that over one-third had been the victims of sexual or aggravated assault or had lost a close friend or relative to homicide. Over 25 percent of the women who had been crime victims had a history of PTSD (Resnick, Kilpatrick, Dansky, & Saunders, 1993).

Studies of rape survivors have found that about 95 percent experience post-traumatic stress symptoms severe enough to qualify for a diagnosis of the disorder in the first 2 weeks following the rape (see Figure 4.4). About 50 percent still qualify for the diagnosis 3 months after the rape. As many as 25 percent still suffer from PTSD 4 to 5 years after the rape (Foa & Riggs, 1995; Girelli, Resick, Marhoefer-Dvorak, & Hutter, 1986; Kilpatrick, Veronen, & Resick, 1979; Resnick, Kilpatrick, Dansky, & Saunders, 1993; Rothbaum, Foa, Riggs, & Murdock, 1992).

Much of what we know about PTSD comes from studies of men and women who have fought in wars and were taken as prisoners of war. There are well-documented cases of "combat fatigue syndrome," "war zone stress," and "shell shock" among soldiers and former prisoners of war of the two world wars and the Korean War, and follow-up studies of some of these people show chronic persistence of post-traumatic stress symptoms for decades after the war (Elder & Clipp, 1989; Sutker, Allain, & Winstead, 1993; Sutker,

Winstead, Galina, & Allain, 1991). The Holocaust left in its wake a generation of PTSD sufferers. One study that examined 124 survivors of the Holocaust 40 years later found that almost half were still suffering from post-traumatic stress disorder (Kuch & Cox, 1992). Survivors who had been in concentration camps were three times more likely to have PTSD as were survivors who had not been in concentration camps.

A study of veterans of the 1991 Persian Gulf War found that about 13 percent were suffering from PTSD

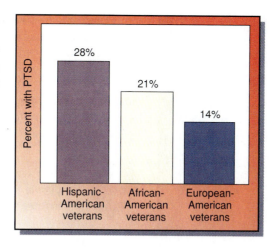

Figure 4.5

Rates of PTSD in Vietnam Veterans. A large study of Vietnam veterans found higher rates of PTSD among veterans of color than among White veterans.
Source: Schlenger et al., 1992.

in the year after the war (Sutker, Davis, Uddo, & Ditta, 1995). The National Vietnam Veterans Readjustment Study found that nearly half a million Vietnam veterans still suffered from PTSD 15 years after their military service. Rates of PTSD are highest among Hispanic veterans, next highest among African-American veterans, and lowest among European-American veterans (see Figure 4.5; Schlenger, Kulka, Fairbank, & Hough, 1992). A separate study of Native American Vietnam veterans found that as many as 70 percent still suffer symptoms of PTSD (Manson et al., 1996).

People from Southeast Asia (Vietnam, Cambodia, Laotians, Hmong, and Mien) have undergone decades of civil war, invasions by other countries, and death at the hands of despots. In the few years that Pol Pot and the Khmer Rouge ruled Cambodia, perhaps one-fourth of Cambodia's 7 million people died. Many others were tortured, starved, and permanently separated from their families. Hundreds of thousands of Southeast Asians fled to Thailand, Europe, the United States, and Canada. Unfortunately, many of these refugees faced further trauma, being imprisoned in refugee camps for years, often separated from their families (Kinzie & Leung, 1993).

Several studies have now been done to determine the psychological scars left by the extreme traumas these people have suffered. Ten percent of Vietnamese, Hmong, Laotian, and Cambodian refugees living in California meet the criteria for PTSD, with the greatest percentage of these being Cambodian (Gong-Guy, 1987). These refugees also suffer from a large number of other psychological problems. Gong-Guy determined that the need for psychiatric services was moderate to severe in 31 percent of the Vietnamese, 54 percent of the Hmong, 50 percent of the Laotians, and 48 percent of the Cambodians.

PTSD can occur following more common events: automobile accidents or other serious accidents; the sudden, unexpected death of a loved one; learning that one's child has a life-threatening disease; or observing someone else being severely injured or killed. One study found that adults who lost children or spouses in fatal car accidents were still experiencing high levels of anxiety and depression 4 to 7 years after their losses, and those who had lost children were more likely than people in a control group to have divorced (Lehman, Wortman, & Williams, 1987).

As these studies illustrate, PTSD symptoms can last a long time after a trauma. About half the people experiencing a trauma appear to recover from PTSD within 3 months of the trauma, but many others continue to experience symptoms for at least 12 months or much longer (APA, 1994).

The people of Southeast Asia have been victims of years of war and oppression.

Theories of Vulnerability to PTSD

The cause of PTSD seems obvious: trauma. However, just what is it about traumatic events that can cause long-term, severe psychological impairment in some people? There are certain basic assumptions about life that can be shattered by a trauma, and it may be the shattering of these assumptions that leads to long-term psychological distress.

Events such as the bombing of the office building and child-care center in Oklahoma City can shatter people's basic assumptions about the goodness of life.

The first is the assumption of *personal invulnerability.* Most people believe that bad things happen to other people, and that they are relatively invulnerable to traumas such as severe car accidents, having their homes destroyed in natural disasters, or being kidnapped or raped. When such events do happen, people lose their illusion of invulnerability. Chronically feeling vulnerable, they are hypervigilant for signs of new traumas and may show signs of chronic anxiety (Janoff-Bulman, 1992).

How adaptive do you think it is for people to have an illusion of personal invulnerability?

The second basic assumption is the assumption that *the world is meaningful and just* and that *things happen for a good reason* (Lerner, 1980). This assumption can be shattered by events that seem senseless, unjust, or perhaps evil, such as the terrorist bombing of a children's day care center.

The third assumption is the assumption that *people who are good, who "play by the rules", do not experience bad things.* Trauma victims will often search for what they did to cause the trauma, in part because they want to know how to prevent it from happening again in the future and in part because their sense of themselves as good people is shattered by their victimization (Janoff-Bulman & Frieze, 1983).

Lenore Terr (1981, 1983) observed the shattering of these assumptions in the child victims of the 1976 Chowchilla school-bus kidnapping, in which 26 children, 5 to 14 years of age, were kidnapped while riding their school bus and then buried underground in a truck trailer. Twenty-seven hours after their kidnapping, the children were freed when two of the boys were able to dig them out of their prison. When the children were interviewed several months later, some could identify events that they believed "caused" their kidnapping or were "warnings" that the kidnapping would happen. Mary, age 9, said, "That day I stepped in a bad luck square. . . . I think if I hadn't have stepped in that square, it would have happened, but not to me!" Five of the children who were kidnapped blamed their parents for failing to recognize "signs" that it would happen. Bob, age 14, was one of the boys who dug the children out of the hole. After the kidnapping, he came to believe he was placed on the bus "by chance" in order to help the other children escape. Bob's vision of himself as the hero later led him to engage in quite dangerous behavior. About 18 months after the kidnapping, Bob shot a stranger who was innocently sitting in his car in front of Bob's family's house, to "protect his family from kidnapping."

It is clear, however, that even in the most severe traumas, there are wide individual differences among people's psychological reactions to trauma. Although most people may feel their basic assumptions about the world have been shattered and experience some symptoms of the PTSD syndrome immediately following a trauma, the severity and duration of these symptoms vary greatly. What makes some people more vulnerable than others to severe, long-term symptoms of PTSD?

The most potent predictors of people's reactions to trauma are the *severity* and *duration* of the trauma and the *proximity* of the individual to the trauma. For example, war veterans are more likely to experience PTSD if they were on the front lines of the war for an extended period of time or if they were taken prisoner of war than if they were not (Schlenger, Kulka, Fairbank, & Hough, 1992). Rape survivors who were violently and repeatedly raped over an extended period are more likely to experience PTSD than are those whose experiences were shorter and less violent (Resick, 1993). Victims of natural disasters who lose their homes or loved ones or are themselves injured are more likely to experience PTSD than are those whose lives were less affected by the natural disaster (Nolen-Hoeksema & Morrow, 1991; Norris & Uhl, 1993).

Another predictor of people's vulnerability to PTSD following trauma is the *social support* they have available to them. People who have others who will support them emotionally through recovery from their traumas, allowing them to discuss their feelings and memories of the traumas, recover more quickly than do those who do not (Kendall-Tackett et al., 1993; La Greca et al., 1996; Sutker et al., 1995). For example, women whose husbands have committed suicide show better physical and emotional health and fewer intrusive thoughts about the suicides if they are able to discuss the suicides with supportive friends than if they had not discussed the suicides with others (Pennebaker & O'Heeron, 1984).

Some events may be more difficult to discuss with others and less likely to engender social support from others because of social stigmas against people who experience such events. Examples are the suicides of family members, sexual assault, and the loss of loved ones to AIDS, particularly if the loved ones were homosexual. Some theorists have argued that veterans of the Vietnam War were more likely than veterans from previous wars to experience PTSD because they received less social support from friends and family members upon returning from combat, due to the social controversy over the war.

The quality of people's social support following a trauma is an important predictor of their psychological reaction to the trauma.

In contrast, events that are experienced by whole communities, such as earthquakes, floods, or hurricanes, might engender less PTSD because individuals can talk with many others who have had experiences similar to their own. For example, following the 7.1 earthquake that hit the San Francisco Bay Area in 1989, almost everyone spoke with friends and neighbors about the earthquake every day for the first two or three weeks after the earthquake (Nolen-Hoeksema & Morrow, 1991). In addition, community leaders mobilized resources to meet people's needs, and there was a spirit of "pitching in" and "supporting each other" that pervaded messages in the media and people's conversations (see also Green, Grace, Lindy, Titchener, & Lindy, 1983; Rachman, 1991).

Another predictor of people's vulnerability to PTSD following a trauma is the level of *distress* they experience *before* the trauma hits. People who are already experiencing increased symptoms of anxiety or depression before encountering a trauma are more likely to experience PTSD (or severe depression) following the trauma than are those who were not anxious or depressed before the trauma (Davidson, Swartz, Storck, Krishnan, & Hammett, 1985; Nolen-Hoeksema & Morrow, 1991).

There is some evidence that people's styles of *coping* with stressful events and with their own symptoms of distress may also influence their vulnerability to PTSD following a trauma. Several studies have shown that combat veterans who use avoidant coping strategies, such as drinking and self-isolation, are more likely to experience PTSD (Fairbank, Hansen, & Fitterling, 1991; Sutker et al., 1995; Wolfe et al., 1993). Unfortunately, these studies took place after the veterans developed PTSD, so it is not clear if their negative coping strategies were the cause or the consequence of the PTSD.

One of the few studies to have gathered data before a trauma happened was conducted around the time of the big 1989 San Francisco earthquake. Fortuitously, researchers had collected information about coping styles and emotional well-being in a group of students shortly before the earthquake. Then, 10 days and again 7 weeks after the earthquake, they assessed depressive symptoms and PTSD symptoms in these same students. They were especially interested in students with ruminative coping styles. People with ruminative coping styles chronically focus on their symptoms of distress and worry about these symptoms without doing anything about them. Students with more ruminative styles of coping were more likely to show symptoms of depression and PTSD both shortly after and 7 weeks after the earthquake than were students with less ruminative coping styles. This was true even after researchers took into account how distressed the students had been before the earthquake and how much stress—property damage, personal injury—they had been exposed to as a result of the earthquake (Nolen-Hoeksema & Morrow, 1991).

Finally, as noted earlier, many studies have found that, following a trauma, most people try to *make sense* of the trauma somehow (Lehman, Wortman, & Williams, 1987; Silver, Boon, & Stones, 1983). They try to find some reason or purpose for the trauma or to understand what the trauma means in their lives. Psychodynamic and existential theorists have argued that searching for meaning in a trauma is a healthy process that can lead people to gain a sense of mastery over their traumas and to integrate their traumas into their understandings of themselves (Frankl, 1963; Freud, 1920; Horowitz, 1976). They suggest that people who are able to "make sense" of their traumas appear less likely to develop PTSD or other chronic emotional problems and may recover more quickly from their traumas than do people who cannot make sense of their traumas (Bulman & Wortman, 1977; Silver et al., 1983). How do people make sense of traumas? Some people have religious or philosophical beliefs that assist them in making sense. For example, recently bereaved people who are religious often say that God needed their loved ones in Heaven or had a special purpose for taking their loved ones and this seems to help them understand their losses (McIntosh, Silver, & Wortman, 1993; Nolen-Hoeksema & Larson, in press). Other people say that the deaths of loved ones made them reevaluate their lives and their relationships with others and make positive changes, and this helped them deal with the loss. Having a confidant with whom to discuss traumas and their meanings appears to facilitate finding meaning (Silver et al., 1983).

 If you have ever experienced a trauma, did you find some meaning in the trauma? If so, how did you do this?

Some people are never able to make sense of their losses or other traumas, and these people are more likely to experience chronic and severe symptoms of PTSD and depression. For example, researchers questioned 77 women who were the survivors of incest, an average 20 years after the incest had ended. They found that 50 percent of the women were still actively searching for meaning in their incest. These women said things such as, "I always ask myself why, over and over, but there is no answer," and, "There is no sense to be made. This should not have happened to me or any child" (Silver et al., 1983). The more actively a woman was still searching for meaning in her incest, the more likely she was to be experiencing recurrent and intrusive ruminations about the incest experience, the more distress she was experiencing, and the lower her level of social functioning was. Because those who search for meaning are ruminating about the past, perhaps they are also less able to focus coping efforts on the present and the future. In trying to understand, they may in effect get "stuck" in the past both voluntarily and through involuntary intrusions of ongoing thought processes. Finding meaning may be particularly difficult in traumas such as sexual assault, in which the nature of the event violates basic moral codes and destroys people's basic trust in others (Resick, 1993; Silver et al., 1983).

Thus, although some traumas may cause almost everyone to experience some symptoms of PTSD, several factors influence an individual's vulnerability to experience more severe and long-lasting symptoms of PTSD. Treating PTSD sufferers can be difficult. Their desire to avoid thinking about their traumas can be so strong that they do not seek treatment. Instead, they may engage in a variety of maladaptive coping behaviors, such as isolating themselves from others, using alcohol and other drugs to dampen their anxiety symptoms, and lashing out at others when their emotions are overwhelming. Relatively new treatments for PTSD, based primarily on behavioral theories, have given PTSD suffers hope that they can overcome their symptoms, however. These treatments are described in the next section.

Treatment for PTSD

Treatments for PTSD generally have three goals: exposing clients to what they fear in order to extinguish that fear, challenging distorted cognitions that are contributing to symptoms, and helping clients manage their ongoing life problems to reduce the stress in their lives.

In systematic desensitization therapy for PTSD, the client identifies those thoughts and situations that create anxiety, ranking them from most anxiety-provoking to least. The therapist then begins to take the client through this hierarchy, using relaxation techniques to quell anxiety. The focus of anxiety in PTSD is the memory of the traumatic event or events and stimuli that remind the person of the event. It is impossible to return to the actual event that triggered the PTSD in many cases, so imagining the event vividly must replace actual exposure to the event: The combat veteran being treated for PTSD imagines the bloody battles and scenes of killing and death that haunt him; the rape survivor imagines the minute details of the assault. The therapist also watches for distorted thinking patterns, such as survivor guilt, and helps the client challenge these thoughts.

Repeatedly and vividly imagining and describing the feared events in the safety of the therapist's office, the client has an opportunity to extinguish his or her fear of the events. Repeatedly imagining and discussing the traumatic events may also allow the client to "work through" them and integrate them into his or her concepts of the self and the world (Horowitz, 1976). Studies of rape survivors and combat veterans have found that this kind of repeated exposure therapy does significantly decrease PTSD symptoms and helps to prevent relapse (Foa et al., 1991; Keane, Gerardi, Quinn, & Litz, 1992; Resick & Schnicke, 1992).

What about those people who are constantly ruminating about their traumas, even years after they are over? Will intensive exposure to thoughts about the traumas help them? Some theorists argue that, for PTSD sufferers who cannot find any meaning in their traumas or "resolve" their traumas, and who experience very frequent intrusive thoughts, it would be more useful to help them find ways of blocking their intrusive thoughts (Horowitz, 1976; Silver et al., 1983). **Thought-stopping techniques** may include the client yelling "No!" loudly when he realizes he is thinking about the trauma or learning to engage in positive activities that distract thoughts away from the trauma (Rachman, 1978). These thought-stopping techniques are often combined with **stress-management interventions** that teach clients skills for overcoming problems in their lives that are increasing their stress and that may be the result of PTSD, such as marital problems or social isolation (Keane et al., 1992). The following case study illustrates the use of several stress-management interventions with a combat veteran suffering from PTSD (Keane et al., 1992, p. 91):

thought-stopping techniques strategy that involves finding ways to stop intrusive thoughts

stress-management interventions strategy that teaches clients to overcome problems in their lives that are increasing their stress

---

Case Study • D. P. was a male Vietnam veteran referred to the PTSD unit of his local DVA [Department of Veterans Affairs] Medical Center. D. P. reported feeling extremely stressed over the past six months because of problems on his job. He complained of sleep disturbance, angry outbursts, intrusive thoughts, nightmares, and avoidance of movies, books, and television shows associated wtih Vietnam. He also was experiencing marital difficulties, constriction of affect, and numbing of emotions. Since his discharge from the military, D. P. had avoided discussing Vietnam (his friends over the past 20 years were unaware that D. P. had even been in the military), and he stated that he did not want to discuss Vietnam in treatment. Respecting his wishes, treatment began by addressing sleep disturbance and interpersonal difficulties. D. P. learned progressive muscle relaxation and began using the technique to prepare for sleep, to get back to sleep after awakening, and at times throughout the day when he felt himself becoming stressed.

Interpersonal difficulties were then addressed in couples sessions using communication and problem-solving skills. D. P. and his wife had developed a relatively noncommunicative style over a number of years. Mrs. P. complained about a lack of intimacy in their relationship and being overburdened with decisions that were better made by both of them. In therapy, the couple learned to listen to one another and to give constructive positive and negative feedback.

As is common among combat veterans with PTSD, D. P. was afraid of his anger, even though he had not been violent in over 17 years. To address this concern, he was taught several strategies for anger control. For example, D. P. was given permission by the therapist to remove himself from a situation or discussion that created stress for him. He was taught to request a time and place to later continue working on that specific problem. This allowed D. P. to work on problem-solving skills while titrating his exposure to aversive, arousing circumstances. Initially, problem solving was conducted only during the session; however, after several weeks, the couple began problem solving at home and reviewed the contracts and solution processes in the following session. As D. P. learned a variety of new skills that enhanced his ability to manage his stress and his interpersonal problems, he became less defensive about Vietnam and began to address those issues more directly in therapy.

Some studies find that these stress-management interventions are helpful both to combat veterans with PTSD and to persons suffering PTSD after rape (Kilpatrick et al., 1979; Meichenbaum & Jaremko, 1983; Veronen & Kilpatrick, 1983). There is still much work to do, however, before we know just how to treat persons with PTSD.

Drug therapies, including the benzodiazepines and antidepressant medications, are used by some clinicians to treat PTSD. These drugs can quell certain symptoms of PTSD, especially the sleep problems, nightmares, and irritability. This may make it easier for the person with PTSD to face his or her memories and extinguish fears of them. The long-term effectiveness of drug therapies for PTSD has not been established, however (Southwick, Bremmer, Krystal, & Charney, 1994).

Finally, some cultures have their own treatments for PTSD-like symptoms. For example, some Native American groups have cleansing rituals that absolve combat veterans from their actions during combat and serve to reintegrate veterans into the community and with the values of his or her group. The Navajo have a healing ceremony called the *Enemy Way*, which is explicitly oriented toward returning combat veterans. The ceremony lasts for seven days and seven nights. The veteran, his or her family and community members, and a tribal healer actively participate in ritual song designed to return balance and harmony to the individual veteran and the entire community (Manson et al., 1996).

Summing Up · Post-Traumatic Stress Disorder

- People with post-traumatic stress disorder repeatedly reexperience the traumatic event, they avoid situations that might arouse memories of their trauma, and they are hypervigilant and chronically aroused.
- PTSD may be most likely to occur following traumas that shatter people's assumptions that they are invulnerable, that the world is a just place, and that bad things do not happen to good people.
- People who experience severe and long-lasting traumas, who have lower levels of social support, who experience socially stigmatizing traumas, who were already depressed or anxious before trauma, or have maladaptive, ruminative coping styles may be at increased risk for PTSD.
- People who are unable to somehow make sense of a trauma appear more likely to have chronic PTSD symptoms.
- The most effective treatment for PTSD involves exposing the person to his or her memories of the trauma, through systematic desensitization and flooding, to extinguish his or her anxiety over these memories.
- Some people cannot tolerate such exposure, however, and may do better with supportive therapy focused on solving current interpersonal difficulties and life problems.

- Benzodiazepines and antidepressant drugs can quell some of the symptoms of PTSD, but these symptoms tend to recur when the drugs are discontinued.

Generalized Anxiety Disorder

The phobias, PTSD, panic, and agoraphobia involve periods of anxiety that are more or less specific to certain situations. In phobias and PTSD, anxiety is aroused by exposure to phobic stimuli or to reminders of a trauma. In agoraphobia and panic, anxiety is aroused by leaving a safe place and going into a place in which one has panicked in the past. Some people are anxious all the time, however, in almost all situations. These people may be diagnosed with a **generalized anxiety disorder (GAD)**.

People with GAD worry about many things in their lives. They may be concerned about their performance on the job, about how their relationships are going, about the health of their children or their parents, and about their own health. They also may worry about minor issues, such as whether they will be late for an appointment, whether the hair stylist will cut their hair the right way, whether they will have time to mop the kitchen floor before the dinner guests arrive. The focus of their worries may shift frequently, and they tend to worry about many different things, instead of just focusing on one issue of concern. Their worry is accompanied by many of the physiological symptoms of anxiety, including muscle tension, sleep disturbances, and a chronic sense of restlessness. They report feeling tired much of the time, probably due to their chronic muscle tension and sleep loss.

GAD is a relatively common type of anxiety disorder, with about 4 percent of the U.S. population experiencing it in any 6-month period (Blazer, George, & Hughes, 1991; Kessler et al., 1994). Many people with this disorder report they have been anxious all their lives.

generalized anxiety disorder (GAD) anxiety disorder characterized by chronic anxiety in daily life

Theories and Treatment of Generalized Anxiety Disorder

Less is known about the causes of and appropriate treatments for generalized anxiety disorder than is known about the other anxiety disorders. Much of the current research focuses on the conscious and unconscious cognitions of people with GAD.

 Given how common GAD is, it might seem strange that so much less is known about it than is about other anxiety disorders. What are some of the features of GAD that you think might make it more difficulty to study?

The conscious cognitions of people with GAD tend to focus on threats (Beck & Emery, 1985). People with GAD worry constantly about being in control and about losing control. Asking people with GAD to engage in relaxation exercises to reduce their anxiety actually heightens their anxiety (Heide & Borkovec, 1984). It seems that in trying to relax, the GAD sufferers feel they are losing control, which just makes them more tense.

Although people with GAD are always anticipating some negative event, they do not tend to think through this anticipated event and vividly imagine it happening to them (Borkovec & Hu, 1990). Indeed, they actively avoid images of what they worry about, perhaps as a way of avoiding the negative emotion associated with those images. By avoiding fully processing those images, while still anticipating something bad is going to happen, people with GAD do not allow themselves to consider ways they might cope with an event if it were to happen or to habituate to the negative emotions associated with the image of an event.

The unconscious cognitions of people with GAD may also be focused on detecting possible threats in the environment (Mathews & MacLeod, 1994). One paradigm in which this has been shown is the Stroop color naming task. In this task, subjects are presented with words printed in color on a computer screen. The subject's task is to say what color the word is printed in. Some of the words have special significance for a person with chronic anxiety, such as *disease* or *failure*, while other words have no special significance. In general, people are slower in naming the color of words that have special significance to them than of nonsignificant words in the Stroop task because they are paying more attention to the content of the significant words than to the color in which the word is printed. One study presented threatening and nonthreatening words to GAD patients and nonpatient controls on the computer screen for only 20 milliseconds, too short a period for the subjects to consciously process the color of the word. The GAD patients were slower in naming the colors of the threatening words than were the nonpatients, but the two groups of subjects did not differ in the time it took them to name the colors of the nonthreatening words. This suggests that people suffering from GAD are always vigilant for signs of impending threat, even at an unconscious level (MacLeod & Mathews, 1994). The goal of new research is to determine whether this constant viligance is due to some type of biological factor or to something about the personalities of people with GAD.

Cognitive-behavioral therapies—focusing on helping people with GAD confront those issues they worry most about, challenge their negative, catastrophizing thoughts, and develop coping strategies—have been shown in some recent studies to be more effective than either benzodiazepine therapy, placebos, or nondirective supportive therapy in the treatment of GAD (Borkovec & Costello, 1993; Butler, Fennell, Robson, & Gelder, 1991; Power, Simpson, Swanson, & Wallace, 1990). One study found that the positive effects of cognitive-behavioral therapies remained in a 1-year follow-up of the GAD clients (Borkovec & Costello, 1993). In contrast, benzodiazepine drugs produce short-term relief from the symptoms of anxiety for some people (Barlow, 1988; Solomon & Hart, 1978). Even people who get some short-term relief with the benodiazepines relapse back into GAD when they discontinue the drugs.

Summing Up	Generalized Anxiety Disorder

- People with generalized anxiety disorder are chronically anxious in most situations.
- People with GAD appear more vigilant for threatening information, even on an unconscious level.
- Benzodiazepines can produce short-term relief for some people with GAD but have not proven effective in the long-term treatment of GAD.
- Cognitive-behavioral therapies focus on changing the catastrophic thinking styles of people with GAD.

Gender Differences in Anxiety Disorders

Women are more prone than men to all of the anxiety disorders we have discussed thus far. Compared to men, women have two or three times the rate of panic with agoraphobia, three or four times more specific phobias, one and one-half times more social phobias, and two times more PTSD (Yonkers & Gurguis, 1995). Why would women be more likely than men to develop these disorders?

First, women may have a greater biological vulnerability to some anxiety disorders than men. Much of the work on women's biological vulnerability to anxiety has focused on panic and agoraphobia. Family history studies of panic disorder with agoraphobia find that the female relatives of people with this disorder are even more likely than the male relatives to also have the disorder (Crowe et al., 1990). The male relatives, on the other hand, are more likely to suffer from alcohol abuse and dependence disorders. This suggests that the genetic vulnerability to panic disorder and agoraphobia is sex-linked. Women may be more likely than men to carry the genetic vulnerability to this disorder. Alternately, women and men may carry an equal genetic vulnerability to some type of disorder, which gets expressed as panic disorder and agoraphobia in women and as alcoholism in men.

Some women with panic disorder report increases in anxiety symptoms during their premenstrual periods and the postpartum period (Yonkers & Gurguis, 1995). In addition, women with a form of mood disorder known as *premenstrual dysphoric disorder* (see Chapter 5), in which they regularly become depressed during the premenstrual phase of their menstrual cycle, appear at increased risk to have full panic attacks when their autonomic nervous systems are aroused. These observations have lead some theorists to argue that the ovarian hormones, particularly progesterone, may play a role in vulnerability to panic attacks. Progesterone can affect activity of both serotonin and GABA neurotransmitter systems. Fluctuations in levels of progesterone with the menstrual cycle or in the postpartum period thus might lead to imbalances or dysfunctioning of the serotonin or GABA systems, thereby influencing susceptibility to panic. In addition, increases in progesterone can induce mild chronic hyperventilation. In women prone to panic attacks, this may be enough to tip the balance in their parasympathetic and sympathetic nervous systems and induce full panic attacks. In women who do not have vulnerability to panic attacks, however, there is little evidence that the hormonal changes of the premenstrual period cause significant anxiety.

Several psychosocial explanations have also been offered for women's greater vulnerability to anxiety disorders compared to men. The psychodynamic explanation is that women are more likely than men to fear separation from others because their self-concepts are more intimately connected to their relationships with others. As a result, women cling to others, play passive and subservient roles in relationships, express a sense of being vulnerable and defenseless, and are hypervigilant to any signs of problems in their relationships. Many women may repeatedly get into relationships with others who reinforce their subservient stance in relationships; for example, many women marry men who want inhibited, servile wives. This suppression of their own desires and fearfulness of loss, however, leaves women chronically anxious, as in generalized anxiety disorder. Panic attacks and phobias are simply extreme expressions of these women's ongoing anxiety. Agoraphobia may be another way to express vulnerability and to conform to the passive role. This intriguing and popular theory has not been extensively studied in empirical research.

A different but related perspective is that sex-role socialization and pressures influence how men and women cope with symptoms of distress and thus whether they develop anxiety disorders. First, norms against men exhibiting anxiety may cause more men than women to confront their phobic objects and their feared situations and thereby extinguish their anxiety. Second, men appear more likely than women to seek medical help for anxiety symptoms, especially panic attacks (Yonkers & Gurguis, 1995). This may suggest that men view these symptoms as annoying medical problems rather than as signs that there is something wrong in their lives or in their personalities. It may also mean that more men than women receive effective treatment in the early stages of possible anxiety disorders. Not all men who have anxiety symptoms seek appropriate help for them, however. Many men who have panic attacks appear to "self-medicate" by consuming large amounts of alcohol to decrease their panic symptoms, a coping behavior that is more acceptable for men than for women (Chambless, Cherney, Caputo, & Rheinstein, 1987; Johannessen, Cowley, Walker, & Jensen, 1989). In contrast, because it is more acceptable for women to remain home and to avoid the kinds of situations that agoraphobics avoid, women may be more likely than men to develop agoraphobia as a way of "coping" with their panic attacks.

Women may also be more likely than men to engage in the catastrophic thinking described by cognitive theories as contributing to anxiety disorders. This hypothesis has not been tested directly, but studies have shown that women are more likely to worry and ruminate about their symptoms of distress than are men (Nolen-Hoeksema, 1990). If this rumination takes the form of the kind of catastrophic thinking the cognitive models of anxiety describe—hypervigilance, misinterpretation of symptoms, snowballing cognitions—it could lead some women who have occasional anxiety symptoms to develop the full syndrome of an anxiety disorder.

Women in many cultures face threats in daily life that quite reasonably would lead them to be chronically anxious and more prone to all of the anxiety disorders. In particular, women are more likely than men to be the targets of physical and sexual abuse. Girls and women who have been physically or sexually abused are at increased risk for most anxiety disorders, especially PTSD (Burnam et al., 1988). In addition, the pervasive threat of violence may leave even women who have not yet been the victims of abuse chronically anxious and thereby prone to generalized anxiety disorders, phobias, and panic attacks.

Summing Up	Gender Differences

- Women may carry a stronger genetic vulnerability to anxiety disorders than men.
- Women with a history of panic attacks have exacerbations of panic symptoms during the premenstrual period, suggesting that fluctuations in hormones can affect anxiety symptoms.
- Women may have certain personality characteristics, particularly an overdependency on others, that predispose them to anxiety. This has not been well-tested in research, however.
- Women's lower status in most cultures and resulting vulnerability to victimization may contribute both to chronic anxiety and to specific anxiety disorders.

Cultural Differences in Anxiety Disorders

ataque de nervios
attack of the nerves, syndrome in Hispanic cultures that closely resembles anxiety and depressive disorders

Manifestations of anxiety may differ across cultures. People in Hispanic cultures report a syndrome known as **ataque de nervios** (attack of the nerves). A typical *ataque de nervios* might include "trembling, heart palpitations, a sense of heat in the chest rising into the head, difficulty moving limbs, loss of consciousness or mind going blank, memory loss, a sensation of needles in parts of the body (paresthesia), chest tightness, difficulty breathing (dyspnea), dizziness, faintness, and spells. Behaviorally, the person begins to shout, swear, and strike out at others. The person then falls to the ground and either experiences convulsive body movements or lies 'as if dead'" (Guarnaccia, Rivera, Franco, Neighbors, & Allende-Ramos, 1996). When *ataque de nervios* comes "out of the blue," it is often attributed to the stresses of daily living or to spiritual causes. Like panic attacks, *ataque de nervios* is more common among recent trauma victims. A study of Puerto Ricans after the 1985 floods and mudslides in Puerto Rico found that 16 percent of the victims reported experiencing *ataque de nervios*. Most of these people could also be diagnosed with anxiety or depressive disorders according to DSM criteria, but they conceptualized their symptoms as *ataque de nervios* and accepting their conceptualization may be more useful and respectful than imposing DSM-IV diagnosis on them (Guarnaccia, Canino, Rubio-Stipec, & Bravo, 1993).

In our discussion of PTSD, we considered that Southeast Asians may be especially vulnerable to this disorder because of the chronic and severe traumas to which many of them have been exposed. When they do seek treatment for psychological distress, Southeast Asians often present with somatic symptoms such as pain, poor sleeping, and stomachaches, rather than the the psychological symptoms of post-traumatic stress disorder. They often do not believe the primary symptoms of PTSD, such as startle reaction, nightmares, reexperiencing the trauma, and irritability, are worth mentioning to a physician, and they steadfastly avoid thinking about or talking about the traumas they experienced (Kinzie & Leung, 1993). Dissociative experiences, such as transient hallucinations or loss of physical functioning for no medical reason, are also common. What follows is a case history of a Cambodian woman with PTSD (adapted from Kinzie & Leung, 1993, p. 292).

Case Study • When originally seen, S. A. was 38 years old. She was a Cambodian refugee brought because she believed she was possessed by her dead mother. During the original evaluation, the patient was so distressed and agitated that no real history could be obtained. A subsequent evaluation showed that she had recently been angry and depressed much of the time and actually felt that her mother had entered her body. This intrusion caused her to become very irritable and angry, and during these episodes, she would lose control.

. . . S. A.'s past history was very disturbing. She was born in a rural area in Cambodia, the third of five children. She worked as a secretary for 1½ years and married at the age of 17. During the Pol Pot regime, she was subjected to 4 years of forced labor. Her father died, and her husband was executed at the time she was in labor with her second child. S. A.'s child died of starvation, and her mother died of disease and starvation. She felt most distressed about the death of her mother, who was the person closest to her and who had helped her with the delivery of her child. In 1979, she left Cambodia and lived in refugee camps for 1½ years before coming to the United States.

. . . At her original presentation, S. A. was extremely agitated and appeared to be in a dissociated state. However, in the second interview, after a week of benzodiazepine treatment, she demonstrated a good fund of knowledge and a good memory for past events. She appeared to be numb and saddened about what she had suffered. Her symptoms included frequent nightmares, intrusive thoughts about the past, startle reaction, irritability, and marked attempts to avoid all memories of the past or any events that would remind her of Cambodia. . . .

Treatment of PTSD in Southeast Asian refugees like S. A. can be especially delicate. They may never have told anyone about the traumas they experienced in their homeland because of strong cultural taboos against discussing these traumas in their families. Thus, therapists must be highly sensitive and supportive in encouraging the refugee to tell his or her own story. The therapist must be careful to avoid any suggestion of interrogating the client as he or she might have been interrogated in the homeland (Kinzie & Leung, 1993). These refugees may need to protect themselves against the agony that memories of their severe traumas arouse and focus more on solving current problems. For example, the therapist treating S. A. might want to ensure that she is getting all the financial support and education available to her to stablize her income and living situation. Although refugees may be having significant problems in their marital and family relationships due to their PTSD symptoms and the amount of stress their families are facing, they may be reluctant to talk to the therapist about these due to cultural taboos against doing so.

In the United States, phobias and PTSD are more common among people in disadvantaged minority groups and those in lower educational and socioeconomic groups than they are among whites and people in higher educational and socioeconomic groups (Blazer et al., 1991; Manson et al., 1996; Schlenger, Kulka, Fairbank, & Hough, 1992; Sheikh, 1992). Recall that people who are chronically distressed are at increased risk of developing phobias. Similarly, people who are already under a great deal of stress before a trauma occurs are at increased risk for PTSD. The stressful environment in which disadvantaged people live may create a chronic and pervasive anxiousness that increases their risk for the development of phobias and of PTSD in the wake of trauma (Barlow, 1988; Manson et al., 1996).

For example, consider a woman living in poverty who is chronically anxious about the unsafe neighborhood in which she lives. Her chronic apprehensiveness could make it easier for even minor events, such as being trapped briefly in the elevator of her apartment building, to create paniclike symptoms. She would then be likely to associate her panic symptoms with elevators or, perhaps more generally, with enclosed spaces. Claustrophobia might develop. Similarly, African-American, Hispanic-American and Native American combat veterans from the Vietnam and Persian Gulf wars may have been more vulnerable than white veterans to PTSD because the veterans of color faced discrimination in the United States both before and after the war, increasing their base levels of distress and making it more likely they would respond to the traumas of combat with PTSD (Manson et al., 1996).

Differences among ethnic or cultural groups in vulnerability to PTSD may also be linked to differences in the social support available to members of these groups before and after traumas. Groups in which individuals have strong social support networks may be less prone to PTSD than those with weaker networks. For example, Southeast Asian refugees who are able to move into existing communities of people from their homeland when emigrating to a new country are less likely to show PTSD than are those who do not have existing communities in their new home (Beiser, 1988).

Summing Up — Cultural Differences

- There are cross-cultural differences in the manifestation of anxiety, with some cultures having conceptualizations of the nature and causes of anxiety that are quite different from those of other cultures.
- Clinicians treating people with anxiety disorders must be sensitive to the extraordinary circumstances that may have lead to these disorders and to cultural norms for what is appropriate to discuss outside one's immediate family or culture.
- Disadvantaged persons may be at increased risk for anxiety disorders because they are chronically stressed and not given adequate social support following traumas.

Obsessive-Compulsive Disorder

obsessive-compulsive disorder (OCD) anxiety disorder characterized by obsessions (persistent thoughts) and compulsions (rituals)

Obsessive-compulsive disorder (OCD) is classified as an anxiety disorder because people with OCD experience anxiety as a result of their obsessional thoughts and when they cannot carry out their compulsive behaviors. However, this disorder has quite a different character than the other anxiety disorders we have discussed and may soon be declassified as an anxiety disorder.

The following two case histories illustrate some of the unusual features of OCD. These case histories are especially interesting because they are written by a young boy with OCD and his father, who also suffered from OCD most of his life but never told anyone until his son was diagnosed (Rapaport, 1990, pp. 43–48):

Case Study • *Zach's Story:* When I was 6 I started doing all these strange things when I swallowed saliva. When I swallowed saliva I had to crouch down and touch the ground. I didn't want to lose any saliva—for a bit I had to sweep the ground with my hand—and later I had to blink my eyes if I swallowed. I was frustrated because I couldn't stop the compulsions. Each time I swallowed I had to do something. For a while I had to touch my shoulders to my chin. I don't know why. I had no reason. I was afraid. It was just so unpleasant if I didn't. If I tried not to do these things, all I got was failure. I had to do it, and no matter how hard I tried, I just *still* had to.

. . . I felt ashamed. I didn't want anyone to know. I wanted it to be just for me to know, no one else.

It wrecked my life. It took away all the time. I couldn't do anything. If you put it all together I did it maybe an hour and a half or sometimes three hours a day.

I had bathroom problems too. I had to take some toilet paper and rip them up a lot of times into teeny pieces that had to be just the right size—only about a millimeter. They had to be torn perfect and then I'd flush them away.

I had to do all kinds of things with my fingers and my mouth. I had to touch all my fingers to my lips a few times if I swallowed saliva. Swallowing was one of the first things. But my elbows were really first. I was afraid of getting my hands dirty. My mind said "Wash them, they're dirty." They *felt* dirty. After I went to the bathroom I had to wash my hands, only mine always felt dirty.

I would forget one thing after another. After I changed one pattern I would completely forget it. I remember one part of one pattern: I had to touch the ends of my thumbs to where the water came out of the faucet. Some other things I don't remember. I couldn't turn off the water with my hands. I was late for school a lot.

Zach's Father's Story: My name is Sam. I am a very successful professional in a very large city, involved with matters of substantial importance and large sums of money, working in a very competitive field. I have a beautiful, loving, understanding wife and three terrific bright children. Times are good . . .

My secretary doesn't know it and the other senior partners don't know it, but my days are not like the days of the others in my office who also handle multimillion-dollar transactions. They are just doing their job. I have two jobs: my profession and battling obsessions. Come enter my thoughts as I prepare to enter that battle . . .

I am very careful as I read a book or newspaper or magazine. I never know what terrible things lie on the next page or the next paragraph or the next sentence. I read slowly. I concentrate on the mantra.

Damn! *Death.* There's that awful word. All right, start to offset it. Be careful. Better to go backwards over what you've already read. Try to remember where the words are. You can't go forward anyway, because forward is the future and you don't want to contaminate the future with eyes that have just beheld a word of such terrible consequence. Go back over what you've read. Go to the past. You can't really harm the past (you don't really believe that)—use it to your advantage. Would anyone in my office believe this if they saw it? Of course not.

I saw the word *death*? Yes. All right, careful. *Life* must be here somewhere. Go back more pages. Where did I see it? *Life*, where are you? There's *living*. No, that won't do. It would work for *dying*, but not *death*. *Death* is the most terrible word. It can only be appeased with *life*. And if *death* was capitalized, try to find *life* capitalized also or find two or three *lifes* to even things out.

Careful.

No-ooo. Damn! *Died.* Now I've got to find *living* or *alive* or *lives* or some such word to offset *died* before I can go back to the first problem. What about *lived*? It's not much better than *died*. Implicit in *lived* is that what was alive is now dead. No, it must be one of the others.

Shit! *Deceased.* Now I've got to offset that before I can offset *died* and then offset *died* before I can offset *death.*

I want to scream out in anger and frustration. This is silly. This is stupid. Why am I doing this? Stay calm. Work through it. Carefully. Slowly. There, *alive*. And there, *lives*. All right, one left to go.

Shit. *Corpse.* I can't go on like this. Why am I doing this? Wait. *Life.* Okay, I'll use that for *corpse*. Now, just one more *life*. Just to be sure.

No! I can't believe he asked me for a sheet of paper, interrupted me, just when I was coming to the end of the search. When I only had one to go. Now I've got to start over. Be calm. He doesn't know what you're doing. Hide it. Don't let on. Why can't I be normal? All these other people don't have to do these things. I'm tired. I can't keep this up. What was the order in which I saw the words? Maybe I just won't do it. But I *have* to do it. Try not to look up with my contaminated eyes until I'm finished with the good words. What time is it?

Damn! Now I've looked at the clock—time, the future—I've contaminated it. Now I've got to offset that against something else. But what? The past. That's it. Find a calendar or book. Here, this old textbook. At the front, there should be a copyright date. Yes, a year long before I was born, so I can use it to free myself of the contamination I created by looking at the clock without affecting myself. I stare at the year and get ready to zap it with my eyes. Wait. What do the numbers in the year add up to? Nineteen. No, I can't believe it. Nineteen was the age of my ex-secretary's son when he was killed in an automobile accident that night she called me at 2:00 A.M., hysterically crying. Block it out. Think mantras. No, find another year, one that adds up to18, to *chai*, to life in Hebrew. Yes, here's another book, another year—18. Relief. Now, don't look at the clock. Don't look at—

I think you have the idea by now.

You may be thinking that the thoughts and behaviors that Zach and Sam describe are "crazy"—that they are so out of touch with reality that they are psychotic. The thoughts and behaviors of people with OCD are not considered psychotic, however, because these people are very aware of how irrational their thoughts and behaviors are.

Obsessions are thoughts, images, ideas, or impulses that are persistent, that the individual feels intrude upon his or her consciousness without control, and that cause significant anxiety or distress. Zach's obsessions involve dirt and being dirty, and his father's obsessions involve death and the possibility of hurting others. The focus of obsessive thoughts seems to be similar across cultures, with the most common type of obsession focusing on contamination (Akhtar et al., 1975; Insel, 1984; Kim, 1993; Rachman & Hodgson, 1980). Other common obsessions include aggressive impulses (e.g., to hurt your child), sexual thoughts (e.g., recurrent pornographic images), impulses to do something against your moral code (e.g., to shout obscenities in church), and repeated doubts (e.g., worrying that you have not turned off the stove). Although thoughts of this kind occur to most people occasionally, most of us can "turn off" these thoughts by dismissing or ignoring them. People with OCD cannot turn off these thoughts. They do not carry out the impulses they have (hurting a baby or shouting obscenities in church), but they are so bothered by the fact that they even have these thoughts that they feel extremely guilty and anxious.

Most people who have severe and persistent obsessions engage in compulsions to try to erase their thoughts and the anxiety the thoughts create. **Compulsions** are repetitive behaviors or mental acts that an individual feels he or she must perform. Sometimes an individual's compulsion is tied to his or her specific obsession by some obvious logic. The compulsive behavior becomes so extreme and repetitive, however, that it is irrational. For example, Zach would wash his hands 35 times a day, until they cracked and bled, to rid himself of contamination obsessions. "Checking" compulsions which are extremely common, are tied to obsessional doubts, as is illustrated in this story (Rapaport, 1990, pp. 21–23).

> I'm driving down the highway doing 55 MPH. I'm on my way to take a final exam. My seat belt is buckled and I'm vigilantly following all the rules of the road. No one is on the highway—not a living soul.
>
> Out of nowhere an obsessive-compulsive disorder (OCD) attack strikes. It's almost magical the way it distorts my perception of reality. While in reality no one is on the road, I'm intruded with the heinous thought that I *might* have hit someone . . . a human being! God knows where such a fantasy comes from. . . .
>
> The pain is a terrible guilt that I have committed an unthinkable, negligent act. At one level, I know this is ridiculous, but there's a terrible pain in my stomach telling me something quite different. . . .
>
> I start ruminating, "Maybe I did hit someone and didn't realize it. . . . Oh, my God! I might have killed somebody! I have to go back and check." Checking is the only way to calm the anxiety. It brings me closer to truth somehow. I can't live with the thought that I actually may have killed someone—I have to check it out. . . .
>
> I've driven 5 miles farther down the road since the attack's onset. I turn the car around and head back to the scene of the mythical mishap. I return to the spot on the road where I "think" it "might" have occurred. Naturally, nothing is there. No police car and no bloodied body. Relieved, I turn around again to get to my exam on time.
>
> Feeling better, I drive for about twenty seconds and then the lingering thoughts and pain start gnawing away again. Only this time they're even more intense. I think, "Maybe I should have pulled *off* the road and checked the side brush where the injured body was thrown and now lies? Maybe I didn't go *far enough* back on the road and the accident occurred a mile farther back."
>
> The pain of my possibly having hurt someone is now so intense that I have no choice—I really see it this way.

obsessions
uncontrollable, persistent thoughts, images, ideas, or impulses that an individual feels intrude upon his or her consciousness and that cause significant anxiety or distress

compulsions
repetitive behaviors or mental acts that the individual feels he or she must perform

I turn the car around a second time and head an extra mile farther down the road to find the corpse. I drive by quickly. Assured that this time I've gone far enough I head back to school to take my exam. But I'm not through yet.

"My God," my attack relentlessly continues, "I didn't get *out* of the car to actually *look* on the side of the road!"

So I turn back a third time. I drive to the part of the highway where I think the accident happened. I park the car on the highway's shoulder. I get out and begin rummaging around the brush.

This man's compulsive checking makes some sense given what he is thinking. However, what he is thinking—that he hit someone on the road without knowing it—is highly improbable. The compulsive checking quells obsessional thoughts briefly, but the obsessional thoughts come back with even more force.

Often, the link between the obsession and compulsion is the result of "magical thinking," as in Sam's feeling that if he found the word *life* he would offset the effects of seeing the word *death*. Similarly, many people with OCD feel compelled to repeat a behavior, a ritual, or a thought a certain number of times, as if there were something magical about the specific number of repetitions. Their rituals often become stereotyped and rigid, and they develop obsessions and compulsions about not performing the rituals correctly. For example, one young woman with obsessions about hurting others had a prayer that she felt compelled to say in order to absolve herself from guilt for having had the obsessional thought. Over time, this developed into a ritual of saying the prayer in multiples of six. If she made even one mistake in this series of six prayers, she had to start over again from the beginning and this time say the prayer 12 times. If she made another mistake, she had to start from the beginning and say the prayer 18 times. Some nights this young woman was up all night trying to get her prayer ritual correct before she could go to bed.

At times, there is no discernible link between the specific obsession a person has and the specific compulsion that helps to dispel the obsession. Recall that Zach engaged in several behaviors, such as touching the floor or touching his shoulders to his chin, when he had an obsession about losing his saliva. He could not even say how these behaviors were related to his obsession; he just knew he had to engage in them. Thus, although compulsions may often seem purposeful, they are not functional.

People with obsessional thoughts about hurting others may fear hitting a person with their car, even if they are miles away from anyone.

People with OCD know that their obsessions and compulsions are irrational, but they feel they cannot stop them. Do you have any thoughts or habits that you know are irrational but that you feel you cannot stop?

OCD often begins when the person is at a young age; the peak age of onset for males is between 6 and 15 years of age, and for females it is between 20 and 29 years of age (APA, 1994; Rasmussen & Eisen, 1990). It tends to be a chronic disorder if left untreated. As the case histories have illustrated, obsessional thoughts are very distressing to people with OCD, and engaging in compulsive behaviors can take a great deal of time and even be dangerous (for example, washing your hands so often that they bleed). As many as 66 percent of people with OCD are also significantly depressed (Edelmann, 1992). Panic attacks, phobias, and substance abuse are also common in OCD.

Estimates of the lifetime prevalence of OCD range from 1.0 to 2.5 percent (Karno & Golding, 1991; Robins et al., 1984). In the United States, whites show a higher prevalence of OCD than do African Americans or Hispanic Americans (Karno & Golding, 1991). The prevalence of OCD does not seem to differ greatly across countries that have been studied, including the United States, Canada, Mexico, England, Norway, Hong Kong, India, Egypt, Japan, and Korea (Escobar, 1993; Insel, 1984; Kim, 1993). Although some studies have found slightly higher rates of OCD in women than in men, there does not appear to be a large or consistent gender difference in OCD (Edelmann, 1992; Karno & Golding, 1991; Rasmussen & Tsuang, 1984, 1986).

Biological Theories of OCD

Some of the most promising research on obsessive compulsive disorder views it as a neurological disorder. Much of this research has focused on a circuit in the brain that is involved in the execution of primitive patterns of behavior, such as aggression, sexuality, and bodily excretion (Baxter et al., 1992; Rapaport, 1990; Swedo et al., 1992). This circuit begins in the orbital region of the frontal cortex, where these impulses arise. These impulses are then carried to a part of the basal ganglia called the *caudate nucleus*, which allows only the strongest of these impulses to carry through to the thalamus. If these impulses reach the thalamus, the person is motivated to think further about and possibly act on these impulses. The action might involve a set of stereotyped behaviors appropriate to the impulse. Once these behaviors are executed, the impulse diminishes. For people with OCD, however, dysfunction in this circuit may result in the inability of the system to turn off these primitive impulses or to turn off the execution of the stereotyped behaviors once they are engaged. For example, most of us when we have the thought that we are dirty will engage in a fairly stereotyped form of cleansing: We wash our hands. People with OCD, however, continue to have the impulse to wash their hands because their brains do not shut off their thoughts about dirt or their behavior when the behavior is no longer necessary. Proponents of this theory have pointed out that many of the obsessions and compulsions of people with OCD have to do with contamination, sex, aggression, and the repetition of patterns of behavior—all issues with which this primitive brain circuit deals.

PET scans of people with OCD show more activity in the areas of the brain involved in this primitive circuit than in people without OCD (Baxter et al., 1990). In addition, people with OCD often get some relief from their symptoms when they take drugs that better regulate the neurotransmitter serotonin; serotonin plays an important role in the proper functioning of this primitive circuit in the brain (Rapaport, 1991). Finally, OCD patients who do respond to serotonin-enhancing drugs tend to show more reductions in the rate of activity in these brain areas than do OCD patients who do not respond well to these drugs (Baxter et al., 1992; Swedo et al., 1992).

Piecing these studies together, researchers have argued that people with OCD have a fundamental dysfunction in the areas of the brain regulating primitive impulses, perhaps due to a functional depletion of serotonin in these systems. As a result, primitive impulses about sex, aggression, and cleanliness break through to their consciousness and motivate the execution of stereotyped behaviors much more often than in people without OCD (Rapaport, 1989, 1991). For now, this theory is mostly just a theory. More evidence is needed for each of the pieces of the theory.

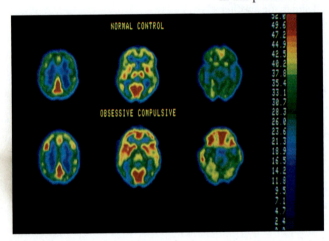

PET scans of people with OCD show more activity in the frontal cortex, basal ganglia, and thalamus than do PET scans of people without OCD.

Psychodynamic Theories of OCD

Psychodynamic theorists suggest that the particular obsessions and compulsions of people with OCD are symbolic of unconscious conflicts that they are guarding against (Freud, 1909). These conflicts create such anxiety for people that they can only confront them indirectly, by displacing the anxiety created by the conflict onto some other more acceptable thought or behavior. The case of Brenda illustrates how OCD might develop, according to psychodynamic theory:

Case Study • Brenda was about 9 years old when her obsessive thoughts and compulsive behaviors began. She had always been a somewhat emotional child, easily becoming anxious when she had to be away from her family for more than a day or so and becoming quite depressed when she did not do as well in school or in sports as she wanted to. When she was 9, Brenda's parents told her they were going to divorce. She had known that her parents fought a lot, but the announcement of the divorce came as a complete surprise.

It also came as a surprise to Brenda that she began to have "bad thoughts," often having to do with someone being hurt. For example, she would see a knife on the kitchen table, and she would have an image of the knife stabbing her brother. Or she would see one of her classmates playing on a swing set and have the thought, "She's going to fall off and die." Brenda felt very guilty for having these thoughts and she worried greatly about the safety of the people in her thoughts. She would say a prayer when she had these thoughts, asking God for forgiveness and to protect the person who was the target of her thoughts. She often did not feel that the prayers "worked" to absolve her of her guilt, however, and she would say the same prayer again, trying this time to feel more contrite as she said the prayer.

She also began having thoughts about germs and disease. She felt almost sick to her stomach if she touched something she felt was contaminated with germs. She would wash her hands many times per day, with extra-strong soap, until eventually her hands cracked and bled. Having open sores on her hands only made her feel more vulnerable to germs, however, and she would wash that much more to rid herself of the invisible germs. Brenda began avoiding situations that she thought would offer an opportunity for contamination, such as playing outdoors or playing with toys that had been touched by other children. She became more isolated from her peers, more withdrawn, and more clinging to her mother.

According to psychodynamic theory, Brenda's obsessions about others being hurt reflected her anger against her parents for splitting up and her desire to hurt her parents for hurting her. Especially because she was a rather dependent, emotional child, Brenda was terrified of her desire to hurt her parents, on whom she was so dependent. Thus, she unconsciously transformed this desire to hurt her parents into a fear that others would be hurt. Her need to be forgiven for thoughts about others being hurt and her obsession with being contaminated and dirty reflected the terrible guilt Brenda experienced over her desire to hurt her parents.

Psychodynamic theory offers an interesting account of both the development of OCD and the specific content of people's obsessions and compulsions. According to this theory, the reason that so many obsessions and compulsions have to do with contamination, sex, and aggression is that unconscious conflicts have to do with sexual and aggressive impulses. Psychodynamic theory suggests that the way to cure people of their OCD is to help them gain insight into the conflicts their obsessions and compulsions symbolize and better resolve these conflicts. This type of therapy actually helped Brenda. When she recognized her anger against her parents and found appropriate ways of expressing that anger, her obsessions and compulsions subsided. Psychodynamic therapy generally is not considered effective for the majority of OCD patients, however.

Cognitive-Behavioral Theories of OCD

It is clear that most people, including people who do *not* have OCD, occasionally have negative, intrusive thoughts. For example, one study found that 84 percent of normal subjects reported sometimes having repetitive, intrusive thoughts (Rachman & deSilva, 1978). People are more prone to have negative, intrusive thoughts and to engage in rigid, ritualistic behaviors when they are distressed (Clark & Purdon, 1993; Rachman & Hodgson, 1980). For example, many new mothers, exhausted from sleep deprivation and the stresses of caring for a newborn, have thoughts about harming their newborn, even though they are horrified by such thoughts and would never carry them out.

According to the cognitive-behavioral theories of OCD, what differentiates people with OCD from people without the disorder is the ability to turn off these negative, intrusive thoughts (Clark, 1988; Rachman & Hodgson, 1980). People who do not develop

OCD are able to turn off their intrusive thoughts by ignoring or dismissing them, attributing them to their distress, and simply letting them subside with the passage of time. People who develop OCD have trouble turning off their thoughts, for several reasons. First, they may be depressed or generally anxious much of the time, so that even minor negative events are more likely to have intrusive, negative thoughts (Clark & Purdon, 1993). Second, people with OCD may have a tendency toward rigid, moralistic thinking (Rachman, 1993; Salkovskis, 1989). They judge the negative, intrusive thoughts they have as more unacceptable than most people would and become more anxious and guilty over having these thoughts. This anxiety then makes it even harder for them to dismiss the thoughts (Clark & deSilva, 1985). In addition, people who feel more responsible for events that happen in their lives and in the lives of others than other people do will have more trouble dismissing thoughts like, "Did I hit someone on the road?", and thus might be more likely to develop OCD. Third, people with OCD appear to believe that they *should* be able to control all thoughts, and have trouble accepting that everyone has horrific thoughts from time to time (Clark & Purdon, 1993; Freeston et al., 1992). They tend to believe that having these thoughts means they are going crazy or they equate having the thoughts with actually engaging in the behaviors (e.g., "If I'm thinking about hurting my child, I'm as guilty as if I actually did hurt my child"). Of course, this just makes them that much more anxious when they have the thoughts, which makes it harder for them to dismiss the thoughts.

How do compulsions develop, according to this theory? They develop largely through operant conditioning. People with anxiety-provoking obsessions discover that if they engage in certain behaviors, their anxiety is reduced. The reduction in anxiety reinforces the behaviors. Each time the obsessions return and they use the behaviors to reduce the obsessions, the behaviors are reinforced. Compulsions are born.

As with the biological theory of OCD, research has supported pieces of the cognitive-behavioral view of OCD, but much more research needs to be done. In particular, because almost all studies investigating the biological and cognitive-behavioral theories of OCD have compared people who already have OCD with those who do not, it is not clear whether the dysfunctions these theories point to are the causes or the consequences of OCD.

Treatment of OCD

Until the 1980s, there were few effective biological treatments for OCD. The antianxiety drugs, the benzodiazepines, were not useful in most cases of OCD, which is one clue that OCD is not like the other anxiety disorders. Then, fortuitously, it was discovered that certain new antidepressant drugs, especially clomipramine (trade name Anafranil) and fluoxetine (trade name Prozac) helped to relieve symptoms of OCD in many patients (Rapaport, 1989, 1991). Controlled studies suggest that 50 to 80 percent of OCD patients experience decreases in their obsessions and compulsions when on these drugs, compared to only 5 percent of patients on placebos (Jenike, 1992; Orloff et al., 1994). These drugs may work by inhibiting the reuptake of the neurotransmitter serotonin, increasing the functional levels of serotonin in the brain. Recall that the latest biological theories of OCD suggest that this disorder involves dysfunctioning of areas of the brain rich in serotonin.

These drugs are not the complete answer for people with OCD, however. Even among people who respond to the drug, obsessions and compulsions are only reduced by about 40 or 50 percent, and they tend to relapse if the drugs are discontinued (De-Veaugh-Geiss et al., 1992; Michelson & Marchione, 1991). The drugs have significant side effects, including drowsiness, constipation, and loss of sexual interest, that prevent many people from taking them. Many clinicians believe that the drugs must be combined with cognitive-behavioral therapies in order to help people recover completely from OCD.

The cognitive-behavioral therapies for OCD focus on repeatedly exposing the client to the focus of the obsession and preventing compulsive responses to the anxiety aroused by the obsession (Rachman & Hodgson, 1980; Marks & Swinson, 1992). The repeated exposure to the content of the obsession is thought to habituate the client to obsession so that it does not arouse as much anxiety as it formerly did. Preventing the person from engaging in compulsive behavior allows this habituation to take place. In addition, the person comes to learn that not engaging in the compulsive behavior does not lead to a terrible result.

To implement this repeated exposure and response prevention, the therapist might first model the behavior he wants the client to practice. For example, if the client has an obsession about contamination and a washing compulsion, the therapist might model rubbing dirt on his hands and then not wash his hands during the therapy session. At the next session, the therapist might again rub dirt on his hands but this time encourage the client to get her hands dirty as well. As the client's compulsion to wash her hands grows, the therapist encourages her not to do so but sits with her and uses relaxation techniques to control her anxiety. After several such sessions, the client may be able to sit with dirty hands without feeling anxious and to control her washing compulsion herself.

The client may also be given homework assignments that help to confront her obsession. For example, early in therapy, she might be assigned to simply refrain from cleaning the house every day of the week, as she normally does, and only clean it every three days. Later in therapy, she might be assigned to drop a cookie on a dirty kitchen floor, and then pick it up and eat it or drop the kitchen knives on the floor, and then use them to prepare food (Emmelkamp, 1982).

These behavioral therapies have been shown to lead to significant improvement in obsessions and compulsive behavior in 60 to 90 percent of OCD clients (Fals-Stewart, Marks, & Schafer, 1993; Marks & Swinson, 1992). Moreover, these improvements are maintained in most clients over periods of up to 6 years (Foa & Kozak, 1993; Marks & Swinson, 1992). Unfortunately, however, this therapy does not tend to eliminate all obsessions and compulsions in OCD patients; in addition, a substantial minority are not helped at all by the therapy. Thus, there remains much work to be done to find a universally and completely effective therapy for OCD. The treatments available now, however, are great improvements over what was available only a few years ago.

 Family members and friends of people with OCD often tell them to just stop their obsessions and compulsions, but this seldom helps. If you had a friend with OCD, how might you respond to him or her?

Summing Up Obsessive-Compulsive Disorder

- Obsessions are thoughts, images, ideas, or impulses that are persistent, are intrusive, and cause distress, and they commonly focus on contamination, sex, violence, and repeated doubts.
- Compulsions are repetitive behaviors or mental acts that the individual feels he or she must perform to somehow erase his or her obsessions.
- Biological theories of OCD speculate that areas of the brain involved in the execution of primitive patterns of behavior, such as washing rituals, may be impaired in people with OCD.
- These areas of the brain are rich in the neurotransmitter serotonin, and drugs that regulate serotonin have proven helpful in the treatment of OCD.
- Psychodynamic theories of OCD suggest that the obsessions and compulsions symbolize unconscious conflict or impulses and that the proper therapy for OCD involves uncovering these unconscious thoughts.
- Cognitive-behavioral theories suggest that people with OCD are chronically distressed, think in rigid and moralistic ways, judge negative thoughts as more acceptable than other people do, and feel more responsible for their thoughts and behaviors. This makes them unable to turn off the negative, intrusive thoughts that most people have occasionally.
- Compulsive behaviors develop through operant conditioning; people are reinforced for compulsive behaviors by the fact that they reduce anxiety.

Biology is clearly involved in the experience of anxiety. Evolution has prepared our bodies to respond to threatening situations with physiological changes that make it easier for us to flee from or fight an attacker. For some people, this natural physiological response may be impaired, leading to chronic arousal, to overreactivity, or to poorly regulated arousal. These people may be more prone to severe anxiety reactions to threatening stimuli and to the anxiety disorders.

Psychological and social factors also clearly play a role in anxiety and the anxiety disorders. People differ in what they perceive as threatening, and these differences in perceptions lead to differences in the level of anxiety people fear when faced with potentially threatening situations. These differences in perceptions may be due to upbringing, as in the case of the child who develops a phobia of dogs because her mother modeled a fearful response to dogs or of the child who is chronically anxious and believes he must be perfect because his parents punish him severely if he makes any type of mistake. Differences in perceptions of what is threatening may also be due to specific traumatic experiences that some people have suffered.

Some of the most successful models of the anxiety disorders are vulnerability-stress models. These models stipulate that a person who will develop an anxiety disorder must have an underlying vulnerability to anxiety, in the form of a poorly regulated autonomic nervous system; chronic, mild anxiety or depression; or a genetic predisposition. For the disorder to develop, the person must also have a tendency to catastrophize situations and his or her own emotional reactions to those situations, to think in absolutist, perfectionist ways, and to be hypervigilant for signs of threat. In the case of PTSD and perhaps phobias, the person must also have experienced a traumatic event. These vulnerability-stress models go far in explaining why some people but not others experience anxiety that is so severe and chronic that it develops into a disorder.

Chapter Summary

There are four types of symptoms of anxiety: physiological or somatic symptoms, emotional symptoms, cognitive symptoms, and behavioral symptoms.

A panic attack is a short, intense experience of several of the physiological symptoms of anxiety, plus cognitions that one is going crazy, losing control, or dying. The diagnosis of panic disorder is given when a person has spontaneous panic attacks frequently, begins to worry about having attacks, and changes ways of living as a result of this worry. About one-third to one-half of people diagnosed with panic disorder also develop agoraphobia. People with agoraphobia fear places from which they might have trouble escaping or where they might have trouble getting help if they should have a panic attack.

One biological theory of panic disorder is that these people have overreactive autonomic nervous systems that put them into a full fight-or-flight response with little provocation. There also is some evidence that panic disorder may be transmitted genetically.

Psychological theories of panic suggest that people who suffer from panic disorder pay very close attention to their bodily sensations, misinterpret bodily sensations in a negative way, and engage in snowballing, catastrophic thinking. This thinking then increases physiological activation, and a full panic attack ensues. Agoraphobia develops when people with panic attacks learn that anxiety is reduced when they remain in "safe" places, and thus the behavior of remaining in these safe places is reinforced.

Antidepressants and benzodiazepines have been effective in reducing panic attacks and agoraphobic behavior, but people tend to relapse into these disorders when they discontinue these drugs. An effective cognitive-behavioral therapy has been developed for panic and agoraphobia. Clients are taught relaxation exercises and then learn to identify and challenge their catastrophic styles of thinking, often while having panic attacks induced in the therapy sessions. Systematic desensitization techniques are used to reduce agoraphobic behavior.

The specific phobias involve fears of specific objects or situations, and most fall into one of four categories: animal type, natural environment type, situational type, and blood-injection-injury type. Social phobia involves fears of being judged or embarrassed.

Freud argued that phobias symbolize unconscious conflicts and fears that have been displaced onto neutral objects. There has been little support for this theory or for psychoanalytic treatment of phobias. Behavioral theories suggest that phobias develop through classical and operant conditioning. The phobic object is a conditioned stimulus that, at some time in the past, was paired with an unconditioned stimulus that elicited fear, leading a person to develop a conditioned response of fear to the phobic object. This fear is maintained because, through operant conditioning, the person has learned that if she avoids the phobic object, her fear is reduced. Phobias can also develop through observational learning. Finally, it appears that through prepared classical conditioning humans develop phobias more readily to objects that our distant ancestors had reason to fear, such as snakes and spiders.

Behavioral treatments focus on extinguishing fear responses to phobic objects and have proven quite effective. People with blood-injection-injury phobias must also learn to tense up when they confront their phobic objects to prevent the decreases in blood pressure and heart rate they experience. Drug therapies have not proven useful for phobias.

Post-traumatic stress disorder occurs after a person experiences a severe trauma. It involves three types of symptoms: first, repeatedly reexperiencing the traumatic event, through intrusive images or thoughts, recurring nightmares, flashbacks, and psychological and physiological reactivity to stimuli that remind the person of the event; second, withdrawal, emotional numbing, and avoidance of anything that might arouse memories of the event; third, hypervigilance and chronic arousal. In addition to having these symptoms, PTSD sufferers report survival guilt.

Traumatic events can shatter people's assumptions that they are invulnerable, that the world is a meaningful and just place, and that they are good people. The more severe and long-lasting a trauma and the more involved a person is in the trauma, the more likely he or she is to show PTSD. People who have lower levels of social support, who experience socially stigmatizing traumas, and who are already depressed or anxious before a trauma may have an increased risk for PTSD. People who have maladaptive, ruminative coping styles may be at increased risk for PTSD. Finally, people who are unable to somehow make sense of a trauma appear more likely to have chronic PTSD symptoms.

The most effective treatment for PTSD involves exposing a person to his or her memories of a trauma, through systematic desensitization and flooding, to extinguish his or her anxiety over these memories. Some people cannot tolerate such exposure, however, and may do better with supportive therapy focused on solving current interpersonal difficulties and life problems. Benzodiazepines and antidepressant drugs can quell some of the symptoms of PTSD, but these symptoms tend to recur when the drugs are discontinued.

People with generalized anxiety disorder are chronically anxious in most situations. People with GAD appear more vigilant for threatening information, even on an unconscious level. Benzodiazepines can produce short-term relief for some people with GAD but have not proven effective in the long-term treatment of GAD. Cognitive-behavioral therapies focus on changing the catastrophic thinking styles of people with GAD.

Women have higher rates of almost all the anxiety disorders than do men. Women may carry a greater genetic vulnerability to anxiety disorders or may experience dysregulation in the neurotransmitters involved in anxiety with changes in their hormone levels. Psychosocial theories of women's greater vulnerability to anxiety are that women are chronically anxious because they fear separation from others or because they truly are in greater danger of sexual or physical abuse than are men. Another theory is that men are punished for exhibiting signs of anxiety whereas women are not, so men cope with their anxiety through adaptive or maladaptive activities, whereas women go on to develop anxiety disorders.

There are cross-cultural differences in the manifestation and conceptualization of anxiety, which must be taken into account when treating people of different cultures. Disadvantaged persons may be more prone to anxiety disorders because the chronic stress they live under leaves them vulnerable. In addition, those who lack social support are more vulnerable to anxiety disorders.

People with obsessive-compulsive disorder experience anxiety when they have obsessions and when they cannot carry out their compulsions. Obsessions are thoughts, images, ideas, or impulses that are persistent, are intrusive, and cause distress. Common obsessions focus on contamination, sex, violence, impulses to do something outside one's moral code, and repeated doubts. Compulsions are repetitive behaviors or mental acts that individuals feel they must perform and that are meant to somehow erase their obsessions. Washing, checking, counting, and stereotyped behavior patterns are common forms of compulsion. OCD is somewhat more common in whites than in African Americans or Hispanic Americans, but there is remarkable consistency across cultures in the prevalence and content of obsessions and compulsions.

One theory of OCD speculates that areas of the brain involved in the execution of primitive patterns of behavior, such as washing rituals, may be impaired in people with OCD. These areas of the brain are rich in the neurotransmitter serotonin, and drugs that regulate serotonin have proven helpful in the treatment of OCD.

Psychodynamic theories of OCD suggest that the obsessions and compulsions symbolize unconscious conflicts or impulses. Psychodynamic therapy, which focuses on helping clients gain insight into these unconscious conflicts or impulses, does not tend to be highly effective with OCD, however.

Cognitive-behavioral theories suggest that people with OCD are chronically distressed, think in rigid and moralistic ways, judge negative thoughts as more acceptable than other people do, and feel more responsible for their thoughts and behaviors. This makes them unable to turn off the negative, intrusive thoughts that most people have occasionally. Compulsive behaviors develop through operant conditioning; people are reinforced for behaviors by the fact that they reduce anxiety.

The most effective drug therapies for OCD are the antidepressants known as serotonin reuptake inhibitors. Cognitive-behavioral therapies have also proven helpful for OCD. These therapies expose OCD clients to the content of their obsessions while preventing compulsive behavior; the anxiety over the obsessions and the compulsions to do the behaviors are extinguished. Unfortunately, neither the drug therapies nor the cognitive-behavioral therapies tend to eliminate the obsessions and compulsions completely. The relapse rate with the drug therapies is high once the drugs are discontinued. Cognitive-behavioral therapies are better at preventing relapse.

Key Terms

fight-or-flight
   response 108
panic attacks 110
panic disorder 111
agoraphobia 111
autonomic nervous
   system 113

sympathetic nervous
   system 113
parasympathetic
   nervous system 113
suffocation false alarm
   theory 113
limbic system 114

brain stem 114
cortex 114
serotonin 114
norepinephrine 114
safety signal
   hypothesis 115

Application   Relaxation Exercises

We have discussed that therapists teach clients with anxiety disorders to use relaxation exercises to quell their anxiety. These exercises can also be used to combat the everyday anxiety and the tension associated with anger that arises in most people's lives. Here are a few exercises that you can use when you feel tense or anxious (taken from Rimm & Masters, 1979; Schafer, 1992).

Six-Second Quieting Response

This is a simple breathing technique that you can use very quickly (it only takes 6 seconds!) and in almost any situation to relax when you feel anxious or angry.

1. Draw a long, deep breath.
2. Hold it for 2 or 3 seconds.
3. Exhale slowly and completely.
4. As you exhale, let your jaw and shoulders drop. Feel relaxation flow into your arms and hands.

Quick Head, Neck, and Shoulder Relaxers

The remainder of the exercises we will describe involve tensing or stretching certain muscles. If you have had a significant injury, such as whiplash or an injured back, you should not try these exercises without first consulting your physician or physical therapist.

Some of the muscles that most commonly tense up when we are anxious or angry are the neck and shoulder muscles. A quick way to release some of this tension is to first tighten the neck and shoulder muscles as much as possible, then hold this for 5 to 10 seconds. Then completely release the muscles. Repeat this a number of times, focusing on the contrast between the tension and the relaxation.

You can also release some neck and shoulder tension by gently rotating your shoulders first forward and then backward. You can also gently rotate your head from side to side and from front to back in a circular motion. Then repeat the movements in the opposite direction. Continue this exercise a number of times until you feel more relaxed. Perform this exercise very slowly and gently or you may strain neck muscles.

The muscles on the forehead are also tensed when you are anxious or angry, and your teeth may be clenched. To relax your forehead, lift your eyebrows gently and release lines of tension or fatigue. Then relax your forehead as you use the breathing exercise described. Check to see if your teeth are clenched and, if so, relax your jaw while breathing deeply and slowly.

Progressive Muscle Relaxation

Progressive muscle relaxation is a set of techniques for successively tensing and then relaxing voluntary muscles in an orderly sequence until all the muscles are relaxed. Before beginning this exercise, you should get as comfortable as possible, sitting down, with any tight clothing loosened. You might also want to begin by using the Six-Second Quieting Response described to start you down the path to relaxation.

Go through each of the next steps in the order given. Spend 10 seconds tensing each muscle group, and then at least 10 to 15 seconds relaxing. Repeat the 10 seconds of tensing that muscle group, followed by another 10 to 15 second relaxing. During the relaxation period, focus on the positive sensations of relaxation and try not to worry about anything else. If you feel that muscle group has relaxed sufficiently, move on to the next one. As you progress through the muscle groups, concentrate hard on tensing only the muscle group you are working on in that step. Try not to let any of the other muscle groups, particularly the ones you have already tensed and relaxed, to be tensed again (the following progression is taken from Rimm & Masters, 1979):

1. *Hands*. Tense your fists, and then relax them. Then extend your fingers as far as possible, and then relax them.
2. *Biceps and Triceps*. Tense your biceps, and then relax. Tense your triceps, and then relax.
3. *Shoulders*. Pull your shoulders back, and then relax. Push your shoulders forward, and then relax.
4. *Neck*. Slowly roll your head on your neck's axis three or four times in one direction, and then in the opposite direction.
5. *Mouth*. Open your mouth as wide as possible, and then relax. Purse your lips in an exaggerated pout, and then relax.
6. *Tongue*. With your mouth open, extend your tongue as far as possible, and then relax. Next, bring your tongue back into

your throat as far as possible, and then relax. Next, dig your tongue into the roof of your mouth as hard as possible, and then relax. Finally, dig your tonge into the floor of your mouth as hard as possible, and then relax.

7. *Eyes and Forehead*. Close your eyes and imagine your are looking at something pleasant far away. Focus your eyes so that you can see and enjoy the distant object. Continue this for about 1 minute.

8. *Breathing*. Take as deep a breath as possible, and then relax.

9. *Back*. With your shoulders resting against a chair, push the trunk of your body forward so as to arch your entire back, and then relax. Do this very slowly, and if you experience any pain, relax immediately and do not repeat this exercise.

10. *Midsection*. Raise your midsection slightly by tensing your buttocks, and then relax. Lower your midsection slightly by digging your buttocks into the seat of your chair, and then relax.

11. *Thighs*. Extend and raise your legs about 6 inches off the floor, trying not to tense your stomach muscles, and then relax. Dig your heels or the back of your feet into the floor, and then relax.

12. *Stomach*. Pull your stomach in as hard as possible, and then relax. Extend your stomach out as much as possible, and then relax.

13. *Calves and feet*. Support your legs, and bend your feet so that your toes are pointed toward your head, and then relax. Next, bend your feet in the opposite direction, and then relax. If your muscles should cramp during this exercise, relax them and shake them loose.

14. *Toes*. With your legs supported and your feet relaxed, dig your toes into the bottom of your shoes, and then relax. Then bend your toes in the opposite direction until they dig into the tops of your shoes, and then relax.

15. *Breathing*. Breathe slowly and deeply for 2 to 3 minutes. Each time you exhale, say the word *calm* to yourself. ∎

chapter 5 Mood Disorders

Unipolar Depressive Disorders

People with unipolar depression experience sadness, loss of interest in their usual activities, changes in sleep and activity levels, and thoughts of worthlessness, hopelessness, and suicide. The several subtypes of unipolar depression have features that distinguish them, including different symptoms and associations with different times of life. Women are more prone to depression than are men, but perhaps surprisingly, older adults seem at lower risk for depression than do younger adults. There are ethnic and cultural differences both in the rates and the presentation of depression. Depression lasts longer and the risk of relapse is greater than was formerly believed.

Bipolar Disorder

People with bipolar disorder experience both periods of depression and periods of mania, during which their mood is elevated or irritable, and they have great energy and self-esteem. Bipolar disorder is much less common than is unipolar depression, and it presents fewer gender and cultural differences. Many important political leaders, artists, and writers have suffered from bipolar disorder. The manifestation of mania can vary substantially across cultures.

Biological Theories of Mood Disorders

There clearly is a heritable component to bipolar disorder, but the evidence is less clear for unipolar depression. Biochemical theories suggest that imbalances in certain neurotransmitters or malfunctioning of receptors for these neurotransmitters contribute to mood disorders. Depressed people show chronic hyperactivity of the system in the body that regulates stress responses. They also show disturbances in sleep patterns and on neuroimaging scans.

Biological Therapies for Mood Disorders

Lithium is useful in the treatment of mood disorders but requires careful monitoring to prevent dangerous side effects. Anticonvulsants, antipsychotics, and calcium channel blockers are also used to treat mania. Tricyclic antidepressants, monoamine oxidase inhibitors, and selective serotonin reuptake inhibitors are all effective in the treatment of depression, although they carry significant side effects. Electroconvulsive therapy is also used to treat serious depressions. Finally, exposure to high intensity lights is an effective therapy for people with a seasonal form of mood disorder.

Psychosocial Theories of Mood Disorders

Chronic, uncontrollable stress may lead some people to feel helpless and become depressed. Cognitive theories suggest that depressed people interpret stressful experiences in negative and distorted ways, also contributing to their depression. Other research suggests, however, that depressed people are actually more realistic about life than are nondepressed people. Psychodynamic theories describe depression as anger turned inward on the self.

Psychosocial Therapies for Depression

Cognitive-behavioral therapies attempt to change depressive thinking and increase behavioral skills. Interpersonal therapy focuses on changing dysfunctional relationships in the lives of depressed people. Comparisons of these two psychosocial therapies and drug therapies show that they are equally effective for most depressions.

The Gender Differences in Depression

Biological theories attribute women's greater vulnerability to depression to hormones, but they have not been strongly supported. Personality explanations suggest that women are more dependent on others and have a more ruminative coping style than do men and these characteristics contribute to their depression. Social theorists argue that women lead more uncontrollable and powerless lives and this contributes to their depression.

Suicide

Sociological theories suggest that various forces within society lead individuals to believe suicide is a rational choice. Psychological factors involved in suicide include hopelessness and substance abuse. Biological theories suggest that low levels of serotonin lead to impulsive suicidal behavior.

Bio-Psycho-Social Integration
Chapter Summary
Key Terms
Application: *Practicing Two Types of Therapy with a Depressed Person*

How much pain have cost us the evils which have never happened.

—Thomas Jefferson, Letter to Thomas Jefferson Smith (February 21, 1825)

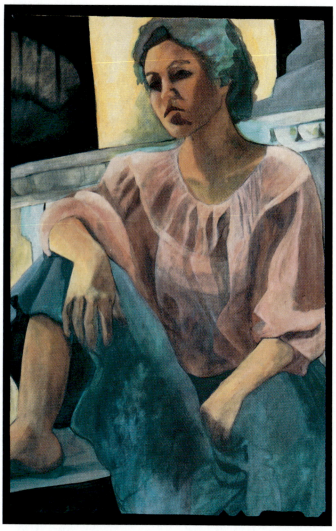

Hyacinth Manning-Carner
Watching from the Steps

I was a senior in high school when I had my first attack. . . . At first, everything seemed so easy. I raced about like a crazed weasel, bubbling with plans and enthusiasms, immersed in sports, and staying up all night, night after night, out with friends, reading everything that wasn't nailed down, filling manuscript books with poems and fragments of plays, and making expansive, completely unrealistic plans for my future. The world was filled with pleasure and promise; I felt great. Not just great, I felt *really* great. I felt I could do anything, that no task was too difficult. My mind seemed clear, fabulously focused, and able to make intuitive mathematical leaps that had up to that point entirely eluded me. Indeed, they elude me still. At the time, however, not only did everything make perfect sense, but it all began to fit into a marvelous kind of cosmic relatedness. My sense of enchantment with the laws of the natural world caused me to fizz over, and I found myself buttonholing my friends to tell them how beautiful it all was. They were less than transfixed by my insights into the webbings and beauties of the universe although considerably impressed at how exhausting it was to be around my enthusiastic ramblings: You're talking too fast, Kay. Slow down, Kay. You're wearing me out, Kay. Slow down, Kay. And those times when they didn't actually come out and say it, I still could see it in their eyes: For God's sake, Kay, slow down.

I did, finally, slow down. In fact, I came to a grinding halt. The bottom began to fall out of my life and my mind. My thinking, far from being clearer than a crystal, was tortuous. I would read the same passage over and over again only to realize that I had no memory at all for what I had just read. My mind had turned on me: It mocked me for my vapid enthusiasms; it laughed at all my foolish plans; it no longer found anything interesting or enjoyable or worthwhile. It was incapable of concentrated thought and turned time and again to the subject of death: I was going to die, what difference did anything make? Life's run was only a short and meaningless one; why live? I was totally exhausted and could scarcely pull myself out of bed in the mornings. It took me twice as long to walk anywhere as it ordinarily did, and I wore the same clothes over and over again, as it was otherwise too much of an effort to make a decision about what to put on. I dreaded having to talk with people, avoided my friends whenever possible, and sat in the school library in the early mornings and late afternoons, virtually inert, with a dead heart and a brain as cold as clay. (Jamison, 1995b, pp. 35–38)

bipolar disorder
disorder marked by cycles between manic episodes and depressive episodes; also called *manic-depression*

mania
state of persistently elevated mood, feelings of grandiosity, overenthusiasm, racing thoughts, rapid speech, and impulsive actions

depression
state marked by either a sad mood or a loss of interest in one's usual activities, as well as feelings of hopelessness, suicidal ideation, psychomotor agitation or retardation, and trouble concentrating

unipolar depression
type of depression consisting of depressive symptoms but without manic episodes

This emotional roller-coaster ride is known as **bipolar disorder** and also *manic depression.* The writer, Kay Jamison, eloquently describes both poles of this disorder. First, she has **mania**, with great energy and enthusiasm for everything, fizzing over with ideas, talking and thinking so fast that her friends cannot keep up with her. Eventually, though, she crashes into a **depression.** Her energy and enthusiasm are gone, and she is slow to think, to talk, to move. The joy has been drained from her life.

Bipolar disorder is one of the two major types of mood disorders. The other type is **unipolar depression.** People with unipolar depression experience only depression and no mania. In this chapter on the mood disorders, we will begin with a discussion of unipolar depression, one of the most common types of psychopathology. Then we will explore the essential features of mania and bipolar disorder.

We will move on to discuss the biological and psychosocial theories of the mood disorders, with a special focus on how these theories explain a startling fact: Women are twice as likely as men to develop depression. We will discuss the highly effective biological and psychosocial therapies for mood disorders that have been developed in recent decades. We will end with a discussion of one of the most troubling outcomes of the mood disorders: suicide.

The mood disorders have a tremendous impact on individuals and on society. In the United States alone, over $40 billion per year goes to cover health care costs for people with mood disorders and losses in their productivity (Goleman, 1993). Fortunately, however, effective treatments are available for most people who suffer from depression and mania, making it possible for these people to live productive lives. Kay Jamison is an excellent example. She is a professor in one of the United States' most prestigious medical schools and a leading researcher in the field of mood disorders.

Unipolar Depressive Disorders

From the time I woke up in the morning until the time I went to bed at night, I was unbearably miserable and seemingly incapable of any kind of joy or enthusiasm. Everything—every thought, word, movement—was an effort. Everything that once was sparkling now was flat. I seemed to myself to be dull, boring, inadequate, thick brained, unlit, unresponsive, chill skinned, bloodless, and sparrow drab. I doubted, completely, my ability to do anything well. It seemed as though my mind had slowed down and burned out to the point of being virtually useless. The wretched, convoluted, and pathetically confused mass of gray worked only well enough to torment me with a dreary litany of my inadequacies and shortcomings in character and to taunt me with the total, the desperate hopelessness of it all. (Jamison, 1995b, p. 110)

Depression takes over the whole person—emotions, bodily functions, behaviors, and thoughts. The most common emotion in depression is *sadness*. This sadness is not the garden-variety type that we all feel sometimes but a deep, unrelenting pain. In addition, many people diagnosed with depression report that they have lost interest in everything in life—a symptom referred to as *anhedonia*. Even when they try to do something enjoyable, they may feel no emotional reaction.

In depression, many bodily functions are disrupted—sleep, appetite, and sexual drive. Depressed people lose the motivation to care for themselves in even the most fundamental ways, as Sylvia Plath describes in *The Bell Jar* (1971):

I hadn't washed my hair for three weeks.

I hadn't slept for seven nights.

My mother told me I must have slept, it was impossible not to sleep in all that time, but if I slept, it was with my eyes wide open, for I had followed the green, luminous course of the second hand and the minute hand and the hour hand of the bedside clock through their circles and semicircles, every night for seven nights without missing a second, or a minute, or an hour.

It seemed silly to wash one day when I would only have to wash again the next. It made me tired just to think of it. (pp. 142–143)

The *changes in appetite, sleep, and activity levels* in depression can take many forms. Some depressed people lose their appetite, but others find themselves eating more, perhaps even binge eating. Some depressed people want to sleep all day. Others find it difficult to sleep and may experience a particular form of insomnia known as *early morning wakening*, as author William Styron describes:

My few hours of sleep were usually terminated at three or four in the morning, when I stared up into yawning darkness, wondering and writing at the devastation taking place in my mind, and awaiting the dawn. . . . (Styron, 1990, p. 49)

Behaviorally, many depressed people are slowed down, a condition known as *psychomotor retardation*. They walk more slowly, gesture more slowly, and perhaps talk more slowly and quietly. They may have more accidents because they cannot react to crises as quickly as necessary to avoid them. Many depressed people *lack energy* and report feeling chronically *fatigued*. A subset of depressed people have *psychomotor agitation* instead of retardation. They feel physically agitated, cannot sit still, and may move around or fidget aimlessly.

The thoughts of depressed people may be filled with themes of *worthlessness, guilt, hopelessness* and even *suicide*. They often have trouble concentrating and making decisions.

Fatigue and problems in concentration are two prominent symptoms in depression.

I seem to be in a perpetual fog and darkness. I cannot get my mind to work; instead of associations "clicking into place" everything is inextricable jumble; instead of seeming to grasp a whole, it seems to remain tied to the actual consciousness of the moment. The whole world of my thought is hopelessly divided into incomprehensible watertight compartments. I could not feel more ignorant, undecided, or inefficient. It is appallingly difficult to concentrate, and writing is a pain and grief to me. (Custance, 1952, p. 62)

Depression takes several forms (see Table 5.1). The DSM-IV recognizes two categories of unipolar depressive disorders: **major depression** and **dysthymic disorder**. The diagnosis of major depression requires that a person experience either depressed mood or loss of interest in usual activities plus at least four other symptoms of depression chronically for at least two weeks. In addition, these symptoms have to be severe enough to interfere with the person's ability to function in everyday life.

Dysthymic disorder is a less severe form of depressive disorder than major depression, but it is more chronic. To be diagnosed with dysthymic disorder, a person must be experiencing depressed mood plus two other symptoms of depression for at least *two years*. During these two years, the person must never have been without the symptoms of

major depression

disorder involving a sad mood or anhedonia, plus four or more of the following symptoms: weight loss or a decrease in appetite, insomnia or hypersomnia, psychomotor agitation or retardation, fatigue, feelings of worthlessness or severe guilt, trouble concentrating, and suicidal ideation; these symptoms must be present for at least two weeks and must produce marked impairments in normal functioning

dysthymic disorder

type of depression that is less severe than major depression but more chronic; diagnosis requires the presence of a sad mood or anhedonia, plus two other symptoms of depression, for at least two years during which symptoms do not remit for two months or longer

Table 5.1 Types of Mood Disorders in the DSM-IV

Unipolar Depressive Disorders

Major Depressive Disorder
Dysthymic Disorder
Premenstrual Dysphoric Disorder (provisional category)

Bipolar Disorders

Bipolar I
Bipolar II
Cyclothymic Disorder

Subtypes That Apply to Major Depression or to the Depressive Phase of Bipolar Disorder

with melancholic features
with atypical features

Subtypes That Apply to Major Depression or to the Depressive or Manic Phases of Bipolar Disorder

with psychotic features
with catatonic features
with postpartum onset
with seasonal onset

depression for more than a two-month period. Said one woman with dysthymic disorder, "It just goes on and on. I never feel really good, I always feel kind of bad, and it seems it's never going to end."

Some unfortunate people experience both major depression and dysthymic disorder. This has been referred to as **double depression**. People with double depression are chronically dysthymic, and then occasionally spike into episodes of major depression. As the major depression passes, however, they return to dysthymia rather than recover to a normal mood. As one might imagine, people with double depression are even more debilitated than are people with major depression or dysthymia alone. They also are less likely to respond to treatments.

Over half of the people diagnosed with major depression or dysthymia also have another psychological disorder. The most common disorders to co-occur with depression are substance abuse (for example, alcohol abuse), anxiety disorders such as panic disorder, and eating disorders (Blazer et al., 1994). Sometimes the depression precedes and perhaps causes the other disorder. Sometimes depression follows and may be the consequence of the other disorder.

Subtypes of Depression

There are several variations on depression—different forms the disorder can take (see Table 5.1). These subtypes apply both to major depression and to the depressive phase of a bipolar disorder.

First, in *depression with melancholic features*, the physiological symptoms of depression are particularly prominent. The diagnosis requires that the person show the inability to experience pleasure plus at least three of the following symptoms: distinct quality of depressed mood, depression that is regularly worse in the morning, early morning awakening, marked psychomotor retardation or agitation, significant anorexia or weight loss, and excessive or inappropriate guilt. Melancholic depressions are thought to be biologically caused rather than caused by environmental events or personality characteristics.

Second, there is *depression with psychotic features*, in which people experience delusions and hallucinations during a major depressive episode. **Delusions** are beliefs with no basis in reality, and **hallucinations** involve seeing, hearing, or feeling things that are not real. The delusions and hallucinations that depressed people experience usually are depressing and negative in content. For example, people have delusions that they have committed a terrible sin, that they are being punished, or that they have killed or hurt someone. They may have auditory hallucinations in which voices accuse them of having committed an atrocity or instructing them to kill themselves.

Third, people with *depression with catatonic features* show a variety of strange behaviors. They may develop **catalepsy**, a condition characterized by trancelike states and a waxy rigidity of the muscles, so that they tend to remain in any position in which they are placed. For example, if one positioned a cataleptic's arm in the air as if he were saying, "halt," he might leave his arm in that position for hours, until it was moved to another position. People in this third category may assume bizarre postures, it may be impossible to move them out of the postures. **Catatonia** can also involve excessive motor activity, such as fidgeting hands, foot tapping, rocking back and forth, and pacing, all without any apparent purpose. Sometimes these activities can be quite peculiar, involving repetitive stereotyped movements such as flapping of hands in the air, bizarre grimacing, or spasmodic imitation of others' behavior, apparently involuntarily. Finally, people with catatonia may show disturbances in their speech, becoming completely mute or only repeating what others say. Catatonia can occur in mania as well as depression; when it does, the diagnosis is Bipolar Disorder with Catatonic Features. It is interesting that catatonia was observed in patients more often in the early part of the twentieth century than it has been observed in the last 20 years. The reasons for this are unclear.

Fourth, there is *depression with atypical features*. The criteria for this subtype are an odd assortment of symptoms. To receive this diagnosis, the individual must show positive mood reactions to positive events and at least two of these four features: significant weight gain or increase in appetite, hypersomnia (sleeping 10 hours or more per day),

double depression
disorder involving a cycle between major depression and dysthymic disorder

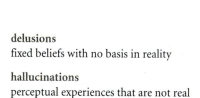

delusions
fixed beliefs with no basis in reality

hallucinations
perceptual experiences that are not real

catalepsy
condition characterized by trancelike states and a waxy rigidity of the muscles

catatonia
disorder of movement involving immobility or excited agitation, often accommpanied by speech disturbances

Some women experience serious depressions during the postpartum period, just after they have had a baby.

seasonal affective disorder (SAD) disorder identified by a two-year period in which a person experiences major depression during winter months and then recovers fully during the summer; some people with this disorder also experience mild mania during summer months

heavy or leaden feelings in the arms or legs, and a long-standing pattern of sensitivity to interpersonal rejection. Author Elizabeth Wurtzel, who vividly describes her own atypical depression in her book *Prozac Nation* (1995), comments:

> The atypically depressed are more likely to be the walking wounded, people like me who are quite functional, whose lives proceed almost as usual, except that they're depressed all the time, almost constantly embroiled in thoughts of suicide even as they go through their paces. Atypical depression is not just a mild malaise—which is known diagnostically as dysthymia—but one that is quite severe and yet still somehow allows an appearance of normalcy because it becomes, over time, a part of life. The trouble is that as the years pass, if untreated, atypical depression gets worse and worse, and its sufferers are likely to commit suicide out of sheer frustration with living a life that is simultaneously productive and clouded by constant despair. (p. 299)

The fifth subtype is *depression with postpartum onset.* This diagnosis is given to women when the onset of a major depressive episode occurs within four weeks of delivery of a child. More rarely, some women develop mania during the postpartum and are given the diagnosis of bipolar disorder with postpartum onset. It is important to distinguish between postpartum mood disorders and what is known as the postpartum blues. The most prominent symptoms of postpartum blues are emotional lability (unstable and quickly shifting moods), frequent crying, irritability, and fatigue. As many as 30 percent of women experience the postpartum blues. For most women, these symptoms are only annoying and pass completely within 2 weeks of the birth. The symptoms may be caused by the massive changes in hormone levels that occur in the first two weeks after birth. They may also be caused, in part, by sleep deprivation and the stress of having a newborn baby.

Women who are diagnosed with major depression with postpartum onset meet the full criteria for a major depressive disorder. This disorder is much less common than the postpartum blues, affecting about 13 percent of women (O'Hara & Swain, 1996). These women often feel very guilty for having depressive feelings, particularly negative feelings toward their baby, at a time when they believe they should be happy. Severe postpartum depression can interfere with a woman's ability to care for her baby and with the development of a positive emotional bond between mother and baby. In extremely rare cases (1 in 500 or 1 in 1,000 births), a woman with major depression with postpartum onset may become psychotic, having delusions that often involve the newborn infant—for example, the woman may believe that the newborn is possessed by the devil, has special powers, or is destined for a terrible fate. The hallucinations can be voices telling the woman to hurt the baby or herself, although again, this is extremely rare.

The diagnosis of postpartum depression is controversial, however. As we shall discuss later in this chapter, several studies suggest that women are at no higher risk for depression during the postpartum period than at other times of their lives (Whiffen & Gotlib, 1993). Those depressions that do occur postpartum do not seem to be qualitatively different from depressions that are not postpartum. Thus, many researchers have questioned the wisdom of singling out postpartum depression with a separate diagnosis and have suggested this pathologizes a normal part of women's lives (Whiffen, 1992).

The final subtype of major depressive disorder is *depression with seasonal pattern,* sometimes referred to as **seasonal affective disorder,** or **SAD.** People with SAD have a history of at least two years of experiencing major depressive episodes and fully recovering from them. The symptoms seem to be tied to the number of hours of daylight in a day. People become depressed when the daylight hours are short and recover when the daylight hours are long. In the northern hemisphere, this means people are depressed November through February and not depressed June through August. Some people with this disorder actually develop mild forms of mania or have full manic episodes during the summer months and are diagnosed with a bipolar disorders with seasonal patterns. In order to be diagnosed with seasonal affective disorder, a person's mood changes cannot be the result of environmental events, such as regularly being unemployed during the winter. Rather, the mood changes must seem to come on without reason or cause. This disorder is more common in latitudes where there are fewer hours of daylight in the winter months. In other words, people in Michigan and Minnesota are more prone to SAD than are people in Louisiana or Texas.

There is one other form of depressive disorder that is not officially included in the main body of the DSM-IV: **premenstrual dysphoric disorder**. Women with this disorder regularly experience increases in depressive symptoms during the premenstrual phase of the menstrual cycle and relief from the symptoms when they begin menstruating. This disorder is controversial for several reasons that we will discuss later in this chapter. The controversies around this disorder led the framers of the DSM-IV to put it in an appendix rather than include it as a recognized diagnosis. Their intention was to provide criteria for a diagnosis of the disorder that could organize future research on the disorder, without officially recognizing it as a disorder.

In summary, there are six recognized subtypes of major depressive disorder: with melancholia, with psychotic features, with catatonia, with atypical features, with postpartum onset, and with seasonal pattern. Each of these subtypes has certain symptoms that are especially prominent. In addition, premenstrual dysphoric disorder is a form of depression that is not officially recognized in the DSM-IV but is the focus of ongoing research.

premenstrual dysphoric disorder syndrome in which a woman experiences an increase in depressive symptoms during the premenstrual period and relief from these symptoms with the onset of menstruation

Gender and Age Differences in Depression

Depression is one of the most common psychological problems. At some time in their lives, 17 percent of Americans experience an episode of major depression, and 6 percent experience dysthymic disorder (Kessler et al., 1994). There are large gender differences and age differences in the prevalence of depression. Let us consider the gender differences first.

Most studies show that women are about twice as likely as men to experience both mild depressive symptoms and severe depressive disorders (Nolen-Hoeksema, 1990). This gender difference in depression has been found in many different countries, in most ethnic groups, and in all adult age groups (see Figure 5.1). Interestingly, children do not show this gender difference in depression, but around age 14 or 15, girls begin to show dramatic increases in their rates of depression, while boys' rates remain quite stable (Nolen-Hoeksema, 1990; Nolen-Hoeksema & Girgus, 1994). One might think that females are just more willing to admit to depression than males. However, the gender difference in depression is found even in studies that use relatively objective measures of depression that do not rely much on self-reports, such as clinicians' ratings of depression, or the reports of family members or friends. Later in the chapter, we will consider explanations for these gender differences.

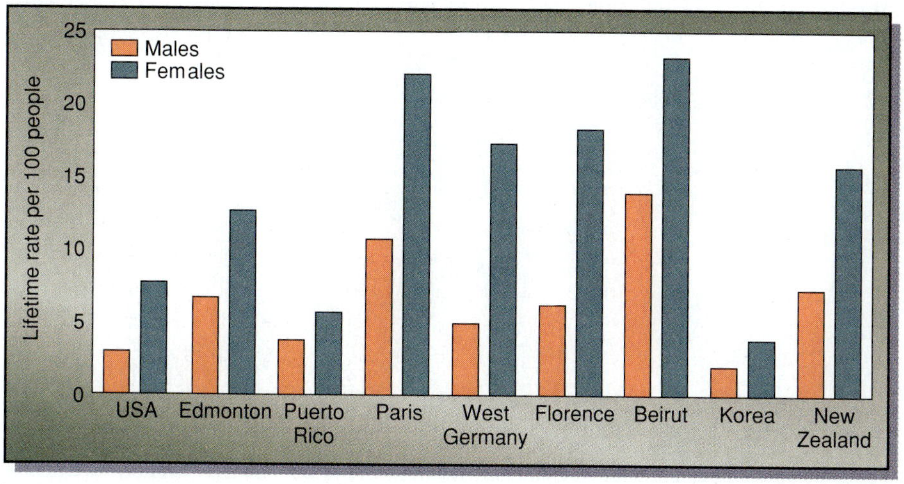

Figure 5.1

Gender Differences in Depression Across Cultures. Across many cultures, more women than men are diagnosed with major depression.
Source: Weissman & Olfson, 1995.

Figure 5.2

Age Differences in Depression. Shown are the percentages of people in each age group who were diagnosed with major depression in a one-month period. Those between 15 and 24 years old have the highest rates of depression and those between 45 and 54 years old have the lowest rates.

Source: Blazer et al., 1994.

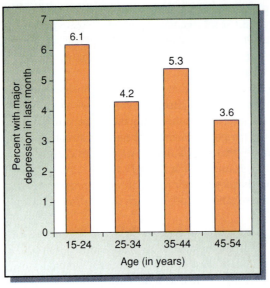

Age also plays a role in people's vulnerability to depression. Among adults, 15 to 24 year olds are most likely to have had a major depressive episode in the past month (see Figure 5.2; Blazer et al., 1994). The lowest rates are among the 45 to 54 year olds, and other studies have found even lower rates in people 55 to 70 years of age (Newmann, 1989).

Perhaps it is surprising that the rate of depression is so low among older adults. Depression may sometimes be underreported by the elderly or misdiagnosed as dementia or some other physical disorder. The rates of depression do go up among the "old-old," those over 85 years of age. Depressions in older people tend to be quite severe and debilitating.

However, researchers have been intrigued with evidence that depression is not as rampant among older adults as was previously believed, and they have introduced several explanations for the relatively low rates of depression in the elderly.

The first is quite grim: Depression appears to interfere with physical health and, as a result, people with a history of depression may be more likely to die before they reach old age (Klerman & Weissman, 1989). The second explanation is more hopeful: As people age, they may develop more adaptive coping skills and a psychologically healthier outlook on life, and this may lead them to experience fewer episodes of depression (Elder, Liker, & Jaworski, 1984).

The third explanation has to do with history rather than age. People born in more recent generations may be at higher risk for depression than are people who were born a few generations ago (Klerman & Weissman, 1989). This is called a *cohort effect:* People born in one historical period are at different risk for a disorder than are people born in another historical period. For example, less than 20 percent of people born before 1915 appear to have experienced episodes of major depression at any time in their lives, whereas over 40 percent of people born after 1955 appear to be at risk for major depression at some time in their lives (see Figure 5.3). Proponents of the cohort explanation suggest that

Some studies suggest people in older generations may have been less prone to depression throughout their lives compared to people in younger generations.

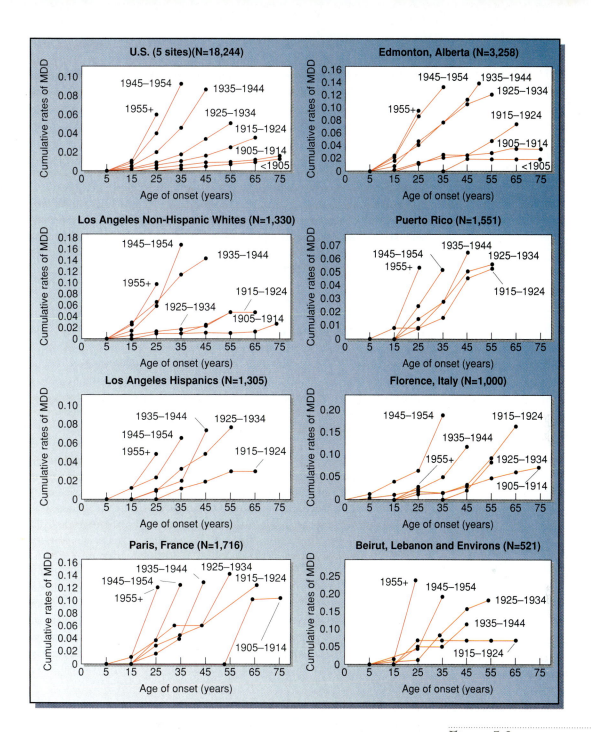

more recent generations have suffered from the disintegration of the family unit and the rapid changes in social values that began in the 1960s (Klerman & Weissman, 1989). This decrease in social support and in identification with common social values may have put younger generations at higher risk for depression than older generations were. Another possible explanation is that younger generations have higher expectations for themselves than did older generations, but these expectations are too high to be met.

Paralleling this cohort effect in rates of depression is a decrease in the age at which people are first becoming depressed. First onsets of depression are occurring at younger and younger ages. These days, half of the people who will eventually develop major depressive disorder experience the onset of their first episode by the age of 25 (Burke, Burke, Regier, & Rae, 1990). The number of youngsters experiencing depression appears to be much higher than was previously thought. Community-based studies of children and

Figure 5.3

Rates of Depression in People Born in Different Historical Periods. These graphs show that in many different countries, people born in more recent historical periods have higher rates of depression and an earlier age of first onset of depression than did people born in earlier historical periods.
Source: Cross National Collaborative Group, 1992.

adolescents find that almost 18 percent experience an episode of major depressive disorder or dysthymic disorder by midadolescence (Lewinsohn et al., 1994). Depressed adolescents and children, like depressed adults, show a wide range of impairments, including problems in school, in interpersonal relationships, in self-esteem, and in their ability to cope with stress (Nolen-Hoeksema & Girgus, 1994). Unfortunately, the younger a person is when he or she has a first episode of depression, the more likely he or she is to have repeated episodes throughout life.

In sum, women are at higher risk for depression among all adult age groups and most ethnic groups in the United States and Europe. The rate of depression is highest for people 15 to 24 years of age and declines with age. Older people may have lower rates of depression than younger people because depression causes early mortality or because people grow better able to cope with the stresses of life as they age. Alternately, older people may have been less prone to depression throughout their lives compared to younger people because they lived in a historical period that provided them with stronger social support and better coping skills.

 Do you think that noting that one group is more prone to a disorder than others stigmatizes that group or validates the experience of that group?

Ethnicity, Culture, and Depression

In one large study done in the United States, people of Hispanic origins showed the highest prevalence of depression in the previous year, followed by whites, with the lowest prevalence among African Americans (Figure 5.4; Blazer et al., 1994). It might seem puzzling that African Americans had the lowest prevalence of depression, given their disadvantaged status in U.S. society. However, African Americans have high rates of anxiety disorders, suggesting that the stress of their societal status may make them especially prone to anxiety disorders rather than to depression. Other studies have found extremely high rates of depression among Native Americans, especially the young (Manson et al., 1990). Depression among these youth is tied to poverty, hopelessness, and alcoholism.

One cultural group within the United States that has especially low prevalence of unipolar depression is the Old Order Amish of central Pennsylvania. The Amish are a religious community of people who maintain a very simple lifestyle oriented around farming and their church and who reject modern conveniences (such as automobiles, electricity, telephones). Essentially, the Amish live as people did in nineteenth-century rural America. Extensive research on the mood disorders among the Amish has suggested that their prevalence of major depression is only one-tenth of that in mainstream groups in the United States (Egeland et al., 1987). Perhaps the simple agrarian lifestyle of the Amish, with its emphasis on family and community, helps to protect its members against depression.

Research among the Old Order Amish of central Pennsylvania suggests they have much lower rates of mood disorders than people in the rest of the United States.

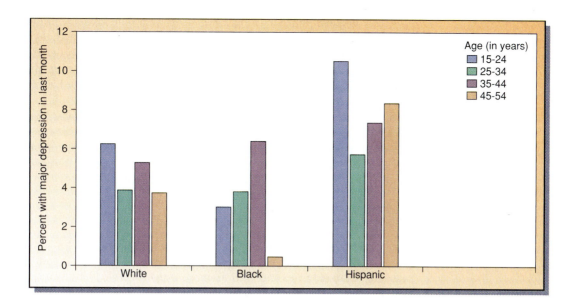

Figure 5.4

Ethnic Differences in Major Depression. These are the percentages of people in each age group and by ethnicity diagnosed with major depression in the previous month. Hispanic Americans show the highest rates across all age groups.

Source: Blazer et al., 1994.

Similarly, cross-national studies have suggested that the prevalence of major depression is lower among less-industrialized and less-modern countries than among more-industrialized and more-modern countries (Cross-National Collaborative Group, 1992). Again, it may be that the fast-paced lifestyles of people in modern industrialized societies, with their lack of stable social support and community values, are toxic to mental health. In contrast, the community- and family-oriented lifestyles of less-modern societies may be beneficial to mental health, despite the physical hardships that many people in these societies face because of their lack of modern conveniences.

Alternately, some researchers have suggested that people in less-modern cultures may tend to manifest depression with physical complaints rather than psychological symptoms of depression, such as sadness, loss of motivation, and hopelessness about the future. In China, people facing severe stress often complain of *neurasthenia*, a collection of physical symptoms such as chronic headaches, pain in the joints, nausea, lack of energy, and palpitations:

Case Study • Lin Hung is a 24-year-old worker in a machine factory who complains of headaches, dizziness, weakness, lack of energy, insomnia, bad dreams, poor memory, and a stiff neck. Pain, weakness, and dizziness, along with bouts of palpitations are his chief symptoms. His symptoms began 6 months ago, and they are gradually worsening. His factory doctors believe he has a heart problem, but repeated electrocardiograms have been normal. He believes he has a serious bodily disorder that is worsened by his work and that interferes with his ability to carry out his job responsibilities.

Until his father retired from the job Lin now occupies, he was a soldier living not far from home. He didn't want to leave the army, but his father was anxious to retire so he could move to a new apartment owned by his factory in another city. Fearing that his son would not be able to stay in the army and thereafter would not find work, Lin's father pressured him to take over his job, a job the younger Lin never liked or wanted for himself. Lin Hung reluctantly agreed but now finds he cannot adjust to the work. He did not want to be a machinist and cries when he recounts that this is what he must be for the rest of his life. Moreover, he is despondent and lonely living so far away from his parents. He has no friends at work and feels lonely living in the dormitory. He has a girlfriend, but he cannot see her regularly anymore, owing to the change in work sites. They wish to marry, but his parents, who have a serious financial problem because of a very low pension, cannot provide the expected furniture, room, or any financial help. The leaders of his work unit are against the marriage because he is too young. They also criticize him for his poor work performance and frequent days missed from work owing to sickness. (adapted from Kleinman & Kleinman, 1985, pp. 454–455).

Upon questioning Lin Hung, psychiatrists trained in "Western" medicine diagnosed major depressive disorder. Like many Chinese, Lin rejected the psychological diagnosis, believing firmly that he was suffering solely from a physical disorder. A psychological diagnosis would not have garnered any sympathy from Lin's coworkers or family, but a physical diagnosis could provide him with an acceptable reason to leave his job and return to his family.

It is difficult to know whether the apparently low rates of depression in less-modern cultures are due to a masking of depression by physical complaints in these cultures. However, in our discussions of many disorders, we will find that some cultures tend to focus on the physical manifestations of disorders, whereas others, such as the dominant U.S. culture, tend to focus on more psychological symptoms of disorders.

The Course of Depression

Depression appears to be a long-lasting and recurrent problem for some people. One study of 423 people who were diagnosed with major depression found that 20 percent were still depressed a year after their diagnosis (Sargeant et al., 1990). Women with less than a high school education and an unstable marital history were even more likely to have persistent depressions: 30 percent of them were still depressed a year after their diagnosis. This study was a natural history study: The researchers did not control whether the participants entered treatment for their depression. Instead, they simply documented the natural course of the depressive episodes. The good news from the study is that once people underwent treatment for their depressions, they tended to recover much more quickly.

Unfortunately, about half of the people who have one episode of major depression will experience another episode at some time in their lives. Most people who relapse into a second episode of depression tend to do so within 2 years of recovering from their first episode. The more episodes of depression people have had, the more likely they are to relapse into further episodes of depression. In addition, people who have inadequate social support from friends and family are more likely to relapse into new episodes of depression (Belsher & Costello, 1988).

Even if they do not relapse into additional major depressive episodes, people with previous episodes of major depression tend to have enduring problems in many areas of their lives (Coryell et al., 1993). Their functioning on the job tends to remain impaired even after their depression subsides, and their interpersonal relationships tend to be conflictual. They report that they are not interested in sex or do not enjoy sex as much as they used to, and there is chronic conflict and dissatisfaction in their intimate relationships (McCabe & Gotlib, 1993).

Summing Up | Unipolar Depressive Disorders

- Depression includes disturbances in emotion (sadness, loss of interest), bodily functions (loss of sleep, appetite, and sexual drive), behaviors (retardation or agitation), and thoughts (worthlessness, guilt, suicidality).
- The two primary categories of unipolar depressive disorders are major depression and dysthymic disorder; in addition, there are several subtypes of major depression.
- Women are twice as likely as men to be depressed.
- Young and middle-aged adults have the highest rates of depression.
- Depression appears less common in less-modern cultures than in more-modern ones, but people in many cultures may also manifest depression through somatic symptoms rather than the symptoms listed in the DSM-IV.
- Many people who become depressed remain so for several months or more and have multiple relapses over their lifetime.

Let us now discuss the other major form of mood disorder: bipolar disorder. Bipolar disorder is much less common than depression, but it is typically a lifelong disorder that left untreated can wreak havoc in the lives of its sufferers and their families.

Bipolar Disorder

There is a particular kind of pain, elation, loneliness, and terror involved in this kind of madness. When you're high it's tremendous. The ideas and feelings are fast and frequent like shooting starts and you follow them until you find better and brighter ones. Shyness goes, the right words and gestures are suddenly there, the power to seduce and captivate others a felt certainty. There are interests found in uninteresting people. Sensuality is pervasive and the desire to seduce and be seduced irresistible. Feelings of ease, intensity, power, well-being, financial omnipotence, and euphoria now pervade one's marrow. But, somewhere, this changes. The fast ideas are far too fast and there are far too many; overwhelming confusion replaces clarity. Memory goes. Humor and absorption on friends' faces are replaced by fear and concern. Everything previously moving with the grain is now against—you are irritable, angry, frightened, uncontrollable, and enmeshed totally in the blackest caves of the mind. You never knew those caves were there. It will never end. (Goodwin & Jamison, 1990, pp. 17–18).

This person is describing an episode of bipolar disorder. When she is manic, she has tremendous energy and vibrancy, her self-esteem is soaring, she is filled with ideas and confidence. Then when she becomes depressed, she is despairing and fearful, she doubts herself and everyone around her, she wishes to die. This alternation between periods of mania and periods of depression is the classic manifestation of bipolar disorder.

We have already discussed the symptoms of depression in detail, so let us focus on the symptoms of mania. The moods of people who are manic can be *elated*, but that elation is often mixed with *irritation* and *agitation*. Said one man,

First and foremost comes a general sense of intense well-being. I know of course that this sense is illusory and transient—Although, however, the restrictions of confinement are apt at times to produce extreme irritation and even paroxysms of anger, the general sense of well-being, the pleasurable and sometimes ecstatic feeling-tone, remains as a sort of permanent background of all experience during a manic period. (Goodwin & Jamison, 1990, pp. 25–26).

The manic person is filled with a *grandiose self-esteem*, and *thoughts* and *impulses* race through the mind. At times, these grandiose thoughts are delusional and may be accompanied by grandiose hallucinations

The condition of my mind for many months is beyond all description. My thoughts ran with lightning-like rapidity from one subject to another. I had an exaggerated feeling of self importance. All the problems of the universe came crowding into my mind, demanding instant discussion and solution—mental telepathy, hypnotism, wireless telegraphy, Christian science, women's rights, and all the problems of medical science, religion, and politics. I even devised means of discovering the weight of the human soul, and had an apparatus constructed in my room for the purpose of weighing my own soul the minute it departed from my body. . . . (Reiss, 1910)

A manic person may *speak rapidly* and *forcefully*, trying to convey the rapid stream of fantastic thoughts he is having. He may become agitated and irritable, particularly with people he perceives as "getting in his way." He may engage in a variety of *impulsive behaviors*, such as ill-advised sexual liaisons or spending sprees. Often he will have *grand plans* and *goals* that he frenetically pursues.

When I am high I couldn't worry about money if I tried. So I don't. The money will come from somewhere, I am entitled, God will provide. Credit cards are disastrous, personal checks worse. Unfortunately, for manics anyway, mania is a natural (if unnatural) extension of the economy. What with credit cards and bank accounts there is little beyond reach. So, I bought 12 snake bite kits, with a sense of urgency and importance. I bought precious stones, elegant and unnecessary furniture, three watches within an hour of one another and totally inappropriate siren-like clothes. During one spree in London I spent several hundred pounds on books having titles or covers that somehow caught my fancy. Once I think I shoplifted a blouse because I could not wait a minute longer for the woman-with-molasses feet in front of me in line. I imagine I must have spent far more than $30,000 during my two major manic episodes, and God only knows how much more during my frequent milder manias. (Jamison, 1995b, p. 74)

Most people who have manic episodes fall into a depressive episode eventually. For some people with bipolar disorder, the depressions are as severe as the major depressive episodes. Other people with bipolar disorder experience mostly the symptoms of mania, with only mild and infrequent episodes of depression. These two forms of bipolar disorder, in which a full manic syndrome is experienced, are known as **Bipolar I Disorder**. Still other people experience only mild episodes of mania, known as *hypomania*, with more severe episodes of major depression. These people are said to have **Bipolar II Disorder.**

Just as dysthymic disorder is the less severe but more chronic form of depressive disorder, there is a less severe but more chronic form of bipolar disorder known as **cyclothymic disorder**. A person with cyclothymic disorder alternates between episodes of mania and depression that are milder than the full manic or depressive episodes but is chronically in a state of either mild mania or depression over at least a 2 year period. During the periods of mild mania, the person may be able to function reasonably well in daily life. Often, however, the periods of depression significantly interfere with daily functioning, although these periods are not as severe as those qualifying as major depressive episodes.

Who Has Bipolar Disorder?

Bipolar disorder is less common than unipolar depression. About 1 or 2 in 100 people will experience at least one episode of bipolar disorder at some time in their lives (Kessler et al., 1994). Men and women seem equally likely to develop the disorder, and there are no consistent differences among ethnic groups in the prevalence of the disorder. Most people who develop bipolar disorder do so in late adolescence or early adulthood (Burke et al., 1990). About half of the people who eventually develop a bipolar disorder experienced their first episode by early adulthood.

About 90 percent of people with bipolar disorder have multiple episodes or cycles during their lifetimes (APA, 1994). The length of an individual episode of bipolar disorder varies greatly from one person to the next. Some people are in a manic state for several weeks or months before moving into a depressed state. More rarely, people switch from mania to depression and back within a matter of days. The number of lifetime episodes also varies tremendously from one person to the next, but a relatively common pattern is for episodes to become more frequent and closer together over time. If a person has four or more cycles of mania and depression within a year, this is known as **rapid cycling bipolar disorder**.

Like people with unipolar depression, people with bipolar disorder often face, between their episodes, chronic problems on the job and in their relationships (Coryell et al., 1993). Some of these problems are due to lingering symptoms of the illness that are not completely obliterated by treatment, and some are the lingering consequences of what the person did while in a manic or depressed state, as Kay Jamison describes:

What then, after the medications, psychiatrist, despair, depression, and overdose? All those incredible feelings to sort through. Who is being too polite to say what? Who knows what? What did I do? Why? and most hauntingly, When will it happen again? Then, too, are the annoyances—-medicine to take, resent, forget, take, resent, and forget, but always to take. Credit cards revoked, bounced checks to cover, explanations due at work, apologies to make, intermittent memories of

Bipolar I Disorder
form of bipolar disorder in which the full symptoms of mania are experienced while depressive aspects may be more infrequent or mild

Bipolar II Disorder
form of bipolar disorder in which only hypomanic episodes are experienced, and the depressive component is more pronounced

cyclothymic disorder
milder but more chronic form of bipolar disorder that consists of alternation between hypomanic episodes and mild depressive episodes over a period of at least two years

rapid cycling bipolar disorder
diagnosis given when a person has four or more cycles of mania and depression within a single year

vague men (what *did* I do?), friendships gone or drained, a ruined marriage. And always, when will it happen again? Which of my feelings are real? Which of the me's is me? The wild, impulsive, chaotic, energetic, and crazy one? Or the shy, withdrawn, desperate, suicidal, doomed, and tired one? Probably a bit of both, hopefully much that is neither. (Jamison, 1995b, p. 68)

The sense that they can never trust their emotions or self-perceptions again haunts many people who have had episodes of mania or depression. Always lurking in their minds is the question, "When will it happen again?" Said poet Robert Lowell (1977) who suffered from bipolar disorder, "If we see a light at the end of the tunnel, it's the light of an oncoming train."

Culture and Bipolar Disorder

Cultures do not seem to differ greatly in the prevalence of bipolar disorder, but they may differ in the manifestation of the disorder. We already discussed the cross-cultural differences in the manifestation of depression. The study of the Old Order Amish described earlier provides a fascinating illustration of how mania can be manifested differently across cultures (Egeland, Hostetter, & Eshleman, 1983). Among the Amish, there are very strict rules against acting in prideful ways that call attention to oneself. Humility and modesty are principle virtues in this society. Thus, behaviors that may seem normal to people from the rest of North American society may seem to indicate grandiosity and inflated self-esteem in Amish society. For example, an Amish person who tells others at length about a recent accomplishment or who dresses in fine modern clothes is violating the norms of his or her society to such a degree that these behaviors might be signs of grandiosity. Similarly, the Amish have strict rules against using modern conveniences, such as telephones or cars, and against giving gifts or planning vacations during certain seasons, because there are only some seasons when gifts and vacations are considered appropriate. So signs that a person might be engaging in manic symptoms include excessive use of a telephone, driving a car, driving one's horse carriage too fast, or giving gifts out of season. Of course, researchers would not diagnose mania in an Amish person simply on the basis of isolated behaviors such as these. The diagnosis would only be made if the person also seemed to fit all the other criteria for a manic episode. This study of the Amish provides striking examples of how social factors can influence the manifestation of a disorder that may be largely biological in its causes.

 Given that there are no biological tests that prove a person has bipolar disorder, how can researchers definitively say that people from other cultures can have bipolar disorder but manifest it with different symptoms from those present in the researchers' own culture?

Leadership, Creativity, and Bipolar Disorder

Could there possibly be anything good about suffering from bipolar disorder? Some theorists have argued that the symptoms of mania—increased self-esteem, a rush of ideas, the courage to pursue these ideas, high energy, little need for sleep, hypervigilance, decisiveness—can actually benefit people in certain occupations, especially highly intelligent or talented people. Indeed, some of the most influential people in history have suffered, and perhaps to some extent benefitted from, bipolar disorder or depression.

Political leaders including Abraham Lincoln, Alexander Hamilton, Winston Churchill, Napoleon Bonaparte, and Benito Mussolini and religious leaders including Martin Luther and George Fox (founder of the Society of Friends, or Quakers) have been posthumously diagnosed by psychiatric biographers as having periods of mania, hypomania, or depression (Goodwin & Jamison, 1990). Although during periods of depression these leaders were often incapacitated, during periods of mania and hypomania they accomplished extraordinary feats. While manic they devised brilliant and daring strategies for winning wars and solving domestic problems and had the energy, self-esteem, and persistence to carry out these strategies. The Duke of Marlborough, a great English military commander, was able to put his chronic hypomania to great use:

> No one can read the whole mass of the letters which Marlborough either wrote, dictated, or signed personally without being astounded at the mental and physical energy which it attests. . . . After 12 or 14 hours in the saddle on the long reconnaissances often under cannon-fire; after endless inspections of troops in camp and garrison; after ceaseless calculations about food and supplies, and all the anxieties of direct command in war, Marlborough would reach his tent and conduct the foreign policy of England, decided the main issues of its Cabinet, and of party politics at home. (Rowse, 1969, pp. 249–250).

Marlborough was an ancestor of Winston Churchill, who was also able to put his cyclothymic temperament to use in his career. However, Churchill's biographer also documented how the grandiosity, scheming, and impulsiveness that are part of mania can be a liability in a leader:

> All those who worked with Churchill paid tribute to the enormous fertility of his new ideas, the inexhaustible stream of invention which poured from him, both when he was Home Secretary, and later when he was Prime Minister and director of the war effort. All who worked with him also agreed that he needed the most severe restraint put upon him, and that many of his ideas, if they had been put into practice, would have been utterly disastrous. (Storr, 1988, pp. 14–15)

 Would you vote for a political leader who was known to have a history of a mood disorder if he or she had been successfully treated and free of symptoms for several years?

Artistic creativity has long been thought to require suffering and a little bit of "madness." Anne Sexton, a Pulitzer Prize-winning poet and sufferer of bipolar disorder who eventually committed suicide, wrote,

> I, myself, alternate between hiding behind my own hands, protecting myself anyway possible, and this other, this seeing, ouching other. I guess I mean that creative people must not avoid the pain they get dealt. . . . Hurt must be examined like a plague. (Sexton & Ames, 1977, p. 105)

Recent studies have documented that writers, artists, and composers of music have a higher than normal prevalence of mania and depression. For example, one study of 36 distinguished British poets found that over half could be diagnosed with bipolar disorder or cyclothymia (Jamison, 1995a). A larger study of 1,005 famous twentieth-century artists, writers, and other professionals found that the artists and writers experienced two to three times the rate of mood disorders, psychosis, and suicide attempts than did comparably successful people in business, science, and public life. The poets in this group were most likely to have been manic (Ludwig, 1992).

Composer Robert Schumann suffered from bipolar disorder, and his productivity closely mirrored his mood state (Figure 5.5). When he was depressed, he composed relatively little and attempted suicide twice. When he was manic or hypomanic, he composed musical scores at an astounding rate and apparently thought little of it: "I cannot see that there is anything remarkable about composing a symphony in a month. Handel wrote a complete oratorio in that time" (Robert Schumann, 1850; quoted in Taylor, 1982, p. 285).

Does mania simply enhance (and depression inhibit) productivity in naturally creative people? Or is there some deeper link between creativity and bipolar disorder? This

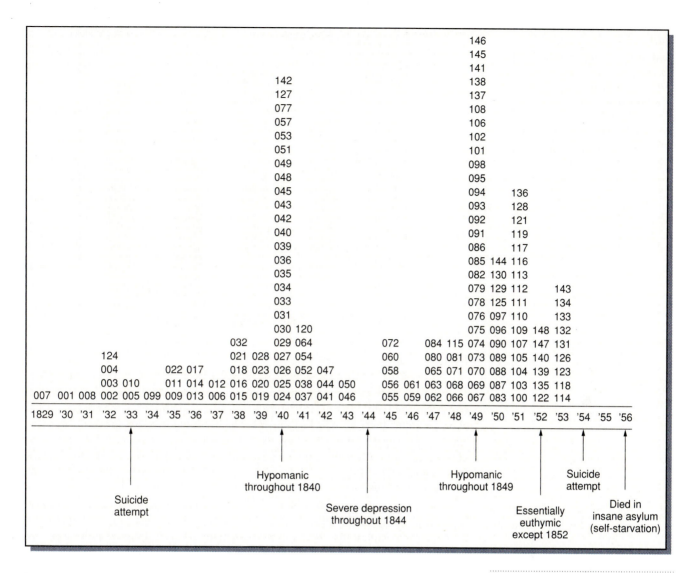

Figure 5.5

Robert Schumann's Productivity Reflects His Periods of Depression and Mania. When Robert Schumann was manic, he produced a phenomenal number of musical scores, but when he was depressed, he produced much less.

Source: Goodwin & Jamison, 1990, p. 348.

is a difficult question to answer by simply examining how many creative people are also manic. However, one study found an ingenious way to address this question. The researchers who conducted this study hypothesized that a genetic vulnerability to bipolar disorder is accompanied by a predisposition to creativity. According to this hypothesis, the close relatives of patients with bipolar disorder should be more creative, even if they do not have bipolar disorder, than the close relatives of people without bipolar disorder. The participants in this study were patients with bipolar disorder or cyclothymia, their first-degree relatives (siblings, parents, and children), a control group of people with no psychiatric disorders, and their first-degree relatives. The relatives in both these groups had no history themselves of mood disorders, so any creativity they evidenced was in the absence of mania or depression.

To measure creativity, the researchers examined the lives of these participants for evidence that they had used their special talents in some original and creative ways. For example, one participant who was rated as extremely creative was an entrepreneur who advanced from a chemist's apprentice to an independent researcher of new products. He then started a major paint manufacturing company, and during the Danish Resistance of World War II, he surreptitiously manufactured and smuggled explosives for the resistance. A participant who was rated as low in creativity had been a bricklayer for 20 years and then inherited a large trust fund and retired to a passive life on a country estate. An advantage of this measure of creativity is that it did not require that a person receive social recognition to be considered creative.

Figure 5.6

A Family Study of Creativity and Bipolar Disorder. Creativity was measured in a control group, healthy family members of bipolar patients, patients with serious bipolar disorder, and patients with cyclothymia. The healthy family members of bipolar patients and the people with cyclothymia had the highest creativity scores.

Source: Richards et al., 1988.

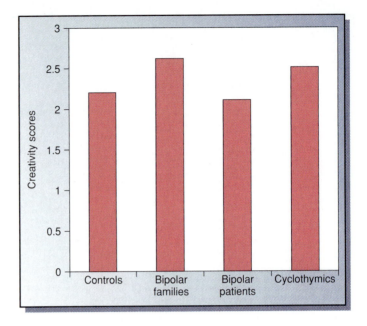

The results of this study suggested that relatives of people with bipolar disorder or cyclothymia were more creative than people with no history of bipolar disorder or cyclothymia or their relatives (see Figure 5.6). The cyclothymics and the normal relatives of people with bipolar disorder had somewhat higher creativity scores than did the patients who had bipolar disorder. This suggests that creativity that is associated with a predisposition toward bipolar disorder is more easily expressed in people who do not suffer from full episodes of mania and depression but may suffer from milder mood swings (Richards et al., 1988).

We should not overemphasize the benefits of bipolar disorder. Although many creative people with bipolar disorder may have been able to learn from their periods of depression and exploit their periods of mania, many also have found the highs and lows of the disorder unbearable and have attempted or completed suicide. As Wurtzel (1995, p. 295) notes,

> While it may be true that a great deal of art finds its inspirational wellspring in sorrow, let's not kid ourselves in how much time each of those people wasted and lost by being mired in misery. So many productive hours slipped by as paralyzing despair took over. This is not to say that we should deny sadness its rightful place among the muses of poetry and of all art forms, but let's stop calling it madness, let's stop pretending that the feeling itself is interesting. Let's call it depression and admit that it is very bleak.

Summing Up | Bipolar Disorder

- The two major diagnostic categories of bipolar mood disorders are bipolar disorder and cyclothymic disorder.
- Bipolar mood disorders are less common than depressive disorders, but are equally common in men and women.
- Cultures do not seem to differ much in rates of bipolar disorder, but cultural norms can affect the manifestation of bipolar disorder.
- The onset of bipolar disorders is most often in late adolescence or early adulthood. Most people with bipolar disorder have multiple episodes.
- There is an intriguing link between mania and creativity.

Biological Theories of Mood Disorders

There are at least four clues that the mood disorders have biological underpinnings (Kraepelin, 1922; Thase & Howland, 1995). First, depression and mania tend to be episodic in nature, as are many physical diseases. Second, many of the symptoms of depression and mania represent disruptions in vital bodily functions, such as sleep, eating, and sexual activity. Third, we have long known that depression and mania run in families, suggesting that they are heritable. Fourth, depression and mania respond to biological treatments, such as drug therapies, and can be induced by certain drugs.

Most of the modern biological theories of the causes of mood disorders focus on genetic abnormalities or dysfunctions in certain neurobiological systems. These two types of theories complement each other: Genetic abnormalities may cause mood disorders by altering a person's neurobiology. In this section, we will first review the evidence for a genetic contribution to depression and mania. Second, we will review the evidence that neurotransmitters play a role in depression and mania. Third, we will explore hypotheses that the neuroendocrine system, which regulates hormones throughout the body, becomes dysregulated in the mood disorders. Fourth, we will examine a variety of neurophysiological abnormalities that have been found in people with mood disorders.

The Role of Genetics in Mood Disorders

Family history studies and twin studies both suggest that the mood disorders can be genetically transmitted. Let us consider bipolar disorder first, because the evidence for a genetic transmission of this disorder is clearer than the evidence regarding unipolar depression. Family history studies of people with bipolar disorder find that their first-degree relatives (that is, parents, children, and siblings) have rates of both bipolar disorder and depressive disorders at least two to three times higher than the rates in relatives of people without bipolar disorder (Gershon, 1990; Keller & Baker, 1991).

One family that appeared to have the "tainted blood" of bipolar disorder was the family of Alfred, Lord Tennyson (see Figure 5.7). Alfred experienced recurrent, debilitating depressions and probably hypomanic spells. His father, his grandfather, two of his great-grandfathers, and five of his seven brothers suffered from bouts of what would be diagnosed today as mania, depression, and psychosis. Alfred's brother Edward was confined to an asylum for nearly 60 years before he died from "manic exhaustion." Lionel Tennyson, one of Alfred's two sons, had a mercurial temperament, as did one of his three grandsons (Jamison, 1995a).

Does this mean that if you have a close relative with bipolar disorder you are destined to develop the disorder? No. Most studies find that less than 10 percent (and often less than 5 percent) of the first-degree relatives of people with bipolar disorder go on to develop the disorder themselves. Thus, the risk is higher for people with a bipolar relative, but still only a minority of them develop the disorder.

Twin studies of bipolar disorder have consistently shown higher concordance rates among monozygotic twins than among dizygotic twins (Faraone & Tsuang, 1990). For example, a Danish study of 69 monozygotic twins and 54 dizygotic twins found concordance rates for bipolar disorder of 69 percent in the monozygotic twins and 19 percent in the dizygotic twins (Bertelsen et al., 1977).

The evidence regarding the heritability of unipolar depression is less consistent. Family history studies do find higher rates of unipolar depression in the first-degree relatives of people with unipolar depression than in control groups (Gershon, 1990; Keller & Baker, 1991). Interestingly, relatives of depressed people do *not* tend to have any greater risk for bipolar disorder than do relatives of people with no mood disorder. This suggests that bipolar disorder has a different genetic basis from unipolar depression.

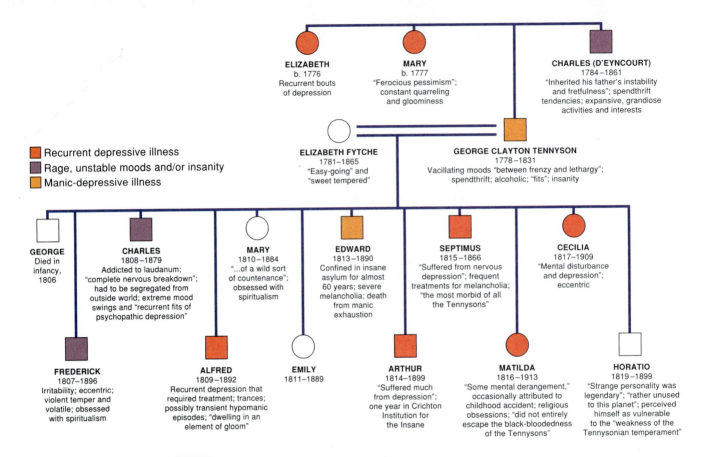

Recurrent depressive illness
Rage, unstable moods and/or insanity
Manic-depressive illness

ELIZABETH
b. 1776
Recurrent bouts
of depression

MARY
b. 1777
"Ferocious pessimism";
constant quarreling
and gloominess

CHARLES (D'EYNCOURT)
1784–1861
"Inherited his father's instability
and fretfulness"; spendthrift
tendencies; expansive, grandiose
activities and interests

ELIZABETH FYTCHE
1781–1865
"Easy-going" and
"sweet tempered"

GEORGE CLAYTON TENNYSON
1778–1831
Vacillating moods "between frenzy and lethargy";
spendthrift; alcoholic; "fits"; insanity

GEORGE
Died in
infancy,
1806

CHARLES
1808–1879
Addicted to laudanum;
"complete nervous breakdown";
had to be segregated from
outside world; extreme mood
swings and "recurrent fits of
psychopathic depression"

MARY
1810–1884
"...of a wild sort
of countenance";
obsessed with
spiritualism

EDWARD
1813–1890
Confined in insane
asylum for almost
60 years; severe
melancholia; death
from manic
exhaustion

SEPTIMUS
1815–1866
"Suffered from nervous
depression"; frequent
treatments for melancholia;
"the most morbid of all
the Tennysons"

CECILIA
1817–1909
"Mental disturbance
and depression";
eccentric

FREDERICK
1807–1896
Irritability; eccentric;
violent temper and
volatile; obsessed
with spiritualism

ALFRED
1809–1892
Recurrent depression that
required treatment; trances;
possibly transient hypomanic
episodes; "dwelling in an
element of gloom"

EMILY
1811–1889

ARTHUR
1814–1899
"Suffered much
from depression";
one year in Crichton
Institution for
the Insane

MATILDA
1816–1913
"Some mental derangement,"
occasionally attributed to
childhood accident; religious
obsessions; "did not entirely
escape the black-bloodedness
of the Tennysons"

HORATIO
1819–1899
"Strange personality was
legendary"; "rather unused
to this planet"; perceived
himself as vulnerable
to the "weakness of the
Tennysonian temperament"

Figure 5.7

The "Tainted Blood" of the Tennysons. Alfred, Lord Tennyson, who himself experienced recurrent, debilitating depressions and probably hypomanic spells, attributed his disorder to the "tainted blood" of the Tennysons. His father, his grandfather, two of his great-grandfathers, and five of his seven brothers suffered from insanity, depression, uncontrollable rage, or bipolar disorder. Lionel Tennyson, one of Alfred's two sons, displayed mood swings, as did one of his three grandsons.
Source: From Jamison, 1995a, p. 62–67.

Twin studies have provided mixed evidence concerning the heritability of unipolar depression. One of the largest twin studies of depressive disorder focused only on female twins (Kendler et al., 1992). The researchers used a twin registry from the state of Virginia to identify 1,033 pairs of twins. They then interviewed the twins to determine whether either or both members of each pair had a history of major depression. They found concordance rates for major depression of 48 percent for monozygotic twins and 42 percent for dizygotic twins. Thus, in this study of all female twins, the concordance rate for major depression was not substantially higher for MZ twins than for DZ twins.

Other studies that included both male and female twin pairs have found larger differences between the concordance rates for MZ and DZ twins (McGuffin et al., 1991; Torgersen, 1986). Unfortunately, however, these studies had much smaller numbers of twin pairs than did the study by Kendler and colleagues (1992). For example, McGuffin and colleagues (1991) had 62 pairs of MZ twins and 72 pairs of DZ twins. They found concordance rates for major depression of 53 percent for MZ twins and 28 percent for DZ twins.

There is a third type of study used to investigate the heritability of disorders: the adoption study. The largest adoption study of mood disorders to date used Danish adoption records and records of people treated in psychiatric hospitals to identify 71 adults who were adopted at birth and later developed some type of mood disorder (bipolar disorder and unipolar depression were not differentiated in this study). The researchers also identified a control group of 71 adults adopted at birth who had never been treated for any psychiatric disorders. The researchers used psychiatric records to trace the biological and adoptive relatives of these adults to determine how many had been treated for mood disorders. The biological relatives of adoptees with mood disorders had significantly higher rates of mood disorders than did their adoptive relatives or the relatives of adoptees with no mood disorder (see Figure 5.8). In addition, the biological relatives of adoptees with mood disorders had significantly higher rates of attempted or completed suicides than did the relatives in the other three groups (Wender et al., 1986).

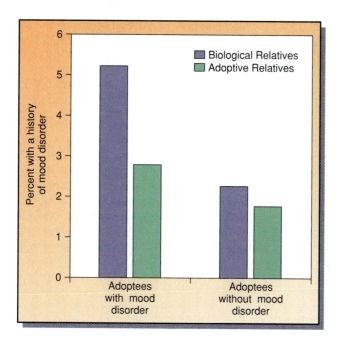

Figure 5.8

Mood Disorders in the Biological and Adoptive Relatives of Adoptees with Mood Disorders. Adoptees with mood disorders had higher rates of mood disorders in their biological relatives than their adoptive relatives, but adoptees with no mood disorders had low rates of mood disorders in both their biological and adoptive relatives.

Source: Wender et al., 1986.

Many people with a mood disorder worry about passing their disorder on to their children through their genes. If you were a person with a mood disorder, how would you feel about this issue, given the data you have just read on the heritability of mood disorders?

The family history studies, twin studies, and adoption studies all suggest that genetics play a role in mood disorders, especially in bipolar disorder. Thus far, researchers have been unable to identify specifically what type of genetic abnormality is involved in mood disorders. Future advances in the technology of genetic research may reveal the specific genetic abnormalities that predispose some people to mood disorders. It is probably the case that there is no single locus on a gene that leads to mood disorders. Many researchers believe that the genetic predisposition to mood disorders is *multifactorial*. That is, a particular configuration of several disordered genes may be necessary to create a mood disorder (Faraone, & Tsuang, 1990).

Neurotransmitter Theories

Most of the biochemical theories of mood disorders have focused on neurotransmitters, those biochemicals that facilitate the transmission of impulses across the synapses between one neuron and another (Figure 5.9). The specific group of neurotransmitters that has been implicated in the mood disorders is called the **monoamines**, and the specific monoamines that have been implicated are **norepinephrine**, **serotonin**, and **dopamine**. These neurotransmitters are found in large concentrations in the limbic system, a part of the brain associated with the regulation of sleep, appetite, and emotional processes. Since depression and mania involve disturbances in sleep, appetite, and emotions, it would make sense that these disorders were caused by dysfunctions in the limbic system.

All of the monoamines have been implicated in mood disorders. Most of the research, however, has focused on norepinephrine and serotonin. The early theory of the roles of these neurotransmitters in mood disorders was that depression is caused by a reduction in the amount of norepinephrine or serotonin in the synapses between neurons (Glassman, 1969; Schildkraut, 1965). This depletion could result from numerous mechanisms: decreased synthesis of the neurotransmitter from its precursors, increased degradation of the neurotransmitter by enzymes, or impaired release or reuptake of the neurotransmitter (see Chapter 3 to review these processes). Mania was thought to be caused by an excess

monoamines
class of neurotransmitters including catecholamines (epinephrine, norepinephrine, and dopamine) and serotonin that have been implicated in the mood disorders

norepinephrine
monoamine neurotransmitter that has been implicated in the mood disorders

serotonin
monoamine neurotransmitter, low levels of which are correlated with depression and aggressive or suicidal behavior

dopamine
monoamine neurotransmitter, low levels of which have been implicated in the mood disorders and high levels of which have been implicated in schizophrenia

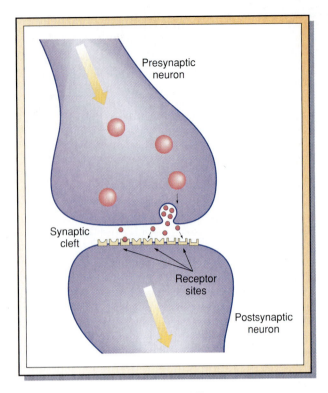

Figure 5.9

Neurotransmitters and the Synapse. Neurotransmitters are released from the presynaptic neuron into the synaptic gap. They then bind to specific receptors, like keys fitting into locks. There are also receptors for the neurotransmitters on the presynaptic neuron.

monoamine theories
theories that low levels of monoamines, particularly norepinephrine and serotonin, cause depression, whereas excessive or imbalanced levels of monoamines, particularly dopamine, cause mania

of the monoamines or perhaps dysregulation of the levels of these amines, especially dopamine. These theories, taken together, are known as the **monoamine theories** of mood disorders (Schildkraut, 1965; Bunney & Davis, 1965).

The level of a neurotransmitter in the brain cannot be measured directly in live human beings. It must be assessed indirectly, usually by measuring levels of the by-products of the neurotransmitter in the blood or urine of subjects. Thousands of studies have now been done comparing people with and without mood disorders on their levels of the by-products of norepinephrine, serotonin, and dopamine. These studies have not consistently found differences between these groups (Thase & Howland, 1995). This may be due in large part to the technical difficulty of accurately measuring the byproducts of the neurotransmitters.

As we have seen throughout this chapter, there are many different forms of depression and mania, and each form may be associated with a different biochemical abnormality. When different types of mood disorder are combined in one study, as is often the case, then it may be impossible to identify consistent differences between people with and without mood disorders. Studies that have attempted to examine the biochemical patterns specific to certain forms of mood disorders have been somewhat successful. For example, one studied suggested that depressed people who have many aggressive and suicidal impulses are especially likely to show evidence of low serotonin levels (see Malone & Mann, 1993).

More recent studies of the monoamine theories have focused on the number and functioning of receptors for the monoamines on neurons in people suffering from mood disorders. Recall from Chapter 3 that neurotransmitters and their receptors interact like locks and keys (see Figure 5.9). Each neurotranmsmitter will fit into a particular type of receptor on the neuronal membrane. If there is the wrong number of receptors for a given type of neurotransmitter or the receptors for that neurotransmitter are too sensitive or not sensitive enough, then the neurons do not efficiently use the neurotransmitter that is available in the synapse.

Several studies suggest that people with major depressive disorder or bipolar disorder may have abnormalities in the number and sensitivity of receptor sites for the monoamine neurotransmitters (e.g., Malone & Mann, 1993; McBride et al., 1994). In major depressive disorder, receptors for serotonin and norepinephrine appear to be too few or insensitive. In bipolar disorder, the picture is less clear, but it is likely that receptors for the monoamines undergo poorly timed changes in sensitivity that are correlated with mood changes (Goodwin & Jamison, 1990). The drugs that relieve depression and mania probably work primarily by changing the sensitivity of neuronal receptors for the monoamines, an effect that takes at least a couple of weeks (Fava & Rosenbaum, 1995).

Most of the neurotransmitter abnormalities found in people with mood disorders are state-dependent. That is, these differences are present when the mood disorder is present but tend to disappear when the mood disorder subsides. Thus, all we know now is that certain neurotransmitter abnormalities may be correlated with, but not necessarily causal of, the mood disorders. As the technology for determining the functioning of neurotransmitters systems develops, our understanding of the relationship between neurotransmitters and mood disorders will no doubt increase.

One intriguing model, known as the *kindling-sensitization model*, suggests that with each episode of depression or mania, these neurotransmitter systems become more easily dysregulated (Post, 1992). The first episode may take a strong stressor to initiate dysregulation, but subsequent episodes require much more mild stressors (environmental or biological) to cause dysregulation. This model helps to explain why, with each new episode of depression or mania, the cumulative risk of new episodes increases. It also helps to explain why the period between episodes decreases over time in many people with mood disorders.

Neuroendocrine Abnormalities

The neuroendocrine system regulates a number of important hormones that, in turn, affect basic functions such as sleep, appetite, sexual drive, and the ability to experience pleasure. These hormones also help the body respond to environmental stressors. Three key components of the neuroendocrine system—the hypothalamus, pituitary, and adrenal cortex—work together in a feedback system that is richly interconnected with the limbic system and the cerebral cortex (see Figure 5.10). This system is often referred to as the *hypothalamic-pituitary-adrenal axis,* or *HPA axis.*

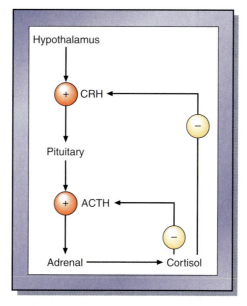

Figure 5.10

The Hypothalamic-Pituitary-Adrenal Axis. The hypothalamus synthesizes corticotrophin-releasing hormone (CRH). CRH is transported to the pituitary gland, where it stimulates the synthesis and release of adrenocorticotrophic hormone (ACTH), which then circulates to the adrenal glands, producing cortisol. Cortisol then inhibits the production of further ACTH and CRH. In normal people, this process prevents too much or too prolonged physiological arousal following a stressor. In major depression, however, people often show abnormal cortisol functioning, suggesting that there is disregulation in this hypothalamic-pituitary-adrenal (HPA) axis.

Normally, when we are confronted with a stressor, the HPA axis becomes more active, increasing levels of hormones like cortisol, which help the body to respond to the stressor by making it possible to fight the stressor or flee from it. Once the stressor is gone, the HPA axis returns to homeostasis.

Depressed people tend to show chronic hyperactivity in the HPA axis and an inability for the HPA axis to return to normal functioning following a stressor (Holsboer, 1992). In turn, the excess hormones produced by heightened HPA activity seem to have an inhibiting effect on receptors for the monoamines. One model for the development of depression is that people exposed to chronic stress may develop poorly regulated neuroendocrine systems. Then when they are exposed even to minor stressors later in life, the HPA axis overreacts and does not easily return to homeostasis. This creates change in the functioning of the monoamine neurotransmitters in the brain, and an episode of depression is likely to ensue (Weiss, 1991).

Neurophysiological Abnormalities

A number of neurophysiological abnormalities have been documented in people with mood disorders, although the significance of these abnormalities is not yet clear (Thase & Howland, 1995). One of the most common neurophysiological abnormalities is altered brain wave activity during sleep. Depressed people have less slow-wave sleep, a type of sleep that helps people feel rested and restored. They go into another form of sleep, rapid eye movement sleep, earlier in the night than do nondepressed people, and they have more of this type of sleep during the night (Figure 5.11). Accompanying these brain wave changes, which can be seen in an electroencephalogram (EEG), are the subjective sleep disturbances of depressed people: They report having trouble going to sleep or remaining asleep, they wake early in the morning and cannot go back to sleep, and they do not feel rested after they sleep.

EEG recordings in awake depressed people also show some abnormalities. It seems that the nondominant side of these people's brains may be overactivated (Banich, Stolar, Heller, & Goldman, 1992). This is interesting because other research on nondepressed people suggests that the nondominant side of the brain (the right side in most people) is particularly active when people are processing information that has a negative emotional tone (Coffey, 1987; Otto, Yeo, & Dougher, 1987). Whether overactivation of the nondominant side of the brain is a cause of depression or simply a symptom of depression is unclear.

Neuroimaging studies using CT scans and MRI scans have found atrophy or deterioration in the cerebral cortex and cerebellum in severe cases of unipolar depression and bipolar disorder (Andreasen, Swayze, Flaum, & Alliger, 1990; Coffey, Wilkinson, Weiner,

Figure 5.11

EEG and Sleep Activity in Normal and Depressed People. (a) The EEG activity of a healthy, 23-year-old female over the course of a night's sleep. (b) the EEG activity of a seriously depressed 63-year-old female over the course of a night. The depressed woman goes into REM sleep much faster than the nondepressed woman and is in and out of REM sleep many more times than the nondepressed woman.
Source: Thase & Howland, 1995, Figure 8.7, p. 236.

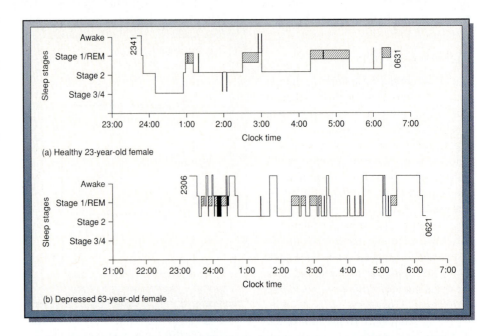

(a) Healthy 23-year-old female

(b) Depressed 63-year-old female

Figure 5.12

Decreased Frontal Cerebral Metabolism in Severely Depressed People. Positron emission tomography (PET) scans show decreased frontal cerebral metabolism in severely depressed people. In the upper- and lower-left and lower-right scans, the abnormality is evident in patients with primary unipolar, primary bipolar, and secondary major depressive syndromes, respectively. Normal brain metabolism is illustrated in the center scans of a healthy control and in the upper right scan of a nondepressed patients with obsessive-compulsive disorder.
Source: From Baxter et al., 1989.

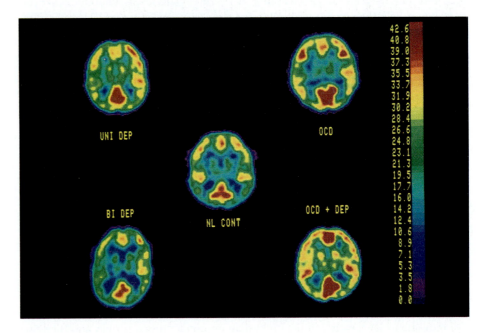

& Ritchie, 1993). PET scans show decreased metabolic activity in the frontal area of the cerebrum of people with severe depression (see Figure 5.12). An interesting study of one person with rapid-cycling bipolar disorder showed that metabolic activity in the brain was highly correlated with how depressed or manic this person was: During manic periods, the metabolism rate was 36 percent greater than during depressed periods (see Figure 5.13; Baxter et al., 1985).

| Summing Up | Biological Theories of Mood Disorders |

- Bipolar disorder is clearly transmitted genetically, although it is somewhat less clear what role genetics play in many forms of unipolar depression.
- The neurotransmitter theories suggest that imbalances in levels of norepinephrine or serotonin or dysregulation of receptors for these neurotransmitters contributes to depression.

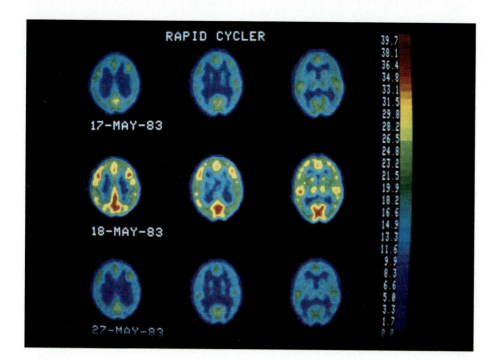

Figure 5.13

Changes in Brain Metabolism from Mania to Depression. The relationship between cerebral metabolism and mood is illustrated in these sequential PET scans of a patient with rapid-cycle bipolar disorder. The whole-brain metabolic rate is 36 percent greater on the hypomanic day (middle row of scans) than on the depressed day (upper and lower rows of scans). Source: Baxter, 1985.

- Depressed people have chronic hyperactivity of the hypothalamic-pituitary-adrenal axis, which helps to regulate the body's response to stress.
- Some depressed people have unusual EEG patterns, disrupted sleep patterns, and abnormalities detectable on CT, PET, and MRI scans.

Biological Therapies for Mood Disorders

Most of the biological treatments for depression and mania are drug treatments. Lithium is the treatment of choice for mania and bipolar disorder, but anticonvulsants, antipsychotics, and calcium channel blockers are also used. There are several classes of antidepressant drugs used to treat depression. In addition to being treated with drugs, some depressed people are treated with electroconvulsive therapy, ECT. Finally, people with the type of depression known as *seasonal affective disorder*, or *SAD*, seem to benefit from a unique type of therapy: exposure to bright lights.

Lithium

The story of the discovery of **lithium** for the treatment of bipolar disorder illustrates the importance of keen observation and the dissemination of scientific findings. An Australian researcher named Cade had been experimenting with the use of lithium to treat gout, a form of arthritis, in the 1940s. His subjects were not people, but pigs—specifically, guinea pigs. Cade noticed that the guinea pigs given lithium became more lethargic and less responsive to their environments. He wondered if lithium might help to calm people who were agitated and overresponsive to their environments. Eventually, he discovered that humans could get some relief from the symptoms of mania with lithium. He published his results in an Australian psychiatry journal in 1949, but because Americans and Europeans did not tend to read that journal, Cade's discovery went unnoticed outside Australia for over a decade.

These days, however, lithium is the most common treatment for bipolar disorder. Older studies suggested that between 80 and 90 percent of patients experience

lithium

most common treatment for bipolar disorder, a drug that reduces levels of certain neurotransmitters and decreases the strength of neuronal firing

significant reductions in their symptoms of bipolar disorder under lithium, but more recent studies suggest the response rate is only 30 to 50 percent (Goodwin & Jamison, 1990; Thase & Kupfer, 1996). Lithium appears to be more effective in reducing the symptoms of mania than the symptoms of depression. People with bipolar disorder are often prescribed lithium to help curb their mania and an antidepressant drug to curb their depression.

Most people with bipolar disorder take lithium even when they have no symptoms of mania or depression, in order to prevent relapses. Approximately 80 percent of patients maintained on adequate doses of lithium do not relapse into new episodes of bipolar disorder (Keller & Baker, 1991). In contrast, the majority of patients not maintained on lithium experience relapses of their disorder.

Although lithium has literally been a lifesaver for many people with bipolar disorder, it poses some problems. First, there are enormous differences among people's rates of absorbing lithium, so the proper dosage varies greatly from one person to the next. Second, the difference between an effective dose of lithium and a toxic dose is small, leaving a very narrow window of therapeutic effectiveness. Thus, people who take lithium must be monitored carefully by physicians who can determine whether the dosage of lithium is adequate to relieve the symptoms of bipolar disorder but not too large to induce toxic side effects.

The side effects of lithium range from annoying to life-threatening. Many patients experience abdominal pain, nausea, vomiting, diarrhea, tremors, and twitches. Says Kay Jamison,

> I found myself beholden to a medication that also caused severe nausea and vomiting many times a month—I often slept on my bathroom floor with a pillow under my head and my warm, woolen St. Andrews gown tucked over me. . . .
> I have been violently ill more places than I choose to remember, and quite embarrassingly so in public places. (Jamison, 1995b, p. 93)

People on lithium complain of blurred vision and problems in concentration and attention that interfere with their ability to work. Lithium can cause a form of diabetes, kidney dysfunction, and birth defects if taken by pregnant women during the first trimester of their pregnancy.

It is not surprising that many people with bipolar disorder will not take lithium or go on and off of it, against their physicians' advice. In addition to experiencing side effects, many patients complain that they miss the positive symptoms of their mania—the elated moods, flowing ideas, and heightened self-esteem—and feel washed out on lithium. Especially during periods of calm, they feel they can manage their illness without lithium and that they can detect when a new episode is coming and go back on the medication then. Usually, however, as a new episode of mania becomes more and more severe, their judgment becomes more impaired, and they do not go back on the lithium.

Studies have shown that combining drug treatment for bipolar disorder with cognitive-behavioral therapy (described below) may reduce the rate at which patients stop taking their medications and may lead more patients to achieve full remission of their symptoms, compared to lithium treatment alone (Miller, Norman, & Keitner, 1989). Psychotherapy can help people with bipolar disorder understand and accept their need for lithium treatment. It also can help them cope with the impact of the disorder on their lives:

> At this point in my existence, I cannot imagine leading a normal life without both taking lithium and having had the benefits of psychotherapy. Lithium prevents my seductive but disastrous highs, diminishes my depressions, clears out the wool and webbing from my disordered thinking, slows me down, gentles me out, keeps me from ruining my career and relationships, keeps me out of a hospital, alive, and makes psychotherapy possible. But, ineffably, psychotherapy *heals*. It makes some sense of the confusion, reins in the terrifying thoughts and feelings, returns some control and hope and possibility of learning from it all. Pills cannot, do not, ease one back into reality; they only bring one back headlong, careening, and faster than

can be endured at times. Psychotherapy is a sanctuary; it is a battleground; it is a place I have been psychotic, neurotic, elated, confused, and despairing beyond belief. But, always, it is where I have believed—or have learned to believe—that I might someday be able to contend with all of this. (Jamison, 1995b, pp. 88–89)

Anticonvulsants, Antipsychotics, and Calcium Channel Blockers

Sometimes lithium does not overcome mania, and even if it is effective, some people cannot tolerate its side effects. Three other classes of drugs, **anticonvulsant drugs, antipsychotic drugs,** and **calcium channel blockers** are alternatives to lithium for the treatment of mania.

The most commonly prescribed anticonvulsant is carbamazepine. Carbamazepine can be highly effective in reducing the symptoms of severe and acute mania, but it does not seem as effective as lithium in the long-term treatment of bipolar disorder (Lerer et al., 1987). The side effects of carbamazepine include dizziness, rash, nausea, and drowsiness (Goodwin & Jamison, 1990). The mechanism by which carbamazepine reduces mania is not yet clear.

The antipsychotic drugs (also referred to as **neuroleptic drugs**) are also used to quell the symptoms of severe mania. These drugs reduce functional levels of dopamine and seem especially useful in the treatment of psychotic manic symptoms. They have many neurological side effects, however, the most severe of which is an irreversible condition known as *tardive dyskinesia*. People with tardive dyskinesia have uncontrollable tics and movements of their face and limbs.

Most recently, drugs known as calcium channel blockers, such as veraparnil, have been shown to be effective in treating mania in small studies (see Thase & Kupfer, 1996). It is not currently known how these drugs work to lower mania.

Tricyclic Antidepressants

The **tricyclic antidepressant drugs** help to reduce the symptoms of depression by preventing the reuptake of norepinephrine or other monoamine neurotransmitters in the synapse or by changing the responsiveness or number of receptors for these neurotransmitters. These drugs are highly effective: 60 to 85 percent of depressed people can get relief with them from their symptoms of depression (Guze & Gitlin, 1994). Some of the most commonly prescribed tricyclic antidepressants are imipramine, amitriptylene, and desipramine.

Unfortunately, however, the tricyclic antidepressants have a number of side effects. The most common ones are dry mouth, excessive perspiration, blurring of vision, constipation, urinary retention, and sexual dysfunction. In addition, some of the tricyclics, especially amitriptylene, can cause weight gain and sedation. These side effects can be beneficial to depressed people who have lost much weight and who have trouble sleeping. However, the weight gain caused by the antidepressants can cause some patients, especially women, to discontinue using them. Another problem with the tricyclic antidepressants is that they can take 4 to 8 weeks to show an effect (Fava & Rosenbaum, 1995). This is an excruciatingly long time to wait for relief from depression. Finally, the tricyclics can be fatal in overdose, and an overdose is only three to four times the average daily prescription for the drug. Thus, physicians are wary of prescribing these drugs, particularly for depressed persons who might be suicidal.

Monamine Oxidase Inhibitors

A second class of drugs used to treat depression is the **monoamine oxidase inhibitors (MAOIs)**. MAO is an enzyme that causes the breakdown of the monoamine neurotransmitters in the synapse. MAO inhibitors decrease the action of MAO and thus result in increases in the levels of the neurotransmitters in the synapse.

anticonvulsant drugs
treatments for mania and alternatives to lithium, effective in reducing mania symptoms but also carrying side effects such as dizziness, rash, nausea, and drowsiness

antipsychotic drugs
treatments for psychotic symptoms, effective by reducing levels of dopamine but also carrying neurological side effects such as tics; also called neuroleptic drugs

calcium channel blockers
treatments for mania

neuroleptic drugs
See **antipsychotic drugs.**

tricyclic antidepressant drugs
treatments for depression that prevent reuptake of monoamines in the synapse while also changing the sensitivity and number of monoamine receptors

monoamine oxidase inhibitors (MAOIs)
treatments for depression that inhibit monoamine oxidase, an enzyme that breaks down monoamines in the synapse, thereby yielding more monoamines

Some studies suggest that the MAOIs are less effective than the tricyclic antidepressants, but this may be because physicians are more conservative in prescribing MAOIs than tricyclic antidepressants, and thus many patients may not be prescribed therapeutic levels of the MAOIs (Fava & Rosenbaum, 1995). The reason physicians are more cautious in prescribing MAOIs is that the side effects of these drugs are potentially more dangerous. When people taking MAOIs ingest food rich in an amino acid called *tyramine*, they can experience a rise in blood pressure that can be fatal. The foods that can interact with MAOIs include aged or ripened cheeses, red wine, beer, and chocolate. The MAOIs can also interact with several drugs, including antihypertension medications and over-the-counter drugs like antihistamines. Finally, MAOIs can cause liver damage, weight gain, severe lowering of blood pressure, and several of the side effects caused by the tricyclic antidepressants.

Selective Serotonin Reuptake Inhibitors

selective serotonin reuptake inhibitors (SSRIs)
treatments for depression that inhibit the reuptake of serotonin by the sending neuron, increasing the amount in the synapse

The newest class of antidepressant drugs is the **selective serotonin reuptake inhibitors**, or **SSRIs**. These drugs are similar in structure to the tricyclic antidepressants, but work more directly to affect serotonin than do the tricyclics. These drugs have become extremely popular in the treatment of depression for several reasons. First, many people begin experiencing relief from their depression after a couple of weeks of using these drugs, whereas it often takes 4 weeks or more for the other drugs to show significant effects. Second, the side effects of the selective serotonin reuptake inhibitors tend to be less severe than the side effects of the other antidepressants. Third, these drugs do not tend to be fatal in overdose and thus are safer than the other antidepressants (Fava & Rosenbaum, 1995).

The SSRIs do have their side effects, however (Fisher, Kent, & Bryant, 1995). One of the most common is increased agitation or nervousness. People on SSRIs often report feeling "jittery" or "hyper" and that they cannot sit still. They may have mild tremors and increased perspiration and feel weak. Others may find themselves becoming angry or hostile more often. Nausea and stomach cramps or gas are common side effects, as is a decrease in appetite. Finally, sexual dysfunction and decreased sexual drive are reported by some people on SSRIs. For many people, these side effects diminish after they have taken the drug for a few weeks, so they may be encouraged to stick with the drug even if they are experiencing side effects, in hopes that the side effects will decrease and the positive effects of the drug will begin to be apparent.

One of the best known selective serotonin reuptake inhibitors is fluoxetine, which goes under the trade name *Prozac*. Prozac was touted as the new "wonder drug" for the treatment of depression in the early 1980s. Clinicians were initially very excited about Prozac because it seemed to work faster and more reliably than the traditional antidepressants and to have fewer side effects. Just a few years after Prozac was declared a wonder drug, some people began calling it a killer drug. Several cases in which depressed patients had become suicidal while on Prozac were reported in the media and medical journals. Controlled empirical studies have found, however, that the rate of suicide among depressed patients on Prozac is not significantly higher than the rate among depressed patients on the other antidepressant drugs (see Thase & Kupfer, 1996).

Other concerns have been raised about the ways the selective serotonin reuptake inhibitors are being used, however. In the United States, over 1 million prescriptions are filled each month for Prozac alone. Most of these prescriptions are filled for people who probably do not meet the diagnostic criteria for a depressive disorder but want some help in dealing with the stresses they are facing or with moderate levels of distress they are experiencing. In addition, some clinicians are promoting the serotonin reuptake inhibitors as drugs that can improve people's personalities (see Figure 5.14). Many people are questioning whether it is appropriate to "change one's personality with a pill" or to use prescription drugs to handle everyday stressors.

While there is now a large selection of drug therapies available for the treatment of depression, there are no consistent rules for determining which of the antidepressant drugs to try first with a depressed patient (Thase & Kupfer, 1996). Many clinicians begin

Figure 5.14

Magazine Cover Illustrating the Controversy over New Uses of the SSRIs. Our society is debating the wisdom of letting people "change their personalities with a pill."

Source: *Beyond Prozac.* (1994, February 7). *Newsweek.*

with the serotonin reuptake inhibitors, because their side effects tend to be less significant. Depressed people often must try several different drugs before finding one that will work well for them and has tolerable side effects. When they find the drug that works for them, it is often as if they have regained their lives:

> And then something just kind of changed in me. Over the next few days, I became all right, safe in my own skin. It happened just like that. One morning I woke up, and I really did want to live, really looked forward to greeting the day, imagined errands to run, phone calls to return, and it was not with a feeling of great dread, not with the sense that the first person who stepped on my toe as I walked through the square may well have driven me to suicide. It was as if the miasma of depression had lifted off me, gone smoothly about its business, in the same way that the fog in San Francisco rises as the day wears on. (Wurtzel, 1995, p. 329)

 Would you want to know how a drug worked before taking it yourself or is it only important that it work?

Electroconvulsive Therapy

Perhaps the most controversial of the biological treatments for depression is **electroconvulsive therapy,** or *ECT*. ECT was introduced in the early twentieth century, originally as a treatment for schizophrenia. Italian physicians Ugo Cerlettii and Lucio Bini decided to experiment with the use of ECT to treat schizophrenics, reasoning that ECT could calm schizophrenics much like experiencing an epileptic seizure would calm and sedate epileptics. Eventually, clinicians found that ECT was not effective for schizophrenia, but it was effective for depression.

ECT consists of a series of treatments in which a brain seizure is induced by passing electrical current through the patient's brain. Patients are first anesthetized and given muscle relaxants so that they are not conscious when they have the seizure and so that their muscles do not jerk violently during the seizure. Metal electrodes are taped to the head, and a current of 70 to 130 volts is passed through one side of the brain for about one-half of a second. Patients typically go into a convulsion, which lasts about 1 minute. The full ECT treatment consists of 6 to 12 sessions.

ECT is most often given to depressed people who have not responded to drug therapies, and it relieves depression in 50 to 60 percent of these people (Thase & Kupfer, 1996). It is not entirely clear how ECT lifts depression. The seizures may increase the permeability of the blood-brain barrier, allowing the antidepressant medications more fully into the brain. When animals are given ECT, they show an acute release of norepinephrine and dopamine. If this also happens in humans, which is unclear, it may be the mechanism by which depression is decreased. Alternately, ECT may work because it causes a severe stimulation of the hypothalamus, a part of the brain that regulates sleep, eating, sexual drive, and emotion. ECT appears to be especially effective for depressed people suffering from weight loss, loss of sexual drive, and insomnia. The most recent theories about how ECT works suggest that it increases the number and sensitivity of a specific type of receptor for serotonin (Extein, 1989).

ECT is controversial for several reasons. First, there were reports in the past of ECT being used as a punishment for patients who were unruly, as was depicted in the movie *One Flew Over the Cuckoo's Nest.* Second, ECT can lead to memory loss and difficulties in learning new information. When ECT was first developed, it was administered to both sides of the brain, and the effects on memory and learning were sometimes severe and permanent. These days, ECT is usually delivered only to one side of the brain, usually the right side because it is less involved in learning and memory. As a result, patients undergoing modern ECT do not tend to experience significant or long-term memory or learning difficulties (Swartz, 1995). Because this unilateral administration is sometimes not

electroconvulsive therapy (ECT) treatment for depression that involves the induction of a brain seizure by passing electrical current through the patient's brain while he or she is anesthetized

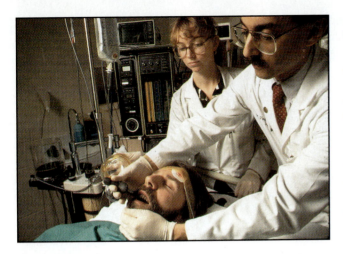

Electroconvulsive therapy is used to treat serious depressions, particularly those that do not respond to drug treatments.

as effective as bilateral administration, some people are still given bilateral ECT. Third, although ECT can be extremely effective in eliminating the symptoms of depression, the relapse rate among people who have undergone ECT is as high as 85 percent (Swartz, 1995). Fourth, perhaps the strongest reason ECT is controversial is that the idea of having electrical current passed through one's brain is very frightening and seems like a primitive form of treatment.

Still, ECT is sometimes the only form of treatment that works for severely depressed patients. Often, ECT is tried as a treatment of last choice for patients who have not responded to a number of antidepressant drugs. In these patients, ECT tends to be effect about 50 percent of the time.

Light Therapy

Would it not be great if depressed people could be cured simply by sitting in the warm sunshine for a few hours a day? It turns out that **light therapy** is just what is needed for people with a subtype of depression, seasonal affective disorder, or SAD. Recall that people with SAD become depressed during the winter months when there are the fewest hours of daylight. If these people are exposed to bright lights for a few hours each day during the winter months, they often experience complete relief from their depression within a couple of days (Rosenthal, 1993).

Exposure to bright lights may help to reduce seasonal affective disorder by resetting depressed people's circadian rhythms. Circadian rhythms are natural cycles of biological activities that occur every 24 hours. The production of several hormones and neurotransmitters varies over the course of the day according to circadian rhythms. These rhythms are regulated by internal clocks but can be affected by environmental stimuli, including light. Depressed people sometimes show disregulation of their circadian rhythms. Light therapy may work by resetting circadian rhythms and thereby normalizing the production of hormones and neurotransmitters (Oren & Rosenthal, 1992; Wehr & Rosenthal, 1989). Another theory is that light therapy works by decreasing levels of the hormone melatonin secreted by the pineal gland. Decreasing melatonin levels can increase levels of norepinephrine and serotonin, thereby reducing the symptoms of depression (Oren & Rosenthal, 1992). Some studies have failed to support the hypothesis that melatonin plays a central role in seasonal affective disorder, however. Finally, recent studies suggest that exposure to bright lights may increase serotonin levels, thereby decreasing depression (Rosenthal, 1995).

Whatever the mechanism, light therapy appears to be highly effective for the subgroup of depressed people whose depressions are clearly tied to the number of hours of daylight per day. Happily, light therapy appears to have few side effects: One cannot get a sunburn from the lights, for example. Light therapy is now portable. The lights can be built into visors that people can wear on their heads, so they do not have to remain in a room under a bank of lights but can go about their daily business while receiving the therapy.

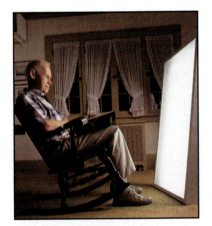

People with seasonal affective disorder can get relief from their depression by sitting under bright lights for some period each day during the winter months.

Summing Up	Biological Therapies for Mood Disorders

- Lithium is useful in the treatment of mood disorders but requires careful monitoring to prevent dangerous side effects.
- Anticonvulsants, antipsychotics, and calcium channel blockers can also help to relieve mania.
- Tricyclic antidepressants are effective in treating depression but have some side effects and can be dangerous in overdose.
- The monoamine oxidase inhibitors also are effective treatments for depression but can interact with certain medications and foods.

- The selective serotonin reuptake inhibitors are effective treatments for depression and have become popular because they are less dangerous and have more tolerable side effects than other drug treatments.
- Electroconvulsive therapy involves inducing seizures in depressed people; it can be quite effective but is controversial.
- Exposure to bright lights can be a highly effective treatment for people with seasonal affective disorder.

Psychosocial Theories of Mood Disorders

Most of the psychosocial theories of mood disorders focus only on the depressive disorders. Psychosocial theorists tend to view bipolar disorder as caused by biological factors, although new episodes of bipolar disorder may be triggered by stressful events or by living in an unsupportive family (Johnson & Roberts, 1995). For the most part, however, the psychosocial theories of mood disorders have focused on characteristics of individuals and their environments that put them at risk to develop depression. Let us turn to the most prominent of these theories.

Stressful life events, particularly the loss of a loved one, are tied to depression.

Behavioral Theories

Many people believe that depression often arises as a reaction to stressful negative events, such as the breakup of a relationship, the death of a loved one, job loss, or a serious medical illness. Sixty-five percent of people with a nonmelancholic type of depression report a negative life event in the six months prior to the onset of their depression (Frank et al., 1994). Depressed people are also more likely to have chronic life stressors, such as financial strain or a bad marriage, than nondepressed people.

The **behavioral theories of depression** suggest that life stress leads to depression because it creates a reduction in positive reinforcers in a person's life (Lewinsohn & Gotlib, 1995). The person begins to withdraw, which only results in further reduction in reinforcers, which leads to more withdrawal, and a self-perpetuating chain is created. For example, imagine that a man is having difficulty in his relationship with his wife. Interactions with her are no longer as positively reinforcing as they formerly were, so he stops initiating these interactions as often. This only worsens the communication between him and his wife, however, so the relationship becomes even worse. He withdraws further and becomes depressed about this area of his life. The behavioral theories suggest that such a pattern is especially likely in people with poor social skills, because they are more likely to experience rejection by others and to withdraw in response to this rejection rather than find ways to overcome the rejection (Lewinsohn, 1974). In addition, these theories suggest that once a person begins engaging in depressive behaviors, these behaviors are reinforced by the sympathy and attention they engender in others.

Another behavioral theory—the **learned helplessness theory**—suggests that the type of stressful event most likely to lead to depression is an uncontrollable negative event. Such an event, especially if frequent or chronic, can lead people to believe that they are helpless to control important outcomes in their environment. In turn, this belief in helplessness leads people to lose their motivation, to reduce actions that might control the environment, and to be unable to learn how to control situations that are controllable. These deficits, known as **learned helplessness deficits**, are similar to the symptoms of depression: low motivation, passivity, indecisiveness (Seligman, 1975).

The initial evidence for the learned helplessness theory came from studies with animals. A group of researchers conducted a series of studies in which dogs were given either controllable shock, uncontrollable shock, or no shock (Overmier and Seligman, 1967; Seligman, & Maier, 1967). The dogs in the controllable shock group could turn off the shock by jumping a short barrier, and they quickly learned how to do so (as did the dogs who

behavioral theories of depression view that depression results from negative life events that represent a reduction in positive reinforcement; sympathetic responses to depressive behavior then serve as positive reinforcement for the depression itself

learned helplessness theory view that exposure to uncontrollable negative events leads to a belief in one's inability to control important outcomes and a subsequent loss of motivation, indecisiveness, and failure of action, symptoms of depression

learned helplessness deficits symptoms such as low motivation, passivity, indecisiveness, and an inability to control outcomes that result from exposure to uncontrollable negative events

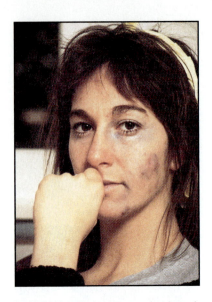

People who live with chronic stress, such as battered women, can develop learned helplessness—the belief that nothing they do can prevent bad events from happening.

had previously received no shock). The dogs in the uncontrollable shock group could not turn off or otherwise escape the shock. The dogs in the controllable and uncontrollable shock conditions received the same total amount of shock. However, when the dogs in the uncontrollable shock group were put into a situation in which they could control the shock, they seemed unable to learn how to do so. They would just sit in the box, passive and whimpering, until the shock went off. Even when the experimenter dragged these dogs across the barrier in an attempt to teach them how to turn off the shock, the dogs did not learn the response. The researchers argued that the dogs in the uncontrollable shock group had learned they were helpless to control the shock, and their passivity and inability to learn to control the shock were the result of this learned helplessness.

In turn, they argued that many human depressions may be helplessness depressions, resulting when people come to believe they are helpless to control important outcomes in their environment. For example, children who lose their mothers may come to believe that important areas of their lives are not under their control. The loss of a mother may not only mean the loss of the person to whom the child is most closely attached. It may also mean years of disruption and instability as the child is moved from one set of relatives to another, if the father is not able to care for the child. Such chronic instability might persuade the child that life truly is uncontrollable, and this may be why childhood bereavement is a predisposing factor for depression. Similarly, women who are frequently battered by their husbands may develop the belief that there is nothing they can do to control their beatings or other parts of their lives, and this may explain the high rates of depression among battered wives (Rounsaville, 1978).

One major problem with the behavioral theories of depression, and more generally with the notion that stressful events are a cause of depression, is that most people who experience uncontrollable, negative events do not become seriously depressed for a significant period of time. In the late 1970s, some psychologists began to argue that the ways people interpret negative events determine whether they will develop depression following the events. We will now turn to these cognitive models of depression.

Cognitive Theories

"Good morning, Eeyore," shouted Piglet.
"Good morning, Little Piglet," said Eeyore. "If it *is* a good morning," he said. "Which I doubt," said he. "Not that it matters," he said. (Milne, 1961, p. 54)

The major argument of the cognitive theories of depression is that the ways people think influence the likelihood they will become depressed. Like poor Eeyore, some people have a chronically gloomy way of interpreting the things that happen to them, and they are more prone to depression. Although there are many individual cognitive theories of depression, we will focus on the two that have had the most impact: Aaron Beck's cognitive distortion theory and the reformulated learned helplessness theory.

cognitive distortion theory
theory that depression results from errors in thinking—such as jumping to conclusions, exaggerating the negative, and ignoring the positive—that lead one to a gloomy view of the self, the world, and the future

One of the first cognitive theories of depression was the **cognitive distortion theory** developed by psychiatrist Aaron Beck. Beck (1967) argued that depressed people commit many types of errors in thinking, such as jumping to negative conclusions on the basis of little evidence, ignoring good events and focusing only on negative events, and exaggerating negative events (see Table 5.2). These errors in thinking tend to perpetuate a negative view of the world, of the future, and of the self in depressed people. Depressed people may not be aware that they hold these negative views or that they make these errors in thinking: Often these negative thoughts are so automatic that depressed people do not realize how they are interpreting situations. Beck's theory led to one of the most widely used and successful therapies for depression, cognitive-behavioral therapy. We will discuss this therapy in detail shortly.

reformulated learned helplessness theory
view that people who attribute negative events to internal, stable, and global causes are more likely than other people to experience learned helplessness deficits following such events and are thus predisposed to depression

First, however, let us focus on another influential cognitive theory of depression, the **reformulated learned helplessness theory**. This theory was proposed to explain how cognitive factors might influence whether a person becomes helpless and depressed following a negative event (Abramson, Seligman, & Teasdale, 1978). This theory focuses

Table 5.2 Errors or Disortions in Thinking in Depression

The cognitive distortions theory of depression suggests that depressed people commit many errors in thinking.

1. *All-or-nothing thinking.* Seeing things in black-or-white, all-or-nothing terms: "If I don't get an A on this test, I'll be a failure."
2. *Overgeneralization.* Seeing a single negative event as part of a large pattern of negative events: "I messed up this relationship and I'll never have a good relationship."
3. *Mental filter.* Focusing only on the negative aspects of a situation: "I can't believe I missed 5 questions on that test (of 100 questions). What an idiot I am."
4. *Disqualifying the positive.* Rejecting positive experiences by discounting them: "Anyone can run a 4-minute mile. That's nothing."
5. *Jumping to conclusions.* Concluding that something negative will happen or is happening with no evidence: "I haven't heard from my friend for over a week. She's probably angry at me for something."
6. *Emotional reasoning.* Assuming that negative emotions necessarily reflect reality: "I feel dumb so I must be dumb."
7. *Should statements.* Putting constant demands on oneself: "I should be a more upbeat person/better student/better lover."
8. *Labeling.* Overgeneralizing by attaching a negative, global label to a person or situation: "I'm a loser." "This situation is hopeless."
9. *Personalization.* Attributing negative events to the self without reason: "The professor is in a bad mood because she doesn't want to deal with me because I ask such stupid questions."

Source: Data from D. D. Burns, *Feeling Good: The New Mood Therapy*, 1980.

on people's causal attributions for events. A **causal attribution** is an explanation of why an event happened. Take, for example, a student who failed an exam. She could explain her failure in many ways: She did not study hard enough, she is not good at that subject, the exam was too hard, the instructor did not give the students enough time to finish the exam, she is generally not a good student. According to the reformulated learned helplessness theory, there are three characteristics of causal attributions that are important in determining whether a person develops learned helplessness deficits (and therefore depressive symptoms) after an event (see Table 5.3).

First, causes can be factors that are *internal* to the individual or that are *external* to the individual. People who attribute negative events to internal causes tend to blame themselves for these events and thus are more likely to show self-esteem loss than are people who attribute negative events to external causes. So if the student who failed the exam attributes her failure to not having studied hard enough, an internal cause, she will be more likely to lose self-esteem than if she attributes her failure to the exam being too hard, an external cause.

Second, causes can be factors that are *stable* in time or *unstable* in time. People who attribute negative events to stable causes expect these negative events to happen again in the future and thus show lowered motivation and other helplessness deficits for a longer time than people who attribute negative events to unstable causes. Again, consider the student who failed the exam. If she attributes the failure to a stable cause, such as having no ability in the subject of the exam, she will expect to fail again in the future and will show longer learned helplessness deficits than if she attributes the failure to an unstable cause, such as the instructor not giving the students enough time.

causal attribution
explanation for why an event occurred that can be internal or external to the individual, stable or unstable in duration, and global or specific in origin

Table 5.3 Attributional Dimensions Important in Depression

The perceived causes of negative events are as follows:

Internal to the person: "It's my fault I failed the exam."
Stable in time: "The reason I failed the exam will occur over and over again."
Global in effect: "This is going to affect my performance in other classes as well."

Students with a pessimistic style of thinking are most distressed when they do poorly on an exam.

Third, causes can be factors that are *global* and affect many areas of one's life or *specific* to just one domain of life. People who attribute negative events to global causes expect negative events to occur in many areas of their lives and thus show learned helplessness deficits in many domains, whereas people who attribute negative events to specific causes only show learned helplessness deficits in that one domain. If the student who failed the exam attributes her failure to her general lack of academic ability, a global cause, she will show learned helplessness in many academic subjects. If she attributes her failure to a lack of ability in just this one academic domain, she will only show learned helplessness deficits in this one domain.

So, according to this theory, people who habitually explain negative events by causes that are internal, stable, and global blame themselves for these negative events, expect negative events to recur in the future, and expect to experience negative events in many areas of their lives. In turn, these expectations lead them to experience long-term learned helplessness deficits plus self-esteem loss in many areas of their lives. Again, researchers equate learned helplessness deficits with depression and argue that an internal-stable-global attributional style for negative events puts people at risk for depression. Most recently, Abramson, Metalsky, and Alloy (1989) argued that a particular form of depression, hopelessness depression, develops when people make pessimistic attributions for the most important events in their lives and perceive they have no way of coping with the consequences of these events.

Many studies have found that the more depressed a person is, the more likely she is to attribute bad events to internal, stable, and global causes (see Peterson & Seligman, 1984, and Sweeney, Anderson, & Bailey, 1986, for reviews). However, we cannot rely on cross-sectional correlational studies to test this theory. Perhaps a pessimistic attributional style is simply a symptom of depression and not a cause.

One study that attempted to test the causal influence of attributional style on depression made use of a naturally occurring stressful event: a midterm examination in an Abnormal Psychology course. The researchers reasoned that students who tended to attribute negative events to internal, stable, and global causes would be more likely to show depressive symptoms if they did poorly on a midterm exam than students who did poorly but tended to attribute negative events to external, unstable, and specific causes. They administered a questionnaire that assessed attributional style to 94 students in an Abnormal Psychology course a couple of weeks before the midterm exam. Also before the exam, the students completed questionnaires that assessed how depressed they were, what grades they hoped to get on the exam, and what grades they would consider a failure. The students' levels of depression were then assessed again the day they received their grades on the exam and two days later (see Figure 5.15).

The researchers found that the only significant predictor of students' levels of depression on the day they received their grades was how well they did on the exam: Students who did more poorly than they wanted to were more depressed than were students who did at least as well as they wanted to, regardless of their attributional styles. However, when the researchers examined depression levels two days after the exam, they found that, among students who did more poorly on the exam than they wanted to, those who had an internal-stable-global attributional style before the exam were significantly more depressed than were students who had a more optimistic attributional style. Again, students who did well on the exam had low levels of depression regardless of their attributional styles (Metalsky, Halberstadt, & Abramson, 1987). The results of this study support an important feature of the reformulated learned helplessness theory: A pessimistic attributional style will lead to depression only when coupled with negative life events. Thus, this theory is a vulnerability-stress theory. The vulnerability factor is a pessimistic attributional style, but a stressor, such as failure on an exam, is also necessary for the development of depression.

Despite the intuitive appeal of and empirical evidence for cognitive theories of depression, there are some problems with these theories. First, some studies suggest that depressed people make pessimistic attributions and have negative automatic thoughts only when they are depressed, but they appear no different in their thoughts before and

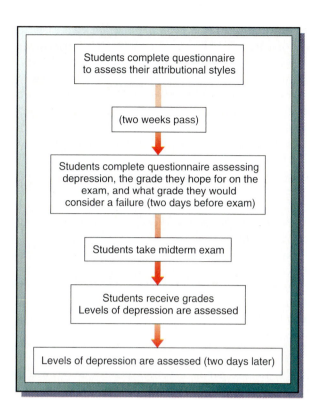

Figure 5.15

The Study of Students in an Abnormal Psychology Course. A study of students taking an Abnormal Psychology course tested the reformulated learned helplessness theory of depression.
Source: *Metalsky et al., 1987.*

after their episodes of depression (see, for example, Hamilton & Abramson, 1983). If negative cognitive styles are a cause of depression, then people who are prone to depression should show these negative cognitive styles when they are not depressed as well as when they are depressed. Beck (see Beck et al., 1979) has suggested that negative cognitions can be latent in people prone to depression when they are not in episodes of depression. That is, these negative cognitions are not on the surface, in consciousness, but they come to the surface in situations that remind the depression-prone person of these thoughts. As these thoughts come to the surface, the person becomes more depressed, and the more depressed the person becomes, the more salient and available these negative thoughts become. There is some experimental evidence in support of this line of argument. Miranda and Persons (1988) induced a mild depressed mood in a group of depression-prone people who were not currently depressed and in another group of people with no history of depression. The depressed mood was induced by having the subjects read a series of increasingly depressing statements. Before the mood induction, the two groups of subjects did not differ in the number of negative thoughts they endorsed. However, under the mood induction, the depression-prone subjects endorsed significantly more negative thoughts than did the subjects with no history of depression. Thus, it may be that negative attributions and cognitions lie beneath the surface of consciousness in depression-prone people when they are not depressed and become activated under certain circumstances, feeding their depressions.

Depressive Distortions or Depressive Realism?

Is it possible that depressed people are not distorted in their negative views of the world but actually are seeing the world realistically for the terrible place that it is? Researchers began investigating this possibility when they stumbled upon a phenomenon that is now referred to as **depressive realism:** When asked to make judgments about how much control they have over situations that are actually uncontrollable, depressed people are quite accurate. In contrast, nondepressed people greatly overestimate the amount of control they have, especially over positive events (Alloy & Abramson, 1979). For example, in one

depressive realism
phenomenon whereby depressed people make more realistic judgments as to whether they can control actually uncontrollable event than do nondepressed people, who exhibit an illusion of control over the same events

study, depressed and nondepressed people were asked to judge to what degree they could control the onset of a green light by pushing a button on a display panel. In truth, none of the subjects had control over the onset of the light. In conditions in which subjects were rewarded whenever the green light came on, the nondepressed people grossly overestimated their control over the onset of the light. In contrast, the depressed subjects accurately judged that they had no control over the onset of the light.

Subsequently, a long line of research has shown that nondepressed people have a robust illusion that they can control all sorts of situations that truly are out of their control and that they have superior skills compared to most people (Taylor & Brown, 1988). For example, nondepressed people believe they can control games of chance like the lottery, that they are more likely than the average person to succeed in life, that they are more immune to car accidents than other people, and that their social skills are better than most people's. In contrast, depressed people do not seem to hold these illusions of control and superiority. Indeed, depressed people seem amazingly accurate in judging the amount of control they have over situations and their skills at various tasks.

This research on illusion of control calls into question the notion that depression results from unrealistic beliefs that one cannot control one's environment or from negative errors in thinking about oneself and the world. Perhaps it is not accurate and realistic thinking that prevents people from becoming depressed but hope and optimism.

 If depressed people are more realistic about life, is it possible or ethical to try to change their outlook through psychotherapy?

Psychodynamic Theories

Some people seem to find themselves in unhealthy and destructive relationships over and over again. Each time these relationships end, they vow never to get into similar relationships again. However, they do and then find themselves depressed over the problems in the relationships or when the relationships inevitably end.

Psychodynamic theorists suggest that such patterns of unhealthy relationships stem from people's childhood experiences that prevented them from developing a strong and positive sense of self reasonably independent of others' evaluations (Arieti & Bemporad, 1980; Bibring, 1953; Blatt & Zuroff, 1992; Freud, 1917). As adults, these people are constantly searching for approval and security in their relationships with others. They are anxious about separation and abandonment and may allow others to take advantage and even abuse them rather than risk losing the relationship by complaining. They are constantly striving to be "perfect" so that they will be loved. Even when they accomplish great things, they do not feel secure or positive about themselves. Eventually, some problem in a close relationship or some failure to achieve perfection occurs, and they plunge into depression.

Many modern psychodynamic theorists still rely on the groundbreaking work of Freud to describe just how depression develops when a person perceives he or she has been abandoned or has failed. Freud pointed out that people who are depressed have many of the symptoms of people who are grieving the death of a loved one: they feel sad, alone, unmotivated, and lethargic. Unlike grieving people, depressed people display severe self-hate and self-blame. Indeed, said Freud, depressed people appear to want to punish themselves, even to the point of killing themselves. Freud argued that depressives are not actually blaming or punishing themselves. Instead, they are blaming or punishing those they perceive have abandoned them. Depressives are so dependent on the approval and love of others that much of their ego or sense of self is made up of their images of these others—what Freud called the "love objects." When they believe others have rejected them, depressives are too frightened to express their rage for this rejection outwardly. Instead, they turn their anger inward on the parts of their own egos that have incorporated the love objects. Their self-blame and punishment is actually blame and punishment of the others who have abandoned them. This is Freud's "introjected hostility" theory of depression.

The case of Giselle illustrates the processes described by the psychodynamic theories of depression.

Case Study • Giselle was raised by two well-meaning but emotionally inhibited parents. The parents had emigrated to the United States from Eastern Europe in the 1970s, fleeing persecution for their anticommunist beliefs. Even after settling in the United States, Giselle's parents remained paranoid about the family's security and constantly told Giselle she had to be "good" or the family would be in danger. Thus, from an early age, Giselle suppressed any childhood willfulness or exuberance. She was not allowed to play with other children; she spent most of her time with the family maid, who had followed them to the United States. Her parents were preoccupied with their uncertain circumstances and also unnecessarily belittled Giselle's childhood concerns. For example, when there was an epidemic of flu at Giselle's school, her mother told her not to worry because only the smart and pretty girls were getting sick. The mother doted on the father when he was in the house, ignoring Giselle. The father payed attention to Giselle only when she was deferential or complimentary.

As a result, Giselle grew up feeling that she was a burden to her parents and had little to offer others; she was greatly desirous of attention and affection yet believed she was too inadequate ever to fulfill her aspirations. The best she could hope for was to be tolerated by others if she worked very hard, did not make trouble, exceeded the expectations of others, and suppressed her own strivings for pleasure. Her vivacity and cheeriness, which she had learned endeared her to others, actually hid a chronic dissatisfaction with herself and a painful insecurity as to her acceptability.

As an adult, Giselle chose to become a nurse because she felt it would gain her acceptance and love by patients. She became the major source of financial support during her marriage, often taking on extra shifts to earn more money. She had done remarkably well in her career because of her hard work and her repeated efforts to please others. She was also the emotional mainstay in her family, being responsible for taking care of the children and for fulfilling the usual responsibilites of running a household. Giselle rarely complained, however. She needed to be certain that everyone liked her and thought well of her and she went to extremes of self-sacrifice to ensure the high regard of others.

Giselle married a man who was somewhat solitary and hypercritical. He was prone to periods of depression and always preoccupied with his own concerns. Giselle saw her husband's psychological liabilities as assets, however, because someone so needy and socially withdrawn would never abandon her or seek the company of another woman. He did leave her, however, telling her that he did not love her any longer and that she no longer gave him any pleasure in his life. In the first few days after her husband announced he was going to leave, Giselle desparately tried to win back his love by indulging his every whim. Eventually, however, they had a violent confrontation during which he walked out. Later that evening, Giselle emptied her medicine cabinet of all drugs, drove to a secluded area, and ingested the drugs in an effort to kill herself. (adapted from Bemporad, 1995)

Some research has supported elements of this psychodynamic perspective on depression. For example, depressed people tend to display many of Giselle's personality traits: They are dependent on others, believe that they must be perfect, have poor self-esteem, and are unable to express anger openly (Riley, Trieber, & Woods, 1989; Sacco & Beck, 1995). In addition, many depressed people describe their parents as having characteristics similar to Giselle's parents: They are cold and neglectful, excessively moralistic and demanding of perfection, or requiring of complete devotion and dependency from their children in exchange for their love (Blatt & Zuroff, 1992). Most of these studies are cross-sectional, however, so we do not know whether these characteristics and views are symptoms of the depression or actual causes of the depression. There are a few longitudinal studies that support elements of the psychodynamic theories. For example, one study of middle-aged women found that those who tended to inhibit any expression of anger and who were unassertive in interpersonal interactions were more likely to become depressed over a 3-year period (Bromberger & Matthews, 1996). For the most part, however, the psychodynamic theories of depression have not been adequately tested in longitudinal studies.

Like the cognitive and behavioral theories, the modern psychodynamic theories that focus on the depressive's patterns of interpersonal relationships have led to an effective therapy for depression. Let us turn now to a discussion of these therapies.

Summing Up | Psychosocial Theories of Depression

- The behavioral theories of depression suggest that stress can induce depression by reducing the number of reinforcers available to people and by leading them to believe that important outcomes are outside of their control.
- The cognitive theories of depression argue that depressed people think in distorted and negative ways, and this leads them to become depressed, particularly in the face of negative events.
- Some research suggests, however, that depressed people may actually be more realistic in their judgments of their own control over situations than are nondepressed people, who tend to maintain an illusion of control.
- The psychodynamic theories posit that depressed people are overly dependent on the evaluations and approval of others for their self-esteem, as a result of poor nurturing by parents.

Psychosocial Therapies for Depression

The behavioral, cognitive, and psychodynamic theories of depression have led to two highly effective treatments for depression: cognitive-behavioral therapy and interpersonal therapy. We explore these therapies in detail here and then examine research comparing the efficacy of these therapies to that of drug therapies for depression.

Cognitive-Behavioral Therapy

cognitive-behavioral therapy
treatment that works by changing negative patterns of thinking and by solving concrete problems through brief sessions in which a therapist helps a client challenge negative thoughts, consider alternative perspectives, and take effective actions

Cognitive-behavioral therapy represents a blending of cognitive and behavioral theories of depression (Beck et al., 1974; Ellis & Harper, 1961; Lewinsohn et al., 1986; Rehm, 1977). There are two general goals in this therapy. First, it aims to change negative, hopeless patterns of thinking described by the cognitive models of depression. Second, it aims to help depressed people solve concrete problems in their lives and develop skills for being more effective in their worlds so that they no longer have the deficits in reinforcers described by behavioral theories of depression.

Cognitive-behavioral therapy is designed to be brief and time-limited. The therapist and client will usually agree on a set of goals that they wish to accomplish in 6 to 12 weeks. These goals focus on specific problems that the client believes are connected to his depression, such as problems in his marriage or dissatisfaction with his job. From the very beginning of therapy, the therapist urges the client to "take charge" of the therapy as much as possible, setting goals and making decisions himself rather than relying on the therapist to give him all the answers.

The first step in cognitive-behavioral therapy is to help a client discover the negative automatic thoughts he habitually has and to understand the link between those thoughts and his depression. Often, the therapist will assign the client the homework of keeping track of times when he feels sad or depressed and writing down on sheets such as the one in Figure 5.16 what is going through his mind at such times. Clients often report that they did not realize the types of thoughts that went through their head when certain types of events would happen. For example, the client whose automatic thought record is given in Figure 5.16 did not realize that she had catastrophic thoughts about losing her job every time her boss was a little cross with her.

The second step in cognitive-behavioral therapy is to help the client challenge his negative thoughts. Depressed people often believe that there is only one way to interpret a situation—their negative way. Therapists will use a series of questions to help the client consider alternative ways of thinking about a situation and the pros and cons of these alternatives. The first question a cognitive therapist might ask a client is, "What is the evidence that you are right in the way you are interpreting this situation?" For example, perhaps a pre-med student thinks that if she fails an upcoming chemistry exam, she will never get into medical school. The therapist might have the following conversation with her.

> Therapist: How do you know you will never get into medical school if you fail this exam?
>
> Student: I don't know, I just worry that it's true, that my grades will be so bad I won't get into medical school.
>
> Therapist: How are your grades now?
>
> Student: Pretty good, mostly A's.
>
> Therapist: So failing one exam might put you out of the running for medical school, even though you have mostly A's right now?
>
> Student: Well, I guess not. But it would still be terrible to flunk this exam.
>
> Therapist: Yes, I agree that it would not be the best thing to flunk this exam. Why do you think you might flunk the exam? Have you done poorly in this class so far?

In cognitive-behavioral therapy, the therapist engages the client actively in challenging his or her dysfunctional thoughts.

Date	Event	Emotion	Automatic thoughts
April 4	Boss seemed annoyed.	Sad, anxious, worried	Oh, what have I done now? If I keep making him mad, I'm going to get fired.
April 5	Husband didn't want to make love.	Sad	I'm so fat and ugly.
April 7	Boss yelled at another employee.	Anxious	I'm next.
April 9	Husband said he's taking a long business trip next month.	Sad, defeated	He's probably got a mistress somewhere. My marriage is falling apart.
April 10	Neighbor brought over some cookies.	A little happy, mostly sad	She probably thinks I can't cook. I look like such a mess all the time. And my house was a disaster when she came in!

Figure 5.16

An Automatic Thoughts Record Used in Cognitive-Behavioral Therapy. In cognitive-behavioral therapy, patients keep records of the negative thoughts that arise when they feel negative emotions. These records are then used in therapy to challenge the patient's depressing thinking.

Student: No, I got an A- on the first exam. I just feel so rotten that I think I might flunk this one.

Therapist: When you are depressed, you do feel rotten. But weren't you already depressed earlier in the semester when you took that first exam? And you did quite well on that one?

Student: You're right. I felt even worse then than I do now, and I still nearly aced the exam. I guess there's really no reason to think I'm going to flunk this exam.

The therapist tried to shake the student's belief that she would flunk the exam by helping her realize the evidence against this belief. Therapists must be careful not to belittle a client's negative beliefs: These beliefs are often firmly held. However, with gentle questioning, the therapist hopes to help the client realize that her negative thoughts are not necessarily true, even if they are compelling.

A second question that cognitive-behavioral therapists ask their clients is, "Are there other ways of looking at this situation?" Let's return to the student about to take the chemistry exam.

Student: I guess the other thought that goes through my mind is that: if I don't continue to get nearly straight A's, I won't get into the good medical schools, and that would be a disaster.

Therapist: A disaster?

Student: Yeah, if I can't go to one of the top medical schools, I might as well not go at all.

Therapist: Is there any other way of looking at this? What do you want most, to go to the top medical school or to be a good doctor?

Student: Well, the most important thing is obviously to be a good doctor. But you need to go to a top medical school to be a good doctor.

Therapist: Is that true? Do you know any good doctors that didn't go to one of the most prestigious medical schools?

Student: Well, I guess there is my uncle. He's considered a really good doctor, and he went to an okay medical school but not a great one.

Therapist: Could you get into your uncle's medical school if your grades were a little lower than they are now?

Student: I think so.

Therapist: Could you be a good doctor if you went to your uncle's medical school?

Student: I suppose if I worked hard, I could be good doctor if I went there.

Therapist: How about any other medical schools that aren't the absolutely most prestigious ones but that you could get into? Are there any that could make you into a good doctor?

Student: Well, there's (Student begins naming other medical schools.)

In this case, the therapist was using a combination of the questions "What's your evidence?" and "Is there another way of thinking about this situation?" to help the student realize she had boxed herself into one narrow and difficult way of looking at her situation when there were other perspectives on her situation that were quite reasonable.

Finally, a cognitive-behavioral therapist will often have to help a client confront her worst fears realistically, by asking her to consider, "What can you do if the worst case scenario comes true?" This is a frightening question for many people (depressed or nondepressed) to consider, but the therapist will try to help the client realize that, even if the worst case scenario materialized, the client could find some way of coping with it.

Therapist: Okay, for a minute now, I want us to think about what would happen for you if you did fail this exam.

Student: Oh . . . (very sad). I, I, I just can't think about that. It would be too horrible.

Therapist: Exactly what do you think would happen, and what could you do about it?

Student: I'd fail the course, I'd drop out of pre-med. There is nothing I could do about it.

Therapist: Nothing? Do you know anyone who has ever failed this chemistry course?

Student: Yeah, lots of people do.

Therapist: Do they all drop out of pre-med?

Student: Well, lots of them do.

Therapist: What about the ones who don't drop out? What do they do?

Student: They take the course over again.

Therapist: And what happens to their failing grade from the first time they took the course?

Student: It's replaced by the grade they get the second time they take the course.

Therapist: So if you fail this course, what could you do other than drop out of pre-med?

Student: I could take the course again. But I'd probably only fail it again.

Therapist: Is there anything you could do to prevent you from failing it again?

Student: I guess I could get a tutor. But that would cost money.

Therapist: Do you think your parents would be willing to pay for a tutor?

Student: Well, yeah. They already said they would if I wanted one.

Therapist: So let's think this through again. What could you do if the worst case scenario happened and you failed this exam?

Student: I could take the course over again with the help of a tutor.

Therapist: And how would that be? How do you feel about that?

Student: I feel a little relieved. I guess it wouldn't be a total disaster if I failed the course. I don't want to fail it, but it wouldn't be a complete disaster.

Of course, these questions that a cognitive-behavioral therapist asks don't always move the client toward more positive ways of thinking about the situation. It is important for the therapist also to be flexible in pursuing a line of questions or comments, dropping approaches that are not helpful and trying new approaches to which the client might respond better.

The third step in cognitive-behavioral therapy is to train the client in new skills she might need to cope better in her life. Often depressed people are unassertive in making requests of other people or in standing up for their rights and needs. This unassertiveness can be the result of their negative automatic thoughts. For example, a person who often thinks, "I can't ask for what I need because the other person might get mad, and that would be horrible," is not likely to make even reasonable requests of other people. The therapist will first help the client recognize the thoughts behind her actions (or lack of action). Then the therapist may work with the client to devise exercises or homework assignments in which the client practices new skills, such as assertiveness skills, between therapy sessions.

The fourth step in cognitive-behavioral therapy is to help the client recognize the deeper, basic beliefs or assumptions she might hold that are feeding her depression. These basic beliefs might be ones such as "If I'm not loved by everyone, I'm a failure" or "If I'm not a complete success at everything, my life is worthless." The therapist will help the client question these beliefs and decide if she truly wants to live her life according to these beliefs.

As noted earlier, cognitive-behavioral therapy has proven quite effective in treating depression. Several studies have shown that about 60 to 70 percent of depressed people experience full relief from their symptoms with 12 weeks of cognitive therapy (Robinson et al., 1990). Cognitive-behavioral therapy has been successfully adapted for the treatment of depressed children and older persons (Futterman, Thompson, Gallagher-Thompson, & Ferris, 1995; Gilham et al., 1995; Lewinsohn, Clarke, Hops, & Andrews, 1990).

Interpersonal Therapy

Although contemporary psychodynamic therapists still subscribe to Freud's basic arguments that a sense of loss is at the core of depression and that depressed people turn their anger at the loss on themselves, most psychodynamic therapists do not treat depression with traditional, long-term psychoanalysis. Depressed people do not respond well to the lack of structure in traditional psychoanalysis. In the 1980s, a new type of therapy based on psychoanalytic theory but designed to be more structured and short-term was introduced for the treatment of depression. This therapy, known as **interpersonal therapy**, focuses on problems in a client's interpersonal relationships that may be contributing to depression (Klerman et al., 1984; Markowitz & Weissman, 1995). The therapy involves helping depressed people gain insight into the types of interpersonal problems contributing to their depression by exploring both current and past relationships. Then the therapist helps clients make decisions about the changes they want to make in current relationships.

There are four types of problems that interpersonal therapists will look for in depressed patients. First, many depressed patients truly are grieving the loss of loved ones, perhaps not from death but from the breakup of important relationships. Interpersonal therapists help clients face such losses and explore their feelings about the losses. Often clients idealize the people they lost, feeling as if they will never have relationships as good. Therapists help clients reconstruct their relationships with the lost loved ones, recognizing both the good and bad aspects of the relationships and developing more balanced views of the relationships. Therapists also help clients let go of the past relationships and begin to invest in new relationships.

The second type of problem interpersonal therapy focuses on is interpersonal role disputes. Such disputes arise when the people in a relationship do not agree on their roles in the relationship. For example, a husband and wife may disagree on the proper roles each should play in relation to their children. Or a college student and a parent may disagree on the extent to which the student should follow the parent's wishes in choosing a career. Interpersonal therapists first help the clients recognize the disputes and then guide clients in making choices about concessions they are or are not willing to make to the other people in the relationships. Therapists may also need to help clients modify and improve their patterns of communicating with others in relationships. For example, a student who resents his parents' intrusions into his private life may tend to withdraw and sulk rather than directly confront his parents about their intrusions. He would be helped in developing more effective ways of communicating his distress over his parents' intrusions.

The third type of problem addressed in interpersonal therapy is role transitions, such as the transition from college to work or from work to full-time motherhood. Sometimes people become depressed out of grief over the roles they must leave behind. Therapists help clients develop more realistic perspectives toward roles that are lost and

interpersonal therapy
structured and short-term version of psychoanalysis consisting of a therapist helping a client understand how role disputes and interpersonal problems can lead to depression, and then helping the client correct these problems by attaining a realistic, balanced view of his or her relationships

help clients regard new roles in more positive manners. If clients feel unsure about their capabilities in new roles, therapists help them develop a sense of mastery in the new roles. Sometimes clients need help in developing new networks of social support within their new roles, to replace the support systems they left behind in old roles.

In interpersonal therapy, the therapist helps clients resolve conflicts in their relationships that are leading to depression.

The fourth type of problem depressed people bring to interpersonal therapy involves deficits in interpersonal skills. Such skill deficits can be the reason that depressed people have inadequate social support networks. Therapists review with clients past relationships, especially important childhood relationships, helping clients understand these relationships and how they might be affecting current relationships. Therapists might also directly teach clients social skills, such as assertiveness.

Interpersonal therapy has been shown to be highly effective in the treatment of depression, with 60 to 80 percent of depressed people recovering during this form of therapy (Markowitz & Weissman, 1995). Like cognitive-behavioral therapy, interpersonal therapy has been successfully adapted for treatment of children and older adults with depression. It can be used both in individual therapy and in group therapy settings.

 Which of these therapies do you think would work best for women? for men? for people of color? Why?

Direct Comparisons of Psychosocial and Drug Therapies

Studies directly comparing cognitive-behavioral therapy, interpersonal therapy, and drug therapies have generally found that they are equally effective for the treatment of most people with depression (see Hollon et al., 1992; Jacobson & Hollon, 1996). The largest study comparing these therapies was the Collaborative Treatment of Depression Study sponsored by the National Institute of Mental Health (Elkin et al., 1989). In this study, 250 patients with major depressive disorders were randomly assigned to undergo interpersonal therapy, cognitive-behavioral therapy, antidepressant therapy (with imipramine), or pill placebo treatment. After 16 weeks of treatment, the patients in all the groups showed significant reductions in depression. Interpersonal therapy, cognitive therapy, and imipramine appeared to work equally well, especially for patients who were less severely depressed.

One of the surprising findings from this study was that the patients in the pill placebo group also tended to improve significantly. Although these patients were not receiving an active drug, they had regular meetings with a psychiatrist who asked them about their symptoms and their lives and gave them advice when asked. The remarkable effectiveness of the placebo treatment suggests that interacting with a warm and caring professional can be quite helpful to a depressed person, even when that professional is not delivering any specific type of therapy. A number of other studies have shown that the relationship between a depressed patient and therapist is an important predictor of recovery: Depressed patients who develop a warm and trusting relationship with their therapists recover faster and more fully than those who do not (Burns & Nolen-Hoeksema, 1992; Orlinsky & Howard, 1986).

Although cognitive-behavioral therapy, interpersonal therapy, and the antidepressant drugs all led to substantial relief for the depressed patients in the NIMH study, the drug therapy tended to work faster than the two psychosocial therapies and was more effective for the severely depressed patients. Yet patients who received cognitive-behavioral therapy or interpersonal therapy were less likely than those who received drug therapy to relapse into new episodes of depression over the 2 years after their treatments had ended (Shea et al., 1992; see also Hollon et al., 1991; Jacobson & Hollon, 1996).

The relapse rates in depression are quite high, even among people whose depressions completely disappear in treatment. This has led many psychiatrists and psychologists to argue that people with a history of recurrent depression should be kept on a maintenance dose of therapy even after their depression is relieved (Hirschfeld, 1994). Usually, the maintenance therapy is a drug therapy; many people remain on antidepressant drugs for years after their initial episodes of depression have passed. Studies of interpersonal therapy and cognitive-behavioral therapy show that maintenance doses of these therapies, usually consisting of once-a-month meetings with therapists, can also substantially reduce relapse (Markowitz & Weissman, 1995; Sacco & Beck, 1995). For example, one study compared the effectiveness of maintenance doses of interpersonal therapy and imipramine in preventing relapse in patients with histories of recurrent depressions (see Figure 5.17). Patients receiving interpersonal therapy avoided relapse for significantly longer than did patients receiving pill placebos. Patients receiving imipramine avoided relapse for even longer than the patients on interpersonal therapy. Patients receiving both imipramine and interpersonal therapy went the longest before relapsing to another episode of depression (Frank, 1991; Frank et al., 1990).

These studies taken together suggest the following conclusions. First, very severely depressed people or those who need faster relief from their depression (perhaps because they are highly suicidal) may benefit more from drug therapies than from the psychosocial therapies in the short-term. Second, patients who are not as severely depressed can benefit from either the drug therapies or psychosocial therapies equally. Third, the psychosocial therapies may more effectively prevent relapse than the drug therapies, if therapies are not maintained after episodes of acute depression have passed. Fourth, maintenance doses of drugs or the psychosocial therapies can reduce the risk of relapse in patients with histories of recurrent depression.

The bottom line in the treatment of depression is that there is a choice in treatments. Drug therapies, cognitive therapy, and interpersonal therapy all seem to be effective for the majority of depressed people. The characteristics of a person's depression—how severe it is, how recurrent it is, what stressors or personal issues are associated with it—probably influence which therapy works best for that individual. In addition, people's beliefs about the causes of their depression and about what type of therapy is most appealing may also influence which therapy is best for them. People who have faith in the type of therapy they are receiving and are willing to go along with their therapist's suggestions recover more fully than do those who are skeptical about the effectiveness of their therapy (Burns & Nolen-Hoeksema, 1991; Frank, 1973; Kazdin, 1986).

Figure 5.17

Effects of Antidepressants and IPT in Preventing Relapse of Depression. Patients maintained on either IPT or antidepressant drugs avoided relapse longer than did patients on placebos.
Source: Frank et al., 1991.

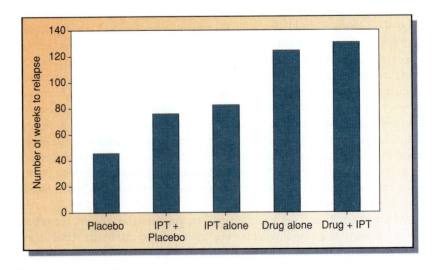

- Cognitive-behavioral therapies for depression are designed to change negative, distorted ways of thinking, and provide the depressed person with behavioral skills to improve his or her life.
- Interpersonal therapies focus on the depressed person's pattern of interpersonal relationships and on correcting dysfunctional patterns that recur.
- Direct comparisons of the psychosocial therapies with drug therapies suggest that all these therapies are equally effective for most depressed people. Severely depressed people seem to respond better to drug therapies than to psychosocial therapies. People who have psychosocial therapy are less prone to relapse than are people who have drug therapy only.

The Gender Differences in Depression

Now that we have discussed the various biological and psychosocial theories of depression, let us return to a question raised at the beginning of this chapter: Why are women so much more likely than men to experience depression? Most of the explanations offered for women's greater vulnerability to depression are similar to the explanations for women's greater vulnerability to anxiety disorders, but the depression explanations have been more extensively researched (McGrath et al., 1990; Nolen-Hoeksema, 1990).

Biological Explanations

The gender differences in depression are remarkably consistent across cultures. This suggests that something about women's biology may predispose them to depression. Do women carry a greater genetic or neurobiological vulnerability to depression than do men? The available evidence suggests that the answer to these questions is no. The genetic vulnerability to depression does not appear to be linked to sex. In addition, women do not seem to have a greater rate of most depression-linked neurobiological abnormalities, such as deficiencies in serotonin levels, than do men (see review by Blehar & Oren, 1995).

Many people have argued over the years that women's greater vulnerability to depression is tied to hormones—specifically, the so-called ovarian hormones, estrogen and progesterone. The main fuel for this idea comes from evidence that women are more prone to depression during the premenstrual period of the menstrual cycle, the postpartum period, menopause, and puberty. These are times when levels of estrogen and progesterone change dramatically. Given how strongly people tend to believe that women's moods are influenced by their hormones, it is remarkable how little evidence there is for this belief.

Let us consider the premenstrual period first. Old studies suggested that the majority of women are regularly incapacitated by depression, anxiety, and physical discomfort during their premenstrual periods (Reid & Yen, 1981). However, these studies relied on faulty methods. They asked women to complete retrospective questionnaires about their experiences of premenstrual mood changes in the past. It turns out that the information women provide on these questionnaires often bears little resemblance to their actual experiences of mood across the menstrual cycle. For example, in one study, women completed daily mood ratings but did not know that the study was investigating the relationship between mood and the menstrual cycle. At the end of the study, the women were asked to report, retrospectively, on their moods during the different phases of their most recent menstrual cycle. On the retrospective questionnaire, the women reported having experienced significantly more negative symptoms during their premenstrual period than during any other period in their last cycle. However, the daily mood ratings of these same women showed no relationship between cycle phase and moods (Abplanap, Haskett, & Rose, 1979; see also Parlee, 1994; Schnurr et al., 1994).

More recent studies have found that it is possible to identify a small group of women who frequently experience increases in depressive symptoms during the premenstrual phase (Endicott, 1994). These women also tend to have a history of frequent major depressive episodes with no connection to the menstrual cycle or of other psychiatric disorders. This suggests that these women have a general vulnerability to depression rather than a specific vulnerability to premenstrual depression (Parry, 1994). This has led many researchers to argue that depressions during the premenstrual period should not be given a separate diagnosis, such as premenstrual dysphoric disorder, but should be considered only exacerbations of major depression or dysthymia. Others argue that we should recognize premenstrual depression separately with its own diagnosis because it is different from depression that has no link with the menstrual cycle and therefore should be studied separately. The DSM-IV dealt with this controversy by putting diagnostic criteria for premenstrual dysphoric disorder in an appendix rather than in the main body of its text with other officially recognized diagnoses.

Some women with histories or general vulnerabilities to depression may become depressed during the postpartum period (the first couple of months after giving birth). However, studies comparing rates of depression in postpartum women and matched groups of women who were not postpartum have tended not to find differences in rates of depression between these two groups (O'Hara & Swain, 1996). Even among women who do become seriously depressed during the postpartum, depressions do not seem to be linked to any specific imbalances in hormones (Gitlin & Pasnau, 1989; Pedersen et al., 1993). Postpartum depressions are most often linked to severe stress in women's lives, such as financial strain, marital difficulties, or lack of social support (O'Hara & Swain, 1996). Another clue that environmental factors contribute to postpartum depression is found in the evidence that adoptive mothers and natural fathers also are at increased risk for depression following the arrival of a new baby (Rees & Lutkins, 1971).

The belief that women were more prone to depression during the menopause was so strong among clinicians that 20 years ago there was a separate diagnostic category in the DSM for menopausal depression. Several studies have found, however, that women are no more likely to show depression around the time of menopause than at any other time in their lives (Matthews et al., 1990).

Finally, let us consider puberty. Girls' rates of depression escalate dramatically in early adolescence, but boys' rates do not. The increase in girls' depressions does not seem to be directly tied to the hormonal changes of puberty, however (Angold & Worthman, 1993). Instead, the observable physical changes of adolescence may have more to do with the emotional development of girls and boys than hormonal development because these characteristics affect boys' and girls' self-esteem differently. Girls appear to value the physical changes that accompany puberty much less than do boys. In particular, girls dislike the weight they gain in fat and their loss of the long, lithe look that is idealized in modern fashions. In contrast, boys like the increase in muscle mass and other pubertal changes their bodies undergo (Dornbusch et al., 1984). Body dissatisfaction appears to be more closely related to low self-esteem and depression in girls than in boys (Allgood-Merten et al., 1990).

One group of girls who seem especially at risk for depression during puberty is girls who mature much earlier than their peers. Girls whose bodies start changing long before their girlfriends' bodies do have higher rates of depression, anxiety disorders, and eating disorders than do girls who mature later in adolescence. Why are early maturing girls at such high risk? First, they have the worst body image of any group of girls, and this may contribute to their vulnerability to depression, anxiety, and eating disorders. Second, these girls seem to become involved in mature dating relationships at a very young age, and they date older boys and become sexually active earlier than do their peers. These relationships may be too difficult for many girls to cope with and may contribute to depression and other problems. Third, because they are becoming sexually mature at a younger age, these girls may be more vulnerable to sexual assault and abuse than are girls who mature later, and as we shall discuss shortly, sexual abuse contributes to depression (Hayward et al., 1993).

In sum, the notion that women's depressions are tied to their hormones has not been well supported. To begin with, there does not seem to be as great an increase in risk for depression during periods of hormonal change as commonly believed. Even among women who do clearly experience serious depression during periods of hormonal change, there has been no consistent evidence of a particular hormonal or biochemical abnormality that distinguishes them from women who do not experience such depressions. Let us look at some other possibilities for the wide difference in depression rates between men and women.

Personality Explanations

I thought I had the perfect relationship. I married Joe when I was 20, thrilled to have "caught" the high school football star, the hunk, the guy that every girl wanted. I settled in to being Mrs. Joe, happy to be freed from the pressure of going to college or getting a job. I never liked competition, never thought I was much good at anything in school. So for the next 15 years, I was just Mrs. Joe. I raised our children and went to enough PTA meetings and such to be a responsible parent. But mostly I stayed home and tried to make it a nice home for Joe and the kids. I lived through their successes. If Joe got a promotion at work or the kids did well at school, I felt good. Of course, if Joe had trouble at work or the kids' grades started falling, I felt bad.

Then, one day, Joe felt sick and stayed home from work. This was really unusual, but I didn't begin to get frightened until he had stayed home a full week and was just getting more sick every day. He went to the doctor, and after many tests, we were told he had leukemia. We were in shock, but we held out hope, through all the tortuous treatments and hospitalizations, that Joe would make it.

But he didn't. He died six months ago. And I can't deal with it. I don't know what to do, who I am, who I'm supposed to be now. I'm so depressed all the time that I'm not even taking care of the kids properly. They're cooking their own food and getting themselves to school. I'm ashamed to be so worthless, but I can't get myself out of bed all day.

Terri, the woman in this story, is the prototype of the depressed woman: She lacks confidence in herself, and she is so highly invested in her relationship with Joe that she loses her sense of self and becomes dependent on him. When he dies, a part of her self-image dies as well, leaving her empty and depressed, feeling completely out of control over her life. The personality theories of women's depressions suggest that, in general, women are more prone than men to be unassertive and dependent on others and that this leads women to experience more helplessness, self-punishment, and depression (Chevron, Quinlan & Blatt , 1978; Jack, 1991; Radloff, 1975).

Women do score lower than men on some measures of assertiveness or self-confidence (see Nolen-Hoeksema, 1990). For example, on questionnaires, women rate themselves as less domineering, less assertive, and less competitive than men rate themselves (Whitley, 1984). These low scores seem to be associated with higher levels of depression.

A specific type of problem with assertiveness may be especially important to the development and maintenance of depression in women. When they feel sad or distressed, women are more likely than men to focus on their distress and passively ruminate about it rather than take action to distract themselves or change their situations (Nolen-Hoeksema, 1990). Laboratory and naturalistic studies have shown that people with such a passive, ruminative style of coping with their periods of depression and distress have longer and more severe periods of depression (see Nolen-Hoeksema, 1995). Thus, women's tendency to ruminate when they feel distressed may be one contributor to their greater rates of serious depression.

Social Explanations

Proponents of the social explanations for women's depressions would read Terri's story and conclude that it wasn't Terri's personality that put her at risk for depression but the fact that she conformed to the traditional sex role for women, which limits women's opportunities and creates conditions that contribute to depression in women (Gove & Herb, 1974). Several studies done in the United States suggest that married women in traditional relationships are at higher risk for depression than are unmarried women or women who spurn traditional sex roles (McGrath et al., 1990). In contrast, married men have lower rates of depression than do unmarried women, and men who conform to the masculine sex role have lower rates of depression than do men who spurn the masculine sex role. It appears that traditional marriages and sex roles are good for men but not for women, in terms of risk for depression.

The most compelling social explanation for women's higher rates of depression, however, is that women's lower social status puts them at high risk for physical and sexual abuse, and these experiences often lead to depression. Women are much more likely than men to be the victims of rape, incest, battering, or sexual harassment (Browne, 1993; Fitzgerald, 1993; Koss, 1993). The rates of these types of violence against women are staggering. Most studies of rape estimate that between 14 and 25 percent of women are raped in their lives, most often before the age of 30 (Koss, 1993). One in eight women reports that she has been physically assaulted by their husband in the last year, and 1.8 million women report having been severely assaulted (punched, kicked, choked, threatened with a gun or knife; Straus & Gelles, 1990). Survivors of physical and sexual assault show high rates of major depression, anxiety disorders, and substance abuse. Thus, it seems likely that at least some of the difference between women's and men's rates of depression may be tied to the higher rates of abuse of women than of men and the resulting depression in female abuse survivors.

 Some studies suggest that there is less of a gender difference in rates of depression among women and men above the age of 65. How would you explain this?

Summing Up	The Gender Differences in Depression

- Although most women's moods probably are not intimately tied to hormonal changes, some women with an underlying predisposition to depression may experience increases in depression at times of great hormonal change.
- Women appear to be less domineering than men and to have a more passive, ruminative coping style than men, and this may contribute to their higher rates of depression.
- Women face a number of obstacles and threats, such as violence, that may contribute to their tendencies toward depression.

Suicide

One of the most frightening aspects of mood disorders is the potential for suicide. Suicide is the ninth leading cause of death in the United States. More than 30,000 people kill themselves each year, which averages to nearly 85 people per day or one person every 17 minutes. In addition, there are approximately 600,000 nonfatal suicide attempts per year (McIntosh, 1991). In truth, these numbers probably underestimate the actual numbers of attempted and completed suicides by two to three times, since many suicide attempts and completions are not reported or are misreported as accidents.

Although females are more likely than males to attempt suicide, males are four times more likely than females to complete suicide (Figure 5.18). This is in part because

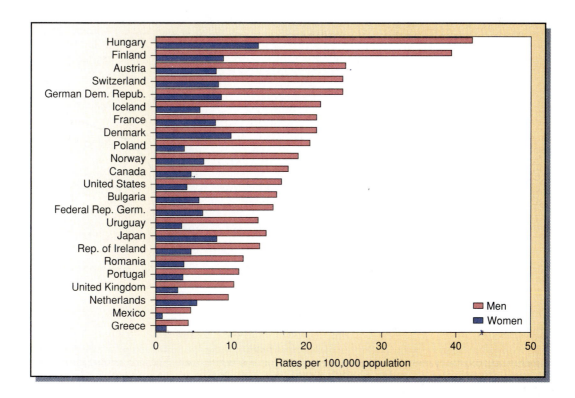

Rates per 100,000 population

males choose more lethal means of suicide than do females (Canetto & Lester, 1995). For example, in the United States, males tend to use guns to attempt suicide whereas females tend to use poisons. Women may also make more suicide attempts that they do not intend to be lethal—these are known as parasuicides.

There are also racial and ethnic differences in suicide rates in the United States (McIntosh, 1991). The highest rates are found among Native Americans, followed by Caucasians, Hispanic Americans, Chinese and Japanese Americans, African Americans, and Filipino Americans. These differences may have to do with cultural and religious norms against suicide.

The overall rate of suicide in the general population has slightly increased over the last 60 years, but the rate among 15 to 24 year olds has skyrocketed by nearly 300 percent (see Figure 5.19). Much of this increase has taken place among African-American youth. In the last decade, the suicide rate has risen by 50 percent for African-American males and by 40 percent for African-American females between 15 and 24 years of age. In contrast, the rate among Caucasian males between 15 and 24 has risen 10 percent in the last decade, and there has been no increase in suicide rates among young Caucasian females. The increase in suicide among African-American youth is probably tied, in part, to their perceptions that there are few opportunities open to them and that they face a constant battle to succeed and be accepted for their talents. The increase in *completed* suicide among young adults is also associated with the increased availability of guns. As it becomes easier for young people to acquire guns, the chances that they will impulsively use the guns to end their lives become greater.

Although there has been a 50 percent decline in suicide rates among the elderly over the last few decades, the elderly still remain at relatively high risk for suicide. When they attempt suicide, older people are much more likely than younger people to be successful. It seems that most older people who attempt suicide fully intend to die. In contrast, most young people who attempt suicide are highly ambivalent. Some older people who commit suicide do so because they cannot tolerate the loss of their spouse or other loved ones. Others suffer from debilitating illnesses and wish to escape their pain and suffering. Most have histories of depression or other psychological problems in their lives and are not suffering from some medical illness (Hendin, 1995).

Figure 5.18

Gender Differences in Completed Suicides in Several Countries. In most countries, men are more likely to complete a suicide than are women, although women are more likely to attempt suicide than are men.
Source: Moscicki, 1995, p. 25.

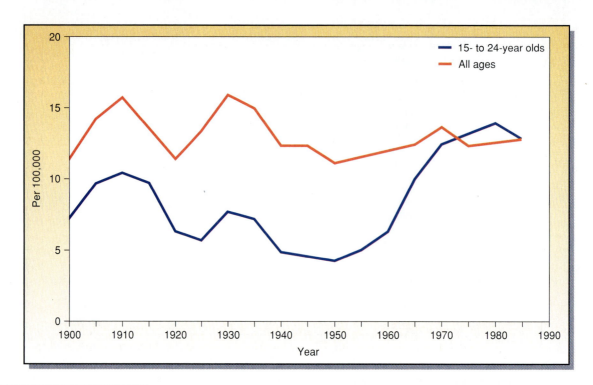

Figure 5.19

Increases in Suicide Among Younger Adults Over Recent Decades. In the last several decades, rates of completed suicide have skyrocketed among 15 to 24 year olds, relative to the rates of suicide in the rest of the population.

Source: Diekstra & Garnefski, 1995, p. 48.

In the United States, the majority of suicides involve guns (Hendin, 1995). Most people who commit suicide by gun do not buy guns expressly to commit suicide. Instead, they use guns that have been in their households for some time. Often, suicide with guns is an impulsive act committed by people under the influence of alcohol: They may be depressed, get drunk, and retrieve family handguns and shoot themselves. Unfortunately, a gunshot to the head is highly likely to end in death, whether or not the person truly intended to commit suicide. Can we reduce the number of such suicides by restricting people's access to guns? The answer may be yes. Some studies have found that suicide rates decrease when cities or states enact strict antigun legislation that limits people's access to guns (see Hendin, 1995). Although people who are intent on committing suicide can find other means to do so if guns are not available, restricting ready access to guns appears to reduce impulsive suicides with guns.

Opponents of gun control may argue that restricting access to guns only makes people more vulnerable to intruders in their homes or to others wishing to do them harm. One study strongly suggests that this is not the case, however. Researchers examined 398 consecutive deaths by gun in homes of families who owned guns (usually handguns). Of these deaths, only 0.5 percent were intruders shot by families protecting themselves, but 83.0 percent of these deaths were suicides of adolescent or adult family members. Another 12 percent were homicides of one adult in the home by another family member, usually in the midst of quarrels. The final 3 percent of deaths were due to accidental gunshots of one of the family members (Kellerman, Rivara, Somes, & Reay, 1992).

Sociological Theories of Suicide

The sociologist Emil Durkheim (1897) proposed that there are three types of suicide, based on his analysis of records of suicide for various countries and across various historical periods. **Egoistic suicide** is committed by people who feel alienated from others, empty of social contacts, alone in an unsupportive world. The schizophrenic patient who kills herself because she is completely isolated from society may be committing egoistic suicide. **Anomic suicide** is committed by people who experience severe disorientation because of some large change in their relationships to society. A man who loses his job after 20 years of service may feel anomie, a complete confusion of his role and worth in society, and

egoistic suicide
suicide committed by people who feel alienated from others and lack social support

anomic suicide
suicide committed by people who experience a severe disorientation and role confusion because of a large change in their relationship to society

may commit anomic suicide. Finally, **altruistic suicide** is committed by people who believe that taking their own lives will benefit society in some way. During the Vietnam War, Buddhist monks burned themselves to death in public suicides to protest the war.

Durkheim's theory suggests that social ties and integration into a society will help to prevent suicide if the society discourages suicide and supports individuals in overcoming negative situations in ways other than suicide. However, if a society supports suicide as an act that benefits the society in some situations, then ties with such a society may actually promote suicide. Similarly, when a well-known member of the society commits suicide, then people who closely identify with that person may see suicide as more acceptable (Hendin, 1995; Stack, 1991). For example, after the suicide of the popular lead singer of the band Nirvana, Kurt Cobain, there were concerns that young people who identified with Cobain and the message in his music would view suicide as an appropriate way of dealing with the social anomie expressed in that music.

Sociological theories of suicide have trouble explaining why some people succumb to societal pressures and other people do not. Psychologists and psychiatrists have tried to identify psychological factors that increase people's risk for suicide.

Kurt Cobain is just one prominent celebrity who committed suicide, leading health care professionals to worry that some devoted fans might do the same.

altruistic suicide
suicide committed by people who believe that taking their own lives will benefit society

Psychological Theories of Suicide

What is going through the minds of people who attempt or complete suicide? Our understanding of why people commit suicide is hampered by the fact that family members and friends of people who commit suicide may, when asked by clinicians or researchers, bias their reports of the situations leading up to the suicide. For example, family members may assume that the person who committed suicide must have been depressed, and they may selectively recall signs of depression before the suicide even when these signs were weak or nonexistent.

One group of researchers was able to conduct a prospective study of people who attempted suicide during a year-long study of 13,673 adults randomly chosen from a community sample. All these adults were interviewed twice, one year apart. A structured clinical interview was used to determine whether each adult qualified for the diagnosis of some type of psychological disorder. Over the year between the two interviews, 40 people in the sample attempted suicide. The researchers randomly chose 40 other people from the rest of the sample who had not attempted suicide to make comparisons with the 40 suicide attempters. The attempters tended to have lower educational levels and were more likely than the nonattempters to be unemployed, separated, or divorced. When the researchers examined the data from the first interview, they found that 53 percent of the suicide attempters had been diagnosed with major depressive disorders, compared to 6 percent of the nonattempters (Petronis, Samuels, Moscicki, & Anthony, 1990).

Perhaps it is surprising that the rate of depression among the suicide attempters was not higher. It is likely that many of the suicide attempters had depressive symptoms that did not quite meet the criteria for a depressive disorder but were nonetheless painful. Still, not everyone who attempts or commits suicide is depressed. Eight percent of the attempters had been diagnosed with mania at the first interview, compared to 0.6 percent of the nonattempters. As many as half the people with bipolar disorder attempt suicide, and perhaps one in five will complete suicide (Goodwin & Jamison, 1990). It might seem strange that a manic person would attempt suicide, because the symptoms of mania include elation and heightened self-esteem. However, often the predominant feelings of mania are agitation and irritation mixed with despair over having the illness or in contemplating falling into a debilitating depression. Kay Jamison (1995b, pp. 113–114) describes one of her suicide attempts, which occurred when she was in a mixed manic and depressive state, and highly agitated:

> In a rage I pulled the bathroom lamp off the wall and felt the violence go through me but not yet out of me. "For Christ's sake," he said, rushing in—and then stopping very quietly. Jesus, I must be crazy, I can see it in his eyes a dreadful mix of concern, terror, irritation, resignation, and why me, Lord? "Are you hurt?" he asks.

Turning my head with its fast-scanning eyes I see in the mirror blood running down my arms. . . . I bang my head over and over against the door. God, make it stop, I can't stand it, I know I'm insane again. He really cares, I think, but within ten minutes he too is screaming, and his eyes have a wild look from contagious madness, from the lightning adrenaline between the two of us. "I can't leave you like this," but I say a few truly awful things and then go for his throat in a more literal way, and he does leave me, provoked beyond endurance and unable to see the devastation and despair inside. I can't convey it and he can't see it; there's nothing to be done. I can't think, I can't calm this murderous cauldron, my grand ideas of an hour ago seem absurd and pathetic, my life is in ruins, and worse still—ruinous; my body is uninhabitable. It is raging and weeping and full of destruction and wild energy gone amok. In the mirror I see a creature I don't know but must live and share my mind with.

I understand why Jekyll killed himself before Hyde had taken over completely. I took a massive overdose of lithium with no regrets.

Another psychological condition that increases risk of suicide attempts is substance abuse. In the prospective study of suicide attempts we have been discussing, 33.0 percent of the attempters were identified as heavy drinkers, compared to 2.5 percent of the nonattempters. Alcohol disinhibits people to engage in impulsive acts, even self-destructive ones like suicide attempts. Also, people with chronic alcohol problems may have a general tendency toward self-destructive acts and may wreck many of their relationships and their careers, making them feel they do not have much reason to live.

Suicide is found among people with all types of psychological disorders. About 10 percent of people with schizophrenia commit suicide (Clark, 1995). They may kill themselves to end the torment of accusatory hallucinations telling them they are evil or to end the excruciating social isolation they may feel. Most suicide attempts among people with schizophrenia happen not when the people are psychotic but when they are lucid but depressed. The schizophrenics who are most likely to commit suicide are young males who have frequent relapses into psychosis but who had a good educational history and high expectations for themselves before they developed schizophrenia. It seems that these young men cannot face a future that is likely to be so much less than what they envisioned for themselves (Hendin, 1995).

One cognitive variable that predicts suicide is hopelessness. One group of researchers examined 207 patients who had been hospitalized while contemplating suicide and found that 89 of them expressed utter hopelessness about their futures. Over the next 5 years, 13 of these 89 hopeless patients committed suicide, compared to only one patient who had not expressed hopelessness (Beck, Steer, Kovacs, & Garrison, 1985). In addition, some research suggests that people who attempt or commit suicide tend to be rigid and inflexible in their thinking (Linehan et al., 1987). This rigidity and inflexibility makes it more difficult for them to consider alternative solutions to their situations or to simply "hold out" until the suicidal feelings pass.

Other emotions frequently expressed by people who attempt suicide are previously unexpressed rage at others and guilt (Hendin, 1995). Teenagers who are enraged at their parents but cannot express it may attempt suicide as a means of punishing their parents. War veterans who feel extreme and unforgivable guilt about actions they took during war, such as shooting civilians or running away from battle, may kill themselves to end their guilt or to punish themselves for their actions.

 How might researchers conduct a study to determine what was on the mind of people just before they committed suicide?

Many people do *not* commit suicide when they are in the depths of despair but instead just as they seem to be getting better. Elizabeth Wurtzel (1995, p. 315) explains:

The suicide attempt startled even me. It seemed to happen out of context, like something that should have taken place months and months ago. It should never have happened within a few days of returning to Cambridge, at a point when, even I had to admit, the fluoxetine (Prozac) was starting to kick in. After all, I was able to get out of bed in the morning, which may not seem like much, but in my life it was up there with Moses parting the Red Sea. . . . Anybody would have thought that these were signs that my mood was on the upswing, and I guess it was. But just as a little bit of knowledge is a dangerous thing, a little bit of energy, in the hands of someone hell-bent on suicide, is a very dangerous thing.

My improved affect did not in any way sway me from the philosophical conviction that life, at its height and depth, basically sucks.

Biological Factors in Suicide

Many studies have found a link between suicide and low serotonin levels (see Goodwin & Jamison, 1990, for a review). For example, postmortem studies of the brains of people who committed suicide find low levels of serotonin. Studies of people who survived suicide attempts find low levels of the major by-product of serotonin in their blood or urine. Low serotonin levels are most strongly associated with impulsive and violent suicides. Although these pieces of evidence do not prove that low serotonin levels cause suicidal behavior, they suggest that people with low serotonin levels may be at high risk for impulsive and violent behavior that sometimes results in suicide.

Is There a Right to Commit Suicide?

Many socieites, including the United States, are currently debating whether people have a right to commit suicide. Some people, such as psychiatrist Thomas Szasz and physician Jack Kevorkian, argue that the right to die as one chooses and when one chooses is a fundamental human right that cannot be regulated by the state. Others note that most people who attempt suicide but do not complete it do not later commit suicide, suggesting that they do not truly wish to die (Hendin, 1995). More generally, most people who contemplate suicide, particularly if they are depressed and not suffering from terminal medical illness, are ambivalent about it, and their suicidal wishes pass after relatively short periods of time. This suggests that preventing suicide is appropriate, at least for people who are mentally but not physically ill, because many people who attempt suicide are not making rational or permanent choices.

These debates will only become more heated as the population of the world ages. Currently, suicides by seriously ill people comprise only about 3 percent of all suicides (Hendin, 1995). That number is likely to increase, however, as more people are living to old age and, as a result, suffering serious illnesses that they may want to end through suicide.

 If one of your family members wanted to commit suicide, are there any conditions that would lead you to support his or her wishes?

What To Do If a Friend Is Suicidal

What should you do if you suspect a friend or family member is suicidal? First, take the situation seriously. Although most people who express suicidal thoughts do not go on to attempt suicide, most people who do commit suicide have communicated their suicidal intentions to friends or family members before attempting suicide (Shneidman, 1976). Unfortunately, friends and family members often do nothing in response to these communications, either because they are too overwhelmed and do not know what to do or because they do not take seriously the communications.

Jack Kevorkian has advocated for severely ill people's rights to commit suicide.

The most important thing to do if you suspect someone is suicidal is get help from mental health professionals as soon as you can, by calling a suicide hotline to ask for help in dealing with the person, calling the local county mental health association, or consulting with a psychologist or psychiatrist at your local health clinic for advice. Even seasoned mental health professionals can find helping a person who is suicidal challenging and unnerving, so you should not expect to be able to deal with a person's suicidality alone.

Summing Up   Suicide

- Although women are more likely than men to *attempt* suicide, men are more likely than women to *commit* suicide.
- Native Americans have higher suicide rates than any other cultural group in the United States.
- The rate of suicide has increased dramatically in the United States in recent decades.
- Sociological theories suggest that people commit suicide when they feel alienated from society or believe the suicide will somehow benefit society.
- Psychological disorders, including depression, mania, substance abuse, and schizophrenia, increase people's risk for suicide, as does a sense of hopelessness or extreme guilt or rage.
- Low levels of serotonin may be involved in impulsive suicidal behaviors.
- Societies are debating whether people have a right to commit suicide.
- The most important thing to do if you suspect a friend is suicidal is seek help from a mental health professional.

Bio-Psycho-Social INTEGRATION

The mood disorders are phenomena of the whole person. Depression and mania involve changes in every aspect of functioning, including biology, cognitions, personality, social skills, and relationships. Some of these changes may be causes of the depression or mania, and some of them may be consequences of the depression or mania. However, the fact that the mood disorders are phenomena of the whole person illustrates the intricate connections among these different aspects of functioning: biology, cognitions, personality, and social interactions. These areas of functioning are so intertwined that major changes in any one area will almost necessarily provoke changes in other areas. Fortunately, the interconnections among these areas of functioning may mean that improving functioning in one area can improve function in other areas. Improving people's biological functioning can improve their cognitive and social functioning and their personality. Improving people's cognitive and social functioning can improve their biological functioning, and so on. Thus, although there may be many pathways into mood disorders (biological, psychological, and social), there may also be many pathways out of the mood disorders, particularly depression.

Chapter Summary

There are two general categories of mood disorder: unipolar depressive disorders and bipolar disorder. People with a unipolar depressive disorder experience only the symptoms of depression (sad mood, loss of interest, disruption in sleep and appetite, retardation or agitation, loss of energy, worthlessness and guilt, suicidality). People with bipolar disorder experience both depression and mania (elated or agitated mood, grandiosity, little need for sleep, racing thoughts and speech, increase in goals and dangerous behavior).

Within the unipolar depressive disorders, the two major diagnostic categories are major depressive episode and dysthymic disorder. In addition, there are several subtypes of major depression: with melancholic features, with psychotic features, with catatonic features, with atypical features, with postpartum onset, with seasonal pattern, and premenstrual dysphoria.

Depression is one of the most common psychological problems. It is most common among young and middle-aged adults. Depressed older adults may often be underdiagnosed or misdiagnosed, but there is evidence that adults from past generations have been less prone to depression throughout their lives than adults from contemporary generations are. People of Hispanic origins show the highest prevalence of depression in the United States, followed by whites and then African Americans. Cross-national studies suggest that rates of depression are lower in less-industrialized and less-modern countries. People in these countries may often express their depression through somatic complaints. Depression is a long-lasting and recurrent problem for many people.

Bipolar disorder is much less common than the depressive disorders. It tends to be a lifelong problem. The length of individual episodes of bipolar disorder varies dramatically from one person to the next and over the life course. Many famous political leaders, artists, composers, and writers have had bipolar disorder. As in depression, the expression of mania may depend on cultural norms.

Genetics probably play a role in determining vulnerability to the mood disorders, especially bipolar disorder. Disordered genes may lead to dysfunction in the monoamine neurotransmitter systems. The neurotransmitters norepinephrine, serotonin, and dopamine have been implicated in the mood disorders. In addition, people with mood disorders show a number of neurophysiological abnormalities, such as unusual brain wave activity during sleep and deterioration of the cerebral cortex and cerebellum, as shown in CT and MRI studies. There is evidence that depressed people have chronic hyperactivity in the hypothalamic-pituitary-adrenal axis, which may make them more susceptible to stress.

Most of the biological therapies for the mood disorders are drug therapies. Lithium is the most effective drug for the treatment of bipolar disorder. It has a number of side effects, including nausea, vomiting, diarrhea, tremors, twitches, kidney dysfunction, and birth defects. Alternatives to lithium include anticonvulsant drugs, antipsychotic drugs and calcium channel blockers.

Three classes of drugs are commonly used to treat depression: tricyclic antidepressants, monoamine oxidase inhibitors, and selective serotonin reuptake inhibitors. Each of these is highly effective in treating depression, but each has significant side effects. Electroconvulsive therapy is used to treat severe depressions, particularly those that do not respond to drugs. Light therapy is used to treat seasonal affective disorder.

Behavioral theories of depression suggest that people with much stress in their lives may have too low a rate of reinforcement and too high a rate of punishment, which then leads to depression. Stressful events can also lead to learned helplessness—the belief that nothing you do can control your environment—which is linked to depression. Most people who are faced with stressful events do not become depressed, however. The cognitive theories of depression argue that the ways people interpret the events in their lives determines whether they become depressed. Some evidence suggests that depressed people are actually quite realistic in their negative views of life, and that nondepressed people are unrealistically optimistic about life. Cognitive-behavioral therapies focus on helping depressed people develop more adaptive ways of thinking and are very effective in treating depression.

Psychodynamic theories of depression suggest that depressed people have chronic patterns of negative relationships and tend to internalize their hostility against others. Interpersonal therapy helps depressed people identify and change their patterns in relationships and is highly effective in treating depression.

Women are twice as likely as men to be diagnosed as depressed. Biological explanations attribute this difference to hormonal dysregulation in women. Personality explanations of this gender difference in depression attribute it to women's tendencies to be unassertive and to base their self-esteem on their relationships with others. Social explanations attribute it to women's lower status in society and their vulnerability to physical and sexual abuse. Each of these explanations has received some support, but there are probably many reasons women are so much more prone to depression than are men.

Between 40 and 60 percent of people who commit suicide have a mood disorder. Women attempt suicide more often than do men, but men complete suicide more often than do women. Older people are more likely to commit suicide than are younger people, but there has been an alarming increase in suicide among young people over the last few decades. Some people commit suicide because they feel isolated and alienated from others, a sense of hopelessness and despair, or guilt over some wrong they have committed. Often, however, suicide is committed just as a depressed person seems to be getting better. The most important thing to do if you suspect a friend might be suicidal is to contact a mental health professional.

Key Terms

bipolar disorder 158
manic 158
depression 158
unipolar depression 158
major depression 160
dysthymic disorder 160
double depression 161
delusions 161
hallucinations 161
catalepsy 161
catatonia 161
seasonal affective disorder (SAD) 162
premenstrual dysphoric disorder 163
Bipolar I Disorder 170
Bipolar II Disorder 170
cyclothymic disorder 170
rapid cycling bipolar disorder 170
monoamines 177

norepinephrine 177
serotonin 177
dopamine 177
monoamine theories 178
lithium 181
anticonvulsant drugs 183
antipsychotic drugs 183
calcium channel blockers 183
neuroleptic drugs 183
tricyclic antidepressant drugs 183
monoamine oxidase inhibitors (MAOIs) 183
selective serotonin reuptake inhibitors (SSRIs) 184
electroconvulsive therapy (ECT) 185
light therapy 186

behavioral theories of depression 187
learned helplessness theory 187
learned helplessness deficits 187
cognitive distortion theory 188
reformulated learned helplessness theory 188
causal attribution 189
depressive realism 191
cognitive-behavioral therapy 194
interpersonal therapy 198
egoistic suicide 206
anomic suicide 206
altruistic suicide 207

Application

Cognitive-behavioral therapists and interpersonal therapists focus on different issues when treating a depressed person. What follows is a case study of a young woman named Elaine who is suffering from depression. What would a cognitive-behavioral therapist say is the reason for Elaine's depression and how would a cognitive-behavioral therapist treat Elaine? How would an interpersonal therapist conceptualize the causes of Elaine's depression and what would an interpersonal therapist focus on in treating Elaine?

Elaine is a 21-year-old senior at a prestigious college, majoring in computer science. She has always received good grades— that is, until this last quarter. For about 2 months, Elaine has been having trouble concentrating, sleeping, and staying motivated to do her work. She has also been feeling sad and down on herself. These feelings seem to have started over winter break, when Elaine had a huge fight with her parents over what she will do after she graduates in June. Her parents want her to move back to her home town on the West Coast and take a job in the local computer software firm. Elaine wants to move to the East Coast to take a job with a large computer firm and live with her best friend.

Elaine's family has always been very close. Elaine always goes home during breaks in the school year and has worked in her hometown every summer. Each member of Elaine's family knows everything about the other members. Elaine has never done anything against her parents' wishes before. Her parents can not understand why she wants to move so far away when she has a good job opportunity near her family. They point out that her father is getting old enough that "he may not be with us for very much longer."

Elaine has been thinking that maybe she is very selfish to want to move to the East Coast. She has also been wondering whether she really wants to make a living in computer science. She is good at it, but she has been having so much trouble lately maintaining her motivation to do her work that she wonders if she really has what it takes to do computer science professionally. Elaine is also beginning to wonder if she will ever have a romantic relationship. She did not have one in college—she did not have time, plus her parents taught her that sex before marriage is a sin, so she decided to avoid relationships so as not to be tempted. Now that she has turned 21 and her college years are almost over, she wonders whether she has missed the opportunity to develop a serious relationship.

Cognitive therapists would focus on the following:

- faulty assumptions or negative schemas: Elaine seems to think she has to please her family, no matter what the cost, and that it is selfish for her to do what she wants to do. A cognitive therapist would see these faulty assumptions as underlying Elaine's depression and would attempt to correct these assumptions.

- negative automatic thoughts: Elaine shows evidence of jumping to conclusions, overgeneralizing, using feelings as facts, and perhaps having a negative attributional style.

Cognitive therapists would recommend the following treatment:

- First, help Elaine to identify and monitor her negative thoughts and to make the connection between these thoughts and her depression. Use homework assignments.

- Next, help Elaine challenge her negative thoughts by asking about the evidence for the thoughts, asking for alternative interpretations, asking her whether she is totally to blame for the situation, and asking how she would deal with the consequences of the worst case scenario.

- Teach Elaine how to replace her negative thoughts with more adaptive, rational responses.

- Use behavioral techniques to increase Elaine's motivation, to teach her assertiveness techniques for dealing with her parents, and to improve her social skills.

Interpersonal therapists would focus on the following:

- Elaine's interpersonal role dispute with her parents and also possibly a conflict over her upcoming role transition (moving from college to work life)

- fundamental deficits in social skills, which contribute to Elaine's lack of a social life.

Interpersonal therapists would recommend the following treatment:

- Help Elaine recognize her role disputes and problems with role transitions, decide how to resolve her conflicts with her parents, and decide how to adjust to her upcoming transitions.

- Help Elaine develop her social skills and broaden her social network. ■

chapter 6 The Schizophrenias

Symptoms of Schizophrenia

People with schizophrenia have delusions (beliefs with little grounding in reality) and hallucinations (unreal perceptual experiences such as hearing voices). Although the fundamental characteristics of delusions and hallucinations are similar across cultures, the specific content has culturally relevant themes. People with schizophrenia also show grossly disorganized thought, speech, and behavior. These are considered the "positive" symptoms of schizophrenia. The "negative" symptoms involve the absence of motivation, affect, and quality communication. Mild to moderate versions of these symptoms are often present before and after acute phases of psychosis and are referred to as *prodromal* and *residual* symptoms.

Types of Schizophrenia

There are four recognized subtypes of schizophrenia. People with paranoid schizophrenia have delusions and hallucinations that are paranoid and grandiose. People with disorganized schizophrenia have severely disorganized thoughts and behaviors and unusual emotional reactions. People with catatonic schizophrenia have motor behaviors that suggest complete unresponsiveness to the environment. People with undifferentiated schizophrenia have a mixture of all symptoms of schizophrenia.

The Prevalence of Schizophrenia Across Cultures and Gender

There is remarkable consistency across cultures in the prevalence of schizophrenia. Men may be more likely to be diagnosed with schizophrenia than women.

Biological Theories of Schizophrenia

There is strong evidence that schizophrenia is transmitted genetically. People with schizophrenia show abnormalities in the prefrontal cortex and ventricles of the brain. Imbalances in the neurotransmitter dopamine are also implicated in schizophrenia.

Psychosocial Contributors to Schizophrenia

Stress probably cannot cause schizophrenia, but it may contribute to relapse in people with the disorder. The communica-tion patterns of families of people with schizophrenia show a variety of oddities that may contribute to relapse. Finally, when the families of people with schizophrenia are high on expressed emotion, there is a greater risk of relapse in the family members with the disorder.

Biological Therapies for Schizophrenia

Drugs referred to as *neuroleptics* have proven very useful in the treatment of schizophrenia. These drugs are most effective in reducing delusions and hallucinations but less effective in reducing the negative symptoms of the disorder. They have significant neurological side effects. A new drug called *clozapine* appears to be effective without inducing as many side effects as previous drugs.

Psychosocial Therapies for Schizophrenia

Psychosocial therapies focus on teaching communication and living skills and reducing isolation in people with schizophrenia. Therapies that involve families also seem effective in reducing risk of relapse in people wtih schizophrenia.

Culture, Gender, and the Prognosis for People with Schizophrenia

People with schizophrenia from developing nations and family oriented cultures have a better prognosis than do people from industrialized countries, and women have a more favorable course of the disorder than do men.

Bio-Psycho-Social Integration
Chapter Summary
Key Terms
Application: *A Personal Account of Schizophrenia*

Whom Fortune wishes to destroy she first makes mad.

—Publilius Syrus, *Moral Sayings* (first century B.C.; translated by Darius Lyman)

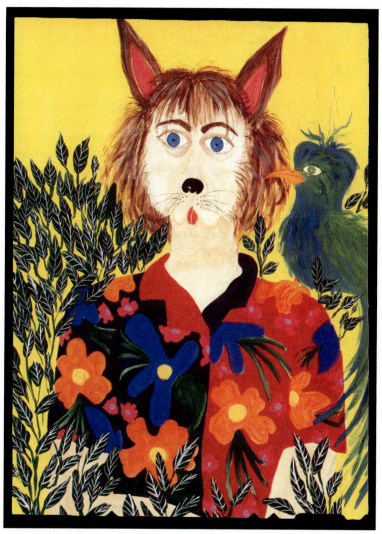

Patricia Schwimmer
My Dog and I Are One

Schizophrenia is one of the most severe and puzzling forms of psychopathology. At times, people with schizophrenia may think and communicate clearly, have an accurate view of reality, and function well in daily life. At other times, their thinking and speech are garbled, they lose touch with reality, and they are not able to care for themselves in even the most basic ways. In the following passage, Julia describes her terrifying descent into schizophrenia (Anonymous, 1992, pp. 333–334):

> My illness began slowly, gradually, when I was between the ages of 15 and 17. During that time reality became distant and I began to wander around in a sort of haze, foreshadowing the delusional world that was to come later. I also began to have visual hallucinations in which people changed into different characters, the change indicating to me their moral value. For example, the mother of a good friend always changed into a witch, and I believed this to be indicative of her evil nature. Another type of visual hallucination I had at this time is exemplified by an occurrence during a family trip through Utah: The cliffs along the side of the road took on a human appearance, and I perceived them as women, bedraggled and weeping.
>
> At the time I didn't know what to make of these changes in my perceptions. On the one hand, I thought they came as a gift from God, but on the other hand, I feared that something was dreadfully wrong. However, I didn't tell anyone what was happening; I was afraid of being called insane. I also feared, perhaps incredibly, that someone would take it lightly and tell me nothing was wrong, that I was just having a rough adolescence, which was what I was telling myself. Anyway, I battled the illness alone until I was 21, at which point, having exhausted all reserves, I decided to leave school and see a psychiatrist. . . .
>
> Also at the time I was very afraid. I had the feeling that I was dissolving and that pieces of me were going out into space; and I feared that I would never be able to find them again. I was also very ashamed and thought people were watching me. I was afraid of people to the extent that I wouldn't come out of my room when people were around. I ate my meals when my family was either gone or asleep. I thought that I must be in hell and that part of the meaning of this particular hell was that no one else around understood that it was hell. . . .

delusions
fixed beliefs with no basis in reality

hallucinations
sensory experiences or perceptions of things that are not real

psychotic symptoms
experiences that involve a loss of contact with reality as well as an inability to differentiate between reality and one's subjective state

schizophrenia
disorder consisting of unreal or disorganized thoughts and perceptions as well as verbal, cognitive, and behavioral deficits

Julia describes two of the core symptoms of schizophrenia. She has **delusions**—beliefs with little grounding in reality—that her body is dissolving and floating into space. She also has **hallucinations**—unreal perceptual experiences—in which people turn into witches and rocks into people. Delusions and hallucinations are often referred to as **psychotic symptoms** because they involve a loss of reality-testing. Schizophrenia involves a variety of other perplexing symptoms, which we will examine shortly.

Schizophrenia has been recognized as a psychological disorder since the early 1800s (Gottesman, 1991). German psychiatrist Emil Kraepelin is credited with the most comprehensive and accurate description of schizophrenia. In 1883, Kraepelin labeled the disorder *dementia praecox* (precocious dementia) because he believed the disorder resulted from premature deterioration of the brain. He viewed the disorder as progressive, irreversible, and chronic. The label **schizophrenia** was introduced by Eugen Bleuler in 1911 and reflected Bleuler's belief that this disorder involved the splitting of usually integrated psychic functions (mental associations, thoughts, and emotions). Contrary to popular belief, Bleuler did not view schizophrenia as the splitting of distinct personalities as in multiple personality disorder nor do modern psychiatrists and psychologists.

In this chapter, we first consider the symptoms of schizophrenia and the different forms that schizophrenia can take, with a focus on cultural and gender differences in the manifestations of schizophrenia. After reviewing the prevalence of schizophrenia, we begin discussing its causes. Most theorists view schizophrenia primarily as a biological disorder, but psychosocial factors can influence how severe this disorder becomes and how often an individual has relapses. Effective biological therapies for schizophrenia have been developed in the last 50 years, as we will learn. These biological therapies are often supplemented by psychosocial therapies that help the person with schizophrenia cope with the impact of the disorder on his or her life, and we will discuss these as well. Finally, we will address the prognosis for people with schizophrenia and the substantial cultural and gender differences in the course of this disorder.

 Why do you think many people are frightened of others whom they see as "crazy" or "out of their minds"?

Symptoms of Schizophrenia

Schizophrenia is a complex disorder that can take many forms. Indeed, many researchers and clinicians talk about "the schizophrenias," reflecting their belief that several different types or forms of schizophrenia are currently captured by the diagnostic criteria for schizophrenia. There are five groups of symptoms that are central to schizophrenia: delusions, hallucinations, disorganized thought and speech, disorganized or catatonic behavior, and the so-called "negative" symptoms of schizophrenia.

Delusions

Delusions are ideas that an individual believes are true but are highly unlikely and often simply impossible. Of course, most people occasionally hold beliefs that are likely to be wrong, such as the belief that they will win the lottery tomorrow. These kinds of *self-deceptions* differ from delusions in at least three ways (Strauss, 1969). First, self-deceptions are not completely implausible, whereas delusions often are. It is possible to win the lottery but it is not possible that Julia's body is dissolving and floating into space. Second, people harboring self-deceptions may think about these beliefs occasionally, but people harboring delusions tend to be preoccupied with them. Delusional people will look for evidence in support of their beliefs, attempt to convince others of these beliefs, and take actions based on them, such as filing lawsuits against the people they believe are trying to control their minds. Third, people holding self-deceptions typically will acknowledge that their beliefs may be wrong, but people holding delusions are usually highly resistant to arguments or compelling facts contradicting their delusions. They may view the arguments of others against their beliefs as a conspiracy to silence them and as evidence for the truth of their beliefs.

Table 6.1 lists some of the most common types of delusions. A **persecutory delusion** is the type of delusion we hear about most often in media depictions of people with schizophrenia and, indeed, is the most common form of delusion. People with persecutory delusions may believe they are being watched or tormented by specific people they know, such as their professors, or by agencies or persons in authority with whom they have never had direct contact, such as the FBI or a particular congressperson. Another common type of delusion, the **delusion of reference**, in which people believe that random events or comments by others are directed at them, is related to persecutory delusions. People with delusions of reference may believe that the newscaster on the local television news is reporting on their movements, or that the comments of a local politician at a rally are directed at them. Sometimes, delusions of reference are part of a grandiose belief system in which all events are meaningful to the believer. For example, one person with schizophrenia was lying in bed feeling cold and shivering when a small earthquake occurred near his house. He believed that he caused the earthquake with his shivering. Delusional beliefs can be simple and transient, such as when a person with schizophrenia believes the pain she just experienced in her stomach was the result of someone across the room shooting a laser beam at her. Delusional beliefs are often complex and elaborate, however, and the schizophrenic person clings to these belief systems for very long periods.

The following account illustrates how several types of delusions—grandiose delusions, persecutory delusions, delusions of reference, and delusions of thought control—

persecutory delusion
false, persistent belief that one is being persecuted by other people

delusion of reference
false belief that external events, such as people's actions or natural disasters, relate somehow to one's self

Paranoia is a prominent symptom in some forms of schizophrenia.

Table 6.1 Types of Delusions

These are several types of delusions that are often woven together in a complex and frightening system of beliefs.

Delusion	Definition	Example
Persecutory delusions	False belief that one's self or one's loved ones are being persecuted, watched, or conspired against by others	Belief that the CIA, FBI, and local police are conspiring to catch you in a "sting" operation
Delusions of being controlled	Belief that one's thoughts, feelings, or behaviors are being imposed or controlled by some external force	Belief that an alien has taken over your body and is controlling your behaviors
Thought broadcasting	Belief that one's thoughts are being broadcast from one's mind for others to hear	Belief that your thoughts are being transmitted via the Internet against your will
Thought insertion	Belief that another person or object is inserting thoughts into one's head	Belief that your spouse is inserting blasphemous thoughts in your mind through the microwave
Thought withdrawal	Belief that thoughts are being removed from one's head by another person or object	Belief that your roommate is stealing all your thoughts while you sleep
Delusions of guilt or sin	False belief that one has committed a terrible act or is responsible for some terrible event	Belief that you have killed someone
Somatic delusions	False belief that one's appearance or part of one's body is diseased or altered	Belief that your intestines have been replaced by snakes
Grandiose delusions	False belief that one has great power, knowledge, or talent or that one is a famous and powerful person	Belief that you are Martin Luther King Jr. reincarnated

can co-occur and work together in one schizophrenic's belief system. Note that, although the following passage is written by a person with schizophrenia about his own experience, he speaks of himself in the third person (Zelt, 1981, pp. 527–531):

> A drama that profoundly transformed David Zelt began at a conference on human psychology. David respected the speakers as scholars and wanted their approval of a paper he had written about telepathy. A week before the conference, David had sent his paper "On the Origins of Telepathy" to one speaker, and the other speakers had all read it. He proposed the novel scientific idea that telepathy could only be optimally studied during the process of birth. . . .
>
> David's paper was viewed as a monumental contribution to the conference and potentially to psychology in general. If scientifically verified, his concept of telepathy, universally present at birth and measurable, might have as much influence as the basic ideas of Darwin and Freud.
>
> Each speaker focused on David. By using allusions and nonverbal communications that included pointing and glancing, each illuminated different aspects of David's contribution. Although his name was never mentioned, the speakers enticed David into feeling that he had accomplished something supernatural in writing the paper. . . .
>
> David was described as having a halo around his head, and the Second Coming was announced as forthcoming. Messianic feelings took hold of him. His mission would be to aid the poor and needy, especially in underdeveloped countries. . . .

David's sensitivity to nonverbal communication was extreme; he was adept at reading people's minds. His perceptual powers were so developed that he could not discriminate between telepathic reception and spoken language by others. He was distracted by others in a way that he had never been before. It was as if the nonverbal behavior of people interacting with him was a kind of code. Facial expressions, gestures, and postures of others often determined what he felt and thought.

Several hundred people at the conference were talking about David. He was the subject of enormous mystery, profound in his silence. Criticism, though, was often expressed by skeptics of the anticipated Second Coming. David felt the intense communication about him as torturous. He wished the talking, nonverbal behavior, and pervasive train of thoughts about him would stop.

David's grandiose delusions were that he discovered the source of telepathy, that all the scientists thought highly of him, and that he might be the Messiah. As is often the case, these grandiose delusions were accompanied by persecutory delusions—that the scientists were criticizing him out of jealousy. David's delusions of reference were that all the scientists were talking about him, directly and indirectly. David believed that he could read others' minds. Finally, he had delusions of thought control, that the scientists were determining what he felt with their facial expressions, gestures, and postures.

Hallucinations

Have you ever had a strange perceptual experience, such as thinking you saw someone when no one was near, thinking you heard a voice talking to you, or feeling as though your body were floating through air? If so, you are not alone. One study found that 15 percent of mentally healthy college students report sometimes hearing voices, such as the voice of God telling them to do something, their "conscience" giving them advice, or two voices (usually both their own) debating a topic (Chapman, Edell, & Chapman, 1980). Six percent of the students believed they had transmitted thoughts into other people's heads at some time. Most of these students probably would not be diagnosed with schizophrenia because their "hallucinations" were occasional and brief, often occurring when they were tired or stressed or under the influence of alcohol or drugs, and did not impair their daily functioning in any way.

The hallucinations of people with schizophrenia tend to be much more bizarre and troubling than the college students' hallucinations, and are precipitated not only by sleep deprivation, stress, or drugs. An **auditory hallucination** (hearing voices, music, and so on)

auditory hallucination
auditory perception of phenomenon that is not real, such as hearing a voice when one is alone

The hallucinations of people with schizophrenia can be very bizzare and frightening.

visual hallucination
visual perception of something that is
not actually present

is the most common hallucination. Often, people hear voices accusing them of evil deeds or threatening them. The voices may also tell them to harm themselves. People with schizophrenia may talk back to the voices, even as they are also trying to talk to people who are actually in a room with them. The second most common hallucination is the **visual hallucination**, often accompanied by auditory hallucinations. For example, a person may see Satan standing at her bedside telling her she is damned and must die. Hallucinations can involve any sensory modality, however. A person with schizophrenia may smell bad smells when no one else does, may have a perpetual metallic taste in the mouth, or may "feel" bugs crawling up his or her back. These hallucinations are often frightening, even terrifying:

> At one point, I would look at my coworkers and their faces would become distorted. Their teeth looked like fangs ready to devour me. Most of the time I couldn't trust myself to look at anyone for fear of being swallowed. I had no respite from the illness. Even when I tried to sleep, the demons would keep me awake, and at times I would roam the house searching for them. I was being consumed on all sides whether I was awake or asleep. I felt I was being consumed by demons. (Long, 1996)

Delusions and Hallucinations Across Cultures

Although the types of delusions and hallucinations we have discussed probably occur in all cultures, the specific content of delusions and hallucinations can differ across cultures. For example, persecutory delusions often focus on intelligence agencies or persons of authority in the schizophrenic person's culture. Urban whites in the United States might fear that the Central Intelligence Agency is after them; Afro-Caribbeans may believe that people are killing them with curses; Asians may believe that ancestor ghosts are pursuing them (Westermeyer, 1993). One study found that, in Japanese people with schizophrenia, delusions of being slandered by others or delusions that others know something terrible about them are relatively common, perhaps due to the emphasis in Japanese culture on how one is thought of by others. In contrast, in German people with schizophrenia, religious delusions of having committed a sin (for example, "Satan orders me to pray to him; I will be punished") are relatively common, perhaps due to the influence of Christianity in Germany (Tateyama, Asai, Kamisada, Hashimoto, Bartels, & Heimann, 1993).

Some theorists argue that odd or impossible beliefs that are part of a culture's shared belief system cannot be considered delusions when these beliefs are held by individuals in that culture (Fabrega, 1993). For example, if a culture believes that the spirits of dead relatives watch over the living, then individuals in that culture who hold that belief are not considered delusional, although people in other cultures might consider such a belief untrue and impossible. The Puerto Rican woman in the following case study was initially diagnosed with schizophrenia because she believed she had special powers to anticipate events and because of her descriptions of what sounded like hallucinations to interviewers who did not know Puerto Rican culture. Later, a Puerto Rican interviewer rejected this diagnosis because this woman's beliefs and experiences were in line with cultural beliefs in Puerto Rico (Guarnaccia, Guevara-Ramos, Gonzales, Canino, & Bird, 1992, pp. 105–106).

Case Study • This case involves a 36-year-old upper-middle-class divorced woman who lives in the metropolitan area of San Juan with her 10-year-old daughter. She acknowledged being very religious and a practicing Catholic. The woman had completed a bachelor's degree in college and worked as a loan processor in a bank. She reported that she was able to read people's minds and to receive messages from other people by a kind of clairvoyance. She also believed she had a "gift" or "power" to anticipate events related to her relatives or to herself and that she could tune in by telepathy if other persons were in danger. The woman stated "God only knows how it really happens." These experiences began occurring when she was 23 years old. For example, she reported, "There are times when I am driving my car, and a voice says stop, reduce your velocity, and I do it immediately. Ahead there is a disastrous accident. Also, when I was sleeping, I heard a voice say, "Get up." There were some men trying to break into the house."

Since around puberty (age 11), she reported having religious visions. "I see images of saints, virgins in the house. I also see the image of Jesus Christ, with the crown of thorns and bleeding." She said she had these kinds of experiences in the night before the interview. The woman also reported sensations of being touched on the shoulder. She consulted a psychiatrist, but no medications were prescribed. She reports that she shares these "powers" and beliefs with a group that occasionally gets together.

This woman was part of a spiritual group common in Latin America that believes in clairvoyance and religious visions, and her experiences were not unusual in this group. In addition, this woman held a good job with responsibility and showed good judgment in most areas of her life. Thus, a diagnosis of schizophrenia seems unwarranted.

However, even theorists who hold cultural relativist positions on delusions tend to view as delusional people who hold extreme manifestations of their culture's shared belief systems. For example, a person who believed that her dead relatives were tormenting her by causing her heart and lungs to rot would be considered delusional, even if she were part of a culture that holds the belief that dead relatives watch over the living. Although the specific content of schizophrenic delusions and hallucinations varies across cultures, the general themes of delusions (for example, persecution, grandiosity, thought control) and of hallucinations (such as accusatory voices) are highly similar across cultures (Jablensky, 1989).

Disorganized Thought and Speech

The disorganized thinking of people with schizophrenia is often referred to as a **formal thought disorder** or *loosening of associations*. One of the most common forms of disorganization in schizophrenia is a tendency to slip from one topic to a seemingly unrelated topic with little coherent transition. For example, one person with schizophrenia posted the following "announcement":

formal thought disorder
state of highly disorganized thinking (also known as *loosening of associations*)

> Things that relate, the town of Antelope, Oregon, Jonestown, Charlie Manson, the Hillside Strangler, the Zodiac Killer, Watergate, King's trial in L.A., and many more. In the last 7 years alone, over 23 Starwars scientists committed suicide for no apparent reason. The Aids coverup, the conference in South America in 87 had over 1000 doctors claim that insects can transmit it. To be able to read one's thoughts and place thoughts in one's mind without the person knowing it's being done. Realization is a reality of bioelectromagnetic control, which is thought transfer and emotional control, recording individual brainwave frequencies of thought, sensation, and emotions.

The person who wrote this announcement saw clear connections among the events he listed in the first half of the paragraph and between these events and his concerns about mind reading and bioelectromagnetic control. However, it is hard for us to see these connections.

A person with schizophrenia may answer questions with comments that are barely related to the questions or completely unrelated to the questions. For example, when asked why he is in the hospital, a man with schizophrenia might answer, "Spaghetti looks like worms. I really think it's worms. Gophers dig tunnels but rats build nests." At times, the schizophrenic person's speech is so disorganized as to be totally incoherent to the listener, when it is often referred to as **word salad**. The person with schizophrenia may make associations between words that are based on the sounds of the words rather than the content, and these are known as **clang associations.** For example, in response to the question, "Is that your dog?" a person with schizophrenia might say, "Dog. Dog is Spog. Frog. Leap. Heap, steep, creep, deep, gotta go beep."

word salad
speech that is so disorganized that a listener cannot comprehend it

clang associations
in schizophrenia, linking together of words based upon their sounds, as opposed to their meanings

The disorganized thinking and speech of people with schizophrenia is associated with a number of cognitive deficits. Many researchers, dating back to Kraepelin and Bleuler, have believed that a fundamental problem in schizophrenia occurs in the deployment and control of basic attentional processes (see Nuechterlein et al., 1992). Much of the research on attentional difficulties in schizophrenia has employed a task called the Continuous Performance Test or CPT (Erlenmeyer-Kimling & Cornblatt, 1987; Nuechterlein et al., 1989). The CPT requires a subject to detect a particular stimulus, such as the letter A, in a series of stimuli presented for very brief periods on a computer screen. The task can be made more difficult by increasing the processing load put on the subject, such as by making the stimulus somewhat blurry or embedding the target stimuli in a group of other stimuli rather than presenting each stimulus separately on the screen. Poor performance on the CPT reflects problems in sustaining attention and in detecting a target stimulus when confronted by distracting stimuli (often referred to as detecting the *signal* among the *noise*). Several studies have shown that people with schizophrenia with acute symptoms perform more poorly on the CPT when the processing load is high than do normal control subjects or persons with other psychiatric disorders (see Cornblatt & Keil, 1994, and Kremen et al., 1994, for reviews). Even more impressive is evidence that people with schizophrenia whose symptoms are in remission continue to show problems in attentional problems on the CPT, and children and siblings of a person with schizophrenia perform more poorly on the CPT than do relatives of normal controls or people with other psychiatric disorders. These children also have more trouble remembering stimuli they have seen if their rehearsal of these stimuli is interrupted by a distraction. In turn, these children who show problems with sustained attention and with detecting signal from noise show more behavioral, social, and emotional problems than do other children (Erlenmeyer-Kimling & Cornblatt, 1992; Erlenmeyer-Kimling, Golden, & Cornblatt, 1989). The attentional problems may overwhelm the children's abilities to cope with the everyday stresses of life. The few studies that have followed these children into adulthood have also found they are more prone to develop early symptoms of schizophrenia (Erlenmeyer-Kimling & Cornblatt, 1992; Erlenmeyer-Kimling et al., 1995). These data suggest that attentional deficits may be a marker for vulnerability to schizophrenia and may indeed lead to the symptoms of schizophrenia.

 Several studies have used "high-risk" designs that identify children who are at risk for schizophrenia because they have parents with schizophrenia. Researchers then follow these children to look for early signs and predictors of schizophrenia. What are some of the advantages and disadvantages of these high-risk designs?

How might deficits in attention contribute to the loose associations and incoherent speech of schizophrenia? All of us tend to think about more than one thing at a time. While you are reading this book, your thoughts probably also are drifting to other issues, such as what you are going to have for dinner tonight or a the content of a conversation you had with a friend this morning. Most of us can differentiate easily between the thoughts that are relevant to our current situations or goals and those that are irrelevant. We can turn off unwanted thoughts. For the person with schizophrenia, this ability to differentiate between relevant and irrelevant and between real and unreal may be gone, and every thought and image may seem as relevant and real as the next. For example, as the person with schizophrenia is trying to hold a conversation with a friend, the thoughts she is having about a television show she watched last night might drift in. Unlike the person without schizophrenia, the person with schizophrenia has trouble differentiating signal (thoughts relevant to the current conversation) from noise (thoughts relevant to the television show she watched last night). In the midst of answering her friend's question about how she is feeling, she might begin to relay her thoughts about the television show, without being aware that she has jumped to a new topic irrelevant to the one being discussed with her friend. In short, it would be very difficult for her to maintain a coherent stream of thought or speech if she could not hold her attention on any particular thought or idea for more than a moment in time.

Spend a few minutes tuning into all the different thoughts going through your head as you read the next few pages. Try to imagine what it would be like to have these thoughts blaring loudly and simultaneously as if several people were trying to talk to you at the same time.

Disorganized or Catatonic Behavior

The disorganized behavior of people with schizophrenia is often what leads others to be afraid of them. The person with schizophrenia may display unpredictable and apparently untriggered agitation, suddenly shouting or swearing or pacing rapidly up and down the street. He may engage in socially disapproved behavior, like public masturbation. He is often disheveled and dirty, sometimes wearing few clothes on a cold day or heavy clothes on a very hot day. Short of these more bizarre behaviors, the person with schizophrenia often has trouble organizing his daily routine to ensure that he bathes, dresses properly, and eats regularly. It is as if all his concentration must be used to accomplish even one simple task, like brushing his teeth, and other tasks just do not get done.

Catatonia is a particular form of disorganized behavior that reflects an extreme lack of responsiveness to the outside world. A person in a **catatonic stupor** is completely unaware of the outside world and will sit motionless for hours if left alone. A person displaying **catatonic posturing** assumes bizarre, inappropriate postures and maintains them for long periods of time. A person in **catatonic excitement** may be wildly agitated for no apparent reason and difficult to subdue. In 1905, Kraepelin gave the following account of a patient showing signs of catatonic excitement (from R. D. Laing, *The Divided Self*, pp. 29–30):

> The patient I will show you today has almost to be carried into the rooms, as he walks in a straddling fashion on the outside of his feet. On coming in, he throws off his slippers, sings a hymn loudly, and then cries twice (in English), "My father, my real father!" He is eighteen years old, and a pupil. . . , tall and rather strongly built, but with a pale complexion, on which there is very often a transient flush. The patient sits with his eyes shut, and pays no attention to his surroundings. He does not look up even when he is spoken to, but answers beginning in a low voice, and gradually screaming louder and louder. When asked where he is, he says, "You want to know that too. I tell you who is being measured and is measured and shall be measured. I know all that, and could tell you, but I do not want to." When asked his name, he screams, "What is your name? What does he shut? He shuts his eyes. What does he hear? He does not understand; he understands not. How? Who? Where? When? What does he mean? When I tell him to look he does not look properly. You there, just look. What is it? What is the matter? Attend; he attends not. I say, what is it, then? Why do you give me no answer? Are you getting impudent again? How can you be so impudent? I'm coming! I'll show you! You don't whore for me. You mustn't be smart either; you're an impudent, lousy fellow, such an impudent, lousy fellow I've never met with. Is he beginning again? You understand nothing at all, nothing at all; nothing at all does he understand. If you follow now, he won't follow, will not follow. Are you getting still more impudent? Are you getting impudent still more? How they attend, they do attend," and so on. At the end, he scolds in quite inarticulate sounds.

This patient's catatonic excitement is infused with angry and agitated outbursts that also have the characteristic disorganization of schizophrenic thought.

Negative Symptoms

Each of the groups of symptoms we have discussed thus far is characterized by the presence of unusual perceptions, thoughts, or behaviors. These symptoms are often referred to as the **positive symptoms** of schizophrenia, or *Type I symptoms*. They are not positive in the sense of being desirable—they are referred to as positive because they represent

People with catatonia will strike strange poses and maintain them for long periods of time without moving.

catatonia
state of behavior that involves a complete lack of responsiveness to the outside world

catatonic stupor
motionless, apathetic state in which one remains oblivious to external stimuli

catatonic posturing
bizarre, inappropriate bodily position of considerable duration in which a person remains oblivious to the outside world

catatonic excitement
state of constant agitation and excitability

positive symptoms
in schizophrenia, hallucinations, delusions, and disorganization in thought and behavior (also called Type I symptoms)

negative symptoms
in schizophrenia, deficits in functioning that indicate the absence of a capacity present in normal people, such as affective flattening (also called Type II symptoms)

affective flattening
negative symptom of schizophrenia that consists of a severe reduction or complete absence of affective responses to the environment

alogia
negative symptom of schizophrenia that consists of a deficit in both the quantity of speech and the quality of its expression

avolition
negative symptom of schizophrenia that consists of an inability to persist at common goal-directed activities

prodromal symptoms
in schizophrenia, experience of milder symptoms prior to an acute phase of the disorder, during which behaviors are unusual and peculiar but not yet psychotic or completely disorganized

residual symptoms
in schizophrenia, experience of milder symptoms following an acute phase of the disorder, during which behaviors are unusual and peculiar but not psychotic or completely disorganized

Avolition—the inability to initiate and maintain activities—is a common symptom in schizophrenia.

the presence of very salient experiences. The **negative symptoms** of schizophrenia, or *Type II symptoms*, involve losses or deficits in certain domains. Three types of negative symptoms are recognized by DSM-IV as core symptoms of schizophrenia. **Affective flattening** is a severe reduction, or even the complete absence, of affective responses to the environment. The person's face may remain immobile most of the time, she may speak in a monotone voice without any emotional expression to her tone, she may not make eye contact with others, and her body language may be unresponsive to what is going on around her. **Alogia**, or poverty of speech, is a reduction in speaking, apparently reflecting a reduction in thinking. The person may not initiate speech with others, and when asked direct questions, she may give brief, empty replies. Finally, **avolition** is an inability to persist at common goal-directed activities, including at work, school, or home. The person has great trouble completing tasks and is disorganized and careless, apparently completely unmotivated. She may sit around all day doing almost nothing.

The negative symptoms of schizophrenia can be difficult to diagnose reliably. First, they involve the absence of behaviors rather than the presence of behaviors, making them more difficult to detect. Second, they lie on a continuum between normal and abnormal, rather than being clearly bizarre behaviors as are the positive symptoms. Third, they can be caused by a host of factors other than schizophrenia, such as depression or social isolation, or may be side effects of medications.

Although the negative symptoms of schizophrenia are less bizarre than the positive symptoms, they are primary causes of the problems people with schizophrenia have in functioning in society. People with schizophrenia with many negative symptoms have lower educational attainments and less success in holding jobs, poorer performance on cognitive tasks, and a poorer prognosis do than those with few negative symptoms and predominantly positive symptoms (Andreasen et al., 1990). In addition, the negative symptoms are less responsive to medication than are the positive symptoms: The person with schizophrenia may be able to overcome the hallucinations, delusions, and thought disturbances with medication but may not be able to overcome the affective flattening, alogia, and avolition. Thus, he may remain chronically unresponsive, unmotivated, and socially isolated, even when he is not acutely psychotic.

Prodromal and Residual Symptoms

The positive and negative symptoms of schizophrenia make up the active or *acute phase* of the illness. People with schizophrenia are not always in this acute phase. Often, they show milder forms of the positive and negative symptoms, which are often referred to as **prodromal** and **residual symptoms**. Prodromal symptoms are present before people go into the acute phase of schizophrenia, and residual symptoms are present after they come out of the acute phase. During the prodromal and residual phases, people with schizophrenia may express beliefs that are not delusional but are unusual or odd. They may have strange perceptual experiences, such as sensing another person in the room, without reporting full-blown hallucinations. They may speak in a somewhat disorganized and tangential way but remain coherent. Their behavior may be peculiar—for example, it may involve collecting scraps of paper—but not grossly disorganized. The negative symptoms are especially prominent in the prodromal and residual phases of the disorder. The person may be withdrawn and uninterested in others or in work or school. During the prodromal phase, family members and friends may experience the person with schizophrenia as "gradually slipping away," much as Julia describes herself at the beginning of this chapter.

Summing Up Symptoms of Schizophrenia

- The positive or Type I symptoms of schizophrenia are delusions, hallucinations, disorganized thinking and speech, and disorganized or catatonic behavior.
- Delusions are beliefs with little grounding in reality.
- Hallucinations are unreal perceptual experiences, such as hearing voices or having visions of objects that are not really present.

- The forms of delusions and hallucinations are relatively similar across cultures, but the specific content varies by culture.
- The negative or Type II symptoms are affective flattening, poverty of speech, and loss of motivation.
- Prodromal symptoms are more moderate positive and negative symptoms that are present before an individual goes into an acute phase of the illness; residual symptoms are symptoms present after an acute phase.

Types of Schizophrenia

There are five types of schizophrenia (APA, 1994). Three of these types, the paranoid, disorganized, and catatonic types, have specific symptoms that differentiate them from each other. The other two, undifferentiated and residual types, are not characterized by specific differentiating symptoms but by a mix of symptoms that are either acute (in the undifferentiated type) or attenuated (in the residual type).

Paranoid Schizophrenia

The best known, and most researched, type of schizophrenia is the paranoid type. People with **paranoid schizophrenia** have prominent delusions and hallucinations that involve themes of persecution and grandiosity. The following letter from a person with paranoid schizophrenia vividly describes his paranoid and grandiose delusions and hallucinations:

paranoid schizophrenia
syndrome marked by delusions and hallucinations that involve themes of persecution and grandiosity

C.I.A. MIND-DRUG EXPERIMENTS FOR "PSYCHOLOGICAL WARFARE," "CREATING JOBS," "TECHNOLOGIES," AND "CRIME" IN THIS MASONIC SYSTEM OF SLAVERY.

The sane (me) vs. the liars, and the stupid (them) in a never ending battle for "truth," "justice" and "freedom" in the American Way. A technocracy disguised as a democracy. Not guilty ever, no lo contendere always.

The mind-controller (whose range is astronomical), synchronizes special microwave frequencies to the brain, creating an electro-magnetic force field in which the natural electro-chemical energy emitted from it: (thoughts or brain-waves): is picked up by remote control and decoded with micro-computer chips for use all over the system of communications. The electronic stimulation not only "forces the brain to release all of its memories," "distorts perception," "induces hypnotic-states," "causes headaches," "ringing in the ears," "any kind of psychosomatic illness imaginable" but it also gives the necessary feeling to make any "suggestions" or "commands" being transmitted (by a para-psychologist) straight into an un-knowing victim's hearing-center, becoming strong impressions on his mind. Those "voices" (which are sometimes accompanied by melodious tones and sounds that either please or irritate the mind) will subliminally change his personality by controlling what kinds of suggestions go into his "sub-conscious memory" to govern how he feels, or mind-boggle him (trick his mind into believing that they are its own thoughts) during these brainwash and thought-control techniques. Psychotropic medications are given to the victims who can "discern the voices" over other sounds in order to keep them ignorant to the real truth about their dilemma, and to enhance the chemical-reaction in the brain to the stimulation as their souls: (minds): are enslaved by computers programmed to "think" for them here in George Orwell's America: (Rev. 2:8–11, 18:11–13). Soledad, has been using a mind-controller on me since Aug. 1980 in hopes of making me "A Punk," "Fool," or "Suicidal" as they've done countless others in the C.D.C. But they failed, and on Mar. 2, 1984, the Judge ordered them to stop (for the record) "A Masonic Conspiracy."

Jesus Christ
A Political Prisoner

Notice that the writer of this letter demonstrates several types of delusions, all with a paranoid theme. He reveals delusions of being controlled, of his thoughts being withdrawn and broadcast, and of thoughts being inserted into his brain and somatic delusions about psychosomatic illnesses. Like many people with paranoid schizophrenia, this man also has a grandiose delusion—that he is Jesus. Finally, this man talks about experiences that are probably auditory hallucinations—the voices and tones he believes are being planted in his brain.

Although the writer of this letter is largely incoherent, people with paranoid schizophrenia often do not show the grossly disorganized speech or behavior that people with other types of schizophrenia show. They may be lucid and articulate, with elaborate stories of how someone is plotting against them.

Not surprisingly, persons with paranoid schizophrenia tend to be angry and anxious. They are highly resistant to any arguments against their delusions and may become very irritated with anyone who argues with them. They may act arrogant and superior to others or remain aloof and suspicious. The combination of persecutory and grandiose delusions can lead people with this type of schizophrenia to be suicidal or violent toward others.

The prognosis for people with paranoid schizophrenia is actually better than the prognosis for people with other types of schizophrenia. They are more likely to be able to live independently and hold down a job, and thus show better cognitive and social functioning (McGlashan & Fenton, 1990). The onset of paranoid schizophrenia tends to occur later in life than the onset of other forms of schizophrenia, and episodes of psychosis are often triggered by stress. In general, paranoid schizophrenia is considered a milder, less insidious form of schizophrenia (McGlashan & Fenton, 1990).

Disorganized (Hebephrenic) Schizophrenia

disorganized schizophrenia
syndrome marked by incoherence in cognition, speech, and behavior as well as flat or inappropriate affect (also called *hebephrenic schizophrenia*)

Unlike people with the paranoid type of schizophrenia, people with **disorganized schizophrenia** do not have well-formed delusions or hallucinations. Instead, their thoughts and behaviors are severely disorganized. People with this type of schizophrenia may speak in word salads, completely incoherent to others. They are prone to odd, stereotyped behaviors like frequent grimacing or mannerisms like flapping their hands. They may be so disorganized that they do not bathe or dress or eat if left on their own.

The emotional experiences and expressions of people with disorganized schizophrenia are also quite disturbed. These people may not show any emotional reactions to anything, or they may have unusual and inappropriate emotional reactions to events, such as laughing uncontrollably at a funeral. When they talk, they may display emotions that are apparently unrelated to what they are saying or to what is going on in the environment. For example, a young woman with disorganized schizophrenia responded in the following manner when asked about her mother, who was recently hospitalized for a serious illness: "Mama's sick. (Giggle.) Sicky, sicky, sicky. (Giggle.) I flipped off a doctor once, did you know that? Flip. I wanta wear my blue dress tomorrow. Dress mess. (Giggle.)"

This type of schizophrenia tends to have an early onset and a continuous course that is often unresponsive to treatment. People with this type of schizophrenia are among the most disabled by the disorder.

Catatonic Schizophrenia

catatonic schizophrenia
syndrome marked by near total unresponsiveness to the environment as well as motor and verbal abnormalities

Catatonic schizophrenia has some of the most distinct features of all the types of schizophrenia. It is very rare, however, and thus has not been well-researched. People with catatonic schizophrenia show a variety of motor behaviors and ways of speaking that suggest almost complete unresponsiveness to their environment. (Many of these behaviors were described earlier.) The diagnostic criteria for catatonic type schizophrenia require two of the following symptoms: (a) catatonic stupor (remaining motionless for long periods of time), (b) catatonic excitement (excessive and purposeless motor activity), (c) the maintenance of rigid postures or being completely mute for long periods of time,

(d) engaging in odd mannerisms like grimacing or hand flapping, and (e) echolalia (senseless repetition of words just spoken by others) or echopraxia (repetitive imitation of the movements of another person).

 The number of people diagnosed with catatonic schizophrenia has declined in the last couple of decades. What might account for this?

Undifferentiated and Residual Schizophrenia

People with **undifferentiated schizophrenia** have symptoms that meet the criteria for schizophrenia (delusions, hallucinations, disorganized speech, disorganized behavior, negative symptoms) but do not meet the criteria for paranoid, disorganized, or catatonic type schizophrenia. This type of schizophrenia tends to have an onset relatively early in life and to be chronic and difficult to treat (McGlashan & Fenton, 1990).

People with **residual schizophrenia** have had at least one episode of acute positive symptoms of schizophrenia but do not currently have any prominent positive symptoms of schizophrenia. They continue to have signs of the disorder, however, including the negative symptoms and mild versions of the positive symptoms. People may have these residual symptoms chronically for several years.

The Prevalence of Schizophrenia Across Cultures and Gender

Estimates of the prevalence of schizophrenia in different countries range from about 0.2 percent to 2.0 percent, but most estimates are between 0.5 and 1.0 percent (see Figure 6.1). Some of the differences between rates of schizophrenia in different countries are due to differences in how narrowly or broadly schizophrenia is defined in those countries. In general, European researchers and clinicians have tended to use more narrow criteria for the diagnosis than have American researchers and clinicians (Gottesman, 1991). Cultural differences in the expression of schizophrenia can complicate comparisons of the rates of schizophrenia across cultures. For example, in determining whether an individual in another culture has flattened or inappropriate affect, we must take into account cultural norms for affective expression, eye contact, and body language. Similarly, there are differences among cultures in what it means to be goal-directed and persistent, which can complicate the assessment of motivation. The assessment of disorganization in speech or of a reduction in speech production must take into account possible language barriers between the assessor and the individual, as well as cultural norms for speaking to persons in authority positions. Finally, there are cultural differences in the content of delusions and hallucinations, which we have discussed. Despite these complications, many clinicians believe that, with some cultural sensitivity, schizophrenia can be diagnosed reliably across cultures (Jablensky, 1989). As we can see in Figure 6.1, there is remarkable consistency across cultures in the estimated prevalence of schizophrenia.

Within the United States, one large epidemiological study found the highest rates of schizophrenia in African Americans, somewhat lower rates in whites, and the lowest rates in Hispanic Americans, although these ethnic differences diminished when socioeconomic status was taken into account (Escobar, 1993). Studies of persons hospitalized for serious mental disorders have found that African Americans are more likely than other groups to be misdiagnosed with schizophrenia, when they are actually suffering from a severe mood disorder (Griffith & Baker, 1993).

There is some evidence that schizophrenia is more common in men than in women, although the gender difference in rates of schizophrenia varies among studies and with the criteria used to diagnose schizophrenia (Goldstein, 1995; Hambrecht, Maurer, Hafner, &

undifferentiated schizophrenia
diagnosis made when a person experiences schizophrenic symptoms, such as delusions and hallucinations, but does not meet criteria for paranoid, disorganized, or catatonic schizophrenia

residual schizophrenia
diagnosis made when a person has already experienced a single acute phase of schizophrenia but currently has milder and less debilitating symptoms

Figure 6.1

Prevalence of Schizophrenia in a Cultural Context. This figure shows us the prevalence of schizophrenia in countries using narrow versus broad definitions of the disorder. Despite differences in definitions, the prevalence of schizophrenia is remarkably similar across countries, ranging from about 0.2 to 2.0 percent.

Source: Gottesman, 1991, p. 80.

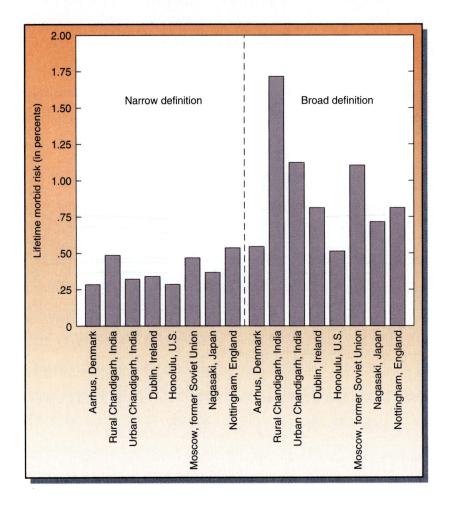

Sartorius, 1992). Men with schizophrenia are more likely than women with the disorder to show severe negative symptoms, such as flattened affect, withdrawal, and loss of motivation. They are also more likely to develop drug or alcohol abuse problems as a result of the disorder. Women are more likely than men to have auditory hallucinations, delusions with themes of persecution, guilt, and sexual morality, and emotional symptoms like severe anxiety and hopelessness.

Women with schizophrenia tend to have better premorbid (predisorder) histories than men. They are more likely to have graduated from high school or college, to have married and had children, and to have developed good social skills. This may be, in part, because the onset of schizophrenia in women tends to be later in life, often in the late 20s or early 30s, than it is for men, who more often develop schizophrenia in their late teens or early 20s.

Biological Theories of Schizophrenia

Given the similarity across cultures and across time in the symptoms and prevalence of schizophrenia, it is not surprising that biological factors have long been thought to play a strong role in the development of schizophrenia. There are three major biological theories of schizophrenia. First, there is good evidence for a genetic transmission of schizophrenia, although genetics do not fully explain who gets this disorder. Second, some people with schizophrenia show structural and functional abnormalities in specific areas of the brain that may contribute to the disorder. Third, the dopamine theory of

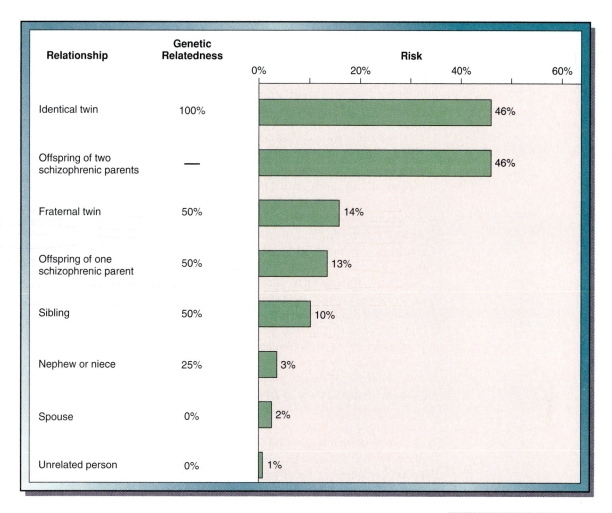

Relationship	Genetic Relatedness	Risk
Identical twin	100%	46%
Offspring of two schizophrenic parents	—	46%
Fraternal twin	50%	14%
Offspring of one schizophrenic parent	50%	13%
Sibling	50%	10%
Nephew or niece	25%	3%
Spouse	0%	2%
Unrelated person	0%	1%

Figure 6.2

Risk of Schizophrenia and Genetic Relatedness. This figure shows that one's risk of developing schizophrenia decreases substantially as one's genetic relationship to a person with schizophrenia becomes more distant.

Source: Gottesman, 1991.

schizophrenia holds that excess levels of the neurotransmitter dopamine play a causal role in schizophrenia.

Genetic Contributors to Schizophrenia

Family, twin, and adoption studies have all provided evidence that genes are involved in the transmission of schizophrenia. Psychologist Irving Gottesman compiled over 40 studies to determine the lifetime risk for developing schizophrenia for people with different familial relationships to a person with schizophrenia. His conclusions are summarized in Figure 6.2. Children of two parents with schizophrenia and monozygotic twins of people with schizophrenia, who share the greatest number of genes with people with schizophrenia, have the greatest risk of developing schizophrenia at some time in their lives. As the genetic similarity to a person with schizophrenia decreases, an individual's risk of developing schizophrenia decreases. Thus, a first-degree relative to a person with schizophrenia, such as a nontwin sibling, who shares about 50 percent of genes with the person with schizophrenia, has about a 9 percent chance of developing schizophrenia. In contrast, a third-degree relative to a person with schizophrenia, such as a first cousin, who shares only about 13 percent of genes with the person with schizophrenia, has only a 2 percent chance of developing schizophrenia, not a significantly greater risk than that to a random person in the general population. This relationship between the degree of genetic similarity between an individual and his or her schizophrenic relative and that individual's own risk of developing schizophrenia strongly suggests that genes play a role in the development of the disorder.

According to Figure 6.2, one of the groups at highest risk for developing the disorder are the biological children of schizophrenic parents. Growing up with a parent with schizophrenia and particularly with two parents with the disorder is likely to mean growing up in a stressful atmosphere. When a parent is psychotic, the child may be exposed to illogical thought, mood swings, and chaotic behavior. Even when the parent is not acutely psychotic, the residual negative symptoms of schizophrenia—the flattening of affect, lack of motivation, and disorganization—may impair the parent's child-care skills. Is it possible that the high risk for developing schizophrenia seen in the children of people with schizophrenia is due, at least in part, to the stress of living with schizophrenic parents?

Adoption studies of children of schizophrenic parents who are adopted shortly after birth and raised by nonschizophrenic parents are a good way to address this question. An early and classic adoption study was conducted by Leonard Heston (1966) in the United States and Canada. He interviewed the adult children of 47 women who had been diagnosed with schizophrenia in the Oregon state mental hospitals in the 1930s. All of these children had been placed in orphanages or with nonmaternal relatives within 3 days of their births. He also interviewed a group of 50 adults who had been adopted shortly after birth but whose mothers had no record of mental illness. If living with a parent with schizophrenia contributes significantly to a child's vulnerability to schizophrenia, then the children of people with schizophrenia who were adopted away from their mothers should have had a lower rate of developing schizophrenia than the 13 percent rate for children who grow up with schizophrenic parents (see Figure 6.2). Heston found, however, that about 17 percent of the adopted-away children of people with schizophrenia developed schizophrenia as adults, a rate even higher than the average rate of 13 percent for children of people with schizophrenia. The rate may be higher for the adopted-away children in the Heston study because the mothers of these children were probably experiencing particularly severe forms of schizophrenia. In contrast, none of the 50 control group children in the Heston study whose mothers had no mental illness developed schizophrenia as adults.

Within Figure 6.2, we also see the compiled results of several twin studies of schizophrenia that suggest that the concordance rate for monozygotic twins is 48 percent, while the concordance rate for dizygotic twins is 17 percent. This difference in concordance rates is statistically significant and is further evidence for a genetic contribution to the development of schizophrenia. Gottesman and Shields (1982) found much higher concordance rates for monozygotic twins of between 75 and 91 percent when they restricted their sample to persons with only the most severe forms of schizophrenia. In comparison, the concordance rates for MZ twins with mild forms of schizophrenia ranged from 17 to 33 percent. This is one of several pieces of evidence that have lead researchers to suggest that people with more severe forms of schizophrenia have a greater genetic loading for the disorder than do people with less severe forms.

What might the genotype for schizophrenia be like? The fact that the concordance rate for schizophrenia among monozygotic twins is not 100 percent and that people can carry the genotype for schizophrenia but never develop the disease argues against a single, major dominant gene for schizophrenia. Some researchers have argued for a polygenic, additive model, in which it takes a certain number and configuration of abnormal genes to create schizophrenia (Gottesman, 1991). The more of these genes an individual is born with, the more likely he or she is to develop schizophrenia and the more serious the disorder will be. Individuals born with some of these genes but not enough to reach the threshold for creating full-blown schizophrenia may still show some of the symptoms of schizophrenia.

The studies we have reviewed thus far make it clear that genetics are involved in the transmission of schizophrenia. The type and location of the gene or genes for schizophrenia are currently unknown, however. One of the greatest hindrances in the search for the genes for schizophrenia is that schizophrenia is not one disorder manifested in the same way across people but a very heterogeneous group of disorders. Each of the different types of schizophrenia may have its own genetic underpinnings. In addition, there may be forms of schizophrenia that are not genetically transmitted, although they may have another form of biological cause such as those described next. As many as 89 percent of people with schizophrenia have no known family history of schizophrenia (Cromwell &

Snyder, 1993). Finally, even when a person carries a genetic risk for schizophrenia, many other biological and environmental factors may influence whether and how he or she manifests the disorder. The classic illustration of this point is found in the Genain quadruplets. These four women, who shared exactly the same genes and grew up in the same family environment, all developed schizophrenia, but the specific symptoms, onset, course, and outcome of the disorder varied substantially among them (Buchsbaum, 1984). Their experiences are evidence that even if we could clone the genes for schizophrenia, we would have a great deal to learn about how this disorder, or group of disorders, emerges out of a genetic predisposition.

The Genain quadruplets all have schizophrenia, but the specific forms of schizophrenia differ among the sisters.

Structural Brain Abnormalities

Clinicians and researchers have long believed that there is something fundamentally different about the workings of the brains of people with schizophrenia compared to the brains of people without schizophrenia. It is only in the last 20 years, with the development of technologies such as positron emission tomography (PET scans), computerized axial tomography (CT scans), and magnetic resonance imaging (MRIs), that scientists have been able to examine in detail the structure and functioning of the brain. The picture of the schizophrenic brain emerging from use of these technologies is not an entirely clear one, again probably because there are many different types of schizophrenia that are often grouped together in studies. However, there is increasing evidence for both major structural and functional deficits in the brains of some schizophrenic people.

First, the **prefrontal cortex** is smaller and shows less activity in some people with schizophrenia than in people without schizophrenia (Figure 6.3; Andreason et al., 1997; Berman, Torrey, Daniel, & Weinberger, 1992; Buchsbaum et al., 1992). The prefrontal cortex is the single largest brain region in human beings, constituting nearly 30 percent of the total cortex, and has connections to all other cortical regions as well as to the limbic system, which is involved in emotion and cognition, and the basal ganglia, which is involved in motor movement. The prefrontal cortex is important in language, emotional expression, planning and producing new ideas, and mediating social interactions. Thus, it seems logical that a person with a prefrontal cortex that is unusually small or inactive would show a wide range of deficits in cognition, emotion, and social interactions, as people with schizophrenia do. Evidence of this lower level of activity is not found in all people with schizophrenia, however. It is more common in people who exhibit predominantly negative symptoms of schizophrenia (low motivation, poor social interactions, blunted affect) than in people who exhibit predominantly positive symptoms (hallucinations and delusions) or a mixed symptom profile (Andreason et al., 1992).

The second major structural brain abnormality found in schizophrenia is enlarged **ventricles** (Figure 6.4; Andreason et al., 1990). The ventricles are fluid-filled spaces in the brain. Enlarged ventricles suggest atrophy or deterioration in other brain tissue. People with schizophrenia with ventricular enlargement also showed reductions in the white matter in the prefrontal areas of the brain and an abnormal connection between the prefrontal cortex and the amygdala and hippocampus. Ventricular enlargement could indicate structural

prefrontal cortex
largest single brain region in humans that facilitates the planning and production of thoughts, language, emotional expression, and actions

ventricles
spaces in the brain filled with cerebrospinal fluid

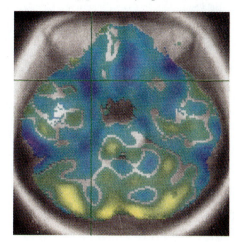

Figure 6.3

Lower Activity in the Prefrontal Cortex in Schizophrenia. This neuroimaging scan shows lower levels of activity in the frontal areas of the brain (as indicated in blue) in schizophrenic patients compared to healthy people.
Source: Andreasen et al., 1997.

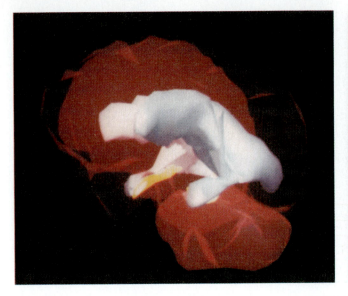
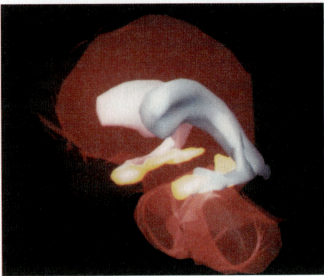

Figure 6.4

Enlarged Ventricles in People with Schizophrenia. The left panel shows the enlarged, fluid-filled ventricles (in gray) of a person with schizophrenia compared to a normal person (right panel). This image was taken by Nancy Andreasen.

Source: Gershon & Rieder, 1992, p. 128.

deficits in many other areas of the brain, however. Indeed, the different areas of the brain that can deteriorate to create ventricular enlargement could lead to different manifestations of schizophrenia (Breier et al., 1992).

People with schizophrenia with ventricular enlargement tend to have poor premorbid histories. That is, they show social, emotional, and behavioral deficits long before they develop the core symptoms of schizophrenia. They also tend to have more severe symptoms than others with schizophrenia and are less responsive to medication, suggesting gross alterations in the functioning of the brain that are difficult to alleviate with treatment. Ventricular enlargement is greater among males with schizophrenia than among females with schizophrenia, although the reason for this gender difference is unknown (Andreasen et al., 1990).

Both low prefrontal activity and ventricular enlargement could have a number of causes, including brain injury due to birth injury, head injury, viral infections, deficiencies in nutrition, deficiencies in cognitive stimulation, or genetic abnormalities. Evidence against a genetic cause for low prefrontal activity and ventricular enlargement has emerged from studies of monozygotic twins who are discordant for schizophrenia—that is, twins of which one has schizophrenia but the other does not (Berman et al., 1992; Suddath et al., 1990). These studies suggest that the schizophrenic twin tends to show low prefrontal activity and/or ventricular enlargement, but the nonschizophrenic twin does not, even though both twins have the identical genetic makeup.

How would you do a study that teased apart the effects of antipsychotic medications on the brains of people with schizophrenia from the effects of the schizophrenia itself?

Epidemiological studies have shown high rates of schizophrenia among persons whose mothers were exposed to the influenza virus while pregnant (see Kirch, 1993). For example, persons whose mothers were exposed to the influenza epidemic that swept Helsinki, Finland, in 1957 were significantly more likely to develop schizophrenia than people in control groups, particularly if their mothers were exposed during the second trimester of pregnancy (Mednick et al., 1988). The second trimester is a crucial period for the development of the central nervous system of the fetus, and disruption in this phase of brain development could cause the major structural deficits found in the brains of some people with schizophrenia. As yet, the specific mechanism by which prenatal exposure to viral infection could lead to schizophrenia or the extent to which prenatal viral exposure contributes to schizophrenia is unknown (Kirch, 1993).

The Dopamine Theory

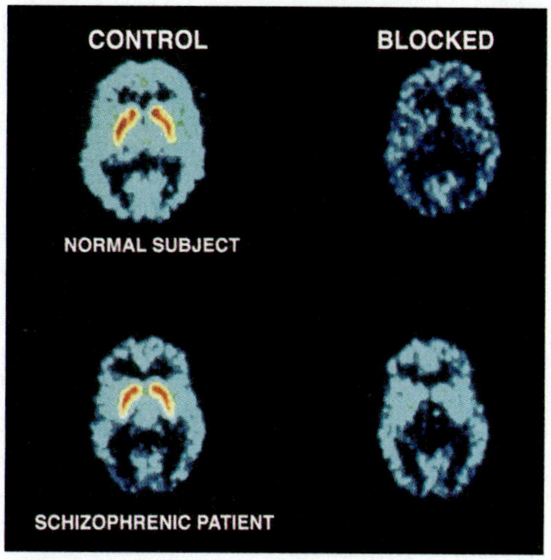

The neurotransmitter dopamine has been thought to play a role in schizophrenia for many years. The original dopamine theory was that schizophrenic symptoms are caused by excess levels of dopamine in the brain, particularly in the frontal lobe and the limbic system. This theory was supported by the following lines of evidence:

Figure 6.5

Greater Dopamine Receptor Activity in Schizophrenia. Schizophrenic people show greater dopamine receptor activity than controls even after taking a drug that blocks these receptors, as indicated by the greater density of blue in the schizophrenic PET scan on the lower right, compared to the control PET scan on the upper right.
Source: Taubes, 1994, p. 1034.

1. Drugs that reduce the functional level of dopamine in the brain tend to reduce the symptoms of schizophrenia. These drugs are commonly referred to as *phenothiazines* or *neuroleptics*.
2. Drugs that increase the functional level of dopamine in the brain, such as amphetamines, tend to increase the psychotic symptoms of schizophrenia.
3. Autopsy and PET scan studies showed more neuronal receptors for dopamine and sometimes higher levels of dopamine in some areas of the brains of people with schizophrenia than in the brains of controls (see Figure 6.5).
4. Levels of a by-product of dopamine, homovanillic acid (HVA), tend to be higher in the blood and cerebrospinal fluid of people with schizophrenia with more severe symptoms than in those with less severe symptoms.
5. Some people with schizophrenia who take phenothiazines to reduce their psychotic symptoms develop motor movement disorders similar to those in Parkinson's disease. It is well-established that Parkinson's disease is caused by a deficiency of dopamine in the brain. Thus, the movement disorders that people with schizophrenia develop as a result of taking phenothiazines are likely to be caused by these drugs reducing the levels of dopamine in their brains.

Now, however, research suggests that the original dopamine theory of schizophrenia was too simple (Davis et al., 1991):

1. Many people with schizophrenia do not respond to the phenothiazines, indicating that neurotransmitter systems other than the dopamine system may be involved in their disorders. Even people with schizophrenia who do respond to phenothiazines tend to experience relief only from their positive symptoms (hallucinations and delusions) and not from their negative symptoms. This suggests that simple dopamine depletion does not explain these negative symptoms.
2. Although persons taking the phenothiazines show reductions in dopamine functioning within hours or days of taking the drugs, their symptoms do not abate for several days after that.
3. Although levels of the dopamine by-product HVA tend to be higher in the blood and cerebrospinal fluid of more severely afflicted people with schizophrenia than of those less severely afflicted, comparisons of people with schizophrenia and normal or psychiatric control groups often find no overall differences in HVA levels, suggesting no overall differences in levels of dopamine in the brain. In fact, some studies find *lower* levels of HVA in people with schizophrenia compared to controls.
4. One of the most effective new drugs for schizophrenia, clozapine, does not work by blocking the same dopamine receptors that the other neuroleptics block. Instead, clozapine appears to bind to a newly discovered type of dopamine receptor, which has been labeled D_4.

Although the original version of the dopamine theory of schizophrenia (that there are generally higher functional levels of dopamine in the brains of people with schizophrenia compared to people without the disorder) is not holding up, it is clear that dopamine is involved in schizophrenia. Let us consider a more complex version of the dopamine theory that can explain both the positive and negative symptoms of schizophrenia (Davis et al., 1991). First, there may be excess dopamine activity in the mesolimbic system, a subcortical part of the brain involved in cognition and emotion. The mesolimbic system is rich with the newly discovered receptors for dopamine, known as D_4 and D_3. High dopamine activity in the mesolimbic system may lead to the positive symptoms of schizophrenia: hallucinations, delusions, and thought disorder. In turn, clozapine may work to reduce the symptoms of schizophrenia by binding to D_4 receptors in the mesolimbic system, blocking the action of dopamine in this system. Second, there may be unusually low dopamine activity in the prefrontal area of the brain, which is involved in attention, motivation, and organization of behavior. Low dopamine activity in the prefrontal area may lead to the negative symptoms of schizophrenia: lack of motivation, inability to care for oneself in daily activities, and blunting of affect. This idea fits well with evidence that structural and functional abnormalities in this part of the brain are associated with the negative symptoms, as discussed. This idea also helps to explain why the phenothiazines, which reduce dopamine activity, do not alleviate the negative symptoms of schizophrenia.

Thus, this more complex dopamine theory of schizophrenia integrates research and clinical findings that, at first glance, seem to contradict one another. It remains to be seen how correct this theory is. Some researchers argue that, while the positive or Type I symptoms of schizophrenia are caused by excess dopamine activity in the brain, the negative or Type II symptoms are not the result of dopamine imbalances but of structural abnormalities in the frontal lobes of the brain.

Summing Up	Biological Theories of Schizophrenia

- There is strong evidence for a genetic contribution to schizophrenia, although genetics do not fully explain who has the disorder.
- Many people with schizophrenia, particularly those with predominantly negative symptoms, show significant structural and functional abnormalities in the brain, including low frontal activity and ventricular enlargement.
- The original dopamine theory of schizophrenia is that the disorder is caused by excessive activity of the dopamine systems in the brain. This theory is probably too simple, but it seems clear that dopamine does play an important role in schizophrenia, especially in the positive symptoms.

Psychosocial Contributors to Schizophrenia

The notion that schizophrenia is caused by stressful events, bad parenting, or some other psychosocial factor has been one of the most controversial in psychology. Psychologists and psychiatrists who subscribe to psychosocial theories of schizophrenia have been accused of blaming the people with schizophrenia and their families for what is a totally biological disorder, out of the control of either patients or their families. There is little evidence that psychosocial factors can cause schizophrenia in otherwise healthy people. There is increasing evidence, however, that psychosocial factors may play an important role in determining the eventual severity of the disorder in people with a biological vulnerability and in triggering new episodes of psychosis.

Stress and Schizophrenia

Although you may have heard of someone having a "nervous breakdown" following a traumatic event, it is rare for someone to develop full-blown schizophrenia in response to a stressful event. Instead, the term *nervous breakdown* often is used to refer to severe depressions or anxiety disorders that develop following trauma.

Still, it is true that people with schizophrenia are more likely than people without schizophrenia to live in chronically stressful circumstances, such as in impoverished inner-city neighborhoods and in low-status occupations or unemployment (Dohrenwend et al., 1987). Most research supports a *social selection* explanation of this link. According to this explanation, the symptoms of schizophrenia interfere with a person's ability to complete an education and hold a job and thus people with schizophrenia tend to drift downward in social class, compared to their families of origin. One of the classic studies showing the process of social selection in schizophrenia tracked the socioeconomic status of men with schizophrenia and compared it with the status of their brothers and fathers (Goldberg & Morrison, 1963). The men with schizophrenia tended to end up in socioeconomic classes that were well below those of their fathers. For example, if their fathers were in the middle class, the men with schizophrenia were likely to be in the lower classes. In contrast, the healthy brothers of people with schizophrenia tended to end up in socioeconomic classes that were equal to or higher than those of their fathers. More recent data also support the social selection theory (Dohrenwend, Levav, Shrout, Schwartz, Naveh, Link, Skodol, & Stueve, 1992).

Stressful circumstances may not cause someone to develop schizophrenia, but they may trigger new episodes in people who are vulnerable to schizophrenia. When researchers looked at the timing of stressful events relative to the onset of new episodes of psychosis, they found higher levels of stress occurring shortly before the onset of a new episode of psychosis as compared to other times in the lives of people with schizophrenia (Norman & Malla, 1993). For example, in one study, researchers followed 30 people with schizophrenia for 1 year, interviewing them every 2 weeks to determine if they had experienced any stressful events and/or any increase in their symptoms. They found that people who experienced relapses of psychosis were more likely than people who did not to experience negative life events in the month before their relapse (Ventura et al., 1989).

 How is it that stress may contribute to relapses in schizophrenia?

It is important not to overstate the link between stressful life events and new episodes of schizophrenia, however. Over half the people in the study who had a relapse of their schizophrenia in the year they were followed had *not* experienced negative life events just before their relapse. In addition, other studies suggest that many of the life events that people with schizophrenia experience in the weeks before they relapse may actually be

People with schizophrenia may have trouble caring for their own daily needs, and end up on the streets.

caused by the prodromal symptoms that occur just before a relapse into psychosis (Dohrenwend et al., 1987). For example, one of the prodromal symptoms of a schizophrenic relapse is social withdrawal; in turn, the negative life events most often preceding a relapse, such as breakup of a relationship or loss of a job, could be caused partially by the social withdrawal of the person with schizophrenia.

Family Interactions and Schizophrenia

Psychoanalysts Freida Fromm-Reichman (1948) and Silvano Arieti (1955) described parenting styles in mothers that could cause their children to become schizophrenic. These *schizophrenogenic mothers* were dominant, cold, and rejecting of their children. Subsequent research comparing the parenting styles of mothers of people with schizophrenia and of mothers of people without the disorder did not confirm this theory.

Another early psychosocial theory of schizophrenia, proposed by Gregory Bateson and colleagues (Bateson, Jackson, Haley, & Weakland, 1956), was that parents (particularly mothers) of children who would become schizophrenic put their children in *double binds* by constantly communicating conflicting messages to the children. Such a mother might physically comfort her child when he falls down and is hurt but at the same time be verbally hostile to and critical of the child. Children chronically exposed to such mixed messages supposedly cannot trust their own feelings or their perceptions of the world and thus develop distorted views of themselves, of others, and of the environment, which contribute to schizophrenia. Again, however, empirical research has not supported the specific predictions of this double bind theory of schizophrenia.

Although the double bind theory of schizophrenia has not been supported, investigations of the *communication patterns* in families of people with schizophrenia have revealed oddities. Most investigators do not believe that these oddities alone cause schizophrenia in children but that they create a stressful environment that makes it more likely that a child with a biological vulnerability to schizophrenia will develop the full syndrome of schizophrenia or that a person with schizophrenia will have more frequent relapses of psychosis.

Margaret Singer and Lyman Wynne (1965) described *communication deviance* within schizophrenic families as involving vague, indefinite communications; misperceptions and misinterpretations; odd or inappropriate word usage; and fragmented, disrupted, and poorly integrated communication. Controlled comparisons of interactions in families with a person with schizophrenia and in families without a person with schizophrenia have found significantly higher levels of communication deviance in the families of people with schizophrenia. Some examples of this would be statements such as, "But the thing is as I said, there's got . . . you can't drive in the alley," and, "It's gonna be up and downwards along the process all the while to go through something like this" (Miklowitz et al., 1991).

Such deviant patterns of communication do not appear to have serious, long-lasting effects on children who do not have family histories of schizophrenia (see Gottesman, 1991). However, among children at risk for schizophrenia because they have family histories of the disorder, those whose families evidenced high levels of communication deviance are more likely to develop schizophrenia than are those whose families have low levels of communication deviance (Goldstein, 1987).

The family interaction style that has received the most attention by researchers of schizophrenia is *expressed emotion.* Families high in expressed emotion are overinvolved with each other, are overprotective of the disturbed family member, and voice self-sacrificing attitudes toward the disturbed family member, while at the same time being critical, hostile, and resentful of the disturbed family member (Brown, Birley, & Wing, 1972; Vaughn & Leff, 1976). Expressed emotion has been assessed through lengthy interviews with people with schizophrenia and their families, through projective tests, and through direct observation of family interactions. A number of studies have shown that people with schizophrenia whose families are high in expressed emotion are three to four times more likely to suffer relapses of psychosis than are those whose families are low in expressed emo-

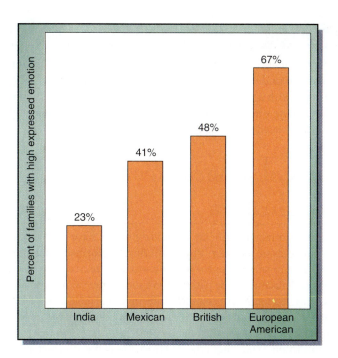

Figure 6.6

Cultural Differences in the Prevalence of Expressed Emotion in Families of Schizophrenics. Families of schizophrenics from developing countries tend to show lower levels of expressed emotion than do families of schizophrenics from developed countries. This may be one reason that schizophrenics from developing countries have fewer relapses than do schizophrenics from developed countries.

Source: Karno & Jenkins, 1993.

tion (Brown, Birley, & Wing, 1972; Kavanagh, 1992; Leff & Vaughn, 1981; Mintz, Lieberman, Miklowitz, & Mintz, 1987; Parker & Hadzi-Pavlovic, 1990). Being in a high expressed-emotion family may create stresses for the person with schizophrenia that overwhelm his or her ability to cope and that trigger new episodes of psychosis.

The link between high levels of family expressed emotion and higher relapse rates has been replicated in several cultures, including European countries, the United States, Mexico, and India. In Mexico and India, however, families of people with schizophrenia tend to score lower on measures of expressed emotion than do their counterparts in Europe or the United States (see Figure 6.6; Karno et al., 1987; Karno & Jenkins, 1993).

Critics of the literature on expressed emotion argue that the hostility and intrusiveness observed in some families of people with schizophrenia might be the result of the symptoms exhibited by the person with schizophrenia rather than contributors to relapse (Parker, Johnston, & Hayward, 1988). Although families are often forgiving of the positive symptoms of schizophrenia (hallucinations, delusions, thought disturbances) because they view them as uncontrollable, they can be unforgiving of the negative symptoms (lack of motivation, blunted affect), viewing them as under the control of the person with schizophrenia (Brewin, MacCarthy, Duda, & Vaughn, 1991; Hooley, Richters, Weintraub, & Neale, 1987). People with schizophrenia who have more of these symptoms may elicit more negative expressed emotion from their families and they may be especially prone to relapse. Another alternative explanation for the link between family expressed emotion and relapse in people with schizophrenia comes from evidence that family members who are particularly high on expressed emotion are themselves more likely to have some form of psychopathology (Goldstein et al., 1992). Thus, it may be that people with schizophrenia in these families have high rates of relapse because they have a greater genetic loading for psychopathology, as evidenced by the presence of psychopathology in their family members, rather than because their family members are high in expressed emotion. Perhaps the best evidence that family expressed emotion actually influences relapse in schizophrenic patients is that interventions that reduce family expressed emotion tend to reduce the relapse rate in schizophrenic family members. These studies will be reviewed shortly.

What would be some of the greatest stresses on the family members of people with schizophrenia?

- There is little evidence that psychosocial factors actually cause schizophrenia in people who have no underlying vulnerability to the disorder.
- Among people with a vulnerability, however, living in stressful circumstances, whether it is living with poverty and violence or living in a family high in expressed emotion, is associated with higher rates of relapse of psychosis.

Biological Therapies for Schizophrenia

Over the centuries, many treatments for schizophrenia have been developed, based on the scientific theories of the time. Physicians have performed brain surgery on people with schizophrenia in an attempt to "fix" or eliminate the part of the brain causing their hallucinations or delusions. These patients were sometimes calmer after their surgeries but often also experienced significant cognitive and emotional deficits as a result of the surgery. *Insulin coma therapy* was used in the 1930s to treat schizophrenia. People with schizophrenia would be given massive doses of insulin—the drug used to treat diabetes—until they went into a coma. When they emerged from this coma, however, patients were rarely much better, and the procedure was a highly dangerous one. *Electroconvulsive therapy*, or ECT, was also used to treat schizophrenia for a time, until it was clear that it had little effect on the symptoms of schizophrenia (although it is effective in treating serious depression).

Mostly, however, people with schizophrenia were simply warehoused. In 1955, one out of every two people in psychiatric hospitals was diagnosed with schizophrenia (Rosenstein, Milazzo-Sayre, & Manderscheid, 1989). These patients received custodial care—they were bathed, fed, and prevented from hurting themselves physically, often with the use of physical restraints—but few received any treatment that actually reduced their symptoms of schizophrenia.

Then, fortuitously, the **phenothiazines** were discovered in the early 1950s. French researchers experimenting with new drugs called *antihistamines* (which are now widely used to treat asthma and allergies) noticed the calming effects these drugs had on patients. French psychiatrists Jean Delay and Pierre Deniker then began experimenting with a close relative of the antihistamines, a phenothiazine called **chlorpromazine**, in the treatment of patients with various mental disorders. They found that patients with schizophrenia had a particularly positive reaction to this drug. Not only did the drug calm agitation, it also appeared to reduce schizophrenic hallucinations and delusions. Chlorpromazine and other related drugs in the class called **neuroleptics** (meaning "taking control of the nerves") revolutionized the treatment of schizophrenia. These drugs appear to work by blocking the receptors for dopamine known as D_1 and D_2 thereby reducing the action of dopamine in the brain. For the first time, many people with schizophrenia could control the positive symptoms of schizophrenia (hallucinations, delusions, thought disturbances) by taking this drug prophylactically (that is, even when they were not experiencing acute symptoms). The need for long-term custodial hospitalization of people with schizophrenia was greatly reduced, so that by 1971, the number of people with schizophrenia who were hospitalized was half of what would have been expected if these drugs had not been available.

The neuroleptic drugs are not without problems, however. First, although these drugs are effective in treating the positive symptoms of schizophrenia, they tend not to reduce the negative symptoms of schizophrenia: the lack of motivation and interpersonal deficits. Thus, many people with schizophrenia who take these drugs, while not actively psychotic still are not able to lead normal lives, holding a job and building positive social relationships. Second, a substantial minority (around 25 percent) of persons with schizophrenia do not respond to these drugs and thus do not get relief even from the positive symptoms of schizophrenia (Liberman et al., 1994). Third, these drugs have significant side

phenothiazines
drugs used to treat schizophrenia that work by blocking postsynaptic receptors for dopamine

chlorpromazine
phenothiazine drug used to treat schizophrenia that blocks certain dopamine receptors in the brain, thereby calming agitation and reducing positive symptoms of schizophrenia

neuroleptics
class of drugs that includes phenothiazines and butyrophenones, which often reduce the positive symptoms of schizophrenia but not the negative ones, and that carries side effects such as akinesia and tardive dyskinesia

effects. These include grogginess, dry mouth, blurred vision, visual disturbances, weight gain or loss, constipation, menstrual disturbances in women, and depression. Another common side effect is called **akinesia** and is characterized by slowed motor activity, monotonous speech, and an expressionless face (Blanchard & Neale, 1992). Patients taking the phenothiazines often show symptoms similar to those seen in Parkinson's disease, including stiffness of muscles, freezing of the facial muscles, tremors and spasms in the extremities, and **akathesis,** an agitation that causes them to pace and be unable to sit still. The fact that Parkinson's disease is caused by a lack of dopamine in the brain suggests that these motoric side effects of the phenothiazines result because these drugs reduce functional levels of dopamine in the brain. One of the most serious side effects is a neurological disorder known as **tardive dyskinesia** and involves involuntary movements of the tongue, face, mouth or jaw. People with this disorder may involuntarily smack their lips, make sucking sounds, stick out their tongues, puff their cheeks, or make other bizarre movements, over and over again. Tardive dyskinesia is often irreversible and may occur in over 20 percent of persons with long-term use of the phenothiazines (Morganstern & Glazer, 1993). Some of the problems of the neuroleptics are described in this personal account:

> My muscles became rigid, my vision blurred, and I slept about 20 hours a day; however, within 2 weeks my symptoms had remitted and I was able to be discharged from the hospital. When I say my symptoms had remitted, I should point out that I am referring to the positive symptoms of schizophrenia, that is the delusions, the hallucinations and the thought disorder. The so-called negative symptoms such as lack of motivation and depression actually got worse and were made more severe by the medication. . . . Another of the side effects of the medication for me was gaining weight. Within 6 months from first starting the treatment I had gained 40 or 50 pounds. This only added to my depression and my poor self-esteem. (Long, 1996)

 If you were taking antipsychotic medications and they were controlling your delusions and hallucinations but giving you significant symptoms of tardive dyskinesia, do you think you would want to discontinue taking these medications or continue taking them? Why or why not?

Physicians prescribing neuroleptics also have to take cultural differences into consideration. There is some evidence that persons of Asian descent need less neuroleptic medication than do persons of European descent to reach desired blood levels of the drug and to show symptom relief (Lin & Shen, 1991). Asians may also show side effects of neuroleptics at lower dosages. It is currently unclear whether these differences in response are due to biological differences or to differences in diet or some other environmental variable.

Fortunately, a relatively new drug seems to be effective in treating schizophrenia without inducing the same serious side effects of the phenothiazines. This drug is called **clozapine**. It has been used in Europe since the 1970s but only recently has been used in North America. It seems to work by binding to a different type of dopamine receptor than the other neuroleptic drugs, known as D_4, although it also influences several other neurotransmitters, including serotonin. Clozapine has been effective with many people with schizophrenia who have never responded to the other neuroleptics, and it appears to reduce negative as well as positive symptoms of schizophrenia in many patients (Wilson & Clausen, 1995). Clozapine does not induce tardive dyskinesia or other neurological side effects. It does have one major, although rare, side effect, however. In perhaps 1 to 2 percent of people who take this drug, a condition called *agranulocytosis* develops. This is a deficiency of granulocytes, which are substances produced by bone marrow that fight infection. This condition can be fatal, so patients taking clozapine must be carefully monitored for the development of this disease.

akinesia
condition marked by slowed motor activity, a monotonous voice, and an expressionless face, resulting from taking neuroleptic drugs

akathesis
agitation caused by neuroleptic drugs

tardive dyskinesia
neurological disorder marked by involuntary movements of the tongue, face, mouth, or jaw, resulting from taking neuroleptic drugs

clozapine
drug used to treat schizophrenia that blocks postsynaptic dopamine receptors other than those blocked by phenothiazines

Despite the potentially serious side effects of the drugs used to treat schizophrenia, many people with schizophrenia and their families regard these drugs as true lifesavers. These drugs have released many people with schizophrenia from lives of psychosis and isolation and have made it possible for them to pursue the everyday activities and goals that most of us take for granted.

 If a person with schiozphrenia says he or she does not want to be medicated and wants to live on the streets, does society have a right or obligation to force him or her to receive treatment?

Psychosocial Therapies for Schizophrenia

With the availability of drugs that control the symptoms of schizophrenia, why would anyone need psychosocial interventions? As this essay written by a woman with schizophrenia illustrates, drugs cannot completely restore the life of a person with schizophrenia:

> A note about becoming "sane": Medicine did not cause sanity; it only made it possible. Sanity came through a minute-by-minute choice of outer reality, which was often without meaning, over inside reality, which was full of meaning. Sanity meant choosing reality that was not real and having faith that someday the choice would be worth the fear involved and that it would someday hold meaning. (Anonymous, 1992, p. 335)

Many individuals who are able to control the acute psychotic symptoms of schizophrenia still experience many of the negative symptoms, particularly problems in motivation and in social interactions. Psychosocial interventions can help them increase their social skills and reduce their isolation and immobility. These interventions can help people with schizophrenia and their families learn to reduce the stress and conflict in their lives, thereby reducing the risk of relapse into psychosis. Psychosocial interventions can help people with schizophrenia understand their disorder and the need to remain on their medications and cope more effectively with the side effects of the medications. Finally, because of the severity of their disorder, many people with schizophrenia have trouble finding or holding jobs, coming up with enough money to feed and shelter themselves, and obtaining necessary medical or psychiatric care. Psychologists, social workers, and other mental health professionals can assist people with schizophrenia in meeting these basic needs by helping them obtain the resources to meet these needs.

Behavioral, Cognitive, and Social Interventions

Most experts in the psychosocial treatment of schizophrenia argue for a comprehensive approach that addresses the wide array of behavioral, cognitive, and social deficits in schizophrenia and that is tailored to the specific deficits of each individual with schizophrenia (see Table 6.2; Liberman, 1994). These treatments are given in addition to medication and can increase everyday functioning and reduce risk of relapse significantly (Benton & Schroeder, 1990).

Behavioral interventions, based on social learning theory (see Chapter 3), include the use of operant conditioning and modeling to teach persons with schizophrenia skills such as initiating and maintaining conversations with others, asking for help or information from physicians, and persisting when they are doing some activity such as cooking or cleaning. Cognitive interventions can include helping people with schizophrenia recognize demoralizing attitudes they may have toward their illness and then change these attitudes so that they will seek out help when needed and participate in society to the extent that they can.

Table 6.2 Skills Often Needed by People with Schizophrenia

These are some of the skills taught to people with schizophrenia as part of intensive skills-training programs.

Skills for Medication Management

To gain an understanding of how these drugs work, why maintenance drug therapy is used, and the benefits of medication

To learn appropriate procedures in taking medication and how to evaluate responses to medication

To learn the side effects of medications and what can be done to alleviate these effects

To practice ways of getting assistance when problems occur with medication

To desensitize fears of injections and learn benefits of biweekly or monthly injectable medication

Skills for Symptom Management

To learn how to identify personal warning signs and monitor them with the assistance of others

To learn specific techniques for managing warning signs and develop emergency plans

To learn how to recognize persistent symptoms and use techniques for coping with them

To learn about the adverse effects of alcohol and illicit drugs and how to avoid them

Basic Conversational Skills

To learn effective verbal and nonverbal listening techniques

To learn the most likely places to meet people and how to determine whether another is willing to engage in conversation

To learn the techniques that sustain conversations

To learn how to end conversations gracefully

To integrate all skill areas into natural and spontaneous conversations

Source: Liberman and Corrigan, 1993, p. 242.

Social interventions include increasing contact between people with schizophrenia and supportive others, often through self-help support groups. These groups meet together to discuss the impact of the disorder on their lives, the frustrations of trying to make people understand their disorder, their fears of relapse, their experiences with various medications, and other concerns they must live with day to day. Group members can also help each other learn social skills and problem-solving skills, such as those described in Table 6.2, by giving each other feedback on problem areas and by providing a forum in which individual members can role-play new skills.

Individual therapy for people with schizophrenia can help them improve their social relationships and cope with the consequences of their illness.

Group homes or **therapeutic communities** are also sometimes established, where people with schizophrenia can live together in a supportive atmosphere, usually with the aid of other residents who are not schizophrenic. One classic example of this is The Lodge, a residential treatment center for people with schizophrenia established by George Fairweather and colleagues (1969). At the Lodge, residents had responsibility for running the household and working with other residents to establish healthy behaviors and discourage inappropriate behaviors. The residents also established their own employment agency to find jobs. Follow-up studies showed that Lodge residents fared much better than people with schizophrenia who were simply discharged from the hospital into the care of their families or less intensive treatment programs (Fairweather, Sanders, Maynard, & Cressler, 1969). For example, Lodge residents were less likely to be rehospitalized and much more likely to hold jobs than were those in the comparison group, even after the Lodge closed.

group home
type of residence for people with mental disorders that serves as an alternative to hospitalization by providing resources and assistance in the least restrictive environment possible

therapeutic community
type of residence where people with mental disorders live with mental health workers and share responsibility for the maintenance of the residence and the development of healthy behavior in one another

Other comprehensive treatment programs provide skills training, vocational rehabilitation, and social support to people with schizophrenia who are living at home. In a model program established in Madison, Wisconsin, mental health professionals worked with chronically disabled people with schizophrenia

1. to help them gain material resources for food, shelter, clothing, and medical care;
2. to help them gain coping skills to meet the demands of community life, such as using public transportation, preparing simple but nutritious meals, and budgeting money;
3. to motivate them to persevere and remain involved with life even when their lives became stressful;
4. to lessen their dependency on family members; and
5. to educate family and community members about the kind of support they need.

These interventions were provided in the homes or communities of patients for 14 months and then the patients were followed for another 28 months. Their progress was compared to that of another group of patients who received standard hospital treatment for their psychotic symptoms. Both groups were treated with antipsychotic medications (Test & Stein, 1980).

The patients who received the home-based intensive skills interventions were less likely than the control group patients to be hospitalized and more likely to be employed both during the treatment and in the 28 months of follow-up (see Figures 6.7 and 6.8). The home-based intervention group also showed lower levels of emotional distress and psychotic symptoms than did the control group during the intervention. The differences in symptoms between the two groups diminished after the intervention period ended, however. In general, the gains that people in skills-based interventions tend to make decline once the interventions end, suggesting that these interventions need to be ongoing (Liberman, 1994). However, the benefits of these interventions can be great. They also are much more cost-effective than hospitalization (Weisbrod, Test, & Stein, 1980).

Family Therapy

We found out earlier in this chapter that communication deviance and high levels of expressed emotion within the family of a person with schizophrenia can substantially increase the risk and frequency of relapse. This increased risk has led many researchers to examine the effectiveness of family oriented therapies for people with schizophrenia. The successful therapies tend to combine basic education on schizophrenia with training of

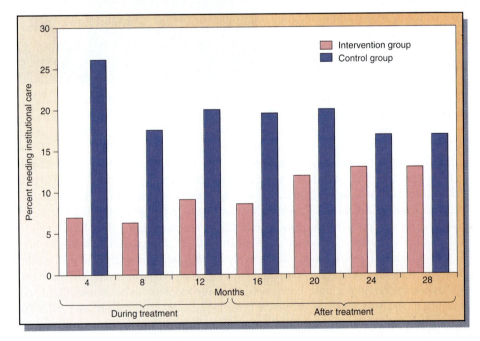

Figure 6.7

Effects of Home-Based Treatment on Need for Institutional Care. When schizophrenic patients received intensive home-based skills training and care, they were much less likely to be hospitalized for psychotic symptoms or to need other types of institutional care.

Source: Test & Stein, 1980.

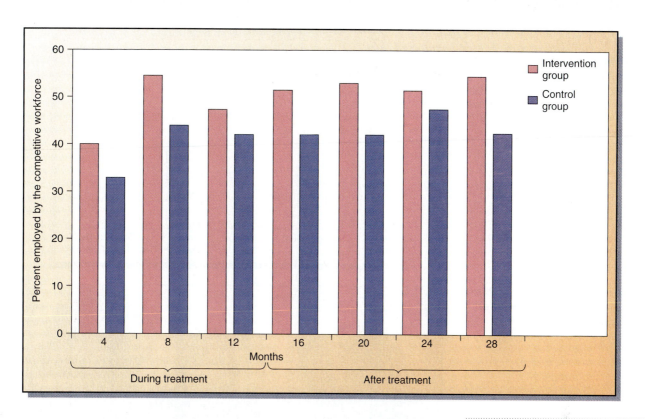

Figure 6.8

Effects of Home-Based Treatment on Employment. Home-based skills interventions also increased the number of schizophrenic patients who were able to maintain employment in the competitive workforce. Source: Test & Stein, 1980.

the family members in coping with the schizophrenic member's inappropriate behaviors and with the impact that the disorder has on their lives (Beels & McFarlane, 1982; Falloon, Brooker, & Graham-Hole, 1992; Halford & Hayes, 1991; Hogarty, 1986; Hogarty et al., 1991; McFarlane et al., 1995; Randolph, Eth, & Glynn, 1994). In the educational portion of these therapies, families are given information about the biological causes of the disorder, the symptoms of the disorder, and neuroleptic medications and their side effects. The hope is that this information will reduce self-blame in the family members, will increase their tolerance for the uncontrollable symptoms of the disorder, and will allow them to monitor their schizophrenic member's use of medication and possible side effects. Family members are also taught good listening and communication skills so as to reduce harsh, conflictual interactions with their schizophrenic member. Family members learn problem-solving skills to manage problems in the family (like lack of money) so as to reduce the overall level of stress in the family. They also learn specific behavioral techniques for encouraging appropriate behavior and discouraging inappropriate behavior in their schizophrenic member.

These family oriented interventions, when combined with drug therapy, appear to be more effective than drug therapy alone (Falloon, Brooker, & Graham-Hole, 1992). For example, Hogarty and colleagues (1986, 1991) compared the effectiveness of four types of intervention for persons with schizophrenia. The first group received medication only. The other three groups received medication plus one of the following types of psychosocial intervention: social skills training for the person with schizophrenia only; family oriented treatment; or a combination of social skills training for the person with schizophrenia and family oriented treatment for his or her family members. In the first year following these treatments, 40 percent of people with schizophrenia in the medication-only group relapsed, compared to only 20 percent in the first two psychosocial intervention groups and no one in the group that received both individual social skills training and family oriented therapy (see Figure 6.9). In the second year of follow-up, the groups that received family oriented therapy continued to fare better than did those who received medication alone. In this study and others, however, the effects of psychosocial interventions diminished with time if the interventions were not continued. Thus, as with the medications for schizophrenia, psychosocial interventions must be ongoing to continue to reduce the chances of relapse in people with schizophrenia.

Figure 6.9

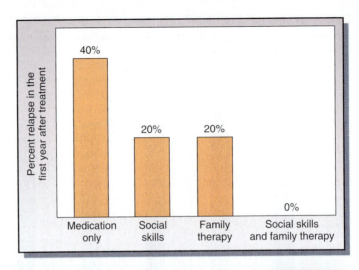

Effects of Psychosocial Intervention (with Medication) on Relapse Rates. Schizophrenic patients who received either social skills training, family therapy, or both in addition to medication had much lower relapse rates in the first year after treatment than did patients who received only medication.
Source: Hogarty et al. 1986.

Family therapy can help the families of people with schizophrenia to reduce stress and understand the symptoms of schizophrenia.

 How would you conduct family therapy with the family of a person with schizophrenia so as not to make the family members feel they were being blamed for their loved one's disorder?

Folk and Religious Treatments for Schizophrenia

In developing or third world countries and in parts of industrialized countries, the symptoms of schizophrenia are sometimes treated by folk or religious healers, according to the cultural beliefs about the meaning and causes of these symptoms. Anthropologists and cultural psychiatrists have described four models that traditional healers tend to follow in treating schizophrenic symptoms (Karno & Jenkins, 1993). According to the *structural model*, there are interrelated levels such as the body, emotion, and cognition or the person, society, and culture, and symptoms arise when the integration between these levels is lost. Healing thus involves reintegrating these levels, through change of diet or environment, prescription of herbal medicines, or rituals. The *social support model* holds that symptoms arise from conflictual social relationships and that healing involves mobilizing a patient's kin to support him or her through this crisis and reintegrating the patient into a positive social support network. The *persuasive model* suggests that rituals can transform the meaning of symptoms for the patient, diminishing the pain of the symptoms. Finally, in the *clinical model*, it is simply the faith that the patient puts in the traditional healer to provide a cure for the symptoms that relieves the symptoms.

In developing countries, care for people with schizophrenia is more likely to be carried out by the extended family rather than by a mental health institution (Karno & Jenkins, 1993). Thus, it may be especially important in these countries that interventions with a person with schizophrenia also include his or her family.

Culture, Gender, and the Prognosis for People with Schizophrenia

Schizophrenia is more chronic and debilitating than most other mental disorders. Between 50 and 80 percent of people who are hospitalized for one schizophrenic episode will be rehospitalized for another episode at some time in their lives (Eaton et al., 1992). The life expectancy of people with schizophrenia is as much as 10 years shorter than that of people without schizophrenia (McGlashan, 1988). People with schizophrenia suffer from infectious and circulatory diseases at a higher rate than do people without the disorder, for reasons that are unclear. Importantly, as many as 10 percent of people with schizophrenia commit suicide (Hendin, 1995). The following account of a schizophrenic woman about her suicidal thoughts gives a sense of the pain that many people with schizophrenia live with and wish to end through suicide (Anonymous, 1992, p. 334).

In cultures where families strongly support their ill family members, the relapse rate for schizophrenia is lower.

> I had major fantasies of suicide by decapitation and was reading up on the construction of guillotines. I had written several essays on the problem of the complete destruction of myself; I thought my inner being to be a deeply poisonous substance. The problem, as I saw it, was to kill myself, but then to get rid of my essence in such a way that it did not harm creation.

Contrary to common views of schizophrenia, however, most people with schizophrenia do not show a progressive deterioration in functioning across the life span. Instead, most stabilize within 5 to 10 years of their first episode, and the number of rehospitalizations declines as the person grows older (Eaton et al., 1992). Studies suggest that between 20 and 30 percent of treated people with schizophrenia recover substantially or completely from their illness within 10 to 20 years of its onset (Breier, Schreiber, Dyer, & Pickar, 1991). One very long-term study that followed people with schizophrenia for an average of 32 years found that 62 percent had completely recovered or showed only minor impairment in functioning at follow-up (Harding, Zubin, & Strauss, 1987). Why does the functioning of people with schizophrenia often improve with age? Perhaps it is because they find treatments that help them stabilize or they and their families learn to recognize the early symptoms of a relapse and seek aggressive treatment before their symptoms become acute. Alternatively, the aging of the brain could somehow reduce the likelihood of new episodes of schizophrenia. It has been speculated that the improvement of people with schizophrenia with age might be related to a reduction of dopamine in the brain with age, and as we learned earlier in this chapter, excess levels of dopamine have been implicated in schizophrenia (Breier, Schreiber, Dyer, & Picker, 1991).

Culture and gender appear to play strong roles in the course of schizophrenia. Schizophrenia tends to have a more benign course in developing countries than in

Figure 6.10

Cultural Differences in the Course of Schizophrenia. People with schizophrenia in developing countries are more likely to have a mild course of the disorder than are people in developed countries, whereas people in developed countries are more likely to have a severe course of the disorder than are people in developing countries.
Source: Jablensky, 1989, p. 521.

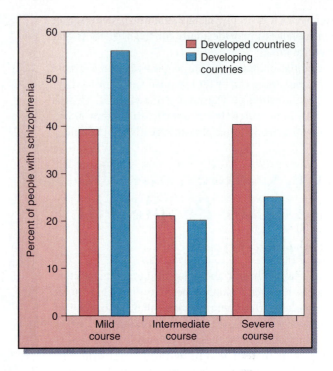

developed countries (Jablensky, 1989; Leff, Sartorius, Jablensky, Korten, & Ernberg, 1992). Cross-national studies conducted in eight countries by the World Health Organization and other studies conducted by individual investigators find that persons who develop schizophrenia in countries such as India, Nigeria, and Colombia are less likely to remain incapacitated by the disorder in the long-term than are persons who develop schizophrenia in countries such as Great Britain, Denmark, and the United States (see Figure 6.10).

The social environment of the person with schizophrenia in developing countries may facilitate adaptation and recovery better than the social environments of people with schizophrenia in developed countries (Karno & Jenkins, 1993). In developing countries, there are broader and closer family networks around the person with schizophrenia, providing more people to care for the person with schizophrenia. This ensures that no one person is solely responsible for the care of the person with schizophrenia, which is risky for both the person with schizophrenia and for the caregiver. Families in some developing countries also score lower on measures of hostility, criticism, and overinvolvement than do families in some developed countries. As noted earlier, low levels of expressed emotion in the families of people with schizophrenia are associated with a lower rate of relapse.

Recent research suggests that cultural differences in family interactions can significantly affect the impact of therapies designed to help families of people with schizophrenia. One study found that behavioral therapies to increase communication in these families actually backfired in some Hispanic families, perhaps because these families already had low levels of expressed emotion and found the techniques suggested by therapists to violate their cultural norms for how family members should interact (Telles et al., 1995). For example, some of the most traditional family members in this study expressed great discomfort during exercises that encouraged them to establish eye contact or express negative feelings to authority figures. These were considered disrespectful actions by these family members. This is just another example of how therapists must take into account the culture of clients in designing appropriate interventions for them.

Across most cultures, women who develop schizophrenia have a more favorable course of the disorder than do men who develop schizophrenia (Hambrecht, Maurer, Hafner, & Sartorius, 1992). Women are hospitalized less often and for briefer periods of time than are men, they show milder negative symptoms between periods of acute positive symptoms, and they have better social adjustment when they are not psychotic (Goldstein, 1995). This may be in part because women tend to develop schizophrenia at a later age than do men, and the later the age of onset of schizophrenia, the more favorable the course of the disorder tends to be (McGlashan, 1988).

Biological factors may contribute to women's better prognosis in schizophrenia. Estrogen may protect women from excessive dopamine turnover, which is thought to play a role in schizophrenia (Seeman, 1983). In addition, the greater hemispheric bilaterality of cognitive function in women may decrease the impact of the brain disturbance of schizophrenia (Flor-Henry, 1985). Neither of these theories has been supported definitively.

Social factors likely contribute to the gender differences in the course of schizophrenia (Mueser et al., 1990). Deviant behavior may be more socially acceptable in women than in men, so women who develop schizophrenia may experience less loss of social support than do men, which helps them cope better with their disorder. Also women with schizophrenia may have better social skills than do men with schizophrenia. These social skills may help women maintain and make use of their social support networks and reduce stress in their lives, thereby reducing their risk of relapse of symptoms.

There is probably more consensus among mental health professionals about the biological roots of schizophrenia than of any other psychopathology we will discuss in this book. The evidence that the fundamental vulnerability to schizophrenia is a biological one is compelling. Yet there is growing consensus that psychosocial factors contribute to the risk for schizophrenia among people with the biological vulnerability. A person with a biological vulnerability to schizophrenia who is raised in a supportive, low-conflict family with good communication skills and who escapes exposure to major stressors may never develop the full syndrome of schizophrenia. On the other hand, a person who has both a biological vulnerability and grows up in an unsupportive, stressful atmosphere is more likely to develop the full syndrome of the disorder. Psychosocial stress also clearly contributes to new episodes of psychosis in schizophrenic people. Finally, there is widespread consensus among mental health professionals that the most effective therapies for schizophrenia are those that address both the biological contributors and the psychosocial contributors to the disorder.

Bio-Psycho-Social INTEGRATION

Chapter Summary

The positive (or Type I) symptoms of schizophrenia include delusions (ideas the individual believes are true but are certainly false), hallucinations (unreal perceptual experiences), thought disturbances (incoherence of thought and speech), and grossly disorganized or catatonic behavior. The negative (or Type II) symptoms include affective flattening, alogia (poverty of speech), and avolition (the inability to initiate and persist in goal-directed activities). Prodromal and residual symptoms are mild versions of the positive and negative symptoms that occur before and after episodes of acute symptoms.

People with the paranoid subtype of schizophrenia have delusions and hallucinations with themes of persecution and grandiosity. This type of schizophrenia tends to begin later in life, and its episodes of psychosis are often triggered by stress. People with this type of schizophrenia have a better prognosis than do people with other types of schizophrenia.

The disorganized (formerly called *hebephrenic*) subtype of schizophrenia shows especially marked disorganization in thought and behavior and either a flattening of affect or frequent inappropriate affect. People with this subtype of schizophrenia are prone to odd, stereotyped behaviors, and their speech is often incoherent. This type of schizophrenia tends to have an early onset and a continuous course that is often unresponsive to treatment.

The catatonic subtype of schizophrenia is characterized by motor behaviors and ways of speaking that suggest the person is completely unresponsive to the environment.

Symptoms include motoric immobility, excessive and purposeless motor activity, extreme negativism, peculiar movements, and echolalia or echopraxia.

People with the undifferentiated subtype of schizophrenia have symptoms that meet the criteria for schizophrenia but do not meet the criteria for paranoid, disorganized, or catatonic schizophrenia.

People with the residual subtype of schizophrenia have had at least one episode of active symptoms but do not currently have prominent positive symptoms of schizophrenia. They continue to have mild positive symptoms and significant negative symptoms.

Estimates of the prevalence of schizophrenia in different countries range from about 0.2 percent to 2.0 percent, but most estimates are between 0.5 and 1.0 percent. There are some slight ethnic differences in rates of schizophrenia, but these may be due to differences in socioeconomic status. The content of delusions and hallucinations changes somewhat across cultures, but the form of these symptoms remains similar across cultures, and many clinicians and researchers believe schizophrenia can be reliably diagnosed across cultures. Men may be more prone to schizophrenia than are women, and there are some differences in symptoms between genders.

Biological theories of schizophrenia have focused on genetics, structural abnormalities in the brain, and neurotransmitters. There is clear evidence for a genetic transmission of schizophrenia, although genetics do not fully account for the disorder. People with schizophrenia show lowered functioning in the prefrontal areas of the brain and enlarged ventricles, suggesting atrophy in parts of the brain. Finally, although the original dopamine theory that schizophrenia is the result of too little dopamine is probably too simple, it is clear that dysfunction in the dopamine system is involved in schizophrenia.

Stressful events probably cannot cause schizophrenia in people who do not have a vulnerability to the disorder, but they may trigger new episodes of psychosis for people with the disorder. Stressful family environments seem to put people with schizophrenia at risk for more frequent relapses into psychosis. In particular, people with schizophrenia who live in families with high levels of communication deviance or expressed emotion tend to relapse more often than do those in families with low levels of these problems.

Drugs known as the phenothiazines were introduced for the treatment of schizophrenia in the 1950s and brought relief to many people with the disorder. The phenothiazines reduce the positive symptoms of schizophrenia but often are not effective with the negative symptoms. These drugs can have major side effects, including tardive dyskinesia, an irreversible neurological disorder characterized by involuntary movements of the tongue, face, mouth, or jaw. A newer drug, clozapine, seems to induce fewer side effects than the phenothiazines and is effective in treating both the positive and the negative symptoms of schizophrenia for many people.

Psychosocial therapies for schizophrenia focus on helping people with schizophrenia reduce stress, improve family interactions, learn social skills, and cope with the impact of the disorder on their lives. People in developing countries tend to show a more positive course of schizophrenia than do people in developed countries, and women tend to have a more positive course than do men.

Key Terms

delusions 216
hallucinations 216
psychotic
 symptoms 216
schizophrenia 216
persecutory
 delusion 217

delusion of
 reference 217
auditory
 hallucination 219
visual hallucination 220
formal thought
 disorder 221

word salad 221
clang associations 221
catatonia 223
catatonic stupor 223
catatonic posturing 223
catatonic
 excitement 223

Application

A Personal Account of Schizophrenia

It is perhaps easy in reading about the major breakthroughs in biological treatments for disorders like schizophrenia to believe that the application of these treatments is rather straightforward. All one has to do is to diagnose the disorder accurately, determine the correct dosage of the proper medication, and monitor for side effects.

Unfortunately, it is not that easy. Even people who are going to respond eventually to an antipsychotic drug or other psychotropic medication must often try different types of drugs at different dosage levels before they find one that provides them with relief from symptoms without inducing intolerable side effects. In the meantime, they must try to keep their lives going as well as possible. The following personal account of a young woman with schizophrenia details how complicated, long, and painful a process finding medications that work often is. This young woman is in school learning to be a pharmacist (Anonymous, 1983, pp. 152–155).

In lectures on antipsychotic drugs I want to tell the faculty and fellow students what it feels like to take these medicines and have to depend on them to function "outside" and what it is like to be titrated as an individual to the proper medication and dosage and the problems involved. I want to talk about schizophrenia and let them know it is not so far removed from them and correct some of the common misconceptions held about people who have schizophrenia.

Let me explain some of the major problems and pressures that schizophrenia has presented to me in getting through pharmacy school.

During my first semester of pharmacy school I was on 2 mg of Haldol (haloperidol) and 2 mg of Cogentin (benztropine, an anticholinergic drug used to reduce such side effects of antipsychotic drugs, such as speech slurring, rigid neck muscles, and fixed gaze) h.s. (at bedtime) as prescribed for me after hospitalization the summer before entry to school. My condition improved psychologically and seemed to be in remission until I entered school. I found I could neither read the board nor my notes; everything was blurred no matter where I sat. I called the psychiatrist who had prescribed the drugs and remembered his suggesting that I should take 2 more mg of Cogentin. (It is not clear whether the psychiatrist misunderstood my reason for calling or whether I misunderstood his advice about Cogentin. However, I later learned that Cogentin makes blurred vision worse, not better.) I complied and the next few days I not only had blurry vision, but I could not even see the lines on my notebook paper nor my writing—it was all one blur. In fact, the paper looked colorless. After 2 to 3 days of this, I called the physician back and told him I just could not take this medicine any more, because I could not read or see with it. I could not even tell if I was taking notes on the lines. This side effect, he said, was as he expected; his recommendation now was to drop down to only 2 mg of Cogentin and switch from Haldol to Stelazine (trifluoperazine) 6 mg every day h.s.

This was a compromise solution because, although I could now read and write, my schizophrenia was not so well-controlled. I wanted to drop out of school 3 weeks into the semester; I was afraid to go outside and felt as though I did not belong in pharmacy school or would not be able to overcome the stresses to be faced there. Fellow students were remarking to me that I seemed to be more impatient, hyperactive, and depressed. I also had problems with what a friend of mine called "the Stelazine stroll"—akathesia (restlessness). I continued to go out of the city once a week to see my psychologist, who helped me with aspects of the pressures I could not face alone or with only the drugs. . . .

In my first semester of my second year . . . I had just restarted Stelazine (after going off it by myself) at 8 mg h.s., an increased dose, and began having what I thought were seizures. In my classes I experienced an aura and then a wave hit me. I felt overstimulated and could hear a lecture but not process the information and take notes. My hand tremor was so bad during these episodes that I could not write. My psychologist suggested a consultation with the psychiatrist who had supervised my previous hospitalizations and prescribed the medications.

Although the psychiatrist was hesitant to give me the label for what was happening, I insisted, and he said it was "transient psychotic episodes." The problem with this development was that it began after I had already been taking an increased amount of the medication. Where could we go from here? The psychiatrist recommended titration, increasing the dose of Stelazine. However, it didn't work. He then suggested taking Stelazine along with another antipsychotic drug with more milligram potency (Navane [thiothixene] 5 mg h.s.), but I was still having acute psychotic episodes in my classes. I had taken to sitting in the back of the classroom, although I could not see the board, because I needed to be able to leave the room when this occurred, at the suggestion of the psychiatrist that I not sit there and suffer through it. I had explained away my change in seating to the other students by saying I felt I was going to have a seizure or by joking and saying I had decided I didn't care to see what teachers were writing on the board anymore.

When I got up in the morning, I could predict that the episodes would occur and where—I had a prodrome (a premonitory symptom). There were many frantic long distance calls to my psychologist after these episodes. I had to tell someone who could help me with what was happening to me. I, at this point, felt scared enough that never again would I have a compliance problem. I didn't want to lose all I had worked for in pharmacy school. I noticed the episodes were worse when emotionally volatile material was discussed in classes, such as antipsychotic agents, characteristics of schizophrenia, depression—all problems I had to cope with daily and that remained unresolved for me. . . .

As a consequence of the psychotic episodes and occasionally having to leave the classroom, I missed a lot of notes in my classes. All this work had to be made up. This increased the pressure I was under, which in turn worsened the schizophrenic symptoms and almost forced me into hospitalization. I did not want to drop out of school or receive too many incomplete grades, which would have been the result of 4 to 8 weeks of hospitalization to get properly titrated on the medication and to decrease disease symptoms. However, most of my instructors had rigid rules about missing exams and taking makeup exams. To reduce the pressure, I told the pro-

fessor with whom I was doing independent study that for medical reasons I would not be able to finish the paper due in that course. I decided to tell him why and he allowed me the Incomplete grade without requiring a medical letter on file, saving me the possible consequences of having this information on written record. And, most importantly, he did not treat me differently as a result of knowing. This reduced my stress and gave me time to make up work and take my final examinations. It also allowed me to work on my independent study paper during vacation and to do a good job on it while I was finally beginning to get a positive response to the medication.

I enjoyed winter break and finished my independent study project without incident, but as second semester approached I began to fear the room we had classes in, all the people and stimulation, and to fear recurrence of these episodes. What scared me most was the fact that this disease could prevent me from doing something I really wanted to do and needed to do, be psychologically healthy—that is, complete pharmacy school—and the knowledge that schizophrenia does this to many people's lives. I could not accept the fact that intellectually I could be capable of something that I may not at times be capable of emotionally.

When classes started, I still felt overstimulated and again had prodromes of psychotic episodes. I could not process information when people were talking; everything just seemed like noise. I was now on 5 mg of Navane b.i.d. (twice daily) and 2 mg of Cogentin h.s. I got enough courage to sit in front of the class again, but I was very fearful. My psychologist explained that I had begun to associate that classroom with these episodes and that extreme anxiety was causing dissociation reactions in me: I felt I was outside my body; I was watching everything. I wanted an antianxiety agent to get rid of these feelings and that constant

impending feeling that a psychotic episode would begin. The psychiatrist prescribed 5 mg of Valium (diazepam) in the morning and at bedtime when necessary. I took it only in the morning when I could not restructure my environment and situation to reduce the anxiety. For the first several weeks I was falling asleep in my first class and had double vision because I could not keep my eyes open. Finally, I became tolerant to the sedative effect.

So this is the answer right now for me: a neuroleptic, an antianxiety agent, an anti-Parkinsonian agent, and intense long-term psychotherapy with my psychologist. And I still look around at my fellow students and say to myself, "They do it without medicine, or doctors, or going to a psychiatric ward," but I needed all these things to cope with the pressure and stress of pharmacy school and life.

What I have been trying to express here is the actual reality of what being "individually titrated to an antipsychotic medicine" and having schizophrenia means to someone personally going through it as opposed to how objectively and easily it is expressed in pharmacy classes. My instructors have stated that "antipsychotics alleviate symptoms but do not cure psychoses," but this matter-of-fact statement has very personal meaning for me. It involves internal conflicts and many complicated adjustments—getting to a psychologist outside the city, or if the necessity of hospitalization occurs, getting hospitalized outside the city so fellow students and the pharmacy school will not have access to that information about me. It means never being able to see well because of the side effects of the medication. It also means enormous medical bills and debts. . . .

Finally, I heard a teacher in one class talk about long-term chronic illness such as schizophrenia in a way that suggested the teacher knew something about the disease and had looked beyond the myths. Through this class, I began to understand a little better my own non-compliance with the psychotropic drugs; how unacceptable my illness was not only to me, but would have been to others if they had known my diagnosis. I didn't take the medicine at times because I didn't want the disease, its problems, and its stigma. I wanted to be normal. And even now in the 1980s, in a professional pharmacy school, it would probably shock many people to know a schizophrenic was in their class, would be a pharmacist, and could do a good job. And knowledge of it could cause loss of many friends and acquaintances. So even now I must write this article anonymously. But I want people to know I have schizophrenia, that I need medicine and psychotherapy, and at some times I have required hospitalization. But, I also want them to know that I have been on the dean's list, and have friends, and expect to receive my pharmacy degree from a major university.

When you think about schizophrenia next time, try to remember me; there are more people like me out there trying to overcome a poorly understood disease and doing the best they can with what medicine and psychotherapy have to offer them. And some of them are making it. ■

chapter 7

Dissociative and Somatoform Disorders

Dissociative Disorders

The dissociative disorders include dissociative identity disorder (formerly called *multiple personality disorder*), dissociative fugue, dissociative amnesia, and depersonalization disorder. In each of these disorders, people experience a fragmentation of their usual sense of self, sometimes develop whole new and separate personalities, and may have amnesia for important facts about themselves.

Dissociative Identity Disorder

People with dissociative identity disorder develop multiple separate personalities. These personalities may have different functions and be of different ages and even of different genders. Dissociative identity disorder may develop in people who experience severe traumas, especially during childhood, and who use self-hypnosis to create "alters" to help them cope with these traumas. Treatment for dissociative identity disorder involves discovering the functions of all the personalities and helping the individual to integrate these personalities and find more adaptive ways of coping with stress.

Dissociative Fugue

People with dissociative fugue move away from home and assume a new identity, with complete amnesia for their previous life. Fugue states may arise following major traumas. Because dissociative fugue disorder is rare, little is known about the causes or appropriate treatments for this disorder.

Dissociative Amnesia

People with dissociative amnesia lose their memories for important facts about their lives and personal identities, apparently for psychological reasons. It is critical to differentiate between psychologically based amnesias and biologically based amnesias. Psychologically based amnesias most frequently occur following traumatic events, such as sexual assaults.

Depersonalization Disorder

Depersonalization experiences involve a sense that one is detached from one's own mental processes or body. Such experiences are common when people are fatigued or under stress. The diagnosis of depersonalization disorder is given when episodes of depersonalization are frequent and severe enough to interfere with a person's functioning.

Somatoform Disorders

The somatoform disorders include conversion disorder, somatization and pain disorder, hypochondriasis, and body dysmorphic disorder. All these disorders involve experiences of significant physical symptoms for which there apparently is no biological cause but that are linked to psychological factors.

Conversion Disorder

People with conversion disorder completely lose functioning in some part of their bodies, apparently for psychological reasons. These disorders arise most commonly in response to extreme stress. Psychodynamic treatments involve helping people make the links between their symptoms and traumatic memories. Behavioral treatments focus on relieving people's anxiety about the initiating traumas through desensitization and exposure treatments.

Somatization and Pain Disorder

People with somatization disorder have histories of multiple physical complaints for which there are no organic causes but for which they have sought a great deal of medical help. People with pain disorder focus their complaints on symptoms of pain. These disorders may represent acceptable ways of expressing distress, especially for people in certain cultures. Cognitive theories of these disorders suggest that they are due to catastrophization of physical symptoms. Treatment for these disorders involves helping people cope more adaptively with the stresses they face.

Hypochondriasis

People with hypochondriasis worry chronically that they may be ill, even when they have no physical symptoms and have been thoroughly checked by medical professionals. The causes and treatments for hypochondriasis are similar to those for somatization disorder.

Body Dysmorphic Disorder

Although body dysmorphic disorder is categorized as a somatoform disorder, it has features that are different from the other somatoform disorders. People with body dysmorphic disorder are excessively preoccupied with some part of their bodies and go to elaborate means to change that part of their bodies. This disorder may be a form of obsessive-compulsive disorder.

Bio-Psycho-Social Integration
Chapter Summary
Key Terms
Application: *It Just Doesn't Add Up*

The image of myself which I try to create in my own mind in order that I may love myself is very different from the image which I try to create in the minds of others in order that they may love me.

—W. H. Auden, "Hic et Ille," *The Dyer's Hand* (1963)

Daniel Nevis
Day Dream

In dissociative disorders, aspects of an individual's personality split apart.

When faced with extremely painful situations or emotions, people often want simply to escape. They may abuse alcohol or some other drug or binge eat in order to avoid distress. In this chapter, we will discuss an extreme form of escape used by some people facing traumatic experiences or intolerable distress. This escape mechanism is known as **dissociation.** Dissociation is a process in which different facets of an individual's identity, memories, or consciousness become split off from one another. The poet Emily Dickinson (1890/1955) describes this process:

a pain
so utter
it swallows substance up
then covers the Abyss with trance
so memory can step around, across, upon it
as one within a swoom goes safely
where an open eye
would drop him
bone by bone.

dissociation
process whereby different facets of an individual's sense of self, memories, or consciousness become split off from one another

The focus of this chapter will be on extreme forms of dissociation in which individuals develop multiple separate personalities or completely lose memory for significant portions of their lives. When these dissociative experiences become chronic and defining features of people's lives, they may be diagnosed with a dissociative disorder. We will also discuss the somatoform disorders, in which affected people appear to develop physiological symptoms that are tied to painful memories or emotions that they are not aware of or are not able to confront. For example, after witnessing the shooting of a child during a robbery, a woman may lose her vision. Many theoreticians believe that dissociative processes are involved in the development of somatoform disorders.

Dissociative Disorders

Mild dissociative experiences are very common. Daydreaming is a dissociative experience. When we daydream, we can lose consciousness of where we are and of what is going on around us. Dissociative experiences are especially common among people who are sleep deprived and under stress. For example, during exam week when they are very tired and stressed, students often have experiences in which they feel their "souls" are floating above their bodies.

Mild dissociative experiences are common when people are stressed or sleep deprived.

Scientific interest in dissociative experiences has waxed and waned over the last few centuries (Ross, 1989). There was a great deal of interest in dissociation in nineteenth-century France and the United States among neurologists and psychologists such as Janet, Charcot, Freud, Jung, and James. French neurologist Pierre Janet viewed dissociation as a process in which systems of ideas are split off from consciousness but available to consciousness in dreams and through hynopsis. One case he investigated was that of a woman named Irene, who had no memory of the fact that her mother had died but who, during her sleep, would physically dramatize the events surrounding her mother's death. Sigmund Freud became fascinated with "hysterical symptoms" that arose out of dissociative processes, such as **glove anesthesia**, in which people lost all feeling in one hand in a manner inconsistent with the anatomy of the nervous system. Freud found that these people tended to regain feeling in their hands when, usually under hypnosis, they recalled painful memories or emotions that had been blocked from consciousness. The study of patients with severe dissociative experiences contributed much to Freud's theory of the structure of the mind and the role of repression in serious psychopathology.

glove anesthesia
a syndrome in which people lose all feeling in one hand in a manner inconsistent with the anatomy of the nervous system, suggesting that the loss of feeling is psychologically caused

After about 1910, interest in dissociative phenomena waned, partly because of the rise of behaviorism and biological approaches within psychology, which rejected the concept of repression and the use of techniques like hypnosis in therapy. Ernest Hilgard (1977, 1986) revitalized interest in dissociation in his experiments on the "hidden observer" phenomenon. He argued that there is an *active mode* to consciousness, which consists of the plans and desires of which we are aware and the voluntary actions we undertake to fulfill these plans and desires. There is also a *receptive mode* to consciousness, which receives stimuli in a relatively passive manner. In this receptive mode, people can register and store information in memory without being aware that the information has been processed, as if hidden observers are watching and recording events in the people's lives without the people being aware. Hilgard and his associates conducted experimental studies in which subjects were hypnotized and given a suggestion that they would feel no pain during a painful procedure but that they would remember the pain when the hypnotist gave them a specific cue. These subjects indeed exhibited no awareness of pain during the procedure but, when cued, recovered memories of the pain in a "matter-of-fact" fashion, as if a "lucid, rational observer" of the event had registered the event for the subject. Other research showed that some surgical patients who had been completely anesthetized during surgery could recall specific pieces of music presented to them through earphones during the surgery when put under hypnosis after surgery. Again, it was as if some "hidden observer" were registering the events of the operations even while the patients were completely unconscious under anesthesia (see also Kihlstrom & Couture, 1992). People who develop dissociative disorders may have chronic disruptions in the integration between active or voluntary consciousness and receptive or involuntary consciousness (Hilgard, 1992; Kihlstrom, 1992). That is, different aspects of consciousness in these people do not communicate with each other in normal ways.

 What do these experiments on the "hidden observer" suggest about the plausibility of attempts to influence people through subliminal perception?

We begin our discussion of specific dissociative disorders with dissociative identity disorder, formerly known as *multiple personality disorder*. We then move to dissociative fugue, dissociative amnesia, and depersonalization disorder. All these disorders involve frequent experiences in which different aspects of a person's "self" are split off from each other, fragmented, and felt as separate. These experiences can be mild enough that the individual is able to keep functioning in society, although with distress and struggling. Or they can be severe enough that the individual is almost completely unable to function in daily life (see Table 7.1).

Table 7.1 Key Features of the Dissociative Disorders

Disorder	Key Features
Dissociative identity disorder	There are separate multiple personalities in the same individual. The personalities may be aware of each other or may have amnesia for each other.
Dissociative fugue	The person moves away and assumes a new identity, with amnesia for the previous identity. There is no switching among personalities as in dissociative identity disorder.
Dissociative amnesia	The person loses memory of important personal facts, including personal identity, for no apparent organic cause.
Depersonalization disorder	There are frequent episodes in which the individual feels detached from his or her mental state or body. The person does not develop new identities or have amnesia for these episodes.

Dissociative Identity Disorder

Eve White was a quiet, proper, and unassuming woman, a full-time homemaker and devoted mother to a young daughter. She sought help from a psychiatrist for painful headaches that were occurring with increasing frequency. The psychiatrist determined that her headaches were related to arguments she was having with her husband over whether to raise their young daughter in the husband's church (which was Catholic) or in her church (which was Baptist). After undergoing some marital therapy, Mrs. White's marriage improved and her headaches subsided for a year or so. Then, her husband recontacted her therapist, alarmed over a recent series of incidents involving his wife. She had gone to visit a favorite cousin in a town 50 miles away and during the visit had behaved in a much more carefree and reckless manner than was customary for her. Mrs. White told her husband over the phone that she was not going to return home, and the two had a terrible fight that ended in an agreement to divorce. When Mrs. White did return home a few days later, however, she said she had no memory of the fight with her husband or, for that matter, of the visit with her cousin. Shortly thereafter, Mrs. White apparently went shopping and bought hundreds of dollars worth of elaborate clothing, which the couple could not afford. When confronted by her husband about her expenditures, Mrs. White claimed to have no memory of buying the clothing.

At the urging of her husband, Mrs. White made an appointment with the therapist whom she had originally consulted about her headaches. In the session, she admitted that her headaches had returned and were much more severe now than before. Eventually, she also tearfully admitted that she had begun to hear a voice other than her own speaking inside her head and that she feared she was going insane. The therapist asked her more questions about the clothes-buying spree, and Mrs. White became more tense and had difficulty getting words out to discuss the incident. Then, as her therapist reported,

> The brooding look in her eyes became almost a stare. Eve seemed momentarily dazed. Suddenly her posture began to change. Her body slowly stiffened until she sat rigidly erect. An alien, inexplicable expression then came over her face. This was suddenly erased into utter blankness. The lines of her countenance seemed to shift in a barely visible, slow, rippling transformation. For a moment there was the impression of something arcane. Closing her eyes, she winced as she put her hands to her temples, pressed hard, and twisted them as if to combat sudden pain. A slight shudder passed over her entire body.
>
> Then the hands lightly dropped. She relaxed easily into an attitude of comfort the physician had never before seen in this patient. A pair of blue eyes popped open. There was a quick reckless smile. In a bright, unfamiliar voice that sparked, the woman said, "Hi, there, Doc!" . . .
>
> Still busy with his own unassimilated surprise, the doctor heard himself say, "How do you feel now?"
>
> "Why just fine—never better! How you doing yourself, Doc?"
>
> Eve looked for a moment straight into his eyes. Her expression was that of one who is just barely able to restrain laughter. Her eyes rolled up and to one side for an instant, then the lids flicked softly before opening wide again. She tossed her head lightly with a little gesture that threw the fine dark hair forward onto her shoulder. A five-year-old might have so reacted to some sudden, unforeseen amusement. In the patient's gesture there was something of pert sauciness, something in which the artless play of a child and a scarcely conscious flirtatiousness mingled. . . .
>
> "She's been having a real rough time. There's no doubt about that," the girl said carelessly. "I feel right sorry for her sometimes. She's such a damn dope though. . . . What she puts up with from that sorry Ralph White—and all her mooning over that little brat . . . ! To hell with it, I say!" . . .
>
> The doctor asked, "Who is 'she'?"

"Why, Eve White, of course. Your long-suffering, saintly, little patient."

"But aren't you Eve White?" he asked.

"That's for laughs," she exclaimed, a ripple of mirth in her tone. . . .

"Why, I'm Eve Black," she said. . . ."I'm me and she's herself," the girl added.
"I like to live and she don't. . . .Those dresses—well, I can tell you about them.
I got out the other day, and I needed some dresses. I like good clothes. So I just
went into town and bought what I wanted. I charged 'em to her husband, too!"
She began to laugh softly. "You ought've seen the look on her silly face when
he showed her what was in the cupboard!" (Reprinted with permission from
C. H. Thigpen and H. M. Cleckley, *The Three Faces of Eve,* Copyright © 1957
McGraw-Hill.)

The movie *Three Faces of Eve* depicted the story of a woman with dissociative identity disorder, who would discover extravagant articles of clothing in her closet that she didn't remember buying.

In later sessions, Eve Black told the psychiatrist of escapades in which she had stayed out all night drinking and then "went back in" in the morning and let Eve White deal with the hangover. At the beginning of therapy, Eve White had no consciousness of Eve Black or of over 20 personalities eventually identified during therapy. This story of the *Three Faces of Eve* is one of the most detailed and gripping accounts of someone diagnosed with dissociative identity disorder. Eve White eventually recovered from her disorder, "integrating" the aspects of her personality represented by Eve Black and her other personalities into one single entity and living a healthy, normal life.

Dissociative identity disorder (**DID**), formerly referred to as *multiple personality disorder,* is one of the most controversial and fascinating disorders recognized in clinical psychology and psychiatry. As the name suggests, people with this disorder have more than one distinct identity or personality. Each personality has different ways of perceiving and relating to the world, and each personality takes control over the individual's behavior on a regular basis. As was true of Eve White/Black, the alternate personalities, or *alters,* can be extremely different from one another, with distinct facial expressions, speech characteristics, physiological responses, gestures, interpersonal styles, and attitudes (Miller, 1989; Putnam, 1991). They often are different ages and different genders and perform specific functions.

dissociative identity disorder (DID) syndrome in which a person develops more than one distinct identity or personality, each of which can have distinct facial and verbal expressions, gestures, interpersonal styles, attitudes, and even physiological responses

Types of Alters

One study of 236 adults with dissociative identity disorder found that *child alters* are the most common (Ross et al., 1989). Childhood trauma is often associated with the development of dissociative identity disorder. A child alter may be created during a traumatic experience to become the victim of the trauma, while the "host" personality escapes into the protection of psychological oblivion. Alternately, an alter may be created as a type of big brother or sister to protect the host personality from traumas. When a child alter is "out" or in control of the individual's behavior, the adult will speak and act in a childlike way.

What might be the relationship between the development of "child alters" by people with dissociative identity disorder and the use of "imaginary playmates" by children who do not go on to develop dissociative identity disorder?

A second type of personality that is very frequent is the *persecutor personality.* These personalities inflict pain or punishment on the other personalities by engaging in self-mutilative behaviors such as self-cutting or burning and suicide attempts (Coons & Milstein, 1990; Ross et al., 1989). A persecutor alter may engage in a dangerous behavior, such as taking an overdose of pills or jumping in front of a truck, and then "go back inside," leaving the host personality to experience the pain. Persecutors may have the delusion that they can harm other personalities without harming themselves. These personalities are often adolescents but sometimes claim to be demons or dead relatives.

A third type of personality is the protector or *helper personality*. The function of this personality is to offer advice to other personalities or to perform functions the host personality is unable to perform, such as engaging in sexual relations or hiding from abusive parents. Protectors sometimes control the switching from one personality to another or may act as passive observers who can report on the thoughts and intentions of all the other personalities (Ross, 1989).

People with dissociative identity disorder typically have significant periods of amnesia or *blank spells*. Some personalities may be completely amnesic for the periods when other personalities are in control. Or there may be one-way amnesia between certain personalities: One personality is aware of what the other is doing, but the second personality is completely amnesic for periods when the first personality is in control. People with dissociative identity disorder may, as with Eve White, suddenly discover unknown objects in their homes, or they may lose objects. People they do not recognize might approach them on the street claiming to know them. They may consistently receive mail or phone calls addressed to someone with a different first or last name.

Like adults, children with dissociative identity disorder exhibit a host of behavioral and emotional problems (Putnam, 1991). Their performance in school may be erratic, sometimes very good and sometimes very poor. They are prone to antisocial behavior, such as stealing, fire-setting, and aggression. They may engage in sexual relations and abuse alcohol or illicit drugs at an early age. They tend to show many symptoms of post-traumatic stress disorder (see Chapter 4), including hypervigilance, flashbacks to traumas they have endured, traumatic nightmares, and an exaggerated startle response. Their emotions are labile, alternating among explosive outbursts of anger, deep depression, and severe anxiety. Most children and many adults with dissociative identity disorder report hearing voices inside their heads. Some report being aware that their actions or words are being controlled by other personalities. For example, Joe, an 8-year-old boy with dissociative identity disorder, described how "a guy inside of me" called B. J. (for Bad Joey) would make him do "bad things" (Hornstein & Putnam, 1992, p. 1081):

> Well, say B. J. hears someone call me names, then he would strike me to do something, like I'd be running at the other kid, but it wouldn't be my legs, I'd be saying to my legs, "no . . . , stop . . . ," but they'd keep going on their own because that's B. J. doing that. Then my arm would be going at the other kid, hitting him, and I could see my arm doing that, but I couldn't stop it, and it wouldn't hurt when my hand hit him, not until later when B. J. goes back in and then my arm is my own arm. Then it starts hurting.

Most people diagnosed with dissociative identity disorder have already been diagnosed with at least three other disorders (Kluft, 1987). Some of the other disorders diagnosed are secondary to or the result of the dissociative identity disorder. For example, more than 80 percent of people with dissociative identity disorder have recurring problems with serious depression or anxiety (Dell & Eisenhower, 1990). Most people with dissociative identity disorder also are diagnosed with a personality disorder (see Chapter 8).

Many of the diagnoses received before the diagnosis of dissociative identity disorder is established may be misdiagnoses of the dissociative symptoms, however. For example, when people with dissociative identity disorder report hearing voices talking inside their heads, they are often misdiagnosed as having the auditory hallucinations of schizophrenia (Kluft, 1987). The voices that people with schizophrenia hear, however, often are experienced as coming from outside their heads. In addition, people with schizophrenia will not evidence full-blown alter personalities, even though they may occasionally have the delusion that they are someone else. That is, when people with schizophrenia believe they are other people, their entire demeanors will not change in the way that the voices, speech, and physical appearances of people with dissociative identity disorder change when they have switched to other personalities. Conversely, people with dissociative identity disorder will not show schizophrenic symptoms such as flat or inappropriate affect or loose or illogical associations.

Are there any assessment tools we discussed in Chapter 2 that might be useful in differentiating between dissociative identity disorder and schizophrenia?

Gender, Historical, and Cultural Differences in Dissociative Identity Disorder

The vast majority of persons diagnosed with this disorder are adult women. It may be that the conditions leading to dissociative identity disorder are more commonly experienced by women than by men (Peterson, 1991). Among children diagnosed with dissociative identity disorder, however, the numbers of females and males appear to be more equal (Dell & Eisenhower, 1990). It may be that boys with dissociative identity disorder are more likely to be taken for treatment than are girls, so as adults, males are less likely to continue to have the disorder than are females (Dell & Eisenhower, 1990). Or girls may be more likely than boys to experience traumas in adolescence that lead to dissociative identity disorder, which continues into adulthood. There are some differences between the characteristics of personalities of male and females with dissociative identity disorder. Males with dissociative identity disorder appear to be more aggressive than females with the disorder. In one study, 29 percent of male dissociative identity patients had been convicted of crimes, compared to 10 percent of female dissociative identity patients (Ross & Norton, 1989). Case reports suggest that females with dissociative identity disorder tend to have more somatic complaints than do males and may engage in more suicidal behavior (Kluft, 1985).

Dissociative identity disorder was rarely diagnosed before about 1980, but there has been a great increase in the number of reported cases since 1980 (Braun, 1986; Coons, 1986). This is due in part to the fact that dissociative identity disorder was first included as a diagnostic category in the *Diagnostic and Statistical Manual of Mental Disorders* of the American Psychiatric Association in the third edition, published in 1980. It is also due to a series of influential papers by psychiatrists describing persons with dissociative identity disorder whom they had treated (Bliss, 1980; Coons, 1980; Greaves, 1980; Rosenbaum, 1980), which aroused interest in the disorder in the psychiatric community. The current estimate of the prevalence of dissociative identity disorder in North America is 1 percent (Ross, 1991).

Dissociative identity disorder is diagnosed much more frequently these days in the United States than in Great Britain, Europe, India, or Japan (Ross, 1989; Saxena & Prasad, 1989; Takahashi, 1990). Some researchers have argued that psychiatrists in the United States are too quick to diagnose dissociative identity disorder, and others argue that psychiatrists in other countries misdiagnose it as some other disorder (Coons et al., 1990; Fahy, 1988). The low rates of dissociative identity disorder in Japan may be tied to the strong orientation to the family in Japanese culture and a low rate of child abuse, which has been linked to the disorder (Takahashi, 1990). Within the United States, dissociative identity disorder is rarely diagnosed in Hispanics (Martinez-Taboas, 1989). Although this may also be due to a strong cultural commitment to the family in this group, dissociative identity disorder in Hispanics may sometimes be misdiagnosed as *ataque de nervios,* a culturally accepted reaction to stress that involves transient periods of loss of consciousness, convulsive movements of a psychological origin, hyperactivity, assaultive behaviors, and impulsive suicidal or homocidal acts (see the discussion of *ataque de nervios* in Chapter 4; Steinberg, 1990). The following case study describes a Hispanic woman believed to experience *ataque de nervios* but later diagnosed with dissociative identity disorder (adapted from Steinberg, 1990, pp. 31–32).

Case Study • Mrs. C., a 40-year-old divorced Hispanic woman, contacted a Hispanic clinic in Connecticut on the suggestion of her previous psychiatrist in Puerto Rico. Over an 18-year period Mrs. C. had made numerous emergency room and follow-up visits to a Puerto Rican psychiatric hospital. Her previous diagnoses included psychotic depression, schizophrenia, post-traumatic stress disorder, schizoaffective disorder, and hysterical personality. A variety of neuroleptics and antidepressants in therapeutic dosages had been prescribed but had provided no relief.

Mrs. C. was the youngest of three daughters born to indigent parents in Puerto Rico and was raised among numerous relatives in an overcrowded setting. Mrs. C. suffered extreme physical and emotional abuse from her mother, including administration of enemas and emetics every other day as punishment "if she was bad." . . . Mrs. C. also recalled being sexually abused by her father and suffered recurrent dreams of this abuse. Married at age 17, she had three children by her first husband, who was physically abusive. After 4 years, Mrs. C. left him and shortly thereafter married another man, whom she described as physically and emotionally abusive. They separated 4 months later. Recently, she moved to Connecticut to be near her grown daughter.

Mrs. C's first presentation in Connecticut was with a classic episode of *ataque*. She described an acute onset of distressing auditory and visual hallucinations, . . . stating that the voices were commanding her to harm herself. The initial diagnostic impression at the clinic was of a psychotic depression and she was given a prescription for an antipsychotic drug. Four days later, in a follow-up visit, she had not used the medication, denied having had auditory or visual hallucinations, and was free of any psychotic symptoms. She described rapid mood swings, "out of body experiences," and amnesic episodes which she had experienced since childhood. At this time, Mrs. C was scheduled for biweekly supportive therapy with a mental health worker. She attended sessions irregularly. Her demeanor, level of functioning, and symptoms fluctuated radically. Several times she spontaneously began acting as though she were a child. Frequently she presented to therapy referring to herself by another name and did not remember previous sessions. During this period, Mrs. C. was brought to the Hispanic clinic by her boyfriend for an emergency consultation due to the acute onset of bizarre behavior. She was childlike and disoriented, suffered auditory and visual hallucinations of suicidal and homicidal nature, and rapidly became restless and agitated. She stated her name was *Rosa*.

At that time the emergency room psychiatrist noted the similarity of her symptoms to the *ataque* and described her presentation: "When she came into the screening area, she took one of the balloons and began to play with it and asked me if I had a doll for her; she also said she was hungry and wanted some cookies and milk." His diagnostic impression was "atypical psychosis." . . . Re-evaluation several hours later revealed a "dramatic change in state." She said she was not Rosa, was not 6 years old, had no interest in playing with a doll, and she did not feel like someone was following her or was telling her to hurt herself. . . .

At this time Mrs. C. began a new course of weekly psychotherapy sessions which she attended fairly regularly. Mrs. C.'s sense of identity, her demeanor, and the content of each session varied significantly. During this treatment, five distinct personalities emerged with different names, ages, memories, and characteristic behaviors. Frequently she would state that she was "unable to remember" what she had discussed in a previous session. Recurrent themes included identity confusion and severe abuse by both parents. Throughout this year she remained off medication. . . .

Severe stress can cause dissociative symptoms, or a syndrome in Latino culture known as *ataque de nervios*.

Mrs. C's acute symptoms were consistent both with the *ataque de nervios* and with dissociative identity disorder: alterations in consciousness, amnesia, disorientation, childlike behaviors, self-mutilation, and psychotic like symptoms. Because Mrs. C. had a long history of episodes such as this and distinct personalities that emerged at different periods, the psychiatrist diagnosed her as having dissociative identity disorder (Steinberg, 1990).

What did it serve to label Mrs. C's symptoms with an "American" psychiatric diagnosis of dissociative identity disorder when she conceived of her symptoms as _ataque de nervios?_

Researchers who are skeptical of the recent increase in reported cases of dissociative identity disorder in the United States argue that the disorder is artificially created in suggestible clients by clinicians who reinforce clients for "admitting" to symptoms of dissociative identity disorder and who induce symptoms of the disorder through hypnotic suggestion (Fahy, 1988). Nicholas Spanos and colleagues (1985) tested this hypothesis in an experiment in which subjects were asked to role-play Harry or Betty, persons who had been accused of murder and who were undergoing a pretrial psychiatric evaluation. In two conditions of this experiment, the subjects underwent a hypnotic induction and then the experimenter asked them a series of leading questions designed to "uncover" dissociative identity disorder. In one condition, the experimenter talked with the subject for a while and then said, "I've talked a bit to Harry/Betty but I think perhaps there might be another part of Harry/Betty that I haven't talked to, another part that maybe feels somewhat differently from the part that I've talked to. And I would like to communicate with that other part. Would you talk to me, Part, by saying, 'I'm here'?" Whatever the subjects' response, the experimenter would say, "Part, are you the same thing as Harry/Betty?" The experimenters called this condition the _Bianchi condition,_ because it was modeled after a series of leading questions put to serial killer Kenneth Bianchi in a pretrial psychiatric evaluation, during which he claimed to have dissociative identity disorder. In the hidden part condition, the experimenter said, "Personality is complex and involves many different ways of thinking and feeling about things. Sometimes part of us thinks about and feels things that other parts of us don't even know about. . . . During hypnosis, it is possible to get behind the mental wall to the blocked off parts of the mind. I am going to put my hand on your shoulder and when I do, I will be in contact with another part of you. I will get behind the wall and will be talking to the part of you that experiences strong feelings and frightening thoughts" (pp. 367–368). In addition, there was a control group of subjects who were not given a hypnotic induction but who were told the same things the subjects in the hidden part condition were told.

The researchers found that most of the subjects in the Bianchi and hidden part conditions but none of the subjects in the control condition displayed symptoms of dissociative identity disorder, including claiming to have at least two separate identities and spontaneous posthypnotic amnesia. The majority of the subjects in the Bianchi condition also assumed different names for their separate parts. Those subjects who did evidence these symptoms of dissociative identity disorder also scored differently on standardized personality tests when they were under the hypnotic suggestion and role-playing the murderer than when they were not, whereas those who did not show symptoms of dissociative identity disorder did not score differently on these personality tests when under hypnosis and when not. Spanos and colleagues noted that the instructions they used to "induce" dissociative identity disorder were extremely similar to those used in psychiatric evaluations of persons thought to have the disorder (e.g., see Ross, 1989). They argued that the disorder is frequently the creation of the misuse of hypnosis and suggestion by therapists.

Others have argued that the fact that Spanos and colleagues could make subjects mimic symptoms of dissociative identity disorder for a short time in a contrived laboratory setting says nothing about the validity of the diagnosis of dissociative identity disorder (Ross, Norton, & Fraser, 1989). In addition, they argue that there is no evidence that the experience of being hypnotized changes the symptoms that people diagnosed with dissociative identity disorder show, as we might expect if therapists were inducing symptoms of the disorder by hypnotizing their patients.

Serial killer Kenneth Bianchi tried to claim he had dissociative identity disorder, but experts proved that he did not.

Children who are abused may dissociate and even develop alter personalities as a way of dealing with their abuse.

Theories of Dissociative Identity Disorder

Theorists who believe that dissociative identity disorder is a valid diagnosis tend to view it as the result of a defense mechanism used by persons faced with intolerable trauma (Bliss, 1986; Kluft, 1987). Most recent studies find that the majority of people diagnosed with dissociative identity disorder self-report having been the victims of sexual or physical abuse during childhood (Coons, 1994; Dell & Eisenhower, 1990; Hornstein & Putnam, 1992). For example, in one study of 100 persons with dissociative identity disorder, 83 percent reported having been sexually abused, 75 percent reported having been repeatedly physically abused, and 68 percent reported having been both sexually and physically abused (Putnam et al., 1986). Similar results have been found in studies in which patients' reports of abuse were corroborated by at least one family member or by emergency room reports (Coons, 1994; Coons & Milstein, 1986). This abuse was most often carried out by parents or other family members and was chronic over an extended period of childhood. Other types of trauma that have been associated with the development of dissociative identity disorder include kidnapping, natural disasters, war, famine, and religious persecution (Ross, 1989).

People who develop dissociative identity disorder tend to be highly suggestible and hypnotizable and may use self-hypnosis to dissociate and escape their traumas. They create the alternate personalities to help them cope with their traumas, much as a child might create imaginary playmates to ease pangs of loneliness. People with dissociative identity disorder become trapped in their own defense mechanisms. Retreating into their alternate personalities or using these personalities to perform frightening functions becomes a chronic way of coping with life.

There is evidence from a few family history studies that dissociative identity disorder may run in some families (Coons, 1984; Dell & Eisenhower, 1990). Perhaps the ability and tendency to dissociate as a defense mechanism is, to some extent, biologically determined. The numbers of families in these studies were quite small, however. Moreover, parents with dissociative identity disorder sometimes abuse their own children or do not protect their children from abuse or harm by others, so their children may be more likely to develop dissociative identity disorder because they are abused, not because they carry a biological predisposition to the disorder (Kluft, 1987).

Treatment of Dissociative Identity Disorder

Treatment of dissociative identity disorder can be extremely challenging (Kluft, 1986; Ross, 1989). The goal of treatment is the integration of all the alter personalities into one coherent personality. This is done by identifying the functions or roles of each personality, helping each personality confront and "work through" the traumas that led to the disorder and the concerns each one has or represents, and negotiating with the personalities for fusion into one personality that has learned adaptive styles of coping with stress. Hypnosis is used heavily in the treatment of dissociative identity disorder to contact alter personalities (Putnam & Lowenstein, 1993). In treatment of children with dissociative identity disorder, it is often necessary to work with parents to improve the family life of the children and sometimes to remove the children from abusive homes (Dell & Eisenhower, 1990). Antidepressants and antianxiety drugs are sometimes used as adjuncts to supportive psychotherapy. Although experts in the treatment of dissociative identity disorder find that such treatment is successful in the majority of cases (Kluft, 1987; Ross, 1989), particularly if the treatment is begun in childhood shortly after a child first develops alternate personalities (Peterson, 1991), controlled outcome data are not available.

Summing Up | Dissociative Identity Disorder

• The core feature of dissociative identity disorder is the presence of two or more separate personalities or identities in the same individual. These personalities may have different ways of speaking and relating to others, be of different ages and genders, and even have different physiological responses.

- Dissociative identity disorder appears more common in women than men and is diagnosed more in the United States than in other countries.
- Skeptics of dissociative identity disorder argue that the symptoms are created in suggestible clients by therapists using hypnosis.
- Proponents of the diagnosis argue that the alter personalities are created by people under conditions of chronic extreme stress, often child abuse.
- Treatment for the disorder most often involves long-term therapy and the use of hypnosis to discover the functions of the personalities and to assist the personalities in "integration."

Dissociative Fugue

A person in the midst of a **dissociative fugue** will suddenly pick up and move to a new place, assume a new identity, and have complete amnesia for his previous identity. He will behave quite normally in his new environment, and it will not seem odd to him that he cannot remember anything from his past. Just as suddenly, he may return to his previous identity and home, resuming his life as if nothing had happened, amnesic for what he did during the fugue. A fugue may last for a matter of days or years, and a person may experience repeated fugue states or a single episode. An extreme and classic case of fugue was that of the Reverend Ansel Bourne, reported by the American philosopher and psychologist William James (1890, Vol. 1, pp. 391–393).

dissociative fugue
disorder in which a person moves away and assumes a new identity, with amnesia for the previous identity.

Case Study • The Rev. Ansel Bourne, of Greene, R.I., was brought up to the trade of a carpenter; but, in consequence of a sudden temporary loss of sight and hearing under very peculiar circumstances, he became converted from Atheism to Christianity just before his thirtieth year, and has since that time for the most part lived the life of an itinerant preacher. He has been subject to headaches and temporary fits of depression of spirits during most of his life, and has had a few fits of unconsciousness lasting an hour or less. He also has a region of somewhat diminished cutaneous sensibility on the left thigh. Otherwise his health is good, and his muscular strength and endurance excellent. He is of a firm and self-reliant disposition, a man whose yea is yea and his nay, nay; and his character for uprightness is such in the community that no person who knows him will for a moment admit the possibility of his case not being perfectly genuine.

On January 17, 1887, he drew 551 dollars from a bank in Providence with which to pay for a certain lot of land in Greene, paid certain bills, and got into a Pawtucket horse-car. This is the last incident which he remembers. He did not return home that day, and nothing was heard of him for two months. He was published in the papers as missing, and foul play being suspected, the police sought in vain his whereabouts. On the morning of March 14th, however, at Norristown, Pennsylvania, a man calling himself A. J. Brown, who had rented a small shop six weeks previously, stocked it with stationery, confectionery, fruit, and small articles, and carried on his quiet trade without seeming to anyone unnatural or eccentric, woke up in a fright and called the people of the house to tell him where he was. He said that his name was Ansel Bourne, that he was entirely ignorant of Norristown, and that he knew nothing of shop-keeping, and that the last thing he remembered—it seemed only yesterday—was drawing the money from the bank, etc. in Providence. He would not believe that two months had elapsed. The people of the house thought him insane; and so, at first, did Dr. Louis H. Read, whom they called in to see him. But on telegraphing to Providence, confirmatory messages came, and presently his nephew, Mr. Andrew Harris, arrived upon the scene, made everything straight, and took him home. He was very weak, having lost apparently over twenty pounds of flesh during his escapade, and had such a horror of the idea of the candy-store that he refused to set foot in it again.

The first two weeks of the period remained unaccounted for, as he had no memory, after he had once resumed his normal personality, of any part of the time, and no one who knew him seems to have seen him after he left home. The remarkable part of the change is, of course, the peculiar occupation which the so-called Brown indulged in. Mr. Bourne has never in his life had the slightest contact with trade. "Brown" was described by the neighbors as taciturn, orderly in his habits, and in no way queer. He went to Philadelphia several times, replenished his stock; cooked for himself in the back shop, where he also slept; went regularly to church; and once at prayer-meeting made what was considered by the hearers as a good address, in the course of which he related an incident which he had witnessed in his natural state of Bourne.

This was all that was known of the case up to June 1890, when I induced Mr. Bourne to submit to hypnotism, so as to see whether, in the hypnotic trance, his "Brown" memory would not come back. It did so with surprising readiness; so much so indeed that it proved quite impossible to make him whilst in the hypnosis remember any of the facts of his normal life. He had heard of Ansel Bourne, but "didn't know as he had ever met the man." When confronted with Mrs. Bourne he said that he had "never seen the woman before," etc. On the other hand, he told of his peregrinations during the lost fortnight, and gave all sorts of details about the Norristown episode. The whole thing was prosaic enough; and the Brown-personality seems to be nothing but a rather shrunken, dejected, and amnesic extract of Mr. Bourne himself. He gives no motive for the wandering except that there was "trouble back there" and "he wanted rest." During the trance he looks old, the corners of his mouth are drawn down, his voice is slow and weak, and he sits screening his eyes and trying vainly to remember what lay before and after the two months of the Brown experience. "I'm all hedged in," he says: "I can't get out at the other end. I don't know what set me down in the Pawtucket horse-car, and I don't know how I ever left that store, or what became of it." His eyes are practically normal, and all his sensibilities (save for tardier response) about the same in hypnosis as in waking. I had hoped by suggestion, etc., to run the two personalities into one, and make the memories continuous, but no artifice would avail to accomplish this, and Mr. Bourne's skill to-day still covers two distinct personal selves.

Some, but not all, persons who experience fugue episodes do so after traumatic events. Many others, such as Rev. Bourne, seem to escape into a fugue state in response to chronic stress in their lives that is within the realm of most people's experience. People are typically depressed before the onset of fugues (Kopelman, 1987). As in dissociative identity disorder, fugue states may be more common in people who are highly hypnotizable. Unlike the person with dissociative identity disorder, however, the person in a fugue state actually leaves the scene of the trauma or stress and leaves his or her former identity behind. Fugue states appear to be more common among people who have previous histories of some type of amnesia, including amnesias due to head injuries (Kopelman, 1987). We do not have an accurate estimate of the prevalence of fugue states, although they appear to be quite rare, and we do not know much about the etiology of fugue states, in part because of their rarity. Clinicians who treat people with this disorder tend to use many of the same techniques used to treat dissociative identity disorder, but again because of the rarity of the disorder, we know little about the outcomes of treatment.

Dissociative Amnesia

In both dissociative identity disorder and dissociative fugue states, individuals may have amnesia for the periods of time when their alternate personalities are in control or when they have been in fugue states. Some people have significant periods of amnesia but do not assume new personalities or identities. People who are simply amnesic cannot remember important facts about their lives and their personal identities and are typically aware

Table 7.2	Differences between Psychogenic and Organic Amnesia	
Psychogenic Amnesia	**Organic Amnesia**
Caused by psychological factors	Caused by biological factors (such as disease, drugs, and blows to the head)
Seldom involves anterograde amnesia (inability to learn new information learned since onset of amnesia)	Often involves anterograde amnesia
Can involve retrograde amnesia (inability to remember events from the past)	Can involve retrograde amnesia
Retrograde amnesia often only for personal information, not for general information	Retrograde amnesia usually for both personal and general information

that there are large gaps in their memory or knowledge of themselves. These people are said to have **dissociative amnesia.**

Amnesia is considered either organic or psychogenic (see Table 7.2). Organic amnesias are caused by brain injury resulting from disease, drugs, accidents (such as blows to the head), or surgery. Organic amnesia often involves the inability to remember new information, known as **anterograde amnesia.** Psychogenic amnesias arise in the absence of any brain injury or disease and are thought to have psychological causes. Psychogenic amnesias rarely involve anterograde amnesia.

The inability to remember information from the past, known as **retrograde amnesia,** can have both organic and psychogenic causes. For example, persons who have been in serious car accidents can have the retrograde amnesia for the few minutes just before the accidents. This retrograde amnesia can be due to brain injury resulting from blows to the head during accidents. Or it can be a motivated forgetting of the events leading up to traumatic accidents. Retrograde amnesia for longer periods of time can also occur. When such amnesias are due to organic causes, people usually forget everything about the past, including personal information, such as where they lived and who they knew, and general information, such as who was president and major historical events of the period. They will typically retain memory of their personal identity, however. Thus, although they may not remember their children, they will know their own names. When long-term retrograde amnesias are due to psychological causes, people typically lose their identities and forget personal information but retain memories for general information. For example, a 35-year-old person with a psychogenic retrograde amnesia that began in 1994 might be unable to remember where she was raised, whom she married, or the birth of her children but will remember who won the World Series each year before 1994 and details of the Persian Gulf War in 1991. The following is a case study of a man with a psychogenic retrograde amnesia (Hilgard, 1986, p. 68):

dissociative amnesia
loss of memory for important facts about a person's own life and personal identity, usually including the awareness of this memory loss

anterograde amnesia
inability to remember new information

retrograde amnesia
inability to remember information from the past

People can have amnesia for the events around a traumatic event, like a traffic accident, for both psychological and biological reasons.

Loss of memory due to alcohol intoxication is common, but usually the person only forgets the events occurring during the period he or she was intoxicated. Severe alcoholics can develop a more global retrograde amnesia, known as *Korsakoff's syndrome* (see Chapter 12), in which they cannot remember much personal or general information for a period of several years or decades. However, the type of retrograde amnesia evidenced in the previous case study, which apparently involved only one episode of heavy drinking and the loss of only personal information, typically has psychological causes.

Psychogenic amnesias may be the result of the use of dissociation as a defense against intolerable memories or stressors. They most frequently occur following traumatic events, such as wars or sexual assaults. Alternately, amnesia for specific events may occur because individuals were in such a high state of arousal during the events they did not encode and store information during the period of the event and thus were unable to retrieve the information later (Kopelman, 1987). A third explanation for amnesias for specific events is that information about events are stored at the time of the events but are associated with a high state of arousal of painful emotions, and after the events people avoid the emotions and therefore do not gain access to the information associated with the emotions (Bower, 1981). Amnesias for specific periods of time around traumas appear to be fairly common, but generalized retrograde amnesias for people's entire pasts and identities appear very rare.

 Imagine that your spouse was in a terrible car accident, sustained a serious head injury, and developed a generalized retrograde amnesia. What would you do?

One complication that arises in diagnosing amnesias is the possibility that amnesias are being faked by people trying to escape punishment for crimes committed during the periods for which they claim to be amnesic. True amnesias can occur in conjunction with the commission of crimes. Many crimes are committed by persons under the influence of alcohol or other drugs, and the drugs can cause blackouts for the periods of intoxication (Kopelman, 1987). Similarly, people who incur head injuries during the commission of crimes—for example, by falling while trying to escape the scene of a crime—can have amnesia for the commission of crimes. Psychogenic amnesias can also occur for the commission of crimes, particularly if the criminals feel extremely guilty about the crimes. For example, a man who beat his wife may feel so guilty for doing so that he develops amnesia for the beating. Amnesia is most often seen in homicide cases, with between 25 and 45 percent of persons arrested for homicide claiming to have amnesia for the killings (Kopelman, 1987). In most of these cases, the victims are closely related to the killers (they are their lovers, spouses, close friends, or family members), the offenses appear to be unpremeditated, and the killers are in states of extreme emotional arousal at the time of the killings. More rarely, the killers appear to have been in psychotic states at the time of the killings. There is no clear-cut way to differentiate true amnesias from feigned ones. Head injuries leading to amnesia may be detectable through CT scans or other examinations

Lorena Bobbitt cut off her husband's penis, after years of experiencing his abuse. She claimed to have amnesia for the act of cutting it off.

of the brain. Some clinicians advocate the use of hypnosis to assist people in remembering events around crimes, if it is suspected that the amnesia is due to psychological causes. However, the possibility that hypnosis will "create" memories through the power of suggestion leads many courts to deny the use of hypnosis in such cases (Kopelman, 1987). In most cases, it can be impossible to determine whether the amnesia is true.

Depersonalization Disorder

The final dissociative disorder is **depersonalization disorder.** People with this disorder have frequent episodes in which they feel detached from their own mental processes or bodies, as if they are outside observers of themselves. Occasional experiences of depersonalization are common, particularly when people are sleep deprived or under the influence of drugs. Depersonalization disorder is diagnosed when episodes of depersonalization are so frequent and distressing that they interfere with individuals' ability to function. We know very little about the causes of this disorder, who is most prone to it, or its prevalence.

depersonalization disorder
syndrome marked by frequent episodes of feeling detached from one's own body and mental processes, as if one were an outside observer of oneself; symptoms must cause significant distress or interference with one's ability to function.

Summing Up — Dissociative Disorders

- The dissociative disorders include dissociative identity disorder, dissociative fugue, dissociative amnesia, and depersonalization disorder.
- In all these disorders, people's conscious experiences of themselves become fragmented, they may lack awareness of core aspects of their selves, and they may experience amnesia for important events.
- The distinct feature of dissociative identity disorder is the development of multiple separate personalities within the same person. The personalities take turns being in control.
- People with dissociative fugue move away from home and assume entirely new identities, with complete amnesia for their previous identities. They do not switch back and forth between different personalities, however.
- People with dissociative amnesia lose important memories due to psychological causes.
- People with depersonalization disorder have frequent experiences of feeling detached from their mental processes or their bodies.
- These disorders are often, although not always, associated with traumatic experiences.
- Therapists often treat these disorders by helping people explore past experiences and feelings that they have blocked from consciousness and by supporting them as they develop more integrated experiences of self and more adaptive ways of coping with stress.

Somatoform Disorders

The **somatoform disorders** are a group of disorders in which people experience significant physical symptoms for which there is no apparent organic cause, that are often inconsistent with possible physiological mechanisms, and in which there is strong reason to believe that psychological factors are involved. People with somatoform disorders do not consciously produce or control the symptoms. Instead, they truly experience the symptoms, and the symptoms only pass when the psychological factors that led to the symptoms are resolved.

Obviously, one of the great difficulties in diagnosing somatoform disorders is the possibility that an individual has a real physical disorder that is simply difficult to detect or diagnose. Many of us have friends or relatives who have complained to their physicians for years about specific physical symptoms that the physicians attributed to "nervousness" or "attention-seeking" but that later were determined to be early symptoms of

somatoform disorders
disorders marked by unpleasant or painful physical symptoms that have no apparent organic cause and that are often not physiologically possible, suggesting that psychological factors are involved

The sympathy and attention of medical professionals can reinforce people with somatoform disorders.

psychosomatic disorders
syndromes marked by identifiable physical illness or defect caused at least partly by psychological factors

malingering
feigning of a symptom or disorder for the purpose of avoiding an unwanted situation, such as military service

factitious disorders
disorders marked by deliberately faking physical or mental illness to gain medical attention

serious disease. The diagnosis of somatoform disorder is made easier when psychological factors leading to the development of the symptoms can clearly be identified, when the characteristics of the symptoms defy what is known about the physiology of the body, or when physical examination can prove that the symptoms cannot be physiologically possible. For example, when a child is perfectly healthy on weekends but has terrible stomachaches in the morning just before going to school, it is likely that the stomachaches are due to distress over going to school. A more extreme example of a clear somatoform disorder is pseudocyesis, or false pregnancy, in which a woman believes she is pregnant, but physical examination and laboratory tests confirm that she is not.

The somatoform disorders must be differentiated from **psychosomatic disorders,** which will be discussed in Chapter 13. Psychological factors are also implicated in the causation of the psychosomatic disorders, but a person with a psychosomatic disorder has an actual physical illness or defect, such as high blood pressure, that can be documented with medical tests, whereas a person with a somatoform disorder does not have any illness or defect that can be documented with tests (see Table 7.3). Somatoform disorders are also different from **malingering,** in which a person fakes a symptom or disorder in order to avoid some unwanted situation, such as military service. Again, the individual with a somatoform disorder subjectively experiences the symptoms, but there is no organic basis for the symptoms. Finally, somatoform disorders are different from **factitious disorders,** in which a person deliberately fakes an illness to gain medical attention.

The somatoform disorders are grouped in this chapter with dissociative disorders because many theorists believe that somatoform disorders are the result of repression or motivated forgetting of painful memories or emotions, as is thought to be the case with dissociative disorders. In somatoform disorders, repressed memories or emotions may re-emerge as or be represented by the physical symptoms the person experiences. Or more simply, the physical symptoms may be an acceptable way for an individual to express psychological distress.

 In the chapters on anxiety and mood disorders, we discussed the fact that people in certain cultures may express severe anxiety and depression through somatic symptoms rather than through psychological symptoms. How would you differentiate between a somatization disorder and an anxiety or mood disorder manifested through physical complaints?

There are four distinct types of somatoform disorders: conversion disorder, somatization and pain disorder, hypochondriasis, and body dysmorphic disorder. Each of these, except body dysmorphic disorder, is characterized by the experience of one or more physical symptoms. Body dysmorphic disorder involves a preoccupation with an imagined defect in one's appearance that is so severe that it interferes with the person's functioning in life. Although this disorder is very different from the other somatoform disorders,

Table 7.3 Distinctions Between Somatoform and Pain Disorders and Related Syndromes			
Somatoform and Pain Disorders	**Psychosomatic Disorders**	**Malingering**	**Factitious Disorder**
Subjective experience of many physical symptoms, with no organic cause (pain disorder involves experience of pain only)	Actual physical illness present and psychological factors seem to be contributing to the illness	Deliberate faking of physical symptoms to avoid an unpleasant situation, such as military duty	Deliberate faking of physical illness to gain medical attention

so much so that its classification as a somatoform disorder is questionable, what we know about this disorder will be reviewed in this chapter.

Conversion Disorder

The most dramatic type of somatoform disorder is **conversion disorder.** People with this disorder lose functioning in some part of their bodies. Some of the most common types of conversion symptoms are paralysis, blindness, mutism, seizures, loss of hearing, severe loss of coordination, and anesthesia in a limb. Conversion disorders typically involve one specific symptom, such as blindness or paralysis, but a person can have repeated episodes of conversion involving different parts of the body. Usually the symptom develops following an extreme psychological stressor and it appears suddenly. A common and fascinating feature of conversion disorders is *la belle indifference,* the beautiful indifference—people may be completely unconcerned about the loss of functioning they are experiencing.

 As a clinician, how would you approach someone with a conversion disorder who showed *la belle indifference*? How could you get him or her to be concerned about the disorder?

Theories of Conversion Disorder

Conversion disorders were formerly referred to as *conversion hysterias,* after the Greek word *hystera,* for womb. Centuries ago, physicians believed that only women developed conversion symptoms and that these symptoms arose when a woman's desires for sexual gratification and children were not fulfilled, causing her womb to dislodge and wander (Veith, 1965). The theory was that the womb would wander into various parts of the body, such as the throat or the leg, causing related symptoms, such as a sensation of choking or paralysis. We know now that conversion symptoms have nothing to do with wandering wombs and that, although they are more common in women than in men, men as well as women can develop these symptoms (Boffeli & Guze, 1992).

Early psychoanalytic theorists were fascinated by conversion symptoms, which were apparently more common in Victorian Europe than they are today in Europe or the United States. They viewed conversion symptoms as results of the transfer of the psychic energy attached to repressed emotions or memories into physical symptoms. The symptoms often symbolized the specific concerns or memories that were being repressed. One of the most famous cases of conversion disorder was that of Anna O., a young Viennese woman who was studied by Josef Breuer and Sigmund Freud (1937). The only daughter in a wealthy family, she became ill in 1880 at the age of 21, around the time of her father's serious illness and eventual death.

Case Study • Up to the onset of the disease, the patient showed no sign of nervousness, not even during pubescence. She had a keen, intuitive intellect, and a craving for psychic fodder, which she did not, however, receive after she left school. She was endowed with a sensitiveness for poetry and fantasy, which was, however, controlled by a very strong and critical mind. . . . Her will was energetic, impenetrable, and perservering, sometimes mounting to selfishness; it relinquished its aim only out of kindness and for the sake of others. . . . Her moods always showed a slight tendency to an excess of merriment or sadness, which made her more or less tempermental. . . . With her puritanically-minded family, this girl of overflowing mental vitality led a most monotonous existence. . . .

Upon her father's illness, in rapid succession there seemingly developed a series of new and severe disturbances.

Left-sided occipital pain; convergent strabismus (diplopia), which was markedly aggravated through excitement. She complained that the wall was falling over (obliquus affection). Profound analyzable visual disturbances, paresis of the anterior muscles of

conversion disorder
syndrome marked by a sudden loss of functioning in some part of the body, usually following an extreme psychological stressor

la belle indifference
feature of conversion disorders involving an odd lack of concern about one's loss of functioning in some area of one's body

Anna O. was a patient of Breuer's and Freud's who had several different conversion symptoms.

the throat, to the extent that the head could finally be moved only if the patient pressed it backward between her raised shoulders and then moved her whole back. Contractures and anesthesia of the right upper extremity, and somewhat later of the right lower extremity. . . . (p. 14)

Breuer treated Anna by asking her to talk about her symptoms under hypnosis, and after 18 months she seemed to be losing her symptoms. After Breuer told Anna he thought she was well and he would not be seeing her again, later that evening he was called back to her house, where he found Anna thrashing around in her bed going through imaginary childbirth. Anna claimed that the baby was Breuer's. He calmed her down by hypnotizing her but soon fled the house in a cold sweat and never saw her again. Anna remained ill intermittently for 6 years but by age 30 she recovered. She did not credit psychoanalysis with any assistance in her recovery from her illness and was very negative about psychoanalysis in her later years.

Conversion symptoms were apparently quite common during the two world wars, when soldiers would become paralyzed or blind inexplicably and therefore unable to return to the front (Ironside & Batchelor, 1945). Their symptoms appeared to be real and not faked. Many of the soldiers seemed unconcerned about their paralysis or blindness, showing *la belle indifference.* Sometimes, the physical symptoms the soldiers experienced represented traumas they had witnessed and perhaps were trying to suppress. For example, a soldier who had stabbed a civilian in the throat might lose the ability to talk.

More recent studies suggest that conversion symptoms may be common among sexual abuse survivors (Anderson, Yasenik, & Ross, 1993). Consider this case of a woman who was raped and later developed both post-traumatic stress disorder (see Chapter 4) and conversion mutism (from Rothbaum & Foa, 1991):

Case Study • At the time she sought treatment, Jane was a 32-year-old divorced black woman living with her 15-year-old son and employed as a lower-level executive. When she was 24, two men entered her home after midnight, held a knife to her throat, and threated to kill her if she made a sound or struggled. They raped her orally and vaginally in front of her son, who was 7 at the time, and then locked them in the basement before leaving. Several weeks after the rape, Jane's mother, to whom she was very close, died of cancer. Jane felt she had to be "the strong one" in the family and prided herself because she "never broke down."

At the age of 31, during an abusive relationship with a live-in boyfriend, Jane developed conversion mutism. In the midst of attempting to ask her boyfriend to leave her house, she was unable to produce any sound. After several months of treatment with a speech therapist, Jane became able to whisper quietly but did not regain her normal speech. The speech therapist referred Jane to a clinic for the treatment of rape-related PTSD.

The pretreatment interview confirmed that Jane suffered from chronic PTSD as a result of the rape. She presented with fears, panicky reactions, nightmares, flashbacks, and intrusive thoughts about the assault. She reported attempts to avoid thinking about the assault and situations that reminded her of it and feelings of detachment from others. She also complained of sleep problems, exaggerated startle, and hyperalertness. Jane was moderately depressed and quite anxious. During the intake interview, Jane indicated that she had never verbally expressed her feelings about the assault and believed that this constriction underlied her inability to speak.

People with conversion disorder tend to have high rates of depression, anxiety, alcohol abuse, and antisocial personality disorder (Bofelli & Guze, 1992; Tomasson, Kent, & Coryell, 1991). They may be depressed or anxious over the same traumas or concerns that led to the conversion disorder. The relationship between conversion disorder and antisocial personality disorder and alcohol abuse may arise because the avoidance of negative emotions leads to impulsive, antisocial behavior, to self-medicating through alcohol abuse, and to conversion symptoms.

Treatment of Conversion Disorder

Psychoanalytic treatment for conversion disorder focuses on the expression of painful emotions and memories and insight into the relationship between these and the conversion symptoms (Gavin, 1985). Recovery is thought to be prompted by the patient drawing the connection between the event and the symptom. Chronic conversion disorder is more difficult to treat. When symptoms are present for more than a month, the person's history often resembles somatization disorder (discussed next) and is treated as such.

Behavioral treatments focus on relieving the person's anxiety around the initial trauma that caused the conversion symptoms. In the case cited, Jane's treatment consisted of nine, twice-weekly, 90-minute sessions that included both systematic desensitization and in vivo exposure therapy (refer to Chapter 4). A hierarchy of situations Jane avoided, mostly situations that reminded her of her rape, was constructed. For the in vivo exposure, Jane was aided in approaching the situations that made her feel anxious, and in progressing up her hierarchy to increasingly more feared situations, while practicing relaxation techniques. During the imagery sessions, Jane recounted the details of the assault first in general terms and later in great detail, including the details of the situation and the details of her physiological and cognitive reactions to the assault. At first, Jane was able to describe the assault in only a whisper, but she cried in full volume. After crying, Jane's speech became increasingly louder, with occasional words uttered in full volume. Eventually, she regained a full-volume voice. Following treatment, Jane's PTSD symptoms also decreased and diminished further over the following year.

People with conversion disorder are difficult to treat because they do not believe there is anything wrong with them psychologically (Krull & Schifferdecker, 1990). If they have *la belle indifference,* they are not even motivated to cooperate with psychological treatment in order to overcome their physical symptoms.

Somatization and Pain Disorder

A person with **somatization disorder** has a long history of complaints about physical symptoms, affecting many different areas of the body, for which medical attention has been sought but that appear to have no physical cause. The most common types of complaints are complaints about chronic pain, including pains in the head, chest, abdomen, and back. People who complain only of chronic pain may be given the diagnosis of **pain disorder.** Since most of what we know about somatization disorder also applies to pain disorder, these two disorders are discussed together in this section.

A person with somatization disorder will have a variety of other physical complaints in addition to pain, including heart palpitations, excessive stomach gas, and gynecological complaints (such as menstrual cramps; Escobar et al., 1987). Obviously, it is extremely important that physicians not assume that an individual has a psychological problem just because they cannot identify the cause of the physical complaints. Somatization disorder should only be diagnosed when the person has a clear history of multiple physical complaints for which no organic causes can be found. These complaints are usually presented in vague, dramatic, or exaggerated ways, and the individual may have insisted on medical procedures, even surgeries, that clearly were not necessary. One study of 191 persons in a general internal medicine outpatient clinic found that about 40 percent who had physical symptoms for which no organic causes could be found met the diagnostic criteria for a somatization disorder, meaning they had long histories of vague and multiple physical complaints with no apparent organic causes (Van Hemert et al., 1993).

Somatization disorder and hypochondriasis (discussed next) are quite similar and indeed may be variations of the same disorder. The primary distinction in the DSM-IV between the two disorders is that the person with somatization disorder actually experiences physical symptoms and seeks help for them, whereas the hypochondriac may just worry that he or she has some disorder. Somatization disorder and conversion disorder also share similarities, and there is a high degree of comorbidity between the two disorders

somatization disorder
syndrome marked by the chronic experience of unpleasant or painful physical symptoms for which no organic cause can be found

pain disorder
syndrome marked by the chronic experience of acute pain that appears to have no physical cause

(Bofelli & Guze, 1992). People with somatization disorder often report loss of functioning in some part of the body, just as do people with conversion disorder. Somatization disorder is diagnosed when the loss of functioning is part of a broader spectrum of symptoms that apparently have psychological causes.

In general, anxiety and depression very frequently are present in people meeting the diagnostic criteria for somatization disorder or pain disorder (Fishbain et al., 1986). One study of somatizers who were particularly high users of medical facilities found that two-thirds had lifetime histories of episodes of major depression (Katon et al., 1990). In addition, men with the disorder sometimes have histories of alcoholism or antisocial personality disorder. As with conversion disorder, people with somatization or pain disorder may be prone to periods of anxiety and depression that they cannot express or cope with adaptively, and they either somatize their distress, or mask the distress in alcohol abuse or antisocial behavior.

Moderate degrees of somatization are apparently quite common, although very few people tend to meet the diagnostic criteria for somatization disorder. For example, one study found that 4.40 percent of a randomly selected sample of adults had a history of significant somatization, but only 0.03 percent met the criteria for somatization disorder (Escobar et al., 1987). Somatization is much more common in women than in men, perhaps because women have more periods of depression and anxiety than do men but are not always comfortable in expressing their distress directly and instead experience it in physical symptoms.

There also appear to be cultural variations in the prevalence of somatization disorder. Studies in China and Puerto Rico and of different ethnic groups in the United States have found that persons from some Latin American countries and persons of Asian heritage appear more likely to have somatization disorder than do Caucasians (Canino, Rubio-Stipec, & Bravo, 1988; Escobar et al., 1987; Jun-mian, 1987; Shrout et al., 1992; Westermeyer, Bouafuely, Neider, & Callies, 1989). Latin and Asian cultures may have higher rates of somatization disorder because of cultural norms of expressing distress in physical complaints rather than admitting to negative emotions.

In the United States, somatization disorder also appears more common in older adults than in middle-aged adults (Grau & Padgett, 1988). The cultural norms with which older adults were raised often prohibited admitting to depression or anxiety, and thus, older adults who are depressed or anxious may be more likely to express their negative emotions in somatic complaints, which are acceptable and expected complaints of old age. Young children also often express their distress in somatic complaints (Garber, Walker, & Zeman, 1991). They may not have the language to express difficult emotions but can say that they feel "bad" or that they have stomachaches or headaches.

Somatization disorder tends to be a long-term problem. In a 2-year study of people with somatization disorder and people with similar physical complaints for which an organic cause could be found, Craig and colleagues (1993) found that the somatizers' symptoms lasted longer than the symptoms of those with medical illnesses. Moreover, changes in the somatizers' symptoms mirrored their emotional well-being: When they were anxious or depressed, they reported more physical complaints than when they were not anxious or depressed.

It can be extremely difficult to differentiate between somatization disorder and organic disorders for which we do not yet have definitive tests. For example, one disorder that is often confused with, or overlaps with, somatization disorder is chronic fatigue syndrome. Chronic fatigue syndrome involves a persistent, debilitating fatigue accompanied by symptoms resembling those of common viral infections (Manu, Lane, & Matthews, 1992). Chronic fatigue syndrome is a real medical syndrome, probably caused by infections and a poorly functioning immune system. It is difficult to diagnose, involves many of the symptoms that people who tend to somatize complain of most often, and has been given considerable attention in the media in recent years. In

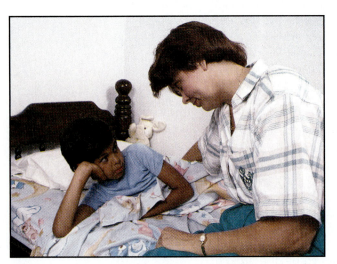

Young children often express psychological distress in somatic complaints.

one study of 100 adults complaining of chronic fatigue syndrome, 15 met the diagnostic criteria of somatization disorder, meaning they had long histories of vague physical complaints involving many parts of their bodies (Manu, Lane, & Mathews, 1989). However, 85 percent had no previous histories of somatic complaints.

 Can you think of other "modern disorders" that may be difficult to differentiate from somatization disorder?

Theories of Somatization and Pain Disorder

Family history studies of somatization and pain disorders find that the disorders run in families, primarily among female relatives (Guze, 1993). Thirty percent of patients with pain disorder have family histories of psychological problems, most often pain disorder in the female relatives and alcoholism in the male relatives (Chaturvedi, 1987). The male relatives of persons with somatization disorder also have higher than usual rates of alcoholism and antisocial personality disorder. It is not clear that the transmission of somatization or pain disorder in families has to do with genetics. The children of parents with these disorders may model their parents' tendencies to somatize distress (Craig et al., 1993). Parents who are somatizers also are more likely to neglect their children, and the children may learn that the only way to receive care and attention is to be ill. In general, the children of parents who are somatizers have increased vulnerability to a wide range of psychological problems, to suicide attempts, and to frequent hospitalizations (Livingston, 1993).

A cognitive theory of somatization or pain disorder suggests that persons with these disorders tend to experience bodily sensations more intensely than do other people, they pay more attention to physical symptoms than do others, and they tend to catastrophize these symptoms (Barsky, 1992). For example, such a person might have a slight case of indigestion but experience it as severe chest pain and interpret the pain as a sure sign of a heart attack. His interpretation of his experience may have a direct influence on his physiological processes, by increasing his heart rate or blood pressure, thereby maintaining and exacerbating his pain. Further, his cognitions will influence the way he presents symptoms to his physician and family. As a result, physicians may prescribe more potent medication or order more diagnostic tests, and family members may express more sympathy, excuse the person from responsibilities, and otherwise encourage passive behavior (Turk & Ruby, 1992). Thus, the person's misinterpretation and catastrophizing of his symptoms are reinforced by the physician and family, increasing the likelihood that he will interpret future symptoms in similar ways.

Somatization disorder may often be part of a post-traumatic stress disorder experienced by a person who has undergone a severe stressor. People with somatization disorder frequently have histories of physical or sexual abuse (Pribor, Yutzy, Dean, & Wetzel, 1993). Refugees and recent immigrants also have an increased risk of somatization disorder. For example, one study found that immigrants to the United States from Central America and Mexico had higher rates of post-traumatic stress disorder and somatization disorder than did U.S.-born Mexican Americans or whites. Moreover, 52 percent of the Central Americans who had fled to the United States to escape war or political unrest had post-traumatic stress disorder and somatization disorder (Cervantes, Salgado de Snyder, & Padilla, 1989). Similarly, a study of Hmong immigrants to the United States, who had fled Cambodia during the Khmer Rouge regime, found 17 percent to have post-traumatic stress disorders characterized by moderate to severe somatizing symptoms (Westermeyer, Bouafuely, Neider, & Callies, 1989).

Treatment of Somatization and Pain Disorder

Convincing people with somatization or pain disorder that they need psychological treatment is not easy. If they do agree to treatment, people with these disorders appear to respond well to intervention that teaches them to express negative feelings or memories and to understand the relationship between their emotions and their physical symptoms (Beutler et al., 1988). Cognitive therapies for these disorders help people learn to interpret their physical symptoms appropriately and to avoid catastrophizing physical symptoms (Turk & Ruby, 1992).

Here is an example of the use of cultural beliefs to treat a Hispanic woman with somatization disorder (adapted from Koss, 1990, p. 22):

> **Case Study •** E was a 45-year-old woman who consulted many doctors for "high fever, vomiting, diarrhea, inability to eat, and rapid weight loss." After numerous negative lab analyses, her doctor told her, "I can't go on with you; go to one of the *espiritistas* or a *curandera*" (traditional healers). A cousin then took her to a Spiritist center "for medicine." She was given herbal remedies: some baths and a tea of *molinillo* to take in the morning before eating. But the treatment focused mainly on the appearance of the spirit of a close friend who had died a month earlier from cancer. The spirit was looking for help from E who had not gone to help during her friend's illness because of her own family problems. The main thrust of the healers' treatment plan was to assist E to understand how she had to deal with the feelings of distress related to the stress of a paralyzed husband and caring for two small daughters without his help. The spirit's influence on E's body was an object lesson that was aimed at increasing her awareness of how her lifestyle was causing her to neglect the care of her own body and feelings much as she had neglected her dying friend.

The spiritual healer in this case recognized the cause of E's somatic complaints as stress, anger, and guilt and helped her link her physical symptoms with these emotions and find ways to cope more adaptively with the emotions. The context for this intervention, rather than being cognitive therapy or some other type of psychotherapy used by the dominant non-Hispanic culture, was the cultural belief system concerning the role of spirits in producing physical symptoms.

 If you were having headaches that you suspected were due to psychological causes, what would you feel would be an appropriate course of action to take to have these headaches treated? What kind of health professional would you contact first?

Hypochondriasis

hypochondriasis
syndrome marked by chronic worry that one has a physical symptom or disease that one clearly does not have

As noted, many of the features of **hypochondriasis** are similar to those of somatization disorder. The primary distinction between people with hypochondriasis and people with somatization disorder is that hypocondriacs may worry that they have a disease but not experience severe physical symptoms suggesting a disease the way people with somatization disorder do.

> **Case Study •** Carlos, a married man of 39, came to the clinic complaining, "I have trouble in my bowels and then it gets me in my head. My bowels just spasm on me, I get constipated, and then my head must get toxic. It seems to poison my system." The patient's complaints dated back 12 years to an attack of "acute indigestion" in which he seemed to bloat up and pains developed in his abdomen and spread in several directions. He traced some of these pathways with his finger as he spoke. Carlos spent a month in bed at this time and then, based on an interpretation of something the doctor said, rested for another 2 months before working again. Words of reassurance from his doctor failed to take effect. He felt "sick, worried, and scared," feeling that he really would never get well again.
>
> For 3 or 4 years after this attack, he took enemas, three a day at first, reducing gradually to one a day. For 8 or 9 years he had taken laxatives and devoted constant atten-

tion to his diet. He described variations in residue with enough detail to indicate conscientious watching of his bowel movements. Four months before coming to the clinic he was discharged from his job as a clerk in a paper mill because of too much sick leave and an unwillingness to do anything he considered outside of his duties. Since that time he has lived with his wife's relatives. . . .

Carlos became very dependent upon the woman he married when he was 22 years old. He left most of the decisions to her and showed little interest in sexual relations. His wife was several years older than he and did not seem to mind his totally passive approach to life. His attack of "acute indigestion" followed her death, 5 years after marriage, by 3 months during which he felt lost and hopeless. In time, he moved to a rural area and remarried. His second wife proved less willing to assume major responsibilities for him than the first, and she made sexual demands upon him that he felt unable to meet. He became more and more preoccupied with his gastrointestinal welfare. In the complete absence of community facilities for psychological assistance where he lived, prognosis for recovery from chronic partially disabling hypochondria was deemed poor. (adapted from Cameron & Rychlak, 1985)

Dial 123-SICK and Reach Out to Your Fellow-Hypochondriacs.
Drawing by Handelsman; © 1989 The New Yorker Magazine Inc.

Most studies of hypochondriasis have grouped people with this disorder with people with somatization disorder, in part because people will often qualify for the diagnosis of both disorders. Thus, most of what was said about the causes of somatization disorder also applies to the causes of hypochondriasis. In particular, people with hypochondriasis appear very prone to chronic depression and anxiety and have family histories of these disorders (Barsky, Wyshak, & Klerman, 1992). Their fears about their health often stem from a general distress and inability to cope with that distress in adaptive ways. As is the case with people with somatization disorder, people with hypochondriasis do not appreciate suggestions that their problems are caused by psychological factors and thus tend not to seek psychological treatment. When they do receive psychological treatment, it focuses on helping them understand the association between their symptoms and emotional distress and on helping them find more adaptive ways of coping with their distress.

Body Dysmorphic Disorder

The final disorder we will consider in this chapter is **body dysmorphic disorder.** People with this disorder are excessively preoccupied with some part of their bodies that they believe is defective. The parts of the body mostly frequently focused on by these people

body dysmorphic disorder
syndrome involving obsessive concern over some part of the body the individual believes is defective

are parts of the face and head (nose, ears, mouth, eyes), arms, legs, and sexual body parts (Hollander, Cohen, & Simeon, 1993). They will spend hours looking at their "deformed" body parts, perhaps in a mirror, and perform elaborate rituals to try to improve the parts or hide them. For example, they may spend hours styling their hair to hide the defects in their ears. People with this disorder also often seek out plastic surgery to change their disliked body parts (Phillips, 1992). Case studies of some people with this disorder indicate that their beliefs that some parts of their bodies are deformed can be so severe and bizarre as to be considered delusional (Phillips, 1991). A study of 30 people with this disorder found that 97 percent avoided social and occupational activities because of their "deformity," 30 percent had become housebound, and 17 percent had attempted suicide (Phillips et al., 1993). The average age of onset of this disorder was 19 years of age, and on average, these people had four or more separate bodily preoccupations.

Most people worry somewhat about their physical appearance, but people with body dysmorphic disorder worry excessively and go to elaborate means to hide or change their "deformed" body parts.

> **Case Study** • Sydney was a popular 17 year old who attended a suburban high school near Washington, D. C. During the spring of her senior year, Sydney became preoccupied with her appearance and began to constantly look for her own image in windows and mirrors. In particular, Sydney began to notice that her nose was abnormally shaped. Her friends all told her that she was crazy when she expressed her concern, so she stopped talking about it to them. She began to apply makeup in an attempt to offset what she believed to be the contemptible contour of her nose. She started wearing her hair loose and holding her head down much of the time so that her face was partially obscured and brushing her hair excessively to encourage it to fall forward around her face. Her distress grew, and she repeatedly begged her parents to let her have surgery to correct the shape of her nose, which by now she regarded as hideous. Her pleas turned to volatile arguments when her parents told her that her nose was fine and that they would not agree to surgery. Sydney started finding excuses not to go out with her friends and refused to date because she could not stand the thought of anyone looking at her up close. She stayed home in her room, staring for hours in the mirror. She refused to attend her senior prom or graduation ceremony.
>
> After high school, Sydney got a job as a night security guard, so she could isolate herself as much as possible and not been seen by others. During the next 7 years, she had five surgeries to correct the shape of her nose. Each time, she became even more dissatisfied and obsessed with her appearance. Although everyone who knew Sydney thought she looked fine, she remained obsessed and tormented by her "defect," which now dominated her life.

Those who seek treatment wait an average of 6 years from the onset of their concerns before seeking treatment. More women than men and more single people than married people seek help for body dysmorphic disorder, but we do not know the prevalence of the disorder in the general population (Phillips, 1991).

Although clinicians in Europe have frequently written about body dysmorphic disorder, it has been relatively ignored by clinicians in the United States (Phillips, 1991). The diagnosis was only introduced in the DSM in the 1987 edition of the manual. Some researchers suggest that body dysmorphic disorder is not a distinct disorder that deserves its own diagnostic category in the DSM (Hollander et al., 1992). Body dissatisfaction is a feature of many other disorders, including depression, the anxiety disorders, and the eating disorders; conversely, perhaps most people with body dysmorphic disorder also have severe levels of depression or anxiety (Hollander, Cohen, & Simeon, 1993). More recent evidence suggests that body dysmorphic disorder may be a form of obsessive-compulsive disorder, in which the person obsesses about some part of her body and engages in compulsive behaviors to change that part of her body (Phillips, 1991).

 Would you say that many teenagers have a mild form of body dysmorphic disorder? Explain.

Treatments for this disorder have included psychoanalytically oriented therapy focused on helping the client gain insight into the real concerns behind her obsession with her body part and systematic desensitization to help the client stop engaging in compulsive behaviors around her body part and to reduce her anxiety over the body part (Hollander et al., 1992). In addition, serotonin reuptake inhibitors have been shown to be effect in some case studies in reducing obsessional thought and compulsive behavior in persons with this disorder (Hollander et al., 1989; Phillips, 1991).

Summing Up | Somatoform Disorders

- The somatoform disorders include conversion disorder, somatization and pain disorder, hypochondriasis, and body dysmorphic disorder.
- People with conversion disorder lose all functioning in some parts of their bodies, for no physiological reason.

- Conversion symptoms most often occur after trauma or stress. Treatment involves helping people express the emotions or memories associated with the symptoms.
- People with somatization disorder have long histories of multiple physical complaints for which there is no organic cause.
- Somatization may be some people's way of expressing distress. People who develop this disorder may also tend to catastrophize physical symptoms. Treatment usually involves helping people find more adaptive ways of coping with their stressors.
- People with hypochondriasis fear they have a disease despite evidence that they do not.
- People with body dysmorphic disorder have an obsessional preoccupation with some parts of their bodies and make elaborate attempts to change these body parts.
- Treatment for body dysmorphic disorder can include psychodynamic therapy to reveal underlying concerns, systematic desensitization therapy to reduce obsessions and compulsions about the body, and serotonin reuptake inhibitors.

Bio-Psycho-Social INTEGRATION

The *mind-body problem* refers to questions philosophers and scientists have raised for centuries about how the mind and body affect each other. Does the mind influence bodily processes? Do changes in the body affect a person's sense of "self?" What are the mechanisms by which the body and mind influence each other?

The dissociative and somatoform disorders are excellent evidence that the mind and body are complexly interwoven. In a person with dissociative identity disorder, different personalities may actually have different physiological characteristics, such as different heart rates or blood pressure, even though they reside in the same body. In conversion disorder, psychological stress causes the person to lose eyesight, hearing, or functioning in some other important physiological system. In somatization and pain disorder, a person under psychological stress experiences physiological symptoms, such as severe headaches.

An underlying theme to these disorders is that it is easier or more acceptable for some people to experience psychological distress through changes in their bodies than to express it more directly as sadness, fear, or anger. We all somatize our distress to some degree—we feel more aches and pains when we are upset about something than when we are happy. People who develop somatoform and perhaps dissociative disorders may somatize their distress to an extreme degree. Their tendency to differentiate between what is going on in their minds and what is going on in their bodies may be low, and they may favor an extreme "bodily" expression of what is going on in their minds.

Chapter Summary

The dissociative disorders are a fascinating group of disorders in which the individual's identity, memories, or consciousness become separated or dissociated from one another. In dissociative identity disorder, the individual develops two or more separate and distinct personalities that alternate in their control over the individual's behavior. Each personality may be amnesic for the other, or some personalities may be aware of the others. The different personalities appear to serve specific functions, such as protecting the "host" personality against harm or inflicting punishment on the host.

Persons with dissociative identity disorder often engage in self-destructive and mutilative behaviors. The vast majority of diagnosed cases of dissociative identity disorder are women, and recent cases tend to have histories of childhood sexual and/or physical abuse. The alternate personalities may have been formed during the traumatic experiences as a way of defending against these experiences, particularly among people who are highly hypnotizable. Some researchers are skeptical about the validity of many cases of dissociative identity disorder, however, arguing that these cases are created by the suggestion of therapists to clients under hypnosis. Treatment of dissociative identity disorder has typically involved helping the different personalities integrate into one functional personality.

Fugue is a disorder in which the person suddenly moves away from home and assumes an entirely new identity, with complete amnesia for the previous identity. Fugue states usually occur in response to some stressor and can remit suddenly, with the person returning to his or her previous identity. Little is known about the prevalence or causes of fugue states.

Dissociative or psychogenic amnesia involves loss of memory due to psychological causes. It must be differentiated from organic amnesia, which is caused by brain injury. With organic amnesia, a person may have difficulty remembering new information, a difficulty known as *anterograde amnesia*, but this is rare in psychogenic amnesia. In addition, with organic amnesia, loss of memory for the past (*retrograde amnesia*) is usually complete, whereas with psychogenic amnesia, it is limited to personal information. Psychogenic amnesia typically occurs following traumatic events. It may be due to motivated forgetting of events, to poor storage of information during events due to hyperarousal, or to avoidance of the emotions experienced during events and to the associated memories of events.

Depersonalization disorder involves frequent episodes in which the individual feels detached from his or her mental processes or body. Transient depersonalization experiences are common, especially under the influence of drugs or sleep deprivation. The causes of depersonalization disorder are unknown.

The somatoform disorders are a group of disorders in which the individual experiences or fears physical symptoms for which no organic cause can be found. These disorders may result from the dissociation of painful emotions or memories and the re-emergence of these emotions or memories as symptoms, as cries for help, or from the secondary gain people receive for these symptoms.

One of the most dramatic somatoform disorders is conversion disorder, in which the individual loses all functioning in some part of his or her body, such as the eyes or legs. Conversion symptoms often occur after trauma or stress. People with conversion disorder tend to have high rates of depression, anxiety, alcohol abuse, and antisocial personality disorder. Treatment for the disorder focuses on the expression of emotions or memories associated with the symptoms.

Somatization disorder involves a long history of multiple physical complaints for which people have sought treatment but of which there is no apparent organic cause. Pain disorder involves only the experience of chronic, unexplainable pain. People with these disorders show high rates of anxiety and depression. The disorders are apparently common and are more common in women, in Asians and Hispanics, and among the elderly and children. Somatization and pain disorders run in families. The cognitive theory of these disorders is that affected people focus excessively on physical symptoms and castrophize these symptoms. People with these disorders often have experienced recent traumas. Treatment involves restructuring the meaning of the traumas and their implications and helping the person find adaptive ways of coping with distress.

Hypochondriasis is a disorder in which the individual fears he or she has some disease, despite medical proof to the contrary. Hypochondriasis shares many of the features and causes of somatization disorder and is typically comorbid with somatization disorder.

The final somatoform disorder is questionably categorized along with the other somatoform disorders. People with body dysmorphic disorder have an obsessional preoccupation with some parts of their bodies, and engage in elaborate behaviors to mask or get rid of these body parts. They are frequently depressed, anxious, and suicidal. This disorder may be a feature of an underlying depression or anxiety disorder or may be a form of obsessive-compulsive disorder. Treatment for the disorder includes psychodynamic therapy to uncover the emotions driving the obsession about the body, systematic desensitization to decrease obsessions and compulsive behaviors focused on the body part, and serotonin reuptake inhibitors to reduce obsessional thought.

Key Terms

Application   It Just Doesn't Add Up

Earlier in this chapter, we briefly examined an unusual disorder related to the somatoform disorders: factitious disorder. People with factitious disorder deliberately fake medical illness to gain attention. Often they will inflict harm on their bodies to create an illness, such as injecting saliva under their skin to create abscesses. They are not simply trying to feign illness to avoid something unpleasant, like military duty or jury duty, as do people accused of malingering. The goal of people with factitious disorder is to take on the sick role and to receive elaborate medical attention. This disorder has also been referred to as *Munchhausen's syndrome.*

In recent years, several cases of *factitious disorder by proxy* have come to light. In these tragic cases, parents have faked or even created illnesses in their children in order to gain attention for themselves. They act as devoted and long-suffering protectors of their children, drawing praise for their dedicated nursing. Their children are subjected to unnecessary and often dangerous medical procedures and may actually die from their parents' attempts to make them ill. Seven-year-old Jennifer Bush may be one victim of factitious disorder by proxy:

Sitting beside Hillary Clinton at a meeting on Capitol Hill two summers ago, Jennifer Bush cut a heart breaking figure. The 7-year-old Coral Springs, Florida, girl with big eyes and a perky red bow atop her little Dutch-boy coif seemed the perfect poster child for the Administration's health-care reform plan. Chronically ill almost from birth, Jennifer had already endured nearly 200 hospitalizations and 40 operations, and her $2 million-plus medical bill had exhausted the family's health-insurance benefits. Not surprisingly, Jennifer became a media darling, appearing on the Today

show and on the front page of many newspapers.

Now it appears that Jennifer's suffering may have been much worse than was ever reported. Florida officials arrested Jennifer's seemingly devoted mother Kathleen Bush and charged her with aggravated child abuse and fraud. According to authorities, Bush, 38, deliberately caused her daughter's ailments by dosing her with unprescribed drugs, tampering with her medications, and even contaminating her feeding tube with fecal bacteria. As a result, say officials, Jennifer was subjected to dozens of needless operations and invasive procedures. Bush has denied all charges.

Almost as shocking as the charges against Jennifer's mother, however, is the fact that it took more than 4 years of warnings before state authorities placed the child under protective custody. Nurses at Coral Springs Medical Center began noticing as early as 1991—when Jennifer was just 4—that her condition seemed to worsen whenever her mother visited. . . .

State officials reopened the investigation last April, after receiving an anonymous complaint. According to the arrest affidavit, once her mother was informed of the inquiry, Jennifer's condition improved dramatically. In the preceding 9 months she had been hospitalized seven times for a total of 83 days. In the 9 months afterward she was admitted just once for 4 days. (Toufexis, 1996, p. 70)

Why would it take so long for authorities to intervene in a case like this? Parents with factitious disorder by proxy may be very adept at hiding what they are doing to their children,

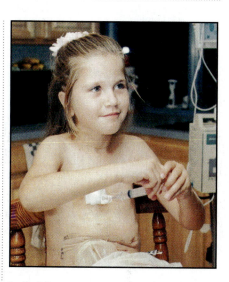

Jennifer Bush has endured hundreds of medical treatments and surgeries in her young life. Her mother is accused of causing Jennifer's illnesses to gain the attention of physicians and the media.

especially if they have medical backgrounds. Also, authorities must be extremely cautious about accusing a parent of causing harm to his or her children because of the great repercussions of falsely accusing parents, including the destruction of reputations, careers, and family relationships.

Thus, like the somatoform disorders, factitious disorder and factitious disorder by proxy raise difficult questions for mental health professionals about when it is appropriate to suggest that symptoms that seem to be the result of medical illness are actually the result of psychological disorder. How much and what types of evidence would you need to decide it was time to make such a suggestion to someone you were treating? ■

8 Personality Disorders

No man can climb out beyond the limitations of his own character.

—John Morley, "Robespierre," *Critical Miscellanies* (1871–1908)

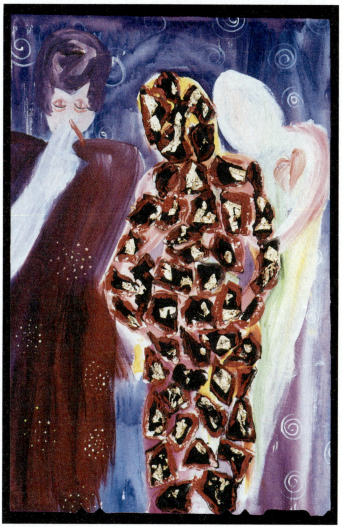

Gayle Ray
The Armour

> **Case Study** • Jimmy has been in trouble all his life. As a kid, he skipped school often, and when he was there, he was prone to starting fights with other kids or getting into arguments with teachers. He was suspended several times for stealing. He was finally expelled at the age of 14 for threatening a teacher, and he essentially never went back to school.
>
> Jimmy is now 29 and has been in and out of jail for the last 15 years. Mostly his crimes have involved small-time burglaries or shoplifting, possession of illegal drugs, or driving while intoxicated. He has never kept a job for more than 6 months at a time. He always gets into fights with his bosses or coworkers, whom he usually considers to be stupid. Then he quits or is fired. When his family members ask Jimmy why he gets into so much trouble, he just shrugs and either blames his predicament on someone else or says he just cannot control his temper.
>
> Jimmy actually talks to his family members only rarely. He has never gotten along with anyone but his mother and has been physically violent toward several family members. Jimmy's romantic relationships have been few and have largely consisted of meeting a woman, having frequent and somewhat violent sex with her for a few weeks, and then leaving her without a good-bye.

personality
habitual and enduring ways of thinking, feeling, and acting that make each of us unique and different from every other person

personality trait
complex pattern of thought, emotion, and behavior that is stable across time and many situations

personality disorder
chronic pattern of maladaptive cognition, emotion, and behavior that begins in adolescence or early adulthood and continues into later adulthood

Does Jimmy have a psychological disorder? Some people would say no, that he is just a "rotten kid" who grew into a "rotten adult." Others would say that Jimmy clearly has been troubled most of his life and that his behaviors fit the concept of a personality disorder quite well.

Personality is all the ways we have of acting, thinking, believing, and feeling that make each of us unique and different from every other person. A **personality trait** is a complex pattern of behavior, thought, and feeling that is stable across time and across many situations.

Defining Personality Disorders

A **personality disorder** is a long-standing pattern of behavior, thought, and feeling that is highly maladaptive for the individual or for people around him or her. By definition, a personality disorder must be present continuously from adolescence or early adulthood into adulthood. The DSM-IV calls special attention to personality disorders and treats them as different in quality from the major acute disorders, such as major depression and schizophrenia, by placing the personality disorders on Axis II of the diagnostic system, instead of on Axis I with the acute disorders (see Chapter 2). People with a personality disorder can experience any of the acute disorders recognized by the DSM, however. Indeed, as we shall discuss later in this chapter, people with personality disorders are at high risk for the acute disorders, and these acute disorders are often what bring them to the attention of clinicians. People with personality disorders tend not to seek therapy until they experience a bout of major depression or their substance abuse lands them in jail or the hospital because they often do not see the behaviors that comprise their personality disorder as maladaptive.

The personality disorders are highly controversial in modern clinical psychology because of problems that exist in the current conceptualization of these disorders and in their assessment. First, the DSM treats these disorders as categories. That is, each disorder is described as if it represents something qualitatively different from a "normal" personality. Yet there is substantial evidence that most of the disorders recognized by the DSM represent the extreme versions of "normal" personality traits (Livesley, Schroeder, Jackson, & Jang, 1994). Second, there is a great deal of overlap in the diagnostic criteria for the different personality disorders, and the majority of people who are diagnosed with one disorder tend to meet the diagnostic criteria for at least one more personality disorder (Morey, 1988). This suggests that there actually may be smaller numbers of personality disorders that adequately account for the variation in personality disorder symptoms.

Third, diagnosing a personality disorder often requires information that is hard for a clinician to obtain, such as accurate information about how an individual treats other people, about how an individual behaves in a wide variety of situations, or about how stable an individual's behaviors have been since childhood or adolescence.

These problems make it difficult for clinicians to be confident of diagnoses of personality disorders. They also make it difficult to do research on personality disorders. Indeed, there is much less research on the epidemiology, etiology, and treatment of the personality disorders than there is on most of the other disorders described in this book. With these caveats in mind, let us turn to what we do know about the personality disorders.

The DSM-IV groups personality disorders into three clusters. *Cluster A* includes three disorders characterized by *odd or eccentric behaviors and thinking:* paranoid personality disorder, schizoid personality disorder, and schizotypal personality disorder. Each of these disorders has some of the features of schizophrenia or paranoid psychotic disorder, but persons with these personality disorders are not psychotic. Their behaviors are simply odd and often inappropriate. *Cluster B* includes four disorders characterized by *dramatic, erratic, and emotional behavior and interpersonal relationships:* antisocial personality disorder, histrionic personality disorder, borderline personality disorder, and narcissistic personality disorder. Persons with these disorders tend to be manipulative, volatile, and uncaring in social relationships and prone to impulsive behaviors. *Cluster C* includes three disorders characterized by *anxious and fearful emotions and chronic self-doubt, leading to maladaptive behaviors:* dependent personality disorder, avoidant personality disorder, and obsessive-compulsive personality disorder.

People with personality disorders have a life-long history of dysfunctional behavior, which may include antisocial behavior.

The Odd-Eccentric Personality Disorders

People with the **odd-eccentric personality disorders** behave in ways that are similar to people with schizophrenia or paranoid psychotic disorder, but they retain their grasp on reality to a greater degree than do people who are psychotic. Still, many researchers consider this group of personality disorders to be part of the "schizophrenia spectrum." That is, these disorders may be precursors to schizophrenia in some people or milder versions of schizophrenia. As we shall see when we discuss the genetic backgrounds of people with odd-eccentric personality disorders, these disorders may often occur in people who have first-degree relatives who have schizophrenia.

odd-eccentric personality disorders category including paranoid, schizotypal, and schizoid personality disorders that is marked by chronic odd and/or inappropriate behavior with mild features of psychosis and/or paranoia

Paranoid Personality Disorder

The defining feature of **paranoid personality disorder** is a pervasive and unwarranted mistrust of others. Persons with this disorder deeply believe that other people are chronically trying to deceive them or to exploit them and are preoccupied with concerns about the loyalty and trustworthiness of others. They are hypervigilant for confirming evidence of their suspicions. They are often penetrating observers of situations, noting details that most other people will miss. For example, they will notice a slight grimace on the face of their boss or an apparently trivial slip of the tongue by their spouse, when these would have gone unnoticed by everyone else. Moreover, paranoid people consider these events highly meaningful and spend a great deal of time trying to decipher these "clues" about other people's true intentions. They are also sensitive to criticism or potential criticism.

Paranoid people misinterpret or overinterpret situations in line with their suspicions. For example, a husband might interpret his wife's cheerfulness one evening as evidence that she is having an affair with a man at work. They are resistant to rational arguments against their suspicions and may take the fact that another person is arguing with them as evidence that this person is part of the conspiracy against them. Some paranoid people become withdrawn from others in an attempt to protect themselves, but others are aggressive and arrogant, sure that their way of looking at the world is right and superior

paranoid personality disorder chronic and pervasive mistrust and suspicion of other people that is unwarranted and maladaptive

and that the best defense against conspiring others is a good offense. Felix, in the following case study, has a paranoid personality disorder:

> **Case Study** • Felix is a 59-year-old construction worker who worries that his coworkers might hurt him. Last week, while he was using a table saw, Felix's hand slipped and his fingers came very close to being cut badly. Felix wonders if someone sabotaged the saw so that somehow the piece of wood he was working with slipped and drew his hand into the saw blade. Since this incident, Felix has observed his coworkers looking at him and whispering to each other. He mentioned his suspicion that the saw had been tampered with to his boss, but the boss told him that was a crazy idea and that Felix obviously had just been careless.
>
> Felix does not have any close friends. Even his brothers and sisters avoid him because he frequently misinterprets things they say as criticisms of him. Felix was married for a few years, but his wife left him when he began to demand that she not see any of her friends or go out without him, because he suspected she was having affairs with other men. Felix lives in a middle-class neighborhood in a small town that has very little crime. Still, he owns three handguns and a shotgun, which are always loaded, in expectation of someone breaking into his house.

People with paranoid personality disorder are suspicious of everyone and everything.

The prevalence of paranoid personality disorder in the general population appears to be between 0.5 and 4.0 percent (Bernstein, Useda, & Siever, 1995). Among clinically referred people, males are three times more likely than females to be diagnosed with this disorder (Fabrega, Ulrich, Pilkonis, & Mezzich, 1991). People with paranoid personality disorder appear to be at increased risk for a number of acute psychological problems, including major depression, anxiety disorders, substance abuse, and psychotic episodes (Bernstein et al., 1995; Fabrega et al., 1991).

Retrospective studies of people with paranoid personality disorder suggest that their prognosis is generally poor, with their symptoms intensifying under stress (Quality Assurance Project, 1990). Not surprisingly, their interpersonal relationships, including intimate relationships, tend to be unstable.

 Can you think of any occupations in which people with paranoid personality disorder might do well? Or do you think their paranoia would be dysfunctional in any occupation? Explain.

Theories of Paranoid Personality Disorder

Both genetic and psychosocial theories of paranoid personality disorder have been offered. Some family history studies suggest that paranoid personality disorder is somewhat more common in the families of people with schizophrenia than in the families of healthy control subjects, suggesting that paranoid personality disorder may be part of the schizophrenic spectrum of disorders (Baron, Gruen, Asnis, & Lord, 1985; Kendler, Neale, Kessler, Heath, & Eaves, 1993; Nigg & Goldsmith, 1994). Twin and adoption studies have not been done to tease apart genetic influences and environmental influences on the development of this disorder, however.

Psychoanalytic theorists argue that paranoid personality disorder is the result of a person's need to deny his or her true feelings about others and to project those feelings onto others (Freud, 1911/1958; Shapiro, 1965). For some paranoid persons, their hostility toward others may come from an exaggerated sense of self-worth, whereas for others, it may come from a poor self-concept and the expectation that others will be critical and blame them for any problems (Millon, 1981). These attitudes can develop in children whose parents are harsh, critical, and intolerant of any weakness but who also emphasize to their children that they are "special" and "different" from others (Millon, 1981; Turkat, 1985). Such parental messages may lead the child to become hypersensitive to evaluations by others and to believe that the world is a hostile place and that he or she is persecuted for being different.

Cognitive theorists see paranoid personality disorder as the result of underlying belief that people are malevolent and deceptive, combined with a lack of self-confidence about being able to defend against others (Beck & Freeman, 1990; Colby, 1981). Thus, the paranoid person must always be vigilant for signs of others' deceit or criticism and must be quick to act against others. Neither the psychoanalytic nor the cognitive theories of the development of paranoid personality disorders have been tested empirically.

Treatment for Paranoid Personality Disorder

People with paranoid personality disorders usually only come into contact with clinicians when they are in crisis. They may seek treatment for severe symptoms of depression or anxiety but often will not feel a need for treatment of their paranoia. In addition, attempts by therapists to challenge their paranoid thinking are likely to be misinterpreted in line with their paranoid belief systems. Obviously, then, it can be quite difficult to treat paranoid personality disorder (Millon, 1981).

In order to gain the trust of a person with a paranoid personality disorder, the therapist must be calm, respectful, and extremely straightforward (Siever & Kendler, 1985). The therapist will behave in a highly professional manner at all times, not attempting to engender a warm, personal relationship with the client that might be misinterpreted. The therapist cannot directly confront the client's paranoid thinking but must rely on more indirect means of raising questions in the client's mind about his or her typical way of interpreting situations. Although many therapists do not expect paranoid clients to achieve full insight into their problems, they hope that by developing at least some degree of trust in the therapist, the client can learn to trust others a bit more, and thereby develop somewhat improved interpersonal relationships.

Cognitive therapy with paranoid individuals focuses on increasing their sense of self-efficacy for dealing with difficult situations, thus decreasing their fear and hostility toward others. As an example, consider this interchange between a cognitive therapist and a woman named Ann, who believed that her coworkers were intentionally trying to annoy her and to turn her supervisor against her (Beck & Freeman, 1990, pp. 111–112):

Therapist: You're reacting as though this is a very dangerous situation. What are the risks you see?

Ann: They'll keep dropping things and making noise to annoy me.

Therapist: Are you sure nothing worse is at risk?

Ann: Yeah.

Therapist: So you don't think there's much chance of them attacking you or anything?

Ann: Nah, they wouldn't do that.

Therapist: If they do keep dropping things and making noises, how bad will that be?

Ann: Like I told you, it's real aggravating. It really bugs me.

Therapist: So it would continue pretty much as it's been going for years now.

Ann: Yeah. It bugs me, but I can take it.

Therapist: And you know that if it keeps happening, at the very least you can keep handling it the way you have been—holding the aggravation in, then taking it out on your husband when you get home. Suppose we could come up with some ways to handle the aggravation even better or to have them get to you less. Is that something you'd be interested in?

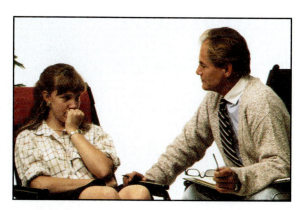

It can be difficult to win the trust of clients who are paranoid.

Ann: Yeah, that sounds good.

Therapist: Another risk you mentioned earlier is that they might talk to your supervisor and turn her against you. As you see it, how long have they been trying to do this?

Ann: Ever since I've been there.

Therapist: How much luck have they had so far in doing that?

Ann: Not much.

Therapist: Do you see any indications that they're going to have any more success now than they have so far?

Ann: No, I don't guess so.

Therapist: So your gut reaction is as though the situation at work is really dangerous. But when you stop and think it through, you conclude that the worst they're going to do is to be really aggravating, and that even if we don't come up with anything new, you can handle it well enough to get by. Does that sound right?

Ann: (Smiling) Yeah, I guess so.

Therapist: And if we can come up with some ways to handle the stress better or handle them better, there will be even less they can do to you.

In this interchange, the therapist did not directly challenge Ann's beliefs about her coworkers' intentions but did try to reduce the sense of danger Ann felt about her workplace by helping her redefine the situation as aggravating rather than threatening. The therapist also enlisted Ann in an effort to develop new coping skills that might further reduce her aggravation.

 Is it ethical for a therapist not to confront irrational thinking in a client but to simply try to help the client feel better by coping better with his or her irrational concerns? Explain.

Schizoid Personality Disorder

schizoid personality disorder syndrome marked by chronic lack of interest in and avoidance of interpersonal relationships as well as emotional coldness in interactions with others

The defining features of **schizoid personality disorder** are a lack of desire to form interpersonal relationships and an emotional coldness in interactions with others. People with this personality disorder are described as aloof, reclusive, and detached and show little emotion in interpersonal interactions. They view relationships with others as unrewarding, messy, and intrusive. Other people experience them as dull, uninteresting, and humorless. The man described next shows several of these symptoms.

> **Case Study** • The patient is a 50-year-old retired police officer who is seeking treatment a few weeks after his dog was run over and died. Since that time he has felt sad, tired, and has had trouble sleeping and concentrating.
>
> The patient lives alone and has for many years had virtually no conversational contacts with other human beings beyond a "Hello" or "How are you?" He prefers to be by himself, finds talk a waste of time, and feels awkward when other people try to initiate a relationship. He occasionally spends some time in a bar but always off by himself and not really following the general conversation. He reads newspapers avidly and is well informed in many areas but takes no particular interest in the people around him. He is employed as a security guard but is known by his fellow workers as a "cold fish" and a "loner." They no longer even notice or tease him, especially since he never seemed to notice or care about their teasing anyway.

> The patient floats through life without relationships except for that with his dog, whom he dearly loved. At Christmas he would buy the dog elaborate gifts and would give himself a wrapped bottle of scotch as if it were a gift from the dog. He believes that dogs are more sensitive and loving than people, and he can express toward them a tenderness and emotion not possible in his relationships with people. The loss of his pets are the only events in his life that have caused him sadness. He experienced the death of his parents without emotion and feels no regret whatever at being completely out of contact with the rest of his family. He considers himself different from other people and regards emotionality in others with bewilderment. (adapted from Spitzer et al., 1981, p. 209)

This man would be diagnosed with schizoid personality disorder because of his long-standing avoidance of relationships with other people and his lack of emotions or emotional understanding. As is often the case with people with personality disorders, he only seeks the help of a clinician when a crisis occurs.

Schizoid personality disorder is quite rare, with about 0.4 to 1.7 percent of adults manifesting the disorder at some time in their lives (Weissman, 1993). Among schizoid persons seeking clinical treatment, males outnumber females about three to one (Fabrega et al., 1991). Schizoid persons can function in society, particularly in occupations that do not require interpersonal interactions.

 If schizoid people generally are not distressed by their own behavior and can function reasonably well in society, what criteria are used to label schizoid personality a disorder?

Theories of Schizoid Personality Disorder

There is a slightly increased rate of schizoid personality disorder in the relatives of persons with schizophrenia, but the link between the two disorders is not clear (Kendler et al., 1993; Nigg & Goldsmith, 1994). Twin studies of personality traits associated with schizoid personality disorder, such as low sociability and low warmth, strongly suggest that these personality traits may be partially inherited (Tellegen, Lykken, Bouchard, & Kimerly, 1988). This is only indirect evidence for the heritability of schizoid personality disorder, however.

Psychoanalytic theorists suggest that schizoid personality disorder develops out of severely disturbed mother-child relationships, in which the child never learns to give or receive love (Bleuler, 1924; Klein, 1952). These children view relationships and emotions as dangerous and thus remain aloof both from other people and from their own feelings.

Cognitive theorists describe the cognitive styles of schizoid persons as impoverished and unresponsive to cues that produce emotions (Beck & Freeman, 1990). Rather than having a particular set of beliefs that lead them to misinterpret situations in specific ways, schizoid persons simply seem disinterested in life around them and only able to acknowledge intellectually that other people experience situations differently from them. As a result, schizoid persons tend to be lethargic and unexpressive and to have poor social skills.

Treatment for Schizoid Personality Disorder

Both psychoanalytic and cognitive treatments for schizoid personality disorder focus on increasing the person's awareness of his or her own feelings and the person's social skills and social contacts (Beck & Freeman, 1990; Quality Assurance Project, 1990). The therapist may model expression of feelings for the client and will help the client identify and express his or her own feelings. Social skills training, done through role-plays with the therapist and through homework assignments in which the client tries out new social skills with other people, is an important component of cognitive therapies. Some thera-

Group therapy can help people with schizoid personality disorder increase their social contacts and social skills.

pists recommend group therapy for people with schizoid personality disorder, so that the group members can model interpersonal relationships and so that the schizoid person can practice new social skills directly with others in the context of group sessions.

Schizotypal Personality Disorder

schizotypal personality disorder
chronic pattern of inhibited or inappropriate emotion and social behavior as well as aberrant cognitions and disorganized speech

Like persons with schizoid personality disorder, persons with **schizotypal personality disorder** tend to be socially isolated, have a restricted range of emotions, and be uncomfortable in interpersonal interactions. The distinguishing characteristics of schizotypal personality disorder are the oddities in cognition, which generally fall into four categories (Beck & Freeman, 1990). The first is *paranoia or suspiciousness.* Much like people with paranoid personality disorder, people with schizotypal personality disorder perceive other people as deceitful and hostile, and much of their social anxiety emerges from this paranoia. The second category of thought is *ideas of reference.* People with schizotypal personality disorder tend to believe that random events or circumstances are related to them. For example, they may think it is highly significant that a fire occurred in a store in which they had shopped only yesterday. The third type of odd cognition is *odd beliefs* and *magical thinking.* For example, they may believe that others know what they are thinking. The fourth category of thought is *illusions* that are just short of hallucinations. For example, they may think they see people in the patterns of wallpaper. In addition to having these oddities of thought, people with schizotypal personality disorder tend to have speech that is tangential, circumstantial, vague, or overelaborate. In interactions with others, they may have inappropriate emotional responses or no emotional responses to what other people say or do. Their behaviors are also odd, sometimes reflecting their odd thoughts. They may be easily distracted or fixate on an object for long periods of time, lost in thought or fantasy. Although the quality of these oddities of thought, speech, and behavior is similar to that in schizophrenia, it is not as severe as in schizophrenia, and people with schizotypal personality disorder maintain basic contact with reality. The woman in the following case study shows many of the oddities of schizotypal personality disorder:

Case Study • The patient is a 32-year-old unmarried, unemployed woman on welfare who complains that she feels "spacey." Her feelings of detachment have gradually become stronger and more uncomfortable. For many hours each day she feels as if she were watching herself move through life, and the world around her seems unreal. She feels especially strange when she looks into a mirror. For many years she has felt able to read people's minds by a "kind of clairvoyance I don't understand." According to her, several people in her family apparently also have this ability. She is preoccupied by the thought that she has some special mission in life but is not sure what it is; she is not particularly religious. She is very self-conscious in public, often feels that people are paying special attention to her, and sometimes thinks that strangers cross the street to avoid her. She is lonely and isolated and spends much of each day lost in fantasies or watching TV soap operas. She speaks in a vague, abstract, digressive manner, generally just missing the point, but she is never incoherent. She seems shy, suspicious, and afraid she will be criticized. She has no gross loss of reality testing, such as hallucinations or delusions. She has never had treatment for emotional problems. She has had occasional jobs but drifts away from them because of lack of interest. (Spitzer et al., 1981, pp. 95–96)

The lifetime prevalence of schizotypal personality disorder is between 0.6 and 5.1 percent (Weissman, 1993). Among clinical samples, it is over twice as commonly diagnosed in males as in females (Fabrega et al., 1991). As with the other odd-eccentric personality disorders, people with schizotypal personality disorder are at increased risk for depression and for schizophrenia or isolated psychotic episodes (Siever, Bernstein, & Silverman, 1995).

For a person to be given a diagnosis of schizotypal personality disorder, his or her odd or eccentric thoughts cannot be part of cultural beliefs, such as cultural belief in magic or specific superstitions. Still, some psychologists have argued that people of color are more often diagnosed with schizophreniclike disorders, such as schizotypal personality disorder, than are whites because white clinicians often misinterpret culturally bound beliefs as evidence of schizotypal thinking (Snowden & Cheung, 1990).

Theories of Schizotypal Personality Disorder

Many more studies of the genetics of schizotypal personality disorder have been conducted than studies of the other odd-eccentric personality disorders. Family history studies, adoption studies, and twin studies all suggest that schizotypal personality disorder is transmitted genetically, at least to some degree (see Nigg & Goldsmith, 1994; Siever et al., 1995). In addition, schizotypal personality disorder is much more common in the first-degree relatives of people with schizophrenia than in the relatives of either psychiatric or healthy control groups (Kendler et al., 1993). Thus, schizotypal personality disorder is often considered a "mild" form of schizophrenia that is transmitted through similar genetic mechanisms as schizophrenia.

Similarly, some of the nongenetic biological factors implicated in schizophrenia are also present in people with schizotypal personality disorder (see Siever et al., 1995; Weston & Siever, 1993). In particular, people with schizotypal personality disorder show problems in the ability to sustain attention on cognitive tasks and deficits in involuntary control of attention similar to those seen in people with schizophrenia (Siever et al., 1990). People with schizotypal personality disorder also tend to show low levels of platelet monoamine oxidase, which could increase levels of dopamine in the brain, and higher levels of homovanillic acid, the major metabolite of dopamine (Baron, Perlman, & Levitt, 1980; Siever et al., 1990). Thus, like people with schizophrenia, people with schizotypal personality disorder may have abnormally high levels of dopamine in their brains. Finally, schizotypal patients show increases in the ventricular regions of the brain, as do schizophrenic patients.

There is little in the psychoanalytic or cognitive theories about schizotypal personality disorder. Perhaps psychological theories have not paid much attention to this disorder because it is so closely tied to schizophrenia, which appears to have strong biological roots, and because it was not added as a diagnostic category to the DSM until relatively recently.

Treatment for Schizotypal Personality Disorder

Schizotypal personality disorder is most often treated with the same neuroleptic drugs as is schizophrenia, such as haloperidol and thiothixene (see Siever et al., 1995). As in schizophrenia, these drugs appear to relieve psychoticlike symptoms, including the schizotypal person's ideas of reference, magical thinking, and illusions. Antidepressants are sometimes used to help people with schizotypal personality disorder who are experiencing significant distress.

Although there are few psychological theories of schizotypal personality disorder, psychological therapies have been developed to help these people overcome some of their symptoms. In psychotherapy, it is especially important for therapists to establish good relationships with schizotypal clients because these clients typically have few close relationships and tend to be paranoid (Beck & Freeman, 1990). The next step in therapy is to help schizotypal clients increase social contacts and learn socially appropriate behaviors through social skills training. Group therapy may be especially helpful in increasing clients' social skills. The crucial component of cognitive therapy with schizotypal clients is teaching them to look for objective evidence in the environment for their thoughts and to disregard bizarre thoughts. For example, a client who often thought that he was not real would be taught to identify that thought as bizarre and to discount the thought when it occurred rather than taking it seriously and acting upon it.

Summing Up The Odd-Eccentric Personality Disorders

- People with the odd-eccentric personality disorders—paranoid, schizoid, and schizotypal personality disorders—have odd thought processes, emotional reactions, and behaviors similar to those of people with schizophrenia, but they retain their grasp on reality.
- People with paranoid personality disorder are chronically suspicious of others but maintain their grasp on reality.
- People with schizoid personality disorder are emotionally cold and distant from others and have great trouble forming interpersonal relationships.
- People with schizotypal personality disorders have a variety of odd beliefs and perceptual experiences but also maintain their grasp on relaity.
- These personality disorders, especially schizotypal personality disorder, have been linked to familial histories of schizophrenia and some of the biological abnormalities of schizophrenia.
- People with these disorders tend not to seek treatment, but when they do, therapists pay close attention to their relationships with them and help them learn to reality-test their unusual thinking.
- Antipsychotics may help schizotypal clients reduce their odd thinking.

The Dramatic-Emotional Personality Disorders

dramatic-emotional personality disorders
category including antisocial, borderline, narcissistic, and histrionic personality disorders that is characterized by dramatic and impulsive behaviors that are maladaptive and dangerous

People with the **dramatic-emotional personality disorders** tend to engage in behaviors that are dramatic and impulsive and often show little regard for their own safety or the safety of others. Two of the disorders in this cluster, antisocial personality disorder and borderline personality disorder, have been the focus of a great deal of research, whereas the other two, narcissistic personality disorder and histrionic personality disorder, have not.

Antisocial Personality Disorder

antisocial personality disorder
pervasive pattern of criminal, impulsive, callous, and/or ruthless behavior, predicated upon disregard for the rights of others and an absence of respect for social norms

Antisocial personality disorder has been recognized under various names as a serious disorder for over two centuries (Sher & Trull, 1994). Pritchard (1837) used the term *moral insanity* to describe people who seemed to have no concern for the rights of others and little self-control but who were not insane, in that they had not lost touch with reality. Later, in 1891, Koch applied the term *psychopathic* to the same individuals. Subsequent writers in the late nineteenth and early twentieth centuries often applied the term *psychopath* to anyone who had a severely maladaptive personality. Today, the label *psychopath* is not part of the official DSM nomenclature, but it is used loosely to refer to people with anti-social personality disorder.

The key features of antisocial personality disorder are an impairment in the ability to form positive relationships with others and a tendency to engage in behaviors that violate basic social norms and values. People with this disorder are cold and callous, gaining pleasure by competing with and humiliating everyone and anyone. They can be cruel and malicious. They often insist on being seen as faultless and are dogmatic in their opinions. However, when they need to, people with antisocial personality disorder may act gracious and cheerful, until they get what they want. They then may revert to being brash and arrogant.

People with antisocial personality disorder tend to have low tolerance for frustration and often act impetuously and impulsively. They often take chances and seek thrills with no concern for danger. They seem unable to anticipate the implications of their behaviors for themselves or others. They are easily bored and restless, unable to endure the tedium of routine or to persist at the day-to-day responsibilities of marriage or a job (Millon, 1981).

A pioneer in the study of people with antisocial personalities, Hervey Cleckley, noted that although these people often ended up in prisons or dead, many of them became successful businesspeople and professionals (see Cleckley, 1941). He suggested that the difference between these successful antisocial personalities and those psychopaths who end up in jail is that the successful ones are better able to maintain an outward appearance of being normal, perhaps because they have superior intelligence and can put on a "mask of sanity" and superficial social charm in order to achieve their goals.

One person with antisocial personality disorder, Gary Gilmore, was eventually sentenced to death for murders he committed. Gilmore became famous because he refused to appeal his death sentence and insisted that it be carried out without delay. He was executed on January 17, 1977, the first person to be executed in the United States since 1966. His life was depicted in *The Executioner's Song* written by Norman Mailer. The following is from a psychologist's evaluation of Gilmore shortly after he was arrested for murder in 1976.

Case Study • The patient grew up in a family that consisted of his father, his mother, and a brother one year older than the patient. He indicated that his family was "a typical family, but there wasn't much closeness in it. I was always left to fend for myself and I got in trouble very early."

Though the patient was obviously bright, he received poor grades in school because "I just wasn't interested." He started "sluffing" school at a young age and at least on two different occasions was temporarily suspended for his truancy and for alleged thefts from his schoolmates. At the age of 14 he was sent to a youth correctional center for stealing a car and was at the reform school for 18 months. Almost immediately after being released, he started burglarizing and was in the county jail on three different occasions, the last two for 1 year each time.

When Gilmore was 20 years of age, he was sent to Oregon State Penitentiary for 18 months for burglary and robbery. Following this, he spent 2 years in a city jail for a "long string of traffic offenses including reckless driving and drunk driving. I started drinking before I was 10 years old." In prison, Gilmore gained a reputation for brutality to other inmates and was known as "the enforcer" and "hammerhead." He also was known as a talented artist and tattoo expert. On a number of occasions, he tattooed obscene words on the backs and forearms of ineffectual and disliked inmates: "I thought it was a good way to get back at the snitches. I would tattoo them on their bodies where they could not watch what I was doing. It wasn't until they looked at their tattoos in the mirror that they saw what I had done to them."

After he was released from jail, he committed armed robbery several times within the next month. He was then sent to Oregon State Penitentiary where he stayed for 11 years and then was transferred to a federal prison in Illinois, where he stayed for another year and a half.

Gilmore indicated he has used almost all types of illicit drugs including heroin, various types of amphetamines, cocaine, and psychedelics. In more recent years, he quit using drugs, partly because they were not as available in prison, and just smoked marijuana. He drank whenever he had the opportunity in prison but said that since he was released he has mainly been drinking just beer. . . .

He was released from prison in April of 1976 and came to Utah to work with his uncle in a shoe repair shop. This did not turn out well, so he briefly tried painting signs and just before his arrest was insulating houses.

He met a woman on May 13 and the very next day moved in with her. He indicated that this was "probably the first close relationship that I ever had with anyone. I just didn't know how to respond to her for any length of time. I was very insensitive to her. I am more accustomed to violence and fighting. I was thoughtless in the way I treated her. She didn't like me to drink and even offered to quit smoking if I would quit drinking, but I never did quit drinking. Also, her two children bugged me and sometimes I would get angry at them and slap them because they were so noisy. And I always ended up in a fight with some other guy whenever we went to a party."

On July 19, just before midnight, "I pulled up near a gas station. I told the service station guy to give me all of his money. I then took him to the bathroom and told him to kneel down and then I shot him in the head twice. The guy didn't give me any trouble but I just felt like I had to do it."

The very next morning, Gilmore left his car at a service station for minor repairs and walked to a motel.

"I went in and told the guy to give me the money. I told him to lay on the floor and then I shot him. I then walked out and was carrying the cash drawer with me. I took the money and threw the cash drawer in a bush and I tried to push the gun in the bush, too. But as I was pushing it in the bush, it went off and that's how come I was shot in the arm. It seems like things have always gone bad for me. It seems like I've always done dumb things that just caused trouble for me. I remember when I was a boy I would feel like I had to do things like sit on a railroad track until just before the train came and then I would dash off. Or I would put my finger over the end of a BB gun and pull the trigger to see if a BB was really in it. Sometimes I would stick my finger in water and then put my finger in a light socket to see if it would really shock me."

Despite Gilmore's anger at being locked up, he was quite willing to tell me the events of his life and the circumstances that led up to his being charged with the murders. Though he said he was sorry that he killed the two victims, it was without depth of feeling, and he appeared actually to be indifferent. (Spitzer et al., 1983, pp. 66–68)

Killer Gary Gilmore had a long history of impulsive behaviors that violated the fundamental rights of others.

Antisocial personality disorder is one of the most common personality disorders, with a lifetime prevalence of between 2.3 and 3.2 percent (Weissman, 1993). Men are five times more likely than women to be diagnosed with this disorder; there are no ethnic/racial differences in rates of diagnosis (Fabrega et al., 1991). People with this personality disorder are somewhat more likely than people with the other personality disorders to have low levels of education (Fabrega et al., 1991).

Like Gilmore, people with antisocial personality disorder are at high risk for substance abuse. One study of persons seeking therapy found that 40 percent of those with antisocial personality disorder also qualified for the diagnosis of substance abuse (Fabrega et al., 1991). People with this disorder are also at somewhat increased risk for suicide attempts (particularly females with the disorder) and for violent death (Perry, 1993).

The tendency to engage in antisocial behaviors is one of the most stable personality characteristics (Perry, 1993). People with antisocial personality disorder typically have shown a disregard for societal norms and a tendency for antisocial behavior since child-

Antisocial tendencies diminish with age, leading some experts to argue that older inmates are probably no threat to society.

hood, and most would have been diagnosed with conduct disorder as children. There is a tendency, however, for their antisocial behavior to diminish as they become older adults. This may be due to some kind of psychological or biological maturation process. Or many people with this disorder may simply be jailed or constrained by society in some other way from acting out their antisocial tendencies.

 Some people argue that criminals who have been in jail for a very long time and are now elderly should be released, even if they have not finished serving their sentences, because the statistics suggest they will have "outgrown" their antisocial tendencies. How do you feel about this argument?

Theories of Antisocial Personality Disorder

There is substantial support for a genetic influence on antisocial behaviors, particularly criminal behaviors (Nigg & Goldsmith, 1994; Robins, 1991). Twin studies find that the concordance rate for criminal behaviors is near 50 percent in MZ twins, compared to 20 percent or lower in DZ twins (Gottesman & Goldsmith, in press; Rutter et al., 1990). Adoption studies find that the criminal records of adopted sons are more similar to the records of their biological fathers than to those of their adoptive fathers (Cloninger & Gottesman, 1987; Mednick, Reznick, Hocevan, & Baker, 1987). Family history studies show that family members of people with antisocial personality disorder show increased rates of this disorder, as well as increased rates of alcoholism and criminal activity (Perry, 1993).

Animal studies suggest that aggressive and impulsive behaviors are linked to low levels of serotonin, leading to the suggestion that people with antisocial personality disorder may also have low levels of serotonin (Coccaro, 1993). Although there is some evidence that impulsiveness and irritability are correlated with low levels of serotonin in humans, the importance of serotonin in the development of antisocial personality disorder is not yet clear.

Many studies have investigated the hypothesis that persons with antisocial personality disorder show low levels of arousability, which then may lead them to seek stimulation and sensation through impulsive and dangerous acts. Low arousability may also make it more difficult for these people to learn from punishment because they will not experience punishment to be as aversive as most people, and they will not be anxious in anticipation of punishment. The results of studies on the arousability of people with antisocial personality disorder have been mixed, however (see Morey, 1993).

One characteristic that people with antisocial personality disorder do tend to show consistently is a difficulty in inhibiting impulsive behaviors (Morey, 1993; Sher & Trull,

Harsh, inconsistent, and negligent parenting can increase chances that a child will develop antisocial behaviors.

1994). Research with children who show antisocial tendencies indicates that a significant percentage, perhaps the majority, have an attention deficit hyperactivity disorder, which involves significant problems with inhibiting impulsive behaviors and with maintaining attention (see Chapter 9). The disruptive behavior of these children leads to frequent punishments and to rejection by peers, teachers, and other adults. These children then become even more disruptive and some become overtly aggressive and antisocial in their behaviors and attitudes. Thus, at least some adults with antisocial personality disorder may have lifelong problems with attentional deficits and hyperactivity, which then contribute to lifelong problems with controlling their behaviors.

Much of the empirical research on the social and personality factors that contribute to antisocial behavior has been conducted with children and is reviewed in detail in the section on children with conduct disorders in Chapter 9. Briefly, children with antisocial tendencies often come from homes in which they have experienced harsh and inconsistent parenting (Patterson, Barbara, & Ramsey, 1989). The parents of these children alternate between being neglectful and being hostile and violent toward their children. These children learn ways of thinking about the world that seem to promote antisocial behavior (Crick & Dodge, 1994). They enter social interactions with the assumption that other children will be aggressive toward them, and interpret the actions of their peers in line with this assumption. As a result, they are quick to engage in aggressive behaviors toward others.

Treatments for Antisocial Personality Disorder

People with antisocial personality disorder do not tend to believe they need treatment. They may submit to therapy when forced to because of marital discord, work conflicts, or incarceration. However, they are prone to blaming others for their current situations rather than accepting responsibility for their actions. As a result, many clinicians do not hold much hope for effectively treating persons with this disorder through psychotherapy (Millon, 1981).

Lithium has been successfully used to control impulsive/aggressive behaviors in people with antisocial personality disorders (Sheard, Marini, Bridges, & Wagner, 1976). More recently, based on the evidence for low levels of serotonin in some animals prone to impulsive and aggressive behavior, researchers have been suggesting the use of drugs that inhibit the reuptake of serotonin into the synapse, such as fluoxetine (Coccaro, 1993). The efficacy of these drugs in treating antisocial personality disorder is not clear yet. Many theorists believe that the only successful cure for antisocial behavior is age.

 If a criminal could prove he has antisocial personality disorder, do you think this should absolve him in any way from responsibility for his criminal acts?

Borderline Personality Disorder

In the following passage, a clinician describes her introduction to a woman later diagnosed with **borderline personality disorder** (adapted from Layton, 1995, pp. 35–36).

> My first appointment with my new client, a referral from a college counseling center, was still several weeks away when I got a message on my answering machine asking me to call her in Minnesota, where she was visiting family. She was in anguish about leaving behind her therapist at the college counseling center and coming to see me. She wanted to know, Was she *that* crazy? I had never even met Vicki face to face, and yet already she had called me, wanting some kind of stability and solace. Here I was, with only the barest notion of what her life was like, not knowing anything of her history, only a wisp of a telephone call to connect the two of us, but in Vicki's heart, I was already on the job.
>
> And I found myself with two distinct reactions, both of which were to continue from that time on to swirl around and shape my work with her: one was a sort of withdrawing shock at how intensely important I already was to Vicki, and the other was a sturdy admiration for this intensity, for this looking to grab and hold on.
>
> Vicki had only been in treatment for a few months at the university counseling center when she revealed to her counselor, Peg, that she often felt so hopeless and so numb that she sometimes cut her leg with scissors. Peg was a trainee, and she realized that she would be unable—both because of the policies of the counseling center and the time limits of her placement there—to provide the long-term relationship she felt Vicki needed. So Peg referred Vicki to me.
>
> Vicki spent her first few months with me perseverating over her attachment to Peg and her panic at her loss. She circled and circled over the events, sometimes finding fresh insults, sometimes reopening old wounds. Anyone who might have overhead Vicki at this time would have thought her reactions were exaggerated, melodramatic, out of sync with the precipitating events. "Get a grip!" they might have said, "Don't be such a victim!" At times, in the beginning of my work with Vicki, I thought as much myself.
>
> But I had worked with enough people in distress to notice something different about the persistent quality of Vicki's suffering. Neither comfort nor humor nor interpretation nor limit setting seemed to be what she needed, and sometimes any intervention at all just inflamed her pain. Even though she seemed profoundly embarrassed to be grinding on this way, in full view of another human being, she still couldn't shift gears. "Stupid" was her word for it, "I know this is stupid, but . . ."
>
> Vicki was also bulimic and heartbreakingly uncertain about who she was, including her sense of herself as a woman. She had marked shifts of mood, including dissociative states. She had chronic and debilitating feelings of emptiness and paralyzing numbness, during which she could only crawl under the covers of her bed and hide. On these days, she was sometimes driven to mutilate her thighs with scissors. Although highly accomplished as a medical student and researcher who had garnered many grants and fellowships, she would sometimes panic and shut down in the middle of a project, creating unbearable pressures on herself to finish the work. While she longed for intimacy and friendship, she was disablingly shy around men.

Vicki's painful symptoms represent some of the benchmarks of borderline personality disorder: out-of-control emotions that cannot be smoothed, a hypersensitivity to abandonment, a tendency to cling too tightly to other people, and a history of hurting oneself.

Lability is a key feature of borderline personality disorder. The *mood* of people with borderline personality disorder is labile, with bouts of severe depression, anxiety, or anger seeming to arise frequently and often without good reason. The *self-concept* of these people is labile, with periods of extreme self-doubt and periods of grandiose self-importance.

borderline personality disorder syndrome characterized by rapidly shifting and unstable mood, self-concept, and interpersonal relationships as well as impulsive behavior and transient dissociative states

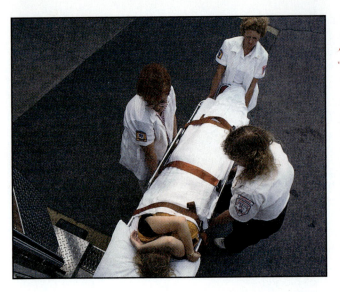
Suicide attempts and self mutilation are common among people with borderline personality disorder.

Their *interpersonal relationships* are extremely labile, and these people can switch from idealizing others to despising them without provocation. Vicki also experienced the desperate emptiness than many people with borderline personality disorder describe. This emptiness leads them to cling to new acquaintances or therapists in hopes that they will fill the tremendous void they experience in themselves. They are nearly paranoid about abandonment and misinterpret other people's innocent actions as abandonment or rejection. For example, if a therapist has to cancel an appointment because she is ill, a client with borderline personality disorder might interpret this as a rejection by the therapist and become extremely depressed or angry. Along with lability of mood, self-concept, and interpersonal relationships comes a tendency toward impulsive self-damaging behaviors, including self-multilating behaviors and suicidal behavior. Vicki's self-mutilating behavior was to cut her thighs with scissors. Finally, people with borderline personality disorder are prone to transient dissociative states, in which they feel unreal, lose track of time, and may even forget who they are.

The variety of symptoms that make up the criteria for diagnosis of borderline personality disorder reflects, to some extent, the complexity of this disorder. The manifestation of this disorder can be quite different from one person to the next and from one day to the next within any one person. The varied list of symptoms also reflects the difficulty that clinicians have had in agreeing on a conceptualization of this disorder (Gunderson, Zanarini, & Kisiel, 1995). The term *borderline* has been used loosely for many years to refer to people who could not be fit easily into existing diagnoses of emotional disorders or psychotic disorders and who were extremely difficult to treat (Millon, 1981). One result of the variety of symptoms listed in the diagnostic criteria for the disorder is that there is a great deal of overlap between the borderline diagnosis and several of the other personality disorders, including paranoid, antisocial, narcissistic, histrionic, and schizotypal personality disorders (Nurnberg, Raskin, Livine, & Pollack, 1991). Indeed, the majority of persons diagnosed with borderline personality disorder will also meet the diagnostic criteria for at least one other personality disorder.

People with borderline personality disorder also tend to receive diagnoses of one of the acute disorders, including substance abuse, depression, and generalized anxiety disorder; simple phobias; agoraphobia; post-traumatic stress disorder; panic disorder; or somatization disoder (Fabrega et al., 1991; Weissman, 1993). About 6 percent of people with this disorder die by suicide (see Perry, 1993). The greatest risk of suicide appears to be in the first year or two after people are diagnosed with borderline personality disorder. This may be because people are often not diagnosed with this disorder until a crisis brings them to the attention of the mental health system.

Epidemiological studies suggest that the lifetime prevalence of borderline personality disorder is between 1 and 2 percent (Weissman, 1993). In clinical settings, borderline personality disorder is much more often diagnosed in women than in men and somewhat more commonly diagnosed in people of color than in whites and in people in lower socioeconomic classes than in other classes (Fabrega et al., 1991; Swartz et al., 1990). People with this disorder are high users of outpatient mental health services; one community study found that 50 percent had used some form of mental health service in the past 6 months (Swartz et al., 1990).

Theories of Borderline Personality Disorder

Several family history studies of borderline personality disorder have been conducted, and the evidence that this specific disorder is transmitted genetically is mixed (Dahl, 1993; Nigg & Goldsmith, 1994). There are high rates of mood disorders in the families of persons diagnosed with borderline personality disorder, however (Kendler et al., 1993). People with borderline personality disorder also show some of the same sleep abnormalities as do people with mood disorders (see Weston & Siever, 1993). Most researchers do not suggest that borderline personality disorder is simply a type of affective disorder, but there clearly are links between the two disorders.

Impulsive behaviors in people with borderline personality disorder are correlated with low levels of serotonin (see Weston & Siever, 1993). Recall that impulsive behaviors in people with antisocial personality disorder have also been linked to low serotonin levels. This suggests that low serotonin is not associated with one diagnostic category but with the category of impulsive behaviors.

Psychoanalytic theorists, particularly those in the objects relations school (see Chapter 3), have been extremely interested in borderline personality disorder (see Kernberg, 1979; Klein, 1952). They suggest that persons with this disorder have just enough reality-testing to retain a foothold in the real world but rely on primitive defenses such as denial. In addition, the borderline person has very poorly developed views of the self and others, stemming from poor early relationships with caregivers. The early caregivers of people with borderline personality disorder are characterized as deriving much gratification from the children's dependence on them early in life. Thus, they do not encourage the children to develop separate senses of self and may punish their attempts at individuation and separation. As a result, the children never learn to fully differentiate their views of themselves and their views of others. This makes them extremely reactive to others' opinions of them and to the possibility of being abandoned by others. When they perceive others as rejecting them, they reject themselves and may engage in self-punishment or self-mutilation. They also have never been able to integrate the positive and negative qualities of either their self-concept or their concept of others, because their early caregivers were comforting and rewarding when they remained dependent and compliant toward them but hostile and rejecting when they tried to individuate from them. They tend to see themselves and other people as either "all good" or "all bad" and vacillate between these two views. This process is referred to as *splitting*. The lability in borderline persons' emotions and interpersonal relationships is due to splitting—their emotions and their perspectives on their interpersonal relationships reflect their vacillation between the "all good" and the "all bad" self or other.

Theodore Millon (1981) argues that people with borderline personality disorder have a fundamental deficit in self-identity, but he attributes this deficit to the intersection of several biological, psychological, and sociological factors rather than only to the individual's early relationships with caregivers. He suggests that the borderline person's lack of a clear sense of self impedes the development of consistent and realistic goals, which in turn results in poorly controlled impulses and a drifting through life. People with this disorder become dependent on others for reassurance and self-worth and very sensitive to signs of possible abandonment by their sources of support. Still, they experience intense conflict regarding their dependency needs. They know they can never entirely trust others or gain the security that they need and harbor intense anger toward others for not fulfilling their needs. Sometimes this anger is expressed directly toward others, but because they are terrified of separation from others and often feel guilt over past attempts at self-assertion and independence, they often turn their anger against themselves in self-criticism and sometimes self-destruction.

Marcia Linehan (1987) argues that people with borderline personality disorder have a deficit in the ability to regulate their emotions, which is probably physiologically based. Their extreme emotional reactions to situations lead to their impulsive actions. In addition, borderline persons have histories of significant others discounting and criticizing their emotional experiences, which make it even harder for them to learn appropriate emotion-regulation skills and to understand and accept their emotional reactions to events. Borderline persons come to rely on others to help them cope with difficult situations but do not have enough self-confidence to ask for help from others in mature ways. Thus, they become manipulative and indirect in trying to gain support from others.

Finally, recent research suggests that many, but not all, persons with borderline personality disorder have histories of physical and sexual abuse during childhood (Coons, 1994). Vicki is one of these people, as she describes here (Layton, 1995, p. 38):

Children who are chronically abused physically or emotionally may be at increased risk for borderline personality disorder.

I remember the night I didn't finish the dishes before I went to bed. My father had been out drinking and when he came in, he saw the frying pan soaking in the sink. My bedroom door flew open, and the doorknob cracked against the wall. He told me to "GET UP!" In a flash I went from sleep to vigilance to terror. I thought this was it, the night we would die. I stood up, and as he berated me, I began to shrink, shrink back inside of myself to protect that little bit of self I had from destruction. He told me to "GET OUT THERE!" The tone in his voice sounded as though he were talking to something so vile that disposing of it would be doing everyone a favor. I stood there frozen, waiting for him to move out of the doorway.

He did not move. He seemed to experience excitement as I submitted to his power, committing the most powerless act walking into the hands of one's executor. All of the life drained from me. My body shook uncontrollably. I felt empty, numb. I walked toward the door. When I got close enough, he knocked me to the ground but told me to get up. I got up. He knocked me down. I can't remember how long this went on. I remember crawling. He would stand on my nightgown while I was trying to get up. Again he would knock me down, beating, punching. I can't remember getting into the kitchen: Everything seemed surreal, but somehow I managed.

While I stood at the sink scrubbing the pan, he pressed his chest up against my shoulder and breathed into my face. Out of the corner of my eye I could see his nostrils flare with rage, as if to let me know that he was deciding if I would live or die. I remember watching my hand make circles in the pan. I was frozen, mesmerized. I couldn't stop, the risk was too great. To this day, I don't know how the pan got in the dish rack. When I was finished, he would not move out of my way, as if he were thrilled at my terror as I chanced getting away. Back in my bed, I moaned—deep, hollow sounds, my body throbbing. I finally rocked myself to sleep, softly calling, "Mommy, Mommy." She never came. The next morning as I left for school, she said, "I told you not to leave any dishes."

Abuse like this could lead to the problems in self-concept that most theorists suggest is at the core of this disorder.

Treatment for Borderline Personality Disorder

Drug treatments for persons with borderline personality disorder have focused on reducing their symptoms of anxiety and depression through antianxiety drugs and antidepressants and on controlling their impulsive behaviors with serotonin reuptake inhibitors (Coccaro, 1993). The effectiveness of these drugs, even in the short term, is not yet clear. Some studies of antidepressants find that people with borderline personality disorder do not improve and some actually become worse on tricyclic antidepressants (Links, Steiner, Boiago, & Irwin, 1990; Soloff , George, Nathan, & Schulz, 1989). Although the serotonin reuptake inhibitor fluoxetine appears to be effective in treating depressed mood and reducing impulsive behaviors in uncontrolled trials of borderline personality disorder, double-blind placebo-controlled studies have not yet been done (Coccaro, 1993).

Psychodynamic treatment for people with borderline personality disorder involves helping clients clarify feelings, confronting clients with their tendency to split images of the self and other, and interpreting clients' transference relationships with therapists (Kernberg, 1989). Many people wtih borderline personality disorder will at times become extremely angry toward their therapists, as they move from idealizing to devaluing them. Therapists can use such times to help clients understand their splitting defenses and to set clear limits on the clients' behaviors. Clients may also be taught more adaptive means of solving everyday problems so that the world does not appear so overwhelming. Self-destructive tendencies are addressed, with therapists helping clients identify the feelings leading to these acts and develop healthy ways of coping with these feelings.

Cognitive behavior therapies focus on helping clients gain a more realistic and positive sense of self, learn adaptive skills for solving problems and regulating emotions, and correct dichotomous thinking (Beck & Freeman, 1990; Linehan, 1987; Millon, 1981). Therapists will teach clients to monitor self-disparaging thoughts and black-or-white evaluations of people and situations and to challenge these thoughts and evaluations. Therapists will also help clients learn appropriate assertiveness skills for close relationships so that they can express their needs and feelings in a mature manner. Clients may learn how to control impulsive behavior by monitoring the situations most likely to lead to such behaviors and learning alternative ways to handle such situations. One study found that cognitive-behavioral therapy significantly reduced suicidal behaviors and the need for hospitalization in 44 women with severe borderline personality disorder (Linehan, Armstrong, Svarez, & Allmon, 1991).

Therapists from all different theoretical perspectives acknowledge the importance of remaining aware of the borderline client's tendency either to idealize a therapist or to completely reject a therapist and of maintaining some emotional distance from the client's effusive praise or damning criticisms. The borderline client finds it very difficult to trust anyone, including a therapist, and is hypersensitive to signs of rejection. It is very important for the therapist to be honest, straightforward, and clear in communicating with the borderline client and to avoid or quickly clarify any misunderstandings that arise in the therapeutic relationship. The therapist must also set limits on the client's behaviors, particularly aggressive behaviors during therapy sessions or frequent requests for special treatment. Change can be slow with borderline clients, and the drop-out rate of borderline clients from therapy is on the order of 60 percent (Shea, 1993).

Given the family dynamics that may contribute to the development of borderline personality disorder, do you think family therapy would be helpful in treating people with this disorder? Or might they do better in a therapy that did not include other family members?

Histrionic Personality Disorder

Histrionic personality disorder shares features with borderline personality disorder, including rapidly shifting emotions and intense and unstable relationships. However, whereas people with borderline personality disorder are often self-effacing in an attempt to win favor from others, people with histrionic personality disorder always want to be the center of attention. They pursue the attention of others by being highly dramatic, being overtly seductive, and emphasizing the positive qualities of their physical appearance. They tend to speak in global terms. Others see them as self-centered and shallow, unable to delay gratification, demanding and overly dependent. Debbie is a person diagnosed with histrionic personality disorder (Beck & Freeman, 1990, pp. 211–212):

histrionic personality disorder syndrome marked by rapidly shifting moods, unstable relationships, and an intense need for attention and approval, which is sought by means of overly dramatic behavior, seductiveness, and dependence

Case Study • Debbie was a 26-year-old woman who worked as a salesclerk in a trendy clothing store and who sought therapy for panic disorder with agoraphobia. She dressed flamboyantly, with an elaborate and dramatic hairdo. Her appearance was especially striking, since she was quite short (under 5 feet tall) and at least 75 pounds overweight. She wore sunglasses indoors throughout the evaluation and constantly fiddled with them, taking them on and off nervously and waving them to emphasize a point. She cried loudly and dramatically at various points in the interview, going through large numbers of tissue. She continually asked for reassurance. ("Will I be OK?" "Can I get over this?") She talked nonstop throughout the evaluation. When gently interrupted by the evaluator, she was very apologetic, laughing and saying, "I know I talk too much"; yet she continued to do so throughout the session.

Flamboyance is one symptom of histrionic personality disorder.

The lifetime prevalence of histrionic personality disorder is between 1.3 and 2.1 percent, and the vast majority of persons diagnosed with this disorder are women (Weissman, 1993). Persons with this disorder are more likely to be separated or divorced than married. They tend to make more medical visits than the average person, and there is an increased rate of suicide gestures and threats in this group (Nestadt, Romanoski, Chahal, & Merchant, 1990). Persons with this disorder most often seek treatment for depression or anxiety (Fabrega et al., 1991).

Theories of Histrionic Personality Disorder

Family history studies indicate that histrionic personality disorder clusters in families along with borderline personality disorder, antisocial personality disorder, and somatization disorder (see Dahl, 1993). It is unclear whether these disorders are genetically related or the results of processes within the family or environment.

Psychodynamic theorists see this disorder as the result of deep dependency needs and repression of emotions, stemming from poor resolution of either the oral stage or the Oedipal stage (Fenichel, 1945; Kernberg, 1975; Millon, 1981; Reich, 1945). Attention-seeking results from the need for approval from others. The shallowness of thought and emotional involvement with others reflects the histrionic person's repression of her own feelings and needs.

Cognitive theories suggest that the underlying assumption driving the histrionic person's behavior is, "I am inadequate and unable to handle life on my own" (Beck & Freeman, 1990). Although this assumption is shared by persons with other disorders, particularly depression, the histrionic person responds to this assumption differently from persons with other disorders. Specifically, she works to get other people to care for her by seeking their attention and approval.

Theodore Millon (1981) argues that histrionic adults may have been born with a high level of energy and need for stimulation. If they were exposed to a series of brief, highly charged, and irregular sources of stimulation, such as a succession of different caretakers in infancy, they may have developed an expectation or need for short, concentrated periods of stimulus from a variety of people. In other words, they may have developed a pattern of intense stimulation-seeking, reliance on others for stimulation, and intolerance for boredom. Their dramatic behaviors and emotional shallowness may have evolved from this pattern. In addition, histrionic people may have learned that parental approval was contingent on some sort of performance, such as "looking pretty" or performing well in some artistic endeavor. They seldom received negative reinforcement from their parents but had to "do something" to get their parents' attention and receive praise.

If Theodore Millon's theory of the development of histrionic personality disorder is correct, would you expect that young people growing up in the last 10 years would be more or less prone to histrionic personality disorder than were their parents and grandparents? Why?

Treatment for Histrionic Personality Disorder

Psychodynamic treatments focus on uncovering histrionic persons' repressed emotions and needs and helping them express these emotions and needs in more socially appropriate ways. Cognitive therapy focuses on identifying histrionic people's assumptions that they cannot function on their own and helping them formulate goals and plans for their lives that do not rely on the approval of others (Beck & Freeman, 1990). Therapists attempt to help clients tone down their dramatic evaluations of situations by challenging these evaluations and suggesting more reasonable evaluations.

Narcissistic Personality Disorder

The characteristics of **narcissistic personality disorder** appear similar to the characteristics of histrionic personality disorder. In both disorders, individuals act in dramatic and grandiose manners, seek admiration from others, and are shallow in their emotional expressions and relationships with others. However, whereas people with histrionic personality disorder look to others for approval, persons with narcissistic personality disorder rely on their own self-evaluations and see dependency on others as weak and dangerous. They are preoccupied with thoughts of their own self-importance and with fantasies of power and success and view themselves as above most others. In interpersonal relationships, they make unreasonable demands for others to follow their wishes, ignore the needs and wants of others, exploit others to gain power, and are arrogant and demeaning.

narcissistic personality disorder syndrome marked by grandiose thoughts and feelings of one's own worth as well as an obliviousness to others' needs and an exploitive, arrogant demeanor

Case Study • David was an attorney in his early 40s when he sought treatment for depressed mood. He cited business and marital problems as the source of his distress and wondered if he was having a midlife crisis.

David appeared to be an outgoing man who paid meticulous attention to his appearance. He made a point of asking for the therapist's admiration of his new designer suit, his winter tan, and his new foreign convertible. He also asked the therapist what kind of car he drove and how many VIP clients he dealt with. David wanted to make sure that he was dealing with someone who was the best in the business. But he was apprehensive of anyone important seeing him at the therapist's office. . . .

David had grown up in a comfortable suburb of a large city, the oldest of three children and the only son of a successful businessman and a former secretary. Always known to have a bit of a temper, David usually provoked his parents and his sisters into giving in to his wishes. Even if they didn't give in to his demands, he reported that he usually went ahead and did what he wanted anyway. David spoke of being an "ace" student and a "super" athlete but could not provide any details that would validate a superior performance in these areas.

David recollected that he had his pick of girlfriends, as most women were "thrilled" to have a date with him. His strategy was to act quite cool initially; nevertheless, he had a pattern of short-lived, intense involvements. If a girl broke off a relationship before he did or if she even showed some interest in someone else, he was apt to respond with a temper tantrum. When he was 17, he slapped a girlfriend for dating another boy, causing some facial bruises . . . she threatened to sue David, and he was stunned that she had the nerve to question his anger.

David went to college, fantasizing about being famous in a high-profile career. He majored in communications, planning to go on to law school and eventually into politics. He met his first wife during college, the year she was the university homecoming queen. They married shortly after their joint graduation. He then went on to law school, and she went to work to support the couple.

During law school, David became a workaholic, fueled by fantasies of brilliant work and international recognition. He spent minimal time with his wife and, after their son was born, even less time with either of them. At the same time, he continued a string of extramarital affairs, mostly brief sexual encounters. He spoke of his wife in an annoyed, devaluing way, complaining about how she just did not live up to his expectations. He waited until he felt reasonably secure in his first job so that he could let go of her financial support and then he sought a divorce. He continued to see his son occasionally, but he rarely paid his stipulated child support.

After his divorce, David decided that he was totally free to just please himself. He loved spending all his money on himself, and he lavishly decorated his condominium and bought an attention-getting wardrobe. He constantly sought the companionship of attractive women. He was very successful at making initial contacts and getting dates, but he rarely found anyone good enough to date more than once or twice. Sometimes he played sexual games to amuse himself, such as seeing how fast he could make sexual contact or how many women would agree to have sex with him. He was somewhat bewildered by the fact that he did not really feel triumphant when he finally managed to "score" five women in one day. David began to long for the convenience and the attention that a single, steady mate could provide. So he screened his dates with a shopping list of requirements, and he eventually married Susan, the daughter of a well-known politician. . . .

David felt worse at work when he had to do routine work and thought that such work was beneath him. He would think about how he really deserved better and how he was not getting appropriate recognition for his talents and aptitudes. Consultations with colleagues often triggered thoughts of their failure to give him appropriate recognition or their "nerve" in saying something even marginally critical about him. David believed that because he was "different" from other people, they had no right to criticize him. But he had every right to criticize others. He also believed that other people were weak and needed contact with someone like him in order to bring direction or pleasure into their lives. He saw no problem in taking advantage of other people if they were "stupid" enough to allow him to do so.

David admitted that the times he felt the worst about his wife, he was usually focusing on some negative aspect of her looks or her intelligence. Typically, he was thinking about her not being worthy of him. Whenever Susan made requests of him, he was apt to become irritated with her. He thought that she was lucky to have him and therefore did not really have the right to make demands. He knew that there would be plenty of other, prettier women who would be glad to cater to his needs.

David felt better when someone flattered him; when he was in a group social situation where he could easily grab the center of attention; and when he could fantasize about obtaining a high-level position, being honored for his great talent, or just being fabulously weathy. (adapted from Beck & Freeman, 1990, pp. 245–247)

Narcissists can be extremely successful in societies that reward self-confidence and assertiveness, such as the United States (Millon, 1981). When narcissists grossly overestimate their abilities, however, they can make poor choices in their careers and may experience many failures. In addition, narcissists annoy other people and can alienate the important people in their lives. Narcissists seek treatment most often for depression and for trouble adjusting to life stressors (Fabrega et al., 1991).

Epidemiological studies suggest that narcissistic personality disorder is rare, with a lifetime prevalence of less than 1 percent (Gunderson, Ronningstam, & Smith, 1995; Weissman, 1993). It is more frequently diagnosed in men.

Theories of Narcissistic Personality Disorder

Sigmund Freud (1914) viewed narcissism as a phase that all children pass through before transferring their love for themselves to significant others. Children could become fixated in this narcissistic phase, however, if they experienced caregivers as untrustworthy and decided that they could only rely on themselves or if they had parents who indulged them and instilled in them a grandiose sense of their abilities and worth (see also Horney, 1939). Later psychodynamic writers (Kernberg, 1975; Kohut, 1971) argued that the narcissist actually suffers from low self-esteem and feelings of emptiness and pain as a result of rejection from parents and that narcissistic behaviors are reaction formations against these problems with self-worth.

From the vantage point of social learning theory, Millon (1969) traced the origin of the narcissistic style to unrealistic overvaluation of a child's worth by parents. The child is unable to live up to his parents' evaluations of himself, but he continues to act as if he

People with narcissistic personality disorder take great pride in their appearance, possessions, and status.

is superior to others and to demand that others see him as superior. Similarly, Beck and Freeman (1990) argued that some narcissists develop assumptions about their self-worth that are unrealistically positive as the result of indulgence and overvaluation by significant others during childhood. Other narcissists develop the belief that they are unique or exceptional in reaction to being singled out as "different" from others due to ethnic, racial, or economic status or as a defense against rejection by important people in their lives.

Treatment for Narcissistic Personality Disorder

People with narcissistic personality disorder do not tend to seek treatment, except when they develop depression or are confronted with severe interpersonal problems (Beck et al., 1990). Cognitive techniques can help these clients develop more sensitivity to the needs of others and more realistic expectations of their own abilities (Millon, 1981). Narcissistic clients often do not remain in therapy once their acute symptoms or interpersonal problems decrease, however.

Summing Up | Dramatic-Emotional Personality Disorders

- People with the dramatic-emotional personality disorders—antisocial, borderline, histrionic, and narcissistic personality disorders—have histories of unstable relationships and emotional experiences and of behaving in dramatic and erratic ways.
- People with antisocial personality disorder regularly violate the basic rights of others and often engage in criminal acts.
- Antisocial personality disorder may have strong biological roots but is also associated with harsh and nonsupportive parenting.
- People with borderline personality disorder vacillate between "all good" and "all bad" evaluations of themselves and others.
- People with histrionic and narcissistic personality disorders act in flamboyant manners. People with histrionic personality disorder are overly dependent and solicitious of others, whereas people with narcissistic personality disorder are dismissive of others.
- None of these personality disorders responds consistently well to current treatments.

The Anxious-Fearful Personality Disorders

The **anxious-fearful personality disorders**—avoidant personality disorder, dependent personality disorder, and obsessive-compulsive personality disorder—are all characterized by a chronic sense of anxiety or fearfulness and behaviors intended to ward off feared situations. What is feared is different in each of the three disorders but people with any one of these three disorders are nervous and not terribly happy.

Avoidant Personality Disorder

Avoidant personality disorder has been the focus of more research than have the other two anxious-fearful personality disorders. People with avoidant personality disorder are extremely anxious about being criticized by others and so avoid interactions with others in which there is any possibility of being criticized. They might choose occupations that are socially isolated, such as being park rangers in the wilderness, and avoid situations in which they must interact with people who may not like them. When they must interact with others, people with avoidant personality disorder are restrained and nervous and hypersensitive to signs of being evaluated or criticized.

anxious-fearful personality disorders category including avoidant, dependent, and obsessive-compulsive personality disorders that is characterized by a chronic sense of anxiety or fearfulness and behaviors intended to ward off feared situations

avoidant personality disorder pervasive anxiety, sense of inadequacy, and fear of being criticized that leads to the avoidance of most social interactions with others and to restraint and nervousness in social interactions

People with avoidant personality disorder may choose professions that allow them to avoid other people.

Case Study • A 27-year-old, single, male bookkeeper was referred to a consulting psychologist because of a recent upsurge in anxiety that seemed to begin when a group of new employees was assigned to his office section. He feared that he was going to be fired, though his work was always highly commended. A clique had recently formed in the office, and, though very much wanting to be accepted into this "in group," the patient hesitated to join the clique unless explicitly asked to do so. Moreover, he "knew he had nothing to offer them" and thought that he would ultimately be rejected anyway.

The patient spoke of himself as having always been a shy, fearful, quiet boy. Although he had two "good friends" whom he continued to see occasionally, he was characterized by fellow workers as a loner, a nice young man who usually did his work efficiently but on his own. They noted that he always ate by himself in the company cafeteria and never joined in the "horsing around." (Spitzer et al., 1981, p. 59)

The lifetime prevalence of avoidant personality disorder is about 1 percent, with no strong gender differences in the prevalence of the disorder (Fabrega et al., 1991; Weissman, 1993). People with this disorder are prone to chronic dysthymia and to bouts of major depression and severe anxiety (Fabrega et al., 1991). There is obvious overlap between the characteristics for avoidant personality disorder and for social phobia (see Chapter 4). The primary distinction between the two is that people with avoidant personality disorder have a pervasive and general fear of being criticized that leads them to avoid most types of social interactions and a general sense of inadequacy, whereas people with social phobia tend to fear specific social situations in which they will be expected to perform (e.g., giving a talk in class) and do not tend to have a general sense of inadequacy. People with schizoid personality disorder also withdraw from social situations, but unlike persons with avoidant personality disorder, they do not view themselves as inadequate and incompetent.

Theories of Avoidant Personality Disorder

Family history studies show that avoidant personality disorder is more common in the first degree relatives of people with the disorder than in the relatives of normal control groups (Dahl, 1993). Studies have not been done to determine whether this is due to a genetic transmission of the disorder or to certain family environments. However, studies of temperamental differences between very young children suggest that some children may be born with a shy, fearful temperament that causes them to avoid most other people (Pilkonis, 1995).

People with avoidant personality disorder may have habitually high levels of physical arousal that make them hypersensitive to their environment and particularly to possible threats (Millon, 1981). As infants, these hypersensitive persons may have been experienced by their parents as troublesome, whining, and difficult to manage. If their parents reacted to the infants with frequent frustration, anger, and criticism, the infants may have begun to develop low self-regard and a sensitivity to criticism. The avoidant personality pattern may be more likely to develop if parental rejection takes the form of belittlement, depreciation, and humiliation of the child and if the child is biologically prone to being apprehensive and timorous (Millon, 1981).

Similarly, cognitive theorists suggest that people with avoidant personality disorder developed dysfunctional beliefs about being worthless as a result of rejection by important others early in life (Beck & Freeman, 1990). They contend that the children whose parents reject them conclude, "I must be a bad person for my mother to treat me so badly," "I must be different or defective," and, "If my parents don't like me, how could anyone?" (p. 261). They assume that they will be rejected by others as they were rejected by their parents and thus avoid interactions with others. Their thoughts are of this sort: "Once people get to know me, they see I'm really inferior." When they must interact with others, they are unassertive and nervous because they think, "I must please this person in every way or she will criticize me." They also tend to discount any positive feedback they receive from others, believing that others are just being nice or do not see how incompetent they really are.

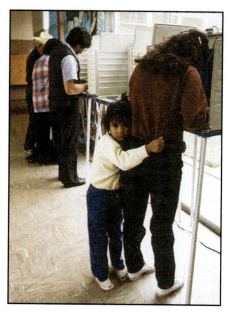

Some children may be born with a shy temperament.

 Several of the personality disorders have been attributed to harsh or inconsistent parenting. What would make some children who receive such parenting develop one type of personality disorder and other children who receive this parenting develop another type of personality disorder?

Treatment for Avoidant Personality Disorder

Cognitive and behavioral therapies have proven helpful for people with avoidant personality disorder (Shea, 1993). These therapies have included graduated exposure to social settings, social skills training, and challenging of negative automatic thoughts about social situations. Persons receiving these therapies show increases in the frequency and range of social contacts, decreases in avoidance behaviors, and increases in comfort and satisfaction in social activities (Alden, 1989; Cappe & Alden, 1986; Stravynski, Marks, & Yule, 1982).

Dependent Personality Disorder

People with **dependent personality disorder** are also anxious about interpersonal interactions, but their anxiety stems from a deep need to be cared for by others rather than a concern that they will be criticized. Their desire to be loved and taken care of by others leads persons with dependent personality disorder to deny any of their own thoughts and feelings that might displease others, to submit to even the most unreasonable demands, and to frantically cling to others. People with this personality disorder cannot make decisions for themselves and do not initiate new activities except in an effort to please others. They deeply fear rejection and abandonment and may allow themselves to be exploited and abused rather than lose relationships.

dependent personality disorder
pervasive selflessness, need to be cared for, and fear of rejection that lead to total dependence on and submission to others

Case Study • Francesca was in a panic because her husband seemed to be getting increasingly annoyed with her. Last night he became very angry when Francesca asked him to cancel an upcoming business trip because she was terrified of being left at home alone. In a rage, her husband shouted, "You can't ever be alone! You can't do anything by yourself! You can't even decide what to have for dinner by yourself! I'm sick of it. Grow up and act like an adult!"

It was true that Francesca had a very difficult time making decisions for herself. While she was in high school, she couldn't decide which courses to take and would talk with her parents and friends for hours about what she should do, finally doing whatever her best friend or her mother told her to do. When she graduated from high school, she didn't feel smart enough to go to college, even though she had good grades in high school. She drifted into a job because her best friend had a job with the same company, and she wanted to remain close to that friend. The friend eventually dumped Francesca, however, because she was tired of Francesca's incessant demands for reassurance. Francesca would frequently buy gifts for the friend and offer to do the friend's laundry or cooking, in obvious attempts to win the friend's favor. But Francesca would also keep the friend for hours in the evening, asking her whether she thought Francesca had made the right decision about some trivial issue, such as what to buy her mother for Christmas, and how she thought Francesca was performing on the job.

Soon after her friend dumped her, Francesca met her husband, and when he showed some interest in her, she quickly tried to form a close relationship with him. She liked the fact that he seemed strong and confident, and when he asked her to marry him, Francesca thought that perhaps finally she would feel safe and secure. But especially since he has begun to get angry with her frequently, Francesca has been worrying constantly that he is going to leave her.

Epidemiological studies put the lifetime prevalence of dependent personality disorder between 1.6 percent and 6.7 percent (Weissman, 1993). Higher rates of the disorder are found when self-report methods are used than when structured clinical interviews are used. More women than men are diagnosed with this disorder in clinical settings (Fabrega et al., 1991). Periods of major depression and chronic anxiety are common in people with the disorder (Fabrega et al., 1991; Millon, 1981).

Causes of Dependent Personality Disorder

Dependent personality disorder runs in families, but again it is unclear whether this is due to genetics or to family environments (Dahl, 1993). Children with histories of anxiety about separation from their parents or of chronic physical illness appear more prone to develop dependent personality disorder (APA, 1994).

Millon (1981) suggests that, as children, persons with dependent personality disorder were gentle but fearful and had warm but overprotective parents. They did not learn to overcome their fearfulness and to be assertive but instead became more and more dependent on others. If such children also have aggressive or abusive siblings or experiences with peers that make them feel unattractive or inadequate, feelings of self-doubt will increase and dependent behaviors may be reinforced by overprotective parents.

Treatment for Dependent Personality Disorder

Unlike people with many of the other personality disorders, persons with dependent personality disorder are disposed to seeking treatment (Millon, 1981). Psychodynamic treatment focuses, of course, on helping clients gain insight into the early experiences with caregivers that led to their dependent behaviors through the use of free association, dream interpretation, and interpretation of the transference process. Nondirective and humanistic therapies may be helpful in fostering autonomy and self-confidence in persons with dependent personality disorder (Millon, 1981).

Cognitive-behavioral therapy for dependent personality disorder includes behavioral techniques designed to increase assertive behaviors and decrease anxiety and cognitive techniques designed to challenge assumptions about the need to rely on others (Beck & Freeman, 1990). Clients might be given graded exposure to anxiety-provoking situations, such as requesting help from a salesperson. Clients may also be taught relaxation skills so they can overcome anxiety enough to engage in homework assignments. They and their therapists might develop a hierarchy of increasingly difficult independent actions that the clients gradually attempt on their own, beginning with deciding what to have for lunch and ending with deciding what job to take. After making each decision, clients are

Parents must strike a balance between giving a child the support and protection he or she needs and encouraging appropriate independence in the child.

encouraged to recognize their competence and challenge the negative thoughts they had about making the decision.

Regardless of what type of psychotherapy is used with clients with dependent personality disorder, therapists must be careful not to reinforce clients' tendency to see therapists as all-powerful people who will provide them with everything they need and to remain passive and submissive in therapy (Beck & Freeman, 1990; Millon, 1981). Clients must be gently encouraged to assume responsibility for their own recovery and to practice assertiveness skills within the context of the therapist-client relationship. Group therapy can be a useful means by which to teach dependent clients skills of assertiveness and decision making and to enhance their confidence in social situations (Millon, 1981).

Obsessive-Compulsive Personality Disorder

The characteristics of self-control, attention to detail, perseverance, and reliability are highly valued in many societies, including U.S. society. Some people, however, carry these traits to an extreme and become rigid, perfectionist, dogmatic, ruminative, and emotionally blocked. These people are said to have **obsessive-compulsive personality disorder**. The obsessive-compulsive personality disorder shares features with obsessive-compulsive disorder (see Chapter 4), but obsessive-compulsive personality disorder represents a more generalized way of interacting with the world than does obsessive-compulsive disorder, which often involves only specific and constrained obsessional thoughts and compulsive behaviors.

People with obsessive-compulsive personality disorder often seem grim and austere, tensely in control of their emotions, and lacking spontaneity (Millon, 1981). They are workaholics and see little need for leisure activities or friendships. Other people experience them as stubborn, stingy, possessive, moralistic, and officious. They tend to relate to others in terms of rank or status and will be ingratiating and deferential to "superiors" but dismissive, demeaning, or authoritarian toward "inferiors." Although they are extremely concerned with efficiency, their perfectionism and obsessions about following rules often interfere with their completion of tasks.

obsessive-compulsive personality disorder
pervasive rigidity in one's activities and interpersonal relationships that includes qualities such as emotional constriction, extreme perfectionism, and anxiety resulting from even slight disruptions in one's routine ways

Case Study • Ronald Lewis is a 32-year-old accountant who is "having trouble holding on to a woman." He does not understand why, but the reasons become very clear as he tells his story. Mr. Lewis is a remarkably neat and well-organized man who tends to regard others as an interference to the otherwise mechanically perfect progression of his life. For many years he has maintained an almost inviolate schedule. On weekdays he arises at 6:47, has two eggs soft-boiled for 2 minutes, 45 seconds, and is at his desk at 8:15. Lunch is at 12:00, dinner at 6:00, bedtime at 11:00. He has separate Saturday and Sunday schedules, the latter characterized by a methodical and thorough trip through *The New York Times*. Any change in schedule causes him to feel varying degrees of anxiety, annoyance, and a sense that he is doing something wrong and wasting time.

Orderliness pervades Mr. Lewis's life. His apartment is immaculately clean and meticulously arranged. His extensive collections of books, records, and stamps are all carefully catalogued, and each item is reassuringly always in the right and familiar place. Mr. Lewis is highly valued at his work because his attention to detail has, at times, saved the company considerable embarrassment. . . . His perfectionism also presents something of a problem, however. He is the slowest worker in the office and probably the least productive. He gets the details right but may fail to put them in perspective. His relationships to coworkers are cordial but formal. He is on a "Mr. and Ms." basis with people he has known for years in an office that generally favors first names.

Mr. Lewis's major problems are with women and follow the same repetitive pattern. At first, things go well. . . . Soon, however, he begins to resent the intrusion upon his schedule a woman inevitably causes. This is most strongly illustrated in the bedtime

arrangements. Mr. Lewis is a light and nervous sleeper with a rather elaborate routine preceding his going to bed. He must spray his sinuses, take two aspirin, straighten up the apartment, do 35 sit-ups and read two pages of the dictionary. The sheets must be of just the right crispness and temperature and the room must be noiseless. Obviously, a woman sleeping over interferes with his inner sanctum and, after sex, Mr. Lewis tries either to have the woman go home or sleep in the living room. No woman has put up with this for very long. (Spitzer et al., 1983, pp. 63–64)

The lifetime prevalence of obsessive-compulsive personality disorder is between 1.7 and 6.4 percent and is more common in men than women (Fabrega et al., 1991; Weissman, 1993).

Theories of Obsessive-Compulsive Personality Disorder

There are no family history, twin, or adoption studies specifically focusing on obsessive-compulsive personality disorder. Perhaps surprisingly, family history and twin studies of obsessive-compulsive disorder do not tend to find a link between this disorder and obsessive-compulsive personality disorder (Insel, Hoover, & Murphy, 1983; Torgersen, 1980).

Early psychodynamic theorists attributed this personality disorder to fixation at the anal stage of development because the patient's parents were overly strict and punitive during toilet training (Freud, 1908/1963). Harry Stack Sullivan (1953) argued that obsessive compulsive personalities arise when children grow up in homes where there is much anger and hate that is hidden behind superficial love and niceness. The children do not develop interpersonal skills and instead avoid intimacy and follow rigid rules to gain a sense of self-esteem and self-control.

Millon (1981) argues that people with this personality disorder had parents who were overcontrolling and punitive when they made mistakes but did not praise or reward them when they did well. Strict limits were set on their behaviors, and as they entered the stage of life when they attempted to assert their desires and resist their parents, the parents responded with firm and harsh discipline. They subsequently retreated and submerged their desire for independence and autonomy, strictly following their parents' rules in order to avoid punishment. They may begin to doubt their own abilities because they have not had the opportunity to test them. Instead, they search for a set of rules and regulations established by others to guide their behaviors.

Treatment for Obsessive-Compulsive Personality Disorder

Supportive therapies may assist people with this disorder in overcoming the crises that bring them in for treatment, and behavioral therapies can be used to decrease compulsive behaviors in persons with this disorder (Beck et al., 1990; Millon, 1981). For example, a client may be given the assignment to alter his usual rigid schedule for the day, first by simply getting up 15 minutes later than he usually does and then gradually changing additional elements of his schedule. The client may be taught to use relaxation techniques to overcome anxiety created by alterations in the schedule. He might also write down the automatic negative thoughts he has about changes in the schedule ("Getting up 15 minutes later is going to put my entire day off"), and in the next therapy session, he and the therapist might discuss the evidence for and against these automatic thoughts.

| Summing Up | The Anxious-Fearful Personality Disorders |

- People with the anxious-fearful personality disorders—avoidant, dependent, and obsessive-compulsive personality disorders—are chronically fearful or concerned.
- People with avoidant personality disorder worry about being critcized.
- People with dependent personality disorder worry about being abandoned.
- People with obsessive-compulsive personality disorder are locked into rigid routines of behavior and become anxious when their routines are violated.
- Some children may be born with temperamental predispositions toward shy and avoidant behaviors, or childhood anxiety may contribute to dependent personalities.
- These disorders may also arise from lack of nurturing parenting and basic fears about one's ability to function competently.

 As a therapist, which of the personality disorders do you think you would find most difficult to treat? Why?

Gender and Cultural Biases in Personality Disorder Diagnoses

One of the greatest controversies in the literature on personality disorders concerns claims that there are substantial gender biases in clinicians' applications of these diagnoses (Widiger, 1995; Widiger & Spitzer, 1991). The diagnoses of histrionic, dependent, and borderline personality disorders have been described as extreme variants of the negative stereotypes of women's personalities (Kaplan, 1983; Walker, 1994). That is, the negative stereotype of women is that they are highly emotional, concerned with their appearance, and dependent on others for self-esteem and that they act seductively to manipulate men. The diagnostic criteria for histrionic, borderline, and dependent personality disorders are extreme versions of these characteristics. This correlation between the stereotypes and the diagnostic criteria may lead clinicians to be too quick to see these characteristics in women clients and to apply these diagnoses. We noted in our earlier discussion of these disorders that women are given these diagnoses more often than are men in clinical settings. There has been little research on whether this difference is due to clinician bias or to a truly higher rate of these disorders in women than in men.

It has also been argued that the diagnostic criteria for antisocial personality disorder represent extremes of negative stereotypes of men, and thus clinicians are biased

Critics of the personality disorders have charged that the diagnostic criteria reflect traditional gender stereotypes of what is a "healthy male" and a "healthy female."

to overapply this diagnosis to men but not to women. However, enough research has been done on antisocial personality disorder in the general population that it seems clear that men do have this disorder, as it is currently defined, more than women do (Kessler et al., 1994).

Yet some researchers have continued to argue that there is a gender bias in the current diagnostic criteria for antisocial personality disorder (Rutherford et al., 1995, 1996). These criteria emphasize overt signs of callous and cruel antisocial behavior, including the commission of crimes against property and people. Women with antisocial personality disorder may be less likely than men with the disorder to engage in such overt antisocial behaviors, because of greater social sanctions against women for doing so. Instead, women with antisocial personality disorder may find more subtle or covert ways of being antisocial, such as acting cruelly toward their children or covertly sabotaging people at work. As we shall see when we discuss childhood disorders in Chapter 9, this same argument has been made about possible gender differences in the expression of the childhood form of antisocial personality disorder: conduct disorder.

Similarly, some theorists have argued that the DSM-IV ignores or downplays possible masculine ways of expressing dependent, histrionic, and borderline personality disorders, and this bias contributes to an underdiagnosis of these disorders in men (see Widiger, Mangine, Corbitt, Ellis, & Thomas, 1995). For example, one of the criteria for histrionic personality disorder is "consistently uses physical appearance to draw attention to the self" (APA, 1994, p. 658). Although the DSM-IV notes that men may express this characteristic by acting "macho" and bragging about their athletic skills, the wording of the criterion brings to mind everyday behaviors more common among women, such as wearing makeup. The DSM-IV makes little mention of how dependency may be expressed in men. For example, many men whose wives die marry again soon after their wives' deaths because they feel a need for women to "take care" of them emotionally and physically (Frances, First, & Pincus, 1995; Kaplan, 1983).

Concerns have also been raised about possible cultural biases in the definitions of personality disorders (Fabrega, 1994). The personality characteristics that make up the personality disorders are considered abnormal because they violate what Western psychiatry views as normal. In particular, Western views of mental health emphasize the importance of autonomy and independence from others—individualism. In contrast, many other societies have more collectivist orientations that value the individual's ability to fit in with the larger society and maintain good relations with others. Thus, it may be that some of the personality characteristics seen as disordered in the DSM-IV, such as those making up the dependent personality disorder, are seen as normal in other cultures.

We have too little research on personality disorders to resolve these controversies. Although the authors of the DSM-IV attempted to weed out gender and cultural biases in the diagnostic criteria for the personality disorders, many theorists argue that they were not completely successful and that future research that uses the DSM-IV criteria will thus be biased (Widiger et al., 1995). In addition, the criteria for personality disorders are inherently more subjective than are the criteria for the other disorders, so they leave considerable room for the biases of individual clinicians to have effects (Hirschfeld, Shea, & Weise, 1991).

Bio-Psycho-Social INTEGRATION

Although empirical research on the personality disorders is too lacking to allow for a clear integration of biological, psychological, and social factors impinging on these disorders, some theoretical models have attempted this integration and are serving as the basis for current research (Millon, 1981; Siever & Davis, 1991). At the root of many of the personality disorders may be a biological predisposition to a certain kind of temperament: an anxious and fearful temperament in the case of avoidant and schizotypal personality disorders, an impulsive and aggressive temperament in the case of borderline and antisocial personality disorders, and a labile, overly emotional temperament in the case of borderline and histrionic personality disorders. Children born with any of these temperaments are difficult to parent effectively, but if parents can be supportive of them and still set appropriate limits on their behavior, the children may never develop severe enough behavioral or emotional problems to be diagnosed with a personality disorder. If parents are unable to counteract children's termperamental vulnerabilities or if they exacerbate these vulnerabilities by engaging in harsh, critical, and unsupportive parenting or over-protective and indulgent parenting, then the children's temperamental vulnerabilities may grow into severe behavioral and emotional problems. These problems will influence how others—teachers, peers, and eventually employers and mates—interact with individuals, perhaps in ways that further exacerbate their temperamental vulnerabilities. Thus, out of the interaction between a child's biologically based temperament and the reactions of others to that temperament may emerge a lifelong pattern of dysfunction that we call a personality disorder.

Chapter Summary

There are three clusters of personality disorders. The odd-eccentric disorders are characterized by odd or eccentric patterns of behavior and thought, including paranoia, extreme social withdrawal or inappropriate social interactions, and magical or illusory thinking. This group of disorders, particularly schizotypal personality disorder, may be linked to schizophrenia genetically and may represent mild variations of schizophrenia. Studies of persons seeking therapy show that these disorders are more common in men than in women, although it is not clear why this is true. People with these disorders tend to have poor social relationships and are at increased risk for some acute psychiatric disorders, especially depression and schizophrenia. Psychoanalytic theorists view paranoid personality disorder as the result of the use of projection as a defense and schizoid personality disorder as the result of extremely dysfunctional parent-child relationships in which the child did not learn to give or receive love. Cognitive theorists view each of the odd-eccentric personality disorders as the result of particular cognitive distortions. Psychoanalytic and cognitive therapies have been devised for these disorders, but they have not been empirically tested for their efficacy. Neuroleptic drugs appear to reduce the odd thinking of people with schizotypal personality disorder.

The dramatic-emotional personality disorders include four disorders characterized by dramatic, erratic, and emotional behavior and interpersonal relationships: antisocial personality disorder, histrionic personality disorder, borderline personality disorder, and narcissistic personality disorder. Persons with these disorders tend to be manipulative, volatile, and uncaring in social relationships and prone to impulsive behaviors. Antisocial personality disorder is one of the most common personality disorders and is more common in men than in women. There is substantial support for a genetic influence on antisocial behaviors, and some studies suggest that people with this personality disorder may suffer from low levels of serotonin, low levels of arousability, an attention deficit disorder, and extreme problems in inhibiting impulsive behaviors. These people tend to have had harsh and inconsistent parenting and to develop a set of assumptions about the world that promotes aggressive responding. Psychotherapy is not considered extremely effective for people with antisocial personality disorder. Lithium and the serotonin reuptake inhibitors may help to control their impulsive behaviors.

People with borderline personality disorder show lability in their moods, self-concept, and interpersonal relationships. This disorder is more common in women than in men. People with the disorder may suffer from low levels of serotonin, which lead to impulsive behaviors. There is little evidence that borderline personality disorder is transmitted genetically, but the family members of people with this disorder show high rates of mood disorders. Psychoanalytic theorists argue that this disorder is the result of poorly developed and integrated views of the self, which result from poor early relationships with caregivers. Cognitive theorists see this disorder as stemming from deficits in self-concept. Many people with this disorder were the victims of physical and sexual abuse in childhood. Drug treatments have not proven very effective for this disorder. Psychoanalytic and cognitive therapies focus on establishing a stronger self-identity in people with this disorder.

Histrionic and narcissistic personality disorders are both characterized by dramatic self-presentations and unstable personal relationships. The person with histrionic personality disorder looks to others for approval, whereas the person with narcissistic personality disorder relies on his or her own self-evaluations. Psychoanalytic theorists see histrionic personality disorder, which is more common in women, as the result of deep dependency needs and repression of emotion, and they see narcissistic personality disorder, which is more common in men, as the result of either fixation at a self-centered stage of self-concept or as a reaction formation against feelings of low self-worth. Cognitive theorists see these disorders as the result of assumptions about one's worth relative to other people.

The anxious-fearful personality disorders include three disorders characterized by anxious and fearful emotions and chronic self-doubt, leading to maladaptive behaviors: dependent personality disorder, avoidant personality disorder, and obsessive-compulsive personality disorder. Dependent personality disorder is more common in women, obsessive-compulsive personality disorder is more common in men, and avoidant personality disorder is equally common in men and women. Dependent and avoidant personality disorders tend to run in families, but it is not clear whether this is due to genetics or to family environments. Psychoanalysts view dependent personality disorder as the result of fixation at the oral stage of development and obsessive-compulsive personality disorder as the result of fixation at the anal stage of development. Cognitive theorists suggest that avoidant personality disorder results from beliefs about being worthless as the result of rejection by others in early life, that dependent personality disorder results from feelings of inadequacy plus parental overprotection, and that obsessive-compulsive disorder results from harsh discipline and parental criticism and beliefs that one must be perfect to be loved.

Some theorists have argued that the DSM-IV definitions of personality disorders are both gender and culturally biased. Some of the personality disorders appear to represent extreme versions of personality characteristics thought to be more common in one gender or the other. This difference may lead clinicians to be too quick to diagnose a client with a personality disorder that is expected for his or her gender. Further, the criteria for personality disorders are based on Western norms for what is a healthy personality and thus may pathologize personality characteristics that are highly valued in other cultures.

Key Terms

personality 282
personality trait 282
personality
   disorder 282
odd-eccentric personality
   disorders 283
paranoid personality
   disorder 283
schizoid personality
   disorder 286
schizotypal
   personality
   disorder 288

dramatic-emotional
   personality
   disorders 290
antisocial personality
   disorder 290
borderline personality
   disorder 295
histrionic personality
   disorder 299
narcissistic personality
   disorder 301

anxious-fearful
   personality
   disorders 303
avoidant personality
   disorder 303
dependent personality
   disorder 305
obsessive-compulsive
   personality
   disorder 307

Application

Seeing Oneself in the Personality Disorders

In Chapter 1, we discussed iatrogenic illness, the tendency for students reading an Abnormal Psychology textbook to see signs of many mental disorders in themselves or in the people in their lives. Students may be especially prone to unjustifiably diagnose personality disorders in themselves or in others. Indeed, people are considerably more likely to diagnose themselves on self-report questionnaires as having a personality disorder than are clinicians to diagnose them in the context of psychiatric interviews (Weissman, 1993). There are at least two possible reasons for this.

First, the criteria for diagnosing personality disorders are more vague than the criteria for many of the other, more acute disorders and thus leave more room for misapplication (Widiger & Costa, 1994). For example, one of the symptoms of dependent personality disorder is "has difficulty expressing disagreement with others because of fear of loss of support or approval." Most of us can probably see signs of this tendency in ourselves or in someone close to us. However, it is unclear from the DSM-IV criteria to what degree this tendency has to be present to be counted as a symptom of dependent personality disorder.

Second, people are prone to attribute behaviors to personality traits and to ignore the influence of situations on those behaviors (see Ross & Nisbett, 1991). This tendency is often referred to as the *fundamental attribution error*. A classic study demonstrating how strongly people discount situational influences over dispositional influences was conducted by Jones and Harris (1967). They asked subjects to read essays presumably written by other subjects. The subjects were told that the persons writing the essays were assigned to present a particular viewpoint on the topic of the essay. For example, they were told that a political science student had been assigned to write an essay defending communism in Cuba or that a debate student had been assigned to attack the proposition that marijuana should be legalized. Despite the fact that the subjects were told that the essay writers were assigned to take a particular viewpoint rather than chose a particular viewpoint, the subjects tended to believe that the essay writers actually held the viewpoint they presented in their essays.

If you think you see signs of one or more personality disorders in yourself or someone close to you, stop and ask yourself the following questions:

1. *What are the situational influences that might be driving my behavior or my friend's or relative's behavior?* For example, let us say that you are concerned that your brother has developed an obsessive-compulsive personality disorder since he entered medical school: He is preoccupied with schedules and always has lists of things to do; he has become a workaholic; he has become a perfectionist to the point of not being able to get things done; and he has become even more moralistic than he was in high school. It is true that certain situations can exaggerate the already dysfunctional behaviors of people with obsessive-compulsive personality disorder. However, consider the possibility that your brother's behaviors, particularly the ones that he has developed since entering medical school, are largely driven by the demands of medical school rather than by some enduring personality traits. Medical school is a 24-hour-per-day job, and many students find it necessary to become hyperefficient workaholics in order to get all their work done. Your brother's preoccupation with lists and schedules and his working 20 hours per day are probably behaviors that he shares with many of his medical school classmates, behaviors that are largely the result of the demands of the situation. In addition, many medical schools weed out a significant percentage of each new class with grueling examinations. This kind of pressure can cause many people to try to be perfectionists but to become so anxious about the possibility of failing that they cannot do their work.

   When you find yourself wondering if you or someone you care about has developed a personality disorder, stop to consider the aspects of the situation that might really be responsible for the behaviors you observe.

2. *Am I selectively remembering behaviors that are signs of a personality disorder and selectively forgetting behaviors that contradict the diagnosis of a personality disorder?* One of the strongest reasons people overestimate the influence of personality traits on the behaviors of themselves and others is that they selectively pay attention to and remember behaviors that are consistent with personality traits and ignore or forget behaviors that are inconsistent with the traits. For example, if you fear that you have a dependent personality disorder, you will probably find it quite easy to remember times in the past when you have had trouble making decisions without much advice from others or have felt uncomfortable and helpless when alone or have been passive in voicing your opinions or needs to others. You will probably forget, however, the many more times when you made decisions with no help from others, actually enjoyed being alone, or spoke up to express your opinions or needs. It can be helpful to try to write down all the times in the recent or distant past when you behaved in ways that contradicted some troubling personality trait you think you have. Or you might want to ask a trusted friend to help you sort out whether your behaviors are always consistent with some negative personality disposition.

3. *Are the behaviors I am observing part of a long-time pattern of behavior or do they only occur occasionally?* Most of us act in dysfunctional or plainly stupid ways occasionally. Sometimes these actions are obviously driven by the situations in which we find ourselves, but sometimes we act in stupid ways even when there is no apparent situational excuse for our actions. A personality disorder is a pattern of behavior that has existed most of a person's life and that the person demonstrates across a range of situations. Occasional lapses into dysfunctional behavior do not constitute a personality disorder.

4. *Are the behaviors I am observing significantly impairing or causing distress in my life or the lives of other people?* In order to qualify as a personality disorder, a set of behaviors has to cause significant distress or impairment in a person's life. We all have our quirks, our tendencies to act in ways we wish we would not. It can be helpful to examine these behaviors and make attempts to change them if they are not in line with our values or if they get us into occasional trouble. However, most quirks are relatively benign.

As always, if you are quite concerned about whether you or someone you care about has a significant psychological problems, it can be helpful to talk it out with a professional mental health specialist who is trained to differentiate between psychological disorders and variations in people's behaviors that are not dangerous or unhealthy. ■

Part Three

Developmental and Health-Related Disorders

The disorders in Part Three tend to develop at certain periods in the life span and can affect people's physical and mental health.

Some behavioral and emotional disorders, mental retardation, and autism begin in childhood. The eating disorders, sexual disorders, and substance use disorders can begin at any age, although the eating disorders and substance use disorders typically begin in adolescence or early adulthood. These disorders involve specific maladaptive behaviors but can have negative effects in many domains of life.

Psychosocial factors are increasingly important in understanding people's physical health as well as mental health. Environmental stress, personality, and coping styles may affect people's vulnerability to illness and their ability to recover from illness across the life span. In old age, a number of disorders arise that involve mental functioning. Although the causes of these disorders are biological, psychosocial factors such as family support may play a role in how well individuals cope with these disorders.

A sound mind in a sound body, is a short but full description of a happy state in this world.

—John Locke, *Some Thoughts Concerning Education* (1963)

Juan Gris
Femme Dans Un Fauteuil

9 Childhood Disorders

Behavior Disorders

The behavior disorders include attention deficit/hyperactivity disorder, conduct disorder, and oppositional defiant disorder. Children with attention deficit/hyperactivity disorder have trouble maintaining attention and controlling impulsive behavior and are hyperactive. These children may suffer from neurological deficits. Treatment for this disorder includes the use of drugs and behavioral therapies. Children with conduct or oppositional defiant disorder engage in frequent antisocial or defiant behavior. They may suffer from neurological deficits, but harsh and inconsistent parenting and a tendency to misinterpret confrontations with others also seem to contribute to these disorders. Treatment for these children uses cognitive-behavioral therapies and drugs.

Emotional Disorders

One of the most common emotional disorders of childhood is separation anxiety disorder, in which children are extremely anxious about any separation from their primary caregivers. These children may have biological predispositions to anxiety disorders, and their parents may model and encourage anxious reactions. Behavioral and cognitive therapies are often used to treat this disorder.

Elimination Disorders

The two elimination disorders are enuresis—uncontrolled wetting—and encopresis—uncontrolled bowel movements. Children with these disorders may have a biological vulnerability to the disorders or may develop the disorders in response to stressful change in their environments. The most effective treatment is a behavioral technique that teaches children to awaken at night when they need to go to the bathroom.

Developmental Disorders

The developmental disorders begin very early in life and are characterized by a broad range of deficits. Children with mental retardation have deficits in cognitive skills that can range from mild to severe. A number of genetic factors and biological traumas in the early years of life can contribute to mental retardation. Sociocultural factors, such as poverty or lack of good education, can also contribute to mental retardation. Autism is another developmental disorder that often involves cognitive deficits but is mostly characterized by a wide array of deficits in communication and social interactions. Autism has biological roots but often responds well to behavioral interventions.

Gender Differences in Childhood Psychopathology

Many disorders are more common in boys than in girls before puberty. This gender difference may occur because boys are more vulnerable biologically or because they are put under greater stress than are girls, which leads to more psychopathology. A switch occurs in early adolescence, however, such that girls become much more prone to certain disorders than are boys.

Bio-Psycho-Social Integration
Chapter Summary
Key Terms
Application: *If Your Parent Has a Psychological Disorder*

od

rs

Youth, even in its sorrows, always has a brilliancy of its own.

—Victor Hugo, "Saint Denis," *Les Miserables* (1962; translated by Charles E. Wilbour)

Daniel Nevins
In the Fields

We like to think of childhood as a time relatively free from stress, when boys and girls can enjoy the simple pleasures of everyday life and are immune from major psychological problems. Yet nearly 20 percent of children and almost 40 percent of adolescents suffer from significant emotional or behavioral disorders (Kessler et al., 1994; Newman, Moffitt, Caspi, & Magdol, 1996). Thus, a substantial minority of children and adolescents are not living carefree existences; instead, they are experiencing distressing symptoms severe enough to warrant attention from mental health professionals.

For some children, psychological symptoms and disorders are linked to major stressors in their environment. A large and growing number of children in the United States and in other countries are faced with severe circumstances that could overwhelm the coping capacities of adults. In the United States, about 1 in 10 children is the victim of severe physical abuse each year, and about 1 in 5 children lives below the poverty line (Wolfner & Gelles, 1993). Children living in the inner city, particularly in the projects where poor families often are housed, are often exposed to violence. For example, in one study of fifth-grade children in a poor area of New Orleans, Louisiana, 91 percent reported witnessing some sort of violence in the last year; 26 percent of the children had witnessed a shooting, 40 percent had seen dead bodies in their neighborhoods, and 49 percent had seen someone wounded. Over half of the children had been the victims of violence (Osofsky, Wewers, Hann, & Fick, 1993). Another study of drive-by shootings in Los Angeles in 1991 found that in that one year, 677 adolescents had been shot at, 429 had suffered gunshot wounds, and 36 had died from their injuries (Hutson, Anglin, & Pratts, 1994).

Children facing any one of these major stressors or risks are more likely than other children to have significant psychological problems (Compas, 1987). A young girl named Melanie who lives in a violence-torn inner-city neighborhood described a recurrent dream (Plantenga, 1991, p. 27):

> I am coming out of a supermarket and a man
> is carrying a gun and tells me to give
> him all my money. I give him my purse
> and my jewelry, but he still shoots me.
> And then I find myself in a funeral home. I
> see my mom, my dad and my brother
> crying and the rest of my family. I go up to
> the coffin and see a person who reminds
> me of me. I see myself. I start to cry and I
> wake up.

Sadly, most children who face one such stressor are beset by multiple stressors. For example, children in poverty are more likely than other children to witness or be the victims of violence, to use illicit drugs, to engage in unprotected sexual intercourse, and to face racial and ethnic discrimination and harassment. These stressors appear to have a cumulative effect on children's risk for psychological problems: The more stressors a child encounters, the more likely he or she is to experience severe psychological symptoms (Osofsky et al., 1993).

What is remarkable is that many, perhaps most, children who face major stressors do *not* develop severe psychological symptoms or disorders. These children have been referred to as *resilient* or *invulnerable* children (Anthony & Cohler, 1987; Garmezy, 1991). We do not know what makes these children so resilient in the face of stress, but having at least one healthy and competent adult that a child can rely on in his or her daily life seems to help. For example, studies of homeless children suggest that those who have high quality interactions with a parent are no more likely to develop psychological problems than are children who are not homeless (Masten, Miliotis, Graham-Bermann, Ramirez, & Neemann, 1993). Conversely, many children who develop psychological disorders do not have any major stressors in their lives to which the development of the disorders can be linked. These children may come from privileged backgrounds in which they have not been exposed to any traumas or chronic problems.

Children, particularly those in urban areas, may be exposed to tremendous violence even at a young age.

It seems that among children, as among adults, most psychological disorders are the result of multiple factors, such as biological predispositions plus environmental stressors. One biological factor that has been implicated in the development of many psychological disorders in children is temperament. *Temperament* refers to a child's arousability and general mood. Children with "difficult" temperaments are highly sensitive to stimulation, become upset easily, and have trouble calming themselves when upset. They also tend to have generally negative moods and trouble adapting to new situations, particularly social situations (Thomas & Chess, 1984). Children with difficult temperaments are more likely than other children to have both minor and major psychological problems during childhood and later in life (Rutter, 1987).

Children who have supportive adults in their lives appear more resilient to stress.

Temperament probably has strong biological roots, including genetic roots (Campos et al., 1989). The link between temperament and the development of psychological problems is not exclusively biological, however. Children with difficult temperaments elicit more negative interactions from others, including their parents. Adults act less affectionately toward children with difficult temperaments, and other children are more likely to be hostile toward these children. It may be the negative environments children with difficult temperments create for themselves that contribute to psychological problems rather than the temperaments per se. Conversely, children with difficult temperaments who receive high quality parenting are not at high risk for psychological problems, whereas children with difficult temperaments who are part of dysfunctional families are at high risk (Rutter, 1987).

Children are even more likely than adults to be diagnosed with multiple psychological disorders if they are diagnosed with any disorders at all. What are some possible explanations for this greater likelihood?

In this chapter, we will review the roles that biology and psychosocial factors play in the development of specific psychological disorders in children. We will discuss four groups of childhood disorders.

The first group is the behavioral disorders, specifically attention deficit/hyperactivity disorder, conduct disorder, and oppositional defiant disorder. Children with these disorders have trouble paying attention and controlling socially inappropriate behaviors.

The second group is the emotional disorders. Although children can suffer from all the mood disorders and anxiety disorders that adults suffer from (see Chapters 4 and 5), we will focus on separation anxiety disorder, because this is a disorder specific to children.

The third group is the elimination disorders, enuresis and encopresis. Children with these disorders have trouble controlling bladder and bowel movements far beyond the age at which most children learn to control them.

The fourth group is the developmental and learning disorders, including mental retardation and autism. Children with these disorders show gross deficits in the development of normal cognitive and social skills.

The study of childhood disorders has expanded greatly in the last decade or so and has grown into a new field known as *developmental psychopathology*. Developmental psychopathologists try to understand when children's behaviors cross the line from the normal perturbations of childhood into unusual or abnormal problems that merit concern. Most children have transient emotional or behavioral problems sometime during childhood. That is, most children will go through periods in which they are unusually fearful or easily distressed or engage in behaviors such as lying or stealing, but these periods pass relatively quickly and are often specific to certain situations. Differentiating these normative periods of distress from signs of a developing psychological disorder is not easy. Developmental psychopathologists also try to understand the impact of normal development on the shape and form that abnormal behaviors will take. That is, children's levels of cognitive, social, and emotional development can affect the types of symptoms they

"We're on vacation, Jeffy. Save that for when we get back to real life."
Reprinted with special permission of King Feature Syndicate.

will show. These developmental considerations make the assessment, diagnosis, and treatment of childhood disorders quite challenging, but helping disturbed children overcome their problems and get back on the path to healthy development can be highly rewarding.

Behavior Disorders

The behavior disorders have been the focus of a great deal of the research on children's disorders, probably because children with these disorders are quite difficult to deal with, and these children's behaviors can exact a heavy toll on society. The three behavior disorders we will discuss are attention deficit/hyperactivity disorder, conduct disorder, and oppositional defiant disorder. These are distinct disorders, but they often co-occur in the same child.

Attention Deficit/Hyperactivity Disorder

"Pay attention! Slow down! You're so hyper today!" These are phrases that most children hear their parents saying to them at least occasionally. A major focus of socialization is helping children learn to pay attention, control their impulses, and organize their behaviors so that they can accomplish long-term goals. Some children have tremendous trouble learning these skills, however, and may be diagnosed with **attention deficit/hyperactivity disorder**, or ADHD (see Table 9.1). Eddie is a young boy with ADHD (adapted from Spitzer et al., 1994, pp. 351–352):

attention deficit/hyperactivity disorder (ADHD)
syndrome marked by deficits in controlling attention, inhibiting impulses, and organizing behavior to accomplish long-term goals

> **Case Study** • Eddie, age 9, was referred to a child psychiatrist at the request of his school because of the difficulties he creates in class. His teacher complains that he is so restless that his classmates are unable to concentrate. He is hardly ever in his seat and mostly roams around the class, talking to other children while they are working. When the teacher is able to get him to stay in his seat, he fidgets with his hands and feet and drops things on the floor. He never seems to know what he is going to do next and may suddenly do something quite outrageous. His most recent suspension from school was for swinging from the fluorescent light fixture over the blackboard. Because he was unable to climb down again, the class was in an uproar.
>
> His mother says that Eddie's behavior has been difficult since he was a toddler and that, as a 3-year-old, he was unbearably restless and demanding. He has always required little sleep and been awake before anyone else. When he was small, "he got into everything," particularly in the early morning, when he would awaken at 4:30 A.M. or 5:00 A.M. and go downstairs by himself. His parents would awaken to find the living room or kitchen "demolished." When he was 4 years old, he managed to unlock the door of the apartment and wander off into a busy main street but, fortunately, was rescued from oncoming traffic by a passerby.
>
> Eddie has no interest in TV and dislikes games or toys that require any concentration or patience. He is not popular with other children and at home prefers to be outdoors, playing with his dog or riding his bike. If he does play with toys, his games are messy and destructive, and his mother cannot get him to keep his things in any order.

Eddie's difficulties in paying attention and his impulsivity go far beyond what is normal for a child his age. Most elementary school-aged children can sit still for some period of time, like to engage in at least some games that require patience and concentration, and can inhibit their impulses to jump up in class and talk to other children or to walk out into busy traffic. Eddie cannot do any of these things. His behavior has a character of being driven and disorganized, following one whim and then the next.

Children like Eddie often do poorly in school. Because they cannot pay attention or quell their hyperactivity, they do not learn the material they are being taught and thus perform below their intellectual capabilities (Henker & Whalen, 1989). In addition, 20 to 25

Table 9.1 **Symptoms of Attention Deficit/Hyperactivity Disorder (ADHD)**

The symptoms of attention deficit/hyperactivity disorder fall into three clusters: inattention, hyperactivity, and impulsivity.

Inattention

Does not pay attention to details and makes careless mistakes
Has difficulty sustaining attention
Does not seem to be listening when others are talking
Does not follow through on instructions or finish tasks
Has difficulty organizing behaviors
Avoids activities that require sustained effort and attention
Loses things frequently
Is easily distracted
Is forgetful

Hyperactivity

Fidgets with hands or feet and squirms in seat
Is restless, leaving his or her seat or running around when it is inappropriate
Has difficulty engaging in quiet activities

Impulsivity

Blurts out responses while others are talking
Has difficulty waiting his or her turn

Reprinted with permission from the *Diagnostic and Statistical Manual of Mental Disorders,* Fourth Edition. Copyright 1994 American Psychiatric Association.

percent of children with ADHD may have serious learning disabilities that make it doubly hard for them to concentrate in school and to learn (Barkley, 1990).

Children with ADHD also have extremely poor relationships with other children and, like Eddie, often are rejected outright by other children (Hinshaw & Melnick, 1995). When interacting with their peers, children with ADHD are disorganized and never finish anything. They are intrusive, irritable, and demanding. They want to play by their own rules and have explosive tempers so when things do not go their way, they may become physically violent (Barkley, Fischer, Edelbrock, & Smallish, 1990). Here is how the classmates of hyperactive boys describe them (Henker & Whalen, 1989, p. 216):

Children usually have a great deal of energy and enthusiasm for life, which can make it difficult to define hyperactivity in children.

> They can't sit still; they don't pay attention to the teacher; they mess around and get into trouble; they try to get others into trouble; they are rude; they get mad when they don't get their way; and they say they can beat everybody up.

The behavioral problems of some children with ADHD are so severe that the children may also be diagnosed with a conduct disorder. As we will discuss shortly, children with conduct disorders grossly violate the norms for appropriate behavior toward others by acting in uncaring and even violent ways. Between 45 and 60 percent of children with ADHD develop conduct disorders, abuse drugs, or become juvenile delinquents (Barkley et al., 1990; Gittelman, Mannuzza, Shenker, & Bonagura, 1985).

Do you think it is the obligation of schools to intervene with children who seem troubled? Explain.

ADHD has become a popular diagnosis to give to children who are disruptive in school or at home, and the media attention on ADHD over the last few years has made it seem that there is an epidemic of this disorder. However, various epidemiological studies indicate that only 1 to 7 percent of children develop ADHD (Hinshaw, 1994; McGee, Feehan, Williams, & Partridge, 1990). Boys are about three times more likely than girls to develop ADHD in childhood and early adolescence (Cohen et al., 1993b). ADHD is found across most cultures and ethnic groups.

The long-term outcomes for children with ADHD vary considerably. The symptoms of ADHD persist from childhood into adolescence for about two-thirds of these children (Hinshaw, 1994). Adults who as children were diagnosed with ADHD are at increased risk for marital problems, traffic accidents, legal infractions, and frequent job changes (Henker & Whalen, 1989). Those children who develop serious conduct problems in addition to ADHD fare worse and tend to have criminal behavior, drug abuse, and emotional problems as adults (Moffitt, 1990). However, many children "grow out" of ADHD. By early adulthood, their symptoms of ADHD have passed and they go on to lead normal and healthy lives (Manuzza, Klein, Bessler, Malloy, & LaPadula, 1993).

In recent years, there has been great public interest in *adult* ADHD (Kelly & Ramundo, 1995; Ratey & Hallowell, 1994). Many adults who have had long histories of underachievement and poor relationships have wondered if they have suffered from ADHD all their lives but were never diagnosed. Because childhood disorders, including ADHD, tended to be underdiagnosed in previous decades, it is likely that many adults who had ADHD as children were not diagnosed. Some of these adults have sought the kinds of treatment for ADHD described next and have found it useful in helping them overcome their current problems on the job and in relationships. However, some studies have suggested that the full syndrome of ADHD in adulthood is quite rare, and ADHD is probably being overdiagnosed currently in adults (Feehan, McGee, & Williams, 1993; Manuzza et al., 1993).

 In what kind of environments might children with ADHD pay better attention and better control their behaviors? What kind of environments might exacerbate attentional and behavioral problems in these children?

Biological Contributors to ADHD

ADHD was formerly referred to as *minimal brain damage,* under the assumption that diagnosed children's attentional deficits and hyperactivity were due to some sort of mild brain damage. Most children who develop ADHD, however, have no histories of brain injury, and most children with some brain injury do not develop ADHD.

Modern studies have shown, however, that ADHD children differ from children with no psychological disorders on a variety of measures of neurological functioning (Anastopoulos & Barkley, 1988). For example, they have lower cerebral blood flow and a variety of abnormalities in EEG readings. It is not yet clear just how these neurological abnormalities are linked to ADHD. One hypothesis is that children with ADHD are neurologically immature—their brains are slower in developing than are other children's—and this is why they are unable to maintain attention and control their behavior at a level that is appropriate for their age. This immaturity hypothesis helps to explain why the symptoms of ADHD decline with age in many children.

The role of genetics in vulnerability to ADHD is not clear. Some studies suggest that children with ADHD come from families in which there are histories of several types of psychological disturbance, most frequently antisocial personality disorder, alcoholism, and hyperactivity (Barkley, 1991; Faraone, Biederman, Keenan, & Tsuang, 1991). Other family history studies have found no higher frequency of psychopathology in the families of children with ADHD than in families of children without the disorder, however (Lahey, Pelham, Schaughency, & Atkins, 1988). The available twin studies and adoption studies do suggest that genetics play a role in vulnerability to ADHD (Cadoret & Stewart, 1991), although it is not clear exactly what aspects of the ADHD syndrome are inherited, whether they be problems with attention, hyperactivity, impulsivity, or aggressivity.

Children with ADHD often have histories of prenatal and birth complications, including maternal ingestion of large amounts of nicotine or barbiturates during pregnancy, low birth weight, premature delivery, and difficult delivery leading to oxygen deprivation (Anastopoulos & Barkley, 1988; Sprich-Buckminster, Biederman, Milberger, & Faraone, 1993). Some investigators suspect that moderate-to-severe drinking by mothers during pregnancy can lead to the kinds of problems in inhibiting behaviors seen in children with ADHD. As preschoolers, some of these children were exposed to high concentrations of lead, when they ingested lead-based paint (Fergusson, Horwood, & Lynskey, 1993). The popular notion that hyperactivity in children is caused by dietary factors, such as the consumption of large amounts of sugar, has not been supported in controlled studies (Milich, Wolrarch, & Lindgren, 1986).

Psychosocial Contributors to ADHD

Children with ADHD are more likely than children without psychological disturbances to belong to families in which there are frequent disruptions, such as changes in residence or parental divorce (Barkley et al., 1990). Their fathers are more prone to antisocial and criminal behavior, and their interactions with their mothers are often marked with hostility and conflict (Barkley et al., 1990). It is unclear, however, whether these family characteristics of children with ADHD are causes or consequences of ADHD or whether both ADHD and these family characteristics result from genetic predispositions to "externalizing behaviors."

Treatments for ADHD

The most common treatment for ADHD in children is the administration of stimulant drugs, such as methylphenidate (trade name Ritalin) and dextroamphetamine. It may seem odd to give a stimulant drug to a hyperactive child, but between 60 and 90 percent of ADHD children respond to these drugs with *decreases* in demanding, disruptive, and noncompliant behavior. They also show increases in positive mood, in the ability to be goal-directed, and in the quality of their interactions with others (Gadow, 1992). The effects of stimulant drugs on the behavior of ADHD children is not as paradoxical as it might seem on the surface. Children without ADHD who are given stimulant drugs also show increases in attention and decreases in disruptive behavior (Rapport et al., 1978).

These drugs have been controversial because some schools and physicians have been too quick to diagnose ADHD and to use drugs to try to control these children (Hinshaw, 1994). In the United States alone, about 750,000 children take Ritalin (Rapport & Kelly, 1991). Stimulant drugs are not benign, and their possible side effects include insomnia, headaches, tics, and nausea (Gadow, 1991, 1992). Thus, it is important that children be accurately diagnosed as having ADHD before being exposed to the these potent drugs.

Unfortunately, the gains made by ADHD children when treated with stimulants alone are short-term (Henker & Whalen, 1989). Longer-term gains can be had by combining stimulant

Stimulant drugs can help hyperactive children control their behaviors.

Behavioral methods, such as giving children "time out" for disruptive behavior, can help children learn to control their behaviors.

therapy with behavioral therapy that focuses on reinforcing attentive, goal-directed, and prosocial behaviors and extinguishing impulsive and hyperactive behaviors (DuPaul & Barkley, 1993). Parents may be taught behavioral methods for promoting positive behaviors and extinguishing maladaptive behaviors in their children. In addition, parents' own psychological problems and the impairments in parenting skills that these problems create may be the focus of psychosocial interventions for children with ADHD.

An ADHD child and his parents might design a contract that says that every time the child complies with a request from his parents to wash his hands, to set the dinner table, and to put away his toys, he earns a chip. At the end of each week, he can exchange his chips for toys or fun activities. Each time the child refuses to comply, however, he loses a chip. If the child throws a tantrum or becomes aggressive, he must go to his room for a time out. Such techniques can help parents break the cycle of arguments with their children that lead to escalations in the children's behaviors that, in turn, lead to more arguments and perhaps physical violence. These techniques also help children learn to anticipate the consequences of their behaviors and make less impulsive choices about their behaviors.

Several studies suggest that the combination of stimulant therapy and psychosocial therapy is more likely to lead to both short-term and long-term improvements than either type of therapy alone (DuPaul & Barkley, 1993; Gadow, 1992). Interventions that focus on promoting parental competence and on treating aggression and defiance in ADHD children very early in childhood appear to lead to the most positive long-term outcomes (Fischer, Barkley, Fletcher, & Smallish, 1993).

Conduct Disorder and Oppositional Defiant Disorder

Have you ever lied? Have you ever stolen something? Have you ever hit someone? Most of us would have to answer *yes* to some and probably all of these questions. Many fewer of us would answer *yes* to the following questions:

- Have you ever pulled a knife or a gun on another person?
- Have you ever forced someone into sexual activity?
- Have you ever deliberately set fire with the hope of doing serious damage to someone else's property?
- Have you ever broken into someone else's car or house with the intention of stealing?

conduct disorder
syndrome marked by chronic disregard for the rights of others, including specific behaviors such as stealing, lying, and engaging in acts of violence

Children who have **conduct disorder** often answer *yes* to these questions and engage in other serious transgressions of societal norms for behavior (see Table 9.2). These children have chronic patterns of unconcern for the basic rights of others. Consider the following case of a boy named Phillip (from Jenkins, 1973, pp. 60–64):

> **Case Study** • Phillip, age 12, was suspended from a small-town Iowa school and referred for psychiatric treatment by his principal, who sent along the following note with Phillip:
>
> > This child has been a continual problem since coming to our school. He does not get along on the playground because he is mean to other children. He disobeys school rules, teases the patrol children, steals from the other children, and defies all authority. Phillip keeps getting into fights with other children on the bus.
> >
> > He has been suspended from cafeteria privileges several times for fighting, pushing, and shoving. After he misbehaved one day at the cafeteria, the teacher

told him to come up to my office to see me. He flatly refused, lay on the floor, and threw a temper tantrum, kicking and screaming.

The truth is not in Phillip. When caught in actual misdeeds, he denies everything and takes upon himself an air of injured innocence. He believes we are picking on him. His attitude is sullen when he is refused anything. He pouts, and when asked why he does these things, he points to his head and says, "Because I'm not right up here."

This boy needs help badly. He does not seem to have any friends. His aggressive behavior prevents the children from liking him. Our school psychologist tested Phillip, and the results indicated average intelligence, but his school achievement is only at the third- and low fourth-grade level.

Table 9.2 Symptoms of Conduct Disorder

The symptoms of conduct disorder include behaviors that violate the basic rights of others and the norms for appropriate social behavior.

Bullies, threatens, or intimidates others
Initiates physical fights
Uses weapons in fights
Engages in theft and burglary
Is physically abusive to people and animals
Forces others into sexual activity
Lies and breaks promises often
Violates parents' rules about staying out at night
Runs away from home
Sets fires deliberately
Vandalizes and destroys others' property deliberately
Often skips school

Reprinted with permission from the *Diagnostic and Statistical Manual of Mental Disorders*, Fourth Edition. Copyright 1994 American Psychiatric Association.

We all have known bullies and children who often get into trouble. Only 3 to 7 percent of children exhibit behaviors serious enough to qualify for a diagnosis of conduct disorder, however (Robins, 1991). Still, the behaviors of children with conduct disorder exact a high cost to society. For example, the cost of vandalism to schools by juveniles in the United States is estimated to be over $600 million per year. Juveniles account for almost 20 percent of all violent-crime arrests (*Newsweek*, August 2, 1993). The average cost per year for caring for an incarcerated juvenile is over $40,000 (Davidson & Redner, 1988).

Unfortunately, many children with conduct disorder continue to have serious difficulty conforming to societal norms in adolescence and adulthood (Offord, Boyle, Racine, & Fleming, 1992). As adolescents, about half of them engage in criminal behavior and drug abuse. As adults, about 75 to 85 percent of them are chronically unemployed, have histories of unstable personal relationships, frequently engage in impulsive physical aggression, or are spouse abusers (Zoccolillo, Pickles, Quinton, & Rutter, 1992). Between 35 and 40 percent of them will be diagnosed with antisocial personality disorder as adults.

The DSM-IV recognizes a less-severe pattern of chronic misbehavior than is seen in conduct disorder. This less-severe pattern is known as **oppositional defiant disorder**. Children with oppositional defiant disorder may be argumentative, negative, irritable, and defiant, but they do not engage in acts as serious as those of children with conduct disorder (see Table 9.3), as can be seen in the case of 9-year-old Jeremy (adapted from Spitzer et al., 1994, p. 343):

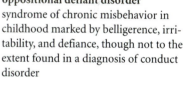

oppositional defiant disorder
syndrome of chronic misbehavior in childhood marked by belligerence, irritability, and defiance, though not to the extent found in a diagnosis of conduct disorder

Grafitti may be art to some people, but it is vandalism to others, and the costs of such antisocial acts to society can be great.

Some oppositional behavior is normal in children, but some children are excessively oppositional.

Case Study • Jeremy has been difficult to manage since nursery school. The problems have slowly escalated. Whenever he is without close supervision, he gets into trouble. At school, he teases and kicks other children, trips them, and calls them names. He is described as bad-tempered and irritable, even though at times he seems to enjoy school. Often he appears to be deliberately trying to annoy other children, though he always claims that others have started the arguments. He does not become involved in serious fights but does occasionally exchange a few blows with another child.

Jeremy sometimes refuses to do what his two teachers tell him to do, and this year has been particularly difficult with one who takes him in the afternoon for arithmetic, art, and science lessons. He gives many reasons why he should not have to do his work and argues when told to do it. At home, Jeremy's behavior is quite variable. On some days he is defiant and rude to his mother, needing to be told to do everything several times before he will do it, though eventually he usually complies. On other days he is charming and volunteers to help, but his unhelpful days predominate. His mother says, "The least little thing upsets him, and then he shouts and screams." Jeremy is described as spiteful and mean with his younger brother, Rickie. His mother also comments that he tells many minor lies though, when pressed, is truthful about important things.

Table 9.3 Symptoms of Oppositional Defiant Disorder

The symptoms of oppositional defiant disorder are not as severe as the symptoms of conduct disorder but have their onset at an earlier age, and oppositional defiant disorder often develops into conduct disorder.

Often loses temper
Often argues with adults
Often refuses to comply with requests or rules
Deliberately tries to annoy others
Blames others for his or her mistakes or misbehaviors
Is touchy or easily annoyed
Is angry and resentful
Is spiteful or vindictive

Reprinted with permission from the *Diagnostic and Statistical Manual of Mental Disorders*, Fourth Edition. Copyright 1994 American Psychiatric Association.

As was the case with Jeremy, the onset of symptoms of oppositional defiant disorder often occurs very early in life, during toddler and preschool years. Many children with oppositional defiant disorder seem to outgrow their behaviors by late childhood or early adolescence. A subset of children with oppositional defiant disorder, particularly those who tend to be aggressive, go on to develop conduct disorder in childhood and adolescence. Indeed, it seems that almost all children who develop conduct disorder during elementary school have had symptoms of oppositional defiant disorder in the earlier years of their lives (Loeber, Green, Keenan, Lahey, 1995).

Boys are about three times more likely than girls to be diagnosed with conduct disorder or oppositional defiant disorder (Cohen et al., 1993). This may be because the causes of these disorders are more frequently present in boys than in girls, as we will discuss later. It may also be because aggressive and antisocial behaviors are tolerated more in boys than in girls, so boys may more frequently than girls develop extremes of these behaviors.

Some researchers have suggested that antisocial aggresive behavior is not more rare in girls than in boys—it just takes a different form (Crick & Grotpeter, 1995; Zahn-Waxler, 1993; Zoccolillo, 1993). Girls' aggression is more likely to be indirect and verbal rather than physical and to involve alienation, ostracism, and character defamation of others. Girls exclude their peers, gossip about them, and collude with others to damage the social status of their targets.

It is clear, however, that girls with conduct and oppositional defiant disorders, like boys with these disorders, are at risk
for severe problems throughout their lives. Long-term studies of
girls diagnosed with conduct disorders find that, as adolescents
and adults, they show high rates of depression and anxiety disorders, severe marital problems, criminal activity, and early
unplanned pregnancies (Kovacs, Krol, & Voti, 1994; Loeber &
Keenan, 1994). Girls with conduct disorders are more likely than
boys with these disorders to marry partners who themselves
engage in antisocial behaviors (Robins, 1991).

Conduct disorders and oppositional defiant disorders are
found more frequently in children in lower socioeconomic classes
and in urban areas than in children in higher socioeconomic
classes and rural areas (Loeber, 1990; Offord, Alder, & Racine,
1986). This tendency may be due to differences between these
groups in some of the environmental causes of antisocial behavior, such as poverty and poor parenting. Alternately, because a
tendency toward antisocial behavior runs in families, as we will discuss next, families with
members who engage in antisocial behavior may experience "downward social drift": The
adults in these families cannot maintain good jobs, and thus the families tend to decline
in socioeconomic status.

Girls may not be overtly aggressive toward others very often, but may use covert forms of
aggression, such as spreading harmful secrets about each other.

**Do you think society should insist that troubled children get
treatment even if their parents object to it?**

Biological Contributors to Conduct Disorder

Antisocial behavior clearly runs in families. Children with conduct disorder are much
more likely than children without this disorder to have parents with antisocial personalities (Edelbrock, Rende, Plomin, & Thompson, 1995; Lahey et al., 1988). Their fathers
are also highly likely to have histories of criminal arrest and alcohol abuse, and their
mothers tend to have histories of depression (Lahey et al., 1988; Robins, 1991).

Twin and adoption studies have focused almost exclusively on criminal behaviors
rather than on conduct disorders specifically. Twin studies find the concordance rate for
criminal behaviors to be between 26 and 51 percent in monozygotic twins, compared to
13 to 22 percent in dizygotic twins (Rutter, Bolton, Harrington, & Couteur, 1990). Adoption
studies find that the criminal records of adopted sons are more similar to the records of
their biological fathers than to their adoptive fathers (Mednick, Moffitt, & Stack, 1987).
It is likely, however, that only children with the most severe cases of conduct disorder
develop criminal records, thus this evidence of a genetic predisposition may apply only
to more severe forms of conduct disorder. One small adoption study specifically focusing on conduct disorder found little evidence for a genetic predisposition to the disorder
(Jary & Stewart, 1985).

Some researchers have suggested that children with conduct disorders have fundamental neurological deficits in the brain systems involved in planning and controlling
behavior (Seguin, Pihl, Harden, & Tremblay, 1995). One piece of evidence that neurological deficits play a role in the development of conduct disorder is the fact that many children with conduct disorder also have attention deficit/hyperactivity disorder (Moffitt &
Silva, 1988). Recall that children with ADHD have trouble maintaining attention and
tend to be irritable and impulsive in their actions. These problems can lead to the development of conduct disorder when they bring about failure in school and therefore to
rejection of school and to poor peer relationships and rejection by peers. Rolf Loeber
(1990) suggests that the path to the development of conduct disorder may begin with a
child being exposed to neurotoxins and drugs while in the womb or during preschool
years, thereby developing a neurological deficit that impairs her ability to maintain

Figure 9.1

One Potential Pathway to the Development of Deliquency. Psychologist Rolf Loeber suggests that many youth who end up as delinquents begin life with neurological impairments that are the result of negative experiences in the womb or early in life. These neurological impairments then contribute to hyperactivity and attention problems, which lead to conduct problems, and eventually a range of problems in school and with peers. These problems culminate in delinquent behavior.

Source: Loeber, 1990, Figure 2, p. 7.

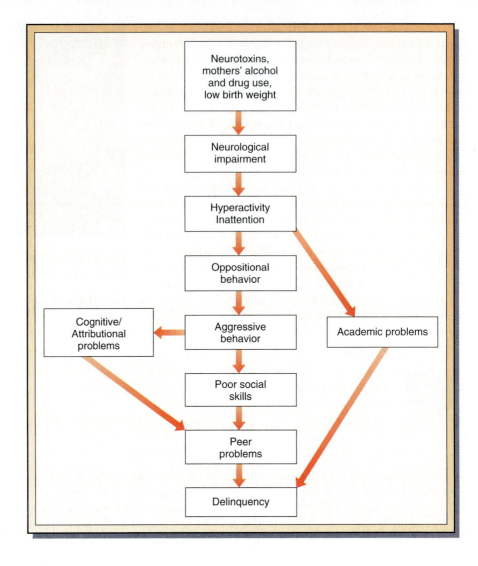

attention and makes her hyperactive (see Figure 9.1). These neurological deficits then lead to oppositional behavior in early childhood, followed by increasingly more aggressive and severe antisocial behavior as the child ages.

Another clue that biological factors are involved in conduct disorder is that there were signs of trouble in diagnosed children even in infancy. Children who develop conduct disorders tend to have been difficult babies and toddlers (Henry, Caspi, Moffitt, & Silva, 1996; Shaw, Keenan, & Vondra, 1994). They were irritable and demanding and did not comply with their parents' requests. They were impulsive, seemed to have little control over their behaviors, and responded to frustration with aggression. This correlation suggests that diagnosed children are born with a particular kind of difficult temperament that portends the antisocial behaviors they will engage in as older children (Seguin et al., 1995).

One way that children learn to control their behavior is by associating punishment with misbehavior and rewards with good behavior. Children with conduct disorders may have more difficulty learning from punishments and rewards because they tend to become less physiologically aroused than other children by reinforcements and punishments they receive for their behaviors (Quay, 1993; Raine, Venables, & Williams, 1996). Dan Olweus (1986) found that boys who were prone to unprovoked aggression, impulsivity, and acting-out behaviors had lower levels of adrenaline in their blood than did boys who were not prone to these behaviors. Olweus suggested that boys with low levels of adrenaline become easily bored and experience a craving for stimulation, for thrills and sensations.

Strong stimuli are not experienced as aversive or disturbing by these boys, making them more likely to take risks. When they engage in aggressive behavior, they may feel pleasant arousal and excitement and thus may seek out situations that foster aggressive behaviors.

Finally, a popular theory of aggressive behavior is that it is linked to the hormone testosterone. Although it is clear that high levels of testosterone are associated with aggressivity in animals, few studies of this association have been done in humans. In one study of 58 boys 15 to 17 years of age, Olweus (1986) found that boys who were more prone to verbal and physical aggression in response to provocation and who were more impatient and irritable had higher blood levels of testosterone.

Although children who develop conduct disorders may have some biological predisposition to these disorders, they are unlikely to develop them unless they are also exposed to environments that promote antisocial behavior (Cadoret & Cain, 1980; Cloninger & Gottesman, 1987). The characteristics of such environments are described in the next section.

Social Contributors to Conduct Disorder

The quality of parenting children receive, particularly children with vulnerability to hyperactivity and conduct disturbances, is strongly related to whether they develop the full syndrome of conduct disorder (Loeber, 1990). One of the best predictors of children's conduct disturbances is parental supervision: Children who frequently are unsupervised or poorly supervised for long periods of time (e.g., left home alone for several hours or even days) are much more likely to develop patterns of delinquent behaviors than are children who are seldom unsupervised. A related variable is parental uninvolvement: Children whose parents are not involved in their everyday lives—for example, children whose parents do not know who their friends are or what they are doing in school—are more likely to develop conduct disturbances. When parents of children with conduct disturbances do interact with their children, these interactions often are characterized by hostility, physical violence, and ridicule (Patterson, DeBaryshe, & Ramsey, 1989). The picture one gets of these families is one in which parents frequently ignore the children or are absent from home, but then when children transgress in some way, the parents lash out at the children violently (Lochman, White, & Wayland, 1991). These parents are more likely to give severe physical punishments to boys than to girls, which may partially account for the higher rate of conduct disturbances in boys (Lytton & Romney, 1991).

What are the critical criteria that should be used to decide when it is appropriate to remove a child from a troubled home?

Children living in such families may turn to their peers for validation and to escape their parents. Unfortunately, these peer groups may be comprised of other children with conduct disturbances. Deviant peer groups tend to encourage delinquent acts, even providing opportunities for such acts (Patterson et al., 1989). For example, the members of a peer group of adolescents may dare a new member to commit a robbery to "show he is a man" and provide him with a weapon and a getaway car to commit the robbery. Children who become part of deviant peer groups are especially likely to begin abusing alcohol and illicit drugs which, in turn, leads to increases in deviant acts (McBride, Joe, & Simpson, 1991). Conversely, adolescents and young adults with conduct disturbances who form close relationships with others who do not have such problems are much more likely to "grow out" of their conduct disturbances. For example, young delinquent men who marry young women with no history of conduct problems tend to cease their delinquent acts and never engage in such acts again (Sampson & Laub, 1992).

The biological factors and family factors that contribute to conduct disorders may often coincide. The neuropsychological problems associated with antisocial behaviors are linked to maternal drug use, poor prenatal nutrition, pre- and postnatal exposure to

Children whose parents use agression to punish them may learn to be aggressive themselves.

The peer groups of aggressive youth can encourage antisocial behaviors and provide opportunities for these behaviors.

toxic agents, child abuse, birth complications, and low birth weight (Moffitt, 1993). Infants and toddlers with these neuropsychological problems are more irritable, impulsive, awkward, overreactive, and inattentive than their peers and slower learners. This makes them difficult for parents to care for, and they are thus at increased risk for maltreatment and neglect. Added to this, the parents of these children are likely to be teenagers and to have psychological problems of their own that contribute to ineffective, harsh, or inconsistent parenting. Thus, children may carry a biological predisposition to disruptive, antisocial behaviors and may experience parenting that contributes to these behaviors. In a study of 536 boys, Terri Moffitt (1990) found that those who had both neuropsychological deficits and adverse home environments scored higher on an aggression scale than did those boys with only neuropsychological deficits or adverse home environments (see also Henry et al., 1996).

Cognitive Contributors to Conduct Disorder

Children with conduct disorder tend to process information about social interactions in ways that promote aggressive reactions to these interactions (Crick & Dodge, 1994). They enter social interactions with assumptions that other children will be aggressive toward them, and they use these assumptions rather than cues from the specific situations to interpret the actions of their peers (Dodge & Tomlin, 1987). For example, when another child accidently bumps into him, a child with a conduct disorder will assume that the bumping was intentional and meant to provoke a fight. In addition, conduct-disordered children tend to believe that any negative actions peers might take against them, such as taking their favorite pencils, are intentional rather than accidental (see Crick & Dodge, 1994). When deciding upon what action to take in response to a perceived provocation by a peer, children with conduct disturbances tend to think of a narrow range of responses, usually including aggression (Pettit, Dodge, & Brown, 1988; Rubin, Daniels-Bierness, & Hayvren, 1982; Spivack & Shure, 1974). When pressed to consider responses other than aggression, these children generate ineffective or vague responses and often consider responses other than aggression to be useless or unattractive (e.g., Crick & Ladd, 1990).

Children who think about their social interactions in these ways are likely to engage in aggressive behaviors toward others. They then may be retaliated against: Other children will hit them, parents and teachers will punish them, and others will perceive them negatively. In turn, these actions by others may feed the children's assumptions that the world is against them, causing them to misinterpret future actions by others. A cycle of interactions can be built that maintains and encourages aggressive, antisocial behaviors in such children. Again, the best evidence that thinking patterns are causes of antisocial behavior in children rather than just correlates comes from studies showing that changing aggressive

Children with conduct problems are prone to interpreting the incorrect actions of others as intentional acts of aggression.

children's thinking patterns can change their tendencies to act aggressively. Let us turn to these interventions and other interventions for children with conduct disorder.

Psychosocial Therapies for Conduct Disorder

Most psychosocial therapies for conduct disorder are derived from social learning theory (see Chapter 3) and focus on changing the children's ways of interpreting interpersonal interactions, teaching them to take the perspectives of others and care about those perspectives, teaching them to use "self-talk" as a way of controlling impulsive behaviors, and teaching them more adaptive ways of solving conflicts than aggression (Chamberlain & Rosicky, 1995; Estrada & Pinsof, 1995; Lochman et al., 1991). The first step in this therapy is to teach children to recognize situations that trigger anger or aggressive behaviors or in which they tend to be impulsive. This is done through observing children in their natural settings and then pointing out to them situations in which they misbehaved or seemed angry, discussing hypothetical situations and how the children would react to them, and having children keep diaries of their feelings and behaviors. The children also are taught to analyze their thoughts in these situations and to consider alternative ways of interpreting situations. Their assumptions that other children or adults act meanly toward them intentionally are challenged, and they are helped to take other people's perspectives on situations. Next, the children may be taught to use "self-talk" to help them avoid negative reactions to situations: They learn to talk to themselves in difficult situations, repeating phrases that help them calm themselves, and consider adaptive ways of coping with situations. For example, a child who tends to respond to provocation by others by immediately beginning to hit and kick might learn to say to himself,

> Slow down, slow down, slow down. Breathe deeply. Count to five. Slow down, slow down, slow down—Think about what to do. Don't want to get mad. Slow down, slow down.

Adaptive problem-solving skills are taught by discussing real and hypothetical problem situations with children and helping the children generate a variety of positive solutions to the problems. These solutions might be modeled by therapists and then practiced by the children in role plays. For example, if a therapist and child are discussing how to respond to another child who has cut in line in the lunchroom at school, the therapist might initially model an assertive (rather than aggressive) response, such as saying, "I would like you to move to the back of the line," to the cutting child. Then, the child in therapy might practice the assertive response and perhaps also pretend to be the child cutting in line in order to gain some perspective on why the child might do this.

Cognitive-behavioral therapies for children with conduct disturbances often are applied in group settings. Lochman and colleagues (1991, pp. 50–51) provided the following example of how group therapy can be especially effective:

> In a recent group session, Bob began talking about an incident that had led to a 5-day suspension from school the prior week. Rather than continue with the scheduled group activity, the bulk of the session was spent in group problem solving about this situation. Bob described how the incident began when he and another boy disagreed over who could sit on a cushion in the library. After a brief exchange of insults took place, the two boys were quiet for the remainder of the library period. However, as the class left the library, Bob got up in the other boy's face and reinitiated the verbal assaults in a more provocative way. When the boy responded with verbal insults, Bob knocked him down and kept hitting him until he was pulled away by the assistant principal. The group discussion included a focus on perspective taking with regard to the other boy's intentions, which did not initially appear to be as purposefully malevolent as Bob had perceived, and with regard to the assistant principal's intentions. In a spirited discussion, the group noted the assistant principal may have been either mean or trying to protect the combatants when he grabbed Bob and swung him around (most group members

eventually decided he was trying to be protective). After several other ways of handling the initial "cushion" problem were suggested to Bob, Bob asked each of the group members how he or she would have handled it. When the group member with the most streetwise demeanor suggested a nonconfrontational solution, Bob tentatively decided to try that strategy in the next conflict. Notable aspects of this discussion included how assaultive incidents often escalate from trivial initial problems, how Bob had great difficulty letting his anger dissipate after the initial provocation, how Bob's anger disrupted his ordinarily adequate social cognitions through preemptive processing, and how the group members were instrumental in providing training in social perspective taking and social problem solving.

Bob was probably more willing to consider a nonconfrontational solution to his problem because it came from one of his peers, an especially "cool" peer, rather than from an adult. All the group members had the opportunity to learn to generate alternative interpretations and solutions to this problem in the nonthreatening context of helping Bob.

Some psychosocial therapies for children with conduct disorder also include parents, particularly if the family dynamics are supporting the children's conduct disorder (Patterson, Reid, Jones, & Conger, 1975). Parents are taught to reinforce positive behaviors in their children and discourage aggressive or antisocial behaviors. Parents are also taught strategies similar to the ones already described for controlling their own angry outbursts and discipline techniques that are not violent. Unfortunately, it can be difficult to get the parents who need the most improvement in parenting skills to participate in therapy (Chamberlain & Rosicky, 1995).

Studies of the therapies based on social learning theory suggest that they can be very effective in reducing aggressive and impulsive behavior in children (see Borduin et al., 1995; Lochman et al., 1991). Unfortunately, many children relapse into conduct disturbances after a while, particularly if their parents have poor parenting skills, alcoholism or drug abuse, or other psychopathology. Interventions are most likely to have long-term positive effects if they are begun early in a disturbed child's life and include his or her parents (Estrada & Pinsof, 1995). Booster sessions of additional therapy sometime after a course of initial therapy has been completed also help a child avoid relapsing into conduct disturbance (Lochman et al., 1991).

Drug Therapies for Conduct Disorder

Children with severely aggressive behavior are sometimes prescribed neuroleptic drugs (Gadow, 1992). Controlled studies suggest that these drugs suppress aggressive behavior in these children (Campbell, Perry, & Green, 1984). It is unclear whether the drugs have any effect on the other symptoms of conduct disorder, such as lying and stealing. Children with both conduct disorder and attention deficit/hyperactivity disorder are frequently prescribed stimulant drugs, and these drugs also suppress aggressive behaviors (Gadow, Nolan, Sverd, Sprafkin, & Paolicelli, 1990). Finally, case reports and controlled studies suggest that lithium may be an effective treatment for children with aggressive conduct disorder (Campbell et al., 1984).

Ethnic/Racial Differences in Interventions for Antisocial Behavior

It appears that the criminal justice system deals differently with ethnic minority adolescents who commit antisocial behaviors than with white adolescents who behave in antisocial ways. Researchers examined the case records of all adolescents who were sent to correctional schools or to state psychiatric hospitals in one area of Connecticut over a year (Lewis, Balla, & Shanok, 1979). The adolescents sent to psychiatric hospitals and those sent to jail were just as likely to have histories of violence and had equal levels of emotional problems. However the adolescents sent to jail were much more likely to be African

American than white, whereas those sent to psychiatric hospitals were much more likely to be white than African American. It appears that disturbed African-American adolescents are incarcerated; whereas disturbed whites are hospitalized.

 Some political leaders have advocated treating juveniles who commit crimes more like adults, in terms of the types of correctional facilities they are sent to and the lengths of their sentences. Given what you have learned about conduct disorder and juvenile delinquency, what do you think about this argument?

African American adolescents with conduct disturbances are often incarcerated, whereas white adolescents with conduct disturbances are more likely to receive counseling.

Summing Up   Behavior Disorders

- The behavior disorders include attention deficit/hyperactivity disorder, conduct disorder, and oppositional defiant disorder.
- Children with attention deficit/hyperactivity disorder are inattentive, impulsive, and overactive. They often do not do well in school, and their relationships with their peers are extremely impaired.
- Many children with attention deficit/hyperactivity disorder grow out of this disorder, but some continue to show the symptoms into adulthood, and they are at high risk for conduct problems and emotional problems throughout their lives.
- The two therapies that are effective in treating ADHD are stimulant drugs and behavioral therapies that teach children how to control their behaviors.
- Children with conduct disorder engage in behaviors that severely violate societal norms, including chronic lying, stealing, and violence toward others.
- Children with oppositional defiant disorder engage in less-severe antisocial behaviors that indicate a negativistic, irritable approach to others.
- Some children outgrow oppositional defiant disorder, but a subset develop full conduct disorder.
- Children who develop conduct disorder often continue to engage in antisocial behaviors into adulthood and have high rates of criminal activity and drug abuse.
- Neurological deficits may be involved in conduct disorder. These deficits may make it more difficult for children with this disorder to learn from reinforcements and punishments and to control their behaviors.
- Children with conduct disorder also tend to have parents that are neglectful much of the time and violent when annoyed with them.
- Children with conduct disorder tend to think about interactions with others in ways that contribute to their aggressive reactions.

 Which childhood behavior problems do you think would pose the greatest difficulty in establishing when the problem crosses the line from a "normal" problem of children to a psychological disorder?

Emotional Disorders

Children can suffer from depression, panic attacks, obsessive-compulsive disorder, generalized anxiety disorder, post-traumatic stress disorder, and phobias. The childhood versions of most of these disorders have been described in the chapters on the individual disorders. One emotional disorder that is specific to childhood is **separation anxiety disorder.**

Many infants, if separated from their primary caregivers, become anxious and upset. They cry loudly and cannot be consoled by anyone but their primary caregivers. This is a normal consequence of an infant's development of the understanding that objects (including mother and father) continue to exist even when they are not in direct sight

separation anxiety disorder
syndrome of childhood and adolescence marked by the presence of abnormal fear or worry over becoming separated from one's caregiver(s) as well as clinging behaviors in the presence of the caregiver(s)

Some separation anxiety is normal in young children, but other children are excessively anxious about leaving their caregivers.

and the infant's attachment to the caregivers. With development, however, most infants come to understand that their caregivers will return and find ways to comfort themselves while their caregivers are away so that they are not excessively anxious.

Some children continue to be extremely anxious when separated from their caregivers, even into childhood and adolescence. They may refuse to go to school because they fear the separation from their caregivers. They cannot sleep at night unless they are with their caregivers. They have nightmares with themes of separation. They may follow their caregivers around the house to be with them. If they are separated from their caregivers, they worry tremendously that something bad will happen to the caregivers. They have exaggerated fears of natural disasters (e.g., tornadoes, earthquakes) and of robbers, kidnappers, and accidents. They may have stomachaches and headaches and become nauseous and vomit if forced to separate from their caregivers. Younger children may cry unconsolably. Older children may avoid activities, such as being on a baseball team, that might take them away from their caregivers, preferring to spend all the time possible with their caregivers.

Many children go through short episodes of a few days of these symptoms after traumatic events, such as getting lost in a shopping mall or the hospitalization of parents for sudden illness. Separation anxiety disorder is not diagnosed unless a child shows symptoms for at least 4 weeks and the symptoms significantly impair the child's ability to function in everyday life. Children with this disorder may be very shy, sensitive, and demanding of adults.

About 2 to 4 percent of preadolescents experience separation anxiety disorder (Anderson, Williams, McGee, & Silva, 1987; Bowen, Offord, & Boyle, 1990). It is much more common in girls than in boys. Left untreated, this disorder can recur frequently throughout childhood and adolescence, significantly interfering with the child's academic progress and peer relationships.

Biological Contributors to Separation Anxiety

Biological factors may be involved in the development of separation anxiety disorder. Children with this disorder tend to have family histories of anxiety disorders (Gittelman & Klein, 1984; Turner, Beidel, & Costello, 1987). There may be a particularly strong link between separation anxiety and panic attacks. The symptoms that children with separation anxiety disorder experience when separated from their parents resemble those of a panic attack. Children with separation anxiety disorder appear at increased risk for developing panic disorder as adults. The children of parents with panic disorder are three times more likely to develop separation anxiety disorder than are the children of parents without panic disorder (Weissman et al., 1984).

Psychosocial Contributors to Separation Anxiety

There is more evidence, however, that psychosocial factors play a role in the development of this disorder than there is evidence for biological contributors. In many cases, separation anxiety disorder develops following traumatic events, such as the following:

Case Study • In the early morning hours, 7-year-old Maria was abruptly awakened by a loud rumbling and violent shaking. She sat upright in bed and called out to her 10-year-old sister, Rosemary, who was leaping out of her own bed 3 feet away. The two girls ran for their mother's bedroom as their toys and books plummeted from shelves and dresser tops. The china hutch in the hallway teetered in front of them and then fell forward with a crash, blocking their path to their mother's room. Mrs. Marshall called out to them to go back and stay in their doorway. They knew the doorway was a place you were supposed to go during an earthquake, so they huddled there together until the shaking finally stopped. Mrs. Marshall climbed over the hutch and broken china to her daughters. Although they were all very shaken and scared, they were unhurt.

Two weeks later, back at school, Maria began to complain every morning of stomachaches, headaches, and dizziness, asking to stay home with her mother. After 4 days, when a medical examination revealed no physical problems, Maria was told she must return to school. She protested tearfully, but her mother insisted, and Rosemary promised to hold her hand all the way to school. In the classroom, Maria could not concentrate on her schoolwork and was often out of her seat looking out the window in the direction of home. She told her teacher she needed to go home to see if her mother was okay. When she was told she couldn't go home, she began to cry and shake so violently the school nurse called Mrs. Marshall who came and picked Maria up and took her home. The next morning, Maria's protests grew stronger and she refused to go to school until her mother promised to go with her and sit in her classroom for the first hour. When Mrs. Marshall began to leave, Maria clung to her, crying, pleading for her not to leave, and following her into the hallway. The next day, Maria refused to leave the house for her Brownie meeting and her dancing lessons or even to play in the front yard. She followed her mother around the house and insisted on sleeping with her at night. "I need to be with you, Mommy, in case something happens," she declared.

Following a trauma, adults need to support children and to model appropriate coping strategies.

Parents may contribute to the development of a separation anxiety disorder in their children by being overprotective and modeling anxious reactions to separations from their children (Kendall, 1992). The families of children with separation anxiety tend to be especially close-knit, not encouraging developmentally appropriate levels of independence in the children.

Treatments for Separation Anxiety

Behavior therapy is often used to treat separation anxiety disorder (Estrada & Pinsof, 1995; Kendall et al., 1991). Children might be taught relaxation exercises to practice during periods of separation, and these periods are increased in duration as the therapy progresses. Parents must be willing to participate in the therapy and to cope with their children's (and their own) reactions to attempts to increase periods of separation. Parents may need to be taught to model nonanxious reactions to separations from their children and to reinforce nonanxious behavior in their children. There is some evidence that adding a cognitive component to this therapy, in which children's fears about separation are challenged and they are taught to use "self-talk" to calm themselves when they become anxious, is useful (Kane & Kendall, 1989). Here is how Maria was treated for her separation anxiety:

Case Study • Mrs. Marshall was instructed to take Maria to school and leave four times during the period she was there. Initially, Mrs. Marshall left for 30 seconds each time. Over time, she gradually increased the amount of time and distance she was away while Maria remained in the classroom. Maria was given a sticker at the end of the school day for each time she remained in her seat while her mother was out of the room. In addition, she was praised by her teacher and her mother, and positive self-statements (e.g., "My mommy will be okay; I'm a big girl and I can stay at school") were encouraged. No response was made when Maria failed to stay in her chair. Maria could exchange her stickers for prizes at the end of each week.

At home, Mrs. Marshall was instructed to give minimal attention to Maria's inquiries about her well-being and to ignore excessive, inappropriate crying. Eventually, Maria was given a sticker and praise each morning for sleeping in her own bed.

The first few times Mrs. Marshall left the classroom, Maria followed her out. Soon she stayed in her chair and received stickers. At home, she remained in her own bed the first night, even though she was told she only had to stay 2 hours to earn her sticker. At her own request, she returned to Brownie meetings and attended summer camp.

Research on drug therapies for separation anxiety disorder is very limited (Gadow, 1991). One study found that the antidepressant drug imipramine reduces symptoms of separation anxiety disorder, particularly children's refusal to go to school (Gittelman-Klein & Klein, 1971), but the results of that study were not replicated in a more recent study (Klein, Koplewicz, & Kanner, 1992).

Elimination Disorders

Case Study • On the morning of her third birthday, Gretchen walked into the kitchen and announced to her mother, "I'm a big girl now, and I'm going to wear big girl underpants. No more diapers." She indeed did wear "big girl underpants" that day, and although she had a couple of accidents during the day, at bedtime Gretchen was extremely proud of herself for being such a big girl. Within a few weeks, she was able to wear big girl underpants all day without any accidents.

Most children gain sufficient control over their bladder and bowel movements by about age 4 that they no longer need to wear diapers during the day or night. Like Gretchen, many children view the ability to control their bladder and bowel movements as a marker of their passage into being "big boys or girls." It is understandable, then, that children who lose this control, particularly when they are far past the preschool years and into middle childhood, can experience shame and distress.

Occasional wetting of the bed at night is common among elementary-school children, particularly during times of stress. Children over age 5 are diagnosed with **enuresis** when they have wet the bed or their clothes at least twice a week for 3 months (APA, 1994). Most children with enuresis wet only at night. A subset wet during the daytime only, most often at school. These children may be socially anxious about using the public toilets at school or prone to becoming preoccupied with other things they are doing. Thus, they do not use the toilet as they need to and tend to have wetting accidents. Enuresis is relatively common, as disorders go, among young children, but the prevalence decreases with age. About 7 percent of boys and 3 percent of girls have enuresis at age 5, but only 3 percent of boys and 2 percent of girls have this disorder at age 10. The prevalence of enuresis among 18 year olds is 1 percent for males and less than 1 percent for females.

Encopresis is a more rare disorder than enuresis, involving repeated defecation into clothing or onto the floor. To be diagnosed with encopresis, children must have at least one such event a month for at least 3 months and must be at least 4 years of age. Only about 1 percent of 5 year olds has encopresis, and it is more common in boys than in girls.

We know much more about the triggers for enuresis than for encopresis. Enuresis runs in families, and approximately 75 percent of children with enuresis have biological relatives who had the disorder. Some of these children may have inherited a biological vulnerability to the disorder in the form of unusually small bladders or lower bladder threshold for involuntary voiding. Psychodynamic and family systems theorists suggest that enuresis is due to conflicts and anxiety due to disruptions or dysfunction in the family (Olmos de Paz, 1990). For example, some children develop enuresis when new babies are born in their families, perhaps because they feel threatened by the attention their parents are giving to the new babies and resentful toward the new babies but cannot express feelings freely. Finally, behaviorists suggest that enuresis may be due to lax or inappropriate toilet training, that

enuresis
diagnosis given to children over 5 years of age who wet the bed or their clothes at lease twice a week for 3 months

encopresis
diagnosis given to children who are at least 4 years old and who defecate inappropriately at least once a month for 3 months

Children are very proud of themselves when they learn to control their bowel and bladder movements, thus loss of control can be very distressing.

enuretic children never learned appropriate bladder control and thus have recurrent problems during childhood (Erickson, 1992).

The most common treatment for enuresis is referred to as the **bell and pad method**. A pad is placed under the child while she sleeps. This pad has a sensory device to detect even small amounts of urine. If the child wets during her sleep, then a bell connected to the pad rings and awakens the child. Through classical conditioning, the child learns to wake up when she has a full bladder and needs to urinate. The bell and pad method is highly effective (Friman & Warzak, 1990; Whelan & Houts, 1990).

Some children with enuresis are given antidepressant medications, which can help to reduce accidental wetting. The benefits of these drugs usually disappear as soon as the children stop taking them, however (Fritz, Rockney, & Young, 1994).

Developmental Disorders

Beginning from the first day home from the hospital, parents eagerly track their children's development, watching for the emergence of cognitive skills, motor skills, and social skills. The first responsive smile from a child, the first tentative steps, and the first babbling words are occasions for major celebrations. Although most parents become anxious at one time or another when it seems their children are not developing some skill "on time" (or perhaps even ahead of other children), their fears usually are allayed as their children's skills eventually emerge.

Sometimes, though, important skills do not emerge or develop fully in a child. A child might not learn to crawl or walk until many months after most children do. Another child might have severe trouble with reading or arithmetic, despite having good teachers. Perhaps most heartbreaking is a child who does not develop socially as other children do, not smiling at others or seeming interested in play with others, not wanting to cuddle with her parents.

Children who have substantial deficits in important cognitive, motor, or social skills are said to have developmental disorders. Some developmental disorders affect only specific skills: **Reading disorder** involves deficits in the ability to read. **Mathematics disorder** involves deficits in the ability to learn math. **Disorder of written expression** involves deficits in the ability to write. **Motor skills disorder** involves deficits in fundamental motor skills, such as walking or running or holding onto objects. **Communication disorder** involves deficits in the ability to communicate verbally, because of a severely limited vocabulary, severe stuttering, or the inability to articulate words correctly. These disorders are diagnosed only if they significantly interfere with a child's progress through school or functioning outside of the classroom.

There are two types of developmental disorders that involve deficits in a wide range of skills: mental retardation and autism. Because these two disorders exact a heavy toll on the children who have them and on their families, the remainder of this chapter will be devoted to these disorders.

Mental Retardation

Mental retardation is defined as significantly subaverage intellectual functioning. A child's level of intellectual functioning may be assessed by standardized tests, usually referred to as *IQ tests* (see Chapter 2 for a discussion of these tests). Low scores on an IQ test do not, by themselves, warrant a diagnosis of mental retardation. This diagnosis requires that a child also show significant problems in performing the tasks of daily life. Specifically, in order to be diagnosed as mentally retarded, a child must show deficits, relative to other children that age, in at least two of the following skill areas: communication, self-care, home living, social and interpersonal, use of community resources (e.g., riding a bus), self-direction, functional academic, work, leisure activity, or protection of one's own health and safety. Mental retardation is not diagnosed unless a child shows evidence of these deficits before age 18.

Parents will closely watch their newborn children for signs they are developing normally.

bell and pad method
treatment for enuresis in which a pad placed under a sleeping child to detect traces of urine sets off a bell when urine is detected, awakening the child to condition him or her to wake up and use the bathroom before urinating

reading disorder
developmental disorder involving deficits in reading ability

mathematics disorder
developmental disorder involving deficits in the ability to learn mathematics

disorder of written expression
developmental disorder involving deficits in the ability to write

motor skills disorder
developmental disorder involving deficits in motor skills such as walking or holding onto objects

communication disorder
developmental disorder involving deficits in communication abilities, such as stuttering or poor articulation

mental retardation
developmental disorder marked by significantly subaverage intellectual functioning, as well as deficits (relative to other children) in life skill areas such as communication, self-care, work, and interpersonal relationships

The severity of mental retardation varies greatly. Children with *mild mental retardation* can feed and dress themselves with minimal help, may have average motor skills, and can learn to talk and write in simple terms. They can get around their own neighborhoods well, although they may not be able to venture beyond their neighborhoods without help. If they are put in special education classes that address their specific deficits, they can achieve high school educations and become self-sufficient. As adults, they can shop for specific items and cook simple meals for themselves. They may be employed in unskilled or semiskilled jobs. Their scores on IQ tests tend to be between about 50 and 70.

Children with *moderate mental retardation* typically have significant delays in language development, such as using only 4 to 10 words by the age of 3. They may be physically clumsy and thus have some trouble dressing and feeding themselves. They typically do not achieve beyond the second grade level in academic skills but, with special education, can acquire simple vocational skills. As adults, they may not be able to travel alone or shop or cook for themselves. Their scores on IQ tests tend to be between about 35 and 50.

Children with *severe mental retardation* have very limited vocabularies and speak in two- to three-word sentences. They may have significant deficits in motor development and may play with toys inappropriately (for example, banging two dolls together rather than having them interact symbolically). As adults, they can feed themselves with spoons and dress themselves if the clothing is not complicated with many buttons or zippers. They cannot travel alone for any distance and cannot shop or cook for themselves. They may be able to learn some unskilled manual labor, but many do not. Their IQ scores tend to run between 20 and 35.

Children and adults with *profound mental retardation* are severely impaired and require full-time custodial care. They cannot dress themselves completely. They may be able to use spoons, but not knives or forks. They tend not to interact with others socially, although they may respond to simple commands. They may achieve vocabularies of 300 to 400 words as adults. Persons with profound mental retardation often suffer from frequent illnesses and their life expectancy is shorter than normal. Their IQ scores tend to be under 20.

Table 9.4 Comparisons of Children with Organic and Cultural-Familial Mental Retardation

Children with organic mental retardation often have an earlier onset of problems, clear histories of biological abnormalities, more severe impairments, and worse prognosis than do children with cultural-familial mental retardation.

Organic Mental Retardation	Cultural-Familial Mental Retardation
It is typically diagnosed in infancy.	It is typically diagnosed at school age.
There is a clear history or indicators of a biological abnormality.	There may be no history or indicators of biological abnormality.
The severity of retardation is profound, severe, or moderate.	The severity of retardation is often mild.
Impairments are generalized across situations.	Impairments are specific to certain situations.
Parents and siblings are likely to have intellectual functioning similar to that of the general population.	Parents and siblings are more likely to have mild retardation.
Socioeconomic status is representative of that of the general population.	Occurs often in lower socioeconomic groups.
Physical health is poorer than in the general population.	Physical health is about the same as that in the general population.
Treatments can improve functioning but not cure the condition.	Treatments may cure the condition entirely.

Source: Data from MacMillan, Gresham, and Siperstein, 1993.

Experts on mental retardation divide this disorder into two types: *organic retardation* and *cultural-familial retardation* (MacMillan, Gresham, & Siperstein, 1993). In cases of organic retardation, there is clear evidence of a biological cause for the disorder, and the level of retardation tends to be more severe. In cases of cultural-familial retardation, there is less evidence for the role of biology and more evidence for the role of environment in the development of the disorder. The severity of the retardation tends to be less severe, and there is a good chance that, with the right intervention, the child will eventually develop normal abilities (see Table 9.4).

There are a large number of biological factors that can cause mental retardation, including chromosomal and gestational disorders, exposure to toxins prenatally and in early childhood, infections, physical trauma, metabolism and nutrition problems, and gross brain disease. We examine these factors first and then turn to the sociocultural factors implicated in mental retardation.

Genetic Contributors to Mental Retardation

Intellectual skills are at least partially inherited. The IQs of adopted children correlate much more strongly with those of their biological parents than with those of their adoptive parents. Similarly, the IQs of monozygotic twins are much more strongly correlated than are the IQs of dizygotic twins, even when the twins are reared apart (Scarr, Weinberg, & Waldman, 1993; Schwartz & Johnson, 1985). Families of children who are mentally retarded tend to have high incidences of a variety of intellectual problems, including the different levels of mental retardation and autism.

Two metabolic disorders that are genetically transmitted and that cause mental retardation are *phenylketonuria* (PKU) and *Tay-Sachs disease*. PKU is carried by a recessive gene and occurs in about 1 in 20,000 births. Children with PKU are unable to metabolize phenylalanine, an amino acid. As a result, phenylalanine and its derivative, phenyl pyruvic acid, build up in the body and cause permanent brain damage. Fortunately, an effective treatment is available, and children who receive this treatment from an early age can develop an average level of intelligence. If untreated, children with PKU typically have IQs below 50.

Tay-Sachs disease also is carried by a recessive gene and occurs primarily in Jewish populations. It usually does not appear until a child is between 3 and 6 months. At this point, a progressive degeneration of the nervous system begins, leading to mental and physical deterioration. These children usually die before the age of 6 years, and there is no effective treatment for this disease.

Several types of chromosomal disorders can lead to mental retardation. Recall from Chapter 3 that children are born with 23 pairs of chromosomes. Twenty-two of these pairs are known as *autosomes*, and the 23rd pair is the sex chromosomes. One of the best-known causes of mental retardation is *Down syndrome,* which is caused when chromosome 21 is present in triplicate rather than in duplicate (for this reason, Down syndrome is also referred to as *Trisomy 21*). Down syndrome occurs in about 1 in every 800 children born in the United States. From childhood, almost all people with Down syndrome are mentally retarded, although the level of their retardation can vary from mild to profound. Children with Down syndrome have round, flat faces and almond-shaped eyes, small noses, slightly protruding lips and tongues, and short square hands. They tend to be short in stature and somewhat obese. Many of these children have congenital heart defects and gastrointestinal difficulties. As adults, they seem to age more rapidly than normal, and their life expectancy is shorter than average. People with Down syndrome have plaques and tangles on the neurons in their brains that resemble those found in Alzheimer's disease. About 25 to 40 percent of them lose their memories and the ability to care for themselves in adulthood.

Fragile X syndrome, which is the second most common cause of mental retardation in males after Down syndrome, is caused when a tip of the X chromosome breaks off. This syndrome is characterized by severe to profound mental retardation, speech defects, and severe deficits in interpersonal interactions. Males with Fragile X syndrome have

Children with Down syndrome have characteristic facial features, including almond shaped eyes, small noses, a slightly protruding lip, and short square hands.

large ears, long faces, and enlarged testes. Two other chromosomal abnormalities that cause mental retardation are *Trisomy 13* (chromosome 13 is present in triplicate) and *Trisomy 18* (chromosome 18 is present in triplicate). Both of these disorders lead to severe retardation and shortened life expectancy. The risk of having a child with Down syndrome or any other chromosomal abnormalities increases the older a woman is when she becomes pregnant. This may be because the older a mother is, the more likely her chromosomes are to have degenerated or been damaged by toxins.

The Prenatal Environment

The intellectual development of a fetus can be profoundly affected by the quality of its prenatal environment. When a pregnant woman contracts the rubella virus (German measles), the herpes virus, or syphilis, there is a risk of physical damage to the fetus that can cause mental retardation. Chronic maternal disorders such as high blood pressure and diabetes can interfere with fetal nutrition and brain development and therefore affect the intellectual capacities of the fetus, although if these disorders are effectively treated throughout the pregnancy, the risk of damage to the fetus is low.

Most drugs that a pregnant woman takes can pass through the placenta to the fetus. It is estimated that 325,000 babies born in the United States each year were exposed to illicit drugs prenatally (Gonzalez & Campbell, 1994). Much media attention has been focused on "crack babies," infants born to women who smoked crack while pregnant. Any form of cocaine constricts the mother's blood vessels, leading to reduced oxygen and blood flow to the fetus, possibly resulting in brain damage and retardation. Crack babies are also characterized as irritable and distractible. Recent studies suggest that mothers who take cocaine during pregnancy differ in many ways from mothers who do not: They are older, more socially disadvantaged, and more likely to use tobacco, alcohol, marijuana, and other illicit drugs (Gonzalez & Campbell, 1994; Richardson & Day, 1994). These other risk factors, in addition to exposure to cocaine, may severely impair intellectual growth in the children of these mothers.

There is increasing evidence that fetuses whose mothers abuse alcohol during pregnancy are at increased risk for mental retardation and a collection of physical defects known as *fetal alcohol syndrome* (Fried & Watkinson, 1990). Children with fetal alcohol syndrome have an average IQ of only 68, along with poor judgment, distractibility, difficulty in perceiving social cues, and the inability to learn from experience. As adolescents, their academic functioning is only at the second to fourth-grade level, and they have great trouble following directions. It is estimated that about 1 in 700 children in the United States is born with fetal alcohol syndrome (Streissguth, Randels, & Smith, 1991). Children born to mothers who drank only moderately during pregnancy may have intellectual deficits that are subtler than those found in fetal alcohol syndrome. Presently, it is not known whether there is a safe amount of alcohol that a woman can ingest during pregnancy.

Birth and the First Years of Life

Infants born several weeks premature are at increased risk for mental retardation because they are more likely to have central nervous system damage (Brooks-Gunn, Klebanov, Liaw, & Spitzer, 1993). Poor prenatal care and cigarette smoking or drug abuse by mothers increases the risk of premature delivery.

Exposure to toxic substances, such as lead, arsenic, and mercury, during early childhood can lead to mental retardation by damaging specific areas of the brain. Children living in lower socioeconomic areas are at increased risk for exposure to lead, because old, run-down buildings often have lead paint, which chips off and is ingested by the children.

Severe head traumas that damage children's brains can lead to mental retardation. *Shaken baby syndrome* is caused when a baby is shaken violently, leading to intracranial injury and retinal hemorrhages (Caffey, 1972). Babies' heads are relatively large and heavy compared to the rest of their bodies, and their neck muscles are too weak to control their

Many toxic substances, if ingested by a pregnant woman, can harm the neurological development of a fetus, causing mental retardation.

heads when they are shaken back and forth in whiplash fashion. The rapid movement of their heads when shaken can lead to their brains being bruised from being banged against the skull wall. Bleeding can also occur in and around the brain and behind the eyes. This can lead to seizures, partial or total blindness, paralysis, mental retardation, or death. Although violent shaking of a baby sometimes is part of a pattern of physical abuse by a parent, it often happens innocently when a frustrated parent does not know that shaking a baby can lead to permanent brain damage, as in the following case of a father of a young infant:

Case Study • Jill's mother was very ill, so she left me with the baby for the day while she went to her mother's house to help her. About 2 o'clock, the baby started crying for some reason. I changed him, I fed him, I rocked him, I sang to him. Nothing would quiet him down. He kept crying and crying, for hours. Finally, around 6 P.M., I got so overwhelmed with his crying that I just shook him, hard, but only for a few seconds. He immediately quieted down, so I thought I had done the right thing. I put him to bed and he seemed to sleep peacefully. But then we had trouble waking him for his feeding. The next day he was listless, just like a rag doll. Jill rushed him to the doctor. They did a series of tests and said that he might have brain damage! That was 4 years ago. Since then, he has been delayed in many areas of his development. The doctors say he will never be normal. I just wish I had known that you aren't supposed to shake a baby.

 Should mental retardation be considered a psychiatric diagnosis, given its strong biological roots? Why or why not?

Sociocultural Factors Associated with Mental Retardation

Children who are mentally retarded are more likely to come from low socioeconomic groups (Gross, Brooks-Gunn, & Spiker, 1992). This may be because their parents are also mentally retarded and thus have not been able to acquire well-paying jobs. The social disadvantages of being poor may also contribute to lower-than-average intellectual development. Poor mothers are less likely to receive good prenatal care, increasing the risk of their children being born prematurely. Poor children are concentrated in the inner city, in poorly funded schools, and this is especially true for poor minority children. Poor children who have lower IQs receive less favorable attention from teachers and fewer learning opportunities, especially if they are also minorities (Alexander, Entwisle, & Thompson, 1987). Poor children are less likely to have parents who read to them, who encourage academic success, and who are involved in their schooling. Although these factors may not cause significant mental retardation, they can substantially affect children's achievement of the highest level of intellectual development of which they are capable (Rodning, Beckwith, & Howard, 1991).

Treatments for the Mentally Retarded

Interventions for mentally retarded children must be comprehensive, intensive, and probably long-term to show benefits. One program showed that premature infants with low birth weight who were at high risk for mental retardation benefited substantially from an intensive intervention that began just after they were born (Gross, et al., 1992). These children went daily to a child development center with specially trained teachers who worked to overcome the children's intellectual and physical deficits. Their mothers were given training in good parenting practices and in ways of facilitating their

Children who do not have access to good nutrition, good schools, and a learning environment in the home, can develop cultural-familial forms of mental retardation.

Some people with Down syndrome live in group homes that specialize in meeting their needs.

children's cognitive development. For example, mothers were taught ways of calming their babies (who tended to be irritable), ways to provide appropriate levels of stimulation and opportunities for self-motivated actions and explorations, and ways of reducing stress in their environments and in their babies' environments. Finally, the program ensured that the children received appropriate medical care for free. At 36 months of age, these children were significantly less likely to have IQ scores in the retarded range than were those in a control group who had the same sociodemographic backgrounds but who received only medical care. Children of African-American mothers benefited even more from this intervention than did children of Caucasian and Hispanic mothers, probably because the African-American families were more disadvantaged than were the other families and thus could not obtain resources as easily on their own (Brooks-Gunn, Klebanov, Liaw, & Spiker, 1993).

The long-term effects of early intervention programs are less clear. Preschool programs for socially disadvantaged children with intellectual deficits, such as the Head Start Program, have positive effects on children's performance in first grade, but these effects appear to diminish with time. This may be because, once these children leave the preschool program, they enter schools that are substandard and receive less favorable treatment than do other children in school (Lee, Brooks-Gunn, Schnur, & Liaw, 1990).

Controversy exists over whether mentally retarded children should be placed in special education classes or *mainstreamed*—that is, put into regular classrooms. Special education classes can concentrate on retarded children's needs, providing them with extra training in skills they lack. Some critics of these classes, however, argue that they stigmatize children and provide them with an education that asks less of them than what they are able to achieve. Critics also have charged that minority children often are placed inappropriately in special education classes because they score lower on culturally biased achievement tests or IQ tests. However, placing retarded children in a classroom with children of average intelligence can put the retarded children at certain disadvantages. One study found that retarded children were viewed by the other children in their classrooms negatively (Gottlieb et al., 1978). Zigler and Hodapp (1991) argue that retarded children who are mainstreamed may often not receive the special training they need. However, studies of the academic progress of retarded children in special education programs and in regular classrooms tend to find little difference in the performance of these two groups.

 If you had a child who had mental retardation, would you want him or her to be mainstreamed into regular classrooms or put in a special needs classroom? Why?

In the past, most retarded children were institutionalized for life. Institutionalization is less common these days, but retarded children with severe physical handicaps or with significant behavior problems, such as problems controlling aggression, may still be institutionalized (Blacher, Hanneman, & Rousey, 1992). African-American and Latino families are less likely to institutionalize their retarded children than are white families (Blacher, et al., 1992). This may be because African-American and Latino families are less likely than white families to have the financial resources to place their children in high quality institutions. It may also be because there is a stronger emphasis placed on caring for ill or disabled family members within the family in African-American and Latino cultures than in white culture.

Many retarded adults live in group homes where they are given assistance in the tasks of daily living (e.g., cooking, cleaning) and training in vocational and social skills. They may work in sheltered workshops during the day, doing unskilled or semiskilled labor. Community-based programs for retarded adults have shown to be effective in enhancing their social and vocational skills in some studies of specific programs.

Summing Up | Mental Retardation

- Mental retardation is defined as subaverage intellectual functioning, indexed by an IQ score of under 70 and deficits in adaptive behavioral functioning.
- There are four levels of mental retardation, ranging from mild to profound.
- A number of biological factors are implicated in mental retardation, including metabolic disorders (PKU, Tay-Sachs disease); chromosomal disorders (Down syndrome, Fragile X, Trisomy 13 and Trisomy 18); prenatal exposure to rubella, herpes, syphilis, or illicit drugs (especially alcohol); premature delivery; and head traumas (such as those arising from being violently shaken).
- There is some evidence that intensive and comprehensive educational interventions, administered very early in an affected child's life, can help to decrease the level of mental retardation.
- Controversy exists over whether mentally retarded children should be put in special education classes with other mentally retarded children or mainstreamed into normal classrooms.

Autism

Autism affects many aspects of a child's development: communication skills, social interactions, cognitive skills, and motor development (see Table 9.5). The most salient features of autism, however, are the impairments in social interaction (Kanner, 1943). Autistic children seem to live in worlds of their own, uninterested in other children or in their own caregivers. Richard is a child with autism (adapted from Spitzer et al., 1994, pp. 336–337):

autism
childhood disorder marked by deficits in social interaction (such as a lack of interest in one's family or other children), communication (such as failing to modulate one's voice to signify emotional expression), and activities and interests (such as engaging in bizarre, repetitive behaviors)

Table 9.5 Symptoms of Autism

The symptoms of autism include a range of deficits in social interactions, communication, and activities. To be diagnosed with autism, children must show these deficits before the age of 3.

Deficits in Social Interactions

Little use of nonverbal behaviors that indicate a social "connection," such as eye-to-eye gazes, facial reactions to others (smiling or frowning at others' remarks as appropriate), body postures that indicate interest in others (leaning toward a person who is speaking), or gestures (waving good-bye to a parent)
Failure to develop peer relationships as other children do
Little expression of pleasure when others are happy
Little reciprocity in social interactions

Deficits in Communication

Delay in, or total absence of, spoken language
In children who do speak, significant trouble in initiating and maintaining conversations
Unusual language, including repetition of certain phrases and pronoun reversal
Lack of make-believe play or imitation of others at a level appropriate for the child's age

Deficits in Activities and Interests

Preoccupation with certain activities or toys and compulsive adherence to routines and rituals
Stereotyped and repetitive movements, such as hand flapping and head banging
Preoccupation with parts of objects (such as the arm of a doll instead of the whole doll) and unusual uses of objects (lining toys up in rows instead of playing "pretend" with them)

Reprinted with permission from the *Diagnostic and Statistical Manual of Mental Disorders,* Fourth Edition. Copyright 1994 American Psychiatric Association.

Case Study • Richard, age 3 1/2, appeared to be self-sufficient and aloof from others. He did not greet his mother in the mornings or his father when he returned from work, though, if left with a baby-sitter, he tended to scream much of the time. He had no interest in other children and ignored his younger brother. His babbling had no conversational intonation. At age 3 he could understand simple practical instructions. His speech consisted of echoing some words and phrases he had heard in the past, with the original speaker's accent and intonation; he could use one or two such phrases to indicate his simple needs. For example, if he said, "Do you want a drink?" he meant he was thirsty. He did not communicate by facial expression or use gesture or mime, except for pulling someone along with him and placing his or her hand on an object he wanted.

He was fascinated by bright lights and spinning objects and would stare at them while laughing, flapping his hands, and dancing on tiptoe. He also displayed the same movements while listening to music, which he liked from infancy. He was intensely attached to a miniature car, which he held in his hand, day and night, but he never played imaginatively with this or any other toy. He could assemble jigsaw puzzles rapidly (with one hand because of the car held in the other), whether the picture side was exposed or hidden. From age 2 he had collected kitchen utensils and arranged them in repetitive patterns all over the floors of the house. These pursuits, together with occasional periods of aimless running around, constituted his whole repertoire of spontaneous activities.

The major management problem was Richard's intense resistance to any attempt to change or extend his interests. Removing his toy car, disturbing his puzzles or patterns, even retrieving, for example, an egg whisk or a spoon for its legitimate use in cooking, or trying to make him look at a picture book precipitated temper tantrums that could last an hour or more, with screaming, kicking, and the biting of himself or others. These tantrums could be cut short by restoring the status quo. Otherwise, playing his favorite music or going for a long car ride were sometimes effective.

His parents had wondered if Richard might be deaf, but his love of music, his accurate echoing, and his sensitivity to some very soft sounds, such as those made by unwrapping chocolate in the next room, convinced them that this was not the cause of his abnormal behavior. Psychological testing gave Richard a mental age of 3 years in non–language-dependent skills (such as assembling objects) but only 18 months in language comprehension.

Autistic children's deficits can be grouped into three categories. The first is deficits in *social interactions*, such as Richard's lack of interaction with his family members. Even as infants, children with autism seem not to connect with other people, including their parents. They may not smile and coo in response to their caregivers or initiate play with their caregivers, as most young infants do. They may not want to cuddle with their parents, even when they are frightened. While most infants love to gaze upon their caregivers as the caregivers gaze adoringly at them, autistic infants may hardly ever make eye-to-eye contact. When they are a bit older, autistic children may not be interested in playing with other children, preferring to remain in solitary play, as Richard did. Autistic children also do not seem to react to other people's emotions. It was formerly thought that autistic children were preoccupied with internal thoughts and fantasies, much as people with schizophrenia might be preoccupied with hallucinations and delusions. Indeed, autism in children formerly was considered a precursor to adult schizophrenia. Studies over the last few decades have shown, however, that autistic children do not develop the classic symptoms of schizophrenia as adults (for example, they show no evidence of hallucinations and delusions) and that adult schizophrenics do not have histories of full autistic disorder as young children. In addition, autism and schizophrenia do not co-occur in families at a high rate, suggesting that they have different genetic causes.

The second group of deficits in autism has to do with *communication*. Approximately 50 percent of autistic children do not develop useful speech (Gillberg, 1991). Those who do develop language may not use it as other children do. Richard showed several of the communication problems of autistic children. Rather than generating his own words, he simply echoed or repeated what he had just heard, in a phenomenon called *echolalia*. He reversed pronouns, using *you* when he meant *I*. When he did try to generate his own words or sentences, he did not modulate his voice for expressiveness, sounding almost like a voice-generating machine.

The third group of deficits concerns the type of *activities and interests* of autistic children. Rather than engaging in symbolic play with toys, they are preoccupied with one part of a toy or object, as Richard was preoccupied with his miniature car. They may engage in bizarre, repetitive behaviors with toys. For example, rather than using two dolls to play "dollies have tea," an autistic child might take the arm off one doll and simply pass it back and forth between her two hands. Routines and rituals are often extremely important to autistic children: When any aspect of the daily routine is changed—for example, if a child's mother stops at the bank on the way to school—they may fly into a rage. Some autistic children perform stereotyped and repetitive behaviors using some parts of their own bodies, such as incessantly flapping their hands or banging their heads against walls. These behaviors are sometimes referred to as *self-stimulatory behaviors*, under the assumption that autistic children engage in these behaviors for self-stimulation. It is not clear, however, that this is the true purpose behind these behaviors.

Some autistic children will hurt themselves by banging their heads against a wall, and thus must wear helmets to be protected against brain damage.

Autistic children often do poorly on measures of intellectual ability, such as IQ tests, with 66 percent scoring below 70 (Ritvo, Jorde, Mason-Brothers, & Freeman, 1989). The deficits of some autistic children, however, are confined to skills that require language and perspective-taking skills, and like Richard, they may score in the average range on subtests that do not require language skills. Much has been made in the popular press about the special talents that some otherwise retarded autistic children have, such as the ability to play music without having been taught or to draw extremely well or exceptional memory and mathematical calculation abilities as was depicted in the movie *Rain Man*. These persons are sometimes referred to as *idiot savants*. These cases are quite rare, however (Gillberg, 1991).

By definition, the symptoms of autism have their onset before the age of 3. However, children with autism are not simply delayed in their development of important skills. When they do develop language or social interaction patterns, there is a deviancy in the nature of these that is striking. It is important to note, though, that there is a wide variation in the severity and outcome of this disorder (Gillberg, 1991). Somewhere between 10 and 20 percent of autistic children "grow out" of autism and eventually are able to function well as adults, hold jobs, and sometimes have families (Gillberg, 1991; Gillbert & Steffenburg, 1987; Szatmari, Bartolucci, Bremner, & Bond, 1989). A substantial portion of these people still have some problems with social interactions, however, remaining aloof and having trouble in normal conversation. One person who apparently had autism as a child but who has recovered from it as an adult is Donna Williams, who wrote two fascinating books on what it is like to be autistic (Williams, 1992, 1994). In her book *Somebody Somewhere*, she wrote,

I felt secure in "my world" and hated anything that tried to call me out of there. I needed no rescue from the heaven of living death. Without "motivation" I would have stayed there. People, no matter how good, had no chance to compete. My reflection in the mirror, with its total predictability and familiarity, was the only person who came close. I would look into her eyes. I would try to touch her hair. Later I would speak to her. But she was stuck forever on the other side of the glass and I couldn't get in. I didn't blame her. It was pretty crappy on this side.

Sleep was not a secure place. Sleep was a place where darkness ate you alive. Sleep was a place without color or light. In the darkness you could not see your reflection. You couldn't get "lost" in sleep. Sleep just came and stole you beyond your control. Anything that robbed me of total control was no friend of mine.

"The world" could force compliance even if it couldn't touch you. A mind that hadn't yet reached out for anything was being force-fed with what others called

Tom Cruise and Dustin Hoffman are shown in a scene from *Rain Man*, in which Hoffman protrays an autistic savant.

"life." The subconscious mind began to store meaning that my conscious mind had not yet learned to reach for. I was still in a state of pure sensing without thought or feeling. Feelings that had not yet met conscious awareness were being triggered. There were no words for them or even knowledge of where they came from. What poured in just sat there. The feelings were not ready.

There was a rip through the center of my soul. Self-abuse was the outward sign of the earthquake nobody saw. I was like an appliance during a power surge. As I blew fuses my hands pulled out my hair and slapped my face. They pulled at my skin and scratched it. My teeth bit my flesh like an animal bites the bars of its cage, not realizing the cage was my own body. My legs took my body around in manic circles as though they could somehow outrun the body they were attached to. My head hit whatever was next to it, like someone trying to crack open a nut that had grown too big for its shell. There was an overwhelming feeling of inner deafness—a deafness to the self that would consume all that was left in a fever pitch of silent screaming. (pp. 8–9)

About two-thirds of autistic people are severely handicapped throughout adult life and must remain completely dependent on families or institutions for daily care (Gillberg, 1991). The remainder of autistic people function somewhere in between, perhaps living in residential facilities with other autistic individuals and a caretaking staff and working in simple jobs. By far, the best predictor of the outcome of autism is a child's IQ and amount of language development before the age of 6 (Gillberg & Steffenburg, 1987; Ritvo et al., 1989; Venter, Lord, & Schopler, 1992). Children who have IQs above 50 and communicative speech before age 6 have a much better prognosis than do those with IQs below 50 and no communicative speech before age 6.

The prevalence of autism is about 4 cases in 10,000 (Pomeroy, 1990; Ritvo et al., 1989). Boys outnumber girls about three to one. The prevalence of autism does not appear to vary by national origin, race/ethnicity, socioeconomic status, or parental education.

 What are some of the greatest stresses you think would exist for the parents of an autistic child? Which of these stresses would affect you most if you had an autistic child? Why?

Contributors to Autism

The psychiatrist who first described autism, Leo Kanner (1943), thought that autism was caused partly by biological factors and partly by poor parenting. He and later psychoanalytic theorists (Bettleheim, 1967) described the parents of autistic children as cold, distant, and uncaring (hence the description, "refrigerator mothers"). The autistic child's symptoms were seen as a retreat inward to a secret world of fantasies in response to unavailable parents. Research over the decades has clearly shown, though, that parenting practices play little or no role in the development of autism. If parents of autistic children differ psychologically at all from parents of nonautistic children, it is because of the stress that having an autistic child places on a parent.

Current theories of the etiology of autism focus on biological causes, and several different types of causes have been implicated. Family and twin studies strongly suggest that genetics play a role in the development of the disorder. Siblings of autistic children are 50 times more likely to also be autistic than are siblings of nonautistic children (Rutter et al., 1990). Twin studies show concordance rates for autism to be much higher for monozygotic twins than for dizygotic twins (Folstein & Rutter, 1977). In addition, about 80 percent of the MZ twins of autistic children have some sort of significant cognitive impairment, compared to 10 percent of DZ twins. Finally, autistic children have a higher-than-average rate of other genetic disorders associated with cognitive impairment, including Fragile X syndrome and PKU. These data suggest that a general vulnerability to several types of cognitive impairment, only one of which is manifested as autism, runs in families.

A variety of structural and functional differences between the central nervous systems of autistic children and nonautistic children have been found (Prior, 1987). Some studies find differences between the electroencephalograph (EEG) readings and between the magnetic resonance imagery (MRI) scans of autistic and nonautistic children. Approximately 30 percent of autistic children develop seizure disorders by adolescence, suggesting a severe neurological dysfunction. This dysfunction could be the result of genetic factors. Alternately, there is a higher-than-average rate of prenatal and birth complications among autistic children, complications that might have created neurological damage. Finally, studies have found differences between autistic and nonautistic children in levels of the neurotransmitters serotonin and dopamine, although the meaning of these differences is not entirely clear (Gilberg & Svennerholm, 1987).

The variety of biological factors implicated in autism may indicate that there are several subtypes of autism, each of which has its own biological cause. With a disorder as rare as autism, it is difficult to study enough autistic children to discover subtypes. Ideally, recent advances in the technology of biomedical research, such as the use of magnetic resonance imagery and genetic mapping, will provide more detailed data on the biology of autism.

Treatments for Autism

A number of drugs have been shown to improve some symptoms autistic children have, such as overactivity, stereotyped behaviors, sleep disturbances, and tension (Gadow, 1992). These drugs include the phenothiazines, fenfluramine (a serotonin inhibitor), lithium, and stimulant drugs. These drugs do not alter the basic autistic disorder, but they may make it easier for autistic persons to participate in school and in other interventions.

Psychosocial therapies for autism combine behavioral techniques and structured educational services. Modeling and reinforcement are used to teach autistic children to speak, to engage in social exchanges with others, and to reduce inappropriate behaviors (such as hand flapping). These techniques are often implemented in highly structured schools designed especially for autistic children. The specific deficits a child has in cognitive, motor, or social skills are targeted, and special materials that reduce possible distractions for autistic children (e.g., reading books that do not have words printed in bright colors) are used. The parents of autistic children may be taught to implement the techniques continually when the children are at home. One study showed that 47 percent of autistic children given this intensive behavioral treatment for at least 40 hours per week for at least 2 years achieved normal intellectual and educational functioning by age 7 compared to only 2 percent of autistic children who received only institutional care (Lovaas, 1987). Several other studies have shown remarkable improvements in cognitive skills and behavioral control in autistic children when they are treated with a comprehensive behavioral therapy administered both by their parents and in their school setting (Estrada & Pinsof, 1995).

Summing Up | Autism

- Autism is characterized by significant interpersonal, communication, and behavioral deficits.
- Two-thirds of autistic children score in the mentally retarded range on IQ tests.
- There is wide variation in the outcome of autism, although the majority of autistic children must have continual care as adults. The best predictors of a good outcome in autism are an IQ above 50 and language development before the age of 6.
- Biological causes of autism may include a genetic predisposition to cognitive impairment, central nervous system damage, prenatal complications, and neurotransmitter imbalances.
- Drugs reduce some behaviors in autism but do not eliminate the core of the disorder.
- Behavioral therapy is used to reduce inappropriate and self-injurious behaviors and to encourage prosocial behaviors in autistic children.

Gender Differences in Childhood Psychopathology

Adults may be less supportive of boys when they are distressed, insisting that the boys "act like a man."

Most of the disorders described in this chapter are more common in boys than in girls. Boys are more likely than girls to have conduct and oppositional defiant disorders, attention deficit/hyperactivity disorder, learning disorders, mental retardation, and autism. In addition, some studies show that before adolescence, boys are more likely than girls to become depressed and to show some types of anxiety disorders (Nolen-Hoeksema, 1990). What accounts for boys' greater vulnerability to psychopathology during childhood?

Boys are more prone than girls to all sorts of physiological problems. For example, male children suffer more birth defects than do female children, 37 percent more males than females die in infancy, and boys are afflicted more than girls by most major childhood diseases. Boys' vulnerability to psychopathology may be an extension of a general biological vulnerability to illness. This may be particularly true of boys' greater vulnerability to psychopathologies that have large neurological components to them, such as mental retardation, learning disorders, autism, and attention deficit/hyperactivity disorder.

A psychological explanation of boys' greater vulnerability to psychopathology is that boys are not given the nurturance and support they need to weather the stresses of childhood as much as girls are, because adults are more reluctant to "baby" boys than girls. Instead, boys are admonished to "act like a man" and be strong rather than cry and ask for reassurance "like a girl" in times of stress. As a result, boys may find maladaptive ways to express their distress, such as aggression.

A different type of psychological explanation is that adults are simply less tolerant of deviance in boys than in girls. As a result, parents more often bring sons' psychopathology to the attention of clinicians than they do daughters' psychopathology, and thus disorders in boys are more likely to be detected than are disorders in girls. For example, one study found that mothers of hyperactive boys were critical, disapproving, unaffectionate, and severe in their punishment of their sons, whereas the mothers of hyperactive girls were not more intolerant of their daughters than were mothers of girls who were not hyperactive (Battle & Lacey, 1972). A variation on this explanation is that girls find ways of expressing their distress and deviance that are more subtle or socially acceptable than the ways boys find. Recall that girls' methods of being aggressive toward their peers tend to be covert and subtle, whereas boys' methods of aggression tend to be physical and overt (Crick & Grotpeter, 1995).

Whatever the reason for boys' greater vulnerability to psychopathology in childhood, there is a dramatic shift in the epidemiology of psychological disorders that occurs in early adolescence: Beginning around age 14 or 15, girls show huge increases in mood disorders and anxiety disorders and the onset of eating disorders (Nolen-Hoeksema & Girgus, 1994). Boys show no such large increases in these disorders at adolescence and may even show decreases in most disorders, except for substance abuse. It may be that girls have vulnerabilities to depression, anxiety, and eating disorders even in preadolescence, but these vulnerabilities do not turn into full-blown disorders until girls face the biological and psychological challenges of puberty and early adolescence. In contrast, puberty and early adolescence seem to be less challenging emotionally and physically for boys and may even be periods when some boys who had psychological problems during childhood "grow out" of these problems.

As noted earlier, the study of psychological disorders in children is often referred to as *developmental psychopathology*. This label explicitly recognizes that, in order to understand psychopathology in children, researchers must understand normal biological, psychological, and social development. Moreover, developmental psychopathologists are concerned with the interdependence of biological, psychological, and social development in children, recognizing that disruptions in any one of these three systems send perturbations through the other systems. The interdependence of these systems is probably even more true in children than in adults, because children are not mature enough to compartmentalize their troubles and are highly dependent on their caregivers and environment even for their most basic needs.

A nice example of the interplay between biology, psychology, and the social environment comes from a study of adopted children (Ge, Conger, Cadoret, & Neiderhiser, 1996). Some of the adopted children in this study had biological parents who had antisocial personalities or histories of substance abuse; the other adopted children had biological parents with no histories of psychological problems. The children whose biological parents had histories of psychopathology were more likely than the other children to be hostile and antisocial themselves. Most researchers who do not adopt a bio-psycho-social approach to childhood disorders would stop with these results and declare the results clear evidence for the genetic inheritance of antisocial and hostile tendencies. The researchers in this study, however, went further and looked at the parenting behaviors of the children's adoptive parents. They found that the adoptive parents of the antisocial/hostile children were more harsh and critical in their parenting than were the adoptive parents of the children who were not antisocial and hostile. It appeared that the antisocial/hostile children drew out harsh and critical behaviors from their adoptive parents. The harsh and critical parenting these children received only exacerbated the children's antisocial behaviors. Thus, the children with biological parents who were antisocial or substance abusers appeared to have a genetic predisposition to being antisocial and hostile. Their genes also created an environment of parenting practices by their adoptive parents that contributed to more antisocial behavior on the part of the children. These children were on a developmental trajectory in which their biology and social environment were acting in synergy to lead them toward serious conduct disturbances. This kind of synergy between biology, psychology, and the social environment is the rule rather than the exception in the development of psychopathology, particularly in children.

Chapter Summary

Nearly 20 percent of children and almost 40 percent of adolescents appear to suffer from serious psychological problems. For these children, some problems are linked to stressful events and others occur in the absence of stressful events, while other children exposed to stressful events appear to be resistant to the development of psychopathology.

The behavioral disorders include attention deficit/hyperactivity disorder (ADHD), conduct disorder, and oppositional defiant disorder. ADHD is characterized by inattentiveness, impulsivity, and hyperactivity. Children with ADHD do poorly in school and in peer relationships and are at increased risk for developing conduct disorder. ADHD is more common in boys than in girls. Biological factors that have been implicated in the development of ADHD include genetics, exposure to toxins prenatally and early in childhood, and abnormalities in neurological functioning. In addition, children with ADHD often come from families in which there are many disruptions, although it is not clear if this is a cause or just a correlate of ADHD. Treatment for ADHD usually involves stimulant drugs and behavior therapy designed to decrease children's impulsivity and hyperactivity and help them control aggression.

Conduct disorder is characterized by extreme antisocial behavior and the violation of other people's rights and of social norms. Conduct disorder is more common in boys than in girls and is highly stable across childhood and adolescence. As adults, people who had conduct disorder are at increased risk for criminal behavior and a host of problems in fitting into society. The milder form of conduct disorder is oppositional defiant disorder. Genetics and neurological problems leading to attention deficits are implicated in the development of conduct disorder. In addition, children with conduct disorder tend to have parents who are harsh and inconsistent in their discipline practices and who model aggressive, antisocial behavior. Psychologically, children with conduct disorder tend to process information in ways that are likely to lead to aggressive reactions to others' behaviors. The treatment for conduct disorder is most often cognitive-behavioral, focusing on changing children's ways of interpreting interpersonal situations and helping them control their angry impulses. Neuroleptic drugs and stimulant drugs are also sometimes used to treat conduct disorder.

Children can develop all the major emotional disorders (mood disorders, anxiety disorders), but separation anxiety is one disorder relatively unique in childhood. The symptoms of separation anxiety include chronic worry about separation from one's parents or about parents' well-being, dreams and fantasies about separation from parents, refusal to go to school, and somatic complaints. This disorder is more common in girls. The disorder runs in families, which may suggest either that genetics play a role in its development or that parents model anxious behavior for their children. Separation anxiety often arises following major traumas, particularly if parents are anxious and overprotective of their children. The therapy for separation anxiety follows behaviorist principles and involves relaxation training and increasing periods of separation from parents.

The elimination disorders are enuresis, the repeated wetting of clothes or bed linens in children over the age of 4, and encopresis, repeated defecation in the clothes or on the floor in children over the age of 5. Enuresis is more common and has been studied more extensively than encopresis and has been linked to psychological stress, inappropriate or lax toilet training, and genetics. Enuresis is often treated with the bell and pad method, which helps children learn to awaken when their bladders are full so they can go to the bathroom. Antidepressants are also used to treat enuresis, but their effects disappear when the children stop taking them.

The two most serious developmental disorders are mental retardation and autism. Mental retardation is defined as subaverage intellectual functioning, indexed by an IQ score below 70 and deficits in adaptive behavioral functioning. There are four levels of mental retardation, ranging from mild to profound. A number of biological factors are implicated in mental retardation, including metabolic disorders (PKU, Tay-Sachs disease); chromosomal disorders (Down syndrome, Fragile X, Trisomy 13 and Trisomy 18); prenatal exposure to rubella, herpes, syphilis, or illicit drugs (especially alcohol), premature delivery; and head traumas (such as those arising from being violently shaken as an infant). There is some evidence that intensive and comprehensive educational interventions, administered very early in an affected child's life, can help to decrease the level of mental retardation. Controversy exists over whether mentally retarded children should be put in special education classes with other mentally retarded children or mainstreamed into normal classrooms.

Autism is characterized by significant interpersonal, communication, and behavioral deficits. Two-thirds of autistic children score in the mentally retarded range on IQ tests. There is wide variation in the outcome of autism, although the majority of people with autism must have continual care even as adults. The best predictors of a good outcome in autism are an IQ above 50 and language development before the age of 6. Biological causes of autism may include a genetic predisposition to cognitive impairment, central nervous system damage, prenatal complications, and neurotransmitter imbalances. Drugs reduce some behaviors in autism but do not eliminate the core of the disorder. Behavioral therapy is used to reduce inappropriate and self-injurious behaviors and to encourage prosocial behaviors.

Boys are more prone than girls to most types of psychopathology. This gender difference may be an extension of boys' greater vulnerability compared to that of girls to many types of physiological disorders. Alternately, parents may be less nurturant and supportive of boys than of girls during stressful times, which would make boys more prone to maladaptive reactions to stress. Finally, parents may be less tolerant of boys' modes of abnormal behavior than of girls' and thus seek help for boys more than for girls.

Key Terms

14

Application   If Your Parent Has a Psychological Disorder

Each of the disorders discussed in this chapter (and in most of the other chapters in this book) runs in families. Sometimes such evidence makes students who have parents with psychological disorders feel that it is inevitable that they will also develop the disorders. This is far from true, however. Only a small minority of the children of parents with psychological disorders also develop the disorders. This is true even for the disorders in which genetics seem to play an especially strong role, such as schizophrenia (Gottesman, 1991). The risk of developing a disorder if your parent has it is small because most psychological disorders probably are not transmitted through dominant genes but through a collection of recessive genes. Recall from Chapter 3 that many genetic theories of psychological disorders suggest that an individual needs to inherit a group of genetic abnormalities in order to have a predisposition to the disorder. Even when the person inherits the entire group of genetic abnormalities, he or she only has a predisposition to the disorder—it is not inevitable that he or she will develop the full-blown disorder.

Although growing up with a parent who has a serious psychological disorder does not make you genetically predestined to have the disorder, there clearly are stresses involved in having a parent who is psychologically impaired. This seems most obvious in the case of schizophrenia. Having a parent who is sometimes psychotic, seeing and hearing things that are not real, espousing strange, sometimes paranoid beliefs, and frequently having long hospitalizations is difficult on children. Studies of the children of schizophrenics show that they experience a wide range of problems related to this stress, including increased levels of depression and anxiety and problems with self-esteem (see Gottesman, 1991). Other research has focused on the children of depressed parents. Depression can affect parenting by reducing a parent's self-esteem, her energy level, and her ability to concentrate on her child and respond to her child. Depressed parents also tend to be more irritable and hostile than nondepressed parents (Nolen-Hoeksema, Wolfson, Mumme, & Guskin, 1994). Since depression is so widespread, especially among women of childbearing age, many young children go through some part of childhood with a seriously depressed parent. These children also seem to be at risk for a range of emotional and behavioral problems, including depressive and anxiety symptoms, academic problems, and problems in regulating their emotions (see Dodge, 1990).

Again, however, it is not inevitable that the children of parents with schizophrenia, depression, or any other serious disorders are going to be negatively influenced by their parents' disorders. There is wide variability in the impact of disorders on parents' functioning as parents. For example, studies of depressed mothers show that some mothers experience serious problems in caring for their children, whereas others are able to function basically normally with their children, despite being clinically depressed (e.g., Hammen, Burge, & Stansbury, 1990; Nolen-Hoeksema et al., 1994). One factor that may determine the impact of parents' disorders on children is whether there are other adults in the children's lives, perhaps the depressed parents' spouses or parents who are healthy and can intervene with children when their parents' psychopathology makes it necessary.

Over the past few decades, a number of organizations have developed to support people who have parents with serious psychological disorders. The best known of these are AlaTeen and AlAnon, which support children, adolescents, and adults who have alcoholic parents. You can find phone numbers for the local chapters of these organizations in the phone book. ■

chapter 10 Eating Disorders

Anorexia Nervosa

Anorexia nervosa is a disorder in which people refuse to maintain body weights that are healthy and normal for their ages and heights. People with anorexia also have distorted body images and intense fears of becoming fat, and women with anorexia lose their menstrual periods.

Bulimia Nervosa

Bulimia nervosa is characterized by uncontrolled binge eating, followed by behaviors designed to prevent weight gain, such as purging, fasting, and excessive exercising.

Binge-Eating Disorder

People with binge-eating disorder compulsively overeat but do not engage in purging, fasting, or excessive exercise to avoid gaining weight.

Dieting and the Eating Disorders

Many people begin disordered eating behaviors simply by going on diets. Dieting may create a number of psychological and physiological stresses that make it difficult for a person to maintain the diet or to return to healthy eating patterns.

Eating Disorders in Athletes

Athletes, particularly those in sports that require or emphasize certain body weights, are at high risk for eating disorders.

Gender Similarities and Differences in the Eating Disorders

Both anorexia and bulimia nervosa are much more common in females than in males, perhaps because thinness is valued more in females than in males. In general, however, the characteristics of eating disorders are similar in males and females.

Cultural Factors in Eating Disorders

People in developed countries, people in upper and middle classes, and whites tend to have higher rates of eating disorders than do other groups.

The Families and Personalities of People with Eating Disorders

Adolescent females who develop eating disorders often appear to come from families that are overcontrolling, require "perfection," and do not allow the expression of negative feelings. Such adolescents may develop eating disorders as one way of controlling their environment. Other theories suggest that bingeing may develop as a way of coping with distress.

Sexual Abuse and the Eating Disorders

Although some women who develop eating disorders have histories of sexual abuse, sexual abuse seems to be a general risk factor for psychological problems rather than a specific risk factor for eating disorders.

Biological Theories of the Eating Disorders

Eating disorders may be, in part, heritable. The families of people with eating disorders also tend to have high rates of depression. People with eating disorders may have disruptions in the hypothalamus, a part of the brain involved in the regulation of eating and emotions.

Psychotherapy for Anorexia Nervosa

People with anorexia nervosa must often be hospitalized and forced to gain weight. Then behavior therapy and family therapy are used to try to help them overcome their disordered eating behaviors and attitudes.

Psychotherapy for Bulimia Nervosa

Cognitive-behavioral therapy and interpersonal therapy have proven useful in the treatment of bulimia nervosa.

Biological Therapies

Antidepressants are helpful in reducing bingeing and purging and in enhancing a sense of control in people with bulimia nervosa. Antidepressants may also prove useful in treating anorexia nervosa, although there are few studies of their effectiveness to date.

Bio-Psycho-Social Integration

Chapter Summary

Key Terms

Application: *What Is So Bad About Being Overweight?*

We love good looks rather than what is practical,
Though good looks may prove destructive.

—La Fontaine, "The Stag and His Reflection," *Fables*
(1668–1694; translated by Marianne Moore)

John S. Bunker
Wednesday's Child

Dear Diary: This morning I had a half of a grapefruit for breakfast, and some coffee—no sugar or cream. For lunch, I had an apple and a diet soda. For dinner, I had some plain white rice and a salad with just some lemon squeezed over it. So I was feeling really good about myself, really virtuous. That is, until Jackie came over, and completely messed up my day. She brought over a movie to watch, which was fine. But then she insisted on ordering a pizza. I told her I didn't want any, that I wasn't hungry (which was a lie, because I was starving). But she ordered it anyway. The pizza arrived, and I thought I could be good and not have any. But it was just sitting there on the table, and I couldn't think of anything except having some. I couldn't concentrate on the movie. I kept smelling the pizza and feeling the emptiness in my stomach. Like a weakling, I reached out and got one piece, a small piece. It was ice cold by then, and kind of greasy, but I didn't care. I ate that piece in about 5 seconds flat. Then I had another piece. And another. I stopped after four pieces. But I still couldn't pay attention to the movie. All I could think about was what a pig I was for eating that pizza, and how I'll never lose the 10 pounds I need to lose to fit into a size smaller dress. Jackie's gone now, and I still keep thinking about how ugly and fat I am, and how I have no willpower. I didn't deserve to have that pizza tonight, because I haven't lost enough weight this month. I'm going to have to skip breakfast and lunch tomorrow, and exercise for a couple of hours, to make up for being a complete pig tonight.

This passage from a young woman's diary probably sounds familiar to many students. Surveys in the United States, Europe, Australia, New Zealand, and Israel have found that the majority of young women and about one-third of young men feel they are overweight and wish they could lose at least a few pounds (Garner & Wooley, 1991; Horm & Anderson, 1993; Sasson, Lewin, & Roth, 1995). For example, at any given time, about 45 percent of women and 25 percent of men in the United States are on diets to control their weight (Williamson, Serdula, Anda, & Levy, 1992). Thirty-one percent of American women between the ages of 19 and 39 diet at least once per month, and 16 percent are perpetual dieters. People are starting to diet at younger ages: Over 70 percent of American girls have dieted by the age of 10 (Hawkins, Turell, & Jackson, 1983). Dieting is hard, however, and almost everyone who loses weight through dieting gains it all back and often more. Many people spend their lives losing and gaining back tens of pounds in a cycle of "yo-yo" dieting. One famous example is the television star Oprah Winfrey, who lost 67 pounds in a heavily publicized liquid fast diet. On her television show, she wheeled 67 pounds of beef fat around the stage in a little red wagon to illustrate what she had left behind. Within a year, however, Winfrey had gained 90 pounds.

Talk-show host Oprah Winfrey has gained attention for her repeated efforts to lose weight and keep it off.

Fashion models have figures that are physically unattainable by the average woman, yet they set the standards for beauty.

Some people turn to more unconventional means of controlling their weight. In 1990, 100,000 people had their jaws wired to prevent them from eating or had liposuction performed to surgically remove fat (LaRosa, 1991). In all, Americans spend over $30 billion per year on weight-loss products, including $8 billion per year on spas and exercise clubs, $382 million on diet books, $10 billion on diet soft drinks, and billions of dollars on low calorie foods and artificial sweeteners. To put this into perspective, consider that the federal government spends about $30 billion per year on all education, training, employment, and social services programs.

Why do people care so much about their weight? There are health concerns that drive the attempt to lose weight. We are told that being overweight can contribute to serious diseases like high blood pressure, heart disease and diabetes and that overweight people have shorter life spans than do people who are not overweight. However, the driving force behind most people's attempts to eat less and lose weight is the desire to be more attractive and increase self-esteem. For at least the last 30 to 40 years, attractiveness, especially for women, has been equated with thinness. Models in fashion magazines, winners of the Miss America and Miss Universe pageants, and Barbie dolls—all icons of beauty for women—have been getting thinner and thinner over the last few decades (Agras & Kirkley, 1986; Garner & Garfinkel, 1980). Indeed, the average model in a fashion magazine these days is pencil thin, with a figure that is physically unattainable by the majority of adult women.

Pressures to be thin do not come just from the media and marketers of Barbie dolls. Studies of adults' perceptions of each other show that women who are thin are rated as more feminine and attractive than are women who are heavier (e.g., Guy, Rankin, & Norvell, 1980). Similarly, women who dare to eat as much food as they wish in public settings (such as a dormitory cafeteria) are rated as less attractive than are women who eat less (Rolls, Fedoroff, & Guthrie, 1991). Women pick up on these cues and modulate their behavior in many ways to conform to societal expectations. For example, women eat less in situations in which they wish to appear desirable and feminine or in situations in which they want to show superiority over other women or compete with other women (Mori, Chaiken, & Pliner, 1987; Pliner & Chaiken, 1990). Many students can attest to the competitions that arise between friends sitting around a dinner table watching what each other eats, comparing calorie counts, and berating the "weaklings" or "traitors" who have dessert.

Men have traditionally not been pressured to be very thin, and being somewhat overweight does not affect men's self-esteem or status with others as much as it does women's self-esteem or status. In recent years, however, there has been increasing emphasis on men attaining a super-fit look, having lean lower bodies and strong, toned upper bodies. The number of articles in men's magazines on achieving such a look has risen dramatically and male television stars reach stardom in part because they have this look

(Nemeroff, Stein, Diehl, & Smilack, 1994). Obviously, this look is more difficult to attain for some men than for others.

 Can you just ignore social pressures to be a certain weight or to have a certain look? Why or why not?

In part as a result of these pressures, for many people food is not simply something they ingest to maintain healthy bodies or because it tastes good and exercise is not just something they do to improve their health. What they eat and how much they exercise become linked to feelings of worth, merit, guilt, sin, rebelliousness, and defiance. Weight and how attractive people feel become an integral part of their self-esteem.

For some people, concerns about eating and weight become so overwhelming and behaviors oriented toward eating or avoiding eating get so out of control that they are said to have eating disorders. There are three specific types of eating disorders: anorexia nervosa, bulimia nervosa, and binge-eating disorder. Anorexia nervosa is characterized by a pursuit for thinness that leads people to starve themselves. Bulimia nervosa is characterized by a cycle of bingeing followed by extreme behaviors to prevent weight gain, such as self-induced vomiting. People with binge-eating disorder regularly binge but do not engage in behaviors to purge what they eat. The eating disorders are the focus of this chapter.

First, we will explore the diagnosis and epidemiology of the eating disorders. This is one group of disorders in which there are huge differences in the rates of the disorder between men and women and between people of different cultures. Next, we will review what we know about the causes of eating disorders. Societal pressures to be thin may create maladaptive attitudes toward weight and body shape in many people, but clearly most people do not develop full eating disorders. We will discuss the psychosocial and biological factors that may lead some people to develop eating disorders. Then we will discuss the most effective treatments for the eating disorders. Some progress has been made in developing effective treatments, especially for bulimia nervosa. In the Application we will explore a controversial question: What is so bad about being overweight?

Anorexia Nervosa

Anorexia nervosa is a disorder in which people refuse to maintain body weights that are healthy and normal for their ages and heights. The DSM-IV criteria for anorexia nervosa require that a person's weight be at least 15 percent below the ideal weight for his or her age and height (APA, 1994). Often an anorexic's weight is much below this. For example, a 5 foot 6 inch young woman with anorexia may weigh 95 pounds, when the healthy weight for a woman this height is between 120 and 159 pounds (see Figure 10.1). In girls and women who have begun menstruating, the weight loss causes them to stop having menstrual periods, a condition known as **amenorrhea**. Despite being emaciated, people with anorexia nervosa have intense fears of becoming fat. They have very distorted images of their bodies, often believing they are fat and need to lose more weight. The self-evaluations of anorexics hinge entirely on their weight and their control over their eating. They believe they are only good and worthwhile when they have complete control over their eating and when they are losing weight. The weight loss causes people with anorexia to be chronically fatigued, yet they will drive themselves to exercise excessively and to keep up a grueling schedule at work or school.

The DSM-IV recognizes two types of anorexia: the restricting type and the binge/purge type. People with the *restricting type* of anorexia nervosa simply refuse to eat as a way of preventing weight gain. Some anorexics who are restrictors attempt to go for days without eating anything. Most will eat very small amounts of food each day, in part simply to stay alive and in part because of pressures from others to eat. An anorexic

Figure 10.1

Height	Small frame	Medium frame	Large frame
		Pounds	
Men (ages 25–59, dressed in 5 pounds of clothes)			
5'2"	128–134	131–141	138–150
5'3"	130–136	133–143	140–153
5'4"	132–138	135–145	142–156
5'5"	134–140	137–148	144–160
5'6"	136–142	139–151	146–164
5'7"	138–145	142–154	149–168
5'8"	140–148	145–157	152–172
5'9"	142–151	148–160	155–176
5'10"	144–154	151–163	158–180
5'11"	146–157	154–166	161–184
6'0"	149–160	157–170	164–188
6'1"	152–164	160–174	168–192
6'2"	155–168	164–178	172–197
6'3"	158–172	167–182	176–202
6'4"	162–176	171–187	181–207
Women (ages 25–59, dressed in 3 pounds of clothes)			
4'10"	102–111	109–121	118–131
4'11"	103–113	109–121	120–134
5'0"	104–115	113–126	122–137
5'1"	106–118	115–129	125–140
5'2"	108–121	118–132	128–143
5'3"	111–124	121–135	131–147
5'4"	114–127	124–138	134–151
5'5"	117–130	127–141	137–155
5'6"	120–133	130–144	140–159
5'7"	123–136	133–147	143–163
5'8"	126–139	136–150	146–167
5'9"	129–142	139–153	149–170
5'10"	132–145	142–156	152–173
5'11"	135–148	145–159	155–176
6'0"	138–151	148–162	158–179

Figure 10.1

1993 Metropolitan Life Insurance Height and Weight Tables. This chart gives one way of viewing what is a "healthy" weight for men and women of different heights and body frames.
Source: Seligman, 1994, p. 176.

may eat only a piece of fruit and a handful of dry cereal or a plain yogurt and a bagel for the day. The other type of anorexia nervosa is the *binge/purge type,* in which people periodically engage in bingeing or purging behaviors (e.g., self-induced vomiting or the misuse of laxatives or diuretics) but also meet the criteria for anorexia. Often a person with the binge/purge type of anorexia nervosa will not engage in real binges in which she eats large amounts of food, but if she eats even a small amount of food, she feels like she has binged and will purge this food.

The following is a case history of a college student with a restricting type of anorexia:

Case Study • Daphne is 5 foot 11 inches tall and weighs 102 pounds. She has felt "large" since her height soared above her schoolmates in the fifth grade. She has been on some type of diet ever since. During her junior year in high school, Daphne decided that she had to take drastic measures to lose more weight. She began by cutting her calorie intake to about 1,000 calories per day. She lost several pounds but not fast enough for her liking. So she cut her intake to 500 calories per day. She also began a vigorous exercise program of cross-country running. Each day, Daphne would not let herself eat until she had run at least 10 miles. Then she would have just a few vegetables and a handful of Cheerios. Later in the day, she might have some more vegetables and some fruit, but she would wait until she was so hungry that she was faint. Daphne dropped to 110 pounds and she stopped menstruating. Her mother expressed some concern about how little Daphne was eating, but since her mother tended to be overweight, she did not discourage Daphne from dieting. When it came time to go to college, Daphne was excited but also frightened, because she had always been a star student in high school

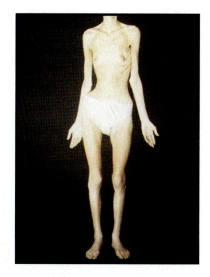

People with anorexia are emaciated but still see themselves as fat.

and wasn't sure she could maintain her straight A's in college. In the first examination period in college, Daphne got mostly A's but one B. She felt very vulnerable, like a failure, and like she was losing control. She also was unhappy with her social life which, by the middle of the first semester, was going nowhere. Daphne decided that things might be better if she lost more weight. So she cut her food intake to two apples and a handful of Cheerios each day. She also ran at least 15 miles each day. By the end of fall semester, she was down to 102 pounds. She was also chronically tired, had trouble concentrating, and occasionally fainted. Still, when Daphne looked in the mirror, she saw a fat, homely young woman who needed to lose more weight.

People with the restricting type of anorexia are more likely than those with the binge/purge type to have deep feelings of mistrust of others and a tendency to deny they have a problem. Binge/purge anorexics are more likely to have problems with unstable moods and controlling their impulses, with alcohol and drug abuse, and with self-mutilation (Garner, Garfinkel, & O'Shaughnessy, 1985). They also tend to have more chronic courses of their disorder.

 Starving oneself to death runs so against all psychological and physiological forces toward self-preservation that some have considered it to represent psychosis. Do you agree?

Epidemiology of Anorexia Nervosa

About 1 percent of people will develop anorexia nervosa at some time in their lives, and between 90 percent and 95 percent of people diagnosed with anorexia nervosa are female (Fairburn, Welch, & Hay, 1993; Strober, 1986). Anorexia nervosa usually begins in adolescence, often after stressful events. The course of the disorder varies greatly from person to person. Long-term studies suggest that as many as half of the women who develop anorexia nervosa recover within 4 years, but perhaps 30 percent still are severely underweight 4 years after the onset of the disorder. The remaining women achieve only intermediate levels of recovery over the 4 years (Hsu, Crisp, & Harding, 1979; Morgan, Purgold, & Wellbourne, 1983; Morgan & Russell, 1975; Szmukler & Russell, 1986).

Anorexia nervosa is a very dangerous disorder physiologically. The death rate among anorexics is 15 percent. Table 10.1 lists just some of the possible physical complications caused by prolonged starvation. Some of the most serious consequences of anorexia are

Table 10.1 Common Medical Complications of Anorexia Nervosa	
Cardiovascular Complications	**Dental Problems**
Slowness of heart rate	Decalcification
Irregular heart beat	Tooth decay
Fluid in the sac enclosing the heart	**Endocrine Complications**
Heart failure	
Metabolic Complications	Amenorrhea
	Lack of sexual interest
Yellowing of the skin	Impotence
Impaired taste	**Gastrointestinal Complications**
Hypoglycemia	
Fluid and Electrolyte Complications	Salivary gland swelling
	Acute expansion of the stomach
Dehydration	Constipation
Weakness	**General Complications**
Tetanus	
Hematological Complications	Weakness
	Hypothermia
Susceptibility to bleeding	
Anemia	

Source: Brownell & Foryet, 1986.

the cardiovascular complications, including bradycardia (extreme slowing of heart rate), arrhythmia (irregular heart beat), and heart failure. Another potentially serious complication of anorexia is acute expansion of the stomach, to the point of rupturing. Kidney damage has been seen in some anorexic patients, and impaired immune system functioning may make anorexics more vulnerable to severe illnesses.

Historical Perspectives on Anorexia Nervosa

There are accounts of self-induced starvation dating from as early as the Middle Ages (Strober, 1986). For example, a nun in Leichester, England, circa 1225, apparently ingested nothing but the wine and wafers of the eucharist for 7 years. The earliest comprehensive description of a syndrome that sounds much like anorexia is credited to Richard Morton in 1694. He described women patients who had decreased appetite, amenorrhea, and aversions to food and were emaciated and hyperactive. Morton was intrigued by the apparent indifference these patients showed to their malnourishment and poor health:

> Mr. Duke's Daughter in St. Mary Axe, in the Year 1684 and the eighteenth Year of her Age, in the month of July fell into a total suppression of her Monthly Courses from a multitude of Cares and Passions of her Mind, but without any Symptom of the Green-Sickness following upon it. From which time her Appetite began to abate, and her Digestion to be bad; her flesh also began to be flaccid and loose, and her looks pale . . . the Winter following, this consumption did seem to be not a little improved; for that she was wont both Day and Night to the injuries of the Air, which was at that time extreamly cold. . . . So from that time loathing all sorts of Medicaments, she wholly neglected the care for her self for two full Years, till at last being brought to the last degree of a Marasmus, or Consumption, and thereupon subjects to Frequent Fainting Fits, she apply'd herself to me for advice.
>
> I do not remember that I did ever in all my Practice see one, that was conversant with the Living so much wasted with the greatest degree of Consumption (like a Skeleton only clad with skin) yet there was no Fever, but on the contrary a coldness of the whole Body. . . . (quoted in Bliss & Branch, 1960, pp. 10–11)

In the latter part of the ninenteenth centruy, Sir William Gull and Charles Lasegue published accounts of anorexic patients, bringing the condition to the widespread attention of the European medical establishment. In 1874, Gull coined the term *anorexia nervosa* for this condition. Gull noted that the onset of the disorder was usually in adolescence and that the disorder was much more likely seen in females than in males. In his 1873 report on "anorexia hysterique," Lasegue noted that girls with this disorder often express morbid beliefs about food being dangerous, that they are characterized by self-doubt and the need for approval from others, and that they seem driven to activity despite being terribly malnourished. Lasegue also described the interactions that arise between an anorexic girl and her family:

> The family has but two methods at its service which it always exhausts—entreaties and menaces, and which both serve as a touchstone. The delicacies of the table are multiplied in the hope of stimulating the appetite; but the more the solicitude increases, the more the appetite diminishes. . . . (pp. 265–266)

The psychoanalyst Hilde Bruch was most influential in the modern conceptualization of anorexia. In 30 years of clinical practice with anorexic patients, Bruch (1970) came to see this disorder as caused by feelings of passivity, ineffectiveness, and lack of control, brought about by maladaptive family dynamics. The anorexic's "relentless pursuit of thinness" helped her gain a sense of efficacy and control over herself and over her relationship with her family. This theory of anorexia nervosa will be discussed more later.

Summing Up — Anorexia Nervosa

- Anorexia nervosa is characterized by self-starvation, a distorted body image, intense fears of becoming fat, and amenorrhea.

- People with the restricting type refuse to eat in order to prevent weight gain.
- People with the binge/purge type periodically engage in bingeing and then purge to prevent weight gain.
- The lifetime prevalence of anorexia is about 1 percent, with 90 to 95 percent of cases being female.
- Anorexia usually begins in adolescence, and the course is variable from one person to another.
- It is a very dangerous disorder, and the death rate among anorexics is 15 percent.

Bulimia Nervosa

bulimia nervosa
eating disorder in which people engage in bingeing (episodes involving a loss of control over eating and consumption of an abnormally large amount of food) as well as behave in ways to prevent weight gain from the binges, such as self-induced vomiting, excessive exercise, or abuse of purging drugs (such as laxatives)

The core characteristics of **bulimia nervosa** are bingeing, followed by behaviors designed to prevent weight gain from the binges. The definition of a binge has been a matter of controversy among clinicians (Fairburn & Wilson, 1993). The DSM-IV defines a binge as occurring in a discrete period of time, such as an hour or two, and involving eating an amount of food that is definitely larger than most people would eat during a similar period of time and in similar circumstances. We often think of a binge as consuming 3 quarts of ice cream, two cakes, and four pizzas in one sitting. There are accounts of bulimic people who frequently consume 15,000 to 20,000 calories in one sitting (Russell, 1979). These people tend to favor fattening, carbohydrate-rich foods during binges. There are tremendous variations among bulimic people in the sizes of their binges, however, and the average binge of a bulimic person is about 1,500 calories. Less than a third of binge episodes contain more than 2,000 calories; one-third of the binge episodes contain only 600 calories, and many people with bulimia will say that they consider eating just one piece of cake a binge. What makes that a binge for them is the sense that they have no control over their eating, that they feel compelled to eat even though they are not hungry. The DSM-IV recognizes this aspect of binges, and the criteria for the diagnosis of bulimia include a sense of lack of control over eating.

The behaviors people with bulimia use to control their weight include self-induced vomiting; the abuse of laxatives, diuretics, or other purging medications; fasting; and excessive exercise. Self-induced vomiting is the behavior people associate most often with bulimia. Many bulimics are discovered by family members, roommates, and friends when they are caught vomiting or when they leave messes after they vomit. Dentists also discover bulimics because frequent vomiting can rot teeth from exposure to stomach acid. People who use self-induced vomiting or purging medications are said to have a *purging type* of bulimia. People who use excessive exercise or fasting to control their weight but do not engage in purging are said to have a *nonpurging type* of bulimia nervosa. Bulimics who use excessive exercise to control their weight can easily hide their bulimia if they are part of a group that values exercise, like students on a college campus.

People with bulimia nervosa are distinguished from people with the binge/purge type of anorexia nervosa primarily by their body weight: The criteria for binge/purge anorexia require that a person be at least 15 percent below normal body weight, whereas there are no weight criteria for bulimia nervosa. People with the restricting type of anorexia nervosa also differ from people with bulimia nervosa in that they do not engage in binges—restrictors severely limit their food intake all of the time. Table 10.2 lays out the differences and similarities in the characteristics of the different eating disorders.

For people with bulimia nervosa, the cycle of bingeing and then purging or other compensatory behaviors to control weight becomes a way of life, as in the case of Alice:

Princess Diana and Jane Fonda are just two public figures who have openly discussed their eating disorders.

Case Study • Alice is a single 17-year-old who lives with her parents, who insisted that she be seen because of binge eating and vomiting. She achieved her greatest weight of 180 pounds at 16 years of age. Her lowest weight since she reached her present height of 5′9″ has been 150 pounds, and her present weight is about 160 pounds. Alice states she has been dieting since age ten and says she has always been . . . slightly chubby.

At age 12 she started binge eating and vomiting. She was a serious competitive swimmer at that time, and it was necessary for her to keep her weight down. She would deprive herself of all food for a few days and then get an urge to eat. She could not control this urge, and would raid the refrigerator and cupboards for ice cream, pastries, and other desserts. She would often do this at night, when nobody was looking, and would eat, for example, a quart of ice cream, an entire pie, and any other desserts she could find. She would eat until she felt physical discomfort and then she would become depressed and fearful of gaining weight, following which she would self-induce vomiting. When she was 15 she was having eating binges and vomiting four days a week. Since age 13 she has gone through only one period of six weeks without gaining weight or eating binges and vomiting. . . . (Spitzer et al., 1981, p. 146)

As with anorexics, the self-evaluations of people with bulimia nervosa are heavily influenced by their body shapes and weights. When they are thin, they feel like a "good person." Bulimics do not tend to show gross distortions in their body images as anorexics do, however. Whereas an anorexic woman who is absolutely emaciated will look in the mirror and see herself as obese, bulimics have more realistic perceptions of their actual body shapes. Still, bulimics are constantly dissatisfied with their shapes and weights and concerned about losing weight.

Table 10.2 Comparisons of Eating Disorders

Characteristics in italics are part of the DSM-IV criteria for the disorder.

Symptom	AN*—Restricting Type	AN—Binge/Purge Type	BN*—Purging Type	BN—Nonpurging Type	Binge-Eating Disorder
Body weight	*Must be <15% underweight*	*Must be <15% underweight*	Often normal or somewhat overweight	Often normal or somewhat overweight	Often significantly overweight
Body image	*Severely disturbed*	*Severely disturbed*	*Overconcern with weight*	*Overconcern with weight*	Often disgusted with overweight
Binges	*No*	Yes	Yes	Yes	Yes
Purges or other compensatory behaviors	*No*	Yes	Yes	*No*	*No*
Sense of lack of control over eating	No	*During binges*	Yes	Yes	Yes
Amenorrhea in females	*Yes*	*Yes*	Not usually	Not usually	No

*AN refers to anorexia nervosa and BN to bulimia nervosa.

Teenagers often feel great pressure to look like the models in magazines or fitness experts in work-out videos.

Epidemiology of Bulimia Nervosa

In the 1970s, the popular media in the United States and Europe became intrigued by the binge-purge cycle of bulimia and afforded it much attention. It was said that there was an epidemic of bulimia on college campuses, with as many as 25 percent of college women using self-induced vomiting to control their weight. Researchers at the University of Pennsylvania investigated this claim in a study of 942 male and 994 female students. They asked the students how frequently they engaged in the behaviors and thoughts required for the diagnosis of bulimia. Many more students engaged in periodic binges than in self-induced vomiting. Among the women, 32 percent engaged in binges at least twice per month, but only 3 percent reported feeling out of control over their eating during those binges. Only 3 percent of the women reported engaging in vomiting after a binge at least once a month; only 1 percent engaged in bingeing and then vomiting twice per week, as required for a diagnosis of bulimia. Among the men, 29 percent engaged in binges at least twice per month, but only about 1 percent reported feeling out of control over their eating. Only 0.3 percent met the criteria for bulimia (Schotte & Stunkard, 1987). Similarly, in a nationwide sample of 1,007 college students, only 1.0 percent of the women and 0.2 percent of the men met the diagnostic criteria for bulimia (Drewnowski, Hopkins, & Kessler, 1988). Thus, although unnecessary concerns about weight control may be common among college students, particularly women students, the full syndrome of bulimia, as defined by clinicians, is relatively uncommon (Schotte & Stunkard, 1987).

As with anorexia nervosa, the onset of bulimia nervosa happens most often during adolescence. The long-term course of bulimia nervosa, left untreated, is unclear. A year-long study of bulimia nervosa on a college campus found that 44 percent of women diagnosed as bulimic in the fall of the academic year were still classified as bulimic in the spring of that year (Drenowski, Yee, & Krahn, 1988). The majority of the remaining women who had been diagnosed as bulimic in the fall still showed some symptoms of bulimia nervosa in the spring, although they did not meet the full diagnostic criteria.

Many people with bulimia nervosa are of normal weight or slightly overweight. You might conclude, then, that bulimia is not a physically dangerous disorder as is anorexia. Although the death rate among bulimic patients is not as high as among anorexic patients, bulimia also has serious medical complications (see Table 10.3). One of the most serious complications is the imbalance in the body's electrolytes that results from fluid loss following excessive and chronic vomiting, laxative abuse, and diuretic abuse. Electrolytes are biochemicals that help to regulate the heart, and imbalances in electrolytes can lead to heart failure.

Table 10.3 Medical Complications of Bulimia Nervosa	
Renal Complications	**Laxative Abuse Complications**
Dehydration	Reduction of blood calcium
Kidney disease	Tetanus
Gastrointestinal Complications	Softening of the bones
	Skin pigmentation
Gastric dilatation	Reduction in magnesium levels
Inflammation of the salivary gland	Fluid retention
Elevations of the enzyme amylase	Malabsorption syndromes
Pancreatic disease	Colon abnormalities
Electrolyte Abnormalities	**Other Abnormalities**
Excess uric acid in the blood	Susceptibility to bleeding
Lowered potassium levels	Electroencephalogram abnormalities
Alkalosis	Abnormal thyroid hormone and growth
Acidosis	hormone responses
Dental Problems	
Tooth decay	
Enamel erosion	

Source: Brownell & Foreyt, 1986.

- Bulimia nervosa is characterized by uncontrolled bingeing followed by behaviors designed to prevent weight gain from the binges.
- People with the purging type use self-induced vomiting, diuretics, or laxatives to prevent weight gain.
- People with the nonpurging type use fasting and exercise to prevent weight gain.
- Although overconcern with weight and occasional bingeing is common among college students, the prevalence of the full syndrome of bulimia nervosa is only about 1.0 percent in women and 0.2 percent in men.
- The onset of bulimia nervosa is most often in adolescence, and its course, if left untreated, is unclear.
- Although people with bulimia nervosa do not tend to be severely underweight, there are a variety of possible medical complications of the disorder.

Do you think the diagnostic criteria for anorexia nervosa and bulimia nervosa should be narrow so that only the most severe behaviors are given a diagnosis or broad so that more moderate types of disordered eating meet the criteria for a diagnosis?

Binge-Eating Disorder

Binge-eating disorder resembles bulimia nervosa in many ways, except that the person with binge-eating disorder does not regularly engage in purging, fasting, or excessive exercise to compensate for his or her binges. People with binge-eating disorder may eat continuously throughout the day with no planned mealtimes. Others engage in discrete binges on large amounts of food, often in response to stress and feelings of anxiety or depression. They may eat very rapidly and be almost in a daze as they eat, as this man describes:

> "The day after New Year's Day I got my check cashed. I usually eat to celebrate the occasion, so I knew it might happen. On the way to the bank I steeled myself against it. I kept reminding myself of the treatment and about my New Year's resolution about dieting. . . .
>
> Then I got the check cashed. And I kept out a hundred. And everything just seemed to go blank. I don't know what it was. All of my good intentions just seemed to fade away. They just didn't seem to mean anything anymore. I just said, 'What the hell,' and started eating, and what I did then was an absolute sin."
>
> He described starting in a grocery store where he bought a cake, several pieces of pie, and boxes of cookies. Then he drove through heavy midtown traffic with one hand, pulling food out of the bag with the other hand and eating as fast as he could.
>
> After consuming all of his groceries, he set out on a furtive round of restaurants, staying only a short time in each and eating only small amounts. Although in constant dread of discovery, he had no idea what "sin" he felt he was committing. He knew only that it was not pleasurable. "I didn't enjoy it at all. It just happened. It's like a part of me just blacked out. And when that happened there was nothing there except the food and me, all alone."
>
> Finally he went into a delicatessen, bought another $20 worth of food and drove home, eating all the way, "until my gut ached." (Stunkard, 1993, pp. 20–21)

People with this disorder are often significantly overweight and say they are disgusted with their bodies and ashamed of their bingeing. They typically have histories of frequent dieting and joining weight-control programs. As many as 30 percent of people currently in weight-loss programs may have binge-eating disorder. In contrast, only about 2 percent of the general population has the disorder (Spitzer, Devlin, Walsh, & Hasin, 1992).

binge-eating disorder
eating disorder in which people compulsively overeat either continuously or on discrete binges but do not behave in ways to compensate for the overeating

As with anorexia and bulimia nervosa, binge-eating disorder is more common in women than in men, in both the general community and among people in weight-loss programs. People with binge-eating disorder have high rates of depression and anxiety and possibly more alcohol abuse and personality disorders (Castonguay, Eldredge, & Agras, 1995).

Binge-eating disorder is not one of the officially recognized forms of eating disorders in the DSM-IV, largely because the authors of the DSM-IV felt there has been too little research on this disorder to sanction the diagnosis. Rather, the diagnostic criteria for binge-eating disorder were placed in the appendix of the DSM-IV for further study.

 If you were prone to bingeing when you were distressed, what are some ways you could overcome this tendency?

Dieting and the Eating Disorders

Most people who develop eating disorders begin their dysfunctional patterns simply by going on diets. Their diets may be innocuous at first, the type of diets most people think are safe and healthy, such as diets that are low in fats and high in fruits and vegetables. The diets may then become more and more extreme, perhaps because the simple and healthy diets do not achieve the desired weight loss. One young woman who became anorexic described it this way:

> At first, I stopped eating meat. But in two weeks, I had only lost a few pounds, so I cut out carbohydrates. The next week I cut out all dairy products. Then I cut out all starchy vegetables, like potatoes. Gradually I was down to water and a couple of pieces of fruit per day.

Even moderate dieting can create a set of psychological and physiological conditions that make it difficult for an individual to maintain healthy eating patterns. Dieting creates chronic frustration, irritability, and emotional reactivity, which can make people more impulsive in their eating patterns (Herman & Polivy, 1975). Dieting also changes people's ability to read their bodies' cues about hunger and satiety and people's attitudes toward food. In a classic study, researchers compared the eating patterns of chronic dieters and of people not dieting. These people were brought into a laboratory and first asked to drink either two milkshakes, one milkshake, or no milkshake. Then they were asked to try three flavors of ice cream and rate the ice cream. People who were not dieting decreased the amount of ice cream they ate as a function of how many milkshakes they had consumed before the rating task: The more milkshakes they had consumed during the "preload," the less ice cream they ate during the rating task. Chronic dieters, however, ate more ice cream during the rating task if they had consumed milkshakes during the preload; those who had consumed two milkshakes during the preload ate even more ice cream during the rating task than did those who had consumed only one milkshake (Herman & Mack, 1975).

The cognitive explanation for these findings is that dieters develop beliefs that if they violate their diets in any way, they might as well violate them totally and binge. One physiological explanation for the findings is that dieting enhances the physiological appeal of "forbidden" foods, making it difficult to resist them especially after a taste of them. Studies have found that people actually prefer sweet-tasting foods more when they are on diets than when they are not (Rodin, Slowchower, & Fleming, 1977).

Another physiological explanation is that each person has a "natural" weight that her body will fight to maintain, even if she attempts to lose weight (Keesey, 1986). This natural weight is often referred to as a **set point.** The set point is determined in part by a person's metabolic rate, which is known to be heavily influenced by genetics (Bouchard et al., 1989). When a person diets, her metabolic rate actually slows down, reducing her body's need for food. Unfortunately, the slowing of the metabolic rate also means that the body is not using up the food she consumes as quickly, making it more likely that

set point
natural body weight determined by a person's metabolic rate, diet, and genetics

this food will turn to fat even though she may be eating much less food than usual. The implication of this *set point theory* is that permanently changing weight may require some people to be on highly restrictive diets permanently.

People rarely stay on restrictive diets or keep their weight off after diets, however. In 1992, *Consumer Reports* did a survey of 95,000 of its readers who had tried to lose weight in the previous 3 years (*Consumer Reports*, June 1993). One in five of these readers had joined commercial weight-loss programs, such as Weight Watchers. Interestingly, 25 percent of these people who had joined commercial weight loss programs were not even moderately overweight at the start. On average, the people who joined commercial weight-loss programs lost 10 to 20 percent of their starting weight, but they gained back half that weight in 6 months and two-thirds of the weight in 2 years. Only 25 percent of them kept the weight off for more than 2 years. A substantial minority of the people responding to this survey had used liquid-fast programs to lose their weight. These liquid fasts did lead to quicker weight loss, but these people gained their weight back just as fast as those who had lost it through other methods. This survey by *Consumer Reports* is not a scientific study, but dozens of well-controlled studies of weight-loss programs, including very low-calorie liquid diets, hospital-based programs, drug therapies, and behavioral therapies for weight loss, confirm that the majority of people can lose weight through these programs, but they tend to gain it back within a couple of years (Garner & Wooley, 1991; Jeffery & Wing, 1995).

Thus, dieting is difficult, and many people who diet engage in at least occasional bingeing. People who go on to develop bulimia do not tend to begin vomiting or using purgatives (laxatives and diuretics) until about 1 year after they began bingeing. Vomiting and the abuse of purgatives are initiated as means of weight control. They also reduce the bulimic's distress and guilt over bingeing and thus are reinforced. Purging allows the bulimic to continue to engage in binges when she is distressed or when she is simply hungry, while avoiding weight gain. The binge-purge pattern eventually becomes a way of life, however, taking up hours of each day and interfering with the bulimic's social life and functioning. As we noted earlier, the binge-purge cycle poses significant risks to the bulimic's health.

People who go on to develop anorexia nervosa often feel that the only way to control their eating is to not eat at all. They become obsessed with following strict rules about eating and exercise, and they build their lives around these rules. Following these rules may give them a sense of control and superiority. Anorexics are often praised for their weight loss early in their illness. They appear to be the successful dieters that we all wish to be, and friends and family will tell them that they envy their ability to lose weight so quickly. Losing weight eventually becomes the anorexic's identity, however, and her self-esteem becomes dependent on her ability to control her food intake.

 How can people watch their diets in ways that improve their health without crossing the line into obsessive concern over what they eat?

Eating Disorders in Athletes

One group that appears to be at increased risk for unhealthy eating habits and full-blown eating disorders is athletes, especially those in sports in which weight is considered an important factor in competitiveness, such as gymnastics, ice skating, dancing, horse racing, wrestling, and bodybuilding. Researchers in Norway assessed all 522 elite female athletes between the ages of 12 and 35 in that country for the presence of eating disorders and found that those in sports classified as "aesthetic" or "weight dependent," including diving, figure skating, gymnastics, dance, judo, karate, and wrestling, were most likely to have anorexia or bulimia nervosa (see Table 10.4; Sundgot-Borgen, 1994). When those women athletes with eating disorders were asked about the triggers for their eating disorders, many said that they felt that the physical changes of puberty came too early for them and decreased their competitive edge, so they had started dieting severely to try

Table 10.4 Rates of Eating Disorders in Elite Women Athletes	
Sport	**Percent with an Eating Disorder**
Aesthetic sports (e.g., figure skating, gymnastics)	35
Weight-dependent sports (e.g., judo, wrestling)	29
Endurance sports (e.g., cycling, running, swimming)	20
Technical sports (e.g., golf, high jumping)	14
Ball game sports (e.g., volleyball, soccer)	12

Source: Data from Sundgot-Borgen, 1993.

to maintain their prepubescent figures (see Table 10.5 for other triggers). The case of Heidi, described here by her therapist, illustrates several of these triggers (adapted from Pipher, 1994, pp. 165–168):

> Heidi arrived in my office after gymnastics practice. Blond and pretty, she was dressed in a shiny red-and-white warm-up suit. We talked about gymnastics, which Heidi had been involved in since she was six. At that time, she was selected to train with the university coaches. Now she trained four hours a day, six days a week. She didn't expect to make an Olympic team, but she anticipated a scholarship to a Big-8 school.
>
> Heidi glowed when she talked about gymnastics, but I noticed her eyes were red and she had a small scar on the index finger of her right hand. (When a hand is repeatedly stuck down the throat, it can be scarred by the acids in the mouth.) I wasn't surprised when she said she was coming in for help with bulimia.
>
> Heidi said, "I've had this problem for two years, but lately it's affecting my gymnastics. I am too weak, particularly on the vault, which requires strength. It's hard to concentrate.
>
> "I blame my training for my eating disorder," Heidi continued. "Our coach has weekly weigh-ins where we count each others' ribs. If they are hard to count we're in trouble."
>
> Heidi explained that since puberty she had had trouble keeping her weight down. After meals, she was nervous that she'd eaten too much. She counted calories; she was hungry but afraid to eat. In class she pinched the fat on her side and freaked out.
>
> I asked when it started.
>
> "After my thirteenth birthday things got tough. I graduated from my neighborhood school and moved into a consolidated school. I made friends there, but I felt under more pressure. School was harder; gymnastics was harder. I gained weight when I started my periods. Coach put me on a diet."

How can a young gymnast ignore pressures to remain very thin and remain competitive?

Sports that require certain body shapes or weights, such as gymnastics or body building, seem to breed eating disorders.

Bodybuilding is an increasingly popular sport, but bodybuilders routinely have substantial weight fluctuations as they try to shape their bodies for competition and then binge in the off seasons. For example, one study of male body builders found that 46 percent reported bingeing after most competitions, and 85 percent reported gaining significant weight (an average of 15 pounds) in the off season. Then they dieted to prepare for competition, losing an average of 14 pounds. A parallel study of female bodybuilders and weight lifters found that 42 percent reported having been anorexic at some time in their lives, 67 percent were terrified of being fat, and 58 percent were obsessed with food (Andersen, Barlett, Morgan, & Brownell, 1995).

Amateur athletes are also at increased risk for disordered eating behaviors. A survey of 4,551 readers of *Runner's World* magazine found that most of the women and many of the men reported dissatisfaction with their bodies, uncontrolled eating, and a preoccupation with food and eating (see Table 10.6; Brownell, Rodin, & Wilmore, 1992). Thus, although participation in athletics is good for the body and soul of many people, it is associated with disordered eating behaviors and attitudes for some people.

Table 10.5 Triggers Mentioned by Athletes with Eating Disorders for the Development of Their Eating Disorders

Trigger	Percent Mentioning
Prolonged periods of dieting/weight fluctuation	37
New coach	30
Injury/illness	23
Casual comments by others about weight	19
Leaving home/failure at school or work	10
Problem in relationship	10
Family problems	7
Illness/injury to family members	7
Death of significant other	4
Sexual abuse	4

Source: Data from Sundgot-Borgen, 1993.

Table 10.6 Body Weight and Dieting Concerns in 4,551 Respondents to Survey in *Runner's World* Magazine

Question	Percent Giving this Response	
	Females (N = 1,911)	Males (N = 2,640)
Do you consciously watch your weight? ("often" or "always")	73	64
How satisfied are you with your current body size and shape? ("moderately satisfied" or worse)	57	37
How easy or difficult is it for you to maintain optimal weight? ("somewhat" or "very" difficult)	52	39
Do you ever feel out of control while you are eating or have the feeling that you won't be able to stop eating? ("sometimes," "often," or "always")		
While in training	43	33
While not training	59	46
In the days before a race	30	20
After a race	38	44
Have you ever eaten a large amount of food rapidly and felt that this incident was excessive and out of control (aside from holiday feasts)	64	45
Questions From Eating Attitudes Test ("often," "usually," or "always")		
I am terrified about being overweight	48	22
I find myself preoccupied with food	36	16
I feel extremely guilty after eating	20	7
I am preoccupied with a desire to be thinner	48	24
I give too much time and thought to food	35	13

From K. D. Brownell and J. Rodin, "The Dieting Maelstrom: Is It Possible and Advisable to Lose Weight" in *American Psychologist*, 49(9):781–791. Copyright © 1994 by the American Psychological Association.

Gender Similarities and Differences in the Eating Disorders

As we have noted, both anorexia nervosa and bulimia nervosa are much more common in females than in males. This gender difference has largely been attributed to the fact that thinness is more valued and encouraged in females than in males. For example, studies of popular women's and men's magazines find 10 times more diet articles in women's magazines than in men's magazines (Andersen & DiDomenico, 1992; Nemeroff et al., 1994). Half of all women report frequent dissatisfaction with their appearance, whereas fewer than one-third of men report the same (*Time Magazine*, June 3, 1996). In recent years, women's magazines have moved somewhat away from articles on dieting only toward articles on fitness and exercise (Nemeroff et al., 1994). Unfortunately, however, women's motivations for exercise are still more likely to be for weight control than are men's motivations, and exercising for weight control is more likely to contribute to eating-disordered behavior than is exercising for health (McDonald & Thompson, 1992).

Others have argued that many adolescent girls and young women develop eating disorders because they are caught between the demands to be a "modern woman"—to be liberated, sexually attractive, and active and successful in traditional male ways—and to fulfill the traditional female role of being nurturant and subservient (Orbach, 1978; Selvini-Palazzoli, 1974). They strive to be perfect in all ways, including in their appearance. They also want to "drop out of the race" and be taken care of, and this is facilitated by becoming sick with an eating disorder. This line of argument may help to explain why bulimia and anorexia nervosa are more common among women in environments that are highly competitive and achievement-oriented. For example, the prevalence of bulimia nervosa in university women is five times greater than the prevalence in working women the same age (Hart & Ollendick, 1985).

Some men do develop eating disorders. Men who develop eating disorders generally display the same symptoms as do women who develop the disorders, including body dissatisfaction and the use of purging and excessive exercise to control their weight. Also, both men and women with eating disorders have high rates of comorbid depression and substance abuse (Olivardia, Pope, Mangweth, & Hudson, 1995).

The following passage was written by a male psychologist who developed bulimia nervosa over a period of years (Wilps, 1990, pp. 19–21). This man grew up viewing food as a source of comfort and bingeing as a way of escaping from overbearing and disapproving parents. He would fast for a day or more after a binge to control his weight. As the pressures of his job and a failed marriage increased, his bulimic pattern of bingeing and then fasting grew more serious:

Men are less likely than women to develop eating disorders, but the features of eating disorders are similar in men and women.

> I would sigh with relief when Sunday evening came, since I had no work responsibilities until the next morning, and I would have just returned my son to his mother's custody. I would then carefully shop at convenience stores for "just right" combinations of cheese, lunch meats, snack chips, and sweets such as chocolate bars. I would also make a stop at a neighborhood newsstand to buy escapist paperback novels (an essential part of the binge) and then settle down for a three-hour session of reading and slow eating until I could barely keep my eyes open. My binges took the place of Sunday dinner, averaging approximately 6,000 kilocalories in size. Following the binge, my stomach aching with distension, I would carefully clean my teeth, wash all the dishes, and fall into a drugged slumber.
>
> I would typically schedule the following day as a heavy working day with evening meetings in order to distract myself from increasing hunger as I fasted. I began running. . . . I would typically run for one hour, four to five days per week, and walked to work as a further weight control measure. . . .
>
> As time went on, I increased the frequency of these binges, probably because of the decreasing structured demands for my time. They went from weekly to twice per week, then I was either bingeing or fasting with no normal days in my

week at all. My sleep patterns were either near-comatose or restless, with either sweating after a binge or shivering after a fast. I became increasingly irritable and withdrawn . . . prompting increased guilt on my part that I resented the intrusion of my friends, my patients, and even my son into my cycle. . . .

The nadir of my life as a bulimic occurred when I found myself calling patients whom I had scheduled for evening appointments, explaining to them that I was ill, then using the freed evening for bingeing . . . I was physically exhausted most of the time, and my hands, feet, and abdomen were frequently puffy and edematous, which I, of course, interpreted as gain in body fat and which contributed to my obsession with weight and food. I weighed myself several times per day in various locations, attending to half pound variations as though my life depended on them.

There are some differences between men and women with eating disorders. Men are more likely than women to have histories of being oveweight and of bingeing before their anorexia or bulimia nervosa developed (Andersen, 1990). There is some evidence that homosexual men are more likely than heterosexual men to have eating disorders but there are no differences between lesbians and heterosexual women in the prevalence of eating disorders (Andersen, 1992; Schneider, O'Leary, & Jenkins, 1995). It may be that the gay male culture encourages concern with weight control as much as do the cultures of both lesbians and heterosexual women.

In general, there are many similarities in the characteristics of eating disorders between men and women. There has been relatively little research, however, investigating the triggers of eating disorders in men.

 Are there any acceptable ways that society might reduce the emphasis in the media on attractiveness? Do you think these ways would help to reduce disordered eating behaviors?

Cultural Factors in Eating Disorders

The prevalence of eating disorders appears to have increased in the United States and Europe over the last few decades (Strober, 1986). In contrast, eating disorders are uncommon in many less developed countries (Davis & Yager, 1992; McCarthy, 1989; Pate, Pumariega, Hester, & Garner, 1992; Sobal & Stunkard, 1989). Psychologists have linked the historical and cross-cultural differences in the prevalence of eating disorders to differences in the standards of beauty for women held at different historical times and in different cultures (Garner & Garfinkel, 1980; McCarthy, 1990; Sobal & Stunkard, 1989). When the most wealthy and influential members of a society value thinness, eating disorders tend to be more prevalent. When a heavier weight is seen as more beautiful, eating disorders are uncommon, but obesity is common. As was noted earlier in this chapter, the ideal shape for women in the United States and Europe has become thinner and thinner over the last few decades. Some writers attribute this to the influence of the weight-control industry and to the media (see Seligman, 1993). In contrast, people in less-developed countries may view heaviness as beautiful because only wealthy people have the means to obtain food and become obese.

Within the United States and Europe, there may be differences among socioeconomic, ethnic, and racial groups in the prevalence of eating disorders. Some studies find that eating disorders are more common among the upper and middle classes than among lower socioeconomic classes. This association between socioeconomic status and eating disorders is found among Caucasians and among African Americans and Hispanics. Perhaps because African Americans and Hispanics are more likely than Caucasians to be in lower socioeconomic groups, the overall rates of eating disorders are lower in African Americans and Hispanics than in Caucasians (Gray, Ford, & Kelly, 1987; Gross & Rosen, 1988; Pate, et al., 1991). Other researchers have argued that the rate of eating disorders is lower in African Americans and Hispanics because they do not accept the thin ideal that is promoted in white culture (Osvold & Sodowsky, 1993). Finally, some researchers have suggested that African-American adolescent girls are more focused than white adolescent girls on work and adult responsibilities, so they are less likely to become preoccupied with physical appearance and dieting than are white girls. The rates of eating disorders in ethnic minority groups in the United States have been rising in recent years, however, and some studies show equal rates across all socioeconomic and ethnic groups in the United States (Davis & Yager, 1992; Pate et al., 1992).

There may be some cultural differences in the symptoms of eating disorders. Whereas fear of becoming fat is one of the defining features of eating disorders among white Europeans and Americans, studies of eating disorder patients in China, Hong Kong, and India find no preoccupation with becoming fat (Khandelwal & Saxena, 1990; Lee, 1995). Anorexic patients in these countries also do not have the distorted body images that are characteristic of anorexia in the United States and Europe and will readily admit that they are very thin. Nonetheless, they stubbornly refuse to eat, as is illustrated by the case of this Chinese woman (adapted from Sing, 1995, pp. 27–29):

> **Case Study** • Miss Y, aged 31, was 5 foot 3 inches. She had formerly weighed 110 pounds but now weighed 48 pounds. Her anorexia began four years previously, when she was suddenly deserted by her boyfriend, who came from a neighboring village. Greatly saddened by his departure for England, Miss Y started to complain of abdominal discomfort and reduced her food intake. She became socially withdrawn and unemployed.
>
> At her psychiatric examination, she wore long hair and was shockingly emaciated—virtually a skeleton. She had sunken eyes, hollow cheeks, and pale, cold skin. She recognized her striking wasting readily but claimed a complete lack of hunger and blamed the weight loss on an unidentifiable abdominal problem. Her concern over the seriousness of her physical condition was perfunctory. When asked whether she consciously tried to restrict the amount she ate, she said, "No." When questioned why she had gone for periods of eight or more waking hours without eating anything, she said it was because she had no hunger and felt distended, pointing to the lower left side of her abdomen. All physical examinations revealed no biological source for her feelings of distension, however.
>
> Miss Y was often in a low mood and became transiently tearful when her grief over the broken relationship was acknowledged. However, she resisted all attempts to discuss this loss in detail and all other psychological and medical treatments. Miss Y later died of cardiac arrest. Postmortem examination revealed no specific pathology other than multiple organ atrophy due to starvation.

If Asians who develop anorexia do not tend to be pursuing thinness and recognize they are too thin, this suggests that the triggers for anorexia nervosa in Asia may be different from those in Europe and the United States. Just what those triggers are for Asian anorexics is not clear, however.

The Families and Personalities of People with Eating Disorders

Earlier in this chapter, we considered evidence that there are strong societal pressures on females in developed countries to be unreasonably and unhealthily thin and increasing pressures on males to have a lean, super-fit look. These pressures lead many people to be unhappy with their current weights and shapes, to diet chronically, and to exercise largely to change their body shapes rather than for health. These pressures are present in the lives of most people in developed countries, but only a minority develop full eating disorders. As the case study of Miss Y illustrates, there are people in developing countries who are not exposed to pressures to be thin or superfit but who still develop eating disorders. What drives some people to develop eating disorders when most people do not?

The following passage written by a young woman with bulimia nervosa describes some of the possible emotional underpinnings of eating disorders:

> I remember deciding not too long ago that if I could just stop bingeing and start eating right, my life would be "perfect." If I could just get control over food, I told myself, bulimia would disappear from my mind and from my life. How very wrong I was.
>
> At that point, I was dealing with my bulimia in the same way as a doctor who would treat a sick person's sneezes rather than her cold. I was trying to treat the symptom of bulimia (overeating) rather than the disease itself.
>
> Bulimia does not deal with food or overeating or bingeing. Food is not the problem. I believe, however, that bulimia does deal with hunger. Each binge is a signal that the bulimic is starving to death and is desparately seeking nourishment. This hunger, however, is one that does not come from physical emptiness but rather arises from an emptiness deep within a person, an emptiness of self. Food is not the problem behind the hunger, and food is not the answer.
>
> I do not deny that I am hungry when my binge voice starts screaming in my ear. I immediately admit that I am terribly hungry. But I then ask myself, "What am I hungry for?" Rarely am I hungry for food. Food is instead a way of feeding emotional hungers that I otherwise do not know how to feed.
>
> Sometimes I realize I am hungry for the approval of others. Sometimes my hunger is for the company of another person when I am lonely. Sometimes my hunger comes from the deprived little girl that still lives within me. Physical hunger is rarely a part of my binge voice. Food is not my problem. Control over food is not my problem. My emotional hungers and my inability to feed those hungers in the right way is my problem.
>
> Never will I be able to eat enough food to fill hungers that are not really crying out for food. I will never get enough of what I do not really want or need. It is only by feeding my true hungers and shedding my food security blanket that I can feel nourished and satisfied. Only when I stop starving myself to death by gorging myself with food will I fully live.

The emotional hungers this young bulimic woman describes are common to people with eating disorders. The need for approval from others, low self-esteem, and frequent feelings of depression and anxiety characterize people with bulimia nervosa, anorexia nervosa, and binge-eating disorder (Herman & Polivy, 1988). Psychosocial theories of eating disorders have attempted to explain how these characteristics develop and when they lead specifically to eating disorders.

A pioneer in psychosocial theorizing about eating disorders is Hilde Bruch (1973, 1982). Her theory is most concerned with girls who develop anorexia nervosa, although it has also been used to understand the development of bulimia nervosa and binge-eating disorder. Bruch noted that anorexia nervosa often occurs in girls who have been unusually "good girls," high achievers, dutiful and compliant daughters who are always trying to please their parents and others by being "perfect." These girls tend to have parents who are overinvested in their daughters' compliance and achievements, who are overcontrolling, and who will not allow the expression of feelings, especially negative feelings. Another pioneer in theorizing about anorexia, Salvador Minuchin, describes the families of anorexics as *enmeshed* (Minuchin, Rosman, & Baker, 1978). There is extreme interdependence and intensity in the family interactions, so that the boundaries between the identities of individual family members are weak and easily crossed.

Throughout their daughters' lives, these parents are ineffective and inappropriate in their parenting, responding primarily to the parents' own schedules and needs rather than to their daughters' needs for food or comfort (Bruch, 1973). As a result, the daughters do not learn to identify and accept their own feelings and desires. Instead, they learn to monitor closely the needs and desires of others and to comply with others' demands, as we can see in the case of Rachel and her family.

> **Case Study** • Rachel is a 16 year old with anorexia nervosa. Her parents are highly educated and very successful, having spent most of their careers in the diplomatic corps. Rachel, her two brothers, and her parents are "very close, as are many families in the diplomatic corps, because we move so much," although the daily care of the children has always been left to nannies. The children had to follow strict rules for appropriate conduct both in the home and outside. These rules were partly driven by the requirements of families of diplomats to "be on the best behavior" in their host country and partly driven by Rachel's parents' very conservative religious beliefs. Rachel, as the only daughter in the family, had always to behave like "a proper lady" to counteract the stereotype of American girls as brash and sexually promiscuous. All the children were required to act mature beyond their years, controlling any emotional outbursts, taking defeats and disappointments without complaint, and happily picking up and moving every couple of years when their parents were reassigned to another country.
>
> Rachel's anorexic behaviors began when her parents announced they were leaving the diplomatic corps to return to the United States. Rachel had grown very fond of their last post in Europe, because she had finally found a group of friends that she liked *and* her parents approved of, and she liked her school. She had always done well in school but often had hated the harshly strict schoolteachers. In her present school, she felt accepted by her teachers as well as challenged by the work. When Rachel told her parents she would like to finish her last year of high school in this school rather than go to the United States with them, they flatly refused to even consider it. Rachel tried to talk with her parents, suggesting she stay with the family of one of her friends, who was willing to have her, but her parents cut her off and told her they would not discuss the idea further. Rachel became sullen and withdrawn and stopped eating shortly after the family arrived in the United States.

As a result of such family dynamics, anorexic girls have fundamental deficits in their senses of self and identities. They experience themselves as always acting in response to others rather than in response to their own wishes and needs. They do not accurately identify their own feelings or desires and thus do not cope appropriately with distress. They do not even accurately identify bodily sensations such as hunger, and this may contribute greatly to their ability to starve themselves for long periods of time.

Why do eating disorders often develop in adolescence? One of the important tasks of adolescence is separation and individuation from one's family. Girls from these families deeply fear separation because they have not developed the ability to act and think independently of their families. They also fear involvement with peers, especially sexual involvement, because they do not understand their feelings or trust their judgment. Yet they recognize at some level their need to separate from their families and take their place among their peers. They harbor rage against their parents for their overcontrol. They become angry, negativistic, defiant, and distrustful. They also discover that controlling their food intake both gives them some sense of control over their lives and elicits concern from their parents. The rigid control of their bodies provides a sense of power over the self and the family that the girls have never had before. It also provides a way of avoiding peer relationships—the girl dons the persona of an anorexic, sickly, distant, untouchable, and superior in her self-control. Other psychoanalytic theorists have taken this argument further to suggest that the anorexic girl is primarily avoiding sexual maturity and relationships by stopping pubertal maturation by self-starvation (Lerner, 1986).

Bingeing may develop as a way of coping with negative emotions (Polivy & Herman, 1993). People who binge tend to be more prone to anxiety, emotionally unstable, and impulsive than are people with restricting anorexia nervosa or no eating disorders. They are easily upset by stressful situations and tend to engage impulsively in bingeing in response to emotional distress (Hsu, 1990). This maladaptive coping response may develop because these people were not allowed to express negative emotions freely in their families and thus did not learn adaptive ways of coping.

Why would girls but not boys in such families develop eating disorders? It may be because, in general, parents tend to appreciate the need for boys to separate from the family in adolescence and give them the freedom to separate. Especially in these enmeshed families, parents are terrified of their girls' independence; the mothers of these girls may need their daughters to remain dependent because their own identities are tied too closely to their daughters (Bruch, 1973; Palazzoli, 1974). Thus, there are tremendous pressures on girls to remain enmeshed with their families, but boys have more opportunity to break free and build their own identities.

Research testing these psychosocial theories has confirmed that the families of girls with eating disorders have high levels of conflict, that expression of negative emotions is discouraged in the families, and that control and perfectionism are key themes in the families (Attie & Brooks-Gunn, 1989; Pike & Rodin, 1991; Strauss & Ryan, 1987). These negative characteristics are not specific to the families of girls with eating disorders, however. They are also prevalent in the families of children with depression, anxiety disorders, and several other forms of psychopathology. What may be crucial in the development of anorexia nervosa is the girls' lack of awareness of their own bodily sensations, which allows them to ignore even the most severe hunger pangs (Leon, Fulkerson, Perry, & Early-Zald, 1995). Girls who come from these troubled families but are not able to completely ignore their hunger may fall into a binge-purge form of anorexia nervosa, or into bulimia nervosa.

Other research on the personalities of people with eating disorders confirms that they are more concerned with the opinions of others, are more conforming to others' wishes, and are more rigid in their evaluations of themselves and others than are other people (Striegel-Moore, Silberstein, & Rodin, 1993; Strober, 1981; Vitousek & Manke, 1994). Studies of the cognitions of people with eating disorders show that they have a dichotomous thinking style, in which everything is either all good or all bad. For example, if they eat one cookie, they may think that they have blown their diets and might as well eat whole boxes of cookies. They will say they cannot break their rigid eating routines or they will completely lose control over their eating. They obsess over their eating routines and plan their days down to the smallest detail around these routines.

 Do you ever feel guilty for eating something? What is the source of this guilt?

Unfortunately, the majority of studies of the families and personality characteristics of anorexics and bulimics have not been prospective but have compared people who already have eating disorders with those who do not (Vitousek & Manke, 1994). As a result, we do not know to what extent these family and personality characteristics are causes of anorexia or bulimia. The controlling nature of parents' behaviors toward their children may be a consequence as well as a cause of the disorder—parents are exerting control to try to save their children's lives. Similarly, many of the personality characteristics of people with eating disorders may be consequences as well as causes of the disorder. Studies of normal people who engage in self-starvation as part of an experiment show that depression, anxiety, rigidity, obsessiveness, irritability, concrete thinking, and social withdrawal appear after a few weeks of self-starvation (Keys, 1950). The success of psychosocial therapies for eating disorders, which we will discuss later, provides more evidence that psychosocial factors are implicated in the development or at least the maintenance of these disorders.

Summing Up | Families and Personalities of People with Eating Disorders

- Psychosocial theories suggest that people who develop eating disorders come from families that are overcontrolling and perfectionistic but discourage the expression of negative emotions. Eating disorders develop as means of gaining some control or coping with negative emotions.

· People who are so unaware of their own bodily sensations that they can starve themselves may develop anorexia nervosa. People who remain aware of their bodily sensations and cannot starve themselves but who are prone to anxiety and impulsivity may develop binge-eating disorder or bulimia nervosa.

· Girls may be more likely than boys to develop eating disorders in adolescence because girls are not given as much freedom as boys to develop independence and their own identities.

Sexual Abuse and the Eating Disorders

A controversial theory that has gained much attention in recent years is that the eating disorders often result from experiences of sexual abuse (see Pope & Hudson, 1992). This theory has been controversial in part because it stemmed from clinical reports of high rates of sexual abuse among persons seeking therapy for eating disorders rather than from controlled studies and because it has led some therapists to urge their clients with eating disorders to search through their pasts for memories of childhood sexual abuse and then take action against their abusors as part of their therapy. Proponents of this theory argue that survivors of sexual abuse develop eating disorders as a symbol of self-loathing and a way of making themselves unattractive in an attempt to prevent further sexual abuse.

In recent years, several careful studies have been done to examine the rates of sexual abuse among women and men with eating disorders and to compare these rates to those of people with other psychological disorders and people with no disorders (Kinzl, Traweger, Guenther, & Biebl, 1994; Pope & Hudson, 1992; Rorty, Yager, & Rossotto, 1994; Welch & Fairburn, 1994). These studies have found that although people with eating disorders tend to have higher rates of sexual abuse than people with no psychological disorders, they do not tend to have higher rates of sexual abuse than do people with other psychological disorders, such as depression or anxiety. Thus, sexual abuse seems to be a general risk factor for psychological problems, including eating disorders, depression, and anxiety, rather than a specific risk factor for eating disorders.

Biological Theories of the Eating Disorders

As is the case with most psychological disorders, anorexia and bulimia nervosa tend to run in families (Kassett et al., 1989; Strober, 1991). One twin study of bulimia nervosa showed a concordance rate among female monozygotic twins of 23 percent, compared to a concordance rate of 9 percent in female dizygotic twins (Kendler, MacLean, Neale, & Kessler, 1991). A twin study of anorexia nervosa showed a concordance rate among female MZ twins of 56 percent, compared to a concordance rate of 5 percent in female DZ twins (Holland, 1984). These data suggest that the eating disorders may be, at least in part, heritable.

The families of people with anorexia and bulimia also have higher than normal rates of depression (Kassett et al., 1988; Kendler et al., 1991). This has led some theorists to argue that the eating disorders are variants of mood disorders. That is, people with eating disorders may have underlying mood disorders that they manifest through bulimia nervosa or anorexia nervosa. Indeed, as many as 75 percent of people with eating disorders can also be diagnosed with mood disorders (APA, 1994). Fueling this perspective is the fact that some of the biological therapies for mood disorders also help to relieve eating disorders in some patients, as we shall discuss in a later section.

It may not be useful to consider the eating disorders only as manifestations of some other underlying disorders, however, because the eating disorders have unique characteristics that must be addressed in therapy even if a patient has a mood disorder as well as an eating disorder (Wilson, 1993). In addition, even if some people with mood disorders develop eating disorders, we would need to understand why these people developed eating disorders while most people with mood disorders do not.

Much of the current research on biological causes of bulimia and anorexia is focusing on the systems in the body that regulate appetite, hunger, satiety, initiation of eating, and cessation of eating. The hypothalamus plays a central role in regulating eating (Blundell & Hill, 1993). It receives messages about the body's recent food consumption and nutrient level and sends messages to cease eating when the body's nutritional needs are met. These messages are carried by a variety of neurotransmitters, including norepinephrine, serotonin, and dopamine, and a number of hormones such as cortisol and insulin. Disordered eating behavior might be caused by imbalances or dysregulation in any of the neurochemicals involved in this system or by structural or functional problems in the hypothalamus. For example, if this system were disrupted, it could cause the individual to have trouble detecting hunger accurately or to stop eating when full, which are both characteristics of people with eating disorders.

There are pieces of evidence that people with eating disorders do have disruptions in the hypothalamus (Study Group on Anorexia Nervosa, 1995). Anorexic persons show lowered functioning of the hypothalamus and abnormalities in the levels or regulation of several different hormones important to the functioning of the hypothalamus (Fava, Copeland, Schweiger, & Herzog, 1989; Mitchell, 1986a, b). It is unclear whether these are causes or consequences of the self-starvation of anorexia. Some studies find that anorexics continue to show abnormalities in hypothalamic and hormonal functioning and in neurotransmitter levels after they gain some weight, whereas others studies show these abnormalities disappear with weight gain.

Many bulimic persons show abnormally low levels of the neurotransmitter serotonin (Mitchell & deZwaan, 1993). Wurtman and others (Wurtman, 1987; Wurtman & Wurtman, 1984) have suggested that this deficiency in serotonin causes the body to crave carbohydrates. Indeed, bulimics often binge on high carbohydrate foods. Bulimic persons may then take up self-induced vomiting or other types of purges in order to avoid gaining weight from eating carbohydrates. Some studies also find that bulimics have lower than normal levels of norepinephrine (Fava et al., 1989). Again, however, it is not clear whether low levels of these neurotransmitters are causes of the bingeing of bulimia or the consequences of the disordered eating patterns of bulimics.

Thus, a number of biological abnormalities are associated with anorexia nervosa and bulimia nervosa. These abnormalities could contribute to disordered eating behavior by causing the body to crave certain foods or by making it difficult for a person to read the body's signals of hunger and fullness. Just why people with eating disorders also develop distorted body images and the other cognitive and emotional problems seen in the eating disorders is not clear, however. In addition, many of the biological abnormalities seen in the eating disorders could be the consequences rather than the causes of the disorders.

Psychotherapy for Anorexia Nervosa

It can be very difficult to engage a person with anorexia nervosa in psychotherapy. Because the anorexic client often feels that others try to control her and that she must maintain absolute control over her own behaviors, she can be extremely resistant to attempts by a therapist to change her behaviors or attitudes. Thus, regardless of what type of psychotherapy a therapist uses with an anorexic client, much work must be done to win the client's trust and participation in the therapy and to maintain this trust and participation as the client begins to gain that dreaded weight.

Winning the anorexic's trust can be especially difficult if the therapist is forced to hospitalize her because she has lost so much weight that her life is in danger. Yet hospitalization and forced refeeding are often necessary to save an anorexic's life. Because people with anorexia nervosa typically do not seek treatment themselves, they often do not come to the attention of therapists until they are so emaciated and malnourished that they have a medical crisis (such as cardiac problems) or their families fear for their lives. The first job of the therapist is obviously to help save the anorexic's life. Because the anorexic will not eat voluntarily, this may mean hospitalizing her and feeding her intravenously. During the hospitalization, the therapist will begin the work of engaging the anorexic in facing and solving the psychological issues causing her to starve herself.

How do you feel about forced hospitalization and refeeding of people with anorexia nervosa? Would you feel differently if the anorexic person was you, a close friend, or your daughter?

The two types of psychotherapy most often used to treat anorexia are behavior therapy and family therapy (Steinhausen, Rauss-Mason, & Seidel, 1991). In behavior therapy, rewards are made contingent upon the anorexic gaining weight. If the client is hospitalized, certain privileges in the hospital are used as rewards, such as watching television, going outside the hospital, or receiving visitors. The client may also be taught relaxation techniques that she can use as she becomes extremely anxious about ingesting food. Studies suggest that the majority of anorexic patients benefit from behavior therapies, gaining weight to within 15 percent of normal body weight (Agras, 1987). The relapse rate with behavior therapies alone is very high, however, and most anorexic patients return to their anorexic eating patterns soon after therapy ends or they are released from

Family therapy is often appropriate when one family member has an eating disorder.

the hospital, unless they are engaged in other therapies that confront some of the emotional issues accompanying their anorexia.

In family therapy, the anorexic and her family are treated as a unit (Minuchin et al., 1978). With some families, therapists must first raise the parents' level of anxiety about their daughters' eating disorders because the parents have been implicitly or explicitly supporting the daughters' avoidance of food. Therapists will identify patterns in the families' interactions that are contributing to the anorexics' sense of being controlled, such as being overprotective while not allowing their daughters the right to express their own needs and feelings. Parents' unreasonable expectations for their daughters are confronted, and families are helped to develop healthy ways of expressing and resolving conflict between the members.

One study of 50 anorexic girls and their families found that family therapy was successful with 86 percent of the cases (Minuchin et al., 1978). These successful girls had normal eating patterns and good relations at home and at school even 2 1/2 years after treatment. This study focused on young girls (of an average age of 14 years) who had only shown anorexic symptoms for a short time. Other studies suggest that anorexics who have shown symptoms for much longer and who are older when they enter treatment are not as likely to benefit from family therapy (Dare, Eisler, Russell, & Szmukler, 1990).

Individual therapy with anorexic persons often focuses on their inability to recognize and trust their own feelings, with the goal of building their self-awareness and independence from others (Bruch, 1973). This can be very difficult, because many anorexic clients are resistant to therapy and suspicious of therapists, whom they think are just other people trying to control their lives. Other anorexic clients may be engaged in therapy but look to therapists to define their feelings for them, just as their parents have done for years. Therapists must convey to clients that their feelings are their own, valuable and legitimate, and the proper focus of attention in therapy. Only when clients can learn to read their feelings accurately will they also read their sensations of hunger and fullness accurately and be able to respond to them.

Another important goal in therapy with anorexic clients is to confront and change their distorted cognitions about their bodies (Bruch, 1973; Garner & Bemis, 1982). Anorexics believe they are fat even when they are emaciated and that if they begin to gain any weight at all, they will become obese. The first step in changing these beliefs is to educate the anorexic person that these beliefs are part of her disorder and not based in reality. A client may be encouraged to write on a card, "Just because I think I'm fat it doesn't really mean I'm fat. It's just part of the anorexia." Then when she becomes anxious about feeling fat, she can read the card for a reality check. A therapist will have an anorexic client gather evidence against these beliefs and weigh the pros and cons of holding these beliefs. One therapist, whose anorexic client described anorexia as "her friend" because it gave her a sense of control and superiority, asked the client, "If anorexia is your friend, why is he making you so tired and weak? Why is he encouraging you to do something that has made your periods stop and your hair fall out?" After several weeks of discussing the benefits and costs of anorexia, the client eventually concluded that her anorexia had "lied" to her: "He promised I would be happy when I was thin, and I'm miserable. He promised I would accomplish great things and I'm too tired to even do what I used to do. He promised I'd be healthy if I ran, and instead my bones ache from the pressure of my body. He promised me friends, and everyone is mad at me. Anorexia has stolen all the fun out of my life." (Pipher, 1994, p. 178).

Psychotherapy can help many anorexic people, but it typically is a long process, often taking years for the anorexic to fully recover. Along the way, many anorexics who have an initial period of recovery, with restoration of their weights to normal levels and their eating to healthy patterns, relapse into bulimic or anorexic behaviors. They often continue to have self-esteem deficits, family problems, and periods of depression and anxiety (Eckert, Halmi, Marchi, & Grove, 1995). The difficulty in helping anorexic people to fully recover may indicate the depth of the psychological issues driving self-starvation. Most therapists combine techniques from different modes of therapy to meet the individual needs of anorexic people.

Psychotherapy for Bulimia Nervosa

A variety of psychotherapies have proven effective in the treatment of bulimia nervosa (Agras, 1993; Fairburn & Hay, 1992). Most controlled studies of psychotherapy for eating disorders have focused on cognitive-behavioral therapy for bulimia (Agras, 1993; Fairburn & Hay, 1992). This therapy is based on the view that the bulimic's extreme concerns about shape and weight are the central features of the disorder. The therapist teaches the client to monitor the cognitions that accompany her eating, particularly her binge episodes and her purging episodes. Then the therapist helps the client confront these cognitions and develop more adaptive attitudes toward her weight and body shape. An interchange between a therapist and client might go like this:

Therapist: What were you thinking just before you began to binge?

Client: I was thinking that I felt really upset and sad about having no social life. I wanted to eat just to feel better.

Therapist: And as you were eating, what were you thinking?

Client: I was thinking that the ice cream tasted really good, that it was making me feel good. But I was also thinking that I shouldn't be eating this, that I'm bingeing again. But then I thought that my life is such a wreck that I deserve to eat what I want to make me feel better.

Therapist: And what were you thinking after you finished the binge?

Client: That I was a failure, a blimp, that I have no control, that this therapy isn't working.

Therapist: Okay, let's go back to the beginning. You said you wanted to eat because you thought it would make you feel better. Did it?

Client: Well, like I said, the ice cream tasted good and it felt good to indulge myself.

Therapist: But in the long run did bingeing make you feel better?

Client: Of course not. I felt terrible afterward.

Therapist: Can you think of anything you might say to yourself the next time you get into such a state, where you want to eat in order to make yourself feel better?

Client: I could remind myself that I'll only feel better for a little while, but then I'll feel terrible.

Therapist: How likely do you think it is that you'll remember to say this to yourself?

Client: Not very likely.

Therapist: Is there any way to increase the likelihood?

Client: Well, I guess I could write it on a card or something and put the card near my refrigerator.

Therapist: That's a pretty good idea. What else could you do to prevent yourself from eating when you feel upset? What other things could you do to relieve your upset, other than eat?

Client: I could call my friend Keisha and talk about how I feel. Or I could go for a walk—someplace away from food—like up in the hills where it's so pretty. Walking up there always makes me feel better.

Therapist: Those are really good ideas. It's important to have a variety of things you can do, other than eat, to relieve bad moods.

The behavioral components of this therapy involve introducing "forbidden foods" (such as bread) back into the client's diet and helping her to confront her irrational thoughts about these foods, such as "if I have just one doughnut, I'm inevitably going to binge." Similarly, the client is taught to eat three healthy meals a day and to challenge the thoughts she has about these meals and the possibility of gaining weight. Cognitive-behavioral therapy for bulimia usually lasts about 3 to 6 months and involves 10 to 20 sessions.

Controlled studies of the efficacy of cognitive-behavioral therapy for bulimia find that about one-half of clients completely stop the binge-purge cycle (see Agras, 1993). Clients undergoing this therapy also show a decrease in depression and anxiety, an increase in social functioning, and a lessening of concern about dieting and weight. Comparisons to drug therapies show that cognitive-behavioral therapy is at least as effective as drug therapies in the short term and more likely to prevent relapse in the long term than are the drug therapies (Fairburn & Hay, 1992).

Other studies of the treatment of bulimia have compared cognitive-behavioral therapy to interpersonal therapy, to supportive-expressive psychodynamic therapy, and to behavior therapy without a focus on cognitions (Fairburn, Jones, Preveler, & Carr, 1991; Fairburn et al., 1995; Garner, Rockert, Davis, & Garner, 1993). In the interpersonal therapy, client and therapist discuss interpersonal problems that are related to the client's eating disorder, and the therapist works actively with the client to develop strategies to solve these interpersonal problems. In supportive-expressive therapy, the therapist encourages the client to talk about problems related to the eating disorder, especially interpersonal problems, but in a highly nondirective manner. In behavior therapy, the client is taught how to monitor her food intake, is reinforced for introducing avoided foods into her diet, and is taught coping techniques for avoiding bingeing. In the studies, all the therapies resulted in significant improvement in the clients' eating behaviors and emotional well-being, with the cognitive-behavioral and interpersonal therapy clients showing the greatest and most enduring improvements. Cognitive-behavioral therapy was better than the other therapies in eliminating disturbed attitudes toward shape and weight and extreme attempts to diet. Clients receiving interpersonal therapy showed the greatest improvements in their relationships. Thus, it appears that cognitive-behavioral therapy and interpersonal therapy may be effective therapies for bulimia.

Biological Therapies

Recall that many people with eating disorders are also depressed or have histories of depression in their families. This connection to depression has led many psychiatrists to use antidepressant drugs to treat the eating disorders, particularly bulimia nervosa (Fairburn & Hay, 1992; Mitchell & Zwaan, 1993). Tricyclic antidepressants are superior to placebos in reducing bingeing and vomiting and in enhancing a sense of control in bulimics (e.g., McCann & Agras, 1990). Bulimic patients often continue to engage in severe dieting, however, and relapse into the binge-purge cycle shortly after stopping the drugs (Mitchell & deZwaan, 1993). The MAO inhibitors also have proven more effective than placebos in the treatment of bulimia but are not typically prescribed because they require severe dietary restrictions to prevent side effects. The serotonin reuptake inhibitors, such as fluoxetine (trade name Prozac), have been the focus of much recent research on biological treatments for the eating disorders. In a large multicenter study of 387 persons with bulimia, the median reduction in the bingeing frequency of persons taking fluoxetine was 67 percent, compared to only 33 percent in the group receiving placebos (FBNC Study Group, 1992).

Tricyclic antidepressants and MAO inhibitors have not proven effective in the treatment of anorexia in controlled clinical trials (Advokat & Kutlesic, 1995; Gadow, 1992). Small-scale studies of fluoxetine, the serotonin reuptake inhibitor, suggest that it may be helpful in treating anorexia (Gwirtsman, Guze, Yager, & Gainsley, 1990; Kaye, Weltzin, Hsu, & Bulik, 1991). Double-blind, placebo control studies are needed before we can be sure of the efficacy of fluoxetine in the treatment of anorexia, however.

There is a high relapse rate in eating disorders, even among people who have been treated for these disorders. Why might relapse rates be particularly high for the eating disorders?

Several experts have suggested that a group of biological, psychological, and social factors interact to create the eating disorders (Agras & Kirkley, 1986; Garner & Garfinkel, 1985; Polivy & Herman, 1993; Striegel-Moore, 1993). Any one of these factors alone may not be enough to push a woman or a man to develop anorexia or bulimia nervosa, but when combined they may.

First, societal pressures for thinness clearly provide a potent impetus for the development of unhealthy attitudes toward eating, especially for women. If these pressures were simply toward achieving a healthy weight and maintaining fitness, they would not be so dangerous. However, as we discussed earlier, the ideal weight for women promoted by beauty symbols in developed countries is much lower than that considered healthy and normal for the average woman. While the ideal weight promoted in these symbols has been getting thinner over the last few decades, the average person in the developed countries has been getting heavier, in part because of the increase in fat in the diet of young people, who eat a great deal of take-out and highly processed foods. Thus, many people find themselves constantly fighting to avoid gaining weight and never quite achieving the slim figures that they wish they had.

Second, biological factors may interact with these societal pressures to make some people more likely than others to develop eating disorders. People who develop eating disorders may have biological predispositions to being overweight or to having poorly regulated eating patterns. They find it extremely difficult to keep weight off without chronically being on severe diets. The societal message that "thin is good" is especially cruel for these people. They want to believe that they can look like the models in fashion magazines if they just try hard enough, when it may be biologically impossible for them to achieve this look and remain physically or psychologically healthy.

Another biological factor that may predispose some people to acquiece to the pressures to diet and be thin is a tendency toward anxiety or mild depression. As noted earlier, many people with eating disorders, especially bulimics, are easily distressed and emotionally labile and tend to eat impulsively in response to their moods. Although problems in mood in people with eating disorders may be the results of environmental circumstances or of the stresses of having eating disorders, they may also be biologically caused in at least some people who develop eating disorders.

Personality factors may also interact with societal pressures to be thin and/or with the biological predispositions described to lead some people to develop eating disorders. Perfectionism, all-or-nothing thinking, and low self-esteem may make people more likely to engage in extreme measures to control their weight in response to unwelcome weight gains or in an attempt to achieve some ideal of attractiveness and therefore increase their self-esteem. These personality characteristics will be more likely to develop in children whose parents are lacking in affection and nurturance and, at the same time, controlling and demanding of perfection.

Thus, it may take some mixture of these factors rather than any single one to lead someone to develop a full eating disorder.

Chapter Summary

The eating disorders include anorexia nervosa, bulimia nervosa, and binge-eating disorder. Anorexia nervosa is characterized by self-starvation, a distorted body image, intense fears of becoming fat, and amenorrhea. People with the restricting type of anorexia nervosa refuse to eat in order to prevent weight gain. People with the binge/purge type periodically engage in bingeing and then purge to prevent weight gain. The lifetime prevalence of anorexia is about 1 percent, with 90 to 95 percent of cases being female. Anorexia nervosa usually begins in adolescence, and the course is variable from one person to another. It is a very dangerous disorder, and the death rate among anorexics is 15 percent.

Bulimia nervosa is characterized by uncontrolled bingeing, followed by behaviors designed to prevent weight gain from the binges. People with the purging type use self-induced vomiting, diuretics, or laxatives to prevent weight gain. People with the nonpurging type use fasting and exercise to prevent weight gain. Although overconcern with weight and occasional bingeing is common among college students, the prevalence of the full syndrome of bulimia nervosa is only about 1.0 percent in women and 0.2 percent in men. The onset of bulimia nervosa is most often in adolescence. Although bulimics do not tend to be underweight, there are several dangerous medical complications in bulimia nervosa.

People with binge-eating disorder engage in bingeing but not in purging or behaviors designed to compensate for the binges. It is more common in women than in men, and people with the disorder tend to be significantly overweight. Binge-eating disorder is not officially recognized by the DSM-IV, but the diagnostic criteria were placed in an appendix for further study.

Many eating disorders begin with diets. Dieting changes people's emotions and attitudes and their bodies' metabolic rates in ways that make it very difficult to maintain diets. Another group besides dieters who are at increased risk are athletes, especially those whose sports require them to maintain certain body shapes or sizes.

Women may be more likely than men to develop eating disorders because the societal ideal for women's but not men's bodies focuses on thinness. Men who develop eating disorders tend to have symptoms very similar to those of women who develop the disorders.

Eating disorders may be more common among whites and in developed countries than among people of color and in developing countries. People in Asia who develop anorexia nervosa may not have the obsession with thinness that anorexics in Europe and the United States have.

Psychosocial theories have suggested that the families of girls with eating disorders are overcontrolling, overprotective, and hostile and do not allow the expression of feelings. Girls with eating disorders tend to have lower self-esteem and greater need for approval than do girls without eating disorders. In addition, girls with bulimia tend to be more anxiety prone, emotionally unstable, and impulsive. In adolescence, these girls may develop eating disorders as a way of exerting control or of coping with negative emotions. Sexual abuse is a risk factor for eating disorders as well as for several other psychological problems.

The biological factors implicated in the development of the eating disorders include genetics, dysregulation of hormonal and neurotransmitter systems, and generally lower functioning in the hypothalamus.

Behavior therapy and family therapy do seem to be effective treatments for anorexia. Cognitive-behavioral therapy has proven as effective as drug therapy in reducing the symptoms of bulimia and more effective in preventing relapse. Interpersonal therapy, supportive expressive therapy, and behavior therapy also appear to be effective for bulimia nervosa. Antidepressants are effective in treating bulimia, but the relapse rate is high. Drug therapies have not proven effective for anorexia.

Key Terms

anorexia nervosa   356   bulimia nervosa   360   set point   364
amenorrhea   356   binge-eating disorder
                                     363

Application

What Is So Bad About Being Overweight?

In this section, we will explore answers to the question, "What is so bad about being overweight?" The stigma against obese people and the assumptions most of us have that obesity is a major health problem may lead you to think this is an absurd question, but psychologists have been hotly debating this question for the last few years, and some of the answers may surprise you (see Brownell & Rodin, 1994; Seligman, 1994).

There are many different ways of defining obesity. One common method is to define it relative to norms for a healthy weight for one's height and body frame. The norms typically used are statistics from the insurance industry about the weights at which people of given heights or body frames are thought to live the longest. People who are 20 to 40 percent above this weight are said to be *mildly obese* or *overweight;* people 41 to 100 percent above this weight are labelled *moderately obese;* people more than 100 percent above this weight are labelled *severely obese.* Another method for defining obesity is application of the body mass index, or BMI. You can calculate your BMI by multiplying your weight in pounds by 700, dividing that by your height in inches, and dividing again by your height. A BMI of 25 or under is considered normal; a BMI of over 25 is considered overweight.

Using definitions such as these, about 30 percent of men and 25 percent of women in the United States are considered at least mildly obese, and about 12 percent of men and women are severely obese (Brownell & Rodin, 1994; Kuczmarski, 1992). In the United States and Europe, obesity is more common in ethnic minority groups and low socioeconomic status groups (Sobal & Stunkard, 1989). It is also more common in older people than in younger people. About 60 percent of African-American women between 45 and 75 years of age are obese (Van Itallie, 1985).

The prevalence of obesity in developed countries has risen since the early 1900s, largely as a result of decreased physical activity and increases in the fat content of our diets (Brownell & Wadden, 1992). The decrease in physical activity is due to changes in the types of occupations people hold. Countries such as the United States were formerly agriculture-based economies, in which most people put in long hard hours of physical labor. Now most developed countries are largely information economies, in which most people sit behind desks at computers all day long. The increase in the fat content of our diets is due in part to changes in shopping and eating habits (Brownell & Wadden, 1992). The consumption of fast foods and high-fat snack items has increased tremendously in the last 30 years. Many of these food items are bought on impulse in the checkout lines of grocery stores or in restaraunts where customers cannot know (and may not want to know) the fat content of food.

Is obesity a problem? Some studies have shown that people who are obese have an increased risk of hypertension, diabetes, and cardiovascular disease (Bray, 1986; Pi-Sunyer, 1991). For example, one study followed over 100,000 American women, 30 to 55 years of age, for 8 years and found that those who were 30 percent or more overweight were 300 percent more likely to develop heart disease (Manson et al., 1990).

Other studies show, however, that mild to moderate obesity is not associated with increased risk of disease (see Garner & Wooley, 1991). For example, Paffenberger and colleagues (1986) followed 16,936 men for a minimum of 35 years and found that those who were overweight were not at higher risk for death due to heart disease or other diseases than were those who were not overweight. Indeed, those who were considerably underweight were at higher risk for death than were those who were normal weight or somewhat overweight. In addition, the men who gained a modest amount of weight during middle age (15 to 24 pounds) actually lived longer than did those who gained less than 15 pounds.

There is one substantial gender difference in the risk of obesity to health. People who carry most of their fat around their waist (the classic apple shape) are at higher risk for heart disease than are people who carry their weight in their hips and thighs (the classic pear shape). Men tend to have the apple shape, whereas women tend to have the pear shape. Thus, being somewhat overweight may be riskier to men than to women. Of course, women are much more likely to try lose their weight than are men.

It may be that something correlated with obesity and not obesity itself is what actually causes health risks. For example, many obese people lead sedentary lifestyles, in part because exercise is more difficult for obese people. Engaging in exercise is a powerful deterrent to illness. Paffenberger and colleagues (1986) found that men who engaged in regular exercise were less likely to die in middle and older age than were those who did not engage in regular exercise, even if they carried other substantial risk factors for heart disease, such as hypertension and a genetic predisposition to heart disease (see also Blair, Lewis, & Booth, 1989). Similarly, obese people may be more likely than nonobese people to have high fat diets, which cause heart disease and cancer or may be more likely to carry genetic risks for heart disease and cancer. Manson and colleagues (1990) found that obesity was related to hypertension, diabetes, and high serum cholesterol levels and that controlling for these factors substantially decreased the relationship between obesity and heart disease.

Does losing weight improve the health of obese people? The existing studies provide inconsistent answers to this question. Some studies of obese people indicate that losing as little as 10 percent of body weight can reduce high blood pressure, reduce cardiovascular disease, and improve diabetes (Blackburn & Kanders, 1987; Wing, Epstein, Nowalk, & Scott, 1987).

There is some evidence that "yo-yo" dieting (losing and then gaining back large amounts of weight) leads to substantial health problems (Garner & Wooley, 1991). In a long-term study of about 5,000 residents of Boston, researchers found that people whose weight fluctuated frequently or by many pounds had a 50 percent higher risk of heart disease than did those whose weight remained stable. As mentioned earlier, dieting tends to lower a person's metabolic rate. As a result, once the person begins gaining weight again, it is more likely that this weight will be stored as fat. In turn, the higher a person's percentage of body fat for his or her weight, the more at risk he or she is for heart disease. Some researchers have argued that the health risks that are typically associated with obesity may actually be due to yo-yo dieting by obese people (Garner & Wooley, 1991).

What's an overweight person to do then? Exercise is one thing. Exercise may be the one way people can overcome the effects of dieting on metabolic rates and keep their weight off. People who exercise regularly increase their basal metabolic rate, so the body burns more calories even when at rest. Thus, people who exercise may be able to maintain lower weights even without continuing to restrict the amount of food they eat. In addition, as mentioned earlier, several studies now show that moderate exercise (i.e., the equivalent of 30 to 60 minutes per day of brisk walking, either in small spurts or all at once) is associated with substantial decreases in health risks and mortality, even among people with genetic predispositions to major diseases, people who smoke, and people who are overweight (Blair et al., 1989; Paffenberger et al., 1986). So even if people do not lose weight through exercise, they may be improving their health and increasing their longevity.

Obesity experts also agree that decreasing the intake of fats and salt and increasing the intake of complex carbohydrates have positive health effects, even if they do not lead to weight loss. Most of us can reduce fats in our diet by switching from whole milk to skim and from high-fat meats to lower-fat meats and fish and by using low-fat dressings and spreads. We can increase carbohydrates by snacking on fruits, vegetables, and whole grains rather than on fatty foods such as potato chips and cookies.

Overweight people who want to lose weight might consider trying to achieve "reasonable" weight loss rather than "ideal" weights (Brownell & Wadden, 1992). The effects of biological factors such as genetics on weight may be strong enough that over-

weight people can never achieve the "ideal" weights they wish to achieve, at least not without chronic self-starvation. Many overweight people find themselves bingeing out of hunger or frustration or yo-yo dieting, both of which harm their self-esteem and possibly their health. If overweight people can adopt healthier diets, exercise regularly, and stablize at weights that are reasonable given their family backgrounds and their histories of weight loss and gain, both their physical and psychological health may improve. ■

chapter 11 Sexual Disorders

Sexual Dysfunctions

The most common sexual disorder is a sexual dysfunction. The sexual dysfunctions include disorders of sexual desire, sexual arousal, orgasm, and sexual pain. Occasional problems in all of these areas are very common. These problems are given a diagnosis when they are persistent, they cause individuals significant distress, and they interfere with people's intimate relationships.

Causes of Sexual Dysfunctions

The sexual dysfunctions can have a host of biological causes, including undiagnosed diabetes, drug use, and hormonal and vascular abnormalities. Possible psychological causes include relationship concerns, traumatic experiences, maladaptive attitudes and cognitions, and an upbringing or cultural milieu that devalues or degrades sex.

Treatment of Sexual Dysfunctions

When a sexual dysfunction has a biological cause, treating the biological cause may reduce the sexual dysfunction. Psychological treatments for sexual dysfunctions focus on the personal concerns of the individual with the dysfunction and on the conflicts between the individual and his or her partner. Sex therapy can decrease people's inhibitions about sex and teach them new techniques for optimal sexual enjoyment.

Paraphilias

People with paraphilias prefer sexual activities that involve non-human objects, nonconsenting adults, the suffering or humiliation of oneself or one's partner, or children. The paraphilias include fetishism, transvestism, sexual sadism and masochism, voyeurism, exhibitionism, frotteurism, and pedophilia. Most paraphilics do not seek treatment for their behavior. Aversion therapy and desensitization therapy may be useful for some paraphilics.

Gender Identity Disorder

Gender identity is one's perception of oneself as male or female. A person with gender identity disorder believes he or she was born with the wrong sex's genitals and is fundamentally a person of the opposite sex. Gender identity disorder in adulthood is also referred to as *transsexualism*. Some transsexuals undergo sex change operations and hormonal treatments.

Bio-Psycho-Social Integration
Chapter Summary
Key Terms
Application: *Practicing Safe Sex*

I don't know whether it's normal or not, but sex has always been something that I take seriously. I would put it higher than tennis on my list of constructive things to do.

—Art Buchwald, *Leaving Home: A Memoir* (1993)

Diana Ong
Shadow of Her Former Self

> **Case Study** • Mallory is distraught. She is very attracted to a man she recently met, named Tom, and he is also attracted to her. They have been on a few dates, and last night they returned to Mallory's apartment and began to make love. Although Mallory was extremely excited about having intercourse with Tom and Tom was a good lover, Mallory did not have an orgasm during intercourse. This was not the first time Mallory did not have an orgasm during a sexual encounter with a man she found attractive, and she is beginning to think there is something terribly wrong with her.

> **Case Study** • Philip likes shoes—women's black patent leather shoes, to be exact. He has hundreds of pairs, which he keeps in a special room in his house. Many nights he will go to that room, undress partially or totally, and lie amidst the shoes as he masturbates. He reaches orgasm quickly and experiences a deep sense of sexual pleasure.

> **Case Study** • David is a pedophile—he prefers to have sex with young children. He was recently arrested when a young boy that David was supposed to be tutoring in mathematics told his parents that David had tried to touch his penis. Under interrogation, David broke down and admitted that he had fondled or exposed himself to a dozen young children and had attempted intercourse with one young girl.

> **Case Study** • Joanne was born with the genitals of a male, but for as long as she can remember, she has considered herself female. She dresses in women's clothes, she wears women's makeup, her voice sounds like a woman's, and thanks to several surgeries and hormonal treatments, she now has a vagina and breasts instead of a penis.

Although the behaviors and concerns of these four people vary greatly, all of them are suffering from some kind of sexual disorder. The one underlying commonality to all the sexual disorders is that they involve sexual behaviors or beliefs that are a source of distress to the individual suffering the disorder or to people around him or her. Sexual disorders fall into three distinct categories. First, sexual dysfunctions involve problems in experiencing sexual arousal or carrying through with a sexual act to the point of sexual satisfaction. Mallory is suffering from a common sexual dysfunction known as *inhibited orgasm*. Second, paraphilias involve sexual activities that are focused on nonhuman objects, children or nonconsenting adults, or on suffering or humiliation. There are several types of paraphilias, and they vary in the severity of their impact on other people. Fetishes like Philip's shoe fetish are relatively benign in that they usually do not affect anyone except the person with the fetish. However, paraphilias that involve nonconsenting adults or children, like David's pedophilia, clearly are not benign. Third, gender identity disorder, also known as *transsexualism,* involves the belief that one has been born with the body of the wrong gender. People with this disorder, like Joanne, feel trapped in the wrong body, wish to be rid of their genitals, and want to live as a member of the other gender.

In this chapter, we will discuss specific sexual disorders within each of these three categories. We will begin with some of the most common disorders that both men and women suffer: sexual dysfunctions. Then we will move to the paraphilias, which are less common and primarily experienced by men. Finally, we will discuss the most uncommon sexual disorder, gender identity disorder.

Sexual Dysfunctions

sexual dysfunctions
problems in experiencing sexual desire or arousal or carrying through with sexual acts to the point of satisfaction

The **sexual dysfunctions** are a set of disorders in which people have trouble engaging in and enjoying sexual relationships with other people. In order to understand the sexual dysfunctions, it is important first to understand something about the human sexual response—what happens in our bodies when we feel sexually aroused, when we engage in sexual intercourse or other forms of sexual stimulation, and when we reach orgasm.

The Sexual Response Cycle

Before the work of William Masters and Virginia Johnson in the 1950s and 1960s, we knew little about what happened in the human body during sexual arousal and activity. Masters and Johnson (1970) observed people engaging in a variety of sexual practices in a laboratory setting and recorded the physiological changes that occurred during sexual activity.

Thanks to the work of Masters and Johnson and later researchers, we now know that the sexual response cycle can be divided into five phases: desire, excitement or arousal, plateau, orgasm, and resolution. **Sexual desire** is the urge to engage in any type of sexual activity. The **arousal** phase or *excitement phase* consists of a psychological experience of arousal and pleasure and the physiological changes known as *vasocongestion* and *myotonia*. **Vasocongestion** is the filling of blood vessels and tissues with blood, also known as *engorgement*. In males, erection of the penis is caused by increases in the flow of blood into the arteries of the penis, accompanied by decreases in the outflow of blood from the penis through the veins. In females, vasocongestion causes the clitoris to enlarge, the labia to swell, and the vagina to moisten. **Myotonia** is muscular tension. During the excitement phase, many muscles in the body may become more tense, culminating in the muscular contractions known as *orgasm*.

Following the excitement phase is the **plateau** phase. During this period, excitement remains at a high but stable level. This period is pleasurable in itself and some people try to extend this period as long as possible before reaching orgasm. During both the excitement and plateau phases, the person may feel tense all over, the skin is flushed, salivation increases, the nostrils flare, the heart pounds, breathing is heavy, and the person may be oblivious to external stimuli or events.

The excitement and plateau phases are followed by **orgasm.** Physiologically, orgasm is the discharge of the neuromuscular tension built up during the excitement and plateau phases. Both males and females experience a sense of the inevitability of orgasm just before it happens.

In males, orgasm involves rhythmic contractions of the prostate, seminal vesicles, vas deferens, and the entire length of the penis and the urethra, accompanied by the ejaculation of semen (see Figure 11.1). In males, a refractory period follows ejaculation. During this period, the male cannot achieve full erection and another orgasm regardless of the type or intensity of sexual stimulation. The refractory period may last anywhere from a few minutes to several hours.

In females, orgasm generally involves rhythmic contractions of the orgasmic platform (see Figure 11.2) and more irregular contractions of the uterus, which are not always felt. Because females do not have a refractory period, they are capable of experiencing additional orgasms immediately following a previous one. However, not all women want to have multiple orgasms or find it easy to be aroused to multiple orgasms.

Following orgasm, the entire musculature of the body relaxes and men and women tend to experience a state of deep relaxation, the stage known as **resolution**. A man loses his erection, and a woman's orgasmic platform subsides.

Both males and females experience these same five phases, regardless of whether orgasm is brought on by masturbation, coitus (insertion of the male penis into the female vagina), or some other activity. There are some differences between the male and female sexual responses, however (Masters, Johnson, & Kolodny, 1993). First, there is greater variability in the female response pattern than in the male response pattern. Sometimes the excitement and plateau phases will be short for a female and she will reach a discernible orgasm quickly. At other times, the excitement and plateau phases are longer, and she may or may not experience a full orgasm. Second, as noted, there typically is a refractory period following orgasm for males but not for females. This refractory period in males becomes longer with age and after successive orgasms during a sexual experience.

If you are sexually active, you may or may not have recognized all these phases in your own sexual response cycle. People vary greatly in the length and distinctiveness of each phase. For example, some people do not notice a distinct plateau phase and feel they go straight from excitement to orgasm. Being aware of how your body reacts to sexual

sexual desire
in the sexual response cycle, urge or inclination to engage in sexual activity

arousal
in the sexual response cycle, psychological experience of arousal and pleasure as well as physiological changes, such as the tensing of muscles and enlargement of blood vessels and tissues (also called the *excitement phase*)

vasocongestion
in the sexual response cycle, filling of blood vessels and tissues with blood, leading to erection of the penis in males and enlargement of the clitoris, swelling of the labia, and vaginal moistening in women (also called *engorgement*)

myotonia
in the sexual response cycle, muscular tension in the body that culminates in contractions during orgasm

plateau
in the sexual response cycle, period between arousal and orgasm during which excitement remains high but stable

orgasm
the discharge of neuromuscular tension built up during sexual activity; in men, entails rhythmic contractions of the prostate, seminal vesicles, vas deferens, and penis and seminal discharge; in women, entails contractions of the orgasmic platform and uterus

resolution
in the sexual response cycle, state of deep relaxation following orgasm in which a man loses his erection and a woman's orgasmic platform subsides

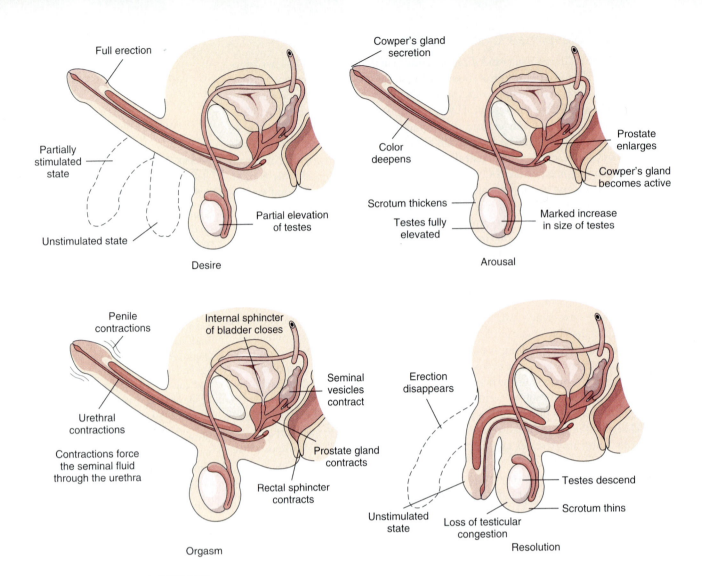

Figure 11.1

The Male Sexual Response Cycle. Males experience characteristic changes in physiology during each phase of their sexual response cycle.
Source: Adapted from Hyde, 1990, p. 199.

stimulation can help you recognize what helps you get the most pleasure from sexual activity and what interferes with that pleasure.

Occasional, transient problems in sexual functioning are extremely common (see Figure 11.3). To qualify for a diagnosis of a sexual dysfunction, a person must be experiencing a problem that causes significant distress or interpersonal difficulty. The DSM-IV divides sexual dysfunctions into four categories: sexual desire disorders, sexual arousal disorders, orgasmic disorders, and sexual pain disorders. In reality, these dysfunctions overlap greatly, and many people who seek treatment for a sexual problem have more than one of these dysfunctions (Segraves & Segraves, 1991).

 As we will discuss shortly, many treatments for sexual dysfunctions include education about the sexual response cycle. Why would such education be useful in the treatment of sexual dysfunctions?

Sexual Desire Disorders

One's level of sexual desire is basically how much he or she wants to have sex. Sexual desire can be manifested in one's sexual thoughts and fantasies, one's interest in initiating or participating in sexual activities, and one's awareness of sexual cues from others (Schiavi & Segraves, 1995). People vary tremendously in their levels of sexual desire, and an individual's level of sexual desire can vary greatly across time (see Tables 11.1 and 11.2). Lack of

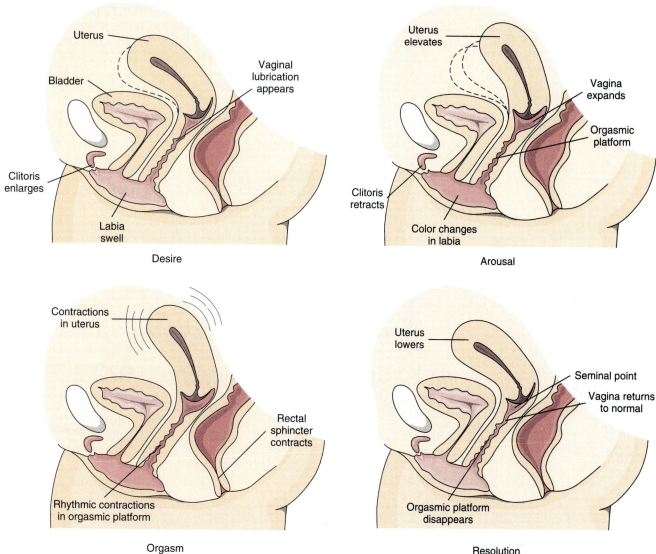

Desire

Arousal

Orgasm

Resolution

Figure 11.2

The Female Sexual Response Cycle. At each phase of the sexual response cycle in females, there are characteristic changes in physiology.
Source: Adapted from Hyde, 1990, p. 200.

Table 11.1	Responses to the Question, "How Often Do You Think About Sex?"		

A national survey found large variation in how often people think about sex and great differences between men and women.

	"Every day" or "several times a day"	"A few times a month" or "a few times a week"	"Less than once a month" or "never"
Men	54%	43%	4%
Women	19	67	14

From R. T. Michael, et al., *Sex in America: A Definitive Survey*. Copyright © 1994 Little, Brown and Company. Reprinted with permission.

sexual desire is the most common complaint of people seeking sex therapy (Segraves & Segraves, 1991).

People who lack sexual desire can be diagnosed with one of two sexual desire disorders: hypoactive sexual desire disorder and sexual aversion disorder. People with **hypoactive sexual desire disorder** have little desire for sex—they do not fantasize about sex or initiate sexual activity—and this lack of sexual desire is causing them marked distress or interpersonal difficulty. In some rare cases, people report never having had much interest in sex, either with other people or privately, as in viewing erotic films, masturbation, or fantasy. In most cases of hypoactive sexual desire, the individual used to enjoy sex but

hypoactive sexual desire disorder condition in which a person's desire for sex is diminished to the point where it causes him or her significant distress or interpersonal difficulties and is not due to transient life circumstances or other sexual dysfunction

Figure 11.3

Percent of People Who Have Had a Sexual Difficulty in the Last Year. A national survey found that many people report having had one or more sexual difficulties in the last year.
Source: Michael et al., 1994, p. 126.

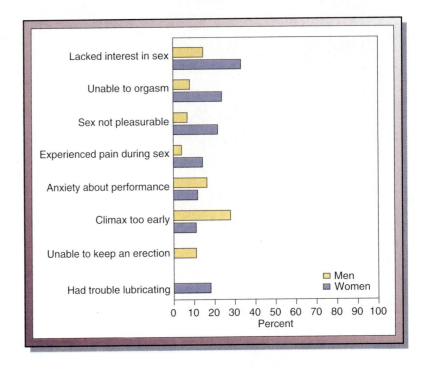

Table 11.2 How Often Do People Have Sex?

A national survey of adults in the United States found a great deal of variation in how frequently people had sex.

	Percentage Reporting	
	Men	**Women**
Two to three times per week	30	26
A few times per month	36	37
A few times per year or not at all	27	30

From E. O. Laumann, et al., *The Social Organization of Sexuality: Sexual Practices in the United States.* Copyright © 1994 University of Chicago Press. Reprinted with permission.

has lost interest in it, despite the presence of a willing and desirable partner. A diagnosis of hypoactive sexual desire is not given if the individual's lack of desire is the result of transient circumstances in his or her life, such as being too busy or fatigued from overwork to care about sex. Also, a diagnosis of sexual desire disorder is not given if lack of desire is actually caused by one of the other problems in sexual functioning, such as the inability to achieve orgasm or pain during intercourse. In such cases, the diagnosis a person receives focuses on the primary dysfunction rather than on the lack of desire that is the result of the primary dysfunction.

Inhibited desire can be either generalized to all partners or situations or specific to certain partners or types of stimulation. A man who has had little desire for sexual activity most of his life would have a *generalized sexual desire disorder.* A woman who lacks desire to have sex with her husband, even though she may love him, but has sexual fantasies about other men may be diagnosed with a *situational sexual desire disorder.* Obviously, the judgment about when a person's sexual desire has been too low for too long is a subjective one. Often, people seek treatment for lack of sexual desire primarily because their partners' sexual desire appears to be considerably greater than their own and the difference is causing conflict in the relationship (Masters et al., 1993).

The other type of sexual desire disorder is **sexual aversion disorder.** People with this disorder do not simply have a passive lack of interest in sex; they actively avoid sexual activities. When they do engage in sex, they may feel sickened by it or experience acute anxiety. Some people experience a generalized aversion to all sexual activities, including kissing and touching.

sexual aversion disorder
condition in which a person actively avoids sexual activities and experiences sex as unpleasant or anxiety provoking

Sexual aversion disorder in women is frequently tied to sexual assault experiences, as in the case of Norma (adapted from Spitzer et al., 1994, p. 213):

Case Study • Norma and Gary were having sex approximately once every 1 to 2 months, and only at Gary's insistence. Their sexual activity consisted primarily of Gary stimulating Norma to orgasm by manually caressing her genitals while he masturbated himself to orgasm.

Norma had always had a strong aversion to looking at or touching her husband's penis. During an interview she explained that she had had no idea of the origin of this aversion until her uncle's recent funeral. At the funeral she was surprised to find herself becoming angry as the eulogy was read. Her uncle had been a world-famous concert musician and was widely respected and admired. As Norma became angrier, she suddenly recalled having been sexually molested by him when she was a child. From the ages of 9 to 12, her uncle had been her music teacher. The lessons included "teaching [her] rhythm" by having her caress his penis in time with the beating of the metronome. This repelled her, but she was frightened to tell her parents about it. She finally refused to continue lessons at age 12 without ever telling her parents why. At some point during her adolescence, she said, she "forgot what he did to me."

Sexual Arousal Disorders

People with **sexual arousal disorders** do not experience the physiological changes that make up the excitement or arousal phase of the sexual response cycle. **Female sexual arousal disorder** involves a recurrent inability to attain or maintain the swelling-lubrication response of sexual excitement. **Male erectile disorder** involves the recurrent inability to attain or maintain an erection until the completion of sexual activity.

Much less is known about female sexual arousal disorder than about male erectile disorder (which was formerly referred to as *impotence*). In general, women's sexual problems have been researched less than men's (Andersen & Cyranowski, 1995). Female sexual arousal disorder is probably common, however. A national survey found that 19 percent of women reported lubrication difficulties during sexual activity (Michael et al., 1994).

Men with the *primary* or *lifelong* form of male erectile disorder have never been able to sustain erections for a desired period of time. Men with the *secondary* or *acquired* form of the disorder were able to sustain erections in the past but no longer can. Occasional problems in gaining or sustaining erections are very common, with as many as 30 million men in the United States having erectile problems at some time in their lives. Such problems do not constitute a disorder until they become persistent and significantly interfere with a man's interpersonal relationships or cause him distress. Only 4 to 9 percent of men will have problems sufficient to warrant a diagnosis of male erectile disorder (Spector & Carey, 1990). Paul Petersen is one of these men (adapted from Spitzer et al., 1994, pp. 198–199):

sexual arousal disorders
conditions in which people do not experience the physiological changes that make up the excitement or arousal phase of the sexual response cycle

female sexual arousal disorder
in women, recurrent inability to attain or maintain the swelling-lubrication response of sexual excitement

male erectile disorder
in men, recurrent inability to attain or maintain an erection until the completion of sexual activity

Case Study • Paul and Petula Petersen have been living together for the last 6 months and are contemplating marriage. Petula describes the problem that has brought them to the sex therapy clinic.

"For the last 2 months he hasn't been able to keep his erection after he enters me."

The psychiatrist learns that Paul, age 26, is a recently graduated lawyer, and that Petula, age 24, is a successful buyer for a large department store. They both grew up in educated, middle class, suburban families. They met through mutual friends and started to have sexual intercourse a few months after they met and had no problems at that time.

Two months later, Paul moved from his family home into Petula's apartment. This was her idea, and Paul was unsure that he was ready for such an important step. Within a few weeks, Paul noticed that although he continued to be sexually aroused and wanted intercourse, as soon as he entered his partner, he began to lose his erection and could not stay inside. They would try again, but by then his desire had waned and he was unable to achieve another erection. Petula would become extremely angry with Paul, but he would just walk away from her.

The psychiatrist learned that sex was not the only area of contention in the relationship. Petula complained that Paul did not spend enough time with her and preferred to go to baseball games with his male friends. Even when he was home, he would watch all the sports events that were available on TV and was not interested in going to foreign movies, museums, or the theater with her. Despite these differences, Petula was eager to marry Paul and was pressuring him to set a date.

Orgasmic Disorders

female orgasmic disorder
in women, recurrent delay in or absence of orgasm after having reached the excitement phase of the sexual response cycle (also called *anorgasmia*)

Women with **female orgasmic disorder,** or *anorgasmia,* experience a recurrent delay in or complete absence of orgasm after having reached the excitement phase of the sexual response cycle. The DSM-IV specifies that this diagnosis should be made only when a woman is unable to achieve orgasm despite receiving adequate stimulation. In truth, many women treated for this disorder (and many women who do not experience orgasms but do not seek treatment) are able to achieve orgasm with certain types of stimulation, particularly clitoral stimulation, but simply cannot achieve orgasm with the type of stimulation they receive from their partners. Studies estimate that 10 percent of women in the United States have never had orgasms during sexual intercourse; about 15 percent of premenopausal and 37 percent of postmenopausal women report usually having some problems reaching orgasm during sexual stimulation (Rosen & Lieblum, 1995; Spector & Carey, 1990). In contrast, about 75 percent of men always have orgasms during sexual stimulation.

premature ejaculation
inability to delay ejaculaton after minimal sexual stimulation or until one wishes to ejaculate, causing significant distress or interpersonal problems

The most common form of orgasmic disorder in males is **premature ejaculation.** Men who have this disorder persistently ejaculate with minimal sexual stimulation before they wish to ejaculate. Between 30 and 40 percent of men have signficant trouble delaying ejaculation at will (Spector & Carey, 1991). Again, it is obviously a judgment call about when premature ejaculation becomes a sexual dysfunction. Premature ejaculation must cause significant distress or interpersonal problems before it is considered a disorder. Some men seeking treatment for this problem simply cannot prevent ejaculation before their partner reaches orgasm. Others do after very little stimulation, long before their partners are fully aroused. Men with significant problems in premature ejaculation seem not to experience the plateau phase of the sexual response cycle.

Men with premature ejaculation resort to applying desensitizing creams to their penises before sex, wearing multiple condoms, distracting themselves by doing complex mathematical problems while making love, not allowing their partners to touch them, and masturbating multiple times shortly before having sex in an attempt to delay their ejaculations (Althof, 1995). These tactics are generally unsuccessful and can make their partners feel shut out of the sexual encounter, as in the following account (McCarthy, 1989, pp. 151–152):

Case Study • Bill and Margaret were a couple in their late 20s who had been married for 2 years. Margaret was 27 and the owner of a hair-styling studio. Bill was 29 and a legislative lobbyist for a financial institution. This was a first marriage for both. They had had a rather tumultuous dating relationship before marriage. Margaret had been in individual and group therapy for 1 1/2 years at a university counseling center before dropping out of school to enroll in a hair-styling program. During their dating period, Margaret reentered individual therapy, and Bill, who had never participated in therapy, attended five conjoint sessions. That therapist helped Bill and Margaret deal with issues in their relationship and increased their commitment to marrying. However, the therapist made an incorrect assumption in stating that with increased intimacy and the commitment of marriage, the ejaculatory control problem would disappear. . . .

Margaret saw the early ejaculation as a symbol of lack of love and caring on Bill's part. As the problem continued over the next 2 years, Margaret became increasingly frustrated and withdrawn. She demonstrated her displeasure by resisting his sexual advances, and their intercourse frequency decreased from three or four times per week to once every 10 days. A sexual and marital crisis was precipitated by Margaret's belief that Bill was acting more isolated and distant when they did have intercourse. When they talked about their sexual relationship, it was usually in bed after intercourse, and the communication quickly broke down into tears, anger, and accusations. Bill was on the defensive and handled the sexual issue by avoiding talking to Margaret, which frustrated her even more.

Unbeknownst to Margaret, Bill had attempted a do-it-yourself technique to gain better control. He had bought a desensitizing cream he'd read about in a men's magazine and applied it to the glans of his penis 20 minutes before initiating sex. He also masturbated the day before couple sex. During intercourse he tried to keep his leg muscles tense and think about sports as a way of keeping his arousal in check. Bill was unaware that Margaret felt emotionally shut out during sex. Bill was becoming more sensitized to his arousal cycle and was worrying about erection. He was not achieving better ejaculatory control, and he was enjoying sex less. The sexual relationship was heading downhill, and miscommuncation and frustration were growing.

Men with **male orgasmic disorder** experience a recurrent delay in or absence of orgasm following the excitement phase of the sexual response cycle. In most cases of this disorder, a man cannot ejaculate during intercourse but can ejaculate with manual or oral stimulation. About 4 to 10 percent of men report persistent problems in reaching orgasm (Spector & Carey, 1991).

male orgasmic disorder
in men, recurrent delay in or absence of orgasm following the excitement phase of the sexual response cycle

Sexual Pain Disorders

The final two sexual dysfunctions are dyspareunia and vaginismus. **Dyspareunia** is genital pain associated with intercourse. It is rare in men, but in community surveys 10 to 15 percent of women report frequent pain during intercourse (Laumann et al., 1994) In women, the pain may be superficial during intromission or deep during penile thrusting. In men, dyspareunia may involve painful erections or pain during thrusting.

Vaginismus only occurs in women and involves the involuntary contraction of the muscles surrounding the outer third of the vagina when vaginal penetration with a penis, finger, tampon, or speculum is attempted. In some women, even the anticipation of vaginal insertion may result in this muscle spasm. It is estimated that 2 to 3 percent of women experience vaginismus (Kolodny et al., 1979).

dyspareunia
genital pain associated with sexual intercourse

vaginismus
in women, involuntary contractions of the muscles surrounding the outer third of the vagina that interfere with penetration and sexual functioning

 Disorders of sexual desire are now the most common problems bringing people to sex therapy. What are some possible reasons for the apparent increase in sexual desire problems in the last decade?

Summing Up | Sexual Disfunctions

- The sexual response cycle includes five phases: desire, excitement or arousal, plateau, orgasm, and resolution.
- People with disorders of sexual desire have little or no desire to engage in sex. These disorders include hypoactive sexual desire disorder and sexual aversion disorder.
- People with sexual arousal disorders do not experience the physiological changes that make up the excitement or arousal phase of the sexual response cycle. These disorders include female sexual arousal disorder and male erectile disorder.
- Women with female orgasmic disorder do not experience orgasm or have greatly delayed orgasm after reaching the excitement phase. Men with premature ejaculation reach ejaculation before they wish. Men with male orgasmic disorder have a recurrent delay in or absence of orgasm following sexual excitement.

- The two sexual pain disorders are dyspareunia, genital pain associated with intercourse, and vaginismus, involuntary contraction of the vaginal muscles in women.
- Occasional problems in all of these areas are common. Such problems do not warrant a diagnosis unless they are persistent, are causing a person significant distress, or are interfering with a person's intimate relationships.

Causes of Sexual Dysfunctions

Most sexual dysfunctions probably have multiple causes, including biological causes and psychosocial causes (Ackerman & Carey, 1995). Perhaps the most common cause of one sexual dysfunction is another sexual dysfunction. For example, one study found about 40 percent of people with hypoactive sexual desire disorder also had a diagnosis of an arousal or orgasmic disorder (Segraves & Segraves, 1991). That is, even when they do engage in sex, these people have difficulty becoming aroused or reaching orgasm. This, in turn, greatly reduces their desire to engage in sexual activity. Similarly, people who experience pain during sexual activity frequently lose all desire for sex.

When people seek help for sexual dysfunctions, clinicians will conduct thorough assessments of their medical conditions, the drugs they are taking, the characteristics of their relationships, their attitudes toward their sexuality, and their sexual practices. Even when one of these factors can be identified as the primary cause of a sexual dysfunction, usually several areas of a person's life have been affected by the dysfunction, including his or her self-concept and relationships, and need to be addressed in treatment.

Biological Causes

Many medical illnesses can cause problems in sexual functioning in both men and women. One of the most common contributors to sexual dysfunction is diabetes, which can lower sexual drive, arousal, enjoyment, and satisfaction, especially in men (Schiavi, Stimmel, Mandeli, & Schreiner-Engel, 1995). Diabetes often goes undiagnosed, so people may believe that psychological factors are causing their sexual dysfunctions, when the cause is really undiagnosed diabetes.

Other diseases that are common causes of sexual dysfunction, particularly in men, are cardiovascular disease, multiple sclerosis, renal failure, vascular disease, spinal cord injury, and injury of the autonomic nervous system by surgery or radiation (APA, 1994; Katchadourian, 1989). As many as 40 percent of cases of male erectile disorder are caused by one of these medical conditions. In men with cardiovascular disease, sexual dysfunction can be caused directly by the disease, which can, for example, reduce the functioning of the vascular system. Sexual dysfunction may be a psychological response to the presence of the disease; for example, a man who recently had a heart attack may fear he will have another if he has sex, and thus he loses his desire for sex.

In men, abnormally low levels of the androgen hormones, especially testosterone, or high levels of the hormones estrogen and prolactin can cause sexual dysfunction. In women, hormones do not seem to have a consistent, direct effect on sexual desire. For example, levels of most reproductive hormones change in women over the menstrual cycle, but there is no consistent effect of these hormones on sexual desire—simply, there is variance among women in what parts of their menstrual cycles they feel the most sexual desire (Beck, 1995; Schiavi & Segraves, 1995). Hormones may have an indirect effect on sexual desire by affecting sexual arousal, however. Low levels of estrogen can cause decreases in vasocongestion and vaginal lubrication, leading to diminished sexual arousal, pain during sexual activity, and, therefore, lowered sexual desire (Sherwin, 1991). Levels of estrogen drop greatly at menopause, and thus postmenopausal women often complain of lowered sexual desire and arousal. Similarly, women who have had radical hysterectomies, which remove the main source of estrogen, the ovaries, can experience reductions in both sexual desire and arousal.

Vaginal dryness or irritation, which causes pain during sex and therefore lowers sexual desire and arousal, can be caused by radiation therapy, endometriosis, antihistamines, douches, tampons, vaginal contraceptives, and infections such as vaginitis or pelvic inflammatory disease. Injuries during childbirth that have healed poorly, such as a poorly repaired episiotomy, can cause coital pain in women (Masters et al., 1993). Biological causes of dyspareunia in men include genital or urinary tract infections, especially prostatitis, and a rare condition called *Peyronie's disease,* which causes deposits of fibrous tissue in the penis.

Although people often drink alcohol to make them feel more "sexy," even small amounts of alcohol can inhibit sexual responsiveness.

Sexual desire, arousal, and activity tend to decrease in men with age, although many men remain sexually active well into their 80s (Schiavi, 1990). It becomes more difficult, however, for many men to maintain erections as they grow old. One study of married men between 60 and 79 years old found that about one-third had difficulty with erections and an additional 15 percent were sexually inactive and unsure about their abilities to maintain erections (Martin, 1981). In many of these cases, the cause of the erectile dysfunction was probably not age per se but one of the medical conditions already listed, which are more common in older men than in younger men. It may also be that normal declines with age in the functioning of the testes, in the production of testosterone, and in the functioning of the vascular system contribute to erectile problems in older men (Schiavi, 1990).

Several drugs can diminish sexual drive and arousal and interfere with orgasm. These include antihypertensive drugs taken by people with high blood pressure, antipsychotic drugs, antidepressants, lithium, and tranquilizers. Many recreational drugs, including marijuana, cocaine, amphetamines, and nicotine, can impair sexual functioning (Schiavi & Segraves, 1995). Even though people often drink alcohol to make them feel more sexy and uninhibited, even small amounts of alcohol can significantly impair sexual functioning, and chronic alcoholics often have diagnosable sexual dysfunctions (Schiavi, 1990).

How can you know if a sexual dysfunction is caused by biological factors or has psychological causes? Certainly, the presence of one of the known biological causes of sexual dysfunctions is a clue that the cause of the dysfunction may be biological; similarly, if dysfunction immediately follows a psychological trauma, there is an increased likelihood that it is psychologically caused. There are some differences among the patterns of symptoms and the courses of biological and psychological sexual dysfunctions as well (Ackerman & Carey, 1995). Biologically caused dysfunctions tend to be global and consistent, whereas psychological disorders are more likely to be situational and inconsistent, occuring, for example, only with certain partners or specific types of sexual activity. Psychological dysfunctions tend to begin suddenly, whereas biologically caused disorders tend to begin more gradually (unless they directly follow accidents or surgery).

For a man with erectile dysfunction, one of the best ways to know if the dysfunction has biological causes is to determine whether he has erections during sleep, as healthy men do. If he is having nocturnal erections, then chances are that his erectile problems have psychological origins, at least in part. If he is not having nocturnal erections, then chances are the erectile problems have biological causes (Ackerman & Carey, 1995). One sign that a man is having nocturnal erections is that he consistently awakens in the morning with an erection. A more thorough assessment of nocturnal erections can be done with devices that directly measure men's erections (Tiefer & Melman, 1989). These devices, which can be used at home, have velcro straps that are wrapped around the man's penis before he goes to sleep. The straps have three connectors that snap with defined penile pressure. A more accurate way of determining if a man is having nocturnal erections is with the help of a sleep laboratory, where strain gauges are attached to the base of the penis to record the magnitude, duration, and pattern of erections, while electroencephalographs record his pattern of sleep. Finally, an alternative home test involves attaching a ring of postage stamps to the base of the man's penis before he goes to sleep. If the ring is broken in the morning, he has probably had an erection during the night.

Women also experience cyclic episodes of vasocongestion during sleep, which can be monitored to determine if a woman experiencing arousal problems has a biological disorder. Vasocongestion in women can be measured with a vaginal photoplethysmograph, a tampon-shaped device inserted into a woman's vagina that records the changes that accompany vasocongestion.

In sum, a number of medical conditions, drugs, and the physiological changes of normal aging can affect sexual desire, arousal, and orgasm. It is critical at the outset of any treatment program to determine if any of these factors are contributing to a sexual dysfunction.

Relationship Factors

Problems in intimate relationships are extremely common among people with sexual dysfunctions. Sometimes these problems are the consequences of sexual dysfunctions, as when a couple cannot communicate about the sexual dysfunction of one of the partners and grow distant from each other. Relationship problems can be direct causes of sexual dysfunctions as well (Beck, 1995).

Conflicts between partners may be about their sexual activities. One partner may want to engage in a type of sexual activity that the other partner is not comfortable with, or one partner may want to engage in sexual activity much more often than the other partner. People with inhibited desire, arousal, or orgasm often have sexual partners who do not know how to arouse them or are not concerned with their arousal and focus on only themselves. Partners often do not communicate with each other about what is arousing, so even if both partners intend to please the other, they do not know what their partner wants them to do (Ackerman & Carey, 1995; Speckens, Hengeveld, Nijeholt, & Hemert, 1995).

Anorgasmia in women is especially likely to be tied to lack of communication between a woman and a male partner about what the woman needs to reach orgasm (Hurlbert, 1991). In sexual encounters between men and women, men still tend to decide when to initiate sex, how long to engage in foreplay, when to penetrate, and what position to use during intercourse. A man's pattern of arousal is often not the same as a woman's pattern of arousal, and he may be making these decisions on the basis of his level of arousal and needs for stimulation rather than hers. Most women have difficulty reaching orgasm by coitus alone and need oral or manual stimulation of the clitoris to become aroused enough to reach orgasm (Hite, 1976; Kaplan, 1974). Many men and women do not know this, however, or believe that men should be able to bring women to orgasm by penile insertion and thrusting alone. Many women thus never receive the stimulation they need to be sufficiently aroused to orgasm. They may feel inhibited from telling their partners that they would like them to stimulate their clitoris more, because they are afraid of hurting their partners' feelings or angering them, or because they believe they do not have the right to ask for the kind of stimulation they want. Some women may fake orgasms to protect their partners' egos. Often their partners know that they are not fully satisfied, however. Communication between partners may break down further, and sex may become a forum for hostility rather than pleasure.

Conflicts between partners that are not directly about their sexual activity can affect their sexual relationship as well, as we saw in the case of Paul and Petula Peterson earlier

CATHY Copyright © Cathy Guisewite. Reprinted with permission of UNIVERSAL PRESS SYNDICATE. All rights reserved.

in this chapter (Beck, 1995; Rosen & Lieblum, 1995). Anger, distrust, and lack of respect for one's partner can greatly interfere with sexual desire and functioning. When one partner suspects that the other partner has been unfaithful or is losing interest in the relationship, all sexual interest may disappear. Often there is an imbalance of power in relationships, and people feel exploited, subjugated, and underappreciated by their partners, leading to problems in their sexual relationships (Rosen & Lieblum, 1995).

Conflict in a relationship is a common cause of sexual dysfunction.

One study of men and women seeking treatment for hypoactive sexual desire disorder found that the women are more likely than men to report problems in their marital relationships, other stressful events in their lives, and higher levels of psychological distress (Donahey & Carroll, 1993). Men seeking treatment are more likely than women to be experiencing other types of sexual dysfunction in addition to low sexual desire, such as erectile dysfunction. Thus, for men, it appeared that issues of sexual functioning precipitate their entry into treatment, whereas for women, lack of sexual desire is linked to a broader array of psychosocial problems.

Why do you think it is so difficult for partners to talk with each other about sex?

Trauma

Reductions in sexual desire and functioning often follow personal traumas, such as the loss of a loved one, the loss of a job, or the diagnosis of severe illness in one's child. Unemployment in men is often tied to declines in sexual desire and functioning (Morokoff & Gillilland, 1993). Traumas such as unemployment can challenge a person's self-esteem and self-concept interfering with his or her sexual self-concept. Traumas can also cause a person to experience a depression that includes a loss of interest in most pleasurable activities, including sex. In such cases, clinicians will typically focus on treatment of the depression, with the expectation that sexual desire will resume once the depression has lifted.

As noted earlier, one type of personal trauma that is often associated with sexual desire disorders in women is sexual assault (Becker, 1989). A woman who has been raped may lose all interest in sex and be disgusted or extremely anxious when anyone, particularly a man, touches her. Her sexual aversion may be tied to a sense of vulnerability and loss of control or to a conditioned aversion to all forms of sexual contact (Lieblum & Rosen, 1989). In addition, male partners of women who have been raped sometimes cannot cope with the rapes and withdraw from sexual encounters with them. This may be more common among men who accept rape myths such as "Women who get raped were asking for it," and "Women enjoy being raped." Women rape survivors may thus feel victimized yet again, and their interest in sex may decline even further.

Attitudes and Cognitions

People who have been taught that sex is dirty, disgusting, sinful, or a "necessary evil" may understandably lack desire to have sex. They may also know so little about their own bodies and sexual responses that they do not know how to make sex pleasurable. Such is the case with Mrs. Booth (adapted from Spitzer et al., 1994, pp. 251–252).

Case Study • Mr. and Mrs. Booth have been married for 14 years and have three children, ages 8 through 12. They are both bright and well-educated. Both are from Scotland, from which they moved 10 years ago because of Mr. Booth's work as an industrial consultant. They present with the complaint that Mrs. Booth has been able to participate passively in sex "as a duty" but has never enjoyed it since they have been married.

Before their marriage, although they had had intercourse only twice, Mrs. Booth had been highly aroused by kissing and petting and felt she used her attractiveness to "seduce" her husband into marriage. She did, however, feel intense guilt about their two episodes of premarital intercourse; during their honeymoon, she began to think of sex as a chore that could not be pleasing. Although she periodically passively complied with intercourse, she had almost no spontaneous desire for sex. She never masturbated, had never reached orgasm, thought of all variations such as oral sex as completely repulsive, and was preoccupied with a fantasy of how disapproving her family would be if she ever engaged in any of these activities.

Mrs. Booth is almost totally certain that no woman she respects in any older generation has enjoyed sex and that despite the "new vogue" of sexuality, only sleazy, crude women let themselves act like "animals." These beliefs have led to a pattern of regular but infrequent sex that at best is accommodating and gives little or no pleasure to her or her husband. Whenever Mrs. Booth comes close to having a feeling of sexual arousal, numerous negative thoughts come into her mind such as, "What am I, a tramp?"; "If I like this, he'll just want it more often"; and "How could I look at myself in the mirror after something like this?" These thoughts almost inevitably are accompanied by a cold feeling and an insensitivity to sensual pleasure. As a result, sex is invariably an unhappy experience. Almost any excuse, such as fatigue or being busy, is sufficient for her to rationalize avoiding intercourse.

Women with severely negative attitudes toward sex like Mrs. Booth's also tend to experience dyspareunia and vaginismus because they have been taught that sex is painful and frightening (Rosen & Lieblum, 1995). Although attitudes toward sex such as Mrs. Booth's may be declining in modern countries among younger people, many younger and older women still report a fear of "letting go" that inteferes with orgasm (Heiman & Grafton-Becker, 1989). They say they fear losing control or acting in some way that will embarrass them. This fear of loss of control may result from distrust of one's partner, a sense of shame about sex, a poor body image, and a host of other factors.

Another set of attitudes that interferes with sexual functioning appears to be rampant among middle-aged and younger adults. These attitudes are often referred to as *performance concerns* or *performance anxiety* (LoPiccolo, 1992; Masters & Johnson, 1970). People worry so much about whether they are going to be aroused and have orgasms that this worry interferes with sexual functioning: "What if I can't get an erection? I'll die of embarrassment!" "I've got to have an orgasm, or he'll think I'm frigid!" "Oh my god, I just can't get aroused tonight!" These worried thoughts are so distracting that people cannot focus on the pleasure that sexual stimulation is giving them and thus do not become as aroused as they want to or need to in order to reach orgasm (Barlow, Sakheim, & Beck, 1983; Cranston-Cuebas & Barlow, 1990). In addition, many people engage in *spectatoring:* They anxiously attend to reactions and performance during sex as if they were spectators (Masters & Johnson, 1970). Spectatoring distracts from sexual pleasure and interferes with sexual functioning. Unfortunately, people who have had some problems in sexual functioning only develop more performance concerns, which then further interfere with their functioning. By the time they seek treatment for sexual dysfunction, they may be so anxious about "performing" sexually that they avoid all sexual activity.

Performance anxiety may also make some men reach orgasm *too* fast. Men with premature ejaculation problems may be so anxious about performing well that they do not pay attention to their level of sexual arousal and do not modulate their levels of self-stimulation or stimulation from their partners enough to control when ejaculation occurs (Grenier & Byers, 1995; Kaplan, 1974; McCarthy, 1989.) Transient problems with premature ejaculation can be caused by anxiety-provoking stressors men encounter on the job or in other areas of their lives, anxiety about being with new sexual partners, or anxiety caused by problems maintaining erections or preventing ejaculation in recent sexual encounters.

More chronic problems can develop from the way young men learn about their own sexual responses during adolescence. Most males, perhaps 90 percent, have their first orgasmic experience during masturbation as adolescents (McCarthy, 1989). Masturbation is usually practiced in an intense, rapid manner, where the only focus is on ejaculation. Many young men do not view masturbation as a positive, healthy exercise in which they are learning about their bodies. Rather, they feel guilty or embarrassed and anxious about being caught masturbating, so they hurry through it, not paying attention to their bodies' levels of arousal and not learning anything about ejaculatory control. In partner sex, they can become aroused without much stimulation from their partners and may fear ejaculating before their partners becomes aroused. Thus, they avoid allowing partners to stimulate them and focus instead on stimulating their partners as quickly as possible so that they can have intercourse. As a result, they come to associate high levels of arousal with anxiety over premature ejaculation, and this anxiety only increases the chance of premature ejaculation.

With experience and maturity, most males gain ejaculatory control through a number of processes, as described by Barry McCarthy (1989, p. 146): "(1) a regular rhythm of being sexual; (2) increased comfort with practice; (3) a more give-and-take 'pleasuring process' rather than goal-oriented foreplay; (4) allowance of more time for the variety of sensations in the sexual experience; (5) greater intimacy and security resulting in increased sexual comfort; (6) partner encouragement for a slower, more tender, rhythmic sexual interchange; and (7) shift of intercourse positions and/or thrusting movements." Men who do not go through the process of gaining ejaculatory control may develop premature ejaculation disorder.

Cultural and Social Factors

Other cultures recognize types of sexual dysfunction not recognized in the DSM-IV. For example, both the traditional Chinese medical system and the Ayurvedic medical system, which is native to India, teach that loss of semen is detrimental to a man's health (Dewaraja & Sasaki, 1991). Masturbation is strongly discouraged, because it results in semen loss without the possibility of conception. A depersonalization syndrome known as *Koro*, thought to result from semen loss, has been reported among Malaysians, Southeast Asians, and southern Chinese. This syndrome involves an acute anxiety state, with a feeling of panic and impending death, and a delusion that the penis is shrinking into the body and disappearing. The patient or his relatives may grab and hold the penis until the attack of Koro is ended to stop the penis from disappearing into the body.

In surveys in the United States, less well-educated and poorer men and women tend to experience more sexual dysfunctions, including pain during sex, not finding sex pleasurable, inability to reach orgasm, lacking interest in sex, and climaxing too early and, for men, trouble in maintaining erections (Laumann et al., 1994). People in lower educational and income groups may have more sexual dysfunctions because they are under more psychological stress, their physical health is worse, or they have not had the benefit of educational programs that teach people about their bodies and healthy social relationships.

If you were the parent of a teenager, how would you talk with your teenager about sex to help him or her develop a healthy perspective on sex?

Summing Up | Causes of Sexual Dysfunctions

- Most sexual dysfunctions probably have multiple causes.
- Biological causes include undiagnosed diabetes or other medical conditions, prescription or recreational drug use, and hormonal or vascular abnormalities.
- Psychosocial causes include problems in intimate relationships, traumatic experiences, maladaptive attitudes and cognitions (especially performance concerns), and an upbringing or cultural milieu that devalues or degrades sex.

Treatment of Sexual Dysfunctions

The proper treatment for a sexual dysfunction obviously is one that is directed at the primary cause of the dysfunction. Because most dysfunctions have multiple causes, however, most treatments must involve a combination of approaches, often including biological interventions, direct sex therapy focusing on the sexual practices of a client and his or her partner, and psychosocial therapy focusing on problems in a relationship or the concerns of an individual client.

Biological Therapies

If a sexual dysfunction is the direct result of another medical condition, such as diabetes, treating the medical condition will often reduce the sexual dysfunction. Similarly, adjusting the dosage of medications that are contributing to a sexual dysfunction or getting a person to stop using recreational drugs that are causing a sexual dysfunction can often cure the dysfunction (Rosen & Ashton, 1993).

A number of drugs have proven useful for the treatment of some of the sexual dysfunctions. Women with vaginal dryness may find that using vaginal lubricants significantly increases their ability to become sexually aroused. Hormone replacement therapy can be very effective for men whose low levels of sexual desire or arousal are linked to low levels of testosterone or for women whose low sexual desire or arousal, or dyspareunia, are linked to low levels of estrogen (Schiavi & Segraves, 1995).

Although some antidepressants can cause sexual dysfunctions, the antidepressant drugs clomipramine (trade name Anafranil) and sertraline (trade name Zoloft) can be useful in reducing premature ejaculation in men (Althof, 1995). For men who have problems obtaining or maintaining erections, two drugs, yohimbine and apomorphine, can increase their ability to have erections (Rosen & Ashton, 1993). Interestingly, yohimbine comes from the bark of the yohimbehe tree, which Africans have chewed for centuries to increase their sexual desire and functioning.

For men, when drugs do not cure erectile disorders, other biological or technical interventions are possible (Ackerman & Carey, 1995). Several drugs can cause penile rigidity when injected into the penis. There are mechanical devices that can cause blood to rush into the penis, causing an erection (Rosen & Lieblum, 1995). The penis is placed in a tube in which a vacuum is created by the device, blood rushes into the penis, and a constricting band at the base of the penis prevents blood from rushing out. Other prosthetic devices can be surgically implanted into the penis to make it erect. One prosthetic is a pair of rods inserted into the penis. The rods create a permanent erection that can be bent up or down against the body. Another type is a hydraulic inflatable device, which allows a man to create an erection by pumping saline into rods inserted in the penis and then to relieve the erection by pumping out the saline.

Sex Therapy

When a sexual dysfunction seems to be due, at least in part, to inadequate sexual practices of the client and his or her partner, then sex therapy focusing on these practices can be useful. Some people have never learned what practices give them or their partners pleasure or have fallen out of the habit of engaging in these practices. Sex therapy teaches these practices and helps partners develop a regular pattern of satisfying sexual encounters.

One of the mainstays of sex therapy is **sensate focus therapy** (Masters & Johnson, 1970). In this therapy, one partner is active, carrying out a set of exercises to stimulate the other partner, while the other partner is the passive recipient, focusing on the pleasure that the exercises bring. Then the partners switch roles, so that each spends time being both the giver and recipient of the stimulation. The exercises should be carried out at quiet, unhurried times that are planned for by the partners. In the early phases of this therapy, partners are instructed *not* to be concerned about or even attempt intercourse. Rather, they

sensate focus therapy
treatment for sexual dysfunction in which partners alternate between giving and receiving stimulaton in a relaxed, openly communicative atmosphere, in order to reduce performance anxiety and concern over achieving orgasm by learning each partner's sexual fulfillment needs

are told to focus intently on the pleasure created by the exercises. These instructions are meant to reduce performance anxiety and concern about achieving orgasm.

In the first phase of sensate focus therapy, partners spend time gently touching each other but not around the genitals. They are instructed to focus on the sensations and to communicate with each other about what does and does not feel good. The goal is to have the partners spend intimate time together communicating, without pressure for intercourse. This first phase may continue for several weeks, until partners feel comfortable with the exercise and have learned what gives each of them pleasure.

In the second phase of sensate focus therapy, partners spend time directly stimulating each others' breasts and genitals but still without attempting to have intercourse. If the problem is a female arousal disorder, a woman will guide her partner to stimulate her in arousing ways. It is acceptable for a woman to be aroused to orgasm during these exercises, but the partners are instructed not to attempt intercourse until she regularly becomes fully aroused by her partner during sensate focus exercises. If the problem is a male erectile disorder, a man will guide his partner in touching him in ways that feel arous-

In sensate focus therapy, people are encouraged to spend time exploring what sexually arouses each other without feeling pressured to reach orgasm.

ing. If he has an erection, he is to let it come and go naturally; intercourse is forbidden until he is able to have erections easily and frequently during the sensate focus exercises. Throughout these exercises, the partner with the problem is instructed to be selfish and to focus only on the arousing sensations and on communicating with his or her partner about what feels good. The touching should proceed in a relaxed and nondemanding atmosphere. Once the partner with the problem regularly experiences arousal with genital stimulation, the partners may begin having intercourse, but the focus remains on enhancing and sustaining pleasure, rather than on orgasm or performance.

Sex therapy often includes teaching or encouraging clients to masturbate (Morokoff & LoPiccolo, 1986). The goals of masturbation are for the people to explore their own bodies to discover what is arousing, and to become less inhibited about their own sexuality. Then individuals are taught to communicate what they have learned they need to partners. This technique can be especially helpful for anorgasmic women who often have never masturbated and have little knowledge of what they need to become aroused.

Two techniques are useful in helping a man with premature ejaculation to gain control over his ejaculations: the *stop-start technique* (Semans, 1956) and the *squeeze technique* (Masters & Johnson, 1970). The stop-start technique can be carried out either through masturbation or with a partner. In the first phase, the man is told to stop stimulating himself or to tell his partner to stop stimulation just before ejaculatory inevitability. He then relaxes and concentrates on the sensations in his body until his level of arousal declines. At that point he or his partner can resume stimulation, again stopping before the point of ejaculatory inevitability. If stimulation stops too late and the man ejaculates, he is encouraged not to feel angry or disappointed but to enjoy the ejaculation and reflect on what he learned about his body and then resume the exercise. If a man is engaging in this exercise with a female partner, they are instructed not to engage in intercourse until he has sufficient control over his ejaculations during her manual stimulation of him. In the second phase of this process, when a female partner is involved, the man lies on his back with his female partner on top of him, and she inserts his penis into her vagina but then remains quiet. Most men with premature ejaculation have intercourse only in the man-on-top position, with quick and short thrusting during intercourse that makes it very difficult for them to exert control over their ejaculations. The goal is for the man to enjoy the sensation of being in the woman's vagina without ejaculating. During the exercise, he is encouraged to touch or massage his partner and to communicate with her about what each is experiencing. If he feels he is reaching ejaculatory inevitability, he can request that she dismount and lie next to him until his arousal subsides. The partners are encouraged to engage in this exercise for at least 10 to 15 minutes, even if they must interrupt it several times to prevent him from ejaculating. In the third phase of the stop-start technique, she creates some thrusting motion while still on top of him but using slow, long strokes. The partners typically reach orgasm and experience the entire encounter as highly intimate and pleasurable. Female partners of men with premature ejaculation often have trouble reaching orgasm themselves because the men lose their erections after ejaculating long before the women are highly aroused, and tension is high between the partners during sex. The stop-start technique can create encounters in which female partners receive the stimulation they need to reach orgasm as well.

The squeeze techinque is used somewhat less often because it is harder to teach to partners (McCarthy, 1989). The man's partner stimulates him to an erection, and then when he signals that ejaculation is imminent, the partner applies a firm but gentle squeeze to his penis, either at the glans or at the base, for 3 to 4 seconds. This results in a partial loss of erection. The partner can then stimulate him again to the point of ejaculation and use the squeeze technique to stop the ejaculation. The goal of this technique, as with the stop-start technique, is for the man with a premature ejaculation disorder to learn to identify the point of ejaculatory inevitability and to control his arousal level at that point.

Vaginismus is often treated by deconditioning the woman's automatic tightening of the muscles of her vagina (Leiblum, Pervin, & Campbell, 1989). She is taught about the muscular tension at the opening of her vagina and the need to learn to relax those muscles. In a safe setting, she is instructed to insert her own fingers into her vagina. She examines her vagina in a mirror and practices relaxation exercises. She may also use silicon or metal vaginal dilators made for this exercise. Gradually, she inserts larger and larger dilators, as she practices relaxation exercises and becomes accustomed to the feel of the dilator in her vagina. If she has a partner, his or her fingers may be used instead of the dilator. If the woman has a male partner, eventually she guides his penis into her vagina, while remaining in control.

In sum, sex therapy techniques include sensate focus therapy, teaching masturbation, the stop-start and squeeze techniques, and deconditioning of vaginal contractions. Each of these techniques has proven successful for the treatment of people with specific sexual dysfunctions (Masters & Johnson, 1970; Rosen & Lieblum, 1995). Again, however, sexual dysfunctions often have multiple causes and may often need other forms of intervention such as the ones we will discuss next.

 If you were experiencing a sexual dysfunction, would you seek sex therapy? Why or why not?

Couples Therapy

Many couples who know how to have pleasurable sex with each other never get around to it or stop giving their sexual relationship the attention it needs leading to declines in sexual desire.

Case Study • Felicia, a middle-aged, upper-middle-class woman, lives with her husband and young son in a luxurious apartment on the Upper East Side of Manhattan. She seems to have it all—a lucrative job, a loving husband, an affluent lifestyle. However, she confessed, she does not have a very active sex life. "My husband and I are very easy with each other," she said. "But the truth is, I seldom feel like doing it. I'm exhausted all the time. So I've got two vibrators. Frankly, I can't remember when the last time I used them was. We make love now, maybe twice a month, if we're lucky. When I fall in bed, I crave sleep, not sex." (Michael et al., 1994, p. 2)

Some couples in long-standing relationships have abandoned the *seduction rituals*—those activities that arouse sexual interest in both partners—they followed when they were first together (Verhulst & Heiman, 1988). Couples in which both partners work may be particularly prone to try to squeeze in sexual encounters late at night when both partners are very tired and not very interested in sex. These encounters may be rushed or not fully satisfying and lead to a gradual decline in interest for any sexual intimacy. A therapist may encourage a couple to set aside enough time so that they can engage in seduction rituals and satisfying sexual encounters. For example, partners may decide to hire a babysitter for their children, have a romantic dinner out, and then go to a hotel where they can have sex without rushing or being interrupted by their children.

Busy people often find little time or energy to engage in seduction rituals with their partners.

Partners often differ in their *scripts* for sexual encounters—their expectations about what will take place during a sexual encounter and about what each partner's responsibilities are. Resolving these differences in scripts may be a useful goal in therapy. For example, if a woman lacks desire for sex because she feels her partner is too rough during sex, a therapist may encourage the partner to slow down and show the woman the kind of gentle intimacy she needs to enjoy sex. In general, therapists will help partners understand what each other wants and needs from sexual interactions and negotiate mutually acceptable and satisfying repertoires of sexual exchange.

When the conflicts between partners involve matters other than their sexual practices, such as an imbalance of power, distrust or hostility, or disagreements over important values or decisions, the therapist will focus on these conflicts primarily and the sexual dysfunction only secondarily. Some therapists use cognitive-behavioral interventions, some use psychodynamic interventions, and some use interventions based on family systems therapy. All of these interventions may have some benefit, although little research has been done to evaluate their effectiveness (Rosen & Lieblum, 1995).

Individual Psychotherapy

Although many therapists prefer to treat people with sexual dysfunctions as members of relationships, this is not always possible. The partner of a person with a dysfunction may refuse to participate in treatment or a person with a dysfunction may not have a partner.

Cognitive-behavioral interventions are being used increasingly to address attitudes and scripts that interfere with sexual functioning (LoPiccolo & Stock, 1986; Rosen & Lieblum, 1995). For example, a man who fears that he will embarrass himself by not sustaining an erection in a sexual encounter may be challenged to examine the evidence for this having happened to him in the past. If this were a common occurrence for this man, his therapist would explore the cognitions surrounding the experience and help the man challenge these cognitions and practice more positive cognitions.

Psychodynamic therapies are used to explore the childhood experiences that contributed to people's negative attitudes toward sex (Kaplan, 1974). For example, some psychodynamic theorists believe that women with vaginismus and dyspareunia are overidentifed with their mothers and have not yet reached the level of personal autonomy they should have reached during adolescence (Hiller, 1996). These women reject involvement in sexual relationships by literally closing their vaginas or experiencing pain during intercourse because they unconsciously equate engaging in intercourse as a rejection of their mothers. Psychotherapy with these women focuses on making the link between their vaginismus and their relationships with their mothers, as in the following case (adapted from Hiller, 1996, pp. 69–70).

Case Study • Sally and Ivan, both in their mid-20s had been married for a year when their physician referred Sally for painful intercourse, which had led to the marriage barely being consummated. Although they had known each other for 4 years, penetration was not attempted until after the wedding. On the few occasions when they tried, the internal pain was too severe for it to be continued.

Both Sally and Ivan were only children of unstable marriages, although neither set of parents had divorced. Sally felt very close to her mother, who confided in her, especially about the fights and marital disharmonies that were regular features of family life. She was acutely aware of wanting to be available when her mother was upset and never wanting to hurt her by letting her know there were differences between them. At the same time, Sally sensed that this prevented her growing, developing, and expressing her own emotions.

Sally believed that her parents' sexual contact had stopped around the time she started school. She was brought up very strictly with the message that boys were only after one thing and that sex before marriage was wrong; otherwise, sexual topics were completely avoided.

Exploring the intense emotional bond with her mother in individual sessions, Sally realized that she had always wanted her mother to feel they were part of one another. This strong mother-daughter tie not only conflicted with her developmental needs but also restricted Sally's involvement with her father—a liked and respected figure—for fear of letting her mother down. I suggested that the anxiety about opening things up with her mother had manifested itself in her ability to open herself up—to expand her own inner space—to allow sexual intercourse to be part of her life when it was no longer part of her mother's life. It seemed as if Sally's lack of full genital arousal maintained the exclusive link of female dependency, thereby preventing the creating of a new (sexual) link with her partner that would represent abandonment of her mother and repeat her earlier loss of significant female relationships. When Sally eventually told her mother about the sexual difficulty and her own therapy, it emerged that her mother had been sexually abused in her teens; she realized she needed help but so far lacked the confidence to embark on therapy for her own marital and sexual problems. Discussing their separate needs for professional help lifted the burden of responsibility from Sally, communication between them became more open.

The focus of couple work with Sally and Ivan was on enabling them to take in a different psychological perspective on their penetration difficulties, in order to counteract their sense of failure and helplessness. Directive intervention, initially involving sensual and sexual pleasuring, facilitated a pattern of foreplay that heightened awareness of their own arousal and the other's needs in the present. During this process, Sally's increased arousal and awareness of emotional change evoked anxiety about being different from her mother and therefore being unloved. Ivan appreciated that Sally needed to address these issues as therapy progressed. Later he became anxious himself, when sexual intimacy moved on to genital stimulation, about failing Sally again by not being able to penetrate. The emerging anxieties were addressed in joint therapy in combination with a behaviorally oriented approach to increasing sexual intimacy. Eventually, comfortable and pleasurable intercourse took place.

Whether a therapist uses a cognitive-behavioral, a psychodynamic, or some other therapeutic approach to addressing the psychological issues involved in a sexual dysfunction, direct sex therapy using the behavioral techniques described earlier often is also a part of therapy. In cognitive-behavioral therapy, the client's cognitions while engaging in new sexual exercises can be evaluated and used as a focus of therapy sessions. For example, a woman who is learning how to masturbate for the first time may realize that she has thoughts such as, "I'm going to get caught and I'll be so embarrassed"; "I shouldn't be doing this, this is sinful;" and "Only pathetic people do this," while masturbating. A therapist can then help the woman address the accuracy of these thoughts and decide whether she wants to maintain this attitude toward masturbation. If the woman is in psycho-dynamic therapy, the therapist might explore the origins of the woman's attitudes about masturbation in her early relationships. Thus, the behavioral techniques of sex therapy not only directly teach the client new sexual skills but also provide material for discussion in therapy sessions.

The Role of Sexual Orientation and Values in Treatment

Most of the treatments described assume that the client is in a heterosexual relationship, but sexual dysfunctions can arise in the context of homosexual relationships as well. Lesbians tend not to complain of dyspareunia or vaginismus as often as do heterosexual women but may be more likely to have aversions to oral sex (Nichols, 1989). In response to the AIDS crisis, gay men have experienced many problems in recent years with low sexual desire and arousal. Some of the sexual therapy treatments described can readily be adapted for gay and lesbian couples and the types of sex that they practice. The therapist treating gay and lesbian clients must also be sensitive to the psychological conflicts and stresses these clients face as a result of society's rejection of their lifestyle (Nichols, 1989).

The treatments for the sexual dysfunctions must also take into account the religious, moral, and cultural values that clients have concerning sex. The treatments described tend to be based on the assumption that men and women should have sex when they wish and enjoy it each time they have it. This assumption is not shared by persons of all backgrounds. Inhibitions about sex based on religious or cultural teachings are often seen as the causes of sexual dysfunctions by sex therapists. The experienced therapist works within the values framework of the sexual partners, first finding out what is in their current repertoire of sexual activity and then building on that according to their comfort.

Summing Up	Treatment of Sexual Dysfunctions

- When the cause of a sexual dysfunction is biological, treatments that eradicate the cause can cure the sexual dysfunction. Alternately, drug therapies or prostheses can be used.
- Sex therapy corrects the inadequate sexual practices of a client and his or her partner. The techniques of sex therapy include sensate focus therapy, teaching masturbation, the stop-start and squeeze techniques, and deconditioning of vaginal contractions.
- Couples therapy focuses on decreasing conflicts between couples over their sexual practices or over other areas of their relationship.
- Individual psychotherapy helps people recognize conflicts or negative attitudes behind their sexual dysfunctions and resolve these.

Paraphilias

People find all sorts of creative ways to fulfill their sexual needs and desires while remaining within the limits set on sexual behavior by their society. Some examples in Western culture might include the use of erotic fantasies, pictures or stories, or sex toys to enhance arousal while engaging in masturbation or sexual encounters with others. People vary greatly in what they do and do not find arousing (see Table 11.3). One person may find oral sex the most stimulating form of activity while another person may be repulsed by oral sex. One man may become extremely aroused while watching a wet T-shirt contest, and another man may experience such a contest as silly. One woman may find men with beards extremely sexy, while another woman may dislike facial hair on men.

Most of the time, these variations in preferences about sexually arousing stimuli simply provide spice to life and to conversations. Societies have always drawn lines, however, between what types of sexual activities they will allow and what types they will not

Table 11.3   What Kinds of Sexual Practices Do People Find Appealing?

A national survey of 18 to 44 year olds found that many different sexual practices appeal to people, with men finding more activities appealing than women do.

	Percent saying "very appealing"	
	Men	Women
Vaginal intercourse	83	78
Watching partner undress	50	30
Receiving oral sex	50	33
Giving oral sex	37	19
Group sex	14	1
Anus stimulated by partner's fingers	6	4
Using dildos/vibrators	5	3
Watching others do sexual things	6	2
Having a same-gender sex partner	4	3
Having sex with a stranger	5	1

From: R. T. Michael et al., *Sex In America: A Definitive Survey*, Copyright © 1994, Little Brown & Company. Reprinted with permission.

allow. Judgments about what are acceptable sexual activities vary by culture and across historical periods. In Western cultures prior to this century and in some Islamic nations today, men are prohibited from seeing most of women's bodies except their faces and hands, for fear that viewing women's legs and perhaps even their arms or their hair could sexually arouse men.

Although we may like to think that in modern Western culture, we only disallow those sexual behaviors that are truly "sick," our judgments about what are normal and abnormal sexual behaviors are still subjective. Consider the following series of behaviors exhibited by three men. The first man goes to a public beach to watch women in skimpy bikinis. The second man pays to see a female topless dancer in a nightclub. The third man stands outside a woman's bedroom window at night secretly watching her undress. The behavior of the first man is not only allowed, but it is promoted in many movies, television shows, and commercials. The behavior of the second man is a form of allowed sexual commerce. Only the behavior of the third man is prohibited both by modern cultural norms and by laws. Yet all three men had the intention of viewing women's partially or fully nude bodies because they found such activity sexually arousing.

Those atypical sexual behaviors that are considered disorders by the DSM-IV are called **paraphilias** (Greek for *besides* and *love*). These behaviors have also been referred to as *perversions*, *deviations*, and *variations* by some. When persons with paraphilias violate laws, they are referred to as *sex offenders*. The paraphilias are sexual activities that involve (1) nonhuman objects, (2) nonconsenting adults, (3) suffering or humiliation of oneself or one's partner, or (4) children.

Many people have occasional paraphilic fantasies. For example, one study of men's sexual fantasies found that 62 percent fanatisized having sex with a young girl, 33 percent fantasized raping a woman, 12 percent fantasized being humiliated during sex, 5 percent fantasized having sexual activity with an animal, and 3 percent fantasized having sexual activity with a young boy (Crepault & Couture, 1980). In a study of male college undergraduates 21 percent reported being sexually attracted to children, 9 percent fantasized having sex with children, 5 percent masturbated to fantasies of having sex with children, and 7 percent indicated they would become sexually involved with children if they could be assured they would never be discovered (Briere & Runtz, 1989). Most of these men would not be diagnosed with paraphilias because their fantasies were not the primary focus of their sexual arousal and they reported making no attempts to act out these fantasies.

For persons diagnosed with paraphilias, atypical sexual acts are their primary forms of sexual arousal. They often feel compelled to engage in their paraphilias, even though they

paraphilias
atypical sexual activities that involve one of the following: (1) nonhuman objects, (2) nonconsenting adults, (3) suffering or humiliation of oneself or one's partner, or (4) children

know they could be punished by law. Their partners in sexual acts are merely vehicles to act out their paraphilic fantasies, not individuals with personalities, needs, or rights. Some paraphilics will pay prostitutes to help them act out their fantasies, because it is difficult to find willing partners. Other paraphilics will force their fantasies on unwilling victims.

As noted at the beginning of this chapter, the paraphilias differ greatly in how severely they affect people other than the paraphilics. We will begin our discussion of the paraphilias with the one that is most benign: fetishism. People with fetishes do not typically impose their atypical sexual practices on other people; indeed, the focus of their sexual activities are nonhuman objects. The second set of paraphilias we will discuss, sadism and masochism, are less benign because they hold the potential for physical harm, even if both partners are engaging in the sexual activity willingly. The third set of paraphilias—voyeurism, exhibitionism, and frotteurism—are not benign because, by definition, they require victims. Finally, the most severe paraphilia is pedophilia, because the victims of pedophiles are the most powerless victims: children.

Fetishism

Fetishism involves the use of inanimate objects as the preferred or exclusive source of sexual arousal or gratification. Soft festishes are objects that are soft, furry, or lacy, such as frilly women's panties, stockings, or garters. Hard fetishes are objects that are smooth, harsh, or black, such as spike-heeled shoes, black gloves, and garments made of leather or rubber. These soft and hard objects are somewhat arousing to many people and, indeed, are promoted as arousing by their manufacturers. For most people, however, the objects simply add to the sexiness of the people wearing them, and their desire is for sex with those people. For the person with a fetish, the desire is for the object itself.

fetishism
paraphilia in which a person uses inanimate objects as the preferred or exclusive source of sexual arousal

Case Study • A 32-year-old, single, male, freelance photographer presented with the chief complaint of "abnormal sex drive." The patient related that although he was somewhat sexually attracted by women, he was far more attracted by "their panties."

To the best of the patient's memory, sexual excitement began at about age 7, when he came upon a pornographic magazine and felt stimulated by pictures of partially nude women wearing panties. His first ejaculation occurred at 13 via masturbation to fantasies of women wearing panties. He masturbated into his older sister's panties, which he had stolen without her knowledge. Subsequently, he stole panties from her friends and from other women he met socially. He found pretexts to "wander" into the bedrooms of women during social occasions and would quickly rummage through their possessions until he found a pair of panties to his satisfaction. He later used these to masturbate into and then "saved them" in a "private cache." The pattern of masturbating into women's underwear had been his preferred method of achieving sexual excitement and orgasm from adolescence until the present consultation.

The patient first had sexual intercourse at 18. Since then he had had intercourse on many occasions, and his preferred partner was a prostitute paid to wear panties, with the crotch area cut away, during the act. On less common occasions when sexual activity was attempted with a partner who did not wear panties, his sexual excitement was sometimes weak.

The patient felt uncomfortable dating "nice women" as he felt that friendliness might lead to sexual intimacy and that they would not understand his sexual needs. He avoided socializing with friends who might introduce him to such women. He recognized that his appearance, social style, and profession all resulted in his being perceived as a highly desirable bachelor. He felt anxious and depressed because his social life was limited by his sexual preference. (adapted from Spitzer et al., 1994, p. 247)

 If a person with a fetish such as a shoe fetish never harms anyone else and is not distressed about his or her behavior, should he or she be diagnosed with a psychological disorder?

Transvestites gain sexual pleasure by dressing in the clothes of the opposite sex.

transvestism
fetish in which a heterosexual man dresses in women's clothing as his primary means of becoming sexually aroused

One elaborate form of fetishism is **transvestism,** also referred to as *cross-dressing,* in which heterosexual men dress in women's clothing as their primary means of becoming sexually aroused. They may surreptitiously wear only one women's garment, such as a pair of women's panties, under their business suits. The complete cross-dresser fully clothes himself in women's garments and applies makeup and a wig. Some men engage in cross-dressing alone, and others participate in transvestite subcultures, in which groups of men gather for drinks, meals, and dancing, while elaborately dressed as women.

Case Study • Mr. A., a 65-year-old security guard, is distressed about his wife's objections to his wearing a nightgown at home in the evening, now that his youngest child has left home. His appearance and demeanor, except when he is dressing in women's clothes, are always masculine, and he is exclusively heterosexual. Occasionally, over the past 5 years, he has worn an inconspicuous item of female clothing even when dressed as a man, sometimes a pair of panties, sometimes an ambiguous pinkie ring. He always carries a photograph of himself dressed as a woman.

His first recollection of an interest in female clothing was putting on his sister's bloomers at age 12, an act accompanied by sexual excitement. He continued periodically to put on women's underpants—an activity that invariably resulted in an erection, sometimes a spontaneous emission, and sometimes masturbation but never accompanied by fantasy. Although he occasionally wished to be a girl, he never fantasized himself as one. During his single years he was always attracted to women but was shy about sex. Following his marriage at age 22, he had his first heterosexual intercourse.

His involvement with female clothes was of the same intensity even after his marriage. Beginning at age 45, after a chance exposure to a magazine called *Transvestia,* he began to increase his cross-dressing activity. He learned there were other men like himself, and he became more and more preoccupied with female clothing in fantasy and progressed to periodically dressing completely as a woman. More recently he has become involved in a transvestite network, writing to other transvestites contacted through the magazine and occasionally attending transvestite parties. These parties have been the only times that he has cross-dressed outside his home.

Although still committed to his marriage, sex with his wife has dwindled over the past 20 years as his waking thoughts and activities have become increasingly centered on cross-dressing. Over time this activity has become less eroticized and more an end in itself, but it still is a source of some sexual excitement. He always has an increased urge to dress as a woman when under stress; it has a tranquilizing effect. If particular circumstances prevent him from cross-dressing, he feels extremely frustrated. (adapted from Spitzer et al., 1994, pp. 257–258)

Some clinicians question whether fetishism should qualify as a psychiatric diagnosis or should simply be considered a variation in human sexual activity. Many, perhaps most, fetishists do not seek therapy or feel particularly disturbed about their behavior, and in most cases, the behavior is socially harmless because it is done in private and does not involve the infliction of harm on others. Fetishism is one of the most common secondary diagnoses of persons with other types of paraphilias, however (Abel & Osborn, 1992). That is, many people who have fetishes also engage in other atypical sexual practices, including pedophilia, exhibitionism, and voyeurism. Thus, for some people, fetishes are part of a larger pattern of atypical sexual behaviors including behaviors that have victims.

Sexual Sadism and Sexual Masochism

sexual sadism
sexual gratification obtained through inflicting pain and humiliation on one's partner

sexual masochism
sexual gratification obtained through experiencing pain and humiliation at the hands of one's partner

sadomasochism
pattern of sexual rituals between a sexually sadistic "giver" and a sexually masochistic "receiver"

Sexual sadism and **masochism** are two separate diagnoses, although sadistic and masochistic sexual practices often are considered together as a pattern referred to as **sadomasochism.** The sexual sadist gains sexual gratification by inflicting pain and humiliation on his or her sex partner. The sexual masochist gains sexual gratification by suffering pain or humiliation during sex. Some people occasionally engage in moderately sadistic or masochistic behaviors during sex or simulate such behaviors without actually carrying through with the infliction of pain or suffering. Persons who are diagnosed as sexual sadists or masochists engage in these behaviors as their preferred or exclusive form of sexual gratification.

The sexual rituals of sadists and masochists typically involve practices of bondage and domination. One partner is bound, gagged, and immobilized and then is subjected by the other partner to sexual acts, beatings, whippings, electrical shock, burning, cutting, stabbing, strangulation, torture, mutilation, and even death. The partner who is the victim in such encounters may be a masochist and a willing victim or may be a nonconsenting victim on whom the sadist carries out his or her wishes. A variety of props may be used in such encounters, including black leather garments, chains, shackles, whips, harnesses, and ropes. Men are much more likely than women to enjoy sadomasochistic sex, both in the roles of sadist and of masochist (Breslow, Evans, & Langlers, 1985). Some women find such activities exciting, but many consent to them only to please their partners or because they are paid to do so, and some are unconsenting victims of sadistic men.

Although sadomasochistic sex between consenting adults typically does not result in physical injury, the activities can get out of control or go too far. Particularly dangerous activities are those that involve sexual arousal by oxygen deprivation, obtained by hanging, by putting plastic bags or masks over the head, or by severe chest compression. Accidents and equipment failure can result in death.

Sadomasochistic practices may be considered just another form of sexual practice by some people, but they can be dangerous.

 What kinds of personality characteristics might differentiate people who find sadomasochistic practices sexually arousing from people who do not?

Voyeurism, Exhibitionism, and Frotteurism

Voyeurism involves secretly watching another person undressing, bathing, doing things in the nude, or engaged in sex as a preferred or exclusive form of sexual arousal. For a diagnosis to be made, the voyeuristic behavior must be repetitive over 6 months and compulsive. The person being observed must be unaware of it and would be upset if he or she knew about it. Almost all voyeurs are men who watch women. They typically masturbate while watching or shortly after watching women. Part of what makes the behavior exciting is the danger of being caught and the knowledge that the women would be frightened or angry if they knew they were being watched.

voyeurism
obtainment of sexual arousal by compulsively and secretly watching another person undressing, bathing, engaging in sex, or being naked

exhibitionism
obtainment of sexual gratification by exposing one's genitals to involuntary observers

Case Study • Benjamin is a peeper. At night he takes out his high-powered binoculars and goes to the roof of his apartment building. From there, he can see into the windows of several other apartments in neighboring buildings. Most nights, he observes at least one event that causes him to be extremely sexually aroused. It might be a woman undressing or taking a bath, a couple engaged in foreplay or intercourse, or an individual masturbating alone. Benjamin will usually masturbate with one hand as he watches through the binoculars with the other hand, until he ejaculates.

Exhibitionism is in some ways the mirror image of voyeurism. The exhibitionist obtains sexual gratification by exposing his or her genitals to involuntary observers who are usually complete strangers. In the vast majority of cases, the exhibitionist is a man who bares all to surprised women. He typically confronts women in a public place, such as a park, a bus, or a subway, either with his genitals already exposed or by flashing open his coat to expose his bare genitals. He then may begin to openly masturbate. His arousal comes from observing the victim's surprise, fear, or disgust or from a fantasy that his victim is becoming sexually aroused. His behavior is often compulsive and impulsive: He feels a sense of excitement, fear, restlessness, and sexual arousal and then feels compelled to find relief by exhibiting himself.

Voyeurs gain sexual pleasure by watching an unknowing victim undress, bathe, or engage in sex.

> **Case Study** • A 27-year-old engineer requested consultation at a psychiatric clinic because of irresistible urges to exhibit his penis to female strangers. At age 18, for reasons unknown to himself, he first experienced an overwhelming desire to engage in exhibitionism. He sought situations in which he was alone with a woman he did not know. As he approached her, he would become sexually excited. He would then walk up to her and display his erect penis. He found that her shock and fear further stimulated him, and usually he would then ejaculate. He also fantasized past encounters while masturbating.
>
> He feels guilty and ashamed after exhibiting himself and vows never to repeat it. Nevertheless, the desire often overwhelms him, and the behavior recurs frequently, usually at periods of tension. (adapted from Spitzer et al., 1994, pp. 117–118)

Exhibitionists are more likely than most sex offenders to get caught, in part because of the public nature of their behavior but also because some of them seem to invite arrest by doing things like repeatedly returning to places where they have already exhibited themselves. It may be that the danger of being caught heightens their arousal. Exhibitionists are also likely to continue their behavior after having been caught.

Frotteurism is another paraphilia that often co-occurs with voyeurism and exhibitionism. The frotteurist gains sexual gratification by rubbing against and fondling parts of the body of a nonconsenting person. Often, the frotteurist engages in this behavior in public places, such as on a bus or subway. Most frotteurists are young men between 15 and 25 years of age, but little else is known about this disorder.

Pedophilia

The most troubling and most common paraphilia is **pedophilia.** Pedophiles are sexually attracted to children and prefer to engage in sex with children rather than with other adults. The diagnosis of pedophilia generally requires that the sexual encounters be with children under the age of 13 and initiated by persons 16 years old or older and at least 5 years older than the children. Laws in most of the United States, however, define child molesting or statutory rape to include adults having sex with persons under the age of 18 (Green, 1993).

Sexual encounters between pedophiles and their child victims are often brief, although they may recur frequently. The contact most often consists of the pedophile exposing and touching the child's genitals (Abel & Osborn, 1992). Other pedophiles perform fellatio (orally stimulating the penis) or cunnilingus (orally stimulating the female genitals) on children or penetrate children's vaginas, mouths, or anuses with their fingers, foreign objects, or penises. Pedophiles often threaten children with harm, physically restrain them, or tell them that they will punish them or loved ones of the children if the children do not comply with the pedophiles' wishes. Pedophiles may try to convince children that they are only showing love to the children through their actions.

Most pedophiles are heterosexual men abusing young girls (Cole, 1992; Finkelhor, 1984). Homosexual men who are pedophiles typically abuse young boys. Women can be pedophiles, but this is much more rare. Sexual abuse of children is not a rare occurrence. The number of children abused in the United States is estimated to be over 400,000 per year (Finkelhor & Dzuiba-Leatherman, 1994). About 60 percent of these children are under 12 years of age. Only about 1 in 10 of these cases is reported to the authorities. Most abusers are family members or acquaintances of the children. Some pedophiles develop elaborate plans for gaining access to the children, such as winning the trust of their mothers or marrying their mothers, trading children with other pedophiles, or in rare cases, abducting children or adopting children from foreign countries (APA, 1994).

> **Case Study** • Dr. Crone, a 35-year-old, single, child psychiatrist, has been arrested and convicted of fondling several neighborhood girls, ages 6 to 12. Friends and colleagues were shocked and dismayed, as he had been considered by all to be particularly caring and supportive of children.

frotteurism
obtainment of sexual gratification by rubbing one's genitals against or fondling the body parts of a nonconsenting person

pedophilia
adult obtainment of sexual gratification by engaging in sexual activities with young children

> Dr. Crone's first sexual experience was at age 6, when a 15-year-old female camp counselor performed fellatio on him several times over the course of the summer—an experience that he had always kept to himself. As he grew older, he was surprised to notice that the age range of girls who attracted him sexually did not change, and he continued to have recurrent erotic urges and fantasies about girls between the ages of 6 and 12. Whenever he masturbated, he would fantasize about a girl in that age range, and on a couple of occasions over the years, he had felt himself to be in love with such a youngster.
>
> Intellectually, Dr. Crone knew that others would disapprove of his many sexual involvements with young girls. He never believed, however, that he had caused any of these youngsters harm, feeling instead that they were simply sharing pleasurable feelings together. He frequently prayed for help and that his actions would go undetected. He kept promising himself that he would stop, but the temptations were such that he could not. (adapted from Spitzer et al., 1994, pp. 187–188)

Many pedophiles have poor interpersonal skills, and feel intimidated when interacting sexually with adults. Others harbor strong hostility toward women and carry out this hostility in antisocial acts toward children (Langevin, 1992). One study found that four of five pedophiles were sexually abused as children (Groth, 1979). They may have learned that it was acceptable for adults to sexually abuse children or may be acting out their childhood traumas in an attempt to gain mastery over those traumas or inflict harm on others the way they were harmed.

Mental health experts are divided over whether pedophiles should be viewed primarily as persons with a psychiatric disorder that needs treating or as criminals who should be incarcerated. Even those who view pedophilia primarily as a disorder to be treated tend to agree that pedophiles should be prevented from their behaviors, often through incarceration. Some clinicians, however, feel unable to empathize with pedophiles to the point of being able to treat them and believe that the resources of the mental health system should be directed toward the victims of the pedophiles rather than the pedophiles themselves.

 How do you stand on this controversy? If pedophiles do have a psychological disorder, should they be held criminally responsible for their behaviors? How should they be dealt with if caught?

The impact on the child victim of the pedophile can be great. The most frequent symptoms shown by sexually abused children are fearfulness, post-traumatic stress disorder, conduct disorder and hyperactivity, sexualized behaviors (promiscuity and sexual behavior inappropriate for their ages), and poor self-esteem (Kendall-Tackett, Williams, & Finkelhor, 1993). More severe symptoms are experienced by children who endure frequent abuse over a long period, who are penetrated by perpetrators, who are abused by family members (typically fathers or stepfathers), and whose mothers do not provide them with support upon learning of the abuse. About two-thirds of victimized children show significant recovery from their symptoms within 12 to 18 months following cessation of the abuse, but significant numbers of abused children continue to experience psychological problems even into adulthood (Burnam, Stein, Golding, & Siegel, 1988; Kendall-Tackett et al., 1993).

Causes of Paraphilias

Many of the paraphilias may have similar causes, which may account for the fact that many paraphilics engage in a number of different paraphilic behaviors. Over 90 percent of paraphilics are men. This may be because paraphilic behavior often involves the acting out of hostile or aggressive impulses, which may be more common in men than in women and certainly are more socially sanctioned for men than for women. Attempts to link paraphilic behavior, particularly sexually aggressive paraphilias, to testosterone abnormalities have met with limited success (Langevin, 1992). Similarly, although some studies have found links between other hormones or endocrine abnormalities and paraphilias, no consistent biological cause of the paraphilias has been found. Alcohol and drug abuse are common among paraphilics (Langevin, 1992). These substances may disinhibit the paraphilic so that he acts out his fantasy. The abuse may also be the consequence of knowing one has unacceptable sexual desires and activities or part of a deeper psychological disturbance that also leads to the paraphilia.

Freud viewed paraphilias as the result of arrested psychological development or regression to childhood forms of sexual arousal (Freud, 1905). He argued that children could be sexually aroused by a myriad of people and objects but that, through proper socialization, they learn to repress their sexual desires for anything except other people. Persons with paraphilias either had been fixated at an early stage of sexual development or regressed back to an earlier stage. Psychoanalyst Robert Stoller (1975) argued that the paraphilias are symbolic reenactments of childhood traumas in which the paraphilic is unconsciously taking revenge on adults who inflicted harm on him as a child.

Behavioral theories of the paraphilias view them as the results of chance classical conditioning (McGuire, Carlisle, & Young, 1965). An adolescent male might be masturbating and notice a picture of a horse on the wall in the room. He fleetingly considers what it might be like to have sex with a horse and becomes more aroused at this thought. The next time he masturbates, he might be more drawn to the picture of the horse because it was arousing the last time and begin to incorporate fantasies about horses into his masturbatory fantasies. If this fantasy becomes so strongly associated with sexual arousal for him, he may find ways to act out the fantasy and thus have a fetish. Because men masturbate more than do women, men would be more likely to develop unusual associations with masturbation and thus to develop paraphilias.

Treatments for the Paraphilias

Most paraphilics do not seek treatment for their behaviors. Treatment is often forced upon those who engage in illegal acts (voyeurism, exhibitionism, frotteurism, pedophilia) after they are arrested for breaking the law by engaging in their behaviors. Simple incarceration does little to change these behaviors, and the recidivism rate among convicted sex offenders is very high.

Drastic biological interventions have been tried, primarily with pedophiles and men who commit rape. These formerly included surgery on the centers of the brain thought to control sexual behavior and surgical castration of the testes. These days, sex offenders might be offered antiandrogen drugs that suppress the functioning of the testes, thereby reducing the production of testosterone and possibly reducing the sex drive. These drugs are typically used in conjunction with psychotherapy and can be useful for hypersexual men who are motivated to change their behavior (Cole, 1992).

Insight-oriented therapies alone have not proven extremely successful in changing paraphilics' behavior. Behavior modification therapies are most commonly used to treat paraphilics and can be successful if paraphilics are willing to change their behavior. **Aversion therapy** is used to extinguish paraphilics' sexual responses to objects or situations they find arousing. During such therapy, paraphilics might receive painful but harmless electric shocks while viewing photographs of what arouse them (such as children) or while actually touching objects that arouse them (such as women's panties). **Desensitization** procedures may be used to reduce paraphilics' anxiety about engaging in normal sexual encounters with other adults. For example, paraphilics might be taught relaxation exercises, which they then use to control their anxiety as they gradually build up fantasies of interacting sexually with other adults in ways that are fulfilling to them and their partners (Wincze, 1989).

Because many paraphilics have deficits in interpersonal and social skills, therapists might teach them skills for approaching and interacting with people they find attractive, in socially acceptable ways (Cole, 1992). Role-plays might be used to allow the paraphilic

aversion therapy
treatment that involves the pairing of unpleasant stimuli with deviant or maladaptive sources of pleasure in order to induce an *aversive* reaction to the formerly pleasurable stimulus

desensitization
treatment used to reduce anxiety by rendering a previously threatening stimulus innocuous by repeated and guided exposure to the stimulus under nonthreatening circumstances

practice in initiating contact and eventually negotiating a positive sexual encounter with another person. Finally, group therapy in which paraphilics come together to support each other through changes in their behavior can be helpful.

Summing Up · Paraphilias

- The paraphilias are a group of disorders in which people's sexual activity is focused on (1) nonhuman objects, (2) nonconsenting adults, (3) suffering or humiliation of oneself or one's partner, or (4) children.
- Fetishism involves the use of inanimate objects (such as panties or shoes) as the preferred or exclusive source of sexual arousal or gratification. One elaborate fetish is transvestism, in which a man dresses in the clothes of a woman to sexually arouse himself.
- Voyeurism involves observing another person nude or engaging in sexual acts, without that person's knowledge or consent, in order to become sexually aroused.
- Exhibitionism involves exposing oneself to another without his or her consent, in order to become sexually aroused.
- Frotteurism involves rubbing up against another without his or her consent, in order to become sexually aroused.
- Sadism and masochism involve physically harming another or allowing oneself to be harmed for sexual arousal.
- Pedophilia involves engaging in sexual acts with a child.
- Most paraphilics are men. Their behavior may represent the acting out of hostile or aggressive impulses.
- Behavioral theories suggest that paraphilics' sexual preferences are the results of chance classical conditioning.
- Treatment of the paraphilias can include biological interventions to reduce sexual drive, behavioral interventions to decondition arousal to paraphillic objects, and training in interpersonal and social skills.

Gender Identity Disorder

For most people, their perception of themselves as male or female, referred to as **gender identity,** is a fundamental component of their self-concept. Gender identity differs from **gender role,** which is a person's belief about how he or she should behave as a male or female in society. Many females choose to engage in behaviors considered part of the masculine gender role, such as playing aggressive sports or pursuing competitive careers, but still have a fundamental sense of themselves as female. Similarly, many males choose to engage in behaviors considered part of the feminine gender role, such as caring for children or cooking and sewing, but still have a fundamental sense of themselves as male.

Gender identity and gender roles differ from **sexual orientation,** which is one's preference for sexual partners of the opposite sex or of the same sex. Most gay men have a fundamental sense of themselves as male and therefore male gender identities; most lesbians have a fundamental sense of themselves as female and therefore female gender identities. Although homosexual men and women are often portrayed as violating stereotypic gender roles, many adhere to traditional roles for their genders, except in their choices of sexual partners.

Gender identity disorder is diagnosed when individuals believe that they were born with the wrong sex's genitals and are fundamentally persons of the opposite sex. Gender identity disorder of childhood is a rare condition in which a child persistently rejects his or her anatomic sex and desires to be or insists he or she is a member of the opposite sex. Girls with this disorder seek masculine-type activities and male peer groups to a degree far beyond that of a "tomboy." Sometimes these girls will express the belief that they will eventually grow penises. Boys with the disorder seek feminine-type activities and

gender identity
one's perception of oneself as male or female

gender role
what society considers to be the appropriate set of behaviors for males or females

sexual orientation
one's preference for partners of the same or opposite sex with respect to attraction and sexual desire

gender identity disorder
condition in which a person believes that he or she was born with the wrong sex's genitals and is fundamentally a person of the opposite sex

transsexualism
condition of chronic discomfort with one's gender and genitals as well as a desire to be rid of one's genitals and to live as a member of the opposite sex

female peer groups and tend to begin cross-dressing in girls' clothes at a very early age. They express disgust with their penises and wish they would disappear (Green, 1986). Boys with gender identity disturbances are more likely to be brought by their parents for counseling than are girls with the disturbance, probably because parents are more concerned about violations of gender roles in boys than in girls.

Gender identity disorder in adulthood is referred to as **transsexualism.** Transsexuals experience a chronic discomfort and sense of inappropriateness with their gender and genitals, wish to be rid of them, and want to live as members of the opposite sex. Transsexuals will often dress in the clothes of the opposite sex, but unlike the transvestite, they do not do this to gain sexual arousal. They simply believe they are putting on the clothes of the gender they really belong to. Transsexuals who can afford it may seek sex-change operations. The sexual preferences of transsexuals vary. Some are asexual, having little interest in either sex, some are heterosexual, and some are homosexual. Transsexualism is rare, with an estimated prevalence of 1 per 30,000 males and 1 per 100,000 females (Katchadourian, 1989).

> **Case Study •** Stephanie was 30 when she first attended our clinic. She gave a history of conviction that she was, in fact, male and wished to rid herself of identifiably female attributes and acquire male traits and features. She said she had been cross-living and employed as a male for about 1 year, following the breakdown of a 10-year marriage. She was taking testosterone prescribed by her family physician. She presented at our clinic with a request for removal of her uterus and ovaries.
>
> She did not give a childhood history of tomboy attitudes, thoughts, or behavior. She said social interaction with other children, boys or girls, was minimal. Desperate for a friend, she fantasized "an articulate and strong" boy, exactly her own age, named Ronan. They were always together and they talked over everything: thoughts and feelings and the events of her life. Cross-dressing in her father's clothing also began during childhood. There was no history of sexual arousal associated with or erotic fantasy involving cross-dressing.
>
> Puberty at age 12 and the accompanying bodily changes apparently did not overly distress Stephanie. Sexual and romantic feelings focused on "slender, feminine-appearing men." At 16, Stephanie met such a man and they were together for 2 years. Her next romantic involvement was with a "male bisexual transvestite." Sexual interaction according to Stephanie, included experimentation with drugs and "role reversals." She and her partner cross-dressed, and Stephanie took the dominant and active role. During vaginal sex, she imagined herself as a male with another male.
>
> At 19, she met a slender, good-looking man. They were compatible and married soon after. The marriage was a success. Stephanie's preferred position for intercourse was with both kneeling, she behind her husband, rubbing her pubic area against him while masturbating him. She would imagine she had a penis and was penetrating him.
>
> Stephanie's marriage broke down after the couple's business failed. She decided to live full-time in the male role as Jacob. While on the West Coast, she started treatment with male hormones. She moved back east and presented at our clinic for assessment. She saw herself as a male, primarily attracted to gay or gay-appearing males. She was uninterested in relationships with women, except perhaps as purely sexual encounters of short duration. (adapted from Dickey & Stephens, 1995, pp. 442–443)

Causes and Treatment of Gender Identity Disorder

Gender identity is the result of a number of biological and social factors, including chromosomes, hormones, and socialization. Gender identity disorder could result from variations in development of any of these factors, although the specific causes of the disorder are unknown. Transsexuals do not consistently show hormonal abnormalities or histories of troubled upbringing. Most transsexuals say they felt they were the wrong gender even as children. Many transsexuals are so disturbed by their misassignment of gender that they develop alcohol and drug-abuse problems and other psychological disorders, but these seem to be consequences rather than causes of their transsexualism (Roback & Lothstein, 1986).

Sex change or sex reassignment requires a series of surgeries and hormone treatments, often taking 2 or more years. Before undertaking any of these medical procedures, patients are usually asked to dress and live in their new gender for a year or two, to ensure that they are confident about their decisions before proceeding. The surgical procedures involve first removing the existing reproductive organs (testes and penis or ovaries and breasts) and then constructing new genitals (vagina or penis), using transplanted tissue from other parts of the body. The construction of male genitals for a female-to-male re-assignment is technically more difficult, and while the artificial penis will allow urination, it cannot achieve a natural erection. Follow-up studies suggest that when patients are carefully selected for such sex reassignment procedures based on their motivation for change and their overall psychological health and given psychological counseling to assist them through the change, the outcome tends to be positive (Lindemalm, Korlin, & Udderberg, 1986). Although many of these patients are unable to experience orgasm during sex, most are satisfied with their sex lives and are psychologically well-adjusted to their new genders.

 Do you think sex-change operations should be covered by insurance policies? Why or why not?

Nowhere is the interplay of biological, psychological, and social forces more apparent than in matters of sexuality. Biological factors influence gender identity, sexual orientation, and sexual functioning. These factors can be greatly moderated by psychological and social factors, however. The meaning to people of a sexual dysfunction, an unusual sexual practice, or an atypical gender identity is heavily influenced by their attitudes toward their sexuality and by the reactions they get from people around them. In addition, as we saw with sexual dysfunctions, purely psychological and social conditions can cause a person's body to stop functioning as it normally would.

Bio-Psycho-Social INTEGRATION

Chapter Summary

The sexual response cycle can be divided into the desire, excitement, plateau, orgasm, and resolution phases. Sexual desire is manifested in sexual thoughts and fantasies, initiation of or participation in sexual activities, and awareness of sexual cues from others. The excitement phase consists of a psychological experience of arousal and pleasure and the physiological changes known as *vasocongestion* (filling of blood vessels and tissues with blood) and *myotonia* (muscle tension). During the plateau phase, excitement remains at a high but stable level. The excitement and plateau phases are followed by orgasm, which involves the discharge of the built-up neuromuscular tension. In males, orgasm involves rhythmic contractions of the prostate, seminal vesicles, vas deferens, and the entire length of the penis and urethra, accompanied by the ejaculation of semen. Males experience a refractory period following orgasm during which they cannot be aroused to another orgasm. In females, orgasm involves rhythmic contractions of the orgasmic platform and more irregular contractions of the uterus. Females do not have a refractory period. Following orgasm, the entire musculature of the body relaxes, and men and women tend to experience a state of deep relaxation, the stage known as *resolution*.

Occasional problems with sexual functioning are extremely common. To qualify for a diagnosis of a sexual dysfunction, a person must be experiencing a problem that causes significant distress or interpersonal difficulty, that is not the result of another

Axis I disorder, and that is not due exclusively to the direct effects of substance use or medical illness. The psychological factors leading to sexual dysfunction most commonly involve negative attitudes toward sex, traumatic or stressful experiences, or conflicts with sexual partners. A variety of biological factors, including medical illnesses, side effects of drugs, nervous system injury, and hormonal deficiencies, can cause sexual dysfunctions.

Sexual desire disorders (hypoactive sexual desire disorder and sexual aversion disorder) are among the most common sexual dysfunctions. Persons with these disorders experience chronically lowered or absent desire for sex. The sexual arousal disorders include female sexual arousal disorder and male erectile disorder (formerly called *impotence*). Women with female orgasmic disorder experience a persistent or recurrent delay in or complete absence of orgasm, after having reached the excitement phase of the sexual response cycle. Men with premature ejaculation persistently experience ejaculation (after minimal sexual stimulation) before, on, or shortly after penetration and before they wish it. Men with male orgasmic disorder experience a persistent or recurrent delay in or absence of orgasm following the excitement phase of the sexual response cycle. The sexual pain disorders include dyspareunia, which is genital pain associated with intercourse, and vaginismus, in which a woman experiences involuntary contraction of the muscles surrounding the outer third of the vaginal when the vagina is penetrated.

Fortunately, most of the sexual dysfunctions can be treated successfully. The psychological treatments combine psychotherapy focused on the personal concerns of the individual with the dysfunction and on the conflicts between the individual and his or her partner and sex therapy designed to decrease inhibitions about sex and to teach new techniques for optimal sexual enjoyment. One important set of techniques is sensate focus exercises. First, partners spend time gently touching each other, focusing on the sensations and communicating what feels good, without touching the genitals. Second, partners spend time in direct genital stimulation but without attempting to have intercourse. Third, partners begin having intercourse but remaining focused on enhancing and sustaining pleasure rather than on orgasm and performance.

Men with premature ejaculation can be helped with the stop-start technique or the squeeze technique. In the stop-start technique, a man repeatedly halts stimulation of his penis just before ejaculation until he can control his level of arousal and the timing of ejaculation. In the squeeze technique, a man's partner squeezes the base or top section of his penis just before ejaculation, again until the man learns to control his level of arousal and timing of ejaculation.

The paraphilias are a group of disorders in which the focus of the individual's sexual urges and activities are (1) nonhuman objects, (2) nonconsenting adults, (3) suffering or humiliation of oneself or one's partner, or (4) children. Pedophiles seek sexual gratification with young children. Most pedophiles are heterosexual men seeking sex with young girls. Many pedophiles have poor interpersonal skills, feel intimidated when interacting sexually with adults, and are victims of childhood sexual abuse. Others harbor strong hostility toward women and carry out this hostility in antisocial acts toward children. The impact of sexual abuse by a pedophile on a child is great, sometimes extending throughout the child's life.

Voyeurism involves secretly watching another person undressing, bathing, doing things in the nude, or engaged in sex as a preferred or exclusive form of sexual arousal. To qualify for a diagnosis, the voyeuristic behavior must be repetitive and compulsive. The person being observed must be unaware of it and would be upset if he or she knew about it. Almost all voyeurs are men who watch women. Voyeurs typically masturbate during or shortly after watching women.

Exhibitionism is in some ways the mirror image of voyeurism. The exhibitionist obtains sexual gratification by exposing his or her genitals to involuntary observers who are usually complete strangers. In the vast majority of cases, the exhibitionist is a man who bares all to surprised women. He typically confronts women in public places, such as a park, a bus, or a subway, either with his genitals already exposed or by flashing open his coat to expose his bare genitals. He then may begin to openly masturbate. His arousal comes from observing the victim's surprise, fear, or disgust. His behavior is often compulsive and impulsive: He feels a sense of excitement, fear, restlessness, and sexual arousal and then feels compelled to find relief by exhibiting himself.

Frotteurism is another paraphilia that often co-occurs with voyeurism and exhibitionism. The frotteurist gains sexual gratification by rubbing against and fondling parts of the body of a nonconsenting person. In order to qualify for a diagnosis, this behavior has to be repetitive and compulsive and represent a preferred way of gaining sexual gratification.

The sexual sadist gains sexual gratification by inflicting pain and humiliation on his or her sex partner. The sexual masochist gains sexual gratification by suffering pain or humiliation during sex. Some people occasionally engage in moderately sadistic or masochistic behaviors during sex or simulate such behaviors without actually carrying through with the infliction of pain or suffering. Persons who are diagnosed as sexual sadists or masochists engage in these behaviors as their preferred or exclusive forms of sexual gratification. The sexual rituals of sadists and masochists typically involve practices of bondage and domination.

The final type of paraphilia is fetishism, which involves the use of isolated body parts or inanimate objects as the preferred or exclusive sources of sexual arousal or gratification. A particular form of fetish is transvestism, in which an individual dresses in clothes of the opposite sex (usually involving a man dressing in women's clothes) in order to become sexually aroused.

Gender identity disorder is diagnosed when an individual believes that he or she was born with the wrong sex's genitals and is fundamentally a person of the opposite sex. Gender identity disorder of childhood is a rare condition in which a child persistently rejects his or her anatomic sex and desires to be or insists he or she is a member of the opposite sex. Gender identity disorder in adulthood is referred to as *transsexualism*. Transsexuals experience a chronic discomfort and sense of inappropriateness with their gender and genitals, wish to be rid of them, and want to live as members of the opposite sex. Transsexuals will often dress in the clothes of the opposite sex, but unlike transvestites, they do not do this to gain sexual arousal.

Key Terms

sexual dysfunctions 386
sexual desire 387
arousal 387
vasocongestion 387
myotonia 387
plateau 387
orgasm 387
resolution 387
hypoactive sexual desire
   disorder 389
sexual aversion
   disorder 390
sexual arousal
   disorders 391
female sexual arousal
   disorder 391

male erectile disorder
   391
female orgasmic
   disorder 392
premature ejaculation
   392
male orgasmic
   disorder 393
dyspareunia 393
vaginismus 393
sensate focus therapy
   400
paraphilias 406
fetishism 407
transvestism 408
sexual sadism 408

sexual masochism 408
sadomasochism 408
voyeurism 409
exhibitionism 409
frotteurism 410
pedophilia 410
aversion therapy 412
desensitization 412
gender identity 413
gender role 413
sexual orientation 413
gender identity
   disorder 413
transsexualism 414

Application

Practicing Safe Sex

Sexually transmitted diseases (STDs) such as AIDS (Acquired Immune Deficiency Syndrome), chlamydia, herpes, genital warts, gonorrhea, and syphilis often have no obvious signs or symptoms, so you cannot know if a potential sexual partner has one by just looking at him or her. Thus, it is essential to practice safe sex if you are going to be sexually active.

What does practicing safe sex mean? Here are some general tips*:

1. Have monogamous sexual relationships: Have sex with only one person who, in turn, is having sex only with you. If you or your partner change sexual partners frequently, your risk of contracting a sexually transmitted disease is increased.

2. Know your partner's sexual history before you engage in sexual activity. It can be very difficult to talk about your partner's history or your own. Volunteer information about your own history and then ask your partner about his or hers. Persist if your partner tries to brush your concerns aside and be prepared to postpone or refuse sexual contact if your partner will not answer your questions.

3. Avoid sexual activity if you or your partner might have been exposed to any sexually transmitted disease. Most of the sexually transmitted diseases can be treated medically, and sex can be resumed when the disease is cured or under control.

4. Wash your genitals after sexual contact; it helps to reduce risk but does not eliminate it.

5. Urinate immediately after intercourse to help flush out some germs.

6. Do not have sex under the influence of alcohol. Alcohol can lead you to practice unsafe sex, it can lead to misunderstandings between partners about what sexual activities are acceptable, and it can impair your ability to resist unwanted sexual activities.

7. Using condoms for vaginal and anal intercourse is the best means of preventing the spread of sexually transmitted diseases:

   • Use a condom EVERY time you have sex.

   • Put condoms on during foreplay, before there is any pre-ejaculatory fluid.

   • After ejaculation and before the penis relaxes, remove the condom by holding it around the base and withdrawing it from the penis.

   • Use another condom if sex is repeated.

   • Store condoms in a cool, dry place (not a wallet or the glove compartment of a car).

   • Never test condoms by inflating them or stretching them.

   • Never use oil-based lubricants like petroleum jelly (Vaseline) on condoms.

   • Never reuse condoms.

8. Oral sex can also spread STDs. Males should wear condoms during oral sex. Partners performing oral sex on women should use dental dams or other latex barriers to protect their mouths from direct exposure to vaginal fluids.

Many people do not practice safe sex because they feel it will reduce spontaneity and excitement in sexual encounters. However, condom use can be eroticized so that it becomes a part of foreplay. Also, knowing that you are practicing safe sex can reduce fear and therefore increase your ability to enjoy sexual encounters. Most importantly, protecting yourself from sexually transmitted diseases, particularly AIDS, should always be a higher priority than having a little more spontaneity in any given sexual encounter. ■

*Adapted from "Breaking the STD Chain," distributed by Cowell Student Health Center and the Office of Residential Education, Stanford University.

chapter 12 Substance Use Disorders

Intoxication, Withdrawal, Abuse, and Dependence

Substance intoxication is a characteristic set of behavioral and psychological symptoms that occur as the direct result of the physiological effects of a substance on the central nervous system. Substance withdrawal is a set of physiological and behavioral symptoms that result when people who have been using substances heavily for prolonged periods of time curtail their use of the substances. Substance abuse is diagnosed when people's recurrent use of substances results in failure to fulfill their important obligations, when they repeatedly use substances in hazardous situations, or when they repeatedly have legal or social problems as a result of substance use. Substance dependence is diagnosed when people show tolerance or withdrawal from substances or when they compulsively use substances despite experiencing significant social, occupational, psychological, or medical problems as a result of their use.

Alcohol

People who abuse or are dependent on alcohol experience a wide range of social and interpersonal problems and are at risk for serious health problems. Women and some groups of Asian descent are less prone to alcohol-related disorders than are men and some other ethnic groups.

Other Depressants: Benzodiazepines, Barbiturates, and Inhalants

The benzodiazepines, barbiturates, and inhalants are depressants of the central nervous system and produce intoxication and withdrawal symptoms similar to those produced by alcohol.

Stimulants: Cocaine and Amphetamines

Cocaine and amphetamines are two central nervous system stimulants that activate the parts of the brain that register reward or pleasure. Symptoms of intoxication with these drugs can include euphoria, self-confidence, and alertness but also agitation and paranoia. Withdrawal symptoms from these drugs can include severe depression. Abuse and dependence can develop quickly with these drugs.

Opioids

Morphine and heroin are common opioids and initially cause euphoria, followed by a state of lethargy and clouded thinking. Withdrawal symptoms can include dysphoria, agitation, and a craving for more opioids

Hallucinogens, PCP, and Cannabis

The hallucinogens, PCP, and cannabis differ somewhat but all produce perceptual illusions and distortions. The other symptoms produced by these drugs depend on the amount taken and can range from a sense of peace and tranquillity to feelings of unreality and violence.

Nicotine

Nicotine is legal for use by adults but is one of the most addictive substances people use. Nicotine causes lung cancer, bronchitis, emphysema, and probably coronary heart disease.

Theories of Substance Use, Abuse, and Dependence

The substances of abuse and dependence have powerful effects on the brain, but most people either never try addictive substances or do not become dependent on them if they do try them. Biological theories of vulnerability to substance disorders attribute this vulnerability largely to genetic predispositions. Other theories see alcoholism and other substance dependencies as manifestations of depression. Psychosocial theories view substance dependence as the result of environments that reinforce substance use, particularly in times of stress, and beliefs that substances can help one cope with stress.

Treatment for Substance Disorders

The first step in the treatment of substance disorders is detoxification. Then drugs may be used to help ease the withdrawal symptoms or to reduce the reinforcing effects of substances. Alcoholics Anonymous provides the most widely used psychosocial treatment for alcoholics. Behavioral treatments can be used to extinguish substance use behaviors, and cognitive therapies can be used to identify those situations and thoughts that motivate substance use.

Gender and Substance Use

Men may be more prone than women to substance disorders because they have a greater genetic vulnerability to the disorders, because they are less sensitive to the intoxicating effects of substances at lower doses, and because they are reinforced more or punished less for substance use.

Cross-Cultural Perspectives on Substance Use and Prevention

Cultures vary greatly in their attitudes toward substance use and in their actions toward people who are substance abusers or dependent. It is not clear that social policies used in one culture can be effective in other cultures.

Bio-Psycho-Social Integration
Chapter Summary
Key Terms
Application: *Promoting Responsible Alcohol Use in Young Adults*

Refrain to-night,
And that shall lend a kind of easiness
To the next abstinence; the next more easy;
For use almost can change the stamp of nature.

—William Shakespeare, *Hamlet* (3:4:165; 1600)

George E. Dunne
The Ferryman's

substance
naturally occurring or synthetically produced product that alters perceptions, thoughts, emotions, and behaviors when ingested, smoked or injected

psychoactive
affecting perceptions, thoughts, emotions, and/or behaviors

drugs
chemicals that alter one's physical and mental state

drug addicts
people who are physically dependent on substances and who suffer from withdrawal when not taking the substances

A **substance** is any natural or synthesized product that has **psychoactive** effects—it changes perceptions, thoughts, emotions, and behaviors. Some of the substances we will discuss in this chapter are cocaine, heroin, and amphetamines. These are popularly referred to as **drugs**, and people who have problems as a result of taking these drugs are often referred to as **drug addicts**. We will use the more neutral term *substance*, however, because some of the disorders we will discuss in this chapter involve substances that you might not normally think of as drugs, such as nicotine and alcohol. Also, as we will see, a person need not be physically dependent on a substance, as is implied by the term *addict*, in order to have problems resulting from taking the substance.

Societies differ in their attitudes about substances with psychoactive effects, some seeing use as a matter of individual choice and others seeing it as a grave public health and security concern. Within the United States, attitudes toward substance use have varied greatly over time and across different subgroups. The American ambivalence toward alcohol use is nicely illustrated in a letter written by former Congressman Billy Mathews in response to a question from one of his constituents: "Dear Congressman, how do you stand on whiskey?" Because the congressman did not know how the constituent stood on alcohol, he fashioned the following safe response (quoted in Marlatt, Larimer, Baer, & Quigley, 1993, p. 462):

> My dear friend, I had not intended to discuss this controversial subject at this particular time. However, I want you to know that I do not shun a controversy. On the contrary, I will take a stand on any issue at any time, regardless of how fraught with controversy it may be. You have asked me how I feel about whiskey. Here is how I stand on the issue.
>
> If when you say whiskey, you mean the Devil's brew; the poison scourge; the bloody monster that defiles innocence, dethrones reason, destroys the home, creates misery, poverty, fear; literally takes the bread from the mouths of little children; if you mean the evil drink that topples the Christian man and woman from the pinnacles of righteous, gracious living into the bottomless pit of degradation and despair, shame and helplessness and hopelessness; then certainly, I am against it with all of my power.
>
> But, if when you say whiskey, you mean the oil of conversation, the philosophic wine, the ale that is assumed when great fellows get together, that puts a song in their hearts and laughter on their lips, and the warm glow of contentment in their eyes; if you mean Christmas cheer; if you mean that stimulating drink that puts the spring in the old gentlemen's step on a frosty morning; if you mean the drink that enables the man to magnify his joy and his happiness and to forget, if only for a little while, life's great tragedies and heartbreaks and sorrows; if you mean that drink, the sale of which pours into our Treasury untold millions of dollars which are used to provide tender care for little crippled children, our blind, our deaf, our pitiful aged and infirm; to build highways, hospitals, and schools; then certainly, I am in favor of it. This is my stand, and I will not compromise. Your congressman.

Many substances come from plants and have been used for medicinal purposes for centuries. As long ago as 1500 B.C., natives in the Andes highlands chewed coca leaves to increase their endurance (Cocores, Pottash, & Gold, 1991). Coca leaves can be manufactured into cocaine. Cocaine was used legally throughout Europe and then America into the twentieth century to relieve fatigue and was an ingredient in the original Coca-Cola drink and over 50 other widely available drinks and elixirs.

Opium, a milky juice produced from the poppy plant, has been used for hundreds of years to relieve pain, particularly in Asian and European countries. The leaves of a plant called *khat* have been chewed in parts of eastern Africa, the Middle East, and South America for hundreds of years to produce a sense of well-being and relief from fatigue. Today, modern derivatives of khat are used to make amphetamines, a class of drugs used to treat attention deficit/hyperactivity disorder, narcolepsy, and obesity and included in over-the-counter cold remedies and appetite suppressants for weight control.

Substances have also been used for religious ceremonies to produce psychological changes important for the ceremonies. For example, the peyote cactus contains a substance that, when chewed, causes people to experience visual hallucinations, in the form of brightly colored lights, or vivid kaleidoscopic visions of geometric forms or of animals and people. The Aztecs and other native groups in Mexico and the Kiowa, Comanche, and other native groups in the United States and Canada have used peyote as part of religious rituals for hundreds of years.

When substances are used not as part of medical treatments or religious or ceremonial rituals but by individuals to change their moods, thoughts, and perceptions, other members of society begin to get nervous. This is because some individuals have great difficulty in using substances in moderation and begin to build their lives around using the substances. Their use of substances may lead to significant problems in their abilities to function in their daily lives—they may shirk their job and family responsibilities, they may act impulsively or bizarrely, and they may endanger their own lives and the lives of others. Such a person is said to have a **substance-related disorder**.

Societies have strong motivations for regulating the use of psychoactive substances. In the United States alone, the use of psychoactive substances for nonmedicinal and nonreligious purposes costs society over $200 billion a year in accidents, crime, health care costs, and lost productivity (Goldstein, 1994). Alcohol alone is associated with over half of the deaths due to accidents, homicides, and suicides.

The prevalence of illegal substance use and abuse increased substantially in the last four decades. In the early 1960s, less than 5 percent of the population of the United States had ever tried an illegal substance such as marijuana, cocaine, or heroin. In the mid-1990s, fully one-third of the U.S. population admitted to having tried an illegal substance at some time in their lives, and over 10 percent had used in the past year (NIDA, 1995). Most people who ever use an illegal substance do so before the age of 20, and the rate of substance use among youth has increased especially dramatically. Recent surveys find that about 20 percent of adolescents have tried an illegal substance by age 17, and 46 percent of young adults have tried an illegal substance by the age of 25 (NIDA, 1995).

Much substance use by adolescents and young adults is experimental—typically, young people try alcohol or marijuana and maybe even heroin or cocaine a few times but do not use them chronically or continue to use them as they grow older. Some substances, however, have such powerful reinforcing effects on the brain that many people who try these substances, even experimentally, find themselves craving more of the substances and have a difficult time resisting taking the substances. This seems especially true of a relatively new form of cocaine: crack. In addition, some people have a greater vulnerability to becoming "hooked" psychologically or physically on substances, so even a little experimentation may be very dangerous for them.

There are four substance-related conditions recognized by the DSM-IV: *substance intoxication, substance withdrawal, substance abuse,* and *substance dependence.* In the first part of this chapter, we will discuss the criteria for each of these conditions. In the remainder of this chapter, we will discuss how these conditions are manifested in the context of the substances most commonly linked to them. These substances can be grouped into the following four categories: (1) central nervous system depressants, including alcohol, barbiturates, benzodiazepines, and inhalants; (2) central nervous system stimulants,

Cocaine was an ingredient in the original Coca-Cola, and its effects were advertised freely.

substance-related disorder
inability to use a substance in moderation and/or the intentional use of a substance to change one's thoughts, feelings, and/or behaviors, leading to impairment in work, academic, personal, or social endeavors

Alcohol and other substances are involved in over half of all traffic accidents.

Table 12.1 Diagnoses Recognized by the DSM-IV for Each Class of Substances				
	Intoxication	Withdrawal	Abuse	Dependence
Alcohol	X	X	X	X
Barbiturates	X	X	X	X
Benzodiazepines	X	X	X	X
Inhalants	X		X	X
Cocaine	X	X	X	X
Amphetamines	X	X	X	X
Caffeine	X			
Opioids	X	X	X	X
Hallucinogens	X		X	X
Phencyclidine	X		X	X
Cannabis	X		X	X
Nicotine		X		X

including cocaine and amphetamines; (3) opioids; and (4) hallucinogens, phencyclidine (PCP), and cannabis. Intoxication, withdrawal, abuse, and dependence can occur with most although not all of these substances (see Table 12.1).

There are many other substances, listed in Table 12.2, that more rarely lead to substance-related disorders. Although most people exposed to the substances listed in Table 12.2 either experience no psychoactive effects or only mild and transient effects, some people experience significant problems in cognition and mood, anxiety, hallucinations, delusions, and seizures when exposed. These people may be given the diagnosis of *other substance-related disorder*.

Two additional substances for which the DSM-IV lists disorders are nicotine and caffeine (see Table 12.1). Although both of these are legal for use (nicotine only for adults), they can have significant negative effects on the users. We will focus on nicotine and address a question that has been raised in recent years: Should this substance be regulated by the government as a drug?

After we discuss specific substances and the disorders associated with them, we will discuss theories of why some people are more prone than others to develop substance-related disorders and what treatments are available for people with substance-related disorders. Most of these theories and treatments focus on people with alcohol-related disorders but have been adapted for people with other disorders. We will also address why there are substantial differences between men and women and among cultures in substance-related disorders. Finally, we will end the chapter discussing ways different

Table 12.2 Other Substances That Can Lead to Substance Use Disorders	
Anesthetics or analgesics	Muscle relaxants
Anticholinergic agents	Nonsteroidal anti-inflammatory medications
Anticonvulsants	Antidepressant medications
Antihistamines	Lead
Blood pressure medications	Rat poisons with strychnine
Antimicrobial medications	Pesticides
Anti-Parkinsonian medications	Nerve gas
Corticosteroids	Antifreeze
Gastrointestinal medications	Carbon monoxide or dioxide

countries have attempted to address the social problems caused by substance use and one program in the United States designed to prevent the development of alcohol-related problems in young people.

Intoxication, Withdrawal, Abuse, and Dependence

Substance intoxication is a set of behavioral and psychological changes that occur as a direct result of the physiological effects of a substance on the central nervous system. When people are intoxicated, their perceptions change and they may see or hear strange things. Their attention is often diminished or they are easily distracted. Their good judgment is gone and they may be unable to "think straight." They cannot control their bodies as well as they normally can, and they may stumble or be too slow or awkward in their reactions. They often either want to sleep a lot or not at all. Their interpersonal interactions change—they may become more gregarious than usual, more withdrawn, or more aggressive and impulsive. People begin to be intoxicated soon after they begin ingesting a substance, and the more they ingest, the more intoxicated they become. Intoxication begins to decline as the amount of substance in people's blood or tissues declines, but symptoms of intoxication may last for hours or days after the substance is no longer detectable in the body.

The specific symptoms of intoxication depend on what substance is taken, how much is taken, how long the substance has been ingested, and the user's tolerance for the substance. Short-term or acute intoxication can produce different symptoms than chronic intoxication. For example, the first time people take a moderate dose of cocaine, they may be outgoing, friendly, and very upbeat. With chronic use over days or weeks, they may begin to withdraw socially and become less gregarious. People's expectations about a substance's effects can also influence the types of symptoms shown. People who expect marijuana to make them relaxed may experience relaxation, whereas people who are frightened of the disinhibition that marijuana creates may experience anxiety, as happened with the woman in the following case study (adapted from Spitzer et al., 1994, pp. 204–205):

substance intoxication
experience of significantly maladaptive behavioral and psychological symptoms due to the effect of a substance on the central nervous system that develops during or shortly after use of the substance

Case Study • In the middle of a rainy October night, a family doctor in a Chicago suburb was awakened by an old friend who begged him to get out of bed and come quickly to a neighbor's house, where he and his wife had been visiting. The caller, Lou Wolff, was very upset because his wife, Sybil, had smoked some marijuana and was "freaking out."

The doctor arrived at the neighbor's house to find Sybil lying on the couch looking quite frantic, unable to get up. She said she was too weak to stand, that she was dizzy, was having palpitations, and could feel her blood "rushing through [her] veins." She kept asking for water because her mouth was so dry she could not swallow. She was sure there was some poison in the marijuana.

Sybil, age 42, was the mother of three teenage boys. She worked as a librarian at a university. She was a very controlled, well-organized woman who prided herself on her rationality. It was she who had asked the neighbors to share some of their high-quality homegrown marijuana with her, because marijuana was a big thing with the students and she "wanted to see what all the fuss was about."

Her husband said that she took four or five puffs on a joint and then wailed, "There's something wrong with me. I can't stand up." Lou and the neighbors tried to calm her, telling her she should just lie down and she would soon feel better; but the more they reassured her, the more convinced she became that something was really wrong with her.

The doctor examined her. The only positive findings were that her heart rate was increased and her pupils dilated. He said to her, "For heaven's sake, Sybil, you're just a little stoned. Go home to bed."

Sybil did go home to bed, where she stayed for 2 days, feeling "spacey" and weak but no longer terribly anxious. She recovered completely and vowed never to smoke marijuana again.

The environment or setting in which the substance is taken can influence the types of symptoms people develop. For example, when people consume a few alcoholic drinks at a party, they may become uninhibited and loud, but when they consume the same amount at home alone, they may become simply tired and depressed. The environment in which people become intoxicated can also influence how maladaptive the intoxication is: People who only drink alcohol at home may be at less risk for causing harm to themselves or others than are people who typically drink at bars and drive home under the influence of alcohol.

Most people have been intoxicated, usually with alcohol, at some time in their lives. The diagnosis of substance intoxication is only given when the behavioral and psychological changes the person experiences are significantly maladaptive in that they cause substantial disruption in the person's social and family relationships, cause occupational or financial problems, or place the individual at significant risk for adverse effects, such as traffic accidents, severe medical complications, or legal problems.

Substance withdrawal involves a set of maladaptive physiological and behavioral symptoms that result when people who have been using substances heavily for prolonged periods of time stop using the substances or greatly reduce their use. The symptoms of withdrawal from a given substance are typically the opposite of the symptoms of intoxication with the same substance. The diagnosis of substance withdrawal is not made unless the withdrawal symptoms cause significant distress or impairment in a person's everyday functioning. For example, although the symptoms of caffeine withdrawal (nervousness, headaches) are annoying to many people, they do not typically cause significant impairment in people's functioning or great distress, and thus caffeine withdrawal is not included as a diagnostic category in the DSM-IV.

The symptoms of withdrawal can begin a few hours after a person stops ingesting a substance or substances that break down quickly in the body, such as alcohol and heroin. The more intense symptoms of withdrawal usually end within a few days to a few weeks. However, withdrawal symptoms, including seizures, may develop several weeks after a person stops taking high doses of substances that take a long time to completely eliminate from the body, such as some antianxiety substances. In addition, subtle physiological signs of withdrawal, such as problems in attention, perception, or motor skills, may be present for many weeks or months after a person stops using a substance.

The diagnosis of **substance abuse** is given when a person's recurrent use of a substance results in significant harmful consequences. There are four categories of harmful consequences that suggest substance abuse (APA, 1994). First, the individual *fails to fulfill important obligations* at work, school, or home. He or she may fail to show up at work or for classes, be unable to concentrate and therefore perform poorly, and perhaps even take the substance at work or at school. Second, the individual *repeatedly uses the substance in situations in which it is physically hazardous to do so*, such as before driving a car or a boat. Third, the individual *repeatedly has legal problems as a result of substance use*, such as arrests for possession of illegal substances or for drunk driving. Fourth, the individual

substance withdrawal
experience of clinically significant distress in social, occupational, or other areas of functioning due to the cessation or reduction of substance use

substance abuse
a diagnosis given when a person's recurrent substance use leads to significant harmful consequences, as manifested by a failure to fulfill obligations at work, school, or home, the use of substances in physically hazardous situations, legal problems, and continued use despite social and legal problems

Each substance causes characteristic symptoms of intoxication and most cause symptoms of withdrawal.

continues to use the substance even though he or she has repeatedly had social or legal prob-lems as a result of the use. A person has to show repeated problems in at least one of these categories within a 12-month period to qualify for a diagnosis of substance abuse. For some people, substance abuse of a particular group of substances evolves into substance dependence on those substances. In such cases, the diagnosis of substance dependence pre-empts the diagnosis of substance abuse, since dependence is considered a more advanced condition than abuse. Some individuals abuse substances for years without ever becom-ing dependent on them, however.

 Do you think the criteria for a diagnosis of abuse are too strict and exclude many people who have serious problems that should be recognized with a diagnosis? Or are they too broad and vague and result in overdiagnosis and pathologizing of drug use behaviors?

The diagnosis of **substance dependence** is closest to what people often refer to as *drug addiction* (see Table 12.3). A person is *physiologically dependent* on a substance when he or she shows either tolerance or withdrawal from the substance. **Tolerance** is present when a person experiences less and less effect from the same dose of a substance and needs greater and greater doses of a substance in order to achieve intoxication. People who have smoked cigarettes for years often smoke more than 20 cigarettes a day, when that same amount would have made them violently ill when they first began smoking. A person who is highly tolerant to a substance may have a very high blood level of the substance with-out being aware of any effects of the substance. For example, people who are highly tol-erant to alcohol may have blood alcohol levels far above those used in the legal definition of intoxication but show few signs of alcohol intoxication. The risk of tolerance varies greatly from one substance to the next. Alcohol, opioids, stimulants, and nicotine have high risks of tolerance, whereas cannabis and PCP appear to have lower risks of tolerance.

People who are physiologically dependent on substances will often show severe withdrawal symptoms when they stop using the substances. The symptoms may be so severe that the substances must be withdrawn gradually in order to prevent the symp-toms from becoming overwhelming or dangerous. These people may take the substances to relieve or avoid withdrawal symptoms. For example, a person dependent on alcohol may have a drink first thing in the morning to relieve a hangover.

Physiological dependence (that is, evidence of tolerance or withdrawal) is not required for a diagnosis of substance dependence, however. The diagnosis can be given when a person compulsively uses a substance, despite experiencing significant social, occupa-tional, psychological, or medical problems as a result of that use. Most people who are dependent on a substance crave the substance and will often do almost anything to get the substance (steal, lie, prostitute themselves) when the craving is strong. Their entire lives

substance dependence
diagnosis given when a person's substance use leads to physiological dependence or significant impairment or distress, as manifested by an inability to use the substance in moderation; decline in social, occupational, or recreational activities; or spending large amounts of time obtaining substances or recovering from their effects

tolerance
the condition of experiencing less and less effect from the same dose of a substance

---

Table 12.3 Symptoms of Substance Dependence

Tolerance to the substance, indicated by a need for increased amounts of the substance to achieve intoxication and/or by a diminished effect of the same amount of substance with continued use, is experienced.

Symptoms of withdrawal from the substance and the use of the substance to relieve or avoid withdrawal symptoms are experienced.

The substance is used over a longer period of time or in larger amounts than was intended.

The person has a persistent desire to cut down on substance use or stop using altogether.

The person spends a great deal of time acquiring or using the substance or recovering from its effects.

The person gives up or reduces important social or job-related activities as a result of substance use.

The person continues to use the substance despite recurrent physical or psychological problems that result from the substance use.

From *Diagnostic and Statistical Manual of Mental Disorders*, 4th ed. (DSM-IV). Copyright © 1994 American Psychiatric Association.

may revolve around obtaining and ingesting the substance. They may have attempted repeatedly to cut back on or quit using the substance, only to find themselves compulsively taking the substance again. Lucy is physically and psychologically dependent on both heroin and crack cocaine (adapted from Inciardi, Lockwood, & Pottieger, 1993, pp. 160–161).

> **Case Study** • By the time Lucy was 18, she was heavily addicted to heroin. Her mother took her to a detoxification program. After the 21-day regimen, Lucy was released but immediately relapsed to heroin use. By age 24, Lucy was mainlining heroin and turning tricks regularly to support both her and a boyfriend's drug habits. Lucy's boyfriend admitted himself to a drug rehabilitation program. When he completed his treatment stay, they both stopped their heroin use. However, they began snorting cocaine. Lucy left this boyfriend not too long afterwards. She went to work in a massage parlor, and the other women there introduced her to crack. This was 1984 and Lucy was 30 years old, a veteran drug addict and prostitute.
>
> Lucy left the massage parlor and began working on the streets. Her crack use increased continually until 1986, when she tried to stop. In her opinion, crack was worse than heroin, so she started injecting narcotics again. But she never stopped using crack.
>
> Because of her crack use, Lucy began doing things she had never even contemplated before, even while on heroin. For instance, she had anal sex and she sold herself for less money than ever before. She even began trading sex for drugs rather than money. Lucy also regularly worked in crack houses. She described them as "disgusting" and crowded. People would smoke and have sex in the same room in front of other people. Lucy insisted that her crack-house tricks rent rooms for sex, refusing to have sex in front of others. After having sex, Lucy would return to the stroll. Lucy would have five to seven customers a night, and most of the sex was oral. During this time, Lucy either stayed with her sister or slept in cars.

 What is your emotional reaction to Lucy's story? Pity? Sadness? Anger? Contempt? What beliefs about substance dependence are influencing your emotional reactions?

The way a substance is administered can be an important factor in determining how rapidly a person will become intoxicated and the likelihood that it will produce withdrawal symptoms or lead to abuse or dependence. Routes of administration that produce rapid and efficient absorption of the substance into the bloodstream lead to more intense intoxication and a greater likelihood of dependence. These include intravenous injection of the substance, smoking the substance, or snorting the substance. These routes of administration are also more likely to lead to overdose. Some substances act more rapidly on the central nervous system and thus lead to faster intoxication and thus are more likely to lead to dependence or abuse. Finally, substances whose effects wear off quickly are more likely to lead to dependence or abuse than are substances whose effects are longer lasting.

Let us turn now to discussing what intoxication, withdrawal, abuse, and dependence look like for the substances associated with substance disorders in the DSM-IV, beginning with the most heavily researched substance, alcohol.

Alcohol

People who are intoxicated with alcohol slur their words, walk with unsteady gaits, have trouble paying attention or remembering things, and are slow and awkward in their physical reactions. They may act inappropriately, such as becoming aggressive or taking off their clothes in public. Their moods may swing from exuberance to despair. With extreme

People dependent on a substance may do anything—including engage in prostitution—to get money to buy their substance.

intoxication, they may fall into stupors or comas. They will often not recognize they are intoxicated or may flatly deny it even though it is obvious. Once sober, they may have amnesia, known as a **blackout**, for the events that occurred while they were intoxicated.

Alcohol is classified as a depressant because of its dampening effects on the central nervous system, seen in the slowing of psychomotor reactions and in the cognitive impairments of people who are intoxicated with alcohol. Yet many people drink alcohol to make them feel good: When drinking, they are more self-confident, more relaxed, and perhaps slightly euphoric. Low doses of alcohol make many people less inhibited, and it may be this disinhibitory effect that many people find attractive. Indeed, people who do not experience the disinhibitory effects of alcohol tend not to drink at all (DeWit, Pierri, & Johanson, 1989). At increasing doses, however, alcohol induces many of the classic symptoms of depression, including fatigue and lethargy, decreased motivation, sleep disturbances, depressed mood, and confusion. Also, although many people take alcohol to feel more sexy (mainly by reducing their sexual inhibitions), even low doses of alcohol can severely impair sexual functioning.

One critical determinant of how quickly people become intoxicated with alcohol is whether their stomachs are full or empty. When the stomach is empty, alcohol is more quickly delivered from the stomach to the small intestine, where it is rapidly absorbed into the body. The person with a full stomach may drink significantly more drinks before reaching a dangerous blood alcohol level or showing clear signs of intoxication. People in countries, such as France, where alcohol is almost always consumed with meals show lower rates of alcohol-related disorders than do people in countries such as the United States, where alcohol is often consumed on empty stomachs.

The legal definition of alcohol intoxication is much more narrow than the criteria for a diagnosis of alcohol intoxication. Most states in the United States consider a person to be under the influence of alcohol if his or her blood alcohol level is above 0.05 or 0.10. As Table 12.4 indicates, it does not take very many drinks for most people to reach this blood alcohol level. Deficits in attention, reaction time, and coordination arise even with the first drink and can interfere with the ability to operate a car or machinery safely and other tasks requiring a steady hand, coordination, clear thinking, and clear vision. These deficits are not always readily observable, even to trained observers (Winger, Hofman, & Woods, 1992). People often leave parties or bars with blood alcohol levels well above the legal limit and dangerous deficits in their ability to drive, without appearing drunk.

Drinking large quantities of alcohol can result in death, even in people who are not chronic abusers of alcohol. About one-third of these deaths occur as a result of

blackout
amnesia for events that occurred during one's intoxication

Drinking alcohol with food leads to slower absorption of the alcohol.

It doesn't take very many drinks for most people to reach the blood alcohol level of 0.05 or 0.10, which are the legal definitions of intoxication in most states.

Absolute Alcohol (ounces)	Beverage Intake*	Blood Alcohol Level (percent)					
		Female (100 lb.)	Male (100 lb.)	Female (150 lb.)	Male (150 lb.)	Female (200 lb.)	Male (200 lb.)
1/2	1 oz. spirits† 1 glass wine 1 can beer	0.045	0.037	0.03	0.025	0.022	0.019
1	2 oz. spirits 2 glasses wine 2 cans beer	0.090	0.075	0.06	0.050	0.045	0.037
2	4 oz. spirits 4 glasses wine 4 cans beer	0.180	0.150	0.12	0.100	0.090	0.070
3	6 oz. spirits 6 glasses wine 6 cans beer	0.270	0.220	0.18	0.150	0.130	0.110
4	8 oz. spirits 8 glasses wine 8 cans beer	0.360	0.300	0.24	0.200	0.180	0.150
5	10 oz. spirits 10 glasses wine 10 cans beer	0.450	0.370	0.30	0.250	0.220	0.180

Source: Data from Ray & Ksir, 1993, p. 194.

* In 1 hour.

†100-proof spirits

respiratory paralysis, usually as a result of a final large dose of alcohol in people who are already intoxicated. Alcohol can also interact fatally with a number of substances (Winger et al., 1992).

Most deaths due to alcohol, however, come from automobile accidents, private plane and boat accidents, and drownings. Nearly half of all fatal automobile accidents and deaths due to falls or fires and over a third of all drownings are alcohol related. More than half of all murderers and their victims are believed to be intoxicated with alcohol at the time of the murders, and people who commit suicide often do so under the influence of alcohol.

Alcohol Withdrawal

Many people who have "a few too many" one night experience the next day what is commonly referred to as a *hangover*, including nausea, vomiting, headaches, and feelings of fatigue and dysphoria. These are symptoms of withdrawal from alcohol. Other symptoms are sweating and a fast pulse, hand tremors, insomnia, transient hallucinations or illusions, agitation, anxiety, and seizures.

People whose alcohol use has been heavy and prolonged can show much more severe alcohol withdrawal symptoms, which can be divided into three stages (Winger et al., 1992). The first stage, which usually begins within a few hours after drinking has been stopped or sharply curtailed, includes tremulousness (the "shakes"), weakness, and profuse perspiration. A person may complain of anxiety (the "jitters"), headache, nausea, and abdominal cramps. He or she may begin to retch and vomit. The person's face is flushed, and he or she is restless and easily startled but alert. The person's EEG pattern may be mildly abnormal. He or she may begin to "see" or "hear" things, at first only with eyes shut but with time also with eyes open. People whose dependence on alcohol is relatively moderate may only experience this first stage of withdrawal, and the symptoms may disappear within a few days. The second stage of withdrawal involves convulsive seizures, which may begin as early as 12 hours after stopping drinking but more often appear during the second or third day. The third phase is characterized by **delirium tremens**, or **DTs**. Auditory, visual, and tactile hallucinations occur. The person may also develop bizarre delusions that are terrifying, such as the belief that monsters are attacking. He or she may sleep little and become severely agitated, continuously active, and completely disoriented. Fever, profuse perspiration, and an irregular heartbeat may develop. Delirium tremens is a fatal condition in approximately 10 percent of cases; death may occur from hyperthermia (greatly increased body temperature) or collapse of the peripheral vascular system. Fortunately, only about 11 percent of individuals with alcohol dependence ever experience seizures or DTs (Schuckit, Tip, Reich, & Hesselbrock, 1995). Seizures and DTs are more common among people who drink large amounts in single sittings and who have additional medical illnesses.

People who make it through the entire withdrawal syndrome can show complete recovery from the withdrawal symptoms. The following is a case study of a man going through delirium tremens after prolonged alcohol dependence, presented by the groundbreaking psychiatrist Emil Kraepelin to medical students in the nineteenth century (Spitzer et al., 1981, pp. 304–305):

> The innkeeper, aged thirty-four, whom I am bringing before you to-day was admitted to the hospital only an hour ago. He understands the questions put to him, but cannot quite hear some of them, and gives a rather absentminded impression. He states his name and age correctly. . . . Yet he does not know the doctors, calls them by the names of his acquaintances, and thinks he has been here for two or three days. It must be the Crown Hotel, or, rather, the "mad hospital." He does not know the date exactly.
>
> . . . He moves about in his chair, looks round him a great deal, starts slightly several times, and keeps on playing with his hands. Suddenly he gets up, and begs to be allowed to play on the piano for a little at once. He sits down again immediately, on persuasion, but then wants to go away "to tell them something else that he has forgotten." He gradually gets more and more excited, saying that his fate is sealed; he must leave the world now; they might telegraph to his wife that her husband is lying at the point of death. We learn, by questioning him, that he is going to be executed by electricity, and also that he will be shot. "The picture is not clearly painted," he says; "every moment someone stands now here, now there, waiting for me with a revolver. When I open my eyes, they vanish." He says that a stinking fluid has been injected into his head and both his toes, which causes the pictures one takes for reality; that is the work of an international society, which makes away with those "who fell into misfortune innocently through false steps." With this he looks eagerly at the window, where he sees houses and trees vanishing and reappearing. With slight pressure on his eyes, he sees first sparks, then a hare, a picture, a head, a washstand-set, a half-moon, and a human head, first dully and then in colours. If you show him a speck on the floor, he tries to pick it up, saying that it is a piece of money. If you shut his hand and ask him what you have given him, he keeps his fingers carefully closed, and guesses that it is a lead-pencil or a piece of indiarubber. The patient's mood is half apprehensive and half amused. His head is much flushed, and his pulse is small, weak, and rather hurried. His face is bloated and his eyes are watery. His breath smells strongly of alcohol and acetone. His tone is thickly furred, and trembles when he puts it out, and his outspread fingers show strong, jerky tremors. The knee-reflexes are somewhat exaggerated.

Alcohol Abuse and Dependence

People given the diagnosis of **alcohol abuse** use alcohol in dangerous situations (such as when driving), fail to meet important obligations at work or at home as a result of their alcohol use, and have recurrent legal or social problems as a result of their alcohol use. People given the diagnosis of **alcohol dependence** typically have all the problems of an alcohol abuser, plus they may show physiological tolerance to alcohol, they spend a great deal

delirium tremens (DTs)
symptoms that result during severe alcohol withdrawal, including hallucinations, delusions, agitation, and disorientation

alcohol abuse
diagnosis given to someone who uses alcohol in dangerous situations, fails to meet obligations at work or at home due to alcohol use, and has recurrent legal or social problems as a result of alcohol use

alcohol dependence
diagnosis given to someone who has a physiological tolerance to alcohol, spends a lot of time intoxicated or in withdrawal, or continues to drink despite significant legal, social, medical, or occupational problems that result from alcohol (often referred to as *alcoholism*)

Table 12.5 Problems Indicated by People Who Are Diagnosed with Alcohol Abuse or Dependence	
Symptom	Percent Saying Yes
Family objected to respondent's drinking	62
Thought himself or herself an excessive drinker	59
Consumed a fifth of liquor in one day	70
Engaged in daily or weekly heavy drinking	80
Told physician about drinking	22
Friends or professionals said drinking too much	39
Wanted to stop drinking but couldn't	21
Made efforts to control drinking	19
Engaged in morning drinking	21
Had job troubles due to drinking	15
Lost job	7
Had trouble driving	35
Was arrested while drinking	31
Had physical fights while drinking	50
Had two or more binges	29
Had blackouts while drinking	57
Had any withdrawal symptom	28
Had any medical complication	22
Continued to drink with serious illness	14
Couldn't do ordinary work without drinking	12

Source: Data from J. E. Helzer, et al., 1992.

of time intoxicated or withdrawing from alcohol, they often organize their lives around drinking, and they continue to drink despite having significant social, occupational, medical, or legal problems that result from drinking. The characteristics of alcohol dependence match what most people associate with the label *alcoholism*. Table 12.5 lists a variety of problems experienced by people who abuse or are dependent on alcohol.

There are at least three distinct patterns of alcohol use by alcohol abusers and dependents. Some people drink large amounts of alcohol every day and plan their days around their drinking. Others abstain from drinking for long periods of time and then go on binges that may last days or weeks. They may stop drinking when faced with crises they must deal with, such as illnesses of their children, or with threats of sanctions for drinking, such as threats of being fired. When they begin drinking again, they may be able to control their drinking for a while, but it may soon escalate until severe problems develop. Still others are sober during the weekdays but drink heavily during the evenings or perhaps only on weekends. Nick and his buddies fit into this third group:

Case Study • Nick began drinking in high school, but his drinking escalated when he moved away from his parents' home to go to college. After just a couple of weeks at college, Nick became friends with a group of guys who liked to party really hard on the weekends. On Thursday nights they would begin to drink beer, often getting quite drunk. They would get a little loud and obnoxious, and sometimes their neighbors in the dormitory would complain to the resident assistant of the dorm about them. They would typically sleep off their hangovers on Friday, missing classes, and then begin drinking again Friday afternoon. They would continue to drink through Saturday, stopping finally on Sunday to sleep and recover.

Nick was able to keep a decent grade average through his first year in college, despite missing many classes. In his sophomore year, however, the classes in his major were getting harder. Nick's drinking was also getting more out of hand. He still would abstain from drinking from about Sunday afternoon until noon on Thursday. But when he would go get the keg of beer for his group of buddies on Thursday afternoon, he'd also pick up a few fifths of vodka or whatever hard liquor was the cheapest. His buddies would stick to the beer, but Nick would mix the beer with shots of hard liquor and was usually extremely drunk by dinner on Thursday. He had started getting really mean and stupid when he was drunk. He punched a hole in the wall of his dorm room one night, and when the resident assistant came up to investigate what was going on, he threatened her, saying he would "smack her across the room" if she didn't shut up and leave. That got him kicked out of his dormitory and off campus. Nick didn't mind being away from the "geeks" who studied all the time and liked having his own apartment where his buddies could come to drink. Nick remained intoxicated from Thursday afternoon until Sunday morning, drinking all day and evening, except when he was passed out. He usually slept through most of his classes on Monday, and even when he did go, he was so hungover that he couldn't pay attention. His grades were falling, and even his drinking buddies were getting disgusted with Nick's behavior.

Family members, friends, and business associates often recognize when an individual is abusing or dependent on alcohol, and they confront the individual. Sometimes this leads the individual to seek help, but denial is strong among alcoholics, and one confrontation or even a series of confrontations often does not motivate an alcohol abuser to change his or her behavior or seek help. Physical aggression, particularly among men, is also common among alcoholics when they are intoxicated. This aggression may be directed at family members. Often, the aggression is random—the alcoholic will take offense at some comment another makes and begin a fight.

 If you drink alcohol, what are some of the situations in which you are most likely to drink? What characteristics of these situations increase your desire to drink?

Heavy and prolonged use of alcohol can have toxic effects on several systems of the body, including the stomach, esophagus, pancreas, and liver (Winger et al., 1992). One of the most common medical conditions associated with alcohol abuse and dependence is low-grade hypertension. This factor, combined with increases in triglycerides and low-density lipoprotein (or "bad") cholesterol, puts alcohol abusers at increased risk for heart disease.

Alcohol abusers and dependents are often malnourished, in part because chronic alcohol ingestion decreases the absorption of critical nutrients from the gastrointestinal system and in part because they tend to "drink their meals." Some alcohol abusers show chronic thiamine deficiencies, which can lead to several disorders of the central nervous system, including numbness and pain in the extremities, deterioration in muscles, and loss of visual acuity for both near and far objects.

Alcohol-induced persisting amnesic disorder, a permanent cognitive disorder caused by damage to the central nervous system, consists of two syndromes. **Wernicke's encephalopathy** involves mental confusion and disorientation and, in severe states, coma. **Korsakoff's psychosis** involves a loss of memory for recent events and problems in recalling distant events. The person may confabulate, telling implausible stories in an attempt to hide his or her ability to remember. **Alcohol-induced dementia** is the loss of intellectual abilities, including memory, abstract thinking, judgment, or problem solving, often accompanied by personality changes, such as increases in paranoia. This syndrome is found in approximately 9 percent of chronic alcohol abusers or dependents and is the second most common cause of adult dementia (Winger et al., 1992). More subtle deficits due to central nervous system damage are observed in many chronic alcohol abusers, even after they have stopped using alcohol.

alcohol-induced persisting amnesic disorder
permanent cognitive disorder caused by damage to the central nervous system, consisting of Wernicke's encephalopathy and Korsakoff's psychosis

Wernicke's encephalopathy
alcohol-induced permanent cognitive disorder involving mental disorientation and confusion and, in severe states, coma

Korsakoff's psychosis
alcohol-induced permanent cognitive disorder involving deficiencies in one's ability to recall both recent and distant events

alcohol-induced dementia
loss of intellectual abilities, including memory, abstract thinking, judgment, and problem solving, often accompanied by changes in personality, such as increases in paranoia

Heavy drinking can be part of the culture of a peer group, but can still lead to alcohol abuse and dependence in some members.

Children of mothers who chronically ingest large amounts of alcohol while pregnant may be born with **fetal alcohol syndrome**. This syndrome is characterized by retarded growth, facial abnormalities, central nervous system damage, mental retardation, motor abnormalities, tremors, hyperactivity, heart defects, and skeletal anomalies. Although the risk of fetal alcohol syndrome is highest among women who are chronic, heavy alcohol users while pregnant, particularly those who abuse alcohol during their first trimester, even moderate intake of alcohol may affect the fetus during any point of pregnancy.

Cultural Differences in Alcohol Disorders

There are marked differences across cultures in the use of alcohol and in rates of alcohol-related problems (see Table 12.6). Low rates of alcohol-related problems in China and Taiwan may be due in part to the absence, in 50 percent of people of Asian descent, of an enzyme that eliminates the first breakdown product of alcohol, acetaldehyde. When these individuals consume alcohol, they experience a flushed face and heart palpitations, and the discomfort of this effect often leads them to avoid alcohol altogether. The low rates of alcohol-related disorders in Asia have also been attributed to the Confucian moral ethic, which discourages drunken behavior, and to the fact that alcohol is seen as appropriate for meals and ceremonial occasions but not for personal indulgence (Helzer & Canino, 1992).

In recent years, however, there have been substantial increases in alcohol use and related problems among businessmen in Asia. This may explain, in part, the high rates of alcohol-related problems in South Korea (see Table 12.6), where drinking among business associates after work is common. These nightly parties often involve drinking contests lasting until some of the contestants have to be carried home.

There also are substantial differences among ethnic groups within the United States in alcohol use and abuse. Notice in Table 12.7 the much higher rate of alcohol abuse and dependence in Mexican Americans born in the United States than in those who immigrated to the United States. Some theorists have argued that the more an immigrant group becomes assimilated to dominant U.S. culture, the more at risk they are for mental health problems in general and particularly for the common mental health problems of this culture (see Gaw, 1993). This is because assimilation robs immigrants of their ties to their heritage and extended social networks and leads immigrants to identify with a culture that will never accept them fully. Mexican Americans born in the United States tend to be more assimilated than are more recent immigrants to the United States, and this may help to explain why they show greater rates of alcohol-related problems.

Differences between white and African-American rates of alcohol problems in the United States vary by age and gender (Helzer et al., 1992). As can be seen in Figure 12.1, there are much higher rates of alcohol problems in young white males than in African-American males but higher rates among older African-American men than older white men. The rates among African-American and white women are similar at all ages.

One group in the United States that appears at high risk for alcohol abuse and dependence are Native Americans (Manson, Shore, Baron, Ackerson, & Neligh, 1992).

Table 12.6 Lifetime Prevalence of Alcohol Dependence in Various Cultures	
Culture	**Percentage**
South Korea	22.00
New Zealand	19.00
Canada	18.00
Germany	13.00
Puerto Rico	13.00
Mainland United States	8.00
Taiwan	6.00
China	0.45

Source: Data from J. E. Helzer et al., 1992.

Heavy drinkers are those who regularly consumed seven or more drinks at least one evening a week for a period of several months but who never had any social, legal, or medical problems related to alcohol or any withdrawal symptoms. Problem drinkers are those who have had at least one alcohol-related problem in their lives but who have not had enough to qualify for a diagnosis of alcohol abuse or dependency.

	Total Abstention	Social Drinkers	Heavy Drinkers	Problem Drinkers	Abuse/ Dependency
All groups	10	61	3	12	14
Mexican Americans born in the United States	7	52	3	14	23
Immigrant Mexican Americans	23	44	1	19	13
Puerto Ricans	20	69	7	10	13

Source: Data from G. J. Canino, et al., 1992.

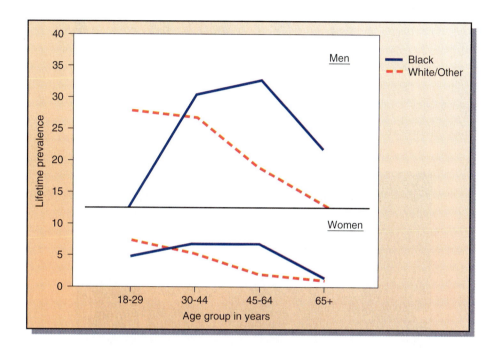

Figure 12.1

Alcohol Abuse and Dependence Among White and Black Men and Women. Men are more likely than women to have alcohol abuse or dependence. Among younger people, whites are more likely to have these disorders than are blacks, but this trend is reversed among older people. The rate of alcohol abuse and dependence decreases with age.
Source: From Helzer, Bucholz, & Robins, 1992, p. 85.

For example, a study of adult members of a Pacific Northwest reservation community found that 27 percent qualified for a diagnosis of alcoholism. Deaths related to alcohol are as much as five times more common among Native Americans than in the general U.S. population (Manson et al., 1992). Hospital records indicate that alcohol-related illnesses are three times higher among Native Americans than among all people in the United States and twice the rates for other ethnic minority groups in the United States. The higher rates of alcohol-related problems among Native Americans have been tied to their excessive rates of poverty and unemployment, lower education, and greater sense of helplessness and hopelessness than those of the general U.S. population.

Gender and Age Differences in Alcohol Disorders

In a community survey done in the United States, 72 percent of adult men said they had consumed at least one alcoholic beverage in the last year, compared to 62 percent of adult women (NIDA, 1995). About 11 percent of American men and 4 percent of American women meet the criteria for alcohol dependence in any given year (Kessler et al., 1994). Males are more likely than females to drink in all cultures, but the size of the gender difference differs by culture (see Figure 12.2; Helzer & Canino, 1992). The gender gap in alcohol use is much greater among men and women who subscribe to traditional gender

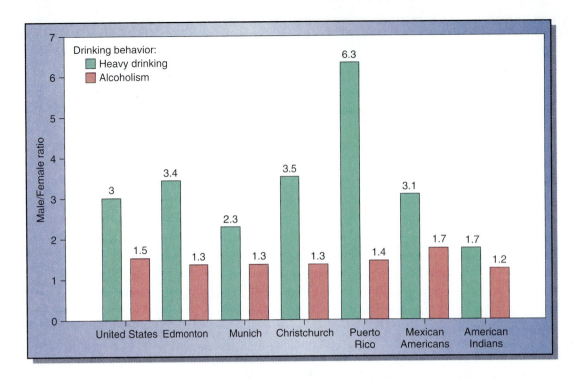

Figure 12.2

Male-to-Female Ratios for People Who Drink Heavily or Are Alcoholics, Across Cultures. Males are more likely than females to be heavy drinkers or alcoholics in most cultures, but the male-to-female ratio varies by culture.
Source: Helzer & Canino, 1992.

High rates of alcoholism among Native Americans have been tied to unemployment and poverty.

roles, which condone drinking for men but not for women (Huselid & Cooper, 1992). Similarly, in ethnic minority groups of the United States in which traditional gender roles are more widely accepted, such as Hispanics and recent Asian immigrants, the gender gap in drinking is greater than it is among whites, due largely to high percentages of women in the minority groups completely abstaining from alcohol.

Elderly people are less likely than others to abuse or be dependent on alcohol, probably for several reasons. First, with age, the liver metabolizes alcohol at a slower rate, and the lower percentage of body water increases the absorption of alcohol. As a result, older people can become intoxicated faster and experience the negative effects of alcohol more severely and quickly. Second, as people grow older, they may become more mature in their choices, including the choice about drinking alcohol to excess. Third, older people have grown up under stronger prohibitions against alcohol use and abuse and in a society in which there was more stigma associated with alcoholism, leading them to curtail their use of alcohol more than younger people do. Finally, people who have used alcohol excessively for many years may die from alcohol-related diseases before they reach old age.

- At low doses, alcohol produces relaxation and a mild euphoria.
- At higher doses, it produces the classic signs of depression and cognitive and motor impairment.
- A large proportion of deaths due to accidents, murders, and suicides are alcohol-related.
- Alcohol withdrawal symptoms can be mild or so severe as to be life threatening.
- Alcohol abusers and dependents experience a wide range of social and interpersonal problems and are at risk for many serious health problems.
- Persons of Asian descent typically are less prone to alcohol-related problems, although exceptions to this include Native Americans and Koreans.
- Women drink less alcohol than do men in most cultures and are less likely to have alcohol-related disorders than are men.

Other Depressants: Benzodiazepines, Barbiturates, and Inhalants

Three other groups of substances that, like alcohol, depress the central nervous system are benzodiazepines, barbiturates, and inhalants. Intoxication with and withdrawal from these substances are quite similar to alcohol intoxication and withdrawal. Users initially may feel euphoric and become disinhibited but then experience depressed moods, lethargy, perceptual distortions, loss of coordination, and other signs of central nervous system depression.

Benzodiazepines (such as Xanax, Valium, Halcion, and Librium) and **barbiturates** (such as Quaalude) are legally manufactured and sold by prescription, usually for the treatment of anxiety and insomnia. In the United States, approximately 90 percent of people hospitalized for medical care or surgery are prescribed sedatives. Large quantities of these substances end up on the illegal black market, however. These substances are especially likely to be taken in combination with other psychoactive substances to produce greater highs or feelings of euphoria or to relieve the agitation created by other substances (Schuckit, 1995).

There are two common patterns in the development of benzodiazapine or barbiturate abuse and dependence (Schuckit, 1995). The most common pattern is followed by the teenager or young adult who begins using these substances "recreationally," often at "bring your own drug" parties, to produce a sense of well-being or euphoria but then escalates to chronic use and physiological dependence. This pattern is especially likely among persons who already have other substance-abuse problems with alcohol, opioids, cocaine, amphetamines, or other substances.

A second pattern is seen in people, particularly women, who initially use sedatives under physicians' care for anxiety or insomnia but then gradually increase their use as tolerance develops, without the knowledge of their physicians. They may obtain prescriptions from several different physicians or even photocopy their prescriptions. When confronted about their sedative use and dependency, they may deny that they use the drugs to produce euphoria or that they are dependent on the sedatives.

Barbiturates and benzodiazepines cause decreases in blood pressure, respiratory rate, and heart rate. In overdose, they can be extremely dangerous and even fatal. Death can occur from respiratory arrest or cardiovascular collapse. Overdose is especially likely to occur when these substances (particularly the benzodiazepines) are taken in combination with alcohol.

Inhalants are solvents such as gasoline, glue, paint thinners, and spray paints. Users may inhale vapors directly from the cans or bottles containing the substances, soak rags with the substances and then hold the rag to their mouths and noses, or place the substances in paper or plastic bags and then inhale the gases from the bags. The chemicals reach the lungs, bloodstream, and brain very rapidly.

benzodiazepines

legally prescribed and manufactured central nervous system depressants that cause initial euphoria and disinhibition yet lead to depressed mood, lethargy, and a loss of coordination

barbiturates

legally available, highly addictive tranquilizers that cause decreases in blood pressure, heart rate, and respiratory rate that are fatal in large doses

inhalants

solvents such as gasoline, glue, or paint thinner that one inhales to produce a high and that can cause permanent central nervous system damage as well as hepatitis and liver and kidney disease

Some women begin taking sedatives by prescription but increase their use dramatically and become physically dependent on these drugs.

The greatest users of inhalants are young boys between 10 and 15 years of age (Schuckit, 1995). Twenty percent of American high school students have reported experimenting with inhalants at least once during high school. One group that appears especially prone to using inhalants are Native American teenagers. Some studies have found that nearly all children on some Native American reservations have experimented with gasoline inhaling. Hispanic American teenagers also appear to have higher rates of inhalant use than other groups of teenagers. Males are three to four times more likely than females to use inhalants.

Chronic users of inhalants may have a variety of respiratory irritations and rashes due to the inhalants. Inhalants can cause permanent damage to the central nervous system, including degeneration and lesions of the brain. Recurrent use can also cause hepatitis and liver and kidney disease. Death can occur from depression of the respiratory or cardiovascular systems; *sudden sniffing death* is due to acute irregularities in the heartbeat or loss of oxygen. Sometimes users suffocate themselves when they go unconscious with plastic bags filled with inhalants firmly placed over their noses and mouths. Users can also die or become seriously injured when the inhalants cause them to have delusions that they can do fantastic things like fly, and they jump off cliffs or tall buildings to try it.

Sniffing inhalants like paint thinner is highly dangerous, but unfortunately it is quite common among young people.

Summing Up   Other Depressants

- Three groups of central nervous system depressants, in addition to alcohol, are benzodiazepines, barbiturates, and inhalants.
- Benzodiazepines and barbiturates are sold legally by prescription for the treatment of anxiety and insomnia.
- Inhalants are solvents such as gasoline or paint thinner.
- These substances can cause an initial rush plus a loss of inhibitions.
- These pleasurable sensations are then followed by depressed mood, lethargy, and physical signs of central nervous system depression.
- Benzodiazepines and barbiturates are dangerous in overdose and when mixed with other substances.
- Inhalants can cause permanent organ and brain damage and accidental deaths due to suffocation or dangerous delusional behavior.

Stimulants:
Cocaine and Amphetamines

The two primary central nervous system stimulants associated with substance disorders, cocaine and amphetamines, can be injected intravenously, taken through the nose (snorting), smoked (freebasing), or swallowed in a pill called *crack* or *rock* in the case of cocaine. Both substances are used by people to get a psychological lift or rush. Both substances cause dangerous increases in blood pressure and heart rate, changes in the rhythm and electrical activity of the heart, and constriction of the blood vessels, which can lead to heart attacks, respiratory arrest, and seizures. In the United States, toxic reactions to cocaine and amphetamines account for 40 percent of all substance-related cases seen in hospital emergency rooms and for 50 percent of sudden deaths in which substances were involved (Goldstein, 1994). These substances are costly, both to users and to society.

Cocaine

Cocaine activates those parts of the brain that register reward or pleasure. It produces a sudden rush of intense euphoria, followed by great self-esteem, alertness, energy, and a general feeling of competence, creativity, and social acceptability. Users often do not feel drugged. Instead, they feel they have become the people they always wanted to be (Winger et al., 1992). When taken at high doses or chronically, however, cocaine leads to grandiosity, impulsiveness, hypersexuality, compulsive behavior, agitation, and anxiety, reaching the point of panic and paranoia. After stopping use of the substance, users may feel exhausted and depressed and sleep a great deal. Users also feel an intense craving for more of the substance, both for its physiological and psychological effects.

Many cocaine abusers and dependents started with heavy alcohol or marijuana use and then graduated to "harder" substances, including cocaine (Miller, 1991). The extraordinarily rapid and strong effects of cocaine on the brain's reward centers, however, seem to make this substance more likely than most illicit substances to result in patterns of abuse and dependence even among people who have never been heavy users of any other substances (Winger et al., 1992).

cocaine
central nervous system stimulant that causes a rush of positive feelings initially but that can lead to impulsiveness, agitation, and anxiety and that can cause withdrawal symptoms of exhaustion and depression

Case Study • Dr. Arnie Rosenthal is a 31-year-old white male dentist, married for 10 years with two children. His wife insisted he see a psychiatrist because of uncontrolled use of cocaine, which over the past year had made it increasingly difficult for him to function as a dentist. During the previous 5 years he used cocaine virtually every day, with only occasional periods of abstinence of 1 or 2 weeks. For the past 4 years he wanted to stop cocaine use, but his desire was overridden by a "compulsion" to take the drug. He estimates having spent $12,000 to $15,000 on cocaine during the past year.

The patient's wife, who accompanied him to the interview, complained primarily about her husband's lack of energy and motivation, which started with his drug use 5 years ago. She complained that "he isn't working; he has no interests outside of me and the kids—not even his music—and he spends all of his time alone watching TV." She is also bothered by his occasional temper outbursts, but that is less troubling to her. . . .

During his second year in dental school he got married, while being supported comfortably by his in-laws. After having been married 1 year he began using marijuana, smoking a joint each day upon coming home from school, and spent the evenings "staring" at TV. When he graduated from dental school his wife was pregnant, and he was "scared to death" at the prospect of being a father. His deepening depression was characterized by social isolation, increased loss of interests, and frequent temper outbursts. He needed to be intoxicated with marijuana, or occasionally sedatives, for sex, relaxation, and socialization. Following the birth of the child he "never felt so crazy," and his marijuana and sedative use escalated. Two years later, a second child was born. Dr. Rosenthal was financially successful, had moved to an expensive suburban home with a swimming pool, and had two cars and "everything my parents wanted for me." He was 27 years old, felt he had nothing to look forward to, felt painfully isolated, and the drugs were no longer providing relief.

He tried cocaine for the first time and immediately felt good. "I was no longer depressed. I used cocaine as often as possible because all my problems seemed to vanish, but I had to keep doing it. The effects were brief and it was very expensive, but I didn't care. When the immediate effects wore off, I'd feel even more miserable and depressed so that I did as much cocaine as I was able to obtain." He is now continuously nervous and irritable. Practicing dentistry has become increasingly difficult. (adapted from Spitzer et al., 1983, pp. 81–83)

Because cocaine has a short half-life, its effects wear off quickly. This means the person dependent on cocaine must take frequent doses of the substance to maintain a high. In addition, tolerance to cocaine can develop, so that the individual must obtain larger and larger amounts of cocaine to experience any high. Cocaine dependents will spend huge amounts of money on the substance and may become involved in theft,

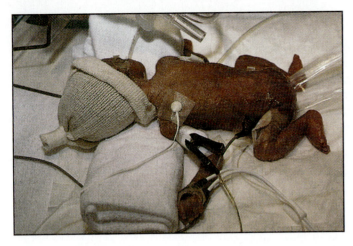

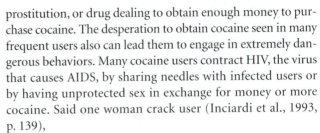

prostitution, or drug dealing to obtain enough money to purchase cocaine. The desperation to obtain cocaine seen in many frequent users also can lead them to engage in extremely dangerous behaviors. Many cocaine users contract HIV, the virus that causes AIDS, by sharing needles with infected users or by having unprotected sex in exchange for money or more cocaine. Said one woman crack user (Inciardi et al., 1993, p. 139),

> If I pulled out a condom in a crack house, I'd be laughed at. If I started to take it out of the wrapper, it would be slapped out of my hand. If I tried to put it on a man's [penis], I'd be slapped across the face, or worse. If I get AIDS, who cares anyway, really?

The babies of mothers who take high levels of crack during pregnancy are at increased risk for being born prematurely and having major birth defects.

Another tragic consequence of cocaine use is its effects on fetuses. Cocaine easily crosses the placenta so that even pregnant women who only occasionally use cocaine put their fetuses at risk. It causes irregularities in placental blood flow, spontaneous abortions, and premature labor and delivery. In addition, pregnant women who are chronic cocaine abusers often are malnourished and abusing other substances, further putting their fetuses at risk. Babies whose mothers have used cocaine tend to be hyperirritable; have small head circumferences; weigh less than normal; and have higher rates of physical malformations, learning disabilities, neurological impairments, and sudden infant death.

Although cocaine began as a wealthy person's substance because of its high cost, a sharp reduction in the cost of cocaine in the 1970s led to its widespread use at all socioeconomic levels. Almost 25 percent of people under the age of 35 have tried cocaine at least once in their lives (NIDA, 1995). Although the monetary cost of cocaine has decreased in recent decades, the human cost of cocaine has risen dramatically. Between 1976 and 1986, cocaine-related emergency room visits, deaths, and admissions to cocaine treatment programs multiplied by 15 (Cocores et al., 1991).

Fortunately, the use and abuse of cocaine has fallen since the mid-1980s. Whereas in 1979, 9 percent of young people said they were using cocaine at least once a month, by the mid-1990s, this number had dropped to less than 2 percent (Goldstein, 1994; NIDA, 1995). This decline may have to do, in part, with antidrug campaigns in schools and in the media and with highly publicized deaths of rock stars and athletes due to cocaine overdose. Decline has occurred primarily among casual users of cocaine; chronic abusers and dependents have continued to use cocaine.

Amphetamines

The symptoms of intoxication with **amphetamines** are similar to the symptoms of cocaine intoxication: euphoria, self-confidence, alertness, agitation, paranoia. Like cocaine, amphetamines can produce perceptual illusions that are frightening. The movement of other people and objects may seem distorted or exaggerated. Users may hear frightening voices making derogatory statements about them, see sores all over their bodies, or feel snakes crawling on their arms. They may have delusions that they are being stalked. They may act out violently against others as a result of their paranoid delusions. Some amphetamine users are aware that these experiences are not real, but some lose their reality-testing and develop *amphetamine-induced psychotic disorders.*

John Belushi and River Phoenix both abused cocaine and other substances and died of overdoses.

Case Study • An agitated 42-year-old businessman was admitted to the psychiatric service after a period of 2 1/2 months in which he found himself becoming increasingly distrustful of others and suspicious of his business associates. He was taking their statements out of context, "twisting" their words, and making inappropriately hostile and accusatory comments; he had, in fact, lost several business deals that had been "virtually sealed." Finally, he fired a shotgun into the backyard late one night when he heard noises that convinced him that intruders were about to break into his house and kill him.

One and one-half years previously, he had been diagnosed as having narcolepsy because of daily irresistible sleep attacks and episodes of sudden loss of muscle tone, and he had been placed on an amphetaminelike stimulant, methylphenidate. His narcolepsy declined and he was able to work quite effectively as the sales manager of a small office-machine company and to participate in an active social life with his family and a small circle of friends.

In the 4 months before this admission, he had been using increasingly large doses of methylphenidate to maintain alertness late at night because of an increasing amount of work that could not be handled during the day. He reported that during this time he could often feel his heart race and he had trouble sitting still. (adapted from Spitzer et al., 1994, pp. 139–140)

After an episode of intense, high-dose use of amphetamines (known as a *speed run*), the withdrawal symptoms may be severe (known as *crashing*). The depressive symptoms may be so severe that the person becomes suicidal. Acute withdrawal symptoms typically subside within a few days, but the chronic user may experience mood instability, memory loss, confusion, paranoid thinking, and perceptual abnormalities for weeks, months, and perhaps even years.

The U.S. pharmaceutical industry alone manufactures 8 to 10 billion doses of amphetamines annually, under names such as Dexedrin and Benzedrine (Miller, 1991). Many of these drugs are used appropriately under the supervision of physicians, but a great many doses are diverted from prescription use to illegal use and abuse. In addition to using them for weight control, many people use them to combat depression or chronic fatigue from overwork or simply to boost their self-confidence and energy (Miller, 1991). Amphetamines provide short-term solutions to these problems but carry many risks for users.

Summing Up   Stimulants: Cocaine and Amphetamines

- The central nervous system stimulants, cocaine and amphetamines, produce a rush of euphoria, followed by increases in self-esteem, alertness, and energy.
- With chronic use, however, they can lead to grandiosity, impulsiveness, hypersexuality, agitation, and paranoia.
- Withdrawal from these substances causes symptoms of depression, exhaustion, and an intense craving for more of the substances.
- Cocaine seems particularly prone to lead to dependence, because it has extraordinarily rapid and strong effects on the brain and its effects wear off quickly.
- The intense activation of the central nervous system caused by cocaine and amphetamines can lead to a number of cardiac, respiratory, and neurological problems, and these substances are responsible for a large percentage of substance-related medical emergencies and deaths.

Opioids

Morphine, heroin, and the synthetic substances resembling morphine are all known as **opioids.** Our bodies actually produce natural opioids, some of which are called *endorphins* and *enkaphalins,* to cope with pain. For example, a sports injury induces the body to produce endorphins to reduce the pain of the injury to avoid shock. Doctors may also prescribe synthetic opioids, such as Percodan, Demerol, or Darvon, to help with the pain.

When used illegally, opioids are often injected directly into veins (*mainlining*), snorted, or smoked. The initial symptom of opioid intoxication is often euphoria. People

Heroin is often injected directly into the veins.

describe a sensation in the abdomen like a sexual orgasm, referring to it as a *thrill, kick,* or *flash* (Winger et al., 1992). They may have a tingling sensation and a pervasive sense of warmth. Their pupils dilate, and they pass into a state of drowsiness during which time they are lethargic, their speech is slurred, and their mind may be clouded. They may experience periods of light sleep, with vivid dreams. Pain is reduced. A person in this state is referred to as being *on the nod.*

Severe intoxication with opioids can lead to unconsciousness, coma, and seizures. These substances can suppress the part of the brain stem controlling the respiratory and cardiovascular systems to the point of death. They are especially dangerous when used in combination with depressants such as alcohol and sedatives.

Withdrawal symptoms can include dysphoria, anxiety, and agitation; an achy feeling in the back and legs; increased sensitivity to pain; and craving for more opioids. The person may be nauseous and vomit and have profuse sweating and goose bumps, diarrhea, and fever. These symptoms usually come on within 8 to 16 hours of the last use of morphine or heroin and peak within 36 to 72 hours. In chronic or heavy users, the symptoms may continue strongly for 5 to 8 days and in a milder form for weeks to months.

Although the opioids are not as toxic in moderate amounts as are many other substances, people dependent on opioids are at very high risk for serious illness and death due to other complications resulting from their opioid use. One of the greatest risks to opioid abusers and dependents is the risk of contracting HIV through contaminated needles or unprotected sex, which many opioid abusers engage in in exchange for more substance. In some areas of the United States, up to 60 percent of chronic heroin users have HIV. Intravenous users also can contract hepatitis, tuberculosis, serious skin abscesses, and deep infections.

Hallucinogens, PCP, and Cannabis

Hallucinogens, phenylcyclidine (PCP), and cannabis differ in their mechanisms of action on the body but produce similar psychological effects, and thus we will consider them together. Most of the substances we have discussed so far can produce perceptual illusions and distortions when taken in large doses. The hallucinogens, PCP, and cannabis produce perceptual changes even in small doses.

Hallucinogens and PCP

hallucinogens
substances, including LSD and MDMA, that produce perceptual illusions and distortions even in small doses

The **hallucinogens** are a mixed group of substances including LSD (lysergic acid diethylamide), MDMA (also called *ecstasy*), and peyote. Perhaps the best-known hallucinogen is LSD, which was first synthesized in 1938 by Swiss chemists. It was not until 1943 that the substance's psychoactive effects were discovered, when Dr. Albert Hoffman accidentally swallowed a minute amount of LSD and experienced visual distortions. He later purposefully swallowed a small amount of LSD and reported the effects (Hoffman, 1968, pp. 185–186):

As far as I remember, the following were the most outstanding symptoms: vertigo, visual disturbances; the faces of those around me appeared as grotesque, colored masks; marked motor unrest, alternating with paresis; an intermittent heavy feeling in the head, limbs, and the entire body, as if they were filled with metal; cramps in the legs, coldness, and loss of feeling in the hands; a metallic taste on the tongue; dry constricted sensation in the throat; feeling of choking; confusion alternating between clear recognition of my condition, in which state I sometimes observed, in the manner of an independent, neutral observer, that I shouted half insanely or babbled incoherent words. Occasionally, I felt as if I were out of my body.

The doctor found a rather weak pulse but an otherwise normal circulation.

Six hours after ingestion of the LSD my condition had already improved considerably. Only the visual disturbances were still pronounced. Everything seemed to sway and the proportions were distorted like the reflections in the surface of moving water. Moreover, all objects appeared in unpleasant, constantly changing colors, the predominant shades being sickly green and blue. When I closed my eyes, an unending series of colorful, very realistic and fantastic images surged in upon me. A remarkable feature was the manner in which all acoustic perceptions (e.g., the noise of a passing car) were transformed into optical effects, every sound causing a corresponding colored hallucination constantly changing in shape and color like pictures in a kaleidoscope.

LSD, part of the psychedelic movement of the 1960s, was not illegal until 1966. By 1967, reports of "bad acid trips," or "bummers," became common, particularly in the Haight-Ashbury district of San Francisco, where many LSD enthusiasts from around the United States congregated (Smith & Seymour, 1994). The symptoms included severe anxiety, paranoia, and loss of control. Some people on bad trips would walk off roofs or jump out windows, believing they could fly, or walk into the sea, believing they were "one with the universe."

Phenylcyclidine (PCP), also known as *angel dust, PeaCePill, Hog,* and *Tranq,* is manufactured as a powder to be snorted or smoked. At lower doses, it produces a sense of intoxication, euphoria or affective dulling, talkativeness, lack of concern, slowed reaction time, vertigo, eye twitching, mild hypertension, abnormal involuntary movements, and weakness. At intermediate doses, it leads to disorganized thinking, distortions of body image (such as feeling one's arms do not belong to the rest of one's body), depersonalization, and feelings of unreality. A user may become hostile, belligerent, and even violent. At higher doses, it produces amnesia and coma, analgesia sufficient to allow surgery, seizures, severe respiratory problems, hypothermia, and hyperthermia. The effects of phenylcyclidine begin immediately after injection, snorting, or smoking, reaching a peak within minutes. The symptoms of severe intoxication can persist for several days. As a result, people with PCP intoxication are often misdiagnosed as having psychotic disorders not related to substance use.

PCP sold well in the 1970s to young, white, polydrug abusers. Use of the substance has declined in recent decades. In 1980, about 13 percent of high school seniors reported having used the substance; this fell to 1 percent by 1994 (NIDA, 1995). It is not used to any great extent outside the United States.

Cannabis

The leaves of the **cannabis** (or hemp) plant can be cut, dried, and rolled into cigarettes or inserted into food and beverages. It is the most widely used illicit substance in the world. In North America, the result is known as *marijuana, pot, grass, reefer,* and *Mary Jane.* Over half the U.S. population under the age of 35 has tried marijuana at some time, and 7 percent use it monthly (NIDA, 1995). It is called *ganja* in Jamaica, *kif* in North Africa, *dagga* in South Africa, *bhang* in India and the Middle East, and *macohna* in South America (Winger et al., 1992). Hashish is a dried resin extract from the cannabis plant sold in cubes in America.

For most people, the psychological effects of marijuana or hashish include feelings of well-being, relaxation, and tranquillity. People who are very anxious, depressed, or angry may become more so under the influence of cannabis, however. Users may feel dizzy, sleepy, or "dreamy." They may become more aware of their environments, and everything may seem funny. They may believe they are thinking profound thoughts, but their short-term memories will be impaired to the point that they cannot remember thoughts long enough to express them in sentences.

phenylcyclidine (PCP)
substance that produces euphoria, slowed reaction times, and involuntary movements at low doses; disorganized thinking, feelings of unreality, and hostility at intermediate doses; and amnesia, analgesia, respiratory problems, and changes in body temperature at high doses

cannabis
substance that causes feelings of well-being, perceptual distortions, and paranoid thinking

Cannabis is categorized as a hallucinogen because at moderate to large doses, users experience perceptual distortions, feelings of depersonalization, and paranoid thinking. Some people experience frank hallucinations and delusions. The changes in perceptions may be experienced as pleasant by some but as very frightening by others. Some users may have severe anxiety episodes resembling panic attacks.

Physiological symptoms of cannabis intoxication include increases in heart rate, an irregular heartbeat, increases in appetite, and dry mouth. Cannabis smoke is irritating and thus increases the risk of chronic cough, sinusitis, bronchitis, and emphysema. It contains even larger amounts of known carcinogens than does tobacco, so it creates a high risk for cancer.

In recent years, several groups have advocated the legalization of marijuana cigarettes for medical uses (Grinspoon & Bakalar, 1995). THC, the active compound in cannabis, can help relieve nausea in cancer patients undergoing chemotherapy and increase appetite in AIDS patients. It also helps in the treatment of asthma and glaucoma. THC can be given in pill form, but some people argue that the level of THC that enters the body is more controllable when it is taken in a marijuana cigarette.

Summing Up	Hallucingens, PCP, and Cannabis

- The hallucinogens (such as LSD, PCP, and cannabis) create perceptual illusions and distortions, sometimes fantastic, sometimes frightening.
- PCP is not widely used these days, but cannabis is the most widely used illicit substance in the world.

Nicotine

All of the substances we have discussed thus far, except alcohol and the inhalants, are illegal for nonprescription use, and there are many laws regulating the use of alcohol. One of the most addictive substances we know, however, is fully legal for use by adults and readily available for use by adolescents.

Nicotine is an alkaloid found in tobacco. Cigarettes are the most popular "nicotine delivery device." In the United States, 55 percent of adults have smoked cigarettes at some time in their lives, and 30 percent currently smoke. Smoking usually begins in the early teens. Among people who continue to smoke through age 20, 95 percent become regular, daily smokers. In general, the use of tobacco has declined in the United States and other industrialized countries over the last few decades. In contrast, its use is increasing in developing countries (Giovini et al., 1994).

Nicotine operates on both the central and peripheral nervous systems. It results in the release of several biochemicals that may have direct reinforcing effects on the brain, including norepinephrine, serotonin, and the endogenous opioids. Although people often say they smoke to reduce stress, the physiological effects of nicotine actually resemble the fight-or-flight syndrome—several systems in the body are aroused in preparation to fight or flee a stressor, including the cardiovascular and respiratory systems.

In 1964, on the basis of a review of 6,000 empirical studies, the Surgeon General of the United States concluded that smoking, particularly cigarette smoking, caused lung cancer, bronchitis, and probably coronary heart disease. Mortality rates for smokers are 70 percent greater than for nonsmokers. This means that a person between 30 and 35 years of age who smokes two packs of cigarettes a day will die 8 to 9 years earlier than will a nonsmoker. The chief causes of increased mortality rates among smokers are coronary heart disease, lung cancer, emphysema, and chronic bronchitis. The babies of women who smoke while pregnant are smaller at birth. The longer a person smokes and the more he or she smokes per day, the greater the health risks.

Increasing attention is being paid to the effects of passive smoking—unintentionally inhaling the smoke from nearby smokers' cigarettes. This smoke contains more tox-

Smoking usually begins in the teen years, and 95 percent of people who continue to smoke through age 20 become regular daily users.

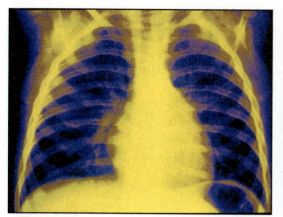

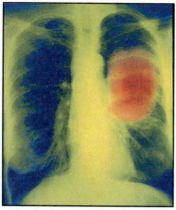

Smoking is a leading cause of lung cancer. The lungs on the left are healthy; the lungs on the right have cancer and are from a smoker.

ins than does the smoke that the smoker actively inhales, although the passive smoker does not inhale the smoke in concentrations as high as the smoker does. Children of parents who smoke have 30 to 80 percent more chronic respiratory problems than do nonsmokers and nearly 30 percent more hospitalizations for bronchitis and pneumonia (Winger et al., 1992).

Tobacco manufacturers still try to claim that nicotine is "not an addictive drug," but it causes most of the core symptoms of physiological and psychological dependence. The best evidence of nicotine dependence is the presence of tolerance to the substance and withdrawal symptoms after quitting. Chronic heavy smokers become so tolerant to nicotine that they show no adverse physiological reactions to a dosage of nicotine that would have made them violently nauseous when they first began smoking. When they try to stop smoking or are prohibited from smoking for an extended period (such as at work or on an airplane), they show severe withdrawal symptoms: They are depressed, irritable, angry, anxious, frustrated, restless, and hungry; they have trouble concentrating; and they desperately crave another cigarette. These symptoms are immediately relieved by smoking another cigarette, another sign of physiological dependence.

Because nicotine is relatively cheap and available, people who are nicotine dependent do not tend to spend large amounts of time trying to obtain nicotine. They may, however, become panicked if they run out of cigarettes and replacements are not available. They may also spend large amounts of their day engaged in smoking or chewing tobacco and continue to use nicotine even though it is damaging their health (such as after they have been diagnosed with emphysema). They may skip social or recreational activities as a result of their habit. For example, people may turn down dinner invitations at the homes of friends who do not allow smoking. Or they may stop playing tennis because they have trouble breathing. With the increasing restrictions on smoking in the workplace, nicotine dependents may even begin to turn down or switch jobs to avoid these restrictions.

Over 80 percent of people who smoke say they wish they could quit. Quitting is difficult, however, in part because the withdrawal syndrome is so difficult to withstand. Only about 45 percent of people who have ever smoked eventually stop smoking. Only 25 percent of these are able to quit the first time they try; most smokers attempt to stop three or four times before they are successful. The craving for cigarettes can remain long after smokers have stopped smoking: 50 percent of people who quit smoking report they have desired cigarettes in the last 24 hours (Goldstein, 1994).

There are increasing calls for the U.S. government to declare nicotine a drug much like marijuana and other substances that produce psychological changes and physiological dependence and are detrimental to health. Such a declaration would then lead to strict governmental regulation of the sale and use of tobacco. Antismoking advocates

The dangers of secondhand smoke have led many businesses to bar smoking inside their buildings, leaving smokers to stand on the street to satisfy their dependency.

argue that nicotine dependence is a negative psychological and physiological condition just as bad as other substance dependencies. Moreover, between the effects of secondary smoke and the health care dollars spent treating diseases due to smoking, nicotine dependence exacts a much bigger toll on people who are not nicotine dependent than do most other substance dependencies. Opponents of the antismoking movement argue that nicotine is not truly a psychoactive substance—nicotine does not cause great changes in mood, thought, or perceptions as does cannabis, cocaine, heroin, or for that matter, alcohol. The negative health effects of smoking are the smoker's business only. People do many things that are not good for their health—they eat high cholesterol foods, they sit in the sun without sunscreen—but these activities are not regulated by the government. Tobacco industry executives argue that science has never actually proven that smoking causes any of the diseases with which it is highly correlated. This debate is likely to rage for some time to come, particularly given the issues of personal freedom and the massive amounts of money involved.

 Given what you know about other substances and the disorders related to them, do you think nicotine is like these other substances and should be regulated by the government? Why or why not?

Theories of Substance Use, Abuse, and Dependence

disease model
view that alcoholism (or drug addiction) is an incurable physical disease, like epilepsy or diabetes, and that only total abstinence can control it

For years, alcoholism was considered the result of a moral deficiency. Alcoholics were simply weak, bad people who would not exert control over their impulses to drink. Since the 1960s, that view has largely been replaced by the **disease model** of alcoholism, which views alcoholism as a incurable physical disease, like epilepsy or diabetes (Jellenick, 1960). This model has been supported somewhat by research on the genetics and biology of alcoholism, but there clearly are social and psychological forces that make some people more prone to alcohol abuse and dependence than are others. In this section, we will discuss the biological, social, and psychological factors that increase people's vulnerability to alcohol abuse and dependence. Most of the theories we will discuss have also been used to

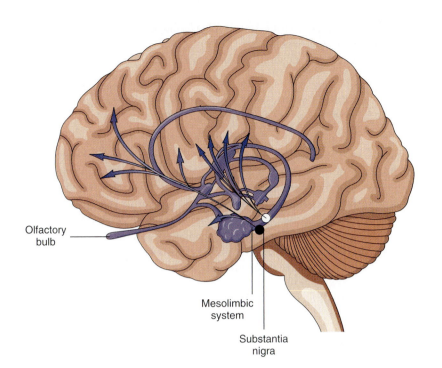

Figure 12.3

The Mesolimbic Dopamine System. The mesolimbic dopamine system may be the "reward center" of the brain where pleasure and displeasure arising from many sources (including psychoactive drugs) is registered.

Olfactory
bulb

Mesolimbic
system

Substantia
nigra

explain the development of abuse of and dependency on substances other than alcohol. However, much more research has been done on alcohol abuse and dependence than on other substance disorders, probably because alcohol-related disorders are more widespread than are the other disorders.

Substances and the Brain

All the substances we have discussed in this chapter affect several biochemicals in the brain, and these chemicals can have direct reinforcing effects on the brain. One area of the brain that may be intimately involved in the effects of psychoactive substances is the **mesolimbic dopamine system** (see Figure 12.3). This system is activated by natural rewards of many kinds, such as the taste of good food and the physical pleasure accompanying sexual stimulation. The same system is activated much more intensely by the psychoactive substances that people abuse or become dependent upon, such as cocaine, amphetamines, and heroin. The activation of this system actually disposes people to want to repeat the events that caused its activation. This occurs when a small bite of tasty food whets one's appetite. It also occurs when one hit of crack causes a user to want another hit (Berridge & Valenstein, 1991).

When the mesolimbic dopamine system is activated by a psychoactive substance, the brain may try to balance this state of activation with processes that have effects that are the opposite of those of the psychoactive substance. These processes are often referred to as *opponent processes* (Solomon, 1980). These opponent processes may remain active even after a person stops taking a psychoactive substance and may cause many of the withdrawal symptoms a person experiences.

Chronic use of psychoactive substances may produce permanent changes in the mesolimbic dopamine system, causing craving for these substances even after withdrawal symptoms pass. The repeated use of substances like cocaine, heroin, and amphetamines causes the neurons in the mesolimbic dopamine system to become hyperactive or sensitized. This sensitization can be permanent, so that these neurons will be activated more highly by subsequent exposure to the psychoactive substance or by stimuli that are associated with the substance (such as the pipe that a cocaine user formerly used to smoke crack). Subjectively, this creates a chronic and strong craving for the substance, which is made worse every time a former user comes into contact with stimuli that remind him or

mesolimbic dopamine system
brain circuit activated by natural rewards as well as psychoactive substances that disposes people to want the same event that led to its activation and that, when activated by chronic substance abuse, can become hypersensitized and lead to chronic and intense cravings

her of the substance. This can create a powerful physiological motivation for relapsing back into substance abuse and dependence (Robinson & Berridge, 1993). Susan, who was dependent on cocaine and alcohol but has been abstinent for 3 months, describes this phenomenon:

> Right now, I mean, I wanna go out and—I mean I want a line so bad, you know, I can taste it. Right now. I know I'm not supposed to. I just want it, though. Coke. (Engel, 1989, p. 40)

Thus, the substances we have discussed in this chapter have powerful effects on the brain, in both the short term and the long term, that can make these substances hard for people to resist once they have used them. Substances like cocaine that have especially rapid and powerful effects on the brain but that also wear off very quickly create great risk for dependency. Even people trying a substance casually can find the rapid, intense, but short-lived high so compelling that they crave more and soon increase their use.

Clearly, however, most people never even try most of the substances discussed in this chapter, and of those who do try them, most do not abuse them or become dependent on them. We turn now to other theories of substance abuse and dependence that have tried to explain individual differences in vulnerability to substance-related disorders.

Biological Theories of Vulnerability to Substance Use Disorders

Family history, adoption, and twin studies all suggest that genetics may play a substantial role in at least some forms of alcohol dependency (Devor, 1994; Schuckit & Smith, 1996). For example, the sons of alcoholic fathers are four to five times more likely to develop alcoholism as are the sons of nonalcoholic fathers. The evidence for a genetic transmission of alcoholism has been much more consistent for males than for females, however. One large-scale study of female twins found evidence for the heritability of alcoholism in women (Kendler, Heath, Neale, Kessler, & Eaves, 1992), but other studies have not. For example, in one study of 356 twins, the concordance rate for alcohol abuse or dependence among the male twins was 0.76 for the MZ twins and 0.53 for the same-sex DZ twins, suggesting heritability (McGue, Pickens, & Svikis, 1992). In contrast, the concordance rates among the female twins were 0.38 for the MZ twins and 0.42 for the same-sex DZ twins, suggesting no heritability. In addition, among the male twins, evidence of heritability was strong only for early-onset alcoholism (with onset of first symptoms before age 20) but not for late-onset alcoholism. These findings suggest that genetics may play the strongest role in early-onset male alcoholism.

What is inherited in this group? When given moderate doses of alcohol, the sons of alcoholics, who are presumably at increased risk for alcoholism, experience less intoxication, subjectively, in their cognitive and motor performance and on some physiological indicators than do the sons of nonalcoholics (Schuckit & Smith, 1996). At high doses of alcohol, however, the sons of alcoholics are just as intoxicated, by both subjective and objective measures, as are the sons of nonalcoholics. This lower reactivity to moderate doses of alcohol among sons of alcoholics may lead them to drink substantially more before they begin to feel drunk; as a result, they may not learn to recognize subtle, early signs of intoxication and may not learn to quit drinking before they become highly intoxicated. They may also develop high physiological tolerance for alcohol, which leads them to ingest more and more alcohol to achieve any level of subjective intoxication. Long-term studies of men with low reactivity to moderate doses of alcohol show that they are significantly more likely to become alcoholics over time than are men with greater reactivity to moderate doses of alcohol (Schuckit & Smith, 1996).

Researchers are searching for possible neurological and biochemical differences between persons with alcohol-related disorders and people without these disorders (Kranzler & Anton, 1994). There is not strong and consistent evidence for any one neurological or biochemical mechanism for the development of alcoholism as yet, but with advances in research technology, more understanding of the nature of biological predispositions to alcoholism is likely to come.

 Can genetic theories of alcoholism explain why many alcoholics also abuse other drugs?

Alcoholism as a Form of Depression

As many as 70 percent of people with alcohol dependency have depressive symptoms severe enough to interfere with daily living (Schuckit, 1991). In addition, early family history studies suggested that alcohol-related disorders and unipolar depression run together in families, with alcoholism more prevalent in male relatives and unipolar depression more prevalent in female relatives (Winokur & Clayton, 1967). These trends have led some researchers to argue that alcoholism and depression are genetically related and that many male alcoholics are actually depressed and denying their depression or "self-medicating" with alcohol (see Williams & Spitzer, 1983).

Although many people with alcohol-related problems appear to use alcohol to cope with daily stresses and emotional distress, it is probably not wise to consider alcoholism simply another form of depression for several reasons. First, although the children of alcoholics do have higher rates of depression than do the children of nonalcoholics, these depressions might result more from the stresses of having alcoholic parents than from genetics (Schuckit, 1995). Second, several family history studies have failed to find higher rates of alcoholism among the offspring of depressed people than among the offspring of nondepressed people, as one would suspect if depression and alcoholism were genetically related (Merikangas, Weissman, & Pauls, 1985). Third, because alcohol is a central nervous system depressant, it can cause the classic symptoms of depression. In addition, the social consequences of alcohol abuse and dependency (loss of relationships, loss of job) can cause depressions. Thus, when depression and alcohol dependency co-occur in individuals, the depression is just as likely to be a consequence as a cause of the alcohol dependency. Fourth, recent studies show that adolescents who are depressed are not more likely to become alcoholics than are adolescents who are not depressed, as we might expect if alcoholism is often a response to depression (Schuckit, 1995). Fifth, simply prescribing antidepressant medications to a person with alcohol abuse or dependency is not enough to help him or her overcome the alcohol-related problems in the long run (Schuckit, 1995). The risk of relapse is high unless he or she also undergoes treatment directly targeted at the drinking. Sixth, depression among alcoholics usually disappears once they become abstinent, even without any antidepressant treatment, again suggesting that the depression is secondary to the alcoholism, rather than its cause (Brown, Inaba, Gillin, & Schuckit, 1995).

Social, Behavioral, and Cognitive Theories

It was great being stoned. It was, you know, it was great. I just could evade all the bull—and just be stoned, do anything stoned. I just wanted to block everything out, is basically what it was. (Engel, 1989, p. 27)

The reinforcing effects of substances—the highs that stimulants produce, the calming and "zoning out" effects of the depressants and opioids—all may be more attractive to people under great psychological stress, particularly those under chronic stress. Thus, we see higher rates of substance abuse

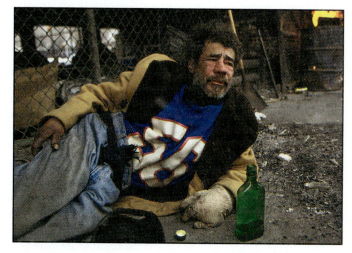

People facing severe chronic stress, like homelessness, may turn to alcohol to "medicate" themselves against their distress.

and dependence among people facing severe chronic stress—people living in poverty and with few hopes, women in abusive relationships, adolescents whose parents fight frequently and violently (Stewart, 1996). For these people, the effects of substances may be especially reinforcing. Plus, they may see few costs to becoming dependent on substances because they feel they have little to lose.

Chronic stress combined with an environment that supports and even promotes the use of substances as an escape is a recipe for widespread substance abuse and dependence. Such was the situation for soldiers fighting in the Vietnam War. The conditions under which they fought and lived created chronic stress. Illegal drugs, especially heroin and marijuana, were readily available, and the culture of the 1960s supported drug experimentation. Only 1 percent of soldiers who served in Vietnam had been dependent on heroin or other hard substances before the war. During the war, half the soldiers used these substances at least occasionally, and 20 percent were dependent on them. Fortunately, once these soldiers left that environment and returned home, their substance use dropped to the same level it was before they went to Vietnam (Robins, Helzer, & Davis, 1975).

 What theories of substance dependence do these data on heroin use in Vietnam soldiers most strongly contradict?

Some people cannot leave their stress behind because the stress is present where they live. Indeed, many people dependent on substances were introduced to these substances by their family members and grew up in horrible conditions from which everyone around them was using substances to escape.

Case Study • LaTisha, 35 years old when interviewed, was born and raised in Miami. Her mother was a barmaid and she never knew her father. She grew up with two brothers and four sisters, all of whom have different fathers. Her mother used pills during LaTisha's childhood, particularly Valium.

LaTisha took her first alcoholic drink when she was 12, introduced to her by her mother. However, she didn't drink regularly until she was 17, although she started sniffing glue at age 13. LaTisha's mother often brought men home from the bar to have sex with them for money. At 14, LaTisha's mother "turned her out" (introduced her to prostitution) by setting her up with "dates" from the bar. LaTisha was not aware until years later that the men had been paying her mother. LaTisha also recalls having been sexually abused by one of her mother's male friends when she was about 8.

When LaTisha was 16, her older brother returned home from the army. He and his friends would smoke marijuana. In an attempt to "be with the crowd," LaTisha also began smoking marijuana. At a party, her brother introduced her to "downers"—prescription sedatives and tranquilizers. LaTisha began taking pills regularly, eventually taking as many as 15 a day for about a year and a half. She was most often using both Valium and Quaalude.

By 17, LaTisha's brother had introduced her to heroin. Almost immediately, she began speedballing—injecting as well as snorting heroin, cocaine, and various amphetamines. During all the phases of LaTisha's injection-substance use, sharing needles was common. By age 24, LaTisha was mainlining heroin and turning tricks every day. (adapted from Inciardi et al., 1993, pp. 160–161)

It does not take conditions as extreme as LaTisha's to create an atmosphere that promotes substance use and abuse. More subtle environmental reinforcements and punishments for substance use and abuse clearly influence people's substance use habits. Some societies discourage any use of alcohol, often as part of religious beliefs, and alcohol abuse and dependence in these societies are rare. Other societies allow drinking of alcohol but strongly discourage excessive drinking or irresponsible behavior while intoxicated. Alcohol-related disorders are less common in these societies than in those with few restrictions, either legal or cultural, on alcohol use (Winger et al., 1992).

Children and adolescents learn alcohol-related behaviors from the modeling of their parents and important others in their culture. Children of parents who abuse alcohol by frequently getting drunk or driving while intoxicated learn that these are acceptable behaviors and are thus more likely to engage in them as well. Because alcohol-related problems are more common among males than females, most of the adults modeling the inappropriate use of alcohol will be male. In turn, because children are more likely to learn from adults who are similar to themselves, male children and male adolescents may be more likely to learn these behaviors from the adults in their world than are female children and female adolescents. Thus, maladaptive patterns of alcohol use may be passed down through the males in a family through modeling (Bandura, 1986).

The cognitive theories of alcohol abuse have focused on people's expectations for the effects of alcohol and their beliefs about the appropriateness of using alcohol to cope with stress (Marlatt, Baer, Donovan, & Kivlahan, 1988). People who expect alcohol to reduce their distress and who do not have other, more adaptive means of coping available to them (such as problem solving or turning to others for support) are more likely than others to drink alcohol when they are upset and more likely to have social problems related to drinking. For example, one study found that both men and women who believed that alcohol helped them relax and handle stress better and who tended to cope with stressful situations with avoidance rather than problem solving drank more often and had more drinking-related problems (Cooper, Russell, Skinner, Frone, & Mudar, 1992). When we explore treatment, we will review therapies that try to change people's beliefs about alcohol as a coping tool and to give people more appropriate strategies for coping with their problems.

 What are your expectations about whether alcohol will help you cope with a stressful situation?

Summing Up	Theories of Substance Use, Abuse, and Dependence

- Psychoactive substances have powerful effects on the parts of the brain that register reward and pleasure, including the mesolimbic dopamine system. Repeated use of a substance may sensitize this system, causing craving for more of the substance.
- Some types of alcoholism, particularly among males, may be genetically transmitted and it may be that men genetically predisposed to alcoholism are less sensitive to the effects of low doses of alcohol.
- Some theorists view alcoholism as a form of depression, although the prevailing evidence suggests that alcoholism and depression are distinct disorders.
- Behavioral theories of alcoholism note that people are reinforced or punished by other people for their alcohol-related behaviors.
- Cognitive theories argue that people who develop alcohol-related problems have strong expectations that alcohol will help them feel better and cope better when they face stressful times.

Treatment for Substance Disorders

The first step in the treatment of people with any substance use disorder is **detoxification**: getting them to stop using the substance and then allowing the substance to eliminate from the body. This is especially important when the substance being used can cause permanent organ or brain damage or is frequently lethal, such as cocaine, amphetamines, and inhalants. Once people stop using the substance and are through the withdrawal process, a variety of biological and psychosocial therapies are used to help them prevent relapse. These therapies are often combined in comprehensive substance treatment programs.

detoxification

first step in treatment for substance-related disorders in which a person stops using the substance and allows it to fully exit the body

People check themselves into these programs where they remain for a few weeks or months until they feel they have gained control over their substance abuse and dependence.

Biological Treatments

Although many substance-dependent people can withstand withdrawal symptoms with emotional support, for other people the symptoms are so severe that drugs may be prescribed to reduce these symptoms (Schuckit, 1996). For people who are alcohol dependent, a benzodiazepine, which has depressant effects similar to those of alcohol, can be prescribed to reduce symptoms of tremor and anxiety, decrease pulse and respiration rates, and stabilize blood pressure. The dosage of the drug is decreased each day so that a patient withdraws from the alcohol slowly but does not become dependent on the benzodiazepine.

Gradual withdrawal from heroin can be achieved with the help of a synthetic drug known as **methadone.** This is an opioid itself, but it has less potent and longer-lasting effects than heroin when taken orally. The heroin dependent will take methadone while discontinuing use of heroin. The methadone will help reduce the extremely negative withdrawal symptoms from heroin. Individuals who take heroin while on methadone do not experience the intense psychological effects of heroin because methadone blocks the receptors for heroin. While the goal of treatment is eventually to withdraw individuals from the methadone, some patients continue to use methadone for years, under physicians' care, rather than taper off their use. These **methadone maintenance programs** are controversial. Some people believe that they allow the heroin dependent simply to transfer dependency to another substance that is legal and provided by a physician. Other people believe that methadone maintenance is the only way to keep some heroin dependents from going back on the street and becoming readdicted. Studies following patients in methadone maintenance programs do find that they are much more likely than patients who try to withdraw from heroin without methadone to remain in psychological treatment and that they are less likely to relapse into heroin use or to become reinvolved in criminal activity (Ball & Ross, 1991).

Heroin dependents are also given other drugs that reduce the reinforcing effects of heroin and thus reduce their desire for the heroin. **Naltrexone** and **naloxone** are opioid antagonists—they block the effects of opioids like heroin. If a person takes heroin while on naltrexone or naloxone, he or she will not experience the positive effects of the heroin.

Naltrexone has also proven useful in blocking the high that can be caused by alcohol. Alcoholics on naltrexone report that their craving for alcohol is diminished and they drink less (Volpicelli, Watson, King, & Sherman, 1995). One drug that can make alcohol actually punishing is **disulfiram**, commonly referred to as *Antabuse* (Petersen, 1992; Schuckit, 1996). Just having one drink can make a person taking disulfiram extremely sick.

Antidepressants are sometimes used to help people weather the withdrawal syndrome so as to continue abstaining from substance use (Giannini, 1991; Schuckit, 1996). Animal studies suggest that the antidepressants known as *serotonin-reuptake inhibitors* can reduce alcohol consumption. Studies with humans have not yet shown the serotonin reuptake inhibitors to be effective in reducing alcohol-seeking behaviors, however. Antidepressant drugs are sometimes used to treat alcoholics who are depressed, but the efficacy of these drugs in treating either the alcohol problems or the depression in the absence of psychotherapy has not been consistently supported (Schuckit, 1996).

Alcoholics Anonymous

Alcoholics Anonymous (AA) is an organization created by and for people with alcohol-related problems. Its interventions are based on the disease model of alcoholism. According to this model, alcoholism is a disease that causes alcoholics to lose all control over their drinking once they have the first drink. The implication of this model is that the only way to control alcoholism is to completely abstain from any alcohol.

methadone
opioid that is less potent and that is longer lasting than heroin, taken by heroin users to decrease their cravings and help them cope with negative withdrawal symptoms

methadone maintenance programs
treatments for heroin abusers that provide doses of methadone to replace heroin use and seek eventually to wean addicted people from the methadone itself

naltrexone
drug that blocks the positive effects of alcohol and heroin and can lead to a decreased desire to drink or use substances

naloxone
drug that blocks the positive effects of heroin and can lead to a decreased desire to use it

disulfiram
drug that produces an aversive physical reaction to alcohol and is used to encourage abstinence; commonly referred to as *Antabuse*

What groups of people (young people, older people, men, women, etc.) do you think might be most resistant to the disease model of alcoholism? Explain.

AA prescribes 12 steps that alcoholics must take toward recovery. The first step is for alcoholics to admit they are alcoholics and powerless to control the effects of alcohol. AA encourages members to seek help from a higher power and to admit to their weaknesses and ask for forgiveness. The goal for all members is complete abstinence. Group members provide moral and social support for each other and make themselves available to each other in times of crisis. Once they are able, group members are expected to devote themselves to helping other alcoholics. AA believes that people are never completely cured of alcoholism—they are always "recovering alcoholics" with the potential of falling back into alcohol dependency with one drink. AA meetings include testimonials from recovering alcoholics about their paths into alcoholism which are meant to motivate others to abstain from alcohol (Spitzer et al., 1983, pp. 87–89):

"I am Duncan. I am an alcoholic." The audience settled deeper into their chairs at these familiar words. Another chronicle of death and rebirth would shortly begin. The Fellowship of Alcoholics Anonymous would reaffirm its mission, celebrate again the saving of a life.

The tall, carefully dressed man continued. "I know that I will always be an alcoholic, that I can never again touch alcohol in any form. It'll kill me if I don't keep away from it. In fact, it almost did." . . . Duncan went on, "Some of you know what I'm talking about don't you? And I think my story'll ring a few bells as well." It was a well-known story to all of them. "I must have been just past my 15th birthday when I had that first drink that everybody talks about. And like so many of them—and you—it was like a miracle. With a little beer in my gut, the world was transformed. I wasn't a weakling anymore, I could lick almost anybody on the block. And girls? Well, you can imagine how a couple of beers made me feel, like I could have any girl I wanted. So, like so many of you, my friends in the Fellowship, alcohol became the royal road to love, respect, and self-esteem. If I couldn't feel good about myself when I wasn't drinking, if I felt stupid or lazy or ugly or misunderstood, all I had to do was belt down a few and everything got better. Of course, I was fooling myself, wasn't I, because I was as ugly and dumb and lazy when I was drunk as when I was sober. But I didn't know it."

Duncan paused, wiped his brow, then started in again. "Though it's obvious to me now that my drinking even then, in high school, and after I got to college, was a problem, I didn't think so at the time. After all, everybody was drinking and getting drunk and acting stupid, and I didn't really think I was different. A couple of minor auto accidents, one conviction for drunken driving, a few fights—nothing out of the ordinary, it seemed to me at the time. True, I was drinking quite a lot, even then, but my friends seemed to be able to down as much beer as I did. I guess the fact that I hadn't really had any blackouts and that I could go for days without having to drink reassured me that things hadn't gotten out of control. And that's the way it went, until I found myself drinking even more—and more often—and suffering more from my drinking, along about my third year of college."

Duncan paused again, took a long draw from his coffee mug, then recalled those earlier days. "My roommate, a friend from high school, started bugging me about my drinking. It wasn't just because I was coming in at all hours or that I was getting sick in the room, and it wasn't even that I'd have to sleep it off the whole next day and miss class, it was that he had begun to hear other friends talking about me, about the fool I'd made of myself at parties. He saw how shaky I was the morning after, and he saw how different I was when I'd been drinking a lot—almost out of my head was the way he put it. And he could count the bottles that I'd leave around the room and he knew what the drinking and the carousing was doing to my grades. So, at his demand, I went to the counseling center, where I was assigned a counselor who totally turned me off to anything a mental health worker could do. All he would say is that my drinking was a sign of deep emotional problems and that I'd have to agree to get into my past and my feelings about my parents and things like that, or I wasn't going to change my drinking. I was totally disenchanted. Partly because I wanted to show this person he was wrong, and partly because I really cared about my roommate and didn't want to lose him as a friend, I did cut down on my drinking by half or more. I only drank on weekends—and then only at night. And I set more-or-less arbitrary limits on how much I would drink, as well as where and when I would drink. And that got me through the rest of college and, actually, through law school as well. I'd drink enough to get very drunk once or twice a week, but only on weekends, and then I'd tough it out through the rest of the week.

"Shortly after getting my law degree, I married my first wife, and with establishing myself in practice and then, a little later, starting a family, I became so preoccupied with interesting things in my life that, for the first time since I started, my drinking was no problem at all. I would go for weeks at a time without touching a drop, so involved was I in my growing practice and family. Then, I'm sorry to say, things got worse again, a lot worse. . . .

"My marriage started to go bad after our second son, our third child, was born. I was very much career-and-success oriented, and I had little time to spend at home with my family. . . . My traveling had increased a lot, there were stimulating people on those trips, and, let's face it, there were some pretty exciting women available, too. So home got to be little else but a nagging, boring wife and children I wasn't very interested in. My drinking had gotten bad again, too, with being on the road so much, having to do a lot of entertaining at lunch when I wasn't away, and trying to soften the hassles at home. I guess I was putting down close to a gallon of very good scotch a week, with one thing or another.

"And as that went on, the drinking began to affect both my marriage and my career. With enough booze in me and under the pressures of guilt over my failure to carry out my responsibilities to my wife and children, I sometimes got kind of rough physically with them. I would break furniture, throw things around, then rush out and drive off in the car. I had a couple of wrecks, lost my license for two years because of one of them. Worst of all was when I tried to stop. By then I was totally hooked, so every time I tried to stop drinking, I'd experience withdrawal in all its horrors. I never had DTs, but I came awfully close many times, with the vomiting and the 'shakes' and being unable to sit still or to lie down. And that would go on for days at a time. . . .

"Then, about four years ago, with my life in ruins, my wife given up on me and the kids with her, out of a job, and way down on my luck, the Fellowship and I found each other. Jim, over there, bless his heart, decided to sponsor me—we'd been friends for a long time, and I knew he'd found sobriety through this group. I've been dry now for a little over two years, and with luck and support, I may stay sober. I've begun to make amends for my transgressions, I've faced my faults squarely again instead of hiding them with booze, and I think I may make it."

The practices and philosophies of AA do not appeal to everyone. The emphases on one's powerlessness, need for a higher power, and complete abstinence turn many people away. In addition, many people who subscribe to AA's philosophy still find it difficult to maintain complete abstinence and "fall off the wagon" at various times throughout their lives. However, thousands of people have found AA very helpful in their recovery from alcohol abuse and dependency. It has been difficult to measure the effectiveness of AA scientifically, because there is self-selection in who goes to AA, and there is controversy over whether to count people who drop out of AA as failures of the program. Still, AA remains the most common source of treatment for people with alcohol-related problems. There are about 23,000 chapters of AA across 90 countries, and it is estimated that 800,000 people currently attend meetings of AA (Goodwin, 1988). Narcotics Anonymous is an organization similar in structure and purpose to AA that focuses on people who abuse substances other than (or in addition to) alcohol.

Behavioral Treatments

Behavioral therapies based on **aversive classical conditioning** are sometimes used to treat alcohol dependency and abuse, either alone or in combination with biological or other psychosocial therapies (Schuckit, 1995). Drugs like disulfiram that make the ingestion of alcoholic unpleasant or toxic are given to alcoholics. If they take drinks of alcohol, the drug interacts with the alcohol to cause nausea and vomiting. Eventually, through classical conditioning, alcoholics develop conditioned responses to the alcohol, namely nausea and vomiting. They then learn to avoid the alcohol, through operant conditioning, in order to avoid the aversive response to the alcohol. Studies have shown such aversive conditioning to be effective in reducing alcohol consumption, at least in the short term (Schuckit, 1995). "Booster" sessions are often needed to reinforce the aversive conditioning, however, because it tends to weaken with time.

An alternative is **covert sensitization therapy** in which alcoholics use imagery to create associations between thoughts of alcohol use and thoughts of highly unpleasant consequences of alcohol use. An example of a sensitization scene that a therapist might take a client through begins as follows (Rimmele, Miller, & Dougher, 1989, p. 135):

> You finish the first sip of beer, and you . . . notice a funny feeling in your stomach. . . . Maybe another drink will help. . . . As you tip back . . . that funny feeling in your stomach is stronger, and you feel like you have to burp. . . . You swallow again, trying to force it down, but it doesn't work. You can feel the gas coming up. . . . You swallow more, but suddenly your mouth is filled with a sour liquid that burns the back of your throat and goes up your nose. . . . [You] spew the liquid all over the counter and sink. . . .

The imagery gets even more graphic from there. Covert sensitization techniques seem effective in creating conditioned aversive responses to the sight and smell of alcohol and in reducing alcohol consumption (Tucker et al., 1992).

Finally, as noted earlier, some alcoholics develop classically conditioned responses to the environmental cues often present when they drink. For example, when they see or smell their favorite alcoholic beverages, they begin to salivate and report cravings to drink. These conditioned responses increase the risk of relapse among alcoholics who are abstinent or trying to quit drinking. A behavioral therapy known as **cue exposure and response prevention** is used to extinguish this conditioned response to cues associated with alcohol intake (Rankin, Hodgson, & Stockwell, 1983). Alcoholics are exposed to their favorite types of alcohol, encouraged to hold glasses to their lips, and smell the alcohol but are prohibited or strongly encouraged not to drink any of the alcohol. Eventually, this procedure has been shown to reduce the desire to drink and increase the ability to avoid drinking when the opportunity arises (Rankin et al., 1983). The procedure probably should be coupled with instructions on strategies for coping with and removing oneself from tempting situations as we shall discuss next.

Cognitively Oriented Treatments

Interventions based on the cognitive models of alcohol abuse and dependency help clients identify those situations in which they are most likely to drink and lose control over their drinking and their expectations that alcohol will help them cope better with those situations (Marlatt & Gordon, 1985). Therapists then work with clients to challenge these expectations by reviewing the negative effects of alcohol on their behavior. For example, a therapist may focus on a recent party at which a client was feeling anxious and thus began to drink heavily. The therapist might have the client recount the embarrassing and socially inappropriate behaviors he engaged in while intoxicated, to challenge the notion that the alcohol helped him cope effectively with his party anxiety. Therapists also help clients learn to anticipate and reduce stress in their lives and to develop more adaptive ways of coping with stressful situations, such as seeking the help of others or active problem solving. Finally, therapists help clients learn to say, "No thanks," when offered drinks and to deal effectively with social pressure to drink by using assertiveness skills.

Behavioral interventions help alcoholics learn to inhibit their impulses to drink.

aversive classical conditioning pairing of alcohol with a substance that will interact with it to cause nausea or vomiting (such as disulfiram) in order to make alcohol itself a conditioned stimulus to be avoided

covert sensitization therapy pairing of mental images of alcohol with other images of highly unpleasant consequences resulting from its use in order to create an aversive reaction to the sight and smell of alcohol and reduce drinking

cue exposure and response prevention therapy to reduce relapse among alcoholics by tempting them with stimuli that induce cravings to drink while preventing them from actually drinking, allowing them to habituate to the cravings and reduce temptation

The following is an excerpt from a discussion between a therapist and a client with alcohol-related problems in which the therapist is helping the client generate strategies for coping with the stress of a possible job promotion (adapted from Sobell & Sobell, 1978, pp. 97–98). The therapist encourages the client to brainstorm coping strategies, without evaluating them for the moment, so that the client feels free to generate as many possible strategies as he can.

Client: I really want this job, and it'll mean a lot more money for me, not only now but also at retirement. Besides, if I refused the promotion, what would I tell my wife or my boss?

Therapist: Rather than worrying about that for the moment, why don't we explore what kinds of possible behavioral options you have regarding this job promotion. Remember, don't evaluate the options now. Alternatives, at this point, can include anything even remotely possible; what we want you to do is come up with a range of possible alternatives. You don't have to carry out an alternative just because you consider it.

Client: You know, I could do what I usually do in these kinds of situations. In fact, being as nervous as I've been these past couple of months, I've done that quite often.

Therapist: You mean drinking?

Client: Yeah, I've been drinking quite heavily some nights when I get home, and my wife is really complaining.

Therapist: Well, OK, drinking is one option. What other ways could you deal with this problem?

Client: Well, I could take the job, and on the side I could take some night courses in business at a local college. That way I could learn how to be a supervisor. But, gee, that would be a lot of work. I don't even know if I have the time. Besides, I don't know if they offer the kind of training I need.

Therapist: At this point, it's really not necessary to worry about how to carry out the options but simply to identify them. You're doing fine. What are some other ways you might handle the situation?

Client: Well, another thing I could do is to simply tell the boss that I'm not sure I'm qualified and either tell him that I don't want the job or ask him if he could give me some time to learn my new role.

Therapist: OK. Go on, you're doing fine.

Client: But what if the boss tells me that I have to take the job, I don't have any choice?

Therapist: Well, what general kinds of things might happen in that case?

Client: Oh, I could take the job and fail. That's one option. I could take the job and learn how to be a supervisor. I could refuse the job, risk being fired, and maybe end up having to look for another job. You know, I could just go and talk to my supervisor right now and explain the problem to him and see what comes of that.

Therapist: Well, you've delineated a lot of options. Let's take some time to evaluate them before you reach any decision.

The therapist then helps the client evaluate the potential effectiveness of each option and anticipate any potential negative consequences of each action. The client decides to accept the promotion but take some courses at the local college to increase his business background. The therapist discusses with the client the stresses of managing a new job and classes, and they generate ways the client can manage these stresses other than by drinking.

In most cases, therapists using these cognitive-behavioral approaches encourage clients to abstain from alcohol, especially when clients have histories of frequent relapses into alcohol abuse. When clients' goals are to learn to drink socially and therapists believe clients have the capability to achieve these goals, then therapists may focus on teaching clients to engage in social, or **controlled, drinking.**

The controlled drinking perspective directly clashes with the idea that alcoholism is a biological disease and that if an alcoholic takes even one sip of alcohol he or she will lose all control and plunge back into full alcoholism (see Pendery, Maltzman, & West, 1982; Sobell & Sobell, 1978). People who have had many alcohol-related problems generally have trouble with controlled social drinking and must remain abstinent in order to avoid relapse into alcohol dependency. Some studies of the natural history of alcoholism find that some proportion of alcoholics spontaneously develop patterns of controlled social drinking, however (Vaillant & Milofsky, 1982). Moreover, more recent studies of controlled drinking programs have suggested that they are at least as beneficial as and sometimes more beneficial than abstinence programs (Marlatt et al., 1993). For example, in a landmark study, Mark and Linda Sobell (1978) found that alcoholics in a controlled drinking program functioned well for 71 percent of the days in the first year following treatment, whereas alcoholics in an abstinence program functioned well for only 35 percent of the days.

 Do you find yourself skeptical that alcoholics can engage in controlled drinking? If so, what beliefs or evidence does this skepticism reflect? If not, why not?

Unfortunately, the relapse rate for people undergoing any kind of treatment for alcohol abuse and dependency is high. The **abstinence violation effect** is a powerful contributor to relapse. There are two components to the abstinence violation effect. The first is a sense of conflict and guilt when an alcoholic who has been abstinent violates the abstinence and has a drink. He or she may then continue to drink to try to suppress the conflict and guilt. The second is a tendency to attribute the violation of abstinence to a lack of willpower and self-control rather than to situational factors. Thus, the person may think, "I'm an alcoholic and there's no way I can control my drinking. The fact I had a drink proves this." This type of thinking may pave the way to continued, uncontrolled drinking.

Relapse prevention programs teach alcoholics to view slips as temporary and situationally caused. Therapists work with clients to identify high-risk situations for relapse and to avoid those situations or exercise effective coping strategies for the situations. For example, a client may identify parties as high-risk situations for relapse. If she decides to go to a party, she may first practice with her therapist assertiveness skills for resisting pressure from friends to drink and write down other coping strategies she can use if she feels tempted to drink, such as starting a conversation with a supportive friend or practicing deep breathing exercises. She may also decide that if the temptation to drink becomes too great, she will ask a supportive friend to leave the party with her and go somewhere for coffee, until the temptation to drink passes.

Only about 10 percent of people who are alcohol dependents or abusers ever seek treatment. Another 40 percent may recover on their own, often as the result of maturation or positive changes in their environment (such as getting a good job or getting married to a supportive person) that help them and motivate them to get control of their drinking. The remainder of people with significant alcohol problems continue to have these problems throughout their lives. Some of these people become physically ill or completely unable to hold jobs or maintain their relationships. Others are able to hide or control their alcohol abuse and dependency enough to keep their jobs and may be in relationships with people who facilitate their alcohol dependency. Often they will have periods, sometimes long periods, of abstinence, but then, perhaps when facing stressful events, they will begin drinking again. This is why preventing the development of alcohol abuse

controlled drinking
controversial goal of therapy that involves people with alcohol problems learning to manage their drinking, usually with the help of therapists, rather than abstaining from drinking completely (as in the disease model)

abstinence violation effect
what happens when a person attempting to abstain from alcohol use ingests alcohol and then endures conflict and guilt by making an internal attribution to explain why he or she drank, thereby making him or her more likely to continue drinking in order to cope with the self-blame and guilt

relapse prevention programs
treatments that seek to offset continued alcohol use by identifying high-risk situations for those attempting to stop or cut down on drinking and teaching them either to avoid those situations or to use assertiveness skills when in them, while viewing setbacks as temporary

Having friends who will engage in activities that do not involve alcohol can help an alcoholic avoid temptations to drink.

and dependency and other substance-related problems is so important. We will focus on one prevention effort in the *Application* at the end of this chapter.

 All of the psychosocial interventions for substance abuse put the major responsibility for stopping substance use on the individual. What are the pros and cons of this?

Summing Up | Treatment for Substance Disorders

- Several drugs can be used to aid substance abusers through withdrawal and to reduce the reinforcing effects of the substances.
- The most common treatment for alcoholism is Alcoholics Anonymous, a self-help group that encourages alcoholics to admit their weaknesses and call on a higher power and other group members to help them remain completely abstinent from alcohol. A related group called *Narcotics Anonymous* is available for people dependent on other substances.
- Behavioral therapies based on aversive classical conditioning are sometimes used to treat alcoholism.
- Treatments based on social learning and cognitive theories focus on training the alcoholic in more adaptive coping skills and challenging his or her positive expectations about the effects of alcohol.
- Many therapists in the behavioral and cognitive tradition reject the disease model of alcoholism and suggest that some alcoholics may learn to engage in controlled social drinking.

Gender and Substance Use

Men are more prone than women to almost all substance use disorders. We have already reviewed evidence that genetics may play a stronger role in male alcoholism than in female alcoholism. This suggests that, if there is a genetic predisposition to alcoholism in a family, the male members are more likely than the female members to be affected.

Another reason women may be less prone than men to alcoholism is that they are much more sensitive than men to the intoxicating effects of alcohol (Lex, 1995). At a given dose of alcohol, about 30 percent more of the alcohol will enter a woman's bloodstream than a man's, because women have less of an enzyme that neutralizes and breaks down alcohol. Thus, a woman will experience the subjective and overt symptoms of alcohol intoxication at lower doses than a man will and may experience more severe withdrawal symptoms (i.e., hangovers) if she drinks too much. These factors may lead many women to drink less than men do. Women who do abuse alcohol, however, may be at more risk for negative health effects of alcohol than are men, because their blood concentrations of alcohol are higher than those of men who abuse.

Most of the theories about the gender differences in substance use disorders, however, have focused on differences in the reinforcements and punishments for substance use between men and women and their resulting attitudes toward their own use (see Gomberg, 1994; Lex, 1995). Substance use, particularly alcohol use, is much more acceptable for men than for women in many societies. Heavy drinking is part of what "masculine" men do and it is modeled by heroes and cultural icons. However, until quite recently, heavy drinking was a sign that a woman was "not a lady." Societal acceptance of heavy drinking by women has increased in recent generations and so has the rate of alcohol use in young women.

Men and women have also tended to have different expectations about the effects of alcohol and perhaps other substances that influence their use. Men are more likely than women to have positive expectations about alcohol helping them cope and to use alcohol to cope. Indeed, some laboratory studies find that women often expect alcohol to interfere with their ability to cope with difficult situations and avoid alcohol when they must deal with stressful situations. Thus, differences between men and women both in expectations about alcohol and the use of alcohol to cope may contribute to the gender differences in alcohol-related problems (Cooper et al., 1992).

Substance abuse and dependence are not just men's problems, however. There are many women substance users, although their patterns of use and reasons for use tend to differ from men's. Whereas men tend to begin using substances in the context of socializing with male friends, women are most often initiated into substance use by family members, partners, or lovers (Boyd & Guthrie, 1996; Gomberg, 1994; Inciardi et al., 1993). One study found that 70 percent of female crack users were living with men who were also substance users, and many were living with multiple abusers (Inciardi et al., 1993).

Male substance abusers often have such severe and long-lasting problems with impulsive and aggressive behavior that they are diagnosed with antisocial personality disorders. In contrast, the most common diagnosis for women substance abusers is depression or anxiety disorder. Also, between 30 and 75 percent of women in treatment for substance abuse have histories of sexual or physical abuse (Miller & Testa, 1993).

These differences in the contexts for men's and women's substance abuse suggest the need for different approaches to treating men and women (Beckman, 1994). For men, treatment may need to focus on challenging the societal supports for their substance use and their view that substance use is an appropriate way to cope. It may also need to focus on men's tendency to act in aggressive and impulsive ways, particularly when intoxicated. For women, treatment may need to focus more on issues of self-esteem and powerlessness and on helping them remove themselves from abusive environments.

Some therapists feel it is harder to treat women substance users than men substance users (see Beckman, 1994). Women who violate social norms so greatly as to become substance abusers may have more severe underlying emotional problems than do men who become substance abusers. In addition, because women substance abusers typically are living with partners and other family members who are also substance abusers, they may not have the necessary support from their environments to stop their substance use. Rarely do husbands or boyfriends participate in the treatment of woman substance users. In contrast, women partners often participate in male substance abusers' treatment (Higgins, Budney, Beckel, & Badger, 1994). Women substance abusers also tend to cut themselves off from women friends, hiding their substance use and feeling they are not like other women (Henderson & Boyd, 1996).

As substance use among women increases, however, treatment programs will have to become more sensitive to the differences in patterns and motives of substance use in women and men and design their programs to meet the need of both genders.

Cross-Cultural Perspectives on Substance Use and Prevention

Countries differ greatly in their attitudes toward substance abuse and dependency, in the laws concerning these problems, and in the ways abusers and dependents are treated (Goldstein, 1994). Many Moslem countries following Islamic law strictly prohibit alcohol and enforce strict penalties on people caught using this or any other substance. When the Communists took over China in the late 1940s, they made it a major goal to eradicate the widespread use of opium. Traffickers were executed, and users were sent to the countryside for rehabilitation and re-education. Today, antidrug laws are still strictly enforced, and punishments for the use or sale of illicit substances remain severe.

In Great Britain, substance addiction is considered a medical disease, and abusers and dependents are treated by physicians. Although traffickers in illegal substances are aggressively prosecuted by the British government, users of illegal substances are more often referred for treatment than arrested for possession of substances. Heroin use is as prevalent as it is in the United States, but physicians in Great Britain are more comfortable with long-term methadone maintenance than are physicians in the United States.

The Dutch make a distinction in their law enforcement between "soft" drugs (such as cannabis) and "hard" drugs (such as cocaine and heroin). Although both types of substances are illegal, possession, use, and sale of cannabis is rarely prosecuted, whereas the importing, manufacture, and sale of the hard substances are subject to heavy penalties that are enforced. The Dutch system is based on the belief that enforcing a strict prohibition of softer drugs would drive users underground, where they would come into contact with persons trafficking in harder drugs and be more likely to begin using these drugs.

Zurich, Switzerland, became famous for its "needle park," where the sale and use of substances including heroin and cocaine were carried out in the open and allowed by authorities, while a doctor employed by the government stood by in a small kiosk to handle any emergencies and to distribute clean needles for injection of substances. Nearby, in a school bus, social workers passed out warm drinks on cold days and were available if anyone requested counseling. The philosophy behind the establishment of this "safe haven" for substance users was that it would reduce some of the negative consequences of substance use and abuse—the risk of infection from used needles, the dangers of interacting with underground substance traffickers, the possibility of overdosing on substances with no medical help available. In addition, by concentrating illicit substance trade and use in one "needle park," the government kept it out of other public areas, such as the railroad stations and shopping malls. Opponents of the park argued that it made it extremely easy for troubled young people to become part of the drug scene and generally legitimized illicit drug use. In 1992, the park was closed because of evidence that addicts from around Europe had poured into the city and crime had soared.

These are but a few examples of the enormous differences in philosophies about and practices of substance use. Which one is best? That is, which approach leads to the least abuse and dependency on substances? These questions do not lend themselves to simple answers (Goldstein, 1994). It is difficult to collect accurate data on the use of substances, particularly illegal substances. Moreover, because cultures differ in their moral philosophies about substances, about personal responsibility, and about individual freedoms, what may work in one culture may not work in another.

What theories of or perspectives on substance abuse and dependence are reflected in the current drug policies of this country?

Bio-Psycho-Social INTEGRATION

The substances we have discussed in this chapter are powerful biological agents. They affect the brain directly, producing changes in mood, thoughts, and perceptions. Some people may find these changes more positive or rewarding than other people do because they are genetically or biochemically predisposed to do so. The rewards and punishments in the environment can clearly affect an individual's choice to pursue the effects of substances, however. Even many long-term chronic substance abusers can abstain from using if they can decide to abstain and receive the strong environmental support for abstention.

The biological and psychosocial pressures that lead some people to develop substance use disorders often co-occur. For example, people who grow up with alcoholic parents may have biological vulnerabilities to alcoholism, may have learned that drinking is an appropriate way to cope with distress, and may have had chaotic childhoods. Actor Gary Crosby, son of singer Bing Crosby and Dixie Lee Crosby, described the wild mood swings of his alcoholic mother (from David, 1994, pp. 230–234). Gary Crosby also became an alcoholic, trying to dull the rage and self-loathing he attributed to his abusive childhood:

> When she wasn't sick she could be a pleasure. My brothers and I would tiptoe into her room in the morning, and she would throw her arms around us and motion us to sit on the bed beside her while she sipped her coffee. She would laugh and joke with us and ask us about our plans for the day. If we didn't have to dash off to school, she might think up a special treat, something she knew we'd enjoy.

But a few hours later her mood was likely to have changed completely. By the time we were ready to leave for the theater, she might not even remember she had told us [we could go].

There was no arguing with her, so that was the end of it. I only hoped she wouldn't think to summon me back to her room later on, because then she was certain to be worse. Even when she was three quarters in the bag, she could still feel the reserve in me pulling away. That would hurt her, then make her angry, and that would set her off yelling and screaming and cursing. I would have to stand there and listen until she was done.

When she got to ranting like that, she slurred and mumbled so badly I could barely make sense of her rage. I was able to decipher that somebody was a "no good sonofabitch," but wasn't sure if it was me or someone else. Whoever it was, when she paused in her tirade, stared me straight in the eye, and asked, "Right?" I knew I had better agree with her. "Right, Mom. Right. Right." Sometimes she ended one of those mumblings with just a question mark and waited for my answer. Then I couldn't fake it. A simple "Right, Mom" wasn't enough, and I didn't know what else to say. That would make her even more furious.

"What's the matter with you? You stupid? What? You must be stupid!"

"Yes, Mom, I'm stupid."

I couldn't explain that I hadn't understood her. Then she would growl, "What's a matter? You deaf? You're not paying attention to me when I talk to you?" Any answer I gave was wrong, so stupid was fine. "OK, I'm stupid." At least that didn't get me a whipping.

It didn't take much to bring one on at those moments. The slightest wrong expression or inflection was enough to trigger her wrath. "I told you not to let me hear that tone of voice!" she would yell, ordering me outside to pick a switch off one of the trees.

Often when I saw her the next morning it was as if nothing had happened. I would sidle into her room expecting the worst and be greeted with outstretched arms and a radiant smile.

"Aw, honey, how are you? It's so good to see you. Come over here and let me give you a hug."

She was all gentleness and warmth then and didn't seem to remember anything at all about how she had raged and cursed and maybe even worked me over less than twenty-four hours before. I think that frightened me even more than the yelling and whipping.

Chapter Summary

A substance is any natural or synthesized product that has psychoactive effects. The four groups of substances most often leading to substance disorders are (1) central nervous system depressants, including alcohol, barbiturates and benzodiazepines, and inhalants; (2) central nervous system stimulants, including cocaine, amphetamines, and caffeine; (3) opioids; and (4) hallucinogens, phencyclidine, and cannabis.

Substance intoxication is indicated by a set of behavioral and psychological changes that occur as a direct result of the physiological effects of a substance on the central nervous system. Substance withdrawal involves a set of physiological and behavioral symptoms that result from the cessation of or reduction in heavy and prolonged use of a substance. The specific symptoms of intoxication and withdrawal depend on the substance being used, the amount of the substance ingested, and the method of ingestion. Substance abuse is indicated when an individual shows persistent problems in one of four categories: (1) failure to fulfill major role obligations at work, school, or home; (2) substance use in situations in which such use is physically hazardous; (3) substance-related legal problems; and (4) continued substance use despite social or interpersonal problems. Substance dependence is characterized by a maladaptive pattern of substance use leading to significant problems in a person's life and usually leading to tolerance to the substance, withdrawal symptoms if the substance is discontinued, and compulsive substance-taking behavior.

Routes of administration that produce rapid and efficient absorption of a substance into the bloodstream (i.e., intravenous injection, smoking, snorting) lead to a more intense intoxication, a greater likelihood of dependence, and a greater risk of overdose. Substances that act more rapidly on the central nervous system and whose effects wear off more quickly (e.g., cocaine) and that lead to faster intoxication are more likely to lead to dependence or abuse.

At low doses, alcohol produces relaxation and a mild euphoria. At higher doses, it produces the classic signs of depression and cognitive and motor impairment. A large proportion of deaths due to accidents, murders, and suicides are alcohol-related. Alcohol withdrawal symptoms can be mild or so severe as to be life threatening. Alcohol abusers and dependents experience a wide range of social and interpersonal problems and are at risk for many serious health problems. Women drink less alcohol than men do in most cultures and are less likely to have alcohol-related problems than are men. Persons of Asian descent typically are less prone to alcohol-related problems.

Benzodiazepines and barbiturates are sold by prescription for the treatment of anxiety and insomnia. One pattern of the development of abuse of or dependence on these substances is reflected by the teenager or young adult who begins using the substances recreationally to produce a sense of well-being or euphoria but then escalates to chronic use and physiological dependence. A second pattern is shown by individuals who begin to use substances under physicians' care for insomnia or anxiety but then escalate their usage without the knowledge of their physicians.

The inhalants are volatile agents that people sniff to produce a sense of euphoria, disinhibition, and increased aggressiveness or sexual performance. The greatest users and abusers of inhalants are young boys, particularly Native American teenagers and Hispanic teenagers. Inhalants are extremely dangerous because they can cause permanent brain damage even with casual use, several major diseases, and suffocation when the user goes unconscious with the plastic bag used for inhaling still over his or her head.

Cocaine activates those parts of the brain that register reward or pleasure and produces a sudden rush of euphoria, followed by increased self-esteem, alertness, and energy and a greater sense of competence, creativity, and social acceptability. The user may also experience frightening perceptual changes. The withdrawal symptoms from cocaine include exhaustion, need for sleep, and depression. The extraordinarily rapid and strong effects of cocaine on the brain's reward centers seem to make this substance more likely than most illicit substances to result in patterns of abuse and dependence.

The amphetamines are readily available by prescription for the treatment of certain disorders but often end up in the black market and used by people to help them keep going through the day or to counteract the effects of depressants or heroin. They can make people feel euphoric, invigorated, self-confident, and gregarious, but they also can make people restless, hypervigilant, anxious, and aggressive and can result in several dangerous physiological symptoms and changes.

The opioids are a group of substances developed from the juice of the poppy plant. The most commonly used illegal opioid is heroin. The initial symptom of opioid intoxication is euphoria; it is followed by a sense of drowsiness, lethargy, and periods of light sleep. Severe intoxication can lead to respiratory difficulties, unconsciousness, coma, and seizures. Withdrawal symptoms include dysphoria, anxiety, agitation, sensitivity to pain, and craving for more substance.

The hallucinogens, phenylcyclidine, and cannabis all produce perceptual changes that can include sensory distortions and hallucinations. For some people, these are pleasant experiences, but for others, they can be extremely frightening. Similarly, some people experience a sense of euphoria or relaxation while on these substances, and others become anxious and agitated.

Nicotine is another widely available substance. While legal, it causes cancer, bronchitis, and coronary heart disease in users and a range of birth defects in the children of women who smoke when pregnant. People can become physiologically dependent on nicotine and undergo difficult withdrawal symptoms when they stop smoking.

The disease model of alcoholism views alcoholism as a biological disorder in which the individual has no control over his or her drinking and therefore must remain abstinent. Other theorists see alcoholism along a continuum of drinking habits, as modifiable through therapy. There is evidence that some types of alcoholism among males may be genetically transmitted and that men genetically predisposed to alcoholism are less sensitive to the effects of low doses of alcohol. Some theorists view alcoholism as a form of depression, although the prevailing evidence suggests that alcoholism and depression are distinct disorders.

Behavioral theories of alcoholism note that people are also reinforced or punished by other people for their alcohol-related behaviors. Cognitive theories argue that people who develop alcohol-related problems have strong expectations that alcohol will help them feel better and cope better when they face stressful times.

Drugs can be used to ease the symptoms of withdrawal from many substances and to reduce craving for substances. The symptoms of withdrawal from opioids can be so severe that dependents are given a drug called *methadone* to curtail the symptoms as they try to discontinue use of heroin. Methadone also blocks the effects of subsequent doses of heroin, reducing people's desire to obtain heroin. Methadone maintenance programs, which continue to administer methadone to former heroin dependents, are controversial.

The most common treatment for alcoholism is Alcoholics Anonymous, a self-help group that encourages alcoholics to admit their weaknesses and call on a higher power and other group members to help them remain completely abstinent from alcohol. Behavioral therapies based on aversive classical conditioning are sometimes used to treat alcoholism. Alcoholics in these therapies use a drug that makes them ill if they ingest alcohol or use imagery to develop a conditioned aversive response to the sight and smell of alcohol. Treatments based on social learning and cognitive theories focus on training alcoholics in more adaptive coping skills and challenging their positive expectations about the effects of alcohol. Many therapists in the behavioral and cognitive tradition reject the disease model of alcoholism and suggest that some alcoholics may learn to engage in controlled social drinking.

Women may lack an enzyme that breaks down alcohol, making them more vulnerable than men to the negative physiological effects of alcohol. This may be one reason women are less prone than men to develop alcoholism. In addition, substance use is more positively reinforced for men than for women, and men expect alcohol to have more positive effects than women do.

Various countries have tried different approaches to control the market for substances and alcohol and to treating substance and alcohol abusers and dependents, ranging from harsh punishment of both users and sellers to near-legalization of illicit substances. No one method clearly works the best.

Key Terms

Application   Promoting Responsible Alcohol Use in Young Adults

In the United States, young adults between 18 and 24 years of age have the highest rates of alcohol consumption and make up the largest proportion of problem drinkers of any age group. College students are even more likely than their peers who are not in college to drink. Among college students, 73 to 98 percent drink alcohol, in response to easy access to alcohol, social activities that focus on drinking, and peer pressure to drink. As many as 20 to 25 percent of college students report having experienced alcohol-related problems. Alcohol-related accidents are the leading causes of death in college students (Marlatt et al., 1993). Heavy drinking is also associated with acute alcohol toxicity (which can be lethal), date rape, unsafe sexual activity, vandalism, and impaired academic performance. The pattern of drinking among college students has shifted over the last decade so that a greater percentage of students abstain completely from alcohol, but those who do drink are more likely to be heavy drinkers (Marlatt et al., 1993). These heavy drinkers are most likely to be binge drinkers, who drink large quantities of alcohol on weekends, typically at social events, often with the intention of getting drunk.

Many colleges are developing programs to reduce drinking and drinking-related problems among students. These programs often emphasize the health-related consequences of drinking, but such long-term concerns do not tend to impress young people who are more likely to be focused on the short-term gains of alcohol use. Simply providing information about the dangers of alcohol abuse and trying to invoke fear of these dangers have little effect. Some college counselors refer students with drinking problems to abstinence programs, such as Alcoholics Anonymous, but college students often find the focus on admitting one's powerlessness and the principle of lifelong abstinence so unattractive that they will not attend these programs.

Psychologist Alan Marlatt and colleagues at the University of Washington (Fromme, Marlatt, Baer, & Kivlahan, 1994; Marlatt et al., 1993) have argued that a more credible approach for college drinkers is to recognize alcohol use as normative behavior among young adults and to focus education on the immediate risks of excessive use of alcohol (such as alcohol-related accidents) and on the payoffs of moderation (such as avoidance of hangovers). They view young drinkers as relatively inexperienced in regulating their use of alcohol and as in need of skills training to prevent abuse of alcohol. Learning to drink safely is compared to learning to drive safely; one must learn to anticipate hazards and avoid "unnecessary accidents."

Their intervention is known as the Alcohol Skills Training Program (ASTP) and consists of eight weekly sessions of 90 minutes. First, participants are taught to be aware of their drinking habits, including when, where, and with whom they are most likely to overdrink, by keeping daily records of their alcohol consumption and the situations in which they drink (see Figure 12.4). They are also taught to calculate their own blood alcohol levels; it often comes as a surprise to people how few drinks it takes to be legally intoxicated. Next, participants' beliefs about the "magical" effects of drinking on social skills and sexual prowess are challenged. They discuss the negative effects of alcohol on social behaviors, on the ability to drive, and on weight gain, and they discuss hangovers. Participants are encouraged to set personal goals for limiting alcohol consumption, based on their maximum blood alcohol levels and their desires to avoid the negative effects of alcohol. They learn skills for limiting consumption, such as alternating alcoholic and nonalcoholic beverages and selecting drinks based on quality rather than quantity (for example, buying two good beers rather than a six-pack of generic beer). In later sessions, members are taught to consider alternatives to drinking alcohol to reduce negative emotional states, such as using relaxation exercises or meditation or reducing sources of stress in their lives. Finally, in role-plays, participants are taught skills for avoiding "high risk situations" in which they are likely to overdrink and for resisting peer pressure to drink.

Evaluations of ASTP have shown that participants do decrease alcohol consumption and problems and increase their social skills in resisting alcohol abuse (Fromme et al., 1994; Marlatt, Baer, & Larimer, 1995). ASTP was designed for a group format, and the use of group pressure to encourage change in individuals and as a forum for role-playing has many advantages. One study suggested that ASTP could be delivered in a written form as a self-help manual with positive effects equal to those of the group administration (Baer, Marlatt, Kivlahan, & Fromme, 1992).

(front of card)

| Card no. | | | | | | | | | | Subject number |

Date	Time	a.m. p.m.	Drink Type	Amount (ozs.)	Where (code)	W/whom (code)	Mood (code)	BAL	Comments

(back of card)

Code for mood states
1. Happy
2. Outgoing
3. Romantic/sexy
4. Relaxed
5. Desire to celebrate
6. Sad/depressed
7. Frustrated
8. Shy/self-conscious
9. Angry
10. Anxious/stressed
11. Restless/bored
12. Other (specify)

Code for with whom
1. Alone
2. Relatives including family
3. Male friend(s)
4. Female friend(s)
5. Friends of both sexes
6. Strangers or people you've met after beginning to drink
7. Other (specify)

Code for where
1. Tavern/bar
2. Restaurant (with meal)
3. Own residence
4. Other's residence
5. Work/school
6. Private club, fraternity, sorority
7. Social event (wedding, party, sports event)
8. In a car
9. Out-of-doors
10. Other (specify)

One drink = 12 ozs. beer, or 4 ozs. wine, or 1 cooler,  or 1 standard cocktail.

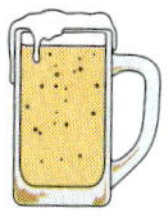

Here are some tips for reducing your own drinking and for preventing problems due to drinking at social events:

1. Set a limit on how much you will drink before you go to a party or other social function. You might want to use Table 12.4 to set your drink limit so that you do not exceed a low-to-moderate blood alcohol limit. Tell a friend what your limit is and get a commitment from that friend that he or she will help you stick to that limit.

2. Alternate between alcohol and nonalcoholic beverages at the party.

3. Eat foods high in protein and carbohydrates before the party and at the party.

4. Designate someone in your group to drive; that person should drink *no* alcoholic beverages at the party.

5. If you are throwing the party, have plenty of nonalcoholic beverages and attractive food and try to focus the party on music or something other than alcohol consumption.

6. If someone at the party appears to be very intoxicated, encourage him or her to stop drinking. Try not to let him or her drive away from the party; call a taxi or have someone who has not been drinking drive him or her home.

7. If a person passes out after drinking heavily, lay the person on his or her side rather than on his or her back, in case of vomiting. Call medical personnel.

8. If you get drunk at a party, after you have recovered, review the reasons for your overdrinking. Were you trying to get rid of a bad mood? Were you nervous and trying to relax? Did certain people push you to drink? Did you tell yourself that you were not drinking that much? Try to develop concrete, realistic plans for avoiding in future situations the reasons you overdrank. ■

Figure 12.4

A Monitoring Card for Daily Alcohol Use. This is a card used in programs to teach young people how to monitor and change their drinking behavior.
Source: From Fromme et al., 1994.

chapter 13

Personality, Behavior, and the Body

Characteristics of Stressful Events

Stress is thought to be a contributor to ill health, but the construct *stress* has been defined in various ways. Events that are perceived as stressful by people are often uncontrollable, are unpredictable, or challenge the limits of our abilities and threaten our self-concepts.

Direct Effects of Stress on Health

Our bodies have a natural physiological response to stress, known as the fight-or-flight response. In the short term, this physiological response is adaptive because it helps the body fight or flee from a threat. When this physiological response is prolonged, however, it causes wear-and-tear on the body, potentially contributing to coronary heart disease, high blood pressure, and impairment of the immune system.

Indirect Effects of Stress on Health

Stress can also affect health indirectly by leading people to engage in less healthy behaviors, such as not sleeping enough.

Personality and Health

Some personality styles that have been linked to poor physical health include dispositional pessimism, the Type A behavior pattern, the repressive coping style, and John Henryism. Each of these may contribute to poor health by causing a chronic hyper-arousal of the fight-or-flight response or by causing people to engage in unhealthy behaviors. In contrast, a coping style involving high quality social support in times of stress is linked to good physical health.

Psychosocial Interventions to Improve Health

Health psychologists have designed a variety of cognitive and behavioral interventions to improve people's physical health, including guided mastery techniques that help people learn healthy behaviors, techniques to reduce catastrophizing cognitions, biofeedback, and time-management techniques.

Bio-Psycho-Social Integration
Chapter Summary
Key Terms
Application: *Stress and the College Student*

If the mind, which rules the body, ever forgets itself so far as to trample upon its slave, the slave is never generous enough to forgive the injury; but will rise and smite its oppressor.

—Longfellow, *Hyperion* (1839)

Daniel Nevins
The Dream Tree

"You're making yourself sick with worry." "If he doesn't slow down, he's going to have a heart attack." "She's so stressed out that she's going to have a stroke."

How many times have we heard or said similar things? Is it true that psychological factors, such as worry or stress, can affect physical health? An entire new field of psychology, known as *health psychology*, has developed over the last 20 or so years to investigate the effects of psychological factors on physical illness. Health psychologists are concerned with the roles of personality factors, coping styles, stressful events, and health-related behaviors (such as maintaining a good diet) in the development and progress of physical disease. They also study whether changing a person's psychology—for example, by teaching stress-reduction techniques—can influence the course of a physical disease and whether diseases can be prevented by helping people adopt healthy lifestyles and attitudes about the world.

The field of health psychology is new, but the questions of whether and how the mind can affect the body and the body affect the mind have been debated for centuries. Such questions are often referred to as the *mind-body question*. Biological theories of mental illness, ranging from the ancient theories through the modern theories of the effects of neurotransmitters and genetics, all suggest that the body has a direct effect on the workings of the mind. There are also ancient theories suggesting that the mind has a direct effect on the workings of the body, such as theories that physical illnesses are the result of sin or possession by spirits. In Eastern medicine to this day, there continues to be an emphasis on the importance of a positive mental state and psychological balance on physical health. In Western medicine, however, the technological advances in identification and treatment of the physical causes of disease have contributed to a dominance of biological models of disease.

In recent decades, interest in the impact of psychological factors has begun to reemerge. There are three models for how psychological factors affect physical disease that drive most of the work in health psychology (see Figure 13.1).

The *direct effects model* suggests that psychological factors, such as stressful experiences or certain personality characteristics, directly cause changes in the physiology of the body that in turn cause or exacerbate disease. As we shall discuss in detail shortly, our bodies have a characteristic physiological response to certain types of stresses or challenges. In the short run, this physiological response is adaptive, but if it is greatly prolonged, it can cause damage to several systems of the body that may then cause or exacerbate disease.

Figure 13.1

Three Models for the Effects of Psychological Factors on Disease. These three models posit quite different pathways by which psychological factors such as stress or personality style might affect physical disease.

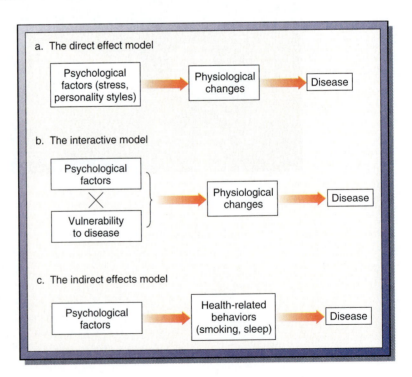

The *interactive model* suggests that psychological factors must interact with a pre-existing biological vulnerability to a disease in order for an individual to develop the disease. According to this model, prolonged stress or a maladaptive personality style will contribute to disease only in people who already have biological vulnerability to the disease or perhaps have already developed mild forms of the disease.

The *indirect effects model* suggests that psychological factors affect disease largely by influencing whether people engage in health-promoting behaviors. For example, our diets, the amount of exercise we get, and whether we smoke, can all influence our vulnerability to certain diseases like heart disease or lung cancer and can influence the progression of many diseases once we have developed them. People under stress or with certain personality characteristics may be less prone to engage in healthy behaviors and more prone to engage in unhealthy behaviors. Thus, according to this model, psychological factors do not directly affect health but affect health indirectly by affecting health-related behaviors.

As already suggested, the two types of psychological factors focused on in many health psychology models are *stress* and *personality styles*. We begin this chapter by discussing what makes some experiences more stressful than others. Then we discuss the body's natural physiological reactions to stress and how these reactions can go awry and contribute to the development of disease or hasten the progression of disease. We also discuss how stress indirectly affects health by increasing people's tendencies to engage in unhealthy behaviors. Then we discuss personality characteristics that may affect health either directly or indirectly. Finally, we will discuss interventions to help people change their attitudes and behaviors in ways that may help them prevent disease or slow existing disease.

Characteristics of Stressful Events

What do we mean by stress? **Stress** is a term that is used loosely in both the popular media and in professional circles. Psychologists have identified three characteristics of events that contribute to their being perceived as stressful: their *controllability*, their *predictability*, and their *level of challenge or threat* to one's capabilities or self-concept.

stress
reaction to events that are perceived as uncontrollable, unpredictable, challenging, and/or threatening

Controllability

Case Study • Tyron was busily doing his job welding small parts onto the frame of a car in the factory where he worked. His foreman told him that the boss wanted to see him. When he entered the boss's office, Tyron knew the news wasn't good. "Tyron," the boss said, "I'm afraid that the plant is undergoing some downsizing. Your job has been eliminated. You've been a good worker, but the new owners of the company want to automatize production in the plant as much as possible and yours is one of the jobs that a computer can do faster and cheaper than a person. I'm sorry to have to give you this news. You can finish out the month here and then you'll get a month's severance pay."

Tyron was stunned. He couldn't talk, he couldn't move. There had never been any indication that the new owners were thinking of firing people. When he was able to think again after several moments. Tyron felt angry, helpless, like the whole world had fallen in on him.

Uncontrollable negative events, such as the loss of a job, sudden death of a loved one, or loss of one's home to a natural disaster, are perceived by most people as stressful. Indeed, a negative event is perceived as more stressful if it is uncontrollable. For example, in one experimental study subjects were shown vivid photographs of victims of violent deaths. One group of subjects, the experimental group, could terminate their viewing by pressing a button. The other group, the control group, could not terminate their viewing by pressing a button. Both groups of subjects saw the same photographs for the same duration of time. The level of anxiety in both groups was measured by their galvanic skin response (GSR), a drop in the electrical resistance of the skin that is an index of physiological arousal. The experimental group showed much less anxiety while viewing the photographs than did the control group, even though the only difference between the groups was their control over their viewing (Geer & Maisel, 1972).

Similarly, a person who has a traffic accident because he or she was not wearing glasses while driving may experience the accident as less stressful than if he or she had not perceived a reason for the accident. An accident that happens because a person forgot to wear glasses can presumably be prevented from happening again by the person wearing glasses. An accident that appears to have no explanation cannot be prevented from happening again in the future.

 Is having complete control over everything in your life necessarily nonstressful? Why or why not?

Unpredictability

Another factor that makes some events especially stressful is unpredictability. Tyron was stunned by his layoff in part because he did not see it coming. Again, experimental studies have confirmed that unpredictable events are more stressful than predictable events. These studies show that both rats and human subjects prefer mild but painful electric shocks or loud bursts of noise that are preceded by a warning tone (and therefore predictable) to electric shocks or noise that are preceded by no warning tone (Abbott, Schoen, & Badia, 1984; Glass & Singer, 1972; Katz & Wykes, 1985). Having sufficient warning of upcoming aversive events may allow people to prepare themselves in ways that reduce the impact of events. For example, knowing that he is about to receive a shot allows a patient to begin distracting himself or practicing breathing exercises to reduce the pain of the shot.

Another reason predictable aversive events may be less stressful is that with predictable events, people know they can relax until they get the warning that the events are about to occur. With unpredictable events, people feel they can never relax because the events may occur at any time; thus, they remain anxious all the time. This explanation has been called the **safety signal hypothesis** (Seligman & Binik, 1977). For example, perhaps a woman's boss occasionally flies into a rage, criticizing her in front of others. If these outbursts are completely unpredictable, then the employee is always on guard and may chronically feel stressed. If, however, she knows these outbursts only happen around the end of each fiscal quarter when her boss is upset because he has to prepare a fiscal account for the firm, then she can relax to some extent during the remainder of the fiscal year. (For more discussion of the safety signal hypothesis, see Chapter 4.)

 What are some conditions or situations that serve as safety signals for you? Why?

One group of people who often feel they are facing events that are both uncontrollable and unpredictable are patients awaiting surgical procedures. They may be terrified that something will go wrong during surgery or that they will be in severe pain or disabled following surgery. Their fears about surgical procedures and about their prognoses are often overblown, based on imagined worst-case scenarios or horror stories that other people have told them or that they have heard on the news. Dozens of studies, sparked by seminal work by psychologist Irving Janis (1958), have now shown that giving surgical patients information about what will happen during surgical procedures, the pain or disability they can expect after procedures, and ways to reduce pain or overcome disability greatly improves their adjustment to surgery. Patients given such information experience less distress before and after surgery, are able to leave the hospital sooner, require less medication, and may experience less pain than patients not given the infor-

Uncontrollable events, such as being laid off a job, are perceived as stressful by many people.

safety signal hypothesis
idea that people will experience more anxiety in situations perceived as unpredictable and less anxiety in situations perceived as predictable

mation. Preoperative information appears to give patients a sense that they can control certain aspects of their experience—for example, by engaging in breathing exercises to reduce their pain—and a sense that, even if they cannot control what will happen to them, what will happen is somewhat predictable. Similar interventions have been used with success with women in childbirth and persons undergoing invasive medical procedures, such as chemotherapy or cardiac catheterization (Ludwick-Rosenthal & Neufeld, 1988).

Challenge or Threat to Capabilities and Self-Concept

Even events that are controllable and predictable may be perceived as stressful if they *challenge the limits of one's capabilities and threaten one's self-concept*. One example is final exam week in college. Even students who know they can do well on their exams and have a good idea of what they must study for exams tend to experience final exams as stressful. They may

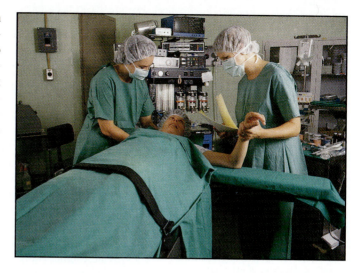

Giving people information about what they can expect and how they can cope following surgery can quicken their recovery.

have to work much harder and for longer hours during exams than at other times of the year and must perform at the peak of their intellectual capabilities even though they may be very weary. Although they are capable of doing well on the exams, their concept of themselves as competent may be threatened by the possibility of doing poorly on the exams.

Any change in life that requires numerous readjustments—even positive changes—can challenge the limits of our capabilities or challenge our self-concepts and thus can be perceived as stressful (Holmes & Rahe, 1967). For example, most people think of marriage as a positive event, but it requires many readjustments in daily life and a change in people's concepts of themselves as they change from single individuals to lifetime partners of other people. However, negative events are more likely than positive events to be perceived as stressful and to have impacts on physical and psychological health (e.g., Sarason, Johnson, & Siegel, 1978). This may be because, although some positive events require people to make adjustments and to change their self-concepts, these changes tend to be for the better: Those affected are gaining something from the events and from the new roles they are taking. In contrast, negative events often involve loss and can threaten self-esteem or sense of mastery of the world (Thoits, 1986).

Summing Up	Characteristics of Stressful Events

- Uncontrollable events are perceived as more stressful than controllable events.
- Unpredictable events are perceived as more stressful than predictable events.
- The safety signal hypothesis suggests that having some signal for when a negative event is going to occur makes it less stressful because it is more predictable and thus can be prepared for better.
- Events that challenge the limits of one's abilities and threaten one's self-concept are more stressful.

Direct Effects of Stress on Health

When the body faces any type of stressor—a saber-toothed tiger, a burglar with a gun, a first bungee jump—it mobilizes to handle the stressor. The liver releases extra sugar (glucose) to fuel muscles, and hormones are released to stimulate the conversion of fats and proteins to sugar. The body's metabolism increases in preparation for expending energy on physical action. Heart rate, blood pressure, and breathing rate increase, and the muscles tense. At the same time, certain unessential activities, such as digestion, are curtailed. Saliva and mucus dry up, thereby increasing the size of air passages to the lungs. The body's natural painkillers, endorphins, are secreted, and the surface blood vessels constrict to reduce bleeding in case of injury. The spleen releases more red blood cells to help carry oxygen.

Most of these physiological changes result from activation of two systems controlled by the hypothalamus, the autonomic nervous system (in particular the sympathetic division of this system) and the adrenal-cortical system (a hormone-releasing system). These physiological responses have developed through evolution to prepare the body to flee a threat or to fight it (e.g., to run away from the saber-toothed tiger or to attack it) and thus have been labeled the **fight-or-flight response**. They are very adaptive when the stressor or threat is immediate and fight or flight is possible and useful. When a stressor is chronic and a person or animal cannot fight it or flee from it, then the chronic arousal of these physiological responses can be severely damaging to the body (see Sapolsky, 1992). Researcher Hans Selye (1978) conducted groundbreaking work showing that animals with prolonged exposure to uncontrollable stressors experienced enlarged adrenal glands, shrunken lymph nodes, and stomach ulcers. In humans, two diseases that have been consistently linked with the body's physiological reactions to stress are coronary heart disease and hypertension. In addition, new research is suggesting that stress can impair humans' immune system, making them more vulnerable to infectious diseases.

Stress and Coronary Heart Disease

fight-or-flight response
physiological changes in the human body that occur in response to a perceived threat, including secretion of glucose, endorphins, and hormones as well as elevation of heart rate, metabolism, blood pressure, breathing, and muscle tension

Case Study • Orrin was so mad he could scream. He had been told at 3:00 that afternoon to prepare a report on the financial status of his division of the company in time for a 9:00 A.M. meeting of the board of directors the next morning. On the way home from work, some idiot rear-ended him at a stop light and caused several hundred dollars in damages to his new car. When he got home from work, there was a message from his wife saying she had been delayed at work and would not be home in time to cook dinner for the children, so Orrin would have to do it. Then at dinner, Orrin's 12-year-old son revealed that he had flunked his math exam that afternoon.

After finishing the dishes, Orrin when to his study to work on the report. The kids had the TV on so loud he couldn't concentrate. Orrin yelled to the kids to turn off the TV but they couldn't hear him. Furious, he stalked into the family room and began yelling at the children about the television and anything else that came to his mind.

Then, suddenly, Orrin began to feel a tremendous pressure on his chest, as if a truck were driving across it. Pain shot through his chest and down his left arm. Orrin felt dizzy and terrified. He collapsed onto the floor. His 7 year old began screaming. Luckily, his 12 year old called 911 for an ambulance.

coronary heart disease (CHD)
chronic illness that is the leading cause of death in the United States, occurring when the blood vessels that supply the heart with oxygen and nutrients are narrowed or closed by plaque, resulting in a myocardial infarction (heart attack) when closed completely

Orrin was having a myocardial infarction—a heart attack. A myocardial infarction is one endpoint of **coronary heart disease**, or **CHD**. CHD occurs when the blood vessels that supply the heart muscles are narrowed or closed by the gradual buildup of a hard, fatty substance called *plaque*, blocking the flow of oxygen and nutrients to the heart. This can lead to pain, called *angina pectoris*, that radiates across the chest and arm. When the oxygen to the heart is completely blocked, it can cause a myocardial infarction.

Coronary heart disease is the leading cause of death and chronic illness in the United States today, accounting for 40 percent of all deaths, most before the age of 75. CHD is also a chronic disease, and millions of people live daily with its symptoms. Men are more prone to CHD than are women, but CHD is still the leading cause of death of women. People with family histories of CHD are more susceptible to CHD. CHD has been linked to high blood pressure, high serum cholesterol, diabetes, smoking, and obesity.

People who live in chronically stressful environments over which they have little control appear to be at increased risk for CHD. For example, one study followed about 900 middle-aged men and women for over 10 years, tracking the emergence of coronary heart disease (Karasek, Russell, & Theorell, 1982). These people worked in a variety of jobs, and the researchers categorized these jobs in terms of how demanding they were and how much control they allowed a worker. Over the 10 years of this study, workers in jobs that were highly demanding but low in control had a risk of coronary heart disease that was 1½ times greater than that of those in other occupations.

The stress of being an immigrant to a new country, particularly a poor immigrant, may contribute to CHD and other illness, as we see in this case study (Mathews, 1996):

> **Case Study** • Heliodoro Bravo worked so hard for so long that, when he dropped dead 2 weeks ago at age 39, what his wife did made sense to their friends: She kept the family restaurant open and kept working.
>
> No time off for a funeral. Only a few scattered hours to mourn. She says she could not even spare the days or money to accompany his body to Mexico, where her husband's parents had a service and burial. "We have always had to go forward, to support the family," says Filomena Bravo, 41. "We always work and work, because we have to pay the bills. We never rest."
>
> "At first, I was astonished to see the Bravos' restaurant open the day he died," said Manuel Alban, publisher of the Spanish-language weekly *El Heraldo*. "But in our community, it was not really a surprise, because if you don't sell, you don't eat."

Coronary heart disease occurs when blood vessels supplying the heart are blocked by plaque; complete blockage causes a myocardial infarction—a heart attack.

The impact on physical health of being an immigrant varies greatly depending on the type of setting a person moves to, however. Some immigrants are able to move with family members into ethnic communities within their new country that provide them with some continuity of culture and help them to adapt. These persons are not at higher risk for CHD or other illness, whereas immigrants who do not have social support systems in their new country may be at increased risk (Kuo & Tsai, 1986).

Stress and Hypertension

Hypertension, or high blood pressure, is a condition in which the supply of blood through the vessels is excessive, putting pressure on the vessel walls. Chronic high blood pressure can cause hardening of the arterial walls and deterioration of the cell tissue, leading eventually to coronary artery disease, kidney failure, and stroke. Approximately 60 million people in the United States have hypertension, and about 16,000 die each year due to hypertensive heart disease. Genetics appear to play a role in the predisposition to hypertension (Smith, Turner, Ford, & Hunt, 1987), but only about 10 percent of cases of hypertension can be traced to genetics or to specific organic causes, such as kidney dysfunction. The other 90 percent of cases are known as **essential hypertension**, meaning the causes are unknown.

Because part of the body's response to stress—the fight-or-flight response—is to increase blood pressure, it is not surprising that people who live in chronically stressful circumstances are more likely to develop hypertension (James, Hartnett, & Kalsbeek, 1983). As an example, persons who move from quiet rural settings to crowded and noisy urban settings show increases in rates of hypertension.

One group that lives in chronically stressful settings and has particularly high rates of hypertension is low-income African Americans. They often do not have adequate financial resources for daily living, are poorly educated and have trouble finding good employment, live in neighborhoods racked with violence, and are frequently exposed to racism. All these conditions have been linked to higher blood pressure.

In addition, African Americans may be genetically prone to a particular pattern of cardiovascular response to stress that contributes to the development of hypertension (Anderson, Lane, Taguchi, & Williams, 1989; Light & Sherwood, 1989). Persons with hypertension and the children of parents with hypertension tend to show a stronger blood pressure response to a wide variety of stressors in experimental situations, including arithmetic problems and immersing their hands in ice water, than do people with no personal or family histories of hypertension (Harrell, 1980). In addition, it takes longer for the blood pressure of persons with hypertension to return to normal following stressors than it does

essential hypertension
condition in which the blood supply through the blood vessels is excessive and can lead to deterioration of the cell tissue and hardening of the arterial walls but cannot be traced to genetics or a specific organic cause

the blood pressure of those without hypertension. This suggests that hypertensives and persons with family/genetic histories of hypertension may have heightened physiological reactivity to stress. If these persons are exposed to chronic stress, then their chronically elevated blood pressure can lead to hardening and narrowing of the arteries, which creates a physiologically based hypertension (Harrell, 1980). Low income African Americans may have both this physiological predisposition to heightened reactivity to stress *and* chronic exposure to stressful environments, making them doubly vulnerable to hypertension.

Stress and the Immune System

The immune system protects the body from disease-causing microorganisms. This system affects our susceptibility to infections diseases, allergies, cancer, and autoimmune disorders in which the immune cells attack normal tissues of the body. There are many components of the immune system and its response to foreign invaders to the body that cause disease, and different investigators have chosen to focus on different components of this response in measuring **immunocompetence,** or the functioning of the immune system. One of the fastest growing areas of health psychology is *psychoneuroimmunology,* the study of the effects of psychological factors on immunocompetence (see Maier, Watkins, & Fleshner, 1994). Stress may affect the immune system through several mechanisms. In particular, some of the biochemicals released as part of the fight-or-flight response may suppress the immune system.

The most controlled research linking stress and immune system functioning has been conducted with animals. They are experimentally exposed to stressors and then the functioning of their immune system is measured directly. Studies have shown that **lymphocytes,** cells of the immune system that attack viruses, are suppressed in animals that have been exposed to loud noise, electric shock, separation from their mothers as infants, separation from peers, and a variety of other stressors (Maier et al., 1994).

Animals are most likely to show impairment of their immune system if exposed to stressors that are uncontrollable. In one experiment, rats were subjected to electric shock that they could turn off by pressing a lever (Laudenslager et al., 1983). Other rats, the yoked control group, received an identical sequence of shocks but could not control the shocks by pressing the lever. A third group received no shock. The investigators examined how well the rats' T-cells multiplied when challenged by invaders. T-cells are lymphocytes that secrete chemicals that kill harmful cells, such as cancer cells. They found that the T-cells in the rats who could control the shock multiplied as well as did those in rats who were not shocked at all (see Figure 13.2). T-cells in rats exposed to uncontrollable shock multiplied only weakly, however. In another study following the same experimental design, investigators implanted tumor cells into rats, gave them controllable or uncontrollable shocks, and examined whether the rats' natural defenses rejected the tumors. Only 27 percent of the rats given uncontrollable shock rejected the tumors, whereas 63 percent of the rats given controllable shock rejected the tumors (Visintainer, Volpicelli, & Seligman, 1982).

Uncontrollable stress also is related to impaired immune system functioning in humans. In a particularly elegant study, investigators exposed about 400 healthy volunteers to a nasal wash containing one of five cold viruses or an innocuous salt solution

immunocompetence
estimation of the robustness or vulnerability of the immune system

lymphocytes
cells of the immune system that attack viruses

Figure 13.2

The Effects of Controllable and Uncontrollable Shock on Rats' Immune Systems. Rats given uncontrollable shock showed less increase in T-cells, which kill harmful cells, that did rats given controllable shock or no shock.
Source: Laudenslager et al., 1983.

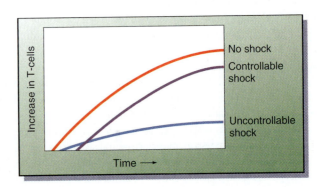

(Cohen, Tyrel, & Smith, 1991). Each participant was assigned a stress score ranging from 3 (lowest stress) to 12 (highest stress), based on the number of stressful events they had experienced in the past year, the degree to which they felt able to cope with daily demands, and their frequency of negative emotions such as anger and depression. The participants were examined daily for cold symptoms and for the presence of cold viruses or virus-specific antibodies in their upper respiratory secretions. The

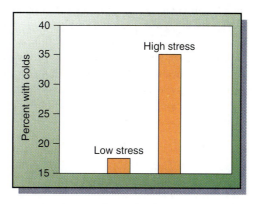

Figure 13.3

The Development of Colds in People with High Stress and Low Stress in Their Lives. People who were leading highly stressful lives were much more likely to develop colds than were people leading low-stress lives when exposed to a cold virus.

Source: Cohen, et al., 1991.

majority of the volunteers exposed to the virus showed some signs of infection, but only about one-third developed colds. Volunteers who reported the highest stress in their lives were more likely to develop infections and much more likely to develop actual colds than were those with the lowest stress scores (see Figure 13.3).

Most other studies of humans simply have compared the immunocompetence of persons undergoing particular stressors, such as exams, bereavement, or marital disruption, with that of persons not undergoing these stressors (see Cohen, 1996). For example, studies have verified the idea that college students and medical students are more prone to infectious illness during exam periods than at other times of the academic year (Glaser et al., 1986). Studies of men whose wives have died from breast cancer show that their immune system functioning declines in the month following their wives' deaths and in some cases remains low for a year thereafter (Schleifer, Keller, McKegney, & Stein, 1979).

Men and women who have recently been separated or divorced show poorer immune functioning than do matched control subjects who are still married (Kiecolt-Glaser et al., 1987, 1988). However, the partner who has more control over the divorce or separation—that is, the partner who initiated the divorce or separation—shows better immune system functioning and better health than does the partner who has less control over the divorce or separation. This is one example of how perceptions of the controllability of a stressor can influence the impact of that stressor on health.

Several studies have examined whether stress can contribute to the development or progression of cancer in humans (see O'Leary, 1990, and Taylor, 1991, for reviews). The results of these studies have been mixed, some showing that people who are more stressed are more vulnerable to develop cancer or have faster progressions of their cancer than do people who are less stressed. Again, it may be that people's perceptions or appraisals of stressors and not the presence of stressors alone determine the impact of the stressors on immune system functioning. For example, one study of women with breast cancer found that those who felt they had little control over their cancer and over other aspects of their lives were more likely to develop new tumors over a 5-year period than were women who felt more in control, even though the two groups of women did not differ in the type or initial seriousness of their cancers (Levy & Heiden, 1991). Similarly, although studies have not shown conclusively that stress contributes to the progression of acquired immune deficiency syndrome (AIDS), perceptions of control may be related to the progression of this disease (O'Leary, 1990). We shall explore these studies in more detail later in this chapter when we discuss the role of personality factors in health.

Summing Up · Direct Effects of Stress on Health

- There is substantial evidence that stress, particularly uncontrollable stress, increases risks for coronary heart disease and hypertension, probably through chronic hyperarousal of the body's fight-or-flight response.
- There is mounting evidence from animal and human studies that stress may also impair the functioning of the immune system, possibly leading to higher rates of infectious diseases.

Indirect Effects of Stress on Health

So far, we have discussed the direct ways stress may affect health. Stress may also indirectly affect health by interfering with a person's ability or tendency to engage in behaviors that promote good health, such as getting a good night's sleep, getting regular physical exercise, eating a balanced diet, and refraining from smoking or excessive alcohol. In the next section, we will focus on one of the most common casualties of stress—sleep.

Stress, Sleep, and Health

In 1993, the National Commission on Sleep Disorders Research estimated that at least one-third of U.S. adults suffer from chronic sleep disturbances, especially chronic sleep deprivation due to busy schedules. Over the past century, the average night's sleep time has declined by more than 20 percent as people try to fit more and more into the 24-hour day. The costs of sleep disorders and sleepiness to society include lost lives, lost income, disabilities, accidents, and family dysfunction. For example, each year in the United States, there are 200,000 sleep-related automobile accidents, and 5,000 of these accidents are fatal. Twenty percent of automobile drivers admit to having fallen asleep at the wheel at least once. Some of the most serious disasters in modern history have been caused by mistakes made by sleepy people (Mitler & Miller, 1995). In 1979, the worst nuclear plant accident in the United States resulted from fatigued workers at Three Mile Island failing to respond to a mechanical problem at the plant. In 1986, the world's worst nuclear disaster happened in Chernobyl in the former Soviet Union while a test was being conducted by an exhausted team of engineers.

Young adults will sleep on average 8.6 hours per day when they have no environmental influences to interfere with sleep patterns. Yet most young adults sleep 7.5 or fewer hours per day. Similarly, most middle-aged adults seem to need at least 7 or 8 hours of sleep per day, but on average get less than 7 hours per day. People who work rotating shifts or in jobs demanding long periods of activity, including nurses, doctors, firefighters, police, and rescue personnel, are often chronically sleep deprived. Even when they have time to sleep, they have trouble doing so, because their bodies' natural rhythms that promote sleep are disrupted by their irregular schedules. The effects of sleep deprivation are cumulative: One builds up an increasing "sleep debt" for every 24-hour period in which one does not get adequate sleep.

Lack of sleep can impair health. People who sleep fewer than 6 hours per night have a 70 percent higher mortality rate than do those sleeping at least 7 or 8 hours per night, probably due both to a greater prevalence of disease and to having more accidents (Kryger, Roth, & Dement, 1994). This is true both for men and for women, for people of many

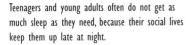

Teenagers and young adults often do not get as much sleep as they need, because their social lives keep them up late at night.

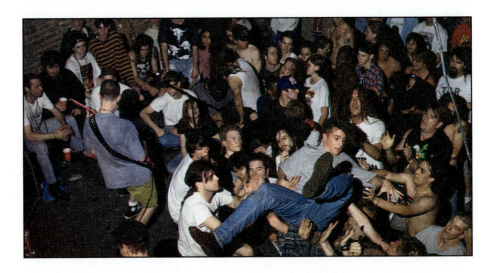

ethnicities, and for people with many different health backgrounds. People who work rotating shifts have higher rates of illness, including cardiovascular and gastrointestinal disease, than do people who do not work shifts.

Sleep deprivation also has a number of psychological effects. Cognitive impairments caused by sleep deprivation include impairments in memory, learning, logical reasoning, arithmetic skills, complex verbal processing, and decision making. For example, reducing one's amount of sleep to 5 hours per night for just two nights significantly reduces performance on math problems and creative thinking tasks. Thus, staying up to study for exams for just a couple of nights can significantly impair one's ability to do as well as possible on those exams. Sleep deprivation also causes irritability, emotional ups and downs, and perceptual distortions such as mild hallucinations (Dinges & Broughton, 1989).

How can people reduce sleepiness and the effects of sleep deprivation? The first answer is by getting enough sleep. Although the social lives of college students often begin at 10 P.M. or later, it is important to keep in mind that the sleep lost on the weekend can affect performance and health for the rest of the week. Students who have families and/or jobs are especially prone to skipping sleep in order to get everything done. Good time-management skills can help people find more time in their days to accomplish all their tasks without having to give up much sleep (tips on time management are given near the end of this chapter). Avoiding alcohol and caffeine in the evening can also help people fall asleep and sleep well when they do go to bed.

Sleep experts emphasize the value of naps during the day, particularly for people who have trouble getting as much sleep as they need during the night. Many people naturally need a short nap in the middle of the day (typically about 8 hours after they have awakened from the night's sleep) to restore them to optimal functioning. The best length for a nap varies from person to person but usually is between 15 and 30 minutes. The important thing is to sleep long enough to restore one's energy and attention but not long enough to make one groggy for the rest of the day.

In addition to its direct positive effects on health, getting adequate sleep helps people feel more in control of the stressful events that befall them during the day. When we are alert and rested, challenging events may not seem so overwhelming because we can marshall our best coping responses. Indeed, when we are rested, we may be better able to prevent stressful events from ever happening because we are alert enough to anticipate them and to take action before they occur. Thus, sleep has both direct effects on our health and indirect effects by enhancing our ability to prevent or cope with stressful events.

 What are your most unhealthy behaviors? Under what conditions are you most likely to engage in these behaviors? What causes you to engage in healthy behaviors even when you recognize them as unhealthy?

Personality and Health

In recent years, psychologists have explored certain personality characteristics and coping strategies that seem to be associated with an increased risk for a variety of diseases. Individuals with these particular characteristics or strategies appraise a wider range of events as stressful or do not readily engage in behaviors that reduce the stressfulness of events. Thus, these persons are more chronically stressed, and their bodies are more chronically in the fight-or-flight response described earlier in this chapter.

Pessimism and Health

In Chapter 5, we explored the relationship between explanatory style—one's habitual way of explaining events—and vulnerability to depression. People who have pessimistic explanatory styles in that they attribute bad events to factors that are internal to them, stable

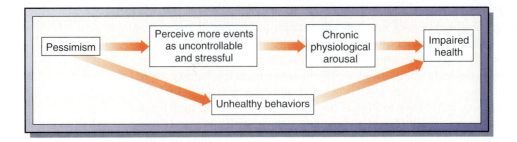

Figure 13.4

Pathways by Which Pessimism Might Impair Health. People who are pessimistic may appraise more events as uncontrollable and stressful, which then leads to chronic arousal of the fight-or-flight syndrome, which impairs health. They may also engage in more unhealthy behaviors that impair health.

in time, and global in their effects, are more prone to becoming depressed when confronted with stressors. Other research has linked a pessimistic explanatory style to poor physical health as well. One study found that students with more pessimistic explanatory styles reported more illness and made more visits to the student health center than did students with more optimistic explanatory styles (Peterson, 1988). Pessimists' vulnerability to illness does not end with college, however. In a long-term study of men in the Harvard classes of 1939 to 1940, men with pessimistic explanatory styles when they were in college were more likely to develop physical illness over the subsequent 35 years than were men with more optimistic explanatory styles (Peterson, Seligman, & Vaillant, 1988).

How does pessimism affect health? People who are pessimistic tend to feel they have less control over their lives than do people who are more optimistic and therefore may appraise more events as stressful. Thus, pessimism may contribute to poor health by causing chronic arousal of the body's fight-or flight response, resulting in the type of physiological damage discussed earlier (see Figure 13.4). One study directly supporting this argument was conducted with older adults (Kamen-Siegel, Rodin, Seligman, & Dwyer, 1991). Those older adults who were pessimistic showed poorer immune system functioning on two biological indices than did those were optimistic, even after the researchers statistically controlled for differences between pessimists and optimists on current health, depression, medication, sleep, and alcohol use.

Another study looked carefully at the types of coping behaviors engaged in by optimists and pessimists and found that a pessimistic outlook may also impair health by leading people to engage in unhealthy behaviors (Taylor, Kemeny, Aspinwall, & Schneider, 1992). The focus of this study was on gay men, some of whom had the virus that causes AIDS (they were HIV positive) and some of whom did not (they were HIV negative). The researchers found that, among both the HIV positive and HIV negative men, those who were more pessimistic and fatalistic in their outlooks were less likely to be engaging in healthy behaviors, such as maintaining proper diets, getting enough sleep, and exercising. These behaviors were particularly important for the HIV positive men, because engaging in these healthy behaviors can reduce the risk of developing AIDS. Thus, a pessimistic outlook may affect health directly by causing hyperarousal of the body's physiological response to stress or indirectly by reducing positive coping strategies and, more specifically, reducing healthy behaviors.

 Some studies suggest that optimists are unrealistically positive in their assessments of themselves. Would you rather be an unrealistic optimist or a realistic pessimist?

Type A Pattern and Health

Like the word *stress*, the term *Type A* is used more or less loosely to describe friends, colleagues, and family members. Let us try to pin down the definition of this important personality style.

The Type A pattern was initially identified by two physicians, Meyer Friedman and Ray Rosenman, who noticed that the chairs in the waiting room of their offices seemed to wear out terribly quickly (Friedman & Rosenman, 1974). Specifically, the edges of the seats would become threadbare, as if their patients were sitting on the edges, anxiously waiting to spring up. These patients were most frequently cardiology patients who had histories of coronary artery disease. Friedman and Rosenman eventually described a personality pattern seen in many of their cardiology patients, which was given the label **Type A behavior pattern.**

Type A behavior pattern
personality pattern characterized by time urgency, hostility, and competitiveness

The three components of the Type A pattern, according to these physicians, are a sense of time urgency, easily aroused hostility, and competitive achievement strivings. People who are Type A are always in a hurry, setting unnecessary deadlines for themselves and trying to do multiple things at once. They are competitive, even in situations in which it is ridiculous to be competitive. For example, they will rush to be the first in line at a restaurant or at the movies, even when the wait would be only 2 or 3 minutes if they were last in line. They are also chronically hostile and will fly into a rage with little provocation. Persons who are not Type A are referred to as *Type B*. They are able to relax without feeling guilty, are able to work without feeling pressured or becoming impatient, and are not easily aroused to hostility.

 What might be the benefits of the Type A behavior pattern for people with this pattern?

One of the most compelling studies to demonstrate the relationship between Type A behavior and coronary heart disease followed more than 3,000 healthy, middle-age men for 8½ years (Rosenman et al., 1976). At the beginning of the study, the men were evaluated for the Type A pattern by means of a cleverly structured interview. The interview was designed to be irritating. The interviewer kept the participant waiting without explanation and then asked a series of questions about being competitive, hostile, and pressed for time: Do you ever feel rushed or under pressure? Do you eat quickly? Would you describe yourself as ambitious and hard driving or relaxed and easygoing? Do you resent it if someone is late? The interviewer interrupted subjects, asked questions in a challenging manner, and threw in non sequiturs. A participant's level of Type A behavior was determined more on the way he behaved in answering the questions and responding to the interviewer's rudeness than on his answers to the questions themselves. For example, a man was labeled as extremely Type A if he spoke loudly in an explosive manner, talked over the interviewer so as not to be interrupted, appeared tense and tight-lipped, and described hostile incidents with great emotional intensity. The Type B men tended to sit in a relaxed manner, spoke slowly and softly, were easily interrupted, and smiled often.

Over the 8½ years of the study, Type A men had twice as many heart attacks or other forms of coronary heart disease than did Type B men. These results held up even after diet, age, smoking, and other variables associated with coronary heart disease were taken into account. Other studies have confirmed this twofold risk and linked Type A behavior to heart disease in both men and women (Haynes, Feinleib, & Kannel, 1980). In addition, Type A behavior correlates with severity of coronary artery blockage as determined at autopsy or in X-ray studies of the inside of coronary blood vessels (Friedman, Rosenhan, Straus, Wurm, & Kositcheck, 1968; Williams, Barefoot, Haney, & Harrell, 1988). Based on such evidence, the American Heart Association classified Type A behavior as a risk factor for coronary heart disease in 1981.

More recent research suggests that the definition of Type A behavior, as originally formulated, is too diffuse. Time urgency and competitiveness do not appear to be the variables that best predict coronary heart disease. Instead, the crucial variable may be hostility, particularly a cynical form of hostility characterized by suspiciousness, resentment, frequent anger, antagonism, and distrust of others (Barefoot, Dodge, Peterson, Dahlstrom, & Williams, 1989; Miller, Smith, Turner, & Guijarro, 1996). Indeed, a person's chronic level of hostility seems to be a better predictor of heart disease than does his or her classification as Type A or Type B (Booth-Kewley & Friedman, 1987; Dembroski, MacDougall, Williams, & Haney, 1985; Thoresen, Telch, & Eagleston, 1981). For example,

People with the Type A behavior pattern are always doing several things at once, trying to cram more and more activity into each day.

a 25-year study of 118 male lawyers found that those who scored high on hostility traits on a personality inventory taken in law school were five times more likely to die before the age of 50 than were classmates who were not hostile (Barefoot, Dodge, Peterson, & Dahlstrom, 1989). Similarly, in a study of physicians, hostility scores obtained in medical school predicted the incidence of coronary heart disease as well as mortality from all causes (Barefoot, Dahlstrom, & Williams, 1983). In both studies, the relationship between hostility and illness was independent of the effects of smoking, age, and high blood pressure.

Although we tend to think of Type A people as angry and aggressive, always fighting to get their way and to accomplish a great deal, there is evidence that they are often anxious and depressed and that these negative emotions may contribute to their risk of disease (Booth-Kewley & Friedman, 1987). Type As may be anxious and depressed because they tend to be dissatisfied with their careers, they tend to spend little time with their families and thus jeopardize their home lives, and their social lives in general are not as satisfying as they might be. Regardless of the source of their negative emotions, it appears that these emotions are risk factors for both coronary heart disease and death as the result of a variety of other diseases.

How does Type A behavior or more specifically hostility and related negative emotions lead to coronary heart disease? Again, one mechanism may have to do with overarousal of the sympathetic nervous system (see Figure 13.5). Type A people show greater physiological arousal in the anticipation of stressors and in the early stages of dealing with stressors (Contrada, Wright, & Glass, 1985): Their heart rates and blood pressures are higher and they have greater secretion of the stress-related biochemicals known as *catecholamines*. They also show slower returns to baseline levels of sympathetic nervous system activity following stressors than do Type Bs. This hyperreactivity may cause wear and tear on the coronary arteries, leading to coronary heart disease. Alternately, the excessive secretion of catecholamines in response to stress seen in Type As may exert a direct chemical effect on blood vessels. The frequent rise and fall of levels of catecholamines may cause frequent changes in blood pressure that reduce the resilience of the blood vessels (Wright, 1984). Type A people and, more generally, hostile people may also engage in behaviors that increase their propensity to heart disease, including smoking, heavy drinking, and maintaining high cholesterol diets (Folsom et al., 1985).

Although the Type A behavior pattern has been linked to coronary heart disease in both men and women, men are more likely to be classified as Type A and more likely to be chronically hostile than are women (Barefoot, Siegler, Nowlin, & Peterson, 1987; Haynes et al., 1980). Men also are more likely than women to carry three other risk factors for CHD: smoking, hypertension, and elevated cholesterol. In turn, men have a much greater rate of CHD than do women: Heart attacks account for 41 percent of the difference between men and women in mortality in early and middle adulthood (Lerner &

Figure 13.5

Pathways by Which Hostility and the Type A Behavior Pattern May Contribute to Coronary Heart Disease. People who are chronically hostile or have the Type A behavior pattern may have chronic or intermittent hyperarousal, which negatively affects the heart, and engage in several behaviors known to increase risk of coronary heart disease.

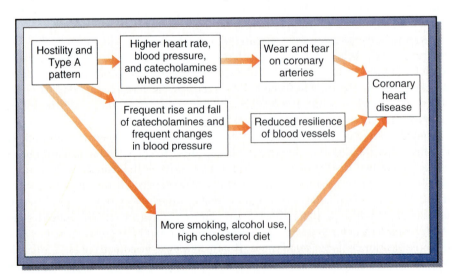

Kannel, 1986). Men's greater tendency to be Type A and hostile may be the result of biological predisposition to physiological reactivity: In several studies, men, particularly Type A men, have been shown to be more physiologically reactive to stressors than have women (see Weidner & Collins, 1993). Most of these studies have used male-stereotyped tasks to induce stress in subjects, however. When more female-stereotyped tasks are used to induce stress (such as taking one's child to the pediatrician), gender differences in physiological reactivity are not found (Weidner & Collins, 1993).

Alternately, because many of the components of the Type A pattern, such as competitiveness and aggressiveness, are behaviors that are valued in males, some men may be reinforced for these behaviors and thus adopt them. Weidner and colleagues (1988) found that sons of Type A fathers were more likely to develop the Type A pattern themselves, perhaps by modeling their fathers' behaviors and by being reinforced for imitating their fathers. Studies of the interactions between Type A children and their parents suggest that Type A children are repeatedly urged by their parents to try harder and to do better but are not given praise when they do well, are often harshly criticized for not performing better than others, and are not given concrete criteria to determine when they have been successful. Thus, they may not learn personal standards to evaluate their own achievements and thus always push harder to do more and do better.

Fortunately, as we will discuss later in this chapter, Type A behavior appears to be changeable through cognitive and behavioral therapies. People who reduce their Type A behaviors reduce their risk of coronary heart disease considerably.

Repressive Coping

Type A people are constantly showing their hostile feelings, much to others' dismay. Some people have the opposite tendency—to bottle up and repress all negative emotions. A person with a **repressive coping style** does not admit when he or she is upset and may not even be aware of his or her own negative emotions.

 How would you differentiate between repressors who deny they experience distress and people who really do not experience much distress?

repressive coping style
tendency to expunge negative emotions from one's awareness, at times to a point at which one is unaware that one is experiencing them at all

Some studies suggest that repressive coping is detrimental to physical health. Laboratory studies find that repressors have higher base levels of cortisol, a hormone that is secreted in response to stress (Brown, Tomarken, Orth, & Loosen, 1996). Repressors also evidence greater autonomic arousal (heart rate, galvanic skin response) while completing sentences with sexual or aggressive content than do people with nonrepressive coping styles (Weinberger, Schwartz, & Davidson, 1979). Repressors are not aware that they are physiologically aroused chronically or in response to challenging tasks, however.

As noted repeatedly in this chapter, chronic physiological arousal or reactivity to situations can cause damage to both the immune and cardiovascular systems. Some naturalistic studies have found links between repressive coping and diseases of the immune or cardiovascular system. For example, studies of students and of elderly adults have found that repressive coping is associated with poorer immune system functioning (Jamner, Schwartz, & Leigh, 1988). Repressive coping styles may be detrimental to health because repressors have no outlets for their negative emotions—they do not recognize them or will not admit to them, so they cannot let go of them. In turn, this may cause the chronic physiological arousal that impairs health. In addition, it may take a great deal of unconscious psychological and physiological work to constantly repress one's emotions, which may take its toll on health.

John Henryism

In general, research has shown that engaging in active strategies to solve one's problems and overcome obstacles is associated with more positive mental and physical health

When people chronically must hold in their negative emotions rather than expressing them, this may be detrimental to health.

African American men who find themselves chronically fighting nearly insurmountable obstacles to their achievement may be at increased risk for hypertension.

John Henryism
pattern of active coping with stressors by trying harder and harder against obstacles that may be insurmountable

(Billings & Moos, 1981). There is an exception to this general conclusion, however. A group of studies has focused on a phenomenon known as *John Henryism*. According to the story, John Henry was an uneducated black laborer who beat a mechanical steam drill in a contest to see which could complete the most work in the shortest period of time. Although John Henry won the battle, he dropped dead after the contest. James and colleagues (1983, 1984) coined the term **John Henryism** for a pattern of active coping with stressors that involves trying harder and harder against obstacles that may be insurmountable and suggested that this coping style may be linked to the high rate of hypertension among African-American men. Subsequent studies found that African-American men in lower socioeconomic groups who had a John Henry way of coping with the obstacles they faced were almost three times more likely to have hypertension than were African-American men in lower socioeconomic classes who did not have the same active coping pattern. In contrast, there was no relationship between John Henryism and health among white men of either high or low socioeconomic status. This suggests that the John Henry coping style is dangerous only for those men who face obstacles that are nearly insurmountable. This research on John Henryism raises the troubling possibility that men who are trying to overcome with hard work and persistence the oppression and hardship they were born into may be putting their health at risk.

Seeking Social Support

We end this section on personality and health on a happier note, focusing on one strategy for coping with negative emotions that appears to help people adjust both emotionally and physically to stressors—seeking emotional support from others. For example, a study of women who had just received surgery for breast cancer found that those who actively sought social support from others had higher natural killer cell activity (Levy, Herberman, Whiteside, & Sanzo, 1990). Killer cells are part of the immune system that aggressively attacks disease. In a large series of studies, James Pennebaker (1990) found that people who simply reveal personal traumas, such as being raped or losing a spouse to suicide, to supportive others tend to show more positive physical health both shortly after traumas and in the long run.

Many people facing stressors, including physical illness, seek support from support groups. A provocative study of breast cancer patients found evidence that support groups may not only help women cope emotionally with their cancer but may also prolong the lives of these women (Spiegel, Bollm, Kraemer, & Gottheil, 1989). Several years ago, researchers began a study in which they randomly assigned women with advanced breast cancer either to a series of weekly support groups or to no support groups. All the women received standard medical care for their cancer. The focus in the groups was on facing death and learning to live one's remaining days to the fullest. The researchers did not expect they could alter the course of the cancer; they only wanted to improve the quality of life for women with advanced cancer. They were quite surprised when, 48 months after the study began, all of the women who had not been in the support groups were dead from their cancer and a third of the women in the support groups were still alive. The average survival from the time the study began for the women in the support groups was about 40 months, compared to about 19 months for the women who were not in the support groups. There were no differences between the groups other than their participation in the weekly support meetings that could explain the differences in the average survival times. It appears that the support groups actually increased the number of months that the women in the support group lived (for similar results, see Richardson, Shelton, Krailo, & Levine, 1990). What can account for this? The women in the support groups had lower levels of emotional distress and they learned how to control their physical pain better than the women who did not participate in the support groups. This lowering of distress may have improved the functioning of their immune systems.

Unfortunately, not all interactions with people are supportive ones. Some friends or relatives can be burdens instead of blessings in times of stress. The quality of the social support a person receives from others following a stressor is more important than the quantity of support received (Rook, 1984). Persons who have a high degree of conflict in their social networks tend to show poorer physical and emotional health following major stressors, such as bereavement (Windholz, Marmar, & Horowitz, 1985). Conflictual social relationships may affect physical health through the immune system. A study of newly-wed couples found that those who became hostile and negative toward each other while discussing marital problems showed more decrements in four indicators of immune system functioning than did couples who remained calm and nonhostile in discussing marital problems. Couples who became hostile during these discussions also showed elevated blood pressure for longer periods of time than did those who did not become hostile (Kiecolt-Glaser, Malarkey, Chee, & Newton, 1993). Thus, the old prescription of talking through troubles with others may only be good if those others can be emotionally supportive when needed.

| Summing Up | Personality and Health |

- People who are chronically pessimistic may show poorer physical health because they appraise more events as uncontrollable or because they engage in poorer health-related behaviors.
- People with the Type A behavior pattern are highly competitive, time urgent, and hostile. The Type A behavior pattern significantly increases risk for coronary heart disease. The most potent component of this pattern is hostility, which alone significantly predicts heart disease.
- People with repressive coping styles deny their negative emotions and may be at increased risk for poor health.
- John Henryism is a coping style in which people work diligently against tremendous obstacles but apparently put their physical health at risk in doing so.
- Seeking high-quality social support is a coping style that may protect people from poor health consequences of stressful events.

Psychosocial Interventions to Improve Health

Most of the interventions designed to improve health have (1) provided people with new health-related skills and opportunity to practice these skills or (2) have attempted to challenge and change negative, self-defeating cognitions that contribute to the development of illness or interfere with recovery or adaptation to illness. We will discuss four types of interventions that have proven useful in improving people's health.

Guided Mastery Techniques

When told what they have to do to protect or improve their health, people often feel unable or unwilling to engage in these behaviors. **Guided mastery techniques** provide people with explicit information about how to engage in positive health-related behaviors and with opportunities to engage in these behaviors in increasingly challenging situations. The goals are to increase people's skills at engaging in the behaviors and their self-efficacy for engaging in the behaviors. For example, a guided mastery program for teaching women how to negotiate safe sexual practices in sexual encounters with men might first provide the women with basic information on safe sexual practices, such as condom use. A counselor might then model how a woman can tell a man that she wants him to use a condom when they have sex. The women would watch the counselor and then practice insisting on condom use in role-plays with the counselor or other group participants. In these role-plays, the women would be presented with increasingly difficult challenges to their insistence on condom use, feedback on effective means for meeting these challenges, and practice in meeting these challenges. The women might also be taught techniques

guided mastery techniques interventions designed to increase health-promoting behaviors by providing explicit information about how to engage in these behaviors as well as opportunities to engage in these behaviors in increasingly challenging situations

Young people may need both information and guided mastery experiences to learn effective ways of negotiating safe sexual practices.

for determining when it was useless to argue with their partners any longer about condom use and skills for withdrawing themselves from sexual encounters in which their partners wanted to practice unsafe sex.

Guided mastery techniques have been successfully used in AIDS prevention programs with African-American female and male adolescents (Jemmott & Jemmott, 1992). In the programs with the young women, researchers gave participants information about the cause, transmission, and prevention of AIDS. The young women then participated in guided mastery exercises such as those described to increase their skills and self-confidence for negotiating condom use by their male partners. The young women were also given instruction on how to eroticize condom use—how to incorporate putting on condoms in foreplay and intercourse in ways that increase positive attitudes toward condoms. Compared to young women who received only information and not guided mastery exercises, these young women showed a greater sense of efficacy in negotiating condom use, more positive expectations for sexual enjoyment with condoms, and stronger intentions to use condoms. These effects were found in a similar program with sexually active African-American female adolescents drawn from the inner city (Jemmott & Jemmott, 1992). In a program with African-American male adolescents, young men also were first given information about the cause, transmission, and prevention of AIDS. Then they participated in guided mastery exercises that taught them how to negotiate condom use with their partners and to eroticize condom use. Follow-up assessments showed that, compared to those in a control group, the adolescents who participated in the program were more knowledgeable about risks for AIDS, less accepting of risky practices, and engaged in lower-risk sexual behavior with fewer sexual partners (Jemmott et al., 1992). Thus, enhancing people's skills to engage in healthy behaviors seems to increase their self-efficacy for engaging in these behaviors and, in turn, increases their intentions to engage in these behaviors and their actual enacting of the behaviors.

Reducing Catastrophizing Cognitions

Many people believe the worst when they are told that they have a serious illness, regardless of what they are told by their physicians about their prognoses. These catastrophizing cognitions cause great distress and can lead people to be fatalistic and to not comply with treatments or engage in behaviors that could prevent future illnesses. For example, a man who has a minor heart attack from which he is expected to recover fully might believe that his physician is trying to shield him from the truth and that he is doomed to die of another heart attack at any minute. Thus, although his physician tells him to quit smoking, reduce the fat in his diet, and begin to exercise regularly, he may decide that all of these changes in his behaviors will do no good, so he will just do what he wants until the next heart attack kills him. Another man might be told he has prostate cancer but that surgeons should be able to remove all the cancer in a routine surgery. Still, upon hearing the word *cancer*, he imagines certain death and becomes so anxious that his blood pressure rises and he begins having panic attacks, which interfere with his preparation for surgery and recovery from the surgery.

 If you were told today that you have a serious illness such as cancer, what thoughts would go through your head? How do you think these thoughts would help or hurt you in dealing with the illness?

Psychologists working with patients who are catastrophizing their illnesses might begin with basic education about their illnesses—the prevalence of the illnesses, the standard procedures for treating the illnesses, the average prognosis for the illnesses, and differences between patients in prognoses. This education may be tailored to the individual patient, in an attempt to make sure that the patient understands all the physician has told him or her about the illness and prognosis. This can be very helpful, because physicians are not always good at speaking to patients about their illnesses in simple, straightforward, understandable language. Much of the catastrophizing patients do about their illnesses comes from misunderstanding what they have been told by their physicians.

Psychologists might also assess the specific catastrophizing thoughts patients have and use standard cognitive therapy techniques to challenge these thoughts (see Chapter 3). For example, a patient who has breast cancer may believe that the lumpectomy that she is going to have to remove the cancer will permanently disfigure her to such a degree that her husband will no longer love her and will leave her. Her psychologist may help her assess the evidence for this belief, perhaps by helping her talk directly with her husband about her fears. The husband might say that he is completely supportive of his wife, that he will love her no matter what surgery she has, and that her fears of his leaving are completely unfounded. Of course, there is always the chance that a patient's fears are realistic—that the husband really is having doubts about his ability to support his wife through her surgery—or that a patient does have an illness that is likely to take her life. In such cases, psychologists must help patients cope as well as possible with reality, such as by finding support in friends and other family members, by getting their affairs in order should death come quickly, and by coming to terms with prognoses.

A recent study demonstrated the efficacy of challenging patients' catastrophizing cognitions about their illnesses (Greene & Blanchard, 1994). The patients in this study had irritable bowel syndrome (IBS), a widespread, chronic illness of the lower gastrointestinal (GI) tract, characterized by abdominal pain or extreme abdominal tenderness and diarrhea or constipation. No pharmacological treatments have proven effective for this condition. In this study, patients with IBS were randomly assigned either to intensive, individualized cognitive therapy (10 sessions over 8 weeks) or to 8 weeks of daily GI symptom reporting. In the cognitive therapy, therapists challenged the patients' negative and irrational cognitions about their condition. Many of these cognitions involved hypervigilance to symptoms and catastrophizing about those symptoms. For example, patients might constantly press against their abdomens, testing for tenderness, and panic at any indication of tenderness, believing that they are beginning to have another episode. The therapists helped patients identify their beliefs and fears about their illness and the ways these fears could exacerbate the illness, "decenter" by labeling their negative self-statements and thereby gain distance from these thoughts, and challenge negative beliefs by engaging in behaviors that disconfirmed their beliefs (e.g., going out in the evening even though they believe that it may trigger a new episode). After treatment, 80 percent of the patients receiving cognitive therapy showed significant improvement in their symptoms of IBS compared to only 10 percent of the patients who simply monitored their symptoms. In the cognitive therapy group, reduction in IBS symptoms was related to reductions in negative, catastrophizing thoughts and to reduction in depression and anxiety. The effects of the cognitive therapy remained strong 3 months following the treatment. Thus, this study demonstrated that cognitive therapy aimed at catastrophizing cognitions not only produced reductions in psychological distress over the illness but also reductions in the actual symptoms of this chronic illness.

Biofeedback

Biofeedback has been used to treat a wide variety of health problems—most frequently migraine headaches, chronic pain, and hypertension. Biofeedback actually comprises several techniques designed to help people change bodily processes by learning to identify signs that the processes are going awry and then learning ways of controlling the processes. For example, a person with hypertension might be hooked up to a machine that converts his heart beats to tones. He sits quietly listening to his heart rate and trying various means to change his heart rate, such as breathing slowly or concentrating on a pleasant image. The goal in biofeedback is for people to detect early signs of dysfunction in their bodies, such as signs that their blood pressure is rising, and to use techniques they learned while hooked up to machines to control their bodies even when they are independent of the machines.

Biofeedback seems to be successful in reducing tension-related headaches (Gannon, Hanes, Cuevas, & Chavez, 1987). Headache sufferers learn to detect when they are tensing the muscles in their heads and techniques for reducing this tension, thus relieving their headaches. Biofeedback also appears to reduce the severity of migraine headaches.

Biofeedback helps people learn to detect when bodily processes are going awry and to counteract these processes.

About 14 percent of adults in the United States suffer from migraines. These are severe headaches that are often accompanied by nausea, irritability, vomiting, and images of bright lights. They appear to be caused by dilation of veins and arteries in the head and can be induced by stress. There are many drugs for the treatment of migraine headaches, but these drugs are often unsuccessful or produce serious unpleasant side effects. Biofeedback is used for migraine sufferers to increase the blood flow to the body's periphery, thereby decreasing the blood flow to the head and thus reducing pressure on the arteries. Migraine patients are hooked up to machines that give them temperature readings to their heads and to their fingers. They are taught to relax fully and to notice the effects that relaxation has on their temperatures. Then they may be encouraged to increase the temperatures of their fingers, using the feedback of the machines as an aid. It is not clear just how patients do this—it is a matter of their using trial and error to find some way of changing their temperatures. Eventually, patients attempt to use the techniques they learned to control headaches at home, noticing when they feel headaches coming on and then warming up their fingers to divert blood flow from the arteries in their heads to the periphery (see Turk, Meichenbaum, & Berman, 1979).

Although biofeedback can be successful in treating hypertension and pain conditions such as headaches, it is not clear that it works the way its proponents believe it works (Turk et al., 1979). For example, although biofeedback can reduce migraine headaches, the evidence that it does so by changing temperature control is mixed. In addition, biofeedback appears to be no more successful than simple relaxation techniques in reducing headaches, pain, and hypertension (see Chapter 4 for a detailed description of relaxation techniques.) Indeed, biofeedback may work largely because individuals often learn relaxation techniques as a part of biofeedback training. Relaxation techniques have the advantage over biofeedback of being much less expensive and time-consuming to learn.

Time Management

A final technique for reducing stress and thereby improving health that we will discuss in this chapter is time management. There are hundreds of books on time management, most of which have been published in the last 25 years, as the pace of life in the industrialized world seems to have quickened and the number of activities people try to jam into each day has seemed to expand greatly. The recommendations of time management experts generally fall into four categories: prioritizing, breaking tasks into small chunks, scheduling, and rewarding oneself.

The first step of time management is determining what activities are worth one's time and what activities are not. Time management experts often distinguish between *important* activities and *urgent* activities. Important activities are activities that have to do with one's central values or goals in life. For example, if one of a person's central goals in life is to become an expert car mechanic and eventually own her own car repair shop, then important activities for her might be taking a course on car repair at the community college, apprenticing at a local car repair shop, or investigating how to buy into a car repair franchise.

Urgent activities are ones that beg to be done *now*. Sometimes these activities are also important activities. For example, if a person's central goal is to become a car mechanic and the deadline for signing up for the course on car repair at the community college is today, then going to the college and signing up today is both an important and an urgent activity. Often, however, urgent activities are not important activities. For example, talking on the phone to a salesperson trying to sell life insurance is an urgent activity (at least the salesperson tries to stress that it is), but it is not an important activity for a person who already has life insurance and whose 2-year-old child is about to pull over the bookshelf. Many of the activities that get labeled urgent involve responding to other people who want one's time or attention *now* but could just as easily be dealt with later. We often make activities into urgent activities when we are trying to avoid important activities that we do not want to do. Cleaning one's dormitory room suddenly becomes an urgent activity during exam week; answering letters ignored for months suddenly becomes an urgent activity when one must decide what courses to take next year; calling one's "best friend" for the first time in a year suddenly becomes an urgent activity when a paper is due the next morning at 9 A.M.

To manage time, one must first decide what activities are important. This involves deciding what one's goals and values are. What would we like to accomplish in the next month, in the next 6 months, in the next year, in the next 5 years? The answers to these questions indicate what our primary goals are, and the activities that help us accomplish these goals are important activities. Which people in our lives do we care about most? Which organizations (e.g., church) or activities (e.g., horseback riding) are most central to our lives? The answers to these questions can help us recognize some of our core values, and the activities that further these values are important activities.

 Pause and ask yourself what you would like to accomplish in the next 6 months, in the next year, and in the next 5 years.

The second step in time management is to break large activities or tasks into smaller ones. It is important to have both distal goals (long-term goals) and proximal goals (short-term goals that move one closer to long-term goals). Any large goal or activity, such as becoming an expert car mechanic, can be broken into a series of smaller activities. It is important to break large goals into small activities because it is necessary to concretely identify the steps that must be taken to accomplish long-term goals in order to begin accomplishing those goals. In addition, the long-term goals can be overwhelming and demoralizing, but breaking these goals into smaller activities can make the tasks seem more manageable. One time management book recommends breaking tasks into 5-minute chunks, if possible (Lakein, 1973). Once that is done, a person can coax himself into getting engaged in the activity by saying to himself, "I'll only work on this for five minutes—I can stand that." Once he has accomplished one 5-minute task, however, he may find himself so engaged in the activity that he moves on to the next 5-minute task and then the next, and soon he has spent an hour on his important activity.

The third step in time management is scheduling important activities. Most of us have to-do lists, and some of us live by them. The to-do lists are often filled with urgent but unimportant activities (*pick up laundry, return five phone calls to unfamiliar people, wash the car*). If important activities do show up on the list, they are often in the form of monolithic tasks, such as *write term paper, look for a new job,* or *save money.* The activities that should be on the to-do list are the important activities broken down into their small components, which was done in step two. So rather than listing *write term paper* on the list, one should write, *discuss ideas for term paper with professor, look in library listings for pertinent materials,* and *begin outline.* In addition, it helps to schedule specific times to do these

It may be tempting to clean a messy room rather than tackling more important activities.

important small activities, rather than leaving to chance the motivation some time in the next week to engage in these activities. So one might write, *after class on Thursday, talk with professor about ideas for term paper*, or *look in library listings on Saturday afternoon for pertinent materials*. When scheduling an important activity for a specific time, it is important to be ruthless about protecting that time from other urgent but unimportant activities, such as chatty phone calls from friends one sees every day. This is not to say that people should schedule every minute of their days. However, by scheduling their important activities people will make it more likely that they will actually accomplish them, which can reduce the stress of worrying about whether and when they are going to work on these activities and reach their goals.

A fourth and final step in time management is rewarding oneself for accomplishing short-term and long-term goals. Few of us can keep up a grueling pace of working on our important activities without taking occasional breaks and patting ourselves on the backs for our accomplishments. These pats on the back may involve doing something social with a close friend, treating oneself to a favorite meal or dessert, or going for a walk in a beautiful place. The key is that we recognize in some way that accomplishing even small activities related to our most important goals is laudable and that we give ourselves praise for this.

Some of us need to reduce the number of activities we try to accomplish in our lives, even if all these activities are important ones. We may be able to reduce the number of important activities we jam into our lives by asking for help from others or by hiring help if we can afford it. For example, a single mother who works full-time might hire someone to clean her house if she can afford it, so that she can spend more of her time away from work with her children. However, we must give up certain goals and activities, in recognition that only a limited number of things can get done well.

Putting It All Together—Interventions for the Type A Behavior Pattern

Many of the interventions we have discussed in this chapter, including biofeedback, cognitive therapy, and time management training, have been used to help people with the Type A behavior pattern change their behaviors and their attitudes toward themselves and the world and thereby reduce their risk of coronary heart disease. In one study, 1,000 men who had had heart attacks were assigned to a cognitive-behavioral treatment to reduce Type A behavior, or to a control group that received no treatment (Friedman et al., 1986). The men in the treatment group were helped to reduce their sense of time urgency by practicing standing in line (a situation Type A individuals find extremely irritating) and using the opportunity to reflect on things they did not normally have time to think about, to watch people, or to strike up conversations with strangers. Treatment also included learning to express themselves without exploding in anger and to alter certain specific behaviors (such as interrupting the speech of others or talking or eating hurriedly). Therapists helped the subjects reevaluate basic beliefs, such as the notion that success depends on the quality of work produced, that might drive much of a Type A person's urgent and hostile behavior. Finally, subjects found ways to make home and work environments less stressful, such as by reducing the number of unnecessary social engagements. When researchers followed up on the treatment and control subjects 4½ years later, they found that the treatment subjects were only about half as likely to have experienced second heart attacks as were the control subjects.

 What do you think might be the most difficult aspects of Type A behavior for a therapist to change?

Summing Up | Psychosocial Interventions to Improve Health

- Guided mastery techniques help people learn positive health-related behaviors, by teaching them the most effective ways of engaging in these behaviors and giving them opportunity to practice the behaviors in increasingly challenging situations.
- Cognitive-behavioral techniques can be used to challenge catastrophizing cognitions people may have about illnesses that maintain high states of physiological arousal.
- Biofeedback is used to help people learn to control their own negative physiological responses.
- Time management techniques can help people reduce the overall levels of stress in their lives, thereby improving their health.
- A variety of cognitive-behavioral techniques have been combined into an effective treatment package to reduce Type A behavior pattern and the risk of further coronary disease in men.

The field of health psychology is based on the notion that the body, the mind, and the environment are intimately connected. Psychological and social factors can have direct effects on the physiology of the body and indirect effects on health by leading people to engage in either health-promoting or health-impairing behaviors. It is clear that our physical health affects our emotional health and self-concept. People with life-threatening or debilitating physical illnesses are at much increased risk for depression and other emotional problems. At a more subtle level, physiology may influence many characteristics we think of as personality, such as how quick we are to react with anger when someone confronts us or how adaptable we are to new situations. Thus, health psychologists begin with the assumption that biology, psychology, and social environment have reciprocal influences on each other. Then they attempt to characterize these influences and determine their importance.

Bio-Psycho-Social
INTEGRATION

Chapter Summary

Health psychologists are concerned with the roles of personality factors, coping styles, stressful events, and health-related behaviors on the development of physical disease and on the progress of disease once it begins. There are three models for explaining how psychological factors affect health. The direct effects model suggests that psychological factors, such as stressful experiences or certain personality characteristics, directly cause changes in the physiology of the body that, in turn, cause or exacerbate disease. The interactive model suggests that psychological factors must interact with preexisting biological vulnerability to disease in order for a disease to develop. The indirect effects model suggests that psychological factors affect disease largely by influencing whether people engage in health-promoting behaviors.

The three characteristics of events that contribute to their being perceived as stressful are their controllability, their predictability, and their level of challenge or threat to the limits of one's capabilities. Stress can have a direct effect on health by causing chronic arousal of the physiological responses that make up the fight-or-flight response. These physiological responses result from the activation of the sympathetic nervous system and the adrenal-cortical system. Although these physiological changes are useful in helping the body fight or flee from a threat, they can cause damage to the body if they are chronically aroused due to stress. Diseases that can result from such chronic arousal include coronary heart disease, hypertension, and possibly impairment of the immune system.

One activity that many of us give up when we are under stress is sleep. There is increasing evidence, however, that the amount and quality of sleep we get on a daily basis have a significant impact on our physical health and our psychological functioning.

Personality characteristics that have been linked to health include explanatory style and optimism. The Type A behavior pattern is strongly related to high risk for coronary heart disease and possibly also to other diseases. People who have the Type A pattern have a sense of time urgency, are easily made hostile, and are competitive in many situations. The component of this pattern that has been most consistently linked to coronary heart disease is a cynical form of hostility. Another important aspect of personality is the way individuals cope with difficult situations. One emotion-focused coping strategy that generally leads to positive health in the face of stress is seeking social support. Two coping strategies that are linked to poor health are repressive coping and John Henryism.

Guided mastery techniques have been effective in increasing self-efficacy for engaging in healthy behaviors and in increasing the actual conduct of healthy behaviors. These techniques include the use of modeling and role-playing to provide people with new skills and opportunities to practice those skills in increasingly challenging circumstances. Cognitive techniques are used to help patients reduce catastrophizing cognitions about their illnesses and stress-inducing self-expectations. Biofeedback is sometimes used to help people gain control over bodily processes that contribute to disease. It is unclear how biofeedback works, but it has been shown to be useful in reducing hypertension and headaches. Finally, time management techniques can help people reduce stress in their lives by identifying important activities, breaking these activities into smaller chunks, scheduling the activities, and rewarding themselves for accomplishing the activities.

These cognitive and behavioral techniques have been combined to reduce the health-damaging behaviors and cognitions of people with the Type A behavior pattern. One study showed that Type A men who underwent cognitive therapy were significantly less likely to have future myocardial infarctions than were Type A men who did not undergo cognitive therapy.

Key Terms

stress 469
safety signal hypothesis 470
fight-or-flight response 472
coronary heart disease (CHD) 472

essential hypertension 473
immunocompetence 474
lymphocytes 474
Type A behavior pattern 479

repressive coping style 481
John Henryism 482
guided mastery techniques 483

Application   Stress and the College Student

If you are a college student, how can you use the stress-management techniques to reduce the stress in your life and possibly improve your health and well-being? The first step involves self-monitoring—monitoring your reactions to events over the course of your day to determine which ones you experience as stressful. You may think that you do not need to do this—that it is obvious what is stressful in your life, such as exams or having too much work to do. However, it is important to do a more fine-grained analysis of exactly what aspects of events make you feel most stressed and/or the cognitions you are having about those events that are increasing your stress level. Keeping a diary or daily log of your emotions and the situations and thoughts connected to those emotions can help. You might discover that it is not exams in general that you are experiencing as stressful but an upcoming math exam in particular. You might further discover that certain cognitions such as, "My parents will kill me if I don't do well in math," "I'm an older student so I can't learn this new math like the younger students," or, "Because I'm a minority, the professor doesn't believe that I can do well in math," are elevating your stress about the exam.

If you identify any cognitions that are contributing to your stress, then use cognitive therapy techniques to challenge these cognitions and determine if they are realistic and the only ways to view your situation. Remember that the four main questions that cognitive therapists ask are (1) what is the evidence for your viewpoint, (2) are there other ways of viewing the situation, (3) what's the worst that could happen in this situation, and (4) how could I cope if the worst case scenario came true? For example, let us say that you are an older person returning to college after a long absence, and you believe that you are incapable of learning math in the way it is taught these days. First, ask yourself what is the evidence for your viewpoint. Have you been completely unable to comprehend any-

thing the professor has taught in this math class? Do your problems have anything to do with your age or are some of the young people in this class also having trouble? Ideally, you will discover evidence against your assumption that you are completely incapable of learning math, which then will lead you to the next question: What is an alternative way of viewing this situation? Is it possible that there are specific skills that you are lacking rather than competence in math? Is it possible that the professor is not very good at teaching math and that the problem lies with her rather than with your capabilities? Although you cannot learn specific new skills or improve your professor's teaching overnight, discovering that the problem is not your general incompetence but something more amenable to change can reduce your sense of stress.

The third question to ask yourself is, what is the worst thing that could happen? The answer in this case is probably that you could flunk the course. What is the consequence of flunking the course? If it is not a required course, then probably the worst thing that could happen would be that you would not know math as well as you might. If it is a required course, then it is time to move to the fourth and final question: How do you cope with the worst case scenario? Perhaps you could find an alternative course that is not as difficult but would still meet the requirement or get some tutoring over the summer and retake the course next fall. If these are not possible coping strategies, then you may need to think of strategies to cope with the reality of your flunking the course, such as changing your major. It can be quite helpful to go through these questions with a trusted friend who can help you generate challenges to your negative cognitions and coping strategies for dealing with the situations that might arise should the worst case scenario come true.

Time management is an especially important component of stress reduction for col-

lege students. Students who are living away from home for the first time may not have the structure and discipline imposed on their lives that their parents provided when they were living at home. At the same time, they may be facing much larger workloads and more difficult course material than they ever dreamed of in high school. The time management strategies discussed earlier in this chapter can go a long way toward structuring their lives around the important activities of doing well in school as well as enjoying a social life. Scheduling of important activities is particularly important for college students who are prone to procrastination. In a college atmosphere, there are endless distractions that can make it easy to put off doing homework assignments or preparing for examinations. Only by scheduling specific times for doing schoolwork and refusing to succumb to these distractions during those times can some college students keep up with their work. Procrastinator college students are very prone to developing the belief that they do their best work when under the pressure of a deadline. This belief is almost always a fantasy that simply justifies procrastination. It is very seldom the case that good papers are written or exams are properly studied for under the influence of sleep deprivation and panic.

Time management is also especially important for students who must work while going to school. Interestingly, these students sometimes are natural time managers and find it easy to impose discipline and schedules on themselves, in part because they have been forced to learn these skills to survive. One type of activity these students sometimes find hardest to work into their schedules are leisure activities that are relaxing and can serve to reward them for all their hard work. These activities are just as important as activities related to school or work, because they can help students keep their stress down and can help them keep a healthy perspective on school and work. ∎

14 The Cognitive Disorders: Dementia, Delirium, and Amnesia

Dementia

Dementia is characterized by memory loss, deterioration in language and the ability to execute voluntary actions, and failure to recognize objects or people. The most common cause of dementia is Alzheimer's disease, but it can also be caused by several other medical conditions and is an effect of chronic intoxication with alcohol and other toxic substances. There is no effective treatment for dementia, but memory aids and drugs to increase cognitive functioning and reduce distress can help.

Delirium

The symptoms of delirium involve disorientation, recent memory loss, and clouding of consciousness. Medical conditions, surgery, many different drugs, high fever, and infections are just some of the causes of delirium. Delirium must be treated quickly to prevent brain damage.

Amnesia

The amnesic disorders can involve retrograde amnesia, which is a loss of memory for past events, and anterograde amnesia, which is the inability to learn new information. Amnesia can result from some medical illnesses, brain damage due to injury, and long-term substance abuse.

Gender and Cultural Issues

Women tend to show greater rates of dementia, perhaps because they live longer than men. People in low socioeconomic groups have higher rates of dementia, but this may be because tests used to diagnose cognitive disorders may favor people with more education.

Bio-Psycho-Social Integration
Chapter Summary
Key Terms
Application: *Tips for the Caregivers of Dementia Patients*

Men are not prisoners of fate, but only prisoners of their own minds.

—Franklin D. Roosevelt, Pan American Day Address (1939)

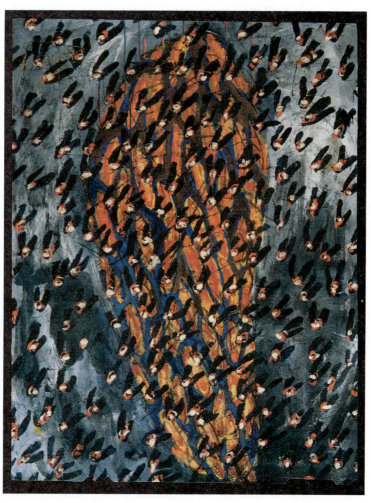

Deborah Schneider
Untitled #4

Case Study • Mariel is a 29-year-old, single, Puerto Rican woman. She has no children and lives with her mother and aunt in the Bronx. Since June 1993, she has been unemployed and supported by her family. Mariel was found to be HIV-positive 8 years ago when she was donating blood. She contracted the virus when raped at age 17 by a family friend. The offender later died of AIDS. For the last 2 years, Mariel was living and working as a store clerk in Puerto Rico. When she developed *Pneumocystis carinii* pneumonia, her mother insisted that she come back to New York City to obtain better medical care.

In the hospital, Mariel was referred for a psychiatric consultation because she was found wandering in a corridor distant from her room. When the psychiatrist arrived in her room, he found her lying on her bed with half her body outside the covers, rocking back and forth while clutching a pink teddy bear, appearing to stare at the television expressionlessly. When asked a series of questions about where she was, what day it was, and so on, she answered correctly, indicating she was oriented to the time and place. But her responses were greatly delayed, and it was almost impossible to engage her in conversation. She said she wanted to leave the hospital to find a place to think. Her mother reported that Mariel had told her she wanted to die.

Over the next few days in the hospital, Mariel became increasingly withdrawn. She would sit motionless for hours, not eating voluntarily, and did not recognize her mother when she came to visit. At times, Mariel would become agitated and appear to be responding to visual hallucinations. When asked to state where she was and her own birthdate, Mariel did not answer and either turned away or became angry and agitated.

As the pneumonia subsided, these acute psychological symptoms dissipated. But Mariel continued to be inattentive, apathetic, and withdrawn and to take a long time to answer simple questions. Suspecting depression, the psychiatrists prescribed an antidepressant medication, but it had little effect on Mariel's symptoms. After being discharged from the hospital, Mariel showed increasing trouble in expressing herself to her mother and in remembering things her mother had told her. She would spend all day in her room, staring out the window, with little interest in the activities her mother would suggest to her.

The impairments that Mariel is experiencing are common in the advanced stages of HIV disease. As we will discuss in this chapter, HIV disease is just one of several progressive diseases that inflict damage on the brain, causing a variety of cognitive and emotional deficits. Mariel shows symptoms of two types of disorders, dementia and delirium. *Dementia* is characterized by the gradual and usually permanent decline of intellectual functioning. In contrast, *delirium* involves a more acute and usually transient disorientation and memory loss.

Dementia and delirium are two of the three disorders often referred to as the **cognitive disorders** (see Table 14.1). The third cognitive disorder is *amnesia*. These disorders are characterized by impairments in cognition caused by a medical condition (such as HIV) or by substance intoxication or withdrawal. The impairments in cognition include memory deficits, language disturbance, perceptual disturbance, impairment in the capacity to plan and organize, and failure to recognize or identify objects. These disorders were formerly called *organic brain disorders*. This label was discontinued in the DSM-IV, however, because it implies that other disorders are *not* caused by biological factors, when it is clear that many disorders recognized by the DSM-IV have biological causes.

The cognitive impairments seen in dementia, delirium, and amnesia can also occur in other psychological disorders. For example, people with schizophrenia have language impairments and perceptual disturbances. People with depression may have problems with concentration and memory. Dementia, delirium, and amnesia are diagnosed when cognitive impairments appear to be the results of nonpsychiatric medical diseases or substance intoxication or withdrawal but not when the cognitive impairments appear only to be symptoms of other psychiatric disorders, such as schizophrenia or depression.

In this chapter, we review the symptoms of, causes of, and treatments for dementia, delirium, and amnesia. We begin with dementia, a disorder that typically involves

cognitive disorders
dementia, delirium, or amnesia characterized by impairments in cognition (such as deficits in memory, language, or planning) and caused by a medical condition or by substance intoxication or withdrawal

Table 14.1	Types of Cognitive Disorders

Dementia
  Dementia due to Alzheimer's disease
  Vascular dementia
  Dementia due to head injury
  Dementia due to Parkinson's disease
  Dementia due to HIV disease
  Dementia due to Huntington's disease
  Dementia due to Pick's disease
  Dementia due to Creutzfeldt-Jakob disease
  Substance-induced persisting dementia
Delirium
  Delirium due to a general medical condition (including illnesses and head injuries)
  Substance intoxication delirium
  Substance withdrawal delirium
  Delirium due to multiple etiologies
Amnesic disorders
  Amnesic disorder due to a general medical condition (including illnesses and head injuries)
  Substance-induced persisting amnesic disorder

Reprinted with permission from the *Diagnostic and Statistical Manual of Mental Disorders,* Fourth Edition. Copyright 1994 American Psychiatric Association.

irreversible loss of intellectual functioning and can devastate the lives of the people suffering from it and their families.

 If the cognitive disorders, by definition, are caused by medical conditions or substance intoxication but not by emotional distress or other psychological problems, should they be considered psychological disorders? Why or why not?

Dementia

Case Study • Aside from sustaining a head injury of uncertain significance while a young man in the service, Mr. Abbot B. Carrington had no medical or psychiatric problems until the age of 56. At that time, employed as an officer of a bank, he began to be forgetful. For example, he would forget to bring his briefcase to work or he would misplace his eyeglasses. His efficiency at work declined. He failed to follow through with assignments. Reports that he prepared were incomplete.

Although still friendly and sociable, Mr. Carrington began to lose interest in many of his usual activities. He ignored his coin collection. He no longer thoroughly perused *The Wall Street Journal* each day. When he discussed economics, it was without his previous grasp of the subject. After about a year of these difficulties, he was gradually eased out of his responsible position at the bank and eventually retired permanently.

At home, he tended to withdraw into himself. He would arise early each morning and go for a long walk, occasionally losing his way if he reached an unfamiliar neighborhood. He needed to be reminded constantly of the time of day, of upcoming events, and of his son's progress in college. He tried to use electric appliances without first plugging them into the socket. He shaved with the wrong side of the razor. Mostly, he remained a quiet, pleasant, and tractable person, but sometimes, particularly at night, he became exceptionally confused, and at these times he might be somewhat irritable, loud, and difficult to control.

Approximately 2 years following the onset of these symptoms, he was seen by a neurologist, who conducted a detailed examination of his mental status. The examiner noted that Mr. Carrington was neatly dressed, polite, and cooperative. He sat passively in the office as his wife described his problems to the doctor. He himself offered very little

Mr. Carrington was slowly losing his ability to remember the most fundamental facts of his life, to express himself through language, and to carry out basic activities of everyday life. This is the picture of **dementia,** the most common cognitive disorder.

There are five types of cognitive deficits in dementia. The most prominent is a *memory deficit*, which is required for the diagnosis of dementia. In the early stages of dementia, the memory lapses may be similar to those that we all experience from time to time—forgetting the name of someone we know casually, our own phone number, or what we went into the next room to get. Most of us eventually remember what we temporarily forgot, either spontaneously or by tricks that jog our memories. The difference with dementia is that memory does not return spontaneously and may not respond to reminders or other memory cues.

 What are your favorite memory aids or cues? Under what conditions or in what areas of your life do you most need memory aids or cues?

People in the early stages of dementia may repeat questions because they do not remember asking them moments ago or they do not remember getting answers. They will misplace items, such as keys or wallets, frequently. They may try to compensate for the memory loss. For example, they may carefully write down their appointments or things they need to do. Eventually, however, they forget to look at their calendars or lists. As the memory problems become more apparent, they may become angry when asked questions or make up answers in an attempt to hide memory loss. Later, as dementia progresses, they may become lost in familiar surroundings and be unable to find their way unaccompanied.

Eventually, long-term memory also becomes impaired. People with dementia will forget the order of major events in their lives, such as graduation from college, marriage, and the birth of their children. After a time, they will be unable to recall the events at all and may not even know their own names.

The second type of cognitive impairment is a deterioration of language, known as **aphasia.** People with dementia will have tremendous difficulty producing the names of objects or people and may often use terms like *thing* or vague references to *them* to hide their inability to produce names. If asked to identify a cup, for example, they may say

dementia
gradual and usually permanent decline of intellectual functioning, including deficits in memory, language, and loss of executive functioning, such as the ability to initiate common voluntary behaviors

aphasia
impaired ability to produce and comprehend language

that it is a *thing for drinking*, but be unable to name it as a cup. They may be unable to understand what another person is saying, and to follow simple requests such as, "Turn on the lights and shut the door." In advanced stages of dementia, people may exhibit *echolalia*—simply repeating back what they hear—or *palialia*—simply repeating sounds or words over and over.

The third cognitive deficit is **apraxia**, an impaired ability to execute common actions, such as waving good-bye or putting on a shirt. This deficit is not caused by problems in motor functioning (i.e., moving the arm), in sensory functioning, or in comprehending what action is required. People with dementia simply are unable to carry out actions that are requested of them or that they wish to carry out.

The fourth cognitive deficit is **agnosia**, the failure to recognize objects or people. People with dementia may not be able to identify common objects such as chairs or tables. At first, they will fail to recognize casual friends or distant family members. With time, they may not recognize their spouses or children or even their own reflections in a mirror.

The fifth cognitive deficit is a *loss of executive functioning*. Executive functioning is the ability to plan, initiate, monitor, and stop complex behaviors. Cooking Thanksgiving dinner requires executive functioning. Each menu item (i.e., the turkey, the stuffing, the pumpkin pie) requires different ingredients and preparation. The cooking of different menu items must be coordinated so that all the items are ready at the same time. People in the early stages of dementia may attempt to cook Thanksgiving dinner but forget important components (like the turkey) or fail to coordinate the dinner, burning certain items while other items remain uncooked. People in later stages of dementia will be unable even to plan or initiate a complex task such as this.

Deficits in executive functioning also involve problems in the kind of abstract thinking required to evaluate novel situations and respond appropriately to these situations. For example, when Mr. Carrington was presented with the proverb, "People who live in glass houses shouldn't throw stones," he was unable to interpret the abstract meaning of the proverb and instead interpreted it concretely to mean, "People don't want their windows broken."

In addition to having these cognitive deficits, people with dementia often show changes in emotional and personality functioning. Shoplifting, exhibitionism, and wandering into traffic are common occurrences caused by declines in judgment and the ability to control impulses. People with dementia may become depressed when they recognize their cognitive deterioration. Often, however, they do not recognize or admit to their cognitive deficits. This can lead them to take unrealistic or dangerous actions, such as starting new businesses when they are not capable of running them, or driving cars when they are too impaired to do so safely. People with dementia may become paranoid and angry with family members and friends, whom they see as thwarting their desires and freedoms. They may accuse others of stealing the belongings they have misplaced. They may believe that others are conspiring against them—the only conclusion left for them when they simply do not remember conversations in which they agreed to some action (such as starting a new medication or moving into a treatment facility for people with dementia). Violent outbursts are not unusual.

 If you had a loved one with dementia, which of the symptoms do you think it would be hardest for you to live with?

Dementia most commonly occurs in late life. The estimated prevalence of the most common type of dementia—that due to Alzheimer's disease—is 2 to 4 percent in people over 65 years of age (APA, 1994). The prevalence of most types

apraxia
impaired ability to initiate common voluntary behaviors

agnosia
impaired ability to recognize objects or people

Losses in executive functioning can make it difficult for a person to accomplish tasks that require much planning and coordination, like preparing an elaborate family dinner.

Severe cognitive decline and physical illness are not inevitable parts of aging.

of dementia increases with age, with an estimated prevalence of 20 percent in people over 85 years of age. Notice, however, that the vast majority of older people do not suffer from dementia. Severe cognitive decline is not an inevitable part of old age.

The amount of news coverage on dementia has increased substantially in recent years, and at times it seems that there is an epidemic of this disorder. Two factors have probably contributed to the increased public attention to dementia. First, there have been substantial advances in our understanding of some types of dementia in the last decade, which have made the news, and which we will review shortly. Second, in previous generations, people died of heart disease, cancer, and infectious diseases at younger ages and, therefore, did not reach the age at which dementia often has its onset. These days, however, people are living long enough for dementia to develop and affect their functioning. The number of people with dementia is expected to double in the next 50 years due to the aging of the general population (Max, 1993). The cost to society in health care and to individuals in time spent caring for demented family members is likely to be staggering.

Dementia has several causes (see Figure 14.1). The most common cause is Alzheimer's disease. Great strides are being made in our understanding of Alzheimer's dementia, and we will discuss this disorder in detail next. Dementia can also be caused by cerebrovascular disease (blockage of blood to the brain), by head injury, by several progressive diseases like Parkinson's disease and HIV disease, and by chronic drug abuse. We will discuss each of these as well.

Dementia of the Alzheimer's Type

In 1995, the family of former President Ronald Reagan announced that he had been diagnosed with Alzheimer's disease. Although the family decided to maintain their privacy concerning the specific manifestations of the disease, their announcement of Reagan's diagnosis helped to bring attention to this disease, which affects nearly four million Americans (Max, 1993).

Dementia due to **Alzheimer's disease** is the most common type of dementia and accounts for approximately 50 percent of all dementias (Maxmen & Ward, 1995). Alzheimer's dementias typically begin with mild memory loss, but as the disease progresses, the memory loss and disorientation quickly become profound. The disease usually begins after the age of 65, but there is an early onset type of Alzheimer's disease that tends to progress more quickly than the late onset type that develops after age 65. On average, people with this disease die within 8 to 10 years of its diagnosis, usually as the result of physical decline or independent diseases common in old age, such as heart disease.

Alzheimer's disease exacts a heavy toll on the family members of patients as well as on the patients. Medical and custodial care for an Alzheimer's patient averages about $47,000 per year (in 1990 dollars), with family members shouldering the majority of this financial burden (Max, 1993). The primary caregiver to an Alzheimer's patient is most often

Alzheimer's disease
progressive neurological disease that is the most common cause of dementia

Figure 14.1

The Leading Causes of Dementia. Alzheimer's disease causes over half of all cases of dementia. Other causes of dementia are chronic alcoholism, nutritional deficiencies, and metabolic imbalances.
Source: Max, 1993.

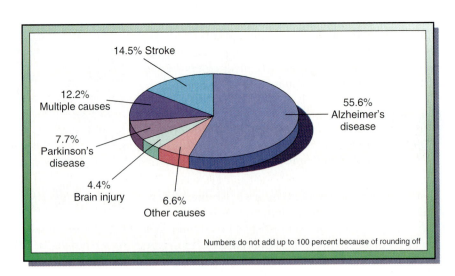

14.5% Stroke

12.2% Multiple causes

7.7% Parkinson's disease

4.4% Brain injury

6.6% Other causes

55.6% Alzheimer's disease

Numbers do not add up to 100 percent because of rounding off

a woman—the daughter, daughter-in-law, or wife of the patient (Mohide, 1993). Often this primary caregiver will also be raising her own children and trying to hold down jobs. This is the *sandwich generation* of women, caught in the middle of caring for young children and for elderly parents or parents-in-law. These primary caregivers show higher rates of depression, anxiety, and physical illness than do controls (see Gallagher-Thompson, Lovett, & Rose, 1991). Some caregivers become so frustrated with their demented family members that they resort to violence and abuse of the family members. Here is an example:

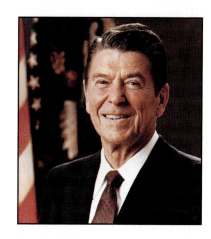

Former President Ronald Reagan has been diagnosed with Alzheimer's disease.

> **Case Study** • Mr. E was a 60-year-old caregiver of a rather frail younger brother (Robert) who had been diagnosed with dementia. Robert had been an alcoholic earlier in life and was the type of person who settled disagreements with verbal and/or physical abuse. Mr. E and his brother had begun sharing a household following the deaths of both their wives about 5 years before. Shortly thereafter, Robert was diagnosed with Alzheimer's disease and eventually developed substantial cognitive and physical deficits. Mr. E felt guilty about doing anything other than keeping his brother in the home with him, although Robert's disabilities were very distressing to him and Robert's increasing hostility and angry verbal outbursts were hard to handle. At the same time, Mr. E was developing a romantic interest and resented not being able to follow through with that as he pleased; instead he felt quite inhibited by his brother's presence in his home. The situation gradually worsened to the point where the two brothers were given to frequent angry outbursts leading, at times, to Mr. E hitting Robert. Afterwards he would feel extremely guilty about this and concerned that he might lose control during one of these episodes and actually hurt his brother. (adapted from Gallagher-Thompson et al., 1991, pp. 68–69)

Support groups for caregivers and therapy focused on developing problem-solving skills for managing the Alzheimer's patient at home have proven effective in reducing caregivers' emotional problems and feelings of burden. For example, Mr. E joined an anger management class and learned new ways of interpreting and reacting to his brother's behaviors. He read about Alzheimer's disease and learned to challenge his beliefs that his brother was intentionally acting in ways to annoy him. He learned to walk away from his brother's angry outbursts. He found other resources in the community to help him care for his brother so that he could pursue his own interests more fully. The Application at the end of this chapter describes other techniques that caregivers can use to manage the stress of caring for demented family members.

 If you have an elderly family member, especially one who has signs of dementia, do you ever find yourself reacting negatively toward that person? How do you or might you prevent yourself from acting negatively toward that person?

Middle-aged women are increasingly finding themselves caring for frail elderly family members while also raising their own children.

Causes of Alzheimer's Dementia

This type of dementia was first described in 1906 by Alois Alzheimer. He observed severe memory loss and disorientation in a 51-year-old female patient. Following her death at age 55, an autopsy revealed that filaments within nerve cells in her brain were twisted and tangled (see Figure 14.2). These **neurofibrillary tangles,** characteristic of Alzheimer's disease, are most prominent in the cerebral cortex and hippocampus, two areas of the brain critical to memory and cognitive functioning (see Figure 14.3). These tangles are common in the brains of Alzheimer's patients but rare in people without cognitive disorders (Beatty, 1995). Another brain abnormality seen in Alzheimer's disease are **plaques**. These are deposits of a class of protein called *amyloid* that accumulate in the extracellular spaces of the cerebral cortex, hippocampus, and other forebrain structures (see Figure 14.4).

There is extensive cell death in the cortex of Alzheimer's patients, resulting in shrinking of the cortex and enlargement of the ventricles of the brain (see Figure 14.5). The

neurofibrillary tangles
twists or tangles of filaments within nerve calls, especially prominent in the cerebral cortex and hippocampus, common in the brains of Alzheimer's disease patients

plaques
deposits of amyloid protein that accumulate in the extracellular spaces of the cerebral cortex, hippocampus, and other forebrain structures in people with Alzheimer's disease

Figure 14.2

Neurofibrillary Tangles in Alzheimer's Disease. The brains of people with Alzheimer's disease show neurofibrillary tangles.
Source: Beatty, 1995.

Figure 14.3

Brain Regions Most Affected in Dementia. The brains of people with Alzheimer's disease have plaques of amyloid beta-protein, indicated here by dots, in specific brain areas.
Source: Selkoe, 1992.

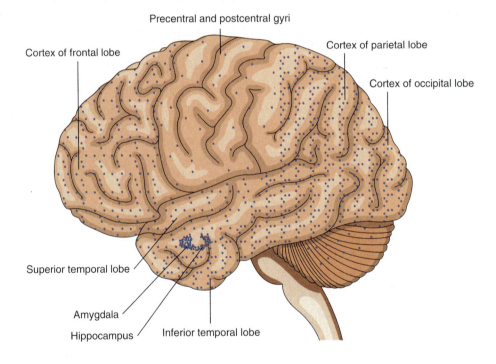

Precentral and postcentral gyri

Cortex of frontal lobe

Cortex of parietal lobe

Cortex of occipital lobe

Superior temporal lobe

Amygdala

Hippocampus

Inferior temporal lobe

remaining cells lose much of their dendrites—the branches of cells that link one cell to other cells (see Figure 14.6). The end result of all these brain abnormalities is profound memory loss and inability to coordinate one's activities.

Typically, Alzheimer's disease cannot be definitively diagnosed until the patient has died and a brain autopsy is performed. The neurofibrillary tangles and plaques can only be detected through a microscope. Advances in neuroimaging techniques (PET, MRI, and CT scans) promise the potential of diagnosing Alzheimer's disease in live patients, however. For example, one study used MRI and single-photon emission computed tomography (SPECT) to examine structural deterioration and diminished blood flow in the brains of people suspected to have Alzheimer's disease and healthy people the same age and gender. These two neuroimaging procedures correctly identified all of the patients later confirmed to have had Alzheimer's (Pearlson, Harris, Powers, & Barta, 1992).

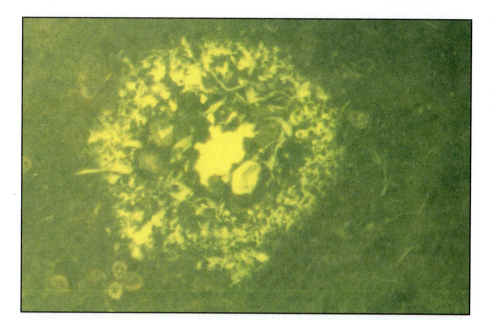

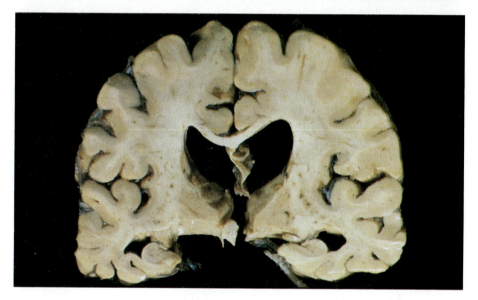

Figure 14.5

Cortical Atrophy in Alzheimer's Disease. Alzheimer's patients show widespread atrophy or shrinkage in the cortex and enlargement in the ventricular areas of the brain.
Source: Beatty, 1995.

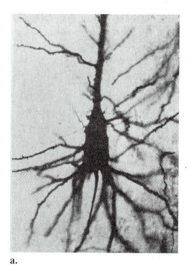
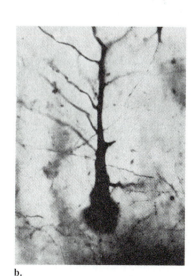

a.   b.

Figure 14.6

Loss of Neuronal Dendrites in Alzheimer's Disease. In panel (a) are dendrites in the brain of a healthy person. In panel (b) are shrunken and deteriorated dendrites in the brain of an Alzheimer's patient.
Source: Beatty, 1995.

What are some of the potential benefits of developing neuro-imaging techniques to diagnose Alzheimer's disease if there currently are no effective treatments for the disorder?

What causes the brain deterioration of Alzheimer's disease? This is an area of tremendous research activity, and new answers to this question emerge each day. Alzheimer's disease has been attributed to viral infections, exposure to toxic levels of aluminum, and head traumas. The most promising lines of research, however, have focused on genes that might transmit a vulnerability to this disorder and on the amyloid proteins that form the plaques found in the brains of almost all Alzheimer's patients.

Three different genes have been linked to Alzheimer's disease. A defective gene on chromosome 19 is associated with an increased risk for the late onset form of Alzheimer's disease, which is the most common form. This gene appears to be responsible for a rare protein known as ApoE4. ApoE4 is one of a group of proteins that transport cholesterol through the blood. ApoE4 binds to the amyloid protein and may play a role in the regulation of amyloid protein. One study found that 64 percent of people with late onset Alzheimer's disease had the ApoE4 gene compared to only 31 percent of people without Alzheimer's disease (Schmechal et al., 1993). Another study found that people with two copies of the ApoE4 gene (one on both of their chromosome 19s) were eight times more likely to have Alzheimer's disease than were people with no copies of the ApoE4 gene on either of their chromosome 19s (Corder, Saunders, & Strittmatter, 1993).

Two other genes are implicated in the development of a less common form of Alzheimer's disease, which begins in middle age and is more strongly familial. The first of these genes is on chromosome 21. The first clue that a defective gene on chromosome 21 may be linked with Alzheimer's disease came from the fact that people with Down syndrome are more likely than people in the general population to develop Alzheimer's disease in late life. Down syndrome is caused by an extra chromosome 21. Researchers hypothesized that the gene responsible for some forms of Alzheimer's disease may be on chromosome 21 and that people with Down syndrome are more prone to Alzheimer's disease because they have an extra chromosome 21 (Mayeux, 1996). This hypothesis has been supported by linkage studies of families with high rates of Alzheimer's disease. These studies have found links between the presence of the disease and the presence of an abnormal gene on chromosome 21. In turn, this abnormal gene on chromosome 21 is near the gene responsible for producing a precursor of the amyloid protein that makes up the plaques in the brains of Alzheimer's patients. It may be that defects along this section of chromosome 21 cause an abnormal production and buildup of amyloid proteins in the brain, resulting in Alzheimer's disease.

More recently, a defective gene on chromosome 14 has been linked to early onset Alzheimer's disease (Sherrington, Rogaev, & Liang, 1995). This discovery is especially exciting because this defective chromosome 14 gene may be responsible for up to 80 percent of early onset Alzheimer's disease. This gene appears to be responsible for a protein on the membranes of cells, known as S182. The link between S182 and the amyloid protein or other processes responsible for Alzheimer's disease is not yet known.

We will likely know much more about the causes of Alzheimer's disease in the next few years, because the technologies to study the genetic and neurological processes of the disease are advancing rapidly and because many researchers are pursuing investigation of this disorder. As many as nine million people in the United States alone may suffer from Alzheimer's disease by the year 2040 (Max, 1993). We can hope that, by then, we will understand the disorder well enough to treat it effectively.

Genetic tests are being developed to identify people who are at risk for developing Alzheimer's disease in old age. If such a test were available, would you want to take it? Why or why not?

Vascular Dementia

The second most common type of dementia, after Alzheimer's dementia, is **vascular dementia** (formerly called *multi-infarct dementia*). To be diagnosed with vascular dementia, a person must have symptoms or laboratory evidence of *cerebrovascular disease*. Cerebrovascular disease occurs when the blood supply to areas of the brain is blocked, causing tissue damage in the brain. Neuroimaging techniques such as PET and MRI can detect areas of tissue damage and reduced blood flow in the brain, confirming cerebrovascular disease (see Figure 14.7).

Sudden damage to an area of the brain due to blockage of blood flow or hemorrhaging is called a *stroke*. Vascular dementia can occur after one large stroke or an accumulation of small strokes. Cerebrovascular disease can also be caused by high blood pressure and the accumulation of fatty deposits in the arteries, which block blood flow to the brain; by diseases that inflame the brain; and by head injuries. The specific cognitive deficits and emotional changes a person experiences will depend on the extent and location of tissue damage to the brain.

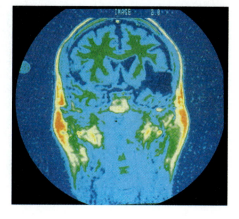

Figure 14.7

Tissue Damage Following a Stroke. This magnetic resonance image shows the tissue damage following a stroke.
Source: Beatty, 1995.

vascular dementia

second most common type of dementia, associated with symptoms of cerebrovascular disease (tissue damage in the brain due to a blockage of blood flow)

Dementia Due to Head Injury

> **Case Study** • A 41-year-old factory worker named Leland was returning home along a rural road one night after work. A drunk driver ran a stop sign and collided at a high rate of speed with the driver's side of Leland's car. Leland was not wearing a seat belt. The collision sent Leland hurling through the windshield and onto the pavement. He lived but sustained substantial injuries to the frontal lobe of his brain as well as many broken bones and contusions. Leland was unconscious for over 2 weeks and then spent another 2 months in the hospital recovering from his injuries.
>
> When he returned home to his family, Leland was not himself. Before the accident he was a quiet man who doted on his family and frequently displayed a wry sense of humor. After the accident, Leland was sullen and chronically irritable. He would scream at his wife or children for the slightest annoyance. He even slapped his wife once when she confronted him about his verbal abuse of the children.
>
> Leland did not fare much better at work. He found he now had great trouble concentrating on his job, and he could not follow his boss's instructions. When his boss approached Leland about his inability to perform his job, Leland could not express much about the trouble he was having. He became angry at his boss and accused him of wanting to fire him. Leland had always been much liked by his coworkers, and they welcomed him back after the accident with sincere joy. But soon he began to lash out at them as he was at his wife and children. He accused a close friend of stealing from him.
>
> These symptoms continued acutely for about 3 months. Gradually they declined. Finally, about 18 months after the accident, Leland's emotional and personality functioning appear to be "back to normal." His cognitive functioning also improved greatly, but he still found it more difficult to pay attention and to complete tasks than he did before the accident.

Leland's symptoms are characteristic of people with traumatic brain injury (see Table 14.2). He showed changes both in his cognitive abilities and in his usual emotional and personality functioning Fortunately, Leland's symptoms subsided after several months. Many victims of brain injury never fully recover (Beatty, 1995).

People engaged in sports like boxing or who do not wear helmets while riding bicycles are at risk for brain injuries that can lead to severe cognitive deficits.

Table 14.2 Symptoms of Frontal Lobe Injuries

Social and Behavioral Changes

- Disorderliness, suspiciousness, argumentativeness, disruptiveness, and anxiousness
- Apathy, lack of concern for others
- Uncharacteristic lewdness, inattention to personal appearance or hygiene
- Intrusiveness, boisterousness, pervasive profanity, talking loudly
- Risk taking, poor impulse control, increased alcohol use

Affective Changes

- Apathy, indifference, shallowness
- Lability of affect, irritability, mania
- Inability to control rage and violent behavior

Intellectual Changes

- Reduced capacity to use language, symbols, and logic
- Reduced ability to use mathematics, to calculate, to process abstract information, and to reason
- Diminished ability to focus, to concentrate, or to be oriented in time and place

Source: Data from R. L. Silver, et al., 1992.

Brain damage can be caused by penetrating injuries, such as those caused by gunshots, or closed head injuries, typically caused by blows to the head. The most common causes of closed head injuries are motor vehicle accidents, followed by falls, blows to the head during violent assault, and sports injuries. Dementias that follow single closed head injuries, such as Leland's, are more likely to dissipate with time than are dementias that follow repeated closed head injuries, such as those experienced by boxers. Young men are most likely to suffer dementia due to head injury because they take more risks associated with head injuries than do other groups.

Dementia Associated with Other Medical Conditions

A variety of other serious medical conditions can produce dementia. *Parkinson's disease* is a degenerative brain disorder that affects about 1 of every 100,000 people (Mayeux, Denaro, Hemenegildo, & Marder, 1992). The primary symptoms of Parkinson's disease are tremors, muscle rigidity, and the inability to initiate movement. About 40 percent of Parkinson's disease patients also develop dementia in the advanced stages of the disorder (Mayeux et al., 1992). Parkinson's disorder results from the death of cells in the brain that produce the neurotransmitter dopamine. The death of these cells can be caused by certain drugs or by inflammation of the brain, but the cause of Parkinson's disease is often unclear.

What other psychiatric disorder is linked to dopamine? What is the link between this disorder and Parkinson's disease?

The *human immunodeficiency virus (HIV)*, the virus that causes AIDS, can cause dementia. HIV probably enters the brain in the early stages of the infection. Memory and concentration become impaired and mental slowing occurs in forms such as difficulty following conversations or plots in movies or taking much longer to organize one's thoughts and complete simple, familiar tasks. Social withdrawal, indifference to familiar people and responsibilities, apathy, and reduced spontaneity are behavioral indicators. The person may complain of fatigue, depression, irritability, agitation, emotional lability, and reduced sex drive. Sometimes, although rarely, psychotic symptoms may be present. Weakness in the legs or hands, clumsiness, loss of balance, and lack of coordination are common complaints. The person may trip more frequently, drop things, or have difficulty writing or eating. If the dementia progresses, the deficits become more global and more severe. Speech becomes increasingly impaired, as does the cognitive processing of language. The ability to walk is lost, and patients are confined to bed, often with indifference to their surroundings and their illness. Incontinence is common, and seizures may occur.

The course of HIV dementia varies from person to person, as does the speed with which it progresses. The San Diego HIV Neurobehavioral Research Center (HNRC) Group has termed the earlier, less severe symptoms of HIV-associated dementia *mild neurocognitive disorder (MND)*. In order to receive a diagnosis of MND, an HIV-infected person must exhibit defects in two or more cognitive areas with mild interference in social/occupational functioning. It is estimated that approximately 50 percent of persons with AIDS will meet the criteria for MND (Heaton, Marcotte, White, & Ross, 1996).

HIV-associated dementia is diagnosed when the deficits and symptoms become more severe and global, with significant disruption of daily activities and functioning. Epidemiological studies estimate that anywhere from 7 percent to 66 percent of HIV-infected persons will become demented (Day, Grant, Atkinson, & Brysk, 1992; McArthur, Hoover, Bacellar, & Miller, 1993). It is possible that the development of treatments, such as the antiviral agent azidobudine (AZT), may have the effect of decreasing the rates of dementia among HIV-infected persons by slowing the progression of the disease.

Huntington's disease is a rare genetic disorder that afflicts people early in life, usually between the ages of 25 and 55. People with this disorder develop severe dementia and chorea—irregular jerks, grimaces, and twitches. Huntington's disease is transmitted by a single dominant gene on chromosome 4 (Gusella, MacDonald, Ambrose, & Duyao, 1993). If one parent has the gene, his or her children have a 50 percent chance of developing the disorder. There are many neurotransmitter changes in the brains of people with Huntington's disease. It is not yet clear which of these changes is responsible for the chorea and the dementia seen in the disorder. Two other rare disorders that can cause dementia are *Pick's disease* and *Creutzfeldt-Jakob disease*.

Finally, chronic heavy use of alcohol, inhalants, and the sedative drugs, especially in combination with nutritional deficiencies, can cause brain damage and dementia. As many as 10 percent of chronic alcohol abusers may develop dementia (Winger et al., 1992). Alcohol-related dementia usually has a slow, insidious onset. It may be slowed with nutritional supplements but is often irreversible.

Treatment for Dementia

To date, there are few widely successful treatments for dementia. People with Alzheimer's disease have reduced levels of the neurotransmitter acetylcholine in their brains, which may contribute to their cognitive impairments. Some Alzheimer's patients show improvement in cognitive functioning when given drugs that increase levels of acetylcholine (Gottlieb & Kumar, 1993). Similarly, since Parkinson's disease is associated with too little dopamine in the brain, some Parkinson's patients are given drugs that increase levels of dopamine

Creutzfeldt-Jakob disease, also known as mad cow disease, can be transmitted through cows. It is a rare disorder that can cause dementia.

and thus experience some relief from their symptoms. For both these diseases, however, the drugs do not work for all patients and have only temporary effects.

Antidepressant and antianxiety drugs may be used to help control the emotional symptoms of people with dementia. Antipsychotic drugs may help to control hallucinations and delusions. In addition, behavioral therapies can be helpful in controlling patients' angry outbursts and emotional lability. Often, family members are given training in behavioral techniques to help them manage patients at home. The Application at the end of this chapter describes some of these techniques.

Summing Up Dementia

- Dementia is typically a permanent deterioration in cognitive functioning, often accompanied by emotional changes.
- The five types of cognitive impairments in dementia are memory impairment, aphasia, apraxia, agnosia, and loss of executive functioning.
- The most common type of dementia is due to Alzheimer's disease.
- The brains of Alzheimer's patients show neurofibrillary tangles, plaques made up of amyloid protein, and cortical atrophy.
- Recent theories of Alzheimer's disease focus on three different genes that might contribute to the buildup of amyloid in the brains of Alzheimer's disease patients.
- Dementia can also be caused by cerebrovascular disorder, head injury, and progressive disorders such as Parkinson's disease, HIV disease, Huntington's disease, Pick's disease, and Creutzfeldt-Jakob disease. Finally, chronic drug abuse and the nutritional deficiencies that often accompany it can lead to dementia.
- There is no effective treatment for dementia, although drugs help to reduce the cognitive symptoms and accompanying depression, anxiety, and psychotic symptoms, in some patients.

Delirium

delirium
cognitive disorder marked by disorientation to time, place, and people as well as recent memory loss and difficulties with focusing, sustaining, or shifting attention

Delirium is characterized by *disorientation, recent memory loss,* and a *clouding of consciousness.* A delirious person will have difficulty focusing, sustaining, or shifting attention. These signs arise suddenly, within several hours or days. They fluctuate over the course of a day and often become worse at night, a condition known as *sundowning.* The duration of these signs is short—rarely more than a month. Delirious patients are often agitated or frightened. They may also experience disrupted sleep-wake cycles, incoherent speech, illusions, and hallucinations.

The signs of delirium usually follow a common progression. Disorientation with regard to time is typically the first sign to appear: If asked, the patient does not know the time of day or the current year or will say it is 6:00 AM when it is 6:00 PM. As the delirium worsens, orientation to place becomes disrupted; for example, the patient may think she is in her childhood home when she is actually in the hospital. If undetected, the delirium progresses, and the person's orientation to familiar people becomes distorted. For example, a delirious patient will misidentify his wife or fail to recognize his child. Immediate memory is the first to be affected, followed by intermediate memory (memories of events occurring in the last 10 minutes), and finally remote or distant memory. When intervals of these symptoms alternate with intervals of lucid functioning and the symptoms become worse at night, a diagnosis of delirium is likely. If the person is not disoriented (to time, place, or person) or recent memory loss is absent, then a diagnosis of delirium is unlikely.

The onset of delirium may be very dramatic, as when a normally quiet person becomes suddenly loud, verbally abusive, and combative or when a compliant hospital patient tries to pull out his IVs and will not be calmed by family or medical staff. Sometimes, though, the onset of delirium is subtle and manifests as an exaggerated form of an individual's normal personality traits. For example, a perfectionist nurse recovering from surgery may complain loudly and harshly about the "inadequate" care she is receiving from the attending nurses. It would be easy for attending staff to regard her irritability as consistent with her personality style and her recovery: "She must be feeling better, she's beginning to complain." In this type of case, the delirium may go unrecognized until severe symptoms of delirium emerge.

Sometimes delirious patients just appear confused. People who know them well say, "He just doesn't seem like himself." These delirious patients may call acquaintances by the wrong names, or forget how to get to familiar locations; for example, they may not remember where their rooms are. In cases like these, often the first indication of delirium comes from the observations of family or medical staff. They will notice that the person seems calm during the day but agitated at night. It is important to monitor such a patient around the clock. Detecting delirium may require frequent testing of the person's orientation. Close monitoring is also important because, with delirium, accidents such as falling out of bed or stepping into traffic are common.

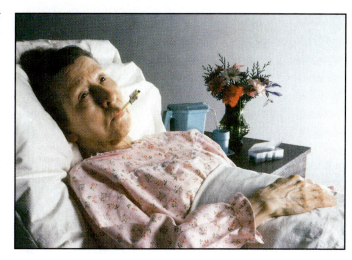

Elderly hospital patients often experience delirium.

Delirium typically is a signal of some serious medical condition. When it is detected and the underlying medical condition treated, delirium is temporary and reversible. The longer delirium continues, however, the more likely the person will suffer permanent brain damage, because the causes of delirium, if left untreated, can induce permanent changes in the functioning of the brain.

Causes of Delirium

There are many causes of delirium. For most patients, an underlying medical, surgical, chemical, or neurological problem causes the delirium. Delirium can be caused by a stroke, congestive heart failure, an infectious disease, a high fever, and AIDS. Drug intoxication or withdrawal can lead to delirium. Other possible causes include fluid and electrolyte imbalances, illicit drugs, medications, and toxic substances (see Table 14.3).

Delirium is probably the most common psychiatric syndrome found in a general hospital, particularly in older people. About 10 percent of older people are delirious upon admission to the hospital for a serious illness, and another 10 to 15 percent develop delirium while in the hospital. Older people often experience delirium following surgery (Fisher & Flowerdew, 1995). The delirium may be the result of the medical disorder of the patient or the effects of medications. It may also result from sensory isolation. There is a syndrome known as *ICU/CCU psychosis* that occurs in intensive care and cardiac care units (Maxmen & Ward, 1995). When patients are kept in unfamiliar surroundings that are strange and monotonous, they may hear noises from machines as human voices, see the walls quiver, or hallucinate that someone is tapping them on the shoulder.

Among the elderly, a high mortality rate is associated with delirium (Byrne, 1994). Typically, this is because the underlying condition or cause of the delirium is very serious. Between 15 and 40 percent of delirious hospital patients die within 1 month as compared to half that rate in nondelirious patients.

Some people are at increased risk for delirium. Risk factors include age (the older the person, the higher the risk), gender (males are more at risk than females), preexisting brain damage or dementia (Gustafson, Brannstrom, Berggren, & Ragnarsson, 1991; Lipowski, 1990; Schor, Levkoff, & Lipsitz, 1992; Williams-Russo, Urquhart, Sharrock, & Charlson, 1992).

Why might men be more prone to delirium than women?

Table 14.3 Substances That Can Induce Delirium

Alcohol	Carbon monoxide
Amphetamines	Cocaine
Anesthetics	Corticosteroids
Analgesics	Gastrointestinal medications
Antiasthmatic agents	Hallucinogens
Anticholinesterase	Inhalants
Anticonvulsants	Muscle relaxants
Antihistamines	Opioids
Antihypertensive and cardiovascular medications	Organophosphate insecticides
	Phencyclidine
Antimicrobials	Psychotropic medications with anticholinergic side effects
Antiparkinsonian drugs	
Cannabis	Sedatives, hypnotics, and anxiolytics
Carbon dioxide	Volatile substances such as fuel or paint

Source: Data from DSM-IV, American Psychiatric Association, 1994.

There are very few data on the prevalence of delirium in the United States (Byrne, 1994). One large epidemiological study of mental disorders in Boston found six cases of delirium in the total sample of 829 adults (Folstein, Bassett, Romanoski, & Nestadt, 1991). Most of these people were over the age of 55. Delirium in these six cases was related to multiple medications, visual impairment, diabetes, brain disease, incontinence, and diuretic use or a combination of these causes. Among nursing home residents, approximately 6 percent have been reported to be delirious (Beinenfeld and Wheeler, 1989).

Treatment of Delirium

It is extremely important that delirium be recognized and treated quickly. If a delirious person is not already hospitalized, an immediate referral to a physician should be made. The first priority is to keep patients alive and to prevent brain damage by removing or alleviating the causes of the delirium. It may also be necessary to prevent people from harming themselves (Maxmen & Ward, 1995). Often, nursing care is required to monitor people's states and to prevent them from wandering off, tripping, or ripping out intravenous tubes and to manage their behavior if they should become noncompliant or violent. In some instances, restraints are necessary.

Psychotropic medications (usually antipsychotics) in small doses initially can help to relieve the patient of psychotic symptoms until the cause of the delirium can be identified and treated. In addition, delirious patients should be oriented frequently—they can be helped by numerous brief contacts with family and staff, reassuring them that they are safe, by having them repeat the date and time, by informing them where they are and who the people around him are, and by giving them detailed descriptions of whatever procedures may be taking place. It may be helpful to place clocks, calendars, and photographs of family members in patients' rooms.

Summing Up Delirium

- Delirium is characterized by disorientation, recent memory loss, and clouding of consciousness.
- The onset of delirium can be either sudden or slow.
- The many causes of delirium include medical diseases, the trauma of surgery, illicit drugs, medications, high fever, and infections.
- Delirium must be treated immediately by treating its underlying causes, to prevent brain damage and to prevent people from hurting themselves.

Amnesia

> **Case Study** • A 46-year-old divorced housepainter is admitted to the hospital with a history of 30 years of heavy drinking. He has had two previous admissions for detoxification, but his family states that he has not had a drink in several weeks, and he shows no signs of alcohol withdrawal. He looks malnourished, however, and appears confused and mistakes one of his physicians for a dead uncle.
>
> Within a week, the patient seems less confused and can find his way to the bathroom without direction. He remembers the names and birthdays of his siblings but has difficulty naming the past five presidents. More strikingly, he has great difficulty in retaining information for longer than a few minutes. He can repeat a list of numbers immediately after he has heard them, but a few minutes later does not recall being asked to perform the task. Shown three objects (keys, comb, ring), he cannot recall them 3 minutes later. He does not seem worried about this. Asked if he can recall the name of his doctor, he replies, "Certainly," and proceeds to call the doctor "Dr. Masters" (not his name), and he claims to have met him in the Korean War. He tells a long untrue story about how he and Dr. Masters served as fellow soldiers. (adapted from Spitzer et al., 1981, pp. 41–42)

In dementia and delirium, people show multiple cognitive deficits, including memory deficits and often language deficits, disorientation, inability to recognize objects or people, and inability to think abstractly or plan and carry through with an activity. In **amnesic disorders**, only memory is affected. A person with **amnesia** will be impaired in the ability to learn new information (**anterograde amnesia**) or to recall previously learned information or past events (**retrograde amnesia**). Amnesic disorders often follow periods of confusion and disorientation and delirium.

The patterns of amnesia represented in television shows and soap operas—with people suddenly losing their memories for everything they previously knew—are unrealistic. Commonly, people with amnesia can remember events from the distant past but not from the recent past. For example, a 60-year-old patient may be able to tell where he went to high school and college but be unable to remember that he was admitted to the hospital yesterday. He will also forget meeting his doctor from one day to the next. In profound amnesia, a person may be completely disoriented about place or time, but rarely does an amnesic person forget his or her own identity.

Often, people with amnesia do not realize they have profound memory deficits and will deny evidence of these deficits. They may seem unconcerned with obvious lapses in memory or may make up stories to cover their lapses in memory, as did the housepainter. They may become agitated with others who point out their memory lapses. They may even accuse others of conspiring against them.

amnesic disorders
cognitive disorders involving deficits in the ability to learn new information and recall previously learned information

amnesia
symptom of cognitive disorders involving impairments in the ability to learn new information or to recall previously learned information or past events

anterograde amnesia
deficit in the ability to learn new information

retrograde amnesia
deficit in the ability to recall previously learned information or past events

 Most people have complete amnesia for events that happened before they were about 3 years of age. Why might this be true?

Causes and Treatment of Amnesic Disorders

Amnesia can be caused by brain damage due to strokes, head injuries, chronic nutritional deficiencies, exposure to toxins (such as through carbon monoxide poisoning), and chronic substance abuse. *Korsakoff's syndrome* is an amnesic disorder caused by damage to the thalamus, a part of the brain that acts as a relay station to other parts of the brain. Chronic and heavy alcohol use is associated with Korsakoff's syndrome, probably because the alcoholic neglects nutrition and thus develops thiamin deficiencies (see Chapter 12).

The course of amnesic disorders depends on the cause. If, for example, a stroke occurs in the hippocampus, the memory loss that results will include events after the date of the stroke. Memories prior to the stroke will remain intact. If the memory loss is caused by alcohol or other toxins, it is often more broad and the onset can be insidious. For some people, remote memory may also become impaired.

The first step in the treatment of amnesic disorders is to remove, if possible, any conditions contributing to the amnesia, such as alcohol use or exposure to toxins. In addition, attention to nutrition and treatment of any accompanying health condition (e.g., hypertension) can help to prevent further deterioration. Lastly, because new surroundings and routines may prove too difficult or impossible for the amnesic person to learn, the environment should be kept as familiar as possible. Often, as with dementia, it can be helpful to have clocks, calendars, photographs, labels, and other kinds of reminders prominent.

Summing Up | Amnesia

- The amnesic disorders are characterized only by memory loss.
- Retrograde amnesia is loss of memory for past events, and anterograde amnesia is the inability to remember new information.
- Amnesia can be caused by brain damage due to strokes, head injuries, chronic nutritional deficiencies, exposure to toxins (such as through carbon monoxide poisoning), and chronic substance abuse.
- Treatment of amnesia can involve removal of the agents contributing to the amnesia and helping the person develop memory aids.

Gender and Cultural Issues

The roles of gender and culture in the prevalence, characteristics, and treatment of the cognitive disorders have received some attention. There are more elderly women than men with dementia, particularly Alzheimer's dementia. This simply may be because women tend to live longer than men and thus live long enough to develop age-related dementias. Among people with dementia, women tend to show greater decline in language skills than do men, even though among people without dementia, women tend to score better on tests of language skills than do men (Buckwalter, Sobel, Dunn, & Diz, 1993). The reason for the greater impact of dementia on language in women compared to men is unknown. Some researchers have speculated that language skills are distributed across both sides of the brain in women but more localized in the left side of the brain for men, and this somehow makes women's language skills more vulnerable to the effects of dementia.

In general, African Americans are more frequently diagnosed with dementia than are whites. The types of dementias that African Americans and whites develop differ, however (de la Monte, Hutchins, & Moore, 1989). African Americans are more likely than whites to be diagnosed with vascular dementia. This may be because African Americans have higher rates of hypertension and cardiovascular disease, which contribute to vascular dementia. African Americans may also have higher rates of delirium than whites because lack of health insurance leads some African Americans not to receive early medical care for serious illnesses; thus, their illnesses may be more likely to become severe enough to cause delirium. In contrast, whites may be more likely than African Americans to have dementias due to Alzheimer's disease and Parkinson's disease. The genetic factors leading to these diseases may be more prevalent in whites than in African Americans.

Perhaps the greatest cross-cultural issue in the cognitive disorders is the impact of culture and education on the validity of instruments used to assess cognitive impairment. One of the most common paper-and-pencil assessment tools is the Mini-Mental State Examination (Folstein, Folstein, & McHugh, 1975). Some items from this questionnaire are presented in Figure 14.8. People with low levels of education tend to perform more poorly on this questionnaire than do people with more education, whether or not they have dementia (Murden, McRae, Kaner, & Bucknam, 1991). This may lead to some elderly people with poor educations being misdiagnosed as having dementia.

Indeed, studies in the United States, Europe, Israel, and China show that people with low levels of education are more likely to be diagnosed with dementia than are peo-

Mini-Mental State Examination
(Add points for each correct response.)

		Score	Points
Orientation			
1. What is the	Year?	——	1
	Season?	——	1
	Date?	——	1
	Day?	——	1
	Month?	——	1
2. Where are we?	State?	——	1
	County?	——	1
	Town or city?	——	1
	Hospital?	——	1
	Floor?	——	1

Registration

3. Name three objects, taking one second to say each. Then ask the patient all three after you have said them. Give one point for each correct anwer. Repeat the answers until patient learns all three. —— 3

Attention and calculation

4. Serial sevens. Give one point for each correct answer. Stop after five answers.
   Alternate: Spell WORLD backwards. —— 5

Recall

5. Ask for names of three objects learned in Q.3. Give one point for each correct answer. —— 3

Language

6. Point to a pencil and a watch. Have the patient name them as you point. —— 2

7. Have the patient repeat 'No ifs, ands or buts.' —— 1

8. Have the patient follow a three-stage command: 'Take a paper in your right hand. Fold the paper in half. Put the paper on the floor.' —— 3

9. Have the patient read and obey the following: 'CLOSE YOUR EYES.' (Write it in large letters.) —— 1

10. Have the patient write a sentence of his or her choice. (The sentence should contain a subject and an object, and should make sense. Ignore spelling errors when scoring.) —— 1

11. Enlarge the design printed below to 1.5 cm per side, and have the patient copy it. (Give one point if all sides and angles are preserved and if the intersecting sides form a quadrangle.) —— 1

———— = Total 30

ple with more education (Katzman, 1993; Stern, Gurland, Tatemichi, & Tang, 1994). The relationship between lower education and dementia is not just a factor of the measures used to assess dementia, however. Neuroimaging studies of people with dementia find that those with less education show more of the brain deterioration associated with dementia than do those with more education. Education and more generally cognitive activity throughout one's life may actually increase brain resources in ways that forestall the development of dementia in people prone to the disorder.

Figure 14.8

The Mini-Mental State Examination. The Mini-Mental State Examination is one of the most commonly used tests to assess patients' cognitive functioning and orientation.
Source: Folstein, Folstein, & McHugh, 1975.

The fact that deterioration or damage to the brain can cause not only cognitive deficits but also personality changes is strong evidence that biological factors have significant impact on psychological characteristics. Do psychological or social factors also have an impact on the cognitive disorders, which by definition, are biologically caused? The answer seems to be "yes." For example, many people in the early stages of dementia become paranoid, irritable, and impulsive. These symptoms may be especially pronounced in people who, even before they developed dementia, were somewhat paranoid, irritable, or impulsive. Social

Bio-Psycho-Social
INTEGRATION

environment can greatly affect the severity of cognitive deficits. If a person who is easily confused or forgetful is further stressed by family members who frequently become annoyed with him or her or expect too much of him or her, then the cognitive deficits can become even more severe. Thus, even though the cognitive disorders are rooted in medical disease or chronic intoxication with substances like alcohol, there are several ways in which psychosocial factors can influence the severity and manifestation of these disorders.

Chapter Summary

Dementia is typically a permanent deterioration in cognitive functioning, often accompanied by emotional changes. The five types of cognitive impairments in dementia are memory impairment, aphasia, apraxia, agnosia, and loss of executive functioning. The most common type of dementia is due to Alzheimer's disease. The brains of Alzheimer's patients show neurofibrillary tangles, plaques made up of amyloid protein, and cortical atrophy. Recent theories of Alzheimer's disease focus on three different genes that might contribute to the buildup of amyloid protein in the brains of Alzheimer's patients.

Dementia can also be caused by cerebrovascular disorder, head injury, and progressive disorders such as Parkinson's disease, HIV disease, Huntington's disease, Pick's disease, and Creutzfeldt-Jakob disease. Finally, chronic drug abuse and the nutritional deficiencies that often accompany it can lead to dementia. There is no effective treatment for dimentia, although drugs help to reduce the cognitive symptoms and accompanying depression, anxiety, and psychotic symptoms in some patients.

Delirium is characterized by disorientation, recent memory loss, and clouding of consciousness. Delirium typically is a signal of a serious medical condition, such as a stroke, congestive heart failure, infectious disease, or high fever, or of drug intoxication or withdrawal. It is a common syndrome in hospitals, particularly among elderly surgery patients. Treating delirium involves treating the underlying condition leading to the delirium and keeping the patient safe until the symptoms subside.

In amnesic disorders, only patients' memories are affected. Anterograde amnesia is the most common form of amnesia and is characterized by the inability to learn or retain new information. Retrograde amnesia is the inability to recall previously learned information or past events. Amnesic disorders can be caused by strokes, head injuries, chronic nutritional deficiencies, exposure to toxins, and chronic substance abuse. The course and treatment of amnesic disorders depend on the cause.

Key Terms

cognitive disorders   494
dementia   496
aphasia   496
apraxia   497
agnosia   497
Alzheimer's disease   498

neurofibrillary
    tangles   499
plaques   499
vascular dementia   503
delirium   506

amnesic disorders   509
amnesia   509
anterograde amnesia   509
retrograde amnesia   509

Application

Tips for the Caregivers of Dementia Patients

There is a good chance that at some time in your life you will be a caregiver to a family member with dementia or some other disease that reduces intellectual and physical functioning. This may be your parent, a loved one who sustains a head injury or has AIDS, or when you are older, your spouse or partner. The Alzheimer's Association has published many practical tips on managing life with a loved one with Alzheimer's disease. These tips are useful for caregivers of anyone who is debilitated by cognitive and emotional deficits. Some of these tips follow. For further information, contact the Alzheimer's Association at 70 E. Lake Street, Chicago, IL 60601-5997 or phone (800) 621-0379.

Activities

People with dementia can have trouble concentrating, following instructions, and initiating or following through with plans. This can lead them to become completely inactive and isolated. Here are some tips for helping your loved one remain as active and involved with others as possible.

Build in structure. Do not be afraid to give activities structure and routine. It is fine for the person to do the same thing at the same time every day. If he has a sense of routine, there is a greater chance that he will look forward to an activity with a positive attitude.

Be flexible. Adjust to the person's level of ability and look for hidden messages. When the person insists that she does not want to do something, it might be her way of telling you that she cannot do it or fears doing it. If an individual patient has problems with one part of a task such as separating dishes and putting them into a cabinet, you might want to take over part of the task and ask the person to hand you dishes one by one.

Stress involvement. Emphasize activities that help the individual feel like a valued part of the household and experience a feeling of success and accomplishment. Working along with you on such tasks as setting the table, wiping countertops, folding napkins, or emptying wastebaskets will help the person feel useful and sociable.

Do not forget the family. Plan for social activities such as family picnics or birthday parties, but make special allowances for the person with the disease. Allow for frequent rest periods and try to prevent family members from overwhelming the individual.

Focus on enjoyment, not achievement. Help the individual find activities that build on remaining skills and talents. A person who was once a professional artist might become frustrated over the declining quality of her work when engaged in an art activity, but someone who never pursued art as a career might enjoy a new opportunity for self-expression.

Combativeness

When a person with dementia becomes combative, angry, or agitated, it may be because of frustration. The individual may feel that he is being pushed to do something that simply cannot be done.

Be on the lookout for frustration. Look for early signs of frustration in such activities as bathing, dressing, or eating and respond in a calm and reassuring tone.

Do not take aggression and combativeness personally. Keep in mind that the person is not necessarily angry at you. Instead, she may misunderstand the situation or be frustrated with her own disabilities.

Avoid teaching. Offer encouragement, but keep in mind the person's capabilities and do not expect more than he can do. Avoid elaborate explanations or arguments.

Learn from previous experiences. Try to avoid situations or experiences that make the person combative. For example, if the individual tires easily when she visits with family members, you might want to limit the length of these visits. Try to identify early signs of agitation. For example, outbursts are sometimes preceded by restlessness, frustration, fidgeting, or blushing.

Restructure tasks and the person's environment. Simplify tasks or plan more difficult tasks for the time of day when the person is at his best. Allow the person to make some choices but limit the total number of choices. Having too many decision to make about what to eat or wear might be confusing or overwhelming. Break down each task into small steps and allow the person to complete one step at a time. Keep the environment calm, quiet, and clutter free.

Feelings

The person with dementia is often on an emotional roller coaster as she attempts to understand and cope with the effects of the disease. Family members can help her express her emotions and cope with them in constructive ways. They can also avoid interactions that induce anger, shame, or sadness in the person with dementia.

Treat the patient as a person. Through words and touch, try to do everything you can to relate to this individual as a valued human being with emotional and spiritual needs. People with dementia are often hurt when caregivers talk about them as if they are not present. Avoid talking about the person in his presence; assume that he understands everything you are saying.

Communicate slowly and calmly. Speak in simple sentences. Slow down your rate of speech and lower the pitch of your voice. Give the person with dementia time to hear your words and prepare a response. Keep in mind that it can take up to a minute for the person with this disease to respond. Keep communication on an adult-to-adult level. Avoid baby talk or demeaning expressions.

Be positive, optimistic, and reassuring to the person. Use comforting and noncontrolling statements. Try to identify feelings rather than argue about facts. For example, instead of arguing with the person about going outside, you can agree by saying, "Yes, it would be fun to go outside." Or put limits on the request by saying, "I want to go outside, too. Let's do it after we eat. I'm hungry!" Give praise for the simplest achievements and successes.

Tell the person what to expect. Prepare the person for what is about to happen. Instead of pulling the patient out of the chair or pushing the patient across the room, say, "We need to get up now." Then gently assist the person out of the chair or across the room.

Help the person remain independent. Avoid taking responsibilities away from the person. Do not assume that the person cannot perform certain tasks; put the emphasis on what the person can do. ■

Part Four

The Methods, Ethics, and Policy of Abnormal Psychology

Mental health professionals conduct research on abnormality and help to form social policy on how people with psychological disorders should be treated. Good research on abnormality conforms to scientific principles of research and treats research participants ethically. Good social policy must balance the needs and rights of individuals with psychological disorders with the needs and rights of others in a society.

When a person with a psychological disorder is accused of a crime, mental health professionals help to determine if the accused is competent to stand trial and was sane at the time the crime was committed. When a person with a psychological disorder needs treatment but refuses it, mental health professionals may seek to have him or her involuntarily committed for treatment. Mental health professionals have a number of other duties to clients and to society, including the duty to provide confidential and competent treatment to clients and the duty to protect others against clients who are threatening them.

It is not enough to do good; one must do it in the right way.

—John Morley, *On Compromise* (1874)

Daniel Nevins
Introspection

chapter 15

The Research Endeavor

The Hypothesis, Independent Variable, and Dependent Variable

An hypothesis is what the researcher believes will happen in a study. The dependent variable is the factor the researcher is attempting to predict in the study. The independent variable is the factor being used to predict the dependent variable.

Defining and Operationalizing Variables

All the variables in a study must be defined and operationalized. An operationalization is a method for measuring or manipulating the variable. In a study, a sample must be drawn that is representative of the population of interest in order for the research to be generalizable to the population of interest. Often, a control group must be defined as well. Matching a control group to the group of primary interest can help to control third variables.

Why Should We Care?

Understanding the research endeavor is important for people who want to become researchers, for practitioners, and for consumers of research and the treatments that derive from research.

Cross-Sectional Comparisons of Two Groups

In a cross-sectional comparison, two or more groups that differ on the variable thought to create the psychopathology are compared. These studies are relatively easy to conduct but cannot separate cause from consequence and represent only a specific slice of time.

Longitudinal Studies

In a longitudinal study, research participants are followed over time to determine whether a certain factor is associated with the onset of psychopathology. These studies allow researchers to assess both long-term and short-term reactions to an event. They are expensive and do not definitively tease apart cause and effect, however.

Correlational Studies

Correlational studies focus on continuous variables. They allow researchers to consider a wider range of experiences among subjects than would be possible by simply comparing two groups. They cannot establish causality, however.

Experimental Study I: Human Laboratory Studies

In human laboratory studies, the variables thought to cause psychopathology are controlled. Participants are randomly assigned to the experimental group, which receives a manipulation, or the control group, which does not. The generalizability and ethics of some human laboratory studies are sometimes questioned.

Experimental Study II: Therapy Outcome Studies

In a therapy outcome study, people with psychopathologies are given therapy meant to reduce their psychopathologies, and their outcomes are compared to those of people who received no therapy or an alternative therapy. Although these studies provide an opportunity to help people, they create several methodological and ethical concerns.

Experimental Study III: Animal Studies

Animal studies are used to test hypotheses that cannot be tested in humans for ethical reasons or that are better tested in animals than in humans. The generalizability of animal studies to humans has been questioned.

Single Case Studies

Case studies of individuals provide rich and detailed information on those individuals but are not often used in science anymore because they cannot be generalized to the wider population.

The Multimethod Approach Revisited

Typically, no single study can address all possible methodological and theoretical concerns. Many researchers therefore take a multimethod approach, applying several different methodologies across different studies to provide converging evidence for a theory.

Special Issues in Cross-Cultural Research

Cross-cultural and cross-gender research requires that researchers gain access to populations that might be reluctant to participate in therapy; to translate theories, concepts, and measures so they are appropriate for all research participants; and to avoid bias in their research that derives from assumptions that one culture or gender is more healthy than another.

Bio-Psycho-Social Integration
Chapter Summary
Key Terms
Application: *How to Write a Report of a Study*

There's no limit to how complicated things can get, on account of one thing always leading to another.

—E. B. White, *Quo Vadimus?* (1939)

Christian Pierre
Global Seat

Headlines like these often appear in newspapers, in magazines, and on radio or television news programs. When you see or hear such headlines, you may ask yourself, "How do they know that?" Sometimes the news story provides detailed information on the study that is being reported. More often, the story only briefly describes the study and, instead, presents the results of the study in a simplified, clear-cut, and occasionally misleading manner.

The results of research studies are seldom simple or clear-cut. Within the scientific community, debates can rage for decades over the appropriate interpretation of research results. This type of complication is true in any discipline—from psychology and sociology to physics, chemistry, and biology. Researchers interested in abnormal behavior face some special challenges that make it particularly difficult to find definitive answers.

First and foremost is that the phenomena of interest—abnormal behaviors and feelings—are extremely difficult to measure accurately. Researchers must often rely on people's self-reports of their internal states or experiences such as hallucinations or delusions because they are the only ones who have access to these experiences. We cannot see or hear or feel other people's emotions, hallucinations, or delusions. There are a number of ways in which people's self-reports can be distorted, intentionally or unintentionally, and therefore we must always question the validity of self-reports. Similarly, relying on an observer's assessments of a target person is inherently problematic. The observer's assessments can be biased by his or her gender and cultural stereotypes, idiosyncratic biases, and lack of information.

A second major challenge in psychological research is that people change, often quickly. Someone who is depressed today may not be depressed tomorrow; and someone who does not hear voices this week may begin hearing voices next week. Such changes are often interesting and, indeed, may be the focus of a psychologist's research. However, they complicate the process of measuring and categorizing people's behaviors.

A third challenge is that most forms of abnormality probably have multiple causes. Thus, unless a single study can capture the biological, psychological, and social causes of the abnormality of interest, it cannot fully explain the causes of that abnormality. Unfortunately, a single study can rarely accomplish so much. This means that we are always left with partial answers to the question of what causes a certain abnormality and must piece together the partial answers from several studies to get a full picture of that abnormality.

 Why could a single study not evaluate all possible biological, psychological, and social causes of a disorder, if the investigators had enough resources?

A fourth challenge is that we often cannot manipulate or control the variables or phenomena of interest in our research, because doing so would require manipulating humans in ways that would be unethical.

We should not be too discouraged about research on abnormality, however, even after considering these daunting challenges researchers face. Tremendous strides have been made in our understanding of many forms of abnormality in the last 40 years or so, thanks to the cleverness and persistence of researchers. Researchers overcome many of the challenges of researching abnormality by using a *multimethod approach,* which means they use a variety of methodologies to research their questions of interest. Each of these methods may have some limitations, but taken together, these different methods can provide convincing evidence for a theory about abnormality.

This chapter discusses the most common methods of testing theories about abnormality, especially psychosocial theories about the causes of abnormality. We will take one simple theory—the theory that stress is a cause of depression—and discuss how different research methods might be used to test this theory. Of course, the research methods we will discuss can be used to test many different theories, but by applying all the methods to one theory, we can see how many tools researchers have at their disposal to test a given theory.

The Hypothesis, Independent Variable, and Dependent Variable

The theory we will be testing is that stress causes depression. Even this simple theory is too broad and abstract to test directly. Thus, we must state an hypothesis based on this theory. An **hypothesis** is a testable statement of what we expect to happen in a research study. To generate a testable hypothesis, we might ask, "What kind of evidence would support the theory that stress causes depression?" Finding that people who had recently experienced stress were more likely to be depressed than people who had not recently experienced stress would support our theory. One hypothesis, then, is that people who have recently experienced stress are more likely to be depressed than people who have not. This proposition is testable by a number of research methods. If we find support for this hypothesis, we will have support for our theory. Our theory will not be proven correct, however. No one study can do that. However, a series of studies supporting our theory will bolster our confidence in the theory, particularly if these studies have different methodologies.

The alternative to our hypothesis is that people who experience stress are *not* more likely to develop depression than are people who do not experience stress. This is called the **null hypothesis** (see Table 15.1). Results often support the null hypothesis instead of the researcher's primary hypothesis. Does this mean that the underlying theory has been disproved? No. The null hypothesis can be supported for many reasons; most importantly, the study may not be designed well enough to provide support for the primary hypothesis. Thus, researchers will often continue to test their primary hypothesis, using a variety of methodologies, even when the results of their initial studies do not support this primary hypothesis. Eventually, however, a good researcher will recognize when the null hypothesis is getting much more support than the primary hypothesis and either modify or drop the primary hypothesis.

Other terms that appear in discussions of any study are *variable, dependent variable,* and *independent variable* (see Table 15.2). A **variable** is a factor or characteristic that can vary within an individual or between individuals. Weight, mood, and attitudes toward one's mother are all factors that can vary over time, so they would be considered variables. Similarly, although height, sex, and ethnicity are not factors that vary for an individual over time, they can vary from one individual to another, so they also would be considered variables. A **dependent variable** is the factor we are trying to predict in our study. In our studies of stress and depression, we will be trying to predict how depressed people are, so depression is our dependent variable. An **independent variable** is the factor we are using to predict the dependent variable. In our studies, stress will be the independent variable.

hypothesis
testable statement about two or more variables and the relationship between them

null hypothesis
alternative to the primary hypothesis, stating that there is no relationship between the independent variable and the dependent variable

variable
measurable factor or characteristic that can vary within an individual, between individuals, or both

dependent variable
factor that one seeks to predict

independent variable
factor that is manipulated by the experimenter or used to predict the dependent variable

Table 15.1 Primary and Null Hypotheses and Their Application to Stress and Depression		
Term	**Definition**	**Application**
Primary hypothesis	Testable statement of what we expect to happen in our study, based on our theory	People who have recently experienced stress are more likely to be depressed than people who have not.
Null hypothesis	What we would expect to happen in our study if our theory is not correct	People who have recently experienced stress are *not* more likely to be depressed than people who have not.

Table 15.2	Dependent Variable, Independent Variable, and Operationalization	
Term	**Definition**	**Application**
Dependent variable	Factor we are trying to predict in our study	Depression
Independent variable	Factor we are using to predict the dependent variable	Stress
Operationalization	Way we measure or manipulate our independent and dependent variables	Questionnaires measuring depression and stress

Defining and Operationalizing Variables

Before we examine ways of researching depression and stress, we must define what we mean by these terms. As discussed in Chapter 5, depression is a syndrome made up of the following symptoms: sadness, loss of interest in one's usual activities, weight loss or gain, insomnia or hypersomnia, agitation or slowing down, fatigue and loss of energy, feelings of worthlessness or excessive guilt, problems in concentration or indecisiveness, and suicidal thoughts (APA, 1994). Some researchers define depressed people as those who meet the criteria in the DSM-IV for one of the depressive disorders. Anyone who has some of these symptoms of depression but does not meet the criteria for one of the depressive disorders would be considered nondepressed. Other researchers focus on the full range of depressive symptoms, from no symptoms to moderate symptoms that do not meet diagnostic criteria for a disorder to the most severe symptoms. They may divide people up into those who show no depressive symptoms, those who show moderately severe depressive symptoms, and those who show severe depressive symptoms.

Stress is a more difficult term to define, because it has been used in so many ways in research and the popular press (see Chapter 13). **Stressor** is used to refer to an *event* that is uncontrollable, is unpredictable, and challenges the limits of people's abilities to cope. *Stress* has been used to refer to people's *emotions and behaviors* in response to stressful events.

Our definition of *depression* or *stress* will influence how we operationalize them. **Operationalization** is the way that we measure or manipulate the variables of interest in a study. If we define depression as symptoms meeting DSM-IV criteria for a depressive disorder, then we will operationalize depression as DSM-IV diagnoses. If we define depression as symptoms along the entire range of severity, then we might operationalize depression as scores on a depression questionnaire.

In operationalizing stress, we must first decide whether we will focus on stressful events or on people's stress reactions to these events. Then we must devise some measure of what we define as stress or some way of manipulating or creating stress so that we can then examine people's reactions to this stress. In this chapter, we will describe several operationalizations of stress as we discuss different research methods.

Why Should We Care?

After reading this rather dry list of definitions, we may be asking ourselves, "Who cares?" There are several reasons it is important to understand how research on abnormality is done.

First, the chapters in this book present the results of dozens of studies purporting to show something important about a disorder: who is most likely to have it, what causes it, what are the most effective treatments for it. We may question or disagree with some of these results. Understanding how the research was done will help us evaluate the support for the claims made in this book.

stressor
an event that is perceived as uncontrollable, unpredictable, challenging, and/or threatening

operationalization
specific manner in which one measures or manipulates variables in a study

Second, people who plan to work in academic settings, teaching and doing research, obviously need to know how research on psychopathology is done so they can do it themselves. Those who plan on being therapists and not doing research may not see the need for understanding research, but just as physicians need basic courses in chemistry, biology, and physics to understand medical diseases and to evaluate new treatments for these diseases, psychotherapists need to understand how psychological research is done so they can evaluate new research findings and proposed treatments relevant to the patients they are treating.

Third, many of us will experience at least one of the disorders described in this book at some time in our lives. We will seek to understand why we are experiencing this disorder and may seek treatment for it. Knowing how research is done will help us evaluate possible explanations for the disorder and treatments that might be recommended.

Let us move, now, to discuss the different methods we might use to test our hypothesis that people who experience stress will be more likely to be depressed than people who do not experience stress.

Cross-Sectional Comparison of Two Groups

Perhaps the most obvious way to test our hypothesis that stress causes depression is to compare a group of people who have experienced recent stressful events with a group who has not. If our hypothesis is correct, the group of people who have experienced stressors should show more depression than the group of people who have not.

So that we can operationalize stress, we must decide what type of stressor our theory says will cause depression—uncontrollable stressors, unpredictable stressors, major traumas, the daily hassles of life. Let us say that our theory states that uncontrollable stressors lead to depression. How are we going to measure uncontrollable stressors? We could develop a list of stressors that we believe are uncontrollable and ask the people in our study whether they have experienced any of these stressors (see Figure 15.1). We could then divide these people into those who had experienced at least one of the stressors on our list and those who had not experienced any of the stressors on our list and then compare these two groups on depression.

Alternately, we can focus on one stressor that most people agree is uncontrollable, such as the loss of a loved one, and compare people who experienced recent losses with people who did not. One advantage of this approach over the list approach is that everyone in the "stress group" will have experienced the same type of stressor. This could be important if some uncontrollable stressors on our list were more likely than others to lead to depression. For example, bereavement is probably more likely to lead to depression than having your plane delayed, though both are uncontrollable stressors. Let us

Instructions: Below is a list of events that may or may not have happened to you recently. Please check any event that you have recently experienced.

_____ Natural disaster
_____ Serious illness
_____ Serious illness in family member
_____ Death of a family member
_____ Fired or laid off from job
_____ Assaulted or robbed
_____ Separated from spouse/partner
_____ House burned down
_____ Other:

Figure 15.1

Questionnaire on Uncontrollable Events. Questionnaires are convenient methods for obtaining data on the stress in people's lives.

therefore compare a group of people who have recently experienced bereavement with a group of people who have not.

What type of depression does our theory say results from uncontrollable stressors? Let us decide to focus on the full range of depressive symptoms and to use observers' ratings of subjects to measure depression.

Now that we have decided on our operationalizations of stress and depression, we must find our sample of people to participate in the study. A **sample** is a group of people taken from our population of interest who participate in our study. In our study, the population of interest is recently bereaved people. Our sample will be some subgroup of all recently bereaved people. Ideally, we will have a **representative sample** of bereaved people. A representative sample is highly similar to the population of interest in terms of sex, ethnicity, age, and other important variables. If a sample is not representative—for example, if there are more women or people of color in our sample of bereaved people than in the general population of bereaved people—then the sample is said to have bias.

The representativeness of a sample is important to the **generalization** we want to make from our study. If our sample represents only a small or unusual group of people, then we cannot generalize the results of our study to the larger population. For example, if all of the people in our study are white, middle-class females, we cannot know whether our results generalize to males, people of color, or people in other socioeconomic classes.

Some methods of recruiting subjects into a study create more representative samples than do others. For example, we could put an advertisement in the local newspaper asking people who had recently experienced loss to volunteer for our study. Some bereaved people could be more likely than others to respond to a newspaper advertisement—perhaps only those who were distressed and looking for help would respond. If our advertisement mentions that the study focuses on depression among the bereaved, it will be even more likely to create a biased sample. In contrast, if we generated our sample by consulting local records of recent deaths and contacting the relatives of all people who died within the last year, we might be less likely to generate a biased sample.

So let us decide to use county records to identify people in our area who have been bereaved in the last year. Of course, not everyone will agree to participate in our study, and there may be important differences between people who participate and people who do not. For example, men tend to be less willing to participate in psychological studies than do women, so we can expect to have more women volunteering for our study than men. Nevertheless, we can try to recruit as representative a sample as possible of all the people who were bereaved in the last year in our area.

 What are some of the motivations people might have for participating in a research study that could affect the representatives of a sample?

We will want to compare levels of depression in our bereaved sample with levels among a group of people who are not recently bereaved. We will seek **matching** of our bereaved group with this comparison group on any variable (other than stress) that we think might influence levels of depression, so that the two groups are alike on these variables. If we do not do this matching process, then any differences we found between the two groups on levels of depression could be attributable to variables for which we did not match. Such a variable is often referred to as a **third variable** (the first and second variables are the independent and dependent variables, respectively). For example, women are generally more likely to be depressed than men, so if we happened to have more women in our bereaved group than in our comparison group, then higher levels of depression in the bereaved group might be attributable to a third variable—the fact that there are more women in that group—and not to the fact that the group had recently been bereaved. Thus, we need to match our bereaved and comparison groups on all third variables that might influence our dependent variable of depression.

Let us decide to match our two groups on sex, age, race or ethnicity, and socioeconomic status. We can generate the comparison group by consulting the local census

sample
group of people taken from a population of interest who participate in a study

representative sample
subgroup taken from a larger population of interest that is similar to the larger sample regarding the prevalence of factors that might affect the results of a study, such as gender, ethnicity, education level, and age

generalization
statement about a large population, the validity and accuracy of which is determined in part by the representativeness of the research sample from which the statement is being made

matching
process of selecting subjects who are identical on all variables that might affect the dependent variable other than the variable of interest

third variable
factor that affects levels of the dependent variable and confounds the results of a study if it is not appropriately controlled for or eliminated

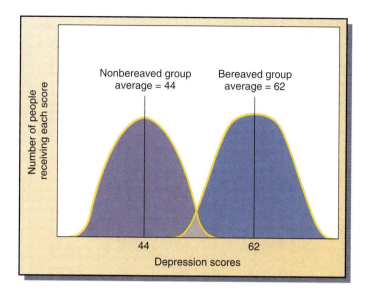

Figure 15.2

Distributions of Scores from Nonbereaved and Bereaved Groups. If the overlap between the scores of two groups is reasonably small and the difference between the average scores of the groups is reasonably large, the two groups may be said to be significantly different.

records and, for every person in our bereaved group, recruit a person of the same sex, age, race, and socioeconomic status from the local area into our comparison group. While not a simple task, this is a good way to generate a matched comparison group.

We now have our two groups—a recently bereaved group and a comparison group of people who are not recently bereaved but are similar to the bereaved group in terms of sex, age, ethnicity, and socioeconomic status. Our observers conduct structured clinical interviews with each person in both groups to determine the levels of depression of each person. Our depression scale ranges from 0 (not at all depressed) to 100 (extremely depressed). Let us assume our bereaved group has an average score of 62 on this scale, and our comparison group has an average score of 44. These two average scores seem quite different, but are they?

We need to conduct a statistical test to determine whether this difference between the two averages occurred simply by chance or is unlikely to have occurred by chance. We will not go into detail about how to conduct this statistical test, which is called a *t-test*. Suffice it to say that this statistic takes into account both the difference between the average scores of the two groups and the amount of overlap in scores between the groups. If the difference between the average scores of the two groups is reasonably large and the amount of overlap in scores of the two groups is reasonably small, then the two groups are said to be **significantly different** (see Figure 15.2). This means that the difference between the scores of the two groups is unlikely to have occurred by chance alone. Many research studies are qualified with statements such as, "This difference was significant at $p < 0.05$." This means that there is less than a 5 in 100 chance that the difference in means between the two groups occurred simply by chance. Researchers typically accept results at this level of significance as support of their hypotheses.

significantly different
difference in scores between two groups that would be unlikely to have occurred if the null hypothesis were true

Many studies have found significantly different levels of depression between recently bereaved and nonbereaved people (see Stroebe & Stroebe, 1987). In one study, researchers looked more closely at different groups of bereaved people to determine if there were significant differences in their levels of depression. These researchers interviewed 253 people who had lost family members to cancer within the last month to determine their levels of depression. Some of the subjects were the spouses or partners of the people who died, some were the adult children of the deceased, some were the adult siblings, and some were the parents of children who had died. Would any of these groups be expected to have higher levels of depression than others? Based on previous studies, the researchers expected that people who had lost spouses or partners and the parents who had lost children would experience their losses as most stressful and would, therefore, be the most depressed.

As you can see in Figure 15.3, however, there were no large differences between the groups in levels of depression. The parents who had lost children had the highest depression scores, but the scores were not significantly higher than those of the other groups. The

Figure 15.3

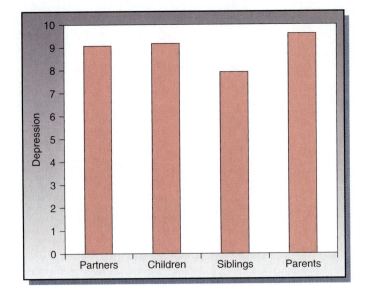

people who had lost siblings had the lowest scores, but again the score were not significantly lower than those of the other groups. Thus, this study supported the null hypothesis that there would be no differences between groups rather than the researchers' primary hypothesis that there would be significant differences between groups. The results of this study are still important because they suggest that anyone who loses a close family member is at risk for depression, even if the survivor is not the partner or parent of the person who died (Nolen-Hoeksema, Parker, & Larson, 1994).

Evaluating Cross-Sectional Studies

One advantage of cross-sectional studies is that they are relatively easy to conduct compared to many other types of studies. In addition, cross-sectional studies have produced valuable information on basic differences between important groups, as in the study of different groups of bereaved people described (Table 15.3).

There are disadvantages to this type of study, however. First, it is often difficult or impossible to match two groups on all third variables that might contribute to the dependent variable. This is in part because we do not always know about all the third variables that could affect our dependent variable. For example, suppose we decided to operationalize uncontrollable stress as experiencing the recent divorce of one's parents rather than as bereavement. We could compare two groups—one group of children whose parents were recently divorced and another group of children of the same sex, age, race/ethnicity, and socioeconomic status whose parents were not divorced. If we found that the children of divorced parents had significantly higher depression scores than did the children whose parents were not divorced, it would be tempting to conclude that parental divorce causes depression in children. It turns out, however, that children whose parents eventually divorce have elevated levels of depression long before the divorce occurs, and this depression is usually linked to the level of conflict between parents rather than to the eventual divorce of the parents (Block, Block, & Gjerde, 1986; Cherlin, Furstenberg,

Studies that have carefully examined families of divorce find that it is probably not the divorce that causes high levels of distress in children, but conflict between their parents, which is present even before the divorce.

Table 15.3 Evaluating Cross-Sectional Studies

Advantages

They are relatively easy to conduct.
They have produced valuable information on differences between important groups.

Disadvantages

It is difficult to match groups on all third variables.
Cause and effect cannot be teased apart.
Vital information can be missed if observations are not made at the right time.

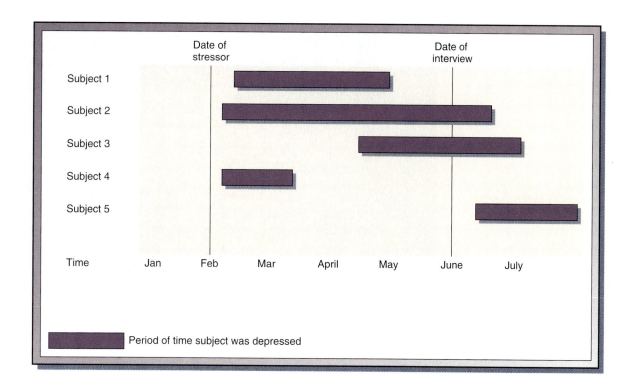

Period of time subject was depressed

Chase-Lansdale, & Kiernan, 1991). In many cases, the divorce actually reduces the conflict between parents and leads to lowering of depression levels in children. Thus, it seems that it is parental conflict, more than parental divorce, that contributes to depression in children (Buchanan, Maccoby, & Dornbusch, 1991; Johnston, Gonzales, & Campbell, 1987).

A second disadvantage of cross-sectional studies is that they cannot tease apart what is a cause and what is a consequence. For example, many stressful events depressed people report may be the consequences of their depression rather than the causes. The symptoms of depression can cause stress by impairing interpersonal skills, interfering with concentration on the job, and causing insomnia. The same problem exists for many types of psychopathology: The symptoms of schizophrenia can disrupt social relationships; alcoholism can lead to unemployment; and so on. Some psychological symptoms may even cause physiological changes in people. For example, people who have recently experienced psychological trauma often develop medical diseases because the traumas reduce the effectiveness of their immune systems, which help to fight disease (Jemmott & Locke, 1984). Thus, simply comparing two groups is an inadequate way to test a theory about the cause of a psychopathology.

A final disadvantage of a cross-sectional study is the potential for bad timing. In our study of bereavement, many of the people in our bereaved group who were not depressed at the time they were interviewed perhaps had already recovered from their depression or had not developed it yet (see Figure 15.4). This potential problem has led many researchers to conduct longitudinal studies, rather than cross-sectional studies, comparing two groups. A **longitudinal study** is simply a study that follows people for an extended period of time rather than just assessing them at one point in time.

Longitudinal Studies

A longitudinal study is often an extension of a cross-sectional study, in which two groups of subjects are followed over time. A more powerful type of longitudinal study is a **prospective longitudinal study**, in which assessments of the two groups are obtained *before* a stressor happens, and the two groups are reassessed *after* the stressor happens.

Figure 15.4

Timing Problem in Cross-Sectional Design. Here is a case in which the timing of a cross-sectional study was a problem. The stressor occurred in February, and the interview for the study occurred in June. The researchers detected depression in Subjects 2 and 3 because they were depressed in June. They missed the depression experienced by Subjects 1, 4, and 5 because these subjects' periods of depression did not happen to overlap with the time of the interview.

longitudinal study
research method that evaluates the same group(s) of people for an extended period of time

prospective longitudinal study
research method that evaluates the same group(s) of people before an event of interest and then again after the event of interest

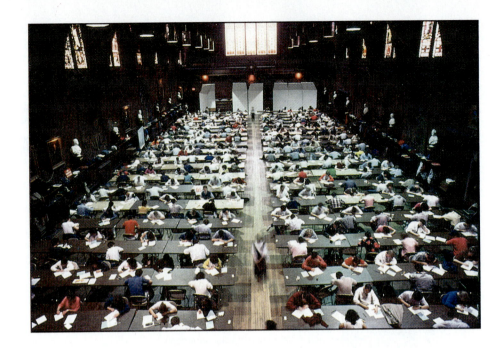

A longitudinal study was able to predict students' emotional reactions to an exam, using information obtained from students before they took the exam.

An example is the midterm study discussed in Chapter 5. A group of researchers took advantage of a stressor they knew was about to happen in the lives of their student subjects: an upcoming midterm examination in an abnormal psychology course. A few days before the examination, they assessed levels of depressed mood in the students, using a self-report questionnaire. They also asked the students what grades they hoped to get on the exam and what grades they would consider failures. One day and three days following the exam, the researchers reassessed the students' levels of depressed mood. The researchers knew what grades the students had received on the exam, so they could divide the students into those who had experienced failure (a grade below what they expected) and those who had experienced success (a grade as good as they expected). Students who had experienced the stress of failure had higher levels of depression after the exam than did those who had experienced success. This finding supports the hypothesis that stress is associated with depression (Metalsky, Halberstadt, & Abramson, 1987).

Evaluating Longitudinal Studies

Prospective longitudinal studies have several advantages over cross-sectional studies. In these studies, researchers can determine whether there are differences between the groups of interest before the crucial event occurs. If there are no differences before the event but significant differences after the event, then they can have more confidence that it was the event that actually lead to the differences between the groups. Longitudinal designs also allow researchers to follow two groups for long enough to assess both short-term and long-term reactions to the event (Table 15.4).

There are some disadvantages to longitudinal studies, however. First, they can be time-consuming and expensive to run. Chapter 6 reports studies in which children at

Table 15.4 Evaluating Longitudinal Studies
Advantages
Differences between groups can be determined before the crucial event occurs.
Groups can be followed long enough to assess both long-term and short-term reactions.
Disadvantages
They are time-consuming and expensive to run.
When the events of interest will happen cannot always be predicted.

high risk for schizophrenia were studied from their preschool years to their early adult years to determine what characteristics could predict who would develop schizophrenia and who would not (Erlenmyer-Kimling, Rock, Squires-Wheeler, & Roberts, 1991). Some of these studies have been going on for over 25 years and have cost millions of dollars. They are producing extremely valuable data but at a high cost in researchers' time and in research dollars.

Second, researchers cannot always predict when the events they are interested in—the experience of a stressor, the onset of depression—will happen. Thus, unless they are constantly assessing their subjects, which is usually not possible, they will miss some of the events of interest.

Correlational Studies

A **correlational study** is any study in which we only observe the relationship between two variables, and do not manipulate one variable to determine its effects on another variable. Thus, both the cross-sectional studies and longitudinal studies we have discussed so far are correlational studies. We observed the relationship between depression and being bereaved or not bereaved and we observed the relationship between failing an exam and depression, but in neither case did we manipulate the variable thought to cause depression.

In each of the studies we have discussed thus far, we have examined differences between two distinct groups of people. Sometimes it is not easy to define two distinct groups of people to compare in a study. We may wish to study people all along a continuum of experiences rather than people who either did or did not have specific experiences. For example, we might hypothesize that it is not the experience of one stressor that leads to depression but the cumulation of multiple stressors that results in depression. To test our hypothesis, we might want to study a large group of people who have experienced varying numbers of stressors, to determine whether the number of stressors experienced is related to the level of depression these people show.

This is the most common type of correlational study done in abnormal psychology—a study of two or more continuous variables. A **continuous variable** is measured along a continuum. For example, on a scale measuring severity of depression, scores might fall along a continuum from 0 (no depression) to 60 (extremely depressed). On a scale measuring number of recent stressors, scores might fall along a continuum from 0 (no stressors) to 20 (20 or more recent stressors).

When researchers conduct a correlational study of two or more continuous variables, they usually represent the relationship between these variables in a statistic called a **correlation**. Figure 15.5 illustrates some possible patterns of correlation. In the top graph of the figure, the correlation is positive, indicating that people who report more stressors have higher levels of depression. In the middle graph, the correlation is negative. If we were still measuring stressors and depression, this would mean that people who report more stressors actually have lower levels of depression. This is an unlikely scenario, but there are many instances of negative correlations between variables. For example, people who have more positive social support from others typically have lower levels of depression. The bottom graph in Figure 15.5 illustrates a case of a zero correlation between two variables. In this case, the two variables show no pattern of going up or down in tandem with each other.

Evaluating Correlational Studies

One advantage of studies using continuous variables is that they take into account the full range of experiences people have, rather than forcing researchers to decide, sometimes arbitrarily, how to divide subjects into two groups. Having information about people's full range of experience provides the researcher with considerable power to test hypotheses about the relationship between two variables.

The major disadvantage of correlational studies, including studies using continuous variables and the cross-sectional and longitudinal comparisons of groups we discussed

correlational study
method in which researchers assess only the relationship between two variables and do not manipulate one variable to determine its effects on another variable

continuous variable
factor that is measured along a continuum (such as 0–100) rather than falling into a discrete category (such as "diagnosed with depression").

correlation
statistic that represents the degree to which two variables are related

Figure 15.5

Some Correlations Between Depression and Other Variables. Correlations can be positive, negative, or zero.

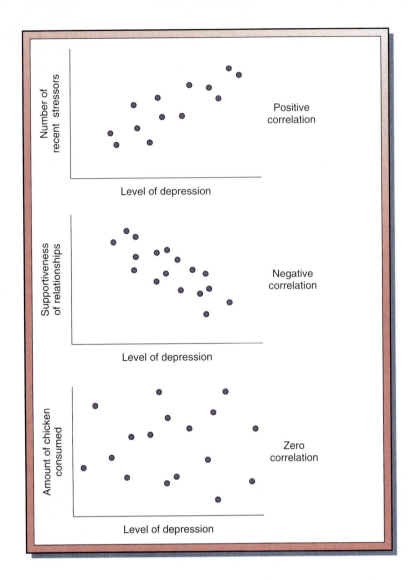

earlier, is that they can only reveal whether the two variables are related. They cannot reveal whether one variable caused the other variable (Table 15.5).

This problem can be addressed, to a certain extent, by conducting longitudinal correlational studies, in which subjects are reassessed at multiple points over time. For example, we might assess subjects' levels of stress and depression three times over the year. We would predict that subjects who experienced stressors between assessment times would show increases in depression between those times. Longitudinal studies allow us to predict which subjects will show depression over time, but they still do not definitively establish that the stressors caused the increases in depression. All correlational studies suffer from the third variable problem. Researchers seldom can measure all the possible influences on their subjects' levels of depression or other psychopathologies.

What do you think is the strongest contributor to anxiety? What might be a third variable that explains the relationship between this contributor and anxiety?

Third variable problems are one of the major reasons researchers turn to experimental studies. The hallmark of such studies is control. Researchers attempt to control all the variables—the independent, the dependent, and any potentially problematic third variable—before they test their hypotheses. We turn now to a discussion of the various types of experimental studies we could do to test our theory that stress leads to depression. We will examine three in particular. The first, the human laboratory study, has the goal of

Table 15.5 Evaluating Correlational Studies
Advantages
They can take into account the range of participants' experiences.
The researcher does not have to form two separate groups of participants.
Disadvantages
Cause cannot be separated from effect.
All third variables cannot be controlled.

inducing the conditions that we theorize will lead to our outcome of interest (i.e., increasing stress to cause depression) in people in a controlled setting. The second, the therapy outcome study, also is conducted with humans but has the opposite focus of the first type of study. In a therapy outcome study, the researcher wants to reduce the conditions leading to the outcome of interest so as to reduce that outcome (i.e., decreasing stress to decrease depression). The third, the animal study, attempts to model what happens in humans by manipulating animals in a laboratory.

Experimental Study I: Human Laboratory Studies

One experimental method for testing our hypothesis that stressors lead to depression is to expose subjects to a stressor in the laboratory and then determine whether it causes an increase in depressed mood. Several studies of this type have been done (see Peterson & Seligman, 1984). The stressor that is often used in this study is some type of unsolvable task or puzzle, such as an unsolvable anagram. If we chose this as the type of stress we would induce, then our operationalization would be participants' exposure to unsolvable anagrams. We are manipulating stress, not just measuring it in this study. This gives us the advantage of knowing precisely what type of stress participants are exposed to and when.

Because we want to know if the unsolvable anagrams cause *changes* in the participants' levels of depression, we need to measure depression both before and after participants complete the anagrams. Does an increase in depression over the period of our experiment necessarily mean that exposure to the unsolvable anagrams caused this increase? Perhaps simply participating in an experiment is a sufficiently negative experience to increase levels of depression. This is basically the same type of third variable problem we encountered in the previous studies. To control third variables, researchers create a **control group** in which participants have all the same experiences as the group of main interest in the study, except that they do not receive the key manipulation—in our case the experience of the unsolvable puzzles. The control group for our study could be made to do puzzles very similar to the unsolvable anagrams the other group works on, but the control group's anagrams could be solvable. Thus, the control group's experience would be identical to that of the other group—the **experimental group**—except that the control group would not receive the stressor of unsolvable anagrams.

What operationalization of depression would be appropriate for this study? It would be cumbersome to have observers conduct structured interviews both before and after participants attempted the anagrams. Also, if the measure of depression were too obvious, participants might guess what hypothesis we were testing. This could create *demand characteristics:* Participants could guess the hypothesis and try to conform their behavior with the hypothesis. To avoid demand characteristics, we could use more subtle measures of depression, such as those illustrated in Figure 15.6, that are embedded in other measures so as to obscure the real purpose of our study. These other measures are often called *filler measures.* Researchers also often use *cover stories:* Participants are told a false story to prevent them from guessing the true purpose of the experiment and changing their behavior accordingly.

control group
in an experimental study, group of subjects whose experience resembles that of the experimental group in all ways, except that they do not receive the key manipulation

experimental group
in an experimental study, group of participants that receives the key manipulation

Figure 15.6

Scales to Measure Depression, Embedded in Other Scales. The researcher may be interested only in subjects' answers on the scales measuring happiness and depression but may embed these scales in other scales to obscure the purpose of the study.

Instructions: On each scale, mark off how you feel right now.

Happy | — — — | — — — | — — — | — — — | — — — | — — — | Unhappy

Curious | — — — | — — — | — — — | — — — | — — — | — — — | Not curious

Thoughtful | — — — | — — — | — — — | — — — | — — — | — — — | Not thoughtful

Depressed | — — — | — — — | — — — | — — — | — — — | — — — | Not depressed

Smart | — — — | — — — | — — — | — — — | — — — | — — — | Not smart

Under what circumstances do you think it would be ethical to deceive research participants? When would it be unethical?

There are a few other techniques we should use in our study to make sure all third variables are controlled. First, we want to insure that our participants for our experimental group (the one that does the unsolvable anagrams) and for our control group (the one that does the solvable anagrams) are *randomly* selected and assigned to the two groups to minimize differences between the two groups before our experiment starts. Second, experimenters who actually interact with the participants should be *unaware* of which condition the participants are in, the experimental condition or control condition, so that they do not give off subtle cues as to what they expect the participants to do in the experiment. For example, if experimenters knew that a participant was in the experimental condition, they might suggest to the participant in subtle ways that the anagrams were unsolvable. This obviously would create demands for the participant to behave in ways he or she otherwise might not have if the experimenters had not subtly communicated their expectations.

We have instituted controls on our study—participants have been randomly selected and assigned, and our experimenters are unaware of the hypothesis of our study and thus to the condition that participants are in. Now the study may be conducted. We find that, as we predicted, participants given the unsolvable anagrams showed greater increases in depressed mood than did participants given the solvable anagrams. What can we conclude about our theory of depression, based on this study? Our experimental controls have helped us rule out third variable explanations, so we can be relatively confident that it was the experience of the uncontrollable stressor that led to the increases in depression in the experimental group. Thus, we can say that we have supported our hypothesis that people exposed to uncontrollable stress will show more depressed mood than will people not exposed to uncontrollable stress.

Evaluating Human Laboratory Studies

As we have already discussed, the primary advantage of human laboratory studies is control. Researchers have more control over third variables, the independent variable, and the dependent variable in these studies than they do in any other type of study they can do with humans. The primary limitation of human laboratory studies is that we cannot know if our results generalize to what happens outside the laboratory. Is being exposed to unsolvable anagrams anything like being exposed to major, real-world, uncontrollable stressors, such as the death of a loved one? Clearly there is a difference in the severity of the two types of experiences, but is this the only important difference? Similarly, do the increases in depressed mood in the participants in our study, which were probably small

Table 15.6 Evaluating Human Laboratory Studies

Advantages

The researcher has more control over variables.
Participants can be randomly assigned to groups.
Appropriate control groups can be created to rule out alternative explanations of important findings.

Disadvantages

Results may not generalize to outside the laboratory.
There are possible ethical limitations.

increases, tell us anything about why some people develop extremely severe, debilitating episodes of depression? Experimental studies such as ours have been criticized for the lack of generalizability of their results to the major psychopathology that occurs in everyday life (see Table 15.6).

A Note on Ethics

Apart from posing the problems of generalizability, human laboratory studies sometimes pose serious ethical issues. Is it ethical to deliberately induce distress, even mild distress, in people? Participants in an experiment can be warned of possible discomfort or distress and told that they can end their participation at any time. Even so, participants rarely stop experiments, even if they are uncomfortable, because of the subtle pressures of the social situation.

What if a participant, even after being told that the stressful experience he had (e.g., being given an unsolvable anagram) was completely out of his control, believes that he should have been able to control the situation or solve the tasks? It turns out that many participants, especially college students, continue to believe that they should have been able to solve unsolvable tasks or that negative feedback they received in an experiment was a true indication of their abilities, even after being told that they were deceived by the experimenter. The researchers who discovered this phenomenon recommended conducting a *process debriefing* with participants following any potentially upsetting experiments (Ross, Lepper, & Hubbard, 1975). In such debriefings, experimenters slowly draw out the particpants' assumptions about the experiments and their performances. They conduct extended conversations with the participants about the purposes and procedures of the experiments, explaining how their behavior was beyond their control and certainly not a reflection of their abilities.

Experimenters must always be aware of the ethical concerns raised by experiments of this sort and take all possible means to limit dangers to participants. All colleges and universities have a human subjects committee that reviews the procedures of studies with humans to insure that the benefits of the study substantially outweigh any risks to participants, and that the risks to participants have been minimized.

 Are there any experiments you have read about in psychology that you think should not have been done in humans for ethical reasons?

Experimental Study II: Therapy Outcome Studies

The ethical concerns of human laboratory studies have led some researchers to advocate studies that attempt to *reduce* psychopathology by reducing the factors believed to cause it. Applying this type of study to our theory would mean intervening with depressed

Figure 15.7

Results of Therapy Outcome Study with Children at Risk for Depression. Children in the therapy group became less depressed after therapy and remained less depressed than did children in the control group through 2 years of follow-up.
Source: Gillham, Reivich, Jaycox, & Seligman, 1995.

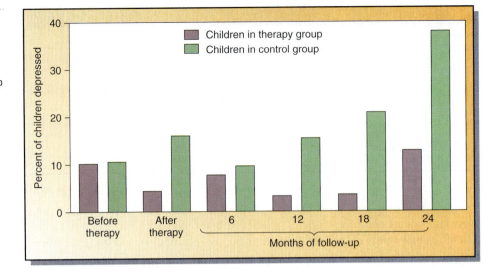

therapy outcome study
experimental study that assesses the effects of an intervention designed to reduce psychopathology in an experimental group, while performing no intervention or a different type of intervention on another group

participants to reduce stress, which should, in turn, decrease depression, according to our theory. This type of study is called a **therapy outcome study**.

Therapy outcome studies are appealing because they involve helping people while, at the same time, providing information. One recent therapy outcome study targeted 142 children at risk for depression because they lived in high stress family environments. These 10 to 13 year olds were randomly assigned either to a therapy group or to a control group. The children in the therapy group were taught more effective ways to cope with the stress in their lives. Specifically, they were taught skills for being more assertive in social situations and for generating good solutions to interpersonal problems. They were also taught how to recognize and change self-defeating ways of thinking about their problems, so that they could be more active in solving their problems. The children in the control group were not given this instruction. The two groups were then followed for 2 years to examine their levels of depression.

As can be seen in Figure 15.7, the children who received the therapy became less depressed over the course of the therapy and remained less depressed than the children in the control group for the next 2 years (Jaycox, Reivich, Gillham, & Seligman, 1994; Gillham, Reivich, Jaycox, & Seligman, 1995). These results are important because they show that depression in children can be alleviated and possibly prevented in the future with therapy that focuses on coping with stressful situations.

Evaluating Therapy Outcome Studies

Although therapy outcome studies might seem the most ethical way of conducting research on people in distress, they carry their own methodological challenges and ethical issues (Table 15.7). First, most psychological therapies involve a package of techniques for responding to people's problems. The children in the study described were taught assertiveness skills, social problem-solving skills, and skills at changing self-defeating thinking. Which of these skills was most responsible for alleviating their depression? Even when a therapy works, researchers often cannot know exactly what it is about the therapy that works. This obviously has practical implications, because we need to know what are the effective elements of a therapy in order to bolster those elements and reduce elements that may be useless or even harmful. It also has important theoretical or scientific implications. If we conduct a therapy outcome study to test a particular theory about the cause of a psychopathology, we need to know whether the therapy works for the reasons we theorized. For example, if we are testing our theory that stress causes depression, we will want to know that our intervention reduced depression because it reduced stress and not because it provided the participants with an opportunity to ventilate their feelings, because it provided them with social support in the form of a therapist, or for some other reason that is not tied to our theory.

Table 15.7	Evaluating Therapy Outcome Studies

Advantages

They provide help to people in distress as research is generated.

Disadvantages

It is difficult to tell which aspect of therapy led to reduction in the psychopathology.
They raise questions about appropriate control groups.
There are ethical considerations about wait list control groups and placebo control groups.
Patients' needs must be balanced with the need to administer standardized therapy.
The generalizability of results to real-world delivery of therapy are unclear.

The second major challenge that researchers face in therapy outcome studies is that if we intervene with people and find that their levels of psychopathology decrease, we cannot rule out that the decrease occurred simply because of the passage of time. Thus, we need to compare our experimental intervention group with a control group of people who did not receive the intervention to see if our participants' improvement in depression had anything to do with our intervention.

In the therapy outcome study described, researchers used a simple control group of children who did not receive the therapy but were tracked for the same period of time as were the children who did receive the therapy. A variation on this simple control group is the **wait list control group**. The participants in this type of group do not receive the intervention when the experimental group does but go onto a wait list to receive the intervention at a later date when the study is completed. Both groups of participants are assessed at the beginning and end of the study, but only the intervention group receives the intervention as part of the study.

Another type of control group is the **placebo control group**. This type of group is used most often in studies of the effectiveness of drugs. The participants in this group have the same interactions with experimenters as do the participants in the experimental group but they take pills that are placebos (inactive substances) rather than the real drug. Usually, both the participants and the experimenters in these studies are unaware what condition the participants are in to prevent demand effects. When this happens, the experiment is known as a **double-blind experiment**.

What type of placebo might be used with a control group in a psychological therapy outcome study? One option is to allow control group participants simple interaction with therapists, minus any experimental therapy. However, some theorists have objected to the idea that interacting with a warm and caring therapist without experiencing any other experimental conditions is a placebo. They suggest that the active ingredient in therapy is receiving unconditional support and encouragement from a warm and caring therapist, not the actual program of therapy (Rogers, 1951). Indeed, psychological placebo interventions have been found to be quite effective with moderately distressed people (Elkin, Shae, Watkins, & Imber, 1989). It seems that a little bit of human caring goes a long way to help people overcome their distress. It also seems it is nearly impossible to construct a true psychological placebo.

There are also ethical problems to using simple control groups, wait list control groups, or placebo control groups in therapy outcome research. Some researchers believe it is unethical to withhold treatment or to provide a treatment they believe is ineffective for people in distress. Many participants assigned to a control group may be in severe distress or in danger of harming themselves or someone else and, therefore, require immediate treatment. In response to this concern, many therapy outcome studies now compare the effectiveness of two or more therapies that are expected to have positive effects. These studies basically are a competition between rival therapies and the theories behind these therapies. Thus, there is some reason to believe that all the participants in such a study will benefit from participation in the study but that the study will yield useful information about the most effective type of therapy for the participants.

A third difficult issue in therapy outcome research is how much a therapy can be modified to respond to a specific participant's needs without compromising the scientific

wait list control group
in a therapy outcome study, group of people that functions as a control group while an experimental group receives an intervention and that then receives the intervention itself after a waiting period

placebo control group
in a therapy outcome study, group of people whose treatment is an inactive substance (to compare with the effects of a drug) or a non–theory-based therapy providing social support (to compare with the effects of psychotherapy)

double-blind experiment
study in which both the researchers and the participants are unaware of which experimental condition the participants are in, in order to prevent demand effects

element of the study. Therapists want to respond to the needs of their participants, varying the dosage of a drug or deviating from a study's protocol for psychological intervention. If they depart too far from the standard therapy, however, there will be great variation in the therapy that participants in the intervention group receive, which could compromise the results of the study.

A fourth, and related, methodological issue has to do with the generalizability of results from therapy outcome studies to the real world. In these studies, the therapeutic intervention is usually delivered to patients in a controlled, high quality atmosphere by the most competent therapists. The patients are usually screened so they fit a narrow set of criteria for being included in the study, and often only the patients who stick with the therapy to its end are included in the final analyses. In the real world, mental health services are not always delivered in controlled, high quality atmospheres by the most competent therapists. Patients are who they are, with their complicated symptom pictures and lives that may not fit neatly into the criteria for an "optimal patient." Patients often leave and return to therapy and may not receive "full trials" of the therapy before they drop out for financial or personal reasons. Thus, there is reason to question the generalizability of many therapy outcome studies to the real world.

One of the most notorious examples of a problem with generalization comes from studies of antidepressant drugs (see Hamilton, 1986). Based on animal studies, researchers believed that the effectiveness of antidepressant drugs varied with a woman's menstrual cycle. Thus, to reduce variation in the responsiveness of depressed subjects to standard doses of antidepressant drugs, researchers regularly excluded women from studies of these drugs. Yet women are twice as likely as men to develop depression, and the majority of seriously depressed people who seek treatment are women. Thus, until relatively recently, researchers did not know much about the effectiveness of antidepressant drugs in the majority of people who develop depression and did not know how to adjust the dosage of these drugs to accommodate a depressed woman's menstrual cycle (see Conrad & Hamilton, 1986). In response to such problems, the National Institutes of Health now require that all studies include representative samples of women and men and people of different ethnicities and socioeconomic classes, so that the results of studies can be generalized to the population at large.

So with all the potential problems in therapy outcome studies, should we stop doing them altogether? These problems make it difficult to use therapy outcome studies to test theories about the causes of psychopathology. Thus, they may not be the best way to test our theory that stress causes depression, because they afford the experimenter much less control than human laboratory studies do over third variables that can affect results. Nevertheless, therapy outcome studies are extremely important to our growing knowledge of how best to intervene with people with various types of psychopathology. They are the best studies for determining what works and what does not to relieve people's distress.

 Suppose you were conducting a therapy outcome study and a participant clearly was not responding to the type of therapy he or she was assigned to. What would you do?

Experimental Study III: Animal Studies

Researchers sometimes try to avoid the ethical issues involved in experimental studies with humans by conducting such studies with animals. Animal research has its own set of ethical issues, which we will discuss shortly. However, many researchers feel it is acceptable to subject animals to situations in the laboratory that would not be ethical to impose on humans. Animal studies thus provide researchers with even more control over laboratory conditions and third variables than is possible in human laboratory studies.

In a well-known series of animal studies designed to investigate depression (alluded to in Chapter 5), Martin Seligman, Bruce Overmier, Steven Maier, and their colleagues subjected mongrel dogs to an uncontrollable stressor in the laboratory (Overmeir & Seligman, 1967; Seligman & Maier, 1967). They did not ask the dogs to do unsolvable anagrams. Instead, they used a stressor over which the researchers could have complete control: a painful electric shock. The experimental group of dogs received a series of uncontrollable shocks. Let us call this *Group E* for *experimental*. In addition, there were two control groups. One control group of dogs received shocks of the same magnitude as the dogs in the experimental group, but they could control the shocks by jumping over a short barrier in their cage. Let us call this *Group J* for *jump*. The dogs in this control group and the dogs in the Group E were yoked, that is, they received exactly the same number and duration of shocks. The only difference between the groups was that the dogs in Group E could not control their shocks, whereas the dogs in control Group J could. The second control group of dogs received no shock. Let us call this *Group N* for *none*.

The results of animal studies on learned helplessness have been used to explain the psychological problems of people living in chronically stressful environments.

Dogs in Group E initially responded to the shocks by jumping around their cages and protesting loudly. Soon, however, the majority became passive and simply hovered in one part of their cages, whimpering. Later, when the researchers provided the dogs with the opportunity to escape the shock by jumping over a barrier, the dogs did not learn to do this. It seemed that they had an expectation that they could not control the shock, so they were unable to recognize opportunities for control that arose. They seemed to have given up. The researchers labeled this set of behaviors *learned helplessness deficits* and argued that the dogs had learned they were helpless to control their situation.

The dogs in the controllable shock Group J, however, quickly learned how to control the shock and did not develop the learned helplessness deficits shown by the dogs in the uncontrollable shock group. The fact that the two groups of dogs experienced the same amount of shock suggests that lack of control and not the shock alone led to the learned helplessness deficits in the experimental group. The dogs in the control Group N that received no shock also did not develop learned helplessness deficits.

Seligman and colleagues likened the learned helplessness deficits shown by their dogs to the symptoms of depression in humans: apathy, low initiation of behavior, and the inability to see opportunities to improve one's environment (see Seligman, 1975). They argued that many human depressions result from people learning they have no control over important outcomes in their lives. This learned helplessness theory of depression seems helpful in explaining the depression and passivity seen in chronically oppressed groups , such as battered wives and some people who grow up in poverty.

A second type of animal study is similar to therapy outcome studies. In studies of the effectiveness of drugs, animals are often given the drugs to determine the effects of the drugs on different bodily systems and behaviors. Sometimes the animals are sacrificed after receiving the drugs so that detailed physiological analyses of the effects of the drugs can be determined. Obviously, such studies could not be done with humans. Animal studies of drugs are particularly useful in the early stages of research, when the possible side effects of the drugs are unknown.

Evaluating Animal Studies

There clearly are problems with animal studies, however (see Table 15.8). First, some people believe it is no more ethical to conduct painful, dangerous, or fatal experiments with animals than it is to do so with humans. Second, from a scientific vantage point, we must

Table 15.8 Evaluating Animal Studies

Advantages

They allow much more control over experiments.

Many people feel it is acceptable to subject animals to manipulations that most people consider unethical for human subjects.

These studies are especially useful in biological research on new drugs or procedures that might be dangerous.

Disadvantages

Treating animals cruelly is considered unethical by many people.

Results may not generalize to humans.

ask whether we can generalize the results of experiments with animals to humans. Are learned helplessness deficits in dogs really analogous to human depression? The debate over the ethical and scientific issues of animal research continues, sometimes leading animal rights advocates to engage in violent measures to stop animal research. Particularly in the case of research on drug effectiveness, however, animal research is crucial to the advancement of our knowledge of how to help people overcome psychopathology.

 What are your beliefs about the ethics of animal research? Where do these beliefs come from?

Single Case Studies

A final type of research methodology deserves mention, although it is not used frequently in scientific research in psychology these days despite its long history. This is the in-depth study of a single individual, referred to as a **single case study**. If we wanted to test in a case study our theory that stress causes depression, we would focus on one individual, interviewing her at length over a long period of time, to discover the links between periods of depression in her life and stressful events. We might also interview her close friends and family to obtain additional information about her history and depression. Based on the information we gathered, we would create a detailed description of the causes of her depressive episodes, with emphasis on the role of stressful events in these episodes.

For example, here is a brief case study of the singer Kurt Cobain of the hit 1990s rock band Nirvana. It was written a week after Cobain committed suicide:

single case study
in-depth analysis of a single individual

> **Case Study •** Cobain always had a fragile constitution (he was subject to bronchitis, as well as the recurrent stomach pains he claimed drove him to a heroin addiction). The image one gets is that of a frail kid batted between warring parents. "[The divorce] just destroyed his life," Wendy O'Connor tells Michael Azerrad in the Nirvana biography *Come As You Are.* "He changed completely. I think he was ashamed. And he became very inward—he just held everything [in]. . . . I think he's *still* suffering." As a teen, Cobain dabbled in drugs and punk rock and dropped out of school. His father persuaded him to pawn his guitar and take an entrance exam for the navy. But Cobain soon returned for the guitar. "To them, I was wasting my life," he told the *Los Angeles Times.* "To me, I was fighting for it." Cobain didn't speak to his father for 8 years. When Nirvana went to the top of the charts, Don Cobain began keeping a scrapbook. "Everything I know about Kurt," he told Azerrad, "I've read in newspapers and magazines."
>
> The more famous Nirvana became, the more Cobain wanted none of it. . . . Nirvana—with their stringy hair, plaid work shirts, and torn jeans—appealed to a mass of young fans who were tired of false idols like Madonna and Michael Jackson and

who'd never had a dangerous rock-and-roll hero to call their own. Unfortunately, the band also appealed to the sort of people Cobain had always hated: poseurs and band-wagoneers, not to mention record-company execs and fashion designers who fell over themselves cashing in on the new sights and sounds. Cobain, who'd grown up as an angry outsider, tried to shake his celebrity. . . .

By 1992, it became clear that Cobain's personal life was as tangled and troubling as his music. The singer married [Courtney] Love in Waikiki—the bride wore a moth-eaten dress once owned by actress Frances Farmer—and the couple embarked on a self-destructive pas de deux widely referred to as a 90s version of *Sid and Nancy*. As Cobain put it, "I was going off with Courtney and we were scoring drugs and we were f-- king up against a wall and stuff . . . and causing scenes just to do it. It was fun to be with someone who would stand up all of a sudden and smash a glass on the table." In September 1992, *Vanity Fair* reported that Love had used heroin while she was pregnant with [their daughter] Frances Bean. She and Cobain denied the story (the baby is healthy). But authorities were reportedly concerned enough to force them to surrender custody of Frances to Love's sister, Jamie, for a month, during which time the couple was, in Cobain's words, "totally suicidal." . . .

. . . [T]hose who knew the singer say there was a real fragility buried beneath the noise of his music and his life. . . . If only someone had heard the alarms ringing at that rambling, gray-shingled home near the lake. Long before there was a void in our hearts, there was a void in Kurt Cobain's. (Giles, 1994, pp. 46–47)

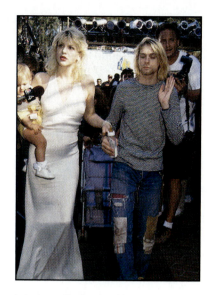

In-depth case histories of troubled people like Kurt Cobain may be rich in detail but not generalizable.

Evaluating Single Case Studies

Case studies are rich in the detail they provide about single individuals. They can help therapists understand how the events in a person's life affect his or her behaviors and emotions. Can we generalize to other populations what we learn in case studies? Do the circumstances leading to Kurt Cobain's death tell us anything about why other people commit suicide? Many researchers would say, "no."

Case studies also suffer from a lack of objectivity on the part of both the subject telling his or her story and the therapist or researcher listening to the story (see Table 15.9). The person telling his story might have biased recollections of his past and may selectively report events that happen to him in the present. The therapist or researcher listening to the story will filter the story through her beliefs and assumptions about the causes of human behavior and feelings and might selectively remember parts of the story that support her beliefs and assumptions and selectively forget parts of the story that do not. This possible lack of objectivity in case studies can result in extraordinary and distorted interpretations of a person's behaviors or feelings. Recall in Chapter 1 the analysis by Dr. Samuel Cartwright of the reasons slaves ran away from their masters in the 1800s. Based on his "case studies," Cartwright concluded that this behavior was due to a mental disorder specific to black people that caused them to desire freedom.

Case studies can still be found occasionally in medical journals, as reports of unusual reactions or side effects that patients have in response to a drug, basically as a warning to

Table 15.9 Evaluating Single Case Studies
Advantages
They provide detailed information about an individual.
They help therapists see how the events in a person's life may affect his or her behavior.
Disadvantages
Self-reports of subjects may be heavily biased.
Researchers' interpretations of participants' stories may be biased.
It is difficult to generalize case studies to other people.

Table 15.10 Methods of Testing Hypotheses: Putting It All Together

	Advantages	Disadvantages
Cross-Sectional Comparisons of Two Groups	They are relatively easy to conduct. They have produced valuable information on differences between important groups.	It is difficult to match groups on all third variables. Cause and effect cannot be teased apart. Vital information can be missed if observations are not made at the right time.
Longitudinal Studies	Differences between groups can be determined before the crucial event occurs. Groups can be followed long enough to assess both long-term and short-term reactions.	They are time-consuming and expensive to run. When the events of interest will happen cannot always be predicted.
Correlational Studies	They can take into account the range of participants' experiences. The researcher does not have to form two separate groups of participants.	Cause cannot be separated from effect. All third variables cannot be controlled.
Experimental Study I: Human Laboratory Studies	The researcher has more control over variables. Subjects can be randomly assigned to groups. Appropriate control groups can be created to rule out alternative explanation of important findings.	Results may not generalize to outside the laboratory. There are possible ethical limitations.
Experimental Study II: Therapy Outcome Studies	They provide help to people in distress as research is generated.	It is difficult to tell which aspect of therapy led to reduction in the psychopathology. They raise questions about appropriate control groups. There are ethical considerations about wait list control groups and placebo control groups. The patients' needs must be balanced with the need to administer standardized therapy. The generalizability of results to real-world delivery of therapy are unclear.
Experimental Study III: Animal Studies	They allow much more control of experiments. Many people feel it is acceptable to subject animals to manipulations that most people consider unethical for human subjects. These studies are especially useful in biological research on new drugs or procedures that might be dangerous.	Treating animals cruelly is considered unethical by many people. Results may not generalize to humans.
Single Case Studies	They provide detailed information about an individual. They help therapists see how the events in a person's life may affect his or her behavior.	Self-reports of subjects may be heavily biased. Researchers' interpretations of participants' stories may be biased. It is difficult to generalize case studies to other people.

other medical researchers and physicians to be aware of the possibility of such reactions. Because of their lack of generalizability and the lack of objectivity, case studies are rarely used these days in scientific research on the causes of psychopathology.

 Do you think case studies are valuable enough that their generalizability should not be as great a concern as it appears to be?

The Multimethod Approach Revisited

Although any one study will have its limitations, a **multimethod approach** that uses several of the research methods described here can build converging evidence in support of an hypothesis that can persuade even the most skeptical of researchers. It takes a systematic program of research, in which alternative explanations of previous findings are ruled out by new studies and gaps in understanding of a phenomenon are addressed, to build a convincing case for an hypothesis.

One good example of the multimethod approach is a program of study conducted by psychologist Laura Carstensen to determine why elderly people decrease their interactions with other people as they grow older. This phenomenon is illustrated in Figure 15.8, which shows that the older a person is, the fewer people he or she interacts with over a given period. Some other researchers had argued that this is the result of poor health or depression among the elderly—they do not interact with others because they do not feel well physically and emotionally. However, Carstensen and her colleagues found that even healthy older people are not very interested in making new friends or interacting with casual acquaintances. Carstensen hypothesized that older people are not avoiding people

multimethod approach investigation of a research question using a variety of research methods, each of which may contain inherent limitations, with the expectation that combining multiple methods may produce convergent evidence

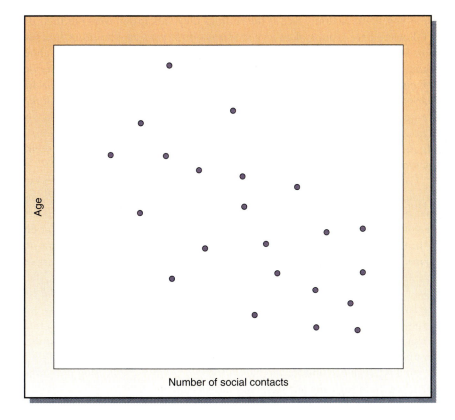

Figure 15.8

Reductions in Social Activity with Increasing Age. As people grow older, they reduce the number of people with whom they have social contact.
Source: Adapted from Carstensen, 1995.

altogether; they are just more choosy about with whom they want to be. They are more choosy because they recognize their time on this earth is short, and they want to maximize the emotional quality of their remaining time. Thus, they focus their time on close family and friends rather than on people they do not know well. Carstensen argues that it is not *age* per se that causes people to become more choosy about their interactions; it is the perception that time is short. Thus, anyone who perceives that the end is near will be choosy about social interactions and will make choices based on the expected emotional quality of those interactions (see Carstensen, 1995).

To test this hypothesis, Carstensen conducted several clever studies with different methodologies—she took a multimethod approach. For example, she conducted cross-sectional studies in which she interviewed young people, older people who were healthy, and older people who were ill. She hypothesized that older people who were ill would perceive the end of their lives as nearer than would the other two groups and thus would be the choosiest about social partners. This is what she found: Older ill people were most concerned with how emotionally positive their interactions with others were and made their choices of social partners based on their expectations of emotional quality. Older healthy people were also quite choosy and focused on emotional quality in their social interactions but not as much as the older ill people. Younger people were the least choosy and concerned with emotional quality in their social interactions. Younger people valued gaining new information from new acquaintances much more than older people did and made some of their choices of social partners accordingly (for example, by choosing to spend their time talking with the author of a book they recently read).

To test her hypothesis that it is not age but perception that the end is near that makes people choosy about social interactions, Carstensen also interviewed young people who perceived the end of their lives as near. These were men who had the HIV virus and active symptoms of AIDS. She compared these men's social choices to those of men who had the HIV virus but no symptoms of AIDS and to those of men without the HIV virus. She found that the HIV positive/symptomatic men were the most likely to focus on emotional quality in their social choices, the HIV positive/asymptomatic men were somewhat less likely, and the HIV negative men were the least likely.

One of Carstensen's colleagues, Barbara Fredrickson (1995), used longitudinal methods to investigate whether anticipated social endings would have similar effects on people's social interactions, even if the endings they anticipated were not their deaths. She followed three groups of college students—first-years, sophomores/juniors, and seniors—for 3 weeks near the end of the school year, asking them each day about the amount of emotional involvement they had with various social partners. Fredrickson found no differences among the groups in their emotional involvement with casual friends. However, the seniors, who were anticipating the ending of their time at college, were more emotionally involved with close friends than were the other two groups even though the groups did not differ in how many close friends they had (see Figure 15.9). These studies are examples of how cross-sectional and longitudinal studies, with all their limitations, can still provide vital information relevant to an hypothesis.

Carstensen conducted numerous human laboratory studies to test her theory. For example, she and her colleagues asked younger and older people to imagine themselves in each others' shoes. The younger people were asked to imagine they only had a short time left before they had to go far away. The older people were asked to imagine their doctors told them they would definitely live another 20 years in good health. Under these manipulations, the younger people made social choices that looked like those older people usually make: They chose to spend their time with close family members and friends. The older people made social choices that looked like those younger people usually make: They chose to spend some of their time meeting new and interesting people. This is a nice example of a human laboratory study in which the researcher controlled third variables and manipulated the independent variable to create changes in the dependent variable, all in a highly ethical manner that imposed no stress on the subjects.

So it is possible to find converging evidence for an hypothesis using a multimethod approach, even though any one study will have its limitations.

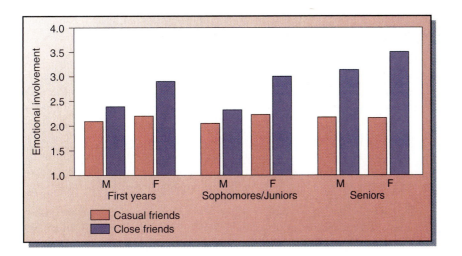

Figure 15.9

Emotional Involvement of College Students. Seniors had greater emotional involvement with close friends than did first years or sophomores/juniors, but there were no groups differences in involvement with casual acquaintances.

Source: Fredrickson, 1995.

Special Issues in Cross-Cultural Research

There is a welcome explosion of cross-cultural research in abnormal psychology. Researchers are investigating the similarities and differences across culture in the nature, causes, and treatment of psychopathology. Cross-cultural researchers face their own special challenges in addition to the ones common to all research (Kleinman & Good, 1985; Lebra, 1972; Rogler, 1989).

First, gaining access to the people one wants to study can be difficult. People who have never participated in research may be wary of cooperating with researchers. In addition, some cultures explicitly shun contact with outsiders. For example, the Old Order Amish, a religious sect who live in Pennsylvania, avoid contact with the "modern" world and live a simple agrarian life much like people lived in the eighteenth century. The Amish use horse and buggy as transportation, most of their homes do not have electricity or telephones, and there is little movement of people into or out of this culture. The Amish have been traditionally unwelcoming to researchers. Researcher Janice Egeland spent 20 years gaining the trust of the Amish, and eventually they allowed her to bring in a research team to study major psychopathology in the culture (Egeland & Hostetter, 1983). The result was some of the most exciting research ever published on cross-cultural similarities and differences in manic-depression. Most of us do not have 20 years to gain the trust of the people we want to study and thus will not chose to study populations that are that difficult to access. Nevertheless, most groups of people will take some time to "warm up" to research. Some things researchers can do to facilitate this "warming up" are to enlist the support of important leaders in the group, provide things that the group needs or wants in exchange for their participation, and learn the customs of the group and adhere to these customs in all interactions with the group.

Second, researchers must be careful in applying theories or concepts that were developed in one culture to another culture. Since the manifestations of disorders can differ across cultures, researchers who insist on narrow definitions of disorders may fail to identify many people suffering from disorders in culturally defined ways. Similarly, theoretical variables can have different meanings or manifestations across cultures. A good example is the variable known as *expressed emotion*. Families high in expressed emotion are highly critical and hostile toward other family members and emotionally over-involved with each other. Several studies of the majority cultures in America and Europe have shown that people with schizophrenia whose families are high in expressed emotion have higher rates of relapse than do those whose families are low in expressed emotion

(Brown, Birley, & Wing, 1972; Vaughn & Leff, 1976). The meaning and manifestation of expressed emotion can differ greatly across cultures, however:

> Criticism within Anglo-American family settings, for example, may focus on allegations of faulty personality traits (e.g., laziness) or psychotic symptom behaviors (e.g., strange ideas). However, in other societies, such as those of Latin America, the same behaviors may not be met with criticism. Among Mexican-descent families, for example, criticism tends to focus on disrespectful or disruptive behaviors that affect the family but not on psychotic symptom behavior and individual personality characteristics. Thus, culture plays a role in creating the content or targets of criticism. Perhaps most importantly, culture is influential in determining *whether* criticism is a prominent part of the familial emotional atmosphere. (Jenkins & Karno, 1992, p. 10)

Thus, today's researchers are more careful to search for culturally specific manifestations of the characteristics of interest in their studies and for the possibility that the characteristics or variables that predict psychopathology in one culture are irrelevant in other cultures.

Third, even if researchers believe they can apply their theories across cultures, they may have difficulty translating their questionnaires or other assessment tools into different languages. A key concept in English may not be precisely translated into another language. Subtle problems can arise because many languages contain variations on pronouns and verbs whose usage is determined by the social relationship between the speaker and the person being addressed. For example, in Spanish, the second-person pronoun *usted* connotes respect, establishes an appropriate distance in a social relationship, and is the correct way for a young interviewer to address an older respondent (Rogler, 1989). By contrast, when a young interviewer addresses a young respondent, the relationship is more informal, and the appropriate form of address is *tú*. If an interviewer violates the social norms implicit in a language, he or she can alienate a respondent and impair the quality of the research.

Fourth, there may be cultural or gender differences in people's responses to the social demands of interacting with researchers. For example, people of Mexican origin, older people, and people of lower socioeconomic class are more likely to answer "yes" to researchers' questions, regardless of the content, and to attempt to answer questions in socially desirable ways than are Anglo-Americans, younger people, and people of higher socioeconomic class. These differences appear to result from differences among groups in deference to authority figures and concern over presenting a proper appearance (Ross & Mirowsky, 1984). Similarly, it is often said that men are less likely than women to admit to "weaknesses" such as symptoms of distress or problems in coping. If researchers do not take biases into account when designing assessment tools and analyzing data, erroneous conclusions can result.

Fifth, researchers may face pressure to designate one culture as the healthy or normative one, and another other culture as the unhealthy or aberrant one. Researchers must constantly guard against such assumptions and must be willing to interpret differences simply as differences, acknowledging that each culture and gender has its healthy and unhealthy characteristics. A good example of a researcher who successfully fought pressure to find one culture deviant and his own culture healthy is psychologist Harold Stevenson. Stevenson studied differences in the educational systems of different countries and the consequences of these differences for children. One stereotype many Americans have of the Japanese educational system is that it drives young children mercilessly to achieve, creating smart but distressed students. Stevenson's extensive research comparing Japan and the United States found, however, that Japanese children were no more anxious, depressed, or unstable than were American children. However, Japanese children were much more advanced in many educational domains than were American children (see Figure 15.10). When Stevenson first began publishing his findings, they were met with protest and disbelief. He stuck to his findings, using various methodologies to provide additional evidence on differences and similarities between Japan, the United States, and other countries. His basic

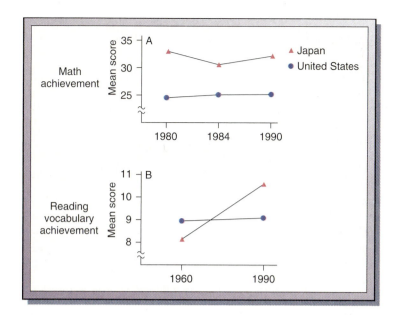

Figure 15.10

Differences Between Japanese and American Students in Math and Reading Achievement. Japanese students performed better than American students on tests of math and reading vocabulary. There were no differences in the emotional health of the two groups (not shown on graph).

Source: Stevenson, Chen, & Lee, 1993.

finding that Japanese children were well-educated *and* relatively happy has been confirmed many times since (Stevenson, Chen, & Lee, 1993). It has led researchers to search for ways that Japanese culture both motivates children to achieve and supports them emotionally.

 Do you think a researcher who is not from the culture he or she is studying can ever truly know what it is like to be a member of that culture?

Bio-Psycho-Social
INTEGRATION

Much of the research on abnormality takes an *interactionist* approach: Researchers assume that abnormality is the result of an interaction between characteristics of the person and characteristics of his or her situation. The characteristics of the person that make him or her more vulnerable to abnormality might include biological characteristics, such as genetic predisposition, or psychological characteristics, such as maladaptive styles of thinking about the world. These personal characteristics must interact with characteristics of the situation or environment to actually create the abnormality, however. For example, a woman with a genetic predisposition to schizophrenia may never develop the disorder in its full form if she has a supportive family and never faces major stressors.

Conducting research that reflects this interactionist perspective on abnormality is not easy. Researchers must gather information about people's biological, psychological, and social vulnerabilities and strengths. This may require specialized equipment or expertise. It may also require following subjects longitudinally to observe what happens when people with vulnerabilities face stressors that may trigger episodes of their disorders. Increasingly, researchers are working together in teams to share their expertise in specialized research methods and to share resources that make possible multidisciplinary longitudinal research. Researchers are also receiving training in disciplines and their methods that are not their primary disciplines. For example, psychologists are learning to use MRIs, PET scans, and other advanced biological methods to investigate abnormality. If you pursue a career researching abnormality, you may find yourself integrating methods from psychology (which have been the focus of this chapter), sociology, and biology to create the most comprehensive picture of the disorder you are investigating. This may seem a daunting task right now, but this integrationist approach holds the possibility of producing breakthroughs that greatly improve the lives of people vulnerable to psychopathology.

Chapter Summary

Researchers of abnormal behavior face certain special challenges. First, abnormal behaviors and feelings are difficult to measure objectively because research must rely to a large extent on people's self-reports. Second, people's behaviors and feelings change, often rapidly, complicating assessment. Third, most forms of abnormality probably have multiple causes, and no one study can investigate all possible causes simultaneously. Fourth, ethical concerns limit researchers' abilities to manipulate variables of interest. These challenges require a multimethod approach, in which a variety of methodologies are used to research questions of interest.

An hypothesis is a statement of what we believe will happen in a study. The primary hypothesis is the one we believe to be true based on our theory. The null hypothesis is the alternative to our primary hypothesis, stating there is no relationship between the independent variable and the dependent variable. The dependent variable is the factor we are trying to predict in our study. The independent variable is the factor we are using to predict the dependent variable.

In any study, the variables of interest must be operationalized: The researcher must decide how to measure or manipulate the variable. A sample is a group of people taken from our population of interest to participate in our study. The samples for the study must be representative of the population of interest, and the research must be generalizable to the population of interest. A control group is a group of people similar in most ways to our primary group of interest, but who do not experience the variable our theory says causes changes in our dependent variable. Matching our control group to our group of primary interest can help to control third variables, which are variables unrelated to our theory that may still have some effect on our dependent variable.

Cross-sectional comparisons of groups are often used to test hypotheses about a psychopathology. The groups being compared may differ on the variable thought to create psychopathology. Statistical tests are used to determine if differences among the groups in the dependent variable are significant. Cross-sectional studies are relatively easy to conduct and have produced valuable information. The disadvantages of cross-sectional studies are that they cannot separate cause from consequence and only represent a specific slice of time, rather than the dynamic process through which many psychopathologies unfold.

Longitudinal studies allow researchers to follow people over time to determine whether certain factors are associated with the onset of psychopathology. These studies allow researchers to follow subjects for long enough to assess both short-term and long-term reactions to events. The disadvantages of longitudinal studies are that they are time-consuming and expensive to run and we cannot always predict when the events we are interested in will happen. In addition, while they allow a researcher to tease apart cause and consequence more than a cross-sectional study does, they still do not allow the researcher to determine definitively whether a factor is the cause of psychopathology.

Correlational studies can be either cross-sectional or longitudinal. Many correlational studies focus on continuous variables, which are variables measured along a continuum. They allow the researcher to consider a wider range of experiences among subjects than do studies simply comparing two groups. However, correlational studies cannot establish causality.

Experimental studies provide more definitive evidence that a given variable causes psychopathology. A human laboratory study has the goal of inducing the conditions that we hypothesize will lead to our outcome of interest (such as increasing stress to cause depression) in people in a controlled setting. People are randomly assigned to either the experimental group, which receives a manipulation, or a control group, which does not. Generalizing experimental studies to real-world phenomena is sometimes not possible, however. In addition, manipulating people who are in distress in an experimental study can create ethical problems.

A special type of experimental study is the therapy outcome study. This type of study allows researchers to test an hypothesis about the causes of a psychopathology while providing a service to subjects. Still, there are several difficult issues researchers face with therapy outcome studies. These include problems in knowing what elements of therapy were effective, questions about the appropriate control groups to use, questions about whether to allow modifications of the therapy to fit individual subjects' needs, and the lack of generalizability of the results of these studies to the real world. In therapy outcome studies, researchers sometimes use wait list control groups, in which control subjects wait to receive the interventions after the studies are completed. Or they may try to construct psychological placebo control groups, in which subjects receive the general support of therapists but none of the elements of the therapy thought to be active. Both of these types of control groups have practical and ethical limitations, however.

Animal studies allow researchers to manipulate their subjects in ways that are not ethically permissible with human subjects, although many people feel that such animal studies are equally unethical. Animal studies suffer from problems in generalizability to humans, however. Single case studies of individuals provide rich and detailed information about their subjects but also suffer from generalizability problems.

In doing cross-cultural or cross-gender research, researchers face other challenges. Access to the populations of interest can be difficult. Theories or concepts that make sense in one culture or gender may not be applicable to other cultures or the other gender. Questionnaires and other assessment tools must be translated accurately. Culture and gender can affect how people respond to the social demands of research. Finally, researchers must be careful not to build into their research assumptions that one culture or gender is the healthy or normal one and another other culture or gender is the deviant one.

Key Terms

hypothesis 519
null hypothesis 519
variable 519
dependent variable 519
independent variable 519
stressor 520
operationalization 520
sample 522
representative sample 522
generalization 522

matching 522
third variable 522
significantly different 523
longitudinal study 525
prospective longitudinal study 525
correlational study 527
continuous variable 527
correlation 527
control group 529
experimental group 529

therapy outcome study 532
wait list control group 533
placebo control group 533
double-blind experiment 533
single case study 536
multimethod approach 539

Application

How to Write a Report of a Study

Once you have conducted a study testing your hypothesis, how do you write a report on the study? You may have looked at research reports in journals of psychology or psychiatry and wondered about the organization and purpose of the various sections of the reports. Following is an outline and description of the major sections of a report of results of a psychology experiment, according to the style approved by the American Psychological Association (APA, 1983).

Title Page

The title page presents the title of your paper, your name and affiliation (your school or the hospital, clinic, foundation, research center, or company you work for), and a running head, or shortened version of your title that will appear in the upper right-hand corner of the remaining pages of your paper. If you are making a presentation of your paper at a conference or your paper has been accepted for publication in a journal, this can be noted near the bottom of the title page. An example of a title page for our study of bereavement and depression follows:

Depression Levels in Recently Bereaved
and Non-bereaved Subjects

Leonor Ruiz and Leslie Howland
The State University

Running Head: Depression-Related
Bereavement

Paper presented to the annual meeting of
the American Psychological Association,
August 14, 1993, Toronto, Ontario.

Abstract

The abstract is a short description of the purpose, design, and results of your study, usually no longer than 200 words. It is presented on a separate page, just after the title page. The abstract for our study of bereavement and depression might read as follows:

Abstract

Levels of depression were assessed by observers through a structured clinical interview in 50 recently bereaved adults identified through county mortality records and a comparison group of 50 adults matched for sex, age, race/ethnicity, and socioeconomic class. The comparison group was identified through census records. The bereaved sample had levels of depression that were significantly higher than the comparison group (Means = 62 and 44, respectively, $p < 0.05$). Similarly, more members of the bereaved group qualified for a diagnosis of a major depressive disorder than members of the comparison group (20% versus 5%, respectively, $p < 0.05$). We discuss the aspects of bereavement that may lead to an elevated risk of depression, and whether bereavement-related depressions should be considered psychopathology or normal reactions.

Introduction

The introduction to your paper begins on the page immediately following the abstract. In the introduction, you review previous studies and theoretical works relevant to your study and justify the need for your study. This justification might be that previous studies have not addressed your specific hypothesis or research question or that the previous studies that have been conducted were flawed in some way that your study will correct. Make sure that you clearly state your hypothesis at some point in the introduction, so readers will know exactly what your study is intended to test.

You should provide citations to all the articles or books you refer to in the body of your paper. If there is only one author of the article or book, simply give the author's last name and the year the book or article was published. If you are using the author's last name as part of the sentence, then only the year of publication goes in parentheses. For example, "Chang (1988) found that recently bereaved people . . .". If the author's name is not part of the sentence, put both the name and the year of publication in parentheses: "One recent study confirmed our results (Chang, 1988)." If there are two authors of the book or article, give both authors' names every time you cite their work: "Chang and Hsu (1988) found that . . ." or "One recent study confirmed our results (Chang & Hsu, 1988)." Note that you use the word *and* between the authors' names when the names are part of the sentence but the symbol & between the authors' names when the names are put in parentheses. When there are three or more authors of a book or article, give all the authors' names the first time you cite their work (unless there are 6 or more authors; then only give the first three, followed by the phrase *et al.*). The remaining citations to their work should provide only the name of the first author, followed by the phrase *et al.* and the year of publication: "Chang, Hsu, and Kuo (1988) found that . . ." (first citation); "Chang et al. (1988) also found that . . . (second citation).

The full references to all the works you cite in your paper should be provided in the references section at the end of the paper.

Method

The method section usually has three subsections. The participants subsection provides a detailed description of the participants in your study (their numbers, ages, genders, socio-economic classes, racial/ethnic distribution) and your methods for recruiting them. The materials subsection provides details of the questionnaires, rating scales, interview questions, tasks, or any other materials you used in your study. The procedures subsection describes how you went about conducting your study. In a questionnaire study, describe where and how participants completed the questionnaires (e.g., as part of a big group or individually in a private room). In an interview study, describe where and how the interviews were conducted and by whom. In an experimental study, describe the details of the manipulations you used and exactly what the participant was made to do over the course of the experiment.

Results

The results section describes the outcome of your study, such as differences between groups on your key variables or correlations between variables, and the results of statistical tests that indicate whether these outcomes were significant (or whether they occurred simply by chance). You might want to present some of your results (e.g., the mean depression scores of your two groups) in a table. A short results section for our study of bereavement and depression might read as follows:

Results
The mean score of the bereaved group on the depression rating scale (M = 62) was

Application continued

significantly higher than the mean score for the comparison groups (M = 44), $p < .05$. In addition, 20% of the bereaved group qualified for a diagnosis of a major depressive episode, whereas only 5% of the comparison group qualified for this diagnosis. Thus, whether depression is indexed as level of symptoms on a continuous scale or as a diagnosis of major depressive episode, the bereaved group showed more depression than the comparison group.

Discussion

In the discussion section, discuss the implications of your findings. Indicate whether your hypothesis was supported by the results of your study and address any alternative explanations for your results. Acknowledge any major weaknesses in your study. Be careful to not draw conclusions from your study that are too generous or extreme. Always remember that no individual study can prove a theory or hypothesis definitively, and there are always questions about the generalizability of any study to the population at large.

References

The formats for referencing some of the most common types of works cited in psychology papers can be found in the *Publication Manual of the American Psychological Association* (APA, 1983). ∎

chapter 16 Society and Mental Health

Judgments About People Accused of Crimes

Mental health professionals are called upon to help determine if accused people are competent to stand trial and if accused people were "sane" at the time crimes were committed. The insanity defense has undergone many changes in recent history, often in response to its use in high profile crimes. It is based on the notion that a person who was mentally incapacitated at the time of a crime should not be held responsible for the crime.

Involuntary Commitment and Patients' Rights

People can be committed involuntarily to psychiatric facilities if they are gravely disabled by psychological disorders or are imminent dangers to themselves or others. These criteria are difficult to apply accurately and consistently. The deinstitutionalization movement led to many long-term psychiatric patients being released, but unfortunately, community-based facilities for helping these people are often inadequate.

Gender and Ethnicity Issues

Women and minority group members are more likely than others to be judged incompetent to stand trial, whereas white people and men are more likely to plead the insanity defense. Violence among mentally ill women may be underestimated by clinicians.

Clinicians' Duties to Clients and Society

Some specific duties clinicians have are the duties to provide competent and appropriate treatment; to avoid multiple relationships, especially sexual relationships, with clients; and to protect clients' confidentiality. Client confidentiality can be broken, however, when clients are threatening others or abusing children or elderly people.

Family Law and Mental Health Professionals

Three areas of family law in which mental health professionals are increasingly involved are child custody disputes between divorcing parents, child maltreatment cases, and adult accusations about their molestation during childhood.

Bio-Psycho-Social Integration
Chapter Summary
Key Terms
Application: *Guidelines for Ethical Service to Culturally Diverse Populations*

All, too, will bear in mind this sacred principle, that though the will of the majority is in all cases to prevail, that will to be rightful must be reasonable; that the minority possess their equal rights, which equal law must protect, and to violate would be oppression.

—Thomas Jefferson, First Inaugural Address (1801)

Paul Klee
Sun and Moon
(Subtitled Starker Traum)

> **Case Study** • A 60-year-old man wanders the streets as the temperature plummets below freezing, talking to imaginary creatures and stripping off his warm clothes. When asked if he wants shelter or food, he curses and turns away. The police apprehend the man and bring him to court. A psychologist is asked to determine whether the man is such a danger to himself that he should be held against his will.
>
> **Case Study** • The parents of two young children are going through a bitter divorce, each claiming that he or she should have custody of the children because the other is an incompetent and abusive parent. The court asks a social worker to assist in determining the best custody arrangement for the children.
>
> **Case Study** • A middle-aged man kills three people in a shooting rampage. When arrested, he says that he was obeying voices telling him to shoot "sinners." A psychiatrist is asked to evaluate whether this man is telling the truth.
>
> **Case Study** • A college student who has been depressed for some time begins to remember events from her childhood that suggest she may have been sexually abused by her father. She seeks out a therapist to determine if these memories are real.

Situations such as these raise fundamental questions about society's values: Do people have the right to conduct their lives as they wish, even if their behaviors pose a risk to their own health and well-being? Under what conditions should people be absolved of responsibility for behaviors that harm others? Does society have a right or an obligation to intervene in troubled families? Should the diagnosis of a psychological disorder entitle a person to special services and protection against discrimination? Questions such as these are concerned with the values of personal freedom, the obligation of society to protect its vulnerable members, the right of society to protect itself against the actions of individuals, and the sanctity of the family.

Mental health professionals are increasingly being brought into such situations to help individuals and society make judgments about the appropriate actions to take. It would be nice if mental health professionals could simply turn to the research literature for "objective" information that indicates which judgment is best in each situation. Frequently, however, there is no research literature relevant to a situation or the research holds conflicting messages. Moreover, at its best, research can only tell us what is *likely* to be right or true in a given situation but not what is *definitely* right or true. That is, the predictions we can make from the research literature are probabilistic—they tell us how likely people are to do something but not that they definitely will do something. Also, we are limited in our ability to generalize from the research literature to individual cases. Finally, because most of such judgments involve conflicts between different values, ethical principles, or moral principles, research and clinical judgment can only tell us so much about the right resolution.

One ethical question facing society is whether we have an obligation to provide mental health services to people who cannot take care of themselves.

In this chapter, we explore some of the tough judgment calls that mental health professionals are asked to help society make with regard to people who may have psychological disorders. This chapter is about the interface between psychology and the law. Throughout this chapter appears a phrase not seen frequently in other chapters of the book: **mentally ill**. We have refrained from using this phrase in most previous chapters because it connotes a medical view of psychological problems, which is only one of several ways to view psychological problems. The literature we will review in this chapter, however, commonly uses phrases such as *mental illness* or *mental disease*. As these phrases suggest, the law has tended to regard at least some psychological disorders as medical illnesses or diseases. We shall see, however, that the law is inconsistent in its view of psychological disorders, and this view has changed quite frequently.

In this chapter, we will first examine how the law regards people charged with crimes who might have psychological disorders. Mental health professionals help legal authorities decide when people's psychological disorders make them incompetent to stand trial and when they should be considered not guilty by reason of insanity. Then we will discuss when a person can be held in a mental health facility against his or her will—a procedure known as *civil commitment*. Over the last 50 years, the criteria for commitment and the rights of committed patients have changed greatly. Next, we will discuss certain duties that courts and professional organizations have argued clinicians have toward clients and society: the duty to provide competent treatment, the duty to avoid multiple relationships with clients, the duty to maintain clients' confidentiality, the duty to protect persons their clients are threatening to harm, and the duty to report suspected child or elder abuse. Finally, we end with a discussion of three areas in which mental health professionals are increasingly becoming involved: child custody disputes in divorce proceedings, child maltreatment cases, and claims by adults that they have recovered repressed memories of childhood sexual abuse.

mentally ill
legal description of an individual who purportedly suffers from a mental illness, which is analogous (in this view) to suffering from a medical disease

Judgments About People Accused of Crimes

Two critical judgments that mental health professionals are asked to make about people accused of crimes are whether they are competent to stand trial and whether they were sane at the time the crimes were committed. Mental health professionals actually do not make the final judgments about the dispensation of people accused of crimes; they only make recommendations to the court. Their recommendations can be influential in judges' or juries' decisions, however.

Competency to Stand Trial

One of the fundamental principles of law is that, in order to stand trial, accused individuals must have a rational understanding of the charges against them and the proceedings of the trial and must be able to participate in their defense. People who do not have an understanding of what is happening to them in a courtroom and who cannot participate in their own defense are said to be **incompetent to stand trial**. Each year, over 25,000 people in the United States and over 5,000 people in Canada are referred to mental health professionals for evaluation of their competency to stand trial (Nicholson & Kugler, 1991). Competency judgments are thus some of the most frequent types of judgments that mental health professionals are asked to make for courts. Judges appear to value the testimony of mental health experts concerning defendants' competency and rarely rule against the experts' recommendations. As a result, the consequences of competency judgments for defendants are great. If they are judged incompetent, trials are postponed as long as there is some reason to believe that they will become competent in the foreseeable future. Incompetent defendants who are wrongly judged competent may not contribute adequately to their defense and may be wrongly convicted and incarcerated.

incompetent to stand trial
legal status of an individual who lacks a rational understanding of the charges against him or her, an understanding of the proceedings of his or her trial, or the ability to participate in his or her own defense

Not surprisingly, defendants with long histories of psychiatric problems are more likely to be referred for competency evaluations (Nicholson & Kugler, 1991). In addition, defendants referred for competency evaluations tend to have lower levels of education and to be poor, unemployed, and unmarried. Over half have been accused of violent offenses.

What determines whether a defendant referred for a competency evaluation is judged competent or incompetent? Psychologists have developed tests of cognitive abilities important to following legal proceedings, and people who perform poorly on these tests are more likely to be judged incompetent to stand trial. These tests are not widely used, however. Instead, judgments of incompetence are usually given to people who have existing diagnoses of psychotic disorders or who have symptoms indicating severe psychopathology, such as gross disorientation, delusions, hallucinations, and thought disorder (Nicholson & Kugler, 1991).

What should happen to someone who continues to be incompetent to stand trial for months or even years after a crime was committed?

Insanity Defense

insanity
legal term denoting a state of mental incapacitation during the time a crime was committed

Insanity is actually a legal term rather than a psychological or medical term, and it has been defined in various ways, as we will explore shortly. All of these definitions reflect the fundamental doctrine that people cannot be held fully responsible for their acts if they are so mentally incapacitated at the time of the acts that they cannot conform to the rules of society. Note that people do not have to be chronically insane for the insanity defense to apply. They only have to be judged to have been insane at the time they committed the acts. Obviously, this can be a difficult judgment to make.

The insanity defense has been one of the most controversial applications of psychology to the law. The lay public often thinks of the insanity defense as a means by which guilty people "get off." When the insanity defense has been used successfully in celebrated cases, as when John Hinckley successfully used this defense after shooting former President Ronald Reagan and the president's press secretary Jim Brady, there have been calls to eliminate the insanity defense altogether. Indeed, these celebrated cases have often led to reappraisals of the insanity defense and redefinitions of the legal meaning of insanity, as we shall consider next.

The insanity defense is used much less often than the public tends to think. As is shown in Table 16.1, fewer than 1 in 100 defendants in felony cases file insanity pleas, and of these only 26 percent result in acquittal (Silver, Cirincione, & Steadman, 1994). Thus, only about 1 in 400 people charged with a felony is judged not guilty by reason of insanity. About two-thirds of these people have diagnoses of schizophrenia, and most have histories of psychiatric hospitalizations and previous crimes (McGreevy, Steadman, & Callahan, 1991).

Even when a defendant is judged not guilty by reason of insanity, it usually is not the case that he or she "gets off." Of those people acquitted because of insanity, about 85 percent are still sent to mental hospitals, and all but 1 percent are put under some type of supervision and care. Of those who are sent to mental hospitals, the average length of stay (or incarceration) in the hospital is almost 3 years when all types of crimes are considered, and over 6 years for those who had been accused (and acquitted by reason of insanity) of murder. John Hinckley, who shot former President Reagan in 1981, has been incarcerated in St. Elizabeth's Hospital since he was found not

John Hinckley was judged not guilty by reason of insanity for shooting President Ronald Reagan. This judgment inspired a reappraisal of the insanity defense.

Table 16.1 Comparison of Public Perceptions of the Insanity Defense with Actual Use and Results

The public perceives that many more accused persons use the insanity defense successfully than is actually the case.

	Public Perception	Reality
Percentage of felony indictments for which an insanity plea is made	37%	1%
Percentage of insanity pleas resulting in "not guilty by reason of insanity"	44%	26%
Percentage of persons "not guilty by reason of insanity" sent to mental hospitals	51%	85%
Percentage of persons "not guilty by reason of insanity" set free	26%	15%
Conditional release		12%
Outpatient treatment		3%
Unconditional release		1%
Length of confinement of persons "not guilty by reason of insanity" (in months)		
All crimes	21.8	32.5
Murder		76.4

Source: Data from R. L. Silver, et al., 1994.

guilty by reason of insanity. Some states require that people judged not guilty by reason of insanity cannot be incarcerated in mental institutions for longer than they would have served prison sentences if they had been judged guilty of their crimes, but not all states have this rule. Thus, there is little evidence that the insanity defense is widely used to help people avoid incarceration for their crimes.

What accounts for the widespread belief in the lay public that many criminals plead the insanity defense successfully and "get off"?

There are five rules that have been used in modern history to evaluate defendants' pleas that they should be judged not guilty by reason of insanity (see Table 16.2). The first is the **M'Naghten Rule**. Daniel M'Naghten lived in England in the mid-1800s and had the delusion that the English Tory party was persecuting him. He set out to kill the Tory prime minister but mistakenly shot the prime minister's secretary. At his trial, the jury judged M'Naghten not guilty by reason of insanity. There was a public outcry at this verdict, leading the House of Lords to formalize a rule for when a person could be absolved from responsibility for his or her acts because of a mental disorder. This rule became known as the *M'Naghten Rule*, and it still is used in many jurisdictions today:

> To establish a defense on the ground of insanity, it must be clearly proved that at the time of committing the act, the party accused was labouring under such a defect of reason, from disease of the mind, as not to know the nature and quality of the act he was doing, or if he did know it, that he did not know he was doing what was wrong.

The M'Naghten rule reflects the doctrine that a person must have a "guilty mind"—in Latin, *mens rea*—or the intention to commit the illegal act in order to be held responsible for the act.

It might seem that applying the M'Naghten Rule is a straightforward matter—one simply determines whether a person suffers from a disease of the mind and whether during the crime he or she understood that his or her actions were wrong. Unfortunately, it

M'Naghten Rule
legal principle stating that an accused criminal must have been suffering from a mental disease at the time he or she committed a crime and have known neither the nature and quality of the act nor that the act was wrong in order to be judged as insane

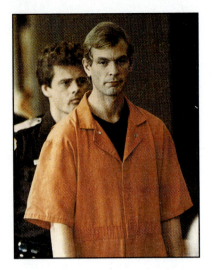

Serial killer Jeffrey Dahmer clearly had psychological problems, but his insanity defense was not accepted because he took care to hide his crimes from the police, suggesting he knew what he was doing was wrong.

Five different criteria have been used for determining whether an individual was insane at the time he or she committed a crime and therefore whether he or she should not be held responsible for the crime.

Rule	The individual is not held responsible for a crime if . . .
M'Naghten Rule	At the time of the crime, the individual was so affected by a disease of the mind that he or she did not know the nature of the act he or she was committing or did not know it was wrong.
Irresistible Impulse Rule	At the time of the crime, the individual was driven by an irresistible impulse to perform the act or had a diminished capacity to resist performing the act.
Durham Rule	The crime was a product of a mental disease or defect.
ALI Rule	At the time of the crime, as a result of mental disease or defect, the person lacked substantial capacity either to appreciate the criminality of the act or to conform his or her conduct to the law.
American Psychiatric Association Definition	At the time of the crime, as a result of mental disease or mental retardation, the person was unable to appreciate the wrongfulness of his or her conduct.

is not that simple. A major problem in applying the M'Naghten Rule emerges in determining what is meant by a "disease of the mind." The law has been unclear and inconsistent in what disorders it recognizes as diseases of the mind. The most consistently recognized diseases are psychoses. It has been relatively easy for the courts and the public to accept that someone experiencing severe delusions and hallucinations is suffering from a disease and, at times, may not know right from wrong. However, defendants have argued that several other disorders, such as alcoholism, severe depression, and post-traumatic stress disorder, are diseases of the mind that impair judgments of right and wrong. It is much more difficult for courts, the lay public, and mental health professionals to agree on these claims.

A second major problem is that the M'Naghten Rule requires that a person have not known right from wrong at the time of the crime in order to be judged not guilty by reason of insanity. This is a difficult judgment to make because it is a retrospective judgment. In addition, even when everyone agrees that a defendant suffers from a severe psychological disorder, this does not necessarily mean that, at the time of the crime, he or she was incapable of knowing "right from wrong" as the M'Naghten Rule requires. For example, the serial killer Jeffrey Dahmer, who tortured, killed, dismembered, and ate his victims, clearly seemed to have a psychological disorder. Nevertheless, the jury denied his insanity defense in part because he took great care to hide his crimes from the local police, suggesting that he knew what he was doing was "wrong" or against the law.

The second rule used to judge the acceptability of the insanity defense is the **irresistible impulse rule**. First applied in Ohio in 1934, the irresistible impulse rule broadened the conditions under which a criminal act could be considered the product of insanity to include "acts of passion." Even if a person knew the act he was committing was wrong, if he was driven by an irresistible impulse to perform the act or had a diminished capacity to resist performing the act, then he could be absolved of responsibility for performing the act. One of the most celebrated applications of the notion of diminished capacity was the "Twinkie Defense" of Dan White. In 1979, Dan White assassinated San Francisco mayor George Moscone and a city council member named Harvey Milk. White argued that he had had diminished capacity to resist the impulse to shoot Moscone and Milk due to the psychological effects of extreme stress and the consumption of large amounts of junk food. Using a particularly broad definition of diminished capacity in force in California law at the time, the jury convicted White of manslaughter instead of first-degree murder.

In 1954, Judge David Bazelon further broadened the criteria for the legal definition of insanity in his ruling on the case *Durham v. United States*, which produced the third rule for defining insanity, the **Durham Rule**. According the Durham Rule, the insanity defense could be accepted for any crimes that were the "product of mental disease or

irresistible impulse rule
legal principle stating that even a person who knowingly performs a wrongful act can be absolved of responsibility if he or she is driven by an irresistible impulse to perform the act or had a diminished capacity to resist performing the act

Durham Rule
legal principle stating that the presence of mental disorder is sufficient to absolve a criminal of responsibility for a crime

mental defect." This allowed defendants to claim that the presence of any disorder recognized by mental health professionals could be the "cause" of their crimes. The Durham Rule did not require that defendants show they were incapacitated by their disorders or that they did not understand that their acts were illegal. The Durham Rule was eventually dropped by almost all jurisdictions by the early 1970s.

The fourth rule for deciding the acceptability of the insanity defense comes from the American Law Institute's Model Penal Code. Motivated by dissatisfaction with the existing legal definitions of insanity, a group of lawyers, judges, and scholars associated with the American Law Institute worked to formulate a better definition, which eventually resulted in what is known as the **ALI rule**:

> A person is not responsible for criminal conduct if at the time of such conduct as the result of mental disease or defect he lacks substantial capacity either to appreciate the criminality (wrongfulness) of his conduct or to conform his conduct to the requirements of the law.

This rule is broader than the M'Naghten Rule because it requires only that the defendant have a lack of appreciation of the criminality of his or her act, not an absence of understanding of the criminality of the act. The defendant's inability to conform his or her conduct to the requirements of the law could come from the emotional symptoms of a psychological disorder as well as from the cognitive deficits caused by the disorder. This expanded understanding incorporates some of the crimes recognized by the irresistible impulse doctrine. The ALI Rule is clearly more restrictive than the Durham Rule, however, because it requires some lack of appreciation of the criminality of one's act rather than merely the presence of a mental disorder. The ALI further restricted the types of mental disorders that could contribute to a successful insanity defense:

> As used in this Article, the term "mental disease or defect" does not include an abnormality manifested only by repeated criminal or otherwise antisocial conduct.

This further restriction prohibited defense attorneys from arguing that a defendant's long history of antisocial acts was itself evidence of the presence of a mental disease or defect. Further, in 1977, in the case *Barrett v. United States*, it was ruled that "temporary insanity created by voluntary use of alcohol or drugs" also did not qualify a defendant for acquittal by reason of insanity.

The ALI was widely adopted in the United States, including in the jurisdiction in which John Hinckley was tried for shooting Ronald Reagan. Hinckley had a longstanding diagnosis of schizophrenia, plus an obsession with the actress Jodi Foster. Letters he wrote to Foster before shooting Reagan indicated that he committed the act under the delusion that this would impress Foster and cause her to return his love. Hinckley's defense attorneys successfully argued that he had a diminished capacity to understand the wrongfulness of shooting Reagan or to conform his behaviors to the requirements of the law. The public outcry over the judgment that Hinckley was "not guilty by reason of insanity" initiated another reappraisal of the legal definition of insanity and the use of the insanity defense.

This reappraisal led to the fifth legal redefinition of insanity, the **Insanity Defense Reform Act,** put into law by Congress in 1984. The Insanity Defense Reform Act adopted a legal definition of insanity proposed by the **American Psychiatric Association definition** of insanity in 1983. This definition dropped the provision in the ALI Rule that absolved people of responsibility for criminal acts if they were unable to conform their behavior to the law and retained the wrongfulness criterion initially proposed in the M'Naghten Rule. This definition reads as follows:

> A person charged with a criminal offense should be found not guilty by reason of insanity if it is shown that, as a result of mental disease or mental retardation, he was unable to appreciate the wrongfulness of his conduct at the time of his offense.

This definition now applies in all cases tried in federal courts and in about half the states. Also following the Hinckley verdict, most states now require that a defendant pleading not

ALI Rule
legal principle stating that a person is not responsible for criminal conduct if he or she lacks the capacity to appreciate the criminality (wrongfulness) of the act or to conform his or her conduct to the requirements of the law as a result of mental disease

Insanity Defense Reform Act
1984 law that affects all federal courts and about half of the state courts that finds a person not guilty by reason of insanity if it is shown that, as a result of mental disease or mental retardation, the accused was unable to appreciate the wrongfulness of his or her conduct at the time of the offense

American Psychiatric Association definition
definition of insanity stating that people cannot be held responsible for their conduct if, at the time they commit crimes, as the result of mental disease or mental retardation they are unable to appreciate the wrongfulness of their conduct

guilty by reason of insanity prove he or she was insane at the time of the crime; previously, the burden of proof had been on the prosecution to prove that the defendant was sane at the time the crime was committed (Steadman et al., 1993).

In a sixth and most recent reform of the insanity defense, some states have adopted as an alternative to the verdict "not guilty by reason of insanity" the verdict **guilty but mentally ill (GBMI).** Defendants convicted as guilty but mentally ill are incarcerated for the normal terms designated for their crimes, with the expectation that they will also receive treatment for their mental illness. Proponents of the GBMI argue that it recognizes the mental illness of defendants while still holding them responsible for their actions. Critics argue that the GBMI verdict is essentially a guilty verdict and a means of eliminating the insanity defense (Tanay, 1992). In addition, juries may believe they are ensuring that a person gets treatment by judging him or her guilty but mentally ill, but there are no guarantees that a person convicted under GBMI will receive treatment. In most states, it is left up to legal authorities to decide whether to incarcerate these people in mental institutions or prisons and, if they are sent to prisons, whether to provide them with treatment for their mental illness.

guilty but mentally ill (GBMI)
verdict that requires a convicted criminal to serve the full sentence designated for his or her crime, with the expectation that he or she will also receive treatment for mental illness

Professional Concerns About the Insanity Defense

Mental health professionals tend to be strong proponents of the notion that psychological disorders can impair people's ability to follow the law and therefore should be taken into consideration when judging an individual's responsibility for his or her actions. Mental health professionals are often called upon to provide expert opinions in such cases. Unfortunately, there can be disagreement among experts about the nature and causes of psychological disorders, the presence or absence of psychological disorders, and the evaluation of defendants' states of mind at the time crimes were committed. This disagreement leads to confusion in judges, juries, and the public.

Mental health professionals have also raised concerns about the rules used to determine the acceptability of the insanity defense. Behind these rules is the assumption that most people, including most people with psychological disorders, have free will and can usually choose how they will act in any given situation. Many current models of both normal and abnormal behavior suggest that people are not that much in control of their behaviors. Because of biological predispositions, early life experiences, or disordered patterns of thinking, people often act in irrational and perhaps uncontrolled ways. This view makes it more difficult to say when a person should or should not be held responsible for his or her behaviors.

Susan Smith drowned her two young sons in 1994. Although she had a troubled history, the public was not prepared to excuse her act because of her history.

This controversy was played out recently in the trial of Susan Smith, the South Carolina woman who drowned her two young sons in 1994. Smith and her lawyers argued that Smith's childhood history of abuse and neglect led her to become desperate for love, impulsive, and self-destructive. She was a young, single mother with few prospects for the future. Moreover, she was in an extreme state of distress in the days before her crime over the breakup of a relationship with a man who said he was not prepared for the responsibility of children. All this culminated, Smith's attorneys initially argued, in Smith's impulsively drowning her sons. Although this scenario is plausible according to many psychological theories, the public and many mental health professionals were very resistant to exonerating Smith from her act because of her background. Smith eventually decided not to use the insanity defense and was convicted of the two murders.

Would you be less likely to accept the insanity defense for someone who killed his or her children than for someone who killed his or her spouse? Why or why not?

Summing Up | Judgments About People Accused of Crimes

- One judgment mental health professionals are asked to make is about an accused person's competency to stand trial.
- Another judgment is whether the accused person was "sane" at the time he or she committed a crime.
- The insanity defense has undergone many changes over recent history, often in response to its use in high profile crimes.
- Five different rules have been used to evaluate the acceptability of a plea of not guilty by reason of insanity: the M'Naghten Rule, the irresistible impulse rule, the Durham Rule, the ALI Rule, and the American Psychiatric Association definition.
- All of these rules require that the defendant be diagnosed with a "mental disease" but do not clearly define *mental disease*.
- Most of these rules also require that the defendant have been unable to understand the criminality of his or her actions or conform his or her actions to the law in order to be judged not guilty by reason of insanity.
- Many states have introduced the alternative verdict of "guilty but mentally ill."

Involuntary Commitment and Patients' Rights

In the best circumstances, people who need treatment for psychological disorders will seek it themselves. They will work with mental health professionals to find the medication or psychotherapy that helps to reduce their symptoms and keeps their disorder under control. Many people who have serious psychological problems do not recognize their need for treatment, however, or may refuse treatment for a variety of reasons. For example, a woman with persecutory delusions and hallucinations may fear treatment, believing that doctors are part of the conspiracy against her. A man in a manic episode may like many of the symptoms he is experiencing—the high energy, inflated self-esteem, and grandiose thoughts—and not want to take medication that will reduce these symptoms. The teenager who is abusing illegal drugs may believe that it is his right to do so and that there is nothing wrong with him. Can these people be forced into mental institutions and to undergo treatment against their will? These are the questions we address in this section.

Civil Commitment

Prior to 1969, in the United States the **need for treatment** was sufficient cause to hospitalize people against their will and force them to undergo treatment. Such involuntary hospitalization is called **civil commitment**. All that was needed for civil commitment was a certificate signed by two physicians stating that a person needed treatment and was not agreeing to it voluntarily. The person could then be confined, often indefinitely, without advice of an attorney, a hearing, or any appeal. In Great Britain and several other countries around the world, need for treatment still is one criterion for civil commitment.

In the United States, however, the need for treatment alone is no longer sufficient legal cause for civil commitment in most states. This change came about as part of the patients' rights movement of the 1960s, in which concerns were raised about the personal freedom and civil liberties of mental patients (Holstein, 1993; Mulvey, Geller, &

need for treatment
legal criterion operationalized as a signed certificate by two physicians stating that a person requires treatment but will not agree to it voluntarily; formerly a sufficient cause to hospitalize the person involuntarily and force him or her to undergo treatment

civil commitment
forcing a person into a mental health facility against his or her will

Roth, 1987). Opponents of the civil commitment process argued that it allowed people to be incarcerated simply for having "alternative lifestyles" or different political or moral values (Szasz, 1963, 1977). Certainly there were many cases in the former Soviet Union and other countries of political dissidents being labeled mentally ill and in need of treatment and then being incarcerated in prisons for years. In the United States, there also were disturbing cases of the misuse of civil commitment proceedings. For example, Mrs. E. P. W. Packard was one of several women involuntarily hospitalized by their husbands for holding "unacceptable" and "sick" political or moral views (Weiner & Wettstein, 1993). Mrs. Packard remained hospitalized for 3 years until she won her release and then began crusading against civil commitment.

The three criteria currently used in the United States and in many other countries to commit someone to a psychiatric facility against his or her will are (1) grave disability, (2) dangerousness to self, and (3) dangerousness to others. In addition, most states require that the danger people pose to themselves or to others be *imminent*—if they are not immediately incarcerated, they or someone else will likely be harmed in the very near future. Finally, all persons committed to psychiatric facilities must be diagnosed with mental disorders.

Criteria for Involuntary Commitment

grave disability
legal criterion for involuntary commitment that is met when a person is so incapacitated by a mental disorder that he or she cannot care for his or her own basic needs such as food, clothing, or shelter and his or her survival is threatened as a result

The **grave disability** criterion requires that people be so incapacitated by mental disorders that they cannot care for their basic needs of food, clothing, and shelter. This criterion is, in theory, much more severe than the need for treatment criterion, because it requires that the person's survival be in immediate danger because of illness. At least 30 states in the United States use the grave disability criterion in civil commitment hearings, and in those states, about 80 percent of persons involuntarily committed are committed on the basis of grave disability (Turkheimer & Parry, 1992).

One might think that the grave disability criterion could be used to hospitalize homeless people on the streets who appear to be psychotic and do not seem able to take care of their basic needs. This is what former New York Mayor Ed Koch thought in the bitter winter of 1988, when he invoked the legal principle of *parens patriae* (sovereign as parent) to have mentally ill homeless people picked up from the streets of New York and taken to mental health facilities. Mayor Koch argued that it was the city's duty to protect these mentally ill homeless people from the ravages of the winter weather because they were unable to do it for themselves. One of the homeless people who was involuntarily taken to a psychiatric facility was 40-year-old Joyce Brown, who was subsequently given a diagnosis of paranoid schizophrenia. Brown had been living on the streets on and off for years, despite efforts by her family to get her into psychiatric treatment. She refused treatment of any kind. When Brown was involuntarily hospitalized in the winter of 1988 as part of Koch's campaign, she and the American Civil Liberties Union contested her commitment and won her release on the grounds that the city had no right to incarcerate Brown if she had no intention of being treated.

One of the legal precedents of Joyce Brown's release is *Donaldson v. O'Connor* (1975). Kenneth Donaldson had been committed to a Florida state hospital for 14 years. It was Donaldson's father who originally had him committed, believing that Donaldson was delusional and therefore a danger to himself. At the time, Florida law allowed people to be committed if their mental disorders might impair their ability to manage their finances or protect themselves against being cheated by others. Throughout his hospitalization, Donaldson refused medication because it violated his Christian Science beliefs. The superintendent, O'Connor, considered this refusal to be a symptom of Donaldson's mental disorder. Even though Donaldson had been caring for himself adequately before his hospitalization and had friends who offered to help care for him if he was released from the hospital, O'Connor and the hospital continually refused Donaldson's requests for release. Donaldson sued, on the grounds that he had received only custodial care during his hospitalization and that he was not a danger to himself. He requested to be released to the care of his friends and family. The Supreme Court agreed and ruled that "a State cannot constitutionally confine . . . a nondangerous individual, who is capable of surviving safely in freedom by himself or with the help of willing and responsible family and friends."

In practice, however, most persons involuntarily committed because of grave disability do not have the American Civil Liberties Union championing their rights or the personal wherewithal to file suit. Often, these are people with few financial resources, friends, or families, who have long histories of serious mental illness. The elderly mentally ill are especially likely to be committed because of grave disability (Turkheimer & Parry, 1992). Often, these people are committed to psychiatric facilities because there are not enough less restrictive treatment facilities available in their communities, and their families do not have the ability to care for them.

The criterion of **dangerousness to self** is most often invoked when it is believed that a person is imminently suicidal. In such cases, the person is often held in an inpatient psychiatric facility for a few days while undergoing further evaluation and possibly treatment. Most states allow short-term commitments without a court hearing in emergency situation such as this. All that is needed is a certification by the attending mental health professionals that the individual is in imminent danger to him- or herself. If the mental health professionals judge that the person needs further treatment but the person does not voluntarily agree to treatment, they can go to court to ask that the person be committed for a longer period of time.

dangerousness to self
legal criterion for involuntary commitment that is met when a person is imminently suicidal or a danger to him- or herself as judged by a mental health professional

 If you were depressed and suicidal, would you want to be committed to a psychiatric facility, even against your will?

Dangerousness to others is the third criterion under which people can be committed involuntarily. If a mentally ill person is going to hurt another if set free, then society has claimed the right to protect itself against this person by holding her against her will. This may seem completely justified. Yet the appropriateness of this criterion rests on our being able to predict who will be dangerous and who will not. Some research has suggested that predictions of dangerousness tend to be wrong more often than they are correct (McNiel & Binder, 1991; Monahan & Walker, 1990). As a tragic example, the serial killer Jeffrey Dahmer was arrested and jailed in 1988 for sexually molesting a 13-year-old boy. He was released in 1990 with only a limited follow-up by mental health professionals, despite concerns raised by his family about his mental health. Dahmer proceeded to drug, molest, kill, and dismember at least 17 additional victims over the next few years before being apprehended.

Recent studies suggest that people with serious psychological disorders have higher rates of violent behavior than do people without disorders (see Table 16.3; Monahan, 1992). Still, only a minority of mentally ill people engage in violent behavior, and mental

dangerousness to others
legal criterion for involuntary commitment that is met when a person would pose a threat or danger to other people if not incarcerated

Table 16.3 Percentage of People Who Have Been Violent in the Past Year, by Psychiatric Diagnosis

Data suggest that people with severe psychiatric disorders are at increased risk for being violent compared to people with no psychiatric diagnosis.

Diagnosis	Percent Violent
No disorder	2.1
Schizophrenia	12.7
Major depression	11.7
Mania or bipolar disorder	11.0
Alcohol abuse/dependence	24.6
Drug abuse/dependence	34.7

Source: Data from Monahan, 1992.

health professionals and the lay public tend to overestimate the likelihood of violence among people with psychological disorders (Steadman & Keveles, 1972).

One of the best predictors of whether people are likely to commit violent acts is their past histories of violence. This is true of both people with psychological disorders and people without disorders. In one study, 728 randomly selected male prisoners who had been convicted of violent crimes were interviewed to determine their rates of psychiatric disorder (Teplin, Abram, & McClelland, 1994). The researchers then followed these men for 6 years to determine if those who had psychiatric disorders were more or less likely to commit subsequent crimes than were those without psychiatric disorders. Nearly 50 percent of the men did commit crimes in the next 6 years, but the researchers found no differences in subsequent arrests for violent crimes between the men with severe mental disorders or substance abuse disorders and those without disorders.

Some recent studies suggest that, given enough information, mental health professionals can make short-term predictions about which individuals are most likely to be violent that are better than chance (Gardner, Lidz, Mulvey, & Shaw, 1996; Lidz, Mulvey, & Gardner, 1993). Three of the best predictors of violence over the short term are a past history of violence, current severe symptoms of psychopathology, and substance abuse (Mulvey, 1994). There still is good reason to be wary of the use of the dangerousness to others criterion to force someone into treatment against his or her will.

Patients' Rights

Procedurally, most states now mandate that persons being considered for involuntary commitment have the right to a public hearing, the right to counsel, the right to call and confront witnesses, the right to appeal decisions, and the right to be placed in the least restrictive treatment setting. In practice, however, attorneys and judges typically defer to the judgment of mental health professionals about a person's mental illness and meeting of the criteria for commitment (Turkheimer & Parry, 1992). Thus, even the attorneys who are supposed to be upholding an individual's rights tend to acquiesce to the judgment of mental health professionals, particularly if the attorney is court-appointed, as is often the case. Again, it appears that many attorneys who are going along with the commitment of their clients are doing so because they believe the clients need treatment and that there are not enough facilities in the community to provide this treatment (Turkheimer & Parry, 1992).

right to treatment
fundamental right of involuntarily committed people to active treatment for their disorders rather than shelter alone

One fundamental right of people who have been committed is the **right to treatment**. In the past, mental patients, including those involuntarily committed and those who sought treatment voluntarily, were often warehoused. The conditions in which they lived were appalling, with little stimulation or pleasantries, let alone treatment for their disorders. In *Wyatt v. Stickney* (1972), patient Ricky Wyatt and others filed a class action suit against a custodial facility in Alabama, charging that they received no useful treatment and lived in minimally acceptable living conditions. They won their case. A federal court ruled that the state could not simply shelter patients who had been civilly committed but had to provide them with active treatment.

right to refuse treatment
right, not recognized by all states, of involuntarily committed people to refuse drugs or other treatment

informed consent
procedure (often legally required prior to treatment administration) in which a patient receives a full and understandable explanation of the treatment being offered and makes a decision about whether to accept or refuse the treatment

Another basic right is the **right to refuse treatment**. One of the greatest fears of people committed against their will is that they will be given drugs or other treatments that rob them of their consciousness, their personality, and their free will. Many states now do not allow mental institutions or prisons to administer treatments without the informed consent of patients. **Informed consent** means that a patient accepts treatment after receiving a full and understandable explanation of the treatment being offered and making a decision based on his or her own judgment of the risks and benefits of the treatment. The right to refuse treatment is not recognized in some states, however, and in most states, this right can be overruled in many circumstances. Particularly if a patient is psychotic or manic, it may be judged that he or she cannot make a reasonable decision about treatment, and thus the decision must be made by others. Patients' psychiatrists and perhaps families may seek court rulings allowing them to administer treatment even if patients refuse treatment. Judges most often agree with the psychiatrists' or families' requests to force treatment on patients (Hargreaves, Shumway, Knutsen, & Weinstein,

One fundamental right of people committed to a mental health facility is the right to be treated rather than just warehoused.

1987). Most cases in which patients refuse treatment never get to court, however. Clinicians and family members pressure and persuade patients to accept treatment, and eventually, most patients agree to treatment after initially refusing it (Cleveland, Mulvey, Appelbaum, & Lidz, 1989).

 Should all committed patients be allowed to refuse all kinds of treatment?

Deinstitutionalization

The patients' rights movement was aimed at stopping the warehousing and dehumanizing of mental patients and reestablishing their personal freedoms and basic legal rights. Patients' rights advocates argued that these patients could recover more fully or live more satisfying lives if they were integrated into the community, with the support of community-based treatment facilities. Many of these patients would continue to need around-the-clock care, but it could be given in halfway houses and group homes based in neighborhoods, rather than in large, impersonal institutions. Thousands of mental patients were released from mental institutions. The number of patients in large state psychiatric hospitals decreased by 75 percent over the period of this movement (Kiesler & Sibulkin, 1987). Many former mental patients who had lived for years in cold, sterile facilities, receiving little useful care, experienced dramatic increases in the quality of life upon their release.

Unfortunately, the resources to care for all the mental patients released from institutions were never adequate. There were not enough halfway houses built or community mental health centers funded to serve the thousands of men and women who were formerly institutionalized or who would have been if the movement had not happened. Instead, these men and women began living in nursing homes or other types of group homes, where they received little mental health treatment, or with their families, who were often ill-equipped to handle serious mental illness (Bachrach, 1987). Some of these people began living on the streets. This situation continues today.

Certainly not all homeless people are mentally ill, but estimates of the rates of serious mental illness among the homeless are typically around 20 to 30 percent (Koegel, Burnam, & Farr, 1988). In emergencies, these people end up in general or private hospitals that are often not equipped to treat them appropriately (Kiesler & Sibulkin, 1983).

Thus, deinstitutionalization began with laudatory goals, but many of these goals were never fully reached, leaving many people who would formerly have been institutionalized in mental hospitals no better off. In recent years, the financial strains on local, state, and federal governments have led to the closing of many more community mental health centers.

The goal of the deinstitutionalization movement was to transfer care of people with mental disorders and disabilities from large state institutions to small community-based mental health facilities.

- People can be held in mental health facilities involuntarily if they are judged to have grave disabilities that make it difficult for them to meet their own basic needs or that pose imminent danger to themselves or to others. Each of the criteria used to make such judgments has its flaws, however, creating concerns about the appropriateness of civil commitment.
- Short-term commitments can occur without court hearings on the certification of mental health professionals that individuals are in emergency situations. Such commitments are most likely to happen for individuals who are actively suicidal.
- Longer-term commitments require court hearings. Patients have the rights to have attorneys and to appeal rulings.
- Other basic rights of patients are the right to be treated while being hospitalized and the right to refuse treatment (at least in some states).
- The deinstitutionalization movement was intended to stop the warehousing of mental patients and to reintegrate them into society through community-based mental health centers. Thousands of patients were subsequently released from long-term mental institutions, but unfortunately, not enough community mental health centers were built and funded to serve all these people's needs.

Gender and Ethnicity Issues

Of those people evaluated for their competency to stand trial, women and members of ethnic minority groups are more likely to be judged incompetent than are men or whites (Nicholson & Kugler, 1991). Women and ethnic minority persons who commit crimes may be more likely to have severe psychological problems that make them incompetent to stand trial than do men or whites who commit crimes. On the other hand, evaluators may have lower thresholds for judging women and ethnic minorities incompetent. In addition, when evaluators do not speak the same languages as ethnic minority defendants, the defendants may not understand the evaluators' questions, evaluators may not understand the defendants' answers to questions, and evaluators may tend to interpret this lack of communication as an indication of defendants' incompetence to stand trial.

 Why might it be that women and minorities who are judged incompetent to stand trial are more seriously disturbed than are white males who are judged incompetent to stand trial?

Almost 90 percent of the people who are acquitted after pleading the insanity defense are male, and two-thirds of them are white (McGreevy et al., 1991). The reasons men and whites are more likely to successfully plead the insanity defense are unclear but may have to do with their greater access to competent attorneys who can effectively argue the insanity defense. In the last decade or two, as society has become more aware of the plight of abused and battered women, increasing numbers of women are pleading the insanity defense after injuring or killing partners who had been abusing them for years. One recent case is that of Lorena and John Bobbitt. According to Lorena Bobbitt, her husband John Bobbitt had sexually and emotionally abused her for years. One night in 1994, John Bobbitt came home drunk and raped Lorena Bobbitt. In what her attorneys described as a brief psychotic episode, Lorena Bobbitt cut off her husband's penis and threw it away. Lorena Bobbitt was acquitted of charges of malicious injury by reason of temporary insanity. She was referred to a mental institution for further evaluation and released a few months later.

Another controversial application of the insanity defense by women has been its use by women who have committed infanticide, supposedly as the result of psychotic postpartum depression (Williamson, 1993). Severe postpartum depression with psychotic symptoms is very rare, afflicting less than 1 percent of postpartum women (Nolen-Hoeksema, 1990). Violence by these women against their newborns is even more rare. When such violence does occur, some courts have accepted that the mothers' behaviors are the result of the postpartum psychosis and have judged these women not guilty by reason of insanity.

Finally, with regard to civil commitment procedures, recent research has suggested that violence by mentally ill women tends to be *underestimated* by clinicians (Coontz, Lidz, & Mulvey, 1994). Clinicians do not expect mentally ill women to be violent to the same degree that they expect mentally ill men to be violent. As a result, they do not probe mentally ill women for evidence regarding violence as much as they probe mentally ill men. In reality, however, mentally ill women are as likely to commit violent acts towards others as are mentally ill men. The victims of mentally ill women's violent acts are most likely to be family members; mentally ill men also are most often violent towards family members, but they commit violent acts against strangers more often than do mentally ill women (Newhill, Mulvey, & Lidz, 1995).

Racial stereotypes lead people to expect that mentally ill persons from ethnic minority groups are more likely to commit acts of violence than are white mentally ill people. There are, however, no differences among the ethnic groups in rates of violence among mentally ill people (Mulvey, 1995).

Clinicians' Duties to Clients and Society

The clinician's primary responsibility to the client is a *duty to provide competent and appropriate treatment* for the client's problems. There are a number of other duties of clinicians that deserve special mention.

First, according to the ethical guidelines that clinicians are expected to follow, there is a *duty not to become involved in multiple relationships* with clients. Thus, therapists should avoid becoming involved in business or social relationships with clients, and therapists should not treat members of their own families. Such multiple relationships can cloud therapists' judgments about the best treatment for their clients. Of greatest concern is potential sexual involvement of therapists with clients. No matter how egalitarian a therapist is, the relationship between a therapist and client is always a relationship of power. The client comes to the therapist, vulnerable and seeking answers. The therapist is in a position to exploit the client's vulnerability. Current professional guidelines for psychologists and psychiatrists assert that it is almost never acceptable for a therapist to become sexually involved with a client, even if the client seems to be consenting to such a liaison voluntarily. Further, a therapist must not become intimately involved with a client for at least 2 years after the therapeutic relationship has ended. Sexual contact between a therapist and client is not just unethical—it is a felony in some states.

Therapists have duties to provide appropriate treatment for their clients, to avoid multiple relationships with clients, and to protect clients' confidentiality.

The vast majority of cases of sexual liaisons between therapists and clients involve male therapists and female clients. Older studies asking therapists (anonymously) if they had ever had sexual contact with their clients suggested that as many as 12 percent of male therapists and 3 percent of female therapists had, at some time in their careers, had such relationships with clients (Holroyd & Brodsky, 1977). Fortunately, the rates of such abuse have decreased dramatically in more recent surveys, which suggest that about 1 to 4 percent of male therapists and less than 1 percent of female therapists have had sexual liaisons with clients (Borys & Pope, 1989; Pope, Tabachnick, & Keith-Spiegel, 1987). The decrease in rates of such liaisons is probably due to a number of factors, including the criminalization of the act, malpractice suits brought against therapists who have become sexually involved with clients, and increased sensitivity to the wrongness of such relationships among professionals and the organizations that govern them. Unfortunately, therapists may be simply less willing to admit to having sexual relationships with their clients now than they were in previous years due to the increased sanctions against such relationships.

Second, therapists have a *duty to protect client confidentiality*. Therapists must not reveal information about their clients, including clients' identities, to anyone except with the clients' permission or under special circumstances. One of those special circumstances occurs when the therapist believes the client needs to be committed involuntarily and must convince a court of this.

Another condition under which therapists can violate their clients' confidentiality happens when they believe clients may harm other people. Based on the decision in *Tarasoff v. Regents of the University of California* (1974), in many jurisdictions clinicians now have a *duty to protect* persons who might be in danger because of their clients. Tatiana Tarasoff was a student at the University of California at Berkeley in the late 1960s. A graduate student named Prosenjit Poddar was infatuated with Tarasoff, who had rejected him. Poddar told his therapist in the student counseling service that he planned to kill Tarasoff when she returned from vacation. The therapist informed the campus police, who picked Poddar up for questioning. Poddar agreed to leave Tarasoff alone, and the campus police released him. Two months later, Poddar killed Tarasoff. Tarasoff's parents sued the University, arguing that the therapist should have protected Tarasoff from Poddar. The California courts agreed and established that therapists have a duty to warn persons who are threatened by their clients during therapy sessions and to take actions to protect these persons.

In addition, in most states, therapists have a *duty to report suspected child abuse* to the proper authorities even when such reports violate their clients' confidentiality. These authorities then are required to investigate these reports and determine whether to file charges and to remove children from potentially abusive situations. In some states, therapists also have a *duty to report suspected abuse of elderly persons*. Confidentiality is considered by therapists one of the most fundamental rights of clients, but in these cases,

the courts have ruled that confidentiality must be broken to protect innocent people that clients might harm or are harming.

Are there any other conditions under which you think it is acceptable for a clinician to violate a client's confidentiality?

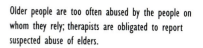

Summing Up   Clinicians' Duties to Clients and Society

- Clinicians must avoid multiple relationships with their clients, particularly sexual relationships.
- They must also protect their clients' confidentiality, except under special circumstances. One of these occurs when therapists believe clients need to be committed involuntarily.
- Two other duties therapists have to society require them to break clients' confidentiality: the duty to protect people clients are threatening to harm and the duty to report suspected child or elder abuse.

Family Law and Mental Health Professionals

In years past, the law had little to say about what could and could not happen within a family. Husbands could beat their wives, parents could beat their children, and the courts tended to turn away from intervening in the "sanctity of the family." Wife battering and child abuse certainly still go on without sufficient intervention by law authorities, but there have been remarkable increases in the rights of individual family members to be protected against the abuses of other family members. Thus, for example, rape within a marriage is now illegal in most jurisdictions, and the law puts limits on the ways that parents can punish or discipline their children. Amidst this revolution in the rights of individual family members has been tremendous change in the structure of families and in what units are recognized as families. The high divorce rate now means that a large percentage of children will live much of their childhoods in single-parent homes with parents who have remarried or being shuttled between their biological parents in complicated joint custody arrangements. In addition, many types of nontraditional families are gaining legal recognition, including homosexual couples and cohabiting (but not married) heterosexual couples and their children.

These many changes in family life and in laws regarding families have led to increases in the number and complexity of court cases requiring decisions that can greatly affect the individual families involved and set precedents that will affect families. Increasingly, the courts have turned to mental health professionals for assistance in formulating and carrying out laws regarding families and children. Here we will consider three areas where mental health professionals have become heavily involved: child custody disputes between divorcing parents, child maltreatment cases, and charges by adults of sexual abuse during their childhoods.

Child Custody Disputes

Ninety percent of the time, parents who are divorcing can agree on the custody arrangements for their children without taking disputes to court (Melton & Wilcox, 1989). If parents cannot agree, however, the court must help determine how much authority each parent will have in decisions for the children and how much contact each parent will have with the children. These decisions obviously can have tremendous impact on a child's daily life. They can determine where a child lives, the financial resources available to the child, the religion the child is raised in, the type of school the child attends, and of course, how much the child sees each parent. The decisions can also have great impact on the lives of the parents. In addition to determining how much contact parents will have with their children, courts can put restraints on parents' freedom to make certain decisions for their children, such as parents' ability to practice Christian Science (which discourages medical intervention for many illnesses) or to move a child to another state where a noncustodial parent will not be able to see the child.

The law requires that custody decisions be made "in the best interest of the child." Determining what custody arrangements are in the best interest of the child can be very difficult. Each parent will often try to convince a judge that he or she is the better parent and that the child would prefer to be with him or her. Each parent can bring family members, friends, and hired mental health professionals to court to try to convince a judge to rule in his or her favor. In the midst of all this highly charged, conflicting information, judges often rely on their own intuitions or theories about what is best for children (Thompson, Tinsley, Scalora, & Parke, 1989).

Alternately, many states have mandated that certain types of custody arrangements be preferred over others in the belief that children usually respond best to a particular type of custody arrangement. For example, the presumption in the law used to be that mothers were the best caregivers for their children, and thus in custody disputes mothers almost always received custody of their children. More recently, however, many states are mandating joint custody of children in the belief that access to both parents is almost always best for children. Another recent trend is to award grandparents visitation rights to children, even when opposed by children's parents, in the belief that children usually benefit from exposure to their grandparents (Thompson et al., 1989). Although it would

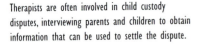

Therapists are often involved in child custody disputes, interviewing parents and children to obtain information that can be used to settle the dispute.

be nice if such mandates were based on solid psychological research, most of the time they are the results of waves of enthusiasm for what "everybody knows" will benefit children and families (Melton & Wilcox, 1989). Moreover, these mandates do not reflect the complexity and idiosyncrasies of individual cases. Thus, recent studies of the wholesale application of the joint custody mandate in California have found that, although many children benefit from exposure to both parents, many children suffer as a result of joint custody (Maccoby & Mnookin, 1992). In particular, children whose parents fought constantly while they were married often continue in such joint custody arrangements to be caught in their parents' conflicts, as their parents are forced to deal with each other to comply with the arrangements. These children might have been better served by single-parent custody arrangements.

Mental health professionals are increasingly being asked to assist courts in making custody decisions. As noted, sometimes mental health professionals are hired by the parents in dispute, but sometimes mental health professionals are brought in by the courts to make independent assessments of what would be "in the best interest of the child." Here are some of the guidelines that the American Psychological Association (1994) recommends that psychologists follow when acting as expert evaluators in child custody proceedings.

- In a child custody evaluation, the child's interests and well-being are paramount. Parents competing for custody, as well as others, may have legitimate concerns, but the child's best interests must prevail.
- The focus of the evaluation is on parenting capacity of the parents, the psychological and developmental needs of the child, and the resulting fit.
- The role of the psychologist is as a professional expert. The psychologist does not act as a judge, who makes the ultimate decision applying the law to all relevant evidence. Neither does the psychologist act as an advocating attorney, who strives to present his or her client's best possible case. The psychologist, in a balanced, impartial manner, informs and advises the court and the prospective custodians of the child of the relevant psychological factors pertaining to the custody issue.
- Psychologists generally avoid conducting child custody evaluations in a case in which they served in therapeutic roles for the children or their immediate families or in which they had other involvements that could compromise their own objectivity.
- The psychologist refrains from drawing conclusions not adequately supported by the data. The psychologist strives to acknowledge to the court any limitations in the methods or data used.
- The psychologist engaging in child custody evaluations is aware of how biases regarding age, gender, race, ethnicity, national origin, religion, sexual orientation, disability, language, culture, and socioeconomic status may interfere with an objective evaluation and recommendations. The psychologist recognizes and strives to overcome any such biases or withdraws from the evaluation.

This last guideline recognizes that all of us, including mental health professionals, have implicit assumptions about what constitutes good parenting, and these assumptions are influenced by the culture in which we are raised. Thus, a person raised in a somewhat stoic, emotionally unexpressive household or culture may be uncomfortable with parents who are highly expressive toward their children, including openly expressing both praise and criticism. If this expressiveness is characteristic of the culture from which the parents and children come, it may be inappropriate for the mental health professional to judge this as "bad parenting." In addition, expectations for how a parent should act toward a child are heavily influenced by the parent's gender. A mother who works 60 to 80 hours per week in a high pressure job may be judged more harshly as neglecting her children than a father who works 60 to 80 hours in a similar job. Mental health professionals must be vigilant that such assumptions or biases do not contaminate their evaluations of parents in custody disputes.

As we shall see, these issues and ethical guidelines also pertain to a mental health professional's role in evaluating children and adults involved in child maltreatment cases.

 Several of the disorders we have discussed in this book are linked to poor parenting. Do you think society should require parents of troubled children to obtain training to become better parents?

Child Maltreatment Cases

Psychologists and other mental health professionals are now involved in every phase of child maltreatment cases. The most recent and controversial change in mental health professionals' roles in child maltreatment cases is the use of mental health professionals to investigate the claims of maltreatment or to determine if maltreatment is likely to happen in the future. A psychologist may interview all the parties involved in a case. The psychologist may administer psychological tests to the parents and children. Then the psychologist may act as an expert witness in court, testifying on what is known about such cases from the research literature.

Although mental health professionals are used to interview children and parents in these highly sensitive cases because they have experience working with troubled children and families, there have been several cases in which mental health professionals appear to have asked leading questions in their interviews, particularly of children, which then have contaminated the evidence for a trial. For example, charges were brought against teachers at the McMartin Preschool in California for sexually molesting children in their care. The charges began with one child reporting strange activities at preschool. Then the other children were interviewed by members of the local police force, members of the prosecutor's office, and mental health professionals. Videotapes of these interviews suggest that some of the children were pressured into "reporting" sexual activities at the preschool. They were told that other children had already admitted that these activities had happened and that these were the "good children." The interviewers made it clear that as soon as a child said what the interviewers were looking for, the interview would be over. At times, words were put directly into the children's mouths. All of this was done by adults who truly believed that abuse had happened and wanted badly to apprehend and punish the people who had perpetrated the abuse. Eventually, many of the children reported extraordinary and bizarre sexual encounters with their preschool teachers. In the end, however, most of the charges had to be dropped against the adults because the evidence was so contaminated by the interview techniques used in the early investigation that it could not be believed.

Other concerns have been raised about mental health professionals providing expert testimony in child maltreatment trials and other types of trials (Melton & Limber, 1989). The least controversial role mental health professionals can play as expert witnesses is to explain behaviors of children or adults that might seem confusing or conflicting with their claims. For example, in child maltreatment cases, children often will not report their abuse to adults until long after the abuse has occurred or has begun, they are often vague or give conflicting information in their reports, and they often retract their accusations when they see the consequences of these accusations. These behaviors might suggest that such children are lying about the accusations. A psychologist can point out (usually for the prosecution) that children who have been abused often exhibit these kinds of behaviors, so they do not necessarily indicate that children are lying.

More concerns have been raised about mental health professionals giving expert opinions about whether the accused fits the profile of the "typical" abuser or the child fits the profile of a "typical" abused child (Melton & Limber, 1989). First, the presence of a similarity between an individual adult or child and some profile does not necessarily mean that an individual is an abuser or is abused. Conversely, if an adult or a child does not fit the abuser or abused profile, it does not necessarily mean that no abuse took place. Second, the profiles described in such testimony are often based on clinical experience rather than on firm research. The statement by an expert witness that someone fits the profile of an abuser or the abused can be taken more seriously than it should by juries and judges who do not understand the probabilistic nature of the kinds of predictions mental health professionals can make. A recent example of controversy over a psychologist providing expert testimony came in the trial of O. J. Simpson for the murders of Nicole Brown Simpson and Ronald Goldman. After interviewing Simpson for 80 hours, a psychologist was willing to testify for the defense that Simpson did not fit the profile of a battering husband with the potential to kill his wife. This psychologist was heavily criticized, in part because her willingness to testify about whether Simpson met the profile of a violent, battering man raised all the concerns mentioned here.

 Should research findings have a strong effect on legal rulings or is each case so individual and idiosyncratic that we cannot apply general research findings to these individual cases? Why?

In recent years, there have been a great deal of discussion and research on proper techniques for interviewing children involved in court cases and on the ethical obligations of mental health professionals serving as expert witnesses. Although some tragic mistakes have been made and there is still much to be learned, mental health professionals do play important and worthwhile roles in legal proceedings, especially those involving families. Mental health professionals have experience in talking with distressed children and adults about sensitive topics. They may be able to gather more information more objectively because of this expertise, without further traumatizing the children and adults being interviewed.

The Repressed/Recovered/False Memory Debate

There has been a profound increase in the last 20 years in public and professional awareness of the sexual and physical abuse of women and children. As a society, we are admitting it happens too frequently, and we are beginning to do something about it. Currently, one of the greatest controversies in clinical psychology is centered on claims by adults, usually women, that they were abused as children but repressed the memories of the abuse for years, only to recover these memories as adults. This phenomenon is variously referred to as the **repressed memory debate**, the *recovered memory debate*, and the *false memory debate*. An example of a claim of a repressed memory follows (Harvey & Herman, 1994, pp. 300–301; this is a compilation of several different cases):

repressed memory debate controversy among psychologists over the existence or nonexistence of repression, the possibility of repressed memories and implanted memories, and the admissibility to legal cases of claims based on such theories

> **Case Study** • Emily B. is a 45-year-old married woman. She and her husband recently relocated to the Boston area where she'd grown up. Emily has two siblings and an aging paternal aunt in this area. She was referred to psychotherapy by a local psychiatric emergency service, where she appeared in a state of confusion and despair following a reunion with her sister, whom she had not seen for many years. . . .
>
> Emily is the youngest of three children raised by their father and two paternal aunts following their mother's untimely death when Emily was 4 years old. The aunts were extraordinarily severe in their approach to punishment and discipline. Emily recalls that she and her siblings were frequently beaten with belts and "other objects," locked in closets, blindfolded for long periods of time, deprived of food, and subjected to verbal assaults and humiliation. Their father did not engage in this abuse, but he also did not protect them. At some point in her childhood—"maybe I was 10 or 11, but maybe I was younger than that"—Emily's father began molesting her. Once the abuse began, it escalated to include oral, anal, and vaginal penetration, and by the time she was 13, it assumed violent and sadistic proportions. As far as Emily knows now, the abuse continued until she ran away at age "15 or 16."
>
> When Emily left home, she cut off all contact with her family. By the time she met and married her husband, she had "completely forgotten" the sexual abuse. "I never forgot the beatings, though." Among the major precipitants to Emily's remem-

brance of the sexual abuse are her return to the geographic area in which she was raised and her renewed contact with an older sister. It was while visiting this sister and hearing "one family horror story after another" that Emily began feeling extremely agitated and fearful. One night, she was awakened with terrifying dreams and for several days afterward was flooded with memories of her father's abuse. Since then, Emily has spent a great deal of time with her sister and has confirmed many of her new memories. She has learned that her sister and brother were also sexually abused by their father.

In nearly 1,000 of such cases, the adults who have remembered such experiences have filed suit against the people they believe abused then. Often, such suits are encouraged by therapists who view this as part of the therapy of empowerment (Bass & Davis, 1988). Many courts will waive the statute of limitations to allow the accused to be tried for such crimes, even though they may have occurred decades ago.

On one side of the controversy over these claims are mental health professionals, often practicing therapists, who believe it is their role to promote the welfare of the women who have been abused by helping them recover their memories of abuse and resolve their feelings about these memories any way possible. These clinicians, many of whom have psychoanalytic orientations, believe strongly in the phenomenon of repression and they see its manifestations every day in their clinical practice.

On the other side of the controversy are mental health professionals, often experimental researchers, who argue there is little or no scientific evidence that repression exists and that many claims of the recovery of repressed memories are due to clients succumbing to suggestions by their therapists (Loftus, 1993). That is, at a time when clients are vulnerable and seeking answers for their current psychological distress, their therapists pressure them directly or indirectly to "recall" memories of the abuse. The clients confabulate—they fill in and create memories of abuse when, in reality, they were never abused.

Both sides in this controversy can marshal evidence in support of their views. Believers in repressed memories often cite three particular studies. The first is by Linda Meyer Williams (1995) who surveyed 129 women who had documented histories of having been sexually abused sometime between 1973 and 1975. These women, who were between 10 months and 12 years old at the time of their abuse, were interviewed about 17 years after their abuse. Williams found that 49 of these 129 women had no memory of or had forgotten about the abuse events that were documented. The second study is by John Briere and Jon Conte (1993) who located 450 therapy patients who identified themselves as abuse victims. Briere and Conte asked these people if there had ever been a time before their 18th birthdays when they "could not remember" their abuse. Fifty-nine percent answered "yes" to this question. In the third study, Judith Herman and Emily Schatzow (1987) asked 53 women who were in therapy groups for abuse survivors to try to find any confirming evidence for their memories of childhood sexual abuse. They reported that over 75 percent of these women did find confirming evidence for their memories.

Nonbelievers in repressed memories first call into question the results of these three studies. First, regarding the Williams (1995) study, it turns out that 33 of the 49 women who said they could not remember the specific abuse incidents they were asked about could remember other abuse incidents during their childhoods. Thus, they had not completely forgotten or repressed all memories of abuse; they simply could not remember the specific incident about which they were being asked. Williams did not give any additional information about the 16 women who could remember no incidents of molestation in their childhoods. They may have been too young to remember these incidents—memory for anything that happens before the age of about 3 tends to be very bad.

Regarding the Briere and Conte study, concerns have been raised about the question they asked their subjects, which required them to report if there ever was a time before they were 18 years old when they could not remember the abuse that occurred. Answering this question requires some fancy retrospection: People were asked not only to remember times when they did not remember events but also to determine whether during those times, they might have been unable to remember events if they had tried. It is not clear that the subjects of this study understood all these nuances in the question they were being asked. A greater problem with this study is that all of the subjects identified themselves, before the study began, as having recovered repressed memories of sexual abuse.

Finally, in the Herman and Schatzow (1987) study the first problem is that it did not focus only on women with repressed memories of sexual abuse. Of the 53 women in the study, 38 percent had never had amnesia for their abuse, 36 percent had had only partial amnesia, and 26 percent had had severe amnesia. We do not know the relative proportions of each of these groups who did and did not find confirming evidence for their abuse. In addition, the quality of the confirming evidence found is not clear. One woman, who had never had any memories of sexual abuse before she joined this group therapy but later remembered extensive abuse by her father, concluded that her new memories must be valid because her sister had asked her a few days previous to the study, "Did Daddy ever try anything funny with you?" This was the full extent of her confirming evidence for her abuse.

Nonbelievers in repressed memories also cite studies indicating that people can be made to believe that things that never happened to them actually did (Ceci, Toglia, & Ross, 1988; Loftus, 1993). For example, Elizabeth Loftus and her colleagues developed a method for instilling a specific childhood memory of being lost on a specific occasion at the age of 5. This method involved a trusted family member engaging the subject in a conversation about the time he or she was lost (Loftus, 1993, p. 532):

Case Study • Chris (14 years old) was convinced by his older brother Jim that he had been lost in a shopping mall when he was 5 years old. Jim told Chris this story as if it were the truth: "It was 1981 or 1982. I remember that Chris was 5. We had gone shopping in the University City shopping mall in Spokane. After some panic, we found Chris being led down the mall by a tall, oldish man (I think he was wearing a flannel shirt). Chris was crying and holding the man's hand. The man explained that he had found Chris walking around crying his eyes out just a few moments before and was trying to help him find his parents."

Just two days later, Chris recalled his feelings about being lost: "That day I was so scared that I would never see my family again. I knew that I was in trouble." On the third day, he recalled a conversation with his mother: "I remember mom telling me never to do that again." On the fourth day: "I also remember that old man's flannel shirt." On the fifth day, he started remembering the mall itself: "I sort of remember the stores." In his last recollection, he could even remember a conversation with the man who found him: "I remember the man asking me if I was lost." . . .

A couple of weeks later, Chris described his false memory and he greatly expanded on it.

> I was with you guys for a second and I think I went over to look at the toy store, the Kay-bee Toy and uh, we got lost and I was looking around and I thought, "Uh-oh, I'm in trouble now." You know. And then I . . . I thought I was never going to see my family again. I was really scared you know. And then this old man, I think he was wearing a blue flannel, came up to me. . . . He was kind of old. He was kind of bald on top. . . . He had like a ring of gray hair . . . and he had glasses.

Believers in repressed memories severely criticize the application of these studies to claims of repressed memories of sexual abuse. First, they argue that people might be willing to go along with experimenters or therapists who try to convince them that they were lost in a shopping mall as a child, but it is unlikely that people would be willing to go along with therapists or experimenters trying to convince them they were sexually abused if this abuse did not happen. Abuse is such a terrible thing to remember, and the social consequences of admitting the abuse and confronting the abuser are so negative that people simply would not claim it were true if it were not true.

In the midst of this controversy are women in pain over what they believe happened to them long ago and families that have been torn apart by allegations of sexual abuse. This is an area where fundamental issues in the science and practice of psychology collide with fundamental issues in the law about how to weigh conflicting and indefinite evidence.

 Given that it is often difficult to objectively determine the truth of accusations of abuse, should we be inclined to believe the accusor or the accused who says she or he did not commit the abuse?

Summing Up | Family Law and Mental Health Professionals

- Psychologists and other mental health professionals can provide a number of services in family law courts hearing cases of custody disputes, charges of child maltreatment, or charges by adults that they were sexually abused as children.
- Mental health professionals can help to investigate cases, employing proper interviewing techniques with great caution to obtain information that is as objective as possible without further traumatizing the parties involved.
- They can act as expert witnesses, providing the court with information about research relevant to a case.
- They can assist in getting family members into appropriate treatment if necessary after a case is decided.
- In each of these areas of involvement, however, there are pitfalls to avoid. In interviewing people for a case, the mental health professional must be careful not to be overly suggestive, leading a person to fabricate a story that is not true or to misremember events.
- In giving expert testimony, the mental health professional must not overstate the research evidence pertinent to a case or make inappropriate generalizations from the research to a specific case being tried.
- In assisting parties in getting treatment, the mental health professional must follow all the ethical guidelines of clinicians, including that of not being involved in multiple relationships with the parties.
- Child custody, child maltreatment, and repressed memory cases create highly charged atmospheres with great potential for further harm of the children and adults involved. Mental health professionals must act with the greatest objectivity and skill to help reduce this harm rather than add to it.

Bio-Psycho-Social INTEGRATION

There has been perhaps less integration of biological, social, and psychological viewpoints in the law's approach to issues of mental health than in the mental health field itself. The rules governing the insanity defense suggest that the law takes a biological perspective on psychological disorders, conforming to the belief that a mental disease is like a medical disease. Similarly, civil commitment rules require certification that a person has a mental disorder or disease before he or she can be committed, further legitimizing psychiatric diagnostic systems that are based on medical models.

The patients' rights movement was led, in part, by people who believed that there was no such thing as a mental disorder and that people said to have such disorders were the victims of their culture's intolerance of anyone different. These critics focused on the social forces driving people's lawful and unlawful behaviors and called upon society to change its behavior and stop treating mental patients as diseased children in need of care by the state.

Finally, psychologists are becoming quite influential in family law cases because they can speak to the ways that societal, biological, and psychological factors influence people's memories for events, their suggestibility under interrogation, and other difficult issues courts face in child custody disputes, child maltreatment cases, and claims of repressed memories of childhood abuse.

In each of the areas discussed in this chapter, however, there are mental health professionals advocating a more integrated and complex view of mental disorders than that traditionally held by the law. These professionals are trying to educate judges, juries, and laypeople that some people have biological, psychological, or social predispositions to disorders and that other biological, psychological, or social factors can interact with predispositions to trigger the onset of disorders or trigger certain manifestations of disorders. What is most difficult to explain is the probabilistic nature of the predictions we can make about mental disorders and the behavior of people with these disorders. That is, a predisposition or certain recent life experiences may make it more likely that a person will develop a disorder or engage in a specific behavior (such as a violent behavior), but they do not determine the disorder or the specific behavior. We all prefer to have predictions about the future that are definite, especially when we are making decisions that will determine a person's freedom or confinement. That kind of definitiveness is not possible, however, given our present knowledge of the ways biological, psychological, and social forces interact to influence people's behavior.

Chapter Summary

One of the fundamental principles of law is that, in order to stand trial, an accused individual must have a reasonable degree of rational understanding of the charges against her and the proceedings of the trial and must be able to participate in her defense. People who do not have an understanding of what is happening to them in a courtroom and who cannot participate in their own defense are said to be incompetent to stand trial. Defendants who have histories of psychotic disorders, who have current symptoms of psychosis, or who perform poorly on tests of important cognitive skills may be judged incompetent to stand trial.

Five different rules for judging the acceptability of the insanity defense have been used in recent history: the M'Naghten Rule, the irresistible impulse rule, the Durham Rule, the ALI Rule, and the American Psychiatric Association definition. Each of these rules requires that the defendant be diagnosed with a mental disorder, and most of the rules require it be shown that the defendant did not appreciate the criminality of his act or could not control his behaviors at the time of the crime. A new verdict, guilty but mentally ill, has been introduced following public uproar over recent uses of the insanity defense in high profile cases. Persons judged guilty but mentally ill are confined for the duration of a regular prison term but with the presumption that they will be given psychiatric treatment. Mental health professionals have raised a number of concerns about the insanity defense. It requires post hoc judgments of a defendant's state of mind at the time of the crime. In addition, the rules governing the insanity defense presume that people have free will and usually can control their actions. These presumptions contradict some models of normal and abnormal behavior that suggest that behavior is strongly influenced by biological, psychological, and social forces.

Civil commitment is the procedure through which a person may be committed for treatment in a mental institution against his or her will. In most jurisdictions, three criteria are used to determine whether individuals may be committed: if they suffer from grave disability that impairs their ability to care for their own basic needs, if they are imminent dangers to themselves, or if they are imminent dangers to others. Each of these criteria requires a subjective judgment on the part of clinicians and often predictions about the future that clinicians may not be that good at making. In particular, the prediction of who will pose a danger to others in the future is a difficult one to make, and it is often made incorrectly.

When being considered for commitment, patients have the right to an attorney, to a public hearing, to call and confront witnesses, to appeal decisions, and to be placed in the least restrictive treatment setting. (The right to a hearing is often waived for short-term commitments in emergency settings.) Once committed, patients have the right to be treated and the right to refuse treatment.

The goal of the deinstitutionalization movement was to move mental patients from custodial mental health facilities, where they were isolated and received little treatment, to community-based mental health centers. Thousands of patients were released from mental institutions. Unfortunately, community-based mental health centers have never been fully funded or supported, leaving many former mental patients with few resources in the community.

Although there has been too little research on the role of gender and ethnicity in the legal system's treatment of people with psychological disorders, a few facts are known. Of those evaluated for competence to stand trial, women and members of ethnic minority groups are more likely to be judged incompetent than are men or whites. Almost 90 percent of those who are judged not guilty of a crime by reason of insanity are men, and two-thirds are white. In civil commitment proceedings, clinicians tend to underestimate the likelihood of violence in mentally ill women. There are no differences among ethnic groups in the United States in propensity to violence among mentally ill people.

Mental health professionals have a number of duties to their clients and to society. They have a duty to provide competent care, to avoid multiple relationships with clients, and to uphold clients' confidentiality, except in unusual circumstances. They have a duty to warn people whom their client is threatening and to report suspected child or elder abuse.

Mental health professionals are becoming increasingly active in family law cases, including child custody disputes, cases of child maltreatment, and charges by adults that they were sexually molested as children. In child custody disputes, the law and professional guidelines require that decisions be made in the best interest of the child. Mental health professionals are often asked by courts to make objective evaluations of the parenting capabilities of both parents and about what would be the best "fit" between parent and child. In child maltreatment cases, mental health professionals must take care not to contaminate the testimony of witnesses, especially children, by being overly suggestive or pressuring witnesses to provide certain types of evidence. Concerns have raised about mental health professionals acting as expert witnesses in such cases, particularly when they provide opinions about whether the accused or the victims fit "typical" profiles of accused people or victims. Finally, there is a recent wave of charges being brought by adults against people they believe sexually abused them in childhood. Their memories of this abuse were repressed most of their lives. These memories are variously known as *repressed memories, recovered memories,* or *false memories.* Believers in repressed memories argue that the experience of child abuse is so terrible that the mind protects itself by repressing memories of the abuse. People who recover memories of abuse as adults must be helped to work through these memories and often to confront their abusers. Nonbelievers in repressed memories argue that there is little scientific evidence for the phenomenon of repression and that false memories of abuse are being created in vulnerable clients by their therapists. Mental health professionals can be found on both sides of this debate.

Key Terms

Application

I n this chapter, we have discussed several sets of guidelines that professional organizations such as the American Psychological Association and the American Psychiatric Association have put forward to guide the conduct of members of their profession. We end this chapter by quoting guidelines from the American Psychological Association for ethical conduct by psychologists treating culturally diverse populations (APA, 1993). These guidelines are meant to inspire psychologists to provide the best possible service and treatment to people who are of ethnicities or cultures different from those of the psychologists. For those of you hoping to become psychologists, these guidelines provide a sense of the competencies you will be expected to gain in your training. For those of you being treated by psychologists, the guidelines provide some expectations you may have of your psychologists, particularly if they are from different ethnicities or cultures.

Preamble: the Guidelines represent general principles that are intended to be aspirational in nature and are designed to provide suggestions to psychologists in working with ethnic, linguistic, and culturally diverse populations.

1. Psychologists educate their clients to the processes of psychological intervention, such as goals and expectations; the scope and, where appropriate, legal limits of confidentiality; and the psychologists' orientations.

2. Psychologists are cognizant of relevant research and practice issues as related to the population being served.
    a. Psychologists acknowledge that ethnicity and culture impact on behavior and take those factors into account when working with various ethnic/racial groups.
    b. Psychologists seek out educational and training experiences to enhance their understanding and thereby address the needs of these populations more appropriately and effectively. These experiences include cultural, social, psychological, political, economic, and historical material specific to the particular ethnic group being served.
    c. Psychologists recognize the limits of their competencies and expertise. Psychologists who do not possess knowledge and training about an ethnic group seek consultation with, and/or make referrals to, appropriate experts as necessary.
    d. Psychologists consider the validity of a given instrument or procedure and interpret resulting data, keeping in mind the cultural and linguistic characteristics of the person being assessed. . . .

3. Psychologists recognize ethnicity and culture as significant parameters in understanding psychological processes.
    a. Psychologists, regardless of ethnic/racial background, are aware of how their own cultural background/ experiences, attitudes, values, and biases influence psychological processes. They make efforts to correct any prejudices and biases. . . .
    b. Psychologists' practice incorporates an understanding of the client's ethnic and cultural background. This includes the client's familiarity and comfort with the majority culture as well as ways in which the client's culture may add to or improve various aspects of the majority culture and/or of society at large. . . .
    c. Psychologists help clients increase their awareness of their own cultural values and norms, and they facilitate discovery of ways client can apply this awareness to their own lives and to society at large. *Illustrative Statement:* Psychologists may be able to help parents distinguish between generational conflict and culture gaps when problems arise between them and their children. In the process, psychologists could help both parents and children to appreciate their own distinguishing cultural values.
    d. Psychologists seek to help a client determine whether a "problem" stems from racism or bias in others so that the client does not inappropriately personalize problems. *Illustrative Statement:* The concept of "healthy paranoia," whereby ethnic minorities may develop defensive behaviors in response to discrimination, illustrates this principle.

4. Psychologists respect the roles of family members and community structures, hierarchies, values, and beliefs within the client's culture.
    a. Psychologists identify resources in the family and the larger community.
    b. Clarification of the role of the psychologist and the expectations of the client precede intervention. . . . *Illustrative Statement:* It is not uncommon for an entire American Indian family to come into the clinic to provide support to the person in distress. Many of the healing practices found in American Indian communities are centered in the family and the whole community.

5. Psychologists respect clients' religious and/or spiritual beliefs and values, including attributions and taboos, since they affect world view, psychosocial functioning, and expressions of distress. . . .

6. Psychologists interact in the language requested by the client and, if this is not feasible, make an appropriate referral.

7. Psychologists consider the impact of adverse social, environmental, and political factors in assessing problems and designing interventions.

8. Psychologists attend to, as well as work to eliminate, biases, prejudices, and discriminatory practices. . . . ■

Glossary

A

abstinence violation effect what happens when a person attempting to abstain from alcohol use ingests alcohol and then endures conflict and guilt by making an internal attribution to explain why he or she drank, thereby making him or her more likely to continue drinking in order to cope with the self-blame and guilt (p. 457)

acculturation extent to which a person identifies with his or her group of origin and its culture or with the mainstream dominant culture (p. 28)

adoption study study of the heritability of a disorder by finding adopted people with a disorder and then determining the prevalence of the disorder among their biological and adoptive relatives, in order to separate out contributing genetic and environmental factors (p. 74)

affective flattening negative symptom of schizophrenia that consists of a severe reduction or complete absence of affective responses to the environment (p. 224)

agnosia impaired ability to recognize objects or people (p. 497)

agoraphobia anxiety disorder characterized by fear of places and situations in which it would be difficult to escape in a panic attack, such as enclosed places, wide open spaces, and crowds (p. 111)

akathesis agitation caused by neuroleptic drugs (p. 239)

akinesia condition marked by slowed motor activity, a monotonous voice, and an expressionless face, resulting from taking neuroleptic drugs (p. 239)

alcohol abuse diagnosis given to someone who uses alcohol in dangerous situations, fails to meet obligations at work or at home due to alcohol use, and has recurrent legal or social problems as a result of alcohol use (p. 431)

alcohol dependence diagnosis given to someone who has a physiological tolerance to alcohol, spends a lot of time intoxicated or in withdrawal, or continues to drink despite significant legal, social, medical, or occupational problems that result from alcohol (often referred to as alcoholism) (p. 431)

alcohol-induced dementia loss of intellectual abilities, including memory, abstract thinking, judgment, and problem solving, often accompanied by changes in personality, such as increases in paranoia (p. 433)

alcohol-induced persisting amnesic disorder permanent cognitive disorder caused by damage to the central nervous system, consisting of Wernicke's encephalopathy and Korsakoff's psychosis (p. 433)

ALI Rule legal principle stating that a person is not responsible for criminal conduct if he or she lacks the capacity to appreciate the criminality (wrongfulness) of the act or to conform his or her conduct to the requirements of the law as a result of mental disease (p. 555)

alogia deficit in both the quantity of speech and the quality of its expression (p. 224)

alternate form reliability extent to which a measure yields consistent results when presented in different forms (p. 30)

altruistic suicide suicide committed by people who believe that taking their own lives will benefit society (p. 207)

Alzheimer's disease progressive neurological disease that is the most common cause of dementia (p. 498)

amenorrhea cessation of the menses (p. 356)

American Psychiatric Association definition definition of insanity stating that people cannot be held responsible for their conduct if, at the time they commit crimes, as the result of mental disease or mental retardation they are unable to appreciate the wrongfulness of their conduct (p. 555)

amnesia impairments in the ability to learn new information or to recall previously learned information or past events (p. 509)

amnesic disorders cognitive disorders involving deficits in the ability to learn new information and recall previously learned information (p. 509)

amphetamines stimulant drugs that can produce symptoms of euphoria, self-confidence, alertness, agitation, paranoia, perceptual illusions, and depression (p. 440)

animal type phobias extreme fear of specific animals that may induce immediate and intense panic attacks and cause the individual to go to great lengths to avoid the animals (p. 120)

anomic suicide suicide committed by people who experience a severe disorientation and role confusion because of a large change in their relationship to society (p. 206)

anorexia nervosa eating disorder in which people fail to maintain body weights that are normal for their ages and heights and suffer from fears of becoming fat, distorted body images, and amenorrhea (p. 356)

anterograde amnesia deficit in the ability to learn new information (pp. 265, 509)

anticonvulsant drugs treatments for mania and alternatives to lithium, effective in reducing mania symptoms but also carrying side effects such as dizziness, rash, nausea, and drowsiness (p. 183)

antidepressant drugs drugs used to treat the symptoms of depression, such as sad mood, negative thinking, and disturbances of sleep and appetite; three common types are monoamine oxidase inhibitors, tricyclics, and serotonin reuptake inhibitors (p. 86)

antipsychotic drugs drugs used to treat psychotic symptoms such as delusions, hallucinations, and disorganized thinking (pp. 86, 183)

antisocial personality disorder pervasive pattern of criminal, impulsive, callous, and/or ruthless behavior, predicated upon disregard for the rights of others and an absence of respect for social norms (p. 290)

anxiety unpleasant state of arousal that consists of symptoms such as rapid heartbeat, perspiration, and feelings of dread (p. 77)

anxious-fearful personality disorders category including avoidant, dependent, and obsessive-compulsive personality disorders that is characterized by a chronic sense of anxiety or fearfulness and behaviors intended to ward off feared situations (p. 303)

aphasia impaired ability to produce and comprehend language (p. 496)

applied tension technique technique used to alleviate blood-injection-injury phobias in which the therapist teaches the client to increase his or her blood pressure and heart rate, thus preventing the client from fainting (p. 126)

apraxia impaired ability to initiate common voluntary behaviors (p. 497)

arousal in the sexual response cycle, psychological experience of arousal and pleasure as well as physiological changes, such as the tensing of muscles and enlargement of blood vessels and tissues (also called the excitement phase) (p. 387)

assessment process of gathering information about a person's symptoms and their possible causes (p. 24)

ataque de nervios attack of the nerves, syndrome in Hispanic cultures that closely resembles anxiety and depressive disorders (p. 140)

attention deficit/hyperactivity disorder (ADHD) syndrome marked by deficits in controlling attention, inhibiting impulses, and organizing behavior to accomplish long-term goals (p. 320)

auditory hallucination auditory perception of phenomena that is not real, such as hearing a voice when one is alone (p. 219)

autism childhood disorder marked by deficits in social interaction (such as a lack of interest in one's family or other children), communication (such as failing to modulate one's voice to signify emotional expression), and activities and interests (such as engaging in bizarre, repetitive behaviors) (p. 343)

automatic thoughts thoughts processed without active effort (p. 84)

autonomic nervous system system that regulates the functions of the adrenals, heart, intestines, and stomach (see also parasympathetic nervous system and sympathetic nervous system) (p. 113)

aversion therapy treatment that involves the pairing of unpleasant stimuli with deviant or maladaptive sources of pleasure in order to induce an aversive reaction to the formerly pleasurable stimulus (p. 412)

aversive classical conditioning pairing of alcohol with a substance that will interact with it to cause nausea or vomiting (such as disulfiram) in order to make alcohol itself a conditioned stimulus to be avoided (p. 455)

avoidant personality disorder pervasive anxiety, sense of inadequacy, and fear of being criticized that leads to the avoidance of most social interactions with others and to restraint and nervousness in social interactions (p. 303)

avolition inability to persist at common goal-directed activities (p. 224)

B

barbiturates drugs used to treat anxiety and insomnia that work by suppressing the central nervous system and decreasing the activity level of certain neurons (pp. 87, 437)

behavioral observation method for assessing the frequency of a client's behaviors and the specific situations in which they occur (p. 42)

behavioral theories of depression view that depression results from negative life events that represent a reduction in positive reinforcement; sympathetic responses to depressive behavior then serve as positive reinforcement for the depression itself (p. 187)

behavior genetics study of the processes by which genes affect behavior and the extent to which personality and abnormality are genetically inherited (p. 71)

bell and pad method treatment for enuresis in which a pad placed under a sleeping child to detect traces of urine sets off a bell when urine is detected, awakening the child to condition him or her to wake up and use the bathroom before urinating (p. 337)

benzodiazepines drugs that reduce anxiety and insomnia (pp. 87, 116, 437)

binge-eating disorder eating disorder in which people compulsively overeat either continuously or on discrete

binges but do not behave in ways to compensate for the overeating (p. 363)

biological approach view that biological factors cause and should be used to treat abnormality (p. 66)

bipolar disorder disorder marked by cycles between manic episodes and depressive episodes; also called manic-depression (p. 158)

Bipolar I Disorder form of bipolar disorder in which the full symptoms of mania are experienced while depressive aspects may be more infrequent or mild (p. 170)

Bipolar II Disorder form of bipolar disorder in which only hypomanic episodes are experienced, and the depressive component is more pronounced (p. 170)

blackout amnesia for events that occurred during one's intoxication (p. 429)

blood-injection-injury type phobias extreme fear of seeing blood or an injury or receiving an injection or other invasive medical procedures, which causes a drop in heart rate and blood pressure and fainting (p. 121)

body dysmorphic disorder syndrome involving obsessive concern over some part of the body the individual believes is defective (p. 275)

borderline personality disorder syndrome characterized by rapidly shifting and unstable mood, self-concept, and interpersonal relationships as well as impulsive behavior and transient dissociative states (p. 295)

brain stem primitive brain structure lying near the core of the brain (p. 114)

bulimia nervosa eating disorder in which people engage in bingeing (episodes involving a loss of control over eating and consumption of an abnormally large amount of food) as well as behave in ways to prevent weight gain from the binges, such as self-induced vomiting, excessive exercise, or abuse of purging drugs (such as laxatives) (p. 360)

C

calcium channel blockers treatments for mania (p. 183)

cannabis substance that causes feelings of well-being, perceptual distortions, and paranoid thinking (p. 443)

catalepsy condition characterized by trancelike states and a waxy rigidity of the muscles (p. 161)

catatonia disorder of movement involving immobility or excited agitation, often accommpanied by speech disturbances (pp. 161, 223)

catatonic excitement state of constant agitation and excitability (p. 223)

catatonic posturing bizarre, inappropriate bodily position of considerable duration in which a person remains oblivious to the outside world (p. 223)

catatonic schizophrenia syndrome marked by near or total unresponsiveness to the environment as well as motor and verbal abnormalities (p. 226)

catatonic stupor motionless, apathetic state in which one remains oblivious to external stimuli (p. 223)

causal attribution explanation for why an event occurred (pp. 82, 189)

cerebrum part of the brain that regulates complex activities such as speech and analytical thinking (p. 68)

chlorpromazine phenothiazine drug used to treat schizophrenia that blocks certain dopamine receptors in the brain, thereby calming agitation and reducing positive symptoms of schizophrenia (p. 238)

civil commitment forcing a person into a mental health facility against his or her will (p. 557)

clang associations in schizophrenia, linking together of words based upon their sounds, as opposed to their meanings (p. 221)

classical conditioning form of learning in which a neutral stimulus becomes associated with a stimulus that naturally elicits a response, thereby making the neutral stimulus itself sufficient to elicit the same response (p. 80)

classification system set of syndromes and criteria for determining whether a client's symptoms constitute a particular syndrome (p. 50)

client-centered therapy (CCT) Carl Rogers's form of psychotherapy that consists of an equal relationship between therapist and client as the client searches for his or her inner self, receiving unconditional positive regard and an empathic understanding from the therapist (p. 88)

clozapine drug used to treat schizophrenia that blocks postsynaptic dopamine receptors other than those blocked by phenothiazines (p. 239)

cocaine central nervous system stimulant that causes a rush of positive feelings initially but that can lead to impulsiveness, agitation, and anxiety and that can cause withdrawal symptoms of exhaustion and depression (p. 439)

cognitions thoughts or beliefs (p. 82)

cognitive-behavioral therapy treatment that works by changing negative patterns of thinking and by solving concrete problems through brief sessions in which a therapist helps a client challenge negative thoughts, consider alternative perspectives, and take effective actions (p. 194)

cognitive disorders dementia, delirium, or amnesia characterized by impairments in cognition (such as deficits in memory, language, or planning) and caused by a medical condition or by substance intoxication or withdrawal (p. 494)

cognitive distortion theory theory that depression results from errors in thinking—such as jumping to conclusions, exaggerating the negative, and ignoring the positive—that lead one to a gloomy view of the self, the world, and the future (p. 188)

cognitive therapy therapeutic approach that focuses on changing people's maladaptive thought patterns (p. 91)

communication disorder developmental disorder involving deficits in communication abilities, such as stuttering or poor articulation (p. 337)

compulsions repetitive behaviors or mental acts that the individual feels he or she must perform (p. 144)

computerized tomography (CT) method of analyzing brain structure by passing narrow X-ray beams through a person's head from several angles to produce measurements from which a computer can construct an image of the brain (p. 31)

concordance rate probability that both twins will develop a disorder if one twin has the disorder (p. 73)

concurrent validity extent to which a test yields the same results as other measures of the same phenomenon (p. 29)

conditioned avoidance response type of behavior in which a person avoids stimuli that he or she associates with anxiety-provoking symptoms, reducing anxiety, which then becomes a positive reinforcer for continuing avoidance (p. 81)

conditioned response (CR) in classical conditioning, response that first followed a natural stimulus but that now follows a conditioned stimulus (p. 80)

conditioned stimulus (CS) in classical conditioning, previously neutral stimulus that when paired with a natural stimulus becomes itself sufficient to elicit a response (p. 80)

conduct disorder syndrome marked by chronic disregard for the rights of others, including specific behaviors such as stealing, lying, and engaging in acts of violence (p. 324)

conscious mental contents and processes of which we are actively aware (p. 76)

construct validity extent to which a test measures only what it is intended to measure (p. 30)

content validity extent to which a measure assesses all the important aspects of a phenomenon that it purports to measure (p. 29)

continuous reinforcement schedule system of behavior modification in which certain behaviors are always rewarded or punished, leading to rapid learning of desired responses (p. 81)

continuous variable factor that is measured along a continuum (such as 0–100) rather than falling into a discrete category (such as "diagnosed with depression") (p. 527)

control group in an experimental study, group of subjects whose experience resembles that of the experimental group in all ways, except that they do not receive the key manipulation (p. 529)

controlled drinking controversial goal of therapy that involves people with alcohol problems learning to manage their drinking, usually with the help of therapists, rather than abstaining from drinking completely (as in the disease model) (p. 457)

control theory cognitive theory that explains people's variance in behavior in certain domains in terms of their beliefs that they can or cannot effectively control situations in that domain (p. 83)

conversion disorder syndrome marked by a sudden loss of functioning in some part of the body, usually following an extreme psychological stressor (p. 269)

coronary heart disease (CHD) chronic illness that is the leading cause of death in the United States, occurring when the blood vessels that supply the heart with oxygen and nutrients are narrowed or closed by plaque, resulting in a myocardial infarction (heart attack) when closed completely (p. 472)

correlation statistic that represents the degree to which two variables are related (p. 527)

correlational study method in which researchers assess only the relationship between two variables and do not manipulate one variable to determine its effects on another variable (p. 527)

cortex surface layer of the cerebral hemispheres (p. 114)

countertransference bias that occurs when a therapist reacts to a client as if the client were a particularly important person in his or her life and incorporates these feelings into his or her assessment of the client (p. 45)

course length of time that a disorder typically lasts and the likelihood that the client will relapse following the current episode of the disorder (p. 51)

covert sensitization therapy pairing of mental images of alcohol with other images of highly unpleasant consequences resulting from its use in order to create an aversive reaction to the sight and smell of alcohol and reduce drinking (p. 455)

cue exposure and response prevention therapy to reduce relapse among alcoholics by tempting them with stimuli that induce cravings to drink while preventing them from actually drinking, allowing them to habituate to the cravings and reduce temptation (p. 455)

cultural relativism view that norms among different cultures set the standard for what counts as normal behavior, which implies that abnormal behavior can only be defined relative to these norms; no universal definition of abnormality is therefore possible; only definitions of abnormality relative to a specific culture are possible (p. 7)

cyclothymic disorder milder but more chronic form of bipolar disorder that consists of alternation between hypomanic episodes and mild depressive episodes over a period of at least two years (p. 170)

D

dangerousness to others legal criterion for involuntary commitment that is met when a person would pose a threat or danger to other people if not incarcerated (p. 559)

dangerousness to self legal criterion for involuntary commitment that is met when a person is imminently suicidal or a danger to him- or herself as judged by a mental health professional (p. 559)

degradation process in which the receiving neuron releases an enzyme into the synapse, breaking down neurotransmitters into other biochemicals (p. 70)

delirium cognitive disorder marked by disorientation to time, place, and people as well as recent memory loss and difficulties with focusing, sustaining, or shifting attention (p. 506)

delirium tremens (DTs) symptoms that result during severe alcohol withdrawal, including hallucinations, delusions, agitation, and disorientation (p. 431)

delusion of reference false belief that external events, such as people's actions or natural disasters, relate somehow to one's self (p. 217)

delusions fixed beliefs with no basis in reality (pp. 161, 216)

dementia gradual and usually permanent decline of intellectual functioning, including deficits in memory, language, and loss of executive functioning, such as the ability to initiate common voluntary behaviors (p. 496)

denial defense mechanism in which a person refuses to perceive or accept reality (p. 77)

dependent personality disorder pervasive selflessness, need to be cared for, and fear of rejection that lead to total dependence on and submission to others (p. 305)

dependent variable factor that one seeks to predict (p. 519)

depersonalization disorder syndrome marked by frequent episodes of feeling detached from one's own body and mental processes, as if one were an outside observer of oneself; symptoms must cause significant distress or interference with one's ability to function. (p. 267)

depression state marked by either a sad mood or a loss of interest in one's usual activities, as well as feelings of hopelessness, suicidal ideation, psychomotor agitation or retardation, and trouble concentrating (p. 158)

depressive realism phenomenon whereby depressed people make more realistic judgments as to whether they can control actually uncontrollable events than do nondepressed people, who exhibit an illusion of control over the same events (p. 191)

desensitization treatment used to reduce anxiety by rendering a previously threatening stimulus innocuous by repeated and guided exposure to the stimulus under nonthreatening circumstances (p. 412)

detoxification first step in treatment for substance-related disorders in which a person stops using the substance and allows it to fully exit the body (p. 451)

diagnosis label affixed to a set of symptoms that tend to occur together (p. 24)

Diagnostic and Statistical Manual of Mental Disorders (DSM) official manual for diagnosing mental disorders in the United States, containing a list of specific criteria for each disorder, how long a person's symptoms must be present to qualify for a diagnosis, and requirements that the symptoms interfere with daily functioning in order to be called disorders (p. 50)

differential diagnosis determination of which of two or more possible diagnoses is most appropriate for a client (p. 26)

disease model view that alcoholism (or drug addiction) is an incurable physical disease, like epilepsy or diabetes, and that only total abstinence can control it (p. 446)

disorder of written expression developmental disorder involving deficits in the ability to write (p. 337)

disorganized schizophrenia syndrome marked by incoherence in cognition, speech, and behavior as well as flat or inappropriate affect (also called hebephrenic schizophrenia) (p. 226)

displacement defense mechanism in which a person discharges unacceptable feelings against someone or something other than the true target of these feelings (p. 77)

dissociation process whereby different facets of an individual's sense of self, memories, or consciousness become split off from one another (p. 254)

dissociative amnesia loss of memory for important facts about a person's own life and personal identity, usually including the awareness of this memory loss (p. 265)

dissociative fugue disorder in which a person moves away and assumes a new identity, with amnesia for the previous identity (p. 263)

dissociative identity disorder (DID) syndrome in which a person develops more than one distinct identity or personality, each of which can have distinct facial and verbal expressions, gestures, interpersonal styles, attitudes, and even physiological responses (p. 257)

disulfiram drug that produces an aversive physical reaction to alcohol and is used to encourage abstinence; commonly referred to as Antabuse (p. 452)

dizygotic (DZ) twins twins who average only 50 percent of their genes in common because they developed from two separate fertilized eggs (p. 73)

dopamine monoamine neurotransmitter, low levels of which have been implicated in the mood disorders and high levels of which have been implicated in schizophrenia (p. 177)

double-blind experiment study in which both the researchers and the participants are unaware of which experimental condition the participants are in, in order to prevent demand effects (p. 533)

double depression disorder involving a cycle between major depression and dysthymic disorder (p. 161)

dramatic-emotional personality disorders category including antisocial, borderline, narcissistic, and histrionic personality disorders that is characterized by dramatic and impulsive behaviors that are maladaptive and dangerous (p. 290)

drug addicts people who are physically dependent on substances and who suffer from withdrawal when not taking the substances (p. 422)

drugs chemicals that alter one's physical and mental state (p. 422)

Durham Rule legal principle stating that the presence of mental disorder is sufficient to absolve a criminal of responsibility for a crime (p. 554)

dysfunctional assumptions fundamental beliefs that are irrational or maladaptive (p. 83)

dyspareunia genital pain associated with sexual intercourse (p. 393)

dysthymic disorder type of depression that is less severe than major depression but more chronic; diagnosis requires the presence of a sad mood or anhedonia, plus two other symptoms of depression, for at least two years during which symptoms do not remit for two months or longer (p. 160)

E

ego part of the psyche that channels libido into activities in accordance superego and within the constraints of reality (p. 76)

egoistic suicide suicide committed by people who feel alienated from others and lack social support (p. 206)

electroconvulsive therapy (ECT) treatment for depression that involves the induction of a brain seizure by passing electrical current through the patient's brain while he or she is anesthetized (p. 185)

electroencephalogram (EEG) graph of the electrical activity in the brain, recorded from electrodes placed on the surface of the scalp (p. 33)

encopresis diagnosis given to children who are at least 4 years old and who

defecate inappropriately at least once a month for 3 months (p. 336)

endocrine system system of glands that produces many different hormones (p. 70)

enuresis diagnosis given to children over 5 years of age who wet the bed or their clothes at least twice a week for 3 months (p. 336)

essential hypertension condition in which the blood supply through the blood vessels is excessive and can lead to deterioration of the cell tissue and hardening of the arterial walls but cannot be traced to genetics or a specific organic cause (p. 473)

event-related potential (ERP) EEG measure of the brain's electrical activity (potentials) as it corresponds to stimuli (events) in the environment (p. 33)

exhibitionism obtainment of sexual gratification by exposing one's genitals to involuntary observers (p. 409)

existential theory view that upholds personal responsibility for discovering one's personal values and meanings in life and then living in accordance with them; people face existential anxiety due to awareness of their life's finitude, and must overcome both this anxiety and obstacles to a life governed by the meanings they give to it, in order to achieve mental health and avoid maladaptive behavior (p. 84)

experimental group in an experimental study, group of participants that receives the key manipulation (p. 529)

extinction abolition of a learned behavior (p. 81)

F

face validity extent to which a measure seems to measure a phenomenon on face value, or intuition (p. 29)

factitious disorders disorders marked by deliberately faking physical or mental illness to gain medical attention (p. 268)

family history study study of the heritability of a disorder involving identifying people with the disorder and people without the disorder and then determining the disorder's frequency within each person's family (p. 73)

family systems therapy psychotherapy that focuses on the family, rather than a single individual, as the source of problems; family therapists challenge communication styles, disrupt pathological family dynamics, and challenge defensive conceptions in order to harmonize relationships among all

members and within each member (p. 92)

female orgasmic disorder in women, recurrent delay in or absence of orgasm after having reached the excitement phase of the sexual response cycle (also called anorgasmia) (p. 392)

female sexual arousal disorder in women, recurrent inability to attain or maintain the swelling-lubrication response of sexual excitement (p. 391)

fetal alcohol syndrome set of symptoms such as mental retardation, central nervous system damage, motor abnormalities, heart defects, and retarded growth that occur in children of mothers who used alcohol during their pregnancy (p. 434)

fetishism paraphilia in which a person uses inanimate objects as the preferred or exclusive source of sexual arousal (p. 407)

field trial way to increase the reliability of diagnostic criteria by testing proposed diagnostic criteria in applied settings to determine their fit with patients' symptoms and consistency across clinicians (p. 52)

fight-or-flight response physiological changes in the human body that occur in response to a perceived threat, including secretion of glucose, endorphins, and hormones as well as elevation of heart rate, metabolism, blood pressure, breathing, and muscle tension (p. 108, 472)

flooding behavioral technique in which a client is intensively exposed to the feared object until the anxiety diminishes (p. 126)

formal thought disorder state of highly disorganized thinking (also known as loosening of associations) (p. 221)

frotteurism obtainment of sexual gratification by rubbing one's genitals against or fondling the body parts of a nonconsenting person (p. 410)

G

gender identity one's perception of oneself as male or female (p. 413)

gender identity disorder condition in which a person believes that he or she was born with the wrong sex's genitals and is fundamentally a person of the opposite sex (p. 413)

gender role what society considers to be the appropriate set of behaviors for males or females (p. 413)

generalization statement about a large population, the validity and accuracy of which is determined in part by the representativeness of the research sample from which the statement is being made (p. 522)

generalized anxiety disorder (GAD) anxiety disorder characterized by chronic anxiety in daily life (p. 137)

global assumptions fundamental beliefs that encompass all types of situations (p. 83)

glove anesthesia syndrome in which people lose all feeling in one hand in a manner inconsistent with the anatomy of the nervous system, suggesting that the loss of feeling is psychologically caused (p. 254)

grave disability legal criterion for involuntary commitment that is met when a person is so incapacitated by a mental disorder that he or she cannot care for his or her own basic needs such as food, clothing, or shelter and his or her survival is threatened as a result (p. 558)

group home type of residence for people with mental disorders that serves as an alternative to hospitalization by providing resources and assistance in the least restrictive environment possible (p. 241)

guided mastery techniques interventions designed to increase health-promoting behaviors by providing explicit information about how to engage in these behaviors as well as opportunities to engage in these behaviors in increasingly challenging situations (p. 483)

guilty but mentally ill (GBMI) verdict that requires a convicted criminal to serve the full sentence designated for his or her crime, with the expectation that he or she will also receive treatment for mental illness (p. 556)

H

hallucinations perceptual experiences that are not real (pp. 161, 216)

hallucinogens substances, including LSD and MDMA, that produce perceptual illusions and distortions even in small doses (p. 442)

histrionic personality disorder syndrome marked by rapidly shifting moods, unstable relationships, and an intense need for attention and approval, which is sought by means of overly dramatic behavior, seductiveness, and dependence (p. 299)

hormone biochemical that sends messages regulating moods, levels of energy, and reactions to stress (p. 70)

humanistic theory view that people strive to develop their innate potential for goodness and self-actualization; abnormality arises as a result of societal pressures to conform to unchosen dictates that clash with a person's self-actualization needs and from an inability to satisfy more basic needs, such as hunger (p. 84)

hypoactive sexual desire disorder condition in which a person's desire for sex is diminished to the point where it causes him or her significant distress or interpersonal difficulties and is not due to transient life circumstances or other sexual dysfunction (p. 389)

hypochondriasis syndrome marked by chronic worry that one has a physical symptom or disease that one clearly does not have (p. 274)

hypothesis testable statement about two or more variables and the relationship between them (p. 519)

hysteria term used by the ancient Greeks and Egyptians to describe what is now referred to as conversion disorder (a disorder in which a person loses functioning in some part of his or her body following a stressful event); the Ancients believed that hysteria was caused by a woman's uterus, which would wander throughout the body and interfere with other organs (p. 11)

I

id most primitive part of the unconscious that consists of drives and impulses seeking immediate gratification (p. 76)

identification defense mechanism in which a person adopts the ideas, values, and tendencies of someone in a superior position in order to elevate self-worth (p. 77)

immunocompetence estimation of the robustness or vulnerability of the immune system (p. 474)

incidence number of new cases of a disorder that develop during a specified period of time (p. 52)

incompetent to stand trial legal status of an individual who lacks a rational understanding of the charges against him or her, an understanding of the proceedings of his or her trial, or the ability to participate in his or her own defense (p. 551)

independent variable factor that is manipulated by the experimenter or used to predict the dependent variable (p. 519)

informed consent procedure (often legally required prior to treatment administration) in which a patient receives a full and understandable explanation of the treatment being offered and makes a decision about whether to accept or refuse the treatment (p. 560)

inhalants solvents such as gasoline, glue, or paint thinner that one inhales to produce a high and that can cause permanent central nervous system damage as well as hepatitis and liver and kidney disease (p. 437)

insanity legal term denoting a state of mental incapacitation during the time a crime was committed (p. 552)

Insanity Defense Reform Act 1984 law that affects all federal courts and about half of the state courts that finds a person not guilty by reason of insanity if it is shown that, as a result of mental disease or mental retardation, the accused was unable to appreciate the wrongfulness of his or her conduct at the time of the offense (p. 555)

intellectualization defense mechanism in which a person adopts a cold, distanced perspective on a matter that actually creates strong unpleasant feelings (p. 77)

internal reliability extent to which a measure yields similar results among its different parts as it measures a single phenomenon (p. 30)

interpersonal therapy (IPT) more structured and short-term version of psychodynamic therapy (pp. 88, 198)

interrater reliability extent to which an observational measure yields similar results across different judges (also called interjudge reliability) (p. 30)

interview method for gathering information from a client and/or his or her family in which a therapist asks questions and examines the content of answers as well as nonverbal behaviors (p. 28)

irresistible impulse rule legal principle stating that even a person who knowingly performs a wrongful act can be absolved of responsibility if he or she is driven by an irresistible impulse to perform the act or had a diminished capacity to resist performing the act (p. 554)

J

John Henryism pattern of active coping with stressors by trying harder and harder against obstacles that may be insurmountable (p. 482)

K

Korsakoff's psychosis alcohol-induced permanent cognitive disorder involving deficiencies in one's ability to recall both recent and distant events (p. 433)

L

la belle indifference   feature of conversion disorders involving an odd lack of concern about one's loss of functioning in some area of one's body (p. 269)

law of effect   Thorndike's observation that behaviors followed by reward are strengthened and behaviors followed by punishment are weakened (p. 81)

learned helplessness   general expectation that one cannot control important events, leading to lowered persistence, motivation, self-esteem, and initiative (p. 83)

learned helplessness deficits   symptoms such as low motivation, passivity, indecisiveness, and an inability to control outcomes that result from exposure to uncontrollable negative events (p. 187)

learned helplessness theory   view that exposure to uncontrollable negative events leads to a belief in one's inability to control important outcomes and a subsequent loss of motivation, indecisiveness, and failure of action, symptoms of depression (p. 187)

libido   psychical energy derived from physiological drives (p. 76)

lifetime prevalence   number of people who will have a disorder at some time in their lives (p. 52)

light therapy   treatment for seasonal affective disorder that involves exposure to bright lights during the winter months (p. 186)

limbic system   part of the brain that relays information from the primitive brain stem about changes in bodily functions to the cortex where the information is interpreted (see also brain stem and cortex) (pp. 69, 114)

lithium   most common treatment for bipolar disorder, a drug that reduces levels of certain neurotransmitters and decreases the strength of neuronal firing (p. 181)

longitudinal study   research method that evaluates the same group(s) of people for an extended period of time (p. 525)

lymphocytes   cells of the immune system that attack viruses (p. 474)

M

magnetic resonance imaging (MRI)   method of measuring both brain structure and function through construction of a magnetic field that affects hydrogen atoms in the brain, emitting signals that

a computer then records and uses to produce a three-dimensional image of the brain (p. 31)

major depression   disorder involving a sad mood or anhedonia, plus four or more of the following symptoms: weight loss or a decrease in appetite, insomnia or hypersomnia, psychomotor agitation or retardation, fatigue, feelings of worthlessness or severe guilt, trouble concentrating, and suicidal ideation; these symptoms must be present for at least two weeks and must produce marked impairments in normal functioning (p. 160)

maladaptive   term referring to behaviors that cause people who have them physical or emotional harm, prevent them from functioning in daily life, and/or indicate that they have lost touch with reality and/or cannot control their thoughts and behavior (also called dysfunctional) (p. 9)

male erectile disorder   in men, recurrent inability to attain or maintain an erection until the completion of sexual activity (p. 391)

male orgasmic disorder   in men, recurrent delay in or absence of orgasm following the excitement phase of the sexual response cycle (p. 393)

malingering   feigning of a symptom or disorder for the purpose of avoiding an unwanted situation, such as military service (p. 268)

mania   state of persistently elevated mood, feelings of grandiosity, overenthusiasm, racing thoughts, rapid speech, and impulsive actions (p. 158)

matching   process of selecting subjects who are identical on all variables that might affect the dependent variable other than the variable of interest (p. 522)

mathematics disorder   developmental disorder involving deficits in the ability to learn mathematics (p. 337)

mental disease or mental illness criterion   view that abnormal behaviors are those that result from a mental illness (p. 9)

mentally ill   legal description of an individual who purportedly suffers from a mental illness, which is analogous (in this view) to suffering from a medical disease (p. 551)

mental retardation   developmental disorder marked by significantly subaverage intellectual functioning, as well as deficits (relative to other children) in life skill areas such as communication, self-care, work, and interpersonal relationships (p. 337)

mesolimbic dopamine system   brain circuit activated by natural rewards as well as psychoactive substances that disposes people to want the same event that led to its activation and that, when activated by chronic substance abuse, can become hypersensitized and lead to chronic and intense cravings (p. 447)

methadone   opioid that is less potent and that is longer lasting than heroin, taken by heroin users to decrease their cravings and help them cope with negative withdrawal symptoms (p. 451)

methadone maintenance programs   treatments for heroin abusers that provide doses of methadone to replace heroin use and seek eventually to wean addicted people from the methadone itself (p. 452)

M'Naghten Rule   legal principle stating that an accused criminal must have been suffering from a mental disease at the time he or she committed a crime and have known neither the nature and quality of the act nor that the act was wrong in order to be judged as insane (p. 553)

modeling   process of learning behaviors by imitating others, especially authority figures or those like oneself (pp. 82, 126)

monoamine oxidase inhibitors (MAOIs)   treatments for depression that inhibit monoamine oxidase, an enzyme that breaks down monoamines, in the synapse, thereby yielding more monoamines (p. 183)

monoamines   class of neurotransmitters including catecholamines (epinephrine, norepinephrine, and dopamine) and serotonin that have been implicated in the mood disorders (p. 177)

monoamine theories   theories that low levels of monoamines, particularly norepinephrine and serotonin, cause depression, whereas excessive or imbalanced levels of monoamines, particularly dopamine, cause mania (p. 178)

monozygotic (MZ) twins   twins who share 100 percent of their genes because they developed from a single fertilized egg (p. 73)

motor skills disorder   developmental disorder involving deficits in motor skills such as walking or holding onto objects (p. 337)

multimethod approach   investigation of a research question using a variety of research methods, each of which may contain inherent limitations, with the expectation that combining multiple methods may produce convergent evidence (p. 539)

myotonia in the sexual response cycle, muscular tension in the body that culminates in contractions during orgasm (p. 387)

N

naloxone drug that blocks the positive effects of heroin and can lead to a decreased desire to use it (p. 452)

naltrexone drug that blocks the positive effects of alcohol and heroin and can lead to a decreased desire to drink or use substances (p. 452)

narcissistic personality disorder syndrome marked by grandiose thoughts and feelings of one's own worth as well as an obliviousness to others' needs and an exploitive, arrogant demeanor (p. 301)

natural environmental type phobia extreme fear of events or situations in the natural environment that causes impairment in one's ability to function normally (p. 121)

need for treatment legal criterion operationalized as a signed certificate by two physicians stating that a person requires treatment but will not agree to it voluntarily; formerly a sufficient cause to hospitalize the person involuntarily and force him or her to undergo treatment (p. 557)

negative symptoms in schizophrenia, deficits in functioning that indicate the absence of a capacity present in normal people, such as affective flattening (also called Type II symptoms) (p. 224)

neurofibrillary tangles twists or tangles of filaments within nerve calls, especially prominent in the cerebral cortex and hippocampus, common in the brains of Alzheimer's disease patients (p. 499)

neuroleptic drugs See antipsychotic drugs. (p. 183)

neuroleptics class of drugs that includes phenothiazines and butyrophenones, which often reduce the positive symptoms of schizophrenia but not the negative ones, and that carries side effects such as akinesia and tardive dyskinesia (p. 238)

neuropsychological test test of cognitive, sensory, and/or motor skills that attempts to differentiate people with deficits in these areas from normal subjects (p. 35)

neurotic paradox situation of a person developing a means of avoiding anxiety that is itself maladaptive (p. 77)

neurotransmitters biochemicals released from a sending neuron that transmit messages to a receiving neuron in the brain and nervous system (p. 70)

norepinephrine neurotransmitter that is involved in the regulation of mood (pp. 114, 177)

null hypothesis alternative to the primary hypothesis, stating that there is no relationship between the independent variable and the dependent variable (p. 519)

O

object relations school group of modern psychodynamic theorists who believe that one develops a self-concept and appraisals of others in a four-stage process during childhood and retains them throughout adulthood; psychopathology consists of an incomplete progression through these stages or an acquisition of poor self-and-other concepts (p. 78)

observational learning learning that occurs when a person observes the rewards and punishments of another's behavior and then behaves in accordance with the same rewards and punishments (p. 82)

obsessions uncontrollable, persistent thoughts, images, ideas, or impulses that an individual feels intrude upon his or her consciousness and that cause significant anxiety or distress (p. 144)

obsessive-compulsive disorder (OCD) anxiety disorder characterized by obsessions (persistent thoughts) and compulsions (rituals) (p. 142)

obsessive-compulsive personality disorder pervasive rigidity in one's activities and interpersonal relationships that includes qualities such as emotional constriction, extreme perfectionism, and anxiety resulting from even slight disruptions in one's routine ways (p. 307)

odd-eccentric personality disorders category including paranoid, schizotypal, and schizoid personality disorders that is marked by chronic odd and/or inappropriate behavior with mild features of psychosis and/or paranoia (p. 283)

Oedipus complex conflict in little boys between their love for their mothers, their jealousy of their fathers, and their fear that their fathers will punish them for loving their mothers (p. 123)

operant conditioning form of learning in which behaviors lead to consequences that either reinforce or punish the organism, leading to an increased or decreased probability of a future response (p. 81)

operationalization specific manner in which one measures or manipulates variables in a study (p. 520)

opioids substances, including morphine and heroin, that produce euphoria followed by a tranquil state; that in severe intoxication can lead to unconsciousness, coma, and seizures; and that can cause withdrawal symptoms of emotional distress and severe nausea, sweating, diarrhea, and fever (p. 441)

oppositional defiant disorder syndrome of chronic misbehavior in childhood marked by belligerence, irritability, and defiance, though not to the extent found in a diagnosis of conduct disorder (p. 325)

orgasm the discharge of neuromuscular tension built up during sexual activity; in men, entails rhythmic contractions of the prostate, seminal vesicles, vas deferens, and penis and seminal discharge; in women, entails contractions of the orgasmic platform and uterus (p. 387)

P

pain disorder syndrome marked by the chronic experience of acute pain that appears to have no physical cause (p. 271)

panic attacks short, intense periods during which an individual experiences physiological and cognitive symptoms of anxiety, characterized by intense fear or discomfort (p. 110)

panic disorder disorder characterized by recurrent, unexpected panic attacks (p. 111)

paranoid personality disorder chronic and pervasive mistrust and suspicion of other people that are unwarranted and maladaptive (p. 283)

paranoid schizophrenia syndrome marked by delusions and hallucinations that involve themes of persecution and grandiosity (p. 225)

paraphilias atypical sexual activities that involve one of the following: (1) nonhuman objects, (2) nonconsenting adults, (3) suffering or humiliation of oneself or one's partner, or (4) children (p. 406)

parasympathetic nervous system part of the autonomic nervous system that lessens physiological arousal (see also autonomic nervous system) (p. 113)

partial reinforcement schedule   form of behavior modification in which a behavior is rewarded or punished only some of the time (p. 81)

pedophilia   adult obtainment of sexual gratification by engaging in sexual activities with young children (p. 410)

persecutory delusion   false, persistent belief that one is being pursued by other people (p. 217)

personality disorder   chronic pattern of maladaptive cognition, emotion, and behavior that begins in adolescence or early adulthood and continues into later adulthood (p. 282)

personality   habitual and enduring ways of thinking, feeling, and acting that make each of us unique and different from every other person (p. 282)

personality trait   complex pattern of thought, emotion, and behavior that is stable across time and many situations (p. 282)

phenothiazines   drugs used to treat schizophrenia that work by blocking postsynaptic receptors for dopamine (p. 238)

phenylcyclidine (PCP)   substance that produces euphoria, slowed reaction times, and involuntary movements at low doses; disorganized thinking, feelings of unreality, and hostility at intermediate doses; and amnesia, analgesia, respiratory problems, and changes in body temperature at high doses (p. 443)

placebo control group   in a therapy outcome study, group of people whose treatment is an inactive substance (to compare with the effects of a drug) or a non–theory-based therapy providing social support (to compare with the effects of psychotherapy) (p. 533)

plaques   deposits of amyloid protein that accumulate in the extracellular spaces of the cerebral cortex, hippocampus, and other forebrain structures in people with Alzheimer's disease (p. 499)

plateau   in the sexual response cycle, period between arousal and orgasm during which excitement remains high but stable (p. 387)

point prevalence   number of people who have a disorder at one given point in time (p. 52)

polygenic   combination of many genes, each of which makes a small contribution to an inherited trait (p. 72)

positive symptoms   in schizophrenia, hallucinations, delusions, and disorganization in thought and behavior (also called Type I symptoms) (p. 223)

positron emission tomography (PET)   method of localizing and measuring brain activity by detecting photons that result from the metabolization of an injected isotope (p. 31)

post-traumatic stress disorder (PTSD)   anxiety disorder characterized by (a) repeated mental images of experiencing a traumatic event, (b) emotional numbing and detachment, and (c) hypervigilance and chronic arousal (p. 128)

preconscious   area of the psyche that contains material from the unconscious before it reaches the conscious mind (p. 76)

predictive validity   extent to which a measure accurately forecasts how a person will think, act, and feel in the future (p. 30)

predisposition   tendency to develop a disorder which must interact with other biological, psychological, or environmental factors for the disorder to develop (p. 72)

prefrontal cortex   largest single brain region in humans that facilitates the planning and production of thoughts, language, emotional expression, and actions (p. 231)

premature ejaculation   inability to delay ejaculaton after minimal sexual stimulation or until one wishes to ejaculate, causing significant distress or interpersonal problems (p. 392)

premenstrual dysphoric disorder   syndrome in which a woman experiences an increase in depressive symptoms during the premenstrual period and relief from these symptoms with the onset of menstruation (p. 163)

prepared classical conditioning   theory that evolution has prepared us to be easily conditioned to fear objects or situations that were dangerous in ancient times (p. 124)

prevalence   number of people who have a disorder during a specified period of time (p. 52)

probands   people who have the disorder under investigation in a family history study (p. 73)

prodromal symptoms   in schizophrenia, experience of milder symptoms prior to an acute phase of the disorder, during which behaviors are unusual and peculiar but not yet psychotic or completely disorganized (p. 224)

projection   defense mechanism in which a person attributes his or her own unacceptable motives or wishes to someone else (p. 77)

projective test   presentation of an ambiguous stimulus, such as an inkblot, to a client, who then projects unconscious motives and issues onto the stimulus in his or her interpretation of its content (p. 43)

prospective longitudinal study   research method that evaluates the same group(s) of people before an event of interest and then again after the event of interest (p. 525)

psychoactive   affecting perceptions, thoughts, emotions, and/or behaviors (p. 422)

psychodynamic theory   theory that explains cognition, emotion, and behavior in terms of a system of unconscious drives; also known as psychoanalytic theory (p. 76)

psychosocial approach   view that psychological characteristics and social events cause abnormality (p. 66)

psychosomatic disorders   syndromes marked by identifiable physical illness or defect caused at least partly by psychological factors (p. 268)

psychotherapy   treatment for abnormality that consists of a therapist and client discussing the client's symptoms and their causes; the therapist's theoretical orientation determines the foci of conversations with the client (p. 86)

psychotic symptoms   experiences that involve a loss of contact with reality as well as an inability to differentiate between reality and one's subjective state (p. 216)

R

rapid cycling bipolar disorder   diagnosis given when a person has four or more cycles of mania and depression within a single year (p. 170)

rationalization   defense mechanism in which a person invents an acceptable motive to explain unacceptably motivated behavior (p. 77)

reaction formation   defense mechanism in which a person adopts a set of attitudes and behaviors that are the opposite of his or her true dispositions (p. 77)

reading disorder   developmental disorder involving deficits in reading ability (p. 337)

reformulated learned helplessness theory   view that people who attribute negative events to internal, stable, and global causes are more likely than other people to experience learned helplessness deficits following such events and are thus predisposed to depression (p. 188)

regression defense mechanism in which a person retreats to a behavior of an earlier developmental period in order to prevent anxiety and satisfy current needs (p. 77)

relapse prevention programs treatments that seek to offset continued alcohol use by identifying high-risk situations for those attempting to stop or cut down on drinking and teaching them either to avoid those situations or to use assertiveness skills when in them, while viewing setbacks as temporary (p. 457)

reliability degree of consistency in a measurement—that is, the extent to which it yields accurate measurements of a phenomenon across several trials, different populations, and in different forms (p. 30)

representative sample subgroup taken from a larger population of interest that is similar to the larger sample regarding the prevalence of factors that might affect the results of a study, such as gender, ethnicity, education level, and age (p. 522)

repressed memory debate controversy among psychologists over the existence or nonexistence of repression, the possibility of repressed memories and implanted memories, and the admissibility to legal cases of claims based on such theories (p. 569)

repression defense mechanism in which the ego pushes anxiety-provoking material back into the unconscious (p. 76)

repressive coping style tendency to expunge negative emotions from one's awareness, at times to a point at which one is unaware that one is experiencing them at all (p. 481)

residual schizophrenia diagnosis made when a person has already experienced a single acute phase of schizophrenia but currently has milder and less debilitating symptoms (p. 227)

residual symptoms in schizophrenia, experience of milder symptoms following an acute phase of the disorder, during which behaviors are unusual and peculiar but not psychotic or completely disorganized (p. 224)

resistance in psychodynamic therapy, material that a client finds difficult or impossible to address; client's resistance signals an unconscious conflict that the therapist then tries to interpret (pp. 45, 88)

resolution in the sexual response cycle, state of deep relaxation following orgasm in which a man loses his erection and a woman's orgasmic platform subsides (p. 387)

retrograde amnesia deficit in the ability to recall previously learned information or past events (pp. 265, 509)

reuptake process in which the sending neuron reabsorbs some of the neurotransmitter in the synapse, decreasing the amount left in the synapse (p. 70)

right to refuse treatment right, not recognized by all states, of involuntarily committed people to refuse drugs or other treatment (p. 560)

right to treatment fundamental right of involuntarily committed people to active treatment for their disorders rather than shelter alone (p. 560)

S

sadomasochism pattern of sexual rituals between a sexually sadistic "giver" and a sexually masochistic "receiver" (p. 408)

safety signal hypothesis the hypothesis that people vividly remember the places in which they have been anxious and associate such locations or situations with symptoms of anxiety, while seeking out situations associated with lowered anxiety (pp. 115, 470)

sample group of people taken from a population of interest who participate in a study (p. 522)

schizoid personality disorder syndrome marked by chronic lack of interest in and avoidance of interpersonal relationships as well as emotional coldness in interactions with others (p. 286)

schizophrenia disorder consisting of unreal or disorganized thoughts and perceptions as well as verbal, cognitive, and behavioral deficits (p. 216)

schizotypal personality disorder chronic pattern of inhibited or inappropriate emotion and social behavior as well as aberrant cognitions and disorganized speech (p. 288)

seasonal affective disorder (SAD) disorder identified by a two-year period in which a person experiences major depression during winter months and then recovers fully during the summer; some people with this disorder also experience mild mania during summer months (p. 162)

selective serotonin reuptake inhibitors (SSRIs) group of drugs that reduces symptoms of depression and anxiety by affecting the functional levels of serotonin (pp. 116, 184)

self-efficacy person's belief that he or she can execute the behaviors necessary to control desired outcomes (pp. 27, 83)

self-monitoring method of assessment in which a client records the number of times per day that he or she engages in a specific behavior and the conditions surrounding the behavior (p. 42)

sensate focus therapy treatment for sexual dysfunction in which partners alternate between giving and receiving stimulaton in a relaxed, openly communicative atmosphere, in order to reduce performance anxiety and concern over achieving orgasm by learning each partner's sexual fulfillment needs (p. 400)

separation anxiety disorder syndrome of childhood and adolescence marked by the presence of abnormal fear or worry over becoming separated from one's caregiver(s) as well as clinging behaviors in the presence of the caregiver(s) (p. 333)

serotonin neurotransmitter that is involved in the regulation of mood and impulsive responses (pp. 114, 177)

set point natural body weight determined by a person's metabolic rate, diet, and genetics (p. 364)

sexual arousal disorders conditions in which people do not experience the physiological changes that make up the excitement or arousal phase of the sexual response cycle (p. 391)

sexual aversion disorder condition in which a person actively avoids sexual activities and experiences sex as unpleasant or anxiety provoking (p. 390)

sexual desire in the sexual response cycle, urge or inclination to engage in sexual activity (p. 387)

sexual dysfunctions problems in experiencing sexual desire or arousal or carrying through with sexual acts to the point of satisfaction (p. 386)

sexual masochism sexual gratification obtained through experiencing pain and humiliation at the hands of one's partner (p. 408)

sexual orientation one's preference for partners of the same or opposite sex with respect to attraction and sexual desire (p. 413)

sexual sadism sexual gratification obtained through inflicting pain and humiliation on one's partner (p. 408)

significantly different difference in scores between two groups that would be unlikely to have occurred if the null hypothesis were true (p. 523)

single case study in-depth analysis of a single individual (p. 536)

situational type phobias extreme fear of stiuations such as public transportation, tunnels, bridges, elevators, flying, driving, and enclosed spaces (p. 121)

social learning theory theory that people learn behaviors by imitating and observing others and learning about the rewards and punishments that follow behaviors (p. 82)

social phobia extreme fear of being judged or embarrassed in front of people that causes the individual to avoid social situations (p. 119)

somatization disorder syndrome marked by the chronic experience of unpleasant or painful physical symptoms for which no organic cause can be found (p. 271)

somatoform disorders disorders marked by unpleasant or painful physical symptoms that have no apparent organic cause and that are often not physiologically possible, suggesting that psychological factors are involved (p. 267)

specific phobia extreme fear of a specific object or situation that causes an individual to routinely avoid that object or situation (p. 119)

splitting in object relations theory, phenomenon wherein a person fails to resolve stages two or three of the self-concept acquisition process and splits conceptions of self and others into either all-good or all-bad categories, neglecting to recognize people's mixed qualities (p. 79)

statistical deviance view that normal behaviors are those performed by a statistical majority of people and that abnormal behaviors are those that deviate from the majority, occurring only rarely or infrequently (p. 8)

stimulants drugs used to increase attention, focus, and self-control (p. 87)

stress reaction to events that are perceived as uncontrollable, unpredictable, challenging, and/or threatening (p. 469)

stress-management interventions strategy that teaches clients to overcome problems in their lives that are increasing their stress (p. 135)

stressor an event that is perceived as uncontrollable, unpredictable, challenging, and/or threatening (p. 520)

structured interview meeting between a clinician and a client or a client's associate(s) in which the clinician asks questions that are standardized, written in advance, and asked of every client (p. 28)

subjective discomfort view that a person must both suffer as a result of a certain behavior and wish to be rid of it in order for it to qualify as abnormal (p. 8)

sublimation defense mechanism in which a person translates wishes and needs into socially acceptable behavior (p. 77)

substance naturally occurring or synthetically produced product that alters perceptions, thoughts, emotions, and behaviors when ingested, smoked or injected (p. 422)

substance abuse diagnosis given when a person's recurrent substance use leads to significant harmful consequences, as manifested by a failure to fulfill obligations at work, school, or home, the use of substances in physically hazardous situations, legal problems, and continued use despite social and legal problems (p. 426)

substance dependence diagnosis given when a person's substance use leads to physiological dependence or significant impairment or distress, as manifested by an inability to use the substance in moderation; decline in social, occupational, or recreational activities; or spending large amounts of time obtaining substances or recovering from their effects (p. 427)

substance intoxication experience of significantly maladaptive behavioral and psychological symptoms due to the effect of a substance on the central nervous system that develops during or shortly after use of the substance (p. 425)

substance-related disorder inability to use a substance in moderation and/or the intentional use of a substance to change one's thoughts, feelings, and/or behaviors, leading to impairment in work, academic, personal, or social endeavors (p. 423)

substance withdrawal experience of clinically significant distress in social, occupational, or other areas of functioning due to the cessation or reduction of substance use (p. 426)

suffocation false alarm theory the theory that people who develop panic disorder are hypersensitive to carbon dioxide and when they are exposed to carbon dioxide (e.g., breathe into a paper bag), their body triggers the autonomic nervous system into a full fight or flight response (p. 113)

superego part of the unconscious that consists of absolute moral standards internalized from one's parents during childhood and one's culture (p. 76)

sympathetic nervous system part of the autonomic nervous system that creates physiological arousal, such as an increased heart rate when experiencing fear (p. 113)

synapse space between the sending neuron and the receiving neuron into which neurotransmitters are first released (also known as the synaptic gap) (p. 70)

syndrome set of symptoms that tend to occur together (p. 49)

systematic desensitization type of behavior therapy that attempts to reduce client anxiety through relaxation techniques and progressive exposure to feared stimuli (pp. 90, 118)

system of diagnosis set of agreed-upon definitions and criteria that mental health professionals use to pinpoint psychological problems for purposes of research and treatment (p. 24)

T

tardive dyskinesia neurological disorder marked by involuntary movements of the tongue, face, mouth, or jaw, resulting from taking neuroleptic drugs (p. 239)

test-retest reliability index of how consistent the results of a test are over time (p. 30)

therapeutic community type of residence where people with mental disorders live with mental health workers and share responsibility for the maintenance of the residence and the development of healthy behavior in one another (p. 241)

therapy outcome study experimental study that assesses the effects of an intervention designed to reduce psychopathology in an experimental group, while performing no intervention or a different type of intervention on another group (p. 532)

third variable factor that affects levels of the dependent variable and confounds the results of a study if it is not appropriately controlled for or eliminated (p. 522)

thought-stopping techniques strategy that involves finding ways to stop intrusive thoughts (p. 135)

token economy application of operant conditioning in which patients receive tokens for exhibiting desired behaviors that are exchangeable for privileges and rewards; these tokens are withheld when a patient exhibits unwanted behaviors (p. 90)

tolerance the condition of experiencing less and less effect from the same dose of a substance (p. 427)

tools of assessment measurements of personality characteristics, cognitive deficits, emotional well-being, and biological functioning that clinicians use to pinpoint psychological problems and their possible causes (p. 24)

transference in psychodynamic therapy, client's reaction to the therapist as if the therapist were an important person in his or her early development; the client's feelings and beliefs about this other person are transferred onto the therapist (p. 88)

transsexualism condition of chronic discomfort with one's gender and genitals as well as a desire to be rid of one's genitals and to live as a member of the opposite sex (p. 414)

transvestism fetish in which a heterosexual man dresses in women's clothing as his primary means of becoming sexually aroused (p. 408)

tricyclic antidepressants group of drugs that reduces symptoms of depression and anxiety by affecting the functional levels of norepinephrine, serotonin, and other neurotransmitters. (pp. 116, 183)

twin study study of the heritability of a disorder by comparing concordance rates between monozygotic and dizygotic twins (p. 73)

Type A behavior pattern personality pattern characterized by time urgency, hostility, and competitiveness (p. 479)

U

unconditioned response (UR) in classical conditioning, response that naturally follows when a certain stimulus appears, as a dog salivating when it smells food (p. 80)

unconditioned stimulus (US) in classical conditioning, stimulus that naturally elicits a reaction, as food elicits salivation in dogs (p. 80)

unconscious area of the psyche where memories, wishes, and needs are stored and where conflicts among the id, ego, and superego are played out (p. 76)

undifferentiated schizophrenia diagnosis made when a person experiences schizophrenic symptoms, such as delusions and hallucinations, but does not meet criteria for paranoid, disorganized, or catatonic schizophrenia (p. 227)

unipolar depression type of depression consisting of depressive symptoms but without manic episodes (p. 158)

unstructured interview meeting between a clinician and a client or a client's associate(s) that consists of open-ended, general questions that are particular to each person interviewed (p. 28)

V

vaginismus in women, involuntary contractions of the muscles surrounding the outer third of the vagina that interfere with penetration and sexual functioning (p. 393)

validity degree of correspondence between a measurement and the phenomenon under study (p. 29)

variable measurable factor or characteristic that can vary within an individual, between individuals, or both (p. 519)

vascular dementia second most common type of dementia, associated with symptoms of cerebrovascular disease (tissue damage in the brain due to a blockage of blood flow) (p. 503)

vasocongestion in the sexual response cycle, filling of blood vessels and tissues with blood, leading to erection of the penis in males and enlargement of the clitoris, swelling of the labia, and vaginal moistening in women (also called engorgement) (p. 387)

ventricles fluid-filled spaces of the brain (pp. 69, 231)

visual hallucination visual perception of something that is not actually present (p. 220)

voyeurism obtainment of sexual arousal by compulsively and secretly watching another person undressing, bathing, engaging in sex, or being naked (p. 409)

W

wait list control group in a therapy outcome study, group of people that functions as a control group while an experimental group receives an intervention and that then receives the intervention itself after a waiting period (p. 533)

Wernicke's encephalopathy alcohol-induced permanent cognitive disorder involving mental disorientation and confusion and, in severe states, coma (p. 433)

word salad speech that is so disorganized that a listener cannot comprehend it (p. 221)

References

A

Abbott, B. B., Schoen, L. S., & Badia, P. (1984). Predictable and unpredictable shock: Behavioral measures of aversion and physiological measures of stress. *Psychological Bulletin, 96,* 45–71.

Abel, G. G., & Osborn, C. (1992). The paraphilias: The extent and nature of sexually deviant and criminal behavior. *Psychiatric Clinics of North America, 15,* 675–687.

Abplanalp, J. M., Haskett, R. F., & Rose, R. M. (1979). Psychoendocrinology of the menstrual cycle: I. Enjoyment of daily activities and moods. *Psychosomatic Medicine, 41,* 587–604.

Abramson, L. Y., Metalsky, G. I., & Alloy, L. B. (1989). Hopelessness depression: A theory-based subtype of depression. *Psychological Review, 96,* 358–372.

Abramson, L. Y., Seligman, M. E. P., & Teasdale, J. (1978). Learned helplessness in humans: Critique and reformulation. *Journal of Abnormal Psychology, 87,* 49–74.

Achenbach, T. M., & Edelbrock, C. (1983). *Manual for the child behavior checklist and revised child behavior profile.* Burlington, VT: Queen City Printers.

Achenbach, T. M., McConaughy, S. H., & Howell, C. T. (1987). Child/adolescent behavioral and emotional problems: Implications of cross-informant correlations for situational specificity. *Psychological Bulletin, 101,* 213–232.

Ackerman, M. D., & Carey, M. P. (1995). Psychology's role in the assessment of erectile dysfunction: Historical perspectives, current knowledge, and methods. *Journal of Consulting & Clinical Psychology, 63,* 862–876.

Advokat, C., & Kutlesic, V. (1995). Pharmacotherapy of the eating disorders: A commentary. *Neuroscience & Biobehavioral Reviews, 19,* 59–66.

Agras, S., Sylvester, D., & Oliveau, D. (1969). The epidemiology of common fears and phobia. *Comprehensive Psychiatry, 10,* 151–156.

Agras, W. S. (1987). *Eating disorders: Management of obesity, bulimia, and anorexia nervosa.* New York: Pergamon Press.

Agras, W. S. (1993). Short term psychological treatments for binge eating. In C. G. Fairburn & G. T. Wilson (Eds.), *Binge eating: Nature, assessment & treatment.* New York: Guilford.

Agras, W. S., & Kirkley, B. G. (1986). Bulimia: Theories of etiology. In K. D. Brownell & J. P. Foreyt (Eds.), *Handbook of eating disorders: Physiology, psychology, and treatment of obesity, anorexia, and bulimia* (pp. 367–378). New York: Basic Books.

Akhtar, S., Pershad, D., & Verma, S. K. (1975). A Rorschach study of obsessional neurosis. *Indian Journal of Clinical Psychology, 2,* 139–143.

Alden, L. (1989). Short-term structured treatment for avoidant personality disorder. *Journal of Consulting & Clinical Psychology, 57,* 756–764.

Alexander, K. L., Entwisle, D. R., & Thompson, M. S. (1987). School performance, status relations, and the structure of sentiment: Bringing the teacher back in. *American Sociological Review, 52,* 665–682.

Allderidge, P. (1979). Hospitals, madhouses and asylums: Cycles in the care of the insane. *British Journal of Psychiatry, 134,* 321–334.

Allgood-Merten, B., Lewinsohn, P. M., & Hops, H. (1990). Sex differences and adolescent depression. *Journal of Abnormal Psychology, 99,* 55–63.

Allison, J., Blatt, S. J., & Zimet, C. N. (1968). *The interpretation of psychological tests.* New York: Harper & Row.

Allison, K. W., Crawford, I., Echemendia, R., & Robinson, L. (1994). Human diversity and professional competence: Training in clinical and counseling psychology revisited. *American Psychologist, 49,* 792–796.

Alloy, L. B., & Abramson, L. Y. (1979). Judgment of contingency in depressed and nondepressed students: Sadder but wiser? *Journal of Experimental Psychology: General, 108,* 441–485.

Altarriba, J., & Santiago-Rivera, A. L. (1994). Current perspectives on using linguistic and cultural factors in counseling the Hispanic client. *Professional Psychology: Research & Practice, 25,* 388–397.

Althof, S. E. (1995). Pharmacologic treatment of rapid ejaculation. *Psychiatric Clinics of North America, 18,* 85–94.

American Psychiatric Association. (1983). *Diagnostic and statistical manual of mental disorders* (3rd ed.). Washington, DC: Author.

American Psychiatric Association (1994). *Diagnostic and statistical manual of mental disorders* (4th ed.). Washington, DC: American Psychiatric Press.

Anastopoulos, A. D., & Barkley, R. A. (1988). Biological factors in attention deficit-hyperactivity disorder. *Behavior Therapist, 11,* 47–53.

Andersen, A. E. (Ed.). (1990). *Males with eating disorders.* New York: Brunner/Mazel.

Andersen, A. E., & DiDomenico, L. (1992). Diet vs. shape content of popular male and female magazines: A dose-response relationship to the incidence of eating disorders? *International Journal of Eating Disorders, 11,* 283–287.

Andersen, B. L., & Cyranowski, J. M. (1995). Women's sexuality: Behaviors, responses, and individual difference. *Journal of Consulting & Clinical Psychology, 63,* 891–906.

Anderson, E. M., & Lambert, M. J. (1995). Short-term dynamically oriented psychotherapy: A review and meta-analysis. *Clinical Psychology Review, 15*, 503–514.

Anderson, G., Yasenik, L., & Ross, C. A. (1993). Dissociative experiences and disorders among women who identify themselves as sexual abuse survivors. *Child Abuse & Neglect, 17*, 677–686.

Anderson, J. C., Williams, S. M., McGee, R., & Silva, P. A. (1987). DSM-III disorders in preadolescent children: Prevalence in a large sample from the general population. *Archives of General Psychiatry, 44*, 69–76.

Anderson, N. B., Lane, J. D., Taguchi, F., & Williams, R. B. (1989). Patterns of cardiovascular responses to stress as a function of race and parental hypertension in men. *Health Psychology, 8*, 525–540.

Anderson, R. E., Bartlett, S. J., Morgan, G. D., & Brownell, K. D. (1995). Weight loss, psychological, and nutritional patterns in competitive male body builders. *International Journal of Eating Disorders, 18*, 49–57.

Andreasen, N. C., Flaum, M., Swayze, V. W., Tyrrell, G., & Arndt, S. (1990). Positive and negative symptoms in schizophrenia: A critical reappraisal. *Archives of General Psychiatry, 47*, 615–621.

Andreasen, N. C., O'Leary, D. S., Flaum, M., Nopoulos, P., Watkins, G. L., Ponto, L. L. B., & Hichwa, R. D. (in press). "Hypofrontality" in schizophrenia: Distributed dysfunctional circuits in neuroleptic naive patients. *Lancet*.

Andreasen, N. C., Rezai, K., Alliger, R., & Swayze, V. W. (1992). Hypofrontality in neuroleptic-naive patients and in patients with chronic schizophrenia: Assessment with xenon 133 single-photon emission computed tomography and the Tower of London. *Archives of General Psychiatry, 49*, 943–958.

Andreasen, N. C., Swayze, V. W., Flaum, M., & Alliger, R. (1990). Ventricular abnormalities in affective disorder; Clinical and demographic correlates. *American Journal of Psychiatry, 147*, 893–900.

Angold, A., & Worthman, C. W. (1993). Puberty onset of gender differences in rates of depression: A developmental, epidemiological and neuroendocrine perspective. *Journal of Affective Disorders, 29*, 145–158.

Anonymous. (1983). First-person account. *Schizophrenia Bulletin, 9*, 152–155.

Anonymous. (1992). First-person account: Portrait of a schizophrenic. *Schizophrenia Bulletin, 18*, 333–334.

Anthony, E. J., & Cohler, B. J. (1987). *The invulnerable child*. New York: Guilford Press.

Arieti, S. (1955). *Interpretation of schizophrenia*. New York: R. Brunner.

Arieti, S., & Bemporad, J. R. (1980). The psychological organization of depression. *American Journal of Psychiatry, 137*, 1360–1365.

Atkinson, D. R. (1983). Ethnic similarity in counseling psychology: A review of the research. *Counseling Psychologist, 11*, 79–92.

Atkinson, D. R., Furlong, M. J., & Poston, W. C. (1986). Afro-American preferences for counselor characteristics. *Journal of Counseling Psychology, 33*, 326–330.

Atkinson, D. R., Maruyama, M., & Matsui, S. (1978). Effects of counselor race and counseling approach on Asian Americans' perceptions of counselor credibility and utility. *Journal of Counseling Psychology, 25*, 76–83.

Attie, I., & Brooks-Gunn, J. (1989). Development of eating problems in adolescent girls: A longitudinal study. *Development Psychology, 25*, 70–79.

B

Bachrach, L. L. (1987). Asylum for chronic mental patients. *New Directions for Mental Health Service, 35*, 5–12.

Baer, J. S., Marlatt, G. A., Kivlahan, D. R., & Fromme, K. (1992). An experimental test of three methods of alcohol risk reduction with young adults. *Journal of Consulting & Clinical Psychology, 60*, 974–979.

Ball, J. C., & Ross, A. (1991). *The effectiveness of methadone maintenance treatment*. New York: Springer-Verlag.

Ballenger, J. C., Burrows, G. D., Dupont, R. L., & Lesser, I. M. (1988). Alprazolam in panic disorder and agoraphobia: Results from a multicenter trial. *Archives of General Psychiatry, 45*, 413–422.

Bandura, A. (1969). *Principles of behavior modification*. New York: Holt, Rinehart & Winston.

Bandura, A. (1977). Self-efficacy: Toward a unifying theory of behavioral change. *Psychological Review, 84*, 191–215.

Bandura, A. (1986). *Social foundations of thought and action*. Englewood Cliffs, NJ: Prentice Hall.

Bandura, A. (1995). *Self-efficacy in changing societies*. New York: Cambridge University Press.

Bandura, A., Adams, N. E., & Beyer, J. (1977). Cognitive processes mediating behavioral change. *Journal of Personality & Social Psychology, 35*, 125–139.

Banich, M. T., Stolar, N., Heller, W., & Goldman, R. B. (1992). A deficit in right-hemisphere performance after induction of a depressed mood. *Neuropsychiatry, Neuropsychology, & Behavioral Neurology, 5*, 20–27.

Barber, J. P., & DeRubeis, R. J. (1989). On second thought: Where the action is in cognitive therapy for depression. *Cognitive Therapy & Research, 13*, 441–457.

Barefoot, J. C., Dahlstrom, W. G., & Williams, R. B. (1983). Hostility, CHD incidence, and total mortality: A 25-yr follow-up study of 255 physicians. *Psychosomatic Medicine, 45*, 59–63.

Barefoot, J. C., Dodge, K. A., Peterson, B. L., Dahlstrom, W. G., & Williams, R. B., Jr. (1989). The Cook-Medley Hostility scale: Item content and ability to predict survival. *Psychosomatic Medicine, 51*, 46–57.

Barefoot, J. C., Siegler, I. C., Nowlin, J. B., & Peterson, B. L. (1987). Suspiciousness, health, and mortality: A follow-up study of 500 older adults. *Psychosomatic Medicine, 49*, 450–457.

Barkley, R. A. (1990). *Attention-deficit hyperactivity disorder: A handbook for diagnosis and treatment*. New York: Guilford Press.

Barkley, R. A. (1991). Attention deficit hyperactivity disorder. *Psychiatric Annals, 21*, 725–733.

Barkley, R. A., Fischer, M., Edelbrock, C. S., & Smallish, L. (1990). The adolescent outcome of hyperactive children diagnosed by research criteria: I. An 8-year prospective follow-up study. *Journal of the American Academy of Child & Adolescent Psychiatry, 29*, 546–557.

Barlow, D. H. (1988). *Anxiety and its disorders: The nature and treatment of anxiety and panic*. New York: Guilford Press.

Barlow, D. H., Brown, T. A., & Craske, M. G. (1994). Definitions of panic attacks and panic disorder in the DSM-IV: Implications for research. *Journal of Abnormal Psychology, 103*, 553–564.

Barlow, D. H., & Craske, M. G. (1994). *Mastery of your anxiety and panic (MAP II)*. Albany, NY: Graywind Publications.

Barlow, D. H., Craske, M. G., Cerny, J. A., & Klosko, J. S. (1989). Behavioral treatment of panic disorder. *Behavior Therapy, 20,* 261–282.

Barlow, D. H., Sakheim, D. K., & Beck, J. G. (1983). Anxiety increases sexual arousal. *Journal of Abnormal Psychology, 92,* 49–54.

Baron, M., Gruen, R., Asnis, L., & Lord, S. (1985). Familial transmission of schizotypal and borderline personality disorders. *American Journal of Psychiatry, 142,* 927–934.

Baron, M., Perlman, R., & Levitt, M. (1980). Paranoid schizophrenia and platelet MAO activity. *American Journal of Psychiatry, 137,* 1465–1466.

Barsky, A. J. (1992). Amplification, somatization, and the somatoform disorders. *Psychosomatics, 33,* 28–34.

Barsky, A. J., Wyshak, G., & Klerman, G. L. (1992). Psychiatric comorbidity in DSM-III-R hypochondriasis. *Archives of General Psychiatry, 49,* 101–108.

Bass, E., & Davis, L. (1988). *The courage to heal: A guide for women survivors of child sexual abuse.* New York: Harper & Row.

Bateson, G., Jackson, D. D., Haley, J., & Weakland, J. (1956). Toward a theory of schizophrenia. *Behavioral Science, 1,* 251–264.

Battle, E. S., & Lacey, B. (1972). A context for hyperactivity in children, over time. *Child Development, 43,* 757–773.

Baxter, L., Schwartz, J., Bergman, K., & Szuba, M. (1992). Caudate glucose metabolic rate changes with both drug and behavior therapy for obsessive-compulsive disorder. *Archives of General Psychiatry, 49,* 681–689.

Baxter, L. R., Jr., Phelps, M. E., Mazziotta, J. C., Schwartz, J. M., Gerner, R. H., Selin, C. E., & Sumida, R. M. (1985). Cerebral metabolic rates for glucose in mood disorders: Studies with positron emission tomography and fluorodeoxyglucose F 18. *Archives of General Psychiatry, 42,* 441–447.

Baxter, L. R., Schwartz, J. M., Guze, B. H., & Bergman, K. (1990). PET imaging in obsessive compulsive disorder with and without depression. *Journal of Clinical Psychiatry, 51,* 61–69.

Baxter, L. R., Schwartz, J. M., Phelps, M. E., & Mazziotta, J. C. (1989). Reduction of prefrontal cortex glucose metabolism common to three types of depression. *Archives of General Psychiatry, 46,* 243–250.

Beatty, J. (1995). *Principles of behavioral neuroscience.* Dubuque, IA: Wm. C. Brown.

Beck, A. T. (1967). *Depression: Clinical, experimental, and theoretical aspects.* New York: Harper & Row.

Beck, A. T. (1976). *Cognitive therapy and the emotional disorders.* New York: International Universities Press.

Beck, A. T., & Beck, R. W. (1972). Screening depressed patients in family practice: A rapid technique. *Postgraduate Medicine, 52,* 81–85.

Beck, A. T., & Emery, G. (1985). *Anxiety disorders and phobias: A cognitive perspective.* New York: Basic Books.

Beck, A. T., & Freeman, A. M. (1990). *Cognitive therapy of personality disorders.* New York: Guilford Press.

Beck, A. T., Rush, A. J., Shaw, B. F., & Emery, G. (1979). *Cognitive therapy of depression.* New York: Guilford Press.

Beck, A. T., Steer, R. A., Kovacs, M., & Garrison, B. (1985). Hopelessness and eventual suicide: A 10-year prospective study of patients hospitalized with suicidal ideation. *American Journal of Psychiatry, 142,* 559–563.

Beck, A. T., Ward, C. H., Mendelson, M., Moch, J. E., & Erbaugh, J. (1962). Reliability of psychiatric diagnosis. II: A study of consistency of clinical judgments and ratings. *American Journal of Psychiatry, 119,* 351–357.

Beck, A. T., Weissman, A., Lester, D., & Trexler, L. (1974). The measurement of pessimism: The Hopelessness Scale. *Journal of Consulting & Clinical Psychology, 42,* 861–865.

Beck, J. G. (1995). Hypoactive sexual desire: An overview. *Journal of Consulting & Clinical Psychology, 63,* 919–927.

Becker, J. V. (1989). Impact of sexual abuse on sexual functioning. In S. R. Leiblum & R. C. Rosen (Eds.), *Principles and practice of sex therapy: Update for the 1990s* (pp. 298–318). New York: Guilford Press.

Beckman, L. J. (1994). Treatment needs of women with alcohol problems. *Alcohol Health & Research World, 18,* 206–211.

Beels, C. C., & McFarlane, W. R. (1982). Family treatments of schizophrenia: Background and state of the art. *Hospital & Community Psychiatry, 33,* 541–550.

Beinenfeld, D., & Wheeler, B. G. (1989). Psychiatric services to nursing homes: A liaison model. *Hospital & Community Psychiatry, 40,* 793–794.

Beiser, M. (1988). Influences of time, ethnicity, and attachment on depression in Southeast Asian refugees. *American Journal of Psychiatry, 145,* 46–51.

Bellack, A. S., Morrison, R. L., & Mueser, K. T. (1992). Behavioral interventions in schizophrenia. In S. M. Turner, K. S. Calhoun, & H. E. Adams (Eds.), *Handbook of clinical behavior therapy* (pp. 135–154). New York: Wiley.

Belsher, G., & Costello, C. G. (1988). Relapse after recovery from unipolar depression: A critical review. *Psychological Bulletin, 104,* 84–96.

Bemporad, J. (1995). Long-term analytic treatment of depression. In E. E. Beckham & W. R. Leber (Eds.), *Handbook of depression,* (2nd ed., pp. 391–403). New York: Guilford.

Bender, L. (1938). *A visual motor gestalt test and its clinical use.* New York: The American Orthopsychiatric Association.

Bennett, A. E. (1947). Mad doctors. *Journal of Nervous & Mental Disorders, 29,* 11–18.

Benton, M. K., & Schroeder, H. E. (1990). Social skills training with schizophrenics: A meta-analytic evaluation. *Journal of Consulting & Clinical Psychology, 58,* 741–747.

Berman, K. F., Torrey, E. F., Daniel, D. G., & Weinberger, D. R. (1992). Regional cerebral blood flow in monozygotic twins discordant and concordant for schizophrenia. *Archives of General Psychiatry, 49,* 927–934.

Bernstein, D. P., Useda, D., & Siever, L. J. (1995). Paranoid personality disorder. In W. J. Livesley (Ed.), *The DSM-IV personality disorders* (pp. 45–57). New York: Guilford Press.

Bernstein, J. G. (1983). *Handbook of drug therapy in psychiatry.* Boston: J. Wright.

Berridge, K. C., & Valenstein, E. S. (1991). What psychological process mediates feeding evoked by electrical stimulation of the lateral hypothalamus? *Behavioral Neuroscience, 105,* 3–14.

Bertelsen, A., Harvald, B., & Hauge, M. A. (1977). A Danish twin study of manic-depressive disorders. *British Journal of Psychiatry, 130,* 330–351.

Bettelheim, B. (1967). *The empty fortress: Infantile autism and the birth of the self.* New York: Free Press.

Beutler, L. F., Daldrup, R., Engle, D., & Guest, P. D. (1988). Family dynamics and emotional expression among patients with chronic pain and depression. *Pain, 32,* 65–72.

Beyond Prozac (1994, February 7). *Newsweek*, p. 123.

Bibring, E. (1953). The mechanism of depression. In P. Greenacre (Ed.), *Affective disorders* (pp. 13–48). New York: International Universities Press.

Billings, A., & Moos, R. H. (1981). The role of coping responses and social resources in attenuating the stress of life events. *Journal of Behavioral Medicine, 4,* 157–189.

Blacher, J. B., Hanneman, R. A., & Rousey, A. B. (1992). Out-of-home placement of children with severe handicaps: A comparison of approaches. *American Journal on Mental Retardation, 96,* 607–616.

Blackburn, G. L., & Kanders, B. S. (1987). Medical evaluation and treatment of the obese patient with cardiovascular disease. *American Journal of Cardiology, 60,* 55G–58G.

Blair, A. J., Lewis, J., & Booth, D. A. (1989). Behavior therapy for obesity: The role of clinicians in the reduction of overweight. *Counseling Psychology Quarterly, 2,* 289–301.

Blanchard, J. J., & Neale, J. M. (1992). Medication effects: Conceptual and methodological issues in schizophrenia research. *Clinical Psychology Review, 12,* 345–361.

Blatt, S. J., & Zuroff, D. C. (1992). Interpersonal relatedness and self-definition: Two prototypes for depression. *Clinical Psychology Review, 12,* 527–562.

Blau, T. H. (1991). *The psychological examination of the child.* New York: John Wiley.

Blazer, D. G., George, L., & Hughes, D. (1991). The epidemiology of anxiety disorders. In C. Salzman & B. Liebowitz (Eds.), *Anxiety disorders in the elderly* (pp. 17–30). New York: Springer-Verlag.

Blazer, D. G., Kessler, R. C., McGonagle, K. A., & Swartz, M. S. (1994). The prevalence and distribution of major depression in a national community sample: The National Comorbidity Study. *American Journal of Psychiatry, 151,* 979–986.

Blehar, M. C., & Oren, D. A. (1995). Women's increased vulnerability to mood disorders: Integrating psychobiology and epidemiology. *Depression, 3,* 3–12.

Bleuler, E. (1924). *Textbook of psychiatry.* New York: Macmillan.

Bliss, E. L. (1980). Multiple personalities: A report of 14 cases with implications for schizophrenia and hysteria. *Archives of General Psychiatry, 37,* 1388–1397.

Bliss, E. L. (1986). *Multiple personality, allied disorders, and hypnosis.* New York: Oxford University Press.

Bliss, E. L., & Branch, C. H. H. (1960). *Anorexia nervosa; its history, psychology, and biology.* New York: Hoeber.

Block, J. H., Block, J., & Gjerde, P. F. (1986). The personality of children prior to divorce: A prospective study. *Child Development, 57,* 827–840.

Blundell, J. E., & Hill, A. (1993). Binge eating: Psychobiological mechanisms. In C. G. Fairburn & G. T. Wilson (Eds.), *Binge eating: Nature, assessment, and treatment* (pp. 15–34). New York: Guilford Press.

Boffeli, T. J., & Guze, S. B. (1992). The simulation of neurologic disease. *Psychiatric Clinics of North America, 15,* 301–310.

Booth-Kewley, S., & Friedman, H. S. (1987). Psychological predictors of heart disease: A quantitative review. *Psychological Bulletin, 101,* 343–362.

Borduin, C. M., Mann, B. J., Cone, L. T., Henggeler, S. W., Fucci, B. R., Blaske, D. M., & Williams, R. A. (1995). Multisystemic treatment of serious juvenile offenders: Long-term prevention of criminality and violence. *Journal of Consulting & Clinical Psychology, 63,* 569–578.

Borkovec, T. D., & Costello, E. (1993). Efficacy of applied relaxation and cognitive-behavioral therapy in the treatment of generalized anxiety disorder. *Journal of Consulting & Clinical Psychology, 61,* 611–619.

Borkovec, T. D., & Hu, S. (1990). The effect of worry on cardiovascular response to phobic imagery. *Behaviour Research & Therapy, 28,* 69–73.

Borys, D. S., & Pope, K. S. (1989). Dual relationships between therapist and client: A national study of psychologists, psychiatrists, and social workers. *Professional Psychology: Research & Practice, 20,* 283–293.

Bouchard, C., Trembley, A., Nadeau, A., Despres, J. P., Theriault, G., Boulay, M. R., Lortie, G., Leblanc, C., & Fournier, G. (1989). Genetic effect in resting and exercise metabolic rates. *Metabolism, 38,* 364–370.

Bouchard, T. J., Lykken, D. T., McGue, M., & Segal, N. L. (1990). Sources of human psychological differences: The Minnesota study of twins reared apart. *Science, 250,* 223–228.

Bourden, K., Boyd, J., Rae, D., & Burns, B. (1988). Gender differences in phobias: Results of the EAC community survey. *Journal of Anxiety Disorders, 2,* 227–241.

Bowen, R. C., Offord, D. R., & Boyle, M. H. (1990). The prevalence of overanxious disorder and separation anxiety disorder: Results of the Ontario Child Health Study. *Journal of the American Academy of Child & Adolescent Psychiatry, 29,* 753–758.

Bower, G. H. (1981). Mood and memory. *American Psychologist, 36,* 129–148.

Boyd, C. J., & Guthrie, B. (1996). Women, their significant others, and crack cocaine. *The American Journal on Addictions, 5,* 156–166.

Braun, B. G. (Ed.). (1986). *Treatment of multiple personality disorder.* Washington, DC: American Psychiatric Press.

Bray, G. A. (1986). Effects of obesity on health and happiness. In K. D. Brownell & J. P. Foreyt (Eds.), *Handbook of eating disorders: Physiology, psychology, and treatment of obesity, anorexia, and bulimia* (pp. 3–44). New York: Basic Books.

Brazier, M. (1960). *The electrical activity of the nervous system: A textbook for students.* London: Pitman Medical Publishing.

Breier, A., Schreiber, J. L., Dyer, J., & Pickar, D. (1991). National Institutes of Mental Health longitudinal study of chronic schizophrenia: Prognosis and predictors of outcome. *Archives of General Psychiatry, 48,* 239–246.

Breier, A., Schreiber, J. L., Dyer, J., & Pickar, D. (1992). Course of illness and predictors of outcome in chronic schizophrenia: Implications for pathophysiology. *British Journal of Psychiatry, 161,* 38–43.

Breslow, N., Evans, L., & Langley, J. (1985). On the prevalence and roles of females in the sadomasochistic subculture: Report of an empirical study. *Archives of Sexual Behavior, 14,* 303–317.

Brewin, C. R., MacCarthy, B., Duda, K., & Vaughn, C. E. (1991). Attribution and expressed emotion in the relatives of patients with schizophrenia. *Journal of Abnormal Psychology, 100,* 546–554.

Briere, J., & Conte, J. R. (1993). Self-reported amnesia for abuse in adults molested as children. *Journal of Traumatic Stress, 6,* 21–31.

Briere, J., & Runtz, M. (1989). University males' sexual interest in children:

Predicting potential indices of "pedophilia" in a nonforensic sample. *Child Abuse & Neglect, 13,* 65–75.

Bromberger, J. T., & Matthews, K. A. (1996). A longitudinal study of the effects of pessimism, trait anxiety, and life stress on depressive symptoms in middle-aged women. *Psychology & Aging, 11,* 207–213.

Brooks-Gunn, J., Klebanov, P. K., Liaw, F., & Spiker, D. (1993). Enhancing the development of low-birthweight, premature infants: Changes in cognition and behavior over the first three years. *Child Development, 64,* 736–753.

Brown, G. W., Birley, J. L., & Wing, J. K. (1972). Influence of family life on the course of schizophrenic disorders: A replication. *British Journal of Psychiatry, 121,* 241–258.

Brown, L. L., Tomarken, A. J., Orth, D. N., & Loosen, P. T. (1996). Individual differences in repressive-defensiveness precit basal salivary cortisol levels. *Journal of Personality & Social Psychology, 70,* 362–371.

Brown, S. A., Inaba, R. K., Gillin, J. C., & Schuckit, M. A. (1995). Alcoholism and affective disorder: Clinical course of depressive symptoms. *American Journal of Psychiatry, 152,* 45–52.

Browne, A. (1993). Violence against women by male partners: Prevalence, outcomes, and policy implications. *American Psychologist, 48,* 1077–1087.

Brownell, K. D., & Foreyt, J. P. (Eds.). (1986). *Handbook of eating disorders.* New York: Basic Books.

Brownell, K. D., & Rodin, J. (1994). The dieting maelstrom: Is it possible and advisable to lose weight? *American Psychologist, 49,* 781–791.

Brownell, K. D., Rodin, J., & Wilmore, J. H. (1992). *Eating, body weight, and performance in athletes: Disorders of modern society.* Philadelphia: Lea & Febiger.

Brownell, K. D., & Wadden, T. A. (1992). Etiology and treatment of obesity: Understanding a serious, prevalent, and refractory disorder. *Journal of Consulting & Clinical Psychology, 60,* 505–517.

Bruch, H. (1970). Instinct and interpersonal experience. *Comprehensive Psychiatry, 11,* 495–506.

Bruch, H. (1973). *Eating disorders: Obesity, anorexia nervosa, and the person within.* New York: Basic Books.

Bruch, H. (1982). Anorexia nervosa: Therapy and theory. *American Journal of Psychiatry, 139,* 1531–1538.

Buchanan, C. M., Maccoby, E. E., & Dornbusch, S. M. (1991). Caught between parents: Adolescent experiences in divorced families. *Child Development, 62,* 1008–1029.

Buckwalter, J., Sobel, E., Dunn, M. E., & Diz, M. M. (1993). Gender differences on a brief measure of cognitive functioning in Alzheimer's disease. *Archives of Neurology, 50,* 757–760.

Bulman, R. J., & Wortman, C. G. (1977). Attributions of blame and coping in the "real world": Severe accident victims react to their lot. *Journal of Personality & Social Psychology, 35,* 351–363.

Bunney, W. E., & Davis, J. M. (1965). Norepinephrine in depressive reactions: A review. *Archives of General Psychiatry, 13,* 483–493.

Burke, K. C., Burke, J. D., Regier, D. A., & Rae, D. S. (1990). Age at onset of selected mental disorders in five community populations. *Archives of General Psychiatry, 47,* 511–518.

Burnam, M. A., Stein, J. A., Golding, J. M., & Siegel, J. M. (1988). Sexual assault and mental disorders in a community population. *Journal of Consulting & Clinical Psychology, 56,* 843–850.

Burns, D. (1980). *Feeling good: The new mood therapy.* New York: Morrow.

Burns, D. D., & Nolen-Hoeksema, S. (1992). Therapeutic empathy and recovery from depression in cognitive-behavioral therapy: A structural equation model. *Journal of Consulting & Clinical Psychology, 60,* 441–449.

Burns, D., & Nolen-Hoeksema, S. (1991). Coping styles, homework assignments and the effectiveness of cognitive-behavioral therapy. *Journal of Consulting & Clinical Psychology, 59,* 305–311.

Buschbaum, M. S. (1984). The Genain quadruplets: Electrophysiological, positron emission, and X-ray tomographic studies. *Psychiatry Research, 13,* 95–108.

Buschbaum, M. S., Haier, R. J., Potkin, S. G., & Nuechterlein, K. (1992). Fronostriatal disorder of cerebral metabolism in never-medicated schizophrenics. *Archives of General Psychiatry, 49,* 935–942.

Butcher, J. N. (1990). *The MMPI-2 in psychological treatment.* New York: Oxford University Press.

Butler, G., Fennell, M., Robson, P., & Gelder, M. (1991). Comparison of behavior therapy and cognitive behavior therapy in the treatment of generalized anxiety disorder. *Journal of Consulting & Clinical Psychology, 59,* 167–175.

Byrne, E. J. (1994). *Confusional states in older people.* Boston: E. Arnold.

C

Cadoret, R. J., & Cain, C. A. (1980). Sex differences in predictors of antisocial behavior in adoptees. *Archives of General Psychiatry, 37,* 1171–1175.

Cadoret, R. J., & Stewart, M. A. (1991). An adoption study of attention deficit/hyperactivity/aggression and their relationship to adult antisocial personality. *Comprehensive Psychiatry, 32,* 73–82.

Caffey, J. (1972). On the theory and practice of shaking infants. *American Journal of Diseases of Children, 124,* 161–172.

Cameron, N., & Rychlak, J. F. (1985). *Personality development and psychopathology: A dynamic approach.* Boston: Houghton Mifflin.

Campbell, M., Perry, R., & Green, W. H. (1984). Use of lithium in children and adolescents. *Psychosomatics, 25,* 95–106.

Canetto, S. S., & Lester, D. (1995). Gender and the primary prevention of suicide mortality. *Suicide & Life Threatening Behavior, 25,* 58–69.

Canino, G. J., Burnam, A., & Caetano, R. (1992). The prevalence of alcohol abuse and/or dependence in two Hispanic communities. In J. E. Helzer & G. J. Canino (Eds.), *Alcoholism in North America, Europe, and Asia* (pp. 131–159). New York: Oxford University Press.

Canino, G. J., Rubio-Stipec, M., & Bravo, M. (1988). Psychiatric diagnostic nosology in transcultural epidemiology research. *Acta Psiquiatrica Psicologica de America Latina, 34,* 251–259.

Caplan, P. J., & Gans, M. (1991). Is there empirical justification for the category of "self-defeating personality disorder"? *Feminism & Psychology, 1,* 263–278.

Cappe, R. F., & Alden, L. E. (1986). A comparison of treatment strategies for clients functionally impaired by extreme shyness and social avoidance. *Journal of Consulting & Clinical Psychology, 54,* 796–801.

Carstensen, L. L. (1995). Evidence for a life-span theory of socioemotional selectivity. *Current Directions in Psychological Science, 4,* 151–156.

Carter, M. M., Hollon, S. D., Carson, R. S., & Shelton, R. C. (1995). Effects of a safe person on induced distress following a biological challenge in panic disorder with agoraphobia. *Journal of Abnormal Psychology, 104,* 156–163.

Castiglioni, A. (1946). *Adventures of the mind.* (1st American ed.). New York: Alfred A. Knopf.

Castonguay, L. G., Eldredge, K. L., & Agras, W. S. (1995). Binge eating disorder: Current state and future directions. *Clinical Psychology Review, 15,* 865–890.

Ceci, S. J., Toglia, M. P., & Ross, D. F. (1988). On remembering . . . more or less: A trace strength interpretation of developmental differences in suggestibility. *Journal of Experimental Psychology: General, 117,* 201–203.

Cervantes, R. C., Salgado de Snyder, V. N., & Padilla, A. M. (1989). Posttraumatic stress in immigrants from Central America and Mexico. *Hospital & Community Psychiatry, 40,* 615–619.

Chamberlain, P., & Rosicky, J. G. (1995). The effectiveness of family therapy in the treatment of adolescents with conduct disorders and delinquency. *Journal of Marital & Family Therapy, 21,* 441–459.

Chambless, D. C., Cherney, J., Caputo, G. C., & Rheinstein, B. J. (1987). Anxiety disorders and alcoholism: A study with inpatient alcoholics. *Journal of Anxiety Disorders, 1,* 29–40.

Chapman, L. J., Edell, W. S., & Chapman, J. P. (1980). Physical anhedonia, perceptual aberration, and psychosis proneness. *Schizophrenia Bulletin, 6,* 639–653.

Chaturvedi, S. K. (1987). Family morbidity in chronic pain patients. *Pain, 30,* 159–168.

Cherlin, A. J., Furstenberg, F. F., Chase-Lansdale, P. L., & Kiernan, K. E. (1991). Longitudinal studies of effects of divorce on children in Great Britain and the United States. *Science, 252,* 1386–1389.

Chevron, E. S., Quinlan, D. M., & Blatt, S. J. (1978). Sex roles and gender differences in the experience of depression. *Journal of Abnormal Psychology, 87,* 680–683.

Clark, D. A., & DeSilva, P. (1985). The nature of depressive and anxious, intrusive thoughts: Distinct or uniform phenomena? *Behaviour Research & Therapy, 23,* 383–393.

Clark, D. A., & Purdon, C. (1993). New perspectives for a cognitive theory of obsessions. *Australian Psychologist, 28,* 161–167.

Clark, D. C. (1995). Epidemiology, assessment, and management of suicide in depressed patients. In E. E. Beckham & W. R. Leber (Eds.), *Handbook of depres-* *sion* (2nd ed., pp. 526–538). New York: Guilford Press.

Clark, D. M. (1988). A cognitive model of panic attacks. In S. Rachman & J. D. Maser (Eds.), *Panic: Psychological perspectives* (pp. 71–89). Hillsdale, NJ: Erlbaum.

Clark, D. M. (1991, September 23–25). *Cognitive therapy for panic disorder.* Paper presented at the NIH Consensus Development Conference on the treatment of panic disorder, Bethesda, Maryland.

Clark, L. A., Watson, D., & Mineka, S. (1994). Temperament, personality, and the mood and anxiety disorders. *Journal of Abnormal Psychology, 103,* 103–116.

Cleckley, H. M. (1941). *The mask of sanity: An attempt to reinterpret the so-called psychopathic personality.* St. Louis: C. V. Mosby.

Cleveland, S., Mulvey, E. P., Appelbaum, P. S., & Lidz, C. W. (1989). Do dangerousness-oriented commitment laws restrict hospitalization of patients who need treatment? A test. *Hospital & Community Psychiatry, 40,* 266–271.

Cloninger, C. R., & Gottesman, I. I. (1987). Genetic and environmental factors in antisocial behavior disorders. In S. A Mednick, T. E. Moffitt, & S. A. Stack (Eds.), *The causes of crime: New biological approaches* (pp. 92–109). New York: Cambridge University Press.

Coccaro, E. F. (1993). Psychopharmacological studies in patients with personality disorders: Review and perspective. *Journal of Personality Disorders* (Spr. Suppl. 1), 181–192.

Cocores, J., Pottash, A. C., & Gold, M. S. (1991). Cocaine. In N. S. Miller (Ed.), *Comprehensive handbook of drug and alcohol addiction* (pp. 341–352). New York: Marcel Dekker.

Coffey, C. E. (1987). Cerebral laterality and emotion: The neurology of depression. *Comprehensive Psychiatry, 28,* 197–219.

Coffey, L. E., Wilkinson, W. E., Weiner, R. D., & Ritchie, J. C. (1993). The dexamethasone suppression test and quantitative cerebral anatomy in depression. *Biological Psychiatry, 33,* 442–449.

Cohen, P., Cohen, J., Kasen, S., Velez, C. N., Hartmark, C., Johnson, J., Rojas, M., Brook, J., & Streuning, E. L. (1993). An epidemiological study of disorders in late adolescence: I. Age- and gender-specific prevalence. *Journal of Child Psychology & Psychiatry, 6,* 851–867.

Cohen, S. (1996). Psychological stress, immunity, and upper respiratory infections. *Current Directions in Psychological Science, 5,* 86–90.

Cohen, S., Tyrrell, D. A. J., & Smith, A. P. (1991). Psychological stress and susceptibility to the common cold. *The New England Journal of Medicine, 325,* 606–612.

Colby, D. M. (1981). Modeling a paranoid mind. *Behavioral & Brain Sciences, 4,* 515–560.

Cole, W. (1992). Incest perpetrators: Their assessment and treatment. *Psychiatric Clinics of North America, 15,* 689–701.

Compas, B. E. (1987). Stress and life events during childhood and adolescence. *Clinical Psychology Review, 7,* 275–302.

Conrad, C. D., & Hamilton, J. A. (1986). Recurrent premenstrual decline in serum lithium concentration: Clinical correlates and treatment implications. *Journal of the American Academy of Child Psychiatry, 25,* 852–853.

Contrada, R. J., Wright, R. A., & Glass, D. C. (1985). Psychophysiologic correlates of Type A behavior: Comments on Houston (1983) and Holmes (1983). *Journal of Research in Personality, 19,* 12–30.

Coons, P. M. (1980). Multiple personality: Diagnostic considerations. *Journal of Clinical Psychiatry, 41,* 330–336.

Coons, P. M. (1984). *Childhood antecedents of multiple personality.* Paper presented at the Meeting of the American Psychiatric Association, Los Angeles, CA.

Coons, P. M. (1986). Treatment progress in 20 patients with multiple personality disorder. *The Journal of Nervous & Mental Disease, 174,* 715–721.

Coons, P. M. (1994). Confirmation of childhood abuse in child and adolescent cases of multiple personality disorder and dissociative disorder not otherwise specified. *Journal of Nervous & Mental Disease, 182,* 461–464.

Coons, P. M., Cole, C., Pellow, T., & Milstein, V. (1990). Symptoms of posttraumatic stress disorder and dissociation in women victims of abuse. In R. P. Kluft (Ed.), *Incest-related syndromes of adult psychopathology* (pp. 205–226). Washington, DC: American Psychiatric Press.

Coons, P. M., & Milstein, V. (1986). Psychosexual disturbances in multiple personality: Characteristics, etiology, and treatment. *Journal of Clinical Psychiatry, 47,* 106–110.

Coons, P. M., & Milstein, V. (1990). Self-mutilation associated with dissociative disorders. *Dissociation: Progress in the Dissociative Disorders, 3*, 81–87.

Coontz, P. D., Lidz, C. W., & Mulvey, E. P. (1994). Gender and the assessment of dangerousness in the psychiatric emergency room. *International Journal of Law & Psychiatry, 17*, 369–376.

Cooper, M. L., Russell, M., Skinner, J. B., Frone, M. R., & Mudar, P. (1992). Stress and alcohol use: Moderating effects of gender, coping, and alcohol expectancies. *Journal of Abnormal Psychology, 101*, 139–152.

Corder, E. H., Saunders, A. M., & Strittmatter, W. J. (1993). Gene dose of apolipoprotein E type 4 allele and the risk of Alzheimer's disease in late onset families. *Science, 261*, 921–923.

Cornblatt, B. A., & Keilp, J. G. (1994). Impaired attention, genetics, and the pathophysiology of schizophrenia. *Schizophrenia Bulletin, 20*, 31–46.

Coryell, W., Scheftner, W., Keller, M., & Endicott, J. (1993). The enduring psychosocial consequences of mania and depression. *American Journal of Psychiatry, 150*, 720–727.

Craig, T. K., Boardman, A. P., Mills, K., & Daly-Jones, O. (1993). The South London Somatisation Study: I. Longitudinal course and the influence of early life experiences. *British Journal of Psychiatry, 163*, 579–588.

Craighead, W. E., Meyers, A. W., & Craighead, L. W. (1985). A conceptual model for cognitive-behavior therapy with children. *Journal of Abnormal Child Psychiatry, 13*, 331–342.

Cranston-Cuebas, M. A., & Barlow, D. H. (1990). Cognitive and affective contributions to sexual functioning. *Annual Review of Sex Research, 1*, 119–161.

Craske, M. G., Brown, T. A., & Barlow, D. H. (1991). Behavioral treatment of panic disorder: A two-year follow-up. *Behavior Therapy, 22*, 289–304.

Crepault, C., & Couture, M. (1980). Men's erotic fantasies. *Archives of Sexual Behavior, 9*, 565–581.

Crick, N. R., & Dodge, K. A. (1994). A review and reformulation of social information-processing mechanisms in children's social adjustment. *Psychological Bulletin, 115*, 74–101.

Crick, N. R., & Grotpeter, J. K. (1995). Relational aggression, gender, and social-psychological adjustment. *Child Development, 66*, 710–722.

Crick, N. R., & Ladd, G. W. (1990). Children's perceptions of the outcomes of social strategies: Do the ends justify being mean? *Developmental Psychology, 26*, 612–620.

Crits-Christoph, P., Baranackie, K., Kurcias, J. S., & Beck, A. T. (1991). Meta-analysis of therapist effects in psychotherapy outcome. *Psychotherapy Research, 1*, 81–91.

Cromwell, R. L., & Snyder, C. R. (Eds.). (1993). *Schizophrenia: Origins, processes, treatment, and outcome.* New York: Oxford University Press.

Cronbach, L. J., & Meehl, P. E. (1955). Construct validity in psychological tests. *Psychological Bulletin, 52*, 281–302.

Cross National Collaborative Group (1992). The changing rate of major depression. *Journal of the American Medical Association, 268*, 3098–3105.

Crowe, R. R. (1990). Panic disorder: Genetic considerations. *Journal of Psychiatric Research, 24*, 129–134.

Crowe, R. R., Noyes, R., Pauls, D. L., & Slymen, D. J. (1983). A family study of panic disorder. *Archives of General Psychiatry, 40*, 1065–1069.

Custance, J. (1952). *Wisdom, madness, and folly: The philosophy of a lunatic.* New York: Straus and Cudahy.

D

D'Andrea, M., & Daniels, J. (1995). Helping students learn to get along: Assessing the effectiveness of a multicultural developmental guidance project. *Elementary School Guidance & Counseling, 30*, 143–154.

Dahl, A. A. (1993). The personality disorders: A critical review of family, twin, and adoption studies. *Journal of Personality Disorders* (Spr. Suppl. 1), 86–99.

Damasio, H., Grabowski, T., Frank, R., Galaburda, A. M., & Damasio, A. R. (1994). The return of Phineas Gage: Clues about the brain from the skull of a famous patient. *Science, 264*, 1102–1105.

Dana, R. H. (1995). *Multicultural assessment perspectives for professional psychology.* Boston: Allyn & Bacon.

Dare, C., Eisler, I., Russell, G. F., & Szmukler, G. I. (1990). The clinical and theoretical impact of a controlled trial of family therapy in anorexia nervosa. *Journal of Marital & Familial Therapy, 16*, 39–57.

David, J. (1994). *The family secret: Adult children of alcoholics tell their stories.* New York: William Morrow.

Davidson, J., Swartz, M., Storck, M., Krishnan, R. R., & Hammett, E. (1985). A diagnostic and family study of post-traumatic stress disorder. *American Journal of Psychiatry, 142*, 90–93.

Davidson, W. S., & Redner, R. (1988). The prevention of juvenile delinquency: Diversion from the juvenile justice system. In E. L. Cowen, R. P. Lorion, & J. Ramos-McKay (Eds.), *Fourteen ounces of prevention: A handbook for practitioners* (pp. 123–137). Washington, DC: American Psychological Association.

Davis, C., & Yager, J. (1992). Transcultural aspects of eating disorders: A critical literature review. *Culture, Medicine & Psychiatry, 16*, 377–394.

Davis, K. L., Kahn, R. S., Ko, G., & Davidson, M. (1991). Dopamine in schizophrenia: A review and conceptualization. *American Journal of Psychiatry, 148*, 1474–1486.

Day, J. J., Grant, I., Atkinson, J. H., & Brysk, L. T. (1992). Incidence of AIDS dementia in a two-year follow-up of AIDS and ARC patients on an initial Phase II AZT placebo-controlled study: San Diego cohort. *Journal of Neuropsychiatry & Clinical Neurosciences, 4*, 15–20.

de la Monte, S. M., Hutchins, G. M., & Moore, G. W. (1989). Racial differences in the etiology of dementia and frequency of Alzheimer lesions in the brain. *Journal of the National Medical Association, 81*, 644–652.

De-Veaugh-Geiss, J., Moroz, G., Biederman, J., & Cantwell, D. P. (1992). Clomipramine hydrochloride in childhood and adolescent obsessive compulsive disorder: A multicenter trial. *Journal of the American Academy of Child & Adolescent Psychiatry, 31*, 45–49.

Deakin, J. W., & Graeff, F. G. (1991). 5-HT and mechanisms of defense. *Journal of Psychopharmacology, 5*, 305–315.

DeHeer, N. D., Wampold, B. E., & Freund, R. D. (1992). Do sex-typed and androgynous subjects prefer counselors on the basis of gender or effectiveness? They prefer the best. *Journal of Counseling Psychology, 39*, 175–184.

Dell, P. F., & Eisenhower, J. W. (1990). Adolescent multiple personality disorder: A preliminary study of eleven cases. *Journal of the American Academy of Child & Adolescent Psychiatry, 29*, 359–366.

Dembroski, T. M., MacDougall, J. M., Williams, J. M., & Haney, T. L. (1985). Components of Type A hostility and anger: Relationship to angiographic findings. *Psychosomatic Medicine, 47,* 219–233.

denBoer, J. A. D., Westenberg, H. G. M., deLeeuw, A. S. D., & vanVliet, I. M. (1995). Biological dissection of anxiety disorders: The clinical role of selective serotonin reuptake inhibitors with particular reference to fluoxetine. *International Clinical Psychopharmacology, 9,* 47–52.

deSilva, P., Rachman, S., & Seligman, M. (1977). Prepared phobias and obsessions. *Behaviour Research & Therapy, 15,* 65–77.

Deutsch, A. (1937). *The mentally ill in America: A history of their care and treatment from colonial times.* Garden City, NY: Doubleday, Doran & Company.

Devor, E. J. (1994). A developmental-genetic model of alcoholism: Implications for genetic research. *Journal of Consulting & Clinical Psychology, 62,* 1108–1115.

Dewaraja, R., & Sasaki, Y. (1991). Semen-loss syndrome: A comparison between Sri Lanka and Japan. *American Journal of Psychotherapy, 45,* 14–20.

DeWit, H., Pierri, J., & Johanson, C. E. (1989). Assessing individual differences in ethanol preference using a cumulative dosing procedure. *Psychopharmacology, 98,* 113–119.

Dickey, R., & Stephens, J. (1995). Female-to-male transsexualism, heterosexual type: Two cases. *Archives of Sexual Behavior, 24,* 439–445.

Dickinson, E. (1955). *Poems: Including variant readings critically compared with all known manuscripts.* Cambridge, MA: Belknap Press.

Diekstra, R., & Garnefski, N. (1995). On the nature, magnitude, and causality of suicidal behavior: An international perspective. *Suicide & Life Threatening Behavior, 25,* 36–57.

Dinges, D. F., & Broughton, R. J. (Eds.). (1989). *Sleep and alertness: Chronobiological, behavioral, and medical aspects of napping.* New York: Raven Press.

Dodge, K. A. (1990). Developmental psychopathology in children of depressed mothers. *Developmental Psychology, 26,* 3–6.

Dodge, K. A., & Tomlin, A. M. (1987). Utilization of self-schemas as a mechanism of interpretational bias in aggressive children. *Social Cognition, 5,* 280–300.

Dohrenwend, B. P., Levav, I., Shrout, P. E., Link, B. G., Skodol, A. E., & Martin, J. L. (1987). Life stress and psychopathology: Progress on research begun with Barbara Snell Dohrenwend. *American Journal of Community Psychology, 15,* 677–715.

Dohrenwend, B. P., Levav, I., Shrout, P. E., Schwartz, S., Naveh, G., Link, B., Skodol, A., & Stueve, A. (1992). Socioeconomic status and psychiatric disorders: The causation-selection issue. *Science, 255,* 946–952.

Donahey, K. M., & Carroll, R. A. (1993). Gender differences in factors associated with hypoactive sexual desire. *Journal of Sex & Marital Therapy, 19,* 25–40.

Dornbusch, S. M., Carlsmith, J. M., Duncan, P. D., Gross, R. T., Martin, J. A., Ritter, P. L., & Siegel-Gorelick, B. (1984). Sexual maturation, social class, and the desire to be thin among adolescent females. *Developmental & Behavioral Pediatrics, 5,* 308–314.

Drewnowski, A., Hopkins, S. A., & Kessler, R. C. (1988). The prevalence of bulimia nervosa in the US college student population. *American Journal of Public Health, 78,* 1322–1325.

Drewnowski, A., Yee, D. K., & Krahn, D. D. (1988). Bulimia in college women: Incidence and recovery rates. 140th Annual Meeting of the American Psychiatric Association (1987, Chicago, Illinois). *American Journal of Psychiatry, 145,* 753–755.

DuPaul, G. J., & Barkley, R. A. (1993). Behavioral contributions to pharmacology: The utility of behavioral methodology in medication treatment of children with attention deficit hyperactivity disorder. *Behavior Therapy, 24,* 47–65.

Durkheim, E. (1897). *Le suicide: Etude de sociologie.* Paris: F. Alcan.

E

Eaton, W. W., Moortensenk, P. B., Herrman, H., & Freeman, H. (1992). Long-term course of hospitalization for schizophrenia: I. Risk for rehospitalization. *Schizophrenia Bulletin, 18,* 217–228.

Eckert, E. D., Halmi, K. A., Marchi, P., & Grove, W. (1995). Ten-year follow-up of anorexia nervosa: Clinical course and outcome. *Psychological Medicine, 25,* 143–156.

Edelbrock, C., Rende, R., Plomin, R., & Thompson, L. A. (1995). A twin study of competence and problem behavior in childhood and adolescence. *Journal of Child Psychology & Psychiatry & Allied Disciplines, 36,* 775–785.

Edelmann, R. J. (1992). *Anxiety: Theory, research, and intervention in clinical and health psychology.* Chichester, NY: Wiley.

Egeland, J. A., Gerhard, D. S., Pauls, D. L., Sussex, J. N., Kidd, K. K., Allen, C. R., Hostetter, A. M., & Housman, D. E. (1987). Bipolar affective disorders linked to DNA markers on Chromosome 11. *Nature, 325,* 783–787.

Egeland, J. A., & Hostetter, S. M. (1983). Amish study: I. Affective disorders among the Amish, 1976–1980. *American Journal of Psychiatry, 140,* 56–61.

Egeland, J. A., Hostetter, A. M., & Eshleman, S. K. (1983). Amish study III: The impact of cultural factors on bipolar diagnosis. *American Journal of Psychiatry, 140,* 67–71.

Ehlers, A. (1995). A 1-year prospective study of panic attacks: Clinical course and factors associated with maintenance. *Journal of Abnormal Psychology, 104,* 164–172.

Ehlers, A., & Breuer, P. (1992). Increased cardiac awareness in panic disorder. *Journal of Abnormal Psychology, 101,* 371–382.

Elder, G. H., & Clipp, E. C. (1989). Combat experience and emotional health: Impairment and resilience in later life. *Journal of Personality, 57,* 311–341.

Elder, G. H., Liker, J. K., & Jaworski, B. J. (1984). Hardship in lives: Depression influences. In K. A. McCluskey & H. W. Reese (Eds.), *Life-span developmental psychology: Historical and generational effects.* Orlando, FL: Academic Press.

Elkin, I., Shea, T., Watkins, J. T., Imber, S. D., Sotsky, S. M., Collins, J. F., Glass, D. R., Pilkonis, P. A., Leber, W. R., Docherty, J. P., Fiester, S. J., & Parloff, M. B. (1989). National Institute of Mental Health treatment of depression collaborative research program: General effectiveness of treatments. *Archives of General Psychiatry, 46,* 971–982.

Ellis, A. (1958). *Rational psychotherapy.* New York: Institute for Rational Living.

Ellis, A., & Harper, R. A. (1961). *A guide to rational living.* Englewood Cliffs, NJ: Prentice Hall.

Emmelkamp, P. M. (1982). *Phobic and obsessive-compulsive disorders.* New York: Plenum.

Endicott, J. (1994). Differential diagnoses and comorbidity. In J. H. Gold & S. K. Severino (Eds.), *Premenstrual dysphorias* (pp. 3–17). Washington, DC: American Psychiatric Association Press.

Engel, J. (1989). *Addicted: Kids talking about drugs in their own words.* New York: T. Doherty.

Erickson, M. T. (1992). *Behavior disorders of children and adolescents.* Englewood Cliffs, NJ: Prentice Hall.

Erikson, K. T. (1976). *Everything in its path: Destruction of community in the Buffalo Creek flood.* New York: Simon & Schuster.

Erlenmeyer-Kimling, L., & Cornblatt, B. (1987). The New York High-Risk Project: A follow-up report. *Schizophrenia Bulletin, 13,* 451–461.

Erlenmeyer-Kimling, L., & Cornblatt, B. A. (1992). A summary of attentional findings in the New York High-Risk Project. *Journal of Psychiatry Research, 26,* 405–426.

Erlenmeyer-Kimling, L., Golden, R. R., & Cornblatt, B. A. (1989). A taxometric analysis of cognitive and neuromotor variables in children at risk for schizophrenia. *Journal of Abnormal Psychology, 98,* 203–208.

Erlenmeyer-Kimling, L., Rock, D., Squires-Wheeler, E., & Roberts, S. (1991). Early life precursors of psychiatric outcomes in adulthood in subjects at risk for schizophrenia or affective disorders. *Psychiatry Research, 39,* 239–256.

Erlenmeyer-Kimling, L., Squires-Wheeler, E., Adamo, U. H., & Bassett, A. S. (1995). The New York High-Risk Project. *Archives of General Psychiatry, 52,* 857–865.

Escobar, J. I. (1993). Psychiatric epidemiology. In A. C. Gaw (Ed.), *Culture, ethnicity, and mental illness* (pp. 43–73). Washington, DC: American Psychiatric Press.

Escobar, J. I., Burnam, M. A., Karno, M., & Forsythe, A. (1987). Somatization in the community. *Archives of General Psychiatry, 44,* 713–718.

Estrada, A. U., & Pinsof, W. M. (1995). The effectiveness of family therapies for selected behavioral disorders of childhood. *Journal of Marital & Family Therapy, 21,* 403–440.

Extein, I. L. (Ed.). (1989). *Treatment of tricyclic-resistant depression.* Washington, DC: American Psychiatric Press.

F

Fabrega, H. (1993). Toward a social theory of psychiatric phenomena. *Behavioral Science, 38,* 75–100.

Fabrega, H. (1994). Personality disorders as medical entities: A cultural interpretation. *Journal of Personality Disorders, 8,* 149–167,

Fabrega, H., Ulrich, R., Pilkonis, P., & Mezzich, J. (1991). On the homogeneity of personality disorder clusters. *Comprehensive Psychiatry, 32,* 373–386.

Fahy, T. A. (1988). The diagnosis of multiple personality disorder: A critical review. *British Journal of Psychiatry, 153,* 597–606.

Fairbank, J. A., Hansen, D. J., & Fitterling, J. M. (1991). Patterns of appraisal and coping across different stressor conditions among former prisoners of war with and without posttraumatic stress disorder. *Journal of Consulting & Clinical Psychology, 59,* 274–281.

Fairburn, C., & Hay, P. J. (1992). Treatment of bulimia nervosa. *Annals of Medicine, 24,* 297–302.

Fairburn, C. G., Jones, R., Peveler, R. C., & Carr, S. J. (1991). Three psychological treatments for bulimia nervosa: A comparative trial. *Archives of General Psychiatry, 48,* 463–469.

Fairburn, C. G., Jones, R., Peveler, R. C., Hope, R. A., & O'Connor, M. (1993). Psychotherapy and bulimia nervosa. *Archives of General Psychiatry, 50,* 419–428.

Fairburn, C. G., Norman, P. A., Welch, S. L., O'Connor, M. E., Doll, H. A., & Peveler, R. C. (1995). A prospective study of outcome in bulimia nervosa and the long-term effects of three psychological treatments. *Archives of General Psychiatry, 52,* 304–312.

Fairburn, C. G., Welch, S. L., & Hay, P. J. (1993). The classification of recurrent overeating: The "binge eating disorder" proposal. Fifth International Conference on Eating Disorders (1992, New York). *International Journal of Eating Disorders, 13,* 155–159.

Fairburn, C. G., & Wilson, G. T. (1993). *Binge eating: Nature, assessment, and treatment.* New York: Guilford Press.

Fairweather, G. W., Sanders, D. H., Maynard, H., & Cressler, D. L. (1969). *Community life for the mentally ill: An alternative to institutional care.* Chicago: Aldine.

Falloon, I. R., Brooker, C., & Graham-Hole, V. (1992). Psychosocial interventions for schizophrenia. *Behavior Change, 9,* 238–245.

Fals-Stewart, W., Marks, A. P., & Schafer, J. (1993). A comparison of behavioral group therapy and individual behavior therapy in treating obsessive-compulsive disorder. *Journal of Nervous & Mental Disease, 181,* 189–193.

Faraone, S. V., Biederman, J., Keenan, K., & Tsuang, M. T. (1991). A family-genetic study of girls with DSM-III attention deficit disorder. *American Journal of Psychiatry, 148,* 112–117.

Faraone, S. V., & Tsuang, M. T. (1990). Genetic transmission of major affective disorders: Quantitative models and linkage analyses. *Psychological Bulletin, 108,* 109–127.

Fava, M., Copeland, P. M., Schweiger, U., & Herzog, D. B. (1989). Neurochemical abnormalities of anorexia nervosa and bulimia nervosa. *American Journal of Psychiatry, 146,* 963–971.

Fava, M., & Rosenbaum, J. F. (1995). Pharmacotherapy and somatic therapies. In E. E. Beckham & W. R. Leber (Eds.), *Handbook of depression* (2nd ed., pp. 280–301). New York: Guilford.

Feehan, M., McGee, R., & Williams, S. (1993). Mental health disorders from age 15 to age 18 years. *Journal of the American Academy of Child & Adolescent Psychiatry, 32,* 1118–1126.

Fenichel, O. (1945). *The psychoanalytic theory of neurosis.* New York: W. W. Norton.

Fennell, M. J. V., & Teasdale, J. D. (1987). Cognitive therapy for depression: Individual differences and the process of change. *Cognitive Therapy & Research, 11,* 253–271.

Fergusson, D. M., Horwood, J. L., & Lynskey, M. T. (1993). Early dentine lead levels and subsequent cognitive and behavioural development. *Journal of Child Psychology & Psychiatry & Allied Disciplines, 34,* 215–227.

Finkelhor, D. (1984). *Child sexual abuse: New theory and research.* New York: Free Press.

Finkelhor, D., & Dzuiba-Leatherman, J. (1994). Victimization of children. *American Psychologist, 49,* 173–183.

Fischer, M., Barkley, R. A., Fletcher, K. E., & Smallish, L. (1993). The adolescent outcome of hyperactive children: Predictors of psychiatric, academic, social, and emotional adjustment. *Journal of the American Academy of Child & Adolescent Psychiatry, 32,* 324–332.

Fishbain, D. A., Goldberg, M., Robert, B., & Steele, R. (1986). Male and female chronic pain patients categorized by DSM-III psychiatric diagnostic criteria. *Pain, 26,* 181–197.

Fisher, B. W., & Flowerdew, G. (1995). A simple model for predicting postoperative delirium in older patients undergoing elective orthopedic surgery. *Journal of the American Geriatrics Society, 43,* 175–178.

Fisher, S., Kent, T. A., & Bryant, S. G. (1995). Postmarketing surveillance by patient self-monitoring: Preliminary data for sertraline versus fluoxetine. *Journal of Clinical Psychiatry, 56,* 288–296.

Fitzgerald, L. F. (1993). Sexual harassment: Violence against women in the workplace. *American Psychologist, 48,* 1070–1076.

Flor-Henry, P. (1985). Psychiatric aspects of cerebral lateralization. *Psychiatric Annals, 15,* 429–434.

Fluoxetine Bulimia Nervosa Collaborative Study Group. (1992). Fluoxetine in the treatment of bulimia nervosa: A multicenter, placebo-controlled, double-blind trial. *Archives of General Psychiatry, 49,* 139–147.

Foa, E. B., Feske, U., Murdock, T. B., & Kozak, M. J. (1991). Processing threat-related information in rape victims. *Journal of Abnormal Psychology, 100,* 156–162.

Foa, E. B., Franklin, M. E., Perry, K. J., & Herbert, J. D. (1996). Cognitive biases in generalized social phobia. *Journal of Abnormal Psychology, 105,* 433–439.

Foa, E., & Kozak, M. (1993). Obsessive-compulsive disorder: Long-term outcome of psychological treatment. In M. Mavissakalian & R. Prien (Eds.), *Long-term treatment of anxiety disorders.* Washington, DC: American Psychiatric Press.

Foa, E. D., & Riggs, D. S. (1995). Posttraumatic stress disorder following assault: Theoretical considerations and empirical findings. *Current Directions in Psychological Science, 4,* 61–65.

Folsom, A. R. (1985). Do Type A men drink more frequently than Type B men? Findings in the Multiple Risk Factor Intervention Trial (MRFIT). *Journal of Behavioral Medicine, 8,* 227–235.

Folstein, M. F., Bassett, S. S., Romanoski, A. J., & Nestadt, G. (1991). The epidemiology of delirium in the community: The Eastern Baltimore Mental Health Survey. *International Psychogeriatrics, 3,* 169–176.

Folstein, M. F., Folstein, S. E., & McHugh, P. R. (1975). Mini-mental state: A practical method for grading the cognitive state of patients for the clinician. *Journal of Psychiatric Research, 12,* 189–198.

Folstein, S., & Rutter, M. (1977). Infantile autism: A genetic study of 21 twin pairs. *Journal of Child Psychology & Psychiatry & Allied Disciplines, 18,* 297–321.

Forehand, R., Lautenschlager, G. J., Faust, J., & Graziano, W. G. (1986). Parent perceptions and parent-child interactions in clinic-referred children: A preliminary investigation of the effects of maternal depressive moods. *Behaviour Research & Therapy, 24,* 73–75.

Frances, A. J., First, M. B., & Pincus, H. A. (1995). *DSM-IV guidebook.* Washington, DC: American Psychiatric Press.

Frank, E. (1991). Interpersonal psychotherapy as a maintenance treatment for patients with recurrent depression. *Psychotherapy, 28,* 259–266.

Frank, E., Anderson, B., Reynolds, C. F., & Ritenour, A. (1994). Life events and the research diagnostic criteria endogenous subtype: A confirmation of the distinction using the Bedford College methods. *Archives of General Psychiatry, 51,* 519–524.

Frank, E., Kupfer, D. J., Perel, J. M., & Cornes, C. (1990). Three-year outcomes for maintenance therapies in recurrent depression. *Archives of General Psychiatry, 47,* 1093–1099.

Frank, E., Kupfer, D., Wagner, E., & McEachran, A. (1991). Efficacy of interpersonal psychotherapy as a maintenance treatment of recurrent depression: Contributing factors. *Archives of General Psychiatry, 48,* 1053–1059.

Frank, J. (1973). *Persuasion and healing: A comparative study of psychotherapy.* Baltimore, MD: The Johns Hopkins University Press.

Frank, J. D. (1978). *Effective ingredients of successful psychotherapy.* New York: Brunner/Mazel.

Frankl, V. E. (1963). *Man's search for meaning: An introduction to logotherapy.* Boston: Beacon Press.

Fraser, M. W., Pecora, P. J., & Haapala, D. A. (Eds.). (1991). *Families in crisis: The impact of intensive family preservation services.* New York: A. de Gruyter.

Fredrickson, B. (1995). Socioemotional behavior at the end of college life. *Journal of Social & Personal Relationships, 12,* 261–276.

Freeston, M. H., Ladouceur, R., Thibodeau, N., & Gagnon, F. (1992). Cognitive intrusions in a non-clinical population: II. Associations with depressive, anxious, and compulsive symptoms. *Behaviour Research & Therapy, 30,* 263–271.

Freud, A. (1937). *The ego and the mechanisms of defense.* London: Hogarth.

Freud, S. (1905). *Collected works.* London: Hogarth Press.

Freud, S. (1909). *Analysis of a phobia of a five-year-old boy.* (Vol. III). New York: Basic Books.

Freud, S. (1914). *Psychopathology of everyday life.* (Authorized English ed.). New York: Macmillan.

Freud, S. (1917). Mourning and melancholia. *Collected works.* London: Hogarth Press.

Freud, S. (1920). *A general introduction to psychoanalysis.* New York: Boni & Liveright.

Freud, S. (1937). *A general selection from the works of Sigmund Freud.* London: Hogarth Press.

Freud, S. (1958). The handling of dream-interpretation in psychoanalysis. In J. Strachey (Ed.), *The standard edition* (Vol. 12, pp. 89–96). London: Hogarth Press.

Freud, S. (1963). *Collected papers. With an introduction by the editor Philip Rieff.* New York: Collier Books.

Fried, P. A., & Watkinson, B. (1990). 36- and 48-month neurobehavioral follow-up of children prenatally exposed to marijuana, cigarettes, and alcohol. *Journal of Developmental & Behavioral Pediatrics, 11,* 49–58.

Friedman, M., & Rosenman, R. H. (1974). *Type A behavior and your heart.* New York: Knopf.

Friedman, M., Rosenman, R. H., Straus, R., Wurm, M., & Kositcheck, R. (1968). The relationship of behavior pattern A to the state of coronary vasculature. *American Journal of Medicine, 44,* 525–537.

Friedman, M., Thoresen, C. E., Gill, J. J., Ulmer, D., Powell, L. H., Price, V. A., Brown, B., Thompson, L., Rabin, D. D., Breall, W. S., Bourg, E., Levy, R., & Dixon, T. (1986). Alteration of Type A behavior and its effect on cardiac recurrences in post myocardial infarction patients: Summary results of the recurrent coronary prevention project. *American Heart Journal, 112,* 653–665.

Friman, P. C., & Warzak, W. J. (1990). Nocturnal enuresis: A prevalent, persistent, yet curable parasomia. *Pediatrician, 17,* 38–45.

Fritz, G. K., Rockney, R. M., & Yeung, A. S. (1994). Plasma levels and efficacy of imipramine treatment for enuresis. *Journal of the American Academy of Child & Adolescent Psychiatry, 33,* 60–64.

Fromm-Reichmann, F. (1948). Notes on the development of treatments of schizophrenia by psychoanalytic psychotherapy. *Psychiatry, 2,* 263–273.

Fromme, K., Marlatt, G. A., Baer, J. S., & Kivlahan, D. R. (1994). The Alcohol Skills Training Program: A group intervention for young adult drinkers. *Journal of Substance Abuse Treatment, 11,* 143–154.

Futterman, A., Thompson, L., Gallagher-Thompson, D., & Ferris, R. (1995). Depression in late life: Epidemiology, assessment, etiology, and treatment. In E. E. Beckham & W. R. Leber (Eds.), *Handbook of depression* (2nd ed., pp. 494–525). New York: Guilford Press.

Fyer, A. J., Liebowitz, M. R., Gorman, J. M., & Campeas, R. (1987). Discontinuation of alprazolam treatment in panic patients. *American Journal of Psychiatry, 144,* 303–308.

Fyer, A. J., Mannuzza, S., Chapman, T. F., & Liebowitz, M. R. (1993). A direct interview family study of social phobia. *Archives of General Psychiatry, 50,* 286–293.

Fyer, A. J., Mannuzza, S., Gallops, M. S., & Martin, L. Y. (1990). Familial transmission of simple phobias and fears: A preliminary report. *Archives of General Psychiatry, 47,* 252–256,

G

Gadow, K. D. (1991). Clinical issues in child and adolescent psychopharmacology. *Journal of Consulting & Clinical Psychology, 59,* 842–852.

Gadow, K. D. (1992). Pediatric psychopharmacology: A review of recent research. *Journal of Child Psychology & Psychiatry & Allied Disciplines, 33,* 153–195.

Gadow, K. D., Nolan, E. E., Sverd, J., Sprafkin, J., & Paolicelli, L. M. (1990). Methylphenidate in aggressive-hyperactive boys: I. Effects on peer aggression in public school settings. *Journal of the American Academy of Child & Adolescent Psychiatry, 29,* 710–718.

Gallagher-Thompson, D., Lovett, S., & Rose, J. (1991). Psychotherapeutic interventions for stressed family caregivers. In W. A. Myers (Ed.), *New techniques in psychotherapy of older patients.*

Washington, DC: American Psychiatric Press.

Gannon, L. R., Haynes, S. N., Cuevas, J., & Chavez, R. (1987). Psychophysiological correlates of induced headaches. *Journal of Behavioral Medicine, 10,* 411–423.

Garber, J., Walker, L. S., & Zeman, J. (1991). Somatization symptoms in a community sample of children and adolescents: Further validation of the Children's Somatization Inventory. *Psychological Assessment, 3,* 588–595.

Gardner, W., Lidz, C. W., Mulvey, E. P., & Shaw, E. C. (1996). Clinical versus actuarial predictions of violence in patients with mental illnesses. *Journal of Consulting & Clinical Psychology, 64,* 602–609.

Garmezy, N. (1991). Resilience and vulnerability to adverse developmental outcomes associated with poverty. *American Behavioral Scientist, 34,* 416–430.

Garner, D. M., & Bemis, K. M. (1982). A cognitive-behavioral approach to anorexia nervosa. *Cognitive Therapy & Research, 6,* 123–150.

Garner, D. M., & Garfinkel, P. E. (1980). Socio-cultural factors in the development of anorexia nervosa. *Psychological Medicine, 10,* 647–656.

Garner, D. M., & Garfinkel, P. E. (Eds.). (1985). *Handbook of psychotherapy for anorexia nervosa and bulimia.* New York: Guilford Press.

Garner, D. M., Garfinkel, P. E., & O'Shaughnessy, M. (1985). The validity of the distinction between bulimia with and without anorexia nervosa. *American Journal of Psychiatry, 142,* 581–587.

Garner, D. M., Rockert, W., Davis, R., & Garner, M. V. (1993). Comparison of cognitive-behavioral and supportive-expressive therapy for bulimia nervosa. *American Journal of Psychiatry, 150,* 37–46.

Garner, D. M., & Wooley, S. C. (1991). Confronting the failure of behavioral and dietary treatments for obesity. *Clinical Psychology Review, 11,* 729–780.

Gavin, A. (1985). Treatment outlines for the management of anxiety states: The Quality Assurance Project. *Australian & New Zealand Journal Psychiatry, 19,* 138–151.

Gaw, A. C. (Ed.). (1993). *Culture, ethnicity, and mental illness.* Washington, DC: American Psychiatric Press.

Ge, X., Conger, R. D., Cadoret, R. J., & Neiderhiser, J. M. (1996). The developmental interface between nature and nurture: A mutual influence model of

child antisocial behavior and parent behaviors. *Developmental Psychology, 32,* 574–589.

Geer, J. H., & Maisel, E. (1972). Evaluating the effects of the prediction-control confound. *Journal of Personality & Social Psychology, 23,* 314–319.

Gershon, E. S. (1990). Genetics. In F. K. Goodwin & K. R. Jamison (Eds.), *Manic-depressive illness* (pp. 373–401). New York: Oxford University Press.

Gershon, E. S., & Rieder, R. O. (1992). Major disorders of mind and brain. *Scientific American, 267,* 128.

Giles, J. (1994, April 18). The poet of alienation. *Newsweek, 123,* 46–47.

Gillberg, C. (1991). Outcome in autism and autistic-like conditions. *Journal of the American Academy of Child & Adolescent Psychiatry, 30,* 375–382.

Gillberg, C., & Steffenburg, S. (1987). Outcome and prognostic factors in infantile autism and similar conditions: A population-based study of 46 cases followed through puberty. *Journal of Autism & Developmental Disorders, 17,* 273–287.

Gillberg, C., & Svennerholm, L. (1987). CSF monoamines in autistic syndromes and other pervasive developmental disorders of early childhood. *British Journal of Psychiatry, 151,* 89–94.

Gillham, J. E., Reivich, K. J., Jaycox, L. H., & Seligman, M. E. P. (1995). Prevention of depressive symptoms in schoolchildren: Two-year follow-up. *Psychological Science, 6,* 343–351.

Gillis, L. S., Elk, R., Ben-Arie, O., & Teggin, A. (1982). The Present State Examination: Experiences with Xhosa-speaking psychiatric patients. *British Journal of Psychiatry, 141,* 143–147.

Giovini, G. A., Schooley, M. W., Zhu, B., Chrismon, J. H., Tomar, S. L., Peddicord, J. P., Merritt, R. K., Husten, C. G., & Eriksen, M. P. (1994). Surveillance for selected tobacco-use behaviors—United States, 1900–1994. *Morbidity & Mortality Weekly Report, 43,* 1–43.

Girelli, S. A., Resick, P. A., Marhoefer-Dvorak, S., & Hutter, C. K. (1986). Subjective distress and violence during rape: Their effects on long-term fear. *Violence & Victims, 1,* 35–46.

Gitlin, M. J., & Pasnau, R. O. (1989). Psychiatric syndromes linked to reproductive function in women: A review of current knowledge. *American Journal of Psychiatry, 146,* 1413–1422.

Gittelman, R., & Klein, D. F. (1984). Relationship between separation anxiety and panic and agoraphobic disorders. *Psychopathology, 17* (Suppl. 1), 56–65.

Gittelman, R., Mannuzza, S., Shenker, R., & Bonagura, N. (1985). Hyperactive boys almost grown up: I. Psychiatric status. *Archives of General Psychiatry, 42,* 937–947.

Gittelman-Klein, R., & Klein, D. F. (1971). Controlled imipramine treatment of school phobia. *Archives of General Psychiatry, 25,* 204–207.

Glaser, R. (1985). Stress-related impairments in cellular immunity. *Psychiatry Research, 16,* 233–239.

Glaser, R., Rice, J., Speicher, C. E., Stout, J. C., & Kiecolt-Glaser, J. C. (1986). Stress depresses interferon production by leukocytes concomitant with a decrease in natural killer cell activity. *Behavioral Neuroscience, 100,* 675–678.

Glass, D. C., & Singer, J. E. (1973). Experimental studies of uncontrollable and unpredictable noise. *Representative Research in Social Psychology, 4,* 165–183.

Glassman, A. (1969). Indoleamines and affective disorders. *Psychosomatic Medicine, 31,* 107–114.

Goldberg, E. M., & Morrison, S. L. (1963). Schizophrenia and social class. *British Journal of Psychiatry, 109,* 785–802.

Goldstein, A. (1994). *Addiction: From biology to drug policy.* New York: W. H. Freeman.

Goldstein, G., & Hersen, M. (Eds.). (1990). *Handbook of psychological assessment.* Elmsford, NY: Pergamon Press.

Goldstein, J. M. (1995). The impact of gender on understanding the epidemiology of schizophrenia. In M. V. Seeman (Ed.), *Gender and psychopathology* (pp. 159–200). Washington, DC: American Psychiatric Press.

Goldstein, M. J. (1987). The UCLA High-Risk Project. *Schizophrenia Bulletin, 13,* 505–514.

Goldstein, M. J., Talovic, S. A., Nuechterlein, K. H., & Fogelson, D. L. (1992). Family interaction versus individual psychopathology: Do they indicate the same processes in the families of schizophrenia? *British Journal of Psychiatry, 161,* 97–102.

Goleman, G. (1993, December 3). Depression costs put at $43 billion. *New York Times,* A-10.

Gomberg, E. S. (1994). Risk factors for drinking over a woman's life span. *Alcohol Health & Research World, 18,* 220–227.

Gong-Guy, E. (1978). *The California Southeast Asian's mental health needs assessment* (California State Department Mental Health Contract #85-7628-2A-2, 1987): California State Department.

Gonzalez, N. M., & Campbell, M. (1994). Cocaine babies: Does prenatal exposure to cocaine affect development? *Journal of the American Academy of Child & Adolescent Psychiatry, 33,* 16–19.

Goodwin, D. W. (1988). *Alcohol and the writer.* Kansas City, MO: Andrews and McMeel.

Goodwin, F. K., & Jamison, K. R. (1990). *Manic-depressive illness.* New York: Oxford University Press.

Gorman, J. M., Liebowitz, M. R., Fyer, A. J., Fyer, M. R., & Klein, D. F. (1986). Possible respiratory abnormalities in panic disorder. *Psychopharmacological Bulletin, 221,* 797–801.

Gottesman, I. I. (1991). *Schizophrenia genesis: The origins of madness.* New York: W. H. Freeman.

Gottesman, I. I., & Goldsmith, H. H. (in press). Developmental psychopathology of antisocial behavior: Inserting genes into its ontogenesis and epigenesis. In C. Nelson (Ed.), *Threats to optimal development: Integrating biological, social, and psychological risk factors* (Vol. 27). Hillsdale, NJ: Erlbaum.

Gottesman, I. I., & Shields, J. (1982). *Schizophrenia, the epigenetic puzzle.* New York: Cambridge University Press.

Gottlieb, G. L., & Kumar, A. (1993). Conventional pharmacologic treatment for patients with Alzheimer's disease. *Neurology, 43,* S56–S63.

Gottlieb, J., Semmel, M. I., & Veldman, D. J. (1978). Correlates of social status among mainstreamed mentally retarded children. *Journal of Educational Psychology, 70,* 396–405.

Gove, W., & Herb, T. (1974). Stress and mental illness among the young: A comparison of the sexes. *Social Forces, 53,* 256–265.

Grau, L., & Padgett, D. (1988). Somatic depression among the elderly: A sociocultural perspective. *International Journal of Geriatric Psychiatry, 3,* 201–207.

Gray, E., & Cosgrove, J. (1985). Ethnocentric perception of childbearing practices in protective services. *Child Abuse and Neglect, 9,* 389–396.

Gray, J. (1982). Precis of the neuropsychology of anxiety: An enquiry into the functions of the septo-hippocampal system. *Behavioral & Brain Sciences, 5,* 469–534.

Gray, J. (1985). A whole and its parts: Behavior, the brain, cognition and emotion. *Bulletin of the British Psychological Society, 38,* 99–112.

Gray, J. J., Ford, K., & Kelly, L. M. (1987). The prevalence of bulimia in a black college population. *International Journal of Eating Disorders, 6,* 733–740.

Greaves, G. B. (1980). Multiple personality: 165 years after Mary Reynolds. *The Journal of Nervous & Mental Disease, 168,* 577–596.

Green, A. H. (1993). Child sexual abuse: Immediate and long-term effects and intervention. *Journal of the American Academy of Child & Adolescent Psychiatry, 32,* 890–902.

Green, B. L., Grace, M. C., Lindy, L. D., Titchener, J. L., & Lindy, J. G. (1983). Levels of functional impairment following a civilian disaster: The Beverly Hills Supper Club fire. *Journal of Consulting & Clinical Psychology, 51,* 573–580.

Green, B. L., Lindy, J. D., Grace, M. C. & Leonard, A. C. (1992). Chronic posttraumatic stress disorder and diagnostic comorbidity in a disaster sample. *Journal of Nervous & Mental Disease, 180,* 760–766.

Green, R. (1986). Gender identity in childhood and later sexual orientation: Follow-up of 78 males. *Annual Progress in Child Psychiatry & Child Development,* 214–220.

Greene, B., & Blanchard, E. B. (1994). Cognitive therapy for irritable bowel syndrome. *Journal of Consulting & Clinical Psychology, 62,* 576–582.

Grenier, G., & Byers, E. S. (1995). Rapid ejaculation: A review of conceptual, etiological, and treatment issues. *Archives of Sexual Behavior, 24,* 447–472.

Griffith, E. E. H., & Baker, F. M. (1993). Psychiatric care of African Americans. In A. C. Gaw (Ed.), *Culture, ethnicity, and mental illness* (pp. 147–173). Washington, DC: American Psychiatric Press.

Grinspoon, L., & Bakalar, J. B. (1995). Marihuana as medicine: A plea for reconsideration. *Journal of the American Medical Association, 273,* 1875–1876.

Gross, J., & Rosen, J. C. (1988). Bulimia in adolescents: Prevalence and psychosocial correlates. *International Journal of Eating Disorders, 7,* 51–61.

Gross, R. T., Brooks-Gunn, J., & Spiker, D. (1992). Efficacy of educational interventions for low birth weight infants: The Infant Health and Development Program. In S. L. Friedman & M. D. Sigman (Eds.), *The psychological devel-*

opment of low birth weight children: Advances in applied developmental psychology. Norwood, NJ: Ablex.

Groth, A. N. (1979). Men who rape: The psychology of the offender. New York: Plenum.

Guarnaccia, P. J., Canino, G., Rubio-Stipec, M., & Bravo, M. (1993). The prevalence of ataques de nervios in the Puerto Rico Disaster Study: The role of culture in psychiatric epidemiology. Journal of Nervous & Mental Disease, 181, 157–165.

Guarnaccia, P. J., Guevara-Ramos, L. M., Gonzales, G., Canino, G. J., & Bird, H. (1992). Cross-cultural aspects of psychiatric symptoms in Puerto Rico. Community & Mental Health, 7, 99–110.

Guarnaccia, P. J., Rivera, M., Franco, F., Neighbors, C., & Allende-Ramos, C. (1996). The experiences of ataques de nervios: Toward an anthropology of emotions in Puerto Rico. Culture, Medicine, & Psychiatry, 15, 139–165.

Gunderson, J. G., Ronningstam, E., & Smith, L. E. (1995a). Narcissistic personality disorder. In W. J. Livesley (Ed.), The DSM-IV personality disorders (pp. 201–212). New York: Guilford Press.

Gunderson, J. G., Zanarini, M. C., & Kisiel, C. L. (1995b). Borderline personality disorder. In W. J. Livesley (Ed.), The DSM-IV personality disorders (pp. 141–157). New York: Guilford Press.

Gusella, J. F., MacDonald, M. E., Ambrose, C. M., & Duyao, M. P. (1993). Molecular genetics of Huntington's disease. Archives of Neurology, 50, 1157–1163.

Gustafson, Y., Brannstrom, B., Berggren, D., & Ragnarsson, J. I. (1991). A geriatric-anesthesiologic program to reduce acute confusional states in elderly patients treated for femoral neck fractures. Journal of the American Geriatrics Society, 39, 655–662.

Guy, R. F., Rankin, B. A., & Norvell, M. J. (1980). The relation of sex role stereotyping to body image. Journal of Psychology, 105, 167–173.

Guze, B. H., & Gitlin, M. (1994). New antidepressants and the treatment of depression. Journal of Family Practice, 38, 49–57.

Guze, S. B. (1993). Genetics of Briquet's syndrome and somatization disorder: A review of family, adoption, and twin studies. Sanibel Island Symposium (1993, Ft. Myers, Florida). Annals of Clinical Psychiatry, 5, 225–230.

Gwirtsman, H. E., Guze, B. H., Yager, J., & Gainsley, B. (1990). Fluoxetine treatment of anorexia nervosa: An open clinical trial. Journal of Clinical Psychiatry, 51, 378–382.

H

Halford, W. K., & Hayes, R. (1991). Psychological rehabilitation of chronic schizophrenic patients: Recent findings on social skills training and family psychoeducation. Clinical Psychology Review, 11, 23–44.

Hambrecht, M., Maurer, K., Hafner, H., & Sartorius, N. (1992). Transnational stability of gender differences in schizophrenia: An analysis based on the WHO study on determinants of outcome of severe mental disorders. European Archives of Psychiatry & Clinical Neuroscience, 242, 6–12.

Hamilton, E. W., & Abramson, L. Y. (1983). Cognitive patterns and major depressive disorder: A longitudinal study in a hospital setting. Journal of Abnormal Psychology, 92, 172–184.

Hamilton, J. A. (1986). An overview of the clinical rationale for advancing gender-related psychopharmacology and drug abuse research. National Institute on Drug Abuse: Research Monograph Series, 65, 14–20.

Hammen, C., Burge, D., & Stansbury, K. (1990). Relationship of mother and child variables to child outcomes in a high-risk sample: A causal modeling analysis. Developmental Psychology, 26, 24–30.

Harding, C. M., Zubin, J., & Strauss, J. S. (1987). Chronicity in schizophrenia: Fact, partial fact, or artifact? Hospital & Community Psychiatry, 38, 477–486.

Hargreaves, W. A., Shumway, M., Knutsen, E. J., & Weinstein, A. (1987). Effects of the Jamison-Farabee consent decree: Due process protection for involuntary psychiatric patients treated with psychoactive medication. American Journal of Psychiatry, 144, 188–192.

Harrell, J. P. (1980). Psychological factors and hypertension: A status report. Psychological Bulletin, 87, 482–501.

Harris, M. J., Milich, R., Corbitt, E. M., & Hoover, D. W. (1992). Self-fulfilling effects of stigmatizing information on children's social interactions. Journal of Personality & Social Psychology, 63, 41–50.

Hart, K. J., & Ollendick, T. H. (1985). Prevalence of bulimia in working and university women. American Journal of Psychiatry, 142, 851–854.

Harter, S. (1983). Developmental perspectives on the self-system. In P. H. Mussen (Ed.), Handbook of child development (pp. 275–385). New York: Wiley.

Harvey, M. R., & Herman, J. L. (1994). Amnesia, partial amnesia, and delayed recall among adult survivors of childhood trauma. Consciousness & Cognition: An International Journal, 3, 295–306.

Hawkins, R. C., Turell, S., & Jackson, L. J. (1983). Desirable and undesirable masculine and feminine traits in relation to student's dieting tendencies and body image dissatisfaction. Sex Roles, 9, 705–718.

Haynes, S. G., Feinleib, M., & Kannel, W. B. (1980). The relationship of psychosocial factors to coronary heart disease in the Framingham study: III. Eight-year incidence of coronary heart disease. American Journal of Epidemiology, 111, 37–58.

Hayward, C., Killen, J. D., Wilson, D. M., Hammer, L. D., Litt, I. F., Kraemer, H. C., Haydel, F., Varady, A., & Taylor, B. C. (1993, October). Timing of puberty and onset of psychiatric symptoms. Paper presented at the American Academy of Child and Adolescent Psychiatry, San Antonio, TX.

Heaton, R. K., Marcotte, T. D., White, D. A., & Ross, D. (1996). Nature and vocational significance of neuropsychological impairment associated with HIV infection. Clinical Neuropsychologist, 10, 1–14.

Hefez, A. (1985). The role of the press and the medical community in the epidemic of "mysterious gas poisoning" in the Jordan West Bank. American Journal of Psychiatry, 142, 833–837.

Heide, F. J., & Borkovec, T. D. (1984). Relaxation-induced anxiety: Mechanisms & theoretical implications. Behaviour Research & Therapy, 22, 1–12.

Heiman, J. R., & Grafton-Becker, V. (1989). Orgasmic disorders in women. In S. R. Leiblum & R. C. Rosen (Eds.), Principles and practice of sex therapy: Update for the 1990s (pp. 51–88). New York: Guilford Press.

Heimberg, R. G., Dodge, C. S., Hope, D. A., & Kennedy, C. R. (1990). Cognitive behavioral group treatment for social phobia: Comparison with a credible placebo control. Cognitive Therapy & Research, 14, 1–23.

Helms, J. E. (1992). Why is there no study of cultural equivalence in standardized cognitive ability testing? *American Psychologist, 47,* 1083–1101.

Helzer, J. E., & Canino, G. J. (1992). *Alcoholism in North America, Europe, and Asia.* New York: Oxford University Press.

Helzer, J. E., Bucholz, K., & Robins, L. N. (1992). Five communities in the United States: Results of the Epidemiologic Catchment Area Survey. In J. E. Helzer & G. J. Canino (Eds.), *Alcoholism in North America, Europe, and Asia.* New York: Oxford University Press.

Henderson, D., & Boyd, C. (1996). *All my buddies was male: Relationship issues of addicted women.* Unpublished manuscript.

Hendin, H. (1995). *Suicide in America.* New York: W. W. Norton.

Henker, B., & Whalen, C. K. (1989). Hyperactivity and attention deficits. *American Psychologist, 44,* 216–223.

Henry, B., Caspi, A., Moffitt, T. E., & Silva, P. A. (1996). Temperamental and familial predictors of violent and nonviolent criminal convictions: Age 3 to age 18. *Developmental Psychology, 32,* 614–623.

Herek, G. M. (1990). Gay people and government security clearances: A social science perspective. *American Psychologist, 45,* 1035–1042.

Herman, C. P., & Mack, D. (1975). Restrained and unrestrained eating. *Journal of Personality, 43,* 647–660.

Herman, C. P., & Polivy, J. (1975). Anxiety, restraint and eating disorder. *Journal of Abnormal Psychology, 84,* 666–672.

Herman, C. P., & Polivy, J. (1988). Psychological factors in the control of appetite. *Current Concepts in Nutrition, 16,* 41–51.

Herman, J. L., & Schatzow, E. (1987). Recovery and verification of memories of childhood sexual trauma. *Psychoanalytic Psychology, 4,* 1–14.

Heston, L., Denney, D., & Pauly, I. (1966). The adult adjustment of persons institutionalized as children. *British Journal of Psychiatry, 112,* 1103–1110.

Higgins, S. T., Budney, A. J., Beckel, W. K., & Badger, G. J. (1994). Participation of significant others in outpatient behavioral treatment predicts greater cocaine abstinence. *American Journal of Drug & Alcohol Abuse, 20,* 47–56.

Hilgard, E. R. (1977/1986). *Divided consciousness: Multiple controls in human thought and action.* New York: Wiley.

Hilgard, E. R. (1992). Divided consciousness and dissociation. *Consciousness and Cognition: An International Journal, 1,* 16–31.

Hiller, J. (1996). Female sexual arousal and its impairment: The psychodynamics of non-organic coital pain. *Sexual & Marital Therapy, 11,* 55–76.

Hinshaw, S. P. (1994). *Attention deficits and hyperactivity in children.* Thousand Oaks, CA: Sage.

Hinshaw, S. P., & Melnick, S. M. (1995). Peer relationships in boys with attention-deficit hyperactivity disorder with and without comorbid aggression. *Development & Psychopathology, 7,* 627–647.

Hirschfeld, R. (1994). Guidelines for the longterm treatment of depression. *Journal of Clinical Psychiatry, 55* (suppl. 12), 59–67.

Hirschfeld, R. M., Shea, M. T., & Wiese, R. E. (1991). Dependent personality disorder: Perspectives for DSM-IV. Special Series: DSM-IV and personality disorders. *Journal of Personality Disorders, 5,* 135–149.

Hite, S. (1976). *The Hite report: A nationwide study on female sexuality.* New York: Macmillan.

Hoffman, A. (1968). Psychotomimetic agents. In A. Burger (Ed.), *Drugs affecting the central nervous system* (Vol. 2). New York: Marcel Dekker.

Hogarty, G. E., Anderson, C. M., Reiss, D. J., Kornblith, S. J., Greenwald, D. P., Jaund, C. D., & Madonia, M. J. (1986). Family psychoeducation, social skills training, and maintenance chemotherapy in the aftercare treatment of schizophrenia: I. One-year effects of a controlled study on relapse and expressed emotion. *Archives of General Psychiatry, 43,* 633–642.

Hogarty, G. E., Anderson, C. M., Reiss, D. J., Kornblith, S. J., Greenwald, D. P., Ulrich, R. F., & Carter, M. (1991). Family psychoeducation, social skills training, and maintenance chemotherapy in the aftercare treatment of schizophrenia: II. Two-year effects of a controlled study on relapse and adjustment. *Archives of General Psychiatry, 48,* 340–347.

Holden, C. (1980). Identical twins reared apart. *Science, 207,* 1323–1328.

Holland, A. J., Hall, A., Murray, R., Russell, G. F. M., & Crisp, A. H. (1984). Anorexia nervosa: A study of 34 twin pairs and one set of triplets. *British Journal of Psychiatry, 145,* 414–419.

Hollander, E., Cohen, L. J., & Simeon, D. (1993). Body dysmorphic disorder. *Psychiatric Annals, 23,* 359–364.

Hollander, E., Liebowitz, M. R., Winchel, R., & Klumker, A. (1989). Treatment of body-dysmorphic disorder with serotonin reuptake blockers. *American Journal of Psychiatry, 146,* 768–770.

Hollander, E., Neville, D., Frenkel, M., & Josephson, S. (1992). Body dysmorphic disorder: Diagnostic issues and related disorders. *Psychosomatics, 33,* 156–165.

Hollon, S. D., DuRubeis, R. J., Evans, M. D., & Wiemer, M. J. (1992). Cognitive therapy and pharmacotherapy for depression: Singly and in combination. *Archives of General Psychiatry, 49,* 774–781.

Hollon, S. D., Shelton, R. C., & Loosen, P. T. (1991). Cognitive therapy and pharmacotherapy for depression. *Journal of Consulting & Clinical Psychology, 59,* 88–99.

Holmes, T. H., & Rahe, R. H. (1967). The social readjustment rating scale. *Journal of Psychosomatic Research, 11,* 213–218.

Holroyd, J. C., & Brodsky, A. M. (1977). Psychologists' attitudes and practices regarding erotic and nonerotic physical contact with patients. *American Psychologist, 32,* 843–849.

Holsboer, F. (1992). The hypothalamic-pituitary-adrenocortical system. In E. S. Paykel (Ed.), *Handbook of affective disorders* (pp. 267–287). New York: Guilford Press.

Holstein, J. A. (1993). *Court-ordered insanity: Interpretive practice and involuntary commitment.* New York: A. de Gruyter.

Hooley, J. M., Richters, J. E., Weintraub, S., & Neale, J. M. (1987). Psychopathology and marital distress: The positive side of positive symptoms. *Journal of Abnormal Psychology, 96,* 27–33.

Horm, J., & Anderson, K. (1993). Who in America is trying to lose weight? *Annals of Internal Medicine, 119,* 672–676.

Horney, K. (1939). *New ways in psychoanalysis.* New York: W. W. Norton.

Hornstein, N. L., & Putnam, F. W. (1992). Clinical phenomenology of child and adolescent dissociative disorders. *Journal of the American Academy of Child & Adolescent Psychiatry, 31,* 1077–1085.

Horowitz, M. J. (1976). *Stress response syndromes.* New York: Aronson.

Hsu, L. G. (1990). Experiential aspects of bulimia nervosa: Implications for cognitive behavioral therapy. *Behavior Modification, 14,* 50–65.

Hsu, L. K., Crisp, A. H., & Harding, B. (1979). Outcome of anorexia nervosa. *Lancet, 1,* 61–65.

Hugdahl, K., & Ohman, A. (1977). Effects of instruction on acquisition and extinction of electrodermal response to fear-relevant stimuli. *Journal of Experimental Psychiatry: Human Learning & Memory, 3,* 608–618.

Hurlbert, D. F. (1991). The role of assertiveness in female sexuality: A comparative study between sexually assertive and sexually nonassertive women. *Journal of Sex & Marital Therapy, 17,* 183–190.

Huselid, R. F., & Cooper, M. L. (1992). Gender roles as mediators of sex differences in adolescent alcohol use and abuse. *Journal of Health & Social Behavior, 33,* 348–362.

Hutson, H. R., Anglin, D., & Pratts, M. J. (1994). Adolescents and children injured or killed in drive-by shootings in Los Angeles. *The New England Journal of Medicine, 330,* 324–327.

Hyde, J. S. (1990). *Understanding human sexuality.* New York: McGraw-Hill.

I

Inciardi, J. A., Lockwood, D., & Pottieger, A. E. (1993). *Women and crack cocaine.* New York: Macmillan.

Insel, T. R. (Ed.). (1984). *New findings in obsessive-compulsive disorder.* Washington, DC: American Psychiatric Press.

Insel, T. R., Hoover, C., & Murphy, D. L. (1983). Parents of patients with obsessive-compulsive disorder. *Psychological Medicine, 13,* 807–811.

Ironside, R. N., & Batchelor, I. R. C. (1945). *Aviation neuro-psychiatry.* Baltimore: Williams & Wilkins.

J

Jablensky, A., (1989). Epidemiology and cross-cultural aspects of schizophrenia. *Psychiatric Annals, 19,* 516–524.

Jack, D. C. (1991). *Silencing the self: Women and depression.* New York: HarperPerennial.

Jacobson, N. S., & Hollon, S. D. (1996). Cognitive-behavior therapy versus pharmacotherapy: Now that the jury's returned its verdict, it's time to present the rest of the evidence. *Journal of Consulting & Clinical Psychology, 64,* 74–80.

James, S. A., Hartnett, S. A., & Kalsbeek, W. D. (1983). John Henryism and blood pressure differences among black men. *Journal of Behavioral Medicine, 6,* 259–278.

James, S. A., LaCroix, A. Z., Kleinbaum, D. G., & Strogatz, D. S. (1984). John Henryism and blood pressure differences among black men: II. The role of occupational stressors. *Journal of Behavioral Medicine, 7,* 259–275.

James, W. (1890). *The principles of psychology.* New York: Henry Holt.

Jamison, K. R. (1995a). Manic-depressive illness and creativity. *Scientific American, 272,* 62–67.

Jamison, K. R. (1995b). *An unquiet mind: A memoir of moods and madness.* New York: Alfred A. Knopf.

Jamner, L. D., Schwartz, G. E., & Leigh, H. (1988). The relationship between repressive and defensive coping styles and monocyte, eosinophile, and serum glucose levels: Support for the opioid peptide hypothesis of repression. *Psychosomatic Medicine, 50,* 567–575.

Janis, I. L. (1958). *Psychological stress: Psychoanalytic and behavioral studies of surgical patients.* New York: Wiley.

Janoff-Bulman, R. (1992). *Shattered assumptions: Toward a new psychology of trauma.* New York: Maxwell Macmillan International.

Janoff-Bulman, R., & Frieze, I. H. (1983). A theoretical perspective for understanding reactions to victimization. *Journal of Social Issues, 39,* 1–17.

Jary, M. L., & Stewart, M. A. (1985). Psychiatric disorder in the parents of adopted children with aggressive conduct disorder. *Neuropsychobiology, 13,* 7–11.

Jaycox, L. H., Reivich, K. J., Gillham, J., & Seligman, M. E. P. (1994). Preventing depressive symptoms in school children. *Behaviour Research & Therapy, 32,* 801–816.

Jeffrey, R. W., & Wing, R. R. (1995). Long-term effects of interventions for weight loss using food provision and monetary incentives. *Journal of Consulting & Clinical Psychology, 63,* 793–796.

Jellenek, E. (1960). *The disease concept of alcoholism.* Highland Park, NJ: Hillhouse.

Jemmott, J. B., Jemmott, L. S., Spears, H., & Hewitt, N. (1992). Self-efficacy, hedonistic expectancies, and condom-use intentions among inner-city black adolescent women: A social cognitive approach to AIDS risk behavior. *Journal of Adolescent Health, 13,* 512–519.

Jemmott, J. B., & Locke, S. E. (1984). Psychosocial factors, immunologic mediation, and human susceptibility to infectious diseases: How much do we really know? *Psychological Bulletin, 95,* 78–108.

Jemmott, L. S., & Jemmott, J. B. (1992). Increasing condom-use intentions among sexually active adolescent women. *Nursing Research, 41,* 273–279.

Jenike, M. A. (1992). Pharmacological treatment of obsessive compulsive disorders. *Psychiatric Clinics of North America, 15,* 895–919.

Jenkins, J. H., & Karno, M. (1992). The meaning of expressed emotion: Theoretical issues raised by cross-cultural research. *American Journal of Psychiatry, 149,* 9–21.

Jenkins, R. L. (1973). *Behavior disorders of childhood and adolescence.* Springfield, IL: Charles C Thomas.

Johannessen, D. J., Cowley, D. S., Walker, D. R., & Jensen, C. F. (1989). Prevalence, onset and clinical recognition of panic states in hospitalized male alcoholics. *American Journal of Psychiatry, 146,* 1201–1203.

Johnson, S. L., & Roberts, J. E. (1995). Life events and bipolar disorder: Implications from biological theories. *Psychological Bulletin, 117,* 434–449.

Johnston, J. R., Gonzales, R., & Campbell, L. E. (1987). Ongoing postdivorce conflict and child disturbance. *Journal of Abnormal Child Psychology, 15,* 493–509.

Jones, E. E. (1978). Effects of race on psychotherapy process and outcome: An exploratory investigation. *Psychotherapy: Theory, Research, & Practice, 15,* 226–236.

Jones, E. E., & Harris, V. A. (1967). The attribution of attitudes. *Journal of Experimental Social Psychology, 3,* 1–24.

Jun-mian, X. (1987). Some issues in the diagnosis of depression in China. *Canadian Journal of Psychiatry, 32,* 368–370.

K

Kamen-Siegel, L., Rodin, J., Seligman, M. E., & Dwyer, J. (1991). Explanatory style and cell-mediated immunity in elderly men and women. *Health Psychology, 10,* 229–235.

Kane, M. T., & Kendall, P. C. (1989). Anxiety disorders in children: A multiple-baseline evaluation of a cognitive-behavioral treatment. *Behavior Therapy, 20,* 499–508.

Kanner, L. (1943). Autistic disturbances of affective contact. *Nervous Child, 21,* 217–250.

Kaplan, H. S. (1974). *The new sex therapy: Active treatment of sexual dysfunction.* New York: Brunner/Mazel.

Kaplan, M. (1983). The issue of sex bias in DSM-III: Comments on the articles by Spitzer, Williams, and Kass. *American Psychologist, 38,* 802–803.

Karasek, R. A., Russell, R. S., & Theorell, T. (1982). Physiology of stress and regeneration in job related cardiovascular illness. *Journal of Human Stress, 8,* 29–42.

Karno, M., & Golding, J. M. (1991). Obsessive compulsive disorder. In L. R. Robins & D. A. Regier (Eds.), *Psychiatric disorders in America: The Epidemiologic Catchment Area Study.* New York: Maxwell Macmillan International.

Karno, M., Hough, R., Burnam, A., Escobar, J. I., Timbers, D. M., Santana, F., & Boyd, J. H. (1987). Lifetime prevalence of specific psychiatric disorders among Mexican Americans and non-Hispanic whites in Los Angeles. *Archives of General Psychiatry, 44,* 695–701.

Karno, M., & Jenkins, J. H. (1993). Cross-cultural issues in the course and treatment of schizophrenia. *Psychiatric Clinics of North America, 16,* 339–350.

Kaslow, N. J., & Racusin, G. R. (1990). Family therapy or child therapy: An open or shut case. *Journal of Family Psychology, 3,* 273–289.

Kassett, J. A., Gwirtsman, H. E., Kaye, W. H., & Brandt, H. A. (1988). Pattern of onset of bulimic symptoms in anorexia nervosa. 140th Annual Meeting of the American Psychiatric Association (1987, Chicago, Illinois). *American Journal of Psychiatry, 145,* 1287–1288.

Katchadourian, H. A. (1989). *Fundamentals of human sexuality* (5th ed.). New York: Holt, Rinehart & Winston.

Katon, W., Korff, M. v., Lin, E., & Lipscomb, P. (1990). Distressed high utilizers of medical care: DSM-III-R diagnoses and treatment needs. *General Hospital Psychiatry, 12,* 355–362.

Katz, R., & Wykes, T. (1985). The psychological difference between temporally predictable and unpredictable stressful events: Evidence for information control theories. *Journal of Personality & Social Psychology, 48,* 781–790.

Katzman, R. (1993). Education and the prevalence of dementia and Alzheimer's disease. *Neurology, 43,* 13–20.

Kavanagh, D. J. (1992). Recent developments in expressed emotion and schizophrenia. *British Journal of Psychiatry, 160,* 601–620.

Kaye, W. H., Weltzin, T. E., Hsu, H. G., & Bulik, C. M. (1991). An open trial of fluoxetine in patients with anorexia nervosa. *Journal of Clinical Psychiatry, 52,* 464–471.

Kazdin, A. E. (1986). Comparative outcome studies of psychotherapy: Methodological issues and strategies. *Journal of Consulting & Clinical Psychology, 54,* 95–105.

Kazdin, A. E. (1991). Effectiveness of psychotherapy with children and adolescents. *Journal of Consulting & Clinical Psychology, 59,* 785–798.

Kazdin, A. E., & Wilcoxon, L. A. (1976). Systematic desensitization and nonspecific treatment effects: A methodological evaluation. *Psychological Bulletin, 83,* 729–758.

Keane, T. M., Gerardi, R. J., Quinn, S. J., & Litz, B. T. (1992). Behavioral treatment of post-traumatic stress disorder. In S. M. Turner, K. S. Calhoun, & H. E. Adams (Eds.), *Handbook of clinical behavior therapy* (pp. 87–97). New York: Wiley.

Keesey, R. E. (1986). A set-point theory of obesity. In K. D. Brownell & J. P. Foreyt (Eds.), *Handbook of eating disorders* (pp. 45–62). New York: Basic Books.

Keesey, R. E., & Powley, T. L. (1986). The regulation of body weight. *Annual Review of Psychology, 37,* 109–133.

Keller, M. B., & Baker, L. A., (1991). Bipolar disorder: Epidemiology, course, diagnosis, and treatment. *Bulletin of the Menninger Clinic, 55,* 172–181.

Kellermann, A. L., Rivara, F. P., Somes, G., & Reay, D. T. (1992). Suicide in the home in relation to gun ownership. *New England Journal of Medicine, 327,* 467–472.

Kelly, K., & Ramundo, P. (1995). *You mean I'm not lazy, stupid, or crazy?!* New York: Charles Scribner's Sons.

Kendall, P. C. (1992). *Anxiety disorders in youth: Cognitive-behavioral interventions.* Boston: Allyn & Bacon.

Kendall, P. C., Hollon, S. D., Beck, A. T., Hammen, C. L., & Ingram, R. E. (1987). Issues and recommendations regarding use of the Beck Depression Inventory. *Cognitive Therapy & Research, 11,* 289–299.

Kendall, P. C., & Morris, R. J. (1991). Child therapy: Issues and recommendations. *Journal of Consulting & Clinical Psychology, 59,* 777–784.

Kendall-Tackett, K. A., Williams, L. M., & Finkelhor, D. (1993). Impact of sexual abuse on children: A review and synthesis of recent empirical studies. *Psychological Bulletin, 113,* 164–180.

Kendler, K. S., Heath, A. C., Neale, M. C., Kessler, R. C., & Eaves, L. J. (1992). A population-based twin study of alcoholism in women. *Journal of the American Medical Association, 268,* 1877–1882.

Kendler, K. S., MacLean, C., Neale, M., & Kessler, R. C. (1991). The genetic epidemiology of bulimia nervosa. *American Journal of Psychiatry, 148,* 1627–1637.

Kendler, K. S., Neale, M. C., Kessler, R. C., & Heath, A. C. (1992). Major depression and generalized anxiety disorder: Same genes, (partly) different environments? *Archives of General Psychiatry, 49,* 716–722.

Kendler, K. S., Neale, M. C., Kessler, R. C., & Heath, A. C. (1993). Panic disorder in women: A population-based twin study. *Psychological Medicine, 23,* 397–406.

Kendler, K. S., Neale, M. C., Kessler, R. C., Heath, A. C., & Eaves, L. J. (1992). A population-based twin study of major depression in women. *Archives of General Psychiatry, 49,* 257–266.

Kendler, K. S., Neale, M. C., Kessler, R. C., Heath, A. C., & Eaves, L. J. (1993). A test of the equal-environment assumption in twin studies of psychiatric illness. *Behavior Genetics, 23,* 21–28.

Kernberg, O. (1975). *Borderline conditions and pathological narcissism.* New York: Jason Aronson.

Kernberg, O. F. (1979). Psychoanalystic profile of the borderline adolescent. *Adolescent Psychiatry, 7,* 234–256.

Kernberg, O. F. (1989). *Psychodynamic psychotherapy of borderline patients.* New York: Basic Books.

Kessler, R. C., McGonagle, K. A., Zhao, S., Nelson, C. B, Hughes, M., Eshleman, S., Wittchen, H., & Kendler, K. S. (1994). Lifetime and 12-month prevalence of DSM-III-R psychiatric disorders in the United States: Results from the National Comorbidity Study. *Archives of General Psychiatry, 51,* 8–19.

Keys, A. B., Brozek, J., Henschel, A., Michelson, O., & Taylor, H. L. (1950). *The biology of human starvation.* Minneapolis: University of Minnesota Press.

Khandelwal, D. K., & Saxena, S. (1990). "Anorexia nervosa in adolescents of Asian extraction": Comment. *British Journal of Psychiatry, 157*, 784.

Kiecolt-Glaser, J. K., Fisher, L. D., Ogrocki, P., & Stout, J. C. (1987). Marital quality, marital disruption, and immune function. *Psychosomatic Medicine, 49*, 13–34.

Kiecolt-Glaser, J. K., Kennedy, S., Malkoff, S., & Fisher, L. (1988). Marital discord and immunity in males. *Psychosomatic Medicine, 50*, 213–229.

Kiecolt-Glaser, J. K., Malarkey, W. B., Chee, M., & Newton, T. (1993). Negative behavior during marital conflict is associated with immunological down-regulation. *Psychosomatic Medicine, 55*, 395–409.

Kiesler, C. A., & Sibulkin, A. E. (1983). Proportion of inpatient days for mental disorders: 1969–1978. *Hospital & Community Psychiatry, 34*, 606–611.

Kiesler, C. A., & Sibulkin, A. E. (1987). *Mental hospitalization: Myths and facts about a national crisis.* Beverly Hills, CA: Sage Publications.

Kihlstrom, J. F. (1992). Dissociation and dissociations: A comment on consciousness and cognition. *Consciousness & Cognition: An International Journal, 1*, 47–53.

Kihlstrom, J. F., & Couture, L. J. (1992). Awareness and information processing in general anesthesia. *Journal of Psychopharmacology, 6*, 410–417.

Kilpatrick, D., Veronen, L., & Resick, P. (1979). The aftermath of rape: Recent empirical findings. *American Journal of Orthopsychiatry, 49*, 658–669.

Kim, L. I. C. (1993). Psychiatric care of Korean Americans. In A. C. Gaw (Ed.), *Culture, ethnicity, and mental illness* (pp. 347–375). Washington, DC: American Psychiatric Press.

Kinney, J., Haapala, D., & Booth, C. (1991). *Keeping families together: The homebuilders model.* New York: A. de Gruyter.

Kinzie, J. D., & Leung, P. K. (1993). Psychiatric care of Indochinese Americans. In A. C. Gaw (Ed.), *Culture, ethnicity, and mental illness* (pp. 281–304). Washington, DC: American Psychiatric Press.

Kinzl, J. F., Traweger, C., Guenther, V., & Biebl, W. (1994). Family background and sexual abuse associated with eating disorders. *American Journal of Psychiatry, 151*, 1127–1131.

Kirch, D. G. (1993). Infection and autoimmunity as etiologic factors in schizo-phrenia: A review and reappraisal. *Schizophrenia Bulletin, 19*, 355–370.

Kirk, S. A., & Kutchins, H. (1992). *The selling of DSM: The rhetoric of science in psychiatry.* New York: A. de Gruyter.

Klein, D. F. (1993). False suffocation alarms, spontaneous panics, and related conditions: An integrative hypothesis. *Archives of General Psychiatry, 50*, 306–317.

Klein, M. (1952). Notes on some schizoid mechanisms. In M. Klein, P. Heimann, S. Isaacs, & J. Riviere (Eds.), *Developments in psychoanalysis.* London: Hogarth Press.

Klein, R. G., Koplewicz, H. S., & Kanner, A. (1992). Imipramine treatment of children with separation anxiety disorder. *Journal of the American Academy of Child & Adolescent Psychiatry, 31*, 21–28.

Kleinman, A., & Good, B. (Eds.). (1985). *Culture and depression: Studies in the anthropology and cross-cultural psychiatry of affect and disorder.* Berkeley: University of California Press.

Kleinman, A., & Kleinman, J. (1985). Somatization: The interconnections in Chinese society among culture, depressive experiences, and meanings of pain. In A. Kleinman, & B. Good (Eds.), *Culture and depression* (pp. 429–490). Berkeley: University of California Press.

Klerman, G. L., & Weissman, M. M. (1989). Increasing rates of depression. *Journal of the American Medical Association, 261*, 2229–2235.

Klerman, G. L., Weissman, M. M., Rounsaville, B., & Chevron, E. (1984). *Interpersonal psychotherapy of depression.* New York: Basic Books.

Kline, P. (1993). *The handbook of psychological testing.* New York: Routledge.

Klosko, J. S., Barlow, D. H., Tassinari, R., & Cerny, J. A. (1990). A comparison of alprazolam and behavior therapy in treatment of panic disorder. *Journal of Consulting & Clinical Psychology, 58*, 77–84.

Kluft, R. P. (1985). The natural history of multiple personality disorder. In R. P. Kluft (Ed.), *Childhood antecedents of multiple personality* (pp. 197–238). Washington, DC: American Psychiatric Press.

Kluft, R. P. (1986). Preliminary observations on age regression in multiple personality disorder patients before and after integration. *American Journal of Clinical Hypnosis, 28*, 147–156.

Kluft, R. P. (1987). Unsuspected multiple personality disorder: An uncommon source of protracted resistance, interruption, and failure in psychoanalysis. *Hillside Journal of Clinical Psychiatry, 9*, 100–115.

Koch, J. L. A. (1891). *The psychopathic inferiorities.* Ravensburg, Germany: Dorn.

Koegel, P., Burnam, M. A., & Farr, R. K. (1988). The prevalence of specific psychiatric disorders among homeless individuals in the inner city of Los Angeles. *Archives of General Psychiatry, 45*, 1085–1092.

Kohut, H. (1971). *The analysis of the self: A systematic approach to the treatment of narcissistic personality disorders.* New York: New York International Universities Press.

Kolodny, R. C., Masters, W. H., & Johnson, V. E. (1979). *Textbook of sexual medicine.* Boston: Little, Brown.

Kopelman, M. D. (1987). Crime and amnesia: A review. *Behavioral Sciences & the Law, 5*, 323–342.

Koss, J. D. (1990). Somatization and somatic complaint syndromes among Hispanics: Overview and ethnopsychological perspectives. *Transcultural Psychiatric Research Review, 27*, 5–29.

Koss, M. P., (1993). Rape: Scope, impact, interventions, and public policy responses. *American Psychologist, 48*, 1062–1069.

Kovacs, M., Krol, R. S., & Voti, L. (1994). Early onset psychopathology and the risk for teenage pregnancy among clinically referred girls. *Journal of the American Academy of Child & Adolescent Psychiatry, 33*, 106–113.

Kraepelin, E. (1922). *Manic-depressive insanity and paranoia.* Edinburgh, Scotland: E. & S. Livingstone.

Kranzler, H. R., & Anton, R. F. (1994). Implications of recent neuropsychopharmacologic research for understanding the etiology and development of alcoholism. *Journal of Consulting & Clinical Psychology, 62*, 1116–1126.

Kremen, W. S., Seidman, L. S., Pepple, J. R., & Lyons, M. J. (1994). Neuropsychological risk indicators for schizophrenia: A review of family studies. *Schizophrenia Bulletin, 20*, 103–119.

Kroll, J. (1973). A reappraisal of psychiatry in the Middle Ages. *Archives of General Psychiatry, 29*, 276–283.

Krull, F., & Schifferdecker, M. (1990). Inpatient treatment of conversion disorder: A clinical investigation of outcome. 14th International Congress of Medical

Psychotherapy: Training in medical psychotherapy: Cross-cultural diversity (1988, Lausanne, Switzerland). *Psychotherapy & Psychosomatics, 53,* 161–165.

Kryger, M. H., Roth, T., & Dement, W. C. (Eds.). (1994). *Principles and practice of sleep medicine.* Philadelphia: Saunders.

Krystal, H. (Ed.). *Massive psychic trauma.* New York: International Universities Press.

Kuch, K., & Cox, B. J. (1992). Symptoms of PTSD in 124 survivors of the Holocaust. *American Journal of Psychiatry, 149,* 337–340.

Kuczmarski, R. J. (1992). Prevalence of overweight and weight gain in the United States. *The American Journal of Clinical Nutrition, 55,* 495–502.

Kuo, W. H., & Tsai, Y. (1986). Social networking, hardiness and immigrant's mental health. *Journal of Health & Social Behavior, 27,* 133–149.

L

LaFromboise, R. D., Trimble, J. E., & Mohatt, G. V. (1990). Counseling intervention and the American Indian tradition: An integrative approach. *The Counseling Psychologist, 18,* 628–654.

LaGreca, A. M., Silverman, W. K., Vernberg, E. M., & Prinstein, M. J. (1996). Symptoms of posttraumatic stress in children after Hurricane Andrew: A prospective study. *Journal of Consulting & Clinical Psychology, 64,* 712–723.

Lahey, B. B., Pelham, W. E., Schaughency, E. A., & Atkins, M. S. (1988). Dimensions and types of attention deficit disorder. *Journal of the American Academy of Child & Adolescent Psychiatry, 27,* 330–335.

Laing, R. D. (1971). *The divided self.* Harmondsworth: Penguin Books.

Lakein, A. (1973). *How to get control of your time and life.* New York: P. H. Wyden.

Lambert, M. C., Knight, F., Overly, K., Weisz, J. R., Desrosiers, M., & Thesiger, C. (1992). Jamaican and American adult perspectives on child psychopathology: Further exploration of the threshold model. *Journal of Consulting & Clinical Psychology, 60,* 146–149.

Langevin, R. (1992). Biological factors contributing to paraphilic behavior. *Psychiatric Annals, 22,* 309–314.

Langone, J. (1985). The war that has no ending. *Discover, 6,* 44–54.

LaRosa, J. (1991). *Dieter beware: The complete consumer guide to weight loss programs.* Valley Stream, NY: Marketdata Enterprises.

Lasegue, C. (1873). On hysterical anorexia. *Medical Times Gazette, 2,* 265–266.

Laudenslager, M. L., Ryan, S. M., Drugan, R. C., Hyson, R. L., & Maier, S. F. (1983). Coping and immunosuppression: Inescapable but not escapable shock suppresses lymphocyte proliferation. *Science, 221,* 569–570.

Laumann, E. O., Gagnon, J. H., Michael, R. T., & Michales, S. (1994). *The social organization of sexuality: Sexual practices in the United States.* Chicago: University of Chicago Press.

Layton, M. (1995, May/June). Emerging from the shadows. *Networker,* 35–41.

Lebra, W. P. (1972). *Transcultural research in mental health: II. Mental health research in Asia and the Pacific.* Honolulu: University of Hawaii Press.

Lee, S. (1995). Self-starvation in context: Towards a culturally sensitive understanding of anorexia nervosa. *Social Science & Medicine, 41,* 25–36.

Lee, V. E., Brooks-Gunn, J., Schnur, E., & Liaw, F. (1990). Are Head Start effects sustained? A longitudinal follow-up comparison of disadvantaged children attending Head Start, no preschool, and other preschool programs. *Child Development, 61,* 495–507.

Leff, J., Sartorius, N., Jablensky, A., Korten, A., & Ernberg, G. (1992). The International Pilot Study of Schizophrenia: Five-year follow-up findings. *Psychological Medicine, 22,* 131–145.

Leff, J. P., & Vaughn, C. E. (1981). The role of maintenance therapy and relatives' expressed emotion in relapse of schizophrenia: A two-year follow-up. *British Journal of Psychiatry, 139,* 102–104.

Lehman, D. R., Wortman, C. B., & Williams, A. F. (1987). Long-term effects of losing a spouse or child in a motor vehicle crash. *Journal of Personality & Social Psychology, 52,* 218–231.

Leiblum, S. R., Pervin, L. A., & Campbell, E. H. (1989). The treatment of vaginismus: Success and failure. In S. R. Leiblum & R. C. Rosen (Eds.), *Principles and practice of sex therapy: Update for the 1990s* (pp. 113–138). New York: Guilford Press.

Leiblum, S. R., & Rosen, R. C. (Eds.). (1989). *Principles and practice of sex therapy: Update for the 1990s.* New York: Guilford Press.

Lemert, E. M. (1967). *Human deviance, social problems, and social control.* Englewood Cliffs, NJ: Prentice Hall.

Leon, G. R., Fulkerson, J. A., Perry, C. L., & Early-Zald, M. B. (1995). Prospective analysis of personality and behavioral vulnerabilities and gender influences in the later development of disordered eating. *Journal of Abnormal Psychology, 104,* 140–149.

Lerer, B., Moore, N., Meyendorff, E., Cho, S.-R., & Gershon, S. (1987). Carbamazepine versus lithium in mania: A double-blind study. *Journal of Clinical Psychiatry, 48,* 89–93.

Lerner, B. (1972). *Therapy in the ghetto: Political impotence and personal disintegration.* Baltimore: The Johns Hopkins Press.

Lerner, D. J., & Kannel, W. B. (1986). Patterns of coronary heart disease morbidity and mortality in the sexes: A 26-year follow-up of the Framington population. *American Heart Journal, 111,* 383–390.

Lerner, H. D. (1986). Current developments in the psychoanalytic psychotherapy of anorexia nervosa and bulimia nervosa. *Clinical Psychologist, 39,* 39–43.

Lerner, M. J. (1980). *The belief in a just world: A fundamental delusion.* New York: Plenum.

Levy, S. M., & Heiden, L. (1991). Depression, distress, and immunity: Risk factors for infectious disease. *Stress Medicine, 7,* 45–51.

Levy, S. M., Herberman, R. B., Whiteside, T., & Sanzo, K. (1990). Perceived social support and tumor estrogen/progesterone receptor status as predictors of natural killer cell activity in breast cancer patients. *Psychosomatic Medicine, 52,* 73–85.

Lewinsohn, P. M. (1974). A behavioral approach to depression. In R. J. Friedman & M. M. Katz (Eds.), *The psychology of depression: Contemporary theory and research.* Washington, DC: Winston-Wiley.

Lewinsohn, P. M., Clark, G. N., Hops, H., & Andrews, J. (1990). Cognitive-behavioral treatment for depressed adolescents. *Behavior Therapy, 21,* 385–401.

Lewinsohn, P. M., Clarke, G. N., Seeley, J. R., & Rhode, P. (1994). Major depression in community adolescents: Age of onset, episode duration, and time to recurrence. *Journal of the American Academy of Child & Adolescent Psychiatry, 33,* 519–526.

Lewinsohn, P. M., & Gotlib, I. H. (1995). Behavioral therapy and treatment of depression. In E. E. Beckham & W. R. Leber (Eds.), *Handbook of depression* (2nd ed., pp. 352–375). New York: Guilford.

Lewinsohn, P. M., Muñoz, R. F., Youngren, M. A., & Zeiss, A. M. (1986). *Control your depression.* Englewood Cliffs, NJ: Prentice Hall.

Lewis, D. O., Balla, D. A., & Shanok, S. S. (1979). Some evidence of race bias in the diagnosis and treatment of the juvenile offender. *American Journal of Orthopsychiatry, 49,* 53–61.

Lex, B. W. (1995). Alcohol and other psychoactive substance dependence in women and men. In M. V. Seeman (Ed.), *Gender and psychopathology* (pp. 311–358). Washington, DC: American Psychiatric Association Press.

Liberman, R. P. (1994). Psychosocial treatments for schizophrenia. *Psychiatry, 57,* 104–114.

Liberman, R. P., Putten, T. V., Marshall, B. D., Mintz, J., Bowen, L., Kuehnel, T. G., Aravagiri, A., & Marder, S. R. (1994). Optimal drug and behavior therapy for treatment-refractory schizophrenic patients. *American Journal of Psychiatry, 151,* 756–759.

Lidz, C. W., Mulvey, E. P., & Gardner, W. (1993). The accuracy of predictions of violence to others. *Journal of the American Medical Association, 269,* 1007–1011.

Liebowitz, M. R., Schneier, F. R., Campeas, R., & Hollander, E. (1992). Phenelzine vs atenolol in social phobia: A placebo-controlled comparison. *Archives of General Psychiatry, 49,* 290–300.

Lieh-Mak, F., Lee, P. W., & Luk, S. L. (1984). Problems encountered in teaching Chinese parents to be behavior therapists. *Psychologia: An International Journal of Psychology in the Orient, 27,* 56–64.

Light, K. C., & Sherwood, A. (1989). Race, borderline hypertension, and hemodynamic responses to behavioral stress before and after beta-adrenergic blockage. *Health Psychology, 8,* 577–595.

Lin, K.-m., & Shen, W. W. (1991). Pharmacotherapy for Southeast Asian psychiatric patients. *Journal of Nervous & Mental Disease, 179,* 346–350.

Lindemalm, G., Korlin, D., & Uddenberg, N. (1986). Long-term follow-up of "sex change" in 13 male-to-female transsexuals. *Archives of Sexual Behavior, 15,* 187–210.

Linehan, M. M. (1987). Dialectical behavior therapy for borderline personality disorder: Theory and method. *Bulletin of the Menninger Clinic, 51,* 261–276.

Linehan, M. M., Armstrong, H. E., Suarez, A., & Allmon, D. (1991). Cognitive-behavioral treatment of chronically parasuicidal borderline patients. *Archives of General Psychiatry, 48,* 1060–1064.

Linehan, M. M., Camper, P., Chiles, J. A., Strosahl, K., & Shearin, E. N. (1987). Interpersonal problem-solving and parasuicide. *Cognitive Therapy & Research, 11,* 1–12.

Links, P. S., Steiner, M., Boiago, I., & Irwin, D. (1990). Lithium therapy for borderline patients: Preliminary findings. *Journal of Personality Disorders, 4,* 173–181.

Lipowski, Z. J. (1990). *Delirium: Acute confusional states.* New York: Oxford University Press.

Livesley, W. J., Schroeder, M. L., Jackson, D. N., & Jang, K. L. (1994). Categorical distinctions in the study of personality disorder: Implications for classification. *Journal of Abnormal Psychology, 103,* 6–17.

Livingston, R. (1993). Children of people with somatization disorder. *Journal of the American Academy of Child & Adolescent Psychiatry, 32,* 536–544.

Lochman, J. E., White, K. J., & Wayland, K. K. (1991). Cognitive-behavioral assessment and treatment with aggressive children. In P. Kendall (Ed.), *Therapy with children and adolescents: Cognitive behavioral procedures.* New York: Guilford Press.

Loeber, R. (1990). Development and risk factors of juvenile antisocial behavior and delinquency. *Clinical Psychology Review, 10,* 1–41.

Loeber, R., Green, S. M., Keenan, K., & Lahey, B. B. (1995). Which boys will fare worse? Early predictors of the onset of conduct disorder in a six-year longitudinal study. *Journal of the American Academy of Child & Adolescent Psychiatry, 34,* 499–509.

Loeber, R., & Keenan, K. (1994). Interaction between conduct disorder and its comorbid conditions. *Clinical Psychology Review, 14,* 497–523.

Loeber, R., Lahey, B. B., & Thomas, C. (1991). Diagnostic conundrum of oppositional defiant disorder and conduct disorder. *Journal of Abnormal Psychology, 100,* 379–390.

Loftus, E. F. (1993). The reality of repressed memories. *American Psychologist, 48,* 518–537.

Long, P. W. (1996). Internet Mental Health. http://www.mentalhealth.com/.

LoPiccolo, J. (1992). Paraphilias. *Nordisk Sexolgi, 10,* 1–14.

Lopiccolo, J., & Stock, W. E. (1986). Treatment of sexual dysfunction. *Journal of Consulting & Clinical Psychology, 54,* 158–167.

Lovaas, O. I. (1987). Behavioral treatment and normal educational and intellectual functioning in young autistic children. *Journal of Consulting & Clinical Psychology, 55,* 3–9.

Lowell, R. (1977). *Day by day.* New York: Farrar, Straus, and Giroux.

Luborksy, L. (1984). *Principles of psychoanalytic psychotherapy: A manual for supportive-expressive treatment.* New York: Basic Books.

Ludwick-Rosenthal, R., & Neufeld, R. W. (1988). Stress management during noxious medical procedures: An evaluative review of outcome studies. *Psychological Bulletin, 104,* 326–342.

Ludwig, A. M. (1992). Creative achievement and psychopathology: Comparison among professions. *American Journal of Psychotherapy, 46,* 330–356.

Luria, A. (1973). *The working brain.* New York: Basic Books.

Luria, A. R. (1976). *Cognitive development: Its cultural and social foundations.* Cambridge, MA: Harvard University Press.

Lydiard, R. B., Brawman-Mintzer, O., & Ballenger, J. C. (1996). Recent developments in the psychopharmacology of anxiety disorders. *Journal of Consulting & Clinical Psychology, 64,* 660–668.

Lykken, D. T., Bouchard, T. J., McGue, M., & Tellegen, A. (1993). Heritability of interests: A twin study. *Journal of Applied Psychology, 78,* 649–661.

Lytton, H., & Romney, D. M. (1991). Parents' differential socialization of boys and girls: A meta-analysis. *Psychological Bulletin, 109,* 267–296.

M

Maccoby, E. E., & Mnookin, R. H. (1992). *Dividing the child: Social and legal dilemmas of custody.* Cambridge, MA: Harvard University Press.

Machover, K. A. (1949). *Personality projection in the drawing of the human figure: A method of personality investigation.* Springfield, IL: Charles C Thomas.

MacMillan, D. L., Gresham, F. M., & Siperstein, G. N. (1993). Conceptual and psychometric concerns about the 1992 AAMR definition of mental retardation. *American Journal on Mental Retardation, 98,* 325–335.

Maier, S. F., Watkins, L. R., & Fleshner, M. (1994). Psychoneuroimmunology: The interface between behavior, brain, and immunity. *American Psychologist, 49,* 1004–1017.

Malone, K., & Mann, J. J. (1993). Serotonin and major depression. In J. J. Mann & D. J. Kupfer (Eds.), *Biology of depressive disorders: Part A. A systems perspective* (pp. 29–49). New York: Plenum.

Mannuzza, S., Klein, R. G., Bessler, A., Malloy, P., & LaPadula, M. (1993). Adult outcome of hyperactive boys: Educational achievement, occupational rank, and psychiatric status. *Archives of General Psychiatry, 50,* 565–576.

Manson, J. E., Colditz, G. A., Stampfer, M. J., Willett, W. C., Rosner, B., Monson, R. R., Speizer, F. E., & Hennekens, C. H. (1990). A prospective study of obesity and risk of coronary heart disease in women. *New England Journal of Medicine, 322,* 882–889.

Manson, S., Beals, J., O'Nell, T., Piasecki, J., Bechtold, D., Keane, E., & Jones, M. (1996). Wounded spirits, ailing hearts: PTSD and related disorders among American Indians. In A. J. Marsella, M. J. Friedman, E. T. Gerrity, & R. M. Scurfield (Eds.), *Ethnocultural aspects of posttraumatic stress disorder* (pp. 255–283). Washington, DC: American Psychiatric Press.

Manson, S. M. (in press). Cross-cultural and multi-ethnic assessment of trauma. In J. P. Wilson & T. M. Keane (Eds.), *Assessing psychological trauma and PTSD: A handbook for practitioners.* New York: Guilford Press.

Manson, S. M., Ackerson, L. M., Dick, R. W., & Baron, A. E. (1990). Depressive symptoms among American Indian adolescents: Psychometric characteristics of the Center for Epidemiologic Studies Depression Scale (CES-D). *Psychological Assessment, 2,* 231–237.

Manson, S. M., Shore, J. H., Baron, A. E., Ackerson, L., & Neligh, G. (1992). Alcohol abuse and dependence among American Indians. In J. E. Helzer & G. J. Canino (Eds.), *Alcoholism in North America, Europe, and Asia* (pp. 113–127). New York: Oxford University Press.

Manu, P., Lane, T. J., & Matthews, D. A. (1989). Somatization disorder in patients with chronic fatigue. *Psychosomatics, 30,* 388–395.

Manu, P., Lane, T. J., & Matthews, D. A. (1992). Chronic fatigue syndromes in clinical practice. *Psychotherapy & Psychosomatics, 58,* 60–68.

Marcos, L. R. (1979). Effects of interpreters on the evaluation of psychopathology in non-English-speaking patients. *American Journal of Psychiatry, 136,* 171–174.

Margraf, J. (1993). Hyperventilation and panic disorder: A psychophysiological connection. *Advances in Behaviour Research & Therapy, 15,* 49–74.

Margraf, J., Barlow, D. H., Clark, D. M., & Telch, M. J. (1993). Psychological treatment of panic: Work in progress on outcome, active ingredients, and follow-up. *Behaviour Research & Therapy, 31,* 1–8.

Markowitz, J. C., & Weissman, M. W. (1995). Interpersonal psychotherapy. In E. E. Beckham & W. R. Leber (Eds.), *Handbook of depression* (2nd ed., pp. 376–390). New York: Guilford.

Marks, I. M., & Swinson, R. (1992). Behavioral and/or drug therapy. In G. D. Burrows, S. M. Roth, & R. Noyes, Jr. (Eds.), *Handbook of Anxiety* (Vol. 5). Oxford: Elsevier.

Marlatt, A., Baer, J. S., & Larimer, M. (1995). Preventing alcohol abuse in college students: A harm reduction approach. In G. M. Boyd, J. Howard, & R. A. Zucker (Eds.), *Alcohol problems among adolescents: Current directions in prevention research* (pp. 147–172). Hillsdale, NJ: Erlbaum.

Marlatt, G. A., Baer, J. S., Donovan, D. M., & Kivlahan, D. R. (1988). Addictive behaviors: Etiology and treatment. *Annual Review of Psychology, 39,* 223–252.

Marlatt, G. A., & Gordon, J. R. (Eds.). (1985). *Relapse prevention: Maintenance strategies in the treatment of addictive behaviors.* New York: Guilford Press.

Marlatt, G. A., Larimer, M. E., Baer, J. S., & Quigley, L. A. (1993). Harm reduction for alcohol problems: Moving beyond the controlled drinking economy. *Behavior Therapy, 24,* 461–503.

Martin, C. E. (1981). Factors affecting sexual functioning in 60–79-year-old married males. *Archives of Sexual Behavior, 10,* 399–420.

Martinez, C. (1993). Psychiatric care of Mexican Americans. In A. C. Gaw (Ed.), *Culture, ethnicity, and mental illness* (pp. 431–466). Washington, DC: American Psychiatric Association Press.

Martinez-Taboas, A. (1989). Preliminary observations on MPD in Puerto Rico. *Dissociation: Progress in the Dissociative Disorders, 2,* 128–131.

Maslow, A. H. (1954). *Motivation and personality.* New York: Harper & Row.

Masten, A. S., Miliotis, D., Graham-Bermann, S. A., & Ramirez, M. (1993). Children in homeless families: Risks to mental health and development. *Journal of Consulting & Clinical Psychology, 61,* 335–343.

Masters, W. H., & Johnson, V. E. (1970). *Human sexual inadequacy.* Boston: Little, Brown.

Masters, W. H., Johnson, V. E., & Kolodny, R. C. (1993). *Biological foundations of human sexuality.* New York: HarperCollins.

Mathews, A., & MacLeod, C. (1994). Cognitive approaches to emotion and emotional disorders. *Annual Review of Psychology, 45,* 25–50.

Mathews. (1996, July 30). *Baltimore Sun.*

Matthews, K. A., Wing, R. R., Kuller, L. H., & Meilhan, E. N. (1990). Influences of natural menopause on psychological characteristics and symptoms of middle-aged healthy women. *Journal of Consulting & Clinical Psychology, 58,* 345–351.

Max, W. (1993). The economic impact of Alzheimer's disease. *Neurology, 43,* S6–S10.

Maxmen, J. S., & Ward, N. G. (1995). *Essential psychopathology and its treatment.* New York: W. W. Norton.

Mayeux, R. (1996). Understanding Alzheimer's disease: Expect more genes and other things. *Annals of Neurology, 39,* 689–690.

Mayeux, R., Denaro, J., Hemenegildo, N., & Marder, K. (1992). A population-based investigation of Parkinson's disease with and without dementia: Relationship to age and gender. *Archives of Neurology, 49,* 492–497.

McArthur, J. C., Hoover, D. R., Bacellar, H., & Miller, E. N. (1993). Dementia in AIDS patients: Incidence and risk factors. *Neurology, 43,* 2245–2252.

McBride, A. A., Joe, G. W., & Simpson, D. D. (1991). Prediction of long-term alcohol use, drug use, and criminality among inhalant users. *Hispanic Journal of Behavioral Sciences, 13,* 315–323.

McBride, P., Brown, R. P., DeMeo, M., & Keilp, J. (1994). The relationship of platelet 5-HT-sub-2 receptor indices to major depressive disorder, personality traits, and suicidal behavior. *Biological Psychiatry, 35,* 295–308.

McCabe, S. B., & Gotlib, I. H. (1993). Interactions of couples with and without a depressed spouse: Self-report and observations of problem-solving situations. *Journal of Social & Personal Relationship, 10,* 589–599.

McCann, U. D., & Agras, W. S. (1990). Successful treatment of nonpurging bulimia nervosa with desipramine: A double-blind, placebo-controlled study. *American Journal of Psychiatry, 147,* 1509–1513.

McCarthy, B. W. (1989). Cognitive-behavioral strategies and techniques in the treatment of early ejaculation. In S. R. Leiblum & R. C. Rosen (Eds.), *Principles and practice of sex therapy: Update for the 1990s* (pp. 141–167). New York: Guilford Press.

McCarthy, M. (1990). The thin ideal, depression and eating disorders in women. *Behaviour Research & Therapy, 28,* 205–215.

McDonald, K., & Thompson, J. K. (1992). Eating disturbance, body image dissatisfaction, and reasons for exercising: Gender differences and correlational findings. *International Journal of Eating Disorders, 11,* 289–292.

McFarlane, W. R., Lukens, E., Link, B., & Dushay, R. (1995). Multiple-family groups and psychoeducation in the treatment of schizophrenia. *Archives of General Psychiatry, 52,* 679–687.

McGee, R., Feehan, M., Williams, S., & Partridge, F. (1990). DSM-III disorders in a large sample of adolescents. *Journal of the American Academy of Child & Adolescent Psychiatry, 29,* 611–619.

McGlashan, T. H. (1988). A selective review of recent North American long-term followup studies of schizophrenia. *Schizophrenia Bulletin, 14,* 515–542.

McGlashan, T. H., & Fenton, W. S. (1991). Classical subtypes for schizophrenia: Literature review for DSM-IV. *Schizophrenia Bulletin, 17,* 609–632.

McGrath, E., Keita, G. P., Strickland, B. R., & Russo, N. F. (1990). *Women and depression: Risk factors and treatment issues.* Washington, DC: American Psychological Association.

McGreevy, M. A., Steadman, H. J., & Callahan, L. A. (1991). The negligible effects of California's 1982 reform of the insanity defense test. *American Journal of Psychiatry, 148,* 744–750.

McGue, M., Pickens, R. W., & Svikis, D. S. (1992). Sex and age effects on the inheritance of alcohol problems: A twin study. *Journal of Abnormal Psychology, 101,* 3–17.

McGuffin, P., Katz, R., & Rutherford, J. (1991). Nature, nurture and depression: A twin study. *Psychological Medicine, 21,* 329–335.

McGuire, R. J., Carlisle, J. M., & Young, B. G. (1965). Sexual deviation as conditioned behavior. *Behavior Research & Therapy, 2,* 185–190.

McIntosh, D. N., Silver, R. C., & Wortman, C. B. (1993). Religion's role in adjustment to a negative life event: Coping with the loss of a child. *Journal of Personality & Social Psychology, 65,* 812–821.

McIntosh, J. L. (1991). Epidemiology of suicide in the United States. In A. A. Leenaars (Ed.), *Life span perspectives of suicide: Time-lines in the suicide process.* New York: Plenum.

McNally, R. J. (1994). *Panic disorder: A critical analysis.* New York: Guilford.

McNiel, D. E., & Binder, R. L. (1991). Clinical assessment of the risk of violence among psychiatric inpatients. *American Journal of Psychiatry, 148,* 1317–1321.

Mednick, B., Reznick, C., Hocevar, D., & Baker, R. (1987). Long-term efffects of parental divorce on young adult male crime. *Journal of Youth & Adolescence, 16,* 31–45.

Mednick, S. A., Machon, R. A., Huttunen, M. O., & Bonett, D. (1988). Adult schizophrenia following prenatal exposure to an influenza epidemic. *Archives of General Psychiatry, 45,* 189–192.

Mednick, S. A., Moffitt, T. E., & Stack, S. A. (Eds.). (1987). *The causes of crime: New biological approaches.* New York: Cambridge University Press.

Meichenbaum, D., & Jaremko, M. (Eds.). (1983). *Stress reduction and prevention.* New York: Plenum.

Melton, G. B., & Limber, S. (1989). Psychologists' involvement in cases of child maltreatment: Limits of role and expertise. *American Psychologist, 44,* 1225–1233.

Melton, G. B., & Wilcox, B. L. (1989). Changes in family law and family life: Challenges for psychology. *American Psychologist, 44,* 1213–1216.

Merikangas, K. R., Weissman, M. M., & Pauls, D. L. (1985). Genetic factors in the sex ratio of major depression. *Psychological Medicine, 15,* 63–69.

Metalsky, G. I., Halberstadt, L. J., & Abramson, L. Y. (1987). Vulnerability to depressive mood reactions: Toward a more powerful test of the diathesis-stress and causal mediation components of the reformulated theory of depression. *Journal of Personality & Social Psychology, 52,* 386–393.

Michael, R. T., Gagnon, J. H., Laumann, E., & Kolata, G. (1994). *Sex in America: A definitive survey.* Boston: Little, Brown.

Michelson, L. K., & Marchione, K. (1991). Behavioral, cognitive, and pharmacological treatments of panic disorder with agoraphobia: Critique and synthesis. *Journal of Consulting & Clinical Psychology, 59,* 100–114.

Miklowitz, D. J., Velligan, D. I., Goldstein, M. J., & Nuechterlein, K. H. (1991). Communication deviance in families of schizophrenic and manic patients. *Journal of Abnormal Psychology, 100,* 163–173.

Milich, R., Wolraich, M. L., & Lindgren, S. (1986). Sugar and hyperactivity: A critical review of empirical findings. *Clinical Psychology Review, 6,* 493–513.

Miller, B. A., Downs, W. R., & Testa, M. (1993). Interrelationships between victimization experiences and women's alcohol use. *Journal of Studies on Alcohol* (suppl. 11), 109–117.

Miller, I. W., Norman, W. H., & Keitner, G. I. (1989). Cognitive-behavioral treatment of depressed inpatients: Six- and twelve-month follow-up. *American Journal of Psychiatry, 146,* 1274–1279.

Miller, N. S. (Ed.). (1991). *Comprehensive handbook of drug and alcohol addiction.* New York: Dekker.

Miller, S. D. (1989). Optical differences in cases of multiple personality disorder. *The Journal of Nervous & Mental Disease, 177,* 480–486.

Miller, T. Q., Smith, T. W., Turner, C. W., & Guijarro, M. L. (1996). Meta-analytic review of research on hostility and physical health. *Psychological Bulletin, 119,* 322–348.

Millon, T. (1969). *Modern psychopathology: A biosocial approach to maladaptive learning and functioning.* Philadelphia: W. B. Saunders.

Millon, T. (1981). *Disorders of personality: DSM-III.* New York: Wiley.

Milne, A. A. (1961). *Winnie-the-Pooh.* New York: E. P. Dutton.

Mineka, S. (1985). Animal models of anxiety based disorders: Their usefulness and limitations. In A. H. Tuma & J. Maser (Eds.), *Anxiety and the anxiety disorders.* Hillsdale, NJ: Erlbaum.

Mineka, S., Davidson, M., Cook, M., & Keir, R. (1984). Observational conditioning of snake fear in rhesus monkeys. *Journal of Abnormal Psychology, 93,* 355–372.

Mintz, L. I., Lieberman, R. P., Miklowitz, D. J., & Mintz, J. (1987). Expressed emotion: A call for partnership among relatives, patients, and professionals. *Schizophrenia Bulletin, 13,* 227–235.

Minuchin, S. (1981). *Family therapy techniques.* Cambridge, MA: Harvard University Press.

Minuchin, S., Rosman, B. L., & Baker, L. (1978). *Psychosomatic families: Anorexia nervosa in context.* Cambridge, MA: Harvard University Press.

Miranda, J., & Persons, J. B. (1988). Dysfunctional attitudes are mood-state dependent. *Journal of Abnormal Psychology, 97,* 76–79.

Mitchell, J. E. (1986). Anorexia nervosa: Medical and physiological aspects. In K. D. Brownell & J. P. Foreyt (Eds.), *Handbook of eating disorders* (pp. 247–265). New York: Basic Books.

Mitchell, J. E., & deZwaan, M. (1993). Pharmacological treatments of binge eating. In C. E. Fairburn & G. T. Wilson (Eds.), *Binge eating: Nature, assessment, & treatment.* New York: Guilford.

Mitler, M. M., & Miller, J. C. (1995). Some practical considerations and policy implications of studies and sleep patterns. *Behavioral Medicine, 21,* 184–185.

Moffitt, T. E. (1990). Juvenile delinquency and attention deficit disorder: Boys' developmental trajectories from age 3 to age 15. *Child Development, 61,* 893–910.

Moffitt, T. E. (1993). The neuropsychology of conduct disorder. *Development and Psychopathology, 5,* 135–151.

Moffitt, T. E., & Silva, P. A. (1988). Self-reported delinquency, neuropsychological deficit, and history of attention deficit disorder. *Journal of Abnormal Child Psychology, 16,* 553–569.

Mohide, E. A. (1993). Informal care of community-dwelling patients with Alzheimer's disease: Focus on the family caregiver. *Neurology, 43,* S16–S19.

Monahan, J. (1992). Mental disorder and violent behavior: Perceptions and evidence. *American Psychologist, 47,* 511–521.

Monahan, J., & Walker, L. (1990). *Social science in law: Cases and materials.* Westbury, NY: Foundation Press.

Morey, L. C. (1988). A psychometric analysis of the DSM-III-R personality disorder criteria. *Journal of Personality Disorders, 2,* 109–124.

Morey, L. C. (1993). Psychological correlates of personality disorder. *Journal of Personality Disorders* (suppl.), 149–166.

Morgan, H. G., Purgold, J., & Welbourne, J. (1983). Management and outcome in anorexia nervosa: A standardized prognostic study. *British Journal of Psychiatry, 143,* 282–287.

Morgan, H. G., & Russell, G. F. M. (1975). Value of family background and clinical features as predictors of long-term outcome in anorexia nervosa: Four-year follow-up study of 41 patients. *Psychological Medicine, 5,* 355–371.

Morgenstern, H., & Glazer, W. M. (1993). Identifying risk factors for tardive dyskinesia among long-term outpatients maintained with neuroleptic medications: Results of the Yale Tardive Dyskinesia Study. *Archives of General Psychiatry, 50,* 723–733.

Mori, D., Chaiken, S., & Pliner, P. (1987). "Eating lightly" and the self-presentation of femininity. *Journal of Personality & Social Psychology, 53,* 693-702.

Morokoff, P. J., & Gillilland, R. (1993). Stress, sexual functioning, and marital satisfaction. *Journal of Sex Research, 30,* 43–53.

Morokoff, P. J., & LoPiccolo, J. (1986). A comparative evaluation of minimal therapist contact and 15-session treatment for female orgasmic dysfunction. *Journal of Consulting & Clinical Psychology, 54,* 294–300.

Moscicki, E. (1995). Epidemiology of suicidal behavior. *Suicide & Life-Threatening Behavior, 25,* 22–35.

Mueser, K. T., Bellack, A. S., Morrison, R. L., & Wade, J. H. (1990). Gender, social competence, and symptomatology in schizophrenia: A longitudinal analysis. *Journal of Abnormal Psychology, 99,* 138–147.

Mukherjee, S., Shukla, S., Woodle, J., Rosen, A. M., & Olarte, S. (1983). Misdiagnosis of schizophrenia in bipolar patients: A multiethnic comparison. *American Journal of Psychiatry, 140,* 1571–1574.

Mulvey, E. P. (1994). Assessing the evidence of a link between mental illness and violence. *Hospital & Community Psychiatry, 45,* 663–668.

Mulvey, E. P. (1995). Personal communication.

Mulvey, E. P., Geller, J. L., & Roth, L. H. (1987). The promise and peril of involuntary outpatient commitment. *American Psychologist, 42,* 571–584.

Murden, R. A., McRae, T. D., Kaner, S., & Bucknam, M. E. (1991). Mini-mental state exam scores vary with education in blacks and whites. *Journal of the American Geriatrics Society, 39,* 149–155.

Murphy, J. M. (1976). Psychiatric labeling in cross-cultural perspective. *Science, 191,* 1019–1028.

Murray, H. A. (1943). *Thematic apperception test manual.* Cambridge, MA: Harvard University Press.

N

National Institute on Drug Abuse. (1995). *National household survey on drug abuse: Population estimates 1994* (SMA 95-3063). Research Triangle Park, NC: U.S. Department of Health and Human Services.

Neighbors, H. W. (1984). Professional help use among black Americans: Implications for unmet need. *American Journal of Community Psychology, 12,* 551–566.

Nemeroff, C. J., Stein, R. I., Diehl, N. S., & Smilack, K. M. (1994). From the Cleavers to the Clintons: Role choices and body orientation as reflected in magazine article content. *International Journal of Eating Disorders, 16,* 167–176.

Nestadt, G., Romanoski, A. J., Chahal, R., & Merchant, A. (1990). An epidemiological study of histrionic personality disorder. *Psychological Medicine, 20,* 413–422.

Neuchterlein, K. H., Dawson, M. E., Gitlin, M., Ventura, J., Goldstein, M. J., Snyder, K. S., Yee, C. M., & Mintz, J. (1992). Developmental processes in schizophrenic disorders: Longitudinal studies of vulnerability and stress. *Schizophrenia Bulletin, 18,* 387–420.

Neugebauer, R. (1979). Medieval and early modern theories of mental illness. *Archives of General Psychiatry, 36,* 477–483.

Newhill, C. E., Mulvey, E. P., & Lidz, C. W. (1995). Characteristics of violence in the community by female patients seen in a psychiatric emergency service. *Psychiatric Services, 46,* 785–789.

Newman, D. L., Moffitt, T. E., Caspi, A., & Magdol, L. (1996). Psychiatric disorder in a birth cohort of young adults: Prevalence, comorbidity, clinical significance, and new case incidence from ages 11–21. *Journal of Consulting and Clinical Psychology, 64,* 552–562.

Newmann, J. P. (1989). Aging and depression. *Psychology & Aging, 4,* 150–165.

Newsweek. (1993, August 2).

Nichols, M. (1989). Sex therapy with lesbians, gay men, and bisexuals. In S. R.

Leiblum & R. C. Rosen (Eds.), *Principles and practice of sex therapy: Update for the 1990s* (pp. 269–297). New York: Guilford Press.

Nicholson, R. A., & Kugler, K. E. (1991). Competent and incompetent criminal defendants: A quantitative review of comparative research. *Psychological Bulletin, 109,* 355–370.

Nigg, J. T., & Goldsmith, H. H. (1994). Genetics of personality disorders: Perspectives from personality and psychopathology research. *Psychological Bulletin, 115,* 346–380.

Nolen-Hoeksema, S. (1990). *Sex differences in depression.* Stanford, CA: Stanford University Press.

Nolen-Hoeksema, S. (1995). Gender differences in coping with depression across the lifespan. *Depression, 3,* 81–90.

Nolen-Hoeksema, S., & Girgus, J. S. (1994). The emergence of gender differences in depression during adolescence. *Psychological Bulletin, 115,* 424–443.

Nolen-Hoeksema, S., & Larson, J. (in press). *Coping with bereavement.* Hillsdale, NJ: Erlbaum.

Nolen-Hoeksema, S., & Morrow, J. (1991). A prospective study of depression and distress following a natural disaster: The 1989 Loma Prieta earthquake. *Journal of Personality & Social Psychology, 61,* 105–121.

Nolen-Hoeksema, S., Parker, L. E., & Larson, J. (1994). Ruminative coping with depressed mood following loss. *Journal of Personality & Social Psychology, 67,* 92–104.

Nolen-Hoeksema, S., Wolfson, A., Mumme, D., & Guskin, K. (1995). Helplessness in children of depressed and nondepressed mothers. *Developmental Psychology, 31,* 377–387.

Norman, R. M., & Malla, A. K. (1993). Stressful life events and schizophrenia: II. Conceptual and methodological issues. *British Journal of Psychiatry, 162,* 166–174.

Norris, F. H., & Uhl, G. A. (1993). Chronic stress as a mediator of acute stress: The case of Hurricane Hugo. *Journal of Applied Social Psychology, 23,* 1263–1284.

Nuechterlein, K. H., Dawson, M. E., Gitlin, M., Ventura, J., Goldstein, M. J., Snyder, K. S., Yee, C. M., & Mintz, J. (1992). Developmental processes in schizophrenic disorders: Longitudinal studies of vulnerability and stress. *Schizophrenia Bulletin, 18,* 387–420.

Nuechterlein, K. H., Goldstein, M. J., Ventura, J., Dawson, M. E., & Doane, J. A. (1989). Patient-environment relationships in schizophrenia. *British Journal of Psychiatry, 155,* 84–89.

Nurnberg, H. G., Raskin, M., Livine, P. E., & Pollack, S. (1991). The comorbidity of borderline personality disorder and other DSM-III-R Axis II personality disorders. *American Journal of Psychiatry, 148,* 1371–1377.

O

Offord, D. R., Alder, R. J., & Boyle, M. H. (1986). Prevalence and sociodemographic correlates of conduct disorder. *American Journal of Social Psychiatry, 4,* 272–278.

Offord, D. R., Boyle, M. H., Racine, Y. A., & Fleming, J. E. (1992). Outcome, prognosis, and risk in a longitudinal follow-up study. *Journal of the American Academy of Child & Adolescent Psychiatry, 31,* 916–923.

O'Hara, M. W., & Swain, A. M. (1996). Rates and risk of postpartum depression—a meta-analysis. *International Review of Psychiatry, 8,* 37–54.

Ohman, A., Fredrikson, M., Hugdahl, K., & Rimmo, P. (1976). The premise of equipotentiality in human classical conditioning: Conditioned electrodermal responses to potentially phobic stimuli. *Journal of Experimental Psychology: General, 105,* 313–337.

O'Leary, A. (1990). Stress, emotion, and human immune function. *Psychological Bulletin, 108,* 363–382.

Olivardia, R., Pope, H. G., Mangweth, B., & Hudson, J. I. (1995). Eating disorders in college men. *American Journal of Psychiatry, 152,* 1279–1285.

Olmos de Paz, T. (1990). Working-through and insight in child psychoanalysis. *Melanie Klein & Object Relations, 8,* 99–112.

Olweus, D. (1986). Aggression and hormones: Behavioral relationship with testosterone and adrenaline. In D. Olweus, J. Block, & M. Radke-Yarrow (Eds.), *Development of antisocial and prosocial behavior: Research, theories, and issues.* Orlando, FL: Academic Press.

Olweus, D., Block, J., & Radke-Yarrow, M. (Eds.). (1986). *Development of antisocial and prosocial behavior: Research, theories, and issues.* Orlando, FL: Academic Press.

Orbach, S. (1978). Social dimensions in compulsive eating in women. *Psychotherapy: Theory, Research & Practice, 15,* 180–189.

Oren, D. A., & Rosenthal, N. E. (1992). Seasonal affective disorders. In E. S. Paykel (Ed.), *Handbook of affective disorders* (pp. 551–567). New York: Guilford Press.

Orlinsky, D. E., & Howard, K. I. (1986). Process and outcome in psychotherapy. In S. L. Garfield & A. E. Bergin (Eds.), *Handbook of psychotherapy and behavior change* (3rd ed., pp. 344–347). New York: Wiley.

Orloff, L. M., Battle, M. A., Baer, L., & Ivanjack, L. (1994). Long-term follow-up of 85 patients with obsessive-compulsive disorder. *American Journal of Psychiatry, 151,* 441–442.

Osofsky, J. D., Wewers, S., Hann, D. M., & Fick, A. C. (1993). Chronic community violence: What is happening to our children? *Psychiatry: Interpersonal & Biological Processes, 56,* 36–45.

Ost, L. (1992). Blood and injection phobia: Background and cognitive, physiological, and behavioral variables. *Journal of Abnormal Psychology, 101,* 68–74.

Ost, L. S., & Sterner, U. (1987). Applied tension: A specific behavioral method for treatment of blood phobia. *Behaviour Research & Therapy, 25,* 25–29.

Osvold, L. L., & Sodowsky, G. R. (1993). Eating disorders of white American, racial and ethnic minority American, and international women. Special issue: Multicultural health issues. *Journal of Multicultural Counseling & Development, 21,* 143–154.

Otto, M. W., Pollack, M. H., Meltzer-Brody, S., & Rosenbaum, J. F. (1992). Cognitive-behavioral therapy for benzodiazepine discontinuation in panic disorder patients. *Psychopharmacology Bulletin, 28,* 123–130.

Otto, M. W., Yeo, R. A., & Dougher, M. J. (1987). Right hemisphere involvement in depression: Toward a neuropsychological theory of negative affective experiences. *Biological Psychiatry, 22,* 1201–1215.

Overmier, B. J., & Seligman, M. E. (1967). Effects of inescapable shock upon subsequent escape and avoidance responding. *Journal of Comparative & Physiological Psychology, 63,* 28–33.

P

Paffenbarger, R. S., Hyde, R. T., Wing, A. L., & Hsieh, C. (1986). Physical activity, all-cause mortality, and longevity of college alumni. *New England Journal of Medicine, 314,* 605–613.

Palazzoli, M. S. (1974). *Self-starvation: From the intrapsychic to the transpersonal approach to anorexia nervosa* (A. Pomerans, Trans.). London: Chaucer.

Parker, G., & Hadzi-Pavlovic, D. (1990). Expressed emotion as a predictor of schizophrenic relapse: An analysis of aggregated data. *Psychological Medicine, 20,* 961–965.

Parker, G., Johnston, P., & Hayward, L. (1988). Parental "expressed emotion" as a predictor of schizophrenic relapse. *Archives of General Psychiatry, 45,* 806–813.

Parker, K. C., Hanson, R., & Hunsley, J. (1988). MMPI, Rorschach, and WAIS: A meta-analytic comparison of reliability, stability, and validity. *Psychological Bulletin, 103,* 367–373.

Parlee, M. B. (1994). Commentary on the literature review. In J. H. Gold & S. K. Severino (Eds.), *Premenstrual dysphorias* (pp. 149–167). Washington, DC: American Psychiatric Association Press.

Parry, B. L. (1994). Biological correlates of premenstrual complaints. In J. H. Gold & S. K. Severino (Eds.), *Premenstrual dysphorias* (pp. 47–66). Washington, DC: American Psychiatric Association Press.

Pate, J. E., Pumariega, A. J., Hester, C., & Garner, D. M. (1992). Cross-cultural patterns in eating disorders: A review. *Journal of the American Academy of Child & Adolescent Psychiatry, 31,* 802–809.

Patterson, G. R., Barbara, D., & Ramsey, E. (1989). A developmental perspective on antisocial behavior. *American Psychologist, 44,* 329–335.

Patterson, G. R., DeBaryshe, B. D., & Ramsey, E. (1989). A developmental perspective on antisocial behavior. *American Psychologist, 44,* 329–335.

Patterson, G. R., Reid, J. B., Jones, R. R., & Conger, R. E. (1975). *A social learning approach to family intervention: Vol. 1. Families with aggressive children.* Eugene, OR: Castalia.

Pearlson, G. D., Harris, G. J., Powers, R. E., & Barta, P. E. (1992). Quantitative changes in mesial temporal volume, regional cerebral blood flow, and cogni-

tion in Alzheimer's disease. *Archives of General Psychiatry, 49,* 402–408.

Pedersen, C. A., Stern, R. A., Pate, J., & Senger, M. A. (1993). Thyroid and adrenal measures during late pregnancy and the puerpérium in women who have been major depressed or who become dysphoric postpartum. *Journal of Affective Disorders, 29,* 201–211.

Pendery, M. L., Maltzman, I. M., & West, L. J. (1982). Controlled drinking by alcoholics? New findings and a reevaluation of a major affirmative study. *Science, 217,* 169–175.

Pennebaker, J. W. (1990). *Opening up: The healing power of confiding in others.* New York: William Morrow.

Pennebaker, J. W., & O'Heeron, R. C. (1984). Confiding in others and illness rates among spouses of suicide and accidental-death victims. *Journal of Abnormal Psychology, 93,* 473–476.

Perry, J. C. (1993). Longitudinal studies of personality disorders. *Journal of Personality Disorders* (Suppl. 1), 63–85.

Petersen, E. N. (1992). The pharmacology and toxicology of disulfiram and its metabolites. *Acta Psychiatrica Scandinavica, 86* (suppl. 369), 7–13.

Peterson, C. (1988). Explanatory style as a risk factor for illness. *Cognitive Therapy & Research, 12,* 119–132.

Peterson, C., & Seligman, M. E. (1984). Causal explanations as a risk factor for depression: Theory and evidence. *Psychological Review, 91,* 347–374.

Peterson, C., Seligman, M. E., & Vaillant, G. E. (1988). Pessimistic explanatory style is a risk factor for physical illness: A thirty-five-year longitudinal study. *Journal of Personality & Social Psychology, 55,* 23–27.

Peterson, G. (1991). Children coping with trauma: Diagnosis of "Dissociation Identity Disorder." *Dissociation: Progress in the Dissociation Disorders, 4,* 152–164.

Petronis, K. R., Samuels, J. F., Moscicki, E. K., & Anthony, J. C. (1990). An epidemiologic investigation of potential risk factors for suicide attempts. *Social Psychiatry & Psychiatric Epidemiology, 25,* 193–199.

Pettit, G. S., Dodge, K. A., & Brown, M. M. (1988). Early family experience, social problem solving patterns, and children's social competence. *Child Development, 59,* 107–120.

Phillips, K. A. (1991). Body dysmorphic disorder: The distress of imagined ugliness. *American Journal of Psychiatry, 148,* 1138–1149.

Phillips, K. A. (1992). "Body dysmorphic disorder: The distress of imagined ugliness": Reply. *American Journal of Psychiatry, 149,* 719.

Phillips, K. A., McElroy, S. L., Keck, P. E., & Pope, H. G. (1993). Body dysmorphic disorder: 30 cases of imagined ugliness. *American Journal of Psychiatry, 150,* 302–308.

Pi-Sunyer, F. X. (1991). Health implications of obesity. *The American Journal of Clinical Nutrition, 53,* 1595–1603.

Pike, K. M., & Rodin, J. (1991). Mothers, daughters, and disordered eating. *Journal of Abnormal Psychology, 100,* 198–204.

Pilkonis, P. A. (1995). Commentary on avoidant personality disorder: Temperament, shame, or both? In W. J. Livesley (Ed.), *The DSM-IV personality disorders* (pp. 234–238). New York: Guilford Press.

Pipher, M. B. (1994). *Reviving Ophelia: Saving the selves of adolescent girls.* New York: Putnam.

Plantenga, B. (1991). *Like open bright windows.* New York: Poets in Public Service.

Plath, S. (1971). *The bell jar.* New York: Harper and Row.

Pliner, P., & Chaiken, S. (1990). Eating, social motives, and self-presentation in women and men. *Journal of Experimental Social Psychology, 26,* 240–254.

Polivy, J., & Herman, C. P. (1993). Etiology of binge eating: Psychological mechanisms. In C. G. Fairburn & G. T. Wilson (Eds.), *Binge eating: Nature, assessment, and treatment.* New York: Guilford Press.

Pomales, J., Claiborn, C. D., & LaFromboise, T. D. (1986). Effects of black students' racial identity on perceptions of white counselors varying in cultural sensitivity. *Journal of Counseling Psychology, 33,* 57–61.

Pope, H. G., & Hudson, J. I. (1992). Is childhood sexual abuse a risk factor for bulimia nervosa? *American Journal of Psychiatry, 149,* 455–463.

Pope, K. S., Tabachnick, B. G., & Keith-Spiegel, P. (1987). Ethics of practice: The beliefs and behaviors of psychologists as therapists. *American Psychologist, 42,* 993–1006.

Post, R. M. (1992). Transduction of psychosocial stress into the neurobiology of recurrent affective disorder. *American Journal of Psychiatry, 149,* 999–1010.

Power, K. G., Simpson, R. J., Swanson, V., & Wallace, L. A. (1990). A controlled comparison of cognitive-behavior therapy, diazepam, and placebo, alone and in combination, for the treatment of generalized anxiety disorder. *Journal of Anxiety Disorders, 4,* 267–292.

Pribor, E. F., Yutzy, S. H., Dean, J. T, & Wetzel, R. D. (1993). Briquet's syndrome, dissociation, and abuse. *American Journal of Psychiatry, 150,* 1507–1511.

Prior, M. R. (1987). Biological and neuropsychological approaches to childhood autism. *British Journal of Psychiatry, 150,* 8–17.

Pritchard, J. C. (1837). *A treatise on insanity and other diseases affecting the mind.* Philadelphia: Harwell, Barrington, and Harwell.

Putnam, F. W. (1991). Recent research on multiple personality disorder. *Psychiatric Clinics of North America, 14,* 489–502.

Putnam, F. W., Guroff, J. J., Silberman, E. K., & Barban, L. (1986). The clinical phenomenology of multiple personality disorder: Review of 100 recent cases. *Journal of Clinical Psychiatry, 47,* 285–293.

Putnam, F. W., & Lowenstein, R. J. (1993). Treatment of multiple personality disorder: A survey of current practices. *American Journal of Psychiatry, 150,* 1048–1052.

Q

Quality Assurance Project (1990). Treatment outlines for paranoid, schizotypal, and schizoid personality disorders. *Australian & New Zealand Journal of Psychiatry, 24,* 339–350.

Quay, H. C. (1993). The psychobiology of undersocialized aggressive conduct disorder: A theoretical perspective. *Development & Psychopathology, 5,* 165–180.

R

Rachman, S. (1978). *Fear and courage.* San Francisco: W. H. Freeman.

Rachman, S. (1991). Neo-conditioning and the classical theory of fear acquisition. *Clinical Psychology Review, 11,* 155–173.

Rachman, S. (1993). Obsessions, responsibility and guilt. *Behaviour Research & Therapy, 31,* 149–154.

Rachman, S., & DeSilva, P. (1978). Abnormal and normal obsessions. *Behaviour Research & Therapy, 16,* 233–248.

Rachman, S. J., & Hodgson, R. J. (1980). *Obsessions and compulsions.* Englewood Cliffs, NJ: Prentice-Hall.

Radloff, L. S. (1975). Sex differences in depression: The effects of occupation and marital status. *Sex Roles, 1,* 249–267.

Raine, A., Venables, P. H., & Williams, M. (1996). Better autonomic conditioning and faster electrodermal half-recovery time at age 15 years as possible protective factors against crime at age 29 years. *Developmental Psychology, 32,* 624–630.

Randolph, E. T., Eth, S., Glynn, S. M., & Paz, G. G. (1994). Behavioural family management in schizophrenia: Outcome of a clinic-based intervention. *British Journal of Psychiatry, 164,* 501–506.

Rankin, H., Hodgson, R., & Stockwell, T. (1983). Cue exposure and response prevention with alcoholics: A controlled trial. *Behaviour Research & Therapy, 21,* 435–446.

Rapaport, J. L. (1989, March). The biology of obsessions and compulsions. *Scientific American,* 83–89.

Rapaport, J. L. (1990). *The boy who couldn't stop washing.* New York: Plume.

Rapaport, J. L. (1991). Recent advances in obsessive-compulsive disorder. *Neuropsychopharmacology, 5,* 1–10.

Rapee, R. M. (1994). Detection of somatic sensations in panic disorder. *Behaviour Research & Therapy, 32,* 825–831.

Rapee, R. M., Brown, T. A., Antony, M. M., & Barlow, D. H. (1992). Response to hyperventilation and inhalation of 5.5% carbon dioxide-enriched air across the DSM III-R anxiety disorders. *Journal of Abnormal Psychology, 101,* 538–552.

Rapport, M. D., Jones, J. T., DuPaul, G. J., Kelly, K. L., Gardner, M. J., Tucker, S. B., & Shea, M. S. (1987). Attention deficit disorder and methylphenidate: Group and single-subject analyses of dose effects on attention in clinic and classroom samples. *Journal of Clinical Child Psychology, 16,* 329–338.

Rapport, M. D., & Kelly, K. L. (1991). Psychostimulant effects of learning and cognitive function: Findings and implications for children with attention deficit hyperactivity disorder. *Clinical Psychology Review, 11,* 61–92.

Rasmussen, S. A., & Eisen, J. L. (1990). Epidemiology of obsessive compulsive disorder. *Journal of Clinical Psychiatry, 51* (Suppl. 2), 10–13.

Rasmussen, S. A., & Tsuang, M. T. (1984). The epidemiology of obsessive compulsive disorder. *Journal of Clinical Psychiatry, 45,* 450–457.

Rasmussen, S. A., & Tsuang, M. T. (1986). Clinical characteristics and family history in DSM-III obsessive-compulsive disorder. *American Journal of Psychiatry, 143,* 317–322.

Ratey, J. J., & Hallowell, N. (1995). *Driven to distraction.* New York: Simon & Schuster.

Ray, O., & Ksir, C. (1993). *Drugs, society, and human behavior.* St. Louis: Mosby.

Rees, W. D., & Lutkins, S. G. (1971). Parental depression before and after childbirth: An assessment with the Beck Depression Inventory. *Journal of the Royal College of General Practitioners, 21,* 26–31.

Rehm, L. P. (1977). A self-control model of depression. *Behavior Therapy, 8,* 787–804.

Reid, R. L., & Yen, S. S. C. (1981). Premenstrual syndrome. *American Journal of Obstetrics & Gynecology, 1,* 85–104.

Reiman, E., Raichle, M., & Robins, E. (1986). The application of positron emission tomography to the study of panic disorder. *American Journal of Psychiatry, 143,* 469–477.

Reiss, E. (1910). *Konstitutionelle Verstimmung und manisch-depressives Irresein: Klinische Untersuchungen uber den Zusammengang von Veranlangung und Psychose.* Berlin: J. Springer.

Reitan, R. M., & Davidson, L. A. (1974). *Clinical neuropsychology: Current status and applications.* Washington, DC: V. H. Winston & Sons.

Resnick, H. S., Kilpatrick, D. G., Dansky, B. S., & Saunders, B. E. (1993). Prevalence of civilian trauma and post-traumatic stress disorder in a representative national sample of women. *Journal of Consulting & Clinical Psychology, 61,* 984–991.

Resick, P. A. (1993). The psychological impact of rape. *Journal of Interpersonal Violence, 8,* 223–255.

Resick, P. A., & Schnicke, M. K. (1992). Cognitive processing therapy for sexual assault victims. *Journal of Consulting & Clinical Psychology, 60,* 748–756.

Richards, R., Kinney, D. K., Lunde, I., & Benet, M. (1988). Creativity in manic-depressives, cyclothymes, their normal relatives, and control subjects. *Journal of Abnormal Psychology, 97,* 281–288.

Richardson, G. A., & Day, N. L. (1994). Detrimental effects of prenatal cocaine exposure: Illusion or reality? *Journal of* the *American Academy of Child & Adolescent Psychiatry, 33,* 28–34.

Richardson, J. L., Shelton, D. R., Krailo, M., & Levine, A. M. (1990). The effect of compliance with treatment in survival among patients with hematologic malignancies. *Journal of Clinical Oncology, 8,* 356.

Riley, W. T., Treiber, F. A., & Woods, M. G. (1989). Anger and hostility in depression. *Journal of Nervous & Mental Disease, 177,* 668–674.

Rimm, D. C., & Masters, J. C. (1979). *Behavior therapy: Techniques and empirical findings* (2nd ed.). New York: Academic Press.

Rimmele, C. T., Miller, W. R., & Dougher, M. J. (1989). Aversion therapies. In R. K. Hester & W. R. Miller (Eds.), *Handbook of alcoholism treatment approaches: Effective alternatives.* New York: Pergamon.

Ritvo, E. A., Jorde, L. B., Mason-Brothers, A., & Freeman, B. J. (1989). The UCLA-University of Utah epidemiologic survey of autism: Recurrence risk estimates and genetic counseling. *American Journal of Psychiatry, 146,* 1032–1036.

Rivera, G. (1988). Hispanic folk medicine utilization in urban Colorado. *Sociology & Social Research, 72,* 237–241.

Roback, H. B., & Lothstein, L. M. (1986). The female mid-life sex change applicant: A comparison with younger female transsexuals and older male sex change applicants. *Archives of Sexual Behavior, 15,* 401–415.

Robins, L. N. (1991). Conduct disorder. *Journal of Child Psychology & Psychiatry & Allied Disciplines, 32,* 193–212.

Robins, L. N., Helzer, J. E., Craghan, J., & Ratcliff, K. S. (1981). National Institute of Mental Health Diagnostic Interview Schedule: Its history, characteristics, and validity. *Archives of General Psychiatry, 38,* 381–389.

Robins, L. N., Helzer, J. E., & Davis, D. H. (1975). Narcotic use in Southeast Asia and afterward: An interview of 898 Vietnam returnees. *Archives of General Psychiatry, 32,* 955–961.

Robins, L. N., Helzer, J. E., Weissman, M. M., Orvaschel, H., Gruenberg, E., Burke, J. D., & Regier, D. A. (1984). Lifetime prevalence of specific psychiatric disorders in three sites. *Archives of General Psychiatry, 41,* 949–958.

Robinson, L. A., Berman, J. S., & Neimeyer, R. A. (1990). Psychotherapy for the treatment of depression: A comprehensive review of controlled outcome research. *Psychological Bulletin, 108,* 30–49.

Robinson, T. E., & Berridge, K. C. (1993). The neural basis of drug craving: An incentive-sensitization theory of addiction. *Brain Research Reviews, 18,* 247–291.

Rockney, R. M., & Lemke, T. (1992). Casualties from a junior-senior high school during the Persian Gulf War: Toxic poisoning or mass hysteria? *Journal of Developmental & Behavioral Pediatrics, 13,* 339–342.

Rodin, J., Slochower, J., & Fleming, B. (1977). Effects of degree of obesity, age of onset, and weight loss on responsiveness to sensory and external stimuli. *Journal of Comparative & Physiological Psychology, 91,* 586–597.

Rodning, C., Beckwith, L., & Howard, J. (1991). Quality of attachment and home environments in children prenatally exposed to PCP and cocaine. *Development & Psychopathology, 3,* 351–366.

Rogers, C. (1951). *Client-centered therapy: Its current practice, implications, and theory.* Boston: Houghton Mifflin.

Rogler, L. H. (1989). The meaning of culturally sensitive research in mental health. *American Journal of Psychiatry, 146,* 296–303.

Rolls, B. J., Fedoroff, I. C., & Guthrie, J. F. (1991). Gender differences in eating behavior and body weight regulation. Special Issue: Gender and health. *Health Psychology, 10,* 133–142.

Rook, K. (1984). The negative side of social interaction: Impact on psychological well-being. *Journal of Personality & Social Psychology, 46,* 1097–1108.

Rorty, M., Yager, J., & Rossotto, E. (1994). Childhood sexual, physical, and psychological abuse in bulimia nervosa. *American Journal of Psychiatry, 151,* 1122–1126.

Rosen, G. (1968). *Madness in society: Chapters in the historical sociology of mental illness.* Chicago: University of Chicago Press.

Rosen, R. C., & Ashton, A. K. (1993). Prosexual drugs: Empirical status of the "new aphrodisiacs." *Archives of Sexual Behavior, 22,* 521–543.

Rosen, R. C., & Leiblum, S. R. (1995). Treatment of sexual disorders in the 1990s: An integrated approach. *Journal of Consulting & Clinical Psychology, 63,* 877–890.

Rosenbaum, J. F., Biederman, J., Bolduc-Murphy, E. A., & Faraone, S. V. (1993). Behavioral inhibition in childhood: A risk factor for anxiety disorders. *Harvard Review of Psychiatry, 1,* 2–16.

Rosenbaum, M. (1980). The role of the term schizophrenia in the decline of the diagnoses of multiple personality. *Archives of General Psychiatry, 37,* 1383–1385.

Rosenhan, D. L. (1973). On being sane in insane places. *Science, 179,* 250–258.

Rosenman, R. H., Brand, R. J., Jenkins, C. D., Friedman, M., Straus, R., & Wrum, M. (1976). Coronary heart disease in the Western Collaborative Group Study: Final follow-up experience of 8 years. *Journal of the American Medical Association, 233,* 877–878.

Rosenstein, M. J., Milazzo-Sayre, L. J., & Manderscheid, R. W. (1989). Care of persons with schizophrenia: A statistical profile. *Schizophrenia Bulletin, 15,* 45–58.

Rosenthal, N. E. (1993). *Winter blues: Seasonal affective disorder: What it is and how to overcome it.* New York: Guilford Press.

Rosenthal, N. E. (1995, October 9–11). *The mechanism of action of light in the treatment of seasonal affective disorder.* Paper presented at the Biologic Effects of Light 1995, Atlanta.

Ross, C. A. (1989). *Multiple personality disorder: Diagnosis, clinical features, and treatment.* New York: Wiley.

Ross, C. A. (1991). Epidemiology of multiple personality disorder and dissociation. *Psychiatric Clinics of North America, 14,* 503–517.

Ross, C. A., & Norton, G. R. (1989). Differences between men and women with multiple personality disorder. *Hospital & Community Psychiatry, 40,* 186–188.

Ross, C. A., Norton, G. R., & Fraser, G. A. (1989). Evidence against the iatrogenesis of multiple personality disorder. *Dissociation: Progress in the Dissociative Disorders, 2,* 61–65.

Ross, C. A., Norton, G. R., & Wozney, K. (1989). Multiple personality disorder: An analysis of 236 cases. *Canadian Journal of Psychiatry, 34,* 413–418.

Ross, C. E., & Mirowsky, J. (1984). Socially-desirable response and acquiescence in a cross-cultural survey of mental health. *Journal of Health & Social Behavior, 25,* 189–197.

Ross, L., Lepper, M. R., & Hubbard, M. (1975). Perseverance in self-perception and social preparation: Biased attributional processes in the debriefing paradigm. *Journal of Personality & Social Psychology, 32,* 880–892.

Ross, L., & Nisbett, R. E. (1991). *The person and the situation: Perspectives of social psychology.* Philadelphia: Temple University Press.

Rothbaum, B. O., & Foa, E. B. (1991). Exposure treatment of PTSD concomitant with conversion mutism: A case study. *Behavior Therapy, 22,* 449–456.

Rothbaum, B. O., Foa, E. D., Riggs, D. S., & Murdock, T. (1992). A prospective examination of post-traumatic stress disorder in rape victims. *Journal of Traumatic Stress, 5,* 455–475.

Rotter, J. B. (1954). *Social learning and clinical psychology.* Englewood Cliffs, NJ: Prentice Hall.

Rounsaville, B. J. (1978). Theories in marital violence: Evidence from a study of battered women. *Victimology, 3,* 11–31.

Rowse, A. L. (1969). *The early Churchills.* Middlesex: Penguin Books.

Rubin, K. H., Daniels-Beirness, T., & Hayvren, M. (1982). Social and social-cognitive correlates of sociometric status in preschool and kindergarten children. *Canadian Journal of Behavioural Science, 14,* 338–349.

Russell, G. (1979). Bulimia nervosa: An ominous variant of anorexia nervosa. *Psychological Medicine, 9,* 429–448.

Rutherford, M. J., Alterman, A. I., Cacciola, J. S., & Snider, E. C. (1995). Gender differences in diagnosing antisocial personality disorder in methadone patients. *American Journal of Psychiatry, 152,* 1309–1316.

Rutherford, M. J., Cacciola, J. S., Alterman, A. I., & McKay, J. R. (1996). Reliability and validity of the Revised Psychopathy Checklist in women methadone patients. *Assessment, 3,* 145–156.

Rutter, M. (1987). Temperament, personality and personality disorder. *British Journal of Psychiatry, 150,* 443–458.

Rutter, M., Bolton, P., Harrington, R., & Couteur, A. I. (1990). Genetic factors in child psychiatric disorder: I. A review of research strategies. *Journal of Child Psychology & Psychiatry & Allied Disciplines, 31,* 3–37.

Rutter, M., MacDonald, H., Couteur, A. L., Harrington, R., Bolton, P., & Bailey, A. (1990). Genetic factors in child psychiatric disorders—II. Empirical findings. *Journal of Child Psychology & Psychiatry, 31,* 39–83.

S

Sacco, W. P., & Beck, A. T. (1995). Cognitive theory and therapy. In E. E. Beckham & W. R. Leber (Eds.), *Handbook of depression* (2nd ed., pp. 329–351). New York: Guilford.

Salkovskis, P. M. (1989). Cognitive-behavioral factors and the persistence of intrusive thoughts in obsessional problems. *Behaviour Research & Therapy, 27,* 677–682.

Sampson, R. J., & Laub, J. H. (1992). Crime and deviance in the life course. *Annual Review of Sociology, 18,* 63–84.

Sanderson, W. C., Rapee, R. M., & Barlow, D. H. (1989). The influence of illusion of control on panic attacks induced via inhalation of 5.5% carbon dioxide-enriched air. *Archives of General Psychology, 46,* 157–162.

Sapolsky, R. M. (1994). *Why zebras don't get ulcers: A guide to stress, stress-related diseases & coping.* New York: W. H. Freeman.

Sarason, I. G., Johnson, J. H., & Siegel, J. M. (1978). Assessing the impact of life changes: Development of the Life Experiences Survey. *Journal of Consulting & Clinical Psychology, 46,* 932–946.

Sarbin, T. R., & Juhasz, J. B. (1967). The historical background of the concept of hallucination. *Journal of the History of the Behavioral Sciences, 3,* 339–358.

Sargeant, J. K., Bruce, M. L., Florio, L. P., & Weissman, M. M. (1990). Factors associated with 1-year outcome of major depression in the community. *Archives of General Psychiatry, 47,* 519–526.

Sasson, A., Lewin, C., & Roth, D. (1995). Dieting behavior and eating attitudes in Israeli children. *International Journal of Eating Disorders, 17,* 67–72.

Satir, V. (1967). Family systems and approaches to family therapy. *Journal of the Fort Logan Mental Health Center, 4,* 81–93.

Sattler, J. (1990). *Assessment of children* (3rd ed.). San Diego, CA: J. Sattler.

Saxena, S., & Prasad, K. V. (1989). DSM-III subclassification of dissociative disorders applied to psychiatric outpatients in India. *American Journal of Psychiatry, 146,* 261–262.

Scarr, S., Weinberg, R. A., & Waldman, I. D. (1993). IQ correlations in transracial adoptive families. *Intelligence, 17,* 541–555.

Schafer, W. (1992). *Stress management for wellness.* Fort Worth: Holt, Rinehart & Winston.

Scheff, T. J. (1966). *Being mentally ill: Sociological theory.* Chicago: Aldine.

Schiavi, R. C. (1990). Sexuality and aging in men. *Annual Review of Sex Research, 1,* 227–249.

Schiavi, R. C., & Segraves, R. T. (1995). The biology of sexual dysfunction. *Psychiatric Clinics of North America, 18,* 7–23.

Schiavi, R. C., Stimmel, B. B., Mandeli, J., & Schreiner-Engel, P. (1995). Diabetes, psychological functioning, and male sexuality. *Journal of Psychosomatic Research, 39,* 305–314.

Schildkraut, J. J. (1965). The catecholamine hypothesis of affective disorder: A review of supporting evidence. *American Journal of Psychiatry, 122,* 509–522.

Schleifer, S. J., Keller, S. E., McKegney, F. P., & Stein, M. (1979). *The influence of stress and other psychosocial factors on human immunity.* Paper presented at the 36th Annual Meeting of the Psychosomatic Society, Dallas, TX.

Schlenger, W. E., Kulka, R. A., Fairbank, J. A., & Hough, R. L. (1992). The prevalence of post-traumatic stress disorder in the Vietnam generation: A multi-method, multisource assessment of psychiatric disorder. *Journal of Traumatic Stress, 5,* 333–363.

Schmechel, D. E., Saunders, A. M., & Strittmatter, W. J. (1993). Increased amyloid b-peptide deposition in cerebral cortex as a consequence of apolipoprotein E genotype in late-onset Alzheimer disease. *Proceedings of the National Academy of Science of the United States of America, 90,* 9649–9653.

Schneider, J. A., O'Leary, A., & Jenkins, S. R. (1995). Gender, sexual orientation, and disordered eating. *Psychology & Health, 10,* 113–128.

Schneidman, E. (1976). *Suicidology: Contemporary developments.* New York: Grune & Stratton.

Schneier, F. R., Johnson, J., Hornig, C. D., & Liebowitz, M. R. (1992). Social phobia: Comorbidity and morbidity in an epidemiologic sample. *Archives of General Psychiatry, 49,* 282–288.

Schnurr, P. P., Hurt, S. W., & Stout, A. L. (1994). Consequences of methodological decisions in the diagnosis of late luteal phase dysphoric disorder. In J. H. Gold & S. K. Severino (Eds.), *Premenstrual dysphorias* (pp. 19–46). Washington, DC: American Psychiatric Association Press.

Schor, J. D., Levkoff, S. E., & Lipsitz, L. A. (1992). Risk factors for delirium in hospitalized elderly. *Journal of the American Medical Association, 267,* 827–831.

Schotte, D. E., & Stunkard, A. J. (1987). Bulimia vs. bulimic behaviors on a college campus. *JAMA: Journal of the American Medical Association, 258,* 1213–1215.

Schuckit, M. A. (1995). *Drug and alcohol abuse: A clinical guide to diagnosis and treatment.* New York: Plenum Medical Book Company.

Schuckit, M. A. (1996). Recent developments in the pharmacotherapy of alcohol dependence. *Journal of Consulting & Clinical Psychology, 64,* 669–676.

Schuckit, M. A., & Smith, T. L. (1996). An 8-year follow-up of 450 sons of alcoholic and control subjects. *Archives of General Psychiatry, 53,* 202–211.

Schuckit, M. A., Tip, J. E., Reich, T., & Hesselbrock, V. M. (1995). The histories of withdrawal convulsions and delirium tremens in 1648 alcohol dependent subjects. *Addiction, 90,* 1335–1347.

Schur, E. M. (1971). *Labeling deviant behavior: Its sociological implications.* New York: Harper & Row.

Seeman, M. V. (1983). Interaction of sex, age and neuroleptic dose. *Comprehensive Psychiatry, 24,* 125–128.

Segraves, K. B., & Segraves, R. T. (1991). Multiple-phase sexual dysfunction. *Journal of Sex Education & Therapy, 17,* 153–156.

Seguin, J. R., Pihl, R. O., Harden, P. W., & Tremblay, R. E. (1995). Cognitive and neuropsychological characteristics of physically aggressive boys. *Journal of Abnormal Psychology, 104,* 614–624.

Seligman, M. (1970). On the generality of the laws of learning. *Psychological Review, 77,* 406–418.

Seligman, M. E. (1993). *What you can change and what you can't: The complete guide to self-improvement.* New York: Alfred A. Knopf.

Seligman, M. E., & Maier, S. F. (1967). Failure to escape traumatic shock. *Journal of Experimental Psychology, 74,* 1–9.

Seligman, M. E. P. (1975). *Helplessness: On depression, development, and death.* San Francisco: Freeman, Cooper.

Seligman, M. E. P. (1995). The effectiveness of psychotherapy: The *Consumer Reports* study. *American Psychologist, 50,* 965–974.

Seligman, M. E. P., & Binik, Y. M. (1977). The safety signal hypothesis. In H. Davis & H. Hurwitz (Eds.), *Pavlovian operant interactions.* Hillsdale, NJ: Erlbaum.

Selkoe, D. (1992). Aging brains, aging mind. *Scientific American, 267,* 134–142.

Selling, L. H. (1940). *Men against madness.* New York: Greenberg.

Selvini-Palazzoli, M. (1974). *Self-starvation: From the intrapsychic to the transpersonal approach to anorexia nervosa* (A. Pomerans, Trans.). London: Chaucer.

Selvini-Palazzoli, M., & Viaro, M. (1988). The anorectic process in the family: A six-stage model as a guide for individual therapy. *Family Process, 27,* 129–148.

Selye, H. (1978). *The stress of life.* New York: McGraw-Hill.

Semans, J. (1956). Premature ejaculation. *Southern Medical Journal, 49,* 352–358.

Sexton, L. G., & Ames, L. (Eds.). *Anne Sexton: A self-portrait in letters.* Boston: Houghton Mifflin.

Shapiro, D. (1965). *Neurotic styles.* New York: Basic Books.

Shaw, D. S., Keenan, K., & Vondra, J. I. (1994). Developmental precursors of externalizing behavior: Ages 1 to 3. *Developmental Psychology, 30,* 355–364.

Shea, M. T. (1993). Psychosocial treatment of personality disorders. *Journal of Personality Disorders* (Spr. Suppl.), 167–180.

Shea, M. T., Elkin, I., Imber, S. D., & Sotsky, S. M. (1992). Course of depressive symptoms over follow-up: Findings from the National Institute of Mental Health Treatment of Depression Collaborative Research Program. *Archives of General Psychiatry, 49,* 782–787.

Sheard, M. H., Marini, J. L., Bridges, C. I., & Wagner, E. (1976). The effect of lithium on impulsive aggressive behavior in man. *American Journal of Psychiatry, 133,* 1409–1413.

Sheikh, J. I. (1992). Anxiety and its disorders in old age. In J. E. Birren, K. Sloan, & G. D. Cohen (Eds.), *Handbook of mental health and aging* (pp. 410–432). New York: Academic Press.

Sher, K. J., & Trull, T. J. (1994). Personality and disinhibitory psychopathology: Alcoholism and antisocial personality disorder. *Journal of Abnormal Psychology, 103,* 92–102.

Sherrington, R., Rogaev, E. I., & Liang, Y. (1995). Cloning of a gene bearing missense mutations in early-onset familial Alzheimer's disease. *Nature, 375,* 754–760.

Sherwin, B. B. (1991). The psychoendocrinology of aging and female sexuality. *Annual Review of Sex Research, 2,* 191–198.

Shneidman, E. (1976). Suicidology: Contemporary developments. New York: Grune & Stratton.

Shrout, P. E., Canino, G. J., Bird, H. R., & Rubio-Stipec, M. (1992). Mental health status among Puerto Ricans, Mexican Americans, and non-Hispanic whites. *American Journal of Community Psychology, 20,* 729–752.

Siever, L. J., Bernstein, D. P., & Silverman, J. M. (1995). Schizotypal personality disorder. In W. J. Livesley (Ed.), *The DSM-IV personality disorders* (pp. 71–90). New York: Guilford Press.

Siever, L. J., & Davis, K. L. (1991). A psychobiological perspective on the personality disorders. *American Journal of Psychiatry, 148,* 1647–1658.

Siever, L. J., Keefe, R., Bernstein, D. P., & Coccaro, E. F. (1990). Eye tracking impairment in clinically identified patients with schizotypal personality disorder. *American Journal of Psychiatry, 147,* 740–745.

Siever, L. J., & Kendler, K. S. (1985). Paranoid personality disorder. In R. Michels, J. Cavenar, & H. Bradley (Eds.), *Psychiatry, Vol. 1. The personality disorders and neuroses* (pp. 1–11). New York: Basic Books.

Silver, E., Cirincione, C., & Steadman, H. J. (1994). Demythologizing inaccurate perceptions of the insanity defense. *Law & Human Behavior, 18,* 63–70.

Silver, R. L., Boon, C., & Stones, M. H. (1983). Searching for meaning in misfortune: Making sense of incest. *Journal of Social Issues, 39,* 81–102.

Silverman, W. K., & Ginsburg, G. S. (1995). Specific phobia and generalized anxiety disorder. In D. P. Cantwell (Ed.), *Anxiety disorders in children and adolescents* (pp. 151–180). New York: Guilford Press.

Sing, L. (1995). Self-starvation in context: Towards a culturally sensitive understanding of anorexia nervosa. *Social Science & Medicine, 41,* 25–36.

Singer, M. T., & Wynne, L. C. (1965). Thought disorder and family relations of schizophrenics: IV. Results and implications. *Archives of General Psychiatry, 12,* 201–212.

Smith, D. E., & Seymour, R. B. (1994). LSD: History and toxicity. *Psychiatric Annals, 24,* 145–147.

Smith, T. W., Turner, C. W., Ford, M. H., & Hunt, S. C. (1987). Blood pressure reactivity in adult male twins. *Health Psychology, 6,* 209–220.

Snowden, L. R., & Cheung, F. K. (1990). Use of inpatient mental health services by members of ethnic minority groups. *American Psychologist, 45,* 347–355.

Sobal, J., & Stunkard, A. J. (1989). Socioeconomic status and obesity: A review of the literature. *Psychological Bulletin, 105,* 260–275.

Sobell, M. B., & Sobell, L. C. (1978). *Behavioral treatment of alcohol problems.* New York: Plenum.

Soloff, P. H., George, A., Nathan, R. S., & Schulz, P. M. (1989). Amitriptyline versus haloperidol in borderlines: Final outcomes and predictors of response. 140th Annual Meeting of the American Psychiatric Association (1987, Chicago). *Journal of Clinical Psychopharmacology, 9,* 238–246.

Solomon, K., & Hart, R. (1978). Pitfalls and prospects in clinical research on antianxiety drugs: Benzodiazepines and placebo: A research review. *Journal of Clinical Psychiatry, 39,* 823–831.

Solomon, R. L. (1980). The opponent-process theory of acquired motivation: The costs of pleasure and the benefits of pain. *American Psychologist, 35,* 691–712.

Southwick, S. M., Bremner, D., Krystal, J. H., & Charney, D. S. (1994). Psychobiologic research in post-traumatic stress disorder. *Psychiatric Clinics of North America, 17,* 251–264.

Spanos, N. P. (1978). Witchcraft in histories of psychiatry: A critical analysis and an alternative conceptualization. *Psychological Bulletin, 85,* 417–439.

Spanos, N. P., Weekes, J. R., & Bertrand, L. D. (1985). Multiple personality: A social psychological perspective. *Journal of Abnormal Psychology, 94,* 362–376.

Speckens, A. E., Hengeveld, M. W., Nijeholt, G. L., & Van Hemert, A. M. (1995). Psychosexual functioning of partners of men with presumed non-organic erectile dysfunction: Causes or consequences of the disorder? *Archives of Sexual Behavior, 24,* 157–172.

Spector, I. P., & Carey, M. P. (1990). Incidence and prevalence of the sexual dysfunctions: A critical review of the empirical literature. *Archives of Sexual Behavior, 19,* 389–408.

Spiegel, D., Bollm, J. R., Kraemer, H. C., & Gottheil, E. (1989). Psychological support for cancer patients. *Lancet, II,* 1447.

Spiegel, D. A., Bruce, T. J., Gregg, S. F. & Nuzzarello, A. (1994). Does cognitive behavior therapy assist slow-taper alprazolam discontinuation in panic disorder? *American Journal of Psychiatry, 151,* 876–881.

Spielberger, C. D., Gorsuch, R. C., & Lushene, R. E. (1970). *Manual for the state-trait anxiety inventory.* Palo Alto, CA: Consulting Psychologists Press.

Spitzer, R. L. (1981). The diagnostic status of homosexuality in DSM-III: A reformulation of the issues. *American Journal of Psychiatry, 138,* 210–215.

Spitzer, R. L., Devlin, M. J., Walsh, B. T., & Hasin, D. (1992). Binge eating disorder: A multisite field trial of the diagnostic criteria. *International Journal of Eating Disorders, 11,* 191–203.

Spitzer, R. L., Gibbon, M., Skodol, A. E., Williams, J. B. W., & First, M. B. (Eds.). (1994). *DSM-IV case book: A learning companion to the Diagnostic and Statistical Manual of Mental Disorders, Fourth Edition.* Washington, DC: American Psychiatric Association Press.

Spitzer, R. L., Skodol, A. E., Gibbon, M., & Williams, J. B. W. (1981). *DSM-III case book: A learning companion to the Diagnostic and Statistical Manual of Mental Disorders* (3rd ed.). Washington, DC: American Psychiatric Association.

Spitzer, R. L., Skodol, A. E., Gibbon, M., & Williams, J. B. W. (1983). *Psychopathology, a case book.* New York: McGraw-Hill.

Spitzer, R. L., Williams, J. B. W., & Gibbon, M. (1987). *Structured clinical interview for DSM-III-R—Non-patient version (SCID-NP4/1/87).* New York: New York State Psychiatric Institute.

Spitzer, R. L., & Williams, J. B. W., Gibbon, M., & First, M. (1992). The Structured Clinical Interview for DSM-III-R (SCID): I. History, rationale, and description. *Archives of General Psychiatry, 49,* 624–636.

Spivack, G., & Shure, M. B. (1974). *Social adjustment of young children: A cognitive approach to solving real-life problems.* San Francisco, CA: Jossey-Bass.

Sprich-Buckminster, S., Biederman, J., Milberger, S., & Faraone, S. V. (1993). Are perinatal complications relevant to the manifestation of ADD? Issues of comorbidity and familiality. *Journal of the American Academy of Child & Adolescent Psychiatry, 32,* 1032–1037.

Stack, S. (1991). Social correlates of suicide by age: Media impacts. In A. A. Leenaars (Ed.), *Life span perspectives of suicide* (pp. 187–213). New York: Plenum.

Steadman, H. J., & Keveles, G. (1972). The community adjustment and criminal activity of the Baxstrom patients: 1966–1970. *American Journal of Psychiatry, 129,* 304–310.

Steadman, H. J., McGreevy, M. A., Morrissey, J. P., Callahan, L. A., Robbins, P. C., & Cirincione, C. (1993). *Before and after Hinckley: Evaluating insanity defense reform.* New York: Guilford Press.

Steinberg, M. (1990). Transcultural issues in psychiatry: The ataque and multiple personality disorder. *Dissociation: Progress in the Dissociative Disorders, 3,* 31–33.

Steinhausen, H. C., Rauss-Mason, C., & Seidel, R. (1991). Follow-up studies of anorexia nervosa: A review of four decades of outcome research. *Psychological Medicine, 21,* 447–454.

Stern, Y., Gurland, B., Tatemichi, T. K., & Tang, M. X. (1994). Influence of education and occupation on the incidence of Alzheimer's disease. *Journal of the American Medical Association, 271,* 1004–1010.

Sternberg, R. J. (1985). *Beyond IQ: A triarchic theory of human intelligence.* New York: Cambridge University Press.

Sternberg, R. J. (1988). *The triarchic mind: A new theory of human intelligence.* New York: Viking Press.

Stevenson, H. W., Chen, C., & Lee, S. (1993). Motivation and achievement of gifted children in East Asia and the United States. *Journal for the Education of the Gifted, 16,* 223–250.

Stewart, S. H. (1996). Alcohol abuse in individuals exposed to trauma: A critical review. *Psychological Bulletin, 120,* 83–112.

Stoller, R. F. (1975). *Perversion: The erotic form of hatred.* New York: Pantheon Books.

Storr, A. (1988). *Churchill's black dog, Kafka's mice, and other phenomena of the human mind.* New York: Grove Press.

Straus, M. A., & Gelles, R. J. (1990). *Physical violence in American families: Risk factors and adaptations to violence in 8,145 families.* New Brunswick, NJ: Transaction.

Strauss, J., & Ryan, R. M. (1987). Autonomy disturbances in subtypes of anorexia nervosa. *Journal of Abnormal Psychology, 96,* 254–258.

Strauss, J. S. (1969). Hallucinations and delusions as points on continua function: Rating scale evidence. *Archives of General Psychiatry, 21,* 581–586.

Stravynski, A., Marks, I., & Yule, W. (1982). Social skills problems in neurotic outpatients: Social skills training with and without cognitive modification. *Archives of General Psychiatry, 39,* 1378–1385.

Streissguth, A. P., Randels, S. P., & Smith, D. F. (1991). A test-retest study of intelligence in patients with fetal alcohol syndrome: Implications for care. *Journal of the American Academy of Child & Adolescent Psychiatry, 30,* 584–587.

Striegel-Moore, R. H. (1993). Etiology of binge eating: A developmental perspective. In C. G. Fairburn & G. T. Wilson (Eds.), *Binge eating: Nature, assessment, and treatment* (pp. 144–172). New York: Guilford Press.

Striegel-Moore, R. H., Silberstein, L. R., & Rodin, J. (1993). The social self in bulimia nervosa: Public self-consciousness, social anxiety, and perceived fradulence. *Journal of Abnormal Psychology, 102,* 297–303.

Strober, M. (1981). The significance of bulimia in juvenile anorexia nervosa: An exploration of possible etiologic factors. *International Journal of Eating Disorders, 1,* 28–43.

Strober, M. (1986). Anorexia nervosa: History and psychological concepts. In K. D. Brownell & J. P. Foreyt (Eds.), *Handbook of eating disorders* (pp. 231–246). New York: Basic Books.

Strober, M. (1991). Family-genetic studies of eating disorders. Annual Meeting of the American Psychiatric Association Symposium: Recent advances in bulimia nervosa (1991, New Orleans, Louisiana). *Journal of Clinical Psychiatry, 52* (Suppl.), 9–12.

Stroebe, W., & Stroebe, M. S. (1987). *Bereavement and health: The psychological and physical consequences of partner loss.* New York: Cambridge University Press.

Study Group on Anorexia Nervosa. (1995). Anorexia nervosa: Directions for future research. *International Journal of Eating Disorders, 17,* 235–241.

Stunkard, A. J. (1993). A history of binge eating. In C. G. Fairburn & G. T. Wilson (Eds.), *Binge eating: Nature, assessment, and treatment* (pp. 15–34). New York: Guilford Press.

Styron, W. (1990). *Darkness visible: A memoir of madness.* New York: Vintage Books.

Suddath, R. L., Christison, G. W., Torrey, E. F., & Casanova, M. F. (1990). Anatomical abnormalities in the brains of monozygotic twins discordant for schizophrenia. *New England Journal of Medicine, 322,* 789–794.

Sue, S. (1988). Psychotherapeutic services for ethnic minorities: Two decades of research findings. *American Psychologist, 43,* 301–308.

Sue, S., Allen, D. B., & Conway, L. (1978). The responsiveness and equality of mental health care to Chicanos and Native Americans. *American Journal of Community Psychology, 6,* 137–146.

Sue, S., & Zane, N. (1987). The role of culture and cultural techniques in psychotherapy: A critique and reformulation. *American Psychologist, 42,* 37–51.

Sullivan, H. S. (1953). *The interpersonal theory of psychiatry.* New York: Norton.

Sundgot-Borgen, J. (1994). Risk and trigger factors for the development of eating disorders in female elite athletes. *Medicine & Science in Sports & Exercise, 26,* 414–419.

Sutker, P. B., Allain, A. N., & Winstead, D. K. (1993). Psychopathology and psychiatric diagnoses of World War II Pacific theater prisoners of war and combat veterans. *American Journal of Psychiatry, 150,* 240–245.

Sutker, P. B., Davis, J. M., Uddo, M., & Ditta, S. R. (1995). Assessment of psychological distress in Persian Gulf troops: Ethnicity and gender comparisons. *Journal of Personality Assessment, 64,* 415–427.

Sutker, P. B., Winstead, D. K., Galina, Z. H., & Allain, A. N. (1991). Cognitive deficits and psychopathology among former prisoners of war and combat veterans of the Korean conflict. *American Journal of Psychiatry, 148,* 67–72.

Swartz, C. (1995). Setting the ECT stimulus. *Psychiatric Times, 12*(6). (Reprint addition)

Swartz, M., Blazer, D., George, L., & Winfield, I. (1990). Estimating the prevalence of borderline personality disorder in the community. *Journal of Personality Disorders, 4,* 257–272.

Swedo, S., Pietrini, P., & Leonard, H. (1992). Cerebral glucose metabolism in childhood-onset obsessive-compulsive disorder. *Archives of General Psychiatry, 49,* 690–694.

Sweeney, P. D., Anderson, K., & Bailey, S. (1986). Attributional style in depression: A meta-analytic review. *Journal of Personality & Social Psychology, 50,* 974–991.

Szasz, T. (1961). *The myth of mental illness.* New York: Hoeber-Harper.

Szasz, T. S. (1963). *Law, liberty, and psychiatry: An inquiry into the social uses of mental health practice.* New York: Collier Books.

Szasz, T. S. (1971). The sane slave: An historical note on the use of medical diagnosis as justificatory rhetoric. *American Journal of Psychotherapy, 25,* 228–239.

Szasz, T. S. (1977). *Psychiatric slavery.* New York: Free Press.

Szatmari, P., Bartolucci, G., Bremner, R., & Bond, S. (1989). A follow-up study of high-functioning autistic children. *Journal of Autism & Developmental Disorders, 19,* 213–225.

Szmukler, G. I., & Russell, G. F. M. (1986). Bulimia: Medical and physiological aspects. In K. D. Brownell & J. P. Foreyt (Eds.), *Handbook of eating disorders* (pp. 283–300). New York: Basic Books.

T

Takahashi, Y. (1990). Is multiple personality disorder really rare in Japan? *Dissociation: Progress in the Dissociative Disorders, 3,* 57–59.

Tanay, E. (1992). The verdict with two names. *Psychiatric Annals, 22,* 571–573.

Tateyama, M., Asai, M., Kamisada, M., Hashimoto, M., Bartels, M., & Heimann, H. (1993). Comparison of schizophrenia delusions between Japan and Germany. *Psychopathology, 26,* 151–158.

Taubes, G. (1994). Will new dopamine receptors offer a key to schizophrenia? *Science, 265,* 1034–1035.

Taylor, R. (1982). *Robert Schumann: His life and work.* London: Granada.

Taylor, S. E. (1991). *Health Psychology.* New York: McGraw-Hill.

Taylor, S. E., & Brown, J. D. (1988). Illusion and well-being: A social psychological perspective on mental health. *Psychological Bulletin, 103,* 193–210.

Taylor, S. E., Kemeny, M. E., Aspinwall, L. G., & Schneider, S. G. (1992). Optimism, coping, psychological distress, and high-risk sexual behavior among men at risk for acquired immunodeficiency syndrome (AIDS). *Journal of Personality & Social Psychology, 63,* 460–473.

Telch, M. J. (1988). Combined pharmacological and psychological treatment for panic sufferers. In S. Rachman & J. D.

Maser (Eds.), *Panic: Psychological perspectives*. Hillsdale, NJ: Erlbaum.

Telch, M. J., Lucas, J. A., & Nelson, P. (1989). Nonclinical panic in college students: An investigation of prevalence and symptomatology. *Journal of Abnormal Psychology, 98,* 300–306.

Tellegen, A., Lykken, D. T., Bouchard, T. J., & Wilcox, K. J. (1988). Personality similarity in twins reared apart or together. *Journal of Personality & Social Psychology, 54,* 1031–1039.

Telles, C. Karno, M., Mintz, J., Paz, G., Arias, M., Tucker, D., & Lopez, S. (1995). Immigrant families coping with schizophrenia. *British Journal of Psychiatry, 167,* 473–479.

Teplin, L. A., Abram, K. M., & McClelland, G. M. (1994). Does psychiatric disorder predict violent crime among released jail detainees? A six-year longitudinal study. *American Psychologist, 49,* 335–342.

Terr, L. C. (1981). Psychic trauma in children: Observations following the Chowchilla school-bus kidnapping. *American Journal of Psychiatry, 138,* 14–19.

Terr, L. C. (1983). Chowchilla revisited: The effects of psychic trauma four years after a school-bus kidnapping. *American Journal of Psychiatry, 140,* 1543–1550.

Test, M. A., & Stein, L. I. (1980). Alternative to mental hospital treatment: III. Social cost. *Archives of General Psychiatry, 37,* 409–412.

Tharp, R. G. (1991). Cultural diversity and treatment of children. *Journal of Consulting & Clinical Psychology, 59,* 799–812.

Thase, M. E., & Howland, R. H. (1995). Biological processes in depression: An updated review and integration. In E. E. Beckham & W. R. Leber (Eds.), *Handbook of depression* (2nd ed., pp. 213–279). New York: Guilford.

Thase, M. E., & Kupfer, D. J. (1996). Recent developments in the pharmacotherapy of mood disorders. *Journal of Consulting & Clinical Psychology, 64,* 646–659.

Thigpen, C. H., & Cleckley, H. M. (1957). *The three faces of Eve.* New York: McGraw-Hill.

Thoits, P. A. (1986). Multiple identities: Examining gender and marital status difference in distress. *American Sociological Review, 51,* 259–272.

Thom, M. (Ed.) (1987). *Letters to Ms.* New York: Henry Holt.

Thomas, A., & Chess, S. (1984). Genesis and evolution of behavioral disorders: From infancy to early adult life. *American Journal of Psychiatry, 141,* 1–9.

Thompson, R. A., Tinsley, B. R., Scalora, M. J., & Parke, R. D. (1989). Grandparents' visitation rights: Legalizing the ties that bind. *American Psychologist, 44,* 1217–1222.

Thoresen, C. E., Telch, M. J., & Eagleston, J. R. (1981). Altering Type A behavior. *Psychosomatics, 8,* 472–482.

Tiefer, L., & Melman, A. (1989). Comprehensive evaluation of erectile dysfunction and medical treatments. In S. R. Leiblum & R. C. Rosen (Eds.), *Principles and practice of sex therapy: Update for the 1990s* (pp. 207–236). New York: Guilford Press.

Tomasson, K., Kent, D., & Coryell, W. (1991). Somatization and conversion disorders: Comorbidity and demographics and presentation. *Acta Psychiatrica Scandinavica, 84,* 288–293.

Torgersen, S. (1980). The oral, obsessive, and hysterical personality syndromes: A study of hereditary and environmental factors by means of the twin method. *Archives of General Psychiatry, 37,* 1272–1277.

Torgersen, S. (1986). Genetic factors in moderately severe and mild affective disorders. *Archives of General Psychiatry, 43,* 222–226.

Toufexis, A. (1996, April 29). Why Jennifer Got Sick. *Time,* 70.

Toufexis, A. (1996, May 13). Diet pills are coming back. *Time, 147,* 78.

Tseng, W. (1973). The development of psychiatric concepts in traditional Chinese medicine. *Archives of General Psychiatry, 29,* 569–575.

Tuma, J. M. (1989). Mental health services for children: The state of the art. *American Psychologist, 44,* 188–199.

Turk, D. C., Meichenbaum, D. H., & Berman, W. H. (1979). Application of biofeedback for the regulation of pain: A critical review. *Psychological Bulletin, 86,* 1322–1338.

Turk, D. C., & Ruby, T. E. (1992). Cognitive factors and persistent pain: A glimpse into Pandora's box. *Cognitive Therapy & Research, 16,* 99–122.

Turkat, I. D. (1985). *Behavioral case formulation.* New York: Plenum.

Turkheimer, E., & Parry, C. D. (1992). Why the gap? Practice and policy in civil commitment hearings. *American Psychologist, 47,* 646–655.

Turner, S. M., Beidel, D. C., & Costello, A. (1987). Psychopathology in the offspring of anxiety disorders patients. *Journal of Consulting & Clinical Psychology, 55,* 229–235.

V

Vaillant, G. E. (1985). An empirically derived hierarchy of adaptive mechanisms and its usefulness as a potential diagnostic axis. *Acta Psychiatrica Scandinavica, 71,* 171–180.

Vaillant, G. E., & Milofsky, E. S. (1982). Natural history of male alcoholism: IV. Paths to recovery. *Archives of General Psychiatry, 39,* 127–133.

Van Hemert, A. M., Hengeveld, M. W., Bolk, J. H., & Rooijmans, H. G. (1993). Psychiatric disorders in relation to medical illness among patients of a general medical outpatient clinic. *Psychological Medicine, 23,* 167–173.

Van Itallie, T. B. (1985). Health implications of overweight and obesity in the United States. *Annals of Internal Medicine, 103,* 983–988.

Vaughn, C. E., & Leff, J. P. (1976). The influence of family and social factors on the course of psychiatric illness: A comparison of schizophrenic and depressed neurotic patients. *British Journal of Psychiatry, 129,* 125–137.

Vazquez-Nuttall, E., Avila-Vivas, Z., & Morales-Barreto, G. (1984). Working with Latin American families. *Family Therapy Collections, 9,* 74–90.

Veith, I. (1965). *Hysteria: The history of a disease.* Chicago, IL: University of Chicago Press.

Venter, A., Lord, C., & Schopler, E. (1992). A follow-up study of high-functioning autistic children. *Journal of Child Psychology & Psychiatry & Allied Disciplines, 33,* 489–507.

Ventura, J., Neuchterlein, K. H., Lukoff, D., & Hardesty, J. P. (1989). A prospective study of stressful life events and schizophrenic relapse. *Journal of Abnormal Psychology, 98,* 407–411.

Verhulst, J., & Heiman, J. (1988). A systems perspective on sexual desire. In S. R. Leiblum & R. C. Rosen (Eds.), *Sexual desire disorders* (pp. 243–270). New York: Guilford Press.

Veronen, L. J., & Kilpatrick, D. G. (1983). Stress management for rape victims. In D. Meichenbaum & M. E. Jaremko (Eds.), *Stress reduction and prevention.* New York: Plenum.

Visintainer, M. A., Volpicelli, J. R., & Seligman, M. E. (1982). Tumor rejection in rats after inescapable or escapable shock. *Science, 216,* 437–439.

Vitousek, K., & Manke, F. (1994). Personality variables and disorders in anorexia nervosa and bulimia nervosa. Special issue: Personality and psychopathology. *Journal of Abnormal Psychology, 103,* 137–147.

Volpicelli, J. R., Watson, N. T., King, A. C., & Sherman, C. E. (1995). Effect of naltrexone on alcohol "high" in alcoholics. *American Journal of Psychiatry, 152,* 613–615.

W

Walker, L. E. A. (1994). Are personality disorders gender biased? In S. A. Kirk & S. D. Einbinder (Eds.), *Controversial issues in mental health* (pp. 22–29). New York: Allyn & Bacon.

Watson, J. B., & Raynor, R. (1920). Conditioned emotional reactions. *Journal of Experimental Psychology, 3,* 1–14.

Wehr, T. A., & Rosenthal, N. E. (1989). Seasonality and affective illness. *American Journal of Psychiatry, 146,* 829–839.

Weidner, G., & Collins, R. L. (1993). Gender, coping, and health. In H. W. Krohne (Ed.), *Attention and avoidance* (pp. 241–265). Seattle: Hogrefe & Huber.

Weidner, G., Sexton, G., Matarazzo, J. D., & Pereira, C. (1988). Type A behavior in children, adolescents, and their parents. *Developmental Psychology, 24,* 118–121.

Weinberger, D. A., Schwartz, G. E., & Davidson, R. J. (1979). Low-anxious, high-anxious, and repressive coping styles: Psychometric patterns and behavioral and physiological responses to stress. *Journal of Abnormal Psychology, 88,* 369–380.

Weiner, B. A., & Wettstein, R. M. (1993). *Legal issues in mental health care.* New York: Plenum.

Weisbrod, B. A., Test, M. A., & Stein, L. I. (1980). Alternative to mental hospital treatment: II. Economic benefit-cost analysis. *Archives of General Psychiatry, 37,* 400–405.

Weiss, B., & Weisz, J. R. (1995). Effectiveness of psychotherapy. *Journal of the American Academy of Child & Adolescent Psychiatry, 34,* 971–972.

Weiss, J. M. (1991). Stress-induced depression: Critical neurochemical and electrophysiological changes. In J. I. Madden (Ed.), *Neurobiology of learning, emotion, and affect* (pp. 123–154). New York: Raven Press.

Weissman, M., & Olfson, M. (1995). Depression in women: Implications for health care research. *Science, 269,* 799–801.

Weissman, M. M. (1993a). Family genetic studies of panic disorder. Conference on panic and anxiety: A decade of progress. *Journal of Psychiatric Research, 27* (suppl. 1), 69–78.

Weissman, M. M. (1993b). The epidemiology of personality disorders: A 1990 update. NIMH Conference: Personality disorders (1990, Williamsburg, Virginia). *Journal of Personality Disorders* (Spr. Suppl. 1), 44–62.

Weissman, M. M., Prusoff, B. A., Gammon, G. D., Merikangas, K. R., Leckman, J. F., & Kidd, K. K. (1984). Psychopathology in children (ages 6–18) of depressed and normal parents. *Journal of the American Academy of Child Psychiatry, 23,* 78–84.

Weisz, J. R., Donenberg, G., Han, S., & Kauneckis, D. (1995). Child and adolescent psychotherapy outcomes in experiments versus clinics: Why the disparity? *Journal of Abnormal Child Psychology, 23,* 83–106.

Weisz, J. R., Weiss, B., Alicke, M. D., & Klotz, M. L. (1987). Effectiveness of psychotherapy with children and adolescents: A meta-analysis for clinicians. *Journal of Consulting & Clinical Psychology, 55,* 542–549.

Welch, S. L., & Fairburn, C. G. (1994). Sexual abuse and bulimia nervosa: Three integrated case control comparisons. 11th National Conference on Eating Disorders (1992, Columbus, Ohio). *American Journal of Psychiatry, 151,* 402–407.

Wender, P. H., Kety, S. S., Rosenthal, D., Schulsinger, F., Ortmann, J., & Lunde, I. (1986). Psychiatric disorders in the biological and adoptive families of adopted individuals with affective disorders. *Archives of General Psychiatry, 43,* 923–929.

Westermeyer, J. (1993). Cross-cultural psychiatric assessment. In A. C. Gaw (Ed.), *Culture, ethnicity, and mental illness* (pp. 125–144). Washington, DC: American Psychiatric Press.

Westermeyer, J., Bouafuely, M., Neider, J., & Callies, A. (1989). Somatization among refugees: An epidemiologic study. *Psychosomatics, 30,* 34–43.

Weston, S. C., & Siever, L. J. (1993). Biologic correlates of personality disorders. NIMH Conference: Personality disorders (1990, Williamsburg, Virginia). *Journal of Personality Disorders* (Suppl. 1), 129–148.

Whelan, J. P., & Houts, A. C. (1990). Effects of a waking schedule on primary enuretic children treated with full-spectrum home training. *Health Psychology, 90,* 164–176.

Whiffen, V. E. (1992). Is postpartum depression a distinct diagnosis? *Clinical Psychology Review, 12,* 485–508.

Whiffen, V. E., & Gotlib, I. H. (1993). Comparison of postpartum and nonpostpartum depression: Clinical presentation, psychiatric history, and psychosocial functioning. *Journal of Consulting & Clinical Psychology, 61,* 485–494.

Widiger, T. A. (1995). Deletion of self-defeating and sadistic personality disorders. In W. J. Livesley (Ed.), *The DSM-IV personality disorders* (pp. 359–376). New York: Guilford Press.

Widiger, T. A., & Costa, P. T. (1994). Personality and personality disorders. Special Issue: Personality and psychopathology. *Journal of Abnormal Psychology, 103,* 78–91.

Widiger, T. A., Mangine, S., Corbitt, E. M., Ellis, C. G., & Thomas, G. V. (1995). *Personality disorder interview-IV. A semistructured interview for the assessment of personality disorders.* Odessa, FL: Psychological Assessment Resources.

Widiger, T. A., & Spitzer, R. L. (1991). Sex biases in the diagnosis of personality disorder: Conceptual and methodological issues. *Clinical Psychological Review, 11,* 1–22.

Williams, D. (1992). *Nobody nowhere: The extraordinary autobiography of an autistic.* New York: Times Books.

Williams, D. (1994). *Somebody somewhere: Breaking free from the world of autism.* New York: Times Books.

Williams, J. B., & Spitzer, R. L. (1983). The issue of sex bias in DSM-III. *American Psychologist, 38,* 793–798.

Williams, L. M. (1995). Recovered memories of abuse in women with documented child sexual victimization histories. *Journal of Traumatic Stress, 8,* 649–673.

Williams, R. B., Barefoot, J. C., Haney, T. L., & Harrell, F. E. (1988). Type A behavior and angiographically documented coronary atherosclerosis in a sample of 2,289 patients. *Psychosomatic Medicine, 50,* 139–152.

Williams-Russo, P., Urquhart, B. L., Sharrock, N. E., & Charlson, M. E. (1992). Post-operative delirium: Predictors and prognosis in elderly orthopedic patients. *Journal of the American Geriatrics Society, 40*, 759–767.

Williamson, D. F., Serdula, M. K., Anda, R. F., & Levy, A. (1992). Weight loss attempts in adults: Goals, duration, and rate of weight loss. *American Journal of Public Health, 82*, 1251–1257.

Williamson, G. L. (1993). Postpartum depression syndrome as a defense to criminal behavior. *Journal of Family Violence, 8*, 151–165.

Wilps, R. F., Jr. (1990). Male bulimia nervosa: An autobiographical case study. In A. E. Andersen (Ed.), *Males with eating disorders* (pp. 9–29). New York: Brunner/Mazel.

Wilson, G. T. (1993). Psychological and pharmacological treatments of bulimia nervosa: A research update. *Applied & Preventive Psychology, 2*, 35–42.

Wilson, W. H., & Clausen, A. M. (1995). 18-month outcome of clozapine treatment for 100 patients in a state psychiatric hospital. *Psychiatric Services, 46*, 386–389.

Wincze, J. P. (1989). Assessment and treatment of atypical sexual behavior. In S. R. Leiblum & R. C. Rosen (Eds.), *Principles and practice of sex therapy: Update for the 1990s* (pp. 382–404). New York: Guilford Press.

Windholz, M. J., Marmar, C. R., & Horowitz, M. J. (1985). A review of the research on conjugal bereavement: Impact on health and efficacy of intervention. *Comprehensive Psychiatry, 26*, 433–447.

Wing, R. R., Epstein, L. H., Nowalk, M. P., & Scott, N. (1987). Family history of diabetes and its effect on treatment outcome in Type II diabetes. *Behavior Therapy, 18*, 283–289.

Winger, G., Hofmann, F. G., & Woods, J. H. (1992). *Handbook on drug and alcohol abuse.* New York: Oxford University Press.

Winokur, G., & Clayton, P. (1967). Family history studies: II. Sex differences and alcoholism in primary affective illness. *British Journal of Psychiatry, 113*, 973–979.

Wolfe, J., Brown, P. J., & Kelley, J. M. (1993). Reassessing war stress: Exposure and the Persian Gulf War. *Journal of Social Issues, 49*, 15–31.

Wolfner, G. D., & Gelles, R. J. (1993). A profile of violence toward children: A national study. *Child Abuse & Neglect, 17*, 197–212.

Wolpe, J. (1969). *The practice of behavior therapy.* Elmsford, New York: Pergamon.

Wright, R. A. (1984). Motivation, anxiety, and the difficulty of avoidant control. *Journal of Personality & Social Psychology, 46*, 1376–1388.

Wurtman, J. J. (1987). Disorders of food intake: Excessive carbohydrate snack intake among a class of obese people. *Annals of the New York Academy of Sciences, 499*, 197–202.

Wurtman, R. J., & Wurtman, J. J. (1984). Nutritional control of central neurotransmitters. In K. M. Pirke & D. Plogg (Eds.), *The psychobiology of anorexia nervosa.* Berlin: Springer-Verlag.

Wurtzel, E. (1995). *Prozac nation.* New York: Berkley.

Y

Yama, M. F. (1990). The usefulness of human figure drawings as an index of overall adjustment. *Journal of Personality Assessment, 54*, 78–86.

Yonkers, K. A., & Gurguis, G. (1995). Gender differences in the prevalence and expression of anxiety disorders. In M. V. Seeman (Ed.), *Gender and psychopathology* (pp. 113–130). Washington, DC: American Psychiatric Press.

Z

Zahn-Waxler, C. (1993). Warriors and worriers: Gender and psychopathology. *Development & Psychopathology, 5*, 79–89.

Zelt, D. (1981). First person account: The Messiah quest. *Schizophrenia Bulletin, 7*, 527–531.

Zigler, E., & Hodapp, R. M. (1991). Behavioral functioning in individuals with mental retardation. *Annual Review of Psychology, 42*, 29–50.

Zilboorg, G., & Henry, G. W. (1941). *A history of medical psychology.* New York: W. W. Norton.

Zoccolillo, M. (1993). Gender and the development of conduct disorder. *Development & Psychopathology, 5*, 65–78.

Zoccolillo, M., Pickles, A., Quinton, D., & Rutter, M. (1992). The outcome of childhood conduct disorder: Implications for defining adult personality disorder and conduct disorder. *Psychological Medicine, 22*, 971–986.

Credits

Photographs

Table of Contents

p. ix: *Heart of the Hunter* by Michelle Puleo, B. 1967, American, Private Collection/ Superstock; p. x: *Grey Clowns* by Diana Ong, B. 1940/Superstock; p. xii: *Femme Dans Un Fauteuil* by Juan Gris. Spanish. Christie's Images, London/Superstock; p. xiv: *Introspection* by Daniel Nevins. American. Private Collection/Superstock.

About the Author

p. xxv: Photograph by Mel Manis.

Part Openers

Part One: *Heart of the Hunter* by Michelle Puleo, B. 1967, American, Private Collection/Superstock; Part Two: *Grey Clowns* by Diana Ong, B. 1940/Superstock; Part Three: *Femme Dans Un Fauteuil* by Juan Gris. Spanish. Christie's Images, London/Superstock; Part Four: *Introspection* by Daniel Nevins. American. Private Collection/Superstock.

Chapter 1

Opener: *People Flying* by Peter Sickles. American/Superstock; p. 6 (top): ©UPI/Corbis-Bettmann, (bottom): ©Mike Mazzaschi/Stock Boston; p. 7 (left): ©Van Bucher/Photo Researchers, (right): ©Steve Lynch/Tony Stone Images; p. 8: ©UPI/Corbis-Bettmann; p. 9: ©Archive Photos; p. 11: ©The Granger Collection; p. 12: ©The Granger Collection; p. 14: ©Corbis-Bettmann; p. 16 (top): ©US National Library of Medicine/Science Photo Library/Photo Researchers, (bottom): ©National Library of Medicine/Photo Researchers; p. 17: ©Belzeaux/Photo Researchers; p. 18 (top): ©Corbis-Bettmann, (bottom): ©Milner/Sygma.

Chapter 2

Opener: *Essor* by Andre Rouillard, 1981/Superstock; p. 27: ©Bob Daemmrich/ Stock Boston; p. 28: ©Michael Newman/ Photo Edit; figure 2.2: ©Science Photo Library/Photo Researchers; figure 2.3: ©Science Source/Photo Researchers; figure 2.4: ©Science Photo Library/Photo Researchers; figure 2.7: ©Joe McNally/ Sygma; p. 42: ©Jeff Greenberg/Photo Edit; figure 2.11: ©Will & Deni McIntyre/Photo Researchers; p. 45: ©Peter L. Chapman/ Stock Boston; p. 47: ©Lawrence Migdale/ Stock Boston; p. 48: ©Michael Newman/ Photo Edit; p. 59: ©Erik Anderson/Stock Boston.

Chapter 3

Opener: *Window of Opportunity* by Christian Pierre. American. Private Collection/Superstock; figure 3.1: From: Damasio, H., Grabowski, T., Frank, R., Galaburda, A. M., Damasio, A. R.: The return of Phineas Gage: Clues about the brain from the skull of a famous patient. *Science*, 264:1102–1105, 1994. Department of Neurology and Image Analysis Facility, University of Iowa; figure 3.4a: Courtesy, Dr. Nancy Andreasen, figure 3.4b: Courtesy, Dr. Nancy Andreasen; figure 3.6: ©L. Willatt/East Anglian Regional Genetics Service/Science Photo Library/Photo Researchers; p. 72 (bottom): ©M. Greenlar/ The Image Works; p. 75: ©Enrico Ferorelli; p. 76: ©Corbis/Bettmann; p. 77 (left): ©Barton Silverman/NYT Pictures, (right): ©Bob Daemmrich/Stock Boston; p. 78: ©Sarah Putnam/The Picture Cube; p. 79 (right): ©Otto Kernberg, p. 79 (left): ©Wellcome Trust; p. 80: ©Corbis/ Bettmann; p. 81 (top): ©Lawrence Migdale/ Stock Boston, (bottom left): ©Archives of the History of American Psychology, (bottom right): ©Christopher Johnson/ Stock Boston; p. 82 (top): Courtesy, Dr. Albert Bandura, p. 82 (bottom left): ©Spencer Grant/Stock Boston, p. 82 (bottom right): ©Bob Daemmrich/Stock Boston; p. 83: ©Doug Menvez/Stock Boston; p. 84 (top): Courtesy, Albert Ellis, (bottom): Courtesy, Aaron T. Beck; p. 85: National Library of Medicine; p. 87: ©Bruce Ayres/Tony Stone Images; p. 92: ©F. Pedrick/The Image Works; p. 94: ©Michael Grecco/Stock Boston.

Chapter 4

Opener: *Birddog* by Diana Ong, B. 1940, Private Collection/Superstock; p. 108: ©Jack Spratt/The Image Works; p. 113 (left): ©Owen Franken/Stock Boston, (right): ©John Elk III/Stock Boston; p. 120: ©John Cancalosi/Stock Boston; p. 127 (left): ©Bob Daemmrich/Stock Boston, (right): ©Howard Grey/Tony Stone Images; p. 129 (top): ©Monika Anderson/Stock Boston, (bottom left): ©William Campbell/ Peter Arnold, (bottom right): ©Peter Menzel/Stock Boston; p. 130: ©AP/ Wide World Photos; p. 131: ©Express Newspapers/Archive Photos; p. 132: ©Bob Daemmrich/Stock Boston; p. 133: ©J. Calson/The Sacramento Bee/Sygma; p. 145: ©John Eastcott/Yva Momatiuk/ Photo Researchers; p. 146: ©Lewis Baxter/Peter Arnold.

Chapter 5

Opener: *Watching from the Steps* by Hyacinth Manning-Carner. African American. Private Collection/Superstock; p. 160: ©Peter Southwick/Stock Boston; p. 162: ©Frank Siteman/Stock Boston; p. 164: ©Bob Daemmrich/Stock Boston; p. 166: ©Joseph Nettis/Stock Boston; figure 5.12: Courtesy, Dr. Lewis R. Baxter, Jr.; figure 5.13: Courtesy, Dr. Lewis R. Baxter, Jr.; figure 5.14: ©1994, Newsweek, Inc. All Rights Reserved. Reprinted by permisson; p. 186 (top): ©Will & Deni McIntyre/Photo Researchers, (bottom): ©Robin Thomas; p. 187: ©Miro Vintoniv/ Stock Boston; p. 188: ©Bill Aron/Photo Edit; p. 190: ©Toni Michaels; p. 195: ©Gale Zucker/Stock Boston; p. 199: ©Bob Daemmrich/Stock Boston; p. 207: ©AP Photo/Robert Sorbo/Wide World Photos; p. 209: ©Corbis/Bettmann.

Chapter 6

Opener: *My Dog and I Are One* by Patricia Schwimmer. Canadian/Superstock; p. 218: ©Judy Allen-Newberry; p. 219: *The Green House* by Sandy Skoglund, 1990, American/ Superstock; p. 223: ©Grunnitus/ Monkmeyer; p. 224: ©Peter Southwick/ Stock Boston; p. 231: Courtesy, The Genain Quadruplets; figure 6.3: Courtesy, Dr. Nancy Andreasen; figure 6.4a: Courtesy, Dr. Nancy Andreasen; figure 6.4b: Courtesy, Dr. Nancy Andreasen; figure 6.5: ©Dr. Dean Wong; p. 235: ©Bob Daemmrich/ Stock Boston; p. 241: ©Ed Lalio/Picture Cube; p. 244: ©Alan Carey/The Image Works; p. 245: ©Rick Smolan/Stock Boston.

Chapter 7

Opener: *Day Dream* by Daniel Nevins. American. Private Collection/Superstock; p. 254 (top): *Le Mois des Venanges* by Rene Magritte. 1959. Private Collection, Paris/Art Resource, (bottom): ©Phyllis Picardizd/ Stock Boston; p. 257: ©The Kobal Collection; p. 260: ©Chris Windsor/ Tony Stone Images; p. 261: ©UPI/ Corbis-Bettmann; p. 262: ©Corbis/ Bettmann;

Line Art & Excerpts
Chapter 2

Opener quote: From the UNICORN AND OTHER POEMS by Anne Morrow Lindbergh. Reprinted by permission of Pantheon Books, a division of Random House, Inc.

Figure 2.1: From Jackson Beatty, *Principles of Behavioral Neuroscience.* Copyright © 1995 The McGraw-Hill Companies, Inc. All Rights Reserved. Reprinted by permission.

Figure 2.5: From M. A. B. Brazier, *The Electrical Activity of the Nervous System: A Textbook for Students,* page 244, Copyright © 1960, from Williams, Wilkins, and Waverly Inc. Reprinted with permission.

Figure 2.6: Reprinted by permission of Hoffman-LaRoche Inc.

Figure 2.8: From J. M. Sattler, *Assessment of Children,* 3e, Copyright © 1992, J. M .Sattler, San Diego, Reprinted with permission.

Figure 2.10: Source: Minnesota Multiphasic Personality Inventory. Copyright © the University of Minnesota, 1942, 1943 (renewed 1970). This form 1948, 1976, 1982. Reprinted by permission of the University of Minnesota Press. "MMPI" and "Minnesota Multiphasic Personality Inventory" are trademarks owned by the University of Minnesota.

Chapter 3

Figure 3.3: From *Psychology,* by E. B. Goldstein, Copyright © 1994, Wadsworth Publishing Company. Reprinted by permission of Brooks/Cole Publishing Co., Pacific Row, CA. A Division of International Thomson Pub. Inc.

p. 98: From: S. Sue and N. Zane, "The Role of Culture and Cultural Techniques in

Psychotherapy: A Critique and Reformulation" in *American Psychologist*, 42(1):42-43, American Psychological Association, 1994; and From: S. Sue and K. K. Morishima, *The Mental Health of Asian Americans*, Copyright © 1994, Jossey-Bass, San Francisco, Reprinted with permission.

p. 103: Adapted from *Finding Help, How to Choose a Psychologist*, Copyright © 1995 by the American Psychological Association. Adapted with permission.

Chapter 4

Figure 4.1: Source: Data from R. M. Rapee, et al., "Response to Hyperventilation and Inhalation of 5.5% Carbon Dioxide-Enriched Air Across the DSM-III-R Anxiety Disorders" in *Journal of Abnormal Psychology*, 101(3):538–552, 1992.

Figure 4.4: Source: Data from E. B. Foa and D. S. Riggs, "Posttraumatic Stress Disorder Following Assault: Theoretical Considerations and Empirical Findings" in *Current Directions in Psychological Science*, 4(2):61–65, 1995.

Figure 4.5: Source: Data from W. E. Schlenger, et al., "The Prevalence of Posttraumatic Stress Disorder in the Vietnam Generation: A Multimethod, Multisource Assessment of Psychiatric Disorder" in *Journal of Traumatic Stress*, 5(3):333–363, 1992.

pp. 142–143: From *The Boy Who Couldn't Stop Washing*, by Dr. Judith Rapaport. Copyright © 1989 by Judith L. Rapaport, M.D. Used by permission of Dutton Signet, a division of Penguin Books USA Inc.

pp. 144–145: From *The Boy Who Couldn't Stop Washing*, by Dr. Judith Rapaport. Copyright © 1989 by Judith L. Rapaport, M.D. Used by permission of Dutton Signet, a division of Penguin Books USA Inc.

p. 153: From D. C. Rimm and J. C. Masters, *Behavior Therapy: Techniques and Empirical Findings*, 2e, Copyright © 1979; Academic Press Inc., Reprinted by permission.

Chapter 5

p. 158: From: K. R. Jamison, *An Unquiet Mind: A Memoir of Moods and Madness*, Copyright © 1995, Alfred A. Knopf, Inc. Reprinted with permission.

p. 159: From: K. R. Jamison, *An Unquiet Mind: A Memoir of Moods and Madness*, Copyright © 1995, Alfred A. Knopf, Inc. Reprinted with permission.

Figure 5.1: Reprinted with permission from M. Weissman and M. Olfson, "Depression In Women: Implications for Health Care Research" in *Science*, 269(5225):799-801. Copyright © 1995 American Association for the Advancement of Science.

Figure 5.2: Source: Data from D. G. Blazer, et al., "The Prevalence and Distribution of Major Depression in a National Community Sample: The National Comorbidity Survey" in *American Journal of Psychiatry*, 151(7):979–986, 1994.

Figure 5.3: From Cross National Collaborative Group, "The Changing Rate of Major Depression" in *Journal of the American Medical Association*, 268(21):3098–3105. Copyright © 1992, American Medical Association. Reprinted with permission.

Figure 5.4: Source: Data from D. G. Blazer, et al., "The Prevalence and Distribution of Major Depression in a National Community Sample: The National Comorbidity Survey" in *American Journal of Psychiatry*, 151(7):979–986, 1994.

pp. 169–170: From: K. R. Jamison, *An Unquiet Mind: A Memoir of Moods and Madness*, Copyright © 1995, Alfred A. Knopf, Inc. Reprinted with permission.

p. 170: From: K. R. Jamison, *An Unquiet Mind: A Memoir of Moods and Madness*, Copyright © 1995, Alfred A. Knopf, Inc. Reprinted with permission.

Figure 5.5: From *Manic-Depressive Illness* by Frederick K. Goodwin and Kay R. Jamison. Copyright © 1990 by Oxford University Press, Inc. Used by permission of Oxford University Press, Inc.

Figure 5.6: Source: Data from R. Richards, et al., "Creativity in Manic-Depressives, Cyclothymes, their Normal Relatives, and Control Subjects" in *Journal of Abnormal Psychology*, 97(3):281–288, 1988.

Figure 5.7: Reprinted with the permission of The Free Press, a division of Simon & Schuster from *Touched With Fire: Manic Depressive Illness and the Artistic Temperament* by Kay Redfield Jamison. Copyright © 1993 by Kay Redfield Jamison.

Figure 5.8: Source: Data from P. H. Wender, et al., "Psychiatric Disorders in the Biological and Adoptive Families of Adopted Individuals With Affective Disorders" in *Archives of General Psychiatry*, 43(10):923–929, 1986.

Figure 5.11: From: M. E. Thase, E. Frank, and D. J. Kupfer, *Biological Processes In Major Depression* in E. E. Beckman/W. R. Leber's *Handbook of Depression*, Dorsey Press, 1985. Reprinted with permission.

p. 182: From: K. R. Jamison, *An Unquiet Mind: A Memoir of Moods and Madness*, Copyright © 1995, Alfred A. Knopf, Inc. Reprinted with permission.

pp. 182–183: From: K. R. Jamison, *An Unquiet Mind: A Memoir of Moods and Madness*, Copyright © 1995, Alfred A. Knopf, Inc. Reprinted with permission.

Figure 5.17: Sources: Data from E. Frank, et al., "Three-Year Outcomes for Maintenance Therapies in Recurrent Depression" in *Archives of General Psychiatry*, 47(12):1093–1099, 1990; and E. Frank, et al., "Efficacy of Interpersonal Psychotherapy as a Maintenance Treatment of Recurrent Depression: Contributing Factors" in *Archives of General Psychiatry*, 48(12):1053–1059, 1991.

Figure 5.18: From E. Moscicki, "Epidemiology of Suicidal Behavior" in *Suicide and Life-Threatening Behavior*, 25(1):22–35. Copyright © 1995 Guildford Publications. Reprinted with permission.

Figure 5.19: From R. Diekstra and N. Garnefksi, "On the Nature, Magnitude, and Causality of Suicidal Behaviors: An International Perspective" in *Suicide and Life-Threatening Behavior*, 25(1):36–57. Copyright © 1995 Guildford Publications.

pp. 207–208: From: K. R. Jamison, *An Unquiet Mind: A Memoir of Moods and Madness*, Copyright © 1995, Alfred A. Knopf, Inc. Reprinted with permission.

Chapter 6

Figure 6.1: Source: Data from I. I. Gottesman, *Schizophrenia Genesis: The Origins of Madness*, Copyright © 1991 Freeman Press, Reprinted with permission.

Figure 6.2: Source: Data from I. I. Gottesman, *Schizophrenia Genesis: The Origins of Madness*, Copyright © 1991 Freeman Press, Reprinted with permission.

Figure 6.6: Source: Data from M. Karno and J. H. Jenkins, "Cross-Cultural Issues in the Course and Treatment of Schizophrenia" in *Psychiatric Clinics of North America*, 16:339–350, 1993.

Figure 6.7: Source: Data from M. A. Test and L. I. Stein, "An Alternative to Mental Hospitals" in *Archives of General Psychiatry*, 37:409–412, 1980.

Figure 6.8: Source: Data from M. A. Test and L. I. Stein, "An Alternative to Mental Hospitals" in *Archives of General Psychiatry*, 37:409–412, 1980.

Figure 6.9: From G. E. Hogarty, et al., "Family Psychoeducation" in *Archives of General Psychiatry*, 43:633–642. Copyright 1986, American Medical Association. Reprinted with permission.

Figure 6.10: From: A. Jablinsky, et al., "Epidemiology and Cross-Cultural Aspects of Schizophrenia" in *Psychiatric Annals*, 19(10):521, Copyright © 1989, Slack, Inc., Reprinted with permission.

p. 249: From: *Schizophrenia Genesis: The Origins of Madness* by Irving I. Gottesman, Copyright © 1991 by Irving I. Gottesman. Used with permission of W. H. Freeman and Company.

Chapter 7

p. 279: From: Toufexis, "Why Jennifer Got Sick," *Time Magazine*, Copyright © 1996 Time Inc. Reprinted by permission.

Chapter 8

pp. 285–286: From: *Child and Adolescent Therapy: Cognitive-Behavioral Procedures*, edited by Philip C. Devidall (1991); New York: Guilford Press.

pp. 286–287: From: R. L. Spitzer, *DSM-III Case Book: A Learning Companion to the Diagnostic and Statistical Manual of Mental Disorders*, 3e, Copyright © 1981, American Psychiatric Association.

pp. 288–289: From: R. L. Spitzer, *DSM-III Case Book: A Learning Companion to the Diagnostic and Statistical Manual of Mental Disorders*, 3e, Copyright © 1981, American Psychiatric Association.

pp. 291–292: From: R. L. Spitzer, *Psychopathology: A Case Book,* Copyright © 1983, McGraw-Hill Companies, Inc., Reprinted with permission.

p. 299: From: A. T. Beck and A. Freeman, *Cognitive Therapy of Personality Disorders,* Copyright © 1990, Guilford Press. Reprinted with permission.

pp. 301–302: From: A. T. Beck and A. Freeman, *Cognitive Therapy of Personality Disorders,* Copyright © 1990, Guilford Press. Reprinted with permission.

p. 304: From: R. L. Spitzer, *DSM-III Case Book: A Learning Companion to the Diagnostic and Statistical Manual of Mental Disorders,* 3e, Copyright © 1981, American Psychiatric Association.

pp. 307–308: From: R. L. Spitzer, *Psychopathology: A Case Book,* Copyright © 1983, McGraw-Hill Companies, Inc., Reprinted with permission.

Chapter 9

Figure 9.1: From: *Diagnostic and Statistical Manual of Mental Disorders,* 4e (DSM-III). Copyright © 1994 American Psychiatric Association.

pp. 331–332: From: J. E. Lochman, et al., "Cognitive-Behavioral Assessment and Treatment With Aggressive Children" in P. Kendall *Therapy With Children And Adolescents: Cognitive Behavioral Procedures,* Copyright © 1991, Guilford Press. Reprinted with permission.

pp. 345–346: From: D. Williams, *Somebody Somewhere: Breaking Free From the World of Autism,* Copyright © 1994 Random House, Reprinted with permission.

Chapter 10

Figure 10.1: From *Statistical Bulletin,* Reprinted with permission from Metropolitan Life Insurance Company. NOTE: Weights at ages 25–59 based on lowest mortality.

pp. 360–361: From: R. L. Spitzer, *DSM-III Case Book: A Learning Companion to the Diagnostic and Statistical Manual of Mental Disorders,* 3e, Copyright © 1981, American Psychiatric Association.

pp. 368–369: From: Anderson: *Males With Eating Disorders,* Copyright © 1990, Brunner/Mazel, Inc. Reprinted with permission.

Chapter 11

Figure 11.1: From: J. S. Hyde, *Understanding Human Sexuality,* 4e, Copyright © 1990, The McGraw-Hill Companies, Inc. Reprinted with permission.

Figure 11.2: From: J. S. Hyde, *Understanding Human Sexuality,* 4e, Copyright © 1990, The McGraw-Hill Companies, Inc. Reprinted with permission.

Figure 11.3: From: R. T. Michael, et al., *Sex In America: A Definitive Survey,* Copyright ©1994, Little, Brown and Company.

Chapter 12

p. 431: From: R. L. Spitzer, *DSM-III Case Book: A Learning Companion to the Diagnostic and Statistical Manual of Mental Disorders,* 3e, Copyright © 1981, American Psychiatric Association.

Figure 12.1: From: J. E. Helzer, et al., "Five Communities in the United States: Results of the Epidemiologic Catchment Area Survey" in *Alcoholism in North America, Europe, and Asia,* 1992.

Figure 12.2: From: J. E. Helzer, et al., "Five Communities in the United States: Results of the Epidemiologic Catchment Area Survey" in *Alcoholism in North America, Europe, and Asia,* 1992.

pp. 453–454: From: R. L. Spitzer, *Psychopathology: A Case Book,* Copyright © 1983, McGraw-Hill Companies, Inc., Reprinted with permission.

pp. 460–461: Excerpt from Crosby and Firestone, *Going My Own Way,* Copyright © 1983 Crosby & Firestone. Used by permission of Doubleday. A division of Bantam Doubleday Dell Publishing Group, Inc.

Figure 12.4: Reprinted from Journal of Substance Abuse Treatment, 11(2):143–154, by K. Fromme, et al., *The Alcohol Skill Training Program: A Group Intervention for Young Adult Drinkers,* Copyright © 1994, with kind permission from Elsevier Science-NL, Sara Burgerhartstraat 25, 1055 KV Amsterdam, The Netherlands.

Chapter 13

Figure 13.2: Source: Data from M. L. Laudenslager, et al., "Coping and Immunosuppression: Inescapable but Not Escapable Shock Suppresses Lymphocyte Proliferation" in *Science,* 221:568–570, 1983.

Figure 13.3: Source: Data from Cohen, Tyrel, and Smith, 1991.

Chapter 14

pp. 495–496: From: R. L. Spitzer, *DSM-III Case Book: A Learning Companion to the Diagnostic and Statistical Manual of Mental Disorders,* 3e, Copyright © 1981, American Psychiatric Association.

Figure 14.1: From: *Diagnostic and Statistical Manual of Mental Disorders,* 4e. (DSM-IV). Copyright © 1994 American Psychiatric Association.

Figure 14.9: Reprinted from Journal of Psychiatric Research, 12(3):189–198, "Mini-Mental State", Copyright © 1975, Elsevier Science Ltd., Oxford, England. Reprinted with permission.

Chapter 15

Figure 15.3: Source: Data from S. Nolen-Hoeksema, "Ruminative Coping With Depressed Mood Following Loss" in *Journal of Personality and Social Psychology,* 67(1):92–104, Copyright © 1994.

Figure 15.7: Data from J. E. Gillham, et al., "Prevention of Depressive Symptoms in Schoolchildren: Two-Year Follow-Up", in *Psychological Science,* 6(6):343–351, 1995.

pp. 536–537: From Newsweek, 4/18/94, Copyright © 1994, Newsweek Inc. All rights reserved. Reprinted by permission.

Figure 15.8: Source: Data from L. L. Carstensen, "Evidence for a Life-Span Theory of Socioemotional Selectivity" in *Current Directions in Psychological Science,* 4(5):151–156, 1995.

Figure 15.9: Source: Data from B. Frederickson, "Socioemotional Behavior at the End of College Life" in *Journal of Social and Personal Relationships,* 12(2):261–276, 1995.

Figure 15.10: Source: Data from H. W. Stevenson, et al., "Motivation and Achievement of Gifted Children in East Asia and the United States" in *Journal for the Education of the Gifted,* 16(3)223–250, 1993.

Chapter 16

p. 567: Reprinted with permission from American Psychological Association.

pp. 569–570: From *Consciousness and Cognition: An International Journal,* 3(3–4):300–301, 1994. Reprinted with permission from Academic Press, M. R. Harvey and J. L. Herman. NOTE: Excerpt is a composite construction.

Name Index

Subject Index